P9-AOK-137

THE MODERN LIBRARY

of the World's Best Books

ELEVEN PLAYS OF HENRIK IBSEN

ELEVEN PLAYS OF HENRIK IBSEN

INTRODUCTION BY

H. L. MENCKEN

THE MODERN LIBRARY

The material inclu'ed in this volume is taken from Everyman's Library.

THE MODERN LIBRARY
IS PUBLISHED BY
RANDOM HOUSE, INC.
BENNETT A. CERF • DONALD S. KLOPFER • ROBERT K. HAAS
Manufactured in the United States of America
Printed by Parkway Printing Company *Bound by H. Wolff*

CONTENTS

INTRODUCTION

By H. L. Mencken

Ibsen, like Wagner and Manet, has lived down his commentators, and is now ready to be examined and enjoyed for what he actually was, namely, a first-rate journeyman dramatist, perhaps the best that ever lived. Twenty years ago he was hymned and damned as anything and everything else: symbolist, seer, prophet, necromancer, maker of riddles, rabble-rouser, cheap shocker, pornographer, spinner of gossamer nothings. Fools belabored him and fools defended him; he was near to being suffocated and done for in the fog of balderdash. I know of no sure cure for all the sorrows of the world, social, political or æsthetic, that was not credited to him, read into him, forced into his baggage. And I know of no crime against virtue, good order and the revelation of God that he was not accused of. The product of all this pawing and bawling was the Ibsen legend, that fabulous picture of a fabulous monster, half Nietzsche and half Dr. Frank Crane, drenching the world with scandalous platitudes from a watch-tower in the chilblained North. The righteous heard of him with creepy shudders; there was bold talk of denying him the use of the mails; he was the Gog and the Magog, the Heliogabalus, nay, the downright Kaiser, of that distant and pious era.

No such Ibsen, of course, ever really existed. The genuine Ibsen was anything but the Anti-Christ thus conjured up by imprudent partisans and terrified opponents. On the contrary, he was a man whose salient quality was precisely his distrust of, and disdain for, any and all such facile heresies; a highly respectable gentleman of the middle class, well-barbered, ease-loving and careful in mind; a very skilful practitioner of a very exacting and lucrative trade; a safe and sane exponent of order, efficiency, honesty and common sense. From end to end of his life there is no record that Ibsen ever wrote a single word or formulated a single idea that might not have been exposed in a newspaper editorial. He believed in all the things that the normal, law-abiding citizen of Christendom believes in, from democracy to romantic love, and from the obligations of duty to the value of virtue, and he always gave them the best of it in his plays. And whenever, mistaking his position, someone charged him with flouting these things or with advocating some notion that stood in opposition to them, he invariably called the plaintiff to book, and denied vehemently that he was guilty, and protested bitterly that it was outrageous to fasten any such wild and naughty stuff upon a reputable man.

Had he been, in truth, the extravagant iconoclast that a misinformed rabbinism tried to make him out, he would have remained, to the end of his career, a mere freak and blank cartridge in the theatre, and of no more influence than such extremists, say, as Max Stirner, Arthur Gobineau and the Marquis de Sade. So long, indeed, as he was generally held to be such an iconoclast, he actually suffered that fate. But when it began to be noticed, first by other dramatists and then by a widening public, that his ideas, after all, were really not extraordinary—that what he said, in the last analysis, was simply what every reasonably intelligent man thought—that his plays, for all their smashing air, were not actually blows at Christian culture—when this began to be understood, then he began to make his way, and all the serious dramatists of Europe began to imitate him. But they saw him, with their keener professional eyes, more clearly than the early and so absurd Ibsenites had seen him. They saw that he was not a brummagem prophet, but a play-maker of astounding skill—one who had a new and better method to teach them. And so, when they set out to follow him, what they imitated was not the imaginary mystifications that foolish fuglemen had read into his dramas, but his direct and adept manner of clothing simple and even self-evident arguments in unusually lucid and brilliant dramatic forms—in brief, his enormously effective technique as a dramatist. He didn't teach them to think extraordinary thoughts; he taught them to put obvious thoughts into sound plays.

All this must be plain to anyone who goes through his so-called social dramas today, despite the confusing memory of all the gabble that went about in the high days of the Ibsen uproar. What ideas does one actually find in them? Such ideas, first and last, as even a Harvard professor might evolve without bursting his brain—for example, that it is unpleasant and degrading for a wife to be treated as a mere mistress and empty-head; that professional patriots and town boomers are frauds; that success in business usually involves doing things that a self-respecting man hesitates to do; that a woman who continues to cohabit with a syphilitic husband may expect to have defective children; that a joint sorrow tends to dampen passion in husband and wife, and so bring them together upon a more secure basis; that a neurotic and lascivious woman is apt to be horrified when she finds that she is pregnant; that a man of 55 or 60 is an ass to fall in love with a flapper of 17; that the world is barbarously cruel to a woman who has violated the Seventh Commandment or a man who has violated the Eighth. If you are discontented with these summaries, then turn to summaries that Ibsen made himself—that is, turn to his notes for his social dramas in his *Nachgelassene Schriften.* Here you will find precisely what he was trying to say. Here you will find, in plain words, the ideas that he started from. They are, without exception, ideas of the utmost simplicity. There is nothing mysterious in them; there is not even anything new in them. Above all, there is no idiotic symbolism in them. They mean just what they say.

As I have said, Ibsen himself was under no delusions about his dramas of ideas. He was a hard-working dramatist and a mere man of sense: he never allowed the grotesque guesses and fantasies of his advocates to corrupt the clarity of his own purpose. Down to the time he lost his mind—he was then at work on "John Gabriel Borkman"—he never wrote a line that had any significance save the obvious one, and he never forgot for an instant that he was writing, not tracts, but stage-plays. When the sentimental German middle classes mistook "A Doll's House" for a revolutionary document against monogamy, and began grouping him with the preachers of free love, he was as indignant as only a respectable family man can be, and even agreed to write a new ending for the play in order to shut off that nonsense. A year later he wrote "Ghosts" to raise a laugh against the alarmed moralists who had swallowed the free lovers' error. The noise of combat continuing, he decided to make an end of it by burlesquing the Ibsenists, and the result was "The Wild Duck," in which the chief figure is a sort of *reductio ad absurdum* of the modern Drama Leaguer. In "The Master Builder" he took a holiday from social ideas, even the most elemental, and put himself into a play, shedding a salt tear over his lost youth. And in "Hedda Gabler," as if to confute the Ibsen talmudists forever, he fashioned a thumping drama out of the oldest, shoddiest materials of Sardou, Scribe and Feuillet, nay, Meilhac and Halévy, as if to prove, once and for all time, that he was a dramatist first and last, and not a windy evangelist and reformer, and that he could meet any other dramatist, however skilful, on equal terms, and dispose of him neatly and completely.

Ibsen's chief interest, from the beginning to the end of his career as a dramatist, was not with the propagation of ethical ideas, but with the solution of æsthetic problems. He was, in brief, not a preacher, but an artist, and not the moony artist of popular legend, but the alert and competent artist of fact, intent upon the technical difficulties of his business. He gave infinitely more thought to questions of practical dramaturgy—to getting his characters on and off the stage, to building up climaxes, to calculating effects—than he ever gave to the ideational content of his dramas. Almost any idea was good enough, so long as it could be converted into a conflict, and the conflict could be worked out straightforwardly and effectively. Read his letters and you will find him tremendously concerned, from the start, with technical difficulties and expedients—and never mentioning morals, lesson, symbols and that sort of thing at all. So early as the time he wrote "The League of Youth" you will find him discussing the details of dramatic machinery with Dr. Georg Brandes, and laying stress on the fact, with no little vanity, that he has "accomplished the feat of doing without a single monologue, in fact, without a single aside." A bit later he began developing the stage direction; go through his plays and observe how he gradually increased its importance, until in the end it almost overshadowed the dialogue. And if you would get, in brief, the full measure of his contribution to the art of the drama, give hard study to "A Doll's House." Here, for the first time, his new technique was in full working. Here he deposed Scribe and company at one blow, and founded an entirely new order of dramaturgy. Other dramatists, long before him, had concocted dramas of ideas—and good ones. The idea in Augier's "Le Mariage d'Olympe" was quite as sound and interesting as that in "A Doll's House;" the idea in Augier's "Les Effrontés" perhaps exceeded it in both ways. But Ibsen got into "A Doll's House" something that Augier and Feuillet and Dumas *fils* and all that crowd of Empire dramatists had never been able to get into their plays, and that was an air of utter and absolute reality, an overwhelming conviction, a complete concealment of the dramatic machinery.

And how did he conceal it? Simply by leaving it out. Scribe had built up an inordinately complex dramaturgy. His plays were elaborate and beautiful mechanisms, but still always mechanisms. He had to sacrifice everything else—reason, probability, human nature—to make the machine run. And Augier, Feuillet and Dumas, better men all, followed docilely in his tracks. They were better observers; they were more keenly interested in the actual life about them; they managed, despite the artificiality of their technique, to get some genuine human beings into their plays. But that technique still hung around their necks; they never quite got rid of it. But Ibsen did. In "A Doll's House" he threw it overboard for all time. Instead of a complicated plot, working beautifully toward a foreordained climax, he presented a few related scenes in the life of a husband and wife. Instead of a finely wrought fabric of suspense and emotion nicely balanced, neatly hanging together, he hit upon an action that was all suspense and all emotion. And instead of carefully calculated explanations, involving the orthodox couriers and prattling chambermaids, he let the story tell itself. The result, as William Archer has said, "was a new order of experience in the theatre." The audience that came to be pleasantly diverted by the old, old tricks found its nerves racked by a glimpse through a terrifying keyhole. This thing was not a stage-play, but a scandal. It didn't caress and soothe; it arrested and shocked. It didn't stay discreetly on the stage; it leaped out over the footlights.

The audience gasped and went out gabbling, and the result was the Ibsen madness, with its twenty years of folderol. But there were dramatists in the house who, with professional eye, saw more clearly what was afoot, and these dramatists, once they could shake off the Scribe tradition, began to imitate Ibsen—Jones and Pinero and later Shaw in England; Hauptmann and Sudermann in Germany; Gorki and many another in Russia; Hervieu, Brieux and their like in France; a swarm of lesser ones in Italy, Scandinavia and Austria. Ibsen, in brief, completely overthrew the well-made play of Scribe, and set up the play that was a direct imitation of reality. He showed that the illusion was not only not helped by the elaborate machinery of Scribe, but that it was actually hindered—that the way to sure and tremendous effects was by the route of simplicity, naturalness, ingenuousness. In "A Doll's House" he abandoned all of the old tricks save two or three; in "Ghosts" he made away with the rest of them, and even managed to do without a plot; by the time he got to "Little Eyolf" there was nothing left of the traditional dramaturgy save the act divisions. It was not, of course, an easy reform to put through. The habits of mind of audiences had to be changed; the lunacies of the Ibsenites had to be lived down, and the moral ire of the anti-Ibsenites; above all, the actors of the time had to be untaught all that they knew about acting, and taught a lot of new things that violated their vanity and hurt their business. But Ibsen's notions had logic behind them, and they had the force of novelty, and there was in them a new and superior opportunity for the dramatist who really had something to say, and so, in the end, they triumphed in the world. Today the methods of Scribe are so archaic that they excite laughter; only the Broadhursts and Kleins of Broadway stoop to them. If an intelligent dramatist were to expose a play built upon the plans of "Verre d'Eau" or "Adrienne Lecouvreur," even the newspaper critics would laugh at him. All that sort of thing now belongs to archeology.

But Ibsen, as I have said, was a dramatist first and last, and not a tin-pot agitator and messiah. He depicted the life of his time and he made use of the ideas of his time; he had no desire to change those ideas, nor even, in the main, to criticise them. "A dramatist's business," he used to say, "is not to answer questions, but merely to ask them." He asked a question in "A Doll's House." He asked another, ironically, in "Ghosts." He asked others in "The Lady from the Sea," "The Wild Duck" and "Little Eyolf." In "The Master Builder," rising, so to speak, to a question of personal privilege, he abandoned his habit and ventured upon a half-answer. But is there any answer in "Hedda Gabler?" Surely not. The play is still chewed and belabored by advocates of this answer or that; the very lack of agreement shows the dramatist's neutrality. "It was not my desire," he once said, "to deal in this play with so-called problems. What I wanted to do was to depict human beings, human emotions, and human destinies, upon a groundwork of certain of the social conditions and principles of the present day." That is to say, here is your state of society, here is your woman, here is what she does—what do you think of it? So, again, in "Pillars of Society." Here is your society, here are your pillars, here are their rascalities—what have you to say of it? Joseph Conrad, another great artist, once put the thing admirably. "My task which I am trying to achieve," he said, "is, by the power of the written word, to make you hear, to make you feel—it is, before all, to make you *see*. That—and no more, and it is everything."

A DOLL'S HOUSE

(1879)

CHARACTERS

TORVALD HELMER.
NORA, *his wife.*
DOCTOR RANK.
MRS. LINDE.
NILS KROGSTAD.
HELMER'S *three young children.*
ANNE, *their nurse.*
A HOUSEMAID.
A PORTER.

The action takes place in HELMER'S *house.*

A DOLL'S HOUSE

ACT I

SCENE.—*A room furnished comfortably and tastefully, but not extravagantly. At the back, a door to the right leads to the entrance hall, another to the left leads to* HELMER'S *study. Between the doors stands a piano. In the middle of the left-hand wall is a door, and beyond it a window. Near the window are a round table, armchairs and a small sofa. In the right-hand wall, at the farther end, another door; and on the same side, nearer the footlights, a stove, two easy chairs and a rocking-chair; between the stove and the door, a small table. Engravings on the walls; a cabinet with china and other small objects; a small book-case with well-bound books. The floors are carpeted, and a fire burns in the stove. It is winter.*

A bell rings in the hall; shortly afterwards the door is heard to open. Enter NORA, *humming a tune and in high spirits. She is in out-door dress and carries a number of parcels; these she lays on the table to the right. She leaves the outer door open after her, and through it is seen a* PORTER *who is carrying a Christmas Tree and a basket, which he gives to the* MAID *who has opened the door.*

Nora. Hide the Christmas Tree carefully, Helen. Be sure the children do not see it till this evening, when it is dressed. *(To the* PORTER, *taking out her purse.)* How much?

Porter. Sixpence.

Nora. There is a shilling. No, keep the change. *(The* PORTER *thanks her, and goes out.* NORA *shuts the door. She is laughing to herself, as she takes off her hat and coat. She takes a packet of macaroons from her pocket and eats one or two; then goes cautiously to her husband's door and listens.)* Yes, he is in.

[*Still humming, she goes to the table on the right.*

Helmer (calls out from his room). Is that my little lark twittering out there?

Nora (busy opening some of the parcels). Yes, it is!

Helmer. Is it my little squirrel bustling about?

Nora. Yes!

Helmer. When did my squirrel come home?

Nora. Just now. *(Puts the bag of macaroons into her pocket and wipes her mouth.)* Come in here, Torvald, and see what I have bought.

Helmer. Don't disturb me. *(A little later, he opens the door and looks into the room, pen in hand.)* Bought, did you say? All these things? Has my little spendthrift been wasting money again?

Nora. Yes, but, Torvald, this year we really can let ourselves go a little. This is the first Christmas that we have not needed to economise.

Helmer. Still, you know, we can't spend money recklessly.

Nora. Yes, Torvald, we may be a wee bit more reckless now, mayn't we? Just a tiny wee bit! You are going to have a big salary and earn lots and lots of money.

Helmer. Yes, after the New Year; but then it will be a whole quarter before the salary is due.

Nora. Pooh! we can borrow till then.

Helmer. Nora! *(Goes up to her and takes her playfully by the ear.)* The same little featherhead! Suppose, now, that I borrowed fifty pounds to-day, and you spent it all in the Christmas week, and then on New Year's Eve a slate fell on my head and killed me, and——

Nora (putting her hands over his mouth). Oh! don't say such horrid things.

Helmer. Still, suppose that happened,—what then?

Nora. If that were to happen, I don't suppose I should care whether I owed money or not.

Helmer. Yes, but what about the people who had lent it?

Nora. They? Who would bother about them? I should not know who they were.

Helmer. That is like a woman! But seriously, Nora, you know what I think about that. No debt, no borrowing. There can be no freedom or beauty about a home life that depends on borrowing and debt. We two have kept bravely on the straight road so far, and we will go on the same way for the short time longer that there need be any struggle.

Nora (moving towards the stove). As you please, Torvald.

Helmer (following her). Come, come, my little skylark must not droop her wings. What is this! Is my little squirrel out of temper? *(Taking out his purse.)* Nora, what do you think I have got here?

Nora (turning round quickly). Money!

Helmer. There you are. *(Gives her some money.)* Do you think I don't know what a lot is wanted for housekeeping at Christmas-time?

Nora (counting). Ten shillings—a pound—two pounds! Thank you, thank you, Torvald; that will keep me going for a long time.

Helmer. Indeed it must.

Nora. Yes, yes, it will. But come here and let me show you what I have bought. And all so cheap! Look, here is a new suit for Ivar, and a sword; and a horse and a trumpet for Bob; and a doll and dolly's bedstead for Emmy, —they are very plain, but anyway she will soon break them in pieces. And here are dress-lengths and handkerchiefs for the maids; old Anne ought really to have something better.

Helmer. And what is in this parcel?

Nora (crying out). No, no! you mustn't see that till this evening.

Helmer. Very well. But now tell me, you extravagant little person, what would you like for yourself?

Nora. For myself? Oh, I am sure I don't want anything.

Helmer. Yes, but you must. Tell me something reasonable that you would particularly like to have.

Nora. No, I really can't think of anything—unless, Torvald——

Helmer. Well?

Nora (playing with his coat buttons, and without raising her eyes to his). If you really want to give me something, you might—you might——

Helmer. Well, out with it!

Nora (speaking quickly). You might give me money, Torvald. Only just as much as you can afford; and then one of these days I will buy something with it.

Helmer. But, Nora——

Nora. Oh, do! dear Torvald; please, please do! Then I will wrap it up in beautiful gilt paper and hang it on the Christmas Tree. Wouldn't that be fun?

Helmer. What are little people called that are always wasting money?

Nora. Spendthrifts—I know. Let us do as you suggest, Torvald, and then I shall have time to think what I am most in want of. That is a very sensible plan, isn't it?

Helmer (smiling). Indeed it is—that is to say, if you were really to save out of the money I give you, and then really buy something for yourself. But if you spend it all on the housekeeping and any number of unnecessary things, then I merely have to pay up again.

Nora. Oh but, Torvald——

Helmer. You can't deny it, my dear little Nora. *(Puts his arm round her waist.)* It's a sweet little spendthrift, but she uses up a deal of money. One would hardly believe how expensive such little persons are!

Nora. It's a shame to say that. I do really save all I can.

Helmer (laughing). That's very true,—all you can. But you can't save anything!

Nora (smiling quietly and happily). You haven't any idea how many expenses we skylarks and squirrels have, Torvald.

Helmer. You are an odd little soul. Very like your father. You always find some new way of wheedling money out of me, and, as soon as you have got it, it seems to melt in your hands. You never know where it has gone. Still, one must take you as you are. It is in the blood; for indeed it is true that you can inherit these things, Nora.

Nora. Ah, I wish I had inherited many of papa's qualities.

Helmer. And I would not wish you to be anything but just what you are, my sweet little skylark. But, do you know, it strikes me that you are looking rather—what shall I say—rather uneasy to-day?

Nora. Do I?

Helmer. You do, really. Look straight at me.

Nora (looks at him). Well?

Helmer (wagging his finger at her). Hasn't Miss Sweet-Tooth been breaking rules in town to-day?

Nora. No; what makes you think that?

Helmer. Hasn't she paid a visit to the confectioner's?

Nora. No, I assure you, Torvald——

Helmer. Not been nibbling sweets?

Nora. No, certainly not.

Helmer. Not even taken a bite at a macaroon or two?

Nora. No, Torvald, I assure you really——

Helmer. There, there, of course I was only joking.

Nora (going to the table on the right). I should not think of going against your wishes.

Helmer. No, I am sure of that! besides, you gave me your word—— *(Going up to her.)* Keep your little Christmas secrets to yourself, my darling. They will all be revealed to-night when the Christmas Tree is lit, no doubt.

Nora. Did you remember to invite Doctor Rank?

Helmer. No. But there is no need; as a matter of course he will come to dinner with us. However, I will ask him when he comes in this morning. I have ordered some good wine. Nora, you can't think how I am looking forward to this evening.

Nora. So am I! And how the children will enjoy themselves, Torvald!

Helmer. It is splendid to feel that one has a perfectly safe appointment, and a big enough income. It's delightful to think of, isn't it?

Nora. It's wonderful?

Helmer. Do you remember last Christmas? For a full three weeks beforehand you shut yourself up every evening till long after midnight, making ornaments for the Christmas Tree and all the other fine things that were to be a surprise to us. It was the dullest three weeks I ever spent!

Nora. I didn't find it dull.

Helmer (smiling). But there was precious little result, Nora.

Nora. Oh, you shouldn't tease me about that again. How could I help the cat's going in and tearing everything to pieces?

Helmer. Of course you couldn't, poor little girl. You had the best of intentions to please us all, and that's the main thing. But it is a good thing that our hard times are over.

Nora. Yes, it is really wonderful.

Helmer. This time I needn't sit here and be dull all

alone, and you needn't ruin your dear eyes and your pretty little hands——

Nora (clapping her hands). No, Torvald, I needn't any longer, need I! It's wonderfully lovely to hear you say so! *(Taking his arm.)* Now I will tell you how I have been thinking we ought to arrange things, Torvald. As soon as Christmas is over—— *(A bell rings in the hall.)* There's the bell. *(She tidies the room a little.)* There's someone at the door. What a nuisance!

Helmer. If it is a caller, remember I am not at home.

Maid (in the doorway). A lady to see you, ma'am,—a stranger.

Nora. Ask her to come in.

Maid (to HELMER*).* The doctor came at the same time, sir.

Helmer. Did he go straight into my room?

Maid. Yes, sir.

[HELMER *goes into his room. The* MAID *ushers in* MRS. LINDE, *who is in travelling dress, and shuts the door.*

Mrs. Linde (in a dejected and timid voice). How do you do, Nora?

Nora (doubtfully). How do you do——

Mrs. Linde. You don't recognise me, I suppose.

Nora. No, I don't know—yes, to be sure, I seem to—— *(Suddenly.)* Yes! Christine! Is it really you?

Mrs. Linde. Yes, it is I.

Nora. Christine! To think of my not recognising you! And yet how could I—— *(In a gentle voice.)* How you have altered, Christine!

Mrs. Linde. Yes, I have indeed. In nine, ten long years——

Nora. Is it so long since we met? I suppose it is. The last eight years have been a happy time for me, I can tell you. And so now you have come into the town, and have taken this long journey in winter—that was plucky of you.

Mrs. Linde. I arrived by steamer this morning.

Nora. To have some fun at Christmas-time, of course. How delightful! We will have such fun together! But take off your things. You are not cold, I hope. *(Helps her.)* Now we will sit down by the stove, and be cosy. No, take this arm-chair; I will sit here in the rocking-chair. *(Takes her hands.)* Now you look like your old self again; it was only the first moment—— You are a little paler, Christine, and perhaps a little thinner.

Mrs. Linde. And much, much older, Nora.

Nora. Perhaps a little older; very, very little; certainly not much. *(Stops suddenly and speaks seriously.)* What a thoughtless creature I am, chattering away like this. My poor, dear Christine, do forgive me.

Mrs. Linde. What do you mean, Nora?

Nora (gently). Poor Christine, you are a widow.

Mrs. Linde. Yes; it is three years ago now.

Nora. Yes, I knew; I saw it in the papers. I assure you, Christine, I meant ever so often to write to you at the time, but I always put it off and something always prevented me.

Mrs. Linde. I quite understand, dear.

Nora. It was very bad of me, Christine. Poor thing, how you must have suffered. And he left you nothing?

Mrs. Linde. No.

Nora. And no children?

Mrs. Linde. No.

Nora. Nothing at all, then?

Mrs. Linde. Not even any sorrow or grief to live upon.

Nora (looking incredulously at her). But, Christine, is that possible?

Mrs. Linde (smiles sadly and strokes her hair). It sometimes happens, Nora.

Nora. So you are quite alone. How dreadfully sad that must be. I have three lovely children. You can't see them just now, for they are out with their nurse. But now you must tell me all about it.

Mrs. Linde. No, no; I want to hear you.

Nora. No, you must begin. I mustn't be selfish to-day; to-day I must only think of your affairs. But there is one thing I must tell you. Do you know we have just had a great piece of good luck?

Mrs. Linde. No, what is it?

Nora. Just fancy, my husband has been made manager of the Bank!

Mrs. Linde. Your husband? What good luck!

Nora. Yes, tremendous! A barrister's profession is such an uncertain thing, especially if he won't undertake unsavoury cases; and naturally Torvald has never been willing to do that, and I quite agree with him. You may imagine how pleased we are! He is to take up his work in the Bank at the New Year, and then he will have a big salary and lots of commissions. For the future we can live quite differently—we can do just as we like. I feel so relieved and so happy, Christine! It will be splendid to have heaps of money and not need to have any anxiety, won't it?

Mrs. Linde. Yes, anyhow I think it would be delightful to have what one needs.

Nora. No, not only what one needs, but heaps and heaps of money.

Mrs. Linde (smiling). Nora, Nora, haven't you learnt sense yet? In our schooldays you were a great spendthrift.

Nora (laughing). Yes, that is what Torvald says now. *(Wags her finger at her.)* But "Nora, Nora" is not so silly as you think. We have not been in a position for me to waste money. We have both had to work.

Mrs. Linde. You too?

Nora. Yes; odds and ends, needlework, crochet-work, embroidery, and that kind of thing. *(Dropping her voice.)* And other things as well. You know Torvald left his office when we were married? There was no prospect of promotion there, and he had to try and earn more than before. But during the first year he overworked himself dreadfully. You see, he had to make money every way he could, and he worked early and late; but he couldn't stand it, and fell dreadfully ill, and the doctors said it was necessary for him to go south.

Mrs. Linde. You spent a whole year in Italy, didn't you?

Nora. Yes. It was no easy matter to get away, I can tell you. It was just after Ivar was born; but naturally we had to go. It was a wonderfully beautiful journey, and it saved Torvald's life. But it cost a tremendous lot of money, Christine.

Mrs. Linde. So I should think.

Nora. It cost about two hundred and fifty pounds. That's a lot, isn't it?

Mrs. Linde. Yes, and in emergencies like that it is lucky to have the money.

Nora. I ought to tell you that we had it from papa.

Mrs. Linde. Oh, I see. It was just about that time that he died, wasn't it?

Nora. Yes; and, just think of it, I couldn't go and nurse him. I was expecting little Ivar's birth every day and I had my poor sick Torvald to look after. My dear, kind father—I never saw him again, Christine. That was the saddest time I have known since our marriage.

Mrs. Linde. I know how fond you were of him. And then you went off to Italy?

Nora. Yes; you see we had money then, and the doctors insisted on our going, so we started a month later.

Mrs. Linde. And your husband came back quite well?

Nora. As sound as a bell!

Mrs. Linde. But—the doctor?

Nora. What doctor?

Mrs. Linde. I thought your maid said the gentleman who arrived here just as I did, was the doctor?

Nora. Yes, that was Doctor Rank, but he doesn't come here professionally. He is our greatest friend, and comes in at least once every day. No, Torvald has not had an hour's illness since then, and our children are strong and healthy and so am I. *(Jumps up and claps her hands.)* Christine! Christine! it's good to be alive and happy!——But how horrid of me; I am talking of nothing but my own affairs. *(Sits on a stool near her, and rests her arms on her knees.)* You mustn't be angry with me. Tell me, is it really true that you did not love your husband? Why did you marry him?

Mrs. Linde. My mother was alive then, and was bedridden and helpless, and I had to provide for my two younger brothers; so I did not think I was justified in refusing his offer.

Nora. No, perhaps you were quite right. He was rich at that time, then?

Mrs. Linde. I believe he was quite well off. But his business was a precarious one; and, when he died, it all went to pieces and there was nothing left.

Nora. And then?——

Mrs. Linde. Well, I had to turn my hand to anything I could find—first a small shop, then a small school, and so on. The last three years have seemed like one long working-day, with no rest. Now it is at an end, Nora. My poor mother needs me no more, for she is gone; and the boys do not need me either; they have got situations and can shift for themselves.

Nora. What a relief you must feel it——

Mrs. Linde. No, indeed; I only feel my life unspeakably empty. No one to live for any more. *(Gets up restlessly.)* That was why I could not stand the life in my little backwater any longer. I hope it may be easier here to find something which will busy me and occupy my thoughts. If only I could have the good luck to get some regular work—office work of some kind——

Nora. But, Christine, that is so frightfully tiring, and you look tired out now. You had far better go away to some watering-place.

Mrs. Linde (walking to the window). I have no father to give me money for a journey, Nora.

Nora (rising). Oh, don't be angry with me.

Mrs. Linde (going up to her). It is you that must not be angry with me, dear. The worst of a position like mine is that it makes one so bitter. No one to work for, and yet obliged to be always on the look-out for chances. One must live, and so one becomes selfish. When you told me of the happy turn your fortunes have taken—you will hardly believe it—I was delighted not so much on your account as on my own.

Nora. How do you mean?—Oh, I understand. You mean that perhaps Torvald could get you something to do.

Mrs. Linde. Yes, that was what I was thinking of.

Nora. He must, Christine. Just leave it to me; I will broach the subject very cleverly—I will think of something that will please him very much. It will make me so happy to be of some use to you.

Mrs. Linde. How kind you are, Nora, to be so anxious to help me! It is doubly kind in you, for you know so little of the burdens and troubles of life.

Nora. I——? I know so little of them?

Mrs. Linde (smiling). My dear! Small household cares and that sort of thing!—You are a child, Nora.

Nora (tosses her head and crosses the stage). You ought not to be so superior.

Mrs. Linde. No?

Nora. You are just like the others. They all think that I am incapable of anything really serious——

Mrs. Linde. Come, come——

Nora. —that I have gone through nothing in this world of cares.

Mrs. Linde. But, my dear Nora, you have just told me all your troubles.

Nora. Pooh!—those were trifles. *(Lowering her voice.)* I have not told you the important thing.

Mrs. Linde. The important thing? What do you mean?

Nora. You look down upon me altogether, Christine—but you ought not to. You are proud, aren't you, of having worked so hard and so long for your mother?

Mrs. Linde. Indeed, I don't look down on any one. But it is true that I am both proud and glad to think that I was privileged to make the end of my mother's life almost free from care.

Nora. And you are proud to think of what you have done for your brothers.

Mrs. Linde. I think I have the right to be.

Nora. I think so, too. But now, listen to this; I too have something to be proud and glad of.

Mrs. Linde. I have no doubt you have. But what do you refer to?

Nora. Speak low. Suppose Torvald were to hear! He mustn't on any account—no one in the world must know, Christine, except you.

Mrs. Linde. But what is it?

Nora. Come here. *(Pulls her down on the sofa beside her.)* Now I will show you that I too have something to be proud and glad of. It was I who saved Torvald's life.

Mrs. Linde. "Saved"? How?

Nora. I told you about our trip to Italy. Torvald would never have recovered if he had not gone there——

Mrs. Linde. Yes, but your father gave you the necessary funds.

Nora (smiling). Yes, that is what Torvald and all the others think, but——

Mrs. Linde. But——

Nora. Papa didn't give us a shilling. It was I who procured the money.

Mrs. Linde. You? All that large sum?

Nora. Two hundred and fifty pounds. What do you think of that?

Mrs. Linde. But, Nora, how could you possibly do it? Did you win a prize in the Lottery?

Nora (contemptuously). In the Lottery? There would have been no credit in that.

Mrs. Linde. But where did you get it from, then?

Nora (humming and smiling with an air of mystery). Hm, hm! Aha!

Mrs. Linde. Because you couldn't have borrowed it.

Nora. Couldn't I? Why not?

Mrs. Linde. No, a wife cannot borrow without her husband's consent.

Nora (tossing her head). Oh, if it is a wife who has any head for business—a wife who has the wit to be a little bit clever——

Mrs. Linde. I don't understand it at all, Nora.

Nora. There is no need you should. I never said I had borrowed the money. I may have got it some other way. *(Lies back on the sofa.)* Perhaps I got it from some other admirer. When anyone is as attractive as I am——

Mrs. Linde. You are a mad creature.

Nora. Now, you know you're full of curiosity, Christine.

Mrs. Linde. Listen to me, Nora dear. Haven't you been a little bit imprudent?

Nora (sits up straight). Is it imprudent to save your husband's life?

Mrs. Linde. It seems to me imprudent, without his knowledge, to——

Nora. But it was absolutely necessary that he should not know! My goodness, can't you understand that? It was necessary he should have no idea what a dangerous condition he was in. It was to me that the doctors came and said that his life was in danger, and that the only thing to save him was to live in the south. Do you suppose I didn't try, first of all, to get what I wanted as if it were for myself? I told him how much I should love to travel abroad like other young wives; I tried tears and entreaties with him; I told him that he ought to remember the condition I was in, and that he ought to be kind and indulgent to me; I even hinted that he might raise a loan. That nearly made him angry, Christine. He said I was thoughtless, and that it was his duty as my husband not to indulge me in my whims and caprices—as I believe he called them. Very well, I thought, you must be saved—and that was how I came to devise a way out of the difficulty——

Mrs. Linde. And did your husband never get to know from your father that the money had not come from him?

Nora. No, never. Papa died just at that time. I had meant to let him into the secret and beg him never to reveal it. But he was so ill then—alas, there never was any need to tell him.

Mrs. Linde. And since then have you never told your secret to your husband?

Nora. Good Heavens, no! How could you think so? A man who has such strong opinions about these things! And besides, how painful and humiliating it would be for Torvald, with his manly independence, to know that he owed me anything! It would upset our mutual relations altogether; our beautiful happy home would no longer be what it is now.

Mrs. Linde. Do you mean never to tell him about it?

Nora (meditatively, and with a half smile). Yes—some day, perhaps, after many years, when I am no longer as nice-looking as I am now. Don't laugh at me! I mean, of course, when Torvald is no longer as devoted to me as he is now; when my dancing and dressing-up and reciting have palled on him; then it may be a good thing to have something in reserve—— *(Breaking off.)* What nonsense! That time will never come. Now, what do you think of my great secret, Christine? Do you still think I am of no use?

I can tell you, too, that this affair has caused me a lot of worry. It has been by no means easy for me to meet my engagements punctually. I may tell you that there is something that is called, in business, quarterly interest, and another thing called payment in instalments, and it is always so dreadfully difficult to manage them. I have had to save a little here and there, where I could, you understand. I have not been able to put aside much from my housekeeping money, for Torvald must have a good table. I couldn't let my children be shabbily dressed; I have felt obliged to use up all he gave me for them, the sweet little darlings!

Mrs. Linde. So it has all had to come out of your own necessaries of life, poor Nora?

Nora. Of course. Besides, I was the one responsible for it. Whenever Torvald has given me money for new dresses and such things, I have never spent more than half of it; I have always bought the simplest and cheapest things. Thank Heaven, any clothes look well on me, and so Torvald has never noticed it. But it was often very hard on me, Christine—because it is delightful to be really well dressed, isn't it?

Mrs. Linde. Quite so.

Nora. Well, then I have found other ways of earning money. Last winter I was lucky enough to get a lot of copying to do; so I locked myself up and sat writing every evening until quite late at night. Many a time I was desperately tired; but all the same it was a tremendous pleasure to sit there working and earning money. It was like being a man.

Mrs. Linde. How much have you been able to pay off in that way?

Nora. I can't tell you exactly. You see, it is very difficult to keep an account of a business matter of that kind. I only know that I have paid every penny that I could scrape together. Many a time I was at my wits' end. *(Smiles.)*

Then I used to sit here and imagine that a rich old gentleman had fallen in love with me——

Mrs. Linde. What! Who was it?

Nora. Be quiet!—that he had died; and that when his will was opened it contained, written in big letters, the instruction: "The lovely Mrs. Nora Helmer is to have all I possess paid over to her at once in cash."

Mrs. Linde. But, my dear Nora—who could the man be?

Nora. Good gracious, can't you understand? There was no old gentleman at all; it was only something that I used to sit here and imagine, when I couldn't think of any way of procuring money. But it's all the same now; the tiresome old person can stay where he is, as far as I am concerned; I don't care about him or his will either, for I am free from care now. *(Jumps up.)* My goodness, it's delightful to think of, Christine! Free from care! To be able to be free from care, quite free from care; to be able to play and romp with the children; to be able to keep the house beautifully and have everything just as Torvald likes it! And, think of it, soon the spring will come and the big blue sky! Perhaps we shall be able to take a little trip—perhaps I shall see the sea again! Oh, it's a wonderful thing to be alive and be happy. *(A bell is heard in the hall.)*

Mrs. Linde (rising). There is the bell; perhaps I had better go.

Nora. No, don't go; no one will come in here; it is sure to be for Torvald.

Servant (at the hall door). Excuse me, ma'am—there is a gentleman to see the master, and as the doctor is with him——

Nora. Who is it?

Krogstad (at the door). It is I, Mrs. Helmer. (MRS. LINDE *starts, trembles, and turns to the window.)*

Nora (takes a step towards him, and speaks in a strained,

low voice). You? What is it? What do you want to see my husband about?

Krogstad. Bank business—in a way. I have a small post in the Bank, and I hear your husband is to be our chief now——

Nora. Then it is——

Krogstad. Nothing but dry business matters, Mrs. Helmer; absolutely nothing else.

Nora. Be so good as to go into the study, then. *(She bows indifferently to him and shuts the door into the hall; then comes back and makes up the fire in the stove.)*

Mrs. Linde. Nora—who was that man?

Nora. A lawyer, of the name of Krogstad.

Mrs. Linde. Then it really was he.

Nora. Do you know the man?

Mrs. Linde. I used to—many years ago. At one time he was a solicitor's clerk in our town.

Nora. Yes, he was.

Mrs. Linde. He is greatly altered.

Nora. He made a very unhappy marriage.

Mrs. Linde. He is a widower now, isn't he?

Nora. With several children. There now, it is burning up.

[*Shuts the door of the stove and moves the rocking-chair aside.*

Mrs. Linde. They say he carries on various kinds of business.

Nora. Really! Perhaps he does; I don't know anything about it. But don't let us think of business; it is so tiresome.

Doctor Rank (comes out of HELMER'S *study. Before he shuts the door he calls to him).* No, my dear fellow, I won't disturb you; I would rather go into your wife for a little while. *(Shuts the door and sees* MRS. LINDE.) I beg your pardon; I am afraid I am disturbing you too.

Nora. No, not at all. *(Introducing him.)* Doctor Rank, Mrs. Linde.

Rank. I have often heard Mrs. Linde's name mentioned here. I think I passed you on the stairs when I arrived, Mrs. Linde?

Mrs. Linde. Yes, I go up very slowly; I can't manage stairs well.

Rank. Ah! some slight internal weakness?

Mrs. Linde. No, the fact is I have been overworking myself.

Rank. Nothing more than that? Then I suppose you have come to town to amuse yourself with our entertainments?

Mrs. Linde. I have come to look for work.

Rank. Is that a good cure for overwork?

Mrs. Linde. One must live, Doctor Rank.

Rank. Yes, the general opinion seems to be that it is necessary.

Nora. Look here, Doctor Rank—you know you want to live.

Rank. Certainly. However wretched I may feel, I want to prolong the agony as long as possible. All my patients are like that. And so are those who are morally diseased; one of them, and a bad case too, is at this very moment with Helmer——

Mrs. Linde (sadly). Ah!

Nora. Whom do you mean?

Rank. A lawyer of the name of Krogstad, a fellow you don't know at all. He suffers from a diseased moral character, Mrs. Helmer; but even he began talking of its being highly important that he should live.

Nora. Did he? What did he want to speak to Torvald about?

Rank. I have no idea; I only heard that it was something about the Bank.

Nora. I didn't know this—what's his name—Krogstad had anything to do with the Bank.

Rank. Yes, he has some sort of appointment there. *(To* MRS. LINDE.) I don't know whether you find also in your part of the world that there are certain people who go zealously snuffing about to smell out moral corruption, and, as soon as they have found some, put the person concerned into some lucrative position where they can keep their eye on him. Healthy natures are left out in the cold.

Mrs. Linde. Still I think the sick are those who most need taking care of.

Rank (shrugging his shoulders). Yes, there you are. That is the sentiment that is turning Society into a sick-house.

[NORA, *who has been absorbed in her thoughts, breaks out into smothered laughter and claps her hands.*

Rank. Why do you laugh at that? Have you any notion what Society really is?

Nora. What do I care about tiresome Society? I am laughing at something quite different, something extremely amusing. Tell me, Doctor Rank, are all the people who are employed in the Bank dependent on Torvald now?

Rank. Is that what you find so extremely amusing?

Nora (smiling and humming). That's my affair! *(Walking about the room.)* It's perfectly glorious to think that we have—that Torvald has so much power over so many people. *(Takes the packet from her pocket.)* Doctor Rank, what do you say to a macaroon?

Rank. What, macaroons? I thought they were forbidden here.

Nora. Yes, but these are some Christine gave me.

Mrs. Linde. What! I?—

Nora. Oh, well, don't be alarmed! You couldn't know that Torvald had forbidden them. I must tell you that he is afraid they will spoil my teeth. But, bah!—once in a way—— That's so, isn't it, Doctor Rank? By your leave? *(Puts a macaroon into his mouth.)* You must have one too, Christine. And I shall have one, just a little one—or at most two. *(Walking about.)* I am tremendously happy. There is just one thing in the world now that I should dearly love to do.

Rank. Well, what is that?

Nora. It's something I should dearly love to say, if Torvald could hear me.

Rank. Well, why can't you say it?

Nora. No, I daren't; it's so shocking.

Mrs. Linde. Shocking?

Rank. Well, I should not advise you to say it. Still, with us you might. What is it you would so much like to say if Torvald could hear you?

Nora. I should just love to say—Well, I'm damned!

Rank. Are you mad?

Mrs. Linde. Nora, dear——!

Rank. Say it, here he is!

Nora (hiding the packet). Hush! Hush! Hush!

[HELMER *comes out of his room, with his coat over his arm and his hat in his hand.*

Nora. Well, Torvald dear, have you got rid of him?

Helmer. Yes, he has just gone.

Nora. Let me introduce you—this is Christine, who has come to town.

Helmer. Christine——? Excuse me, but I don't know ——

Nora. Mrs. Linde, dear; Christine Linde.

Helmer. Of course. A school friend of my wife's, I presume?

Mrs. Linde. Yes, we have known each other since then.

Nora. And just think, she has taken a long journey in order to see you.

Helmer. What do you mean?

Mrs. Linde. No, really, I——

Nora. Christine is tremendously clever at book-keeping, and she is frightfully anxious to work under some clever man, so as to perfect herself——

Helmer. Very sensible, Mrs. Linde.

Nora. And when she heard you had been appointed manager of the Bank—the news was telegraphed, you know—she travelled here as quick as she could, Torvald, I am sure you will be able to do something for Christine, for my sake, won't you?

Helmer. Well, it is not altogether impossible. I presume you are a widow, Mrs. Linde?

Mrs. Linde. Yes.

Helmer. And have had some experience of book-keeping?

Mrs. Linde. Yes, a fair amount.

Helmer. Ah! well, it's very likely I may be able to find something for you——

Nora (clapping her hands). What did I tell you? What did I tell you?

Helmer. You have just come at a fortunate moment, Mrs. Linde.

Mrs. Linde. How am I to thank you?

Helmer. There is no need. *(Puts on his coat.)* But to-day you must excuse me——

Rank. Wait a minute; I will come with you.

[*Brings his fur coat from the hall and warms it at the fire.*

Nora. Don't be long away, Torvald dear.

Helmer. About an hour, not more.

Nora. Are you going too, Christine?

Mrs. Linde (putting on her cloak). Yes, I must go and look for a room.

Helmer. Oh, well then, we can walk down the street together.

Nora (helping her). What a pity it is we are so short of space here: I am afraid it is impossible for us——

Mrs. Linde. Please don't think of it! Good-bye, Nora dear, and many thanks.

Nora. Good-bye for the present. Of course you will come back this evening. And you too, Dr. Rank. What do you say? If you are well enough? Oh, you must be! Wrap yourself up well.

[*They go to the door all talking together. Children's voices are heard on the staircase.*

Nora. There they are. There they are! *(She runs to open the door. The* NURSE *comes in with the children.)* Come in! Come in! *(Stoops and kisses them.)* Oh, you sweet blessings! Look at them, Christine! Aren't they darlings?

Rank. Don't let us stand here in the draught.

Helmer. Come along, Mrs. Linde; the place will only be bearable for a mother now!

[RANK, HELMER *and* MRS. LINDE *go downstairs. The* NURSE *comes forward with the children;* NORA *shuts the hall door.*

Nora. How fresh and well you look! Such red cheeks! —like apples and roses. *(The children all talk at once while she speaks to them.)* Have you had great fun? That's splendid! What, you pulled both Emmy and Bob along on the sledge?—both at once?—that *was* good. You are a clever boy, Ivar. Let me take her for a little, Anne. My sweet little baby doll! *(Takes the baby from the* MAID *and dances it up and down.)* Yes, yes, mother will dance with Bob too. What! Have you been snowballing? I wish I had been there too! No, no, I will take their things off, Anne; please let me do it, it is such fun. Go in now, you look half frozen. There is some hot coffee for you on the stove.

[*The* NURSE *goes into the room on the left.* NORA *takes off the children's things and throws them about, while they all talk to her at once.*

Nora. Really! Did a big dog run after you? But it didn't bite you? No, dogs don't bite nice little dolly children. You mustn't look at the parcels, Ivar. What are they? Ah, I daresay you would like to know. No, no—it's something nasty! Come, let us have a game! What shall we play at? Hide and Seek? Yes, we'll play Hide and Seek. Bob shall hide first. Must I hide? Very well, I'll hide first.

[*She and the children laugh and shout, and romp in and out of the room; at last* NORA *hides under the table, the children rush in and look for her, but do not see her; they hear her smothered laughter, run to the table, lift up the cloth and find her. Shouts of laughter. She crawls forward and pretends to frighten them. Fresh laughter. Meanwhile there has been a knock at the hall door, but none of them has noticed it. The door is half opened, and* KROGSTAD *appears. He waits a little; the game goes on.*

Krogstad. Excuse me, Mr. Helmer.

Nora (with a stifled cry, turns round and gets up on to her knees). Ah! what do you want?

Krogstad. Excuse me, the outer door was ajar; I suppose someone forgot to shut it.

Nora (rising). My husband is out, Mr. Krogstad.

Krogstad. I know that.

Nora. What do you want here, then?

Krogstad. A word with you.

Nora. With me?— *(to the children, gently.)* Go in to nurse. What? No, the strange man won't do mother any harm. When he has gone we will have another game. *(She takes the children into the room on the left, and shuts the door after them.)* You want to speak to me?

Krogstad. Yes, I do.

Nora. To-day? It is not the first of the month yet.

Krogstad. No, it is Christmas Eve, and it will depend on yourself what sort of a Christmas you will spend.

Nora. What do you want? To-day it is absolutely impossible for me——

Krogstad. We won't talk about that till later on. This is something different. I presume you can give me a moment?

Nora. Yes—yes, I can—although——

Krogstad. Good. I was in Olsen's Restaurant and saw your husband going down the street——

Nora. Yes?

Krogstad. With a lady.

Nora. What then?

Krogstad. May I make so bold as to ask if it was a Mrs. Linde?

Nora. It was.

Krogstad. Just arrived in town?

Nora. Yes, to-day.

Krogstad. She is a great friend of yours, isn't she?

Nora. She is. But I don't see——

Krogstad. I knew her too, once upon a time.

Nora. I am aware of that.

Krogstad. Are you? So you know all about it; I thought as much. Then I can ask you, without beating about the bush—is Mrs. Linde to have an appointment in the Bank?

Nora. What right have you to question me, Mr. Krogstad?—You, one of my husband's subordinates! But since you ask, you shall know. Yes, Mrs. Linde *is* to have an appointment. And it was I who pleaded her cause, Mr. Krogstad, let me tell you that.

Krogstad. I was right in what I thought, then.

Nora (walking up and down the stage). Sometimes one has a tiny little bit of influence, I should hope. Because one is a woman, it does not necessarily follow that——. When anyone is in a subordinate position, Mr. Krogstad, they should really be careful to avoid offending anyone who—who——

Krogstad. Who has influence?

Nora. Exactly.

Krogstad (changing his tone). Mrs. Helmer, you will be so good as to use your influence on my behalf.

Nora. What? What do you mean?

Krogstad. You will be so kind as to see that I am allowed to keep my subordinate position in the Bank.

Nora. What do you mean by that? Who proposes to take your post away from you?

Krogstad. Oh, there is no necessity to keep up the pretence of ignorance. I can quite understand that your friend is not very anxious to expose herself to the chance of rubbing shoulders with me; and I quite understand, too, whom I have to thank for being turned off.

Nora. But I assure you——

Krogstad. Very likely; but, to come to the point, the time has come when I should advise you to use your influence to prevent that.

Nora. But, Mr. Krogstad, I *have* no influence.

Krogstad. Haven't you? I thought you said yourself just now——

Nora. Naturally I did not mean you to put that construction on it. I! What should make you think I have any influence of that kind with my husband?

Krogstad. Oh, I have known your husband from our student days. I don't suppose he is any more unassailable than other husbands.

Nora. If you speak slightingly of my husband, I shall turn you out of the house.

Krogstad. You are bold, Mrs. Helmer.

Nora. I am not afraid of you any longer. As soon as the New Year comes, I shall in a very short time be free of the whole thing.

Krogstad (controlling himself). Listen to me, Mrs. Helmer. If necessary, I am prepared to fight for my small post in the Bank as if I were fighting for my life.

Nora. So it seems.

Krogstad. It is not only for the sake of the money; indeed, that weighs least with me in the matter. There is another reason—well, I may as well tell you. My position is this. I daresay you know, like everybody else, that once, many years ago, I was guilty of an indiscretion.

Nora. I think I have heard something of the kind.

Krogstad. The matter never came into court; but every way seemed to be closed to me after that. So I took to the business that you know of. I had to do something; and, honestly, I don't think I've been one of the worst. But now I must cut myself free from all that. My sons are growing up; for their sake I must try and win back as much respect as I can in the town. This post in the Bank was like the first step up for me—and now your husband is going to kick me downstairs again into the mud.

Nora. But you must believe me, Mr. Krogstad; it is not in my power to help you at all.

Krogstad. Then it is because you haven't the will; but I have means to compel you.

Nora. You don't mean that you will tell my husband that I owe you money?

Krogstad. Hm!—suppose I were to tell him?

Nora. It would be perfectly infamous of you. *(Sobbing.)* To think of his learning my secret, which has been my joy and pride, in such an ugly, clumsy way—that he should learn it from you! And it would put me in a horribly disagreeable position——

Krogstad. Only disagreeable?

Nora (impetuously). Well, do it, then!—and it will be the worse for you. My husband will see for himself what a blackguard you are, and you certainly won't keep your post then.

Krogstad. I asked you if it was only a disagreeable scene at home that you were afraid of?

Nora. If my husband does get to know of it, of course he will at once pay you what is still owing, and we shall have nothing more to do with you.

Krogstad (coming a step nearer). Listen to me, Mrs. Helmer. Either you have a very bad memory or you know very little of business. I shall be obliged to remind you of a few details.

Nora. What do you mean?

Krogstad. When your husband was ill, you came to me to borrow two hundred and fifty pounds.

Nora. I didn't know any one else to go to.

Krogstad. I promised to get you that amount——

Nora. Yes, and you did so.

Krogstad. I promised to get you that amount, on certain conditions. Your mind was so taken up with your husband's illness, and you were so anxious to get the money for your journey, that you seem to have paid no attention to the conditions of our bargain. Therefore it will not be amiss if I remind you of them. Now, I promised to get the money on the security of a bond which I drew up.

Nora. Yes, and which I signed.

Krogstad. Good. But below your signature there were a few lines constituting your father a surety for the money; those lines your father should have signed.

Nora. Should? He did sign them.

Krogstad. I had left the date blank; that is to say your father should himself have inserted the date on which he signed the paper. Do you remember that?

Nora. Yes, I think I remember——

Krogstad. Then I gave you the bond to send by post to your father. Is that not so?

Nora. Yes.

Krogstad. And you naturally did so at once, because five

or six days afterwards you brought me the bond with your father's signature. And then I gave you the money.

Nora. Well, haven't I been paying it off regularly?

Krogstad. Fairly so, yes. But--to come back to the matter in hand—that must have been a very trying time for you, Mrs. Helmer?

Nora. It was, indeed.

Krogstad. Your father was very ill, wasn't he?

Nora. He was very near his end.

Krogstad. And died soon afterwards?

Nora. Yes.

Krogstad. Tell me, Mrs. Helmer, can you by any chance remember what day your father died?—on what day of the month, I mean.

Nora. Papa died on the 29th of September.

Krogstad. That is correct; I have ascertained it for myself. And, as that is so, there is a discrepancy *(taking a paper from his pocket)* which I cannot account for.

Nora. What discrepancy? I don't know——

Krogstad. The discrepancy consists, Mrs. Helmer, in the fact that your father signed this bond three days after his death.

Nora. What do you mean? I don't understand——

Krogstad. Your father died on the 29th of September. But, look here; your father has dated his signature the 2nd of October. It is a discrepancy, isn't it? *(*NORA *is silent.)* Can you explain it to me? *(*NORA *is still silent.)* It is a remarkable thing, too, that the words "2nd of October," as well as the year, are not written in your father's handwriting but in one that I think I know. Well, of course it can be explained; your father may have forgotten to date his signature, and someone else may have dated it haphazard before they knew of his death. There is no harm in that. It all depends on the signature of the name; and *that* is genuine, I suppose, Mrs. Helmer? It was your father himself who signed his name here?

Nora (after a short pause, throws her head up and looks defiantly at him). No, it was not. It was I that wrote papa's name.

Krogstad. Are you aware that is a dangerous confession?

Nora. In what way? You shall have your money soon.

Krogstad. Let me ask you a question; why did you not send the paper to your father?

Nora. It was impossible; papa was so ill. If I had asked him for his signature, I should have had to tell him what the money was to be used for; and when he was so ill himself I couldn't tell him that my husband's life was in danger—it was impossible.

Krogstad. It would have been better for you if you had given up your trip abroad.

Nora. No, that was impossible. That trip was to save my husband's life; I couldn't give that up.

Krogstad. But did it never occur to you that you were committing a fraud on me?

Nora. I couldn't take that into account; I didn't trouble myself about you at all. I couldn't bear you, because you put so many heartless difficulties in my way, although you knew what a dangerous condition my husband was in.

Krogstad. Mrs. Helmer, you evidently do not realise clearly what it is that you have been guilty of. But I can assure you that my one false step, which lost me all my reputation, was nothing more or nothing worse than what you have done.

Nora. You? Do you ask me to believe that you were brave enough to run a risk to save your wife's life.

Krogstad. The law cares nothing about motives.

Nora. Then it must be a very foolish law.

Krogstad. Foolish or not, it is the law by which you will be judged, if I produce this paper in court.

Nora. I don't believe it. Is a daughter not to be allowed to spare her dying father anxiety and care? Is a wife not to be allowed to save her husband's life? I don't know much about law; but I am certain that there must be laws permitting such things as that. Have you no knowledge of such laws—you who are a lawyer? You must be a very poor lawyer, Mr. Krogstad.

Krogstad. Maybe. But matters of business—such business as you and I have had together—do you think I don't understand that? Very well. Do as you please. But let me tell you this—if I lose my position a second time, you shall lose yours with me.

[*He bows, and goes out through the hall.*

Nora (appears buried in thought for a short time, then tosses her head). Nonsense! Trying to frighten me like that!—I am not so silly as he thinks. *(Begins to busy herself putting the children's things in order.)* And yet——? No, it's impossible! I did it for love's sake.

The Children (in the doorway on the left). Mother, the stranger man has gone out through the gate.

Nora. Yes, dears, I know. But, don't tell anyone about the stranger man. Do you hear? Not even papa.

Children. No, mother; but will you come and play again?

Nora. No, no,—not now.

Children. But, mother, you promised us.

Nora. Yes, but I can't now. Run away in; I have such a lot to do. Run away in, my sweet little darlings. *(She gets them into the room by degrees and shuts the door on them; then sits down on the sofa, takes up a piece of needlework and sews a few stitches, but soon stops.)* No! *(Throws down the work, gets up, goes to the hall door and calls out.)* Helen! bring the Tree in. *(Goes to the table on the left, opens a drawer, and stops again.)* No, no! it is quite impossible!

Maid (coming in with the Tree). Where shall I put it, ma'am?

Nora. Here, in the middle of the floor.

Maid. Shall I get you anything else?

Nora. No, thank you. I have all I want. [*Exit* MAID.

Nora (begins dressing the tree). A candle here—and flowers here——. The horrible man! It's all nonsense—there's nothing wrong. The Tree shall be splendid! I will do everything I can think of to please you, Torvald!—I will sing for you, dance for you—*(*HELMER *comes in with some papers under his arm.)* Oh! are you back already?

Helmer. Yes. Has anyone been here?

Nora. Here? No.

Helmer. That is strange. I saw Krogstad going out of the gate.

Nora. Did you? Oh yes, I forgot, Krogstad was here for a moment.

Helmer. Nora, I can see from your manner that he has been here begging you to say a good word for him.

Nora. Yes.

Helmer. And you were to appear to do it of your own accord; you were to conceal from me the fact of his having been here; didn't he beg that of you too?

Nora. Yes, Torvald, but——

Helmer. Nora, Nora, and you would be a party to that sort of thing? To have any talk with a man like that, and give him any sort of promise? And to tell me a lie into the bargain?

Nora. A lie——?

Helmer. Didn't you tell me no one had been here? *(Shakes his finger at her.)* My little song-bird must never do that again. A song-bird must have a clean beak to chirp with—no false notes! *(Puts his arm round her waist.)* That is so, isn't it? Yes, I am sure it is. *(Lets her go.)* We will say no more about it. *(Sits down by the stove.)* How warm and snug it is here!

[*Turns over his papers.*

Nora (after a short pause, during which she busies herself with the Christmas Tree). Torvald!

Helmer. Yes.

Nora. I am looking forward tremendously to the fancy dress ball at the Stenborgs' the day after to-morrow.

Helmer. And I am tremendously curious to see what you are going to surprise me with.

Nora. It was very silly of me to want to do that.

Helmer. What do you mean?

Nora. I can't hit upon anything that will do; everything I think of seems so silly and insignificant.

Helmer. Does my little Nora acknowledge that at last?

Nora (standing behind his chair with her arms on the back of it). Are you very busy, Torvald?

Helmer. Well——

Nora. What are all those papers?

Helmer. Bank business.

Nora. Already?

Helmer. I have got authority from the retiring manager to undertake the necessary changes in the staff and in the rearrangement of the work; and I must make use of the Christmas week for that, so as to have everything in order for the new year.

Nora. Then that was why this poor Krogstad——

Helmer. Hm!

Nora (leans against the back of his chair and strokes his hair). If you hadn't been so busy I should have asked you a tremendously big favour, Torvald.

Helmer. What is that? Tell me.

Nora. There is no one has such good taste as you. And I do so want to look nice at the fancy-dress ball. Torvald couldn't you take me in hand and decide what I shall go as, and what sort of a dress I shall wear?

Helmer. Aha! so my obstinate little woman is obliged to get someone to come to her rescue?

Nora. Yes, Torvald, I can't get along a bit without your help.

Helmer. Very well, I will think it over, we shall manage to hit upon something.

Nora. That *is* nice of you. *(Goes to the Christmas Tree. A short pause.)* How pretty the red flowers look ——. But, tell me, was it really something very bad that this Krogstad was guilty of?

Helmer. He forged someone's name. Have you any idea what that means?

Nora. Isn't it possible that he was driven to do it by necessity?

Helmer. Yes; or, as in so many cases, by imprudence. I am not so heartless as to condemn a man altogether because of a single false step of that kind.

Nora. No you wouldn't, would you, Torvald?

Helmer. Many a man has been able to retrieve his character, if he has openly confessed his fault and taken his punishment.

Nora. Punishment——?

Helmer. But Krogstad did nothing of that sort; he got himself out of it by a cunning trick, and that is why he has gone under altogether.

Nora. But do you think it would——?

Helmer. Just think how a guilty man like that has to lie and play the hypocrite with everyone, how he has to wear a mask in the presence of those near and dear to him, even before his own wife and children. And about the children—that is the most terrible part of it all, Nora.

Nora. How?

Helmer. Because such an atmosphere of lies infects and poisons the whole life of a home. Each breath the children take in such a house is full of the germs of evil.

Nora (coming nearer him). Are you sure of that?

Helmer. My dear, I have often seen it in the course of my life as a lawyer. Almost everyone who has gone to the bad early in life has had a deceitful mother.

Nora. Why do you only say—mother?

Helmer. It seems most commonly to be the mother's influence, though naturally a bad father's would have the same result. Every lawyer is familiar with the fact. This Krogstad, now, has been persistently poisoning his own children with lies and dissimulation; that is why I say he has lost all moral character. *(Holds out his hands to her.)* That is why my sweet little Nora must promise me not to plead his cause. Give me your hand on it. Come, come, what is this? Give me your hand. There now, that's settled. I assure you it would be quite impossible for me to work with him; I literally feel physically ill when I am in the company of such people.

Nora (takes her hand out of his and goes to the opposite side of the Christmas Tree). How hot it is in here; and I have such a lot to do.

Helmer (getting up and putting his papers in order). Yes, and I must try and read through some of these before dinner; and I must think about your costume, too. And it is just possible I may have something ready in gold paper to hang up on the Tree. *(Puts his hand on her head.)* My precious little singing-bird!

[*He goes into his room and shuts the door after him.*

Nora (after a pause, whispers). No, no—it isn't true It's impossible; it must be impossible.

[*The* NURSE *opens the door on the left.*

Nurse. The little ones are begging so hard to be allowed to come in to mamma.

Nora. No, no, no! Don't let them come in to me! You stay with them, Anne.

Nurse. Very well, ma'am. [*Shuts the door.*

Nora (pale with terror). Deprave my little children? Poison my home? *(A short pause. Then she tosses her head.)* It's not true. It can't possibly be true.

ACT II

THE SAME SCENE.—*The Christmas Tree is in the corner by the piano, stripped of its ornaments and with burnt-down candle-ends on its dishevelled branches.* NORA'S *cloak and hat are lying on the sofa. She is alone in the room, walking about uneasily. She stops by the sofa and takes up her cloak.*

Nora (drops the cloak). Someone is coming now! *(Goes to the door and listens.)* No—it is no one. Of course, no one will come to-day, Christmas Day—nor to-morrow either. But, perhaps—*(opens the door and looks out).* No, nothing in the letter-box; it is quite empty. *(Comes forward.)* What rubbish! of course he can't be in earnest about it. Such a thing couldn't happen; it is impossible—I have three little children.

[*Enter the* NURSE *from the room on the left, carrying a big cardboard box.*

Nurse. At last I have found the box with the fancy dress.

Nora. Thanks; put it on the table.

Nurse (doing so). But it is very much in want of mending.

Nora. I should like to tear it into a hundred thousand pieces.

Nurse. What an idea! It can easily be put in order—just a little patience.

Nora. Yes, I will go and get Mrs. Linde to come and help me with it.

Nurse. What, out again? In this horrible weather? You will catch cold, ma'am, and make yourself ill.

Nora. Well, worse than that might happen. How are the children?

Nurse. The poor little souls are playing with their Christmas presents, but——

Nora. Do they ask much for me?

Nurse. You see, they are so accustomed to have their mamma with them.

Nora. Yes, but, nurse, I shall not be able to be so much with them now as I was before.

Nurse. Oh well, young children easily get accustomed to anything.

Nora. Do you think so? Do you think they would forget their mother if she went away altogether?

Nurse. Good heavens!—went away altogether?

Nora. Nurse, I want you to tell me something I have often wondered about—how could you have the heart to put your own child out among strangers?

Nurse. I was obliged to, if I wanted to be little Nora's nurse.

Nora. Yes, but how could you be willing to do it?

Nurse. What, when I was going to get such a good place by it? A poor girl who has got into trouble should be glad to. Besides, that wicked man didn't do a single thing for me.

Nora. But I suppose your daughter has quite forgotten you.

Nurse. No, indeed she hasn't. She wrote to me when she was confirmed, and when she was married.

Nora (putting her arms round her neck). Dear old Anne, you were a good mother to me when I was little.

Nurse. Little Nora, poor dear, had no other mother but me.

Nora. And if my little ones had no other mother, I am sure you would—— What nonsense I am talking! *(Opens the box.)* Go in to them. Now I must——. You will see to-morrow how charming I shall look.

Nurse. I am sure there will be no one at the ball so charming as you, ma'am.

[*Goes into the room on the left.*

Nora (begins to unpack the box, but soon pushes it away from her). If only I dared go out. If only no one would come. If only I could be sure nothing would happen here in the meantime. Stuff and nonsense! No one will come. Only I mustn't think about it. I will brush my muff. What lovely, lovely gloves! Out of my thoughts, out of my thoughts! One, two, three, four, five, six—— *(Screams.)* Ah! there is someone coming——.

[*Makes a movement towards the door, but stands irresolute.*

[*Enter* Mrs. Linde *from the hall, where she has taken off her cloak and hat.*

Nora. Oh, it's you, Christine. There is no one else out there, is there? How good of you to come!

Mrs. Linde. I heard you were up asking for me.

Nora. Yes, I was passing by. As a matter of fact, it is something you could help me with. Let us sit down here on the sofa. Look here. To-morrow evening there is to be a fancy-dress ball at the Stenborgs', who live above us; and Torvald wants me to go as a Neapolitan fisher-girl, and dance the Tarantella that I learnt at Capri.

Mrs. Linde. I see; you are going to keep up the character.

Nora. Yes, Torvald wants me to. Look, here is the dress; Torvald had it made for me there, but now it is all so torn, and I haven't any idea——

Mrs. Linde. We will easily put that right. It is only some of the trimming come unsewn here and there. Needle and thread? Now then, that's all we want.

Nora. It *is* nice of you.

Mrs. Linde (sewing). So you are going to be dressed up to-morrow, Nora. I will tell you what—I shall come in for a moment and see you in your fine feathers. But I have completely forgotten to thank you for a delightful evening yesterday.

Nora (gets up, and crosses the stage). Well I don't think yesterday was as pleasant as usual. You ought to have come to town a little earlier, Christine. Certainly Torvald does understand how to make a house dainty and attractive.

Mrs. Linde. And so do you, it seems to me; you are not your father's daughter for nothing. But tell me, is Doctor Rank always as depressed as he was yesterday?

Nora. No; yesterday it was very noticeable. I must tell you that he suffers from a very dangerous disease. He has consumption of the spine, poor creature. His father was a horrible man who committed all sorts of excesses; and that is why his son was sickly from childhood, do you understand?

Mrs. Linde (dropping her sewing). But, my dearest Nora, how do you know anything about such things?

Nora (walking about). Pooh! When you have three children, you get visits now and then from—from married women, who know something of medical matters, and they talk about one thing and another.

Mrs. Linde (goes on sewing. A short silence). Does Doctor Rank come here every day?

Nora. Every day regularly. He is Torvald's most intimate friend, and a great friend of mine too. He is just like one of the family.

Mrs. Linde. But tell me this—is he perfectly sincere? I mean, isn't he the kind of man that is very anxious to make himself agreeable?

Nora. Not in the least. What makes you think that?

Mrs. Linde. When you introduced him to me yesterday, he declared he had often heard my name mentioned in this house; but afterwards I noticed that your husband hadn't the slightest idea who I was. So how could Doctor Rank ——?

Nora. That is quite right, Christine. Torvald is so absurdly fond of me that he wants me absolutely to himself, as he says. At first he used to seem almost jealous if I mentioned any of the dear folk at home, so naturally I gave up doing so. But I often talk about such things with Doctor Rank, because he likes hearing about them.

Mrs. Linde. Listen to me, Nora. You are still very like a child in many things, and I am older than you in many ways and have a little more experience. Let me tell you this—you ought to make an end of it with Doctor Rank.

Nora. What ought I to make an end of?

Mrs. Linde. Of two things, I think. Yesterday you talked some nonsense about a rich admirer who was to leave you money——

Nora. An admirer who doesn't exist, unfortunately! But what then?

Mrs. Linde. Is Doctor Rank a man of means?

Nora. Yes, he is.

Mrs. Linde. And has no one to provide for?

Nora. No, no one; but——

Mrs. Linde. And comes here every day?

Nora. Yes, I told you so.

Mrs. Linde. But how can this well-bred man be so tactless?

Nora. I don't understand you at all.

Mrs. Linde. Don't prevaricate, Nora. Do you suppose I don't guess who lent you the two hundred and fifty pounds?

Nora. Are you out of your senses? How can you think of such a thing! A friend of ours, who comes here every day! Do you realise what a horribly painful position that would be?

Mrs. Linde. Then it really isn't he?

Nora. No, certainly not. It would never have entered into my head for a moment. Besides, he had no money to lend then; he came into his money afterwards.

Mrs. Linde. Well, I think that was lucky for you, my dear Nora.

Nora. No, it would never have come into my head to ask Doctor Rank. Although I am quite sure that if I had asked him——

Mrs. Linde. But of course you won't.

Nora. Of course not. I have no reason to think it could possibly be necessary. But I am quite sure that if I told Doctor Rank——

Mrs. Linde. Behind your husband's back?

Nora. I must make an end of it with the other one, and that will be behind his back too. I *must* make an end of it with him.

Mrs. Linde. Yes, that is what I told you yesterday, but——

Nora (walking up and down). A man can put a thing like that straight much easier than a woman——

Mrs. Linde. One's husband, yes.

Nora. Nonsense! *(Standing still.)* When you pay off a debt you get your bond back, don't you?

Mrs. Linde. Yes, as a matter of course.

Nora. And can tear it into a hundred thousand pieces, and burn it up—the nasty dirty paper!

Mrs. Linde (looks hard at her, lays down her sewing and gets up slowly). Nora, you are concealing something from me.

Nora. Do I look as if I were?

Mrs. Linde. Something has happened to you since yesterday morning. Nora, what is it?

Nora (going nearer to her). Christine! *(Listens.)* Hush! there's Torvald come home. Do you mind going in to the children for the present? Torvald can't bear to see dressmaking going on. Let Anne help you.

Mrs. Linde (gathering some of the things together). Certainly—but I am not going away from here till we have had it out with one another.

[*She goes into the room on the left, as* HELMER *comes in from the hall.*

Nora (going up to HELMER*).* I have wanted you so much, Torvald dear.

Helmer. Was that the dressmaker?

Nora. No, it was Christine; she is helping me to put my dress in order. You will see I shall look quite smart.

Helmer. Wasn't that a happy thought of mine, now?

Nora. Splendid! But don't you think it is nice of me, too, to do as you wish?

Helmer. Nice?—because you do as your husband wishes? Well, well, you little rogue, I am sure you did not mean it in that way. But I am not going to disturb you; you will want to be trying on your dress, I expect.

Nora. I suppose you are going to work.

Helmer. Yes. *(Shows her a bundle of papers.)* Look at that. I have just been into the bank.

[*Turns to go into his room.*

Nora. Torvald.

Helmer. Yes.

Nora. If your little squirrel were to ask you for something very, very prettily——?

Helmer. What then?

Nora. Would you do it?

Helmer. I should like to hear what it is, first.

Nora. Your squirrel would run about and do all her tricks if you would be nice, and do what she wants.

Helmer. Speak plainly.

Nora. Your skylark would chirp about in every room, with her song rising and falling——

Helmer. Well, my skylark does that anyhow.

Nora. I would play the fairy and dance for you in the moonlight, Torvald.

Helmer. Nora—you surely don't mean that request you made of me this morning?

Nora (going near him). Yes, Torvald, I beg you so earnestly——

Helmer. Have you really the courage to open up that question again?

Nora. Yes, dear, you *must* do as I ask; you *must* let Krogstad keep his post in the Bank.

Helmer. My dear Nora, it is his post that I have arranged Mrs. Linde shall have.

Nora. Yes, you have been awfully kind about that; but you could just as well dismiss some other clerk instead of Krogstad.

Helmer. This is simply incredible obstinacy! Because you chose to give him a thoughtless promise that you would speak for him, I am expected to——

Nora. That isn't the reason, Torvald. It is for your own sake. This fellow writes in the most scurrilous newspapers; you have told me so yourself. He can do you an unspeakable amount of harm. I am frightened to death of him——

Helmer. Ah, I understand; it is recollections of the past that scare you.

Nora. What do you mean?

Helmer. Naturally you are thinking of your father.

Nora. Yes—yes, of course. Just recall to your mind what these malicious creatures wrote in the papers about papa, and how horribly they slandered him. I believe they would have procured his dismissal if the Department had not sent you over to inquire into it, and if you had not been so kindly disposed and helpful to him.

Helmer. My little Nora, there is an important difference between your father and me. Your father's reputation as a public official was not above suspicion. Mine is, and I hope it will continue to be so, as long as I hold my office.

Nora. You never can tell what mischief these men may contrive. We ought to be so well off, so snug and happy here in our peaceful home, and have no cares—you and I and the children, Torvald! That is why I beg you so earnestly——

Helmer. And it is just by interceding for him that you make it impossible for me to keep him. It is already known at the Bank that I mean to dismiss Krogstad. Is it to get about now that the new manager has changed his mind at his wife's bidding——

Nora. And what if it did?

Helmer. Of course!—if only this obstinate little person can get her way! Do you suppose I am going to make myself ridiculous before my whole staff, to let people think that I am a man to be swayed by all sorts of outside influence? I should very soon feel the consequences of it, I can tell you! And besides, there is one thing that makes it quite impossible for me to have Krogstad in the Bank as long as I am manager.

Nora. Whatever is that?

Helmer. His moral failings I might perhaps have overlooked, if necessary——

Nora. Yes, you could—couldn't you?

Helmer. And I hear he is a good worker, too. But I knew him when we were boys. It was one of those rash friendships that so often prove an incubus in after life. I may as well tell you plainly, we were once on very intimate terms with one another. But this tactless fellow lays no restraint on himself when other people are present. On the contrary, he thinks it gives him the right to adopt a familiar tone with me, and every minute it is "I say, Helmer, old fellow!" and that sort of thing. I assure you it is extremely painful for me. He would make my position in the Bank intolerable.

Nora. Torvald, I don't believe you mean that.

Helmer. Don't you? Why not?

Nora. Because it is such a narrow-minded way of looking at things.

Helmer. What are you saying? Narrow-minded? Do you think I am narrow-minded?

Nora. No, just the opposite, dear—and it is exactly for that reason.

Helmer. It's the same thing. You say my point of view is narrow-minded, so I must be so too. Narrow-minded! Very well—I must put an end to this. *(Goes to the hall-door and calls.)* Helen!

Nora. What are you going to do?

Helmer (looking among his papers). Settle it. *(Enter* MAID.*)* Look here; take this letter and go downstairs with it at once. Find a messenger and tell him to deliver it, and be quick. The address is on it, and here is the money.

Maid. Very well, sir. [*Exit with the letter*

Helmer (putting his papers together). Now then, little Miss Obstinate.

Nora (breathlessly). Torvald—what was that letter?

Helmer. Krogstad's dismissal.

Nora. Call her back, Torvald! There is still time. Oh Torvald, call her back! Do it for my sake—for your own sake—for the children's sake! Do you hear me, Torvald? Call her back! You don't know what that letter can bring upon us.

Helmer. It's too late.

Nora. Yes, it's too late.

Helmer. My dear Nora, I can forgive the anxiety you are in, although really it is an insult to me. It is, indeed Isn't it an insult to think that I should be afraid of a starving quill-driver's vengeance? But I forgive you nevertheless, because it is such eloquent witness to your great love for me. *(Takes her in his arms.)* And that is as it should be, my own darling Nora. Come what will, you may be sure I shall have both courage and strength if they be needed. You will see I am man enough to take everything upon myself.

Nora (in a horror-stricken voice). What do you mean by that?

Helmer. Everything, I say——

Nora (recovering herself). You will never have to do that.

Helmer. That's right. Well, we will share it, Nora, as man and wife should. That is how it shall be. *(Caressing her.)* Are you content now? There! there!—not these frightened dove's eyes! The whole thing is only the wildest fancy!—Now, you must go and play through the Tarantella and practise with your tambourine. I shall go into the inner office and shut the door, and I shall hear nothing; you can make as much noise as you please. *(Turns back at the door.)* And when Rank comes, tell him where he will find me.

[*Nods to her, takes his papers and goes into his room, and shuts the door after him.*

Nora (bewildered with anxiety, stands as if rooted to the spot, and whispers). He was capable of doing it. He will do it. He will do it in spite of everything.—No, not that! Never, never! Anything rather than that! Oh, for some help, some way out of it! *(The door-bell rings.)* Doctor Rank! Anything rather than that—anything, whatever it is!

[*She puts her hands over her face, pulls herself together, goes to the door and opens it.* RANK *is standing without, hanging up his coat. During the following dialogue it begins to grow dark.*

Nora. Good-day, Doctor Rank. I knew your ring. But you mustn't go into Torvald now; I think he is busy with something.

Rank. And you?

Nora (brings him in and shuts the door after him). Oh, you know very well I always have time for you.

Rank. Thank you. I shall make use of as much of it as I can.

Nora. What do you mean by that? As much of it as you can?

Rank. Well, does that alarm you?

Nora. It was such a strange way of putting it. Is anything likely to happen?

Rank. Nothing but what I have long been prepared for. But I certainly didn't expect it to happen so soon.

Nora (gripping him by the arm). What have you found out? Doctor Rank, you must tell me.

Rank (sitting down by the stove). It is all up with me. And it can't be helped.

Nora (with a sigh of relief). Is it about yourself?

Rank. Who else? It is no use lying to one's self. I am the most wretched of all my patients, Mrs. Helmer. Lately I have been taking stock of my internal economy. Bankrupt! Probably within a month I shall lie rotting in the churchyard.

Nora. What an ugly thing to say!

Rank. The thing itself is cursedly ugly, and the worst of it is that I shall have to face so much more that is ugly before that. I shall only make one more examination of myself; when I have done that, I shall know pretty certainly when it will be that the horrors of dissolution will begin. There is something I want to tell you. Helmer's refined nature gives him an unconquerable disgust at everything that is ugly; I won't have him in my sick-room.

Nora. Oh, but, Doctor Rank——

Rank. I won't have him there. Not on any account. I bar my door to him. As soon as I am quite certain that the worst has come, I shall send you my card with a black cross on it, and then you will know that the loathsome end has begun.

Nora. You are quite absurd to-day. And I wanted you so much to be in a really good humour.

Rank. With death stalking beside me?—To have to pay this penalty for another man's sin! Is there any justice in that? And in every single family, in one way or another, some such inexorable retribution is being exacted——

Nora (putting her hands over her ears). Rubbish! Do talk of something cheerful.

Rank. Oh, it's a mere laughing matter, the whole thing. My poor innocent spine has to suffer for my father's youthful amusements.

Nora (sitting at the table on the left). I suppose you mean that he was too partial to asparagus and pâté de foie gras, don't you.

Rank. Yes, and to truffles.

Nora. Truffles, yes. And oysters too, I suppose?

Rank. Oysters, of course, that goes without saying.

Nora. And heaps of port and champagne. It is sad that all these nice things should take their revenge on our bones.

Rank. Especially that they should revenge themselves on the unlucky bones of those who have not had the satisfaction of enjoying them.

Nora. Yes, that's the saddest part of it all.

Rank (with a searching look at her). Hm!——

Nora (after a short pause). Why did you smile?

Rank. No, it was you that laughed.

Nora. No, it was you that smiled, Doctor Rank!

Rank (rising). You are a greater rascal than I thought.

Nora. I am in a silly mood to-day.

Rank. So it seems.

Nora (putting her hands on his shoulders). Dear, dear Doctor Rank, death mustn't take you away from Torvald and me.

Rank. It is a loss you would easily recover from. Those who are gone are soon forgotten.

Nora (looking at him anxiously). Do you believe that?

Rank. People form new ties, and then——

Nora. Who will form new ties?

Rank. Both you and Helmer, when I am gone. You

yourself are already on the high road to it, I think. What did that Mrs. Linde want here last night?

Nora. Oho!—you don't mean to say you are jealous of poor Christine?

Rank. Yes, I am. She will be my successor in this house. When I am done for, this woman will—

Nora. Hush! don't speak so loud. She is in that room.

Rank. To-day again. There, you see.

Nora. She has only come to sew my dress for me. Bless my soul, how unreasonable you are! (*Sits down on the sofa.*) Be nice now, Doctor Rank, and to-morrow you will see how beautifully I shall dance, and you can imagine I am doing it all for you—and for Torvald too, of course. *(Takes various things out of the box.)* Doctor Rank, come and sit down here, and I will show you something.

Rank (sitting down). What is it?

Nora. Just look at those!

Rank. Silk stockings.

Nora. Flesh-coloured. Aren't they lovely? It is so dark here now, but to-morrow—. No, no, no! you must only look at the feet. Oh well, you may have leave to look at the legs too.

Rank. Hm!—

Nora. Why are you looking so critical? Don't you think they will fit me?

Rank. I have no means of forming an opinion about that.

Nora (looks at him for a moment). For shame! *(Hits him lightly on the ear with the stockings.)* That's to punish you. *(Folds them up again.)*

Rank. And what other nice things am I to be allowed to see?

Nora. Not a single thing more, for being so naughty. *(She looks among the things, humming to herself.)*

Rank (after a short silence). When I am sitting here,

talking to you as intimately as this, I cannot imagine for a moment what would have become of me if I had never come into this house.

Nora (smiling). I believe you do feel thoroughly at home with us.

Rank (in a lower voice, looking straight in front of him). And to be obliged to leave it all——

Nora. Nonsense, you are not going to leave it.

Rank (as before). And not be able to leave behind one the slightest token of one's gratitude, scarcely even a fleeting regret—nothing but an empty place which the first comer can fill as well as any other.

Nora. And if I asked you now for a—? No!

Rank. For what?

Nora. For a big proof of your friendship——

Rank. Yes, yes!

Nora. I mean a tremendously big favour——

Rank. Would you really make me so happy for once?

Nora. Ah, but you don't know what it is yet.

Rank. No—but tell me.

Nora. I really can't, Doctor Rank. It is something out of all reason; it means advice, and help, and a favour——

Rank. The bigger a thing it is the better. I can't conceive what it is you mean. Do tell me. Haven't I your confidence?

Nora. More than anyone else. I know you are my truest and best friend, and so I will tell you what it is. Well, Doctor Rank, it is something you must help me to prevent. You know how devotedly, how inexpressibly deeply Torvald loves me; he would never for a moment hesitate to give his life for me.

Rank (leaning towards her). Nora—do you think he is the only one——?

Nora (with a slight start). The only one—?

Rank. The only one who would gladly give his life for your sake.

Nora (sadly). Is that it?

Rank. I was determined you should know it before I went away, and there will never be a better opportunity than this. Now you know it, Nora. And now you know, too, that you can trust me as you would trust no one else.

Nora (rises, deliberately and quietly). Let me pass.

Rank (makes room for her to pass him, but sits still) Nora!

Nora (at the hall door). Helen, bring in the lamp. *(Goes over to the stove.)* Dear Doctor Rank, that was really horrid of you.

Rank. To have loved you as much as anyone else does? Was that horrid?

Nora. No, but to go and tell me so. There was really no need——

Rank. What do you mean? Did you know—? *(*MAID *enters with lamp, puts it down on the table, and goes out.)* Nora—Mrs. Helmer—tell me, had you any idea of this?

Nora. Oh, how do I know whether I had or whether I hadn't? I really can't tell you— To think you could be so clumsy, Doctor Rank! We were getting on so nicely.

Rank. Well, at all events you know now that you can command me, body and soul. So won't you speak out?

Nora (looking at him). After what happened?

Rank. I beg you to let me know what it is.

Nora. I can't tell you anything now.

Rank. Yes, yes. You mustn't punish me in that way. Let me have permission to do for you whatever a man may do.

Nora. You can do nothing for me now. Besides, I really don't need any help at all. You will find that the whole thing is merely fancy on my part. It really is so—of course it is! *(Sits down in the rocking-chair, and looks at him with a smile.)* You are a nice sort of man, Doctor Rank!—don't you feel ashamed of yourself, now the lamp has come?

Rank. Not a bit. But perhaps I had better go—for ever?

Nora. No, indeed, you shall not. Of course you must come here just as before. You know very well Torvald can't do without you.

Rank. Yes, but you?

Nora. Oh, I am always tremendously pleased when you come.

Rank. It is just that, that put me on the wrong track. You are a riddle to me. I have often thought that you would almost as soon be in my company as in Helmer's.

Nora. Yes—you see there are some people one loves best, and others whom one would almost always rather have as companions.

Rank. Yes, there is something in that.

Nora. When I was at home, of course I loved papa best. But I always thought it tremendous fun if I could steal down into the maid's room, because they never moralised at all, and talked to each other about such entertaining things.

Rank. I see—it is *their* place I have taken.

Nora (jumping up and going to him). Oh, dear, nice Doctor Rank, I never meant that at all. But surely you can understand that being with Torvald is a little like being with papa——

[*Enter* MAID *from the hall.*

Maid. If you please, ma'am. *(Whispers and hands her a card.)*

Nora (glancing at the card). Oh! *(Puts it in her pocket.)*

Rank. Is there anything wrong?

Nora. No, no, not in the least. It is only something—it is my new dress——

Rank. What? Your dress is lying there.

Nora. Oh, yes, that one; but this is another. I ordered it Torvald mustn't know about it——

Rank. Oho! Then that was the great secret.

Nora. Of course. Just go in to him; he is sitting in the inner room. Keep him as long as——

Rank. Make your mind easy; I won't let him escape. *(Goes into* HELMER's *room.)*

Nora (to the MAID). And he is standing waiting in the kitchen?

Maid. Yes; he came up the back stairs.

Nora. But didn't you tell him no one was in?

Maid. Yes, but it was no good.

Nora. He won't go away?

Maid. No; he says he won't until he has seen you, ma'am.

Nora. Well, let him come in—but quietly. Helen, you mustn't say anything about it to anyone. It is a surprise for my husband.

Maid. Yes, ma'am, I quite understand. [*Exit.*

Nora. This dreadful thing is going to happen! It will happen in spite of me! No, no, no, it can't happen—it shan't happen!

[*She bolts the door of* HELMER'S *room. The* MAID *opens the hall door for* KROGSTAD *and shuts it after him. He is wearing a fur coat, high boots and a fur cap.*

Nora (advancing towards him.) Speak low—my husband is at home.

Krogstad. No matter about that.

Nora. What do you want of me?

Krogstad. An explanation of something.

Nora. Make haste then. What is it?

Krogstad. You know, I suppose, that I have got my dismissal.

Nora. I couldn't prevent it, Mr. Krogstad. I fought as hard as I could on your side, but it was no good.

Krogstad. Does your husband love you so little, then? He knows what I can expose you to, and yet he ventures——

Nora. How can you suppose that he has any knowledge of the sort?

Krogstad. I didn't suppose so at all. It would not be the least like our dear Torvald Helmer to show so much courage—

Nora. Mr. Krogstad, a little respect for my husband, please.

Krogstad. Certainly— all the respect he deserves. But since you have kept the matter so carefully to yourself, I make bold to suppose that you have a little clearer idea, than you had yesterday, of what it actually is that you have done?

Nora. More than you could ever teach me.

Krogstad. Yes, such a bad lawyer as I am.

Nora. What is it you want of me?

Krogstad. Only to see how you were, Mrs. Helmer. I have been thinking about you all day long. A mere cashier, a quill-driver, a—well, a man like me—even he has a little of what is called feeling, you know.

Nora. Show it, then; think of my little children.

Krogstad. Have you and your husband thought of mine? But never mind about that. I only wanted to tell you that you need not take this matter too seriously. In the first place there will be no accusation made on my part.

Nora. No, of course not; I was sure of that.

Krogstad. The whole thing can be arranged amicably; there is no reason why anyone should know anything about it. It will remain a secret between us three.

Nora. My husband must never get to know anything about it.

Krogstad. How will you be able to prevent it? Am I to understand that you can pay the balance that is owing?

Nora. No, not just at present.

Krogstad. Or perhaps that you have some expedient for raising the money soon?

Nora. No expedient that I mean to make use of.

Krogstad. Well, in any case, it would have been of no use to you now. If you stood there with ever so much money in your hand, I would never part with your bond.

Nora. Tell me what purpose you mean to put it to.

Krogstad. I shall only preserve it—keep it in my possession. No one who is not concerned in the matter shall have the slightest hint of it. So that if the thought of it has driven you to any desperate resolution——

Nora. It has.

Krogstad. If you had it in your mind to run away from your home——

Nora. I had.

Krogstad. Or even something worse——

Nora. How could you know that?

Krogstad. Give up the idea.

Nora. How did you know I had thought of *that?*

Krogstad. Most of us think of that at first. I did, too—but I hadn't the courage.

Nora (faintly). No more had I.

Krogstad (in a tone of relief). No, that's it, isn't it—you hadn't the courage either?

Nora. No, I haven't—I haven't.

Krogstad. Besides, it would have been a great piece of folly. Once the first storm at home is over—. I have a letter for your husband in my pocket.

Nora. Telling him everything?

Krogstad. In as lenient a manner as I possibly could.

Nora (quickly). He mustn't get the letter. Tear it up. I will find some means of getting money.

Krogstad. Excuse me, Mrs. Helmer, but I think I told you just now——

Nora. I am not speaking of what I owe you. Tell me what sum you are asking my husband for, and I will get the money.

Krogstad. I am not asking your husband for a penny.

Nora. What do you want, then?

Krogstad. I will tell you. I want to rehabilitate myself, Mrs. Helmer; I want to get on; and in that your husband must help me. For the last year and a half I have not had a hand in anything dishonourable, and all that time I have been struggling in most restricted circumstances. I was content to work my way up step by step. Now I am turned out, and I am not going to be satisfied with merely being taken into favour again. I want to get on, I tell you. I want to get into the Bank again, in a higher position. Your husband must make a place for me——

Nora. That he will never do!

Krogstad. He will; I know him; he dare not protest. And as soon as I am in there again with him, then you will see! Within a year I shall be the manager's right hand. It will be Nils Krogstad and not Torvald Helmer who manages the Bank.

Nora. That's a thing you will never see!

Krogstad. Do you mean that you will——?

Nora. I have courage enough for it now.

Krogstad. Oh, you can't frighten me. A fine, spoilt lady like you——

Nora. You will see, you will see.

Krogstad. Under the ice, perhaps? Down into the cold, coal-black water? And then, in the spring, to float up to the surface, all horrible and unrecognisable, with your hair fallen out——

Nora. You can't frighten me.

Krogstad. Nor you me. People don't do such things, Mrs. Helmer. Besides, what use would it be? I should have him completely in my power all the same.

Nora. Afterwards? When I am no longer——

Krogstad. Have you forgotten that it is I who have the keeping of your reputation? *(Nora stands speechlessly looking at him.)* Well, now, I have warned you. Do not do anything foolish. When Helmer has had my letter, I shall expect a message from him. And be sure you remember that it is your husband himself who has forced me into such ways as this again. I will never forgive him for that. Good-bye, Mrs. Helmer. [*Exit through the hall.*

Nora (goes to the hall door, opens it slightly and listens). He is going. He is not putting the letter in the box. Oh no, no! that's impossible! *(Opens the door by degrees.)* What is that? He is standing outside. He is not going downstairs. Is he hesitating? Can he——

[*A letter drops into the box; then* KROGSTAD'S *footsteps are heard, till they die away as he goes downstairs.* NORA *utters a stifled cry and runs across the room to the table by the sofa. A short pause.*

Nora. In the letter-box. *(Steals across to the hall door.)* There it lies—Torvald, Torvald, there is no hope for us now!

[MRS. LINDE *comes in from the room on the left, carrying the dress.*

Mrs. Linde. There, I can't see anything more to mend now. Would you like to try it on——?

Nora (in a hoarse whisper). Christine, come here.

Mrs. Linde (throwing the dress down on the sofa). What is the matter with you? You look so agitated!

Nora. Come here. Do you see that letter? There, look—you can see it through the glass in the letter-box.

Mrs. Linde. Yes, I see it.

Nora. That letter is from Krogstad.

Mrs. Linde. Nora—it was Krogstad who lent you the money!

Nora. Yes, and now Torvald will know all about it.

Mrs. Linde. Believe me, Nora, that's the best thing for both of you.

Nora. You don't know all. I forged a name.

Mrs. Linde. Good heavens——!

Nora. I only want to say this to you, Christine—you must be my witness.

Mrs. Linde. Your witness? What do you mean? What am I to—?

Nora. If I should go out of my mind—and it might easily happen——

Mrs. Linde. Nora!

Nora. Or if anything else should happen to me—anything, for instance, that might prevent my being here—

Mrs. Linde. Nora! Nora! you are quite out of your mind.

Nora. And if it should happen that there were someone who wanted to take all the responsibility, all the blame, you understand——

Mrs. Linde. Yes, yes—but how can you suppose—?

Nora. Then you must be my witness, that it is not true, Christine. I am not out of my mind at all; I am in my right senses now, and I tell you no one else has known anything about it; I, and I alone, did the whole thing. Remember that.

Mrs. Linde. I will, indeed. But I don't understand all this.

Nora. How should you understand it? A wonderful thing is going to happen.

Mrs. Linde. A wonderful thing?

Nora. Yes, a wonderful thing!—But it is so terrible, Christine; it *mustn't* happen, not for all the world.

Mrs. Linde. I will go at once and see Krogstad.

Nora. Don't go to him; he will do you some harm.

Mrs. Linde. There was a time when he would gladly do anything for my sake.

Nora. He?

Mrs. Linde. Where does he live?

Nora. How should I know—? Yes *(feeling in her pocket.)* here is his card. But the letter, the letter——!

Helmer (calls from his room, knocking at the door). Nora!

Nora (cries out anxiously). Oh, what's that? What do you want?

Helmer. Don't be so frightened. We are not coming in; you have locked the door. Are you trying on your dress?

Nora. Yes, that's it. I look so nice, Torvald.

Mrs. Linde (who has read the card). I see he lives at the corner here.

Nora. Yes, but it's no use. It is hopeless. The letter is lying there in the box.

Mrs. Linde. And your husband keeps the key?

Nora. Yes, always.

Mrs. Linde. Krogstad must ask for his letter back unread, he must find some pretence——

Nora. But it is just at this time that Torvald generally——

Mrs. Linde. You must delay him. Go in to him in the meantime. I will come back as soon as I can.

[*She goes out hurriedly through the hall door.*

Nora (goes to HELMER's *door, opens it and peeps in).* Torvald!

Helmer (from the inner room). Well? May I venture at last to come into my own room again? Come along, Rank, now you will see— *(Halting in the doorway.)* But what is this?

Nora. What is what, dear?

Helmer. Rank led me to expect a splendid transformation.

Rank (in the doorway). I understood so, but evidently I was mistaken.

Nora. Yes, nobody is to have the chance of admiring me in my dress until to-morrow.

Helmer. But, my dear Nora, you look so worn out. Have you been practising too much?

Nora. No, I have not practised at all.

Helmer. But you will need to—

Nora. Yes, indeed I shall, Torvald. But I can't get on a bit without you to help me; I have absolutely forgotten the whole thing.

Helmer. Oh, we will soon work it up again.

Nora. Yes, help me, Torvald. Promise that you will! I am so nervous about it—all the people—. You must give yourself up to me entirely this evening. Not the tiniest bit of business—you mustn't even take a pen in your hand. Will you promise, Torvald dear?

Helmer. I promise. This evening I will be wholly and absolutely at your service, you helpless little mortal. Ah, by the way, first of all I will just——

[*Goes towards the hall door.*

Nora. What are you going to do there?

Helmer. Only see if any letters have come.

Nora. No, no! don't do that, Torvald!

Helmer. Why not?

Nora. Torvald, please don't. There is nothing there.

Helmer. Well, let me look. *(Turns to go to the letter-box.* NORA, *at the piano, plays the first bars of the Tarantella.* HELMER *stops in the doorway.)* Aha!

Nora. I can't dance to-morrow if I don't practise with you.

Helmer (going up to her). Are you really so afraid of it, dear.

Nora. Yes, so dreadfully afraid of it. Let me practise at once; there is time now, before we go to dinner. Sit down and play for me, Torvald dear; criticise me, and correct me as you play.

Helmer. With great pleasure, if you wish me to.

[*Sits down at the piano.*

Nora (takes out of the box a tambourine and a long variegated shawl. She hastily drapes the shawl round her. Then she springs to the front of the stage and calls out). Now play for me! I am going to dance!

[HELMER *plays and* NORA *dances.* RANK *stands by the piano behind* HELMER *and looks on.*

Helmer (as he plays). Slower, slower!

Nora. I can't do it any other way.

Helmer. Not so violently, Nora!

Nora. This is the way.

Helmer (stops playing). No, no—that is not a bit right.

Nora (laughing and swinging the tambourine). Didn't I tell you so?

Rank. Let me play for her.

Helmer (getting up). Yes, do. I can correct her better then.

[RANK *sits down at the piano and plays.* NORA *dances more and more wildly.* HELMER *has taken up a position beside the stove, and during her dance gives her frequent instructions. She does not seem to hear him; her hair comes down and falls over her shoulders; she pays no attention to it, but goes on dancing. Enter* MRS. LINDE.

Mrs. Linde (standing as if spell-bound in the doorway). Oh!——

Nora (as she dances). Such fun, Christine!

Helmer. My dear darling Nora, you are dancing as if your life depended on it.

Nora. So it does.

Helmer. Stop, Rank; this is sheer madness. Stop, I tell you! (RANK *stops playing, and* NORA *suddenly stands still.* HELMER *goes up to her.)* I could never have believed it. You have forgotten everything I taught you.

Nora (throwing away the tambourine). There, you see.

Helmer. You will want a lot of coaching.

Nora. Yes, you see how much I need it. You must coach me up to the last minute. Promise me that, Torvald!

Helmer. You can depend on me.

Nora. You must not think of anything but me, either

to-day or to-morrow; you mustn't open a single letter—not even open the letter-box——

Helmer. Ah, you are still afraid of that fellow——

Nora. Yes, indeed I am.

Helmer. Nora, I can tell from your looks that there is a letter from him lying there.

Nora. I don't know; I think there is; but you must not read anything of that kind now. Nothing horrid must come between us till this is all over.

Rank (whispers to HELMER*).* You mustn't contradict her.

Helmer (taking her in his arms). The child shall have her way. But to-morrow night, after you have danced——

Nora. Then you will be free.

[*The* MAID *appears in the doorway to the right.*

Maid. Dinner is served, ma'am.

Nora. We will have champagne, Helen.

Maid. Very good, ma'am. [*Exit.*

Helmer. Hullo!—are we going to have a banquet?

Nora. Yes, a champagne banquet till the small hours. *(Calls out.)* And a few macaroons, Helen—lots, just for once!

Helmer. Come, come, don't be so wild and nervous. Be my own little skylark, as you used.

Nora. Yes, dear, I will. But go in now and you too, Doctor Rank. Christine, you must help me to do up my hair.

Rank (whispers to HELMER *as they go out).* I suppose there is nothing—she is not expecting anything?

Helmer. Far from it, my dear fellow; it is simply nothing more than this childish nervousness I was telling you of.

[*They go into the right-hand room.*

Nora. Well!

Mrs. Linde. Gone out of town.

Nora. I could tell from your face.

Mrs. Linde. He is coming home to-morrow evening. I wrote a note for him

Nora. You should have let it alone; you must prevent nothing. After all, it is splendid to be waiting for a wonderful thing to happen.

Mrs. Linde. What is it that you are waiting for?

Nora. Oh, you wouldn't understand. Go in to them, I will come in a moment. (MRS. LINDE *goes into the dining-room.* NORA *stands still for a little while, as if to compose herself. Then she looks at her watch.)* Five o'clock. Seven hours till midnight; and then four-and-twenty hours till the next midnight. Then the Tarantella will be over. Twenty-four and seven? Thirty-one hours to live.

Helmer (from the doorway on the right). Where's my little skylark?

Nora (going to him with her arms outstretched). Here she is!

ACT III

THE SAME SCENE. *The table has been placed in the middle of the stage, with chairs round it. A lamp is burning on the table. The door into the hall stands open. Dance music is heard in the room above.* MRS. LINDE *is sitting at the table idly turning over the leaves of a book; she tries to read, but does not seem able to collect her thoughts. Every now and then she listens intently for a sound at the outer door.*

Mrs. Linde (looking at her watch). Not yet—and the time is nearly up. If only he does not—. *(Listens again.)* Ah, there he is. *(Goes into the hall and opens the outer door carefully. Light footsteps are heard on the stairs. She whispers.)* Come in. There is no one here.

Krogstad (in the doorway). I found a note from you at home. What does this mean?

Mrs. Linde. It is absolutely necessary that I should have a talk with you.

Krogstad. Really? And is it absolutely necessary that it should be here?

Mrs. Linde. It is impossible where I live; there is no private entrance to my rooms. Come in; we are quite alone. The maid is asleep, and the Helmers are at the dance upstairs.

Krogstad (coming into the room). Are the Helmers really at a dance to-night?

Mrs. Linde. Yes, why not?

Krogstad. Certainly—why not?

Mrs. Linde. Now, Nils, let us have a talk.

Krogstad. Can we two have anything to talk about?

Mrs. Linde. We have a great deal to talk about.

Krogstad. I shouldn't have thought so.

Mrs. Linde. No, you have never properly understood me.

Krogstad. Was there anything else to understand except what was obvious to all the world—a heartless woman jilts a man when a more lucrative chance turns up?

Mrs. Linde. Do you believe I am as absolutely heartless as all that? And do you believe that I did it with a light heart?

Krogstad. Didn't you?

Mrs. Linde. Nils, did you really think that?

Krogstad. If it were as you say, why did you write to me as you did at the time?

Mrs. Linde. I could do nothing else. As I had to break with you, it was my duty also to put an end to all that you felt for me.

Krogstad (wringing his hands). So that was it. And all this—only for the sake of money!

Mrs. Linde. You must not forget that I had a helpless mother and two little brothers. We couldn't wait for you, Nils; your prospects seemed hopeless then.

Krogstad. That may be so, but you had no right to throw me over for any one else's sake.

Mrs. Linde. Indeed I don't know. Many a time did I ask myself if I had the right to do it.

Krogstad (more gently). When I lost you, it was as if all the solid ground went from under my feet. Look at me now—I am a shipwrecked man clinging to a bit of wreckage.

Mrs. Linde. But help may be near.

Krogstad. It *was* near; but then you came and stood in my way.

Mrs. Linde. Unintentionally, Nils. It was only to-day that I learnt it was your place I was going to take in the Bank.

Krogstad. I believe you, if you say so. But now that you know it, are you not going to give it up to me?

Mrs. Linde. No, because that would not benefit you in the least.

Krogstad. Oh, benefit, benefit—I would have done it whether or no.

Mrs. Linde. I have learnt to act prudently. Life, and hard, bitter necessity have taught me that.

Krogstad. And life has taught me not to believe in fine speeches.

Mrs. Linde. Then life has taught you something very reasonable. But deeds you must believe in?

Krogstad. What do you mean by that?

Mrs. Linde. You said you were like a shipwrecked man clinging to some wreckage.

Krogstad. I had good reason to say so.

Mrs. Linde. Well, I am like a shipwrecked woman clinging to some wreckage—no one to mourn for, no one to care for.

Krogstad. It was your own choice.

Mrs. Linde. There was no other choice—then.

Krogstad. Well, what now?

Mrs. Linde. Nils, how would it be if we two shipwrecked people could join forces?

Krogstad. What are you saying?

Mrs. Linde. Two on the same piece of wreckage would stand a better chance than each on their own.

Krogstad. Christine!

Mrs. Linde. What do you suppose brought me to town?

Krogstad. Do you mean that you gave me a thought?

Mrs. Linde. I could not endure life without work. All my life, as long as I can remember, I have worked, and it has been my greatest and only pleasure. But now I am quite alone in the world—my life is so dreadfully empty and I feel so forsaken. There is not the least pleasure in working for one's self. Nils, give me someone and something to work for.

Krogstad. I don't trust that. It is nothing but a woman's overstrained sense of generosity that prompts you to make such an offer of yourself.

Mrs. Linde. Have you ever noticed anything of the sort in me?

Krogstad. Could you really do it? Tell me—do you know all about my past life?

Mrs. Linde. Yes.

Krogstad. And do you know what they think of me here?

Mrs. Linde. You seemed to me to imply that with me you might have been quite another man.

Krogstad. I am certain of it.

Mrs. Linde. Is it too late now?

Krogstad. Christine, are you saying this deliberately? Yes, I am sure you are. I see it in your face. Have you really the courage, then—?

Mrs. Linde. I want to be a mother to someone, and your children need a mother. We two need each other. Nils, I have faith in your real character—I can dare anything together with you.

Krogstad (grasps her hands). Thanks, thanks, Christine! Now I shall find a way to clear myself in the eyes of the world. Ah, but I forgot——

Mrs. Linde (listening). Hush! The Tarantella! Go, go!

Krogstad. Why? What is it?

Mrs. Linde. Do you hear them up there? When that is over, we may expect them back.

Krogstad. Yes, yes—I will go. But it is all no use. Of course you are not aware what steps I have taken in the matter of the Helmers.

Mrs. Linde. Yes, I know all about that.

Krogstad. And in spite of that have you the courage to—?

Mrs. Linde. I understand very well to what lengths a man like you might be driven by despair.

Krogstad. If I could only undo what I have done!

Mrs. Linde. You cannot. Your letter is lying in the letter-box now.

Krogstad. Are you sure of that?

Mrs. Linde. Quite sure, but——

Krogstad (with a searching look at her). Is that what it all means?—that you want to save your friend at any cost? Tell me frankly. Is that it?

Mrs. Linde. Nils, a woman who has once sold herself for another's sake, doesn't do it a second time.

Krogstad. I will ask for my letter back.

Mrs. Linde. No, no.

Krogstad. Yes, of course I will. I will wait here till Helmer comes; I will tell him he must give me my letter back—that it only concerns my dismissal—that he is not to read it——

Mrs. Linde. No, Nils, you must not recall your letter.

Krogstad. But, tell me, wasn't it for that very purpose that you asked me to meet you here?

Mrs. Linde. In my first moment of fright, it was. But twenty-four hours have elapsed since then, and in that time I have witnessed incredible things in this house. Helmer must know all about it. This unhappy secret must be disclosed; they must have a complete understanding between them, which is impossible with all this concealment and falsehood going on.

Krogstad. Very well, if you will take the responsibility. But there is one thing I can do in any case, and I shall do it at once.

Mrs. Linde (listening). You must be quick and go! The dance is over; we are not safe a moment longer.

Krogstad. I will wait for you below.

Mrs. Linde. Yes, do. You must see me back to my door.

Krogstad. I have never had such an amazing piece of good fortune in my life.

[*Goes out through the outer door. The door between the room and the hall remains open.*

Mrs. Linde (tidying up the room and laying her hat and cloak ready). What a difference! what a difference! Someone to work for and live for—a home to bring comfort into. That I will do, indeed. I wish they would be quick and come— *(Listens.)* Ah, there they are now. I must put on my things.

[*Takes up her hat and cloak.* HELMER'S *and* NORA'S *voices are heard outside; a key is turned, and* HELMER *brings* NORA *almost by force into the hall. She is in an Italian costume with a large black shawl round her; he is in evening dress and a black domino which is flying open.*

NORA *(hanging back in the doorway, and struggling with him).* No, no, no!—don't take me in. I want to go upstairs again; I don't want to leave so early.

Helmer. But, my dearest Nora——

Nora. Please, Torvald dear—please, *please*—only an hour more.

Helmer. Not a single minute, my sweet Nora. You know that was our agreement. Come along into the room; you are catching cold standing there.

[*He brings her gently into the room, in spite of her resistance.*

Mrs. Linde. Good evening.

Nora. Christine!

Helmer. You here, so late, Mrs. Linde?

Mrs. Linde. Yes, you must excuse me; I was so anxious to see Nora in her dress.

Nora. Have you been sitting here waiting for me?

Mrs. Linde. Yes, unfortunately I came too late, you

had already gone upstairs; and I thought I couldn't go away again without having seen you.

Helmer (taking off NORA's *shawl).* Yes, take a good look at her. I think she is worth looking at. Isn't she charming, Mrs. Linde?

Mrs. Linde. Yes, indeed she is.

Helmer. Doesn't she look remarkably pretty? Everyone thought so at the dance. But she is terribly self-willed, this sweet little person. What are we to do with her? You will hardly believe that I had almost to bring her away by force.

Nora. Torvald, you will repent not having let me stay, even if it were only for half an hour.

Helmer. Listen to her, Mrs. Linde! She had danced her Tarantella, and it had been a tremendous success, as it deserved—although possibly the performance was a trifle too realistic—a little more so, I mean, than was strictly compatible with the limitations of art. But never mind about that! The chief thing is, she had made a success—she had made a tremendous success. Do you think I was going to let her remain there after that, and spoil the effect? No indeed! I took my charming little Capri maiden—my capricious little Capri maiden, I should say—on my arm; took one quick turn round the room; a curtsey on either side, and, as they say in novels, the beautiful apparition disappeared. An exit ought always to be effective, Mrs. Linde; but that is what I cannot make Nora understand. Pooh! this room is hot. *(Throws his domino on a chair and opens the door of his room.)* Hullo! it's all dark in here. Oh, of course—excuse me——.

[*He goes in and lights some candles.*

Nora (in a hurried and breathless whisper). Well?

Mrs. Linde (in a low voice). I have had a talk with him.

Nora. Yes, and——

Mrs. Linde. Nora, you must tell your husband all about it.

Nora (in an expressionless voice). I knew it.

Mrs. Linde. You have nothing to be afraid of as far as Krogstad is concerned; but you must tell him.

Nora. I won't tell him.

Mrs. Linde. Then the letter will.

Nora. Thank you, Christine. Now I know what I must do. Hush——!

Helmer (coming in again). Well, Mrs. Linde, have you admired her?

Mrs. Linde. Yes, and now I will say good-night.

Helmer. What, already? Is this yours, this knitting?

Mrs. Linde (taking it). Yes, thank you, I had very nearly forgotten it.

Helmer. So you knit?

Mrs. Linde. Of course.

Helmer. Do you know, you ought to embroider.

Mrs. Linde. Really? Why?

Helmer. Yes, it's far more becoming. Let me show you. You hold the embroidery thus in your left hand, and use the needle with the right—like this—with a long, easy sweep. Do you see?

Mrs. Linde. Yes, perhaps——

Helmer. But in the case of knitting—that can never be anything but ungraceful; look here—the arms close together, the knitting-needles going up and down—it has a sort of Chinese effect—. That was really excellent champagne they gave us.

Mrs. Linde. Well,—good-night, Nora, and don't be self-willed any more.

Helmer. That's right, Mrs. Linde.

Mrs. Linde. Good-night, Mr. Helmer.

Helmer (accompanying her to the door). Good-night, good-night. I hope you will get home all right. I should be very happy to—but you haven't any great distance to go. Good-night, good-night. *(She goes out; he shuts the door after her, and comes in again.)* Ah!—at last we have got rid of her She is a frightful bore, that woman.

Nora. Aren't you very tired, Torvald?

Helmer. No, not in the least.

Nora. Nor sleepy?

Helmer. Not a bit. On the contrary, I feel extraordinarily lively. And you?—you really look both tired and sleepy.

Nora. Yes, I am very tired. I want to go to sleep at once.

Helmer. There, you see it was quite right of me not to let you stay there any longer.

Nora. Everything you do is quite right, Torvald.

Helmer (kissing her on the forehead). Now my little skylark is speaking reasonably. Did you notice what good spirits Rank was in this evening?

Nora. Really? Was he? I didn't speak to him at all.

Helmer. And I very little, but I have not for a long time seen him in such good form. *(Looks for a while at her and then goes nearer to her.)* It is delightful to be at home by ourselves again, to be all alone with you—you fascinating, charming little darling!

Nora. Don't look at me like that, Torvald.

Helmer. Why shouldn't I look at my dearest treasure?—at all the beauty that is mine, all my very own?

Nora (going to the other side of the table). You mustn't say things like that to me to-night.

Helmer (following her). You have still got the Tarantella in your blood, I see. And it makes you more captivating than ever. Listen—the guests are beginning to go now. *(In a lower voice.)* Nora—soon the whole house will be quiet.

Nora. Yes, I hope so.

Helmer. Yes, my own darling Nora. Do you know, when I am out at a party with you like this, why I speak so little to you, keep away from you, and only send a stolen glance in your direction now and then?—do you know why I do that? It is because I make believe to myself that we are secretly in love, and you are my secretly promised bride, and that no one suspects there is anything between us.

Nora. Yes, yes—I know very well your thoughts are with me all the time.

Helmer. And when we are leaving, and I am putting the shawl over your beautiful young shoulders—on your lovely neck—then I imagine that you are my young bride and that we have just come from the wedding, and I am bringing you for the first time into our home—to be alone with you for the first time—quite alone with my shy little darling! All this evening I have longed for nothing but you. When I watched the seductive figures of the Tarantella, my blood was on fire; I could endure it no longer, and that was why I brought you down so early——

Nora. Go away, Torvald! You must let me go. I won't——

Helmer. What's that? You're joking, my little Nora! You won't—you won't? Am I not your husband—?

[*A knock is heard at the outer door.*

Nora (starting). Did you hear——?

Helmer (going into the hall). Who is it?

Rank (outside). It is I. May I come in for a moment?

Helmer (in a fretful whisper). Oh, what does he want now? *(Aloud.)* Wait a minute? *(Unlocks the door.)* Come, that's kind of you not to pass by our door.

Rank. I thought I heard your voice, and felt as if I should like to look in. *(With a swift glance round.)* Ah, yes!—these dear familiar rooms. You are very happy and cosy in here, you two.

Helmer. It seems to me that you looked after yourself pretty well upstairs too.

Rank. Excellently. Why shouldn't I? Why shouldn't

one enjoy everything in this world?—at any rate as much as one can, and as long as one can. The wine was capital——

Helmer. Especially the champagne.

Rank. So you noticed that too? It is almost incredible how much I managed to put away!

Nora. Torvald drank a great deal of champagne tonight, too.

Rank. Did he?

Nora. Yes, and he is always in such good spirits afterwards.

Rank. Well, why should one not enjoy a merry evening after a well-spent day?

Helmer. Well spent? I am afraid I can't take credit for that.

Rank (clapping him on the back). But I can, you know!

Nora. Doctor Rank, you must have been occupied with some scientific investigation to-day.

Rank. Exactly.

Helmer. Just listen!—little Nora talking about scientific investigations!

Nora. And may I congratulate you on the result?

Rank. Indeed you may.

Nora. Was it favourable, then?

Rank. The best possible, for both doctor and patient—certainty.

Nora (quickly and searchingly). Certainty?

Rank. Absolute certainty. So wasn't I entitled to make a merry evening of it after that?

Nora. Yes, you certainly were, Doctor Rank.

Helmer. I think so too, so long as you don't have to pay for it in the morning.

Rank. Oh well, one can't have anything in this life without paying for it.

Nora. Doctor Rank—are you fond of fancy-dress balls?

Rank. Yes, if there is a fine lot of pretty costumes.

Nora. Tell me—what shall we two wear at the next?

Helmer. Little featherbrain!—are you thinking of the next already?

Rank. We two? Yes, I can tell you. You shall go as a good fairy——

Helmer. Yes, but what do you suggest as an appropriate costume for that?

Rank. Let your wife go dressed just as she is in everyday life.

Helmer. That was really very prettily turned. But can't you tell us what you will be?

Rank. Yes, my dear friend, I have quite made up my mind about that.

Helmer. Well?

Rank. At the next fancy dress ball I shall be invisible.

Helmer. That's a good joke!

Rank. There is a big black hat—have you never heard of hats that make you invisible? If you put one on, no one can see you.

Helmer (suppressing a smile). Yes, you are quite right.

Rank. But I am clean forgetting what I came for. Helmer, give me a cigar—one of the dark Havanas.

Helmer. With the greatest pleasure.

[*Offers him his case.*

Rank (takes a cigar and cuts off the end). Thanks.

Nora (striking a match). Let me give you a light.

Rank. Thank you. *(She holds the match for him to light his cigar.)* And now good-bye!

Helmer. Good-bye, good-bye, dear old man!

Nora. Sleep well, Doctor Rank.

Rank. Thank you for that wish.

Nora. Wish me the same.

Rank. You? Well, if you want me to sleep well! And thanks for the light.

[*He nods to them both and goes out.*

Helmer (in a subdued voice). He has drunk more than he ought.

Nora (absently). Maybe. *(*HELMER *takes a bunch of keys out of his pocket and goes into the hall.)* Torvald! what are you going to do there?

Helmer. Empty the letter-box; it is quite full; there will be no room to put the newspaper in to-morrow morning.

Nora. Are you going to work to-night?

Helmer. You know quite well I'm not. What is this? Some one has been at the lock.

Nora. At the lock—?

Helmer. Yes, someone has. What can it mean? I should never have thought the maid—. Here is a broken hairpin. Nora, it is one of yours.

Nora (quickly). Then it must have been the children—

Helmer. Then you must get them out of those ways. There, at last I have got it open. *(Takes out the contents of the letter-box, and calls to the kitchen.)* Helen!—Helen, put out the light over the front door. *(Goes back into the room and shuts the door into the hall. He holds out his hand full of letters.)* Look at that—look what a heap of them there are. *(Turning them over.)* What on earth is that?

Nora (at the window). The letter—No! Torvald, no!

Helmer. Two cards—of Rank's.

Nora. Of Doctor Rank's?

Helmer (looking at them). Doctor Rank. They were on the top. He must have put them in when he went out.

Nora. Is there anything written on them?

Helmer. There is a black cross over the name. Look there—what an uncomfortable idea! It looks as if he were announcing his own death.

Nora. It is just what he is doing.

Helmer. What? Do you know anything about it? Has he said anything to you?

Nora. Yes. He told me that when the cards came it

would be his leave-taking from us. He means to shut himself up and die.

Helmer. My poor old friend. Certainly I knew we should not have him very long with us. But so soon! And so he hides himself away like a wounded animal.

Nora. If it has to happen, it is best it should be without a word—don't you think so, Torvald?

Helmer (walking up and down). He had so grown into our lives. I can't think of him as having gone out of them. He, with his sufferings and his loneliness, was like a cloudy background to our sunlit happiness. Well, perhaps it is best so. For him, anyway. *(Standing still.)* And perhaps for us too, Nora. We two are thrown quite upon each other now. *(Puts his arms round her.)* My darling wife, I don't feel as if I could hold you tight enough. Do you know, Nora, I have often wished that you might be threatened by some great danger, so that I might risk my life's blood, and everything, for your sake.

Nora (disengages herself, and says firmly and decidedly). Now you must read your letters, Torvald.

Helmer. No, no; not to-night. I want to be with you, my darling wife.

Nora. With the thought of your friend's death——

Helmer. You are right, it has affected us both. Something ugly has come between us—the thought of the horrors of death. We must try and rid our minds of that. Until then—we will each go to our own room.

Nora (hanging on his neck). Good-night, Torvald—Good-night!

Helmer (kissing her on the forehead). Good-night, my little singing-bird. Sleep sound, Nora. Now I will read my letters through.

[*He takes his letters and goes into his room, shutting the door after him.*

Nora (gropes distractedly about, seizes HELMER'S *domino, throws it round her, while she says in quick, hoarse, spas-*

modic whispers). Never to see him again. Never! Never! *(Puts her shawl over her head.)* Never to see my children again either—never again. Never! Never!—Ah! the icy, black water—the unfathomable depths—If only it were over! He has got it now—now he is reading it. Good-bye, Torvald and my children!

[*She is about to rush out through the hall, when* HELMER *opens his door hurriedly and stands with an open letter in his hand.*

Helmer. Nora!

Nora. Ah!——

HELMER. What is this? Do you know what is in this letter?

Nora. Yes, I know. Let me go! Let me get out!

Helmer (holding her back). Where are you going?

Nora (trying to get free). You shan't save me, Torvald!

Helmer (reeling). True? Is this true, that I read here? Horrible! No, no—it is impossible that it can be true.

Nora. It is true. I have loved you above everything else in the world.

Helmer. Oh, don't let us have any silly excuses.

Nora (taking a step towards him). Torvald——!

Helmer. Miserable creature—what have you done?

Nora. Let me go. You shall not suffer for my sake. You shall not take it upon yourself.

Helmer. No tragedy airs, please. *(Locks the hall door.)* Here you shall stay and give me an explanation. Do you understand what you have done? Answer me? Do you understand what you have done?

Nora (looks steadily at him and says with a growing look of coldness in her face). Yes, now I am beginning to understand thoroughly.

Helmer (walking about the room). What a horrible awakening! All these eight years—she who was my joy and pride—a hypocrite, a liar—worse, worse—a criminal!

The unutterable ugliness of it all! For shame! For shame! (*Nora is silent and looks steadily at him. He stops in front of her.*) I ought to have suspected that something of the sort would happen. I ought to have foreseen it. All your father's want of principle—be silent!—all your father's want of principle has come out in you. No religion, no morality, no sense of duty—. How I am punished for having winked at what he did! I did it for your sake, and this is how you repay me.

Nora. Yes, that's just it.

Helmer. Now you have destroyed all my happiness. You have ruined all my future. It is horrible to think of! I am in the power of an unscrupulous man; he can do what he likes with me, ask anything he likes of me, give me any orders he pleases—I dare not refuse. And I must sink to such miserable depths because of a thoughtless woman!

Nora. When I am out of the way, you will be free.

Helmer. No fine speeches, please. Your father had always plenty of those ready, too. What good would it be to me if you were out of the way, as you say? Not the slightest. He can make the affair known everywhere; and if he does, I may be falsely suspected of having been a party to your criminal action. Very likely people will think I was behind it all—that it was I who prompted you! And I have to thank you for all this—you whom I have cherished during the whole of our married life. Do you understand now what it is you have done for me?

Nora (coldly and quietly). Yes.

Helmer. It is so incredible that I can't take it in. But we must come to some understanding. Take off that shawl. Take it off, I tell you. I must try and appease him some way or another. The matter must be hushed up at any cost. And as for you and me, it must appear as if everything between us were just as before—but naturally only in the eyes of the world. You will still remain in my house, that is a matter of course. But I shall not allow you to bring up the children; I dare not trust them to you. To think that I should be obliged to say so to one whom I have loved so dearly, and whom I still——. No, that is all over. From this moment happiness is not the question; all that concerns us is to save the remains, the fragments, the appearance——

[*A ring is heard at the front-door bell.*

Helmer (with a start). What is that? So late! Can the worst——? Can he——? Hide yourself, Nora. Say you are ill.

[NORA *stands motionless.* HELMER goes and unlocks the hall door.

Maid (half-dressed, comes to the door). A letter for the mistress.

Helmer. Give it to me. *(Takes the letter, and shuts the door.)* Yes, it is from him. You shall not have it; I will read it myself.

Nora. Yes, read it.

Helmer (standing by the lamp). I scarcely have the courage to do it. It may mean ruin for both of us. No, I must know. *(Tears open the letter, runs his eye over a few lines, looks at a paper enclosed and gives a shout of joy.)* Nora! *(She looks at him questioningly.)* Nora!—No, I must read it once again——. Yes, it is true! I am saved! Nora, I am saved!

Nora. And I?

Helmer. You too, of course; we are both saved, both you and I. Look, he sends you your bond back. He says he regrets and repents—that a happy change in his life—never mind what he says! We are saved, Nora! No one can do anything to you. Oh, Nora, Nora!—no, first I must destroy these hateful things. Let me see——. *(Takes a look at the bond.)* No, no, I won't look at it. The whole thing shall be nothing but a bad dream to me. *(Tears up the bond and both letters, throws them all into the stove, and watches them burn.)* There—now it doesn't exist any longer. He says that since Christmas Eve you——. These must have been three dreadful days for you, Nora.

Nora. I have fought a hard fight these three days.

Helmer. And suffered agonies, and seen no way out but——. No, we won't call any of the horrors to mind. We will only shout with joy, and keep saying, "It's all over! It's all over!" Listen to me, Nora. You don't seem to realise that it is all over. What is this?—such a cold, set face! My poor little Nora, I quite understand; you don't feel as if you could believe that I have forgiven you. But it is true, Nora, I swear it; I have forgiven you everything. I know that what you did, you did out of love for me.

Nora. That is true.

Helmer. You have loved me as a wife ought to love her husband. Only you had not sufficient knowledge to judge of the means you used. But do you suppose you are any the less dear to me, because you don't understand how to act on your own responsibility? No, no; only lean on me; I will advise you and direct you. I should not be a man if this womanly helplessness did not just give you a double attractiveness in my eyes. You must not think any more about the hard things I said in my first moment of consternation, when I thought everything was going to overwhelm me. I have forgiven you, Nora; I swear to you I have forgiven you.

Nora. Thank you for your forgiveness.

[*She goes out through the door to the right.*

Helmer. No, don't go——. *(Looks in.)* What are you doing in there?

Nora (from within). Taking off my fancy dress.

Helmer (standing at the open door). Yes, do. Try and calm yourself, and make your mind easy again, my frightened little singing-bird. Be at rest, and feel secure; I have broad wings to shelter you under. *(Walks up and down by the door.)* How warm and cosy our home is, Nora. Here is shelter for you; here I will protect you like a hunted dove that I have saved from a hawk's claws. I will bring peace to your poor beating heart. It will come, little by little, Nora, believe me. Tomorrow morning you will look upon it all quite differently; soon everything will be just as it was before. Very soon you won't need me to assure you that I have forgiven you; you will yourself feel the certainty that I have done so. Can you suppose I should ever think of such a thing as repudiating you, or even reproaching you? You have no idea what a true man's heart is like, Nora. There is something so indescribably sweet and satisfying, to a man, in the knowledge that he has forgiven his wife—forgiven her freely, and with all his heart. It seems as if that had made her, as it were, doubly his own; he has given her a new life, so to speak; and she has in a way become both wife and child to him. So you shall be for me after this, my little scared, helpless darling. Have no anxiety about anything, Nora; only be frank and open with me, and I will serve as will and conscience both to you——. What is this? Not gone to bed? Have you changed your things?

Nora (in everyday dress). Yes, Torvald, I have changed my things now.

Helmer. But what for?—so late as this.

Nora. I shall not sleep to-night.

Helmer. But, my dear Nora——

Nora (looking at her watch). It is not so very late. Sit down here, Torvald. You and I have much to say to one another.

[*She sits down at one side of the table.*

Helmer. Nora—what is this?—this cold, set face?

Nora. Sit down. It will take some time; I have a lot to talk over with you.

Helmer (sits down at the opposite side of the table). You alarm me, Nora!—and I don't understand you.

Nora. No, that is just it. You don't understand me, and I have never understood you either—before to-night. No, you mustn't interrupt me. You must simply listen to what I say. Torvald, this is a settling of accounts.

Helmer. What do you mean by that?

Nora (after a short silence). Isn't there one thing that strikes you as strange in our sitting here like this?

Helmer. What is that?

Nora. We have been married now eight years. Does it not occur to you that this is the first time we two, you and I, husband and wife, have had a serious conversation?

Helmer. What do you mean by serious?

Nora. In all these eight years—longer than that—from the very beginning of our acquaintance, we have never exchanged a word on any serious subject.

Helmer. Was it likely that I would be continually and for ever telling you about worries that you could not help me to bear?

Nora. I am not speaking about business matters. I say that we have never sat down in earnest together to try and get at the bottom of anything.

Helmer. But, dearest Nora, would it have been any good to you?

Nora. That is just it; you have never understood me. I have been greatly wronged, Torvald—first by papa and then by you.

Helmer. What! By us two—by us two, who have loved you better than anyone else in the world?

Nora (shaking her head). You have never loved me. You have only thought it pleasant to be in love with me.

Helmer. Nora, what do I hear you saying?

Nora. It is perfectly true, Torvald. When I was at home with papa, he told me his opinion about everything, and so I had the same opinions; and if I differed from him I concealed the fact, because he would not have liked it. He called me his doll-child, and he played with me just as I used to play with my dolls. And when I came to live with you——

Helmer. What sort of an expression is that to use about our marriage?

Nora (undisturbed). I mean that I was simply transferred from papa's hands into yours. You arranged everything according to your own taste, and so I got the same tastes as you—or else I pretended to, I am really not quite sure which—I think sometimes the one and sometimes the other. When I look back on it, it seems to me as if I had been living here like a poor woman—just from hand to mouth. I have existed merely to perform tricks for you, Torvald. But you would have it so. You and papa have committed a great sin against me. It is your fault that I have made nothing of my life.

Helmer. How unreasonable and how ungrateful you are, Nora! Have you not been happy here?

Nora. No, I have never been happy. I thought I was, but it has never really been so.

Helmer. Not—not happy!

Nora. No, only merry. And you have always been so kind to me. But our home has been nothing but a playroom. I have been your doll-wife, just as at home I was papa's doll-child; and here the children have been my dolls. I thought it great fun when you played with me, just as they thought it great fun when I played with them. That is what our marriage has been, Torvald.

Helmer. There is some truth in what you say—exaggerated and strained as your view of it is. But for the future it shall be different. Playtime shall be over, and lesson-time shall begin.

Nora. Whose lessons? Mine, or the children's?

Helmer. Both yours and the children's, my darling Nora.

Nora. Alas, Torvald, you are not the man to educate me into being a proper wife for you.

Helmer. And you can say that!

Nora. And I—how am I fitted to bring up the children?

Helmer. Nora!

Nora. Didn't you say so yourself a little while ago—that you dare not trust me to bring them up?

Helmer. In a moment of anger! Why do you pay any heed to that?

Nora. Indeed, you were perfectly right. I am not fit for the task. There is another task I must undertake first. I must try and educate myself—you are not the man to help me in that. I must do that for myself. And that is why I am going to leave you now.

Helmer (springing up). What do you say?

Nora. I must stand quite alone, if I am to understand myself and everything about me. It is for that reason that I cannot remain with you any longer.

Helmer. Nora! Nora!

Nora. I am going away from here now, at once. I am sure Christine will take me in for the night——

Helmer. You are out of your mind! I won't allow it! I forbid you!

Nora. It is no use forbidding me anything any longer. I will take with me what belongs to myself. I will take nothing from you, either now or later.

Helmer. What sort of madness is this!

Nora. To-morrow I shall go home—I mean, to my old home. It will be easiest for me to find something to do there.

Helmer. You blind, foolish woman!

Nora. I must try and get some sense, Torvald.

Helmer. To desert your home, your husband and your children! And you don't consider what people will say!

Nora. I cannot consider that at all. I only know that it is necessary for me.

Helmer. It's shocking. This is how you would neglect your most sacred duties.

Nora. What do you consider my most sacred duties?

Helmer. Do I need to tell you that? Are they not your duties to your husband and your children?

Nora. I have other duties just as sacred.

Helmer. That you have not. What duties could those be?

Nora. Duties to myself.

Helmer. Before all else, you are a wife and a mother.

Nora. I don't believe that any longer. I believe that before all else I am a reasonable human being, just as you are—or, at all events, that I must try and become one. I know quite well, Torvald, that most people would think you right, and that views of that kind are to be found in books; but I can no longer content myself with what most people say, or with what is found in books. I must think over things for myself and get to understand them.

Helmer. Can you not understand your place in your own home? Have you not a reliable guide in such matters as that?—have you no religion?

Nora. I am afraid, Torvald, I do not exactly know what religion is.

Helmer. What are you saying?

Nora. I know nothing but what the clergyman said when I went to be confirmed. He told us that religion was this, and that, and the other. When I am away from all this, and am alone, I will look into that matter too. I will see if what the clergyman said is true, or at all events if it is true for me.

Helmer. This is unheard of in a girl of your age! But if religion cannot lead you aright, let me try and awaken your conscience. I suppose you have some moral sense? Or—answer me—am I to think you have none?

Nora. I assure you, Torvald, that is not an easy question to answer. I really don't know. The thing perplexes me altogether. I only know that you and I look at it in quite a different light. I am learning, too, that the law is quite another thing from what I supposed; but I find it impossible to convince myself that the law is right. According to it a woman has no right to spare her old dying father, or to save her husband's life. I can't believe that.

Helmer. You talk like a child. You don't understand the conditions of the world in which you live.

Nora. No, I don't. But now I am going to try. I am going to see if I can make out who is right, the world or I.

Helmer. You are ill, Nora; you are delirious; I almost think you are out of your mind.

Nora. I have never felt my mind so clear and certain as to-night.

Helmer. And is it with a clear and certain mind that you forsake your husband and your children?

Nora. Yes, it is.

Helmer. Then there is only one possible explanation.

Nora. What is that?

Helmer. You do not love me any more.

Nora. No, that is just it.

Helmer. Nora!—and you can say that?

Nora. It gives me great pain, Torvald, for you have always been so kind to me, but I cannot help it. I do not love you any more.

Helmer (regaining his composure). Is that a clear and certain conviction too?

Nora. Yes, absolutely clear and certain. That is the reason why I will not stay here any longer.

Helmer. And can you tell me what I have done to forfeit your love?

Nora. Yes, indeed I can. It was to-night, when the wonderful thing did not happen; then I saw you were not the man I had thought you.

Helmer. Explain yourself better—I don't understand you.

Nora. I have waited so patiently for eight years; for, goodness knows, I knew very well that wonderful things don't happen every day. Then this horrible misfortune came upon me; and then I felt quite certain that the wonderful thing was going to happen at last. When Krogstad's letter was lying out there, never for a moment did I imagine that you would consent to accept this man's conditions. I was so absolutely certain that you would say to him: Publish the thing to the whole world. And when that was done——

Helmer. Yes, what then?—when I had exposed my wife to shame and disgrace?

Nora. When that was done, I was so absolutely certain, you would come forward and take everything upon yourself, and say: I am the guilty one.

Helmer. Nora——!

Nora. You mean that I would never have accepted such a sacrifice on your part? No, of course not. But what would my assurances have been worth against yours? That was the wonderful thing which I hoped for and feared; and it was to prevent that, that I wanted to kill myself.

Helmer. I would gladly work night and day for you, Nora—bear sorrow and want for your sake. But no man would sacrifice his honour for the one he loves.

Nora. It is a thing hundreds of thousands of women have done.

Helmer. Oh, you think and talk like a heedless child.

Nora. Maybe. But you neither think nor talk like the man I could bind myself to. As soon as your fear was over—and it was not fear for what threatened me, but for what might happen to you—when the whole thing was past, as far as you were concerned it was exactly as if nothing at all had happened. Exactly as before, I was your little skylark, your doll, which you would in future treat with doubly gentle care, because it was so brittle and fragile. *(Getting up.)* Torvald—it was then it dawned upon me that for eight years I had been living here with a strange man, and had borne him three children——. Oh, I can't bear to think of it! I could tear myself into little bits!

Helmer (sadly). I see, I see. An abyss has opened between us—there is no denying it. But, Nora, would it not be possible to fill it up?

Nora. As I am now, I am no wife for you.

Helmer. I have it in me to become a different man.

Nora. Perhaps—if your doll is taken away from you.

Helmer. But to part!—to part from you! No, no, Nora, I can't understand that idea.

Nora (going out to the right). That makes it all the more certain that it must be done.

[*She comes back with her cloak and hat and a small bag which she puts on a chair by the table.*

Helmer. Nora, Nora, not now! Wait till to-morrow.

Nora (putting on her cloak). I cannot spend the night in a strange man's room.

Helmer. But can't we live here like brother and sister——?

Nora (putting on her hat). You know very well that would not last long. *(Puts the shawl round her.)* Good-bye, Torvald. I won't see the little ones. I know they are in better hands than mine. As I am now, I can be of no use to them.

Helmer. But some day, Nora—some day?

Nora. How can I tell? I have no idea what is going to become of me.

Helmer. But you are my wife, whatever becomes of you.

Nora. Listen, Torvald. I have heard that when a wife deserts her husband's house, as I am doing now, he is legally freed from all obligations towards her. In any case I set you free from all your obligations. You are not to feel yourself bound in the slightest way, any more than I shall. There must be perfect freedom on both sides. See here is your ring back. Give me mine.

Helmer. That too?

Nora. That too.

Helmer. Here it is.

Nora. That's right. Now it is all over. I have put the keys here. The maids know all about everything in the house—better than I do. To-morrow, after I have left her,

Christine will come here and pack up my own things that I brought with me from home. I will have them sent after me.

Helmer. All over! All over!—Nora, shall you never think of me again?

Nora. I know I shall often think of you and the children and this house.

Helmer. May I write to you, Nora?

Nora. No—never. You must not do that.

Helmer. But at least let me send you——

Nora. Nothing—nothing——

Helmer. Let me help you if you are in want.

Nora. No. I can receive nothing from a stranger.

Helmer. Nora—can I never be anything more than a stranger to you?

Nora (taking her bag). Ah, Torvald, the most wonderful thing of all would have to happen.

Helmer. Tell me what that would be!

Nora. Both you and I would have to be so changed that——. Oh, Torvald, I don't believe any longer in wonderful things happening.

Helmer. But I will believe in it. Tell me? So changed that——?

Nora. That our life together would be a real wedlock. Good-bye.

[*She goes out through the hall.*

Helmer (sinks down on a chair at the door and buries his face in his hands). Nora! Nora! *(Looks round, and rises.)* Empty. She is gone. *(A hope flashes across his mind.)* The most wonderful thing of all——?

[*The sound of a door shutting is heard from below.*

GHOSTS
(1881)

CHARACTERS

MRS. ALVING, *a widow.*
OSWALD ALVING, *her son, an artist.*
MANDERS, *the Pastor of the parish.*
ENGSTRAND, *a carpenter.*
REGINA ENGSTRAND, *his daughter, in Mrs. Alving's service.*

The action takes place at MRS. ALVING'S *house on one of the larger fjords of western Norway.*

GHOSTS

ACT I

SCENE.—*A large room looking upon a garden. A door in the left-hand wall, and two in the right. In the middle of the room, a round table with chairs set about it, and books, magazines and newspapers upon it. In the foreground on the left, a window, by which is a small sofa with a work-table in front of it. At the back the room opens into a conservatory rather smaller than the room. From the right-hand side of this a door leads to the garden. Through the large panes of glass that form the outer wall of the conservatory, a gloomy fjord landscape can be discerned, half obscured by steady rain.*

ENGSTRAND *is standing close up to the garden door. His left leg is slightly deformed, and he wears a boot with a clump of wood under the sole.* REGINA, *with an empty garden-syringe in her hand, is trying to prevent his coming in.*

Regina (below her breath). What is it you want? Stay where you are. The rain is dripping off you.

Engstrand. God's good rain, my girl.

Regina. The Devil's own rain, that's what it is!

Engstrand. Lord, how you talk, Regina. *(Takes a few limping steps forward.)* What I wanted to tell you was this——

Regina. Don't clump about like that, stupid! The young master is lying asleep upstairs.

Engstrand. Asleep still? In the middle of the day?

Regina. Well, it's no business of yours.

Engstrand. I was out on the spree last night——

Regina. I don't doubt it.

Engstrand. Yes, we are poor weak mortals, my girl——

Regina. We are indeed.

Engstrand. —and the temptations of the world are manifold, you know—but, for all that, here I was at my work at half-past five this morning.

Regina. Yes, yes, but make yourself scarce now. I am not going to stand here as if I had a *rendez-vous* with you.

Engstrand. As if you had a what?

Regina. I am not going to have any one find you here: so now you know, and you can go.

Engstrand (coming a few steps nearer). Not a bit of it! Not before we have had a little chat. This afternoon I shall have finished my job down at the school house, and I shall be off home to town by to-night's boat.

Regina (mutters). Pleasant journey to you!

Engstrand. Thanks, my girl. To-morrow is the opening of the Orphanage, and I expect there will be a fine kick-up here and plenty of good strong drink, don't you know. And no one shall say of Jacob Engstrand that he can't hold off when temptation comes in his way.

Regina. Oho!

Engstrand. Yes, because there will be a lot of fine folk here to-morrow. Parson Manders is expected from town, too.

Regina. What is more, he's coming to-day.

Engstrand. There you are! And I'm going to be precious careful he doesn't have anything to say against me, do you see?

Regina. Oh, that's your game, is it?

Engstrand. What do you mean?

Regina (with a significant look at him). What is it you want to humbug Mr. Manders out of, this time?

Engstrand. Sh! Sh! Are you crazy? Do you suppose *I* would want to humbug Mr. Manders? No, no—Mr. Manders has always been too kind a friend for me to do that. But what I wanted to talk to you about, was my going back home to-night.

Regina. The sooner you go, the better I shall be pleased.

Engstrand. Yes, only I want to take you with me, Regina.

Regina (open-mouthed). You want to take me——? What did you say?

Engstrand. I want to take you home with me, I said.

Regina (contemptuously). You will never get me home with you.

Engstrand. Ah, we shall see about that.

Regina. Yes, you can be quite certain we *shall* see about that. I, who have been brought up by a lady like Mrs. Alving?—I, who have been treated almost as if I were her own child?—do you suppose I am going home with *you?*—to such a house as yours? Not likely!

Engstrand. What the devil do you mean? Are you setting yourself up against your father, you hussy?

Regina (mutters, without looking at him). You have often told me I was none of yours.

Engstrand. Bah!—why do you want to pay any attention to that?

Regina. Haven't you many and many a time abused me and called me a——? For shame!

Engstrand. I'll swear I never used such an ugly word.

Regina. Oh, it doesn't matter what word you used.

Engstrand. Besides, that was only when I was a bit fuddled—hm! Temptations are manifold in this world, Regina.

Regina. Ugh!

Engstrand. And it was when your mother was in a nasty temper. I had to find some way of getting my knife into her, my girl. She was always so precious genteel.

(Mimicking her.) "Let go, Jacob! Let me be! Please to remember that I was three years with the Alvings at Rosenvold, and they were people who went to Court!" *(Laughs.)* Bless my soul, she never could forget that Captain Alving got a Court appointment while she was in service here.

Regina. Poor mother—you worried her into her grave pretty soon.

Engstrand (shrugging his shoulders). Of course, of course; I have got to take the blame for everything.

Regina (beneath her breath, as she turns away). Ugh—that leg, too!

Engstrand. What are you saying, my girl?

Regina. *Pied de mouton.*

Engstrand. Is that English?

Regina. Yes.

Engstrand. You have had a good education out here, and no mistake; and it may stand you in good stead now, Regina.

Regina (after a short silence). And what was it you wanted me to come to town for?

Engstrand. Need you ask why a father wants his only child? Ain't I a poor lonely widower?

Regina. Oh, don't come to me with that tale. Why do you want me to go?

Engstrand. Well, I must tell you I am thinking of taking up a new line now.

Regina (whistles). You have tried that so often—but it has always proved a fool's errand.

Engstrand. Ah, but this time you will just see, Regina! Strike me dead if——

Regina (stamping her feet). Stop swearing!

Engstrand. Sh! Sh!—you're quite right, my girl, quite right! What I wanted to say was only this, that I have put by a tidy penny out of what I have made by working at this new Orphanage up here.

Regina. Have you? All the better for you.

Engstrand. What is there for a man to spend his money on, out here in the country?

Regina. Well, what then?

Engstrand. Well, you see, I thought of putting the money into something that would pay. I thought of some kind of an eating-house for seafaring folk——

Regina. Heavens!

Engstrand. Oh, a high-class eating-house, of course,—not a pigsty for common sailors. Damn it, no; it would be a place ships' captains and first mates would come to; really good sort of people, you know.

Regina. And what should I——?

Engstrand. You would help there. But only to make a show, you know. You wouldn't find it hard work, I can promise you, my girl. You should do exactly as you liked

Regina. Oh, yes, quite so!

Engstrand. But we must have some women in the house; that is as clear as daylight. Because in the evening we must make the place a little attractive—some singing and dancing, and that sort of thing. Remember they are sea-folk—wayfarers on the waters of life! *(Coming nearer to her.)* Now don't be a fool and stand in your own way, Regina. What good are you going to do here? Will this education, that your mistress has paid for, be of any use? You are to look after the children in the new Home, I hear. Is that the sort of work for you? Are you so frightfully anxious to go and wear out your health and strength for the sake of these dirty brats?

Regina. No, if things were to go as I want them to then——. Well, it may happen; who knows? It may happen!

Engstrand. What may happen?

Regina. Never you mind. Is it much that you have put by, up here?

Engstrand. Taking it all round, I should say about forty or fifty pounds.

Regina. That's not so bad.

Engstrand. It's enough to make a start with, my girl.

Regina. Don't you mean to give me any of the money?

Engstrand. No, I'm hanged if I do.

Regina. Don't you mean to send me as much as a dress-length of stuff, just for once?

Engstrand. Come and live in the town with me and you shall have plenty of dresses.

Regina. Pooh!—I can get that much for myself, if I have a mind to.

Engstrand. But it's far better to have a father's guiding hand, Regina. Just now I can get a nice house in Little Harbour Street. They don't want much money down for it—and we could make it like a sort of seamen's home, don't you know.

Regina. But I have no intention of living with you! I have nothing whatever to do with you. So now, be off!

Engstrand. You wouldn't be living with me long, my girl. No such luck—not if you knew how to play your cards. Such a fine wench as you have grown this last year or two——

Regina. Well——?

Engstrand. It wouldn't be very long before some first mate came along—or perhaps a captain.

Regina. I don't mean to marry a man of that sort. Sailors have no *savoir-vivre*.

Engstrand. What haven't they got?

Regina. I know what sailors are, I tell you. They aren't the sort of people to marry.

Engstrand. Well, don't bother about marrying them. You can make it pay just as well. *(More confidentially.)* That fellow—the Englishman—the one with the yacht—he gave seventy pounds, he did; and she wasn't a bit prettier than you.

Regina (advancing towards him). Get out!

Engstrand (stepping back). Here! here!—you're not going to hit me, I suppose?

Regina. Yes! If you talk like that of mother, I will hit you. Get out, I tell you! *(Pushes him up to the garden door.)* And don't bang the doors. Young Mr. Alving——

Engstrand. Is asleep—I know. It's funny how anxious you are about young Mr. Alving. *(In a lower tone.)* Oho! is it possible that it is *he* that——?

Regina. Get out, and be quick about it! Your wits are wandering, my good man. No, don't go that way; Mr. Manders is just coming along. Be off down the kitchen stairs.

Engstrand (moving towards the right). Yes, yes—all right. But have a bit of a chat with him that's coming along. He's the chap to tell you what a child owes to its father. For I am your father, anyway, you know. I can prove it by the Register.

[*He goes out through the farther door which* REGINA *has opened. She shuts it after him, looks hastily at herself in the mirror, fans herself with her handkerchief and sets her collar straight; then busies herself with the flowers.* MANDERS *enters the conservatory through the garden door. He wears an overcoat, carries an umbrella and has a small travelling-bag slung over his shoulder on a strap.*

Manders. Good morning, Miss Engstrand.

Regina (turning round with a look of pleased surprise). Oh, Mr. Manders, good morning. The boat is in, then?

Manders. Just in. *(Comes into the room.)* It is most tiresome, this rain every day.

Regina (following him in). It's a splendid rain for the farmers, Mr. Manders.

Manders. Yes, you are quite right. We town-folk think so little about that.

[*Begins to take off his overcoat.*

Regina. Oh, let me help you. That's it. Why, how wet it is! I will hang it up in the hall. Give me your umbrella, too; I will leave it open, so that it will dry.

[*She goes out with the things by the farther door on the right.* MANDERS *lays his bag and his hat down on a chair.* REGINA *re-enters.*

Manders. Ah, it's very pleasant to get indoors. Well, is everything going on well here?

Regina. Yes, thanks.

Manders. Properly busy, though, I expect, getting ready for to-morrow?

Regina. Oh, yes, there is plenty to do.

Manders. And Mrs. Alving is at home, I hope?

Regina. Yes, she is. She has just gone upstairs to take the young master his chocolate.

Manders. Tell me—I heard down at the pier that Oswald had come back.

Regina. Yes, he came the day before yesterday. We didn't expect him till to-day.

Manders. Strong and well, I hope?

Regina. Yes, thank you, well enough. But dreadfully tired after his journey. He came straight from Paris without a stop—I mean, he came all the way without breaking his journey. I fancy he is having a sleep now, so we must talk a little bit more quietly, if you don't mind.

Manders. All right, we will be very quiet.

Regina (while she moves an armchair up to the table). Please sit down, Mr. Manders, and make yourself at home. *(He sits down; she puts a footstool under his feet.)* There! Is that comfortable?

Manders. Thank you, thank you. That is most comfortable. *(Looks at her.)* I'll tell you what, Miss Engstrand, I certainly think you have grown since I saw you last

Regina. Do you think so? Mrs. Alving says, too, that I have developed.

Manders. Developed? Well, perhaps a little—just suitably. [*A short pause.*

Regina. Shall I tell Mrs. Alving you are here?

Manders. Thanks, there is no hurry, my dear child.—Now tell me, Regina my dear, how has your father been getting on here?

Regina. Thank you, Mr. Manders, he is getting on pretty well.

Manders. He came to see me, the last time he was in town.

Regina. Did he? He is always so glad when he can have a chat with you.

Manders. And I suppose you have seen him pretty regularly every day?

Regina. I? Oh, yes, I do—whenever I have time, that is to say.

Manders. Your father has not a very strong character, Miss Engstrand. He sadly needs a guiding hand.

Regina. Yes, I can quite believe that.

Manders. He needs someone with him that he can cling to, someone whose judgment he can rely on. He acknowledged that freely himself, the last time he came up to see me.

Regina. Yes, he has said something of the same sort to me. But I don't know whether Mrs. Alving could do without me—most of all just now, when we have the new Orphanage to see about. And I should be dreadfully unwilling to leave Mrs. Alving, too; she has always been so good to me.

Manders. But a daughter's duty, my good child——. Naturally we should have to get your mistress' consent first.

Regina. Still I don't know whether it would be quite the thing, at my age, to keep house for a single man.

Manders. What!! My dear Miss Engstrand, it is your own father we are speaking of!

Regina. Yes, I dare say, but still——. Now, if it were in a good house and with a real gentleman——

Manders. But, my dear Regina——

Regina. ——one whom I could feel an affection for, and really feel in the position of a daughter to——

Manders. Come, come—my dear good child——

Regina. I should like very much to live in town. Out here it is terribly lonely; and you know yourself, Mr. Manders, what it is to be alone in the world. And, though I say it, I really am both capable and willing. Don't you know any place that would be suitable for me, Mr. Manders?

Manders. I? No, indeed I don't.

Regina. But, dear Mr. Manders—at any rate don't forget me, in case——

Manders (getting up). No, I won't forget you, Miss Engstrand.

Regina. Because, if I——

Manders. Perhaps you will be so kind as to let Mrs. Alving know I am here?

Regina. I will fetch her at once, Mr. Manders.

[*Goes out to the left.* MANDERS *walks up and down the room once or twice, stands for a moment at the farther end of the room with his hands behind his back and looks out into the garden. Then he comes back to the table, takes up a book and looks at the title page, gives a start and looks at some of the others.*

Manders. Hm!—Really!

[MRS. ALVING *comes in by the door on the left. She is followed by* REGINA, *who goes out again at once through the nearer door on the right.*

Mrs. Alving (holding out her hand). I am very glad to see you, Mr. Manders.

Manders. How do you do, Mrs. Alving. Here I am, as I promised.

Mrs. Alving. Always punctual!

Manders. Indeed, I was hard put to it to get away. What with vestry meetings and committees——

Mrs. Alving. It was all the kinder of you to come in such good time; we can settle our business before dinner. But where is your luggage?

Manders (quickly). My things are down at the village shop. I am going to sleep there to-night.

Mrs. Alving (repressing a smile). Can't I really persuade you to stay the night here this time?

Manders. No, no; many thanks all the same; I will put up there, as usual. It is so handy for getting on board the boat again.

Mrs. Alving. Of course you shall do as you please. But it seems to me quite another thing, now we are two old people——

Manders. Ha! ha! You will have your joke! And it's natural you should be in high spirits to-day—first of all there is the great event to-morrow, and also you have got Oswald home.

Mrs. Alving. Yes, am I not a lucky woman! It is more than two years since he was home last, and he has promised to stay the whole winter with me.

Manders. Has he, really? That is very nice and filial of him; because there must be many more attractions in his life in Rome or in Paris, I should think.

Mrs. Alving. Yes, but he has his mother here, you see. Bless the dear boy, he has got a corner in his heart for his mother still.

Manders. Oh, it would be very sad if absence and preoccupation with such a thing as Art were to dull the natural affections.

Mrs. Alving. It would, indeed. But there is no fear of that with him, I am glad to say. I am quite curious to see if you recognise him again. He will be down directly; he is just lying down for a little on the sofa upstairs. But do sit down, my dear friend.

Manders. Thank you. You are sure I am not disturbing you?

Mrs. Alving. Of course not.

[*She sits down at the table.*

Manders. Good. Then I will show you——. *(He goes to the chair where his bag is lying and takes a packet of papers from it; then sits down at the opposite side of the table and looks for a clear space to put the papers down.)* Now first of all, here is—*(breaks off).* Tell me, Mrs. Alving, what are these books doing here?

Mrs. Alving. These books? I am reading them.

Manders. Do you read this sort of thing?

Mrs. Alving. Certainly I do.

Manders. Do you feel any the better or the happier for reading books of this kind?

Mrs. Alving. I think it makes me, as it were, more self-reliant.

Manders. That is remarkable. But why?

Mrs. Alving. Well, they give me an explanation or a confirmation of lots of different ideas that have come into my own mind. But what surprises me, Mr. Manders, is that, properly speaking, there is nothing at all new in these books. There is nothing more in them than what most people think and believe. The only thing is, that most people either take no account of it or won't admit it to themselves.

Manders. But, good heavens, do you seriously think that most people——?

Mrs. Alving. Yes, indeed, I do.

Manders. But not here in the country at any rate? Not here amongst people like ourselves?

Mrs. Alving. Yes, amongst people like ourselves too.

Manders. Well, really, I must say——!

Mrs. Alving. But what is the particular objection that you have to these books?

Manders. What objection? You surely don't suppose that I take any particular interest in such productions?

Mrs. Alving. In fact, you don't know anything about what you are denouncing?

Manders. I have read quite enough about these books to disapprove of them.

Mrs. Alving. Yes, but your own opinion——

Manders. My dear Mrs. Alving, there are many occasions in life when one has to rely on the opinion of others. That is the way in this world, and it is quite right that it should be so. What would become of society, otherwise?

Mrs. Alving. Well, you may be right.

Manders. Apart from that, naturally I don't deny that literature of this kind may have a considerable attraction. And I cannot blame you, either, for wishing to make yourself acquainted with the intellectual tendencies which I am told are at work in the wider world in which you have allowed your son to wander for so long. But——

Mrs. Alving. But——?

Manders (lowering his voice). But one doesn't talk about it, Mrs. Alving. One certainly is not called upon to account to every one for what one reads or thinks in the privacy of one's own room.

Mrs. Alving. Certainly not. I quite agree with you.

Manders. Just think of the consideration you owe to this Orphanage, which you decided to build at a time when your thoughts on such subjects were very different from what they are now—as far as I am able to judge.

Mrs. Alving. Yes, I freely admit that. But it was about the Orphanage——

Manders. It was about the Orphanage we were going to talk; quite so. Well—walk warily, dear Mrs. Alving! And now let us turn to the business in hand. *(Opens an envelope and takes out some papers.)* You see these?

Mrs. Alving. The deeds?

Manders. Yes, the whole lot—and everything in order. I can tell you it has been no easy matter to get them in time. I had positively to put pressure on the authorities; they are almost painfully conscientious when it is a question of settling property. But here they are at last. *(Turns over the papers.)* Here is the deed of conveyance of that part of the Rosenvold estate known as the Solvik property, together with the buildings newly erected thereon—the school, the masters' houses and the chapel. And here is the legal sanction for the statutes of the institution. Here, you see—*(reads)* "Statutes for the Captain Alving Orphanage."

Mrs. Alving (after a long look at the papers). That seems all in order.

Manders. I thought "Captain" was the better title to use, rather than your husband's Court title of "Chamberlain." "Captain" seems less ostentatious.

Mrs. Alving. Yes, yes; just as you think best.

Manders. And here is the certificate for the investment of the capital in the bank, the interest being earmarked for the current expenses of the Orphanage.

Mrs. Alving. Many thanks; but I think it will be most convenient if you will kindly take charge of them.

Manders. With pleasure. I think it will be best to leave the money in the bank for the present. The interest is not very high, it is true; four per cent at six months' call. Later on, if we can find some good mortgage—of course it must be a first mortgage and on unexceptionable security—we can consider the matter further.

Mrs. Alving. Yes, yes, my dear Mr. Manders, you know best about all that.

Manders. I will keep my eye on it, anyway. But there is one thing in connection with it that I have often meant to ask you about.

Mrs. Alving. What is that?

Manders. Shall we insure the buildings, or not?

Mrs. Alving. Of course we must insure them.

Manders. Ah, but wait a moment, dear lady. Let us look into the matter a little more closely.

Mrs. Alving. Everything of mine is insured—the house and its contents, my livestock—everything.

Manders. Naturally. They are your own property. I do exactly the same, of course. But this, you see, is quite a different case. The Orphanage is, so to speak, dedicated to higher uses.

Mrs. Alving. Certainly, but——

Manders. As far as I am personally concerned, I can conscientiously say that I don't see the smallest objection to our insuring ourselves against all risks.

Mrs. Alving. That is exactly what I think.

Manders. But what about the opinion of the people hereabouts?

Mrs. Alving. Their opinion——?

Manders. Is there any considerable body of opinion here —opinion of some account, I mean—that might take exception to it?

Mrs. Alving. What, exactly, do you mean by opinion of some account?

Manders. Well, I was thinking particularly of persons of such independent and influential position that one could hardly refuse to attach weight to their opinion.

Mrs. Alving. There are a certain number of such people here, who might perhaps take exception to it if we——

Manders. That's just it, you see. In town there are lots of them. All my fellow-clergymen's congregations, for instance! It would be so extremely easy for them to interpret it as meaning that neither you nor I had a proper reliance on Divine protection.

Mrs. Alving. But as far as you are concerned, my dear friend, you have at all events the consciousness that——

Manders. Yes, I know, I know; my own mind is quite easy about it, it is true. But we should not be able to prevent a wrong and injurious interpretation of our action. And that sort of thing, moreover, might very easily end in exercising a hampering influence on the work of the Orphanage.

Mrs. Alving. Oh, well, if that is likely to be the effect of it——

Manders. Nor can I entirely overlook the difficult—indeed, I may say, painful—position I might possibly be placed in. In the best circles in town the matter of this Orphanage is attracting a great deal of attention. Indeed the Orphanage is to some extent built for the benefit of the town too, and it is to be hoped that it may result in the lowering of our poor-rate by a considerable amount. But as I have been your adviser in the matter and have taken charge of the business side of it, I should be afraid that it would be I that spiteful persons would attack first of all——

Mrs. Alving. Yes, you ought not to expose yourself to that.

Manders. Not to mention the attacks that would undoubtedly be made upon me in certain newspapers and reviews——

Mrs. Alving. Say no more about it, dear Mr. Manders; that quite decides it.

Manders. Then you don't wish it to be insured?

Mrs. Alving. No, we will give up the idea.

Manders (leaning back in his chair). But suppose, now, that some acident happened?—one can never tell—would you be prepared to make good the damage?

Mrs. Alving. No; I tell you quite plainly I would not do so under any circumstances.

Manders. Still, you know, Mrs. Alving—after all, it is a serious responsibility that we are taking upon ourselves.

Mrs. Alving. But do you think we can do otherwise?

Manders. No, that's just it. We really can't do otherwise. We ought not to expose ourselves to a mistaken judgment; and we have no right to do anything that will scandalise the community.

Mrs. Alving. You ought not to, as a clergyman, at any rate.

Manders. And, what is more, I certainly think that we may count upon our enterprise being attended by good fortune—indeed, that it will be under a special protection.

Mrs. Alving. Let us hope so, Mr. Manders.

Manders. Then we will leave it alone?

Mrs. Alving. Certainly.

Manders. Very good. As you wish. *(Makes a note.)* No insurance, then.

Mrs. Alving. It's a funny thing that you should just have happened to speak about that to-day——

Manders. I have often meant to ask you about it——

Mrs. Alving. ——because yesterday we very nearly had a fire up there.

Manders. Do you mean it!

Mrs. Alving. Oh, as a matter of fact it was nothing of any consequence. Some shavings in the carpenter's shop caught fire.

Manders. Where Engstrand works?

Mrs. Alving. Yes. They say he is often so careless with matches.

Manders. He has so many things on his mind, poor fellow—so many anxieties. Heaven be thanked, I am told he is really making an effort to live a blameless life.

Mrs. Alving. Really? Who told you so?

Manders. He assured me himself that it is so. He's a good workman, too.

Mrs. Alving. Oh, yes, when he is sober.

Manders. Ah, that sad weakness of his! But the pain in his poor leg often drives him to it, he tells me. The last time he was in town, I was really quite touched by him. He came to my house and thanked me so gratefully for getting him work here, where he could have the chance of being with Regina.

Mrs. Alving. He doesn't see very much of her.

Manders. But he assured me that he saw her every day.

Mrs. Alving. Oh well, perhaps he does.

Manders. He feels so strongly that he needs some one who can keep a hold on him when temptations assail him. That is the most winning thing about Jacob Engstrand; he comes to one like a helpless child and accuses himself and confesses his frailty. The last time he came and had a talk with me——. Suppose now, Mrs. Alving, that it were really a necessity of his existence to have Regina at home with him again——

Mrs. Alving (standing up suddenly). Regina!

Manders. ——you ought not to set yourself against him.

Mrs. Alving. Indeed, I set myself very definitely against that. And, besides, you know Regina is to have a post in the Orphanage.

Manders. But consider, after all he is her father——

Mrs. Alving. I know best what sort of a father he has been to her. No, she shall never go to him with my consent.

Manders (getting up). My dear lady, don't judge so hastily. It is very sad how you misjudge poor Engstrand. One would really think you were afraid——

Mrs. Alving (more calmly). That is not the question. I have taken Regina into my charge, and in my charge she remains. *(Listens.)* Hush, dear Mr. Manders, don't say any more about it. *(Her face brightens with pleasure.)* Listen! Oswald is coming downstairs. We will only think about him now.

[OSWALD ALVING, *in a light overcoat, hat in hand and smoking a big meerschaum pipe, comes in by the door on the left.*

Oswald (standing in the doorway). Oh, I beg your pardon, I thought you were in the office. *(Comes in.)* Good morning, Mr. Manders.

Manders (staring at him). Well! It's most extraordinary——

Mrs. Alving. Yes, what do you think of him, Mr. Manders?

Manders. I—I—no, can it possibly be——?

Oswald. Yes, it really is the prodigal son, Mr. Manders.

Manders. Oh, my dear young friend——

Oswald. Well, the son come home, then.

Mrs. Alving. Oswald is thinking of the time when you were so opposed to the idea of his being a painter.

Manders. We are only fallible, and many steps seem to us hazardous at first, that afterwards—*(grasps his hand).* Welcome, welcome! Really, my dear Oswald—may I still call you Oswald?

Oswald. What else would you think of calling me?

Manders. Thank you. What I mean, my dear Oswald, is that you must not imagine that I have any unqualified disapproval of the artist's life. I admit that there are many who, even in that career, can keep the inner man free from harm.

Oswald. Let us hope so.

Mrs. Alving (beaming with pleasure). I know one who has kept both the inner and the outer man free from harm. Just take a look at him, Mr. Manders.

Oswald (walks across the room). Yes, yes, mother dear, of course.

Manders. Undoubtedly—no one can deny it. And I hear you have begun to make a name for yourself. I have often seen mention of you in the papers—and extremely favourable mention, too. Although, I must admit, latterly I have not seen your name so often.

Oswald (going towards the conservatory). I haven't done so much painting just lately.

Mrs. Alving. An artist must take a rest sometimes, like other people.

Manders. Of course, of course. At those times the artist is preparing and strengthening himself for a greater effort.

Oswald. Yes. Mother, will dinner soon be ready?

Mrs. Alving. In half an hour. He has a fine appetite, thank goodness.

Manders. And a liking for tobacco too.

Oswald. I found father's pipe in the room upstairs, and ——

Manders. Ah, that is what it was!

Mrs. Alving. What?

Manders. When Oswald came in at that door with the pipe in his mouth, I thought for the moment it was his father in the flesh.

Oswald. Really?

Mrs. Alving. How can you say so! Oswald takes after me.

Manders. Yes, but there is an expression about the corners of his mouth—something about the lips—that reminds me so exactly of Mr. Alving—especially when he smokes.

Mrs. Alving. I don't think so at all. To my mind, Oswald has much more of a clergyman's mouth.

Manders. Well, yes—a good many of my colleagues in the church have a similar expression.

Mrs. Alving. But put your pipe down, my dear boy. I don't allow any smoking in here.

Oswald (puts down his pipe). All right, I only wanted to try it, because I smoked it once when I was a child.

Mrs. Alving. You?

Oswald. Yes; it was when I was quite a little chap. And I can remember going upstairs to father's room one evening when he was in very good spirits.

Mrs. Alving. Oh, you can't remember anything about those days.

Oswald. Yes, I remember plainly that he took me on his knee and let me smoke his pipe. "Smoke, my boy," he said, "have a good smoke, boy!" And I smoked as hard as I could, until I felt I was turning quite pale and the perspiration was standing in great drops on my forehead. Then he laughed—such a hearty laugh——

Manders. It was an extremely odd thing to do.

Mrs. Alving. Dear Mr. Manders, Oswald only dreamt it.

Oswald. No indeed, mother, it was no dream. Because —don't you remember—you came into the room and carried me off to the nursery, where I was sick, and I saw that you were crying. Did father often play such tricks?

Manders. In his young days he was full of fun——

Oswald. And, for all that, he did so much with his life—so much that was good and useful, I mean—short as his life was.

Manders. Yes, my dear Oswald Alving, you have inherited the name of a man who undoubtedly was both energetic and worthy. Let us hope it will be a spur to your energies——

Oswald. It ought to be, certainly.

Manders. In any case it was nice of you to come home for the day that is to honour his memory.

Oswald. I could do no less for my father.

Mrs. Alving. And to let me keep him so long here—that's the nicest part of what he has done.

Manders. Yes, I hear you are going to spend the winter at home.

Oswald. I am here for an indefinite time, Mr. Manders. —Oh, it's good to be at home again!

Mrs. Alving (beaming). Yes, isn't it?

Manders (looking sympathetically at him). You went out into the world very young, my dear Oswald.

Oswald. I did. Sometimes I wonder if I wasn't too young.

Mrs. Alving. Not a bit of it. It is the best thing for an active boy, and especially for an only child. It's a pity when they are kept at home with their parents and get spoilt.

Manders. That is a very debatable question, Mrs. Alving. A child's own home is, and always must be, his proper place.

Oswald. There I agree entirely with Mr. Manders.

Manders. Take the case of your own son. Oh yes, we can talk about it before him. What has the result been in his case? He is six or seven and twenty, and has never yet had the opportunity of learning what a well-regulated home means.

Oswald. Excuse me, Mr. Manders, you are quite wrong there.

Manders. Indeed? I imagined that your life abroad had practically been spent entirely in artistic circles.

Oswald. So it has.

Manders. And chiefly amongst the younger artists.

Oswald. Certainly.

Manders. But I imagined that those gentry, as a rule, had not the means necessary for family life and the support of a home.

Oswald. There are a considerable number of them who have not the means to marry, Mr. Manders.

Manders. That is exactly my point.

Oswald. But they can have a home of their own, all the same; a good many of them have. And they are very well-regulated and very comfortable homes, too.

[MRS. ALVING, *who has listened to him attentively, nods assent, but says nothing.*

Manders. Oh, but I am not talking of bachelor establishments. By a home I mean family life—the life a man lives with his wife and children.

Oswald. Exactly, or with his children and his children's mother.

Manders (starts and clasps his hands). Good heavens!

Oswald. What is the matter?

Manders. Lives with—with—his children's mother!

Oswald. Well, would you rather he should repudiate his children's mother?

Manders. Then what you are speaking of are those unprincipled conditions known as irregular unions!

Oswald. I have never noticed anything particularly unprincipled about these people's lives.

Manders. But do you mean to say that it is possible for a man of any sort of bringing up, and a young woman, to reconcile themselves to such a way of living—and to make no secret of it, either?

Oswald. What else are they to do? A poor artist, and a poor girl—it costs a good deal to get married. What else are they to do?

Manders. What are they to do? Well, Mr. Alving, I will tell you what they ought to do. They ought to keep away from each other from the very beginning—that is what they ought to do!

Oswald. That advice wouldn't have much effect upon hot-blooded young folk who are in love.

Mrs. Alving. No, indeed it wouldn't.

Manders (persistently). And to think that the authorities tolerate such things! That they are allowed to go on, openly! *(Turns to* Mrs. Alving.*)* Had I so little reason, then, to be sadly concerned about your son? In circles where open immorality is rampant—where, one may say, it is honoured——

Oswald. Let me tell you this, Mr. Manders. I have been a constant Sunday guest at one or two of these "irregular" households——

Manders. On Sunday, too!

Oswald. Yes, that is the day of leisure. But never have I heard one objectionable word there, still less have I ever seen anything that could be called immoral. No; but do you know when and where I *have* met with immorality in artists' circles?

Manders. No, thank heaven, I don't!

Oswald. Well, then, I shall have the pleasure of telling you. I have met with it when some one or other of your model husbands and fathers have come out there to have a bit of a look round on their own account, and have done the artists the honour of looking them up in their humble quarters. Then we had a chance of learning something, I can tell you. These gentlemen were able to instruct us about places and things that we had never so much as dreamt of.

Manders. What? Do you want me to believe that honourable men when they get away from home will——

Oswald. Have you never, when these same honourable men come home again, heard them deliver themselves on the subject of the prevalence of immorality abroad?

Manders. Yes, of course, but——

Mrs. Alving. I have heard them, too.

Oswald. Well, you can take their word for it, unhesitatingly. Some of them are experts in the matter. *(Putting his hands to his head.)* To think that the glorious freedom of the beautiful life over there should be so besmirched!

Mrs. Alving. You mustn't get too heated, Oswald; you gain nothing by that.

Oswald. No, you are quite right, mother. Besides, it isn't good for me. It's because I am so infernally tired, you know. I will go out and take a turn before dinner. I beg your pardon, Mr. Manders. It is impossible for you to realise the feeling; but it takes me that way.

[*Goes out by the farther door on the right.*

Mrs. Alving. My poor boy!

Manders. You may well say so. This is what it has brought him to! (MRS. ALVING *looks at him, but does not speak.)* He called himself the prodigal son. It's only too true, alas—only too true! (MRS. ALVING *looks steadily at him.)* And what do you say to all this?

Mrs. Alving. I say that Oswald was right in every single word he said.

Manders. Right? Right? To hold such principles as that?

Mrs. Alving. In my loneliness here I have come to just

the same opinions as he, Mr. Manders. But I have never presumed to venture upon such topics in conversation. Now there is no need; my boy shall speak for me.

Manders. You deserve the deepest pity, Mrs. Alving. It is my duty to say an earnest word to you. It is no longer your business man and adviser, no longer your old friend and your dead husband's old friend, that stands before you now. It is your priest that stands before you, just as he did once at the most critical moment of your life.

Mrs. Alving. And what is it that my priest has to say to me?

Manders. First of all I must stir your memory. The moment is well chosen. To-morrow is the tenth anniversary of your husband's death; to-morrow the memorial to the departed will be unveiled; to-morrow I shall speak to the whole assembly that will be met together. But to-day I want to speak to you alone.

Mrs. Alving. Very well, Mr. Manders, speak!

Manders. Have you forgotten that after barely a year of married life you were standing at the very edge of a precipice?—that you forsook your house and home?—that you ran away from your husband—yes, Mrs. Alving, ran away, ran away—and refused to return to him in spite of his requests and entreaties?

Mrs. Alving. Have you forgotten how unspeakably unhappy I was during that first year?

Manders. To crave for happiness in this world is simply to be possessed by a spirit of revolt. What right have we to happiness? No! we must do our duty, Mrs. Alving. And your duty was to cleave to the man you had chosen and to whom you were bound by a sacred bond.

Mrs. Alving. You know quite well what sort of a life my husband was living at that time—what excesses he was guilty of.

Manders. I know only too well what rumour used to say of him; and I should be the last person to approve of his conduct as a young man, supposing that rumour spoke the truth. But it is not a wife's part to be her husband's judge. You should have considered it your bounden duty humbly to have borne the cross that a higher will had laid upon you. But, instead of that, you rebelliously cast off your cross, you deserted the man whose stumbling footsteps you should have supported, you did what was bound to imperil your good name and reputation, and came very near to imperilling the reputation of others into the bargain.

Mrs. Alving. Of others? Of one other, you mean.

Manders. It was the height of imprudence, your seeking refuge with me.

Mrs. Alving. With our priest? With our intimate friend?

Manders. All the more on that acount. You should thank God that I possessed the necessary strength of mind—that I was able to turn you from your outrageous intention, and that it was vouchsafed to me to succeed in leading you back into the path of duty and back to your lawful husband.

Mrs. Alving. Yes, Mr. Manders, that certainly was your doing.

Manders. I was but the humble instrument of a higher power. And is it not true that my having been able to bring you again under the yoke of duty and obedience sowed the seeds of a rich blessing on all the rest of your life? Did things not turn out as I foretold to you? Did not your husband turn from straying in the wrong path as a man should? Did he not, after all, live a life of love and good report with you all his days? Did he not become a benefactor to the neighbourhood? Did he not so raise you up to his level, so that by degrees you became his fellow-worker in all his undertakings—and a noble fellow-worker, too, I know, Mrs. Alving; that praise I will give you.—But now I come to the second serious false step in your life.

Mrs. Alving What do you mean?

Manders. Just as once you forsook your duty as a wife, so, since then, you have forsaken your duty as a mother.

Mrs. Alving. Oh——!

Manders. You have been overmastered all your life by a disastrous spirit of wilfulness. All your impulses have led you towards what is undisciplined and lawless. You have never been willing to submit to any restraint. Anything in life that has seemed irksome to you, you have thrown aside recklessly and unscrupulously, as if it were a burden that you were free to rid yourself of if you would. It did not please you to be a wife any longer, and so you left your husband. Your duties as a mother were irksome to you, so you sent your child away among strangers.

Mrs. Alving. Yes, that is true; I did that.

Manders. And that is why you have become a stranger to him.

Mrs. Alving. No, no, I am not that!

Manders. You are; you must be. And what sort of a son is it that you have got back? Think over it seriously, Mrs. Alving. You erred grievously in your husband's case —you acknowledge as much, by erecting this memorial to him. Now you are bound to acknowledge how much you have erred in your son's case; possibly there may still be time to reclaim him from the paths of wickedness. Turn over a new leaf, and set yourself to reform what there may still be that is capable of reformation in him. Because *(with uplifted forefinger)* in very truth, Mrs. Alving, you are a guilty mother!—That is what I have thought it my duty to say to you.

[*A short silence.*

Mrs. Alving (speaking slowly and with self-control). You have had your say, Mr. Manders, and to-morrow you will be making a public speech in memory of my husband. I shall not speak to-morrow. But now I wish to speak to you for a little, just as you have been speaking to me.

Manders. By all means; no doubt you wish to bring forward some excuses for your behaviour——

Mrs. Alving. No. I only want to tell you something.

Manders. Well?

Mrs. Alving. In all that you said just now about me and my husband, and about our life together after you had, as you put it, led me back into the path of duty—there was nothing that you knew at first hand. From that moment you never again set foot in our house—you, who had been our daily companion before that.

Manders. Remember that you and your husband moved out of town immediately afterwards.

Mrs. Alving. Yes, and you never once came out here to see us in my husband's lifetime. It was only the business in connection with the Orphanage that obliged you to come and see me.

Manders (in a low and uncertain voice). Helen—if that is a reproach, I can only beg you to consider——

Mrs. Alving. ——the respect you owed to your calling?—yes. All the more as I was a wife who had tried to run away from her husband. One can never be too careful to have nothing to do with such reckless women.

Manders. My dear—Mrs. Alving, you are exaggerating dreadfully——

Mrs. Alving. Yes, yes,—very well. What I mean is this, that when you condemn my conduct as a wife you have nothing more to go upon than ordinary public opinion.

Manders. I admit it. What then?

Mrs. Alving. Well—now, Mr. Manders, now I am going to tell you the truth. I had sworn to myself that you should know it one day—you, and you only!

Manders. And what may the truth be?

Mrs. Alving. The truth is this, that my husband died just as great a profligate as he had been all his life.

Manders (feeling for a chair). What are you saying?

Mrs. Alving. After nineteen years of married life, just

as profligate—in his desires at all events—as he was before you married us.

Manders. And can you talk of his youthful indiscretions —his irregularities—his excesses, if you like—as a profligate life!

Mrs. Alving. That was what the doctor who attended him called it.

Manders. I don't understand what you mean.

Mrs. Alving. It is not necessary you should.

Manders. It makes my brain reel. To think that your marriage—all the years of wedded life you spent with your husband—were nothing but a hidden abyss of misery.

Mrs. Alving. That and nothing else. Now you know.

Manders. This—this bewilders me. I can't understand it! I can't grasp it! How in the world was it possible——? How could such a state of things remain concealed?

Mrs. Alving. That was just what I had to fight for incessantly, day after day. When Oswald was born, I thought I saw a slight improvement. But it didn't last long. And after that I had to fight doubly hard—fight a desperate fight so that no one should know what sort of a man my child's father was. You know quite well what an attractive manner he had; it seemed as if people could believe nothing but good of him. He was one of those men whose mode of life seems to have no effect upon their reputations. But at last, Mr. Manders—you must hear this too—at last something happened more abominable than everything else.

Manders. More abominable than what you have told me!

Mrs. Alving. I had borne with it all, though I knew only too well what he indulged in in secret, when he was out of the house. But when it came to the point of the scandal coming within our four walls——

Manders. Can you mean it! Here?

Mrs. Alving. Yes, here, in our own home. It was in there *(pointing to the nearer door on the right)* in the dining-room that I got the first hint of it. I had something to do in there and the door was standing ajar. I heard our maid come up from the garden with water for the flowers in the conservatory.

Manders. Well——?

Mrs. Alving. Shortly afterwards I heard my husband come in too. I heard him say something to her in a low voice. And then I heard—*(with a short laugh)*—oh, it rings in my ears still, with its mixture of what was heart-breaking and what was so ridiculous—I heard my own servant whisper: "Let me go, Mr. Alving! Let me be!"

Manders. What unseemly levity on his part! But surely nothing more than levity, Mrs. Alving, believe me.

Mrs. Alving. I soon knew what to believe. My husband had his will of the girl—and that intimacy had consequences, Mr. Manders.

Manders (as if turned to stone). And all that in this house! In this house!

Mrs. Alving. I have suffered a good deal in this house. To keep him at home in the evening—and at night—I have had to play the part of boon companion in his secret drinking-bouts in his room up there. I have had to sit there alone with him, have had to hobnob and drink with him, have had to listen to his ribald senseless talk, have had to fight with brute force to get him to bed——

Manders (trembling). And you were able to endure all this!

Mrs. Alving. I had my little boy, and endured it for his sake. But when the crowning insult came—when my own servant—then I made up my mind that there should be an end of it. I took the upper hand in the house, absolutely—both with him and all the others. I had a weapon to use against him, you see; he didn't dare to speak. It was then that Oswald was sent away. He was about seven then, and was beginning to notice things and ask questions as children will. I could endure all that, my friend. It seemed to me that the child would be poisoned if he breathed the air of this polluted house. That was why I sent him away. And now you understand, too, why he never set foot here as long as his father was alive. No one knows what it meant to me.

Manders. You have indeed had a pitiable experience.

Mrs. Alving. I could never have gone through with it, if I had not had my work. Indeed, I can boast that I have worked. All the increase in the value of the property, all the improvements, all the useful arrangements that my husband got the honour and glory of—do you suppose that he troubled himself about any of them? He, who used to lie the whole day on the sofa reading old Official Lists! No, you may as well know that too. It was I that kept him up to the mark when he had his lucid intervals; it was I that had to bear the whole burden of it when he began his excesses again or took to whining about his miserable condition.

Manders. And this is the man you are building a memorial to!

Mrs. Alving. There you see the power of an uneasy conscience.

Manders. An uneasy conscience? What do you mean?

Mrs. Alving. I had always before me the fear that it was impossible that the truth should not come out and be believed. That is why the Orphanage is to exist, to silence all rumours and clear away all doubt.

Manders. You certainly have not fallen short of the mark in that, Mrs. Alving.

Mrs. Alving. I had another very good reason. I did not wish Oswald, my own son, to inherit a penny that belonged to his father.

Manders. Then it is with Mr. Alving's property——

Mrs. Alving. Yes. The sums of money that, year after year, I have given towards this Orphanage, make up the amount of property—I have reckoned it carefully—which in the old days made Lieutenant Alving a catch.

Manders. I understand.

Mrs. Alving. That was my purchase money. I don't wish it to pass into Oswald's hands. My son shall have everything from me, I am determined.

[OSWALD *comes in by the farther door on the right. He has left his hat and coat outside.*

Mrs. Alving. Back again, my own dear boy?

Oswald. Yes, what can one do outside in this everlasting rain? I hear dinner is nearly ready. That's good!

[REGINA *comes in from the dining-room, carrying a parcel.*

Regina. This parcel has come for you, ma'am.

[*Gives it to her.*

Mrs. Alving (glancing at MANDERS*).* The ode to be sung to-morrow, I expect.

Manders. Hm——!

Regina. And dinner is ready.

Mrs. Alving. Good. We will come in a moment. I will just—*(begins to open the parcel).*

Regina (to OSWALD*).* Will you drink white or red wine, sir?

Oswald. Both, Miss Engstrand.

Regina. *Bien*—very good, Mr. Alving.

[*Goes into the dining-room.*

Oswald. I may as well help you to uncork it——.

[*Follows her into the dining-room, leaving the door ajar after him.*

Mrs. Alving. Yes, I thought so. Here is the ode, Mr. Manders.

Manders (clasping his hands). How shall I ever have the courage to-morrow to speak the address that——

Mrs. Alving. Oh, you will get through it.

Manders (in a low voice, fearing to be heard in the dining-room). Yes, we must raise no suspicions.

Mrs. Alving (quietly but firmly). No; and then this long dreadful comedy will be at an end. After to-morrow,

I shall feel as if my dead husband had never lived in this house. There will be no one else here then but my boy and his mother.

[*From the dining-room is heard the noise of a chair falling; then* REGINA'S *voice is heard in a loud whisper:* Oswald! Are you mad? Let me go!

Mrs. Alving (starting in horror). Oh——!

[*She stares wildly at the half-open door.* OSWALD *is heard coughing and humming, then the sound of a bottle being uncorked.*

Manders (in an agitated manner). What's the matter? What is it, Mrs. Alving?

Mrs. Alving (hoarsely). Ghosts. The couple in the conservatory—over again.

Manders. What are you saying! Regina——? Is she——?

Mrs. Alving. Yes. Come. Not a word——!

[*Grips* MANDERS *by the arm and walks unsteadily with him into the dining-room.*

ACT II

The same scene. The landscape is still obscured by mist. MANDERS *and* MRS. ALVING *come in from the dining-room.*

Mrs. Alving (calls into the dining-room from the doorway). Aren't you coming in here, Oswald?

Oswald. No, thanks; I think I will go out for a bit.

Mrs. Alving. Yes, do; the weather is clearing a little. *(She shuts the dining-room door, then goes to the hall door and calls.)* Regina!

Regina (from without). Yes, ma'am?

Mrs. Alving. Go down into the laundry and help with the garlands.

Regina. Yes, ma'am.

[MRS. ALVING *satisfies herself that she has gone, then shuts the door.*

Manders. I suppose he can't hear us?

Mrs. Alving. Not when the door is shut. Besides, he is going out.

Manders. I am still quite bewildered. I don't know how I managed to swallow a mouthful of your excellent dinner.

Mrs. Alving (walking up and down, and trying to control her agitation). Nor I. But what are we to do?

Manders. Yes, what are we to do? Upon my word I don't know; I am so completely unaccustomed to things of this kind.

Mrs. Alving. I am convinced that nothing serious has happened yet.

Manders. Heaven forbid! But it is most unseemly behaviour, for all that.

Mrs. Alving. It is nothing more than a foolish jest of Oswald's, you may be sure.

Manders. Well, of course, as I said, I am quite inexperienced in such matters; but it certainly seems to me——

Mrs. Alving. Out of the house she shall go—and at once. That part of it is as clear as daylight——

Manders. Yes, that is quite clear.

Mrs. Alving. But where is she to go? We should not be justified in——

Manders. Where to? Home to her father, of course.

Mrs. Alving. To whom, did you say?

Manders. To her——. No, of course Engstrand isn't ——. But, great heavens, Mrs. Alving, how is such a thing possible? You surely may have been mistaken, in spite of everything.

Mrs. Alving. There was no chance of mistake, more's the pity. Joanna was obliged to confess it to me—and my husband couldn't deny it. So there was nothing else to do but to hush it up.

Manders. No, that was the only thing to do.

Mrs. Alving. The girl was sent away at once, and was given a tolerably liberal sum to hold her tongue. She looked after the rest herself when she got to town. She renewed an old acquaintance with the carpenter Engstrand; gave him a hint, I suppose, of how much money she had got, and told him some fairy tale about a foreigner who had been here in his yacht in the summer. So she and Engstrand were married in a great hurry. Why, you married them yourself!

Manders. I can't understand it——. I remember clearly Engstrand's coming to arrange about the marriage. He was full of contrition, and accused himself bitterly for the light conduct he and his fiancée had been guilty of.

Mrs. Alving. Of course he had to take the blame on himself.

Manders. But the deceitfulness of it! And with me, too! I positively would not have believed it of Jacob Engstrand. I shall most certainly give him a serious talking to.—And the immorality of such a marriage! Simply for the sake of the money——! What sum was it that the girl had?

Mrs. Alving. It was seventy pounds.

Manders. Just think of it—for a paltry seventy pounds to let yourself be bound in marriage to a fallen woman!

Mrs. Alving. What about myself, then?—I let myself be bound in marriage to a fallen man.

Manders. Heaven forgive you! what are you saying? A fallen man?

Mrs. Alving. Do you suppose my husband was any purer, when I went with him to the altar, than Joanna was when Engstrand agreed to marry her?

Manders. The two cases are as different as day from night——

Mrs. Alving. Not so very different, after all. It is true there was a great difference in the price paid, between a paltry seventy pounds and a whole fortune.

Manders. How can you compare such totally different things! I presume you consulted your own heart—and your relations.

Mrs. Alving (looking away from him). I thought you understood where what you call my heart had strayed to at that time.

Manders (in a constrained voice). If I had understood anything of the kind, I would not have been a daily guest in your husband's house.

Mrs. Alving. Well, at any rate this much is certain, that I didn't consult myself in the matter at all.

Manders. Still you consulted those nearest to you, as was only right—your mother, your two aunts.

Mrs. Alving. Yes. that is true. The three of them settled the whole matter for me. It seems incredible to me now, how clearly they made out that it would be sheer folly to reject such an offer. If my mother could only see what all that fine prospect has led to!

Manders. No one can be responsible for the result of it. Anyway, there is this to be said, that the match was made in complete conformity with law and order.

Mrs. Alving (going to the window). Oh, law and order! I often think it is that that is at the bottom of all the misery in the world.

Manders. Mrs. Alving, it is very wicked of you to say that.

Mrs. Alving. That may be so; but I don't attach importance to those obligations and considerations any longer. I cannot! I must struggle for my freedom.

Manders. What do you mean?

Mrs. Alving (tapping on the window panes). I ought never to have concealed what sort of a life my husband led. But I had not the courage to do otherwise then—for my own sake, either. I was too much of a coward.

Manders. A coward?

Mrs. Alving. If others had known anything of what happened, they would have said: "Poor man, it is natural enough that he should go astray, when he has a wife that has run away from him."

Manders. They would have had a certain amount of justification for saying so.

Mrs. Alving (looking fixedly at him). If I had been the woman I ought, I would have taken Oswald into my confidence and said to him: "Listen, my son, your father was a dissolute man"——

Manders. Miserable woman——

Mrs. Alving. ——and I would have told him all I have told you, from beginning to end.

Manders. I am almost shocked at you, Mrs. Alving.

Mrs. Alving. I know. I know quite well! I am shocked at myself when I think of it. *(Comes away from the window.)* I am coward enough for that.

Manders. Can you call it cowardice that you simply did your duty! Have you forgotten that a child should love and honour his father and mother?

Mrs. Alving. Don't let us talk in such general terms. Suppose we say: "Ought Oswald to love and honour Mr. Alving?"

Manders. You are a mother—isn't there a voice in your heart that forbids you to shatter your son's ideals?

Mrs. Alving. And what about the truth?

Manders. What about his ideals?

Mrs. Alving. Oh—ideals, ideals! If only I were not such a coward as I am!

Manders. Do not spurn ideals, Mrs. Alving—they have a way of avenging themselves cruelly. Take Oswald's own case, now. He hasn't many ideals, more's the pity. But this much I have seen, that his father is something of an ideal to him.

Mrs. Alving. You are right there.

Manders. And his conception of his father is what you inspired and encouraged by your letters.

Mrs. Alving. Yes, I was swayed by duty and consideration for others; that was why I lied to my son, year in and year out. Oh, what a coward—what a coward I have been!

Manders. You have built up a happy illusion in your son's mind, Mrs. Alving—and that is a thing you certainly ought not to undervalue.

Mrs. Alving. Ah, who knows if that is such a desirable thing after all!—But anyway I don't intend to put up with any goings on with Regina. I am not going to let him get the poor girl into trouble.

Manders. Good heavens, no—that would be a frightful thing!

Mrs. Alving. If only I knew whether he meant it seriously, and whether it would mean happiness for him——

Manders. In what way? I don't understand.

Mrs. Alving. But that is impossible; Regina is not equal to it, unfortunately.

Manders. I don't understand. What do you mean?

Mrs. Alving. If I were not such a miserable coward, I would say to him: "Marry her, or make any arrangement you like with her—only let there be no deceit in the matter."

Manders. Heaven forgive you! Are you actually suggesting anything so abominable, so unheard of, as a marriage between them!

Mrs. Alving. Unheard of, do you call it? Tell me honestly, Mr. Manders, don't you suppose there are plenty of married couples out here in the country that are just as nearly related as they are?

Manders. I am sure I don't understand you.

Mrs. Alving. Indeed you do.

Manders. I suppose you are thinking of cases where possibly——. It is only too true, unfortunately, that family life is not always as stainless as it should be. But as for the sort of thing you hint at—well, it's impossible to tell, at all events with any certainty. Here, on the other hand—for you, a mother, to be willing to allow your——

Mrs. Alving. But I am not willing to allow it. I would not allow it for anything in the world; that is just what I was saying.

Manders. No, because you are a coward, as you put it. But, supposing you were not a coward——! Great heavens—such a revolting union!

Mrs. Alving. Well, for the matter of that, we are all descended from a union of that description, so we are told. And who was it that was responsible for this state of things Mr. Manders?

Manders. I can't discuss such questions with you, Mrs. Alving; you are by no means in the right frame of mind for that. But for you to dare to say that it is cowardly of you——!

Mrs. Alving. I will tell you what I mean by that. I am frightened and timid, because I am obsessed by the presence of ghosts that I never can get rid of.

Manders. The presence of what?

Mrs. Alving. Ghosts. When I heard Regina and Oswald in there, it was just like seeing ghosts before my eyes. I am half inclined to think we are all ghosts, Mr. Manders. It is not only what we have inherited from our fathers and mothers that exists again in us, but all sorts of old dead ideas and all kinds of old dead beliefs and things of that kind. They are not actually alive in us; but there they are dormant, all the same, and we can never be rid of them. Whenever I take up a newspaper and read it, I fancy I see ghosts creeping between the lines. There must be ghosts all over the world. They must be as countless as the grains of the sands, it seems to me. And we are so miserably afraid of the light, all of us.

Manders. Ah!—there we have the outcome of your reading. Fine fruit it has borne—this abominable, subversive, free-thinking literature!

Mrs. Alving. You are wrong there, my friend. You are the one who made me begin to think; and I owe you my best thanks for it.

Manders. I!

Mrs. Alving. Yes, by forcing me to submit to what you called my duty and my obligations; by praising as right and just what my whole soul revolted against, as it would against something abominable. That was what led me to examine your teachings critically. I only wanted to unravel one point in them; but as soon as I had got that unravelled, the whole fabric came to pieces. And then I realised that it was only machine-made.

Manders (softly, and with emotion). Is that all I accomplished by the hardest struggle of my life?

Mrs. Alving. Call it rather the most ignominious defeat of your life.

Manders. It was the greatest victory of my life, Helen; victory over myself.

Mrs. Alving. It was a wrong done to both of us.

Manders. A wrong?—wrong for me to entreat you as a wife to go back to your lawful husband, when you came to me half distracted and crying: "Here I am, take me!" Was that a wrong?

Mrs. Alving. I think it was.

Manders. We two do not understand one another.

Mrs. Alving. Not now, at all events.

Manders. Never—even in my most secret thoughts—have I for a moment regarded you as anything but the wife of another.

Mrs. Alving. Do you believe what you say?

Manders. Helen——!

Mrs. Alving. One so easily forgets one's own feelings.

Manders. Not I. I am the same as I always was.

Mrs. Alving. Yes, yes—don't let us talk any more about the old days. You are buried up to your eyes now in committees and all sorts of business; and I am here, fighting with ghosts both without and within me.

Manders. I can at all events help you to get the better of those without you. After all that I have been horrified to hear from you to-day, I cannot conscientiously allow a young defenceless girl to remain in your house.

Mrs. Alving. Don't you think it would be best if we could get her settled?—by some suitable marriage, I mean.

Manders. Undoubtedly. I think, in any case, it would have been desirable for her. Regina is at an age now that —well, I don't know much about these things, but——

Mrs. Alving. Regina developed very early.

Manders. Yes, didn't she. I fancy I remember thinking she was remarkably well developed, bodily, at the time I prepared her for Confirmation. But, for the time being she must in any case go home. Under her father's care—no, but of course Engstrand is not——. To think that he, of all men, could so conceal the truth from me!

[*A knock is heard at the hall door.*

Mrs. Alving. Who can that be? Come in!

[ENGSTRAND, *dressed in his Sunday clothes, appears in the doorway.*

Engstrand. I humbly beg pardon, but——

Manders. Aha! Hm!——

Mrs. Alving. Oh, it's you, Engstrand!

Engstrand. There were none of the maids about, so I took the great liberty of knocking.

Mrs. Alving. That's all right. Come in. Do you want to speak to me?

Engstrand (coming in). No, thank you very much, ma'm. It was Mr. Manders I wanted to speak to for a moment.

Manders (walking up and down). Hm!—do you. You want to speak to me, do you?

Engstrand. Yes, sir, I wanted so very much to——

Manders (stopping in front of him). Well, may I ask what it is you want?

Engstrand. It's this way, Mr. Manders. We are being paid off now. And many thanks to you, Mrs. Alving. And now the work is quite finished, I thought it would be so nice and suitable if all of us, who have worked so honestly together all this time, were to finish up with a few prayers this evening.

Manders. Prayers? Up at the Orphanage?

Engstrand. Yes, sir, but if it isn't agreeable to you, then——

Manders. Oh, certainly——but—hm!——

Engstrand. I have made a practice of saying a few prayers there myself each evening——

Mrs. Alving. Have you?

Engstrand. Yes, ma'am, now and then—just as a little

edification, so to speak. But I am only a poor common man, and haven't rightly the gift, alas—and so I thought that as Mr. Manders happened to be here, perhaps——

Manders. Look here, Engstrand. First of all I must ask you a question. Are you in a proper frame of mind for such a thing? Is your conscience free and untroubled?

Engstrand. Heaven have mercy on me a sinner! My conscience isn't worth our speaking about, Mr. Manders.

Manders. But it is just what we must speak about. What do you say to my question?

Engstrand. My conscience? Well—it's uneasy sometimes, of course.

Manders. Ah, you admit that at all events. Now will you tell me, without any concealment—what is your relationship to Regina?

Mrs. Alving (hastily). Mr. Manders!

Manders (calming her).—Leave it to me!

Engstrand. With Regina? Good Lord, how you frightened me! *(Looks at* Mrs. Alving.*)* There is nothing wrong with Regina, is there?

Manders. Let us hope not. What I want to know is, what is your relationship to her? You pass as her father, don't you?

Engstrand (unsteadily). Well—hm!—you know, sir, what happened between me and my poor Joanna.

Manders. No more distortion of the truth! Your late wife made a full confession to Mrs. Alving, before she left her service.

Engstrand. What!—do you mean to say——? Did she do that after all?

Manders. You see it has all come out, Engstrand.

Engstrand. Do you mean to say that she, who gave me her promise and solemn oath——

Manders. Did she take an oath?

Engstrand. Well, no—she only gave me her word, but as seriously as a woman could.

Manders. And all these years you have been hiding the truth from me—from me, who have had such complete and absolute faith in you.

Engstrand. I am sorry to say I have, sir.

Manders. Did I deserve that from you, Engstrand? Haven't I been always ready to help you in word and deed as far as lay in my power? Answer me! Is it not so?

Engstrand. Indeed there's many a time I should have been very badly off without you, sir.

Manders. And this is the way you repay me—by causing me to make false entries in the church registers, and afterwards keeping back from me for years the information which you owed it both to me and to your sense of the truth to divulge. Your conduct has been absolutely inexcusable, Engstrand, and from to-day everything is at an end between us.

Engstrand (with a sigh). Yes, I can see that's what it means.

Manders. Yes, because how can you possibly justify what you did?

Engstrand. Was the poor girl to go and increase her load of shame by talking about it? Just suppose, sir, for a moment that your reverence was in the same predicament as my poor Joanna——

Manders. I!

Engstrand. Good Lord, sir, I don't mean the same predicament. I mean, suppose there were something your reverence were ashamed of in the eyes of the world, so to speak. We men oughtn't to judge a poor woman too hardly, Mr. Manders.

Manders. But I am not doing so at all. It is you I am blaming.

Engstrand. Will your reverence grant me leave to ask you a small question?

Manders. Ask away.

Engstrand. Shouldn't you say it was right for a man to raise up the fallen?

Manders. Of course it is.

Engstrand. And isn't a man bound to keep his word of honour?

Manders. Certainly he is; but——

Engstrand. At the time when Joanna had her misfortune with this Englishman—or maybe he was an American or a Russian, as they call 'em—well, sir, then she came to town. Poor thing, she had refused me once or twice before; she only had eyes for good-looking men in those days, and I had this crooked leg then. Your reverence will remember how I had ventured up into a dancing-saloon where seafaring men were revelling in drunkenness and intoxication, as they say. And when I tried to exhort them to turn from their evil ways——

Mrs. Alving (coughs from the window). Ahem!

Manders. I know, Engstrand, I know—the rough brutes threw you downstairs. You have told me about that incident before. The affliction to your leg is a credit to you.

Engstrand. I don't want to claim credit for it, your reverence. But what I wanted to tell you was that she came then and confided in me with tears and gnashing of teeth. I can tell you, sir, it went to my heart to hear her.

Manders. Did it, indeed, Engstrand? Well, what then?

Engstrand. Well, then I said to her: "The American is roaming about on the high seas, he is. And you, Joanna," I said, "you have committed a sin and are a fallen woman. But here stands Jacob Engstrand," I said, "on two strong legs"—of course that was only speaking in a kind of metaphor, as it were, your reverence.

Manders. I quite understand. Go on.

Engstrand. Well, sir, that was how I rescued her and made her my lawful wife, so that no one should know how recklessly she had carried on with the stranger.

Manders. That was all very kindly done. The only thing I cannot justify was your bringing yourself to accept the money——

Engstrand. Money? I? Not a farthing.

Manders (to Mrs. Alving, *in a questioning tone).* But——

Engstrand. Ah, yes!—wait a bit; I remember now. Joanna did have a trifle of money, you are quite right. But I didn't want to know anything about that. "Fie," I said, "on the mammon of unrighteousness, it's the price of your sin; as for this tainted gold"—or notes, or whatever it was—"we will throw it back in the American's face," I said. But he had gone away and disappeared on the stormy seas, your reverence.

Manders. Was that how it was, my good fellow?

Engstrand. It was, sir. So then Joanna and I decided that the money should go towards the child's bringing-up, and that's what became of it; and I can give a faithful account of every single penny of it.

Manders. This alters the complexion of the affair very considerably.

Engstrand. That's how it was your reverence. And I make bold to say that I have been a good father to Regina—as far as was in my power—for I am a poor erring mortal, alas!

Manders. There, there, my dear Engstrand——

Engstrand. Yes, I do make bold to say that I brought up the child, and made my poor Joanna a loving and careful husband, as the Bible says we ought. But it never occurred to me to go to your reverence and claim credit for it or boast about it because I had done one good deed in this world. No; when Jacob Engstrand does a thing like that, he holds his tongue about it. Unfortunately it doesn't often happen, I know that only too well. And whenever I do come to see your reverence, I never seem to have anything but trouble and wickedness to talk about. Because, as I said just now—and I say it again—conscience can be very hard on us sometimes.

Manders. Give me your hand, Jacob Engstrand.

Engstrand. Oh, sir, I don't like——

Manders. No nonsense. *(Grasps his hand.)* That's it!

Engstrand. And may I make bold humbly to beg your reverence's pardon——

Manders. You? On the contrary it is for me to beg your pardon——

Engstrand. Oh no, sir.

Manders. Yes, certainly it is, and I do it with my whole heart. Forgive me for having so much misjudged you. And I assure you that if I can do anything for you to prove my sincere regret and my goodwill towards you——

Engstrand. Do you mean it, sir?

Manders. It would give me the greatest pleasure.

Engstrand. As a matter of fact, sir, you could do it now. I am thinking of using the honest money I have put away out of my wages up here, in establishing a sort of Sailors' Home in the town.

Mrs. Alving. You?

Engstrand. Yes, to be a sort of Refuge, as it were. There are such manifold temptations lying in wait for sailor men when they are roaming about on shore. But my idea is that in this house of mine they should have a sort of parental care looking after them.

Manders. What do you say to that, Mrs. Alving!

Engstrand. I haven't much to begin such a work with, I know; but Heaven might prosper it, and if I found any helping hand stretched out to me, then——

Manders. Quite so; we will talk over the matter further. Your project attracts me enormously. But in the meantime go back to the Orphanage and put everything tidy and light the lights, so that the occasion may seem a little solemn.

And then we will spend a little edifying time together, my dear Engstrand, for now I am sure you are in a suitable frame of mind.

Engstrand. I believe I am, sir, truly. Good-bye, then, Mrs. Alving, and thank you for all your kindness; and take good care of Regina for me. *(Wipes a tear from his eye.)* Poor Joanna's child—it is an extraordinary thing, but she seems to have grown into my life and to hold me by the heartstrings. That's how I feel about it, truly.

[*Bows and goes out.*

Manders. Now then, what do you think of him, Mrs. Alving! That was quite another explanation that he gave us.

Mrs. Alving. It was, indeed.

Manders. There, you see how exceedingly careful we ought to be in condemning our fellow-men. But at the same time it gives one genuine pleasure to find that one was mistaken. Don't you think so?

Mrs. Alving. What I think is that you are, and always will remain, a big baby, Mr. Manders.

Manders. I?

Mrs. Alving (laying her hands on his shoulders). And I think that I should like very much to give you a good hug.

Manders (drawing back hastily). No, no, good gracious! What an idea!

Mrs. Alving (with a smile). Oh, you needn't be afraid of me.

Manders (standing by the table). You choose such an extravagant way of expressing yourself sometimes. Now I must get these papers together and put them in my bag. *(Does so.)* That's it. And now good-bye, for the present. Keep your eyes open when Oswald comes back. I will come back and see you again presently.

[*He takes his hat and goes out by the hall door.* MRS ALVING *sighs, glances out of the window, puts one or two things tidy in the room and turns to go into the dining-room. She stops in the doorway with a stifled cry.*

Mrs. Alving. Oswald, are you still sitting at table!

Oswald (from the dining-room). I am only finishing my cigar.

Mrs. Alving. I thought you had gone out for a little turn.

Oswald (from within the room). In weather like this? *(A glass is heard clinking.* Mrs. Alving *leaves the door open and sits down with her knitting on the couch by the window.)* Wasn't that Mr. Manders that went out just now?

Mrs. Alving. Yes, he has gone over to the Orphanage.

Oswald. Oh.

[*The clink of a bottle on a glass is heard again.*

Mrs. Alving (with an uneasy expression). Oswald, dear, you should be careful with that liqueur. It is strong.

Oswald. It's a good protective against the damp.

Mrs. Alving. Wouldn't you rather come in here?

Oswald. You know you don't like smoking in there.

Mrs. Alving. You may smoke a cigar in here, certainly.

Oswald. All right; I will come in, then. Just one drop more. There! *(Comes in, smoking a cigar, and shuts the door after him. A short silence.)* Where has the parson gone?

Mrs. Alving. I told you he had gone over to the Orphanage.

Oswald. Oh, so you did.

Mrs. Alving. You shouldn't sit so long at table, Oswald.

Oswald (holding his cigar behind his back). But it's so nice and cosy, mother dear. *(Caresses her with one hand.)* Think what it means to me—to have come home; to sit at my mother's own table, in my mother's own room, and to enjoy the charming meals she gives me.

Mrs. Alving. My dear, dear boy!

Oswald (a little impatiently, as he walks up and down smoking.) And what else is there for me to do here? I have no occupation——

Mrs. Alving. No occupation?

Oswald. Not in this ghastly weather, when there isn't a blink of sunshine all day long. *(Walks up and down the floor.)* Not to be able to work, it's——!

Mrs. Alving. I don't believe you were wise to come home.

Oswald. Yes, mother; I had to.

Mrs. Alving. Because I would ten times rather give up the happiness of having you with me, sooner than that you should——

Oswald (standing still by the table). Tell me, mother—is it really such a great happiness for you to have me at home?

Mrs. Alving. Can you ask?

Oswald (crumpling up a newspaper). I should have thought it would have been pretty much the same to you whether I were here or away.

Mrs. Alving. Have you the heart to say that to your mother, Oswald?

Oswald. But you have been quite happy living without me so far.

Mrs. Alving. Yes, I have lived without you—that is true.

[*A silence. The dusk falls by degrees.* OSWALD *walks restlessly up and down. He has laid aside his cigar.*

Oswald (stopping beside MRS. ALVING*).* Mother, may I sit on the couch beside you?

Mrs. Alving. Of course, my dear boy.

Oswald (sitting down). Now I must tell you something, mother.

Mrs. Alving (anxiously). What?

Oswald (staring in front of him). I can't bear it any longer.

Mrs. Alving. Bear what? What do you mean?

Oswald (as before). I couldn't bring myself to write to you about it; and since I have been at home——

Mrs. Alving (catching him by the arm). Oswald, what is it?

Oswald. Both yesterday and to-day I have tried to push my thoughts away from me—to free myself from them. But I can't.

Mrs. Alving (getting up). You must speak plainly, Oswald!

Oswald (drawing her down to her seat again). Sit still, and I will try and tell you. I have made a great deal of the fatigue I felt after my journey——

Mrs. Alving. Well, what of that?

Oswald. But that isn't what is the matter. It is no ordinary fatigue——

Mrs. Alving (trying to get up). You are not ill, Oswald!

Oswald (pulling her down again). Sit still, mother. Do take it quietly. I am not exactly ill—not ill in the usual sense. *(Takes his head in his hands.)* Mother, it's my mind that has broken down—gone to pieces—I shall never be able to work any more!

[*Buries his face in his hands and throws himself at her knees in an outburst of sobs.*

Mrs. Alving (pale and trembling). Oswald! Look at me! No, no, it isn't true!

Oswald (looking up with a distracted expression). Never to be able to work any more! Never—never! A living death! Mother, can you imagine anything so horrible!

Mrs. Alving. My poor unhappy boy? How has this terrible thing happened?

Oswald (sitting up again). That is just what I cannot possibly understand. I have never lived recklessly, in any sense. You must believe that of me, mother! I have never done that.

Mrs. Alving. I haven't a doubt of it, Oswald.

Oswald. And yet this comes upon me all the same!—this terrible disaster!

Mrs. Alving. Oh, but it will all come right again, my dear precious boy. It is nothing but overwork. Believe me, that is so.

Oswald (dully). I thought so too, at first; but it isn't so.

Mrs. Alving. Tell me all about it.

Oswald. Yes, I will.

Mrs. Alving. When did you first feel anything?

Oswald. It was just after I had been home last time and had got back to Paris. I began to feel the most violent pains in my head—mostly at the back, I think. It was as if a tight band of iron was pressing on me from my neck upwards.

Mrs. Alving. And then?

Oswald. At first I thought it was nothing but the headaches I always used to be so much troubled with while I was growing.

Mrs. Alving. Yes, yes——

Oswald. But it wasn't; I soon saw that. I couldn't work any longer. I would try and start some big new picture; but it seemed as if all my faculties had forsaken me, as if all my strength were paralysed. I couldn't manage to collect my thoughts; my head seemed to swim—everything went round and round. It was a horrible feeling! At last I sent for a doctor—and from him I learnt the truth.

Mrs. Alving. In what way, do you mean?

Oswald. He was one of the best doctors there. He made me describe what I felt, and then he began to ask me a whole heap of questions which seemed to me to have nothing to do with the matter. I couldn't see what he was driving at——

Mrs. Alving. Well?

Oswald. At last he said: "You have had the canker of

disease in you practically from your birth"—the actual word he used was *"vermoulu."*

Mrs. Alving (anxiously). What did he mean by that?

Oswald. I couldn't understand, either—and I asked him for a clearer explanation. And then the old cynic said—*(clenching his fist.)* Oh!——

Mrs. Alving. What did he say?

Oswald. He said: "The sins of the fathers are visited on the children."

Mrs. Alving (getting up slowly). The sins of the fathers——!

Oswald. I nearly struck him in the face——

Mrs. Alving (walking across the room). The sins of the fathers——!

Oswald (smiling sadly). Yes, just imagine! Naturally I assured him that what he thought was impossible. But do you think he paid any heed to me? No, he persisted in his opinion; and it was only when I got out your letters and translated to him all the passages that referred to my father——

Mrs. Alving. Well, and then?

Oswald. Well, then of course he had to admit that he was on the wrong tack; and then I learnt the truth—the incomprehensible truth! I ought to have had nothing to do with the joyous happy life I had lived with my comrades. It had been too much for my strength. So it was my own fault!

Mrs. Alving. No, no, Oswald! Don't believe that!

Oswald. There was no other explanation of it possible, he said. That is the most horrible part of it. My whole life incurably ruined—just because of my own imprudence. All that I wanted to do in the world—not to dare to think of it any more—not to be *able* to think of it! Oh! if only I could live my life over again—if only I could undo what I have done!

[*Throws himself on his face on the couch.* MRS. ALVING *wrings her hands and walks up and down silently fighting with herself.*

Oswald (looks up after a while, raising himself on his elbows). If only it had been something I had inherited—something I could not help. But, instead of that, to have disgracefully, stupidly, thoughtlessly thrown away one's happiness, one's health, everything in the world—one's future, one's life——

Mrs. Alving. No, no, my darling boy; that is impossible! *(Bending over him.)* Things are not so desperate as you think.

Oswald. Ah, you don't know——. *(Springs up.)* And to think, mother, that I should bring all this sorrow upon you! Many a time I have almost wished and hoped that you really did not care so very much for me.

Mrs. Alving. I, Oswald? My only son! All that I have in the world! The only thing I care about!

Oswald (taking hold of her hands and kissing them). Yes, yes, I know that is so. When I am at home I know that is true. And that is one of the hardest parts of it to me. But now you know all about it; and now we won't talk any more about it to-day. I can't stand thinking about it long at a time. *(Walks across the room.)* Let me have something to drink, mother!

Mrs. Alving. To drink? What do you want?

Oswald. Oh, anything you like. I suppose you have got some punch in the house.

Mrs. Alving. Yes, but my dear Oswald——!

Oswald. Don't tell me I mustn't, mother. Do be nice! I must have something to drown these gnawing thoughts. *(Goes into the conservatory.)* And how—how gloomy it is here! (MRS. ALVING *rings the bell.)* And this incessant rain. It may go on week after week—a whole month. Never a ray of sunshine. I don't remember ever having seen the sunshine once when I have been at home.

Mrs. Alving. Oswald—you are thinking of going away from me!

Oswald. Hm!—*(sighs deeply)*. I am not thinking about anything. I *can't* think about anything! *(In a low voice.)* I have to let that alone.

Regina (coming from the dining-room). Did you ring, ma'am?

Mrs. Alving. Yes, let us have the lamp in.

Regina. In a moment, ma'am; it is all ready lit.

[*Goes out.*

Mrs. Alving (going up to OSWALD*).* Oswald, don't keep anything back from me.

Oswald. I don't, mother. *(Goes to the table.)* It seems to me I have told you a good lot.

[REGINA *brings the lamp and puts it upon the table.*

Mrs. Alving. Regina, you might bring us a small bottle of champagne.

Regina. Yes, ma'am. [*Goes out.*

Oswald (taking hold of his mother's face). That's right. I knew my mother wouldn't let her son go thirsty.

Mrs. Alving. My poor dear boy, how could I refuse you anything now?

Oswald (eagerly). Is that true, mother? Do you mean it?

Mrs. Alving. Mean what?

Oswald. That you couldn't deny me anything?

Mrs. Alving. My dear Oswald——

Oswald. Hush!

[REGINA *brings in a tray with a small bottle of champagne and two glasses, which she puts on the table.*

Regina. Shall I open the bottle?

Oswald. No, thank you, I will do it.

[REGINA *goes out.*

Mrs. Alving (sitting down at the table). What did you mean, when you asked if I could refuse you nothing?

Oswald (busy opening the bottle). Let us have a glass first—or two.

[*He draws the cork, fills one glass and is going to fill the other.*

Mrs. Alving (holding her hand over the second glass). No, thanks—not for me.

Oswald. Oh, well, for me then!

[*He empties his glass, fills it again and empties it; then sits down at the table.*

Mrs. Alving (expectantly). Now, tell me.

Oswald (without looking at her). Tell me this; I thought you and Mr. Manders seemed so strange—so quiet—at dinner.

Mrs. Alving. Did you notice that?

Oswald. Yes. Ahem! *(After a short pause.)* Tell me —What do you think of Regina?

Mrs. Alving. What do I think of her?

Oswald. Yes, isn't she splendid!

Mrs. Alving. Dear Oswald, you don't know her as well as I do——

Oswald. What of that?

Mrs. Alving. Regina was too long at home, unfortunately. I ought to have taken her under my charge sooner.

Oswald. Yes, but isn't she splendid to look at, mother? [*Fills his glass.*

Mrs. Alving. Regina has many serious faults——

Oswald. Yes, but what of that? [*Drinks.*

Mrs. Alving. But I am fond of her, all the same; and I have made myself responsible for her. I wouldn't for the world she should come to any harm.

Oswald (jumping up). Mother, Regina is my only hope of salvation!

Mrs. Alving (getting up). What do you mean?

Oswald. I can't go on bearing all this agony of mind alone.

Mrs. Alving. Haven't you your mother to help you to bear it?

Oswald. Yes, I thought so; that was why I came home to you. But it is no use; I see that it isn't. I cannot spend my life here.

Mrs. Alving. Oswald!

Oswald. I must live a different sort of life, mother; so I shall have to go away from you. I don't want you watching it.

Mrs. Alving. My unhappy boy! But, Oswald, as long as you are ill like this——

Oswald. If it was only a matter of feeling ill, I would stay with you, mother. You are the best friend I have in the world.

Mrs. Alving. Yes, I am that, Oswald, am I not?

Oswald (walking restlessly about). But all this torment —the regret, the remorse—and the deadly fear. Oh—this horrible fear!

Mrs. Alving (following him). Fear? Fear of what? What do you mean?

Oswald. Oh, don't ask me any more about it. I don't know what it is. I can't put it into words. *(*MRS. ALVING *crosses the room and rings the bell.)* What do you want?

Mrs. Alving. I want my boy to be happy, that's what I want. He mustn't brood over anything. *(To* REGINA, *who has come to the door.)* More champagne—a large bottle.

Oswald. Mother!

Mrs. Alving. Do you think we country people don't know how to live?

Oswald. Isn't she splendid to look at? What a figure! And the picture of health!

Mrs. Alving (sitting down at the table). Sit down, Oswald, and let us have a quiet talk.

Oswald (sitting down). You don't know, mother, that I owe Regina a little reparation.

Mrs. Alving. You!

Oswald. Oh, it was only a little thoughtlessness—call it what you like. Something quite innocent, anyway. The last time I was home——

Mrs. Alving. Yes?

Oswald. ——she used often to ask me questions about Paris, and I told her one thing and another about the life there. And I remember saying one day: "Wouldn't you like to go there yourself?"

Mrs. Alving. Well?

Oswald. I saw her blush, and she said: "Yes, I should like to very much." "All right," I said, "I daresay it might be managed"—or something of that sort.

Mrs. Alving. And then?

Oswald. I naturally had forgotten all about it; but the day before yesterday I happened to ask her if she was glad I was to be so long at home——

Mrs. Alving. Well?

Oswald. ——and she looked so queerly at me, and asked: "But what is to become of my trip to Paris?"

Mrs. Alving. Her trip!

Oswald. And then I got it out of her that she had taken the thing seriously, and had been thinking about me all the time, and had set herself to learn French——

Mrs. Alving. So that was why——

Oswald. Mother—when I saw this fine, splendid, handsome girl standing there in front of me—I had never paid any attention to her before then—but now, when she stood there as if with open arms ready for me to take her to myself——

Mrs. Alving. Oswald!

Oswald. ——then I realised that my salvation lay in her, for I saw the joy of life in her.

Mrs. Alving (starting back). The joy of life——? Is there salvation in that?

Regina (coming in from the dining-room with a bottle of champagne). Excuse me for being so long; but I had to go to the cellar.

[*Puts the bottle down on the table.*

Oswald. Bring another glass, too.

Regina (looking at him in astonishment). The mistress's glass is there, sir.

Oswald. Yes, but fetch one for yourself, Regina. (REGINA *starts, and gives a quick shy glance at* MRS. ALVING.) Well?

Regina (in a low and hesitating voice). Do you wish me to, ma'am?

Mrs. Alving. Fetch the glass, Regina.

[REGINA *goes into the dining-room.*

Oswald (looking after her). Have you noticed how well she walks?—so firmly and confidently!

Mrs. Alving. It cannot be, Oswald.

Oswald. It is settled. You must see that. It is no use forbidding it. (REGINA *comes in with a glass, which she holds in her hand.*) Sit down, Regina.

[REGINA *looks questioningly at* MRS. ALVING.

Mrs. Alving. Sit down. (REGINA *sits down on a chair near the dining-room door, still holding the glass in her hand.*) Oswald, what was it you were saying about the joy of life?

Oswald. Ah, mother—the joy of life! You don't know very much about that at home here. I shall never realise it here.

Mrs. Alving. Not even when you are with me?

Oswald. Never at home. But you can't understand that.

Mrs. Alving. Yes, indeed I almost think I do understand you—now.

Oswald. That—and the joy of work. They are really

the same thing at bottom. But you don't know anything about that either.

Mrs. Alving. Perhaps you are right. Tell me some more about it, Oswald.

Oswald. Well, all I mean is that here people are brought up to believe that work is a curse and a punishment for sin, and that life is a state of wretchedness and that the sooner we can get out of it the better.

Mrs. Alving. A vale of tears, yes. And we quite conscientiously make it so.

Oswald. But the people over there will have none of that. There is no one there who really believes doctrines of that kind any longer. Over there the mere fact of being alive is thought to be a matter for exultant happiness. Mother, have you noticed that everything I have painted has turned upon the joy of life?—always upon the joy of life, unfailingly. There is light there, and sunshine, and a holiday feeling—and people's faces beaming with happiness. That is why I am afraid to stay at home here with you.

Mrs. Alving. Afraid? What are you afraid of here, with me?

Oswald. I am afraid that all these feelings that are so strong in me would degenerate into something ugly here.

Mrs. Alving (looking steadily at him). Do you think that is what would happen?

Oswald. I am certain it would. Even if one lived the same life at home here, as over there—it would never really be the same life.

Mrs. Alving (who has listened anxiously to him, gets up with a thoughtful expression and says:) Now I see clearly how it all happened.

Oswald. What do you see?

Mrs. Alving. I see it now for the first time. And now I can speak.

Oswald (getting up). Mother, I don't understand you.

Regina (who has got up also). Perhaps I had better go.

Mrs. Alving. No, stay here. Now I can speak. Now, my son, you shall know the whole truth. Oswald! Regina!

Oswald. Hush!—here is the parson——

[MANDERS *comes in by the hall door.*

Manders. Well, my friends, we have been spending an edifying time over there.

Oswald. So have we.

Manders. Engstrand must have help with his Sailors' Home. Regina must go home with him and give him her assistance.

Regina. No, thank you, Mr. Manders.

Manders (perceiving her for the first time). What——? you in here?—and with a wineglass in your hand!

Regina (putting down the glass hastily). I beg your pardon——!

Oswald. Regina is going away with me, Mr. Manders.

Manders. Going away! With you!

Oswald. Yes, as my wife—if she insists on that.

Manders. But, good heavens——!

Regina. It is not my fault, Mr. Manders.

Oswald. Or else she stays here if I stay.

Regina (involuntarily). Here!

Manders. I am amazed at you, Mrs. Alving.

Mrs. Alving. Neither of those things will happen, for now I can speak openly.

Manders. But you won't do that! No, no, no!

Mrs. Alving. Yes, I can and I will. And without destroying any one's ideals.

Oswald. Mother, what is it that is being concealed from me?

Regina (listening). Mrs. Alving! Listen! They are shouting outside.

[*Goes into the conservatory and looks out.*

Oswald (going to the window on the left). What can be the matter? Where does that glare come from?

Regina (calls out). The Orphanage is on fire!

Mrs. Alving (going to the window). On fire?

Manders. On fire? Impossible. I was there just a moment ago.

Oswald. Where is my hat? Oh, never mind that. Father's Orphanage——!

[*Runs out through the garden door.*

Mrs. Alving. My shawl, Regina! The whole place is in flames.

Manders. How terrible! Mrs. Alving, that fire is a judgment on this house of sin!

Mrs. Alving. Quite so. Come, Regina.

[*She and* REGINA *hurry out.*

Manders (clasping his hands). And no insurance!

[*Follows them out.*

ACT III

The same scene. All the doors are standing open. The lamp is still burning on the table. It is dark outside, except for a faint glimmer of light seen through the windows at the back. MRS. ALVING, *with a shawl over her head, is standing in the conservatory, looking out.* REGINA, *also wrapped in a shawl, is standing a little behind her.*

Mrs. Alving. Everything burnt—down to the ground.

Regina. It is burning still in the basement.

Mrs. Alving. I can't think why Oswald doesn't come back. There is no chance of saving anything.

Regina. Shall I go and take his hat to him?

Mrs. Alving. Hasn't he even got his hat?

Regina (pointing to the hall). No, there it is, hanging up.

Mrs. Alving. Never mind. He is sure to come back soon. I will go and see what he is doing.

[*Goes out by the garden door.* MANDERS *comes in from the hall.*

Manders. Isn't Mrs. Alving here?

Regina. She has just this moment gone down into the garden.

Manders. I have never spent such a terrible night in my life.

Regina. Isn't it a shocking misfortune, sir!

Manders. Oh, don't speak about it. I scarcely dare to think about it.

Regina. But how can it have happened?

Manders. Don't ask me, Miss Engstrand! How should I know? Are you going to suggest too——? Isn't it enough that your father——?

Regina. What has he done?

Manders. He has nearly driven me crazy.

Engstrand (coming in from the hall). Mr. Manders——!

Manders (turning round with a start). Have you even followed me here!

Engstrand. Yes, God help us all——! Great heavens! What a dreadful thing, your reverence!

Manders (walking up and down). Oh dear, oh dear!

Regina. What do you mean?

Engstrand. Our little prayer-meeting was the cause of it all, don't you see? *(Aside, to* REGINA.*)* Now we've got the old fool, my girl. *(Aloud.)* And to think it is my fault that Mr. Manders should be the cause of such a thing!

Manders. I assure you, Engstrand——

Engstrand. But there was no one else carrying a light there except you, sir.

Manders (standing still). Yes, so you say. But I have no clear recollection of having had a light in my hand.

Engstrand. But I saw quite distinctly your reverence take a candle and snuff it with your fingers and throw away the burning bit of wick among the shavings.

Manders. Did you see that?

Engstrand. Yes, distinctly.

Manders. I can't understand it at all. It is never my habit to snuff a candle with my fingers.

Engstrand. Yes, it wasn't like you to do that, sir. But who would have thought it could be such a dangerous thing to do?

Manders (walking restlessly backwards and forwards). Oh, don't ask me!

Engstrand (following him about). And you hadn't insured it either, had you, sir?

Manders. No, no, no; you heard me say so.

Engstrand. You hadn't insured it— and then went and set light to the whole place! Good Lord, what bad luck!

Manders (wiping the perspiration from his forehead). You may well say so, Engstrand.

Engstrand. And that it should happen to a charitable institution that would have been of service both to the town and the country, so to speak! The newspapers won't be very kind to your reverence, I expect.

Manders. No, that is just what I am thinking of. It is almost the worst part of the whole thing. The spiteful attacks and accusations—it is horrible to think of!

Mrs. Alving (coming in from the garden). I can't get him away from the fire.

Manders. Oh, there you are, Mrs. Alving.

Mrs. Alving. You will escape having to make your inaugural address now, at all events, Mr. Manders.

Manders. Oh, I would so gladly have——

Mrs. Alving (in a dull voice). It is just as well it has happened. This Orphanage would never have come to any good.

Manders. Don't you think so?

Mrs. Alving. Do you?

Manders. But it is none the less an extraordinary piece of ill luck.

Mrs. Alving. We will discuss it simply as a business matter.—Are you waiting for Mr. Manders, Engstrand?

Engstrand (at the hall door). Yes, I am.

Mrs. Alving. Sit down then, while you are waiting.

Engstrand. Thank you, I would rather stand.

Mrs. Alving (to MANDERS*).* I suppose you are going by the boat?

Manders. Yes. It goes in about an hour.

Mrs. Alving. Please take all the documents back with you. I don't want to hear another word about the matter. I have something else to think about now——

Manders. Mrs. Alving——

Mrs. Alving. Later on I will send you a power of attorney to deal with it exactly as you please.

Manders. I shall be most happy to undertake that. I am afraid the original intention of the bequest will have to be entirely altered now.

Mrs. Alving. Of course.

Manders. Provisionally, I should suggest this way of disposing of it. Make over the Solvik property to the parish. The land is undoubtedly not without a certain value; it will always be useful for some purpose or another. And as for the interest on the remaining capital that is on deposit in the bank, possibly I might make suitable use of that in support of some undertaking that promises to be of use to the town.

Mrs. Alving. Do exactly as you please. The whole thing is a matter of indifference to me now.

Engstrand. You will think of my Sailors' Home, Mr. Manders?

Manders. Yes, certainly, that is a suggestion. But we must consider the matter carefully.

Engstrand (aside). Consider!—devil take it! Oh Lord.

Manders (sighing). And unfortunately I can't tell how much longer I may have anything to do with the matter—whether public opinion may not force me to retire from it altogether. That depends entirely upon the result of the enquiry into the cause of the fire.

Mrs. Alving. What do you say?

Manders. And one cannot in any way reckon upon the result beforehand.

Engstrand (going nearer to him). Yes, indeed one can; because here stand I, Jacob Engstrand.

Manders. Quite so, but——

Engstrand (lowering his voice). And Jacob Engstrand isn't the man to desert a worthy benefactor in the hour of need, as the saying is.

Manders. Yes, but, my dear fellow—how——?

Engstrand. You might say Jacob Engstrand is an angel of salvation, so to speak, your reverence.

Manders. No, no, I couldn't possibly accept that.

Engstrand. That's how it will be, all the same. I know some one who has taken the blame for some one else on his shoulders before now, I do.

Manders. Jacob! *(Grasps his hand.)* You are one in a thousand! You shall have assistance in the matter of your Sailors' Home, you may rely upon that.

[ENGSTRAND *tries to thank him, but is prevented by emotion.*

Manders (hanging his wallet over his shoulder). Now we must be off. We will travel together.

Engstrand (by the dining-room door, says aside to REGINA*).* Come with me, you hussy! You shall be as cosy as the yolk in an egg!

Regina (tossing her head). Merci!

[*She goes out into the hall and brings back* MANDER'S *luggage.*

Manders. Good-bye, Mrs. Alving! And may the spirit of order and of what is lawful speedily enter into this house.

Mrs. Alving. Good-bye, Mr. Manders.

[*She goes into the conservatory, as she sees* OSWALD *coming in by the garden door.*

Engstrand (as he and REGINA *are helping* MANDERS *on with his coat).* Good-bye, my child. And if anything should happen to you, you know where Jacob Engstrand is to be found. *(Lowering his voice.)* Little Harbour Street, ahem——! *(To* MRS. ALVING *and* OSWALD.*)* And my house for poor seafaring men shall be called the "Alving Home," it shall. And, if I can carry out my own ideas about it, I shall make bold to hope that it may be worthy of bearing the late Mr. Alving's name.

Manders (at the door). Ahem—ahem! Come along, my dear Engstrand. Good-bye—good-bye!

[*He and* ENGSTRAND *go out by the hall door*

Oswald (going to the table). What house was he speaking about?

Mrs. Alving. I believe it is some sort of a Home that he and Mr. Manders want to start.

Oswald. It will be burnt up just like this one.

Mrs. Alving. What makes you think that?

Oswald. Everything will be burnt up; nothing will be left that is in memory of my father. Here am I being burnt up, too. [REGINA *looks at him in alarm.*

Mrs. Alving. Oswald! You should not have stayed so long over there, my poor boy.

Oswald (sitting down at the table). I almost believe you are right.

Mrs. Alving. Let me dry your face, Oswald; you are all wet. [*Wipes his face with her handkerchief.*

Oswald (looking straight before him, with no expression in his eyes). Thank you, mother.

Mrs. Alving. And aren't you tired, Oswald? Don't you want to go to sleep?

Oswald (uneasily). No, no—not to sleep! I never sleep; I only pretend to. *(Gloomily.)* That will come soon enough.

Mrs. Alving (looking at him anxiously). Anyhow you are really ill, my darling boy.

Regina (intently). Is Mr. Alving ill?

Oswald (impatiently). And do shut all the doors! This deadly fear——

Mrs. Alving. Shut the doors, Regina. *(*REGINA *shuts the doors and remains standing by the hall door.* MRS. ALVING *takes off her shawl;* REGINA *does the same.* MRS. ALVING *draws up a chair near to* OSWALD'S *and sits down beside him.)* That's it! Now I will sit beside you——

Oswald. Yes, do. And Regina must stay in here too. Regina must always be near me. You must give me a helping hand, you know, Regina. Won't you do that?

Regina. I don't understand——

Mrs. Alving. A helping hand?

Oswald. Yes—when there is need for it.

Mrs. Alving. Oswald, have you not your mother to give you a helping hand?

Oswald. You? *(Smiles.)* No, mother, you will never give me the kind of helping hand I mean. *(Laughs grimly.)* You? Ha, ha! *(Looks gravely at her.)* After all, you have the best right. *(Impetuously.)* Why don't you call me by my Christian name, Regina? Why don't you say Oswald?

Regina (in a low voice). I did not think Mrs. Alving would like it.

Mrs. Alving It will not be long before you have the right to do it. Sit down here now beside us, too. *(*REGINA *sits down quietly and hesitatingly at the other side of the table.)* And now, my poor tortured boy, I am going to take the burden off your mind——

Oswald. You, mother?

Mrs. Alving. ——all that you call remorse and regret and self-reproach.

Oswald. And you think you can do that?

Mrs. Alving. Yes, now I can, Oswald. A little while ago you were talking about the joy of life, and what you said seemed to shed a new light upon everything in my whole life.

Oswald (shaking his head). I don't in the least understand what you mean.

Mrs. Alving. You should have known your father in his young days in the army. He was full of the joy of life, I can tell you.

Oswald. Yes, I know.

Mrs. Alving. It gave me a holiday feeling only to look at him, full of irrepressible energy and exuberant spirits.

Oswald. What then?

Mrs. Alving. Well, then this boy, full of the joy of life —for he was just like a boy, then—had to make his home in a second-rate town which had none of the joy of life to offer him, but only dissipations. He had to come out here and live an aimless life; he had only an official post. He had no work worth devoting his whole mind to; he had nothing more than official routine to attend to. He had not a single companion capable of appreciating what the joy of life meant; nothing but idlers and tipplers——

Oswald. Mother——!

Mrs. Alving. And so the inevitable happened!

Oswald. What was the inevitable?

Mrs. Alving. You said yourself this evening what would happen in your case if you stayed at home.

Oswald. Do you mean by that, that father——?

Mrs. Alving. Your poor father never found any outlet for the overmastering joy of life that was in him. And I brought no holiday spirit into his home, either.

Oswald. You didn't, either?

Mrs. Alving. I had been taught about duty, and the sort of thing that I believed in so long here. Everything seemed to turn upon duty—my duty, or his duty—and I am afraid I made your poor father's home unbearable to him, Oswald.

Oswald. Why did you never say anything about it to me in your letters?

Mrs. Alving. I never looked at it as a thing I could speak of to you, who were his son.

Oswald. What way did you look at it, then?

Mrs. Alving. I only saw the one fact, that your father was a lost man before ever you were born.

Oswald (in a choking voice). Ah——!

[*He gets up and goes to the window.*

Mrs. Alving. And then I had the one thought in my mind, day and night, that Regina in fact had as good a right in this house—as my own boy had.

Oswald (turns round suddenly). Regina——?

Regina (gets up and asks in choking tones). I——?

Mrs. Alving. Yes, now you both know it.

Oswald. Regina!

Regina (to herself). So mother was one of that sort too.

Mrs. Alving. Your mother had many good qualities, Regina.

Regina. Yes, but she was one of that sort too, all the same. I have even thought so myself, sometimes, but——. Then, if you please, Mrs. Alving, may I have permission to leave at once?

Mrs. Alving. Do you really wish to, Regina?

Regina. Yes, indeed, I certainly wish to.

Mrs. Alving. Of course you shall do as you like, but——

Oswald (going to Regina*).* Leave now? This is your home.

Regina. *Merci,* Mr. Alving—oh, of course I may say Oswald now, but that is not the way I thought it would become allowable.

Mrs. Alving. Regina, I have not been open with you——

Regina. No, I can't say you have! If I had known Oswald was ill——. And now that there can never be anything serious between us——. No, I really can't stay here in the country and wear myself out looking after invalids.

Oswald. Not even for the sake of one who has so near a claim on you?

Regina. No, indeed I can't. A poor girl must make some use of her youth, otherwise she may easily find herself out in the cold before she knows where she is. And I have got the joy of life in me, too, Mrs. Alving!

Mrs. Alving. Yes, unfortunately; but don't throw yourself away, Regina.

Regina. Oh, what's going to happen will happen. If Oswald takes after his father, it is just as likely I take after my mother, I expect.—— May I ask, Mrs. Alving, whether Mr. Manders knows this about me?

Mrs. Alving. Mr. Manders knows everything.

Regina (putting on her shawl). Oh, well then, the best thing I can do is to get away by the boat as soon as I can. Mr. Manders is such a nice gentleman to deal with; and it certainly seems to me that I have just as much right to some of that money as he—as that horrid carpenter.

Mrs. Alving. You are quite welcome to it, Regina.

Regina (looking at her fixedly). You might as well have brought me up like a gentleman's deaughter; it would have been more suitable. *(Tosses her head.)* Oh, well—never mind! *(With a bitter glance at the unopened bottle.)* I daresay some day I shall be drinking champagne with gentlefolk, after all.

Mrs. Alving. If ever you need a home, Regina, come to me.

Regina. No, thank you, Mrs. Alving. Mr. Manders takes an interest in me, I know. And if things should go very badly with me, I know one house at any rate where I shall feel at home.

Mrs. Alving. Where is that?

Regina. In the "Alving Home."

Mrs. Alving. Regina—I can see quite well—you are going to your ruin!

Regina. Pooh!—good-bye.

[*She bows to them and goes out through the hall.*

Oswald (standing by the window and looking out). Has she gone?

Mrs. Alving. Yes.

Oswald (muttering to himself). I think it's all wrong.

Mrs. Alving (going up to him from behind and putting her hands on his shoulders). Oswald, my dear boy—has it been a great shock to you?

Oswald (turning his face towards her). All this about father, do you mean?

Mrs. Alving. Yes, about your unhappy father. I am so afraid it may have been too much for you.

Oswald. What makes you think that? Naturally it has taken me entirely by surprise; but, after all, I don't know that it matters much to me.

Mrs. Alving (drawing back her hands). Doesn't matter! —that your father's life was such a terrible failure!

Oswald. Of course I can feel sympathy for him, just as I would for anyone else, but——

Mrs. Alving. No more than that! For your own father!

Oswald (impatiently). Father—father! I never knew anything of my father. I don't remember anything else about him except that he once made me sick.

Mrs. Alving. It is dreadful to think of!—But surely a child should feel some affection for his father, whatever happens?

Oswald. When the child has nothing to thank his father for? When he has never known him? Do you really cling to that antiquated superstition—you, who are so broad-minded in other things?

Mrs. Alving. You call it nothing but a superstition!

Oswald. Yes, and you can see that for yourself quite well, mother. It is one of those beliefs that are put into circulation in the world, and——

Mrs. Alving. Ghosts of beliefs!

Oswald (walking across the room). Yes, you might call them ghosts.

Mrs. Alving (with an outburst of feeling). Oswald—then you don't love me either.

Oswald. You I know, at any rate——

Mrs. Alving. You know me, yes; but is that all?

Oswald. And I know how fond you are of me, and I ought to be grateful to you for that. Besides, you can be so tremendously useful to me, now that I am ill.

Mrs. Alving. Yes, can't I, Oswald! I could almost bless your illness, as it has driven you home to me. For I see quite well that you are not my very own yet; you must be won.

Oswald (impatiently). Yes, yes, yes; all that is just a way of talking. You must remember I am a sick man, mother. I can't concern myself much with anyone else; I have enough to do, thinking about myself.

Mrs. Alving (gently). I will be very good and patient.

Oswald. And cheerful too, mother!

Mrs. Alving. Yes, my dear boy, you are quite right. *(Goes up to him.)* Now have I taken away all your remorse and self-reproach?

Oswald. Yes, you have done that. But who will take away the fear?

Mrs. Alving. The fear?

Oswald (crossing the room). Regina would have done it for one kind word.

Mrs. Alving. I don't understand you. What fear do you mean—and what has Regina to do with it?

Oswald. Is it very late, mother?

Mrs. Alving. It is early morning. *(Looks out through the conservatory windows.)* The dawn is breaking already on the heights. And the sky is clear, Oswald. In a little while you will see the sun.

Oswald. I am glad of that. After all, there may be many things yet for me to be glad of and to live for——

Mrs. Alving. I should hope so!

Oswald. Even if I am not able to work——

Mrs. Alving. You will soon find you are able to work again now, my dear boy. You have no longer all those painful depressing thoughts to brood over.

Oswald. No, it is a good thing that you have been able to rid me of those fancies. If only, now, I could overcome this one thing——. *(Sits down on the couch.)* Let us have a little chat, mother.

Mrs. Alving. Yes, let us.

[*Pushes an armchair near to the couch and sits down beside him.*

Oswald. The sun is rising—and you know all about it; so I don't feel the fear any longer.

Mrs. Alving. I know all about what?

Oswald (without listening to her). Mother, isn't it the case that you said this evening there was nothing in the world you would not do for me if I asked you?

Mrs. Alving. Yes, certainly I said so.

Oswald. And will you be as good as your word, mother?

Mrs. Alving. You may rely upon that, my own dear boy. I have nothing else to live for, but you.

Oswald. Yes, yes; well, listen to me, mother. You are very strong-minded, I know. I want you to sit quite quiet when you hear what I am going to tell you.

Mrs. Alving. But what is this dreadful thing——?

Oswald. You mustn't scream. Do you hear? Will you promise me that? We are going to sit and talk it over quite quietly. Will you promise me that, mother?

Mrs. Alving. Yes, yes, I promise—only tell me what it is.

Oswald. Well, then, you must know that this fatigue of mine—and my not being able to think about my work—all that is not really the illness itself——

Mrs. Alving. What is the illness itself?

Oswald. What I am suffering from is hereditary; it—*(touches his forehead, and speaks very quietly)*—it lies here.

Mrs. Alving (almost speechless). Oswald! No—no!

Oswald. Don't scream; I can't stand it. Yes, I tell you, it lies here, waiting. And any time, any moment, it may break out.

Mrs. Alving. How horrible——!

Oswald. Do keep quiet. That is the state I am in——

Mrs. Alving (springing up). It isn't true, Oswald! It is impossible! It can't be that!

Oswald. I had one attack while I was abroad. It passed off quickly. But when I learnt the condition I had been in, then this dreadful haunting fear took possession of me.

Mrs. Alving. That was the fear, then——

Oswald. Yes, it is so indescribably horrible, you know.

If only it had been an ordinary mortal disease——. I am not so much afraid of dying; though, of course, I should like to live as long as I can.

Mrs. Alving. Yes, yes, Oswald, you must!

Oswald. But this is so appallingly horrible. To become like a helpless child again—to have to be fed, to have to be——. Oh, it's unspeakable!

Mrs. Alving. My child has his mother to tend him.

Oswald (jumping up). No, never; that is just what I won't endure! I dare not think what it would mean to linger on like that for years—to get old and grey like that. And you might die before I did. *(Sits down in* MRS. ALVING'S *chair.)* Because it doesn't necessarily have a fatal end quickly, the doctor said. He called it a kind of softening of the brain—or something of that sort. *(Smiles mournfully.)* I think that expression sounds so nice. It always makes me think of cherry-coloured velvet curtains—something that is soft to stroke.

Mrs. Alving (with a scream). Oswald!

Oswald (jumps up and walks about the room). And now you have taken Regina from me! If I had only had her. She would have given me a helping hand, I know.

Mrs. Alving (going up to him). What do you mean, my darling boy? Is there any help in the world I would not be willing to give you?

Oswald. When I had recovered from the attack I had abroad, the doctor told me that when it recurred—and it will recur—there would be no more hope.

Mrs. Alving. And he was heartless enough to——

Oswald. I insisted on knowing. I told him I had arrangements to make——. *(Smiles cunningly.)* And so I had. *(Takes a small box from his inner breast-pocket.)* Mother, do you see this?

Mrs. Alving. What is it?

Oswald. Morphia powders.

Mrs. Alving (looking at him in terror). Oswald—my boy!

Oswald. I have twelve of them saved up——

Mrs. Alving (snatching at it). Give me the box, Oswald!

Oswald. Not yet, mother.

[*Puts it back in his pocket.*

Mrs. Alving. I shall never get over this!

Oswald. You must. If I had had Regina here now, I would have told her quietly how things stand with me—and asked her to give me this last helping hand. She would have helped me, I am certain.

Mrs. Alving. Never!

Oswald. If this horrible thing had come upon me and she had seen me lying helpless, like a baby, past help, past saving, past hope—with no chance of recovering——

Mrs. Alving. Never in the world would Regina have done it.

Oswald. Regina would have done it. Regina was so splendidly light-hearted. And she would very soon have tired of looking after an invalid like me.

Mrs. Alving. Then thank heaven Regina is not here!

Oswald. Well, now you have got to give me that helping hand, mother.

Mrs. Alving (with a loud scream). I!

Oswald. Who has a better right than you?

Mrs. Alving. I? Your mother!

Oswald. Just for that reason.

Mrs. Alving. I, who gave you your life!

Oswald. I never asked you for life. And what kind of a life was it that you gave me? I don't want it! You shall take it back!

Mrs. Alving. Help! Help!

[*Runs into the hall*

Oswald (following her). Don't leave me! Where are you going?

Mrs. Alving (in the hall). To fetch the doctor to you, Oswald! Let me out!

Oswald (going into the hall). You shan't go out. And no one shall come in.

[*Turns the key in the lock.*

Mrs. Alving (coming in again). Oswald! Oswald!—my child!

Oswald (following her). Have you a mother's heart—and can bear to see me suffering this unspeakable terror?

Mrs. Alving (controlling herself, after a moment's silence). There is my hand on it.

Oswald. Will you——?

Mrs. Alving. If it becomes necessary. But it shan't become necessary. No, no—it is impossible it should!

Oswald. Let us hope so. And let us live together as long as we can. Thank you, mother.

[*He sits down in the armchair, which* MRS. ALVING *had moved beside the couch. Day is breaking; the lamp is still burning on the table.*

Mrs. Alving (coming cautiously nearer). Do you feel calmer now?

Oswald. Yes.

Mrs. Alving (bending over him). It has only been a dreadful fancy of yours, Oswald. Nothing but fancy. All this upset has been bad for you. But now you will get some rest, at home with your own mother, my darling boy. You shall have everything you want, just as you did when you were a little child.—There, now. The attack is over. You see how easily it passed off! I knew it would.—And look, Oswald, what a lovely day we are going to have? Brilliant sunshine. Now you will be able to see your home properly.

[*She goes to the table and puts out the lamp. It is sunrise. The glaciers and peaks in the distance are seen bathed in bright morning light.*

Oswald (who has been sitting motionless in the armchair,

with his back to the scene outside, suddenly says:) Mother, give me the sun.

Mrs. Alving (standing at the table, and looking at him in amazement). What do you say?

Oswald (repeats in a dull, toneless voice). The sun—the sun.

Mrs. Alvin (going up to him). Oswald, what is the matter with you? *(*Oswald *seems to shrink up in the chair; all his muscles relax; his face loses its expression, and his eyes stare stupidly.* Mrs. Alving *is trembling with terror.)* What is it! *(Screams.)* Oswald! What is the matter with you! *(Throws herself on her knees beside him and shakes him.)* Oswald! Oswald! Look at me! Don't you know me!

Oswald (in an expressionless voice, as before). The sun—the sun.

Mrs. Alving (jumps up despairingly, beats her head with her hands, and screams). I can't bear it! *(Whispers as though paralysed with fear.)* I can't bear it! Never! *(Suddenly.)* Where has he got it? *(Passes her hand quickly over his coat.)* Here! *(Draws back a little way and cries:)* No, no, no!—Yes!—no, no!

[*She stands a few steps from him, her hands thrust into her hair, and stares at him in speechless terror.*

Oswald (sitting motionless, as before). The sun—the sun.

AN ENEMY OF THE PEOPLE
(1882)

CHARACTERS

DR. THOMAS STOCKMANN, *Medical Officer of the Municipal Baths.*

MRS. STOCKMANN, *his wife.*

PETRA, *their daughter, a teacher.*

EJLIF } *their sons (aged 13 and 10 respectively).*
MORTEN }

PETER STOCKMANN, *the Doctor's elder brother; Mayor of the Town and Chief Constable, Chairman of the Baths' Committee, etc., etc.*

MORTEN KIIL, *a tanner (*MRS. STOCKMANN'S *adoptive father).*

HOVSTAD, *editor of the "People's Messenger."*

BILLING, *sub-editor.*

CAPTAIN HORSTER.

ASLAKSEN, *a printer.*

MEN *of various conditions and occupations, some few women, and a troop of schoolboys—the audience at a public meeting.*

The action takes place in a coast town in southern Norway.

AN ENEMY OF THE PEOPLE

ACT I

SCENE.—DR. STOCKMANN'S *sitting-room. It is evening. The room is plainly but neatly appointed and furnished. In the right-hand wall are two doors; the farther leads out to the hall, the nearer to the doctor's study. In the left-hand wall, opposite the door leading to the hall, is a door leading to the other rooms occupied by the family. In the middle of the same wall stands the stove, and, further forward, a couch with a looking-glass hanging over it and an oval table in front of it. On the table, a lighted lamp, with a lampshade. At the back of the room, an open door leads to the dining-room.* BILLING *is seen sitting at the dining table, on which a lamp is burning. He has a napkin tucked under his chin, and* MRS. STOCKMANN *is standing by the table handing him a large plate-full of roast beef. The other places at the table are empty, and the table somewhat in disorder, a meal having evidently recently been finished.*

Mrs. Stockmann. You see, if you come an hour late, Mr. Billing, you have to put up with cold meat.

Billing (as he eats). It is uncommonly good, thank you —remarkably good.

Mrs. Stockmann. My husband makes such a point of having his meals punctually, you know——

Billing. That doesn't affect me a bit. Indeed, I almost

think I enjoy a meal all the better when I can sit down and eat all by myself and undisturbed.

Mrs. Stockmann. Oh well, as long as you are enjoying it——. *(Turns to the hall door, listening.)* I expect that is Mr. Hovstad coming too.

Billing. Very likely.

[PETER STOCKMANN *comes in. He wears an overcoat and his official hat, and carries a stick.*

Peter Stockmann. Good evening, Katherine.

Mrs. Stockmann (coming forward into the sitting-room). Ah, good evening—is it you? How good of you to come up and see us!

Peter Stockmann. I happened to be passing, and so—*(looks into the dining-room).* But you have company with you, I see.

Mrs. Stockmann (a little embarrassed). Oh, no—it was quite by chance he came in. *(Hurriedly.)* Won't you come in and have something, too?

Peter Stockmann. I! No, thank you. Good gracious—hot meat at night! Not with my digestion.

Mrs. Stockmann. Oh, but just once in a way——

Peter Stockmann. No, no, my dear lady; I stick to my tea and bread and butter. It is much more wholesome in the long run—and a little more economical, too.

Mrs. Stockmann (smiling). Now you mustn't think that Thomas and I are spendthrifts.

Peter Stockmann. Not you, my dear; I would never think that of you. *(Points to the Doctor's study.)* Is he not at home?

Mrs. Stockmann. No, he went out for a little turn after supper—he and the boys.

Peter Stockmann. I doubt if that is a wise thing to do. *(Listens.)* I fancy I hear him coming now.

Mrs. Stockmann. No, I don't think it is he. *(A knock is heard at the door.)* Come in! (HOVSTAD *comes in from the hall.)* Oh, it is you, Mr. Hovstad!

Hovstad. Yes, I hope you will forgive me, but I was delayed at the printer's. Good evening, Mr. Mayor.

Peter Stockmann (bowing a little distantly). Good evening. You have come on business, no doubt.

Hovstad. Partly. It's about an article for the paper.

Peter Stockmann. So I imagined. I hear my brother has become a prolific contributor to the "People's Messenger."

Hovstad. Yes, he is good enough to write in the "People's Messenger" when he has any home truths to tell.

Mrs. Stockmann (to HOVSTAD*).* But won't you——?

[*Points to the dining-room.*

Peter Stockmann. Quite so, quite so. I don't blame him in the least, as a writer, for addressing himself to the quarters where he will find the readiest sympathy. And, besides that, I personally have no reason to bear any ill will to your paper, Mr. Hovstad.

Hovstad. I quite agree with you.

Peter Stockmann. Taking one thing with another, there is an excellent spirit of toleration in the town—an admirable municipal spirit. And it all springs from the fact of our having a great common interest to unite us—an interest that is in an equally high degree the concern of every right-minded citizen——

Hovstad. The Baths, yes.

Peter Stockmann. Exactly—our fine, new, handsome Baths. Mark my words, Mr. Hovstad—the Baths will become the focus of our municipal life! Not a doubt of it!

Mrs. Stockmann. That is just what Thomas says.

Peter Stockmann. Think how extraordinarily the place has developed within the last year or two! Money has been flowing in, and there is some life and some business doing in the town. Houses and landed property are rising in value every day.

Hovstad. And unemployment is diminishing.

Peter Stockmann. Yes, that is another thing. The burden of the poor rates has been lightened, to the great relief of the propertied classes; and that relief will be even greater if only we get a really good summer this year, and lots of visitors—plenty of invalids, who will make the Baths talked about.

Hovstad. And there is a good prospect of that, I hear.

Peter Stockmann. It looks very promising. Enquiries about apartments and that sort of thing are reaching us every day.

Hovstad. Well, the doctor's article will come in very suitably.

Peter Stockmann. Has he been writing something just lately?

Hovstad. This is something he wrote in the winter; a recommendation of the Baths—an account of the excellent sanitary conditions here. But I held the article over, temporarily.

Peter Stockmann. Ah,—some little difficulty about it, I suppose?

Hovstad. No, not at all; I thought it would be better to wait till the spring, because it is just at this time that people begin to think seriously about their summer quarters.

Peter Stockmann. Quite right; you were perfectly right, Mr. Hovstad.

Hovstad. Yes, Thomas is really indefatigable when it is a question of the Baths.

Peter Stockmann. Well—remember, he is the Medical Officer to the Baths.

Hovstad. Yes, and what is more, they owe their existence to him.

Peter Stockmann. To him? Indeed! It is true I have heard from time to time that some people are of that opinion. At the same time I must say I imagined that I took a modest part in the enterprise.

Mrs. Stockman. Yes, that is what Thomas is always saying.

Hovstad. But who denies it, Mr. Stockmann? You set the thing going and made a practical concern of it; we all know that. I only meant that the idea of it came first from the doctor.

Peter Stockmann. Oh, ideas—yes! My brother has had plenty of them in his time—unfortunately. But when it is a question of putting an idea into practical shape, you have to apply to a man of different mettle, Mr. Hovstad. And I certainly should have thought that in this house at least——

Mrs. Stockmann. My dear Peter——

Hovstad. How can you think that——?

Mrs. Stockmann. Won't you go in and have something, Mr. Hovstad? My husband is sure to be back directly.

Hovstad. Thank you, perhaps just a morsel.

[*Goes into the dining-room.*

Peter Stockmann (lowering his voice a little). It is a curious thing that these farmers' sons never seem to lose their want of tact.

Mrs. Stockmann. Surely it is not worth bothering about! Cannot you and Thomas share the credit as brothers?

Peter Stockmann. I should have thought so; but apparently some people are not satisfied with a share.

Mrs. Stockmann. What nonsense! You and Thomas get on so capitally together. *(Listens.)* There he is at last, I think.

[*Goes out and opens the door leading to the hall.*

Dr. Stockmann (laughing and talking outside). Look here—here is another guest for you, Katherine. Isn't that jolly! Come in, Captain Horster; hang your coat up on this peg. Ah, you don't wear an overcoat. Just think, Katherine; I met him in the street and could hardly persuade him to come up! (CAPTAIN HORSTER *comes into the room and greets* MRS. STOCKMANN. *He is followed by* DR. STOCKMANN.*)* Come along in, boys. They are ravenously hungry again, you know. Come along, Captain Horster; you must have a slice of beef.

[*Pushes* HORSTER *into the dining-room.* EJLIF *and* MORTEN *go in after them.*

Mrs. Stockmann. But, Thomas, don't you see——?

Dr. Stockmann (turning in the doorway). Oh, is it you, Peter? *(Shakes hands with him.)* Now that is very delightful.

Peter Stockmann. Unfortunately I must go in a moment——

Dr. Stockmann. Rubbish! There is some toddy just coming in. You haven't forgotten the toddy, Katherine?

Mrs. Stockmann. Of course not; the water is boiling now.

[*Goes into the dining-room.*

Peter Stockmann. Toddy too!

Dr. Stockmann. Yes, sit down and we will have it comfortably.

Peter Stockmann. Thanks, I never care about an evening's drinking.

Dr. Stockmann. But this isn't an evening's drinking.

Peter Stockmann. It seems to me——. *(Looks towards the dining-room.)* It is extraordinary how they can put away all that food.

Dr. Stockmann (rubbing his hands). Yes, isn't it splendid to see young people eat? They have always got an appetite, you know! That's as it should be. Lots of food—to build up their strength! They are the people who are going to stir up the fermenting forces of the future, Peter.

Peter Stockmann. May I ask what they will find here to "stir up," as you put it?

Dr. Stockmann. Ah, you must ask the young people that—when the times comes. We shan't be able to see it, of course. That stands to reason—two old fogies, like us——

Peter Stockmann. Really, really! I must say that is an extremely odd expression to——

Dr. Stockmann. Oh, you mustn't take me too literally, Peter. I am so heartily happy and contented, you know. I think it is such an extraordinary piece of good fortune to be in the middle of all this growing, germinating life. It is a splendid time to live in! It is as if a whole new world were being created around one.

Peter Stockmann. Do you really think so?

Dr. Stockmann. Ah, naturally you can't appreciate it as keenly as I. You have lived all your life in these surroundings, and your impressions have got blunted. But I, who have been buried all these years in my little corner up north, almost without ever seeing a stranger who might bring new ideas with him—well, in my case it has just the same effect as if I had been transported into the middle of a crowded city.

Peter Stockmann. Oh, a city——!

Dr. Stockmann. I know, I know; it is all cramped enough here, compared with many other places. But there is life here—there is promise—there are innumerable things to work for and fight for; and that is the main thing *(Calls.)* Katherine, hasn't the postman been here?

Mrs. Stockmann (from the dining-room). No.

Dr. Stockmann. And then to be comfortably off, Peter! That is something one learns to value, when one has been on the brink of starvation, as we have.

Peter Stockmann. Oh, surely——

Dr. Stockmann. Indeed I can assure you we have often been very hard put to it, up there. And now to be able to live like a lord! To-day, for instance, we had roast beef for dinner—and, what is more, for supper too. Won't you come and have a little bit? Or let me show it you, at any rate? Come here——

Peter Stockmann. No, no—not for worlds!

Dr. Stockmann. Well, but just come here then. Do you see, we have got a table-cover?

Peter Stockmann. Yes, I noticed it.

Dr. Stockmann. And we have got a lamp-shade too. Do you see? All out of Katherine's savings! It makes the room so cosy. Don't you think so? Just stand here for a moment—no, no, not there—just here, that's it! Look now, when you get the light on it altogether—I really think it looks very nice, doesn't it?

Peter Stockmann. Oh, if you can afford luxuries of this kind——

Dr. Stockmann. Yes, I can afford it now. Katherine tells me I earn almost as much as we spend.

Peter Stockmann. Almost—yes!

Dr. Stockmann. But a scientific man must live in a little bit of style. I am quite sure an ordinary civil servant spends more in a year than I do.

Peter Stockmann. I daresay. A civil servant—a man in a well-paid position——

Dr. Stockmann. Well, any ordinary merchant, then! A man in that position spends two or three times as much as——

Peter Stockmann. It just depends on circumstances.

Dr. Stockmann. At all events I assure you I don't waste money unprofitably. But I can't find it in my heart to deny myself the pleasure of entertaining my friends. I need that sort of thing, you know. I have lived for so long shut out of it all, that it is a necessity of life to me to mix with young, eager, ambitious men, men of liberal and active minds; and that describes every one of those fellows who are enjoying their supper in there. I wish you knew more of Hovstad——

Peter Stockmann. By the way, Hovstad was telling me he was going to print another article of yours.

Dr. Stockmann. An article of mine?

Peter Stockmann. Yes, about the Baths. An article you wrote in the winter.

Dr. Stockmann. Oh, that one! No, I don't intend that to appear just for the present.

Peter Stockmann. Why not? It seems to me that this would be the most opportune moment.

Dr. Stockmann. Yes, very likely—under normal conditions. [*Crosses the room.*

Peter Stockmann (following him with his eyes). Is there anything abnormal about the present conditions?

Dr. Stockmann (standing still). To tell you the truth, Peter, I can't say just at this moment—at all events not to-night. There may be much that is very abnormal about the present conditions—and it is possible there may be nothing abnormal about them at all. It is quite possible it may be merely my imagination.

Peter Stockmann. I must say it all sounds most mysterious. Is there something going on that I am to be kept in ignorance of? I should have imagined that I, as Chairman of the governing body of the Baths——

Dr. Stockmann. And I should have imagined that I——. Oh, come, don't let us fly out at one another, Peter.

Peter Stockmann. Heaven forbid! I am not in the habit of flying out at people, as you call it. But I am entitled to request most emphatically that all arrangements shall be made in a business-like manner, through the proper channels, and shall be dealt with by the legally constituted authorities. I can allow no going behind our backs by any roundabout means.

Dr. Stockmann. Have I ever at any time tried to go behind your backs!

Peter Stockmann. You have an ingrained tendency to take your own way, at all events; and that is almost equally inadmissible in a well-ordered community. The individual ought undoubtedly to acquiesce in subordinating himself to the community—or, to speak more accurately, to the authorities who have the care of the community's welfare.

Dr. Stockmann. Very likely. But what the deuce has all this got to do with me?

Peter Stockmann. That is exactly what you never appear to be willing to learn, my dear Thomas. But, mark my words, some day you will have to suffer for it—sooner or later. Now I have told you. Good-bye.

Dr. Stockmann. Have you taken leave of your senses? You are on the wrong scent altogether.

Peter Stockmann. I am not usually that. You must excuse me now if I—*(calls into the dining-room).* Good night, Katherine. Good night, gentlemen. [*Goes out.*

Mrs. Stockmann (coming from the dining-room). Has he gone?

Dr. Stockmann. Yes, and in such a bad temper.

Mrs. Stockmann. But, dear Thomas, what have you been doing to him again?

Dr. Stockmann. Nothing at all. And, anyhow, he can't oblige me to make my report before the proper time.

Mrs. Stockmann. What have you got to make a report to him about?

Dr. Stockmann. Hm! Leave that to me, Katherine. ——It is an extraordinary thing that the postman doesn't come.

[HOVSTAD, BILLINGS *and* HORSTER *have got up from the table and come into the sitting-room.* EJLIF *and* MORTEN *come in after them.*

Billing (stretching himself). Ah!—one feels a new man after a meal like that.

Hovstad. The mayor wasn't in a very sweet temper to-night, then.

Dr. Stockmann. It is his stomach; he has a wretched digestion.

Hovstad. I rather think it was us two of the "People's Messenger" that he couldn't digest.

Mrs. Stockmann. I thought you came out of it pretty well with him.

Hovstad. Oh yes; but it isn't anything more than a sort of truce.

Billing. That is just what it is! That word sums up the situation.

Dr. Stockmann. We must remember that Peter is a lonely man, poor chap. He has no home comforts of any kind; nothing but everlasting business. And all that infernal weak tea wash that he pours into himself! Now then, my boys, bring chairs up to the table. Aren't we going to have that toddy, Katherine?

Mrs. Stockmann (going into the dining-room). I am just getting it.

Dr. Stockmann. Sit down here on the couch beside me, Captain Horster. We so seldom see you——. Please sit down, my friends.

[*They sit down at the table.* MRS. STOCKMANN *brings a tray, with a spirit-lamp, glasses, bottles, etc., upon it.*

Mrs. Stockmann. There you are! This is arrack, and this is rum, and this one is the brandy. Now every one must help himself.

Dr. Stockmann (taking a glass). We will. *(They all mix themselves some toddy.)* And let us have the cigars. Ejlif, you know where the box is. And you, Morten, can fetch my pipe. *(The two boys go into the room on the right.)* I have a suspicion that Ejlif pockets a cigar now and then!—but I take no notice of it. *(Calls out.)* And my smoking-cap too, Morten. Katherine, you can tell him where I left it. Ah, he has got it. *(The boys bring the various things.)* Now, my friends. I stick to my pipe, you know. This one has seen plenty of bad weather with me up north. *(Touches glasses with them.)* Your good health! Ah! it is good to be sitting snug and warm here.

Mrs. Stockmann (who sits knitting). Do you sail soon, Captain Horster?

Horster. I expect to be ready to sail next week.

Mrs. Stockmann. I suppose you are going to America?

Horster. Yes, that is the plan.

Mrs. Stockmann. Then you won't be able to take part in the coming election.

Horster. Is there going to be an election?

Billing. Didn't you know?

Horster. No, I don't mix myself up with those things.

Billing. But do you not take an interest in public affairs?

Horster. No, I don't know anything about politics.

Billing. All the same, one ought to vote, at any rate.

Horster. Even if one doesn't know anything about what is going on?

Billing. Doesn't know! What do you mean by that? A community is like a ship; every one ought to be prepared to take the helm.

Horster. May be that is all very well on shore; but on board ship it wouldn't work.

Hovstad. It is astonishing how little most sailors care about what goes on on shore.

Billing. Very extraordinary.

Dr. Stockmann. Sailors are like birds of passage; they feel equally at home in any latitude. And that is only an additional reason for our being all the more keen, Hovstad. Is there to be anything of public interest in to-morrow's "Messenger"?

Hovstad. Nothing about municipal affairs. But the day after to-morrow I was thinking of printing your article——

Dr. Stockmann. Ah, devil take it—my article! Look here, that must wait a bit.

Hovstad. Really? We had just got convenient space for it, and I thought it was just the opportune moment——

Dr. Stockmann. Yes, yes, very likely you are right; but it must wait all the same. I will explain to you later.

[PETRA *comes in from the hall, in hat and cloak and with a bundle of exercise books under her arm.*

Petra. Good evening.

Dr. Stockmann. Good evening, Petra; come along.

[*Mutual greetings;* PETRA *takes off her things and puts them down on a chair by the door.*

Petra. And you have all been sitting here enjoying yourselves, while I have been out slaving!

Dr. Stockmann. Well, come and enjoy yourself too!

Billing. May I mix a glass for you?

Petra (coming to the table). Thanks, I would rather do it; you always mix it too strong. But I forgot, father—I have a letter for you.

[*Goes to the chair where she has laid her things.*

Dr. Stockmann. A letter? From whom?

Petra (looking in her coat pocket). The postman gave it to me just as I was going out——

Dr. Stockmann (getting up and going to her). And you only give to me now!

Petra. I really had not time to run up again. There it is!

Dr. Stockmann (seizing the letter). Let's see, let's see, child! *(Looks at the address.)* Yes, that's all right!

Mrs. Stockmann. Is it the one you have been expecting so anxiously, Thomas?

Dr. Stockmann. Yes, it is. I must go to my room now and——. Where shall I get a light, Katherine? Is there no lamp in my room again?

Mrs. Stockmann. Yes, your lamp is all ready lit on your desk.

Dr. Stockmann. Good, good. Excuse me for a moment——. [*Goes into his study.*

Petra. What do you suppose it is, mother?

Mrs. Stockmann. I don't know; for the last day or two he has always been asking if the postman has not been.

Billing. Probably some country patient.

Petra. Poor old dad!—he will overwork himself soon. *(Mixes a glass for herself.)* There, that will taste good!

Hovstad. Have you been teaching in the evening school again to-day?

Petra (sipping from her glass). Two hours.

Billing. And four hours of school in the morning——

Petra. Five hours.

Mrs. Stockmann. And you have still got exercises to correct, I see.

Petra. A whole heap, yes.

Horster. You are pretty full up with work too, it seems to me.

Petra. Yes—but that is good. One is so delightfully tired after it.

Billing. Do you like that?

Petra. Yes, because one sleeps so well then.

Morten. You must be dreadfully wicked, Petra.

Petra. Wicked?

Morten. Yes, because you work so much. Mr. Rörlund says work is a punishment for our sins.

Ejlif. Pooh, what a duffer you are, to believe a thing like that!

Mrs. Stockmann. Come, come, Ejlif!

Billing (laughing). That's capital!

Hovstad. Don't you want to work as hard as that, Morten?

Morten. No, indeed I don't.

Hovstad. What do you want to be, then?

Morten. I should like best to be a Viking.

Ejlif. You would have to be a pagan then.

Morten. Well, I could become a pagan, couldn't I?

Billing. I agree with you, Morten! My sentiments, exactly.

Mrs. Stockmann (signalling to him). I am sure that is not true, Mr. Billing.

Billing. Yes, I swear it is! I am a pagan, and I am proud of it. Believe me, before long we shall all be pagans.

Morten. And then shall be allowed to do anything we like?

Billing. Well, you see, Morten——.

Mrs. Stockmann. You must go to your room now, boys; I am sure you have some lessons to learn for to-morrow.

Ejlif. I should like so much to stay a little longer——

Mrs. Stockmann. No, no; away you go, both of you.

[*The boys say good-night and go into the room on the left.*

Hovstad. Do you really think it can do the boys any harm to hear such things?

Mrs. Stockmann. I don't know; but I don't like it.

Petra. But you know, mother, I think you really are wrong about it.

Mrs. Stockmann. Maybe, but I don't like it—not in our own home.

Petra. There is so much falsehood both at home and at school. At home one must not speak, and at school we have to stand and tell lies to the children.

Horster. Tell lies?

Petra. Yes, don't you suppose we have to teach them all sorts of things that we don't believe?

Billing. That is perfectly true.

Petra. If only I had the means I would start a school of my own, and it would be conducted on very different lines.

Billing. Oh, bother the means——!

Horster. Well if you are thinking of that, Miss Stockmann, I shall be delighted to provide you with a schoolroom. The great big old house my father left me is standing almost empty; there is an immense dining-room downstairs——

Petra (laughing). Thank you very much; but I am afraid nothing will come of it.

Hovstad. No, Miss Petra is much more likely to take to journalism, I expect. By the way, have you had time to do anything with that English story you promised to translate for us?

Petra. No, not yet; but you shall have it in good time.

[DR. STOCKMANN *comes in from his room with an open letter in his hand.*

Dr. Stockmann (waving the letter). Well, now the town will have something new to talk about, I can tell you!

Billing. Something new?

Mrs. Stockmann. What is this?

Dr. Stockmann. A great discovery, Katherine.

Hovestad. Really?

Mrs. Stockmann. A discovery of yours?

Dr. Stockmann. A discovery of mine. *(Walks up and down.)* Just let them come saying, as usual, that it is all fancy and a crazy man's imagination! But they will be careful what they say this time, I can tell you!

Petra. But, father, tell us what it is.

Dr. Stockmann. Yes, yes—only give me time, and you shall know all about it. If only I had Peter here now! It just shows how we men can go about forming our judgments, when in reality we are as blind as any moles——

Hovstad. What are you driving at, Doctor?

Dr. Stockmann (standing still by the table). Isn't it the universal opinion that our town is a healthy spot?

Hovstad. Certainly.

Dr. Stockmann. Quite an unusually healthy spot, in fact—a place that deserves to be recommended in the warmest possible manner either for invalids or for people who are well——

Mrs. Stockmann. Yes, but my dear Thomas——

Dr. Stockmann. And we have been recommending it and praising it—I have written and written, both in the "Messenger" and in pamphlets——

Hovstad. Well, what then?

Dr. Stockmann. And the Baths—we have called them the "main artery of the town's life-blood," the "nerve-centre of our town," and the devil knows what else——

Billing. "The town's pulsating heart" was the expression I once used on an important occasion——

Dr. Stockmann. Quite so. Well, do you know what they really are, these great, splendid, much praised Baths, that have cost so much money—do you know what they are?

Hovstad. No, what are they?

Mrs. Stockmann. Yes, what are they?

Dr. Stockmann. The whole place is a pesthouse!

Petra. The Baths, father?

Mrs. Stockmann (at the same time). Our Baths!

Hovstad. But, Doctor——

Billing. Absolutely incredible!

Dr. Stockmann. The whole Bath establishment is a whited, poisoned sepulchre, I tell you—the gravest possible danger to the public health! All the nastiness up at Mölledal, all that stinking filth, is infecting the water in the conduit-pipes leading to the reservoir; and the same cursed, filthy poison oozes out on the shore too——

Horster. Where the bathing-place is?

Dr. Stockmann. Just there.

Hovstad. How do you come to be so certain of all this, Doctor?

Dr. Stockmann. I have investigated the matter most conscientiously. For a long time past I have suspected something of the kind. Last year we had some very strange cases of illness among the visitors—typhoid cases, and cases of gastric fever——

Mrs. Stockmann. Yes, that is quite true.

Dr. Stockmann. At the time, we supposed the visitors had been infected before they came; but later on, in the winter, I began to have a different opinion; and so I set myself to examine the water, as well as I could.

Mrs. Stockmann. Then that is what you have been so busy with?

Dr. Stockmann. Indeed I have been busy, Katherine. But here I had none of the necessary scientific apparatus; so I sent samples, both of the drinking-water and of the sea-water, up to the University, to have an accurate analysis made by a chemist.

Hovstad. And have you got that?

Dr. Stockmann (showing him the letter). Here it is! It proves the presence of decomposing organic matter in the water—it is full of infusoria. The water is absolutely dangerous to use, either internally or externally.

Mrs. Stockmann. What a mercy you discovered it in time.

Dr. Stockmann. You may well say so.

Hovstad. And what do you propose to do now, Doctor?

Dr. Stockmann. To see the matter put right—naturally.

Hovstad. Can that be done?

Dr. Stockmann. It must be done. Otherwise the Baths will be absolutely useless and wasted. But we need not anticipate that; I have a very clear idea what we shall have to do.

Mrs. Stockmann. But why have you kept this all so secret, dear?

Dr. Stockmann. Do you suppose I was going to run about the town gossiping about it, before I had absolute proof? No, thank you. I am not such a fool.

Petra. Still, you might have told us——

Dr. Stockmann. Not a living soul. But to-morrow you may run round to the old Badger——

Mrs. Stockmann. Oh, Thomas! Thomas!

Dr. Stockmann. Well, to your grandfather, then. The

old boy will have something to be astonished at! I know he thinks I am cracked—and there are lots of other people think so too, I have noticed. But now these good folks shall see—they shall just see——! *(Walks about, rubbing his hands.)* There will be a nice upset in the town, Katherine; you can't imagine what it will be. All the conduit-pipes will have to be relaid.

Hovstad (getting up). All the conduit-pipes——?

Dr. Stockmann. Yes, of course. The intake is too low down; it will have to be lifted to a position much higher up.

Petra. Then you were right after all.

Dr. Stockmann. Ah, you remember, Petra—I wrote opposing the plans before the work was begun. But at that time no one would listen to me. Well, I am going to let them have it, now! Of course I have prepared a report for the Baths Committee; I have had it ready for a week, and was only waiting for this to come. *(Shows the letter.)* Now it shall go off at once. *(Goes into his room and comes back with some papers.)* Look at that! Four closely written sheets!—and the letter shall go with them. Give me a bit of paper, Katherine—something to wrap them up in. That will do! Now give it to—to—*(stamps his foot)*—what the deuce is her name?—give it to the maid, and tell her to take it at once to the Mayor.

[MRS. STOCKMAN *takes the packet and goes out through the dining-room.*

Petra. What do you think uncle Peter will say, father?

Dr. Stockmann. What is there for him to say? I should think he would be very glad that such an important truth has been brought to light.

Hovstad. Will you let me print a short note about your discovery in the "Messenger?"

Dr. Stockmann. I shall be very much obliged if you will.

Hovstad. It is very desirable that the public should be informed of it without delay.

Dr. Stockmann. Certainly.

Mrs. Stockmann (coming back). She has just gone with it.

Billing. Upon my soul, Doctor, you are going to be the foremost man in the town!

Dr. Stockmann (walking about happily). Nonsense! As a matter of fact I have done nothing more than my duty. I have only made a lucky find—that's all. Still, all the same——

Billing. Hovstad, don't you think the town ought to give Dr. Stockmann some sort of testimonial?

Hovstad. I will suggest it, anyway.

Billing. And I will speak to Aslaksen about it.

Dr. Stockmann. No, my good friends, don't let us have any of that nonsense. I won't hear of anything of the kind. And if the Baths Committee should think of voting me an increase of salary, I will not accept it. Do you hear, Katherine?—I won't accept it.

Mrs. Stockmann. You are quite right, Thomas.

Petra (lifting her glass). Your health, father!

Hovstad and Billing. Your health, Doctor! Good health!

Horster (touches glasses with DR. STOCKMANN*).* I hope it will bring you nothing but good luck.

Dr. Stockmann. Thank you, thank you, my dear fellows! I feel tremendously happy! It is a splendid thing for a man to be able to feel that he has done a service to his native town and to his fellow-citizens. Hurrah, Katherine!

[*He puts his arms round her and whirls her round and round, while she protests with laughing cries. They all laugh, clap their hands and cheer the* DOCTOR. *The boys put their heads in at the door to see what is going on.*

ACT II

SCENE.—*The same. The door into the dining-room is shut It is morning.* MRS. STOCKMANN, *with a sealed letter in her hand, comes in from the dining-room, goes to the door of the* DOCTOR'S *study and peeps in.*

Mrs. Stockmann. Are you in, Thomas?

Dr. Stockmann (from within his room). Yes, I have just come in. *(Comes into the room.)* What is it?

Mrs. Stockmann. A letter from your brother.

Dr. Stockmann. Aha, let us see! *(Opens the letter and reads:)* "I return herewith the manuscript you sent me"—*(reads on in a low murmur)* Hm!——

Mrs. Stockmann. What does he say?

Dr. Stockmann (putting the papers in his pocket). Oh, he only writes that he will come up here himself about midday.

Mrs. Stockmann. Well, try and remember to be at home this time.

Dr. Stockmann. That will be all right; I have got through all my morning visits.

Mrs. Stockmann. I am extremely curious to know how he takes it.

Dr. Stockmann. You will see he won't like it's having been I, and not he, that made the discovery.

Mrs. Stockmann. Aren't you a little nervous about that?

Dr. Stockmann. Oh, he really will be pleased enough, you know. But, at the same time, Peter is so confoundedly afraid of anyone's doing any service to the town except himself.

Mrs. Stockmann. I will tell you what, Thomas—you should be good-natured, and share the credit of this with him. Couldn't you make out that it was he who set you on the scent of this discovery?

Dr. Stockmann. I am quite willing. If only I can get the thing set right. I——

[MORTEN KIIL *puts his head in through the door leading from the hall, looks round in an enquiring manner and chuckles.*

Morten Kiil (slyly). Is it—is it true?

Mrs. Stockmann (going to the door). Father!—is it you?

Dr. Stockmann. Ah, Mr. Kiil—good morning, good morning!

Mrs. Stockmann. But come along in.

Morten Kiil. If it is true, I will; if not, I am off.

Dr. Stockmann. If what is true?

Morten Kiil. This tale about the water-supply. Is it true?

Dr. Stockmann. Certainly it is true. But how did you come to hear it?

Morten Kiil (coming in). Petra ran in on her way to the school——

Dr. Stockmann. Did she?

Morten Kiil. Yes; and she declares that——. I thought she was only making a fool of me, but it isn't like Petra to do that.

Dr. Stockmann. Of course not. How could you imagine such a thing!

Morten Kiil. Oh well, it is better never to trust anybody; you may find you have been made a fool of before you know where you are. But it is really true, all the same?

Dr. Stockmann. You can depend upon it that it is true. Won't you sit down? *(Settles him on the couch.)* Isn't it a real bit of luck for the town——

Morten Kiil (suppressing his laughter). A bit of luck for the town?

Dr. Stockmann. Yes, that I made the discovery in good time.

Morten Kiil (as before). Yes, yes, yes!—But I should never have thought you the sort of man to pull your own brother's leg like this!

Dr. Stockmann. Pull his leg!

Mrs. Stockmann. Really, father dear——

Morten Kiil (resting his hands and his chin on the handle of his stick and winking slyly at the DOCTOR*).* Let me see, what was the story? Some kind of beast that had got into the water-pipes, wasn't it?

Dr. Stockmann. Infusoria—yes.

Morten Kiil. And a lot of these beasts had got in, according to Petra—a tremendous lot.

Dr. Stockmann. Certainly; hundreds of thousands of them, probably.

Morten Kiil. But no one can see them—isn't that so?

Dr. Stockmann. Yes; you can't see them.

Morten Kiil (with a quiet chuckle.). Damme—it's the finest story I have ever heard!

Dr. Stockmann. What do you mean?

Morten Kiil. But you will never get the Mayor to believe a thing like that.

Dr. Stockmann. We shall see.

Morten Kiil. Do you think he will be fool enough to——?

Dr. Stockmann. I hope the whole town will be fools enough.

Morten Kiil. The whole town! Well, it wouldn't be a bad thing. It would just serve them right, and teach them a lesson. They think themselves so much cleverer than we old fellows. They hounded me out of the council; they did, I tell you—they hounded me out. Now they shall pay for it. You pull their legs too, Thomas!

Dr. Stockmann. Really, I——

Morten Kiil. You pull their legs! *(Gets up.)* If you can work it so that the Mayor and his friends all swallow the same bait, I will give ten pounds to a charity—like a shot!

Dr. Stockmann. That is very kind of you.

Morten Kiil. Yes, I haven't got much money to throw away, I can tell you; but if you can work this, I will give five pounds to a charity at Christmas.

[HOVSTAD *comes in by the hall door.*

Hovstad. Good morning! *(Stops.)* Oh, I beg your pardon——

Dr. Stockmann. Not at all; come in.

Morten Kiil (with another chuckle). Oho!—is he in this too?

Hovstad. What do you mean?

Dr. Stockmann. Certainly he is.

Morten Kiil. I might have known it! It must get into the papers. You know how to do it, Thomas! Set your wits to work. Now I must go.

Dr. Stockmann. Won't you stay a little while?

Morten Kiil. No, I must be off now. You keep up this game for all it is worth; you won't repent it, I'm damned if you will!

[*He goes out;* MRS. STOCKMANN *follows him into the hall.*

Dr. Stockmann (laughing). Just imagine—the old chap doesn't believe a word of all this about the water-supply.

Hovstad. Oh that was it, then?

Dr. Stockmann. Yes, that was what we were talking about. Perhaps it is the same thing that brings you here?

Hovstad. Yes, it is. Can you spare me a few minutes, Doctor?

Dr. Stockmann. As long as you like, my dear fellow.

Hovstad. Have you heard from the Mayor yet?

Dr. Stockmann. Not yet. He is coming here later.

Hovstad. I have given the matter a great deal of thought since last night.

Dr. Stockmann. Well?

Hovstad. From your point of view, as a doctor and a man of science, this affair of the water-supply is an isolated matter. I mean, you do not realise that it involves a great many other things.

Dr. Stockmann. How, do you mean?—Let us sit down my dear fellow. No, sit here on the couch. (HOVSTAD *sits down on the couch,* DR. STOCKMANN *on a chair on the other side of the table.)* Now then. You mean that——?

Hovstad. You said yesterday that the pollution of the water was due to impurities in the soil.

Dr. Stockmann. Yes, unquestionably it is due to that poisonous morass up at Mölledal.

Hovstad. Begging your pardon, doctor, I fancy it is due to quite another morass altogether.

Dr. Stockmann. What morass?

Hovstad. The morass that the whole life of our town is built on and is rotting in.

Dr. Stockmann. What the deuce are you driving at, Hovstad?

Hovstad. The whole of the town's interests have, little by little, got into the hands of a pack of officials.

Dr. Stockmann. Oh, come!—they are not all officials.

Hovstad. No, but those that are not officials are at any rate the officials' friends and adherents; it is the wealthy folk, the old families in the town, that have got us entirely in their hands.

Dr. Stockmann. Yes, but after all they are men of ability and knowledge.

Hovstad. Did they show any ability or knowledge when they laid the conduit-pipes where they are now?

Dr. Stockmann. No, of course that was a great piece of

stupidity on their part. But that is going to be set right now.

Hovstad. Do you think that will be all such plain sailing?

Dr. Stockmann. Plain sailing or no, it has got to be done, anyway.

Hovstad. Yes, provided the press takes up the question.

Dr. Stockmann. I don't think that will be necessary, my dear fellow, I am certain my brother——

Hovstad. Excuse me, doctor; I feel bound to tell you I am inclined to take the matter up.

Dr. Stockmann. In the paper?

Hovstad. Yes. When I took over the "People's Messenger" my idea was to break up this ring of self-opinionated old fossils who had got hold of all the influence.

Dr. Stockmann. But you know you told me yourself what the result had been; you nearly ruined your paper.

Hovstad. Yes, at the time we were obliged to climb down a peg or two, it is quite true; because there was a danger of the whole project of the Baths coming to nothing if they failed us. But now the scheme has been carried through, and we can dispense with these grand gentlemen.

Dr. Stockmann. Dispense with them, yes; but we owe them a great debt of gratitude.

Hovstad. That shall be recognised ungrudgingly. But a journalist of my democratic tendencies cannot let such an opportunity as this slip. The bubble of official infallibility must be pricked. This superstition must be destroyed, like any other.

Dr. Stockmann. I am whole-heartedly with you in that, Mr. Hovstad; if it is a superstition, away with it!

Hovstad. I should be very reluctant to bring the Mayor into it, because he is your brother. But I am sure you will agree with me that truth should be the first consideration.

Dr. Stockmann. That goes without saying. *(With sudden emphasis.)* Yes, but—but——

Hovstad. You must not misjudge me. I am neither more self-interested nor more ambitious than most men.

Dr. Stockmann. My dear fellow—who suggests anything of the kind?

Hovstad. I am of humble origin, as you know; and that has given me opportunities of knowing what is the most crying need in the humbler ranks of life. It is that they should be allowed some part in the direction of public affairs, Doctor. That is what will develop their faculties and intelligence and self-respect——

Dr. Stockmann. I quite appreciate that.

Hovstad. Yes—and in my opinion a journalist incurs a heavy responsibility if he neglects a favourable opportunity of emancipating the masses—the humble and oppressed. I know well enough that in exalted circles I shall be called an agitator, and all that sort of thing; but they may call what they like. If only my conscience doesn't reproach me, then ——

Dr. Stockmann. Quite right! Quite right, Mr. Hovstad. But all the same—devil take it! *(A knock is heard at the door.)* Come in!

[ASLAKSEN *appears at the door. He is poorly but decently dressed, in black, with a slightly crumpled white neckcloth; he wears gloves and has a felt hat in his hand.*

Aslaksen (bowing). Excuse my taking the liberty, Doctor——

Dr. Stockmann (getting up). Ah, it is you, Aslaksen!

Aslaksen. Yes, Doctor.

Hovstad (standing up). Is it me you want, Aslaksen?

Aslaksen. No; I didn't know I should find you here. No, it was the Doctor I——

Dr. Stockmann. I am quite at your service. What is it?

Aslaksen. Is what I heard from Mr. Billing true, sir—that you mean to improve our water-supply?

Dr. Stockmann. Yes, for the Baths.

Aslaksen. Quite so, I understand. Well, I have come to say that I will back that up by every means in my power.

Hovstad (to the Doctor*).* You see!

Dr. Stockmann. I shall be very grateful to you, but——

Aslaksen. Because it may be no bad thing to have us small tradesmen at your back. We form, as it were, a compact majority in the town—if we choose. And it is always a good thing to have the majority with you, Doctor.

Dr. Stockmann. That is undeniably true; but I confess I don't see why such unusual precautions should be necessary in this case. It seems to me that such a plain, straightforward thing——

Aslaksen. Oh, it may be very desirable, all the same. I know our local authorities so well; officials are not generally very ready to act on proposals that come from other people. That is why I think it would not be at all amiss if we made a little demonstration.

Hovstad. That's right.

Dr. Stockmann. Demonstration, did you say? What on earth are you going to make a demonstration about?

Aslaksen. We shall proceed with the greatest moderation, Doctor. Moderation is always my aim; it is the greatest virtue in a citizen—at least, I think so.

Dr. Stockmann. It is well known to be a characteristic of yours, Mr. Aslaksen.

Aslaksen. Yes, I think I may pride myself on that. And this matter of the water-supply is of the greatest importance to us small tradesmen. The Baths promise to be a regular gold-mine for the town. We shall all make our living out of them, especially those of us who are householders. That is why we will back up the project as strongly as possible. And as I am at present Chairman of the Householders' Association——

Dr. Stockmann. Yes——?

Aslaksen. And, what is more, local secretary of the Temperance Society—you know, sir, I suppose, that I am a worker in the temperance cause?

Dr. Stockmann. Of course, of course.

Aslaksen. Well, you can understand that I come into contact with a great many people. And as I have the reputation of a temperate and law-abiding citizen—like yourself, Doctor—I have a certain influence in the town, a little bit of power, if I may be allowed to say so.

Dr. Stockmann. I know that quite well, Mr. Aslaksen.

Aslaksen. So you see it would be an easy matter for me to set on foot some testimonial, if necessary.

Dr. Stockmann. A testimonial?

Aslaksen. Yes, some kind of an address of thanks from the townsmen for your share in a matter of such importance to the community. I need scarcely say that it would have to be drawn up with the greatest regard to moderation, so as not to offend the authorities—who, after all, have the reins in their hands. If we pay strict attention to that, no one can take it amiss, I should think!

Hovstad. Well, and even supposing they didn't like it——

Aslaksen. No, no, no; there must be no discourtesy to the authorities, Mr. Hovstad. It is no use falling foul of those upon whom our welfare so closely depends. I have done that in my time, and no good ever comes of it. But no one can take exception to a reasonable and frank expression of a citizen's views.

Dr. Stockmann (shaking him by the hand). I can't tell you, dear Mr. Aslaksen, how extremely pleased I am to find such hearty support among my fellow-citizens. I am delighted—delighted! Now, you will take a small glass of sherry, eh?

Aslaksen. No, thank you; I never drink alcohol of that kind.

Dr. Stockmann. Well, what do you say to a glass of beer, then?

Aslaksen. Nor that either, thank you, Doctor. I never drink anything as early as this. I am going into town now to talk this over with one or two householders, and prepare the ground.

Dr. Stockmann. It is tremendously kind of you, Mr. Aslaksen; but I really cannot understand the necessity for all these precautions. It seems to me that the thing should go of itself.

Aslaksen. The authorities are somewhat slow to move, Doctor. Far be it from me to seem to blame them——

Hovstad. We are going to stir them up in the paper tomorrow, Aslaksen.

Aslaksen. But not violently, I trust, Mr. Hovstad. Proceed with moderation, or you will do nothing with them. You may take my advice; I have gathered my experience in the school of life. Well, I must say good-bye, Doctor. You know now that we small tradesmen are at your back at all events, like a solid wall. You have the compact majority on your side, Doctor.

Dr. Stockmann. I am very much obliged, dear Mr. Aslaksen. *(Shakes hands with him.)* Good-bye, good-bye.

Aslaksen Are you going my way, towards the printing-office, Mr. Hovstad?

Hovstad. I will come later; I have something to settle up first.

Aslaksen. Very well.

[*Bows and goes out;* STOCKMANN *follows him into the hall.*

Hovstad (as STOCKMANN *comes in again).* Well, what do you think of that, Doctor? Don't you think it is high time we stirred a little life into all this slackness and vacillation and cowardice?

Dr. Stockmann. Are you referring to Aslaksen?

Hovstad. Yes, I am. He is one of those who are floundering in a bog—decent enough fellow though he may be, otherwise. And most of the people here are in just the same case—see-sawing and edging first to one side and then to the other, so overcome with caution and scruple that they never dare to take any decided step.

Dr. Stockmann. Yes, but Aslaksen seemed to me so thoroughly well-intentioned.

Hovstad. There is one thing I esteem higher than that; and that is for a man to be self-reliant and sure of himself.

Dr. Stockmann. I think you are perfectly right there.

Hovstad. That is why I want to seize this opportunity, and try if I cannot manage to put a little virility into these well-intentioned people for once. The idol of Authority must be shattered in this town. This gross and inexcusable blunder about the water-supply must be brought home to the mind of every municipal voter.

Dr. Stockmann. Very well; if you are of opinion that it is for the good of the community, so be it. But not until I have had a talk with my brother.

Hovstad. Anyway, I will get a leading article ready; and if the Mayor refuses to take the matter up——

Dr. Stockmann. How can you suppose such a thing possible?

Hovstad. It is conceivable. And in that case——

Dr. Stockmann. In that case I promise you——. Look here, in that case you may print my report—every word of it.

Hovstad. May I? Have I your word for it?

Dr. Stockmann (giving him the MS.). Here it is; take it with you. It can do no harm for you to read it through, and you can give it me back later on.

Hovstad. Good, good! That is what I will do. And now good-bye, Doctor.

Dr. Stockmann. Good-bye, good-bye. You will see everything will run quite smoothly, Mr. Hovstad—quite smoothly.

Hovstad. Hm!—we shall see. [*Bows and goes out.*

Dr. Stockmann (opens the dining-room door and looks in). Katherine! Oh, you are back, Petra?

Petra (coming in). Yes, I have just come from the school.

Mrs. Stockmann (coming in). Has he not been here yet?

Dr. Stockmann. Peter? No. But I have had a long talk with Hovstad. He is quite excited about my discovery. I find it has a much wider bearing than I at first imagined. And he has put his paper at my disposal if necessity should arise.

Mrs. Stockmann. Do you think it will?

Dr. Stockmann. Not for a moment. But at all events it makes me feel proud to know that I have the liberal-minded independent press on my side. Yes, and—just imagine—I have had a visit from the Chairman of the Householders' Association!

Mrs. Stockmann. Oh! What did he want?

Dr. Stockmann. To offer me his support too. They will support me in a body if it should be necessary. Katherine—do you know what I have got behind me?

Mrs. Stockmann. Behind you? No, what have you got behind you?

Dr. Stockmann. The compact majority.

Mrs. Stockmann. Really? Is that a good thing for you, Thomas?

Dr. Stockmann. I should think it was a good thing. *(Walks up and down rubbing his hands.)* By Jove, it's a fine thing to feel this bond of brotherhood between oneself and one's fellow-citizens!

Petra. And to be able to do so much that is good and useful, father!

Dr. Stockmann. And for one's own native town into the bargain, my child!

Mrs. Stockmann. That was a ring at the bell.

Dr. Stockmann. It must be he, then. *(A knock is heard at the door.)* Come in!

Peter Stockmann (comes in from the hall). Good morning.

Dr. Stockmann. Glad to see you, Peter!

Mrs. Stockmann. Good morning, Peter. How are you?

Peter Stockmann. So so, thank you. *(To* DR. STOCKMANN.*)* I received from you yesterday, after office-hours, a report dealing with the condition of the water at the Baths.

Dr. Stockmann. Yes. Have you read it?

Peter Stockmann. Yes, I have.

Dr. Stockmann. And what have you to say to it?

Peter Stockmann (with a sidelong glance). Hm!——

Mrs. Stockmann. Come along, Petra.

[*She and* PETRA *go into the room on the left.*

Peter Stockmann (after a pause). Was it necessary to make all these investigations behind my back?

Dr. Stockmann. Yes, because until I was absolutely certain about it——

Peter Stockmann. Then you mean that you are absolutely certain now?

Dr. Stockmann. Surely you are convinced of that.

Peter Stockmann. Is it your intention to bring this document before the Baths Committee as a sort of official communication?

Dr. Stockmann. Certainly. Something must be done in the matter—and that quickly.

Peter Stockmann. As usual, you employ violent expressions in your report. You say, amongst other things, that what we offer visitors in our Baths is a permanent supply of poison.

Dr. Stockmann. Well, can you describe it any other way, Peter? Just think—water that is poisonous, whether you drink it or bathe in it! And this we offer to the poor sick folk who come to us trustfully and pay us at an exorbitant rate to be made well again!

Peter Stockmann. And your reasoning leads you to this conclusion, that we must build a sewer to draw off the alleged impurities from Mölledal and must relay the water-conduits.

Dr. Stockmann. Yes. Do you see any other way out of it? I don't.

Peter Stockmann. I made a pretext this morning to go and see the town engineer, and, as if only half seriously, broached the subject of these proposals as a thing we might perhaps have to take under consideration some time later on.

Dr. Stockmann. Some time later on!

Peter Stockmann. He smiled at what he considered to be my extravagance, naturally. Have you taken the trouble to consider what your proposed alterations would cost? According to the information I obtained, the expenses would probably mount up to fifteen or twenty thousand pounds.

Dr. Stockmann. Would it cost so much?

Peter Stockmann. Yes; and the worst part of it would be that the work would take at least two years.

Dr. Stockmann. Two years? Two whole years?

Peter Stockmann. At least. And what are we to do with the Baths in the meantime? Close them? Indeed we should be obliged to. And do you suppose any one would come near the place after it had got about that the water was dangerous?

Dr. Stockmann. Yes, but, Peter, that is what it is.

Peter Stockmann. And all this at this juncture—just as the Baths are beginning to be known. There are other towns in the neighbourhood with qualifications to attract visitors for bathing purposes. Don't you suppose they would immediately strain every nerve to divert the entire stream of strangers to themselves? Unquestionably they would; and then where should we be? We should probably have to abandon the whole thing, which has cost us so much money—and then you would have ruined your native town.

Dr. Stockmann. I—should have ruined——!

Peter Stockmann. It is simply and solely through the

Baths that the town has before it any future worth mentioning. You know that just as well as I.

Dr. Stockmann. But what do you think ought to be done, then?

Peter Stockmann. Your report has not convinced me that the condition of the water at the Baths is as bad as you represent it to be.

Dr. Stockmann. I tell you it is even worse!—or at all events it will be in summer, when the warm weather comes.

Peter Stockmann. As I said, I believe you exaggerate the matter considerably. A capable physician ought to know what measures to take—he ought to be capable of preventing injurious influences or of remedying them if they become obviously persistent.

Dr. Stockmann. Well? What more?

Peter Stockmann. The water-supply for the Baths is now an established fact, and in consequence must be treated as such. But probably the Committee, at its discretion, will not be disinclined to consider the question of how far it might be possible to introduce certain improvements consistently with a reasonable expenditure.

Dr. Stockmann. And do you suppose that I will have anything to do with such a piece of trickery as that?

Peter Stockmann. Trickery!!

Dr. Stockmann. Yes, it would be a trick—a fraud, a lie, a downright crime towards the public, towards the whole community!

Peter Stockmann. I have not, as I remarked before, been able to convince myself that there is actually any imminent danger.

Dr. Stockmann. You have! It is impossible that you should not be convinced. I know I have represented the facts absolutely truthfully and fairly. And you know it very well, Peter, only you won't acknowledge it. It was owing to your action that both the Baths and the water-conduits were built where they are; and that is what you won't acknowledge—that damnable blunder of yours. Pooh!—do you suppose I don't see through you?

Peter Stockmann. And even if that were true? If I perhaps guard my reputation somewhat anxiously, it is in the interests of the town. Without moral authority I am powerless to direct public affairs as seems, to my judgment, to be best for the common good. And on that account—and for various other reasons, too—it appears to me to be a matter of importance that your report should not be delivered to the Committee. In the interests of the public, you must withhold it. Then, later on, I will raise the question and we will do our best, privately; but nothing of this unfortunate affair—not a single word of it—must come to the ears of the public.

Dr. Stockmann. I am afraid you will not be able to prevent that now, my dear Peter.

Peter Stockmann. It must and shall be prevented.

Dr. Stockmann. It is no use, I tell you. There are too many people that know about it.

Peter Stockmann. That know about it? Who? Surely you don't mean those fellows on the "People's Messenger"?

Dr. Stockmann. Yes, they know. The liberal-minded independent press is going to see that you do your duty.

Peter Stockmann (after a short pause). You are an extraordinarily independent man, Thomas. Have you given no thought to the consequences this may have for yourself?

Dr. Stockmann. Consequences?—for me?

Peter Stockmann. For you and yours, yes.

Dr. Stockmann. What the deuce do you mean?

Peter Stockmann. I believe I have always behaved in a brotherly way to you—have always been ready to oblige or to help you?

Dr. Stockmann. Yes, you have, and I am grateful to you for it.

Peter Stockmann. There is no need. Indeed, to some

extent I was forced to do so—for my own sake. I always hoped that, if I helped to improve your financial position, I should be able to keep some check on you.

Dr. Stockmann. What!! Then it was only for your own sake——!

Peter Stockmann. Up to a certain point, yes. It is painful for a man in an official position to have his nearest relative compromising himself time after time.

Dr. Stockmann. And do you consider that I do that?

Peter Stockmann. Yes, unfortunately, you do, without even being aware of it. You have a restless, pugnacious, rebellious disposition. And then there is that disastrous propensity of yours to want to write about every sort of possible and impossible thing. The moment an idea comes into your head, you must needs go and write a newspaper article or a whole pamphlet about it.

Dr. Stockmann. Well, but is it not the duty of a citizen to let the public share in any new ideas he may have?

Peter Stockmann. Oh, the public doesn't require any new ideas. The public is best served by the good, old-established ideas it already has.

Dr. Stockmann. And that is your honest opinion?

Peter Stockmann. Yes, and for once I must talk frankly to you. Hitherto I have tried to avoid doing so, because I know how irritable you are; but now I must tell you the truth, Thomas. You have no conception what an amount of harm you do yourself by your impetuosity. You complain of the authorities, you even complain of the government—you are always pulling them to pieces; you insist that you have been neglected and persecuted. But what else can such a cantankerous man as you expect?

Dr. Stockmann. What next! Cantankerous, am I?

Peter Stockmann. Yes, Thomas, you are an extremely cantankerous man to work with—I know that to my cost. You disregard everything that you ought to have consideration for. You seem completely to forget that it is me you have to thank for your appointment here as medical officer to the Baths——

Dr. Stockmann. I was entitled to it as a matter of course!—I and nobody else! I was the first person to see that the town could be made into a flourishing watering-place, and I was the only one who saw it at that time. I had to fight single-handed in support of the idea for many years; and I wrote and wrote——

Peter Stockmann. Undoubtedly. But things were not ripe for the scheme then—though, of course, you could not judge of that in your out-of-the-way corner up north. But as soon as the opportune moment came I—and the others—took the matter into our hands——

Dr. Stockmann. Yes, and made this mess of all my beautiful plan. It is pretty obvious now what clever fellows you were!

Peter Stockmann. To my mind the whole thing only seems to mean that you are seeking another outlet for your combativeness. You want to pick a quarrel with your superiors—an old habit of yours. You cannot put up with any authority over you. You look askance at anyone who occupies a superior official position; you regard him as a personal enemy, and then any stick is good enough to beat him with. But now I have called your attention to the fact that the town's interests are at stake—and, incidentally, my own too. And therefore I must tell you, Thomas, that you will find me inexorable with regard to what I am about to require you to do.

Dr. Stockmann. And what is that?

Peter Stockmann. As you have been so indiscreet as to speak of this delicate matter to outsiders, despite the fact that you ought to have treated it as entirely official and confidential, it is obviously impossible to hush it up now. All sorts of rumours will get about directly, and everybody who has a grudge against us will take care to embellish these rumours. So it will be necessary for you to refute them publicly.

Dr. Stockmann. I! How? I don't understand.

Peter Stockmann. What we shall expect is that, after making further investigations, you will come to the conclusion that the matter is not by any means as dangerous or as critical as you imagined in the first instance.

Dr. Stockmann. Oho!—so that is what you expect!

Peter Stockmann. And, what is more, we shall expect you to make public profession of your confidence in the Committee and in their readiness to consider fully and conscientiously what steps may be necessary to remedy any possible defects.

Dr. Stockmann. But you will never be able to do that by patching and tinkering at it—never! Take my word for it, Peter; I mean what I say, as deliberately and emphatically as possible.

Peter Stockmann. As an officer under the Committee, you have no right to any individual opinion.

Dr. Stockmann (amazed). No right?

Peter Stockmann. In your official capacity, no. As a private person, it is quite another matter. But as a subordinate member of the staff of the Baths, you have no right to express any opinion which runs contrary to that of your superiors.

Dr. Stockmann. This is too much! I, a doctor, a man of science, have no right to——!

Peter Stockmann. The matter in hand is not simply a scientific one. It is a complicated matter, and has its economic as well as its technical side.

Dr. Stockmann. I don't care what it is! I intend to be free to express my opinion on any subject under the sun.

Peter Stockmann. As you please—but not on any subject concerning the Baths. That we forbid.

Dr. Stockmann (shouting). You forbid——! You! A pack of——

Peter Stockmann. I forbid it—I, your chief; and if I forbid it, you have to obey.

Dr. Stockmann (controlling himself). Peter—if you were not my brother——

Petra (throwing open the door). Father, you shan't stand this!

Mrs. Stockmann (coming in after her). Petra, Petra!

Peter Stockmann. Oh, so you have been eavesdropping.

Mrs. Stockmann. You were talking so loud, we couldn't help——

Petra. Yes, I was listening.

Peter Stockmann. Well, after all, I am very glad——

Dr. Stockmann (going up to him). You were saying something about forbidding and obeying?

Peter Stockmann. You obliged me to take that tone with you.

Dr. Stockmann. And so I am to give myself the lie, publicly?

Peter Stockmann. We consider it absolutely necessary that you should make some such public statement as I have asked for.

Dr. Stockmann. And if I do not—obey?

Peter Stockmann. Then we shall publish a statement ourselves to reassure the public.

Dr. Stockmann. Very well; but in that case I shall use my pen against you. I stick to what I have said; I will show that I am right and that you are wrong. And what will you do then?

Peter Stockmann. Then I shall not be able to prevent your being dismissed.

Dr. Stockmann. What——?

Petra. Father—dismissed!

Mrs. Stockmann. Dismissed!

Peter Stockmann. Dismissed from the staff of the Baths. I shall be obliged to propose that you shall immediately be given notice, and shall not be allowed any further participation in the Baths' affairs.

Dr. Stockmann. You would dare to do that!

Peter Stockmann. It is you that are playing the daring game.

Petra. Uncle, that is a shameful way to treat a man like father!

Mrs. Stockmann. Do hold your tongue, Petra!

Peter Stockmann (looking at PETRA*).* Oh, so we volunteer our opinions already, do we? Of course. *(To* MRS. STOCKMANN.*)* Katherine, I imagine you are the most sensible person in this house. Use any influence you may have over your husband, and make him see what this will entail for his family as well as——

Dr. Stockmann. My family is my own concern and nobody else's!

Peter Stockmann. ——for his own family, as I was saying, as well as for the town he lives in.

Dr. Stockmann. It is I who have the real good of the town at heart! I want to lay bare the defects that sooner or later must come to the light of day. I will show whether I love my native town.

Peter Stockmann. You, who in your blind obstinacy want to cut off the most important source of the town's welfare?

Dr. Stockmann. The source is poisoned, man! Are you mad? We are making our living by retailing filth and corruption! The whole of our flourishing municipal life derives its sustenance from a lie!

Peter Stockmann. All imagination—or something even worse. The man who can throw out such offensive insinuations about his native town must be an enemy of our community.

Dr. Stockmann (going up to him). Do you dare to——!

Mrs. Stockmann (throwing herself between them). Thomas!

Petra (catching her father by the arm). Don't lose your temper, father!

Peter Stockmann. I will not expose myself to violence. Now you have had a warning; so reflect on what you owe to yourself and your family. Good-bye. [*Goes out.*

Dr. Stockmann (walking up and down). Am I to put up with such treatment as this? In my own house, Katherine! What do you think of that!

Mrs. Stockmann. Indeed it is both shameful and absurd, Thomas——

Petra. If only I could give uncle a piece of my mind——

Dr. Stockmann. It is my own fault. I ought to have flown out at him long ago!—shown my teeth!—bitten! To hear him call me an enemy to our community! Me! I shall not take that lying down, upon my soul!

Mrs. Stockmann. But, dear Thomas, your brother has power on his side——

Dr. Stockmann. Yes, but I have right on mine, I tell you.

Mrs. Stockmann. Oh yes, right—right. What is the use of having right on your side if you have not got might?

Petra. Oh, mother!—how can you say such a thing!

Dr. Stockmann. Do you imagine that in a free country it is no use having right on your side? You are absurd, Katherine. Besides, haven't I got the liberal-minded, independent press to lead the way, and the compact majority behind me? That is might enough, I should think!

Mrs. Stockmann. But, good heavens, Thomas, you don't mean to——?

Dr. Stockmann. Don't mean to what?

Mrs. Stockmann. To set yourself up in opposition to your brother.

Dr. Stockmann. In God's name, what else do you suppose I should do but take my stand on right and truth?

Petra. Yes, I was just going to say that.

Mrs. Stockmann. But it won't do you any earthly good. If they won't do it, they won't.

Dr. Stockmann. Oho, Katherine! Just give me time, and you will see how I will carry the war into their camp.

Mrs. Stockmann. Yes, you carry the war into their camp, and you get your dismissal—that is what you will do.

Dr. Stockmann. In any case I shall have done my duty towards the public—towards the community. I, who am called its enemy!

Mrs. Stockmann. But towards your family, Thomas? Towards your own home! Do you think that is doing your duty towards those you have to provide for?

Petra. Ah, don't think always first of us, mother.

Mrs. Stockmann. Oh, it is easy for you to talk; you are able to shift for yourself, if need be. But remember the boys, Thomas; and think a little, too, of yourself, and of me——

Dr. Stockmann. I think you are out of your senses, Katherine! If I were to be such a miserable coward as to go on my knees to Peter and his damned crew, do you suppose I should ever know an hour's peace of mind all my life afterwards?

Mrs. Stockmann. I don't know anything about that; but God preserve us from the peace of mind we shall have, all the same, if you go on defying him! You will find yourself again without the means of subsistence, with no income to count upon. I should think we had had enough of that in the old days. Remember that, Thomas; think what that means.

Dr. Stockmann (collecting himself with a struggle and clenching his fists). And this is what this slavery can bring upon a free, honourable man! Isn't it horrible, Katherine?

Mrs. Stockmann. Yes, it is sinful to treat you so, it is perfectly true. But, good heavens, one has to put up with so much injustice in this world.—There are the boys,

Thomas! Look at them! What is to become of them? Oh, no, no, you can never have the heart——.

[EJLIF *and* MORTEN *have come in while she was speaking, with their school books in their hands.*

Dr. Stockmann. The boys——! *(Recovers himself suddenly.)* No, even if the whole world goes to pieces, I will never bow my neck to this yoke!

[*Goes towards his room.*

Mrs. Stockmann (following him). Thomas—what are you going to do!

Dr. Stockmann (at his door). I mean to have the right to look my sons in the face when they are grown men.

[*Goes into his room.*

Mrs. Stockmann (bursting into tears). God help us all!

Petra. Father is splendid! He will not give in.

[*The boys look on in amazement;* PETRA *signs to them not to speak.*

ACT III

SCENE.—*The editorial office of the "People's Messenger." The entrance door is on the left-hand side of the back wall; on the right-hand side is another door with glass panels through which the printing-room can be seen. Another door in the right-hand wall. In the middle of the room is a large table covered with papers, newspapers and books. In the foreground on the left a window, before which stand a desk and a high stool. There are a couple of easy chairs by the table, and other chairs standing along the wall. The room is dingy and uncomfortable; the furniture is old, the chairs stained and torn. In the printing-room the compositors are seen at work, and a printer is working a hand-press.* HOVSTAD *is sitting at the desk, writing.* BILLING *comes in from the right with* DR. STOCKMANN'S *manuscript in his hand.*

Billing. Well, I must say!

Hovstad (still writing). Have you read it through?

Billing (laying the MS. on the desk). Yes, indeed I have.

Hovstad. Don't you think the Doctor hits them pretty hard?

Billing. Hard? Bless my soul, he's crushing! Every word falls like—how shall I put it?—like the blow of a sledgehammer.

Hovstad. Yes, but they are not the people to throw up the sponge at the first blow.

Billing. That is true; and for that reason we must strike blow upon blow until the whole of this aristocracy tumbles to pieces. As I sat in there reading this, I almost seemed to see a revolution in being.

Hovstad (turning round). Hush!—Speak so that Aslaksen cannot hear you.

Billing (lowering his voice). Aslaksen is a chicken-hearted chap, a coward; there is nothing of the man in him. But this time you will insist on your own way, won't you? You will put the Doctor's article in?

Hovstad. Yes, and if the Mayor doesn't like it——

Billing. That will be the devil of a nuisance.

Hovstad. Well, fortunately we can turn the situation to good account, whatever happens. If the Mayor will not fall in with the Doctor's project, he will have all the small tradesmen down on him—the whole of the Householders' Association and the rest of them. And if he does fall in with it, he will fall out with the whole crowd of large shareholders in the Baths, who up to now have been his most valuable supporters——

Billing. Yes, because they will certainly have to fork out a pretty penny——

Hovstad. Yes, you may be sure they will. And in this way the ring will be broken up, you see, and then in every issue of the paper we will enlighten the public on the Mayor's incapability on one point and another, and make it clear that all the positions of trust in the town, the whole control of municipal affairs, ought to be put in the hands of the Liberals.

Billing. That is perfectly true! I see it coming—I see it coming; we are on the threshold of a revolution!

[*A knock is heard at the door.*

Hovstad. Hush! *(Calls out.)* Come in! *(*DR. STOCKMANN *comes in by the street door.* HOVSTAD *goes to meet him.)* Ah, it is you, Doctor! Well?

Dr. Stockmann. You may set to work and print it, Mr. Hovstad!

Hovstad. Has it come to that, then?

Billing. Hurrah!

Dr. Stockmann. Yes, print away. Undoubtedly it has come to that. Now they must take what they get. There is going to be a fight in the town, Mr. Billing!

Billing. War to the knife, I hope! We will get our knives to their throats, Doctor!

Dr. Stockmann. This article is only a beginning. I have already got four or five more sketched out in my head. Where is Aslaksen?

Billing (calls into the printing-room). Aslaksen, just come here for a minute!

Hovstad. Four or five more articles, did you say? On the same subject?

Dr. Stockmann. No—far from it, my dear fellow. No, they are about quite another matter. But they all spring from the question of the water-supply and the drainage. One thing leads to another, you know. It is like beginning to pull down an old house, exactly.

Billing. Upon my soul, it's true; you find you are not done till you have pulled all the old rubbish down.

Aslaksen (coming in). Pulled down? You are not thinking of pulling down the Baths surely, Doctor?

Hovstad. Far from it, don't be afraid.

Dr. Stockmann. No, we meant something quite different. Well, what do you think of my article, Mr. Hovstad?

Hovstad. I think it is simply a masterpiece——

Dr. Stockmann. Do you really think so? Well, I am very pleased, very pleased.

Hovstad. It is so clear and intelligible. One need have no special knowledge to understand the bearing of it. You will have every enlightened man on your side.

Aslaksen. And every prudent man too, I hope?

Billing. The prudent and the imprudent—almost the whole town.

Aslaksen. In that case we may venture to print it.

Dr. Stockmann. I should think so!

Hovstad. We will put it in to-morrow morning.

Dr. Stockmann. Of course—you must not lose a single day. What I wanted to ask you, Mr. Aslaksen, was if you would supervise the printing of it yourself.

Aslaksen. With pleasure.

Dr. Stockmann. Take care of it as if it were a treasure! No misprints—every word is important. I will look in again a little later; perhaps you will be able to let me see a proof. I can't tell you how eager I am to see it in print, and see it burst upon the public——

Billing. Burst upon them—yes, like a flash of lightning!

Dr. Stockmann. ——and to have it submitted to the judgment of my intelligent fellow-townsmen. You cannot imagine what I have gone through to-day. I have been threatened first with one thing and then with another; they have tried to rob me of my most elementary rights as a man——

Billing. What! Your rights as a man!

Dr. Stockmann. ——they have tried to degrade me, to make a coward of me, to force me to put personal interests before my most sacred convictions——

Billing. That is too much—I'm damned if it isn't.

Hovstad. Oh, you mustn't be surprised at anything from that quarter.

Dr. Stockmann. Well, they will get the worst of it with me; they may assure themselves of that. I shall consider the "People's Messenger" my sheet-anchor now, and every single day I will bombard them with one article after another, like bomb-shells——

Aslaksen. Yes, but——

Billing. Hurrah!—it is war, it is war!

Dr. Stockmann. I shall smite them to the ground—I shall crush them—I shall break down all their defences, before the eyes of the honest public! That is what I shall do!

Aslaksen. Yes, but in moderation, Doctor—proceed with moderation——

Billing. Not a bit of it, not a bit of it! Don't spare the dynamite!

Dr. Stockmann. Because it is not merely a question of water-supply and drains now, you know. No—it is the whole of our social life that we have got to purify and disinfect——

Billing. Spoken like a deliverer!

Dr. Stockmann. All the incapables must be turned out, you understand—and that in every walk of life! Endless vistas have opened themselves to my mind's eye to-day. I cannot see it all quite clearly yet, but I shall in time. Young and vigorous standard-bearers—those are what we need and must seek, my friends; we must have new men in command at all our outposts.

Billing. Hear, hear!

Dr. Stockmann. We only need to stand by one another, and it will all be perfectly easy. The revolution will be launched like a ship that runs smoothly off the stocks. Don't you think so?

Hovstad. For my part I think we have now a prospect of getting the municipal authority into the hands where it should lie.

Aslaksen. And if only we proceed with moderation, I cannot imagine that there will be any risk.

Dr. Stockmann. Who the devil cares whether there is any risk or not! What I am doing, I am doing in the name of truth and for the sake of my conscience.

Hovstad. You are a man who deserves to be supported, Doctor.

Aslaksen. Yes, there is no denying that the Doctor is a true friend to the town—a real friend to the community, that he is.

Billing. Take my word for it, Aslaksen, Dr. Stockmann is a friend of the people.

Aslaksen. I fancy the Householders' Association will make use of that expression before long.

Dr. Stockmann (affected, grasps their hands). Thank you, thank you, my dear staunch friends. It is very refreshing to me to hear you say that; my brother called me something quite different. By Jove, he shall have it back, with interest! But now I must be off to see a poor devil ——. I will come back, as I said. Keep a very careful eye on the manuscript, Aslaksen, and don't for worlds leave out any of my notes of exclamation! Rather put one or two more in! Capital, capital! Well, good-bye for the present—good-bye, good-bye!

[*They show him to the door, and bow him out.*

Hovstad. He may prove an invaluably useful man to us.

Aslaksen. Yes, so long as he confines himself to this matter of the Baths. But if he goes farther afield, I don't think it would be advisable to follow him.

Hovstad. Hm!—that all depends——

Billing. You are so infernally timid, Aslaksen!

Aslaksen. Timid? Yes, when it is a question of the local authorities, I am timid, Mr. Billing; it is a lesson I have learnt in the school of experience, let me tell you. But try me in higher politics, in matters that concern the government itself, and then see if I am timid.

Billing. No, you aren't, I admit. But this is simply contradicting yourself.

Aslaksen. I am a man with a conscience, and that is the whole matter. If you attack the government, you don't do the community any harm, anyway; those fellows pay no attention to attacks, you see—they go on just as they are, in spite of them. But *local* authorities are different; they *can* be turned out, and then perhaps you may get an ignorant lot into office who may do irreparable harm to the householders and everybody else.

Hovstad. But what of the education of citizens by self-government—don't you attach any importance to that?

Aslaksen. When a man has interests of his own to protect, he cannot think of everything, Mr. Hovstad.

Hovstad. Then I hope I shall never have interests of my own to protect!

Billing. Hear, hear!

Aslaksen (with a smile). Hm! *(Points to the desk.)* Mr. Sheriff Stensgaard was your predecessor at that editorial desk.

Billing (spitting). Bah! That turncoat.

Hovstad. I am not a weathercock—and never will be.

Aslaksen. A politician should never be too certain of anything, Mr. Hovstad. And as for you, Mr. Billing, I should think it is time for you to be taking in a reef or two in your sails, seeing that you are applying for the post of secretary to the Bench.

Billing. I——!

Hovstad. Are you, Billing?

Billing. Well, yes—but you must clearly understand I am doing it only to annoy the bigwigs.

Aslaksen. Anyhow, it is no business of mine. But if I am to be accused of timidity and of inconsistency in my principles, this is what I want to point out: my political past is an open book. I have never changed, except perhaps to become a little more moderate, you see. My heart is still with the people; but I don't deny that my reason has a certain bias towards the authorities—the local ones, I mean.

[*Goes into the printing-room.*

Billing. Oughtn't we to try and get rid of him, Hovstad?

Hovstad. Do you know anyone else who will advance the money for our paper and printing bill?

Billing. It is an infernal nuisance that we don't possess some capital to trade on.

Hovstad (sitting down at his desk). Yes, if we only had that, then——

Billing. Suppose you were to apply to Dr. Stockmann?

Hovstad (turning over some papers). What is the use? He has got nothing.

Billing. No, but he has got a warm man in the back.

ground, old Morten Kiil—"the Badger," as they call him.

Hovstad (writing). Are you so sure *he* has got anything?

Billing. Good Lord, of course he has! And some of it must come to the Stockmanns. Most probably he will do something for the children, at all events.

Hovstad (turning half round). Are you counting on that?

Billing. Counting on it? Of course I am not counting on anything.

Hovstad. That is right. And I should not count on the secretaryship to the Bench either, if I were you; for I can assure you—you won't get it.

Billing. Do you think I am not quite aware of that? My object is precisely *not* to get it. A slight of that kind stimulates a man's fighting power—it is like getting a supply of fresh bile—and I am sure one needs that badly enough in a hole-and-corner place like this, where it is so seldom anything happens to stir one up.

Hovstad (writing). Quite so, quite so.

Billing. Ah, I shall be heard of yet!—Now I shall go and write the appeal to the Householders' Association.

[*Goes into the room on the right.*

Hovstad (sitting at his desk, biting his penholder, says slowly). Hm!—that's it, is it? *(A knock is heard.)* Come in! *(*PETRA *comes in by the outer door.* HOVSTAD *gets up.)* What, you!—here?

Petra. Yes, you must forgive me——

Hovstad (pulling a chair forward). Won't you sit down?

Petra. No, thank you; I must go again in a moment.

Hovstad. Have you come with a message from your father, by any chance?

Petra. No, I have come on my own account. *(Takes a book out of her coat pocket.)* Here is the English story.

Hovstad. Why have you brought it back?

Petra. Because I am not going to translate it.

Hovstad. But you promised me faithfully——

Petra. Yes, but then I had not read it. I don't suppose you have read it either?

Hovstad. No, you know quite well I don't understand English; but——

Petra. Quite so. That is why I wanted to tell you that you must find something else. *(Lays the book on the table.)* You can't use this for the "People's Messenger."

Hovstad. Why not?

Petra. Because it conflicts with all your opinions.

Hovstad. Oh, for that matter——

Petra. You don't understand me. The burden of this story is that there is a supernatural power that looks after the so-called good people in this world and makes everything happen for the best in their case—while all the so-called bad people are punished.

Hovstad. Well, but that is all right. That is just what our readers want.

Petra. And are you going to be the one to give it to them? For myself, I do not believe a word of it. You know quite well that things do not happen so in reality.

Hovstad. You are perfectly right; but an editor cannot always act as he would prefer. He is often obliged to bow to the wishes of the public in unimportant matters. Politics are the most important thing in life—for a newspaper, anyway; and if I want to carry my public with me on the path that leads to liberty and progress, I must not frighten them away. If they find a moral tale of this sort in the serial at the bottom of the page, they will be all the more ready to read what is printed above it; they feel more secure, as it were.

Petra. For shame! You would never go and set a snare like that for your readers; you are not a spider!

Hovstad (smiling). Thank you for having such a good opinion of me. No; as a matter of fact that is Billing's idea and not mine.

Petra. Billing's!

Hovstad. Yes; anyway he propounded that theory here one day. And it is Billing who is so anxious to have that story in the paper; I don't know anything about the book.

Petra. But how can Billing, with his emancipated views——

Hovstad. Oh, Billing is a many-sided man. He is applying for the post of secretary to the Bench, too, I hear.

Petra. I don't believe it, Mr. Hovstad. How could he possibly bring himself to do such a thing?

Hovstad. Ah, you must ask him that.

Petra. I should never have thought it of him.

Hovstad (looking more closely at her). No? Does it really surprise you so much?

Petra. Yes. Or perhaps not altogether. Really, I don't quite know——

Hovstad. We journalists are not much worth, Miss Stockmann.

Petra. Do you really mean that?

Hovstad. I think so sometimes.

Petra. Yes, in the ordinary affairs of everyday life, perhaps; I can understand that. But now, when you have taken a weighty matter in hand——

Hovstad. This matter of your father's, you mean?

Petra. Exactly. It seems to me that now you must feel you are a man worth more than most.

Hovstad. Yes, to-day I do feel something of that sort.

Petra. Of course you do, don't you? It is a splendid vocation you have chosen—to smooth the way for the march of unappreciated truths, and new and courageous lines of thought. If it were nothing more than because you stand fearlessly in the open and take up the cause of an injured man——

Hovstad. Especially when that injured man is—ahem! —I don't rightly know how to——

Petra. When that man is so upright and so honest, you mean?

Hovstad (more gently). Especially when he is your father, I meant.

Petra (suddenly checked). That?

Hovstad. Yes, Petra—Miss Petra.

Petra. Is it *that,* that is first and foremost with you? Not the matter itself? Not the truth?—not my father's big generous heart?

Hovstad. Certainly—of course—that too.

Petra. No, thank you; you have betrayed yourself, Mr. Hovstad, and now I shall never trust you again in anything.

Hovstad. Can you really take it so amiss in me that it is mostly for your sake——?

Petra. What I am angry with you for, is for not having been honest with my father. You talked to him as if the truth and the good of the community were what lay nearest to your heart. You have made fools of both my father and me. You are not the man you made yourself out to be. And that I shall never forgive you—never!

Hovstad. You ought not to speak so bitterly, Miss Petra—least of all now.

Petra. Why not now, especially?

Hovstad. Because your father cannot do without my help.

Petra (looking him up and down). Are you that sort of man too? For shame!

Hovstad. No, no, I am not. This came upon me so unexpectedly—you must believe that.

Petra. I know what to believe. Good-bye.

Aslaksen (coming from the printing-room, hurriedly and with an air of mystery). Damnation, Hovstad!—*(Sees* PETRA.*)* Oh, this is awkward——

Petra. There is the book; you must give it to some one else. [*Goes towards the door.*

Hovstad (following her). But, Miss Stockmann——

Petra. Good-bye. [*Goes out.*

Aslaksen. I say—Mr. Hovstad——

Hovstad. Well, well!—what is it?

Aslaksen. The Mayor is outside in the printing-room.

Hovstad. The Mayor, did you say?

Aslaksen. Yes, he wants to speak to you. He came in by the back door—didn't want to be seen, you understand.

Hovstad. What can he want? Wait a bit—I will go myself. [*Goes to the door of the printing-room, opens it, bows and invites* PETER STOCKMANN *in.)* Just see, Aslaksen, that no one——

Aslaksen. Quite so. [*Goes into the printing-room.*

Peter Stockmann. You did not expect to see me here, Mr. Hovstad?

Hovstad. No, I confess I did not.

Peter Stockmann (looking round). You are very snug in here—very nice indeed.

Hovstad. Oh——

Peter Stockmann. And here I come, without any notice, to take up your time!

Hovstad. By all means, Mr. Mayor. I am at your service. But let me relieve you of your—— *(takes* STOCKMANN'S *hat and stick and puts them on a chair).* Won't you sit down?

Peter Stockmann (sitting down by the table). Thank you. (HOVSTAD *sits down.)* I have had an extremely annoying experience to-day, Mr. Hovstad.

Hovstad. Really? Ah well, I expect with all the various business you have to attend to——

Peter Stockmann. The Medical Officer of the Baths is responsible for what happened to-day.

Hovstad. Indeed? The Doctor?

Peter Stockmann. He has addressed a kind of report to the Baths Committee on the subject of certain supposed defects in the Baths.

Hovstad. Has he indeed?

Peter Stockmann. Yes—has he not told you? I thought he said——

Hovstad. Ah, yes—it is true he did mention something about——

Aslaksen (coming from the printing-room). I ought to have that copy——

Hovstad (angrily). Ahem!—there it is on the desk.

Aslaksen (taking it). Right.

Peter Stockmann. But look there—that is the thing I was speaking of!

Aslaksen. Yes, that is the Doctor's article, Mr. Mayor.

Hovstad. Oh, is *that* what you were speaking about?

Peter Stockmann. Yes, that is it. What do you think of it?

Hovstad. Oh, I am only a layman—and I have only taken a very cursory glance at it.

Peter Stockmann. But you are going to print it?

Hovstad. I cannot very well refuse a distinguished man——

Aslaksen. I have nothing to do with editing the paper Mr. Mayor——

Peter Stockmann. I understand.

Aslaksen. I merely print what is put into my hands.

Peter Stockmann. Quite so.

Aslaksen. And so I must——

[*Moves off towards the printing-room.*

Peter Stockmann. No, but wait a moment, Mr. Aslaksen. You will allow me, Mr. Hovstad?

Hovstad. If you please, Mr. Mayor.

Peter Stockmann. You are a discreet and thoughtful man, Mr. Aslaksen.

Aslaksen. I am delighted to hear you think so, sir.

Peter Stockmann. And a man of very considerable influence.

Aslaksen. Chiefly among the small tradesmen, sir.

Peter Stockmann. The small tax-payers are the majority —here as everywhere else.

Aslaksen. That is true.

Peter Stockmann. And I have no doubt you know the general trend of opinion among them, don't you?

Aslaksen. Yes, I think I may say I do, Mr. Mayor.

Peter Stockmann. Yes. Well, since there is such a praiseworthy spirit of self-sacrifice among the less wealthy citizens of our town——

Aslaksen. What?

Hovstad. Self-sacrifice?

Peter Stockmann. It is pleasing evidence of a public-spirited feeling, extremely pleasing evidence. I might almost say I hardly expected it. But you have a closer knowledge of public opinion than I.

Aslaksen. But, Mr. Mayor——

Peter Stockmann. And indeed it is no small sacrifice that the town is going to make.

Hovstad. The town?

Aslaksen. But I don't understand. Is it the Baths——?

Peter Stockmann. At a provisional estimate, the alterations that the Medical Officer asserts to be desirable will cost somewhere about twenty thousand pounds.

Aslaksen. That is a lot of money, but——

Peter Stockmann. Of course it will be necessary to raise a municipal loan.

Hovstad (getting up). Surely you never mean that the town must pay——?

Aslaksen. Do you mean that it must come out of the municipal funds?—out of the ill-filled pockets of the small tradesmen?

Peter Stockmann. Well, my dear Mr. Aslaksen, where else is the money to come from?

Aslaksen. The gentlemen who own the Baths ought to provide that.

Peter Stockmann. The proprietors of the Baths are not in a position to incur any further expense.

Aslaksen. Is that absolutely certain, Mr. Mayor?

Peter Stockmann. I have satisfied myself that it is so. If the town wants these very extensive alterations, it will have to pay for them.

Aslaksen. But, damn it all—I beg your pardon—this is quite another matter, Mr. Hovstad!

Hovstad. It is, indeed.

Peter Stockmann. The most fatal part of it is that we shall be obliged to shut the Baths for a couple of years.

Hovstad. Shut them? Shut them altogether?

Aslaksen. For two years?

Peter Stockmann. Yes, the work will take as long as that —at least.

Aslaksen. I'm damned if we will stand that, Mr. Mayor! What are we householders to live upon in the meantime?

Peter Stockmann. Unfortunately, that is an extremely difficult question to answer, Mr. Aslaksen. But what would you have us do? Do you suppose we shall have a single visitor in the town, if we go about proclaiming that our water is polluted, that we are living over a plague spot, that the entire town——

Aslaksen. And the whole thing is merely imagination?

Peter Stockmann. With the best will in the world, I have not been able to come to any other conclusion.

Aslaksen. Well then I must say it is absolutely unjustifiable of Dr. Stockmann—I beg your pardon, Mr. Mayor——

Peter Stockmann. What you say is lamentably true, Mr. Aslaksen. My brother has, unfortunately, always been a headstrong man.

Aslaksen. After this, do you mean to give him your support, Mr. Hovstad?

Hovstad. Can you suppose for a moment that I——?

Peter Stockmann. I have drawn up a short *résumé* of the situation as it appears from a reasonable man's point of view. In it I have indicated how certain possible defects might suitably be remedied without outrunning the resources of the Baths Committee.

Hovstad. Have you got it with you, Mr. Mayor?

Peter Stockmann (fumbling in his pocket). Yes, I brought it with me in case you should——

Aslaksen. Good Lord, there he is!

Peter Stockmann. Who? My brother?

Hovstad. Where? Where?

Aslaksen. He has just gone through the printing-room.

Peter Stockmann. How unlucky! I don't want to meet him here, and I had still several things to speak to you about.

Hovstad (pointing to the door on the right). Go in there for the present.

Peter Stockmann. But——?

Hovstad. You will only find Billing in there.

Aslaksen. Quick, quick, Mr. Mayor—he is just coming.

Peter Stockmann. Yes, very well; but see that you get rid of him quickly.

[*Goes out through the door on the right, which* Aslaksen *opens for him and shuts after him.*

Hovstad. Pretend to be doing something, Aslaksen.

[*Sits down and writes.* Aslaksen *begins foraging among a heap of newspapers that are lying on a chair.*

Dr. Stockmann (coming in from the printing-room). Here I am again. [*Puts down his hat and stick.*

Hovstad (writing). Already, Doctor? Hurry up with what we were speaking about, Aslaksen. We are very pressed for time to-day.

Dr. Stockmann (to Aslaksen*).* No proof for me to see yet, I hear.

Aslaksen (without turning round). You couldn't expect it yet, Doctor.

Dr. Stockmann. No, no; but I am impatient, as you can understand. I shall not know a moment's peace of mind till I see it in print.

Hovstad. Hm!—it will take a good while yet, won't it, Aslaksen?

Aslaksen. Yes, I am almost afraid it will.

Dr. Stockmann. All right, my dear friends; I will come back. I do not mind coming back twice if necessary. A matter of such great importance—the welfare of the town at stake—it is no time to shirk trouble. *(Is just going, but stops and comes back.)* Look here—there is one thing more I want to speak to you about.

Hovstad. Excuse me, but could it not wait till some other time?

Dr. Stockmann. I can tell you in half a dozen words. It is only this. When my article is read to-morrow and it is realised that I have been quietly working the whole winter for the welfare of the town——

Hovstad. Yes, but, Doctor——

Dr. Stockmann. I know what you are going to say. You don't see how on earth it was any more than my duty—my obvious duty as a citizen. Of course it wasn't; I know that as well as you. But my fellow-citizens, you know——! Good Lord, think of all the good souls who think so highly of me——!

Aslaksen. Yes, our townsfolk have had a very high opinion of you so far, Doctor.

Dr. Stockmann. Yes, and that is just why I am afraid they——. Well, this is the point; when this reaches them, especially the poorer classes, and sounds in their ears like a summons to take the town's affairs into their own hands for the future——

Hovstad (getting up). Ahem! Doctor, I won't conceal from you the fact——

Dr. Stockmann. Ah!—I knew there was something in

the wind! But I won't hear a word of it. If anything of that sort is being set on foot——

Hovstad. Of what sort?

Dr. Stockmann. Well, whatever it is—whether it is a demonstration in my honour, or a banquet, or a subscription list for some presentation to me—whatever it is, you must promise me solemnly and faithfully to put a stop to it. You too, Mr. Aslaksen; do you understand?

Hovstad. You must forgive me, Doctor, but sooner or later we must tell you the plain truth——

[*He is interrupted by the entrance of* MRS. STOCKMANN, *who comes in from the street door.*

Mrs. Stockmann (seeing her husband). Just as I thought!

Hovstad (going towards her). You too, Mrs. Stockmann?

Dr. Stockmann. What on earth do *you* want here, Katherine?

Mrs. Stockmann. I should think you know very well what I want.

Hovstad. Won't you sit down? Or perhaps——

Mrs. Stockmann. No, thank you; don't trouble. And you must not be offended at my coming to fetch my husband; I am the mother of three children, you know.

Dr. Stockmann. Nonsense!—we know all about that.

Mrs. Stockmann. Well, one would not give you credit for much thought for your wife and children to-day; if you had had that, you would not have gone and dragged us all into misfortune.

Dr. Stockmann. Are you out of your senses, Katherine! Because a man has a wife and children, is he not to be allowed to proclaim the truth—is he not to be allowed to be an actively useful citizen—is he not to be allowed to do a service to his native town!

Mrs. Stockmann. Yes, Thomas—in reason.

Aslaksen. Just what I say. Moderation is everything.

Mrs. Stockmann. And that is why you wrong us, Mr. Hovstad, in enticing my husband away from his home and making a dupe of him in all this.

Hovstad. I certainly am making a dupe of no one——

Dr. Stockmann. Making a dupe of me! Do you suppose *I* should allow myself to be duped!

Mrs. Stockmann. It is just what you do. I know quite well you have more brains than anyone in the town, but you are extremely easily duped, Thomas. *(To* HOVSTAD.*)* Please to realise that he loses his post at the Baths if you print what he has written——

Aslaksen. What!

Hovstad. Look here, Doctor——

Dr. Stockmann (laughing). Ha—ha!—just let them try! No, no—they will take good care not to. I have got the compact majority behind me, let me tell you!

Mrs. Stockmann. Yes, that is just the worst of it—your having any such horrid thing behind you.

Dr. Stockmann. Rubbish, Katherine!—Go home and look after your house and leave me to look after the community. How can you be so afraid, when I am so confident and happy? *(Walks up and down, rubbing his hands.)* Truth and the People will win the fight, you may be certain! I see the whole of the broad-minded middle class marching like a victorious army——! *(Stops beside a chair.)* What the deuce is that lying there?

Aslaksen. Good Lord!

Hovstad. Ahem!

Dr. Stockmann. Here we have the topmost pinnacle of authority!

[*Takes the Mayor's official hat carefully between his finger-tips and holds it up in the air.*

Mrs. Stockmann. The Mayor's hat!

Dr. Stockmann. And here is the staff of office too. How in the name of all that's wonderful——?

Hovstad. Well, you see——

Dr. Stockmann. Oh, I understand. He has been here trying to talk you over. Ha—ha!—he made rather a mistake there! And as soon as he caught sight of me in the printing-room——. *(Bursts out laughing.)* Did he run away. Mr. Aslaksen?

Aslaksen (hurriedly). Yes, he ran away, Doctor.

Dr. Stockmann. Ran away without his stick or his——. Fiddlesticks! Peter doesn't run away and leave his belongings behind him. But what the deuce have you done with him? Ah!—in there, of course. Now you shall see, Katherine.

Mrs. Stockmann. Thomas—please don't——!

Aslaksen. Don't be rash, Doctor.

[DR. STOCKMANN *has put on the Mayor's hat and taken his stick in his hand. He goes up to the door, opens it and stands with his hand to his hat at the salute.* PETER STOCKMANN *comes in, red with anger.* BILLING *follows him.*

Peter Stockmann. What does this tomfoolery mean?

Dr. Stockmann. Be respectful, my good Peter. I am the chief authority in the town now. [*Walks up and down.*

Mrs. Stockmann (almost in tears). Really, Thomas!

Peter Stockmann (following him about). Give me my hat and stick.

Dr. Stockmann (in the same tone as before). If you are chief constable, let me tell you that I am the Mayor—I am the master of the whole town, please understand!

Peter Stockmann. Take off my hat, I tell you. Remember it is part of an official uniform.

Dr. Stockmann. Pooh! Do you think the newly awakened lion-hearted people are going to be frightened by an official hat? There is going to be a revolution in the town to-morrow, let me tell you. You thought you could turn me out; but now I shall turn you out—turn you out of all your various offices. Do you think I cannot? Listen to me. I have triumphant social forces behind me. Hovstad and Billing will thunder in the "People's Messenger," and Aslaksen will take the field at the head of the whole Householders' Association——

Aslaksen. That I won't, Doctor.

Dr. Stockmann. Of course you will——

Peter Stockmann. Ah!—may I ask then if Mr. Hovstad intends to join this agitation?

Hovstad. No, Mr. Mayor.

Aslaksen. No, Mr. Hovstad is not such a fool as to go and ruin his paper and himself for the sake of an imaginary grievance.

Dr. Stockmann (looking round him). What does this mean?

Hovstad. You have represented your case in a false light, Doctor, and therefore I am unable to give you my support.

Billing. And after what the Mayor was so kind as to tell me just now, I——

Dr. Stockmann. A false light! Leave that part of it to me. Only print my article; I am quite capable of defending it.

Hovstad. I am not going to print it. I cannot and will not and dare not print it.

Dr. Stockmann. You dare not? What nonsense!—you are the editor; and an editor controls his paper, I suppose!

Aslaksen. No, it is the subscribers, Doctor.

Peter Stockmann. Fortunately, yes.

Aslaksen. It is public opinion—the enlightened public—householders and people of that kind; they control the newspapers.

Dr. Stockmann (composedly). And I have all these influences against me?

Aslaksen. Yes, you have. It would mean the absolute ruin of the community if your article were to appear.

Dr. Stockmann. Indeed.

Peter Stockmann. My hat and stick, if you please. *(*Dr. Stockmann *takes off the hat and lays it on the table with the stick.* Peter Stockmann *takes them up.)* Your authority as mayor has come to an untimely end.

Dr. Stockmann. We have not got to the end yet. *(To* Hovstad.*)* Then it is quite impossible for you to print my article in the "People's Messenger"?

Hovstad. Quite impossible—out of regard for your family as well.

Mrs. Stockmann. You need not concern yourself about his family, thank you, Mr. Hovstad.

Peter Stockmann (taking a paper from his pocket). It will be sufficient, for the guidance of the public, if this appears. It is an official statement. May I trouble you?

Hovstad (taking the paper). Certainly; I will see that it is printed.

Dr. Stockmann. But not mine. Do you imagine that you can silence me and stifle the truth! You will not find it so easy as you suppose. Mr. Aslaksen, kindly take my manuscript at once and print it as a pamphlet—at my expense. I will have four hundred copies—no, five—six hundred.

Aslaksen. If you offered me its weight in gold, I could not lend my press for any such purpose, Doctor. It would be flying in the face of public opinion. You will not get it printed anywhere in the town.

Dr. Stockmann. Then give it me back.

Hovstad (giving him the MS.) Here it is.

Dr. Stockmann (taking his hat and stick). It shall be made public all the same. I will read it out at a mass meeting of the townspeople. All my fellow-citizens shall hear the voice of truth!

Peter Stockmann. You will not find any public body in the town that will give you the use of their hall for such a purpose.

Aslaksen. Not a single one, I am certain.

Billing. No, I'm damned if you will find one.

Mrs. Stockmann. But this is too shameful! Why should every one turn against you like that?

Dr. Stockmann (angrily). I will tell you why. It is because all the men in this town are old women—like you; they all think of nothing but their families, and never of the community.

Mrs. Stockmann (putting her arm into his). Then I will show them that an—an old woman can be a man for once. I am going to stand by you, Thomas!

Dr. Stockmann. Bravely said, Katherine! It shall be made public—as I am a living soul! If I can't hire a hall, I shall hire a drum, and parade the town with it and read it at every street-corner.

Peter Stockmann. You are surely not such an arrant fool as that!

Dr. Stockmann. Yes, I am.

Aslaksen. You won't find a single man in the whole town to go with you.

Billing. No, I'm damned if you will.

Mrs. Stockmann. Don't give in, Thomas. I will tell the boys to go with you.

Dr. Stockmann. That is a splendid idea!

Mrs. Stockmann. Morten will be delighted; and Ejlif will do whatever he does.

Dr. Stockmann. Yes, and Petra!—and you two, Katherine!

Mrs. Stockmann. No, I won't do that; but I will stand at the window and watch you, that's what I will do.

Dr. Stockmann (puts his arms round her and kisses her). Thank you, my dear! Now you and I are going to try a fall, my fine gentlemen! I am going to see whether a pack of cowards can succeed in gagging a patriot who wants to purify society!

[*He and his wife go out by the street door.*

Peter Stockmann (shaking his head seriously). Now he has sent *her* out of her senses, too.

ACT IV

SCENE. *A big old-fashioned room in* CAPTAIN HORSTER'S *house. At the back folding-doors, which are standing open, lead to an ante-room. Three windows in the left-hand wall. In the middle of the opposite wall a platform has been erected. On this is a small table with two candles, a water-bottle and glass, and a bell. The room is lit by lamps placed between the windows. In the foreground on the left there is a table with candles and a chair. To the right is a door and some chairs standing near it. The room is nearly filled with a crowd of townspeople of all sorts, a few women and schoolboys being amongst them. People are still streaming in from the back, and the room is soon filled.*

1st Citizen (meeting another). Hullo, Lamstad! You here too?

2nd Citizen. I go to every public meeting, I do.

3rd Citizen. Brought your whistle too, I expect!

2nd Citizen. I should think so. Haven't you?

3rd Citizen. Rather! And old Evensen said he was going to bring a cow-horn, he did.

2nd Citizen. Good old Evensen!

[*Laughter among the crowd.*

4th Citizen (coming up to them). I say, tell me what is going on here to-night.

2nd Citizen. Dr. Stockmann is going to deliver an address attacking the Mayor.

4th Citizen. But the Mayor is his brother.

1st Citizen. That doesn't matter; Dr. Stockmann's not the chap to be afraid.

3rd Citizen. But he is in the wrong; it said so in the "People's Messenger."

2nd Citizen. Yes, I expect he must be in the wrong this time, because neither the Householders' Association nor the Citizens' Club would lend him their hall for his meeting.

1st Citizen. He couldn't even get the loan of the hall at the Baths.

2nd Citizen. No, I should think not.

A Man in another part of the crowd. I say—who are we to back up in this?

Another Man, beside him. Watch Aslaksen, and do as he does.

Billing (pushing his way through the crowd, with a writing-case under his arm). Excuse me, gentlemen—do you mind letting me through? I am reporting for the "People's Messenger." Thank you very much!

[*He sits down at the table on the left.*

A Workman. Who was that?

Second Workman. Don't you know him? It's Billing, who writes for Aslaksen's paper.

[CAPTAIN HORSTER *brings in* MRS. STOCKMANN *and* PETRA *through the door on the right.* EJLIF *and* MORTEN *follow them in.*

Horster. I thought you might all sit here; you can slip out easily from here, if things get too lively.

Mrs. Stockmann. Do you think there will be a disturbance?

Horster. One can never tell—with such a crowd. But sit down, and don't be uneasy.

Mrs. Stockmann (sitting down). It was extremely kind of you to offer my husband the room.

Horster. Well, if nobody else would——

Petra (who has sat down beside her mother). And it was a plucky thing to do, Captain Horster.

Horster. Oh, it is not such a great matter as all that.

[HOVSTAD *and* ASLAKSEN *make their way through the crowd.*

Aslaksen (going up to HORSTER*).* Has the Doctor not come yet?

Horster. He is waiting in the next room.

[*Movement in the crowd by the door at the back.*

Hovstad. Look—here comes the Mayor!

Billing. Yes, I'm damned if he hasn't come after all!

[PETER STOCKMANN *makes his way gradually through the crowd, bows courteously and takes up a position by the wall on the left. Shortly afterwards* DR. STOCKMANN *comes in by the right-hand door. He is dressed in a black frock-coat, with a white tie. There is a little feeble applause, which is hushed down. Silence is obtained.*

Dr. Stockmann (in an undertone). How do you feel, Katherine?

Mrs. Stockmann. All right, thank you. *(Lowering her voice.)* Be sure not to lose your temper, Thomas.

Dr. Stockmann. Oh, I know how to control myself. *(Looks at his watch, steps on to the platform and bows.)* It is a quarter past—so I will begin.

[*Takes his M.S. out of his pocket*

Aslaksen. I think we ought to elect a chairman first.

Dr. Stockmann. No, it is quite unnecessary.

Some of the Crowd. Yes—yes!

Peter Stockmann. I certainly think, too, that we ought to have a chairman.

Dr. Stockmann. But I have called this meeting to deliver a lecture, Peter.

Peter Stockmann. Dr. Stockmann's lecture may possibly lead to a considerable conflict of opinion.

Voices in the Crowd. A chairman! A chairman!

Hovstad. The general wish of the meeting seems to be that a chairman should be elected.

Dr. Stockmann (restraining himself). Very well—let the meeting have its way.

Aslaksen. Will the Mayor be good enough to undertake the task?

Three Men (clapping their hands). Bravo! Bravo!

Peter Stockmann. For various reasons, which you will easily understand, I must beg to be excused. But fortunately we have amongst us a man who I think will be acceptable to you all. I refer to the President of the Householders' Association, Mr. Aslaksen.

Several Voices. Yes—Aslaksen! Bravo Aslaksen!

[DR. STOCKMANN *takes up his MS. and walks up and down the platform.*

Aslaksen. Since my fellow-citizens choose to entrust me with this duty, I cannot refuse.

[*Loud applause.* ASLAKSEN *mounts the platform.*

Billing (writing). "Mr. Aslaksen was elected with enthusiasm."

Aslaksen. And now, as I am in this position, I should like to say a few brief words. I am a quiet and peaceable man, who believes in discreet moderation, and—and—in moderate discretion. All my friends can bear witness to that.

Several Voices. That's right! That's right, Aslaksen!

Aslaksen. I have learnt in the school of life and experience that moderation is the most valuable virtue a citizen can possess——

Peter Stockmann. Hear, hear!

Aslaksen. ——And moreover that discretion and moderation are what enable a man to be of most service to the community. I would therefore suggest to our esteemed fellow-citizen, who has called this meeting, that he should strive to keep strictly within the bounds of moderation.

A Man by the door. Three cheers for the Moderation Society!

A Voice. Shame!

Several Voices. Sh!—Sh!

Aslaksen. No interruptions, gentlemen, please! Does anyone wish to make any remarks?

Peter Stockmann. Mr. Chairman.

Aslaksen. The Mayor will address the meeting.

Peter Stockmann. In consideration of the close relationship in which, as you all know, I stand to the present Medical Officer of the Baths, I should have preferred not to speak this evening. But my official position with regard to the Baths and my solicitude for the vital interests of the town compel me to bring forward a motion. I venture to presume that there is not a single one of our citizens present who considers it desirable that unreliable and exaggerated accounts of the sanitary condition of the Baths and the town should be spread abroad.

Several Voices. No, no! Certainly not! We protest against it!

Peter Stockmann. Therefore I should like to propose that the meeting should not permit the Medical Officer either to read or to comment on his proposed lecture.

Dr. Stockmann (impatiently). Not permit——! What the devil——!

Mrs. Stockmann (coughing). Ahem!—ahem!

Dr. Stockmann (collecting himself). Very well. Go ahead!

Peter Stockmann. In my communication to the "People's Messenger," I have put the essential facts before the public in such a way that every fair-minded citizen can easily form his own opinion. From it you will see that the main result of the Medical Officer's proposals—apart from their constituting a vote of censure on the leading men of the town—would be to saddle the ratepayers with an unnecessary expenditure of at least some thousands of pounds.

[*Sounds of disapproval among the audience, and some cat-calls.*

Aslaksen (ringing his bell). Silence, please, gentlemen! I beg to support the Mayor's motion. I quite agree with him that there is something behind this agitation started by the Doctor. He talks about the Baths; but it is a revolution he is aiming at—he wants to get the administration of the town put into new hands. No one doubts the honesty of the Doctor's intentions—no one will suggest that there can be any two opinions as to that. I myself am a believer in self-government for the people, provided it does not fall too heavily on the ratepayers. But that would be the case here; and that is why I will see Dr. Stockmann damned—I beg your pardon—before I go with him in the matter. You can pay too dearly for a thing sometimes; that is my opinion.

[*Loud applause on all sides.*

Hovstad. I, too, feel called upon to explain my position. Dr. Stockmann's agitation appeared to be gaining a certain amount of sympathy at first, so I supported it as impartially as I could. But presently we had reason to suspect that we had allowed ourselves to be misled by misrepresentation of the state of affairs——

Dr. Stockmann. Misrepresentation——!

Hovstad. Well, let us say a not entirely trustworthy representation. The Mayor's statement has proved that I hope no one here has any doubt as to my liberal principles; the attitude of the "People's Messenger" towards important political questions is well known to every one. But the advice of experienced and thoughtful men has convinced me that in purely local matters a newspaper ought to proceed with a certain caution.

Aslaksen. I entirely agree with the speaker.

Hovstad. And, in the matter before us, it is now an undoubted fact that Dr. Stockmann has public opinion against him. Now, what is an editor's first and most obvious duty, gentlemen? Is it not to work in harmony with his readers?

Has he not received a sort of tacit mandate to work persistently and assiduously for the welfare of those whose opinions he represents? Or is it possible I am mistaken in that?

Voices from the crowd. No, no! You are quite right!

Hovstad. It has cost me a severe struggle to break with a man in whose house I have been lately a frequent guest—a man who till to-day has been able to pride himself on the undivided goodwill of his fellow-citizens—a man whose only, or at all events whose essential, failing is that he is swayed by his heart rather than his head.

A few scattered voices. That is true! Bravo, Stockmann!

Hovstad. But my duty to the community obliged me to break with him. And there is another consideration that impels me to oppose him, and, as far as possible, to arrest him on the perilous course he has adopted; that is, consideration for his family——

Dr. Stockmann. Please stick to the water-supply and drainage!

Hovstad. ——consideration, I repeat, for his wife and his children for whom he has made no provision.

Morten. Is that us, mother?

Mrs. Stockmann. Hush!

Aslaksen. I will now put the Mayor's proposition to the vote.

Dr. Stockmann. There is no necessity! To-night I have no intention of dealing with all that filth down at the Baths. No; I have something quite different to say to you.

Peter Stockmann (aside). What is coming now?

A Drunken Man (by the entrance door). I am a ratepayer! And therefore I have a right to speak too! And my entire—firm—inconceivable opinion is——

A number of voices. Be quiet, at the back there!

Others. He is drunk! Turn him out!

[*They turn him out.*

Dr. Stockmann. Am I allowed to speak?

Aslaksen (ringing his bell). Dr. Stockmann will address the meeting.

Dr. Stockmann. I should like to have seen anyone, a few days ago, dare to attempt to silence me as has been done to-night! I would have defended my sacred rights as a man, like a lion! But now it is all one to me; I have something of even weightier importance to say to you.

[*The crowd presses nearer to him,* MORTEN KIIL *conspicuous among them.*

Dr. Stockmann (continuing). I have thought and pondered a great deal, these last few days—pondered over such a variety of things that in the end my head seemed too full to hold them——

Peter Stockmann (with a cough). Ahem!

Dr. Stockmann. ——but I got them clear in my mind at last, and then I saw the whole situation lucidly. And that is why I am standing here to-night. I have a great revelation to make to you, my fellow-citizens! I will impart to you a discovery of a far wider scope than the trifling matter that our water-supply is poisoned and our medicinal Baths are standing on pestiferous soil.

A number of voices (shouting). Don't talk about the Baths! We won't hear you! None of that!

Dr. Stockmann. I have already told you that what I want to speak about is the great discovery I have made lately—the discovery that all the sources of our *moral* life are poisoned and that the whole fabric of our civic community is founded on the pestiferous soil of falsehood.

Voices of disconcerted Citizens. What is that he says?

Peter Stockmann. Such an insinuation——!

Aslaksen (with his hand on his bell). I call upon the speaker to moderate his language.

Dr. Stockmann. I have always loved my native town as a man only can love the home of his youthful days. I was not old when I went away from here; and exile, longing and memories cast, as it were, an additional halo over both the town and its inhabitants. *(Some clapping and applause.)* And there I stayed, for many years, in a horrible hole far away up north. When I came into contact with some of the people that lived scattered about among the rocks, I often thought it would of been more service to the poor half-starved creatures if a veterinary doctor had been sent up there, instead of a man like me.

[*Murmurs among the crowd.*

Billing (laying down his pen). I'm damned if I have ever heard——!

Hovstad. It is an insult to a respectable population!

Dr. Stockmann. Wait a bit! I do not think anyone will charge me with having forgotten my native town up there. I was like one of the eider-ducks brooding on its nest, and what I hatched was—the plans for these Baths. *(Applause and protests.)* And then when fate at last decreed for me the great happiness of coming home again—I assure you, gentlemen, I thought I had nothing more in the world to wish for. Or rather, there was one thing I wished for—eagerly, untiringly, ardently—and that was to be able to be of service to my native town and the good of the community.

Peter Stockmann (looking at the ceiling). You chose a strange way of doing it—ahem!

Dr. Stockmann. And so, with my eyes blinded to the real facts, I revelled in happiness. But yesterday morning—no, to be precise, it was yesterday afternoon—the eyes of my mind were opened wide, and the first thing I realised was the colossal stupidity of the authorities——.

[*Uproar, shouts and laughter.* MRS. STOCKMANN *coughs persistently.*

Peter Stockmann. Mr. Chairman!

Aslaksen (ringing his bell). By virtue of my authority——!

Dr. Stockmann. It is a petty thing to catch me up on a word, Mr. Aslaksen. What I mean is only that I got scent of the unbelievable piggishness our leading men had been responsible for down at the Baths. I can't stand leading men at any price!—I have had enough of such people in my time. They are like billy-goats in a young plantation; they do mischief everywhere. They stand in a free man's way, whichever way he turns, and what I should like best would be to see them exterminated like any other vermin——.

[*Uproar.*

Peter Stockmann. Mr. Chairman, can we allow such expressions to pass?

Aslaksen (with his hand on his bell). Doctor——!

Dr. Stockmann. I cannot understand how it is that I have only now acquired a clear conception of what these gentry are, when I had almost daily before my eyes in this town such an excellent specimen of them—my brother Peter—slow-witted and hide-bound in prejudice——.

[*Laughter, uproar and hisses.* MRS. STOCKMANN *sits coughing assiduously.* ASLAKSEN *rings his bell violently.*

The Drunken Man (who has got in again). Is it me he is talking about? My name's Petersen, all right—but devil take me if I——

Angry Voices. Turn out that drunken man! Turn him out. [*He is turned out again.*

Peter Stockmann. Who was that person?

1st Citizen. I don't know who he is, Mr. Mayor.

2nd Citizen. He doesn't belong here.

3rd Citizen. I expect he is a navvy from over at (*the rest is inaudible*).

Aslaksen. He had obviously had too much beer.—Proceed, Doctor; but please strive to be moderate in your language.

Dr. Stockmann. Very well, gentlemen, I will say no more about our leading men. And if anyone imagines, from what I have just said, that my object is to attack these people this evening, he is wrong—absolutely wide of the mark.

For I cherish the comforting conviction that these parasites—all these venerable relics of a dying school of thought—are most admirably paving the way for their own extinction; they need no doctor's help to hasten their end. Nor is it folk of that kind who constitute the most pressing danger to the community. It is not they who are most instrumental in poisoning the sources of our moral life and infecting the ground on which we stand. It is not they who are the most dangerous enemies of truth and freedom amongst us.

Shouts from all sides. Who then? Who is it? Name! Name!

Dr. Stockmann. You may depend upon it I shall name them! That is precisely the great discovery I made yesterday. *(Raises his voice.)* The most dangerous enemy of truth and freedom amongst us is the compact majority—yes, the damned compact Liberal majority—that is it! Now you know!

[*Tremendous uproar. Most of the crowd are shouting, stamping and hissing. Some of the older men among them exchange stolen glances and seem to be enjoying themselves.* MRS. STOCKMANN *gets up, looking anxious.* EJLIF *and* MORTEN *advance threateningly upon some schoolboys who are playing pranks.* ASLAKSEN *rings his bell and begs for silence.* HOVSTAD *and* BILLING *both talk at once, but are inaudible. At last quiet is restored.*

Aslaksen. As chairman, I call upon the speaker to withdraw the ill-considered expressions he has just used.

Dr. Stockmann. Never, Mr. Aslaksen! It is the majority in our community that denies me my freedom and seeks to prevent my speaking the truth.

Hovstad. The majority always has right on its side.

Billing. And truth too, by God!

Dr. Stockmann. The majority *never* has right on its side. Never, I say! That is one of these social lies against which an independent, intelligent man must wage war. Who is it that constitute the majority of the population in a country? Is it the clever folk or the stupid? I don't imagine you will dispute the fact that at present the stupid people are in an absolutely overwhelming majority all the world over. But, good Lord!—you can never pretend that it is right that the stupid folk should govern the clever ones! *(Uproar and cries.)* Oh, yes—you can shout me down, I know! but you cannot answer me. The majority has *might* on its side—unfortunately; but *right* it has *not*. I am in the right—I and a few other scattered individuals. The minority is always in the right. [*Renewed uproar.*

Hovstad. Aha!—so Dr. Stockmann has become an aristocrat since the day before yesterday!

Dr. Stockmann. I have already said that I don't intend to waste a word on the puny, narrow-chested, short-winded crew whom we are leaving astern. Pulsating life no longer concerns itself with them. I am thinking of the few, the scattered few amongst us, who have absorbed new and vigorous truths. Such men stand, as it were, at the outposts, so far ahead that the compact majority has not yet been able to come up with them; and there they are fighting for truths that are too newly-born into the world of consciousness to have any considerable number of people on their side as yet.

Hovstad. So the Doctor is a revolutionary now!

Dr. Stockmann. Good heavens—of course I am, Mr. Hovstad! I propose to raise a revolution against the lie that the majority has the monopoly of the truth. What sort of truths are they that the majority usually supports? They are truths that are of such advanced age that they are beginning to break up. And if a truth is as old as that, it is also in a fair way to become a lie, gentlemen. *(Laughter and mocking cries.)* Yes, believe me or not, as you like; but truths are by no means as long-lived as Methuselah—as some folk imagine. A normally constituted truth lives, let us say, as a rule seventeen or eighteen, or at most twenty years; seldom longer. But truths as aged as that are always worn frightfully thin, and nevertheless it is only then that the majority recognises them and recommends them to the community as wholesome moral nourishment. There is no great nutritive value in that sort of fare, I can assure you; and, as a doctor, I ought to know. These "majority truths" are like last year's cured meat—like rancid, tainted ham; and they are the origin of the moral scurvy that is rampant in our communities.

Aslaksen. It appears to me that the speaker is wandering a long way from his subject.

Peter Stockmann. I quite agree with the Chairman.

Dr. Stockmann. Have you gone clean out of your senses, Peter? I am sticking as closely to my subject as I can; for my subject is precisely this, that it is the masses, the majority—this infernal compact majority—that poisons the sources of our moral life and infects the ground we stand on.

Hovstad. And all this because the great, broad-minded majority of the people is prudent enough to show deference only to well-ascertained and well-approved truths?

Dr. Stockmann. Ah, my good Mr. Hovstad, don't talk nonsense about well-ascertained truths! The truths of which the masses now approve are the very truths that the fighters at the outposts held to in the days of our grandfathers. We fighters at the outposts nowadays no longer approve of them; and I do not believe there is any other well-ascertained truth except this, that no community can live a healthy life if it is nourished only on such old marrowless truths.

Hovstad. But instead of standing there using vague generalities, it would be interesting if you would tell us what these old marrowless truths are, that we are nourished on.

[*Applause from many quarters.*

Dr. Stockmann. Oh, I could give you a whole string of such abominations; but to begin with I will confine myself to one well-approved truth, which at bottom is a foul lie, but upon which nevertheless Mr. Hovstad and the "People's Messenger" and all the "Messenger's" supporters are nourished.

Hovstad. And that is——?

Dr. Stockmann. That is, the doctrine you have inherited from your forefathers and proclaim thoughtlessly far and wide—the doctrine that the public, the crowd, the masses are the essential part of the population—that they constitute the People—that the common folk, the ignorant and incomplete element in the community, have the same right to pronounce judgment and to approve, to direct and to govern, as the isolated, intellectually superior personalities in it.

Billing. Well, damn me if ever I——

Hovstad (at the same time, shouting out). Fellow-citizens, take good note of that!

A number of voices (angrily). Oho!—we are not the People! Only the superior folks are to govern, are they!

A Workman. Turn the fellow out, for talking such rubbish!

Another. Out with him!

Another (calling out). Blow your horn, Evensen!

[*A horn is blown loudly, amidst hisses and an angry uproar.*

Dr. Stockmann (when the noise has somewhat abated). Be reasonable! Can't you stand hearing the voice of truth for once? I don't in the least expect you to agree with me all at once; but I must say I did expect Mr. Hovstad to admit I was right, when he had recovered his composure a little. He claims to be a freethinker——

Voices (in murmurs of astonishment). Freethinker, did he say? Is Hovstad a freethinker?

Hovstad (shouting). Prove it, Dr. Stockmann! When have I said so in print?

Dr. Stockmann (reflecting). No, confound it, you are right!—you have never had the courage to. Well, I won't put you in a hole, Mr. Hovstad. Let us say it is I that am the freethinker, then. I am going to prove to you, scientifically, that the "People's Messenger" leads you by the nose in a shameful manner when it tells you that you—that the common people, the crowd, the masses are the real essence of the People. That is only a newspaper lie, I tell you! The common people are nothing more than the raw material of which a People is made. *(Groans, laughter and uproar.)* Well, isn't that the case? Isn't there an enormous difference between a well-bred and an ill-bred strain of animals? Take, for instance, a common barn-door hen. What sort of eating do you get from a shrivelled up old scrag of a fowl like that? Not much, do you! And what sort of eggs does it lay? A fairly good crow or a raven can lay pretty nearly as good an egg. But take a well-bred Spanish or Japanese hen, or a good pheasant or a turkey—then you will see the difference. Or take the case of dogs, with whom we humans are on such intimate terms. Think first of an ordinary common cur—I mean one of the horrible, coarse-haired, low-bred curs that do nothing but run about the streets and befoul the walls of the houses. Compare one of these curs with a poodle whose sires for many generations have been bred in a gentleman's house, where they have had the best of food and had the opportunity of hearing soft voices and music. Do you not think that the poodle's brain is developed to quite a different degree from that of the cur? Of course it is. It is puppies of well-bred poodles like that, that showmen train to do incredibly clever tricks—things that a common cur could never learn to do even if it stood on its head. [*Uproar and mocking cries.*

A Citizen (calls out). Are you going to make out we are dogs, now?

Another Citizen. We are not animals, Doctor!

Dr. Stockmann. Yes, but, bless my soul, we *are,* my friend! It is true we are the finest animals anyone could wish for; but, even amongst us, exceptionally fine animals are rare. There is a tremendous difference between poodle-men and cur-men. And the amusing part of it is, that Mr. Hovstad quite agrees with me as long as it is a question of four-footed animals——

Hovstad. Yes, it is true enough as far as they are concerned.

Dr. Stockmann. Very well. But as soon as I extend the principle and apply it to two-legged animals, Mr. Hovstad stops short. He no longer dares to think independently, or to pursue his ideas to their logical conclusion; so he turns the whole theory upside down and proclaims in the "People's Messenger" that it is the barn-door hens and street curs that are the finest specimens in the menagerie. But that is always the way, as long as a man retains the traces of common origin and has not worked his way up to intellectual distinction.

Hovstad. I lay no claim to any sort of distinction. I am the son of humble countryfolk, and I am proud that the stock I come from is rooted deep among the common people he insults.

Voices. Bravo, Hovstad! Bravo! Bravo!

Dr. Stockmann. The kind of common people I mean are not only to be found low down in the social scale; they crawl and swarm all around us—even in the highest social positions. You have only to look at your own fine, distinguished Mayor! My brother Peter is every bit as plebeian as anyone that walks in two shoes——

[*Laughter and hisses.*

Peter Stockmann. I protest against personal allusions of this kind.

Dr. Stockmann (imperturbably). ——and that, not because he is, like myself, descended from some old rascal of a pirate from Pomerania or thereabouts—because that is who we are descended from——

Peter Stockmann. An absurd legend. I deny it!

Dr. Stockmann. ——but because he thinks what his superiors think and holds the same opinions as they. People who do that are, intellectually speaking, common people; and that is why my magnificent brother Peter is in reality so very far from any distinction—and consequently also so far from being liberal-minded.

Peter Stockmann. Mr. Chairman——!

Hovstad. So it is only the distinguished men that are liberal-minded in this country? We are learning something quite new! [*Laughter.*

Dr. Stockmann. Yes, that is part of my new discovery too. And another part of it is that broad-mindedness is almost precisely the same thing as morality. That is why I maintain that it is absolutely inexcusable in the "People's Messenger" to proclaim, day in and day out, the false doctrine that it is the masses, the crowd, the compact majority that have the monopoly of broad-mindedness and morality—and that vice and corruption and every kind of intellectual depravity are the result of culture, just as all the filth that is draining into our Baths is the result of the tanneries up at Mölledal! *(Uproar and interruptions.* DR. STOCKMANN *is undisturbed, and goes on, carried away by his ardour, with a smile.)* And yet this same "People's Messenger" can go on preaching that the masses ought to be elevated to higher conditions of life! But, bless my soul, if the "Messenger's" teaching is to be depended upon, this very raising up the masses would mean nothing more or less than setting them straightway upon the paths of depravity! Happily the theory that culture demoralises is only an old falsehood that our forefathers believed in and we have inherited. No, it is ignorance, poverty, ugly conditions of life that do the devil's work! In a house which does not get aired and swept every day—my wife Katherine maintains that the floor ought to be scrubbed as well, but that is a debatable question—in such a house, let me tell you, people will lose within two or three years the power of thinking or acting in a moral manner. Lack of oxygen weakens the conscience. And there must be a plentiful lack of oxygen in very many houses in this town, I should think, judging from the fact that the whole compact majority can be unconscientious enough to wish to build the town's prosperity on a quagmire of falsehood and deceit.

Aslaksen. We cannot allow such a grave accusation to be flung at a citizen community.

A Citizen. I move that the Chairman direct the speaker to sit down.

Voices (angrily). Hear, hear! Quite right! Make him sit down!

Dr. Stockmann (losing his self-control). Then I will go and shout the truth at every street corner! I will write it in other towns' newspapers! The whole country shall know what is going on here!

Hovstad. It almost seems as if Dr. Stockmann's intention were to ruin the town.

Dr. Stockmann. Yes, my native town is so dear to me that I would rather ruin it than see it flourishing upon a lie.

Aslaksen. This is really serious.

[*Uproar and cat-calls.* MRS. STOCKMANN *coughs, but to no purpose; her husband does not listen to her any longer.*

Hovstad (shouting above the din). A man must be a public enemy to wish to ruin a whole community!

Dr. Stockmann (with growing fervour). What does the destruction of a community matter, if it lives on lies! It ought to be razed to the ground, I tell you! All who live by lies ought to be exterminated like vermin! You will end by infecting the whole country; you will bring about such a state of things that the whole country will deserve to be ruined. And if things come to that pass, I shall say from the bottom of my heart: Let the whole country perish, let all these people be exterminated!

Voices from the crowd. That is talking like an out-and-out enemy of the people!

Billing. There sounded the voice of the people, by all that's holy!

The whole crowd (shouting). Yes, yes! He is an enemy of the people! He hates his country! He hates his own people!

Aslaksen. Both as a citizen and as an individual, I am profoundly disturbed by what we have had to listen to. Dr. Stockmann has shown himself in a light I should never have dreamed of. I am unhappily obliged to subscribe to the opinion which I have just heard my estimable fellow-citizens utter; and I propose that we should give expression to that opinion in a resolution. I propose a resolution as follows: "This meeting declares that it considers Dr. Thomas Stockmann, Medical Officer of the Baths, to be an enemy of the people."

[*A storm of cheers and applause. A number of men surround the* DOCTOR *and hiss him.* MRS. STOCKMANN *and* PETRA *have got up from their seats.* MORTEN *and* EJLIF *are fighting the other schoolboys for hissing; some of their elders separate them.*

Dr. Stockmann (to the men who are hissing him). Oh, you fools! I tell you that——

Aslaksen (ringing his bell). We cannot hear you now, Doctor. A formal vote is about to be taken; but, out of regard for personal feelings, it shall be by ballot and not verbal. Have you any clean paper, Mr. Billings?

Billing. I have both blue and white here.

Aslaksen (going to him). That will do nicely; we shall get on more quickly that way. Cut it up into small strips—yes, that's it. *(To the meeting.)* Blue means no; white means yes. I will come round myself and collect votes.

[PETER STOCKMANN *leaves the hall.* ASLAKSEN *and one or two others go round the room with the slips of paper in their hats.*

1st Citizen (to Hovstad*).* I say, what has come to the Doctor? What are we to think of it?

Hovstad. Oh, you know how headstrong he is.

2nd Citizen (to Billing*).* Billing, you go to their house —have you ever noticed if the fellow drinks?

Billings. Well I'm hanged if I know what to say. There are always spirits on the table when you go.

3rd Citizen. I rather think he goes quite off his head sometimes.

1st Citizen. I wonder if there is any madness in his family?

Billing. I shouldn't wonder if there were.

4th Citizen. No, it is nothing more than sheer malice; he wants to get even with somebody for something or other.

Billing. Well certainly he suggested a rise in his salary on one occasion lately, and did not get it.

The Citizens (together). Ah!—then it is easy to understand how it is!

The Drunken Man (who has got amongst the audience again). I want a blue one, I do! And I want a white one too!

Voices. It's that drunken chap again! Turn him out!

Morten Kiil (going up to Dr. Stockmann*).* Well, Stockmann, do you see what these monkey tricks of yours lead to?

Dr. Stockmann. I have done my duty.

Morten Kiil. What was that you said about the tanneries at Mölledal?

Dr. Stockmann. You heard well enough. I said they were the source of all the filth.

Morten Kiil. My tannery too?

Dr. Stockmann. Unfortunately your tannery is by far the worst.

Morten Kiil. Are you going to put that in the papers?

Dr. Stockmann. I shall conceal nothing.

Morten Kiil. That may cost you dear, Stockmann.

[*Goes out.*

A Stout Man (going up to Captain Horster, *without taking any notice of the ladies).* Well, Captain, so you lend your house to enemies of the people?

Horster. I imagine I can do what I like with my own possessions, Mr. Vik.

The Stout Man. Then you can have no objection to my doing the same with mine.

Horster. What do you mean, sir?

The Stout Man. You shall hear from me in the morning.

[*Turns his back on him and moves off*

Petra. Was that not your owner, Captain Horster?

Horster. Yes, that was Mr. Vik the ship-owner.

Aslaksen (with the voting-papers in his hands, gets up on to the platform and rings his bell). Gentlemen, allow me to announce the result. By the votes of every one here except one person——

A Young Man. That is the drunk chap!

Aslaksen. By the votes of every one here except a tipsy man, this meeting of citizens declares Dr. Thomas Stockmann to be an enemy of the people. *(Shouts and applause.)* Three cheers for our ancient and honourable citizen community! *(Renewed applause.)* Three cheers for our able and energetic Mayor, who has so loyally suppressed the promptings of family feeling! *(Cheers.)* The meeting is dissolved.

[*Gets down.*

Billing. Three cheers for the Chairman!

The whole crowd. Three cheers for Aslaksen! Hurrah!

Dr. Stockmann. My hat and coat, Petra! Captain, have you room on your ship for passengers to the New World?

Horster. For you and yours we will make room, Doctor.

Dr. Stockmann (as Petra *helps him into his coat).* Good. Come, Katherine! Come, boys!

Mrs. Stockmann (in an undertone). Thomas, dear, let us go out by the back way.

Dr. Stockmann. No back ways for me, Katherine. *(Raising his voice.)* You will hear more of this enemy of the people, before he shakes the dust off his shoes upon you! I am not so forgiving as a certain Person; I do not say: "I forgive you, for ye know not what ye do."

Aslaksen (shouting). That is a blasphemous comparison, Dr. Stockmann!

Billing. It is, by God! It's dreadful for an earnest man to listen to.

A Coarse Voice. Threatens us now, does he!

Other Voices (excitedly). Let's go and break his windows! Duck him in the fjord!

Another Voice. Blow your horn, Evensen! Pip, pip!

[*Horn-blowing, hisses and wild cries.* DR. STOCKMANN *goes out through the hall with his family,* HORSTER *elbowing a way for them.*

The Whole Crowd (howling after them as they go). Enemy of the People! Enemy of the People!

Billing (as he puts his papers together). Well, I'm damned if I go and drink toddy with the Stockmanns tonight!

[*The crowd press towards the exit. The uproar continues outside; shouts of* "Enemy of the People!" *are heard from without.*

ACT V

SCENE.—DR. STOCKMANN'S *study. Bookcases, and cabinets containing specimens, line the walls. At the back is a door leading to the hall; in the foreground on the left, a door leading to the sitting-room. In the right-hand wall are two windows, of which all the panes are broken. The* DOCTOR'S *desk, littered with books and papers, stands in the middle of the room, which is in disorder. It is morning.* DR. STOCKMANN *in dressing-gown, slippers and a smoking-cap, is bending down and raking with an umbrella under one of the cabinets After a little while he rakes out a stone.*

Dr. Stockmann (calling through the open sitting-room door). Katherine, I have found another one.

Mrs. Stockmann (from the sitting-room). Oh, you will find a lot more yet, I expect.

Dr. Stockmann (adding the stone to a heap of others on the table). I shall treasure these stones as relics. Ejlif and Morten shall look at them every day, and when they are grown up they shall inherit them as heirlooms. *(Rakes about under a bookcase.)* Hasn't—what the deuce is her name?—the girl, you know—hasn't she been to fetch the glazier yet?

Mrs. Stockmann (coming in). Yes, but he said he didn't know if he would be able to come to-day.

Dr. Stockmann. You will see he won't dare to come.

Mrs. Stockmann. Well, that is just what Randine thought—that he didn't dare to, on account of the neighbours. *(Calls into the sitting-room.)* What is it you want,

Randine? Give it to me. *(Goes in, and comes out again directly.)* Here is a letter for you, Thomas.

Dr. Stockmann. Let me see it. *(Opens and reads it.)* Ah!—of course.

Mrs. Stockmann. Who is it from?

Dr. Stockmann. From the landlord. Notice to quit.

Mrs. Stockmann. Is it possible? Such a nice man——

Dr. Stockmann (looking at the letter). Does not dare do otherwise, he says. Doesn't like doing it, but dare not do otherwise—on account of his fellow-citizens—out of regard for public opinion. Is in a dependent position—dare not offend certain influential men——

Mrs. Stockmann. There, you see, Thomas!

Dr. Stockmann. Yes, yes, I see well enough; the whole lot of them in the town are cowards; not a man among them dares do anything for fear of the others. *(Throws the letter on to the table.)* But it doesn't matter to us, Katherine. We are going to sail away to the New World, and——

Mrs. Stockmann. But, Thomas, are you sure we are well advised to take this step?

Dr. Stockmann. Are you suggesting that I should stay here, where they have pilloried me as an enemy of the people—branded me—broken my windows! And just look here, Katherine—they have torn a great rent in my black trousers too!

Mrs. Stockmann. Oh, dear!—and they are the best pair you have got!

Dr. Stockmann. You should never wear your best trousers when you go out to fight for freedom and truth. It is not that I care so much about the trousers, you know; you can always sew them up again for me. But that the common herd should dare to make this attack on me, as if they were my equals—that is what I cannot, for the life of me, swallow!

Mrs. Stockmann. There is no doubt they have behaved very ill to you, Thomas; but is that sufficient reason for our leaving our native country for good and all?

Dr. Stockmann. If we went to another town, do you suppose we should not find the common people just as insolent as they are here? Depend upon it, there is not much to choose between them. Oh, well, let the curs snap—that is not the worst part of it. The worst is that, from one end of this country to the other, every man is the slave of his Party. Although, as far as that goes, I daresay it is not much better in the free West either; the compact majority, and liberal public opinion, and all that infernal old bag of tricks are probably rampant there too. But there things are done on a larger scale, you see. They may kill you, but they won't put you to death by slow torture. They don't squeeze a free man's soul in a vice, as they do here. And, if need be, one can live in solitude. *(Walks up and down.)* If only I knew where there was a virgin forest or a small South Sea island for sale, cheap——

Mrs. Stockmann. But think of the boys, Thomas.

Dr. Stockmann (standing still). What a strange woman you are, Katherine! Would you prefer to have the boys grow up in a society like this? You saw for yourself last night that half the population are out of their minds; and if the other half have not lost their senses, it is because they are mere brutes, with no sense to lose.

Mrs. Stockmann. But, Thomas dear, the imprudent things you said had something to do with it, you know.

Dr. Stockmann. Well, isn't what I said perfectly true? Don't they turn every idea topsy-turvy? Don't they make a regular hotch-potch of right and wrong? Don't they say that the things I know are true, are lies? The craziest part of it all is the fact of these "liberals," men of full age, going about in crowds imagining that they are the broad-minded party! Did you ever hear anything like it, Katherine!

Mrs. Stockmann. Yes, yes, it's mad enough of them, certainly; but—— (PETRA *comes in from the sitting-room).* Back from school already?

Petra. Yes. I have been given notice of dismissal.

Mrs. Stockmann. Dismissal?

Dr. Stockmann. You too?

Petra. Mrs. Busk gave me my notice; so I thought it was best to go at once.

Dr. Stockmann. You were perfectly right, too!

Mrs. Stockmann. Who would have thought Mrs. Busk was a woman like that!

Petra. Mrs. Busk isn't a bit like that, mother; I saw quite plainly how it hurt her to do it. But she didn't dare do otherwise, she said; and so I got my notice.

Dr. Stockmann (laughing and rubbing his hands). She didn't dare do otherwise, either! It's delicious!

Mrs. Stockmann. Well, after the dreadful scenes last night——

Petra. It was not only that. Just listen to this, father!

Dr. Stockmann. Well?

Petra. Mrs. Busk showed me no less than three letters she received this morning——

Dr. Stockmann. Anonymous, I suppose?

Petra. Yes.

Dr. Stockmann. Yes, because they didn't dare to risk signing their names, Katherine!

Petra. And two of them were to the effect that a man, who has been our guest here, was declaring last night at the Club that my views on various subjects are extremely emancipated——

Dr. Stockmann. You did not deny that, I hope?

Petra. No, you know I wouldn't. Mrs. Busk's own views are tolerably emancipated, when we are alone together; but now that this report about me is being spread, she dare not keep me on any longer.

Mrs. Stockmann. And some one who had been a guest of

ours! That shows you the return you get for your hospitality, Thomas!

Dr. Stockmann. We won't live in such a disgusting hole any longer. Pack up as quickly as you can, Katherine; the sooner we can get away, the better.

Mrs. Stockmann. Be quiet—I think I hear some one in the hall. See who it is, Petra.

Petra (opening the door). Oh, it's you, Captain Horster! Do come in.

Horster (coming in). Good morning. I thought I would just come in and see how you were.

Dr. Stockmann (shaking his hand). Thanks—that is really kind of you.

Mrs. Stockmann. And thank you, too, for helping us through the crowd, Captain Horster.

Petra. How did you manage to get home again?

Horster. Oh, somehow or other. I am fairly strong and there is more sound than fury about these folk.

Dr. Stockmann. Yes, isn't their swinish cowardice astonishing? Look here, I will show you something! There are all the stones they have thrown through my windows. Just look at them! I'm hanged if there are more than two decently large bits of hardstone in the whole heap; the rest are nothing but gravel—wretched little things. And yet they stood out there bawling and swearing that they would do me some violence; but as for *doing* anything—you don't see much of that in this town.

Horster. Just as well for you this time, doctor!

Dr. Stockmann. True enough. But it makes one angry all the same; because if some day it should be a question of a national fight in real earnest, you will see that public opinion will be in favour of taking to one's heels, and the compact majority will turn tail like a flock of sheep, Captain Horster. That is what is so mournful to think of; it gives me so much concern, that——. No, devil take it, it is ridiculous to care about it! They have called me an enemy of the people, so an enemy of the people let me be!

Mrs. Stockmann. You will never be that, Thomas.

Dr. Stockmann. Don't swear to that, Katherine. To be called an ugly name may have the same effect as a pin-scratch in the lung. And that hateful name—I can't get quit of it. It is sticking here in the pit of my stomach, eating into me like a corrosive acid. And no magnesia will remove it.

Petra. Bah!—you should only laugh at them, father.

Horster. They will change their minds some day, Doctor.

Mrs. Stockmann. Yes, Thomas, as sure as you are standing here.

Dr. Stockmann. Perhaps, when it is too late. Much good may it do them! They may wallow in their filth then and rue the day when they drove a patriot into exile. When do you sail, Captain Horster?

Horster. Hm!—that was just what I had come to speak about——

Dr. Stockmann. Why, has anything gone wrong with the ship?

Horster. No; but what has happened is that I am not to sail in it.

Petra. Do you mean that you have been dismissed from your command?

Horster (smiling). Yes, that's just it.

Petra. You too.

Mrs. Stockmann. There, you see, Thomas!

Dr. Stockmann. And that for the truth's sake! Oh, if I had thought such a thing possible——

Horster. You mustn't take it to heart; I shall be sure to find a job with some ship-owner or other, elsewhere.

Dr Stockmann. And that is this man Vik—a wealthy man, independent of every one and everything——! Shame on him!

Horster. He is quite an excellent fellow otherwise; he

told me himself he would willingly have kept me on, if only he had dared——

Dr. Stockmann. But he didn't dare? No, of course not.

Horster. It is not such an easy matter, he said, for a party man——

Dr. Stockmann. The worthy man spoke the truth. A party is like a sausage machine; it mashes up all sorts of heads together into the same mincemeat—fatheads and blockheads, all in one mash!

Mrs. Stockmann. Come, come, Thomas dear!

Petra (to Horster*).* If only you had not come home with us, things might not have come to this pass.

Horster. I do not regret it.

Petra (holding out her hand to him). Thank you for that!

Horster (to Dr. Stockmann*).* And so what I came to say was that if you are determined to go away, I have thought of another plan——

Dr. Stockmann. That's splendid!—if only we can get away at once.

Mrs. Stockmann. Hush!—wasn't that some one knocking?

Petra. That is uncle, surely.

Dr. Stockmann. Aha! *(Calls out.)* Come in!

Mrs. Stockmann. Dear Thomas, promise me definitely——

[Peter Stockmann *comes in from the hall.*

Peter Stockmann. Oh, you are engaged. In that case, I will——

Dr. Stockmann. No, no, come in.

Peter Stockmann. But I wanted to speak to you alone.

Mrs. Stockmann. We will go into the sitting-room in the meanwhile.

Horster. And I will look in again later.

Dr. Stockmann. No, go in there with them, Captain Horster; I want to hear more about——.

Horster. Very well, I will wait, then.

[*He follows* MRS. STOCKMANN *and* PETRA *into the sitting-room.*

Dr. Stockmann. I daresay you find it rather draughty here to-day. Put your hat on.

Peter Stockmann. Thank you, if I may. *(Does so.)* I think I caught cold last night; I stood and shivered——

Dr. Stockmann. Really? I found it warm enough.

Peter Stockmann. I regret that it was not in my power to prevent those excesses last night.

Dr. Stockmann. Have you anything particular to say to me besides that?

Peter Stockmann (taking a big letter from his pocket). I have this document for you, from the Baths Committee.

Dr. Stockmann. My dismissal?

Peter Stockmann. Yes, dating from to-day. *(Lays the letter on the table.)* It gives us pain to do it; but, to speak frankly, we dared not do otherwise on account of public opinion.

Dr. Stockmann (smiling). Dared not? I seem to have heard that word before, to-day.

Peter Stockmann. I must beg you to understand your position clearly. For the future you must not count on any practice whatever in the town.

Dr. Stockmann. Devil take the practice! But why are you so sure of that?

Peter Stockmann. The Householders' Association is circulating a list from house to house. All right-minded citizens are being called upon to give up employing you; and I can assure you that not a single head of a family will risk refusing his signature. They simply dare not.

Dr. Stockmann. No, no; I don't doubt it. But what then?

Peter Stockmann. If I might advise you, it would be best to leave the place for a little while——

Dr. Stockmann. Yes, the propriety of leaving the place *has* occurred to me.

Peter Stockmann. Good. And then, when you have had six months to think things over, if, after mature consideration, you can persuade yourself to write a few words of regret, acknowledging your error——

Dr. Stockmann. I might have my appointment restored to me, do you mean?

Peter Stockmann. Perhaps. It is not at all impossible.

Dr. Stockmann. But what about public opinion, then? Surely you would not dare to do it on account of public feeling.

Peter Stockmann. Public opinion is an extremely mutable thing. And, to be quite candid with you, it is a matter of great importance to us to have some admission of that sort from you in writing.

Dr. Stockmann. Oh, that's what you are after, is it! I will just trouble you to remember what I said to you lately about foxy tricks of that sort!

Peter Stockmann. Your position was quite different then. At that time you had reason to suppose you had the whole town at your back——

Dr. Stockmann. Yes, and now I feel I have the whole town *on* my back—*(flaring up)* I would not do it if I had the devil and his dam on my back——! Never—never, I tell you!

Peter Stockmann. A man with a family has no right to behave as you do. You have no right to do it, Thomas.

Dr. Stockmann. I have no right! There is only one single thing in the world a free man has no right to do. Do you know what that is?

Peter Stockmann. No.

Dr. Stockmann. Of course you don't, but I will tell you. A free man has no right to soil himself with filth; he has no right to behave in a way that would justify his spitting in his own face.

Peter Stockmann. This sort of thing sounds extremely plausible, of course; and if there were no other explanation for your obstinacy——. But as it happens that there is.

Dr. Stockmann. What do you mean?

Peter Stockmann. You understand very well what I mean. But, as your brother and as a man of discretion, I advise you not to build too much upon expectations and prospects that may so very easily fail you.

Dr. Stockmann. What in the world is all this about?

Peter Stockmann. Do you really ask me to believe that you are ignorant of the terms of Mr. Kiil's will?

Dr. Stockmann. I know that the small amount he possesses is to go to an institution for indigent old workpeople. How does that concern me?

Peter Stockmann. In the first place, it is by no means a small amount that is in question. Mr. Kiil is a fairly wealthy man.

Dr. Stockmann. I had no notion of that!

Peter Stockmann. Hm!—hadn't you really? Then I suppose you had no notion, either, that a considerable portion of his wealth will come to your children, you and your wife having a life-rent of the capital. Has he never told you so?

Dr. Stockmann. Never, on my honour! Quite the reverse; he has consistently done nothing but fume at being so unconscionably heavily taxed. But are you perfectly certain of this, Peter?

Peter Stockmann. I have it from an absolutely reliable source.

Dr. Stockmann. Then, thank God, Katherine is provided for—and the children too! I must tell her this at once—*(calls out)* Katherine, Katherine!

Peter Stockmann (restraining him). Hush, don't say a word yet!

Mrs. Stockmann (opening the door). What is the matter?

Dr. Stockmann. Oh, nothing, nothing; you can go back. *(She shuts the door.* DR. STOCKMANN *walks up and down in his excitement.)* Provided for!——Just think of it, we are all provided for! And for life! What a blessed feeling it is to know one is provided for!

Peter Stockmann. Yes, but that is just exactly what you are not. Mr. Kiil can alter his will any day he likes.

Dr. Stockmann. But he won't do that, my dear Peter. The "Badger" is much too delighted at my attack on you and your wise friends.

Peter Stockmann (starts and looks intently at him). Ah, that throws a light on various things.

Dr. Stockmann. What things?

Peter Stockmann. I see that the whole thing was a combined manœuvre on your part and his. These violent, reckless attacks that you have made against the leading men of the town, under the pretence that it was in the name of truth——

Dr. Stockmann. What about them?

Peter Stockmann. I see that they were nothing else than the stipulated price for that vindictive old man's will.

Dr. Stockmann (almost speechless). Peter—you are the most disgusting plebeian I have ever met in all my life.

Peter Stockmann. All is over between us. Your dismissal is irrevocable—we have a weapon against you now [*Goes out*

Dr. Stockmann. For shame! For shame! *(Calls out.)* Katherine, you must have the floor scrubbed after him! Let—what's her name—devil take it, the girl who has always got soot on her nose——

Mrs. Stockmann (in the sitting-room). Hush, Thomas, be quiet!

Petra (coming to the door). Father, grandfather is here, asking if he may speak to you alone.

Dr. Stockmann. Certainly he may. *(Going to the door.)* Come in, Mr. Kiil. *(*MORTEN KIIL *comes in.* DR.

STOCKMANN *shuts the door after him.)* What can I do for you? Won't you sit down?

Morten Kiil. I won't sit. *(Looks around.)* You look very comfortable here to-day, Thomas.

Dr. Stockmann. Yes, don't we!

Morten Kiil. Very comfortable—plenty of fresh air. I should think you have got enough to-day of that oxygen you were talking about yesterday. Your conscience must be in splendid order to-day, I should think.

Dr. Stockmann. It is.

Morten Kiil. So I should think. *(Taps his chest.)* Do you know what I have got here?

Dr. Stockmann. A good conscience, too, I hope.

Morten Kiil. Bah!—No, it is something better than that.

[*He takes a thick pocket-book from his breast-pocket, opens it, and displays a packet of papers.*

Dr. Stockmann (looking at him in astonishment). Shares in the Baths?

Morten Kiil. They were not difficult to get to-day.

Dr. Stockmann. And you have been buying——?

Morten Kiil. As many as I could pay for.

Dr. Stockmann. But, my dear Mr. Kiil—consider the state of the Baths' affairs!

Morten Kiil. If you behave like a reasonable man, you can soon set the Baths on their feet again.

Dr. Stockmann. Well, you can see for yourself that I have done all I can, but——. They are all mad in this town!

Morten Kiil. You said yesterday that the worst of this pollution came from my tannery. If that is true, then my grandfather and my father before me, and I myself, for many years past, have been poisoning the town like three destroying angels. Do you think I am going to sit quiet under that reproach?

Dr. Stockmann. Unfortunately, I am afraid you will have to.

Morten Kiil. No, thank you. I am jealous of my name and reputation. They call me "the Badger," I am told. A badger is a kind of pig, I believe; but I am not going to give them the right to call me that. I mean to live and die a clean man.

Dr. Stockmann. And how are you going to set about it?

Morten Kiil. You shall cleanse me, Thomas.

Dr. Stockmann. I!

Morten Kiil. Do you know what money I have bought these shares with? No, of course you can't know—but I will tell you. It is the money that Katherine and Petra and the boys will have when I am gone. Because I have been able to save a little bit after all, you know.

Dr. Stockmann (flaring up). And you have gone and taken Katherine's money for *this!*

Morten Kiil. Yes, the whole of the money is invested in the Baths now. And now I just want to see whether you are quite stark, staring mad, Thomas! If you still make out that these animals and other nasty things of that sort come from my tannery, it will be exactly as if you were to flay broad strips of skin from Katherine's body, and Petra's, and the boys'; and no decent man would do that—unless he were mad.

Dr. Stockmann (walking up and down). Yes, but I *am* mad; I *am* mad!

Morten Kiil. You cannot be so absurdly mad as all that, when it is a question of your wife and children.

Dr. Stockmann (standing still in front of him). Why couldn't you consult me about it, before you went and bought all that trash?

Morten Kiil. What is done cannot be undone.

Dr. Stockmann (walks about uneasily). If only I were not so certain about it——! But I am absolutely convinced that I am right.

Morten Kiil (weighing the pocket-book in his hand).

If you stick to your mad idea, this won't be worth much, you know. *(Puts the pocket-book in his pocket.)*

Dr. Stockmann. But, hang it all! it might be possible for science to discover some prophylactic, I should think—or some antidote of some kind——

Morten Kiil. To kill these animals, do you mean?

Dr. Stockmann. Yes, or to make them innocuous.

Morten Kiil. Couldn't you try some rat's-bane?

Dr. Stockmann. Don't talk nonsense! They all say it is only imagination, you know. Well, let it go at that! Let them have their own way about it! Haven't the ignorant, narrow-minded curs reviled me as an enemy of the people?—and haven't they been ready to tear the clothes off my back too?

Morten Kiil. And broken all your windows to pieces!

Dr. Stockmann. And then there is my duty to my family. I must talk it over with Katherine; she is great on those things.

Morten Kiil. That is right; be guided by a reasonable woman's advice.

Dr. Stockmann (advancing towards him). To think you could do such a preposterous thing! Risking Katherine's money in this way, and putting me in such a horribly painful dilemma! When I look at you, I think I see the devil himself——.

Morten Kiil. Then I had better go. But I must have an answer from you before two o'clock—yes or no. If it is no, the shares go to a charity, and that this very day.

Dr. Stockmann. And what does Katherine get?

Morten Kiil. Not a halfpenny. *(The door leading to the hall opens, and* HOVSTAD *and* ASLAKSEN *make their appearance.)* Look at those two!

Dr. Stockmann (staring at them). What the devil!—have *you* actually the face to come into my house?

Hovstad. Certainly.

Aslaksen. We have something to say to you, you see.

Morten Kiil (in a whisper). Yes or no—before two o'clock.

Aslaksen (glancing at HOVSTAD*).* Aha!

[MORTEN KIIL *goes out.*

Dr. Stockmann. Well, what do you want with me? Be brief.

Hovstad. I can quite understand that you are annoyed with us for our attitude at the meeting yesterday——

Dr. Stockmann. Attitude, do you call it? Yes, it was a charming attitude! I call it weak, womanish—damnably shameful!

Hovstad. Call it what you like, we could not do otherwise.

Dr. Stockmann. You *dared* not do otherwise—isn't that it?

Hovstad. Well, if you like to put it that way.

Aslaksen. But why did you not let us have word of it beforehand?—just a hint to Mr. Hovstad or to me?

Dr. Stockmann. A hint? Of what?

Aslaksen. Of what was behind it all.

Dr. Stockmann. I don't understand you in the least.

Aslaksen (with a confidential nod). Oh, yes, you do, Dr. Stockmann.

Hovstad. It is no good making a mystery of it any longer.

Dr. Stockmann (looking first at one of them and then at the other). What the devil do you both mean?

Aslaksen. May I ask if your father-in-law is not going round the town buying up all the shares in the Baths?

Dr. Stockmann. Yes, he has been buying Baths' shares to-day; but——

Aslaksen. It would have been more prudent to get some one else to do it—some one less nearly related to you.

Hovstad. And you should not have let your name appear

in the affair. There was no need for anyone to know that the attack on the Baths came from you. You ought to have consulted me, Dr. Stockmann.

Dr. Stockmann (looks in front of him; then a light seems to dawn on him and he says in amazement:) Are such things conceivable? Are such things possible?

Aslaksen (with a smile). Evidently they are. But it is better to use a little *finesse,* you know.

Hovstad. And it is much better to have several persons in a thing of that sort; because the responsibility of each individual is lessened, when there are others with him.

Dr. Stockmann (composedly). Come to the point, gentlemen. What do you want?

Aslaksen. Perhaps Mr. Hovstad had better——

Hovstad. No, you tell him, Aslaksen.

Aslaksen. Well, the fact is that, now we know the bearings of the whole affair, we think we might venture to put the "People's Messenger" at your disposal.

Dr. Stockmann. Do you dare do that now? What about public opinion? Are you not afraid of a storm breaking upon our heads?

Hovstad. We will try to weather it.

Aslaksen. And you must be ready to go off quickly on a new tack, Doctor. As soon as your invective has done its work——

Dr. Stockmann. Do you mean, as soon as my father-in-law and I have got hold of the shares at a low figure?

Hovstad. Your reasons for wishing to get the control of the Baths are mainly scientific, I take it.

Dr. Stockmann. Of course; it was for scientific reasons that I persuaded the old "Badger" to stand in with me in the matter. So we will tinker at the conduit-pipes a little, and dig up a little bit of the shore, and it shan't cost the town a sixpence. That will be all right—eh?

Hovstad. I think so—if you have the "People's Messenger" behind you.

Aslaksen. The Press is a power in a free community, Doctor.

Dr. Stockmann. Quite so. And so is public opinion. And you, Mr. Aslaksen—I suppose you will be answerable for the Householders' Association?

Aslaksen. Yes, and for the Temperance Society. You may rely on that.

Dr. Stockmann. But, gentlemen—I really am ashamed to ask the question—but, what return do you——?

Hovstad. We should prefer to help you without any return whatever, believe me. But the "People's Messenger" is in rather a shaky condition; it doesn't go really well; and I should be very unwilling to suspend the paper now, when there is so much work to do here in the political way.

Dr. Stockmann. Quite so; that would be a great trial to such a friend of the people as you are. *(Flares up.)* But I am an enemy of the people, remember! *(Walks about the room.)* Where have I put my stick? Where the devil is my stick?

Hovstad. What's that?

Aslaksen. Surely you never mean——?

Dr. Stockmann (standing still). And suppose I don't give you a single penny of all I get out of it? Money is not very easy to get out of us rich folk, please to remember!

Hovstad. And you please to remember that this affair of the shares can be represented in two ways!

Dr. Stockmann. Yes, and you are just the man to do it. If I don't come to the rescue of the "People's Messenger," you will certainly take an evil view of the affair; you will hunt me down, I can well imagine—pursue me—try to throttle me as a dog does a hare.

Hovstad. It is a natural law; every animal must fight for its own livelihood.

Aslaksen. And get its food where it can, you know.

Dr. Stockmann (walking about the room). Then you go and look for yours in the gutter; because I am going to show you which is the strongest animal of us three! *(Finds an umbrella and brandishes it above his head.)* Ah, now——!

Hovstad. You are surely not going to use violence!

Aslaksen. Take care what you are doing with that umbrella.

Dr. Stockmann. Out of the window with you, Mr. Hovstad!

Hovstad (edging to the door). Are you quite mad!

Dr. Stockmann. Out of the window, Mr. Aslaksen! Jump, I tell you! You will have to do it, sooner or later.

Aslaksen (running round the writing-table). Moderation, Doctor—I am a delicate man—I can stand so little—*(calls out.)* help, help!

[MRS. STOCKMANN, PETRA *and* HORSTER *come in from the sitting-room.*

Mrs. Stockmann. Good gracious, Thomas! What is happening?

Dr. Stockmann (brandishing the umbrella). Jump out, I tell you! Out into the gutter!

Hovstad. An assault on an unoffending man! I call you to witness, Captain Horster.

[*Hurries out through the hall.*

Aslaksen (irresolutely). If only I knew the way about here——. [*Steals out through the sitting-room.*

Mrs. Stockmann (holding her husband back). Control yourself, Thomas!

Dr. Stockmann (throwing down the umbrella). Upon my soul, they have escaped after all.

Mrs. Stockmann. What did they want you to do?

Dr. Stockmann. I will tell you later on; I have something else to think about now. *(Goes to the table and writes something on a calling-card.)* Look there, Katherine; what is written there?

Mrs. Stockmann. Three big No's; what does that mean?

Dr. Stockmann. I will tell you that too, later on. *(Holds out the card to* PETRA.*)* There, Petra; tell sooty-face to run over to the "Badger's" with that, as quickly as she can. Hurry up!

[PETRA *takes the card and goes out to the hall.*

Dr. Stockmann. Well, I think I have had a visit from every one of the devil's messengers to-day! But now I am going to sharpen my pen till they can feel its point; I shall dip it in venom and gall; I shall hurl my ink-pot at their heads!

Mrs. Stockmann. Yes, but we are going away, you know, Thomas.

[PETRA *comes back.*

Dr. Stockmann. Well?

Petra. She has gone with it.

Dr. Stockmann. Good.——Going away, did you say? No, I'll be hanged if we are going away! We are going to stay where we are, Katherine!

Petra. Stay here?

Mrs. Stockmann. Here, in the town?

Dr. Stockmann. Yes, here. This is the field of battle—this is where the fight will be. This is where I shall triumph! As soon as I have had my trousers sewn up I shall go out and look for another house. We must have a roof over our heads for the winter.

Horster. That you shall have in my house.

Dr. Stockmann. Can I?

Horster. Yes, quite well. I have plenty of room, and I am almost never at home.

Mrs. Stockmann. How good of you, Captain Horster!

Petra. Thank you!

Dr. Stockmann (grasping his hand). Thank you, thank you! That is one trouble over! Now I can set to work in earnest at once. There is an endless amount of things to look through here, Katherine! Luckily I shall have all my time at my disposal; because I have been dismissed from the Baths, you know.

Mrs. Stockmann (with a sigh). Oh, yes, I expected that

Dr. Stockmann. And they want to take my practice away from me, too. Let them! I have got the poor people to fall back upon, anyway—those that don't pay anything; and, after all, they need me most, too. But, by Jove, they will have to listen to me; I shall preach to them in season and out of season, as it says somewhere.

Mrs. Stockmann. But, dear Thomas, I should have thought events had showed you what use it is to preach.

Dr. Stockmann. You are really ridiculous, Katherine. Do you want me to let myself be beaten off the field by public opinion and the compact majority and all that devilry? No, thank you! And what I want to do is so simple and clear and straightforward. I only want to drum into the heads of these curs the fact that the liberals are the most insidious enemies of freedom—that party programmes strangle every young and vigorous truth—that considerations of expediency turn morality and justice upside down—and that they will end by making life here unbearable. Don't you think, Captain Horster, that I ought to be able to make people understand that?

Horster. Very likely; I don't know much about such things myself.

Dr. Stockmann. Well, look here—I will explain! It is the party leaders that must be exterminated. A party leader is like a wolf, you see—like a voracious wolf. He requires a certain number of smaller victims to prey upon every year, if he is to live. Just look at Hovstad and Aslaksen! How many smaller victims have they not put an end to—or at any rate maimed and mangled until they are fit for nothing except to be householders or subscribers to the "People's Messenger"! *(Sits down on the edge of the table.)* Come here, Katherine—look how beautifully the sun shines to-day! And this lovely spring air I am drinking in!

Mrs. Stockmann. Yes, if only we could live on sunshine and spring air, Thomas.

Dr. Stockmann. Oh, you will have to pinch and save a bit—then we shall get along. That gives me very little concern. What is much worse is that I know of no one who is liberal-minded and high-minded enough to venture to take up my work after me.

Petra. Don't think about that, father; you have plenty of time before you.——Hullo, here are the boys already!

[EJLIF *and* MORTEN *come in from the sitting-room.*

Mrs. Stockmann. Have you got a holiday?

Morten. No; but we were fighting with the other boys between lessons——

Ejlif. That isn't true; it was the other boys were fighting with us.

Morten. Well, and then Mr. Rörlund said we had better stay at home for a day or two.

Dr. Stockmann (snapping his fingers and getting up from the table). I have it! I have it, by Jove! You shall never set foot in the school again!

The Boys. No more school!

Mrs. Stockmann. But, Thomas——

Dr. Stockmann. Never, I say. I will educate you myself; that is to say, you shan't learn a blessed thing——

Morten. Hooray!

Dr. Stockmann. ——but I will make liberal-minded and high-minded men of you. You must help me with that, Petra.

Petra. Yes, father, you may be sure I will.

Dr. Stockmann. And my school shall be in the room where they insulted me and called me an enemy of the people. But we are too few as we are; I must have at least twelve boys to begin with.

Mrs. Stockmann. You will certainly never get them in this town.

Dr. Stockmann. We shall. *(To the boys.)* Don't you know any street urchins—regular ragamuffins——?

Morten. Yes, father, I know lots!

Dr. Stockmann. That's capital! Bring me some specimens of them. I am going to experiment with curs, just for once; there may be some exceptional heads amongst them.

Morten. And what are we going to do, when you have made liberal-minded and high-minded men of us?

Dr. Stockmann. Then you shall drive all the wolves out of the country, my boys!

[EJLIF *looks rather doubtful about it;* MORTEN *jumps about crying* "Hurrah!"

Mrs. Stockmann. Let us hope it won't be the wolves that will drive you out of the country, Thomas.

Dr. Stockmann. Are you out of your mind, Katherine? Drive me out! Now—when I am the strongest man in the town!

Mrs. Stockmann. The strongest—now?

Dr. Stockmann. Yes, and I will go so far as to say that now I am the strongest man in the whole world.

Morten. I say!

Dr. Stockmann (lowering his voice). Hush! You mustn't say anything about it yet; but I have made a great discovery.

Mrs. Stockmann. Another one?

Dr. Stockmann. Yes. *(Gathers them round him, and says confidentially:)* It is this, let me tell you—that the strongest man in the world is he who stands most alone.

Mrs. Stockmann (smiling and shaking her head). Oh, Thomas, Thomas!

Petra (encouragingly, as she grasps her father's hands). Father!

THE MASTER BUILDER

(1892)

CHARACTERS

HALVARD SOLNESS, *Master Builder.*
ALINE SOLNESS, *his wife.*
DOCTOR HERDAL, *physician.*
KNUT BROVIK, *formerly an architect, now in* SOLNESS'S *employment.*
RAGNER BROVIK, *his son, draughtsman.*
KAIA FOSLI, *his niece, book-keeper.*
MISS HILDA WANGEL.
Some Ladies.
A Crowd in the street.

The action passes in and about SOLNESS'S *house.*

THE MASTER BUILDER

ACT I

A plainly furnished work-room in the house of HALVARD SOLNESS. *Folding doors on the left lead out to the hall. On the right is the door leading to the inner rooms of the house. At the back is an open door into the draughtsmen's office. In front, on the left, a desk with books, papers and writing materials. Further back than the folding-door, a stove. In the right-hand corner, a sofa, a table and one or two chairs. On the table a water-bottle and glass. A smaller table, with a rocking-chair and arm-chair, in front on the right. Lighted lamps, with shades, on the table in the draughtsmen's office, on the table in the corner and on the desk.*

In the draughtsmen's office sit KNUT BROVIK *and his son* RAGNAR, *occupied with plans and calculations. At the desk in the outer office stands* KAIA FOSLI, *writing in the ledger.* KNUT BROVIK *is a spare old man with white hair and beard. He wears a rather threadbare but well-brushed black coat, spectacles and a somewhat discoloured white neckcloth.* RAGNAR BROVIK *is a well-dressed, light-haired man in his thirties, with a slight stoop.* KAIA FOSLI *is a slightly built girl, a little over twenty, carefully dressed and delicate-looking. She has a green shade over her eyes.——All three go on working for some time in silence.*

Knut Brovik (rises suddenly, as if in distress, from the

table; breathes heavily and laboriously as he comes forward into the doorway). No, I can't bear it much longer!

Kaia (going up to him). You are feeling very ill this evening, are you not, uncle?

Brovik. Oh, I seem to get worse every day.

Ragnar (has risen and advances). You ought to go home, father. Try to get a little sleep——

Brovik (impatiently). Go to bed, I suppose? Would you have me stifled outright?

Kaia. Then take a little walk.

Ragnar. Yes, do. I will come with you.

Brovik (with warmth). I will not go till he comes! I am determined to have it out this evening with—*(in a tone of suppressed bitterness)*—with him—with the chief.

Kaia (anxiously). Oh no, uncle—do wait awhile before doing that.

Ragnar. Yes, better wait, father!

Brovik (draws his breath laboriously). Ha—ha——! I haven't much time for waiting.

Kaia (listening). Hush! I hear him on the stairs.

[*All three go back to their work. A short silence.*

[HALVARD SOLNESS *comes in through the hall door. He is a man no longer young, but healthy and vigorous, with close-cut curly hair, dark moustache and dark thick eyebrows. He wears a greyish-green buttoned jacket with an upstanding collar and broad lapels. On his head he wears a soft grey felt hat, and he has one or two light portfolios under his arm.*

Solness (near the door, points towards the draughtsmen's office, and asks in a whisper:) Are they gone?

Kaia (softly, shaking her head). No.

[*She takes the shade off her eyes.* SOLNESS *crosses the room, throws his hat on a chair, places the portfolios on the table by the sofa and ap-*

proaches the desk again. KAIA *goes on writing without intermission, but seems nervous and uneasy.*

Solness (aloud). What is that you are entering, Miss Fosli?

Kaia (starts). Oh, it is only something that——

Solness. Let me look at it, Miss Fosli. *(Bends over her, pretends to be looking into the ledger, and whispers:)* Kaia!

Kaia (softly, still writing). Well?

Solness. Why do you always take that shade off when I come?

Kaia (as before). I look so ugly with it on.

Solness (smiling). Then you don't like to look ugly, Kaia?

Kaia (half glancing up at him.) Not for all the world. Not in your eyes.

Solness (stroking her hair gently). Poor, poor little Kaia——

Kaia (bending her head). Hush—they can hear you.

[SOLNESS *strolls across the room to the right, turns and pauses at the door of the draughtsmen's office.*

Solness. Has any one been here for me?

Ragnar (rising). Yes, the young couple who want a villa built, out at Lövstrand.

Solness (growling). Oh, those two! They must wait. I am not quite clear about the plans yet.

Ragnar (advancing, with some hesitation). They were very anxious to have the drawings at once.

Solness (as before). Yes, of course—so they all are.

Brovik (looks up). They say they are longing so to get into a house of their own.

Solness. Yes, yes—we know all that! And so they are content to take whatever is offered them. They get a—a roof over their heads—an address—but nothing to call a home. No thank you! In that case, let them apply to somebody else. Tell them that, the next time they call.

Brovik (pushes his glasses up on to his forehead and looks in astonishment at him.) To somebody else? Are you prepared to give up the commission?

Solness (impatiently). Yes, yes, yes, devil take it! If that is to be the way of it——. Rather that, than build away at random. *(Vehemently.)* Besides, I know very little about these people as yet.

Brovik. The people are safe enough. Ragnar knows them. He is a friend of the family. Perfectly safe people.

Solness. Oh, safe—safe enough! That is not at all what I mean. Good Lord—don't you understand me either? *(Angrily.)* I won't have anything to do with these strangers. They may apply to whom they please, so far as I am concerned.

Brovik (rising). Do you really mean that?

Solness (sulkily). Yes I do,—For once in a way.

[*He comes forward.*

[BROVIK *exchanges a glance with* RAGNAR, *who makes a warning gesture. Then* BROVIK *comes into the front room.*

Brovik. May I have a few words with you?

Solness. Certainly.

Brovik (to KAIA*).* Just go in there for a moment, Kaia.

Kaia (uneasily). Oh, but uncle——

Brovik. Do as I say, child. And shut the door after you.

[KAIA *goes reluctantly into the draughtsmen's office, glances anxiously and imploringly at* SOLNESS, *and shuts the door.*

Brovik (lowering his voice a little). I don't want the poor children to know how ill I am.

Solness. Yes, you have been looking very poorly of late.

Brovik. It will soon be all over with me. My strength is ebbing—from day to day.

Solness. Won't you sit down?

Brovik. Thanks—may I?

Solness (placing the arm-chair more conveniently). Here —take this chair.—And now?

Brovik (has seated himself with difficulty). Well, you see, it's about Ragnar. That is what weighs most upon me. What is to become of him?

Solness. Of course your son will stay with me as long as ever he likes.

Brovik. But that is just what he does not like. He feels that he cannot stay here any longer.

Solness. Why, I should say he was very well off here. But if he wants more money, I should not mind——

Brovik. No, no! It is not that. *(Impatiently.)* But sooner or later he, too, must have a chance of doing something on his own account.

Solness (without looking at him). Do you think that Ragnar has quite talent enough to stand alone?

Brovik. No, that is just the heartbreaking part of it—I have begun to have my doubts about the boy. For you have never said so much as—as one encouraging word about him. And yet I cannot but think there must be something in him—he can't be without talent.

Solness. Well, but he has learnt nothing—nothing thoroughly, I mean. Except, of course, to draw.

Brovik (looks at him with covert hatred and says hoarsely). You had learned little enough of the business when you were in my employment. But that did not prevent you from setting to work—*(breathing with difficulty)*—and pushing your way up and taking the wind out of my sails— mine, and so many other people's.

Solness. Yes, you see—circumstances favoured me.

Brovik. You are right there. Everything favoured you

But then how can you have the heart to let me go to my grave—without having seen what Ragnar is fit for? And of course I am anxious to see them married, too—before I go.

Solness (sharply). Is it she who wishes it?

Brovik. Not Kaia so much as Ragnar—he talks about it every day. *(Appealingly.)* You must—you must help him to get some independent work now! I must see something that the lad has done. Do you hear?

Solness (peevishly). Hang it, man, you can't expect me to drag commissions down from the moon for him!

Brovik. He has the chance of a capital commission at this very moment. A big bit of work.

Solness (uneasily, startled). Has he?

Brovik. If you would give your consent.

Solness. What sort of work do you mean?

Brovik (with some hesitation). He can have the building of that villa out at Lövstrand.

Solness. That! Why, I am going to build that myself.

Brovik. Oh, you don't much care about doing it.

Solness (flaring up). Don't care! I? Who dares to say that?

Brovik. You said so yourself just now.

Solness. Oh, never mind what I say.—Would they give Ragnar the building of that villa?

Brovik. Yes. You see, he knows the family. And then—just for the fun of the thing—he has made drawings and estimates and so forth——

Solness. Are they pleased with the drawings? The people who will have to live in the house?

Brovik. Yes. If you would only look through them and approve of them.

Solness. Then they would let Ragnar build their home for them?

Brovik. They were immensely pleased with his idea. They thought it exceedingly original, they said.

Solness. Oho! Original! Not the old-fashioned stuff that *I* am in the habit of turning out!

Brovik. It seemed to them different.

Solness (with suppressed irritation). So it was to see Ragnar that they came here—whilst I was out!

Brovik. They came to call upon you—and at the same time to ask whether you would mind retiring——

Solness (angrily). Retire? I?

Brovik. In case you thought that Ragnar's drawings——

Solness. I? Retire in favour of your son!

Brovik. Retire from the agreement, they meant.

Solness. Oh, it comes to the same thing. *(Laughs angrily.)* So that is it, is it? Halvard Solness is to see about retiring now! To make room for younger men! For the very youngest, perhaps! He must make room! Room! Room!

Brovik. Why, good heavens! there is surely room for more than one single man——

Solness. Oh, there's not so very much room to spare either. But, be that as it may—I will never retire! I will never give way to anybody! Never of my own free will. Never in this world will I do that!

Brovik (rises with difficulty). Then I am to pass out of life without any certainty? Without a gleam of happiness? Without any faith or trust in Ragnar? Without having seen a single piece of work of his doing? Is that to be the way of it?

Solness (turns half aside and mutters). H'm—don't ask more just now.

Brovik. I must have an answer to this one question. Am I to pass out of life in such utter poverty?

Solness (seems to struggle with himself; finally he says, in a low but firm voice:) You must pass out of life as best you can.

Brovik. Then be it so. [*He goes up the room.*

Solness (following him, half in desperation). Don't you understand that I cannot help it? I am what I am, and I cannot change my nature!

Brovik. No, no; I suppose you can't. *(Reels and supports himself against the sofa-table.)* May I have a glass of water?

Solness. By all means.

[*Fills a glass and hands it to him.*

Brovik. Thanks.

[*Drinks and puts the glass down again.*

[SOLNESS *goes up and opens the door of the draughtsmen's office.*

Solness. Ragnar—you must come and take your father home.

[RAGNAR *rises quickly. He and* KAIA *come into the work-room.*

Ragnar. What is the matter, father?

Brovik. Give me your arm. Now let us go.

Ragnar. Very well. You had better put your things on, too, Kaia.

Solness. Miss Fosli must stay—just for a moment. There is a letter I want written.

Brovik (looks at SOLNESS*).* Good night. Sleep well—if you can.

Solness. Good night.

[BROVIK *and* RAGNAR *go out by the hall door.* KAIA *goes to the desk.* SOLNESS *stands with bent head, to the right, by the armchair.*

Kaia (dubiously). Is there any letter——?

Solness (curtly). No, of course not. *(Looks sternly at her.)* Kaia!

Kaia (anxiously, in a low voice). Yes!

Solness (points imperatively to a spot on the floor). Come here! At once!

Kaia (hesitatingly). Yes.

Solness (as before). Nearer!

Kaia (obeying). What do you want with me?

Solness (looks at her for a while). Is it you I have to thank for all this?

Kaia. No, no, don't think that!

Solness. But confess now—you want to get married!

Kaia (softly). Ragnar and I have been engaged for four or five years, and so——

Solness. And so you think it time there were an end to it. Is not that so?

Kaia. Ragnar and Uncle say I must. So I suppose I shall have to give in.

Solness (more gently). Kaia, don't you really care a little bit for Ragnar, too?

Kaia. I cared very much for Ragnar once—before I came here to you.

Solness. But you don't now? Not in the least?

Kaia (passionately, clasping her hands and holding them out towards him). Oh, you know very well there is only one person I care for now! One, and one only, in all the world! I shall never care for any one else.

Solness. Yes, you say that. And yet you go away from me—leave me alone here with everything on my hands.

Kaia. But could I not stay with you, even if Ragnar——?

Solness (repudiating the idea). No, no, that is quite impossible. If Ragnar leaves me and starts work on his own account, then of course he will need you himself.

Kaia (wringing her hands). Oh, I feel as if I could not be separated from you! It's quite, quite impossible!

Solness. Then be sure you get those foolish notions out of Ragnar's head. Marry him as much as you please—*(alters his tone.)*—I mean—don't let him throw up his good situation with me. For then I can keep you, too, my dear Kaia.

Kaia. Oh yes, how lovely that would be, if it could only be managed!

Solness (clasps her head with his two hands and whispers). For I cannot get on without you, you see. I must have you with me every single day.

Kaia (in nervous exaltation). My God! My God!

Solness (kisses her hair). Kaia—Kaia!

Kaia (sinks down before him). Oh, how good you are to me! How unspeakably good you are!

Solness (vehemently). Get up! For goodness' sake get up! I think I hear some one!

[*He helps her to rise. She staggers over to the desk.*

[MRS. SOLNESS *enters by the door on the right. She looks thin and wasted with grief, but shows traces of bygone beauty. Blonde ringlets. Dressed with good taste, wholly in black. Speaks somewhat slowly and in a plaintive voice.*

Mrs. Solness (in the doorway). Halvard!

Solness (turns). Oh, are you there, my dear——?

Mrs. Solness (with a glance at KAIA*).* I am afraid I am disturbing you.

Solness. Not in the least. Miss Fosli has only a short letter to write.

Mrs. Solness. Yes, so I see.

Solness. What do you want with me, Aline?

Mrs. Solness. I merely wanted to tell you that Dr. Herdal is in the drawing-room. Won't you come and see him, Halvard?

Solness (looks suspiciously at her). H'm—is the doctor so very anxious to talk to me?

Mrs. Solness. Well, not exactly anxious. He really came to see me; but he would like to say how-do-you-do to you at the same time.

Solness (laughs to himself). Yes, I daresay. Well, you must ask him to wait a little.

Mrs. Solness. Then you will come in presently?

Solness. Perhaps I will. Presently, presently, dear. In a little while.

Mrs. Solness (glancing again at Kaia*).* Well, now, don't forget, Halvard.

[*Withdraws and closes the door behind her.*

Kaia (softly). Oh dear, oh dear—I am sure Mrs. Solness thinks ill of me in some way!

Solness. Oh, not in the least. Not more than usual, at any rate. But all the same, you had better go now, Kaia.

Kaia. Yes, yes, now I must go.

Solness (severely). And mind you get that matter settled for me. Do you hear?

Kaia. Oh, if it only depended on me——

Solness. I will have it settled, I say! And to-morrow too—not a day later!

Kaia (terrified). If there's nothing else for it, I am quite willing to break off the engagement.

Solness (angrily). Break it off? Are you mad? Would you think of breaking it off?

Kaia (distracted). Yes, if necessary. For I must—I must stay here with you! I can't leave you! That is utterly—utterly impossible!

Solness (with a sudden outburst). But deuce take it—how about Ragnar then! It's Ragnar that I——

Kaia (looks at him with terrified eyes). It is chiefly on Ragnar's account, that—that you——

Solness (collecting himself). No, no, of course not! You don't understand me either. (*Gently and softly.*) Of course it is you I want to keep—you above everything, Kaia. But for that very reason, you must prevent Ragnar, too, from throwing up his situation. There, there,—now go home.

Kaia. Yes, yes—good-night, then.

Solness. Good-night. *(As she is going.)* Oh, stop a moment! Are Ragnar's drawings in there?

Kaia. I did not see him take them with him.

Solness. Then just go and find them for me. I might perhaps glance over them, after all.

Kaia (happy). Oh yes, please do!

Solness. For your sake, Kaia dear. Now, let me have them at once, please.

[KAIA *hurries into the draughtsmen's office, searches anxiously in the table-drawer, finds a portfolio and brings it with her.*

Kaia. Here are all the drawings.

Solness. Good. Put them down there on the table.

Kaia (putting down the portfolio). Good-night, then. *(Beseechingly.)* And please, please think kindly of me.

Solness. Oh, that I always do. Good-night, my dear little Kaia. *(Glances to the right.)* Go, go now!

[MRS. SOLNESS *and* DR. HERDAL *enter by the door on the right. He is a stoutish, elderly man, with a round, good-humoured face, clean shaven, with thin, light hair, and gold spectacles.*

Mrs. Solness (still in the doorway). Halvard, I cannot keep the doctor any longer.

Solness. Well then, come in here.

Mrs. Solness (to KAIA, *who is turning down the desk-lamp).* Have you finished the letter already, Miss Fosli?

Kaia (in confusion). The letter——?

Solness. Yes, it was quite a short one.

Mrs. Solness. It must have been very short.

Solness. You may go now, Miss Fosli. And please come in good time to-morrow morning.

Kaia. I will be sure to. Good-night, Mrs. Solness.

[*She goes out by the hall door.*

Mrs. Solness. She must be quite an acquisition to you, Halvard, this Miss Fosli.

Solness. Yes, indeed. She is useful in all sorts of ways.

Mrs. Solness. So it seems.

Dr. Herdal. Is she good at book-keeping too?

Solness. Well—of course she has had a good deal of practice during these two years. And then she is so nice and willing to do whatever one asks of her.

Mrs. Solness. Yes, that must be very delightful——

Solness. It is. Especially when one is not too much accustomed to that sort of thing.

Mrs. Solness (in a tone of gentle remonstrance). Can you say that, Halvard?

Solness. Oh, no, no, my dear Aline; I beg your pardon.

Mrs. Solness. There's no occasion.—Well then, doctor, you will come back later on and have a cup of tea with us?

Dr. Herdal. I have only that one patient to see and then I'll come back.

Mrs. Solness. Thank you.

[*She goes out by the door on the right*

Solness. Are you in a hurry, doctor?

Dr. Herdal. No, not at all.

Solness. May I have a little chat with you?

Dr. Herdal. With the greatest of pleasure.

Solness. Then let us sit down. *(He motions the doctor to take the rocking-chair and sits down himself in the arm-chair. Looks searchingly at him.)* Tell me—did you notice anything odd about Aline?

Dr. Herdal. Do you mean just now, when she was here?

Solness. Yes, in her manner to me. Did you notice anything?

Dr. Herdal (smiling). Well, I admit—one couldn't well avoid noticing that your wife—h'm——

Solness. Well?

Dr. Herdal. ——that your wife is not particularly fond of this Miss Fosli.

Solness. Is that all? I have noticed that myself.

Dr. Herdal. And I must say I am scarcely surprised at it.

Solness. At what?

Dr. Herdal. That she should not exactly approve of your seeing so much of another woman, all day and every day.

Solness. No, no, I suppose you are right there—and Aline too. But it's impossible to make any change.

Dr. Herdal. Could you not engage a clerk?

Solness. The first man that came to hand? No, thank you—that would never do for me.

Dr. Herdal. But now, if your wife——? Suppose, with her delicate health, all this tries her too much?

Solness. Even then—I might almost say—it can make no difference. I must keep Kaia Fosli. No one else could fill her place.

Dr. Herdal. No one else?

Solness (curtly). No, no one.

Dr. Herdal (drawing his chair closer). Now listen to me, my dear Mr. Solness. May I ask you a question, quite between ourselves?

Solness. By all means.

Dr. Herdal. Women, you see—in certain matters, they have a deucedly keen intuition——

Solness. They have, indeed. There is not the least doubt of that. But——?

Dr. Herdal. Well, tell me now—if your wife can't endure this Kaia Fosli——?

Solness. Well, what then?

Dr. Herdal. ——may she not have just—just the least little bit of reason for this instinctive dislike?

Solness (looks at him and rises). Oho!

Dr. Herdal. Now don't be offended—but hasn't she?

Solness (with curt decision). No.

Dr. Herdal. No reason of any sort?

Solness. No other reason than her own suspicious nature.

Dr. Herdal. I know you have known a good many women in your time.

Solness. Yes, I have.

Dr. Herdal. And have been a good deal taken with some of them, too.

Solness. Oh, yes, I don't deny it.

Dr. Herdal. But as regards Miss Fosli, then? There is nothing of that sort in the case?

Solness. No; nothing at all—on my side.

Dr. Herdal. But on her side?

Solness. I don't think you have any right to ask that question, doctor.

Dr. Herdal. Well, you know, we were discussing your wife's intuition.

Solness. So we were. And for that matter—*(lowers his voice)*—Aline's intuition, as you call it—in a certain sense, it has not been so far astray.

Dr. Herdal. Aha! there we have it!

Solness (sits down). Doctor Herdal—I am going to tell you a strange story—if you care to listen to it.

Dr. Herdal. I like listening to strange stories.

Solness. Very well then. I daresay you recollect that I took Knut Brovik and his son into my employment—after the old man's business had gone to the dogs.

Dr. Herdal. Yes, so I have understood.

Solness. You see, they really are clever fellows, these two. Each of them has talent in his own way. But then the son took it into his head to get engaged; and the next thing, of course, was that he wanted to get married—and begin to build on his own account. That is the way with all these young people.

Dr. Herdal (laughing). Yes, they have a bad habit of wanting to marry.

Solness. Just so. But of course that did not suit my plans; for I needed Ragnar myself—and the old man, too. He is exceedingly good at calculating bearing-strains and cubic contents—and all that sort of devilry, you know.

Dr. Herdal. Oh, yes, no doubt that's indispensable.

Solness. Yes, it is. But Ragnar was absolutely bent on setting to work for himself. He would hear of nothing else.

Dr. Herdal. But he has stayed with you all the same.

Solness. Yes, I'll tell you how that came about. On

day this girl, Kaia Fosli, came to see them on some errand or other. She had never been here before. And when I saw how utterly infatuated they were with each other, the thought occurred to me: if I could only get her into the office here, then perhaps Ragnar, too, would stay where he is.

Dr. Herdal. That was not at all a bad idea.

Solness. Yes, but at the time I did not breathe a word of what was in my mind. I merely stood and looked at her—and kept on wishing intently that I could have her here. Then I talked to her a little, in a friendly way—about one thing and another. And then she went away.

Dr. Herdal. Well?

Solness. Well, then, next day, pretty late in the evening, when old Brovik and Ragnar had gone home, she came here again and behaved as if I had made an arrangement with her.

Dr. Herdal. An arrangement? What about?

Solness. About the very thing my mind had been fixed on. But I hadn't said one single word about it.

Dr. Herdal. That was most extraordinary.

Solness. Yes, was it not? And now she wanted to know what she was to do here—whether she could begin the very next morning, and so forth.

Dr. Herdal. Don't you think she did it in order to be with her sweetheart?

Solness. That was what occurred to me at first. But no, that was not it. She seemed to drift quite away from him—when once she had come here to me.

Dr. Herdal. She drifted over to you, then?

Solness. Yes, entirely. If I happen to look at her when her back is turned, I can tell that she feels it. She quivers and trembles the moment I come near her. What do you think of that?

Dr. Herdal. H'm—that's not very hard to explain.

Solness. Well, but what about the other thing? That she believed I had said to her what I had only wished and willed—silently—inwardly—to myself? What do you say to that? Can you explain that, Dr. Herdal?

Dr. Herdal. No, I won't undertake to do that.

Solness. I felt sure you would not; and so I have never cared to talk about it till now. But it's a cursed nuisance to me in the long run, you understand. Here I have to go on day after day pretending——. And it's a shame to treat her so, too, poor girl. *(Vehemently.)* But I cannot do anything else. For if she runs away from me—then Ragnar will be off too.

Dr. Herdal. And you have not told your wife the rights of the story?

Solness. No.

Dr. Herdal. Then why on earth don't you?

Solness (looks fixedly at him, and says in a low voice:) Because I seem to find a sort of—of salutary self-torture in allowing Aline to do me an injustice.

Dr. Herdal (shakes his head). I don't in the least understand what you mean.

Solness. Well, you see—it is like paying off a little bit of a huge, immeasurable debt——

Dr. Herdal. To your wife?

Solness. Yes; and that always helps to relieve one's mind a little. One can breathe more freely for a while, you understand.

Dr. Herdal. No, goodness knows, I don't understand at all——

Solness (breaking off, rises again). Well, well, well—then we won't talk any more about it. *(He saunters across the room, returns and stops beside the table. Looks at the doctor with a sly smile.)* I suppose you think you have drawn me out nicely now, doctor?

Dr. Herdal (with some irritation). Drawn you out? Again I have not the faintest notion what you mean, Mr. Solness.

Solness. Oh come, out with it; I have seen it quite clearly, you know.

Dr. Herdal. What have you seen?

Solness (in a low voice, slowly). That you have been quietly keeping on eye upon me.

Dr. Herdal. That *I* have! And why in all the world should I do that?

Solness. Because you think that I—— *(Passionately.)* Well, devil take it—you think the same of me as Aline does.

Dr. Herdal. And what does she think about you?

Solness (having recovered his self-control). She has begun to think that I am—that I am—ill.

Dr. Herdal. Ill! You! She has never hinted such a thing to me. Why, what can she think is the matter with you?

Solness (leans over the back of the chair and whispers). Aline has made up her mind that I am mad. That is what she thinks.

Dr. Herdal (rising). Why, my dear good fellow——!

Solness. Yes, on my soul she does! I tell you it is so. And she has got you to think the same! Oh, I can assure you, doctor, I see it in your face as clearly as possible. You don't take me in so easily, I can tell you.

Dr. Herdal (looks at him in amazement). Never, Mr. Solness—never has such a thought entered my mind.

Solness (with an incredulous smile). Really? Has it not?

Dr. Herdal. No, never! Nor your wife's mind either, I am convinced. I could almost swear to that.

Solness. Well, I wouldn't advise you to. For, in a certain sense, you see, perhaps—perhaps she is not so far wrong in thinking something of the kind.

Dr. Herdal. Come now, I really must say——

Solness (interrupting, with a sweep of his hand). Well, well, my dear doctor—don't let us discuss this any further.

We had better agree to differ. *(Changes to a tone of quiet amusement.)* But look here now, doctor—h'm——

Dr. Herdal. Well?

Solness. Since you don't believe that I am—ill—and crazy, and mad, and so forth——

Dr. Herdal. What then?

Solness. Then I daresay you fancy that I am an extremely happy man.

Dr. Herdal. Is that mere fancy?

Solness (laughs). No, no—of course not! Heaven forbid! Only think—to be Solness the master builder! Halvard Solness! What could be more delightful?

Dr. Herdal. Yes, I must say it seems to me you have had the luck on your side to an astounding degree.

Solness (suppresses a gloomy smile). So I have, I can't complain on that score.

Dr. Herdal. First of all that grim old robbers' castle was burnt down for you. And that was certainly a great piece of luck.

Solness (seriously). It was the home of Aline's family. Remember that.

Dr. Herdal. Yes, it must have been a great grief to her.

Solness. She has not got over it to this day—not in all these twelve or thirteen years.

Dr. Herdal. Ah, but what followed must have been the worst blow for her.

Solness. The one thing with the other.

Dr. Herdal. But you—yourself—you rose upon the ruins. You began as a poor boy from a country village—and now you are at the head of your profession. Ah, yes, Mr. Solness, you have undoubtedly had the luck on your side.

Solness (looking at him with embarrassment). Yes, but that is just what makes me so horribly afraid.

Dr. Herdal. Afraid? Because you have the luck on your side!

Solness. It terrifies me—terrifies me every hour of the day. For sooner or later the luck must turn, you see.

Dr. Herdal. Oh nonsense! What should make the luck turn?

Solness (with firm assurance). The younger generation.

Dr. Herdal. Pooh! The younger generation! You are not laid on the shelf yet, I should hope. Oh no—your position here is probably firmer now than it has ever been.

Solness. The luck will turn. I know it—I feel the day approaching. Some one or other will take it into his head to say: Give me a chance! And then all the rest will come clamouring after him, and shake their fists at me and shout: Make room—make room—make room! Yes, just you see, doctor—presently the younger generation will come knock at my door——

Dr. Herdal (laughing). Well, and what if they do?

Solness. What if they do? Then there's an end of Halvard Solness.

[*There is a knock at the door on the left.*

Solness (starts). What's that? Did you not hear something?

Dr. Herdal. Some one is knocking at the door.

Solness (loudly). Come in.

[HILDA WANGEL *enters by the hall door. She is of middle height, supple and delicately built. Somewhat sunburnt. Dressed in a tourist costume, with skirt caught up for walking, a sailor's collar open at the throat and a small sailor hat on her head. Knapsack on back, plaid in strap, and alpenstock.*

Hilda (goes straight up to SOLNESS, *her eyes sparkling with happiness).* Good evening!

Solness (looks doubtfully at her). Good evening——

Hilda (laughs). I almost believe you don't recognise me!

Solness. No—I must admit that—just for the moment ——

Dr. Herdal (approaching). But I recognise you, my dear young lady——

Hilda (pleased). Oh, is it you that——

Dr. Herdal. Of course it is. *(To* Solness.*)* We met at one of the mountain stations this summer. *(To* Hilda.*)* What became of the other ladies?

Hilda. Oh, they went westward.

Dr. Herdal. They didn't much like all the fun we used to have in the evenings.

Hilda. No, I believe they didn't.

Dr. Herdal (holds up his finger at her). And I am afraid it can't be denied that you flirted a little with us.

Hilda. Well that was better fun than to sit there knitting stockings with all those old women.

Dr. Herdal (laughs). There I entirely agree with you.

Solness. Have you come to town this evening?

Hilda. Yes, I have just arrived.

Dr. Herdal. Quite alone, Miss Wangel?

Hilda. Oh, yes!

Solness. Wangel? Is your name Wangel?

Hilda (looks in amused surprise at him). Yes, of course it is.

Solness. Then you must be a daughter of the district doctor up at Lysanger?

Hilda (as before). Yes, who else's daughter should I be?

Solness. Oh, then I suppose we met up there, that summer when I was building a tower on the old church.

Hilda (more seriously). Yes, of course it was then we met.

Solness. Well, that is a long time ago.

Hilda (looks hard at him). It is exactly ten years.

Solness. You must have been a mere child then, I should think.

Hilda (carelessly). Well, I was twelve or thirteen.

Dr. Herdal. Is this the first time you have ever been up to town, Miss Wangel?

Hilda. Yes, it is indeed.

Solness. And don't you know any one here?

Hilda. Nobody but you. And of course, your wife.

Solness. So you know her, too?

Hilda. Only a little. We spent a few days together at the sanatorium.

Solness. Ah, up there?

Hilda. She said I might come and pay her a visit if ever I came up to town. *(Smiles.)* Not that that was necessary.

Solness. Odd that she should never have mentioned it.

[HILDA *puts her stick down by the stove, takes off the knapsack and lays it and the plaid on the sofa.* DR. HERDAL *offers to help her.* SOLNESS *stands and gazes at her.*

Hilda (going towards him). Well, now I must ask you to let me stay the night here.

Solness. I am sure there will be no difficulty about that.

Hilda. For I have no other clothes than those I stand in, except a change of linen in my knapsack. And that has to go to the wash, for it's very dirty.

Solness. Oh, yes, that can be managed. Now I'll just let my wife know——

Dr. Herdal. Meanwhile I will go and see my patient.

Solness. Yes, do; and come again later on.

Dr. Herdal (playfully, with a glance at HILDA*).* Oh, that I will, you may be very certain! *(Laughs.)* So your prediction has come true, Mr. Solness!

Solness. How so?

Dr. Herdal. The younger generation did come knocking at your door.

Solness (cheerfully). Yes, but in a very different way from what I meant.

Dr. Herdal. Very different, yes. That's undeniable.

[*He goes out by the hall door.* SOLNESS *opens the door on the right and speaks into the side room.*

Solness. Aline! Will you come in here, please. Here is a friend of yours—Miss Wangel.

Mrs. Solness (appears in the doorway). Who do you say it is? *(Sees* HILDA.*)* Oh, is it you, Miss Wangel? *(Goes up to her and offers her hand.)* So you have come to town after all.

Solness. Miss Wangel has this moment arrived; and she would like to stay the night here.

Mrs. Solness. Here with us? Oh yes, certainly.

Solness. Till she can get her things a little in order, you know.

Mrs. Solness. I will do the best I can for you. It's no more than my duty. I suppose your trunk is coming on later?

Hilda. I have no trunk.

Mrs. Solness. Well, it will be all right, I daresay. In the meantime, you must excuse my leaving you here with my husband, until I can get a room made a little comfortable for you.

Solness. Can we not give her one of the nurseries? They are all ready as it is.

Mrs. Solness. Oh, yes. There we have room and to spare. *(To* HILDA.*)* Sit down now, and rest a little.

[*She goes out to the right.*

[HILDA, *with her hands behind her back, strolls about the room and looks at various objects.* SOLNESS *stands in front, beside the table, also with his hands behind his back, and follows her with his eyes.*

Hilda (stops and looks at him). Have you several nurseries?

Solness. There are three nurseries in the house.

Hilda. That's a lot. Then I suppose you have a great many children?

Solness. No. We have no child. But now you can be the child here, for the time being.

Hilda. For to-night, yes. I shall not cry. I mean to sleep as sound as a stone.

Solness. Yes, you must be very tired, I should think.

Hilda. Oh, no! But all the same—— It's so delicious to lie and dream.

Solness. Do you dream much of nights?

Hilda. Oh, yes! Almost always.

Solness. What do you dream about most?

Hilda. I shan't tell you to-night. Another time, perhaps.

[*She again strolls about the room, stops at the desk and turns over the books and papers a little.*

Solness (approaching). Are you searching for anything?

Hilda. No, I am merely looking at all these things. (*Turns.*) Perhaps I mustn't?

Solness. Oh, by all means.

Hilda. Is it you that write in this great ledger?

Solness. No, it's my book-keeper.

Hilda. Is it a woman?

Solness (smiles). Yes.

Hilda. One you employ here, in your office?

Solness. Yes.

Hilda. Is she married?

Solness. No, she is single.

Hilda. Oh, indeed!

Solness. But I believe she is soon going to be married.

Hilda. That's a good thing for her.

Solness. But not such a good thing for me. For then I shall have nobody to help me.

Hilda. Can't you get hold of some one else who will do just as well?

Solness. Perhaps you would stay here and write in the ledger?

Hilda (measures him with a glance). Yes, I daresay! No, thank you—nothing of that sort for me.

[*She again strolls across the room and sits down in the rocking-chair.* SOLNESS, *too, goes to the table.*

Hilda (continuing). For there must surely be plenty of other things to be done here. *(Looks smiling at him.)* Don't you think so, too?

Solness. Of course. First of all, I suppose, you want to make a round of the shops and get yourself up in the height of fashion.

Hilda (amused). No, I think I shall let that alone!

Solness. Indeed.

Hilda. For you must know I have run through all my money.

Solness (laughs). Neither trunk nor money, then.

Hilda. Neither one nor the other. But never mind—it doesn't matter now.

Solness. Come now, I like you for that.

Hilda. Only for that?

Solness. For that among other things. *(Sits in the arm-chair.)* Is your father alive still?

Hilda. Yes, father's alive.

Solness. Perhaps you are thinking of studying here?

Hilda. No, that hadn't occurred to me.

Solness. But I suppose you will be staying for some time?

Hilda. That must depend upon circumstances.

[*She sits awhile rocking herself and looking at him, half seriously, half with a suppressed smile. Then she takes off her hat and puts it on the table in front of her.*

Hilda. Mr. Solness!

Solness. Well?

Hilda. Have you a very bad memory?

Solness. A bad memory? No, not that I am aware of.

Hilda. Then have you nothing to say to me about wha' happened up there?

Solness (in momentary surprise). Up at Lysanger? *(Indifferently.)* Why, it was nothing much to talk about, it seems to me.

Hilda (looks reproachfully at him). How can you sit there and say such things?

Solness. Well, then, you talk to me about it.

Hilda. When the tower was finished, we had grand doings in the town.

Solness. Yes, I shall not easily forget that day.

Hilda (smiles). Will you not? That comes well from you.

Solness. Comes well?

Hilda. There was music in the churchyard—and many, many hundreds of people. We school-girls were dressed in white; and we all carried flags.

Solness. Ah yes, those flags—I can tell you I remember them!

Hilda. Then you climbed right up the scaffolding, straight to the very top; and you had a great wreath with you; and you hung that wreath right away up on the weather-vane.

Solness (curtly interrupting). I always did that in those days. It was an old custom.

Hilda. It was so wonderfully thrilling to stand below and look up at you. Fancy, if he should fall over! He—the master builder himself!

Solness (as if to divert her from the subject). Yes, yes, yes, that might very well have happened, too. For one of those white-frocked little devils,—she went on in such a way, and screamed up at me so——

Hilda (sparkling with pleasure). "Hurrah for Master Builder Solness!" Yes!

Solness. ——and waved and flourished with her flag, so that I—so that it almost made me giddy to look at it.

Hilda (in a lower voice, seriously). That little devil—that was *I*.

Solness (fixes his eyes steadily upon her). I am sure of that now. It must have been you.

Hilda (lively again). Oh, it was so gloriously thrilling! I could not have believed there was a builder in the whole world that could build such a tremendously high tower. And then, that you yourself should stand at the very top of it, as large as life! And that you should not be the least bit dizzy! It was that above everything that made one—made one dizzy to think of.

Solness. How could you be so certain that I was not ——?

Hilda (scouting the idea). No indeed! Oh, no! I knew that instinctively. For if you had been, you could never have stood up there and sung.

Solness (looks at her in astonishment). Sung? Did *I* sing?

Hilda. Yes, I should think you did.

Solness (shakes his head). I have never sung a note in my life.

Hilda. Yes indeed, you sang then. It sounded like harps in the air.

Solness (thoughtfully). This is very strange—all this.

Hilda (is silent awhile, looks at him and says in a low voice:) But then,—it was after that—and the real thing happened.

Solness. The real thing?

Hilda (sparkling with vivacity). Yes, I surely don't need to remind you of that?

Solness. Oh, yes, do remind me a little of that, too.

Hilda. Don't you remember that a great dinner was given in your honour at the Club?

Solness. Yes, to be sure. It must have been the same afternoon, for I left the place next morning.

Hilda. And from the Club you were invited to come round to our house to supper.

Solness. Quite right, Miss Wangel. It is wonderful how

all these trifles have impressed themselves on your mind.

Hilda. Trifles! I like that! Perhaps it was a trifle, too, that I was alone in the room when you came in?

Solness. Were you alone?

Hilda (without answering him). You didn't call me a little devil then?

Solness. No, I suppose I did not.

Hilda. You said I was lovely in my white dress, and that I looked like a little princess.

Solness. I have no doubt you did, Miss Wangel.—And besides—I was feeling so buoyant and free that day——

Hilda. And then you said that when I grew up I should be your princess.

Solness (laughing a little). Dear, dear—did I say that, too?

Hilda. Yes, you did. And when I asked how long I should have to wait, you said that you would come again in ten years—like a troll and carry me off—to Spain or some such place. And you promised you would buy me a kingdom there.

Solness (as before). Yes, after a good dinner one doesn't haggle about the halfpence. But did I really say all that?

Hilda (laughs to herself). Yes. And you told me, too, what the kingdom was to be called.

Solness. Well, what was it?

Hilda. It was to be called the kingdom of Orangia,* you said.

Solness. Well, that was an appetising name.

Hilda. No, I didn't like it a bit; for it seemed as though you wanted to make game of me.

Solness. I am sure that cannot have been my intention.

Hilda. No, I should hope not—considering what you did next——

Solness. What in the world did I do next?

* In the original "Appelsinia," "appelsin" meaning "orange."

Hilda. Well, that's the finishing touch, if you have forgotten that, too. I should have thought no one could help remembering such a thing as that.

Solness. Yes, yes, just give me a hint, and then perhaps —— Well——

Hilda (looks fixedly at him). You came and kissed me, Mr. Solness.

Solness (open-mouthed, rising from his chair). I did!

Hilda. Yes, indeed you did. You took me in both your arms, and bent my head back and kissed me—many times.

Solness. Now really, my dear Miss Wangel——!

Hilda (rises). You surely cannot mean to deny it?

Solness. Yes, I do. I deny it altogether!

Hilda (looks scornfully at him). Oh, indeed!

[*She turns and goes slowly close up to the stove, where she remains standing motionless, her face averted from him, her hands behind her back Short pause.*

Solness (goes cautiously up behind her). Miss Wangel ——!

Hilda (is silent and does not move).

Solness. Don't stand there like a statue. You must have dreamt all this. *(Lays his hand on her arm.)* Now just listen——

Hilda (makes an impatient movement with her arm).

Solness (as a thought flashes upon him). Or——! Wait a moment! There is something under all this, you may depend!

Hilda (does not move).

Solness (in a low voice, but with emphasis). I must have thought all that. I must have wished it—have willed it—have longed to do it. And then——. May not that be the explanation?

Hilda (is still silent).

Solness (impatiently). Oh very well, deuce take it all—then I did it, I suppose.

Hilda (turns her head a little, but without looking at him). Then you admit it now?

Solness. Yes—whatever you like.

Hilda. You came and put your arms around me?

Solness. Oh, yes!

Hilda. And bent my head back?

Solness. Very far back.

Hilda. And kissed me?

Solness. Yes, I did.

Hilda. Many times?

Solness. As many as ever you like.

Hilda (turns quickly towards him and has once more the sparkling expression of gladness in her eyes). Well, you see, I got it out of you at last!

Solness (with a slight smile). Yes—just think of my forgetting such a thing as that.

Hilda (again a little sulky, retreats from him). Oh, you have kissed so many people in your time, I suppose.

Solness. No, you mustn't think that of me. *(*HILDA *seats herself in the armchair.* SOLNESS *stands and leans against the rocking-chair. Looks observantly at her.)* Miss Wangel!

Hilda. Yes!

Solness. How was it now? What came of all this—between us two?

Hilda. Why, nothing more came of it. You know that quite well. For then the other guests came in, and then—bah!

Solness. Quite so! The others came in. To think of my forgetting that, too!

Hilda. Oh, you haven't really forgotten anything: you are only a little ashamed of it all. I am sure one doesn't forget things of that kind.

Solness. No, one would suppose not.

Hilda (lively again, looks at him). Perhaps you have even forgotten what day it was?

Solness. What day——?

Hilda. Yes, on what day did you hang the wreath on the tower? Well? Tell me at once!

Solness. H'm—I confess I have forgotten the particular day. I only knew it was ten years ago. Sometime in the autumn.

Hilda (nods her head slowly several times). It was ten years ago—on the 19th of September.

Solness. Yes, it must have been about that time. Fancy your remembering that, too! *(Stops.)* But wait a moment——! Yes—it's the 19th of September to-day.

Hilda. Yes, it is; and the ten years are gone. And you didn't come—as you promised me.

Solness. Promised you? Threatened, I suppose you mean?

Hilda. I don't think there was any sort of threat in that.

Solness. Well then, a little bit of fun.

Hilda. Was that all you wanted? To make fun of me?

Solness. Well, or to have a little joke with you. Upon my soul, I don't recollect. But it must have been something of that kind; for you were a mere child then.

Hilda. Oh, perhaps I wasn't quite such a child either. Not such a mere chit as you imagine.

Solness (looks searchingly at her). Did you really and seriously expect me to come again?

Hilda (conceals a half-teasing smile). Yes, indeed; I did expect that of you.

Solness. That I should come back to your home and take you away with me?

Hilda. Just like a troll—yes.

Solness. And make a princess of you?

Hilda. That's what you promised.

Solness. And give you a kingdom as well?

Hilda (looks up at the ceiling). Why not? Of course it need not have been an actual, every-day sort of kingdom.

Solness. But something else just as good?

Hilda. Yes, at least as good. *(Looks at him a moment.)* I thought, if you could build the highest church-towers in the world, you could surely manage to raise a kingdom of one sort or another as well.

Solness (shakes his head). I can't quite make you out, Miss Wangel.

Hilda. Can you not? To me it seems all so simple.

Solness. No, I can't make up my mind whether you mean all you say, or are simply having a joke with me.

Hilda (smiles). Making fun of you, perhaps? I, too?

Solness. Yes, exactly. Making fun—of both of us. *(Looks at her.)* Is it long since you found out that I was married?

Hilda. I have known it all along. Why do you ask me that?

Solness (lightly). Oh, well, it just occurred to me. *(Looks earnestly at her and says in a low voice.)* What have you come for?

Hilda. I want my kingdom. The time is up.

Solness (laughs involuntarily). What a girl you are!

Hilda (gaily). Out with my kingdom, Mr. Solness! *(Raps with her fingers.)* The kingdom on the table!

Solness (pushing the rocking-chair nearer and sitting down). Now, seriously speaking—what have you come for? What do you really want to do here?

Hilda. Oh, first of all, I want to go around and look at all the things that you have built.

Solness. That will give you plenty of exercise.

Hilda. Yes, I know you have built a tremendous lot.

Solness. I have indeed—especially of late years.

Hilda. Many church-towers among the rest? Immensely high ones?

Solness. No. I build no more church-towers now. Nor churches either.

Hilda. What do you build, then?

Solness. Homes for human beings.

Hilda (reflectively). Couldn't you build a little—a little bit of a church-tower over these homes as well?

Solness (starting). What do you mean by that?

Hilda. I mean—something that points—points up into the free air. With the vane at a dizzy height.

Solness (pondering a little). Strange that you should say that—for that is just what I am most anxious to do.

Hilda (impatiently). Why don't you do it, then?

Solness (shakes his head). No, the people will not have it.

Hilda. Fancy their not wanting it!

Solness (more lightly). But now I am building a new home for myself—just opposite here.

Hilda. For yourself?

Solness. Yes. It is almost finished. And on that there is a tower.

Hilda. A high tower?

Solness. Yes.

Hilda. Very high?

Solness. No doubt people will say it is too high—too high for a dwelling-house.

Hilda. I'll go out and look at that tower the first thing to-morrow morning.

Solness (sits resting his cheek on his hand and gazes at her). Tell me, Miss Wangel—what is your name? Your Christian name, I mean?

Hilda. Why, Hilda, of course.

Solness (as before). Hilda? Indeed?

Hilda. Don't you remember that? You called me Hilda yourself—that day when you misbehaved.

Solness. Did I really?

Hilda. But then you said "little Hilda"; and I didn't like that.

Solness. Oh, you didn't like that, Miss Hilda?

Hilda. No, not at such a time as that. But—"Princess Hilda"—that will sound very well, I think.

Solness. Very well indeed. Princess Hilda of—of—what was to be the name of the kingdom?

Hilda. Pooh! I won't have anything to do with that stupid kingdom. I have set my heart upon quite a different one!

Solness (has leaned back in the chair, still gazing at her). Isn't it strange——? The more I think of it now, the more it seems to me as though I had gone about all these years torturing myself with—h'm——

Hilda. With what?

Solness. With the effort to recover something—some experience, which I seemed to have forgotten. But I never had the least inkling of what it could be.

Hilda. You should have tied a knot in your pockethandkerchief, Mr. Solness.

Solness. In that case, I should simply have had to go racking my brains to discover what the knot could mean.

Hilda. Oh, yes, I suppose there are trolls of that kind in the world, too.

Solness (rises slowly). What a good thing it is that you have come to me now.

Hilda (looks deeply into his eyes). Is it a good thing?

Solness. For I have been so lonely here. I have been gazing so helplessly at it all. *(In a lower voice.)* I must tell you—I have begun to be so afraid—so terribly afraid of the younger generation.

Hilda (with a little snort of contempt). Pooh—is the younger generation a thing to be afraid of?

Solness. It is indeed. And that is why I have locked and barred myself in. *(Mysteriously.)* I tell you the younger generation will one day come and thunder at my door! They will break in upon me!

Hilda. Then I should say you ought to go out and open the door to the younger generation.

Solness. Open the door?

Hilda. Yes. Let them come in to you on friendly terms, as it were.

Solness. No, no, no! The younger generation—it means retribution, you see. It comes, as if under a new banner, heralding the turn of fortune.

Hilda (rises, looks at him and says with a quivering twitch of her lips). Can I be of any use to you, Mr. Solness?

Solness. Yes, you can indeed! For you, too, come—under a new banner, it seems to me. Youth marshalled against youth——!

[DR. HERDAL *comes in by the hall-door.*

Dr. Herdal. What—you and Miss Wangel here still?

Solness. Yes. We have had no end of things to talk about.

Hilda. Both old and new.

Dr. Herdal. Have you really?

Hilda. Oh, it has been the greatest fun. For Mr. Solness—he has such a miraculous memory. All the least little details he remembers instantly.

[MRS. SOLNESS *enters by the door on the right.*

Mrs. Solness. Well, Miss Wangel, your room is quite ready for you now.

Hilda. Oh, how kind you are to me!

Solness (to MRS. SOLNESS*)*. The nursery?

Mrs. Solness. Yes, the middle one. But first let us go in to supper.

Solness (nods to HILDA*)*. Hilda shall sleep in the nursery, she shall.

Mrs. Solness (looks at him). Hilda?

Solness. Yes, Miss Wangel's name is Hilda. I knew her when she was a child.

Mrs. Solness. Did you really, Halvard? Well, shall we go? Supper is on the table.

[*She takes* DR. HERDAL'S *arm and goes out with*

him to the right. HILDA *has meanwhile been collecting her travelling things.*

Hilda (softly and rapidly to SOLNESS*).* Is it true, what you said? Can I be of use to you?

Solness (takes the things from her). You are the very being I have needed most.

Hilda (looks at him with happy, wondering eyes and clasps her hands). But then, great heavens——!

Solness (eagerly). What——?

Hilda. Then I have my kingdom!

Solness (involuntarily). Hilda——!

Hilda (again with the quivering twitch of her lips). Almost—I was going to say.

[*She goes out to the right,* SOLNESS *follows her.*

ACT II

A prettily furnished small drawing-room in SOLNESS'S *house. In the back, a glass door leading out to the verandah and garden. The right-hand corner is cut off transversely by a large bay-window, in which are flower-stands. The left-hand corner is similarly cut off by a transverse wall, in which is a small door papered like the wall. On each side, an ordinary door. In front, on the right, a console table with a large mirror over it. Well-filled stands of plants and flowers. In front, on the left, a sofa with a table and chairs. Further back, a bookcase. Well forward in the room, before the bay window, a small table and some chairs. It is early in the day.*

SOLNESS *sits by the little table with* RAGNAR BROVIK'S *portfolio open in front of him. He is turning the drawings over and closely examining some of them.* MRS. SOLNESS *moves about noiselessly with a small watering-pot, attending to her flowers. She is dressed in black as before. Her hat, cloak and parasol lie on a chair near the mirror. Unobserved by her,* SOLNESS *now and again follows her with his eyes. Neither of them speaks.*

KAIA FOSLI *enters quietly by the door on the left.*

Solness (turns his head, and says in an off-hand tone of indifference). Well, is that you?

Kaia. I merely wished to let you know that I have come.

Solness. Yes, yes, that's all right. Hasn't Ragnar come, too?

Kaia. No, not yet. He had to wait a little while to see the doctor. But he is coming presently to hear——

Solness. How is the old man to-day?

Kaia. Not well. He begs you to excuse him; he is obliged to keep his bed to-day.

Solness. Why, of course; by all means let him rest. But now, get to work.

Kaia. Yes. *(Pauses at the door.)* Do you wish to speak to Ragnar when he comes?

Solness. No—I don't know that I have anything particular to say to him.

[KAIA *goes out again to the left.* SOLNESS *remains seated, turning over the drawings.*

Mrs. Solness (over beside the plants). I wonder if he isn't going to die now, as well?

Solness (looks up to her). As well as who?

Mrs. Solness (without answering). Yes, yes—depend upon it, Halvard, old Brovik is going to die, too. You'll see that he will.

Solness. My dear Aline, ought you not to go out for a little walk?

Mrs. Solness. Yes, I suppose I ought to.

[*She continues to attend to the flowers.*

Solness (bending over the drawings). Is she still asleep?

Mrs. Solness (looking at him). Is it Miss Wangel you are sitting there thinking about?

Solness (indifferently). I just happened to recollect her.

Mrs. Solness. Miss Wangel was up long ago.

Solness. Oh, was she?

Mrs. Solness. When I went in to see her, she was busy putting her things in order.

[*She goes in front of the mirror and slowly begins to put on her hat.*

Solness (after a short pause). So we have found a use for one of our nurseries after all, Aline.

Mrs. Solness. Yes, we have.

Solness. That seems to me better than to have them all standing empty.

Mrs. Solness. That emptiness is dreadful; you are right there.

Solness (closes the portfolio, rises and approaches her). You will find that we shall get on far better after this, Aline. Things will be more comfortable. Life will be easier—especially for you.

Mrs. Solness (looks at him). After this?

Solness. Yes, believe me, Aline——

Mrs. Solness. Do you mean—because she has come here?

Solness (checking himself). I mean, of course— when once we have moved into the new house.

Mrs. Solness (takes her cloak). Ah, do you think so, Halvard? Will it be better then?

Solness. I can't think otherwise. And surely you think so, too?

Mrs. Solness. I think nothing at all about the new house.

Solness (cast down). It's hard for me to hear you say that; for you know it is mainly for your sake that I have built it.

[*He offers to help her on with her cloak.*

Mrs. Solness (evades him). The fact is, you do far too much for my sake.

Solness (with a certain vehemence). No, no, you really mustn't say that, Aline! I cannot bear to hear you say such things!

Mrs. Solness. Very well, then I won't say it, Halvard.

Solness. But I stick to what *I* said. You'll see that things will be easier for you in the new place.

Mrs. Solness. O heavens—easier for me——!

Solness (eagerly). Yes, indeed they will! You may be quite sure of that! For you see—there will be so very, very much there that will remind you of your own home——

Mrs. Solness. The home that used to be father's and mother's—and that was burnt to the ground——

Solness (in a low voice). Yes, yes, my poor Aline. That was a terrible blow for you.

Mrs. Solness (breaking out in lamentation). You may build as much as ever you like, Halvard—you can never build up again a real home for me!

Solness (crosses the room). Well, in heaven's name, let us talk no more about it, then.

Mrs. Solness. Oh, yes, Halvard, I understand you very well. You are so anxious to spare me—and to find excuses for me, too—as much as ever you can.

Solness (with astonishment in his eyes). You! Is it you—yourself, that you are talking about, Aline?

Mrs. Solness. Yes, who else should it be but myself?

Solness (involuntarily to himself). That, too!

Mrs. Solness. As for the old house, I wouldn't mind so much about that. When once misfortune was in the air—why——

Solness. Ah, you are right there. Misfortune will have its way—as the saying goes.

Mrs. Solness. But it's what came of the fire—the dreadful thing that followed——! That is the thing! That, that, that!

Solness (vehemently). Don't think about that, Aline!

Mrs. Solness. Ah, that is exactly what I cannot help thinking about. And now, at last, I must speak about it, too; for I don't seem able to bear it any longer. And then never to be able to forgive myself——

Solness (exclaiming). Yourself——!

Mrs. Solness. Yes, for I had duties on both sides—both towards you and towards the little ones. I ought to have hardened myself—not to have let the horror take such hold upon me—nor the grief for the burning of my old home. *(Wrings her hands.)* Oh, Halvard, if I had only had the strength!

Solness (softly, much moved, comes closer). Aline—you

must promise me never to think these thoughts any more.—Promise me that, dear!

Mrs. Solness. Oh, promise, promise! One can promise anything.

Solness (clenches his hands and crosses the room). Oh, but this is hopeless, hopeless! Never a ray of sunlight! Not so much as a gleam of brightness to light up our home!

Mrs. Solness. This is no home, Halvard.

Solness. Oh no, you may well say that. *(Gloomily).* And God knows whether you are not right in saying that it will be no better for us in the new house, either.

Mrs. Solness. It will never be any better. Just as empty—just as desolate—there as here.

Solness (vehemently). Why in all the world have we built it then? Can you tell me that?

Mrs. Solness. No; you must answer that question for yourself.

Solness (glances suspiciously at her). What do you mean by that, Aline?

Mrs. Solness. What do I mean?

Solness. Yes, in the devil's name! You said it so strangely—as if you had hidden some meaning in it.

Mrs. Solness. No, indeed, I assure you——

Solness (comes closer). Oh, come now—I know what I know. I have both my eyes and my ears about me, Aline—you may depend upon that!

Mrs. Solness. Why, what are you talking about? What is it?

Solness (places himself in front of her). Do you mean to say you don't find a kind of lurking, hidden meaning in the most innocent word I happen to say?

Mrs. Solness. *I,* do you say? *I* do that?

Solness (laughs). Ho-ho-ho! It's natural enough, Aline! When you have a sick man on your hands——

Mrs. Solness (anxiously). Sick? Are you ill, Halvard?

Solness (violently). A half-mad man then! A crazy man! Call me what you will.

Mrs. Solness (feels blindly for a chair and sits down). Halvard—for God's sake——

Solness. But you are wrong, both you and the doctor. I am not in the state you imagine.

[*He walks up and down the room.* MRS. SOLNESS *follows him anxiously with her eyes. Finally he goes up to her.*

Solness (calmly). In reality there is nothing whatever the matter with me.

Mrs. Solness. No, there isn't, is there? But then what is it that troubles you so?

Solness. Why this, that I often feel ready to sink under this terrible burden of debt——

Mrs. Solness. Debt, do you say? But you owe no one anything, Halvard!

Solness (softly, with emotion). I owe a boundless debt to you—to you—to you, Aline.

Mrs. Solness (rises slowly). What is behind all this? You may just as well tell me at once.

Solness. But there is nothing behind it; I have never done you any wrong—not wittingly and wilfully, at any rate. And yet—and yet it seems as though a crushing debt rested upon me and weighed me down.

Mrs. Solness. A debt to me?

Solness. Chiefly to you.

Mrs. Solness. Then you are—ill after all, Halvard.

Solness (gloomily). I suppose I must be—or not far from it. *(Looks towards the door to the right, which is opened at this moment.)* Ah! now it grows lighter.

[HILDA WANGEL *comes in. She has made some alteration in her dress and let down her skirt.*

Hilda. Good morning, Mr. Solness!

Solness (nods). Slept well?

Hilda. Quite deliciously! Like a child in a cradle. Oh —I lay and stretched myself like—like a princess!

Solness (smiles a little). You were thoroughly comfortable then?

Hilda. I should think so.

Solness. And no doubt you dreamed, too.

Hilda. Yes, I did. But that was horrid.

Solness. Was it?

Hilda. Yes, for I dreamed I was falling over a frightfully high, sheer precipice. Do you never have that kind of dream?

Solness. Oh yes—now and then——

Hilda. It's tremendously thrilling—when you fall and fall——

Solness. It seems to make one's blood run cold.

Hilda. Do you draw your legs up under you while you are falling?

Solness. Yes, as high as ever I can.

Hilda. So do I.

Mrs. Solness (takes her parasol). I must go into town now, Halvard. *(To* Hilda.*)* And I'll try to get one or two things that you may require.

Hilda (making a motion to throw her arms round her neck). Oh, you dear, sweet Mrs. Solness! You are really much too kind to me! Frightfully kind——

Mrs. Solness (deprecatingly, freeing herself). Oh, not at all. It's only my duty, so I am very glad to do it.

Hilda (offended, pouts). But really, I think I am quite fit to be seen in the streets—now that I've put my dress to rights. Or do you think I am not?

Mrs. Solness. To tell you the truth, I think people would stare at you a little.

Hilda (contemptuously). Pooh! Is that all? That only amuses me.

Solness (with suppressed ill-humour). Yes, but people

might take it into their heads that you were mad, too, you see.

Hilda. Mad? Are there so many mad people here in town, then?

Solness (points to his own forehead). Here you see one, at all events.

Hilda. You—Mr. Solness!

Mrs. Solness. Oh, don't talk like that, my dear Halvard!

Solness. Have you not noticed that yet?

Hilda. No, I certainly have not. *(Reflects and laughs a little.)* And yet—perhaps in one single thing.

Solness. Ah, do you hear that, Aline?

Mrs. Solness. What is that one single thing, Miss Wangel?

Hilda. No, I won't say.

Solness. Oh, yes, do!

Hilda. No, thank you—I am not so mad as that.

Mrs. Solness. When you and Miss Wangel are alone, I daresay she will tell you, Halvard.

Solness. Ah—you think she will?

Mrs. Solness. Oh, yes, certainly. For you have known her so well in the past. Ever since she was a child—you tell me.

[*She goes out by the door on the left.*

Hilda (after a little while). Does your wife dislike me very much?

Solness. Did you think you noticed anything of the kind?

Hilda. Did you not notice it yourself?

Solness (evasively). Aline has become exceedingly shy with strangers of late years.

Hilda. Has she really?

Solness. But if only you could get to know her thoroughly——! Ah! she is so good—so kind—so excellent a creature——

Hilda (impatiently). But if she is all that—what made her say that about her duty?

Solness. Her duty?

Hilda. She said that she would go out and buy something for me, because it was her duty. Oh, I can't bear that ugly, horrid word!

Solness. Why not?

Hilda. It sounds so cold and sharp and stinging. Duty —duty—duty. Don't you think so, too? Doesn't it seem to sting you?

Solness. H'm—haven't thought much about it.

Hilda. Yes, it does. And if she is so good—as you say she is—why should she talk in that way?

Solness. But, good Lord, what would you have had her say, then?

Hilda. She might have said she would do it because she had taken a tremendous fancy to me. She might have said something like that—something really warm and cordial, you understand.

Solness (looks at her). Is that how you would like to have it?

Hilda. Yes, precisely. *(She wanders about the room, stops at the bookcase and looks at the books.)* What a lot of books you have.

Solness. Yes, I have got together a good many.

Hilda. Do you read them all, too?

Solness. I used to try to. Do you read much?

Hilda. No, never! I have given it up. For it all seems so irrelevant.

Solness. That is just my feeling.

[HILDA *wanders about a little, stops at the small table, opens the portfolio and turns over the contents.*

Hilda. Are all these drawings yours?

Solness. No, they are drawn by a young man whom I employ to help me.

Hilda. Some one you have taught?

Solness. Oh, yes, no doubt he has learnt something from one, too.

Hilda (sits down). Then I suppose he is very clever. *(Looks at a drawing.)* Isn't he?

Solness. Oh, he might be worse. For my purpose——

Hilda. Oh, yes—I'm sure he is frightfully clever.

Solness. Do you think you can see that in the drawings?

Hilda. Pooh—these scrawlings! But if he has been learning from you——

Solness. Oh, so far as that goes—there are plenty of people that have learnt from me and have come to little enough for all that.

Hilda (looks at him and shakes her head). No, I can't for the life of me understand how you can be so stupid.

Solness. Stupid? Do you think I am so very stupid?

Hilda. Yes, I do indeed. If you are content to go about here teaching all these people——

Solness (with a slight start). Well, and why not?

Hilda (rises, half serious, half laughing). No indeed, Mr. Solness! What can be the good of that? No one but you should be allowed to build. You should stand quite alone—do it all yourself. Now you know it.

Solness (involuntarily). Hilda——!

Hilda. Well!

Solness. How in the world did that come into your head?

Hilda. Do you think I am so very far wrong, then?

Solness. No, that's not what I mean. But now I'll tell you something.

Hilda. Well?

Solness. I keep on—incessantly—in silence and alone—brooding on that very thought.

Hilda. Yes, that seems to me perfectly natural.

Solness (looks somewhat searchingly at her). Perhaps you have noticed it already?

Hilda. No, indeed I haven't.

Solness. But just now—when you said you thought I was—off my balance? In one thing, you said——

Hilda. Oh, I was thinking of something quite different.

Solness. What was it?

Hilda. I am not going to tell you.

Solness (crosses the room). Well, well—as you please. *(Stops at the bow-window.)* Come here, and I will show you something.

Hilda (approaching). What is it?

Solness. Do you see—over there in the garden——?

Hilda. Yes?

Solness (points). Right above the great quarry——?

Hilda. That new house, you mean?

Solness. The one that is being built, yes. Almost finished.

Hilda. It seems to have a very high tower.

Solness. The scaffolding is still up.

Hilda. Is that your new house?

Solness. Yes.

Hilda. The house you are soon going to move into?

Solness. Yes.

Hilda (looks at him). Are there nurseries in that house, too?

Solness. Three, as there are here.

Hilda. And no child,

Solness. And there never will be one.

Hilda (with a half-smile). Well, isn't it just as I said——?

Solness. That——?

Hilda. That you are a little—a little mad after all.

Solness. Was that what you were thinking of?

Hilda. Yes, of all the empty nurseries I slept in.

Solness (lowers his voice). We have had children—Aline and I.

Hilda (looks eagerly at him). Have you——?

Solness. Two little boys. They were of the same age.

Hilda. Twins, then.

Solness. Yes, twins. It's eleven or twelve years ago now.

Hilda (cautiously). And so both of them——? You have lost both the twins, then?

Solness (with quiet emotion). We kept them only about three weeks. Or scarcely so much. *(Bursts forth.)* Oh, Hilda, I can't tell you what a good thing it is for me that you have come! For now at last I have some one I can talk to!

Hilda. Can you not talk to—her, too?

Solness. Not about this. Not as I want to talk and must talk. *(Gloomily.)* And not about so many other things, either.

Hilda (in a subdued voice). Was that all you meant when you said you needed me?

Solness. That was mainly what I meant—at all events, yesterday. For to-day I am not so sure——*(Breaking off.)* Come here and let us sit down, Hilda. Sit there on the sofa—so that you can look into the garden. *(*HILDA *seats herself in the corner of the sofa.* SOLNESS *brings a chair closer.)* Should you like to hear about it?

Hilda. Yes, I shall love to sit and listen to you.

Solness (sits down). Then I will tell you all about it.

Hilda. Now I can see both the garden and you, Mr. Solness. So now, tell away! Begin!

Solness (points towards the bow-window). Out there on the rising ground—where you see the new house——

Hilda. Yes?

Solness. Aline and I lived there in the first years of our married life. There was an old house up there that had belonged to her mother; and we inherited it, and the whole of the great garden with it.

Hilda. Was there a tower on that house, too?

Solness. No, nothing of the kind. From the outside it

looked like a great, dark, ugly wooden box; but all the same, it was snug and comfortable enough inside.

Hilda. Then did you pull down the ramshackle old place?

Solness. No, it burnt down.

Hilda. The whole of it?

Solness. Yes.

Hilda. Was that a great misfortulne for you?

Solness. That depends on how you look at it. As a builder, the fire was the making of me——

Hilda. Well, but——?

Solness. It was just after the birth of the two little boys——

Hilda. The poor little twins, yes.

Solness. They came healthy and bonny into the world. And they were growing too—you could see the difference from day to day.

Hilda. Little children do grow quickly at first.

Solness. It was the prettiest sight in the world to see Aline lying with the two of them in her arms.—But then came the night of the fire——

Hilda (excitedly). What happened? Do tell me! Was any one burnt?

Solness. No, not that. Every one got safe and sound out of the house——

Hilda. Well, and what then——?

Solness. The fright had shaken Aline terribly. The alarm—the escape—the break-neck hurry—and then the ice-cold night air—for they had to be carried out just as they lay—both she and the little ones.

Hilda. Was it too much for them?

Solness. Oh no, they stood it well enough. But Aline fell into a fever, and it affected her milk. She would insist on nursing them herself; because it was her duty, she said. And both our little boys, they—*(clenching his hands.)*—they—oh!

Hilda. They did not get over that?

Solness. No, that they did not get over. That was how we lost them.

Hilda. It must have been terribly hard for you.

Solness. Hard enough for me; but ten times harder for Aline. *(Clenching his hands in suppressed fury.)* Oh, that such things should be allowed to happen here in the world! *(Shortly and firmly.)* From the day I lost them, I had no heart for building churches.

Hilda. Did you not like the church-tower in our town?

Solness. I didn't like it. I know how free and happy I felt when the tower was finished.

Hilda. *I* know that, too.

Solness. And now I shall never—never build anything of that sort again! Neither churches nor church-towers.

Hilda (nods slowly). Nothing but houses for people to live in.

Solness. Homes for human beings, Hilda.

Hilda. But homes with high towers and pinnacles upon them.

Solness. If possible. *(Adopts a lighter tone.)* But, as I said before, that fire was the making of me—as a builder, I mean.

Hilda. Why don't you call yourself an architect, like the others?

Solness. I have not been systematically enough taught for that. Most of what I know, I have found out for myself.

Hilda. But you succeeded all the same.

Solness. Yes, thanks to the fire. I laid out almost the whole of the garden in villa lots; and there I was able to build after my own heart. So I came to the front with a rush.

Hilda (looks keenly at him). You must surely be a very happy man, as matters stand with you.

Solness (gloomily). Happy? Do you say that, too—like all the rest of them?

Hilda. Yes, I should say you must be. If you could only cease thinking about the two little children——

Solness (slowly). The two little children—they are not so easy to forget, Hilda.

Hilda (somewhat uncertainly). Do you still feel their loss so much—after all these years?

Solness (looks fixedly at her, without replying). A happy man you said——

Hilda. Well, now, are you not happy—in other respects?

Solness (continues to look at her). When I told you all this about the fire—h'm——

Hilda. Well?

Solness. Was there not one special thought that you—that you seized upon?

Hilda (reflects in vain). No. What thought should that be?

Solness (with subdued emphasis). It was simply and solely by that fire that I was enabled to build homes for human beings. Cosy, comfortable, bright homes, where father and mother and the whole troop of children can live in safety and gladness, feeling what a happy thing it is to be alive in the world—and most of all to belong to each other—in great things and in small.

Hilda (ardently). Well, and is it not a great happiness for you to be able to build such beautiful homes?

Solness. The price, Hilda! The terrible price I had to pay for the opportunity!

Hilda. But can you never get over that?

Solness. No. That I might build homes for others, I had to forego—to forego for all time—the home that might have been my own. I mean a home for a troop of children—and for father and mother, too.

Hilda (cautiously). But need you have done that? For all time, you say?

Solness (nods slowly). That was the price of this happiness that people talk about. *(Breathes heavily.)* This happiness—h'm—this happiness was not to be bought any cheaper, Hilda.

Hilda (as before). But may it not come right even yet?

Solness. Never in this world—never. That is another consequence of the fire—and of Aline's illness afterwards.

Hilda (looks at him with an indefinable expression). And yet you build all these nurseries?

Solness (seriously). Have you never noticed, Hilda, how the impossible—how it seems to beckon and cry aloud to one?

Hilda (reflecting). The impossible? *(With animation.)* Yes, indeed! Is that how you feel too?

Solness. Yes, I do.

Hilda. There must be—a little of the troll in you, too.

Solness. Why of the troll?

Hilda. What would you call it, then?

Solness (rises). Well, well, perhaps you are right. *(Vehemently).* But how can I help turning into a troll, when this is how it always goes with me in everything—in everything!

Hilda. How do you mean?

Solness (speaking low, with inward emotion). Mark what I say to you, Hilda. All that I have succeeded in doing, building, creating—all the beauty, security, cheerful comfort—ay, and magnificence, too—*(Clenches his hands.)* Oh, is it not terrible even to think of——!

Hilda. What is so terrible?

Solness. That all this I have to make up for, to pay for —not in money, but in human happiness. And not with my own happiness only, but with other people's, too. Yes, yes, do you see that, Hilda? That is the price which my position as an artist has cost me—and others. And every single day I have to look on while the price is paid for me anew. Over again, and over again—and over again for ever!

Hilda (rises and looks steadily at him). Now I can see that you are thinking of—of her.

Solness. Yes, mainly of Aline. For Aline—she, too, had her vocation in life, just as much as I had mine. *(His voice quivers.)* But her vocation has had to be stunted, and crushed and shattered—in order that mine might force its way to—to a sort of great victory. For you must know that Aline—she, too, had a talent for building.

Hilda. She! For building?

Solness (shakes his head). Not houses and towers, and spires—not such things as I work away at——

Hilda. Well, but what then?

Solness (softly, with emotion). For building up the souls of little children, Hilda. For building up children's souls in perfect balance, and in noble and beautiful forms. For enabling them to soar up into erect and full-grown human souls. That was Aline's talent. And there it all lies now—— unused and unusable for ever—of no earthly service to any one—just like the ruins left by a fire.

Hilda. Yes, but even if this were so——?

Solness. It is so! It is so! I know it!

Hilda. Well, but in any case it is not your fault.

Solness (fixes his eyes on her and nods slowly). Ah, that is the great, terrible question. That is the doubt that is gnawing me—night and day.

Hilda. That?

Solness. Yes. Suppose the fault was mine—in a certain sense.

Hilda. Your fault! The fire!

Solness. All of it; the whole thing. And yet, perhaps—I may not have had anything to do with it.

Hilda (looks at him with a troubled expression). Oh, Mr. Solness—if you can talk like that, I am afraid you must be—ill, after all.

Solness. H'm—I don't think I shall ever be of quite sound mind on that point.

[Ragnar Brovik *cautiously opens the little door in the left-hand corner.* Hilda *comes forward.*

Ragnar (when he sees HILDA*).* Oh. I beg pardon, Mr. Solness— [*He makes a movement to withdraw.*

Solness. No, no, don't go. Let us get it over.

Ragnar. Oh, yes—if only we could.

Solness. I hear your father is no better?

Ragnar. Father is fast growing weaker—and therefore I beg and implore you to write a few kind words for me on one of the plans! Something for father to read before he——

Solness (vehemently). I won't hear anything more about those drawings of yours!

Ragnar. Have you looked at them?

Solness. Yes—I have.

Ragnar. And they are good for nothing? And *I* am good for nothing, too?

Solness (evasively). Stay here with me, Ragnar. You shall have everything your own way. And then you can marry Kaia and live at your ease—and happily, too, who knows? Only don't think of building on your own account.

Ragnar. Well, well, then I must go home and tell father what you say—I promised I would.—Is this what I am to tell father—before he dies?

Solness (with a groan). Oh tell him—tell him what you will, for me. Best to say nothing at all to him! *(With a sudden outburst).* I cannot do anything else, Ragnar!

Ragnar. May I have the drawings to take with me?

Solness. Yes, take them—take them by all means! They are lying there on the table.

Ragnar (goes to the table). Thanks.

Hilda (puts her hand on the portfolio). No, no; leave them here.

Solness. Why?

Hilda. Because I want to look at them, too.

Solness. But you have been—— *(To* RAGNAR*).* Well, leave them here, then.

Ragnar. Very well.

Solness. And go home at once to your father.

Ragnar. Yes. I suppose I must.

Solness (as if in desperation). Ragnar—you must not ask me to do what is beyond my power! Do you hear, Ragnar? You must not!

Ragnar. No, no. I beg your pardon——

[*He bows and goes out by the corner door.* HILDA *goes over and sits down on a chair near the mirror.*

Hilda (looks angrily at SOLNESS*).* That was a very ugly thing to do.

Solness. Do you think so, too?

Hilda. Yes, it was horrible ugly—and hard and bad and cruel as well.

Solness. Oh, you don't understand my position.

Hilda. No matter——. I say you ought not to be like that.

Solness. You said yourself, only just now, that no one but *I* ought to be allowed to build.

Hilda. *I* may say such things—but you must not.

Solness. I most of all, surely, who have paid so dear for my position.

Hilda. Oh yes—with what you call domestic comfort—and that sort of thing.

Solness. And with my peace of soul into the bargain.

Hilda (rising). Peace of soul! *(With feeling.)* Yes, yes, you are right in that! Poor Mr. Solness—you fancy that——

Solness (with a quiet, chuckling laugh). Just sit down again, Hilda, and I'll tell you something funny.

Hilda (sits down; with intent interest). Well?

Solness. It sounds such a ludicrous little thing; for, you see, the whole story turns upon nothing but a crack in a chimney.

Hilda. No more than that?

Solness. No, not to begin with.

[*He moves a chair nearer to* Hilda *and sits down.*

Hilda (impatiently, taps on her knee). Well, now for the crack in the chimney!

Solness. I had noticed the split in the flue long, long before the fire. Every time I went up into the attic, I looked to see if it was still there.

Hilda. And it was?

Solness. Yes; for no one else knew about it.

Hilda. And you said nothing?

Solness. Nothing.

Hilda. And did not think of repairing the flue either?

Solness. Oh, yes, I thought about it—but never got any further. Every time I intended to set to work, it seemed just as if a hand held me back. Not to-day, I thought—to-morrow; and nothing ever came of it.

Hilda. But why did you keep putting it off like that?

Solness. Because I was revolving something in my mind. *(Slowly, and in a low voice.)* Through that little black crack in the chimney, I might, perhaps, force my way upwards—as a builder.

Hilda (looking straight in front of her). That must have been thrilling.

Solness. Almost irresistible—quite irresistible. For at that time it appeared to me a perfectly simple and straightforward matter. I would have had it happen in the winter-time—a little before midday. I was to be out driving Aline in the sleigh. The servants at home would have made huge fires in the stoves.

Hilda. For, of course, it was to be bitterly cold that day?

Solness. Rather biting, yes—and they would want Aline to find it thoroughly snug and warm when she came home.

Hilda. I suppose she is very chilly by nature?

Solness. She is. And as we drove home, we were to see the smoke.

Hilda. Only the smoke?

Solness. The smoke first. But when we came up to the

garden gate, the whole of the old timber-box was to be a rolling mass of flames.—That is how I wanted it to be, you see.

Hilda. Oh why, why could it not have happened so!

Solness. You may well say that, Hilda.

Hilda. Well, but now listen, Mr. Solness. Are you perfectly certain that the fire was caused by that little crack in the chimney?

Solness. No, on the contrary—I am perfectly certain that the crack in the chimney had nothing whatever to do with the fire.

Hilda. What?

Solness. It has been clearly ascertained that the fire broke out in a clothes-cupboard—in a totally different part of the house.

Hilda. Then what is all this nonsense you are talking about the crack in the chimney?

Solness. May I go on talking to you a little, Hilda?

Hilda. Yes, if you'll only talk sensibly——

Solness. I will try. [*He moves his chair nearer.*

Hilda. Out with it, then, Mr. Solness.

Solness (confidentially). Don't you agree with me, Hilda, that there exist special, chosen people who have been endowed with the power and faculty of desiring a thing, craving for a thing, willing a thing—so persistently and so—so inexorably—that at last it has to happen? Don't you believe that?

Hilda (with an indefinable expression in her eyes). If that is so, we shall see, one of these days, whether *I* am one of the chosen.

Solness. It is not one's self alone that can do such great things. Oh, no—the helpers and the servers—they must do their part, too, if it is to be of any good. But they never come of themselves. One has to call upon them very persistently—inwardly, you understand.

Hilda. What are these helpers and servers?

Solness. Oh, we can talk about that some other time. For the present, let us keep to this business of the fire.

Hilda. Don't you think that fire would have happened all the same—even without your wishing for it?

Solness. If the house had been old Knut Brovik's, it would never have burnt down so conveniently for him. I am sure of that; for he does not know how to call for the helpers—no, nor for the servers, either. *(Rises in unrest.)* So you see, Hilda—it is my fault, after all, that the lives of the two little boys had to be sacrificed. And do you think it is not my fault, too, that Aline has never been the woman she should and might have been—and that she most longed to be?

Hilda. Yes, but if it is all the work of those helpers and servers——?

Solness. Who called for the helpers and servers? It was I! And they came and obeyed my will. *(In increasing excitement.)* That is what people call having the luck on your side; but I must tell you what this sort of luck feels like! It feels like a great raw place here on my breast. And the helpers and servers keep on flaying pieces of skin off other people in order to close my sore!— But still the sore is not healed—never, never! Oh, if you knew how it can sometimes gnaw and burn.

Hilda (looks attentively at him). You are ill, Mr. Solness. Very ill, I almost think.

Solness. Say mad; for that is what you mean.

Hilda. No, I don't think there is much amiss with your intellect.

Solness. With what then? Out with it!

Hilda. I wonder whether you were not sent into the world with a sickly conscience.

Solness. A sickly conscience? What devilry is that?

Hilda. I mean that your conscience is feeble—too delicately built, as it were—hasn't strength to take a grip of things—to lift and bear what is heavy.

Solness (growls). H'm! May I ask, then, what sort of conscience one ought to have?

Hilda. I should like your conscience to be—to be thoroughly robust.

Solness. Indeed? Robust, eh? Is your own conscience robust, may I ask?

Hilda. Yes, I think it is. I have never noticed that it wasn't.

Solness. It has not been put very severely to the test, I should think.

Hilda (with a quivering of the lips). Oh, it was no such simple matter to leave father—I am so awfully fond of him.

Solness. Dear me! for a month or two——

Hilda. I think I shall never go home again.

Solness. Never? Then why did you leave him?

Hilda (half-seriously, half-banteringly). Have you forgotten that the ten years are up?

Solness. Oh nonsense. Was anything wrong at home? Eh?

Hilda (quite seriously). It was this impulse within me that urged and goaded me to come—and lured and drew me on, as well.

Solness (eagerly). There we have it! There we have it, Hilda! There is a troll in you, too, as in me. For it's the troll in one, you see—it is that that calls to the powers outside us. And then you must give in—whether you will or no.

Hilda. I almost think you are right, Mr. Solness.

Solness (walks about the room). Oh, there are devils innumerable abroad in the world, Hilda, that one never sees!

Hilda. Devils, too?

Solness (stops). Good devils and bad devils; light-haired devils and black-haired devils. If only you could always tell whether it is the light or dark ones that have got hold of you! *(Paces about.)* Ho-ho! Then it would be simple enough.

Hilda (follows him with her eyes). Or if one had a really vigorous, radiantly healthy conscience—so that one dared to do what one would.

Solness (stops beside the console table). I believe, now, that most people are just as puny creatures as I am in that respect.

Hilda. I shouldn't wonder.

Solness (leaning against the table). In the sagas—— Have you read any of the old sagas?

Hilda. Oh, yes! When I used to read books, I——

Solness. In the sagas you read about vikings, who sailed to foreign lands, and plundered and burned and killed men——

Hilda. And carried off women——

Solness. ——and kept them in captivity——

Hilda. ——took them home in their ships——

Solness. ——and behaved to them like—like the very worst of trolls.

Hilda (looks straight before her, with a half-veiled look). I think that must have been thrilling.

Solness (with a short, deep laugh). To carry off women,

Hilda. To be carried off.

Solness (looks at her a moment). Oh, indeed.

Hilda (as if breaking the thread of the conversation). But what made you speak of these vikings, Mr. Solness?

Solness. Why, those fellows must have had robust consciences, if you like! When they got home again, they could eat, and drink and be as happy as children. And the women, too! They often would not leave them on any account. Can you understand that, Hilda?

Hilda. Those women I can understand exceedingly well.

Solness. Oho! Perhaps you could do the same yourself?

Hilda. Why not?

Solness. Live—of your own free will—with a ruffian like that?

Hilda. If it was a ruffian I had come to love——

Solness. Could you come to love a man like that?

Hilda. Good heavens, you know very well one can't choose whom one is going to love.

Solness (looks meditatively at her). Oh, no, I suppose it is the troll within one that's responsible for that.

Hilda (half-laughing). And all those blessed devils, that you know so well—both the light-haired and the dark-haired ones.

Solness (quietly and warmly). Then I hope with all my heart that the devils will choose carefully for you, Hilda.

Hilda. For me they have chosen already—once and for all.

Solness (looks earnestly at her). Hilda—you are like a wild bird of the woods.

Hilda. Far from it. I don't hide myself away under the bushes.

Solness. No, no. There is rather something of the bird of prey in you.

Hilda. That is nearer it—perhaps. *(Very earnestly.)* And why not a bird of prey? Why should not *I* go a-hunting—I, as well as the rest. Carry off the prey I want—if only I can get my claws into it and do with it as I will.

Solness. Hilda—do you know what you are?

Hilda. Yes, I suppose I am a strange sort of bird.

Solness. No. You are like a dawning day. When I look at you—I seem to be looking towards the sunrise.

Hilda. Tell me, Mr. Solness—are you certain that you have never called me to you? Inwardly, you know?

Solness (softly and slowly). I almost think I must have.

Hilda. What did you want with me?

Solness. You are the younger generation, Hilda.

Hilda (smiles). That younger generation that you are so afraid of?

Solness (nods slowly). And which, in my heart, I yearn towards so deeply.

[Hilda *rises, goes to the little table and fetches* Ragnar Brovik's *portfolio.*

Hilda (holds out the portfolio to him). We were talking of these drawings——

Solness (shortly, waving them away). Put those things away! I have seen enough of them.

Hilda. Yes, but you have to write your approval on them.

Solness. Write my approval on them? Never!

Hilda. But the poor old man is lying at death's door! Can't you give him and his son this pleasure before they are parted? And perhaps he might get the commission to carry them out, too.

Solness. Yes, that is just what he would get. He has made sure of that—has my fine gentleman!

Hilda. Then, good heavens—if that is so—can't you tell the least little bit of a lie for once in a way?

Solness. A lie? *(Raging.)* Hilda—take those devil's drawings out of my sight!

Hilda (draws the portfolio a little nearer to herself). Well, well, well—don't bite me.—You talk of trolls—but I think you go on like a troll yourself. *(Looks around.)* Where do you keep your pen and ink?

Solness. There is nothing of the sort in here.

Hilda (goes towards the door). But in the office where that young lady is——

Solness. Stay where you are, Hilda!—I ought to tell a lie, you say. Oh, yes, for the sake of his old father I might well do that—for in my time I have crushed him, trodden him under foot——

Hilda. Him, too?

Solness. I needed room for myself. But this Ragnar—he must on no account be allowed to come to the front.

Hilda. Poor fellow, there is surely no fear of that. If he has nothing in him——

Solness (comes closer, looks at her and whispers). If

Ragnar Brovik gets his chance, he will strike me to the earth. Crush me—as I crushed his father.

Hilda. Crush you? Has he the ability for that?

Solness. Yes, you may depend upon it he has the ability! He is the younger generation that stands ready to knock at my door—to make an end of Halvard Solness.

Hilda (looks at him with quiet reproach). And yet you would bar him out. Fie, Mr. Solness!

Solness. The fight I have been fighting has cost heart's blood enough.—And I am afraid, too, that the helpers and servers will not obey me any longer.

Hilda. Then you must go ahead without them. There is nothing else for it.

Solness. It is hopeless, Hilda. The luck is bound to turn. A little sooner or a little later. Retribution is inexorable.

Hilda (in distress, putting her hands over her ears). Don't talk like that! Do you want to kill me? To take from me what is more than my life?

Solness. And what is that?

Hilda. The longing to see you great. To see you, with a wreath in your hand, high, high up upon a church-tower. *(Calm again.)* Come, out with your pencil now. You must have a pencil about you?

Solness (takes out his pocket-book). I have one here.

Hilda (lays the portfolio on the sofa-table). Very well. Now let us two sit down here, Mr. Solness. *(*SOLNESS *seats himself at the table.* HILDA *stands behind him, leaning over the back of the chair.)* And now we will write on the drawings. We must write very, very nicely and cordially—for this horrid Ruar—or whatever his name is.

Solness (writes a few words, turns his head and looks at her). Tell me one thing, Hilda.

Hilda. Yes!

Solness. If you have been waiting for me all these ten years——

Hilda. What then?

Solness. Why have you never written to me? Then I could have answered you.

Hilda (hastily). No, no, no! That was just what I did not want.

Solness. Why not?

Hilda. I was afraid the whole thing might fall to pieces. —But we were going to write on the drawings, Mr. Solness.

Solness. So we were.

Hilda (bends forward and looks over his shoulder while he writes). Mind now, kindly and cordially! Oh how I hate —how I hate this Ruald——

Solness (writing). Have you never really cared for any one, Hilda?

Hilda (harshly). What do you say?

Solness. Have you never cared for any one?

Hilda. For any one else, I suppose you mean?

Solness (looks up at her). For any one else, yes. Have you never? In all these ten years? Never?

Hilda. Oh, yes, now and then. When I was perfectly furious with you for not coming.

Solness. Then you did take an interest in other people, too?

Hilda. A little bit—for a week or so. Good heavens, Mr. Solness, you surely know how such things come about.

Solness. Hilda—what is it you have come for?

Hilda. Don't waste time talking. The poor old man might go and die in the meantime.

Solness. Answer me, Hilda. What do you want of me?

Hilda. I want my kingdom.

Solness. H'm——

[*He gives a rapid glance towards the door on the left and then goes on writing on the drawings. At the same moment* Mrs. Solness *enters; she has some packages in her hand.*

Mrs. Solness. Here are a few things I have got for you, Miss Wangel. The large parcels will be sent later on.

Hilda. Oh, how very, very kind of you!

Mrs. Solness. Only my simple duty. Nothing more than that.

Solness (reading over what he has written). Aline!

Mrs. Solness. Yes?

Solness. Did you notice whether the—the book-keeper was out there?

Mrs. Solness. Yes, of course, she was out there.

Solness (puts the drawings in the portfolio). H'm——

Mrs. Solness. She was standing at the desk, as she always is—when *I* go through the room.

Solness (rises). Then I'll give this to her and tell her that——

Hilda (takes the portfolio from him). Oh, no, let me have the pleasure of doing that! *(Goes to the door, but turns.)* What is her name?

Solness. Her name is Miss Fosli.

Hilda. Pooh, that sounds too cold! Her Christian name, I mean?

Solness. Kaia—I believe.

Hilda (opens the door and calls out). Kaia, come in here! Make haste! Mr. Solness wants to speak to you.

[KAIA FOSLI *appears at the door.*

Kaia (looking at him in alarm). Here I am——?

Hilda (handing her the portfolio). See here, Kaia! You can take this home; Mr. Solness has written on them now.

Kaia. Oh, at last!

Solness. Give them to the old man as soon as you can.

Kaia. I will go straight home with them.

Solness. Yes, do. Now Ragnar will have a chance of building for himself.

Kaia. Oh, may he come and thank you for all——?

Solness (harshly). I won't have any thanks! Tell him that from me.

Kaia. Yes, I will——

Solness. And tell him at the same time that henceforward I do not require his services—nor yours either.

Kaia (softly and quiveringly). Not mine either?

Solness. You will have other things to think of now and to attend to; and that is a very good thing for you. Well, go home with the drawings now, Miss Fosli. At once! Do you hear?

Kaia (as before). Yes, Mr. Solness.

[*She goes out.*

Mrs. Solness. Heavens! what deceitful eyes she has.

Solness. She? That poor little creature?

Mrs. Solness. Oh—I can see what I can see, Halvard. —— Are you really dismissing them?

Solness. Yes.

Mrs. Solness. Her as well?

Solness. Was not that what you wished?

Mrs. Solness. But how can you get on without her——? Oh, well, no doubt you have some one else in reserve, Halvard.

Hilda (playfully). Well, I for one am not the person to stand at that desk.

Solness. Never mind, never mind—it will be all right, Aline. Now all you have to do is to think about moving into our new home—as quickly as you can. This evening we will hang up the wreath—*(Turns to Hilda.)*—right on the very pinnacle of the tower. What do you say to that, Miss Hilda?

Hilda (looks at him with sparkling eyes). It will be splendid to see you so high up once more.

Solness. Me!

Mrs. Solness. For heaven's sake, Miss Wangel, don't imagine such a thing! My husband!—when he always gets so dizzy!

Hilda. He get dizzy! No, I know quite well he does not!

Mrs. Solness. Oh, yes, indeed he does.

Hilda. But I have seen him with my own eyes right up at the top of a high church-tower!

Mrs. Solness. Yes, I hear people talk of that; but it is utterly impossible——

Solness (vehemently). Impossible—impossible, yes! But there I stood all the same!

Mrs. Solness. Oh, how can you say so, Halvard? Why, you can't even bear to go out on the second-story balcony here. You have always been like that.

Solness. You may perhaps see something different this evening.

Mrs. Solness (in alarm). No, no, no! Please God I shall never see that. I will write at once to the doctor—and I am sure he won't let you do it.

Solness. Why, Aline——!

Mrs. Solness. Oh, you know you're ill, Halvard. This proves it! Oh God—Oh God!

[*She goes hastily out to the right.*

Hilda (looks intently at him). Is it so, or is it not?

Solness. That I turn dizzy?

Hilda. That my master builder dares not—cannot—climb as high as he builds?

Solness. Is that the way you look at it?

Hilda. Yes.

Solness. I believe there is scarcely a corner in me that is safe from you.

Hilda (looks towards the bow-window). Up there, then. Right up there——

Solness (approaches her). You might have the topmost room in the tower, Hilda—there you might live like a princess.

Hilda (indefinably, between earnest and jest). Yes, that is what you promised me.

Solness. Did I really?

Hilda. Fie, Mr. Solness! You said I should be a princess, and that you would give me a kingdom. And then you went and——Well!

Solness (cautiously). Are you quite certain that this is not a dream—a fancy, that has fixed itself in your mind?

Hilda (sharply). Do you mean that you did not do it?

Solness. I scarcely know myself. *(More softly.)* But now I know so much for certain, that I——

Hilda. That you——? Say it at once!

Solness. —that I ought to have done it.

Hilda (exclaims with animation). Don't tell me you can ever be dizzy!

Solness. This evening, then, we will hang up the wreath —Princess Hilda.

Hilda (with a bitter curve of the lips). Over your new home, yes.

Solness. Over the new house, which will never be a home for me.

[*He goes out through the garden door.*

Hilda (looks straight in front of her with a far-away expression and whispers to herself. The only words audible are) —frightfully thrilling——

ACT III

The large, broad verandah of SOLNESS'S *dwelling-house. Part of the house, with outer door leading to the verandah, is seen to the left. A railing along the verandah to the right. At the back, from the end of the verandah, a flight of steps leads down to the garden below. Tall old trees in the garden spread their branches over the verandah and towards the house. Far to the right, in among the trees, a glimpse is caught of the lower part of the new villa, with scaffolding round so much as is seen of the tower. In the background the garden is bounded by an old wooden fence. Outside the fence, a street with low, tumble-down cottages.*

Evening sky with sun-lit clouds.

On the verandah, a garden bench stands along the wall of the house, and in front of the bench a long table. On the other side of the table, an arm-chair and some stools. All the furniture is of wicker-work.

MRS. SOLNESS, *wrapped in a large white crape shawl, sits resting in the arm-chair and gazes over to the right. Shortly after,* HILDA WANGEL *comes up the flight of steps from the garden. She is dressed as in the last act and wears her hat. She has in her bodice a little nosegay of small common flowers.*

Mrs. Solness (turning her head a little). Have you been round the garden, Miss Wangel?

Hilda. Yes, I have been taking a look at it.

Mrs. Solness. And found some flowers, too, I see.

Hilda. Yes, indeed! There are such heaps of them in among the bushes.

Mrs. Solness. Are there really? Still? You see I scarcely ever go there.

Hilda (closer). What! Don't you take a run down into the garden every day, then?

Mrs. Solness (with a faint smile). I don't "run" anywhere, nowadays.

Hilda. Well, but do you not go down now and then to look at all the lovely things there?

Mrs. Solness. It has all become so strange to me. I am almost afraid to see it again.

Hilda. Your own garden!

Mrs. Solness. I don't feel that it is mine any longer.

Hilda. What do you mean——?

Mrs. Solness. No, no, it is not—not—not as it was in my mother's and father's time. They have taken away so much—so much of the garden, Miss Wangel. Fancy—they have parcelled it out—and built houses for strangers—people that I don't know. And they can sit and look in upon me from their windows.

Hilda (with a bright expression). Mrs. Solness!

Mrs. Solness. Yes!

Hilda. May I stay here with you a little?

Mrs. Solness. Yes, by all means, if you care to.

[HILDA *moves a stool close to the arm-chair and sits down.*

Hilda. Ah—here one can sit and sun oneself like a cat.

Mrs. Solness (lays her hand softly on HILDA'S *neck).* It is nice of you to be willing to sit with me. I thought you wanted to go in to my husband.

Hilda. What should I want with him?

Mrs. Solness. To help him, I thought.

Hilda. No, thank you. And besides, he is not in. He is over there with the workmen. But he looked so fierce that I did not care to talk to him.

Mrs. Solness. He is so kind and gentle in reality.

Hilda. He!

Mrs. Solness. You do not really know him yet, Miss Wangel.

Hilda (looks affectionately at her). Are you pleased at the thought of moving over to the new house?

Mrs. Solness. I ought to be pleased; for it is what Halvard wants——

Hilda. Oh, not just on that account, surely.

Mrs. Solness. Yes, yes, Miss Wangel; for it is only my duty to submit myself to him. But very often it is dreadfully difficult to force one's mind to obedience.

Hilda. Yes, that must be difficult indeed.

Mrs. Solness. I can tell you it is—when one has so many faults as I have——

Hilda. When one has gone through so much trouble as you have——

Mrs. Solness. How do you know about that?

Hilda. Your husband told me.

Mrs. Solness. To me he very seldom mentions these things.——Yes, I can tell you I have gone through more than enough trouble in my life, Miss Wangel.

Hilda (looks sympathetically at her and nods slowly). Poor Mrs. Solness. First of all there was the fire——

Mrs. Solness (with a sigh). Yes, everything that was mine was burnt.

Hilda. And then came what was worse.

Mrs. Solness (looking inquiringly at her). Worse?

Hilda. The worst of all.

Mrs. Solness. What do you mean?

Hilda (softly). You lost the two little boys.

Mrs. Solness. Oh, yes, the boys. But, you see, that was a thing apart. That was a dispensation of Providence; and in such things one can only bow in submission—yes, and be thankful, too.

Hilda. Then you are so?

Mrs. Solness. Not always, I am sorry to say. I know well enough that it is my duty—but all the same I cannot.

Hilda. No, no, I think that is only natural.

Mrs. Solness. And often and often I have to remind myself that it was a righteous punishment for me——

Hilda. Why?

Mrs. Solness. Because I had not fortitude enough in misfortune.

Hilda. But I don't see that——

Mrs. Solness. Oh, no, no, Miss Wangel—do not talk to me any more about the two little boys. We ought to feel nothing but joy in thinking of them; for they are so happy —so happy now. No, it is the small losses in life that cut one to the heart—the loss of all that other people look upon as almost nothing.

Hilda (lays her arms on MRS. SOLNESS's *knees and looks up at her affectionately).* Dear Mrs. Solness—tell me what things you mean!

Mrs. Solness. As I say, only little things. All the old portraits were burnt on the walls. And all the old silk dresses were burnt, that had belonged to the family for generations and generations. And all mother's and grandmother's lace—that was burnt, too. And only think—the jewels, too! *(Sadly.)* And then all the dolls.

Hilda. The dolls?

Mrs. Solness (choking with tears). I had nine lovely dolls.

Hilda. And they were burnt, too?

Mrs. Solness. All of them. Oh, it was hard—so hard for me.

Hilda. Had you put by all these dolls, then? Ever since you were little?

Mrs. Solness. I had not put them by. The dolls and I had gone on living together.

Hilda. After you were grown up?

Mrs. Solness. Yes, long after that.

Hilda. After you were married, too?

Mrs. Solness. Oh, yes, indeed. So long as he did not see it——. But they were all burnt up, poor things. No one thought of saving them. Oh, it is so miserable to think of. You mustn't laugh at me, Miss Wangel.

Hilda. I am not laughing in the least.

Mrs. Solness. For you see, in a certain sense, there was life in them, too. I carried them under my heart—like little unborn children.

[DR. HERDAL, *with his hat in his hand, comes out through the door and observes* MRS. SOLNESS *and* HILDA.

Dr. Herdal. Well, Mrs. Solness, so you are sitting out here catching cold?

Mrs. Solness. I find it so pleasant and warm here to-day.

Dr. Herdal. Yes, yes. But is there anything going on here? I got a note from you.

Mrs. Solness (rises). Yes, there is something I must talk to you about.

Dr. Herdal. Very well; then perhaps we had better go in. *(To* HILDA.*)* Still in your mountaineering dress, Miss Wangel?

Hilda (gaily, rising). Yes—in full uniform! But to-day I am not going climbing and breaking my neck. We two will stop quietly below and look on, doctor.

Dr. Herdal. What are we to look on at?

Mrs. Solness (softly, in alarm, to HILDA*).* Hush, hush—for God's sake! He is coming. Try to get that idea out of his head. And let us be friends, Miss Wangel. Don't you think we can?

Hilda (throws her arms impetuously round MRS. SOLNESS'S *neck).* Oh, if we only could!

Mrs. Solness (gently disengages herself). There, there, there! There he comes, doctor. Let me have a word with you.

Dr. Herdal. Is it about him?

Mrs. Solness. Yes, to be sure it's about him. Do come in.

[*She and the doctor enter the house. Next moment* SOLNESS *comes up from the garden by the flight of steps. A serious look comes over* HILDA'S *face.*

Solness (glances at the house-door, which is closed cautiously from within). Have you noticed, Hilda, that as soon as I come, she goes?

Hilda. I have noticed that as soon as you come, you make her go.

Solness. Perhaps so. But I cannot help it. *(Looks observantly at her.)* Are you cold, Hilda? I think you look cold.

Hilda. I have just come up out of a tomb.

Solness. What do you mean by that?

Hilda. That I have got chilled through and through, Mr. Solness.

Solness (slowly). I believe I understand——

Hilda. What brings you up here just now?

Solness. I caught sight of you from over there.

Hilda. But then you must have seen her too?

Solness. I knew she would go at once if I came.

Hilda. Is it very painful for you that she should avoid you in this way?

Solness. In one sense, it's a relief as well.

Hilda. Not to have her before your eyes?

Solness. Yes.

Hilda. Not to be always seeing how heavily the loss of the little boys weighs upon her?

Solness. Yes. Chiefly that.

[HILDA *drifts across the verandah with her hands behind her back, stops at the railing and looks out over the garden.*

Solness (after a short pause). Did you have a long talk with her?

[HILDA *stands motionless and does not answer.*

Solness. Had you a long talk, I asked?

[HILDA *is silent as before.*

Solness. What was she talking about, Hilda?

[HILDA *continues silent.*

Solness. Poor Aline! I suppose it was about the little boys.

Hilda (a nervous shudder runs through her; then she nods hurriedly once or twice).

Solness. She will never get over it—never in this world. *(Approaches her.)* Now you are standing there again like a statue; just as you stood last night.

Hilda (turns and looks at him, with great serious eyes). I am going away.

Solness (sharply). Going away!

Hilda. Yes.

Solness. But I won't allow you to!

Hilda. What am I to do here now?

Solness. Simply to be here, Hilda!

Hilda (measures him with a look). Oh, thank you. You know it wouldn't end there.

Solness (heedlessly). So much the better!

Hilda (vehemently). I cannot do any harm to one whom I know! I can't take away anything that belongs to her.

Solness. Who wants you to do that?

Hilda (continuing). A stranger, yes! for that is quite a different thing! A person I have never set eyes on. But one that I have come into close contact with——! Oh, no! Oh, no! Ugh!

Solness. Yes, but I never proposed you should.

Hilda. Oh, Mr. Solness, you know quite well what the end of it would be. And that is why I am going away.

Solness. And what is to become of me when you are gone? What shall I have to live for then?—After that?

Hilda (with the indefinable look in her eyes). It is surely not so hard for you. You have your duties to her. Live for those duties.

Solness. Too late. These powers—these—these——

Hilda. —devils——

Solness. Yes, these devils! And the troll within me as well—they have drawn all the life-blood out of her. *(Laughs in desperation.)* They did it for my happiness! Yes, yes! *(Sadly.)* And now she is dead—for my sake. And I am chained alive to a dead woman. *(In wild anguish.)* *I—I* who cannot live without joy in life!

[HILDA *moves round the table and seats herself on the bench, with her elbows on the table, and her head supported by her hands.*

Hilda (sits and looks at him awhile). What will you build next?

Solness (shakes his head). I don't believe I shall build much more.

Hilda. Not those cosy, happy homes for mother and father, and for the troop of children?

Solness. I wonder whether there will be any use for such homes in the coming time.

Hilda. Poor Mr. Solness! And you have gone all these ten years—and staked your whole life—on that alone.

Solness. Yes, you may well say so, Hilda.

Hilda (with an outburst). Oh, it all seems to me so foolish—so foolish!

Solness. All what?

Hilda. Not to be able to grasp at your own happiness—at your own life! Merely because some one you know happens to stand in the way!

Solness. One whom you have no right to set aside.

Hilda. I wonder whether one really has not the right! And yet, and yet——. Oh, if one could only sleep the whole thing away!

[*She lays her arms flat on the table, rests the left*

side of her head on her hands and shuts her eyes.

Solness (turns the arm-chair and sits down at the table). Had you a cosy, happy home—up there with your father, Hilda?

Hilda (without stirring, answers as if half asleep). I had only a cage.

Solness. And you are determined not to go back to it?

Hilda (as before). The wild bird never wants to go into the cage.

Solness. Rather range through the free air——

Hilda (still as before). The bird of prey loves to range——

Solness (lets his eyes rest on her). If only one had the viking-spirit in life——

Hilda (in her usual voice; opens her eyes but does not move). And the other thing? Say what that was!

Solness. A robust conscience.

[HILDA *sits erect on the bench, with animation. Her eyes have once more the sparkling expression of gladness.*

Hilda (nods to him). I know what you are going to build next!

Solness. Then you know more than I do, Hilda.

Hilda. Yes, builders are such stupid people.

Solness. What is it to be then?

Hilda (nods again). The castle.

Solness. What castle?

Hilda. My castle, of course.

Solness. Do you want a castle now?

Hilda. Don't you owe me a kingdom, I should like to know?

Solness. You say I do.

Hilda. Well—you admit you owe me this kingdom. And you can't have a kingdom without a royal castle, I should think!

Solness (more and more animated). Yes, they usually go together.

Hilda. Good! Then build it for me! This moment!

Solness (laughing). Must you have that on the instant, too?

Hilda. Yes, to be sure! For the ten years are up now, and I am not going to wait any longer. So—out with the castle, Mr. Solness!

Solness. It's no light matter to owe you anything, Hilda.

Hilda. You should have thought of that before. It is too late now. So—*(tapping the table)*—the castle on the table! It is my castle! I will have it at once!

Solness (more seriously, leans over towards her, with his arms on the table). What sort of castle have you imagined, Hilda?

[*Her expression becomes more and more veiled. She seems gazing inwards at herself.*

Hilda (slowly). My castle shall stand on a height—on a very great height—with a clear outlook on all sides, so that I can see far—far around.

Solness. And no doubt it is to have a high tower!

Hilda. A tremendously high tower. And at the very top of the tower there shall be a balcony. And I will stand out upon it——

Solness (involuntarily clutches at his forehead). How can you like to stand at such a dizzy height——?

Hilda. Yes, I will, right up there will I stand and look down on the other people—on those that are building churches, and homes for mother and father and the troop of children. And you may come up and look on at it, too.

Solness (in a low tone). Is the builder to be allowed to come up beside the princess?

Hilda. If the builder will.

Solness (more softly). Then I think the builder will come.

Hilda (nods). The builder—he will come.

Solness. But he will never be able to build any more. Poor builder!

Hilda (animated). Oh yes, he will! We two will set to work together. And then we will build the loveliest—the very loveliest—thing in all the world.

Solness (intently). Hilda—tell me what that is!

Hilda (looks smilingly at him, shakes her head a little, pouts and speaks as if to a child). Builders—they are such very—very stupid people.

Solness. Yes, no doubt they are stupid. But now tell me what it is—the loveliest thing in the world—that we two are to build together?

Hilda (is silent a little while, then says with an indefinable expression in her eyes). Castles in the air.

Solness. Castles in the air?

Hilda (nods). Castles in the air, yes! Do you know what sort of thing a castle in the air is?

Solness. It is the loveliest thing in the world, you say.

Hilda (rises with vehemence and makes a gesture of repulsion with her hand). Yes, to be sure it is! Castles in the air—they are so easy to take refuge in. And so easy to build, too—*(looks scornfully at him)*—especially for the builders who have a—a dizzy conscience.

Solness (rises). After this day we two will build together, Hilda.

Hilda (with a half-dubious smile). A real castle in the air?

Solness. Yes. One with a firm foundation under it.

[Ragnar Brovik *comes out from the house. He is carrying a large, green wreath with flowers and silk ribbons.*

Hilda (with an outburst of pleasure). The wreath! Oh, that will be glorious!

Solness (in surprise). Have you brought the wreath, Ragnar?

Ragnar. I promised the foreman I would.

Solness (relieved). Ah, then I suppose your father is better?

Ragnar. No.

Solness. Was he not cheered by what I wrote?

Ragnar. It came too late.

Solness. Too late!

Ragnar. When she came with it he was unconscious. He had had a stroke.

Solness. Why, then, you must go home to him! You must attend to your father!

Ragnar. He does not need me any more.

Solness. But surely you ought to be with him.

Ragnar. She is sitting by his bed.

Solness (rather uncertainly). Kaia?

Ragnar (looking darkly at him). Yes—Kaia.

Solness. Go home, Ragnar—both to him and to her. Give me the wreath.

Ragnar (suppresses a mocking smile). You don't mean that you yourself——?

Solness. I will take it down to them myself. *(Takes the wreath from him.)* And now you go home; we don't require you to-day.

Ragnar. I know you do not require me any more; but to-day I shall remain.

Solness. Well, remain then, since you are bent upon it.

Hilda (at the railing). Mr. Solness, I will stand here and look on at you.

Solness. At me!

Hilda. It will be fearfully thrilling.

Solness (in a low tone). We will talk about that presently, Hilda.

[*He goes down the flight of steps with the wreath and away through the garden.*

Hilda (looks after him, then turns to Ragnar*).* I think you might at least have thanked him.

Ragnar. Thanked him? Ought I to have thanked him?

Hilda. Yes, of course you ought!

Ragnar. I think it is rather you I ought to thank.

Hilda. How can you say such a thing?

Ragnar (without answering her). But I advise you to take care, Miss Wangel! For you don't know him rightly yet.

Hilda (ardently). Oh, no one knows him as I do!

Ragnar (laughs in exasperation). Thank him, when he has held me down year after year! When he made father disbelieve in me—made me disbelieve in myself! And all merely that he might——!

Hilda (as if divining something). That he might——? Tell me at once!

Ragnar. That he might keep her with him.

Hilda (with a start towards him). The girl at the desk.

Ragnar. Yes.

Hilda (threateningly, clenching her hands). That is not true! You are telling falsehoods about him!

Ragnar. I would not believe it either until to-day—when she said so herself.

Hilda (as if beside herself). What did she say? I will know! At once! at once!

Ragnar. She said that he had taken possession of her mind—her whole mind—centred all her thoughts upon himself alone. She says that she can never leave him—that she will remain here, where he is——

Hilda (with flashing eyes). She will not be allowed to!

Ragnar (as if feeling his way). Who will not allow her?

Hilda (rapidly). He will not either!

Ragnar. Oh no—I understand the whole thing now. After this, she would merely be—in the way.

Hilda. You understand nothing—since you can talk like that! No, *I* will tell you why he kept hold of her.

Ragnar. Well then, why?

Hilda. In order to keep hold of you.

Ragnar. Has he told you so?

Hilda. No, but it is so. It must be so! *(Wildly.)* I will—I will have it so!

Ragnar. And at the very moment when you came—he let her go.

Hilda. It was you—you that he let go. What do you suppose he cares about strange women like her?

Ragnar (reflects). Is it possible that all this time he has been afraid of me?

Hilda. He afraid! I would not be so conceited if I were you.

Ragnar. Oh, he must have seen long ago that I had something in me, too. Besides—cowardly—that is just what he is, you see.

Hilda. He! Oh, yes, I am likely to believe that!

Ragnar. In a certain sense he is cowardly—he, the great master builder. He is not afraid of robbing others of their life's happiness—as he has done both for my father and for me. But when it comes to climbing up a paltry bit of scaffolding—he will do anything rather than that.

Hilda. Oh, you should just have seen him high, high up—at the dizzy height where I once saw him.

Ragnar. Did you see that?

Hilda. Yes, indeed I did. How free and great he looked as he stood and fastened the wreath to the church-vane!

Ragnar. I know that he ventured that, once in his life—one solitary time. It is a legend among us younger men. But no power on earth would induce him to do it again.

Hilda. To-day he will do it again!

Ragnar (scornfully). Yes, I daresay!

Hilda. We shall see it!

Ragnar. That neither you nor I will see.

Hilda (with uncontrollable vehemence). I will see it! I will and must see it!

Ragnar. But he will not do it. He simply dare not do it. For you see he cannot get over this infirmity—master builder though he be.

[Mrs. Solness *comes from the house on to the verandah.*

Mrs. Solness (looks around). Is he not here? Where has he gone to?

Ragnar. Mr. Solness is down with the men.

Hilda. He took the wreath with him.

Mrs. Solness (terrified). Took the wreath with him! Oh, God! oh, God! Brovik—you must go down to him! Get him to come back here!

Ragnar. Shall I say you want to speak to him, Mrs. Solness?

Mrs. Solness. Oh, yes, do!—No, no—don't say that *I* want anything! You can say that somebody is here, and that he must come at once.

Ragnar. Good. I will do so, Mrs. Solness.

[*He goes down the flight of steps and away through the garden.*

Mrs. Solness. Oh, Miss Wangel, you can't think how anxious I feel about him.

Hilda. Is there anything in this to be so terribly frightened about?

Mrs. Solness. Oh, yes; surely you can understand. Just think, if he were really to do it! If he should take it into his head to climb up the scaffolding!

Hilda (eagerly). Do you think he will?

Mrs. Solness. Oh, one can never tell what he might take into his head. I am afraid there is nothing he mightn't think of doing.

Hilda. Aha! Perhaps you too think that he is—well——?

Mrs. Solness. Oh, I don't know what to think about him now. The doctor has been telling me all sorts of things; and putting it all together with several things I have heard him say——

[Dr. Herdal *looks out, at the door*

Dr. Herdal. Is he not coming soon?

Mrs. Solness. Yes, I think so. I have sent for him at any rate.

Dr. Herdal (advancing). I am afraid you will have to go in, my dear lady——

Mrs. Solness. Oh, no! Oh, no! I shall stay out here and wait for Halvard.

Dr. Herdal. But some ladies have just come to call on you——

Mrs. Solness. Good heavens, that too! And just at this moment!

Dr. Herdal. They say they positively must see the ceremony.

Mrs. Solness. Well, well, I suppose I must go to them after all. It is my duty.

Hilda. Can't you ask the ladies to go away?

Mrs. Solness. No, that would never do. Now that they are here, it is my duty to see them. But do you stay out here in the meantime—and receive him when he comes.

Dr. Herdal. And try to occupy his attention as long as possible——

Mrs. Solness. Yes, do, dear Miss Wangel. Keep a firm hold of him as ever you can.

Hilda. Would it not be best for you to do that?

Mrs. Solness. Yes; God knows that is my duty. But when one has duties in so many directions——

Dr. Herdal (looks towards the garden). There he is coming.

Mrs. Solness. And I have to go in!

Dr. Herdal (to Hilda). Don't say anything about my being here.

Hilda. Oh, no! I daresay I shall find something else to talk to Mr. Solness about.

Mrs. Solness. And be sure you keep firm hold of him. I believe you can do it best.

[MRS. SOLNESS *and* DR. HERDAL *go into the house.*

HILDA *remains standing on the verandah.* SOLNESS *comes from the garden, up the flight of steps.*

Solness. Somebody wants me, I hear.

Hilda. Yes; it is I, Mr. Solness.

Solness. Oh, is it you, Hilda? I was afraid it might be Aline or the Doctor.

Hilda. You are very easily frightened, it seems!

Solness. Do you think so?

Hilda. Yes; people say that you are afraid to climb about—on the scaffoldings, you know.

Solness. Well, that is quite a special thing.

Hilda. Then it is true that you are afraid to do it?

Solness. Yes, I am.

Hilda. Afraid of falling down and killing yourself?

Solness. No, not of that.

Hilda. Of what, then?

Solness. I am afraid of retribution, Hilda.

Hilda. Of retribution? *(Shakes her head.)* I don't understand that.

Solness. Sit down and I will tell you something.

Hilda. Yes, do! At once!

[*She sits on a stool by the railing and looks expectantly at him.*

Solness (throws his hat on the table). You know that I began by building churches.

Hilda (nods). I know that well.

Solness. For, you see, I came as a boy from a pious home in the country; and so it seemed to me that this church-building was the noblest task I could set myself.

Hilda. Yes, yes.

Solness. And I venture to say that I built those poor little churches with such honest and warm and heartfelt devotion that—that——

Hilda. That——? Well?

Solness. Well, that I think that he ought to have been pleased with me.

Hilda. He? What he?

Solness. He who was to have the churches, of course! He to whose honour and glory they were dedicated.

Hilda. Oh, indeed! But are you certain, then, that—that he was not—pleased with you?

Solness (scornfully). He pleased with me! How can you talk so, Hilda? He who gave the troll in me leave to lord it just as it pleased. He who bade them be at hand to serve me, both day and night—all these—all these——

Hilda. Devils——

Solness. Yes, of both kinds. Oh, no, he made me feel clearly enough that he was not pleased with me. *(Mysteriously.)* You see, that was really the reason why he made the old house burn down.

Hilda. Was that why?

Solness. Yes, don't you understand? He wanted to give me the chance of becoming an accomplished master in my own sphere—so that I might build all the more glorious churches for him. At first I did not understand what he was driving at; but all of a sudden it flashed upon me.

Hilda. When was that?

Solness. It was when I was building the church-tower up at Lysanger.

Hilda. I thought so.

Solness. For you see, Hilda—up there, amidst those new surroundings, I used to go about musing and pondering within myself. Then I saw plainly why he had taken my little children from me. It was that I should have nothing else to attach myself to. No such thing as love and happiness, you understand. I was to be only a master builder—nothing else. And all my life long I was to go on building for him. *(Laughs.)* But I can tell you nothing came of that!

Hilda. What did you do, then?

Solness. First of all, I searched and tried my own heart——

Hilda. And then?

Solness. Then I did the impossible—I no less than he.

Hilda. The impossible?

Solness. I had never before been able to climb up to a great, free height. But that day I did it.

Hilda (leaping up). Yes, yes, you did!

Solness. And when I stood there, high over everything, and was hanging the wreath over the vane, I said to him: Hear me now, thou Mighty One! From this day forward I will be a free builder—I, too, in my sphere—just as thou in thine. I will never more build churches for thee—only homes for human beings.

Hilda (with great sparkling eyes). That was the song that I heard through the air!

Solness. But afterwards his turn came.

Hilda. What do you mean by that?

Solness (looks despondently at her). Building homes for human beings—is not worth a rap, Hilda.

Hilda. Do you say that now?

Solness. Yes, for now I see it. Men have no use for these homes of theirs—to be happy in. And I should not have had any use for such a home, if I had had one. *(With a quiet, bitter laugh.)* See, that is the upshot of the whole affair, however far back I look. Nothing really built; nor anything sacrificed for the chance of building. Nothing, nothing! the whole is nothing.

Hilda. Then you will never build anything more?

Solness (with animation). On the contrary, I am just going to begin!

Hilda. What, then? What will you build? Tell me at once!

Solness. I believe there is only one possible dwelling-place for human happiness—and that is what I am going to build now.

Hilda (looks fixedly at him). Mr. Solness—you mean our castle?

Solness. The castles in the air—yes.

Hilda. I am afraid you would turn dizzy before we got half-way up.

Solness. Not if I can mount hand in hand with you, Hilda.

Hilda (with an expression of suppressed resentment). Only with me? Will there be no others of the party?

Solness. Who else should there be?

Hilda. Oh—that girl—that Kaia at the desk. Poor thing—don't you want to take her with you, too?

Solness. Oho! Was it about her that Aline was talking to you?

Hilda. Is it so—or is it not?

Solness (vehemently). I will not answer such a question. You must believe in me, wholly and entirely!

Hilda. All these ten years I have believed in you so utterly—so utterly.

Solness. You must go on believing in me!

Hilda. Then let me see you stand free and high up!

Solness (sadly). Oh Hilda—it is not every day that I can do that.

Hilda (passionately). I will have you do it! I will have it! *(Imploringly.)* Just once more, Mr. Solness! Do the impossible once again!

Solness (stands and looks deep into her eyes). If I try it, Hilda, I will stand up there and talk to him as I did that time before.

Hilda (in rising excitement). What will you say to him?

Solness. I will say to him: Hear me, Mighty Lord—thou may'st judge me as seems best to thee. But hereafter I will build nothing but the loveliest thing in the world——

Hilda (carried away). Yes—yes—yes!

Solness. —build it together with a princess, whom I love——

Hilda. Yes, tell him that! Tell him that!

Solness. Yes. And then I will say to him: Now I shall go down and throw my arms round her and kiss her——

Hilda. —many times! Say that!

Solness. —many, many times, I will say.

Hilda. And then——?

Solness. Then I wiil wave my hat—and come down to the earth—and do as I said to him.

Hilda (with outstretched arms). Now I see you again as I did when there was song in the air.

Solness (looks at her with his head bowed). How have you become what you are, Hilda?

Hilda. How have you made me what I am?

Solness (shortly and firmly). The princess shall have her castle.

Hilda (jubilant, clapping her hands). Oh, Mr. Solness——! My lovely, lovely castle. Our castle in the air!

Solness. On a firm foundation.

[*In the street a crowd of people has assembled, vaguely seen through the trees. Music of wind-instruments is heard far away behind the new house.*

[MRS. SOLNESS, *with a fur collar round her neck,* DOCTOR HERDAL *with her white shawl on his arm, and some ladies, come out on the verandah.* RAGNAR BROVIK *comes at the same time up from the garden.*

Mrs. Solness (to RAGNAR*).* Are we to have music, too?

Ragnar. Yes. It's the band of the Mason's Union. *(To* SOLNESS.*)* The foreman asked me to tell you that he is ready now to go up with the wreath.

Solness (takes his hat). Good. I will go down to him myself.

Mrs. Solness (anxiously). What have you to do down there, Halvard?

Solness (curtly). I must be down below with the men.

Mrs. Solness. Yes, down below—only down below.

Solness. That is where I always stand—on everyday occasions.

[*He goes down the flight of steps and away through the garden.*

Mrs. Solness (calls after him over the railing). But do beg the man to be careful when he goes up? Promise me that, Halvard!

Dr. Herdal (to Mrs. Solness*).* Don't you see that I was right? He has given up all thought of that folly.

Mrs. Solness. Oh, what a relief! Twice workmen have fallen, and each time they were killed on the spot. *(Turns to* Hilda.*)* Thank you, Miss Wangel, for having kept such a firm hold upon him. I should never have been able to manage him.

Dr. Herdal (playfully). Yes, yes, Miss Wangel, you know how to keep firm hold on a man, when you give your mind to it.

[Mrs. Solness *and* Dr. Herdal *go up to the ladies, who are standing nearer to the steps and looking over the garden.* Hilda *remains standing beside the railing in the foreground.* Ragnar *goes up to her.*

Ragnar (with suppressed laughter, half whispering). Miss Wangel—do you see all those young fellows down in the street?

Hilda. Yes.

Ragnar. They are my fellow-students, come to look at the master.

Hilda. What do they want to look at him for?

Ragnar. They want to see how he daren't climb to the top of his own house.

Hilda. Oh, that is what those boys want, is it?

Ragnar (spitefully and scornfully). He has kept us down so long—now we are going to see him keep quietly down below himself.

Hilda. You will not see that—not this time.

Ragnar (smiles). Indeed! Then where shall we see him?

Hilda. High—high up by the vane! That is where you will see him!

Ragnar (laughs). Him! Oh, yes, I daresay!

Hilda. His will is to reach the top—so at the top you shall see him.

Ragnar. His will, yes; that I can easily believe. But he simply cannot do it. His head would swim round, long, long before he got half-way. He would have to crawl down again on his hands and knees.

Dr. Herdal (points across). Look! There goes the foreman up the ladders.

Mrs. Solness. And of course he has the wreath to carry, too. Oh, I do hope he will be careful!

Ragnar (stares incredulously and shouts). Why, but it's——

Hilda (breaking out in jubilation). It is the master builder himself!

Mrs. Solness (screams with terror). Yes, it is Halvard! Oh, my great God——! Halvard! Halvard!

Dr. Herdal. Hush! Don't shout to him!

Mrs. Solness (half beside herself). I must go to him! I must get him to come down again!

Dr. Herdal (holds her). Don't move, any of you! Not a sound!

Hilda (immovable, follows Solness *with her eyes).* He climbs and climbs. Higher and higher! Higher and higher! Look! Just look!

Ragnar (breathless). He must turn now. He can't possibly help it.

Hilda. He climbs and climbs. He will soon be at the top now.

Mrs. Solness. Oh, I shall die of terror. I cannot bear to see it.

Dr. Herdal. Then don't look up at him.

Hilda. There he is standing on the topmost planks. Right at the top!

Dr. Herdal. Nobody must move! Do you hear?

Hilda (exulting, with quiet intensity). At last! At last! Now I see him great and free again!

Ragnar (almost voiceless). But this is im——

Hilda. So I have seen him all through these ten years. How secure he stands! Frightfully thrilling all the same. Look at him! Now he is hanging the wreath round the vane.

Ragnar. I feel as if I were looking at something utterly impossible.

Hilda. Yes, it is the impossible that he is doing now! *(With the indefinable expression in her eyes.)* Can you see any one else up there with him?

Ragnar. There is no one else.

Hilda. Yes, there is one he is striving with.

Ragnar. You are mistaken.

Hilda. Then do you hear no song in the air, either?

Ragnar. It must be the wind in the tree-tops.

Hilda. *I* hear a song—a mighty song! *(Shouts in wild jubilation and glee.)* Look, look! Now he is waving his hat! He is waving it to us down here! Oh, wave, wave back to him. For now it is finished! *(Snatches the white shawl from the Doctor, waves it and shouts up to* SOLNESS.*)* Hurrah for Master Builder Solness!

Dr. Herdal. Stop! Stop! For God's sake——!

[*The ladies on the verandah wave their pocket-handkerchiefs, and the shouts of "Hurrah" are taken up in the street below. Then they are suddenly silenced, and the crowd bursts out into a shriek of horror. A human body, with planks and fragments of wood, is vaguely perceived crashing down behind the trees.*

Mrs. Solness and the Ladies (at the same time). He is falling! He is falling!

[MRS. SOLNESS *totters, falls backwards, swooning, and is caught, amid cries and confusion, by the ladies. The crowd in the street breaks down the fence and storms into the garden. At the same time* DR. HERDAL, *too, rushes down thither. A short pause.*

Hilda (stares fixedly upwards and says, as if petrified). My Master Builder.

Ragnar (supports himself, trembling, against the railing). He must be dashed to pieces—killed on the spot.

One of the Ladies (whilst MRS. SOLNESS *is carried into the house).* Run down for the doctor——

Ragnar. I can't stir a foot——

Another Lady. Then call to some one!

Ragnar (tries to call out). How is it? Is he alive?

A Voice (below in the garden). Mr. Solness is dead!

Other Voices (nearer). The head is all crushed.——He fell right into the quarry.

Hilda (turns to RAGNAR *and says quietly).* I can't see him up there now.

Ragnar. This is terrible. So, after all, he could not do it.

Hilda (as if in quiet spell-bound triumph). But he mounted right to the top. And I heard harps in the air. *(Waves her shawl in the air, and shrieks with wild intensity.)* My—my Master Builder!

PILLARS OF SOCIETY
(1877)

CHARACTERS

KARSTEN BERNICK, *a shipbuilder.*
MRS. BERNICK, *his wife.*
OLAF, *their son, thirteen years old.*
MARTHA BERNICK, *Karsten Bernick's sister.*
JOHAN TÖNNESEN, *Mrs. Bernick's younger brother.*
LONA HESSEL, *Mrs. Bernick's elder half-sister.*
HILMAR TÖNNESEN, *Mrs. Bernick's cousin.*
DINA DORF, *a young girl living with the Bernicks.*
RÖRLUND, *a schoolmaster.*
RUMMEL, *a merchant.*
VIGELAND } *tradesmen.*
SANDSTAD }
KRAP, *Bernick's confidential clerk.*
AUNE, *foreman of Bernick's shipbuilding yard.*
MRS. RUMMEL.
HILDA RUMMEL, *her daughter.*
MRS. HOLT.
NETTA HOLT, *her daughter.*
MRS. LYNGE.
Townsfolk and visitors, foreign sailors, steamboat passengers, etc., etc.

The action takes place at the BERNICKS' *house in one of the smaller coast towns in Norway.*

PILLARS OF SOCIETY

ACT I

SCENE.—*A spacious garden room in the* BERNICKS' *house. In the foreground on the left is a door leading to* BERNICK'S *business room; farther back in the same wall, a similar door. In the middle of the opposite wall is a large entrance door, which leads to the street. The wall in the background is almost wholly composed of plate-glass; a door in it opens upon a broad flight of steps which lead down to the garden; a sun-awning is stretched over the steps. Below the steps a part of the garden is visible, bordered by a fence with a small gate in it. On the other side of the fence runs a street, the opposite side of which is occupied by small wooden houses painted in bright colours. It is summer, and the sun is shining warmly. People are seen, every now and then, passing along the street and stopping to talk to one another; others going in and out of a shop at the corner; etc., etc.*

In the room a gathering of ladies is seated round a table. MRS. BERNICK *is presiding; on her left side are* MRS. HOLT *and her daughter* NETTA, *and next to them* MRS. RUMMEL *and* HILDA RUMMEL. *On* MRS. BERNICK'S *right are* MRS. LYNGE, MARTHA BERNICK *and* DINA DORF. *All the ladies are busy working. On the table lie great piles of linen garments and other articles of clothing, some half finished and some merely cut out. Farther back, at a small table on which two pots of flowers and a glass of sugared water are standing,* Rörlund *is sitting, reading aloud from a book with gilt edges, but only loud enough for the spectators to catch a word now and then. Out in the garden* Olaf Bernick *is running about and shooting at a target with a toy crossbow.*

After a moment Aune *comes in quietly through the door on the right. There is a slight interruption in the reading.* Mrs. Bernick *nods to him and points to the door on the left.* Aune *goes quietly across, knocks softly at the door of* Bernick's *room and, after a moment's pause, knocks again.* Krap *comes out of the room, with his hat in his hand and some papers under his arm.*

Krap. Oh, it was you knocking?

Aune. Mr. Bernick sent for me.

Krap. He did; but he cannot see you. He has deputed me to tell you——

Aune. Deputed you? All the same, I would much rather——

Krap. ——deputed me to tell you what he wanted to say to you. You must give up these Saturday lectures of yours to the men.

Aune. Indeed? I supposed I might use my own time ——

Krap. You must not use your own time in making the men useless in working hours. Last Saturday you were talking to them of the harm that would be done to the workmen by our new machines and the new working methods at the yard. What makes you do that?

Aune. I do it for the good of the community.

Krap. That's curious, because Mr. Bernick says it is disorganising the community.

Aune. My community is not Mr. Bernick's, Mr. Krap! As president of the Industrial Association, I must——

Krap. You are, first and foremost, president of Mr. Bernick's shipbuilding yard; and, before everything else, you have to do your duty to the community known as the firm of Bernick & Co.; that is what every one of us lives for. Well, now you know what Mr. Bernick had to say to you.

Aune. Mr. Bernick would not have put it that way, Mr. Krap! But I know well enough whom I have to thank for this. It is that damned American boat. Those fellows expect to get work done here the way they are accustomed to it over there, and that——

Krap. Yes, yes, but I can't go into all these details. You know now what Mr. Bernick means, and that is sufficient. Be so good as to go back to the yard; probably you are needed there. I shall be down myself in a little while.—Excuse me, ladies!

[*Bows to the ladies and goes out through the garden and down the street.* AUNE *goes quietly out to the right.* RÖRLUND, *who has continued his reading during the foregoing conversation, which has been carried on in low tones, has now come to the end of the book and shuts it with a bang.*

Rörlund. There, my dear ladies, that is the end of it.

Mrs. Rummel. What an instructive tale!

Mrs. Holt. And such a good moral!

Mrs. Bernick. A book like that really gives one something to think about.

Rörlund. Quite so; it presents a salutary contrast to what, unfortunately, meets our eyes every day in the newspapers and magazines. Look at the gilded and painted exterior displayed by any large community, and think what it really conceals!—emptiness and rottenness, if I may say so; no foundation of morality beneath it. In a word, these large communities of ours now-a-days are whited sepulchres.

Mrs. Holt. How true! How true!

Mrs. Rummel. And for an example of it we need look

no farther than at the crew of the American ship that is lying here just now.

Rörlund. Oh, I would rather not speak of such offscourings of humanity as that. But even in higher circles—what is the case there? A spirit of doubt and unrest on all sides; minds never at peace, and instability characterising all their behaviour. Look how completely family life is undermined over there! Look at their shameless love of casting doubt on even the most serious truths!

Dina (without looking up from her work). But are there not many big things done there too?

Rörlund. Big things done——? I do not understand ——.

Mrs. Holt (in amazement). Good gracious, Dina——!

Mrs. Rummel (in the same breath). Dina, how can you——?

Rörlund. I think it would scarcely be a good thing for us if such "big things" became the rule here. No, indeed, we ought to be only too thankful that things are as they are in this country. It is true enough that tares grow up amongst our wheat here, too, alas; but we do our best conscientiously to weed them out as well as we are able. The important thing is to keep society pure, ladies—to ward off all the hazardous experiments that a restless age seeks to force upon us.

Mrs. Holt. And there are more than enough of them in the wind, unhappily.

Mrs. Rummel. Yes, you know last year we only by a hair's breadth escaped the project of having a railway here.

Mrs. Bernick. Ah, my husband prevented that.

Rörlund. Providence, Mrs. Bernick. You may be certain that your husband was the instrument of a higher Power when he refused to have anything to do with the scheme.

Mrs. Bernick. And yet they said such horrible things about him in the newspapers! But we have quite forgotten to thank you, Mr. Rörlund. It is really more than friendly of you to sacrifice so much of your time to us.

Rörlund. Not at all. This is holiday time, and——

Mrs. Bernick. Yes, but it is a sacrifice all the same, Mr. Rörlund.

Rörlund (drawing his chair nearer). Don't speak of it, my dear lady. Are you not all of you making some sacrifice in a good cause?—and that willingly and gladly? These poor fallen creatures for whose rescue we are working may be compared to soldiers wounded on the field of battle; you, ladies, are the kind-hearted sisters of mercy who prepare the lint for these stricken ones, lay the bandages softly on their wounds, heal them and cure them——

Mrs. Bernick. It must be a wonderful gift to be able to see everything in such a beautiful light.

Rörlund. A good deal of it is inborn in one—but it can be to a great extent acquired, too. All that is needful is to see things in the light of a serious mission in life. *(To* MARTHA:*)* What do you say, Miss Bernick? Have you not felt as if you were standing on firmer ground since you gave yourself up to your school work?

Martha. I really do not know what to say. There are times, when I am in the schoolroom down there, that I wish I were far away out on the stormy seas.

Rörlund. That is merely temptation, dear Miss Bernick. You ought to shut the doors of your mind upon such disturbing guests as that. By the "stormy seas"—for of course you do not intend me to take your words literally—you mean the restless tide of the great outer world, where so many are shipwrecked. Do you really set such store on the life you hear rushing by outside? Only look out into the street. There they go, walking about in the heat of the sun, perspiring and tumbling about over their little affairs. No, we undoubtedly have the best of it, who are able to sit here in the cool and turn our backs on the quarter from which disturbance comes.

Martha. Yes, I have no doubt you are perfectly right——

Rörlund. And in a house like this—in a good and pure home, where family life shows in its fairest colours—where peace and harmony rule—— *(To* MRS. BERNICK:*)* What are you listening to, Mrs. Bernick?

Mrs. Bernick (who has turned towards the door of BERNICK'S *room).* They are talking very loud in there.

Rörlund. Is there anything particular going on?

Mrs. Bernick. I don't know. I can hear that there is somebody with my husband.

[HILMAR TÖNNESEN, *smoking a cigar, appears in the doorway on the right, but stops short at the sight of the company of ladies.*

Hilmar. Oh, excuse me—— [*Turns to go back.*

Mrs. Bernick. No, Hilmar, come along in; you are not disturbing us. Do you want something?

Hilmar. No, I only wanted to look in here.—Good morning, ladies. *(To* MRS. BERNICK.*)* Well, what is the result?

Mrs. Bernick. Of what?

Hilmar. Karsten has summoned a meeting, you know.

Mrs. Bernick. Has he? What about?

Hilmar. Oh, it is this railway nonsense over again.

Mrs. Rummel. Is it possible?

Mrs. Bernick. Poor Karsten, is he to have more annoyance over that?

Rörlund. But how do you explain that, Mr. Tönnesen? You know that last year Mr. Bernick made it perfectly clear that he would not have a railway here.

Hilmar. Yes, that is what I thought, too; but I met Krap, his confidential clerk, and he told me that the railway project had been taken up again, and that Mr. Bernick was in consultation with three of our local capitalists.

Mrs. Rummel. Ah, I was right in thinking I heard my husband's voice.

Hilmar. Of course Mr. Rummel is in it, and so are Sandstad and Michael Vigeland—"Saint Michael," as they call him.

Rörlund. Ahem!

Hilmar. I beg your pardon, Mr. Rörlund?

Mrs. Bernick. Just when everything was so nice and peaceful.

Hilmar. Well, as far as I am concerned, I have not the slightest objection to their beginning their squabbling again. It will be a little diversion, anyway.

Rörlund. I think we can dispense with that sort of diversion.

Hilmar. It depends how you are constituted. Certain natures feel the lust of battle now and then. But, unfortunately, life in a country town does not offer much in that way, and it isn't given to every one to—*(turns the leaves of the book* RÖRLUND *has been reading).* "Woman as the Handmaid of Society." What sort of drivel is this?

Mrs. Bernick. My dear Hilmar, you must not say that. You certainly have not read the book.

Hilmar. No, and I have no intention of reading it, either.

Mrs. Bernick. Surely you are not feeling quite well today.

Hilmar. No, I am not.

Mrs. Bernick. Perhaps you did not sleep well last night?

Hilmar. No, I slept very badly. I went for a walk yesterday evening for my health's sake; and I finished up at the club and read a book about a Polar expedition. There is something bracing in following the adventures of men who are battling with the elements.

Mrs. Rummel. But it does not appear to have done you much good, Mr. Tönnesen.

Hilmar. No, it certainly did not. I lay all night tossing about, only half asleep, and dreamt that I was being chased by a hideous walrus.

Olaf (who meanwhile has come up the steps from the garden). Have you been chased by a walrus, uncle?

Hilmar. I dreamt it, you duffer! Do you mean to say you are still playing about with that ridiculous bow? Why don't you get hold of a real gun.

Olaf. I should like to, but——

Hilmar. There is some sense in a thing like that; it is always an excitement every time you fire it off.

Olaf. And then I could shoot bears, uncle. But daddy won't let me.

Mrs. Bernick. You really mustn't put such ideas into his head, Hilmar.

Hilmar. Hm!—it's a nice breed we are educating up now-a-days, isn't it! We *talk* a great deal about manly sports, goodness knows—but we only play with the question, all the same; there is never any serious inclination for the bracing discipline that lies in facing danger manfully. Don't stand pointing your crossbow at me, blockhead—it might go off.

Olaf. No, uncle, there is no arrow in it.

Hilmar. You don't know that there isn't—there may be, all the same. Take it away, I tell you!—Why on earth have you never gone over to America on one of your father's ships? You might have seen a buffalo hunt then, or a fight with Red Indians.

Mrs. Bernick. Oh, Hilmar——!

Olaf. I should like that awfully, uncle; and then perhaps I might meet Uncle Johan and Aunt Lona.

Hilmar. Hm!—Rubbish.

Mrs. Bernick. You can go down into the garden again now, Olaf.

Olaf. Mother, may I go out into the street, too?

Mrs. Bernick. Yes, but not too far, mind.

[OLAF *runs down into the garden and out through the gate in the fence.*

Rörlund. You ought not to put such fancies into the child's head, Mr. Tönnesen.

Hilmar. No, of course he is destined to be a miserable stay-at-home, like so many others.

Rörlund. But why do you not take a trip over there yourself?

Hilmar. I? With my wretched health? Of course I get no consideration on that account. But putting that out of the question, you forget that one has certain obligations to perform towards the community of which one forms a part. There must be *some one* here to hold aloft the banner of the Ideal.—Ugh, there he is shouting again!

The Ladies. Who is shouting?

Hilmar. I am sure I don't know. They are raising their voices so loud in there that it gets on my nerves.

Mrs. Bernick. I expect it is my husband, Mr. Tönnesen. But you must remember he is so accustomed to addressing large audiences——

Rörlund. I should not call the others low-voiced, either.

Hilmar. Good Lord, no!—not on any question that touches their pockets. Everything here ends in these petty material considerations. Ugh!

Mrs. Bernick. Anyway, that is a better state of things than it used to be when everything ended in mere frivolity.

Mrs. Lynge. Used things really to be as bad as that here?

Mrs. Rummel. Indeed they were, Mrs. Lynge. You may think yourself lucky that you did not live here then.

Mrs. Holt. Yes, times have changed, and no mistake. When I look back to the days when I was a girl——

Mrs. Rummel. Oh, you need not look back more than fourteen or fifteen years. God forgive us, what a life we led! There used to be a Dancing Society and a Musical Society——

Mrs. Bernick. And the Dramatic Club. I remember it very well.

Mrs. Rummel. Yes, that was where your play was performed, Mr. Tönnesen?

Hilmar (from the back of the room). What, what?

Rörlund. A play by Mr. Tönnesen?

Mrs. Rummel. Yes, it was long before you came here, Mr. Rörlund. And it was only performed once.

Mrs. Lynge. Was that not the play in which you told me you took the part of a young man's sweetheart, Mrs. Rummel?

Mrs. Rummel (glancing towards RÖRLUND*).* I? I really cannot remember, Mrs. Lynge. But I remember well all the riotous gaiety that used to go on.

Mrs. Holt. Yes, there were houses I could name in which two large dinner-parties were given in one week.

Mrs. Lynge. And surely I have heard that a touring theatrical company came here, too?

Mrs. Rummel. Yes, that was the worst thing of the lot ——

Mrs. Holt (uneasily). Ahem!

Mrs. Rummel. Did you say a theatrical company? No, I don't remember that at all.

Mrs. Lynge. Oh, yes, and I have been told they played all sorts of mad pranks. What is really the truth of those stories?

Mrs. Rummel. There is practically no truth in them, Mrs. Lynge.

Mrs. Holt. Dina, my love, will you give me that linen?

Mrs. Bernick (at the same time). Dina, dear, will you go and ask Katrine to bring us our coffee?

Martha. I will go with you, Dina.

[DINA *and* MARTHA *go out by the farther door on the left.*

Mrs. Bernick (getting up). Will you excuse me for a few minutes? I think we will have our coffee outside

[*She goes out to the verandah and sets to work to lay a table.* RÖRLUND *stands in the doorway talking to her.* HILMAR *sits outside, smoking.*

Mrs. Rummel (in a low voice). My goodness, Mrs. Lynge, how you frightened me!

Mrs. Lynge. I?

Mrs. Holt. Yes, but you know it was you that began it, Mrs. Rummel.

Mrs. Rummel. I? How can you say such a thing, Mrs. Holt? Not a syllable passed my lips!

Mrs. Lynge. But what does it all mean?

Mrs. Rummel. What made you begin to talk about——? Think—did you not see that Dina was in the room?

Mrs. Lynge. Dina? Good gracious, is there anything wrong with——?

Mrs. Holt. And in this house, too! Did you not know it was Mrs. Bernick's brother——?

Mrs. Lynge. What about him? I know nothing about it at all; I am quite new to the place, you know.

Mrs. Rummel. Have you not heard that——? Ahem! *(To her daughter.)* Hilda, dear, you can go for a little stroll in the garden.

Mrs. Holt. You go, too, Netta. And be very kind to poor Dina when she comes back.

[HILDA *and* NETTA *go out into the garden.*

Mrs. Lynge. Well, what about Mrs. Bernick's brother?

Mrs. Rummel. Don't you know the dreadful scandal about him?

Mrs. Lynge. A dreadful scandal about Mr. Tönnesen?

Mrs. Rummel. Good Heavens, no. Mr. Tönnesen is her cousin, of course, Mrs. Lynge. I am speaking of her brother——

Mrs. Holt. The wicked Mr. Tönnesen——

Mrs. Rummel. His name was Johan. He ran away to America.

Mrs. Holt. Had to run away, you must understand.

Mrs. Lynge. Then it is he the scandal is about?

Mrs. Rummel. Yes; there was something—how shall I

put it?—there was something of some kind between him and Dina's mother. I remember it all as if it were yesterday. Johan Tönnesen was in old Mrs. Bernick's office then; Karsten Bernick had just come back from Paris—he had not yet become engaged——

Mrs. Lynge. Yes, but what was the scandal?

Mrs. Rummel. Well, you must know that Möller's company were acting in the town that winter——

Mrs. Holt. And Dorf, the actor, and his wife were in the company. All the young men in the town were infatuated with her.

Mrs. Rummel. Yes, goodness knows how they could think *her* pretty. Well, Dorf came home late one evening——

Mrs. Holt. Quite unexpectedly.

Mrs. Rummel. And found his——. No, really it isn't a thing one can talk about.

Mrs. Holt. After all, Mrs. Rummel, he didn't find anything, because the door was locked on the inside.

Mrs. Rummel. Yes, that is just what I was going to say—he found the door locked. And—just think of it—the man that was in the house had to jump out of the window.

Mrs. Holt. Right down from an attic window.

Mrs. Lynge. And that was Mrs. Bernick's brother?

Mrs. Rummel. Yes, it was he.

Mrs. Lynge. And that was why he ran away to America?

Mrs. Holt. Yes, he had to run away, you may be sure.

Mrs. Rummel. Because something was discovered afterwards that was nearly as bad; just think—he had been making free with the cash-box——

Mrs. Holt. But, you know, no one was certain of that, Mrs. Rummel; perhaps there was no truth in the rumour.

Mrs. Rummel. Well, I must say——! Wasn't it known all over the town? Did not old Mrs. Bernick nearly go bankrupt as the result of it? However, God forbid *I* should be the one to spread such reports.

Mrs. Holt. Well, anyway, Mrs. Dorf didn't get the money, because she——

Mrs. Lynge. Yes, what happened to Dina's parents afterwards?

Mrs. Rummel. Well, Dorf deserted both his wife and his child. But madam was impudent enough to stay here a whole year. Of course she had not the face to appear at the theatre any more, but she kept herself by taking in washing and sewing——

Mrs. Holt. And then she tried to set up a dancing school.

Mrs. Rummel. Naturally that was no good. What parents would trust their children to such a woman? But it did not last very long. The fine madam was not accustomed to work; she got something wrong with her lungs and died of it.

Mrs. Lynge. What a horrible scandal!

Mrs. Rummel. Yes, you can imagine how hard it was upon the Bernicks. It is the dark spot among the sunshine of their good fortune, as Rummel once put it. So never speak about it in this house, Mrs. Lynge.

Mrs. Holt. And for heaven's sake never mention the step-sister, either!

Mrs. Lynge. Oh, so Mrs. Bernick has a step-sister, too?

Mrs. Rummel. *Had,* luckily; for the relationship between them is all over now. She was an extraordinary person, too! Would you believe it, she cut her hair short and used to go about in men's boots in bad weather!

Mrs. Holt. And when her step-brother—the black sheep—had gone away, and the whole town naturally was talking about him—what do you think she did? She went out to America to him!

Mrs. Rummel. Yes, but remember the scandal *she* caused before she went, Mrs. Holt!

Mrs. Holt. Hush, don't speak of it.

Mrs. Lynge. My goodness, did she create a scandal, too?

Mrs. Rummel. I think you ought to hear it, Mrs. Lynge

Mr. Bernick had just got engaged to Betty Tönnesen, and the two of them went arm in arm into her aunt's room to tell her the news——

Mrs. Holt. The Tönnesens' parents were dead, you know——

Mrs. Rummel. When, suddenly, up got Lona Hessel from her chair and gave our refined and well-bred Karsten Bernick such a box on the ear that his head swam.

Mrs. Lynge. Well, I am sure I never——

Mrs. Holt. It is absolutely true.

Mrs. Rummel. And then she packed her box and went away to America.

Mrs. Lynge. I suppose she had had her eye on him for herself.

Mrs. Rummel. Of course she had. She imagined that he and she would make a match of it when he came back from Paris.

Mrs. Holt. The idea of her thinking such a thing! Karsten Bernick—a man of the world and the pink of courtesy—a perfect gentleman—the darling of all the ladies——

Mrs. Rummel. And, with it all, such an excellent young man, Mrs. Holt—so moral.

Mrs. Lynge. But what has this Miss Hessel made of herself in America?

Mrs. Rummel. Well, you see, over that (as my husband once put it) has been drawn a veil which one should hesitate to lift.

Mrs. Lynge. What do you mean?

Mrs. Rummel. She no longer has any connection with the family, as you may suppose; but this much the whole town knows, that she has sung for money in drinking saloons over there——

Mrs. Holt. And has given lectures in public——

Mrs. Rummel. And has published some mad kind of book.

Mrs. Lynge. You don't say so!

Mrs. Rummel. Yes, it is true enough that Lona Hessel is one of the spots on the sun of the Bernick family's good fortune. Well, now you know the whole story, Mrs. Lynge. I am sure I would never have spoken about it except to put you on your guard.

Mrs. Lynge. Oh, you may be sure I shall be most careful. But that poor child Dina Dorf! I am truly sorry for her.

Mrs. Rummel. Well, really it was a stroke of good luck for her. Think what it would have meant if she had been brought up by such parents! Of course we did our best for her, every one of us, and gave her all the good advice we could. Eventually Miss Bernick got her taken into this house.

Mrs. Holt. But she has always been a difficult child to deal with. It is only natural—with all the bad example she had had before her. A girl of that sort is not like one of our own; one must be lenient with her.

Mrs. Rummel. Hush—here she comes. *(In a louder voice.)* Yes, Dina is really a clever girl. Oh, is that you, Dina? We are just putting away the things.

Mrs. Holt. How delicious your coffee smells, my dear Dina. A nice cup of coffee like that——.

Mrs. Bernick (calling in from the verandah). Will you come out here?

[*Meanwhile* MARTHA *and* DINA *have helped the maid to bring out the coffee. All the ladies seat themselves on the verandah and talk with a great show of kindness to* DINA. *In a few moments* DINA *comes back into the room and looks for her sewing.*

Mrs. Bernick (from the coffee table). Dina, won't you ——?

Dina. No, thank you.

[*Sits down to her sewing.* MRS. BERNICK *and* RÖRLUND *exchange a few words; a moment aft-*

erwards he comes back into the room, makes a pretext for going up to the table and begins speaking to DINA *in low tones.*

Rörlund. Dina.

Dina. Yes?

Rörlund. Why don't you want to sit with the others?

Dina. When I came in with the coffee, I could see from the strange lady's face that they had been talking about me.

Rörlund. But did you not see as well how agreeable she was to you out there?

Dina. That is just what I will not stand!

Rörlund. You are very self-willed, Dina.

Dina. Yes.

Rörlund. But why?

Dina. Because it is my nature.

Rörlund. Could you not try to alter your nature?

Dina. No.

Rörlund. Why not?

Dina (looking at him). Because I am one of the "poor fallen creatures," you know.

Rörlund. For shame, Dina.

Dina. So was my mother.

Rörlund. Who has spoken to you about such things?

Dina. No one; they never do. Why don't they? They all handle me in such a gingerly fashion, as if they thought I should go to pieces if they—— Oh, how I hate all this kind-heartedness.

Rörlund. My dear Dina, I can quite understand that you feel repressed here, but——

Dina. Yes; if only I could get right away from here. I could make my own way quite well, if only I did not live amongst people who are so—so——

Rörlund. So what?

Dina. So proper and so moral.

Rörlund. Oh but, Dina, you don't mean that.

Dina. You know quite well in what sense I mean it.

Hilda and Netta come here every day, to be exhibited to me as good examples. I can never be so beautifully behaved as they; I don't *want* to be. If only I were right away from it all, I should grow to be worth something.

Rörlund. But you are worth a great deal, Dina dear.

Dina. What good does that do me here?

Rörlund. Get right away, you say? Do you mean it seriously?

Dina. I would not stay here a day longer, if it were not for you.

Rörlund. Tell me, Dina—why is it that you are fond of being with me?

Dina. Because you teach me so much that is beautiful.

Rörlund. Beautiful? Do you call the little I can teach you, beautiful?

Dina. Yes. Or perhaps, to be accurate, it is not that you teach me anything; but when I listen to you talking I see beautiful visions.

Rörlund. What do you mean exactly when you call a thing beautiful?

Dina. I have never thought it out.

Rörlund. Think it out now, then. What do you understand by a beautiful thing?

Dina. A beautiful thing is something that is great—and far off.

Rörlund. Hm!—Dina, I am so deeply concerned about you, my dear.

Dina. Only that?

Rörlund. You know perfectly well that you are dearer to me than I can say.

Dina. If I were Hilda or Netta, you would not be afraid to let people see it.

Rörlund. Ah, Dina, you can have no idea of the number of things I am forced to take into consideration. When it is a man's lot to be a moral pillar of the community he lives in, he cannot be too circumspect. If only I could be certain that people would interpret my motives properly—— But no matter for that; you must, and shall be, helped to raise yourself. Dina, is it a bargain between us that when I come—when circumstances allow me to come—to you and say: "Here is my hand," you will take it and be my wife? Will you promise me that, Dina?

Dina. Yes.

Rörlund. Thank you, thank you! Because for my part, too—oh, Dina, I love you so dearly. Hush! Some one is coming. Dina—for my sake—go out to the others.

[*She goes out to the coffee table. At the same moment* RUMMEL, SANDSTAD *and* VIGELAND *come out of* BERNICK'S *room, followed by* BERNICK, *who has a bundle of papers in his hand.*

Bernick. Well, then, the matter is settled.

Vigeland. Yes, I hope to goodness it is.

Rummel. It is settled, Bernick. A Norseman's word stands as firm as the rocks on Dovrefjeld, you know!

Bernick. And no one must falter, no one give way, no matter what opposition we meet with.

Rummel. We will stand or fall together, Bernick.

Hilmar (coming in from the verandah). Fall? If I may ask, isn't it the railway scheme that is going to fall?

Bernick. No, on the contrary, it is going to proceed——

Rummel. Full steam, Mr. Tönnesen.

Hilmar (coming nearer). Really?

Rörlund. How is that?

Mrs. Bernick (at the verandah door). Karsten dear, what is it that——?

Bernick. My dear Betty, how can it interest you? *(To the three men.)* We must get out lists of subscribers, and the sooner the better. Obviously our four names must head the list. The positions we occupy in the community make it our duty to make ourselves as prominent as possible in the affair.

Sandstad. Obviously, Mr. Bernick.

Rummel. The thing *shall* go through, Bernick; I swear it shall.

Bernick. Oh, I have not the least anticipation of failure. We must see that we work, each one among the circle of his own acquaintances; and if we can point to the fact that the scheme is exciting a lively interest in all ranks of society, then it stands to reason that our Municipal Corporation will have to contribute its share.

Mrs. Bernick. Karsten, you really must come out here and tell us——

Bernick. My dear Betty, it is an affair that does not concern ladies at all.

Hilmar. Then you are really going to support this railway scheme after all?

Bernick. Yes, naturally.

Rörlund. But last year, Mr. Bernick——

Bernick. Last year it was quite another thing. At that time is was a question of a line along the coast——

Vigeland. Which would have been quite superfluous, Mr. Rörlund; because, of course, we have our steamboat service——

Sandstad. And would have been quite unreasonably costly——

Rummel. Yes, and would have absolutely ruined certain important interests in the town.

Bernick. The main point was that it would not have been to the advantage of the community as a whole. That is why I opposed it, with the result that the inland line was resolved upon.

Hilmar. Yes, but surely that will not touch the towns about here.

Bernick. It will eventually touch *our* town, my dear Hilmar, because we are going to build a branch line here.

Hilmar. Aha—a new scheme, then?

Rummel. Yes, isn't it a capital scheme? What?

Rörlund. Hm!——

Vigeland. There is no denying that it looks as though Providence had just planned the configuration of the country to suit a branch line.

Rörlund. Do you really mean it, Mr. Vigeland?

Bernick. Yes, I must confess it seems to me as if it had been the hand of Providence that caused me to take a journey on business this spring, in the course of which I happened to traverse a valley through which I had never been before. It came across my mind like a flash of lightning that this was where we could carry a branch line down to our town. I got an engineer to survey the neighbourhood, and have here the provisional calculations and estimate; so there is nothing to hinder us.

Mrs. Bernick (who is still with the other ladies at the verandah door). But, my dear Karsten, to think that you should have kept it all a secret from us!

Bernick. Ah, my dear Betty, I knew you would not have been able to grasp the exact situation. Besides, I have not mentioned it to a living soul till to-day. But now the decisive moment has come, and we must work openly and with all our might. Yes, even if I have to risk all I have for its sake, I mean to push the matter through.

Rummel. And we will back you up, Bernick; you may rely upon that.

Rörlund. Do you really promise us so much, then, from this undertaking, gentlemen?

Bernick. Yes, undoubtedly. Think what a lever it will be to raise the status of our whole community. Just think of the immense tracts of forest-land that it will make accessible; think of all the rich deposits of minerals we shall be able to work; think of the river with one waterfall above another! Think of the possibilities that open out in the way of manufactories!

Rörlund. And you are not afraid that an easier intercourse with the depravity of the outer world——?

Bernick. No, you may make your mind quite easy on that score, Mr. Rörlund. Our little hive of industry rests now-a-days, God be thanked, on such a sound moral basis; we have all of us helped to drain it, if I may use the expression; and that we will continue to do, each in his degree. You, Mr. Rörlund, will continue your richly blessed activity in our schools and our homes. We, the practical men of business, will be the support of the community by extending its welfare within as wide a radius as possible; and our women—yes, come nearer, ladies, you will like to hear it—our women, I say, our wives and daughters—you, ladies, will work on undisturbed in the service of charity and moreover will be a help and a comfort to your nearest and dearest, as my dear Betty and Martha are to me and Olaf—— *(Looks round him.)* Where is Olaf to-day?

Mrs. Bernick. Oh, in the holidays it is impossible to keep him at home.

Bernick. I have no doubt he is down at the shore again. You will see he will end by coming to some harm there.

Hilmar. Bah! A little sport with the forces of nature ——

Mrs. Rummel. Your family affection is beautiful, Mr. Bernick!

Bernick. Well, the family is the kernel of society. A good home, honoured and trusty friends, a little snug family circle where no disturbing elements can cast their shadow ——

[KRAP *comes in from the right, bringing letters and papers.*

Krap. The foreign mail, Mr. Bernick—and a telegram from New York.

Bernick (taking the telegram). Ah—from the owners of the "Indian Girl."

Rummel. Is the mail in? Oh, then you must excuse me.

Vigeland. And me, too.

Sandstad. Good day, Mr. Bernick.

Bernick. Good day, good day, gentlemen. And remember, we have a meeting this afternoon at five o'clock.

The Three Men. Yes—quite so—of course.

[*They go out to the right.*

Bernick (who has read the telegram). This is thoroughly American! Absolutely shocking!

Mrs. Bernick. Good gracious, Karsten, what is it?

Bernick. Look at this, Krap! Read it!

Krap (reading). "Do the least repairs possible. Send over 'Indian Girl' as soon as she is ready to sail; good time of year; at a pinch her cargo will keep her afloat." Well, I must say——

Rörlund. You see the state of things in these vaunted great communities!

Bernick. You are quite right; not a moment's consideration for human life, when it is a question of making a profit. *(To* KRAP:*)* Can the "Indian Girl" go to sea in four—or five—days?

Krap. Yes, if Mr. Vigeland will agree to our stopping work on the "Palm Tree" meanwhile.

Bernick. Hm—he won't. Well, be so good as to look through the letters. And look here, did you see Olaf down at the quay?

Krap. No, Mr. Bernick. [*Goes into* BERNICK'S *room.*

Bernick (looking at the telegram again). These gentlemen think nothing of risking eight men's lives——

Hilmar. Well, it is a sailor's calling to brave the elements: it must be a fine tonic to the nerves to be like that, with only a thin plank between one and the abyss——

Bernick. I should like to see the ship-owner amongst us who would condescend to such a thing! There is not one that would do it—not a single one! *(Sees* OLAF *coming up to the house.)* Ah, thank Heaven, here he is, safe and sound.

[OLAF, *with a fishing-line in his hand, comes run-*

ning up the garden and in through the verandah.

Olaf. Uncle Hilmar, I have been down and seen the steamer.

Bernick. Have you been down to the quay again?

Olaf. No, I have only been out in a boat. But just think, Uncle Hilmar, a whole circus company has come on shore, with horses and animals; and there were such lots of passengers.

Mrs. Rummel. No, are we really to have a circus?

Rörlund. We? I certainly have no desire to see it.

Mrs. Rummel. No, of course I don't mean *we,* but——

Dina. I should like to see a circus very much.

Olaf. So should I.

Hilmar. You are a duffer. Is that anything to see? Mere tricks. No, it would be something quite different to see the Gaucho careering over the Pampas on his snorting mustang. But, Heaven help us, in these wretched little towns of ours——

Olaf (pulling at MARTHA's *dress).* Look, Aunt Martha! Look, there they come!

Mrs. Holt. Good Lord, yes—here they come.

Mrs. Lynge. Ugh, what horrid people!

[*A number of passengers and a whole crowd of townsfolk are seen coming up the street.*

Mrs. Rummel. They *are* a set of mountebanks, certainly. Just look at that woman in the grey dress, Mrs. Holt—the one with a knapsack over her shoulder.

Mrs. Holt. Yes—look—she has slung it on the handle of her parasol. The manager's wife, I expect.

Mrs. Rummel. And there is the manager himself, no doubt! He looks a regular pirate. Don't look at him, Hilda!

Mrs. Holt. Nor you, Netta!

Olaf. Mother, the manager is bowing to us.

Bernick. What?

Mrs. Bernick. What are you saying, child?

Mrs. Rummel. Yes, and—good heavens—the woman is bowing to us, too.

Bernick. That is a little *too* cool!

Martha (exclaims involuntarily). Ah——!

Mrs. Bernick. What is it, Martha?

Martha. Nothing, nothing. I thought for a moment——

Olaf (shrieking with delight). Look, look, there are the rest of them, with the horses and animals! And there are the Americans, too! All the sailors from the "Indian Girl"!

[*The strains of "Yankee Doodle," played on a clarinet and a drum, are heard.*

Hilmar (stopping his ears). Ugh, ugh, ugh!

Rörlund. I think we ought to withdraw ourselves from sight a little, ladies; we have nothing to do with such goings on. Let us go to our work again.

Mrs. Bernick. Do you think we had better draw the curtains?

Rörlund. Yes, that is exactly what I meant.

[*The ladies resume their places at the work-table;* RÖRLUND *shuts the verandah door and draws the curtains over it and over the windows, so that the room becomes half dark.*

Olaf (peeping out through the curtains). Mother, the manager's wife is standing by the fountain now, washing her face.

Mrs. Bernick. What? In the middle of the market-place?

Mrs. Rummel. And in broad daylight, too!

Hilmar. Well, I must say if I were travelling across a desert waste and found myself beside a well, I am sure I should not stop to think whether—— Ugh, that frightful clarinet!

Rörlund. It is really high time the police interfered.

Bernick. Oh, no! we must not be too hard on foreigners. Of course these folk have none of the deep-seated instincts of decency which restrain us within proper bounds. Suppose they do behave outrageously, what does it concern us? Fortunately this spirit of disorder, that flies in the face of all that is customary and right, is absolutely a stranger to our community, if I may say so—— What is this!

[LONA HESSEL *walks briskly in from the door on the right.*

The Ladies (in low, frightened tones). The circus woman! The manager's wife!

Mrs. Bernick. Heavens, what does this mean!

Martha (jumping up). Ah——!

Lona. How do you do, Betty dear! How do you do, Martha! How do you do, brother-in-law!

Mrs. Bernick (with a cry). Lona——!

Bernick (stumbling backwards). As sure as I am alive ——!

Mrs. Holt. Mercy on us——!

Mrs. Rummel. It cannot possibly be——!

Hilmar. Well! Ugh!

Mrs. Bernick. Lona——! Is it really——?

Lona. Really me? Yes, indeed it is; you may fall on my neck if you like.

Hilmar. Ugh, ugh!

Mrs. Bernick. And coming back here as——?

Mrs. Holt. And actually mean to appear in——?

Lona. Appear? Appear in what?

Bernick. Well, I mean—in the circus——

Lona. Ha, ha, ha! Are you mad, brother-in-law? Do you think I belong to the circus troupe? No; certainly I have turned my hand to a good many things, and made a fool of myself in a good many ways——

Mrs. Rummel. Hm!——

Lona. But I have never tried circus riding.

Bernick. Then you are not——?

Mrs. Bernick. Thank Heaven!

Lona. No, we travelled like other respectable folk—second-class, certainly, but we are accustomed to that.

Mrs. Bernick. We, did you say?

Bernick (taking a step forward). Whom do you mean by "we"?

Lona. I and the child, of course.

The Ladies (with a cry). The child!

Hilmar. What!

Rörlund. I really must say——!

Mrs. Bernick. But what do you mean, Lona?

Lona. I mean John, of course; I have no other child, as far as I know, but John—or Johan, as you used to call him.

Mrs. Bernick. Johan!

Mrs. Rummel (in an undertone, to MRS. LYNGE*).* The scapegrace brother!

Bernick (hesitatingly). Is Johan with you?

Lona. Of course he is; I certainly would not come without him. Why do you look so tragical? And why are you sitting here in the gloom, sewing white things? There has not been a death in the family, has there?

Rörlund. Madam, you find yourself in the Society for Fallen Women——

Lona (half to herself). What? Can these nice, quiet-looking ladies possibly be——?

Mrs. Rummel. Well, really——!

Lona. Oh, I understand! But, bless my soul, that is surely Mrs. Rummel? And Mrs. Holt sitting there, too! Well, we three have not grown younger since the last time we met. But listen now, good people; let the Fallen Women wait for a day—they will be none the worse for that. A joyful occasion like this——

Rörlund. A home-coming is not always a joyful occasion.

Lona. Indeed? How do you read your Bible, Mr. Parson?

Rörlund. I am not a parson.

Lona. Oh, you will grow into one, then. But—faugh! —this moral linen of yours smells tainted—just like a winding-sheet. I am accustomed to the air of the prairies, let me tell you.

Bernick (wiping his forehead). Yes, it certainly is rather close in here.

Lona. Wait a moment; we will resurrect ourselves from this vault. *(Pulls the curtains to one side.)* We must have broad daylight in here when the boy comes. Ah, you will see a boy then that has washed himself——

Hilmar. Ugh!

Lona (opening the verandah door and window). I should say, *when* he has washed himself up at the hotel—for on the boat he got piggishly dirty.

Hilmar. Ugh, ugh!

Lona. Ugh! Why, surely isn't that——? *(Points at* HILMAR *and asks the others:)* Is *he* still loafing about here saying "Ugh"?

Hilmar. I do not loaf; it is the state of my health that keeps me here.

Rörlund. Ahem! Ladies, I do not think——

Lona (who has noticed OLAF*).* Is he yours, Betty? Give me a paw, my boy! Or are you afraid of your ugly old aunt?

Rörlund (putting his book under his arm). Ladies, I do not think any of us is in the mood for any more work to-day. I suppose we are to meet again to-morrow?

Lona (while the others are getting up and taking their leave). Yes, let us. I shall be on the spot.

Rörlund. You? Pardon me, Miss Hessel, but what do you propose to do in *our* Society?

Lona. I will let some fresh air into it, Mr. Parson.

ACT II

SCENE.—*The same room.* MRS. BERNICK *is sitting alone at the work-table, sewing.* BERNICK *comes in from the right, wearing his hat and gloves and carrying a stick.*

Mrs. Bernick. Home already, Karsten?

Bernick. Yes, I have made an appointment with a man.

Mrs. Bernick (with a sigh). Oh, yes, I suppose Johan is coming up here again.

Bernick. With a *man,* I said. *(Lays down his hat.)* What has become of all the ladies to-day?

Mrs. Bernick. Mrs. Rummel and Hilda hadn't time to come.

Bernick. Oh!—did they send any excuse?

Mrs. Bernick. Yes, they had so much to do at home.

Bernick. Naturally. And of course the others are not coming either?

Mrs. Bernick. No, something has prevented them to-day, too.

Bernick. I could have told you that, beforehand. Where is Olaf?

Mrs. Bernick. I let him go out a little with Dina.

Bernick. Hm—she is a giddy little baggage. Did you see how she at once started making a fuss of Johan yesterday?

Mrs. Bernick. But, my dear Karsten, you know Dina knows nothing whatever of——

Bernick. No, but in any case Johan ought to have had sufficient tact not to pay her any attention. I saw quite well, from his face, what Vigeland thought of it.

Mrs. Bernick (laying her sewing down on her lap). Karsten, can you imagine what his object is in coming here?

Bernick. Well—I know he has a farm over there, and I fancy he is not doing particularly well with it; *she* called attention yesterday to the fact that they were obliged to travel second-class——

Mrs. Bernick. Yes, I am afraid it must be something of that sort. But to think of her coming with him? She! After the deadly insult she offered him!

Bernick. Oh, don't think about that ancient history.

Mrs. Bernick. How can I help thinking of it just now? After all, he is my brother—still, it is not on his account that I am distressed, but because of all the unpleasantness it would mean for you. Karsten, I am so dreadfully afraid——

Bernick. Afraid of what?

Mrs. Bernick. Isn't it possible that they may send him to prison for stealing that money from your mother?

Bernick. What rubbish! Who can prove that the money *was* stolen?

Mrs. Bernick. The whole town knows it, unfortunately; and you know you said yourself——

Bernick. I said nothing. The town knows nothing whatever about the affair; the whole thing was no more than idle rumour.

Mrs. Bernick. How magnanimous you are, Karsten!

Bernick. Do not let us have any more of these reminiscences, please! You don't know how you torture me by raking up all that. *(Walks up and down; then flings his stick away from him.)* And to think of their coming home now—just now, when it is particularly necessary for me that I should stand well in every respect with the town and with the Press. Our newspaper men will be sending paragraphs to the papers in the other towns about here. Whether I receive them well, or whether I receive them ill, it will all be discussed and talked over. They will rake up all those old stories—as you do. In a community like ours —*(Throws his gloves down on the table.)* And I have not a soul here to whom I can talk about it and to whom I can go for support.

Mrs. Bernick. No one at all, Karsten?

Bernick. No—who is there? And to have them on my shoulders just at this moment! Without a doubt they will create a scandal in some way or another—she, in particular. It is simply a calamity to be connected with such folk in any way!

Mrs. Bernick. Well, *I* can't help their——

Bernick. What can't you help? Their being your relations? No, that is quite true.

Mrs. Bernick. And I did not ask them to come home.

Bernick. That's it—go on! "I did not ask them to come home; I did not write to them; I did not drag them home by the hair of their heads!" Oh, I know the whole rigmarole by heart.

Mrs. Bernick (bursting into tears). You need not be so unkind——

Bernick. Yes, that's right—begin to cry, so that our neighbours may have that to gossip about, too. Do stop being so foolish, Betty. Go and sit outside; some one may come in here. I don't suppose you want people to see the lady of the house with red eyes? It would be a nice thing, wouldn't it, if the story got about that—— There, I hear some one in the passage. *(A knock is heard at the door.)* Come in!

[MRS. BERNICK *takes her sewing and goes out down the garden steps.* AUNE *comes in from the right.*

Aune. Good morning, Mr. Bernick.

Bernick. Good morning. Well, I suppose you can guess what I want you for?

Aune. Mr. Krap told me yesterday that you were not pleased with——

Bernick. I am displeased with the whole management of

the yard, Aune. The work does not get on as quickly as it ought. The "Palm Tree" ought to have been under sail long ago. Mr. Vigeland comes here every day to complain about it; he is a difficult man to have with one as part owner.

Aune. The "Palm Tree" can go to sea the day after tomorrow.

Bernick. At last. But what about the American ship, the "Indian Girl," which has been laid up here for five weeks and——

Aune. The American ship? I understood that, before everything else, we were to work our hardest to get your own ship ready.

Bernick. I gave you no reason to think so. You ought to have pushed on as fast as possible with the work on the American ship also; but you have not.

Aune. Her bottom is completely rotten, Mr. Bernick; the more we patch it, the worse it gets.

Bernick. That is not the reason. Krap has told me the whole truth. You do not understand how to work the new machines I have provided—or rather, you will not try to work them.

Aune. Mr. Bernick, I am well on in the fifties; and ever since I was a boy I have been accustomed to the old way of working——

Bernick. We cannot work that way now-a-days. You must not imagine, Aune, that it is for the sake of making profit; I do not need that, fortunately; but I owe consideration to the community I live in, and to the business I am at the head of. I must take the lead in progress, or there would never be any.

Aune. I welcome progress, too, Mr. Bernick.

Bernick. Yes, for your own limited circle—for the working class. Oh, I know what a busy agitator you are; you make speeches, you stir people up; but when some concrete instance of progress presents itself—as now, in the case of our machines—you do not want to have anything to do with it; you are afraid.

Aune. Yes, I really am afraid, Mr. Bernick. I am afraid for the number of men who will have the bread taken out of their mouths by these machines. You are very fond, sir, of talking about the consideration we owe to the community; it seems to me, however, that the community has its duties, too. Why should science and capital venture to introduce these new discoveries into labour, before the community has had time to educate a generation up to using them?

Bernick. You read and think too much, Aune; it does you no good, and that is what makes you dissatisfied with your lot.

Aune. It is not, Mr. Bernick; but I cannot bear to see one good workman dismissed after another, to starve because of these machines.

Bernick. Hm! When the art of printing was discovered, many a quill-driver was reduced to starvation.

Aune. Would you have admired the art so greatly if you had been a quill-driver in those days, sir?

Bernick. I did not send for you to argue with you. I sent for you to tell you that the "Indian Girl" must be ready to put to sea the day after to-morrow.

Aune. But, Mr. Bernick——

Bernick. The day after to-morrow, do you hear?—at the same time as our own ship, not an hour later. I have good reasons for hurrying on the work. Have you seen to-day's papers? Well, then you know the pranks these American sailors have been up to again. The rascally pack is turning the whole town upside down. Not a night passes without some brawling in the taverns or the streets—not to speak of other abominations.

Aune. Yes, they certainly are a bad lot.

Bernick. And who is it that has to bear the blame for all this disorder? It is I! Yes, it is I who have to suffer for it. These newspaper fellows are making all sorts of covert insinuations because we are devoting all our energies to the "Palm Tree." I, whose task in life it is to influence my fellow-citizens by the force of example, have to endure this sort of thing cast in my face. I am not going to stand that. I have no fancy for having my good name smirched in that way.

Aune. Your name stands high enough to endure that and a great deal more, sir.

Bernick. Not just now. At this particular moment I have need of all the respect and good-will my fellow-citizens can give me. I have a big undertaking on the stocks, as you probably have heard; but if it should happen that evil-disposed persons succeeded in shaking the absolute confidence I enjoy, it might land me in the greatest difficulties. That is why I want, at any price, to avoid these shameful innuendoes in the papers, and that is why I name the day after to-morrow as the limit of the time I can give you.

Aune. Mr. Bernick, you might just as well name this afternoon as the limit.

Bernick. You mean that I am asking an impossibility?

Aune. Yes, with the hands we have now at the yard.

Bernick. Very good; then we must look about elsewhere.

Aune. Do you really mean, sir, to discharge still more of your old workmen?

Bernick. No, I am not thinking of that.

Aune. Because I think it would cause bad blood against you both among the townsfolk and in the papers, if you did that.

Bernick. Very probably; therefore we will not do it. But, if the "Indian Girl" is not ready to sail the day after to-morrow, I shall discharge *you.*

Aune (with a start). Me! *(He laughs.)* You are joking, Mr. Bernick.

Bernick. I should not be so sure of that, if I were you.

Aune. Do you mean that you can contemplate discharging *me?*—Me, whose father and grandfather worked in your yard all their lives, as I have done myself——?

Bernick. Who is it that is forcing me to do it?

Aune. You are asking what is impossible, Mr. Bernick.

Bernick. Oh, where there's a will there's a way. Yes or no; give me a decisive answer, or consider yourself discharged on the spot.

Aune (coming a step nearer to him). Mr. Bernick, have you ever realised what discharging an old workman means? You think he can look about for another job. Oh, yes, he can do that; but does that dispose of the matter? You should just be there once, in the house of a workman who has been discharged, the evening he comes home bringing all his tools with him.

Bernick. Do you think I am discharging you with a light heart? Have I not always been a good master to you?

Aune. So much the worse, Mr. Bernick. Just for that very reason those at home will not blame *you;* they will say nothing to me, because they dare not; but they will look at me when I am not noticing and think that I must have deserved it. You see, sir, that is—that is what I cannot bear. I am a mere nobody, I know; but I have always been accustomed to stand first in my own home. My humble home is a little community, too, Mr. Bernick—a little community which I have been able to support and maintain because my wife has believed in me and because my children have believed in me. And now it is all to fall to pieces.

Bernick. Still, if there is nothing else for it, the lesser must go down before the greater; the individual must be sacrificed to the general welfare. I can give you no other answer; and that, and no other, is the way of the world. You are an obstinate man, Aune! You are opposing me, not because you cannot do otherwise, but because you will not exhibit the superiority of machinery over manual labour.

Aune. And you will not be moved, Mr. Bernick, because

you know that if you drive me away you will at all events have given the newspapers proof of your good-will.

Bernick. And suppose that were so? I have told you what it means for me—either bringing the Press down on my back, or making them well-disposed to me at a moment when I am working for an object which will mean the advancement of the general welfare. Well, then, can I do otherwise than as I am doing? The question, let me tell you, turns upon this—whether your home is to be supported, as you put it, or whether hundreds of new homes are to be prevented from existing—hundreds of homes that will never be built, never have a fire lighted on their hearth, unless I succeed in carrying through the scheme I am working for now. That is the reason why I have given you your choice.

Aune. Well, if that is the way things stand, I have nothing more to say.

Bernick. Hm—my dear Aune, I am extremely grieved to think that we are to part.

Aune. We are not going to part, Mr. Bernick.

Bernick. How is that?

Aune. Even a common man like myself has something he is bound to maintain.

Bernick. Quite so, quite so—then I presume you think you may promise——?

Aune. The "Indian Girl" shall be ready to sail the day after to-morrow. [*Bows and goes out to the right.*

Bernick. Ah, I have got the better of that obstinate fellow! I take it as a good omen.

[HILMAR *comes in through the garden door, smoking a cigar.*

Hilmar (as he comes up the steps to the verandah). Good morning, Betty! Good morning, Karsten!

Mrs. Bernick. Good morning.

Hilmar. Ah, I see you have been crying, so I suppose you know all about it, too?

Mrs. Bernick. Know all about what?

Hilmar. That the scandal is in full swing. Ugh!

Bernick. What do you mean?

Hilmar (coming into the room). Why, that our two friends from America are displaying themselves about the streets in the company of Dina Dorf.

Mrs. Bernick (coming in after him). Hilmar, is it possible?

Hilmar. Yes, unfortunately, it is quite true. Lona was even so wanting in tact as to call after me, but of course I appeared not to have heard her.

Bernick. And no doubt all this has not been unnoticed.

Hilmar. You may well say that. People stood still and looked at them. It spread like wildfire through the town—just like a prairie fire out West. In every house people were at the windows waiting for the procession to pass, cheek by jowl behind the curtains—ugh! Oh, you must excuse me, Betty, for saying "ugh"—this has got on my nerves. If it is going on, I shall be forced to think about getting right away from here.

Mrs. Bernick. But you should have spoken to him and represented to him that——

Hilmar. In the open street? No, excuse me, I could not do that. To think that the fellow should dare to show himself in the town at all! Well, we shall see if the Press doesn't put a stopper on him; yes—forgive me, Betty, but——

Bernick. The Press, do you say? Have you heard a hint of anything of the sort?

Hilmar. There *are* such things flying about. When I left here yesterday evening I looked in at the club, because I did not feel well. I saw at once, from the sudden silence that fell when I went in, that our American couple had been the subject of conversation. Then that impudent newspaper fellow, Hammer, came in and congratulated me at the top of his voice on the return of my rich cousin.

Bernick. Rich?

Hilmar. Those were his words. Naturally I looked him up and down in the manner he deserved and gave him to understand that I knew nothing about Johan Tönnesen's being rich. "Really," he said, "that is very remarkable. People usually get on in America when they have something to start with, and I believe your cousin did not go over there quite empty-handed."

Bernick. Hm—now will you oblige me by——

Mrs. Bernick (distressed). There, you see, Karsten——

Hilmar. Anyhow, I have spent a sleepless night because of them. And here he is, walking about the streets as if nothing were the matter. Why couldn't he disappear for good and all? It really is insufferable how hard some people are to kill.

Mrs. Bernick. My dear Hilmar, what are you saying?

Hilmar. Oh, nothing. But here this fellow escapes with a whole skin from railway accidents and fights with Californian grizzlies and Blackfoot Indians—has not even been scalped—— Ugh, here they come!

Bernick (looking down the street). Olaf is with them, too!

Hilmar. Of course! They want to remind everybody that they belong to the best family in the town. Look there!—look at the crowd of loafers that have come out of the chemist's to stare at them and make remarks. My nerves really won't stand it; how a man is to be expected to keep the banner of the Ideal flying under such circumstances, I——

Bernick. They are coming here. Listen, Betty; it is my particular wish that you should receive them in the friendliest possible way.

Mrs. Bernick. Oh, may I, Karsten?

Bernick. Certainly, certainly—and you, too, Hilmar. It is to be hoped they will not stay here very long; and when we are quite by ourselves—no allusions to the past; we must not hurt their feelings in any way.

Mrs. Bernick. How magnanimous you are, Karsten!

Bernick. Oh, don't speak of that.

Mrs. Bernick. But you must let me thank you; and you must forgive me for being so hasty. I am sure you had every reason to——

Bernick. Don't talk about it, please!

Hilmar. Ugh!

[JOHAN TÖNNESEN *and* DINA *come up through the garden, followed by* LONA *and* OLAF.

Lona. Good morning, dear people!

Johan. We have been out having a look round the old place, Karsten.

Bernick. So I hear. Greatly altered, is it not?

Lona. Mr. Bernick's great and good works everywhere. We have been up into the Recreation Ground you have presented to the town——

Bernick. Have you been *there?*

Lona. "The gift of Karsten Bernick," as it says over the gateway. You seem to be responsible for the whole place here.

Johan. Splendid ships you have got, too. I met my old schoolfellow, the captain of the "Palm Tree."

Lona. And you have built a new school-house too; and I hear that the town has to thank you for both the gas-supply and the water-supply.

Bernick. Well, one ought to work for the good of the community one lives in.

Lona. That is an excellent sentiment, brother-in-law; but it is a pleasure, all the same, to see how people appreciate you. I am not vain, I hope; but I could not resist reminding one or two of the people we talked to that we were relations of yours.

Hilmar. Ugh!

Lona. Do you say "ugh" to that?

Hilmar. No, I said "ahem."

Lona. Oh, poor chap, you may say that if you like. But are you all by yourselves to-day?

Bernick. Yes, we are by ourselves to-day.

Lona. Ah, yes, we met a couple of members of your Morality Society up at the market; they made out they were very busy. You and I have never had an opportunity for a good talk yet. Yesterday you had your three pioneers here, as well as the parson——

Hilmar. The schoolmaster.

Lona. I call him the parson. But now tell me what you think of *my* work during these fifteen years? Hasn't he grown a fine fellow? Who would recognise the madcap that ran away from home?

Hilmar. Hm!

Johan. Now, Lona, don't brag too much about me.

Lona. Well, I can tell you I am precious proud of him. Goodness knows it is about the only thing I have done in my life; but it does give me a sort of right to exist. When I think, Johan, how we two began over there with nothing but our four bare fists——

Hilmar. Hands.

Lona. I say fists; and they were dirty fists——

Hilmar. Ugh!

Lona. And empty, too.

Hilmar. Empty? Well, I must say——

Lona. What must you say?

Bernick. Ahem!

Hilmar. I must say—ugh!

[*Goes out through the garden.*

Lona. What is the matter with the man?

Bernick. Oh, do not take any notice of him; his nerves are rather upset just now. Would you not like to take a look at the garden? You have not been down there yet, and I have got an hour to spare.

Lona. With pleasure. I can tell you my thoughts have been with you in this garden many and many a time.

Mrs. Bernick. We have made a great many alterations there, too, as you will see.

[BERNICK, MRS. BERNICK *and* LONA *go down to the garden, where they are visible every now and then during the following scene.*

Olaf (coming to the verandah door). Uncle Hilmar, do you know what uncle Johan asked me? He asked me if I would go to America with him.

Hilmar. You, you duffer, who are tied to your mother's apron strings——!

Olaf. Ah, but I won't be that any longer. You will see, when I grow big——

Hilmar. Oh, fiddlesticks! You have no really serious bent towards the strength of character necessary to——

[*They go down to the garden.* DINA *meanwhile has taken off her hat and is standing at the door on the right, shaking the dust off her dress.*

Johan (to DINA*).* The walk has made you pretty warm.

Dina. Yes, it was a splendid walk. I have never had such a splendid walk before.

Johan. Do you not often go for a walk in the morning?

Dina. Oh, yes—but only with Olaf.

Johan. I see.—Would you rather go down into the garden than stay here?

Dina. No, I would rather stay here.

Johan. So would I. Then shall we consider it a bargain that we are to go for a walk like this together every morning?

Dina. No, Mr. Tönnesen, you mustn't do that.

Johan. What mustn't I do? You promised, you know.

Dina. Yes, but—on second thoughts—you mustn't go out with me.

Johan. But why not?

Dina. Of course, you are a stranger—you cannot understand; but I must tell you——

Johan. Well?

Dina. No, I would rather not talk about it.

Johan. Oh, but you must; you can talk to me about whatever you like.

Dina. Well, I must tell you that I am not like the other young girls here. There is something—something or other about me. That is why you mustn't.

Johan. But I do not understand anything about it. You have not done anything wrong?

Dina. No, not I, but—— No, I am not going to talk any more about it now. You will hear about it from the others, sure enough.

Johan. Hm!

Dina. But there is something else I want very much to ask you.

Johan. What is it?

Dina. I suppose it is easy to make a position for oneself over in America?

Johan. No, it is not always easy; at first you often have to rough it and work very hard.

Dina. I should be quite ready to do that.

Johan. You?

Dina. I can work now; I am strong and healthy; and Aunt Martha taught me a lot.

Johan. Well, hang it, come back with us!

Dina. Ah, now you are only making fun of me; you said that to Olaf, too. But what I wanted to know is if people are so very—so very moral over there?

Johan. Moral?

Dina. Yes; I mean are they as—as proper and as well-behaved as they are here?

Johan. Well, at all events they are not so bad as people here make out. You need not be afraid on that score.

Dina. You don't understand me. What I want to hear is just that they are *not* so proper and so moral.

Johan. Not? What would you wish them to be, then?

Dina. I would wish them to be natural.

Johan. Well, I believe that is just what they are.

Dina. Because in that case I should get on if I went there.

Johan. You would, for certain!—and that is why you must come back with us.

Dina. No, I don't want to go with you; I must go alone. Oh, I would make something of my life; I would get on——

Bernick (speaking to LONA *and his wife at the foot of the garden steps).* Wait a moment—I will fetch it, Betty dear; you might so easily catch cold.

[*Comes into the room and looks for his wife's shawl.*

Mrs. Bernick (from outside). You must come out, too, Johan; we are going down to the grotto.

Bernick. No, I want Johan to stay here. Look here, Dina; you take my wife's shawl and go with them. Johan is going to stay here with me, Betty dear. I want to hear how he is getting on over there.

Mrs. Bernick. Very well—then you will follow us; you know where you will find us.

[MRS. BERNICK, LONA *and* DINA *go out through the garden, to the left.* BERNICK *looks after them for a moment, then goes to the farther door on the left and locks it, after which he goes up to* JOHAN, *grasps both his hands and shakes them warmly.*

Bernick. Johan, now that we are alone, you must let me thank you.

Johan. Oh, nonsense!

Bernick. My home and all the happiness that it means to me—my position here as a citizen—all these I owe to you.

Johan. Well, I am glad of it, Karsten; some good came of that mad story after all, then.

Bernick (grasping his hands again). But still you must let me thank you! Not one in ten thousand would have done what you did for me.

Johan. Rubbish! Weren't we, both of us, young and thoughtless? One of us had to take the blame, you know.

Bernick. But surely the guilty one was the proper one to do that?

Johan. Stop! At the moment the innocent one happened to be the proper one to do it. Remember, I had no ties—I was an orphan; it was a lucky chance to get free from the drudgery of the office. You, on the other hand, had your old mother still alive; and, besides that, you had just become secretly engaged to Betty, who was devoted to you. What would have happened between you and her if it had come to her ears?

Bernick. That is true enough, but still——

Johan. And wasn't it just for Betty's sake that you broke off your acquaintance with Mrs. Dorf? Why, it was merely in order to put an end to the whole thing that you were up there with her that evening.

Bernick. Yes, that unfortunate evening when that drunken creature came home! Yes, Johan, it was for Betty's sake; but, all the same, it was splendid of you to let all the appearances go against you and to go away.

Johan. Put your scruples to rest, my dear Karsten. We agreed that it should be so; you had to be saved, and you were my friend. I can tell you, I was uncommonly proud of that friendship. Here was I, drudging away like a miserable stick-in-the-mud, when you came back from your grand tour abroad, a great swell who had been to London and to Paris; and you chose me for your chum, although I was four years younger than you—it is true it was because you were courting Betty, I understand that now—but I *was* proud of it! Who would not have been? Who would not willingly have sacrificed himself for you?—especially as it only meant a month's talk in the town and enabled me to get away into the wide world.

Bernick. Ah, my dear Johan, I must be candid and tell you that the story is not so completely forgotten yet.

Johan. Isn't it? Well, what does that matter to me, once I am back over there on my farm again?

Bernick. Then you mean to go back?

Johan. Of course.

Bernick. But not immediately, I hope?

Johan. As soon as possible. It was only to humour Lona that I came over with her, you know.

Bernick. Really? How so?

Johan. Well, you see, Lona is no longer young, and lately she began to be obsessed with home-sickness; but she never would admit it. *(Smiles.)* How could she venture to risk leaving such a flighty fellow as me alone, who before I was nineteen had been mixed up in——

Bernick. Well, what then?

Johan. Well, Karsten, now I am coming to a confession that I am ashamed to make.

Bernick. You surely haven't confided the truth to her?

Johan. Yes. It was wrong of me, but I could not do otherwise. You can have no conception what Lona has been to me. You never could put up with her; but she has been like a mother to me. The first year we were out there, when things went so badly with us, you have no idea how she worked! And when I was ill for a long time, and could earn nothing and could not prevent her, she took to singing ballads in taverns and gave lectures that people laughed at; and then she wrote a book that she has both laughed and cried over since then—all to keep the life in me. Could I look on when in the winter she, who had toiled and drudged for me, began to pine away? No, Karsten, I couldn't. And so I said, "You go home for a trip, Lona; don't be afraid for me, I am not so flighty as you think." And so—the end of it was that she had to know.

Bernick. And how did she take it?

Johan. Well, she thought, as was true, that as I knew I was innocent nothing need prevent me from taking a trip over here with her. But make your mind easy; Lona will let nothing out, and I shall keep my mouth shut as I did before.

Bernick. Yes, yes—I rely on that.

Johan. Here is my hand on it. And now we will say no more about that old story; luckily it is the only mad prank either of us has been guilty of, I am sure. I want thoroughly to enjoy the few days I shall stay here. You cannot think what a delightful walk we had this morning. Who would have believed that that little imp, who used to run about here and play angels' parts on the stage——! But tell me, my dear fellow, what became of her parents afterwards?

Bernick. Oh, my boy, I can tell you no more than I wrote to you immediately after you went away. I suppose you got my two letters?

Johan. Yes, yes, I have them both. So that drunken fellow deserted her?

Bernick. And drank himself to death afterwards.

Johan. And *she* died soon afterwards, too?

Bernick. She was proud; she betrayed nothing and would accept nothing.

Johan. Well, at all events you did the right thing by taking Dina into your house.

Bernick. I suppose so. As a matter of fact it was Martha that brought that about.

Johan. So it was Martha? By the way, where is she to-day?

Bernick. She? Oh, when she hasn't her school to look after, she has her sick people to see to.

Johan. So it was Martha who interested herself in her.

Bernick. Yes, you know Martha has always had a certain liking for teaching; so she took a post in the Board-school. It was very ridiculous of her.

Johan. I thought she looked very worn yesterday; I should be afraid her health was not good enough for it.

Bernick. Oh, as far as her health goes, it is all right

enough. But it is unpleasant for me; it looks as though I, her brother, were not willing to support her.

Johan. Support her? I thought she had means enough of her own.

Bernick. Not a penny. Surely you remember how badly off our mother was when you went away? She carried things on for a time with my assistance, but naturally I could not put up with that state of affairs permanently. I made her take me into the firm, but even then things did not go well. So I had to take over the whole business myself, and when we made up our balance-sheet it became evident that there was practically nothing left as my mother's share. And when mother died soon afterwards, of course Martha was left penniless.

Johan. Poor Martha!

Bernick. Poor! Why? You surely do not suppose I let her want for anything? No, I venture to say I am a good brother. Of course she has a home here with us; her salary as a teacher is more than enough for her to dress on; what more could she want?

Johan. Hm—that is not our idea of things in America.

Bernick. No, I dare say not—in such a revolutionary state of society as you find there. But in our small circle—in which, thank God, depravity has not gained a footing, up to now at all events—women are content to occupy a seemly, as well as modest, position. Moreover, it is Martha's own fault; I mean, she might have been provided for long ago, if she had wished.

Johan. You mean she might have married?

Bernick. Yes, and married very well, too. She has had several good offers—curiously enough, when you think that she is a poor girl, no longer young, and, besides, quite an insignificant person.

Johan. Insignificant?

Bernick. Oh, I am not blaming her for that. I most certainly would not wish her otherwise. I can tell you it is always a good thing to have a steady-going person like that in a big house like this—some one you can rely on in any contingency.

Johan. Yes, but what does *she*——?

Bernick. She? How? Oh, well, of course *she* has plenty to interest herself in; she has Betty and Olaf and me. People should not think first of themselves—women least of all. We have all got some community, great or small, to work for. That is my principle, at all events. *(Points to* KRAP, *who has come in from the right.)* Ah, here is an example of it, ready to hand. Do you suppose that it is my own affairs that are absorbing me just now? By no means. *(Eagerly to* KRAP.*)* Well?

Krap (in an undertone, showing him a bundle of papers). Here are all the sale contracts, completed.

Bernick. Capital! Splendid!—Well, Johan, you must really excuse me for the present. *(In a low voice, grasping his hand.)* Thanks, Johan, thanks! And rest assured that anything I can do for you—— Well, of course you understand. Come along, Krap. [*They go into* BERNICK'S *room.*

Johan (looking after them for a moment). Hm! *(Turns to go down to the garden. At the same moment* MARTHA *comes in from the right, with a little basket over her arm.)* Martha!

Martha. Ah, Johan—is it you?

Johan. Out so early?

Martha. Yes. Wait a moment; the others are just coming. [*Moves towards the door on the left.*

Johan. Martha, are you always in such a hurry?

Martha. I?

Johan. Yesterday you seemed to avoid me, so that I never managed to have a word with you—we two old playfellows.

Martha. Ah, Johan; that is many, many years ago.

Johan. Good Lord—why, it is only fifteen years ago, no more and no less. Do you think I have changed so much?

Martha. You? Oh yes, you have changed too, although——

Johan. What do you mean?

Martha. Oh, nothing.

Johan. You do not seem to be very glad to see me again.

Martha. I have waited so long, Johan—too long.

Johan. Waited? For me to come?

Martha. Yes.

Johan. And why did you think I would come?

Martha. To atone for the wrong you had done.

Johan. I?

Martha. Have you forgotten that it was through you that a woman died in need and in shame? Have you forgotten that it was through you that the best years of a young girl's life were embittered?

Johan. And you can say such things to me? Martha, has your brother never——?

Martha. Never what?

Johan. Has he never—oh, of course, I mean has he never so much as said a word in my defence?

Martha. Ah, Johan, you know Karsten's high principles.

Johan. Hm—! Oh, of course; I know my old friend Karsten's high principles! But really this is—— Well, well. I was having a talk with him just now. He seems to me to have altered considerably.

Martha. How can you say that? I am sure Karsten has always been an excellent man.

Johan. Yes, that was not exactly what I meant—but never mind. Hm! Now I understand the light you have seen me in; it was the return of the prodigal that you were waiting for.

Martha. Johan, I will tell you what light I have seen you in. *(Points down to the garden.)* Do you see that girl playing on the grass down there with Olaf? That is Dina. Do you remember that incoherent letter you wrote me when you went away? You asked me to believe in you.

I have believed in you, Johan. All the horrible things that were rumoured about you after you had gone must have been done through being led astray—from thoughtlessness,

Johan. What do you mean?

Martha. Oh, you understand me well enough—not a word more of that. But of course you had to go away and begin afresh—a new life. Your duties here which you never remembered to undertake—or never were able to undertake—I have undertaken for you. I tell you this, so that you shall not have that also to reproach yourself with. I have been a mother to that much-wronged child; I have brought her up as well as I was able.

Johan. And have wasted your whole life for that reason.

Martha. It has not been wasted. But you have come late, Johan.

Johan. Martha—if only I could tell you—— Well, at all events let me thank you for your loyal friendship.

Martha (with a sad smile). Hm.—Well, we have had it out now, Johan. Hush, some one is coming. Good-bye, I can't stay now.

[*Goes out through the farther door on the left.* LONA *comes in from the garden, followed by* MRS. BERNICK.

Mrs. Bernick. But, good gracious, Lona—what are you thinking of?

Lona. Let me be, I tell you! I must and will speak to him.

Mrs. Bernick. But it would be a scandal of the worst sort! Ah, Johan—still here?

Lona. Out with you, my boy; don't stay here indoors; go down into the garden and have a chat with Dina.

Johan. I was just thinking of doing so.

Mrs. Bernick. But——

Lona. Look here, Johan—have you had a good look at Dina?

Johan. I should think so!

Lona. Well, look at her to some purpose, my boy. That would be somebody for *you!*

Mrs. Bernick. But, Lona!

Johan. Somebody for me?

Lona. Yes, to look at, I mean. Be off with you!

Johan. Oh, I don't need any pressing.

[*Goes down into the garden.*

Mrs. Bernick. Lona, you astound me! You cannot possibly be serious about it?

Lona. Indeed I am. Isn't she sweet and healthy and honest? She is exactly the wife for Johan. She is just what he needs over there; it will be a change from an old step-sister.

Mrs. Bernick. Dina? Dina Dorf? But think——

Lona. I think first and foremost of the boy's happiness, because help him I must; he has not much idea of that sort of thing; he has never had much of an eye for girls or women.

Mrs. Bernick. He? Johan? Indeed I think we have had only too sad proofs that——

Lona. Oh, devil take all those stupid stories! Where is Karsten? I mean to speak to him.

Mrs. Bernick. Lona, you must not do it, I tell you!

Lona. I am going to. If the boy takes a fancy to her—and she to him—then they shall make a match of it. Karsten is such a clever man, he must find some way to bring it about.

Mrs. Bernick. And do you think these American indecencies will be permitted here?

Lona. Bosh, Betty!

Mrs. Bernick. Do you think a man like Karsten, with his strictly moral way of thinking——

Lona. Pooh! he is not so terribly moral.

Mrs. Bernick. What have you the audacity to say?

Lona. I have the audacity to say that Karsten is not any more particularly moral than anybody else.

Mrs. Bernick. So you still hate him as deeply as that! But what are you doing here, if you have never been able to forget that? I cannot understand how you dare look him in the face after the shameful insult you put upon him in the old days.

Lona. Yes, Betty, that time I did forget myself badly.

Mrs. Bernick. And to think how magnanimously he has forgiven you—he, who had never done any wrong! It was not *his* fault that you encouraged yourself with hopes. But since then you have always hated me, too. *(Bursts into tears.)* You have always grudged me my good fortune. And now you come here to heap all this on my head—to let the whole town know what sort of family I have brought Karsten into. Yes, it is me that it all falls upon, and that is what you want. Oh, it is abominable of you.

[*Goes out by the door on the left, in tears.*

Lona (looking after her). Poor Betty!

[BERNICK *comes in from his room. He stops at the door to speak to* KRAP.

Bernick. Yes, that is excellent, Krap—capital! Send twenty pounds to the fund for dinners to the poor. *(Turns round.)* Lona! *(Comes forward.)* Are you alone? Is Betty not coming in?

Lona. No. Would you like me to call her?

Bernick. No, no—not at all. Oh, Lona, you don't know how anxious I have been to speak openly to you—after having begged for your forgiveness.

Lona. Look here, Karsten—do not let us be sentimental; it doesn't suit us.

Bernick. You *must* listen to me, Lona. I know only too well how much appearances are against me, as you have learnt all about that affair with Dina's mother. But I swear to you that it was only a temporary infatuation; I was really, truly and honestly, in love with you once.

Lona. Why do you think I have come home?

Bernick. Whatever you have in your mind, I entreat you

to do nothing until I have exculpated myself. I can do that Lona; at all events I can excuse myself.

Lona. Now you are frightened. You once were in love with me, you say. Yes, you told me that often enough in your letters; and perhaps it was true, too—in a way—as long as you were living out in the great, free world which gave you the courage to think freely and greatly. Perhaps you found in me a little more character and strength of will and independence than in most of the folk at home here. And then we kept it secret between us; nobody could make fun of your bad taste.

Bernick. Lona, how can you think——?

Lona. But when you came back—when you heard the gibes that were made at me on all sides—when you noticed how people laughed at what they called my absurdities——

Bernick. You were regardless of people's opinion at that time.

Lona. Chiefly to annoy the petticoated and trousered prudes that one met at every turn in the town. And then, when you met that seductive young actress——

Bernick. It was a boyish escapade—nothing more; I swear to you that there was no truth in a tenth part of the rumours and gossip that went about.

Lona. Maybe. But then, when Betty came home—a pretty young girl, idolised by every one—and it became known that she would inherit all her aunt's money and that I would have nothing——

Bernick. That is just the point, Lona; and now you shall have the truth without any beating about the bush. I did not love Betty then; I did not break off my engagement with you because of any new attachment. It was entirely for the sake of the money. I needed it; I *had* to make sure of it.

Lona. And you have the face to tell me that?

Bernick. Yes, I have. Listen, Lona.

Lona. And yet you wrote to me that an unconquerable passion for Betty had overcome you—invoked my magnanimity—begged me, for Betty's sake, to hold my tongue about all that had been between us.

Bernick. I *had* to, I tell you.

Lona. Now, by Heaven, I don't regret that I forgot myself as I did that time!

Bernick. Let me tell you the plain truth of how things stood with me then. My mother, as you remember, was at the head of the business, but she was absolutely without any business ability whatever. I was hurriedly summoned home from Paris; times were critical, and they relied on me to set things straight. What did I find? I found—and you must keep this a profound secret—a house on the brink of ruin. Yes—as good as on the brink of ruin, this old respected house which had seen three generations of us. What else could I—the son, the only son—do than look about for some means of saving it?

Lona. And so you saved the house of Bernick at the cost of a woman.

Bernick. You know quite well that Betty was in love with me.

Lona. But what about me?

Bernick. Believe me, Lona, you would never have been happy with me.

Lona. Was it out of consideration for my happiness that you sacrificed me?

Bernick. Do you suppose I acted as I did from selfish motives? If I had stood alone then, I would have begun all over again with cheerful courage. But you do not understand how the life of a man of business, with his tremendous responsibilities, is bound up with that of the business which falls to his inheritance. Do you realise that the prosperity or the ruin of hundreds—of thousands—depends on him? Can you not take into consideration the fact that the whole community in which both you and I were born would have been affected to the most dangerous extent if the house of Bernick had gone to smash?

Lona. Then is it for the sake of the community that you have maintained your position these fifteen years upon a lie?

Bernick. Upon a lie?

Lona. What does Betty know of all this that underlies her union with you?

Bernick. Do you suppose that I would hurt her feelings to no purpose by disclosing the truth?

Lona. To no purpose, you say? Well, well—you are a man of business; you ought to understand what is to the purpose. But listen to me, Karsten—*I* am going to speak the plain truth now. Tell me, are you really happy?

Bernick. In my family life, do you mean?

Lona. Yes.

Bernick. I am, Lona. You have not been a self-sacrificing friend to me in vain. I can honestly say that I have grown happier every year. Betty is good and willing; and if I were to tell you how, in the course of years, she has learnt to model her character on the lines of my own——

Lona. Hm!

Bernick. At first, of course, she had a whole lot of romantic notions about love; she could not reconcile herself to the idea that, little by little, it must change into a quiet comradeship.

Lona. But now she is quite reconciled to that?

Bernick. Absolutely. As you can imagine, daily intercourse with me has had no small share in developing her character. Every one, in their degree, has to learn to lower their own pretensions, if they are to live worthily of the community to which they belong. And Betty, in her turn, has gradually learnt to understand this; and that is why our home is now a model to our fellow-citizens.

Lona. But your fellow-citizens know nothing about the lie?

Bernick. The lie?

Lona. Yes—the lie you have persisted in for these fifteen years.

Bernick. Do you mean to say that you call that——?

Lona. I call it a lie—a threefold lie; first of all there is the lie towards me, then the lie towards Betty, and then the lie towards Johan.

Bernick. Betty has never asked me to speak.

Lona. Because she has known nothing.

Bernick. And *you* will not demand it—out of consideration for her.

Lona. Oh, no—I shall manage to put up with their gibes well enough; I have broad shoulders.

Bernick. And Johan will not demand it either; he has promised me that.

Lona. But you yourself, Karsten. Do you feel within yourself no impulse urging you to shake yourself free of this lie?

Bernick. Do you suppose that of my own free will I would sacrifice my family happiness and my position in the world?

Lona. What right have you to the position you hold?

Bernick. Every day during these fifteen years I have earned some little right to it—by my conduct, and by what I have achieved by my work.

Lona. True, you have achieved a great deal by your work, for yourself as well as for others. You are the richest and most influential man in the town; nobody in it dares do otherwise than defer to your will, because you are looked upon as a man without spot or blemish; your home is regarded as a model home, and your conduct as a model of conduct. But all this grandeur, and you with it, is founded on a treacherous morass. A moment may come and a word may be spoken—and you and all your grandeur will be engulfed in the morass, if you do not save yourself in time.

Bernick. Lona—what is your object in coming here?

Lona. I want to help you to get firm ground under your feet, Karsten.

Bernick. Revenge!—you want to revenge yourself! I

suspected it. But you won't succeed! There is only one person here that can speak with authority, and he will be silent.

Lona. You mean Johan?

Bernick. Yes, Johan. If any one else accuses me, I shall deny everything. If any one tries to crush me, I shall fight for my life. But you will never succeed in that, let me tell you! The one who could strike me down will say nothing—and is going away.

[RUMMEL *and* VIGELAND *come in from the right.*

Rummel. Good morning, my dear Bernick, good morning. You must come up with us to the Commercial Association. There is a meeting about the railway scheme, you know.

Bernick. I cannot. It is impossible just now.

Vigeland. You really must, Mr. Bernick.

Rummel. Bernick, you must. There is an opposition to us on foot. Hammer, and the rest of those who believe in a line along the coast, are declaring that private interests are at the back of the new proposals.

Bernick. Well, then, explain to them——

Vigeland. Our explanations have no effect, Mr. Bernick.

Rummel. No, no, you must come yourself. Naturally, no one would dare to suspect you of such duplicity.

Lona. I should think not.

Bernick. I cannot, I tell you; I am not well. Or, at all events, wait—let me pull myself together.

[RÖRLUND *comes in from the right.*

Rörlund. Excuse me, Mr. Bernick, but I am terribly upset.

Bernick. Why, what is the matter with you?

Rörlund. I must put a question to you, Mr. Bernick. Is it with your consent that the young girl who has found a shelter under your roof shows herself in the open street in the company of a person who——

Lona. What person, Mr. Parson?

Rörlund. With the person from whom, of all others in the world, she ought to be kept farthest apart!

Lona. Ha! ha!

Rörlund. Is it with your consent, Mr. Bernick?

Bernick (looking for his hat and gloves). I know nothing about it. You must excuse me; I am in a great hurry. I am due at the Commercial Association.

[HILMAR *comes up from the garden and goes over to the farther door on the left.*

Hilmar. Betty, Betty, I want to speak to you.

Mrs. Bernick (coming to the door). What is it?

Hilmar. You ought to go down into the garden and put a stop to the flirtation that is going on between a certain person and Dina Dorf! It has quite got on my nerves to listen to them.

Lona. Indeed! And what has the certain person been saying?

Hilmar. Oh, only that he wishes she would go off to America with him. Ugh!

Rörlund. Is it possible?

Mrs. Bernick. What do you say?

Lona. But that would be perfectly splendid!

Bernick. Impossible! You cannot have heard aright.

Hilmar. Ask him yourself, then. Here comes the pair of them. Only, leave me out of it, please.

Bernick (to RUMMEL *and* VIGELAND*).* I will follow you —in a moment.

[RUMMEL *and* VIGELAND *go out to the right.* JOHAN *and* DINA *come up from the garden.*

Johan. Hurrah, Lona, she is going with us!

Mrs. Bernick. But, Johan— are you out of your senses?

Rörlund. Can I believe my ears! Such an atrocious scandal! By what arts of seduction have you——?

Johan. Come, come, sir—what are you saying?

Rörlund. Answer me, Dina; do you mean to do this—entirely of your own free will?

Dina. I must get away from here.

Rörlund. But with *him!*—with *him!*

Dina. Can you tell me of any one else here who would have the courage to take me with him?

Rörlund. Very well, then—you shall learn who he is.

Johan. Do not speak!

Bernick. Not a word more!

Rörlund. If I did not, I should be unworthy to serve a community of whose morals I have been appointed a guardian and should be acting most unjustifiably towards this young girl, in whose upbringing I have taken a material part, and who is to me——

Johan. Take care what you are doing!

Rörlund. She *shall* know! Dina, this is the man who was the cause of all your mother's misery and shame.

Bernick. Mr. Rörlund——?

Dina. He! *(To* JOHAN.*)* Is this true?

Johan. Karsten, you answer.

Bernick. Not a word more! Do not let us say another word about it to-day.

Dina. Then it is true.

Rörlund. Yes, it is true. And more than that—this fellow, whom you were going to trust, did not run away from home empty-handed; ask him about old Mrs. Bernick's cash-box—Mr. Bernick can bear witness to that!

Lona. Liar!

Bernick. Ah!——

Mrs. Bernick. My God! my God!

Johan (rushing at RÖRLUND *with uplifted arm.)* And you dare to——

Lona (restraining him.) Do not strike him, Johan!

Rörlund. That is right, assault me! But the truth will out; and it *is* the truth—Mr. Bernick has admitted it, and the whole town knows it. Now, Dina, you know him.

[*A short silence.*

Johan (softly, grasping Bernick *by the arm).* Karsten, Karsten, what have you done?

Mrs. Bernick (in tears). Oh, Karsten, to think that I should have mixed you up in all this disgrace!

Sandstad (coming in hurriedly from the right and calling out, with his hand still on the door-handle). You positively *must* come now, Mr. Bernick. The fate of the whole railway is hanging by a thread.

Bernick (abstractedly). What is it? What have I to——

Lona (earnestly and with emphasis). You have to go and be a pillar of society, brother-in-law.

Sandstad. Yes, come along; we need the full weight of your moral excellence on our side.

Johan (aside to Bernick*).* Karsten, we will have a talk about this to-morrow.

[*Goes out through the garden.* Bernick, *looking half dazed, goes out to the right with* Sandstad.

ACT III

SCENE. *The same room.* BERNICK, *with a cane in his hand and evidently in a great rage, comes out of the farther room on the left, leaving the door half-open behind him.*

Bernick (speaking to his wife, who is in the other room). There! I have given it him in earnest now; I don't think he will forget that thrashing! What do you say?—And *I* say that you are an injudicious mother! You make excuses for him and countenance any sort of rascality on his part.—Not rascality? What do you call it, then? Slipping out of the house at night, going out in a fishing boat, staying away till well on in the day and giving me such a horrible fright when I have so much to worry me! And then the young scamp has the audacity to threaten that he will run away! Just let him try it!—You? No, very likely; you don't trouble yourself much about what happens to him. I really believe that if he were to get killed——! Oh, really? Well, *I* have work to leave behind me in the world; I have no fancy for being left childless.—Now, do not raise objections, Betty; it shall be as I say—he is confined to the house. *(Listens.)* Hush; do not let any one notice anything.

[KRAP *comes in from the right.*

Krap. Can you spare me a moment, Mr. Bernick?

Bernick (throwing away the cane). Certainly, certainly. Have you come from the yard?

Krap. Yes. Ahem——!

Bernick. Well? Nothing wrong with the "Palm Tree," I hope?

Krap. The "Palm Tree" can sail to-morrow, but——

Bernick. It is the "Indian Girl," then? I had a suspicion that that obstinate fellow——

Krap. The "Indian Girl" can sail to-morrow, too; but I am sure she will not get very far.

Bernick. What do you mean?

Krap. Excuse me, sir; that door is standing ajar, and I think there is some one in the other room——

Bernick (shutting the door). There, then! But what is this that no one else must hear?

Krap. Just this—that I believe Aune intends to let the "Indian Girl" go to the bottom with every mother's son on board.

Bernick. Good God!—what makes you think that?

Krap. I cannot account for it any other way, sir.

Bernick. Well, tell me as briefly as you can——

Krap. I will. You know yourself how slowly the work has gone on in the yard since we got the new machines and the new inexperienced hands?

Bernick. Yes, yes.

Krap. But this morning, when I went down there, I noticed that the repairs to the American boat had made extraordinary progress; the great hole in the bottom—the rotten patch, you know——

Bernick. Yes, yes—what about it?

Krap. Was completely repaired—to all appearance, at any rate—covered up—looked as good as new. I heard that Aune himself had been working at it by lantern light the whole night.

Bernick. Yes, yes—well?

Krap. I turned it over in my head for a bit; the hands were away at breakfast, so I found an opportunity to have a look round the boat, both outside and in, without any one's seeing me. I had a job to get down to the bottom through the cargo, but I learnt the truth. There is something very suspicious going on, Mr. Bernick.

Bernick. I cannot believe it, Krap. I cannot and will not believe such a thing of Aune.

Krap. I am very sorry—but it is the simple truth. Something very suspicious is going on. No new timbers put in, as far as I could see, only stopped up and tinkered at, and covered over with sailcloth and tarpaulins and that sort of thing—an absolute fraud. The "Indian Girl" will never get to New York; she will go to the bottom like a cracked pot.

Bernick. This is most horrible! But what can be his object, do you suppose?

Krap. Probably he wants to bring the machines into discredit—wants to take his revenge—wants to force you to take the old hands on again.

Bernick. And to do this he is willing to sacrifice the lives of all on board.

Krap. He said the other day that there were no men on board the "Indian Girl"—only wild beasts.

Bernick. Yes, but—apart from that—has he no regard for the great loss of capital it would mean?

Krap. Aune does not look upon capital with a very friendly eye, Mr. Bernick.

Bernick. That is perfectly true; he is an agitator and a fomenter of discontent; but such an unscrupulous thing as this—— Look here, Krap; you must look into the matter once more. Not a word of it to any one. The blame will fall on our yard if any one hears anything of it.

Krap. Of course, but——

Bernick. When the hands are away at their dinner you must manage to get down there again; I must have absolute certainty about it.

Krap. You shall, sir; but, excuse me, what do you propose to do?

Bernick. Report the affair, naturally. We cannot, of course, let ourselves become accomplices in such a crime. I could not have such a thing on my conscience. Moreover, it will make a good impression, both on the Press and on the public in general, if it is seen that I set all personal interests aside and let justice take its course.

Krap. Quite true, Mr. Bernick.

Bernick. But first of all I must be absolutely certain. And meanwhile, do not breathe a word of it——

Krap. Not a word, sir. And you shall have your certainty. [*Goes out through the garden and down the street.*

Bernick (half aloud). Shocking!—But no, it is impossible!—inconceivable!

[*As he turns to go into his room,* HILMAR *comes in from the right.*

Hilmar. Good morning, Karsten. Let me congratulate you on your triumph at the Commercial Association yesterday.

Bernick. Thank you.

Hilmar. It was a brilliant triumph, I hear; the triumph of intelligent public spirit over selfishness and prejudice—something like a raid of French troops on the Kabyles. It is astonishing that after that unpleasant scene here, you could——

Bernick. Yes, yes—quite so.

Hilmar. But the decisive battle has not been fought yet.

Bernick. In the matter of railway, do you mean?

Hilmar. Yes; I suppose you know the trouble that Hammer is brewing?

Bernick (anxiously). No, what is that?

Hilmar. Oh, he is greatly taken up with the rumour that is going round and is preparing to dish up an article about it.

Bernick. What rumour?

Hilmar. About the extensive purchase of property along the branch line, of course.

Bernick. What? Is there such a rumour as that going about?

Hilmar. It is all over the town. I heard it at the club when I looked in there. They say that one of our lawyers has quietly bought up, on commission, all the forest-land, all the mining-land, all the waterfalls——

Bernick. Don't they say whom it was for?

Hilmar. At the club they thought it must be for some company, not connected with this town, that has got a hint of the scheme you have in hand, and has made haste to buy before the price of these properties went up. Isn't it villainous?—ugh!

Bernick. Villainous?

Hilmar. Yes, to have strangers putting their fingers into our pie—and one of our own local lawyers lending himself to such a thing! And now it will be outsiders that will get all the profits!

Bernick. But, after all, it is only an idle rumour.

Hilmar. Meanwhile people are believing it, and to-morrow or next day I have no doubt Hammer will nail it to the counter as a fact. There is a general sense of exasperation in the town already. I heard several people say that if the rumour were confirmed they would take their names off the subscription lists.

Bernick. Impossible!

Hilmar. Is it? Why do you suppose these mercenary-minded creatures were so willing to go into the undertaking with you? Don't you suppose they have scented profit for themselves——

Bernick. It is impossible, I am sure; there is so much public spirit in our little community——

Hilmar. In our community? Of course you are a confirmed optimist, and so you judge others by yourself. But I, who am a tolerably experienced observer——! There isn't a single soul in the place—excepting ourselves, of course—not a single soul in the place who holds up the banner of the Ideal. *(Goes towards the verendah.)* Ugh, I can see them there!

Bernick. See whom?

Hilmar. Our two friends from America. *(Looks out to*

the right.) And who is that they are walking with? As I am alive, if it is not the captain of the "Indian Girl." Ugh!

Bernick. What can they want with *him?*

Hilmar. Oh, he is just the right company for them. He looks as if he had been a slave-dealer or a pirate; and who knows what the other two may have been doing all these years.

Bernick. Let me tell you that it is grossly unjust to think such things about them.

Hilmar. Yes—you are an optimist. But here they are, bearing down upon us again; so I will get away while there is time.

[*Goes towards the door on the left.* LONA *comes in from the right.*

Lona. Oh, Hilmar, am I driving you away?

Hilmar. Not at all; I am in rather a hurry! I want to have a word with Betty.

[*Goes into the farthest room on the left.*

Bernick (after a moment's silence). Well, Lona?

Lona. Yes?

Bernick. What do you think of me to-day?

Lona. The same as I did yesterday. A lie more or less——

Bernick. I must enlighten you about it. Where has Johan gone?

Lona. He is coming; he had to see a man first.

Bernick. After what you heard yesterday, you will understand that my whole life will be ruined if the truth comes to light.

Lona. I can understand that.

Bernick. Of course, it stands to reason that *I* was not guilty of the crime there was so much talk about here.

Lona. That stands to reason. But who was the thief?

Bernick. There was no thief. There was no money stolen—not a penny.

Lona. How is that?

Bernick. Not a penny, I tell you.

Lona. But those rumours? How did that shameful rumour get about that Johan——

Bernick. Lona, I think I can speak to you as I could to no one else. I will conceal nothing from you. *I* was partly to blame for spreading the rumour.

Lona. You? You could act in that way towards a man who for your sake——!

Bernick. Do not condemn me without bearing in mind how things stood at that time. I told you about it yesterday. I came home and found my mother involved in a mesh of injudicious undertakings; we had all manner of bad luck—it seemed as if misfortunes were raining upon us, and our house was on the verge of ruin. I was half reckless and half in despair. Lona, I believe it was mainly to deaden my thoughts that I let myself drift into that entanglement that ended in Johan's going away.

Lona. Hm——

Bernick. You can well imagine how every kind of rumour was set on foot after he and you had gone. People began to say that it was not his first piece of folly—that Dorf had received a large sum of money to hold his tongue and go away; other people said that she had received it. At the same time it was obvious that our house was finding it difficult to meet its obligations. What was more natural than that scandal-mongers should find some connection between these two rumours? And as the woman remained here, living in poverty, people declared that he had taken the money with him to America; and every time rumour mentioned the sum, it grew larger.

Lona. And you, Karsten——?

Bernick. I grasped at the rumour like a drowning man at a straw.

Lona. You helped to spread it?

Bernick. I did not contradict. Our creditors had begun to be pressing, and I had the task of keeping them quiet.

The result was the dissipating of any suspicion as to the stability of the firm; people said that we had been hit by a temporary piece of ill-luck—that all that was necessary was that they should not press us—only give us time and every creditor would be paid in full.

Lona. And every creditor was paid in full?

Bernick. Yes, Lona, that rumour saved our house and made me the man I now am.

Lona. That is to say, a lie has made you the man you now are.

Bernick. Whom did it injure at the time? It was Johan's intention never to come back.

Lona. You ask whom it injured. Look into your own heart and tell me if it has not injured you.

Bernick. Look into any man's heart you please, and you will always find, in every one, at least one black spot which he has to keep concealed.

Lona. And you call yourselves pillars of society!

Bernick. Society has none better.

Lona. And of what consequence is it whether such a society be propped up or not? What does it all consist of? Show and lies—and nothing else. Here are you, the first man in the town, living in grandeur and luxury, powerful and respected—you, who have branded an innocent man as a criminal.

Bernick. Do you suppose I am not deeply conscious of the wrong I have done him? And do you suppose I am not ready to make amends to him for it?

Lona. How? By speaking out?

Bernick. Would you have the heart to insist on that?

Lona. What else can make amends for such a wrong?

Bernick. I am rich, Lona; Johan can demand any sum he pleases——

Lona. Yes, offer him money, and you will hear what he will say.

Bernick. Do you know what he intends to do?

Lona. No; since yesterday he has been dumb. He looks as if this had made a grown man of him all at once.

Bernick. I must talk to him.

Lona. Here he comes.

[JOHAN *comes in from the right.*

Bernick (going towards him). Johan——!

Johan (motioning him away). Listen to me first. Yesterday morning I gave you my word that I would hold my tongue.

Bernick. You did.

Johan. But then I did not know——

Bernick. Johan, only let me say a word or two to explain the circumstances——

Johan. It is unnecessary; I understand the circumstances perfectly. The firm was in a dangerous position at the time; I had gone off, and you had my defenceless name and reputation at your mercy. Well, I do not blame you so very much for what you did; we were young and thoughtless in those days. But now I have need of the truth, and now you must speak.

Bernick. And just now I have need of all my reputation for morality, and therefore I *cannot* speak.

Johan. I don't take much account of the false reports you spread about me; it is the other thing that you must take the blame of. I shall make Dina my wife, and here—here in your town—I mean to settle down and live with her.

Lona. Is that what you mean to do?

Bernick. With Dina? Dina as your wife?—in this town?

Johan. Yes, here and nowhere else. I mean to stay here to defy all these liars and slanderers. But before I can win her you must exonerate me.

Bernick. Have you considered that, if I confess to the one thing, it will inevitably mean making myself responsible for the other as well? You will say that I can show by our books that nothing dishonest happened? But I cannot;

our books were not so accurately kept in those days. And even if I could, what good would it do? Should I not in any case be pointed at as the man who had once saved himself by an untruth and for fifteen years had allowed that untruth and all its consequences to stand without having raised a finger to demolish it? You do not know our community very much, or you would realise that it would ruin me utterly.

Johan. I can only tell you that I mean to make Mrs. Dorf's daughter my wife and live with her in this town.

Bernick (wiping the perspiration from his forehead). Listen to me, Johan—and you, too, Lona. The circumstances I am in just now are quite exceptional. I am situated in such a way that if you aim this blow at me you will not only destroy me, but will also destroy a great future, rich in blessings, that lies before the community which, after all, was the home of your childhood.

Johan. And if I do not aim this blow at you, I shall be destroying all my future happiness with my own hand.

Lona. Go on, Karsten.

Bernick. I will tell you, then. It is mixed up with the railway project, and the whole thing is not quite so simple as you think. I suppose you have heard that last year there was some talk of a railway line along the coast? Many influential people backed up the idea—people in the town and the suburbs, and especially the Press; but I managed to get the proposal quashed, on the ground that it would have injured our steamboat trade along the coast.

Lona. Have you any interest in the steamboat trade?

Bernick. Yes. But no one ventured to suspect me on that account; my honoured name fully protected me from that. For the matter of that, I could have stood the loss; but the place could not have stood it. So the inland line was decided upon. As soon as that was done, I assured myself—without saying anything about it—that a branch line could be laid to the town.

Lona. Why did you say nothing about it, Karsten?

Bernick. Have you heard the rumours of extensive buying up of forest-lands, mines and waterfalls——?

Johan. Yes, apparently it is some company from another part of the country——

Bernick. As these properties are situated at present, they are as good as valueless to their owners, who are scattered about the neighbourhood; they have therefore been sold comparatively cheap. If the purchaser had waited till the branch line began to be talked of, the proprietors would have asked exorbitant prices.

Lona. Well—what then?

Bernick. Now I am going to tell you something that can be construed in different ways—a thing to which, in our community, a man could only confess provided he had an untarnished and honoured name to take his stand upon.

Lona. Well?

Bernick. It is I that have bought up the whole of them.

Lona. You?

Johan. On your own account?

Bernick. On my own account. If the branch line becomes an accomplished fact, I am a millionaire; if it does not, I am ruined.

Lona. It is a big risk, Karsten.

Bernick. I have risked my whole fortune on it.

Lona. I am not thinking of your fortune; but if it comes to light that——

Bernick. Yes, that is the critical part of it. With the unblemished and honoured name I have hitherto borne, I can take the whole thing upon my shoulders, carry it through and say to my fellow-citizens: "See, I have taken this risk for the good of the community."

Lona. Of the community?

Bernick. Yes; and not a soul will doubt my motives.

Lona. Then some of those concerned in it have acted

more openly—without any secret motives or considerations.

Bernick. Who?

Lona. Why, of course Rummel and Sandstad and Vigeland.

Bernick. To get them on my side I was obliged to let them into the secret.

Lona. And they?

Bernick. They have stipulated for a fifth part of the profits as their share.

Lona. Oh, these pillars of society!

Bernick. And isn't it society itself that forces us to use these underhand means? What would have happened, if I had not acted secretly? Everybody would have wanted to have a hand in the undertaking; the whole thing would have been divided up, mismanaged and bungled. There is not a single man in the town except myself who is capable of directing so big an affair as this will be. In this country, almost without exception, it is only foreigners who have settled here who have the aptitude for big business schemes. That is the reason why my conscience acquits me in the matter. It is only in my hands that these properties can become a real blessing to the many who have to make their daily bread.

Lona. I believe you are right there, Karsten.

Johan. But I have no concern with the many, and my life's happiness is at stake.

Bernick. The welfare of your native place is also at stake. If things come out which cast reflections on my earlier conduct, then all my opponents will fall upon me with united vigour. A youthful folly is never allowed to be forgotten in our community. They would go through the whole of my previous life, bring up a thousand little incidents in it, interpret and explain them in the light of what has been revealed; they would crush me under the weight of humours and slanders. I should be obliged to abandon the railway scheme; and, if I take my hand off that, it will come to nothing, and I shall be ruined and my life as a citizen will be over.

Lona. Johan, after what we have just heard, you must go away from here and hold your tongue.

Bernick. Yes, yes—Johan—you must!

Johan. Yes, I will go away, and I will hold my tongue; but I shall come back, and then I shall speak.

Bernick. Stay over there, Johan; hold your tongue, and I am willing to share with you——

Johan. Keep your money, but give me back my name and reputation.

Bernick. And sacrifice my own!

Johan. You and your community must get out of that the best way you can. I must and shall win Dina for my wife. And therefore I am going to sail to-morrow in the "Indian Girl"——

Bernick. In the "Indian Girl"?

Johan. Yes. The captain has promised to take me. I shall go over to America, as I say; I shall sell my farm and set my affairs in order. In two months I shall be back.

Bernick. And then you will speak?

Johan. Then the guilty man must take his guilt on himself.

Bernick. Have you forgotten that, if I do that, I must also take on myself guilt that is not mine?

Johan. Who is it that for the last fifteen years has benefited by that shameful rumour?

Bernick. You will drive me to desperation! Well, if you speak, I shall deny everything! I shall say it is a plot against me—that you have come here to blackmail me!

Lona. For shame, Karsten!

Bernick. I am a desperate man, I tell you, and I shall fight for my life. I shall deny everything—everything!

Johan. I have your two letters. I found them in my

box among my other papers. This morning I read them again; they are plain enough.

Bernick. And will you make them public?

Johan. If it becomes necessary.

Bernick. And you will be back here in two months?

Johan. I hope so. The wind is fair. In three weeks I shall be in New York—if the "Indian Girl" does not go to the bottom.

Bernick (with a start). Go to the bottom? Why should the "Indian Girl" go to the bottom?

Johan. Quite so—why should she?

Bernick (scarcely audibly). Go to the bottom?

Johan. Well, Karsten, now you know what is before you. You must find your own way out. Good-bye! You can say good-bye to Betty for me, although she has not treated me like a sister. But I must see Martha. She shall tell Dina—she shall promise me——

[*Goes out through the farther door on the left.*

Bernick (to himself). The "Indian Girl"——? *(Quickly.)* Lona, you *must* prevent that!

Lona. You see for yourself, Karsten—I have no influence over him any longer.

[*Follows* JOHAN *into the other room.*

Bernick (a prey to uneasy thoughts). Go to the bottom——?

[AUNE *comes in from the right.*

Aune. Excuse me, sir, but if it is convenient——

Bernick (turning round angrily). What do you want?

Aune. To know if I may ask you a question, sir.

Bernick. Be quick about it, then. What is it?

Aune. I wanted to ask if I am to consider it as certain—absolutely certain—that I should be dismissed from the yard if the "Indian Girl" were not ready to sail to-morrow?

Bernick. What do you mean? The ship *is* ready to sail.

Aune. Yes—it is. But suppose it were not, should I be discharged?

Bernick. What is the use of asking such idle questions?

Aune. Only that I should like to know, sir. Will you answer me that?—should I be discharged?

Bernick. Am I in the habit of keeping my word or not?

Aune. Then to-morrow I should have lost the position I hold in my house and among those near and dear to me—lost my influence over men of my own class—lost all opportunity of doing anything for the cause of the poorer and needier members of the community?

Bernick. Aune, we have discussed all that before.

Aune. Quite so—then the "Indian Girl" will sail.

[*A short silence.*

Bernick. Look here—it is impossible for me to have my eyes everywhere—I cannot be answerable for everything. You can give me your assurance, I suppose, that the repairs have been satisfactorily carried out?

Aune. You gave me very short grace, Mr. Bernick.

Bernick. But I understand you to warrant the repairs?

Aune. The weather is fine, and it is summer.

[*Another pause.*

Bernick. Have you anything else to say to me?

Aune. I think not, sir.

Bernick. Then—the "Indian Girl" will sail——

Aune. To-morrow?

Bernick. Yes.

Aune. Very good.

[*Bows and goes out.* BERNICK *stands for a moment irresolute; then walks quickly towards the door, as if to call* AUNE *back; but stops, hesitatingly, with his hand on the door-handle. At that moment the door is opened from without, and* KRAP *comes in.*

Krap (in a low voice). Aha, he has been here. Has he confessed?

Bernick. Hm—have you discovered anything?

Krap. What need of that, sir? Could you not see the evil conscience looking out of the man's eyes?

Bernick. Nonsense—such things don't show. Have you discovered anything, I want to know?

Krap. I could not manage it; I was too late. They had already begun hauling the ship out of the dock. But their very haste in doing that plainly shows that——

Bernick. It shows nothing. Has the inspection taken place, then?

Krap. Of course; but——

Bernick. There, you see! And of course they found nothing to complain of?

Krap. Mr. Bernick, you know very well how much this inspection means, especially in a yard that has such a good name as ours has.

Bernick. No matter—it takes all responsibility off us.

Krap. But, sir, could you really not tell from Aune's manner that——?

Bernick. Aune has completely reassured me, let me tell you.

Krap. And let me tell you, sir, that I am morally certain that——

Bernick. What does this mean, Krap? I see plainly enough that you want to get your knife into this man; but if you want to attack him you must find some other occasion. You know how important it is to me—or, I should say, to the owners—that the "Indian Girl" should sail to-morrow.

Krap. Very well—so be it; but if ever we hear of *that* ship again—hm!

[VIGELAND *comes in from the right.*

Vigeland. I wish you a very good morning, Mr. Bernick. Have you a moment to spare?

Bernick. At your service, Mr. Vigeland.

Vigeland. I only want to know if you are also of opinion that the "Palm Tree" should sail to-morrow?

Bernick. Certainly; I thought that was quite settled.

Vigeland. Well, the captain came to me just now and told me that storm-signals have been hoisted.

Bernick. Oh! Are we to expect a storm?

Vigeland. A stiff breeze, at all events; but not a contrary wind—just the opposite.

Bernick. Hm—well, what do you say?

Vigeland. I say, as I said to the captain, that the "Palm Tree" is in the hands of Providence. Besides, they are only going across the North Sea at first; and in England freights are running tolerably high just now, so that——

Bernick. Yes, it would probably mean a loss for us if we waited.

Vigeland. Besides, she is a stout ship and fully insured as well. It is more risky, now, for the "Indian Girl"——

Bernick. What do you mean?

Vigeland. She sails to-morrow, too.

Bernick. Yes, the owners have been in such a hurry, and, besides——

Vigeland. Well, if that old hulk can venture out—and with such a crew, into the bargain—it would be a disgrace to us if we——

Bernick. Quite so. I presume you have the ship's papers with you.

Vigeland. Yes, here they are.

Bernick. Good; then will you go in with Mr. Krap?

Krap. Will you come in here, sir, and we will dispose of them at once.

Vigeland. Thank you—And the issue we leave in the hands of the Almighty, Mr. Bernick.

[*Goes with* KRAP *into* BERNICK'S *room.* RÖRLUND *comes up from the garden.*

Rörlund. At home at this time of day, Mr. Bernick?

Bernick (lost in thought). As you see.

Rörlund. It was really on your wife's account I came. I thought she might be in need of a word of comfort.

Bernick. Very likely she is. But I want to have a little talk with you, too.

Rörlund. With the greatest of pleasure, Mr. Bernick. But what is the matter with you? You look quite pale and upset.

Bernick. Really? Do I? Well, what else could you expect—a man so loaded with responsibilities as I am? There is all my own big business—and now the planning of this railway.——But tell me something, Mr. Rörlund; let me put a question to you.

Rörlund. With pleasure, Mr. Bernick.

Bernick. It is about a thought that has occurred to me. Suppose a man is face to face with an undertaking which will concern the welfare of thousands, and suppose it should be necessary to make a sacrifice of one——?

Rörlund. What do you mean?

Bernick. For example, suppose a man were thinking of starting a large factory. He knows for certain—because all his experience has taught him so—that sooner or later a toll of human life will be exacted in the working of that factory.

Rörlund. Yes, that is only too probable.

Bernick. Or, say a man embarks on a mining enterprise. He takes into his service fathers of families and young men in the first flush of their youth. Is it not quite safe to predict that all of them will not come out of it alive?

Rörlund. Yes, unhappily that is quite true.

Bernick. Well—a man in that position will know beforehand that the undertaking he proposes to start must undoubtedly, at some time or other, mean a loss of human life. But the undertaking itself is for the public good; for every man's life that it costs, it will undoubtedly promote the welfare of many hundreds.

Rörlund. Ah, you are thinking of the railway—of all the dangerous excavating and blasting, and that sort of thing——

Bernick. Yes—quite so—I am thinking of the railway.

And, besides, the coming of the railway will mean the starting of factories and mines. But do not think, nevertheless——

Rörlund. My dear Mr. Bernick, you are almost overconscious. What I think is that, if you place the affair in the hands of Providence——

Bernick. Yes—exactly; Providence—

Rörlund. You are blameless in the matter. Go on and build your railway hopefully.

Bernick. Yes, but now I will put a special instance to you. Suppose a charge of blasting-powder had to be exploded in a dangerous place, and that unless it were exploded the line could not be constructed? Suppose the engineer knew that it would cost the life of the workman who lit the fuse, but that it had to be lit, and that it was the engineer's duty to send a workman to do it?

Rörlund. Hm——

Bernick. I know what you will say. It would be a splendid thing if the engineer took the match himself and went and lit the fuse. But that is out of the question, so he must sacrifice a workman.

Rörlund. That is a thing no engineer here would ever do.

Bernick. No engineer in the bigger countries would think twice about doing it.

Rörlund. In the bigger countries? No, I can quite believe it. In those depraved and unprincipled communities——

Bernick. Oh, there is a good deal to be said for those communities.

Rörlund. Can you say that?—you, who yourself——

Bernick. In the bigger communities a man finds space to carry out a valuable project—finds the courage to make some sacrifice in a great cause; but here a man is cramped by all kinds of petty considerations and scruples.

Rörlund. Is human life a petty consideration?

Bernick. When that human life threatens the welfare of thousands.

Rörlund. But you are suggesting cases that are quite inconceivable, Mr. Bernick! I do not understand you at all to-day. And you quote the bigger countries—well, what do they think of human life there? They look upon it simply as part of the capital they have to use. But *we* look at things from a somewhat different moral standpoint, I should hope. Look at our respected shipping industry! Can you name a single one of our ship-owners who would sacrifice a human life for the sake of paltry gain? And then think of those scoundrels in the bigger countries, who for the sake of profit send out freights in one unseaworthy ship after another——

Bernick. I am not talking of unseaworthy ships!

Rörlund. But I am, Mr. Bernick.

Bernick. Yes, but to what purpose? They have nothing to do with the question.——Oh, these small, timid considerations! If a General from this country were to take his men under fire and some of them were shot, I suppose he would have sleepless nights after it! It is not so in other countries. You should hear what that fellow in there says——

Rörlund. He? Who? The American——?

Bernick. Yes. You should hear how in America——

Rörlund. He, in there? And you did not tell me? I shall at once——

Bernick. It's no use; you won't be able to do anything with him.

Rörlund. We shall see. Ah, here he comes.

[JOHAN *comes in from the other room.*

Johan (talking back through the open door). Yes, yes, Dina—as you please; but I do not mean to give you up, all the same. I shall come back, and then everything will come right between us.

Rörlund. Excuse me, but what did you mean by that? What is it you propose to do?

Johan. I propose that that young girl, before whom you blackened my character yesterday, shall become my wife.

Rörlund. Your wife? And can you really suppose that——?

Johan. I mean to marry her.

Rörlund. Well, then you shall know the truth. *(Goes to the half-open door.)* Mrs. Bernick, will you be so kind as to come and be a witness—and you, too, Miss Martha. And let Dina come. *(Sees* LONA *at the door.)* Ah, you here, too?

Lona. Shall I come, too?

Rörlund. As many as you please—the more the better.

Bernick. What are you going to do?

[LONA, MRS. BERNICK, MARTHA, DINA *and* HILMAR *come in from the other room.*

Mrs. Bernick. Mr. Rörlund, I have tried my hardest, but I cannot prevent him——

Rörlund. I shall prevent him, Mrs. Bernick. Dina, you are a thoughtless girl, but I do not blame you so greatly. You have too long lacked the necessary moral support that should have sustained you. I blame myself for not having afforded you that support.

Dina. You mustn't speak now!

Mrs. Bernick. What is it?

Rörlund. It is now that I *must* speak, Dina, although your conduct yesterday and to-day has made it ten times more difficult for me. But all other considerations must give way to the necessity for saving you. You remember that I gave you my word; you remember what you promised you would answer when I judged that the right time had come. Now I dare not hesitate any longer, and therefore——. *(Turns to* JOHAN.*)* This young girl, whom you are persecuting, is my betrothed.

Mrs. Bernick. What?

Bernick. Dina!

Johan. She? Your——?

Martha. No, no, Dina!

Lona. It is a lie!

Johan. Dina—is this man speaking the truth?

Dina (after a short pause). Yes.

Rörlund. I hope this has rendered all your arts of seduction powerless. The step I have determined to take for Dina's good I now wish openly proclaimed to every one. I cherish the certain hope that it will not be misinterpreted. And now, Mrs. Bernick, I think it will be best for us to take her away from here and try to bring back peace and tranquillity to her mind.

Mrs. Bernick. Yes, come with me. Oh, Dina—what a lucky girl you are!

[*Takes* DINA *out to the left;* RÖRLUND *follows them.*

Martha. Good-bye, Johan!

[*Goes out.*

Hilmar (at the verandah door). Hm—I really must say——

Lona (who has followed DINA *with her eyes, to* JOHAN*).* Don't be downhearted, my boy! I shall stay here and keep my eye on the parson.

[*Goes out to the right.*

Bernick. Johan, you won't sail in the "Indian Girl" now?

Johan. Indeed I shall.

Bernick. But you won't come back?

Johan. I am coming back.

Bernick. After this? What have you to do here after this?

Johan. Revenge myself on you all; crush as many of you as I can.

[*Goes out to the right.* VIGELAND *and* KRAP *come in from* BERNICK'S *room.*

Vigeland. There, now the papers are in order, Mr. Bernick.

Bernick. Good, good.

Krap (in a low voice). And I suppose it is settled that the "Indian Girl" is to sail to-morrow?

Bernick. Yes.

[*Goes into his room.* VIGELAND *and* KRAP *go out to the right.* HILMAR *is just going after them, when* OLAF *puts his head carefully out of the door on the left.*

Olaf. Uncle! Uncle Hilmar!

Hilmar. Ugh, is it you? Why don't you stay upstairs? You know you are confined to the house.

Olaf (coming a step or two nearer). Hush! Uncle Hilmar, have you heard the news?

Hilmar. Yes, I have heard that you got a thrashing to-day.

Olaf (looking threateningly towards his father's room). He shan't thrash me any more. But have you heard that Uncle Johan is going to sail to-morrow with the Americans?

Hilmar. What has that got to do with you? You had better run upstairs again.

Olaf. Perhaps I shall be going for a buffalo hunt, too, one of these days, uncle.

Hilmar. Rubbish! A coward like you——

Olaf. Yes—just wait! You will learn something to-morrow!

Hilmar. Duffer!

[*Goes out through the garden.* OLAF *runs into the room again and shuts the door, as he sees* KRAP *coming in from the right.*

Krap (going to the door of BERNICK'S *room and opening it slightly).* Excuse my bothering you again, Mr. Bernick; but there is a tremendous storm blowing up. *(Waits a moment, but there is no answer.)* Is the "Indian Girl" to sail, for all that?

[*After a short pause, the following is heard.*

Bernick (from his room). The "Indian Girl" is to sail, for all that.

[KRAP *shuts the door and goes out again to the right.*

ACT IV

SCENE.—*The same room. The work-table has been taken away. It is a stormy evening and already dusk. Darkness sets in as the following scene is in progress. A man-servant is lighting the chandelier, two maids bring in pots of flowers, lamps and candles, which they place on tables and stands along the walls.* RUMMEL, *in dress clothes, with gloves and a white tie, is standing in the room giving instructions to the servants.*

Rummel. Only every other candle, Jacob. It must not look as if it were arranged for the occasion—it has to come as a surprise, you know. And all these flowers——? Oh, well, let them be; it will probably look as if they stood there every day.

[BERNICK *comes out of his room.*

Bernick (stopping at the door). What does this mean?

Rummel. Oh dear, is it you! *(To the servants.)* Yes, you might leave us for the present.

[*The servants go out.*

Bernick. But, Rummel, what is the meaning of this?

Rummel. It means that the proudest moment of your life has come. A procession of his fellow-citizens is coming to do honour to the first man of the town.

Bernick. What!

Rummel. In procession—with banners and a band! We ought to have had torches, too; but we did not like to risk that in this stormy weather. There will be illuminations—and that always sounds well in the newspapers.

Bernick. Listen, Rummel—I won't have anything to do with this.

Rummel. But it is too late now; they will be here in half-an-hour.

Bernick. But why did you not tell me about this before?

Rummel. Just because I was afraid you would raise objections to it. But I consulted your wife; she allowed me to take charge of the arrangements, while she looks after the refreshments.

Bernick (listening). What is that noise? Are they coming already? I fancy I hear singing.

Rummel (going to the verandah door). Singing? Oh, that is only the Americans. The "Indian Girl" is being towed out.

Bernick. Towed out? Oh, yes. No, Rummel, I cannot this evening; I am not well.

Rummel. You certainly do look bad. But you must pull yourself together; devil take it—you *must!* Sandstad and Vigeland and I all attach the greatest importance of carrying this thing through. We have got to crush our opponents under the weight of as complete an expression of public opinion as possible. Rumours are getting about the town; our announcement about the purchase of the property cannot be withheld any longer. It is imperative that this very evening—after songs and speeches, amidst the clink of glasses—in a word, in an ebullient atmosphere of festivity—you should inform them of the risk you have incurred for the good of the community. In such an ebullient atmosphere of festivity—as I just now described it—you can do an astonishing lot with the people here. But you must have that atmosphere, or the thing won't go.

Bernick. Yes, yes——

Rummel. And especially when so delicate and ticklish a point has to be negotiated. Well, thank goodness, you have a name that will be a tower of strength, Bernick.

But listen now; we must make our arrangements, to some extent. Mr. Hilmar Tönnesen has written an ode to you. It begins very charmingly with the words: "Raise the Ideal's banner high!" And Mr. Rörlund has undertaken the task of making the speech of the evening. Of course you must reply to that.

Bernick. I cannot to-night, Rummel. Couldn't you——?

Rummel. It is impossible, however willing I might be; because, as you can imagine, his speech will be especially addressed to you. Of course, it is possible he may say a word or two about the rest of us; I have spoken to Vigeland and Sandstad about it. Our idea is that, in replying, you should propose the toast of "Prosperity to our Community"; Sandstad will say a few words on the subject of harmonious relations between the different strata of society; then Vigeland will express the hope that this new undertaking may not disturb the sound moral basis upon which our community stands; and I propose, in a few suitable words, to refer to the ladies, whose work for the community, though more inconspicuous, is far from being without its importance. But you are not listening to me——

Bernick. Yes—indeed I am. But, tell me, do you think there is a very heavy sea running outside?

Rummel. Why, are you nervous about the "Palm Tree"? She is fully insured, you know.

Bernick. Yes, she is insured; but——

Rummel. And in good repair—and that is the main thing.

Bernick. Hm—— Supposing anything does happen to a ship, it doesn't follow that human life will be in danger, does it? The ship and the cargo may be lost—and one might lose one's boxes and papers——

Rummel. Good Lord—boxes and papers are not of much consequence.

Bernick. Not of much consequence! No, no; I only meant—— Hush—I hear voices again.

Rummel. It is on board the "Palm Tree."

[VIGELAND *comes in from the right.*

Vigeland. Yes, they are just towing the "Palm Tree" out. Good evening, Mr. Bernick.

Bernick. And you, as a seafaring man, are still of opinion that——

Vigeland. I put my trust in Providence, Mr. Bernick. Moreover, I have been on board myself and distributed a few small tracts which I hope may carry a blessing with them.

[SANDSTAD *and* KRAP *come in from the right.*

Sandstad (to some one at the door). Well, if that gets through all right, anything will. *(Comes in.)* Ah, good evening, good evening!

Bernick. Is anything the matter, Krap?

Krap. I say nothing, Mr. Bernick.

Sandstad. The entire crew of the "Indian Girl" are drunk; I will stake my reputation on it that they won't come out of it alive.

[LONA *comes in from the right.*

Lona. Ah, now I can say his good-byes for him.

Bernick. Is he on board already?

Lona. He will be directly, at any rate. We parted outside the hotel.

Bernick. And he persists in his intention?

Lona. As firm as a rock.

Rummel (who is fumbling at the window). Confound these new-fangled contrivances; I cannot get the curtains drawn.

Lona. Do you want them drawn? I thought, on the contrary——

Rummel. Yes, drawn at first, Miss Hessel. You know what is in the wind, I suppose?

Lona. Yes. Let me help you. *(Takes hold of the cords.)* I will draw down the curtains on my brother-in-law—though I would much rather draw them up.

Rummel. You can do that, too, later on. When the garden is filled with a surging crowd, then the curtains shall be drawn back, and they will be able to look in upon a surprised and happy family. Citizens' lives should be such that they can live in glass houses!

[BERNICK *opens his mouth, as though he were going to say something; but he turns hurriedly away and goes into his room.*

Rummel. Come along, let us have a final consultation. Come in, too, Mr. Krap; you must assist us with information on one or two points of detail.

[*All the men go into* BERNICK'S *room.* LONA *has drawn the curtains over the windows, and is just going to do the same over the open glass door, when* OLAF *jumps down from the room above on to the garden steps; he has a wrap over his shoulders and a bundle in his hand.*

Lona. Bless me, child, how you frightened me!

Olaf (hiding his bundle). Hush, aunt!

Lona. Did you jump out of the window? Where are you going?

Olaf. Hush!—don't say anything. I want to go to Uncle Johan—only on to the quay, you know—only to say good-bye to him. Good-night, aunt!

[*Runs out through the garden.*

Lona. No—stop! Olaf—Olaf!

[JOHAN, *dressed for his journey, with a bag over his shoulder, comes warily in by the door on the right.*

Johan. Lona!

Lona (turning round). What! Back again?

Johan. I have still a few minutes. I must see her once more; we cannot part like this.

[*The farther door on the left opens, and* Martha *and* Dina, *both with cloaks on, and the latter carrying a small travelling-bag in her hand, come in.*

Dina. Let me go to him! Let me go to him!

Martha. Yes, you shall go to him, Dina!

Dina. There he is!

Johan. Dina!

Dina. Take me with you!

Johan. What——!

Lona. You mean it?

Dina. Yes, take me with you. The other has written to me that he means to announce to every one this evening——

Johan. Dina—you do not love him?

Dina. I have never loved the man! I would rather drown myself in the fjord than be engaged to him! Oh, how he humiliated me yesterday with his condescending manner! How clear he made it that he felt he was lifting up a poor despised creature to his own level! I do not mean to be despised any longer. I mean to go away. May I go with you?

Johan. Yes, yes—a thousand times, yes!

Dina. I will not be a burden to you long. Only help me to get over there; help me to go the right way about things at first——

Johan. Hurrah, it is all right after all, Dina!

Lona (pointing to Bernick's *door).* Hush!—gently, gently!

Johan. Dina, I shall look after you.

Dina. I am not going to let you do that. I mean to look after myself; over there, I am sure I can do that. Only let me get away from here. Oh, these women!—you don't know—they have written to me to-day, too—exhorting me to realise my good fortune—impressing on me how magnanimous he has been. To-morrow, and every day afterwards, they would be watching me to see if I were making myself worthy of it all. I am sick and tired of all this goodness!

Johan. Tell me, Dina—is that the only reason you are coming away? Am I nothing to you?

Dina. Yes, Johan, you are more to me than any one else in the world.

Johan. Oh, Dina——!

Dina. Every one here tells me I ought to hate and detest you—that it is my duty; but I cannot see that it is my duty and shall never be able to.

Lona. No more you shall, my dear!

Martha. No, indeed you shall not; and that is why you shall go with him as his wife.

Johan. Yes, yes!

Lona. What? Give me a kiss, Martha. I never expected that from *you!*

Martha. No, I dare say not; I would not have expected it myself. But I was bound to break out some time! Ah, what we suffer under the tyranny of habit and custom! Make a stand against that, Dina. Be his wife. Let me see you defy all this convention.

Johan. What is your answer, Dina?

Dina. Yes, I will be your wife.

Johan. Dina!

Dina. But first of all I want to work—to make something of myself—as you have done. I am not going to be merely a thing that is taken.

Lona. Quite right—that is the way.

Johan. Very well; I shall wait and hope——

Lona. And win, my boy! But now you must get on board!

Johan. Yes, on board! Ah, Lona, my dear sister, just one word with you. Look here——

[*He takes her into the background and talks hurriedly to her.*

Martha. Dina, you lucky girl, let me look at you, and kiss you once more—for the last time.

Dina. Not for the last time; no, my darling aunt, we shall meet again.

Martha. Never! Promise me, Dina, never to come back! *(Grasps her hands and looks at her.)* Now go to your happiness, my dear child—across the sea. How often, in my schoolroom, I have yearned to be over there! It must be beautiful; the skies are loftier than here—a freer air plays about your head——

Dina. Oh, Aunt Martha, some day you will follow us.

Martha. I? Never—never. I have my little vocation here, and now I really believe I can live to the full the life that I ought.

Dina. I cannot imagine being parted from you.

Martha. Ah, one can part from much, Dina. *(Kisses her.)* But I hope you may never experience that, my sweet child. Promise me to make him happy.

Dina. I will promise nothing; I hate promises; things must happen as they will.

Martha. Yes, yes, that is true; only remain what you are—true and faithful to yourself.

Dina. I will, aunt.

Lona (putting into her pocket some papers that JOHAN *has given her).* Splendid, splendid, my dear boy. But now you must be off.

Johan. Yes, we have no time to waste now. Good-bye, Lona, and thank you for all your love. Good-bye, Martha, and thank you, too, for your loyal friendship.

Martha. Good-bye, Johan! Good-bye, Dina! And may you be happy all your lives!

[*She and* LONA *hurry them to the door at the back.* JOHAN *and* DINA *go quickly down the steps and through the garden.* LONA *shuts the door and draws the curtains over it.*

Lona. Now we are alone, Martha. You have lost her and I him.

Martha. You—lost him?

Lona. Oh, I had already half lost him over there. The boy was longing to stand on his own feet; that was why I pretended to be suffering from homesickness.

Martha. So that was it? Ah, then I understand why you came. But he will want you back, Lona.

Lona. An old step-sister—what use will he have for her now? Men break many very dear ties to win their happiness.

Martha. That sometimes is so.

Lona. But we two will stick together, Martha.

Martha. Can I be anything to you?

Lona. Who more so? We two foster-sisters—haven't we both lost our children? Now we are alone.

Martha. Yes, alone. And therefore you ought to know this, too—I loved him more than anything in the world.

Lona. Martha! *(Grasps her by the arm.)* Is that true?

Martha. All my existence lies in those words. I have loved him and waited for him. Every summer I waited for him to come. And then he came—but he had no eyes for me.

Lona. You loved him! And it was you yourself that put his happiness into his hands.

Martha. Ought I not to be the one to put his happiness into his hands, since I loved him? Yes, I have loved him. All my life has been for him, ever since he went away. What reason had I to hope, you mean? Oh, I think I had some reason, all the same. But when he came back—then it seemed as if everything had been wiped out of his memory. He had no eyes for me.

Lona. It was Dina that overshadowed you, Martha?

Martha. And it is a good thing she did. At the time he went away, we were of the same age; but when I saw him again—oh, that dreadful moment!—I realised that now I was ten years older than he. He had gone out into the bright sparkling sunshine and breathed in youth and health with every breath; and here I sat meanwhile, spinning and spinning——

Lona. Spinning the thread of his happiness, Martha.

Martha. Yes, it was a golden thread I spun. No bitterness! We have been two good sisters to him, haven't we, Lona?

Lona (throwing her arms round her). Martha!

[BERNICK *comes in from his room.*

Bernick (to the other men, who are in his room). Yes, yes, arrange it any way you please. When the time comes, I shall be able to—— *(Shuts the door.)* Ah, you are here. Look here, Martha—I think you had better change your dress; and tell Betty to do the same. I don't want anything elaborate, of course—something homely, but neat. But you must make haste.

Lona. And a bright, cheerful face, Martha; your eyes must look happy.

Bernick. Olaf is to come downstairs, too; I will have him beside me.

Lona. Hm! Olaf——

Martha. I will give Betty your message.

[*Goes out by the farther door on the left.*

Lona. Well, the great and solemn moment is at hand.

Bernick (walking uneasily up and down). Yes, it is.

Lona. At such a moment I should think a man would feel proud and happy.

Bernick (looking at her). Hm!

Lona. I hear the whole town is to be illuminated.

Bernick. Yes, they have some idea of that sort.

Lona. All the different clubs will assemble with their banners—your name will blaze out in letters of fire—to-night the telegraph will flash the news to every part of the country: "In the bosom of his happy family, Mr. Bernick received the homage of his fellow-citizens as one of the pillars of society."

Bernick. That is so; and they will begin to cheer outside, and the crowd will shout in front of my house until I shall be obliged to go out and bow to them and thank them.

Lona. Obliged to?

Bernick. Do you suppose I shall feel happy at that moment?

Lona. No, I don't suppose you will feel so very happy.

Bernick. Lona, you despise me.

Lona. Not yet.

Bernick. And you have no right to; no right to *despise* me! Lona, you can have no idea how utterly alone I stand in this cramped and stunted community—where I have had, year after year, to stifle my ambition for a fuller life. My work may seem many-sided, but what have I really accomplished? Odds and ends—scraps. They would not stand anything else here. If I were to go a step in advance of the opinions and views that are current at the moment, I should lose all my influence. Do you know what we are —we who are looked upon as pillars of society? We are nothing more nor less than the tools of society.

Lona. Why have you only begun to realise that now?

Bernick. Because I have been thinking a great deal lately—since you came back—and this evening I have thought more seriously than ever before. Oh, Lona, why did not I really know you then—in the old days, I mean?

Lona. And if you had?

Bernick. I should never have let you go; and, if I had had you, I should not be in the position I am in to-night.

Lona. And do you never consider what *she* might have been to you—she whom you chose in my place?

Bernick. I know, at all events, that she has been nothing to me of what I needed.

Lona. Because you have never shared your interests

with her; because you have never allowed her full and frank exchange of thoughts with you; because you have allowed her to be borne under by self-reproach for the shame you cast upon one who was dear to her.

Bernick. Yes, yes; it all comes from lying and deceit.

Lona. Then why not break with all this lying and deceit?

Bernick. Now? It is too late now, Lona.

Lona. Karsten, tell me—what gratification does all this show and deception bring you?

Bernick. It brings *me* none. I must disappear some day, and all this community of bunglers with me. But a generation is growing up that will follow us; it is my son that I work for—I am providing a career for *him.* There will come a time when truth will enter into the life of the community, and on that foundation he shall build up a happier existence than his father.

Lona. With a lie at the bottom of it all? Consider what sort of inheritance it is that you are leaving to your son.

Bernick (in tones of suppressed despair). It is a thousand times worse than you think. But surely some day the curse must be lifted; and yet—nevertheless—— *(Vehemently.)* How could I bring all this upon my own head! Still, it is done now; I must go on with it now. You *shall* not succeed in crushing me!

[HILMAR *comes in hurriedly and agitatedly from the right, with an open letter in his hand.*

Hilmar. But this is—— Betty, Betty!

Bernick. What is the matter? Are they coming already?

Hilmar. No, no—but I must speak to some one immediately.

[*Goes out through the farther door on the left.*

Lona. Karsten, you talk about our having come here to crush you. So let me tell you what sort of stuff this prodigal son, whom your moral community shuns as if he had the plague, is made of. He can do without any of you—for he is away now.

Bernick. But he said he meant to come back——

Lona. Johan will never come back. He is gone for good, and Dina with him.

Bernick. Never come back?—and Dina with him?

Lona. Yes, to be his wife. That is how these two strike your virtuous community in the face, just as I did once—but never mind that.

Bernick. Gone—and she, too—in the "Indian Girl"——

Lona. No; he would not trust so precious a freight to that rascally crew. Johan and Dina are on the "Palm Tree."

Bernick. Ah! Then it is all in vain—— *(Goes hurriedly to the door of his room, opens it and calls in.)* Krap, stop the "Indian Girl"—she must not sail to-night!

Krap (from within). The "Indian Girl" is already standing out to sea, Mr. Bernick.

Bernick (shutting the door and speaking faintly). Too late—and all to no purpose——

Lona. What do you mean?

Bernick. Nothing, nothing. Leave me alone!

Lona. Hm!—look here, Karsten. Johan was good enough to say that he entrusted to me the good name and reputation that he once lent to you, and also the good name that you stole from him while he was away. Johan will hold his tongue; and I can act just as I please in the matter. See, I have two letters in my hand.

Bernick. You have got them! And you mean now—this very evening—perhaps when the procession comes——

Lona. I did not come back here to betray you, but to stir your conscience so that you should speak of your own free will. I did not succeed in doing that—so you must remain as you are, with your life founded upon a lie. Look, I am tearing your two letters in pieces. Take the wretched things—there you are. Now there is no evidence against you, Karsten. You are safe now; be happy, too—if you can.

Bernick (much moved). Lona—why did you not do that sooner! Now it is too late; life no longer seems good to me; I cannot live on after to-day.

Lona. What has happened?

Bernick. Do not ask me—— But I *must* live on, nevertheless! I *will* live—for Olaf's sake. He shall make amends for everything—expiate everything——

Lona. Karsten——!

[HILMAR *comes hurriedly back.*

Hilmar. I cannot find any one; they are all out—even Betty!

Bernick. What is the matter with you?

Hilmar. I daren't tell you.

Bernick. What is it? You *must* tell me!

Hilmar. Very well—Olaf has run away on board the "Indian Girl."

Bernick (stumbling back). Olaf—on board the "Indian Girl"! No, no!

Lona. Yes, he is! Now I understand—I saw him jump out of the window.

Bernick (calls in through the door of his room in a despairing voice). Krap, stop the "Indian Girl" at any cost!

Krap. It is impossible, sir. How can you suppose——?

Bernick. We *must* stop her; Olaf is on board!

Krap. What!

Rummel (coming out of BERNICK'S *room).* Olaf run away? Impossible!

Sandstad (following him). He will be sent back with the pilot, Mr. Bernick.

Hilmar. No, no; he has written to me. *(Shows the letter.)* He says he means to hide among the cargo till they are in the open sea.

Bernick. I shall never see him again!

Rummel. What nonsense!—a good strong ship, newly repaired——

Vigeland (who has followed the others out of BERNICK'S *room).* And in your own yard, Mr. Bernick!

Bernick. I shall never see him again, I tell you. I have lost him, Lona; and—I see it now—he never was really mine. *(Listens.)* What is that?

Rummel. Music. The procession must be coming.

Bernick. I cannot take any part in it—I will not.

Rummel. What are you thinking of! That is impossible.

Sandstad. Impossible, Mr. Bernick; think what you have at stake.

Bernick. What does it all matter to me now? What have I to work for now?

Rummel. Can you ask? You have us and the community.

Vigeland. Quite true.

Sandstad. And surely, Mr. Bernick, you have not forgotten that we——

[MARTHA *comes in through the farther door to the left. Music is heard in the distance, down the street.*

Martha. The procession is just coming, but Betty is not in the house. I don't understand where she——

Bernick. Not in the house! There, you see, Lona—no support to me, either in gladness or in sorrow.

Rummel. Draw back the curtains! Come and help me, Mr. Krap—and you, Mr. Sandstad. It is a thousand pities that the family should not be united just now; it is quite contrary to the programme.

[*They draw back all the curtains. The whole street is seen to be illuminated. Opposite the house is a large transparency, bearing the words:* "Long live Karsten Bernick, Pillar of our Society"!

Bernick (shrinking back). Take all that away! I don't want to see it! Put it out, put it out!

Rummel. Excuse me, Mr. Bernick, but are you not well?

Martha. What is the matter with him, Lona?

Lona. Hush!

[*Whispers to her.*

Bernick. Take away those mocking words, I tell you! Can't you see that all these lights are grinning at us?

Rummel. Well, really, I must confess——

Bernick. Oh, how could you understand——! But, I, I——! It is all like candles in a dead-room!

Rummel. Well, let me tell you that you are taking the thing a great deal too seriously.

Sandstad. The boy will enjoy a trip across the Atlantic, and then you will have him back.

Vigeland. Only put your trust in the Almighty, Mr. Bernick.

Rummel. And in the vessel, Bernick; it is not likely to sink, I know.

Krap. Hm——

Rummel. Now if it were one of those floating coffins that one hears are sent out by men in the bigger countries——

Bernick. I am sure my hair must be turning grey!

[MRS. BERNICK *comes in from the garden, with a shawl thrown over her head.*

Mrs. Bernick. Karsten, Karsten, do you know——?

Bernick. Yes, I know; but you—you, who see nothing that is going on—you, who have no mother's eyes for your son——!

Mrs. Bernick. Listen to me, do!

Bernick. Why did you not look after him? Now I have lost him. Give him back to me, if you can.

Mrs. Bernick. I can! I have got him!

Bernick. You have got him!

The Men. Ah!

Hilmar. Yes, I thought so.

Martha. You have got him back, Karsten!

Lona. Yes—make him your own, now.

Bernick. You have got him! Is that true? Where is he?

Mrs. Bernick. I shall not tell you, till you have forgiven him.

Bernick. Forgiven! But how did you know——?

Mrs. Bernick. Do you not think a mother sees? I was in mortal fear of your getting to know anything about it. Some words he let fall yesterday—and then his room was empty, and his knapsack and clothes missing——

Bernick. Yes, yes?

Mrs. Bernick. I ran and got hold of Aune; we went out in his boat; the American ship was on the point of sailing. Thank God, we were in time—got on board—searched the hold—found him! Oh, Karsten, you must not punish him!

Bernick. Betty!

Mrs. Bernick. Nor Aune, either!

Bernick. Aune? What do you know about him? Is the "Indian Girl" under sail again?

Mrs. Bernick. No, that is just it.

Bernick. Speak, speak!

Mrs. Bernick. Aune was just as agitated as I was; the search took us some time; it had grown dark, and the pilot made objections; and so Aune took upon himself—in your name——

Bernick. Well?

Mrs. Bernick. To stop the ship's sailing till to-morrow.

Krap. Hm——

Bernick. Oh, how glad I am!

Mrs. Bernick. You are not angry?

Bernick. I cannot tell you how glad I am, Betty!

Rummel. You really take things far too seriously.

Hilmar. Oh, yes, as soon as it is a question of a little struggle with the elements—ugh!

Krap (going to the window). The procession is just coming through your garden gate, Mr. Bernick.

Bernick. Yes, they can come now.

Rummel. The whole garden is full of people.

Sandstad. The whole street is crammed.

Rummel. The whole town is afoot, Bernick. It really is a moment that makes one proud.

Vigeland. Let us take it in a humble spirit, Mr. Rummel.

Rummel. All the banners are out! What a procession! Here comes the committee, with Mr. Rörlund at their head.

Bernick. Yes, let them come in!

Rummel. But, Bernick—in your present agitated frame of mind——

Bernick. Well, what?

Rummel. I am quite willing to speak instead of you, if you like.

Bernick. No, thank you; I will speak for myself tonight.

Rummel. But are you sure you know what to say?

Bernick. Yes, make your mind easy, Rummel—I know now what to say.

[*The music grows louder. The verandah door is opened.* RÖRLUND *comes in, at the head of the Committee, escorted by a couple of hired waiters, who carry a covered basket. They are followed by townspeople of all classes, as many as can get into the room. An apparently endless crowd of people, waving banners and flags, are visible in the garden and the street.*

Rörlund. Mr. Bernick! I see, from the surprise depicted upon your face, that it is as unexpected guests that we are intruding upon your happy family circle and your peaceful fireside, where we find you surrounded by honoured and energetic fellow-citizens and friends. But it is our hearts that have bidden us come to offer you our homage—not for the first time, it is true, but for the first time on such a comprehensive scale. We have on many occasions given you our thanks for the broad moral foundation upon which you have, so to speak, reared the edifice of our community. On this occasion we offer our homage especially to the clear-sighted, indefatigable, unselfish—nay, self-sacrificing—citizen who has taken the initiative in an undertaking which, we are assured on all sides, will give a powerful impetus to the temporal prosperity and welfare of our community.

Voices. Bravo, bravo!

Rörlund. You, sir, have for many years been a shining example in our midst. This is not the place for me to speak of your family life, which has been a model to us all; still less to enlarge upon your unblemished personal character. Such topics belong to the stillness of a man's own chamber, not to a festal occasion such as this! I am here to speak of your public life as a citizen, as it lies open to all men's eyes. Well-equipped vessels sail away from your shipyard and carry our flag far and wide over the seas. A numerous and happy band of workmen look up to you as to a father. By calling new branches of industry into existence, you have laid the foundation of the welfare of hundreds of families. In a word—you are, in the fullest sense of the term, the mainstay of our community.

Voices. Hear, hear! Bravo!

Rörlund. And, sir, it is just that disinterestedness, which colours all your conduct, that is so beneficial to our community—more so than words can express—and especially at the present moment. You are now on the point of procuring for us what I have no hesitation in calling bluntly by its prosaic name—a railway!

Voices. Bravo, bravo!

Rörlund. But it would seem as though the undertaking

were beset by certain difficulties, the outcome of narrow and selfish considerations.

Voices. Hear, hear!

Rörlund. For the fact has come to light that certain individuals, who do not belong to our community, have stolen a march upon the hard-working citizens of this place and have laid hands on certain sources of profit which by rights should have fallen to the share of our town.

Voices. That's right! Hear, hear!

Rörlund. This regrettable fact has naturally come to your knowledge also, Mr. Bernick. But it has not had the slightest effect in deterring you from proceeding steadily with your project, well knowing that a patriotic man should not solely take local interests into consideration.

Voices. Oh!—No, no!——Yes, yes!

Rörlund. It is to such a man—to the patriot citizen, whose character we all should emulate—that we bring our homage this evening. May your undertaking grow to be a real and lasting source of good fortune to this community! It is true enough that a railway may be the means of our exposing ourselves to the incursion of pernicious influences from without; but it gives us also the means of quickly expelling them from within. For even we, at the present time, cannot boast of being entirely free from the danger of such outside influences; but as we have, on this very evening—if rumour is to be believed—fortunately got rid of certain elements of that nature, sooner than was to be expected——

Voices. Order, order!

Rörlund. I regard the occurrence as a happy omen for our undertaking. My alluding to such a thing at such a moment only emphasises the fact that the house in which we are now standing is one where the claims of morality are esteemed even above ties of family.

Voices. Hear, hear! Bravo!

Bernick (at the same moment). Allow me——

Rörlund. I have only a few more words to say, Mr. Bernick. What you have done for your native place we all know has not been done with any underlying ideas of its bringing tangible profit to yourself. But, nevertheless, you must not refuse to accept a slight token of grateful appreciation at the hands of your fellow-citizens—least of all at this important moment when, according to the assurances of practical men, we are standing on the threshold of a new era.

Voices. Bravo! Hear, hear!

[RÖRLUND *signs to the servants, who bring forward the basket. During the following speech, members of the Committee take out and present the various objects mentioned.*

Rörlund. And so, Mr. Bernick, we have the pleasure of presenting you with this silver coffee-service. Let it grace your board when in the future, as so often in the past, we have the happiness of being assembled under your hospitable roof.

You, too, gentlemen, who have so generously seconded the leader of our community, we ask to accept a small souvenir. This silver goblet is for you, Mr. Rummel. Many a time have you, amidst the clink of glasses, defended the interests of your fellow-citizens in well-chosen words; may you often find similar worthy opportunities to raise and empty this goblet in some patriotic toast! To you, Mr. Sandstad, I present this album containing photographs of your fellow-citizens. Your well-known and conspicuous liberality has put you in the pleasant position of being able to number your friends amongst all classes of society. And to you, Mr. Vigeland, I have to offer this book of Family Devotions, printed on vellum and handsomely bound, to grace your study table. The mellowing influence of time has led you to take an earnest view of life; your zeal in carrying out your daily duties has, for a long period of years, been purified and ennobled by thoughts of higher and holier things. *(Turns to the crowd.)* And now, friends, three cheers for Mr. Bernick and his fellow-workers! Three cheers for the Pillars of our Society!

The whole crowd. Bernick! Pillars of Society! Hurrah—hurrah—hurrah!

Lona. I congratulate you, brother-in-law!

[*An expectant hush follows.*

Bernick (speaking seriously and slowly). Fellow-citizens—your spokesman said just now that to-night we are standing on the threshold of a new era. I hope that will prove to be the case. But before that can come to pass, we must lay fast hold of *Truth*—truth which, till to-night, has been altogether and in all circumstances a stranger to this community of ours. *(Astonishment among the audience.)* To that end, I must begin by deprecating the praises with which you, Mr. Rörlund, according to custom on such occasions, have overwhelmed me. I do not deserve them; because, until to-day, my actions have by no means been disinterested. Even though I may not always have aimed at pecuniary profit, I at all events recognise now that a craving for power, influence and position has been the moving spirit of most of my actions.

Rummel (half aloud). What next!

Bernick. Standing before my fellow-citizens, I do not reproach myself for that; because I still think I am entitled to a place in the front rank of our capable men of affairs.

Voices. Yes, yes, yes!

Bernick. But what I charge myself with is that I have so often been weak enough to resort to deceitfulness, because I knew and feared the tendency of the community to espy unclean motives behind everything a prominent man here undertakes. And now I am coming to a point which will illustrate that.

Rummel (uneasily). Hm—hm!

Bernick. There have been rumours of extensive purchases of property outside the town. These purchases have been made by me—by me alone, and by no one else. *(Murmurs are heard:* "What does he say?—He?—Bernick?") The properties are, for the time being, in my hands. Naturally I have confided in my fellow-workers, Mr. Rummel, Mr. Vigeland and Mr. Sandstad, and we are all agreed that——

Rummel. It is not true! Prove it—prove it!

Vigeland. We are not all agreed about anything!

Sandstad. —Well, really I must say——!

Bernick. That is quite true—we are not yet agreed upon the matter I was going to mention. But I confidently hope that these three gentlemen will agree with me when I announce to you that I have to-night come to the decision that these properties shall be exploited as a company of which the shares shall be offered for public subscription; any one that wishes can take shares.

Voices. Hurrah! Three cheers for Bernick!

Rummel (in a low voice, to BERNICK*).* This is the basest treachery——!

Sandstad (also in an undertone). So you have been fooling us——!

Vigeland. Well, then, devil take——! Good lord, what am I saying?

[*Cheers are heard without.*

Bernick. Silence, gentlemen. I have no right to this homage you offer me; because the decision I have just come to does not represent what was my first intention. My intention was to keep the whole thing for myself; and, even now, I am of opinion that these properties would be worked to best advantage if they remained in one man's hands. But you are at liberty to choose. If you wish it, I am willing to administer them to the best of my abilities.

Voices. Yes, yes, yes!

Bernick. But, first of all, my fellow-townsmen must know me thoroughly. And let each man seek to know himself thoroughly, too; and so let it really come to pass that to-night we begin a new era. The old era—with its affectation, its hypocrisy and its emptiness, its pretence of virtue and its miserable fear of public opinion—shall be for us like a museum, open for purposes of instruction; and to that museum we will present—shall we not, gentlemen?—the coffee service, and the goblet, and the album and the Family Devotions printed on vellum and handsomely bound.

Rummel. Oh, of course.

Vigeland (muttering). If you have taken everything else, then——

Sandstad. By all means.

Bernick. And now for the principal reckoning I have to make with the community. Mr. Rörlund said that certain pernicious elements had left us this evening. I can add what you do not yet know. The man referred to did not go away alone; with him, to become his wife, went——

Lona (loudly). Dina Dorf!

Rörlund. What?

Mrs. Bernick. What?

[*Great commotion.*

Rörlund. Fled? Run away—with him! Impossible!

Bernick. To become his wife, Mr. Rörlund. And I will add more. *(In a low voice, to his wife.)* Betty, be strong to bear what is coming. *(Aloud.)* This is what I have to say: hats off to that man, for he has nobly taken another's guilt upon his shoulders. My friends, I want to have done with falsehood; it has very nearly poisoned every fibre of my being. You shall know all. Fifteen years ago, *I* was the guilty man.

Mrs. Bernick (softly and tremblingly). Karsten!

Martha (similarly). Ah, Johan——!

Lona. Now at last you have found yourself!

[*Speechless consternation among the audience.*

Bernick. Yes, friends, I was the guilty one, and he went away. The vile and lying rumours that were spread abroad afterwards, it is beyond human power to refute now; but I have no right to complain of that. For fifteen years I have climbed up the ladder of success by the help of those rumours; whether now they are to cast me down again, or not, each of you must decide in his own mind.

Rörlund. What a thunderbolt! Our leading citizen——! *(In a low voice, to* Betty.*)* How sorry I am for you, Mrs. Bernick!

Hilmar. What a confession! Well, I must say——!

Bernick. But come to no decision to-night. I entreat every one to go home—to collect his thoughts—to look into his own heart. When once more you can think calmly, then it will be seen whether I have lost or won by speaking out. Good-bye! I have still much—very much—to repent of; but that concerns my own conscience only. Good-night! Take away all these signs of rejoicing. We must all feel that they are out of place here.

Rörlund. That they certainly are. *(In an undertone to* Mrs. Bernick.*)* Run away! So then she was completely unworthy of me. *(Louder, to the Committee.)* Yes, gentlemen, after this I think we had better disperse as quietly as possible.

Hilmar. How, after this, any one is to manage to hold the Ideal's banner high—— Ugh!

[*Meantime the news has been whispered from mouth to mouth. The crowd gradually disperses from the garden.* Rummel, Sandstad *and* Vigeland *go out, arguing eagerly but in a low voice.* Hilmar *slinks away to the right. When silence is restored, there only remain in the room* Bernick, Mrs. Bernick, Martha, Lona *and* Krap.

Bernick. Betty, can you forgive me?

Mrs. Bernick (looking at him with a smile). Do you know, Karsten, that you have opened out for me the happiest prospect I have had for many a year?

Bernick. How?

Mrs. Bernick. For many years I have felt that once you were mine and that I had lost you. Now I know that you never have been mine yet; but I shall win you.

Bernick (folding her in his arms). Oh, Betty, you *have* won me. It was through Lona that I first learned really to know you. But now let Olaf come to me.

Mrs. Bernick. Yes, you shall have him now. Mr. Krap——!

[*Talks softly to* KRAP *in the background. He goes out by the garden door. During what follows the illuminations and lights in the houses are gradually extinguished.*

Bernick (in a low voice). Thank you, Lona—you have saved what was best in me—and for me.

Lona. Do you suppose I wanted to do anything else?

Bernick. Yes, was that so—or not? I cannot quite make you out.

Lona. Hm——

Bernick. Then it was not hatred? Not revenge? Why did you come back, then?

Lona. Old friendship does not rust.

Bernick. Lona.

Lona. When Johan told me about the lie, I swore to myself that the hero of my youth should stand free and true.

Bernick. What a wretch I am!—and how little I have deserved it of you!

Lona. Oh, if we women always looked for what we deserve, Karsten——!

[AUNE *comes in with* OLAF *from the garden.*

Bernick (going to meet them). Olaf!

Olaf. Father, I promise I will never do it again——

Bernick. Never run away?

Olaf. Yes, yes, I promise you, father.

Bernick. And I promise you, you shall never have reason to. For the future you shall be allowed to grow up, not as the heir to *my* life's work, but as one who has his own life's work before him.

Olaf. And shall I be allowed to be what I like, when I grow up?

Bernick. Yes.

Olaf. Oh, thank you! Then I won't be a pillar of society.

Bernick. No? Why not?

Olaf. No—I think it must be so dull.

Bernick. You shall be yourself, Olaf; the rest may take care of itself.——And you, Aune——

Aune. I know, Mr. Bernick; I am dismissed.

Bernick. We remain together, Aune; and forgive me——

Aune. What? The ship has not sailed to-night.

Bernick. Nor will it sail to-morrow, either. I gave you too short grace. It must be looked to more thoroughly.

Aune. It shall, Mr. Bernick—and with the new machines!

Bernick. By all means—but thoroughly and conscientiously. There are many among us who need thorough and conscientious repairs, Aune. Well, good-night.

Aune. Good-night, sir—and thank you, thank you.

[*Goes out.*

Mrs. Bernick. Now they are all gone.

Bernick. And we are alone. My name is not shining in letters of fire any longer; all the lights in the windows are out.

Lona. Would you wish them lit again?

Bernick. Not for anything in the world. Where have I been! You would be horrified if you knew. I feel now as if I had come back to my right senses, after being poisoned. But I feel this—that I *can* be young and healthy again. Oh, come nearer—come closer round me. Come, Betty! Come, Olaf, my boy! And you, Martha—it seems to me as if I had never seen you all these years.

Lona. No, I can believe that. Your community is a community of bachelor souls; you do not see women.

Bernick. That is quite true; and for that very reason—this is a bargain, Lona—you must not leave Betty and me.

Mrs. Bernick. No, Lona, you must not.

Lona. No, how could I have the heart to go away and leave you young people who are just setting up housekeeping? Am I not your foster-mother? You and I, Martha, the two old aunts—— What are you looking at?

Martha. Look how the sky is clearing, and how light it is over the sea. The "Palm Tree" is going to be lucky.

Lona. It carries its good luck on board.

Bernick. And we—we have a long earnest day of work ahead of us; I most of all. But let it come; only keep close round me, you true, loyal women. I have learnt *this,* too, in these last few days; it is you women that are the pillars of society.

Lona. You have learnt a poor sort of wisdom, then, brother-in-law. *(Lays her hand firmly upon his shoulder.)* No, my friend; the spirit of truth and the spirit of freedom—they are the pillars of society.

HEDDA GABLER

(1890)

CHARACTERS

GEORGE TESMAN.*
HEDDA TESMAN, *his wife.*
MISS JULIANA TESMAN, *his aunt.*
MRS. ELVSTED.
JUDGE† BRACK.
EILERT LÖVBORG.
BERTA, *searvant at the Tesmans.*

The scene of the action is Tesman's villa, in the west end of Christiania.

* Tesman, whose Christian name in the original is "Jörgen," is described as "stipendiat i kulturhistorie"—that is to say, the holder of a scholarship for purposes of research into the History of Civilisation.

† In the original "Assessor."

HEDDA GABLER

ACT I

A spacious, handsome, and tastefully furnished drawing-room, decorated in dark colours. In the back, a wide doorway with curtains drawn back, leading into a smaller room decorated in the same style as the drawing-room. In the right-hand wall of the front room, a folding door leading out to the hall. In the opposite wall, on the left, a glass door, also with curtains drawn back. Through the panes can be seen part of a verandah outside and trees covered with autumn foliage. An oval table, with a cover on it, and surrounded by chairs, stands well forward. In front, by the wall on the right, a wide stove of dark porcelain, a high-backed arm-chair, a cushioned foot-rest and two foot-stools. A settee, with a small round table in front of it, fills the upper right-hand corner. In front, on the left, a little way from the wall, a sofa. Further back than the glass door, a piano. On either side of the doorway at the back a whatnot with terra-cotta and majolica ornaments.—Against the back wall of the inner room a sofa, with a table, and one or two chairs. Over the sofa hangs the portrait of a handsome elderly man in a General's uniform. Over the table a hanging lamp, with an opal glass shade.—A number of bouquets are arranged about the drawing-room, in vases and glasses. Others lie upon the tables. The floors in both rooms are cov-

ered with thick carpets.—Morning light. The sun shines in through the glass door.

MISS JULIANA TESMAN, *with her bonnet on and carrying a parasol, comes in from the hall, followed by* BERTA, *who carries a bouquet wrapped in paper.* MISS TESMAN *is a comely and pleasant-looking lady of about sixty-five. She is nicely but simply dressed in a grey walking-costume.* BERTA *is a middle-aged woman of plain and rather countrified appearance.*

Miss Tesman (stops close to the door, listens and says softly). Upon my word, I don't believe they are stirring yet!

Berta (also softly). I told you so, Miss. Remember how late the steamboat got in last night. And then, when they got home!—good Lord, what a lot the young mistress had to unpack before she could get to bed.

Miss Tesman. Well, well—let them have their sleep out. But let us see that they get a good breath of the fresh morning air when they do appear.

[*She goes to the glass door and throws it open.*

Berta (beside the table, at a loss what to do with the bouquet in her hand). I declare there isn't a bit of room left. I think I'll put it down here, Miss.

[*She places it on the piano.*

Miss Tesman. So you've got a new mistress now, my dear Berta. Heaven knows it was a wrench to me to part with you.

Berta (on the point of weeping). And do you think it wasn't hard for me, too, Miss? After all the blessed years I've been with you and Miss Rina.*

Miss Tesman. We must make the best of it, Berta. There was nothing else to be done. George can't do without you, you see—he absolutely can't. He has had you to look after him ever since he was a little boy.

* Pronounced Reena.

Berta. Ah but, Miss Julia, I can't help thinking of Miss Rina lying helpless at home there, poor thing. And with only that new girl, too! She'll never learn to take proper care of an invalid.

Miss Tesman. Oh, I shall manage to train her. And of course, you know, I shall take most of it upon myself. You needn't be uneasy about my poor sister, my dear Berta.

Berta. Well, but there's another thing, Miss. I'm so mortally afraid I shan't be able to suit the young mistress.

Miss Tesman. Oh well—just at first there may be one or two things——

Berta. Most like she'll be terrible grand in her ways.

Miss Tesman. Well, you can't wonder at that—General Gabler's daughter! Think of the sort of life she was accustomed to in her father's time. Don't you remember how we used to see her riding down the road along with the General? In that long black habit—and with feathers in her hat?

Berta. Yes, indeed—I remember well enough——! But good Lord, I should never have dreamt in those days that she and Master George would make a match of it.

Miss Tesman. Nor I.—But, by-the-bye, Berta—while I think of it: in future you mustn't say Master George. You must say Dr. Tesman.

Berta. Yes, the young mistress spoke of that, too—last night—the moment they set foot in the house. Is it true then, Miss?

Miss Tesman. Yes, indeed it is. Only think, Berta—some foreign university has made him a doctor—while he has been abroad, you understand. I hadn't heard a word about it, until he told me himself upon the pier.

Berta. Well, well, he's clever enough for anything, he is. But I didn't think he'd have gone in for doctoring people, too.

Miss Tesman. No, no, it's not that sort of doctor he is. *(Nods significantly.)* But let me tell you, we may have to call him something still grander before long.

Berta. You don't say so! What can that be, Miss?

Miss Tesman (smiling). H'm—wouldn't you like to know! *(With emotion.)* Ah, dear, dear—if my poor brother could only look up from his grave now and see what his little boy has grown into! *(Looks around.)* But bless me, Berta—why have you done this? Taken the chintz covers off all the furniture?

Berta. The mistress told me to. She can't abide covers on the chairs, she says.

Miss Tesman. Are they going to make this their everyday sitting-room then?

Berta. Yes, that's what I understood—from the mistress. Master George—the doctor—he said nothing.

[GEORGE TESMAN *comes from the right into the inner room, humming to himself, and carrying an unstrapped empty portmanteau. He is a middle-sized, young-looking man of thirty-three, rather stout, with a round, open, cheerful face, fair hair and beard. He wears spectacles and is somewhat carelessly dressed in comfortable indoor clothes.*

Miss Tesman. Good morning, good morning, George.

Tesman (in the doorway between the rooms). Aunt Julia! Dear Aunt Julia! *(Goes up to her and shakes hands warmly.)* Come all this way—so early! Eh?

Miss Tesman. Why, of course I had to come and see how you were getting on.

Tesman. In spite of your having had no proper night's rest?

Miss Tesman. Oh, that makes no difference to me.

Tesman. Well, I suppose you got home all right from the pier? Eh?

Miss Tesman. Yes, quite safely, thank goodness. Judge Brack was good enough to see me right to my door.

Tesman. We were so sorry we couldn't give you a seat

in the carriage. But you saw what a pile of boxes Hedda had to bring with her.

Miss Tesman. Yes, she had certainly plenty of boxes.

Berta (to TESMAN*).* Shall I go in and see if there's anything I can do for the mistress?

Tesman. No, thank you, Berta—you needn't. She said she would ring if she wanted anything.

Berta (going towards the right). Very well.

Tesman. But look here—take this portmanteau with you.

Berta (taking it). I'll put it in the attic.

[*She goes out by the hall door.*

Tesman. Fancy, Auntie—I had the whole of that portmanteau chock full of copies of documents. You wouldn't believe how much I have picked up from all the archives I have been examining—curious old details that no one has had any idea of——

Miss Tesman. Yes, you don't seem to have wasted your time on your wedding trip, George.

Tesman. No, that I haven't. But do take off your bonnet, Auntie. Look here! Let me untie the strings—eh?

Miss Tesman (while he does so). Well, well—this is just as if you were still at home with us.

Tesman (with the bonnet in his hand, looks at it from all sides). Why, what a gorgeous bonnet you've been investing in!

Miss Tesman. I bought it on Hedda's account.

Tesman. On Hedda's account? Eh?

Miss Tesman. Yes, so that Hedda needn't be ashamed of me if we happened to go out together.

Tesman (patting her cheek). You always think of everything, Aunt Julia. *(Lays the bonnet on a chair beside the table.)* And now, look here—suppose we sit comfortably on the sofa and have a little chat, till Hedda comes.

[*They seat themselves. She places her parasol in the corner of the sofa.*

Miss Tesman (takes both his hands and looks at him). What a delight it is to have you again, as large as life, before my very eyes, George! My George—my poor brother's own boy!

Tesman. And it's a delight for me, too, to see you again, Aunt Julia! You, who have been father and mother in one to me.

Miss Tesman. Oh, yes, I know you will always keep a place in your heart for your old aunts.

Tesman. And what about Aunt Rina? No improvement—eh?

Miss Tesman. Oh, no—we can scarcely look for any improvement in her case, poor thing. There she lies, helpless, as she has lain for all these years. But heaven grant I may not lose her yet awhile! For if I did, I don't know what I should make of my life, George—especially now that I haven't you to look after any more.

Tesman (patting her back). There, there, there——!

Miss Tesman (suddenly changing her tone). And to think that here are you a married man, George!—And that you should be the one to carry off Hedda Gabler—the beautiful Hedda Gabler! Only think of it—she, that was so beset with admirers!

Tesman (hums a little and smiles complacently). Yes, I fancy I have several good friends about town who would like to stand in my shoes—eh?

Miss Tesman. And then this fine long wedding-tour you have had! More than five—nearly six months——

Tesman. Well, for me it has been a sort of tour of research as well. I have had to do so much grubbing among old records—and to read no end of books, too, Auntie.

Miss Tesman. Oh, yes, I suppose so. *(More confidentially, and lowering her voice a little.)* But listen now, George—have you nothing—nothing special to tell me?

Tesman. As to our journey?

Miss Tesman. Yes.

Tesman. No, I don't know of anything except what I have told you in my letters. I had a doctor's degree conferred on me—but that I told you yesterday.

Miss Tesman. Yes, yes, you did. But what I mean is—haven't you any—any—expectations——?

Tesman. Expectations?

Miss Tesman. Why, you know, George—I'm your old auntie!

Tesman. Why, of course I have expectations.

Miss Tesman. Ah!

Tesman. I have every expectation of being a professor one of these days.

Miss Tesman. Oh, yes, a professor——

Tesman. Indeed, I may say I am certain of it. But my dear Auntie—you know all about that already!

Miss Tesman (laughing to herself). Yes, of course I do. You are quite right there. *(Changing the subject.)* But we were talking about your journey. It must have cost a great deal of money, George?

Tesman. Well, you see—my handsome travelling-scholarship went a good way.

Miss Tesman. But I can't understand how you can have made it go far enough for two.

Tesman. No, that's not so easy to understand—eh?

Miss Tesman. And especially travelling with a lady—they tell me that makes it ever so much more expensive.

Tesman. Yes, of course—it makes it a little more expensive. But Hedda had to have this trip, Auntie! She really had to. Nothing else would have done.

Miss Tesman. No, no, I suppose not. A wedding-tour seems to be quite indispensable nowadays.—But tell me now—have you gone thoroughly over the house yet?

Tesman. Yes, you may be sure I have. I have been afoot ever since daylight.

Miss Tesman. And what do you think of it all?

Tesman. I'm delighted! Quite delighted! Only I can't

think what we are to do with the two empty rooms between this inner parlour and Hedda's bedroom.

Miss Tesman (laughing). Oh, my dear George, I daresay you may find some use for them—in the course of time.

Tesman. Why of course you are quite right, Aunt Julia! You mean as my library increases—eh?

Miss Tesman. Yes, quite so, my dear boy. It was your library I was thinking of.

Tesman. I am specially pleased on Hedda's account. Often and often, before we were engaged, she said that she would never care to live anywhere but in Secretary Falk's villa.*

Miss Tesman. Yes, it was lucky that this very house should come into the market, just after you had started.

Tesman. Yes, Aunt Julia, the luck was on our side, wasn't it—eh?

Miss Tesman. But the expense, my dear George! You will find it very expensive, all this.

Tesman (looks at her, a little cast down). Yes, I suppose I shall, Aunt!

Miss Tesman. Oh, frightfully!

Tesman. How much do you think? In round numbers? —Eh?

Miss Tesman. Oh, I can't even guess until all the accounts come in.

Tesman. Well, fortunately, Judge Brack has secured the most favourable terms for me,—so he said in a letter to Hedda.

Miss Tesman. Yes, don't be uneasy, my dear boy.—Besides, I have given security for the furniture and all the carpets.

Tesman. Security? You? My dear Aunt Julia—what sort of security could you give?

Miss Tesman. I have given a mortgage on our annuity.

* In the original, "Statsradinde Falks villa"—showing that it had belonged to the widow of a cabinet minister.

Tesman (jumps up). What! On your—and Aunt Rina's annuity!

Miss Tesman. Yes, I knew of no other plan, you see.

Tesman (placing himself before her). Have you gone out of your senses, Auntie! Your annuity—it's all that you and Aunt Rina have to live upon.

Miss Tesman. Well, well, don't get so excited about it. It's only a matter of form you know—Judge Brack assured me of that. It was he that was kind enough to arrange the whole affair for me. A mere matter of form, he said.

Tesman. Yes, that may be all very well. But nevertheless——

Miss Tesman. You will have your own salary to depend upon now. And, good heavens, even if we did have to pay up a little——! To eke things out a bit at the start——! Why, it would be nothing but a pleasure to us.

Tesman. Oh, Auntie—will you never be tired of making sacrifices for me!

Miss Tesman (rises and lays her hands on his shoulders). Have I any other happiness in this world except to smooth your way for you, my dear boy? You, who have had neither father nor mother to depend on. And now we have reached the goal, George! Things have looked black enough for us, sometimes; but, thank heaven, now you have nothing to fear.

Tesman. Yes, it is really marvellous how everything has turned out for the best.

Miss Tesman. And the people who opposed you—who wanted to bar the way for you—now you have them at your feet. They have fallen, George. Your most dangerous rival—his fall was the worst.—And now he has to lie on the bed he has made for himself—poor misguided creature.

Tesman. Have you heard anything of Eilert? Since I went away, I mean.

Miss Tesman. Only that he is said to have published a new book.

Tesman. What! Eilert Lövborg! Recently—eh?

Miss Tesman. Yes, so they say. Heaven knows whether it can be worth anything! Ah, when your new book appears—that will be another story, George! What is it to be about?

Tesman. It will deal with the domestic industries of Brabant during the Middle Ages.

Miss Tesman. Fancy—to be able to write on such a subject as that!

Tesman. However, it may be some time before the book is ready. I have all these collections to arrange first, you see.

Miss Tesman. Yes, collecting and arranging—no one can beat you at that. There you are my poor brother's own son.

Tesman. I am looking forward eagerly to setting to work at it; especially now that I have my own delightful home to work in.

Miss Tesman. And, most of all, now that you have got the wife of your heart, my dear George.

Tesman (embracing her). Oh, yes, yes, Aunt Julia. Hedda—she is the best part of it all! *(Looks towards the doorway.)* I believe I hear her coming—eh?

[HEDDA *enters from the left through the inner room. She is a woman of nine-and-twenty. Her face and figure show refinement and distinction. Her complexion is pale and opaque. Her steel-grey eyes express a cold, unruffled repose. Her hair is of an agreeable medium brown, but not particularly abundant. She is dressed in a tasteful, somewhat loose-fitting morning gown.*

Miss Tesman [going to meet HEDDA*).* Good morning, my dear Hedda! Good morning, and a hearty welcome.

Hedda (holds out her hand). Good morning, dear Miss Tesman! So early a call! That is kind of you.

Miss Tesman (with some embarrassment). Well—has the bride slept well in her new home?

Hedda. Oh, yes, thanks. Passably.

Tesman (laughing). Passably! Come, that's good, Hedda! You were sleeping like a stone when I got up.

Hedda. Fortunately. Of course one has always to accustom one's self to new surroundings, Miss Tesman—little by little. *(Looking towards the left.)* Oh—there the servant has gone and opened the verandah door and let in a whole flood of sunshine.

Miss Tesman (going towards the door). Well, then, we will shut it.

Hedda. No, no, not that! Tesman, please draw the curtains. That will give a softer light.

Tesman (at the door). All right—all right. There now, Hedda, now you have both shade and fresh air.

Hedda. Yes, fresh air we certainly must have, with all these stacks of flowers—— But—won't you sit down, Miss Tesman?

Miss Tesman. No, thank you. Now that I have seen that everything is all right here—thank heaven!—I must be getting home again. My sister is lying longing for me, poor thing.

Tesman. Give her my very best love, Auntie; and say I shall look in and see her later in the day.

Miss Tesman. Yes, yes, I'll be sure to tell her. But by-the-bye, George—*(feeling in her dress pocket)*—I had almost forgotten—I have something for you here.

Tesman. What is it, Auntie? Eh?

Miss Tesman (produces a flat parcel wrapped in newspaper and hands it to him). Look here, my dear boy.

Tesman (opening the parcel). Well, I declare!—Have you really saved them for me, Aunt Julia! Hedda! isn't this touching—eh?

Hedda (beside the whatnot on the right). Well, what is it?

Tesman. My old morning-shoes! My slippers.

Hedda. Indeed. I remember you often spoke of them while we were abroad.

Tesman. Yes, I missed them terribly. *(Goes up to her.)* Now you shall see them, Hedda!

Hedda (going towards the stove). Thanks, I really don't care about it.

Tesman (following her). Only think—ill as she was, Aunt Rina embroidered these for me. Oh, you can't think how many associations cling to them.

Hedda (at the table). Scarcely for me.

Miss Tesman. Of course not for Hedda, George.

Tesman. Well, but now that she belongs to the family, I thought——

Hedda (interrupting). We shall never get on with this servant, Tesman.

Miss Tesman. Not get on with Berta?

Tesman. Why, dear, what puts that in your head? Eh?

Hedda (pointing). Look there! She has left her old bonnet lying about on a chair.

Tesman (in consternation, drops the slippers on the floor.) Why, Hedda——

Hedda. Just fancy, if any one should come in and see it!

Tesman. But Hedda—that's Aunt Julia's bonnet.

Hedda. Is it!

Miss Tesman (taking up the bonnet). Yes, indeed it's mine. And, what's more, it's not old, Madam Hedda.

Hedda. I really did not look closely at it, Miss Tesman.

Miss Tesman (trying on the bonnet). Let me tell you it's the first time I have worn it—the very first time.

Tesman. And a very nice bonnet it is, too—quite a beauty!

Miss Tesman. Oh, it's no such great things, George. *(Looks around her.)* My parasol——? Ah, here. *(Takes it.)* For this is mine, too—*(mutters)*—not Berta's.

Tesman. A new bonnet and a new parasol! Only think, Hedda!

Hedda. Very handsome indeed.

Tesman. Yes, isn't it? Eh? But Auntie, take a good look at Hedda before you go! See how handsome she is!

Miss Tesman. Oh, my dear boy, there's nothing new in that. Hedda was always lovely.

[*She nods and goes towards the right.*

Tesman (following). Yes, but have you noticed what splendid condition she is in? How she has filled out on the journey?

Hedda (crossing the room). Oh, do be quiet——!

Miss Tesman (who has stopped and turned). Filled out?

Tesman. Of course you don't notice it so much now that she has that dress on. But I, who can see——

Hedda (at the glass door, impatiently). Oh, you can't see anything.

Tesman. It must be the mountain air in the Tyrol——

Hedda (curtly, interrupting). I am exactly as I was when I started.

Tesman. So you insist; but I'm quite certain you are not. Don't you agree with me, Auntie?

Miss Tesman (who has been gazing at her with folded hands). Hedda is lovely—lovely—lovely. *(Goes up to her, takes her head between both hands, draws it downwards and kisses her hair.)* God bless and preserve Hedda Tesman—for George's sake.

Hedda (gently freeing herself). Oh——! Let me go.

Miss Tesman (in quiet emotion). I shall not let a day pass without coming to see you.

Tesman. No, you won't, will you, Auntie? Eh?

Miss Tesman. Good-bye—good-bye!

[*She goes out by the hall door.* TESMAN *accompanies her. The door remains half open.* TESMAN *can be heard repeating his message to* AUNT RINA *and his thanks for the slippers.*

[*In the meantime,* HEDDA *walks about the room, raising her arms and clenching her hands as if in desperation. Then she flings back the curtains from the glass door and stands there looking out.*

[*Presently* TESMAN *returns and closes the door behind him.*

Tesman (picks up the slippers from the floor). What are you looking at, Hedda?

Hedda (once more calm and mistress of herself). I am only looking at the leaves. They are so yellow—so withered.

Tesman (wraps up the slippers and lays them on the table). Well you see, we are well into September now.

Hedda (again restless). Yes, to think of it!—Already in —in September.

Tesman. Don't you think Aunt Julia's manner was strange, dear? Almost solemn? Can you imagine what was the matter with her? Eh?

Hedda. I scarcely know her, you see. Is she not often like that?

Tesman. No, not as she was today.

Hedda (leaving the glass door). Do you think she was annoyed about the bonnet?

Tesman. Oh, scarcely at all. Perhaps a little, just at the moment——

Hedda. But what an idea, to pitch her bonnet about in the drawing-room! No one does that sort of thing.

Tesman. Well, you may be sure Aunt Julia won't do it again.

Hedda. In any case, I shall manage to make my peace with her.

Tesman. Yes, my dear, good Hedda, if you only would.

Hedda. When you call this afternoon, you might invite her to spend the evening here.

Tesman. Yes, that I will. And there's one thing more you could do that would delight her heart.

Hedda. What is it?

Tesman. If you could only prevail on yourself to say *du** to her. For my sake, Hedda? Eh?

Hedda. No, no, Tesman—you really mustn't ask that of me. I have told you so already. I shall try to call her "Aunt"; and you must be satisfied with that.

Tesman. Well, well. Only I think now that you belong to the family, you——

Hedda. H'm—I can't in the least see why——

[*She goes up towards the middle doorway.*

Tesman (after a pause). Is there anything the matter with you, Hedda? Eh?

Hedda. I'm only looking at my old piano. It doesn't go at all well with all the other things.

Tesman. The first time I draw my salary, we'll see about exchanging it.

Hedda. No, no—no exchanging. I don't want to part with it. Suppose we put it there in the inner room and then get another here in its place. When it's convenient, I mean.

Tesman (a little taken aback). Yes—of course we could do that.

Hedda (takes up the bouquet from the piano). These flowers were not here last night when we arrived.

Tesman. Aunt Julia must have brought them for you.

Hedda (examining the bouquet). A visiting-card. *(Takes it out and reads:)* "Shall return later in the day." Can you guess whose card it is?

Tesman. No. Whose? Eh?

Hedda. The name is "Mrs. Elvsted."

Tesman. Is it really? Sheriff Elvsted's wife? Miss Rysing that was.

Hedda. Exactly. The girl with the irritating hair, that she was always showing off. An old flame of yours I've been told.

Tesman (laughing). Oh, that didn't last long; and it

* Du-thou; Tesman means, "If you could persuade yourself to tutoyer her."

was before I knew you, Hedda. But fancy her being in town!

Hedda. It's odd that she should call upon us. I have scarcely seen her since we left school.

Tesman. I haven't seen her either for—heaven knows how long. I wonder how she can endure to live in such an out-of-the-way hole—eh?

Hedda (after a moment's thought says suddenly). Tell me, Tesman—isn't it somewhere near there that he—that—Eilert Lövborg is living?

Tesman. Yes, he is somewhere in that part of the country.

[BERTA *enters by the hall door.*

Berta. That lady, ma'am, that brought some flowers a little while ago, is here again. *(Pointing.)* The flowers you have in your hand, ma'am.

Hedda. Ah, is she? Well, please show her in.

[BERTA *opens the door for* MRS. ELVSTED *and goes out herself.*—MRS. ELVSTED *is a woman of fragile figure, with pretty, soft features. Her eyes are light blue, large, round, and somewhat prominent, with a startled, inquiring expression. Her hair is remarkably light, almost flaxen, and unusually abundant and wavy. She is a couple of years younger than* HEDDA. *She wears a dark visiting dress, tasteful, but not quite in the latest fashion.*

Hedda (receives her warmly). How do you do, my dear Mrs. Elvsted? It's delightful to see you again.

Mrs. Elvsted (nervously, struggling for self-control). Yes, it's a very long time since we met.

Tesman (gives her his hand). And we, too—eh?

Hedda. Thanks for your lovely flowers——

Mrs. Elvsted. Oh, not at all—— I would have come straight here yesterday afternoon; but I heard that you were away——

Tesman. Have you just come to town? Eh?

Mrs. Elvsted. I arrived yesterday, about midday. Oh, I was quite in despair when I heard that you were not at home.

Hedda. In despair! How so?

Tesman. Why, my dear Mrs. Rysing—I mean Mrs. Elvsted——

Hedda. I hope that you are not in any trouble?

Mrs. Elvsted. Yes, I am. And I don't know another living creature here that I can turn to.

Hedda (laying the bouquet on the table). Come—let us sit here on the sofa——

Mrs. Elvsted. Oh, I am too restless to sit down.

Hedda. Oh no, you're not. Come here.

[*She draws* MRS. ELVSTED *down upon the sofa and sits at her side.*

Tesman. Well? What is it, Mrs. Elvsted?

Hedda. Has anything particular happened to you at home?

Mrs. Elvsted. Yes—and no. Oh—I am so anxious you should not misunderstand me——

Hedda. Then your best plan is to tell us the whole story, Mrs. Elvsted.

Tesman. I suppose that's what you have come for—eh?

Mrs. Elvsted. Yes, yes—of course it is. Well, then, I must tell you—if you don't already know—that Eilert Lövborg is in town, too.

Hedda. Lövborg——!

Tesman. What! Has Eilert Lövborg come back? Fancy that, Hedda!

Hedda. Well, well—I hear it.

Mrs. Elvsted. He has been here a week already. Just fancy—a whole week! In this terrible town, alone! With so many temptations on all sides.

Hedda. But my dear Mrs. Elvsted—how does he concern you so much?

Mrs. Elvsted (looks at her with a startled air and says rapidly). He was the children's tutor.

Hedda. Your children's?

Mrs. Elvsted. My husband's. I have none.

Hedda. Your step-children's, then?

Mrs. Elvsted. Yes.

Tesman (somewhat hesitatingly). Then was he—I don't know how to express it—was he—regular enough in his habits to be fit for the post? Eh?

Mrs. Elvsted. For the last two years his conduct has been irreproachable.

Tesman. Has it indeed? Fancy that, Hedda!

Hedda. I hear it.

Mrs. Elvsted. Perfectly irreproachable, I assure you! In every respect. But all the same—now that I know he is here—in this great town—and with a large sum of money in his hands—I can't help being in mortal fear for him.

Tesman. Why did he not remain where he was? With you and your husband? Eh?

Mrs. Elvsted. After his book was published he was too restless and unsettled to remain with us.

Tesman. Yes, by-the-bye, Aunt Julia told me he had published a new book.

Mrs. Elvsted. Yes, a big book, dealing with the march of civilisation—in broad outline, as it were. It came out about a fortnight ago. And since it has sold so well, and been so much read—and made such a sensation——

Tesman. Has it indeed? It must be something he has had lying by since his better days.

Mrs. Elvsted. Long ago, you mean?

Tesman. Yes.

Mrs. Elvsted. No, he has written it all since he has been with us—within the last year.

Tesman. Isn't that good news, Hedda? Think of that.

Mrs. Elvsted. Ah, yes, if only it would last!

Hedda. Have you seen him here in town?

Mrs. Elvsted. No, not yet. I have had the greatest difficulty in finding out his address. But this morning I discovered it at last.

Hedda (looks searchingly at her). Do you know, it seems to me a little odd of your husband—h'm——

Mrs. Elvsted (starting nervously). Of my husband! What?

Hedda. That he should send you to town on such an errand—that he does not come himself and look after his friend.

Mrs. Elvsted. Oh, no, no—my husband has no time. And besides, I—I had some shopping to do.

Hedda (with a slight smile). Ah, that is a different matter.

Mrs. Elvsted (rising quickly and uneasily). And now I beg and implore you, Mr. Tesman—receive Eilert Lövborg kindly if he comes to you! And that he is sure to do. You see, you were such great friends in the old days. And then you are interested in the same studies—the same branch of science—so far as I can understand.

Tesman. We used to be, at any rate.

Mrs. Elvsted. That is why I beg so earnestly that you—you, too—will keep a sharp eye upon him. Oh, you will promise me that, Mr. Tesman—won't you?

Tesman. With the greatest of pleasure, Mrs. Rysing——

Hedda. Elvsted.

Tesman. I assure you I shall do all I possibly can for Eilert. You may rely upon me.

Mrs. Elvsted. Oh, how very, very kind of you! *(Presses his hands.)* Thanks, thanks, thanks! *(Frightened.)* You see, my husband is so very fond of him!

Hedda (rising). You ought to write to him, Tesman. Perhaps he may not care to come to you of his own accord.

Tesman. Well, perhaps it would be the right thing to do, Hedda? Eh?

Hedda. And the sooner the better. Why not at once?

Mrs. Elvsted (imploringly). Oh, if you only would!

Tesman. I'll write this moment. Have you his address, Mrs.—Mrs. Elvsted.

Mrs. Elvsted. Yes. *(Takes a slip of paper from her pocket and hands it to him.)* Here it is.

Tesman. Good, good. Then I'll go in—— *(Looks about him.)* By-the-bye,—my slippers? Oh, here.

[*Takes the packet and is about to go.*

Hedda. Be sure you write him a cordial, friendly letter. And a good long one, too.

Tesman. Yes, I will.

Mrs. Elvsted. But please, please don't say a word to show that I have suggested it.

Tesman. No, how could you think I would? Eh?

[*He goes out to the right, through the inner room.*

Hedda (goes up to Mrs. Elvsted, *smiles and says in a low voice).* There! We have killed two birds with one stone.

Mrs. Elvsted. What do you mean?

Hedda. Could you not see that I wanted him to go?

Mrs. Elvsted. Yes, to write the letter——

Hedda. And that I might speak to you alone.

Mrs. Elvsted (confused). About the same thing?

Hedda. Precisely.

Mrs. Elvsted (apprehensively). But there is nothing more, Mrs. Tesman! Absolutely nothing!

Hedda. Oh, yes, but there is. There is a great deal more—I can see that. Sit here—and we'll have a cosy, confidential chat.

[*She forces* Mrs. Elvsted *to sit in the easy-chair beside the stove and seats herself on one of the footstools.*

Mrs. Elvsted (anxiously, looking at her watch). But, my dear Mrs. Tesman—I was really on the point of going.

Hedda. Oh, you can't be in such a hurry.—Well? Now tell me something about your life at home.

Mrs. Elvsted. Oh, that is just what I care least to speak about.

Hedda. But to me, dear——? Why, weren't we schoolfellows?

Mrs. Elvsted. Yes, but you were in the class above me. Oh, how dreadfully afraid of you I was then!

Hedda. Afraid of me?

Mrs. Elvsted. Yes, dreadfully. For when we met on the stairs you used always to pull my hair.

Hedda. Did I, really?

Mrs. Elvsted. Yes, and once you said you would burn it off my head.

Hedda. Oh, that was all nonsense, of course.

Mrs. Elvsted. Yes, but I was so silly in those days.—And since then, too—we have drifted so far—far apart from each other. Our circles have been so entirely different.

Hedda. Well, then, we must try to drift together again. Now listen! At school we said *du* to each other; and we called each other by our Christian names——

Mrs. Elvsted. No, I am sure you must be mistaken.

Hedda. No, not at all! I can remember quite distinctly. So now we are going to renew our old friendship. *(Draws the footstool closer to* MRS. ELVSTED.*)* There now! *(Kisses her cheek.)* You must say *du* to me and call me Hedda.

Mrs. Elvsted (presses and pats her hands). Oh, how good and kind you are! I am not used to such kindness.

Hedda. There, there, there! And I shall say *du* to you, as in the old days, and call you my dear Thora.

Mrs. Elvsted. My name is Thea.*

Hedda. Why, of course! I meant Thea. *(Looks at her compassionately.)* So you are not accustomed to goodness and kindness, Thea? Not in your own home?

Mrs. Elvsted. Oh, if I only had a home! But I haven't any; I have never had a home.

* Pronounce *Tora* and *Taya*.

Hedda (looks at her for a moment). I almost suspected as much.

Mrs. Elvsted (gazing helplessly before her). Yes—yes—yes.

Hedda. I don't quite remember—was it not as housekeeper that you first went to Mr. Elvsted's?

Mrs. Elvsted. I really went as governess. But his wife—his late wife—was an invalid,—and rarely left her room. So I had to look after the housekeeping as well.

Hedda. And then—at last—you became mistress of the house.

Mrs. Elvsted (sadly). Yes, I did.

Hedda. Let me see—about how long ago was that?

Mrs. Elvsted. My marriage?

Hedda. Yes.

Mrs. Elvsted. Five years ago.

Hedda. To be sure; it must be that.

Mrs. Elvsted. Oh, those five years——! Or at all events the last two or three of them! Oh, if you* could only imagine——

Hedda (giving her a little slap on the hand). De? Fie, Thea!

Mrs. Elvsted. Yes, yes, I will try—— Well, if—you could only imagine and understand——

Hedda (lightly). Eilert Lövborg has been in your neighbourhood about three years, hasn't he?

Mrs. Elvsted (looks at her doubtfully). Eilert Lövborg? Yes—he has.

Hedda. Had you known him before, in town here?

Mrs. Elvsted. Scarcely at all. I mean—I knew him by name of course.

Hedda. But you saw a good deal of him in the country?

Mrs. Elvsted. Yes, he came to us every day. You see,

* Mrs. Elvsted here uses the formal pronoun *De,* whereupon Hedda rebukes her. In her next speech Mrs. Elvsted says *du.*

he gave the children lessons; for in the long run I couldn't manage it all myself.

Hedda. No, that's clear.—And your husband——? I suppose he is often away from home?

Mrs. Elvsted. Yes. Being sheriff, you know, he has to travel about a good deal in his district.

Hedda (leaning against the arm of the chair). Thea—my poor, sweet Thea—now you must tell me everything—exactly as it stands.

Mrs. Elvsted. Well, then, you must question me.

Hedda. What sort of man is your husband, Thea? I mean—you know—in everyday life. Is he kind to you?

Mrs. Elvsted (evasively). I am sure he means well in everything.

Hedda. I should think he must be altogether too old for you. There is at least twenty years' difference between you, is there not?

Mrs. Elvsted (irritably). Yes, that is true, too. Everything about him is repellent to me! We have not a thought in common. We have no single point of sympathy—he and I.

Hedda. But is he not fond of you all the same? In his own way?

Mrs. Elvsted. Oh, I really don't know. I think he regards me simply as a useful property. And then it doesn't cost much to keep me. I am not expensive.

Hedda. That is stupid of you.

Mrs. Elvsted (shakes her head). It cannot be otherwise—not with him. I don't think he really cares for any one but himself—and perhaps a little for the children.

Hedda. And for Eilert Lövborg, Thea.

Mrs. Elvsted (looking at her). For Eilert Lövborg? What puts that into your head?

Hedda. Well, my dear—I should say, when he sends you after him all the way to town—— *(Smiling almost imperceptibly.)* And besides, you said so yourself, to Tesman.

Mrs. Elvsted (with a little nervous twitch). Did I? Yes, I suppose I did. *(Vehemently, but not loudly.)* No—I may just as well make a clean breast of it at once! For it must all come out in any case.

Hedda. Why, my dear Thea——?

Mrs. Elvsted. Well, to make a long story short: My husband did not know that I was coming.

Hedda. What! Your husband didn't know it!

Mrs. Elvsted. No, of course not. For that matter, he was away from home himself—he was travelling. Oh, I could bear it no longer, Hedda! I couldn't indeed—so utterly alone as I should have been in future.

Hedda. Well? And then?

Mrs. Elvsted. So I put together some of my things—what I needed most—as quietly as possible. And then I left the house.

Hedda. Without a word?

Mrs. Elvsted. Yes—and took the train straight to town.

Hedda. Why, my dear, good Thea—to think of you daring to do it!

Mrs. Elvsted (rises and moves about the room). What else could I possibly do?

Hedda. But what do you think your husband will say when you go home again?

Mrs. Elvsted (at the table, looks at her). Back to him?

Hedda. Of course.

Mrs. Elvsted. I shall never go back to him again.

Hedda (rising and going towards her). Then you have left your home—for good and all?

Mrs. Elvsted. Yes. There was nothing else to be done.

Hedda. But then—to take flight so openly.

Mrs. Elvsted. Oh, it's impossible to keep things of that sort secret.

Hedda. But what do you think people will say of you, Thea?

Mrs. Elvsted. They may say what they like, for aught I

care. *(Seats herself wearily and sadly on the sofa.)* I have done nothing but what I had to do.

Hedda (after a short silence). And what are your plans now? What do you think of doing?

Mrs. Elvsted. I don't know yet. I only know this, that I must live here, where Eilert Lövborg is—if I am to live at all.

Hedda (takes a chair from the table, seats herself beside her and strokes her hands). My dear Thea—how did this—this friendship—between you and Eilert Lövborg come about?

Mrs. Elvsted. Oh, it grew up gradually. I gained a sort of influence over him.

Hedda. Indeed?

Mrs. Elvsted. He gave up his old habits. Not because I asked him to, for I never dared do that. But of course he saw how repulsive they were to me; and so he dropped them.

Hedda (concealing an involuntary smile of scorn). Then you have reclaimed him—as the saying goes—my little Thea.

Mrs. Elvsted. So he says himself, at any rate. And he, on his side, has made a real human being of me—taught me to think and to understand so many things.

Hedda. Did he give you lessons, too, then?

Mrs. Elvsted. No, not exactly lessons. But he talked to me—talked about such an infinity of things. And then came the lovely, happy time when I began to share in his work—when he allowed me to help him!

Hedda. Oh, he did, did he?

Mrs. Elvsted. Yes! He never wrote anything without my assistance.

Hedda. You were two good comrades, in fact?

Mrs. Elvsted (eagerly). Comrades! Yes, fancy, Hedda—that is the very word he used!—Oh, I ought to feel perfectly happy; and yet I cannot; for I don't know how long it will last.

Hedda. Are you no surer of him than that?

Mrs. Elvsted (gloomily). A woman's shadow stands between Eilert Lövborg and me.

Hedda (looks at her anxiously). Who can that be?

Mrs. Elvsted. I don't know. Some one he knew in his —in his past. Some one he has never been able wholly to forget.

Hedda. What has he told you—about this?

Mrs. Elvsted. He has only once—quite vaguely—alluded to it.

Hedda. Well. And what did he say?

Mrs. Elvsted. He said that when they parted, she threatened to shoot him with a pistol.

Hedda (with cold composure). Oh, nonsense! No one does that sort of thing here.

Mrs. Elvsted. No. And that is why I think it must have been that red-haired singing-woman whom he once——

Hedda. Yes, very likely.

Mrs. Elvsted. For I remember they used to say of her that she carried loaded firearms.

Hedda. Oh—then of course it must have been she.

Mrs. Elvsted (wringing her hands). And now just fancy, Hedda—I hear that this singing-woman—that she is in town again! Oh, I don't know what to do——

Hedda (glancing towards the inner room). Hush! Here comes Tesman. *(Rises and whispers.)* Thea—all this must remain between you and me.

Mrs. Elvsted (springing up). Oh, yes, yes! for heaven's sake——!

[George Tesman, *with a letter in his hand, comes from the right through the inner room.*

Tesman. There now—the epistle is finished.

Hedda. That's right. And now Mrs. Elvsted is just going. Wait a moment—I'll go with you to the garden gate.

Tesman. Do you think Berta could post the letter, Hedda dear?

Hedda (takes it). I will tell her to.

[BERTA *enters from the hall.*

Berta. Judge Brack wishes to know if Mrs. Tesman will receive him.

Hedda. Yes, ask Judge Brack to come in. And look here—put this letter in the post.

Berta (taking the letter). Yes, ma'am.

[*She opens the door for* JUDGE BRACK *and goes out herself.* BRACK *is a man of forty-five; thick-set, but well-built and elastic in his movements. His face is roundish with an aristocratic profile. His hair is short, still almost black, and carefully dressed. His eyes are lively and sparkling. His eyebrows thick. His moustaches are also thick, with short-cut ends. He wears a well-cut walking-suit, a little too youthful for his age. He uses an eye-glass, which he now and then lets drop.*

Judge Brack (with his hat in his hand, bowing). May one venture to call so early in the day?

Hedda. Of course one may.

Tesman (presses his hand). You are welcome at any time. *(Introducing him.)* Judge Brack—Miss Rysing——

Hedda. Oh——!

Brack (bowing). Ah—delighted——

Hedda (looks at him and laughs). It's nice to have a look at you by daylight, Judge!

Brack. Do you find me—altered?

Hedda. A little younger, I think.

Brack. Thank you so much.

Tesman. But what do you think of Hedda—eh? Doesn't she look flourishing? She has actually——

Hedda. Oh, do leave me alone. You haven't thanked Judge Brack for all the trouble he has taken——

Brack. Oh, nonsense—it was a pleasure to me——

Hedda. Yes, you are a friend indeed. But here stands

Thea all impatience to be off—so *au revoir* Judge. I shall be back again presently.

[*Mutual salutations.* MRS. ELVSTED *and* HEDDA *go out by the hall door.*

Brack. Well,—is your wife tolerably satisfied——

Tesman. Yes, we can't thank you sufficiently. Of course she talks of a little re-arrangement here and there; and one or two things are still wanting. We shall have to buy some additional trifles.

Brack. Indeed!

Tesman. But we won't trouble you about these things. Hedda says she herself will look after what is wanting.—Shan't we sit down? Eh?

Brack. Thanks, for a moment. *(Seats himself beside the table.)* There is something I wanted to speak to you about, my dear Tesman.

Tesman. Indeed? Ah, I understand! *(Seating himself.)* I suppose it's the serious part of the frolic that is coming now. Eh?

Brack. Oh, the money question is not so very pressing; though, for that matter, I wish we had gone a little more economically to work.

Tesman. But that would never have done, you know! Think of Hedda, my dear fellow! You, who know her so well——. I couldn't possibly ask her to put up with a shabby style of living!

Brack. No, no—that is just the difficulty.

Tesman. And then—fortunately—it can't be long before I receive my appointment.

Brack. Well, you see—such things are often apt to hang fire for a time.

Tesman. Have you heard anything definite? Eh?

Brack. Nothing exactly definite—— *(Interrupting himself.)* But, by-the-bye—I have one piece of news for you.

Tesman. Well?

Brack. Your old friend, Eilert Lövborg, has returned to town.

Tesman. I know that already.

Brack. Indeed! How did you learn it?

Tesman. From that lady who went out with Hedda.

Brack. Really? What was her name? I didn't quite catch it.

Tesman. Mrs. Elvsted.

Brack. Aha—Sheriff Elvsted's wife? Of course—he has been living up in their regions.

Tesman. And fancy—I'm delighted to hear that he is quite a reformed character!

Brack. So they say.

Tesman. And then he has published a new book—eh?

Brack. Yes, indeed he has.

Tesman. And I hear it has made some sensation!

Brack. Quite an unusual sensation.

Tesman. Fancy—isn't that good news! A man of such extraordinary talents—— I felt so grieved to think that he had gone irretrievably to ruin.

Brack. That was what everybody thought.

Tesman. But I cannot imagine what he will take to now! How in the world will he be able to make his living? Eh?

[*During the last words,* HEDDA *has entered by the hall door.*

Hedda (to BRACK, *laughing with a touch of scorn).* Tesman is for ever worrying about how people are to make their living.

Tesman. Well, you see, dear—we were talking about poor Eilert Lövborg.

Hedda (glancing at him rapidly). Oh, indeed? *(Seats herself in the arm-chair beside the stove and asks indifferently:)* What is the matter with him?

Tesman. Well—no doubt he has run through all his property long ago; and he can scarcely write a new book every year—eh? So I really can't see what is to become of him.

Brack. Perhaps I can give you some information on that point.

Tesman. Indeed!

Brack. You must remember that his relations have a good deal of influence.

Tesman. Oh, his relations, unfortunately, have entirely washed their hands of him.

Brack. At one time they called him the hope of the family.

Tesman. At one time, yes! But he has put an end to all that.

Hedda. Who knows? *(With a slight smile.)* I hear they have reclaimed him up at Sheriff Elvsted's——

Brack. And then this book that he has published——

Tesman. Well, well, I hope to goodness they may find something for him to do. I have just written to him. I asked him to come and see us this evening, Hedda dear.

Brack. But, my dear fellow, you are booked for my bachelors' party this evening. You promised on the pier last night.

Hedda. Had you forgotten, Tesman?

Tesman. Yes, I had utterly forgotten.

Brack. But it doesn't matter, for you may be sure he won't come.

Tesman. What makes you think that? Eh?

Brack (with a little hesitation, rising and resting his hands on the back of his chair). My dear Tesman—and you, too, Mrs. Tesman—I think I ought not to keep you in the dark about something that—that——

Tesman. That concerns Eilert——?

Brack. Both you and him.

Tesman. Well, my dear Judge, out with it.

Brack. You must be prepared to find your appointment deferred longer than you desired or expected.

Tesman (jumping up uneasily). Is there some hitch about it? Eh?

Brack. The nomination may perhaps be made conditional on the result of a competition——

Tesman. Competition! Think of that, Hedda!

Hedda (leans farther back in the chair). Aha—aah!

Tesman. But who can my competitor be? Surely not ——?

Brack. Yes, precisely—Eilert Lövborg.

Tesman (clasping his hands). No, no—it's quite inconceivable! Quite impossible! Eh?

Brack. H'm—that is what it may come to, all the same.

Tesman. Well, but, Judge Brack—it would show the most incredible lack of consideration for me. *(Gesticulates with his arms.)* For—just think—I'm a married man! We have married on the strength of these prospects, Hedda and I; and run deep into debt; and borrowed money from Aunt Julia, too. Good heavens, they had as good as promised me the appointment. Eh?

Brack. Well, well, well—no doubt you will get it in the end; only after a contest.

Hedda (immovable in her arm-chair). Fancy, Tesman, there will be a sort of sporting interest in that.

Tesman. Why, my dearest Hedda, how can you be so indifferent about it.

Hedda (as before). I am not at all indifferent. I am most eager to see who wins.

Brack. In any case, Mrs. Tesman, it is best that you should know how matters stand. I mean—before you set about the little purchases I hear you are threatening.

Hedda. This can make no difference.

Brack. Indeed! Then I have no more to say. Goodbye! *(To* TESMAN.*)* I shall look in on my way back from my afternoon walk and take you home with me.

Tesman. Oh, yes, yes—your news has quite upset me.

Hedda (reclining, holds out her hand). Good-bye, Judge; and be sure you call in the afternoon.

Brack. Many thanks. Good-bye, good-bye!

Tesman (accompanying him to the door). Good-bye, my dear Judge! You must really excuse me——

[JUDGE BRACK *goes out by the hall door.*

Tesman (crosses the room). Oh, Hedda—one should never rush into adventures. Eh?

Hedda (looks at him, smiling). Do you do that?

Tesman. Yes, dear—there is no denying—it was adventurous to go and marry and set up house upon mere expectations.

Hedda. Perhaps you are right there.

Tesman. Well—at all events, we have our delightful home, Hedda! Fancy, the home we both dreamed of—the home we were in love with, I may almost say. Eh?

Hedda (rising slowly and wearily). It was part of our compact that we were to go into society—to keep open house.

Tesman. Yes, if you only knew how I had been looking forward to it! Fancy—to see you as hostess—in a select circle! Eh? Well, well, well—for the present we shall have to get on without society, Hedda—only to invite Aunt Julia now and then.—Oh, I intended you to lead such an utterly different life, dear——!

Hedda. Of course I cannot have my man in livery just yet.

Tesman. Oh, no, unfortunately. It would be out of the question for us to keep a footman, you know.

Hedda. And the saddle-horse I was to have had——

Tesman (aghast). The saddle-horse!

Hedda. ——I suppose I must not think of that now.

Tesman. Good heavens, no!—that's as clear as daylight.

Hedda (goes up the room). Well, I shall have one thing at least to kill time with in the meanwhile.

Tesman (beaming). Oh, thank heaven for that! What is it, Hedda? Eh?

Hedda (in the middle doorway, looks at him with covert scorn). My pistols, George.

Tesman (in alarm). Your pistols!

Hedda (with cold eyes). General Gabler's pistols.

[*She goes out through the inner room, to the left.*

Tesman (rushes up to the middle doorway and calls after her:) No, for heaven's sake, Hedda darling—don't touch those dangerous things! For my sake, Hedda! Eh?

ACT II

The room at the TESMANS' *as in the first Act, except that the piano has been removed, and an elegant little writing-table with book-shelves put in its place. A smaller table stands near the sofa on the left. Most of the bouquets have been taken away.* MRS. ELVSTED'S *bouquet is upon the large table in front.—It is afternoon.*

HEDDA, *dressed to receive callers, is alone in the room. She stands by the open glass door, loading a revolver. The fellow to it lies in an open pistol-case on the writing-table.*

Hedda (looks down the garden, and calls:) So you are here again, Judge!

Brack (is heard calling from a distance). As you see, Mrs. Tesman!

Hedda (raises the pistol and points). Now I'll shoot you, Judge Brack!

Brack (calling unseen). No, no, no! Don't stand aiming at me!

Hedda. This is what comes of sneaking in by the back way.* [*She fires.*

Brack (nearer). Are you out of your senses——!

Hedda. Dear me— did I happen to hit you?

Brack (still outside). I wish you would let these pranks alone!

Hedda. Come in then, Judge.

[JUDGE BRACK, *dressed as though for a men's*

* "Bagveje" means both "back ways" and "underhand courses."

party, enters by the glass door. He carries a light overcoat over his arm.

Brack. What the deuce—haven't you tired of that sport yet? What are you shooting at?

Hedda. Oh, I am only firing in the air.

Brack (gently takes the pistol out of her hand). Allow me, madam! *(Looks at it.)* Ah—I know this pistol well! *(Looks around.)* Where is the case? Ah, here it is. *(Lays the pistol in it and shuts it.)* Now we won't play at that game any more to-day.

Hedda. Then what in heaven's name would you have me do with myself?

Brack. Have you had no visitors?

Hedda (closing the glass door). Not one. I suppose all our set are still out of town.

Brack. And is Tesman not at home either?

Hedda (at the writing-table, putting the pistol-case in a drawer which she shuts). No. He rushed off to his aunt's directly after lunch; he didn't expect you so early.

Brack. H'm—how stupid of me not to have thought of that!

Hedda (turning her head to look at him). Why stupid?

Brack. Because if I had thought of it I should have come a little—earlier.

Hedda (crossing the room). Then you would have found no one to receive you; for I have been in my room changing my dress ever since lunch.

Brack. And is there no sort of little chink that we could hold a parley through?

Hedda. You have forgotten to arrange one.

Brack. That was another piece of stupidity.

Hedda. Well, we must just settle down here—and wait. Tesman is not likely to be back for some time yet.

Brack. Never mind; I shall not be impatient.

[HEDDA *seats herself in the corner of the sofa.* BRACK *lays his overcoat over the back of the nearest chair and sits down, but keeps his hat in his hand. A short silence. They look at each other.*

Hedda. Well?

Brack (in the same tone). Well?

Hedda. I spoke first.

Brack (bending a little forward). Come, let us have a cosy little chat, Mrs. Hedda.*

Hedda (leaning further back in the sofa). Does it not seem like a whole eternity since our last talk? Of course I don't count those few words yesterday evening and this morning.

Brack. You mean since our last confidential talk? Our last *tête-à-tête?*

Hedda. Well, yes—since you put it so.

Brack. Not a day has passed but I have wished that you were home again.

Hedda. And I have done nothing but wish the same thing.

Brack. You? Really, Mrs. Hedda? And I thought you had been enjoying your tour so much!

Hedda. Oh, yes, you may be sure of that!

Brack. But Tesman's letters spoke of nothing but happiness.

Hedda. Oh, Tesman! You see, he thinks nothing so delightful as grubbing in libraries and making copies of old parchments, or whatever you call them.

Brack (with a spice of malice). Well, that is his vocation in life—or part of it, at any rate.

Hedda. Yes, of course; and no doubt when it's your

* As this form of address is contrary to English usage, and as the note of familiarity would be lacking in "Mrs. Tesman," Brack may, in stage representation, say "Miss Hedda," thus ignoring her marriage and reverting to the form of address no doubt customary between them of old.

vocation—— But *I!* Oh, my dear Mr. Brack, how mortally bored I have been.

Brack (sympathetically). Do you really say so? In downright earnest?

Hedda. Yes, you can surely understand it——! To go for six whole months without meeting a soul that knew anything of our circle, or could talk about the things we are interested in.

Brack. Yes, yes—I too should feel that a deprivation.

Hedda. And then, what I found most intolerable of all——

Brack. Well?

Hedda. ——was being everlastingly in the company of —one and the same person——

Brack (with a nod of assent). Morning, noon, and night, yes—at all possible times and seasons.

Hedda. I said "everlastingly."

Brack. Just so. But I should have thought, with our excellent Tesman, one could——

Hedda. Tesman is—a specialist, my dear Judge.

Brack. Undeniably.

Hedda. And specialists are not at all amusing to travel with. Not in the long run at any rate.

Brack. Not even—the specialist one happens to love?

Hedda. Faugh—don't use that sickening word!

Brack (taken aback). What do you say, Mrs. Hedda?

Hedda (half laughing, half irritated). You should just try it! To hear of nothing but the history of civilisation, morning, noon, and night——

Brack. Everlastingly.

Hedda. Yes, yes, yes! And then all this about the domestic industry of the middle ages——! That's the most disgusting part of it!

Brack (looks searchingly at her). But tell me—in that case, how am I to understand your——? H'm——

Hedda. My accepting George Tesman, you mean?

Brack. Well, let us put it so.

Hedda. Good heavens, do you see anything so wonderful in that?

Brack. Yes and no—Mrs. Hedda.

Hedda. I had positively danced myself tired, my dear Judge. My day was done—— *(With a slight shudder.)* Oh, no—I won't say that; nor think it either!

Brack. You have assuredly no reason to.

Hedda. Oh, reasons—— *(Watching him closely.)* And George Tesman—after all, you must admit that he is correctness itself.

Brack. His correctness and respectability are beyond all question.

Hedda. And I don't see anything absolutely ridiculous about him.—Do you?

Brack. Ridiculous? N—no—I shouldn't exactly say so——

Hedda. Well—and his powers of research, at all events, are untiring.—I see no reason why he should not one day come to the front, after all.

Brack (looks at her hesitatingly). I thought that you, like every one else, expected him to attain the highest distinction.

Hedda (with an expression of fatigue). Yes, so I did.—And then, since he was bent, at all hazards, on being allowed to provide for me—I really don't know why I should not have accepted his offer?

Brack. No—if you look at it in that light——

Hedda. It was more than my other adorers were prepared to do for me, my dear Judge.

Brack (laughing). Well, I can't answer for all the rest; but as for myself, you know quite well that I have always entertained a—a certain respect for the marriage tie—for marriage as an institution, Mrs. Hedda.

Hedda (jestingly). Oh, I assure you I have never cherished any hopes with respect to you.

Brack. All I require is a pleasant and intimate interior, where I can make myself useful in every way and am free to come and go as—as a trusted friend——

Hedda. Of the master of the house, do you mean?

Brack (bowing). Frankly—of the mistress first of all; but of course of the master, too, in the second place. Such a triangular friendship—if I may call it so—is really a great convenience for all parties, let me tell you.

Hedda. Yes, I have many a time longed for some one to make a third on our travels. Oh—those railway-carriage *tête-à-têtes*——!

Brack. Fortunately your wedding journey is over now.

Hedda (shaking her head). Not by a long—long way. I have only arrived at a station on the line.

Brack. Well, then the passengers jump out and move about a little, Mrs. Hedda.

Hedda. I never jump out.

Brack. Really?

Hedda. No—because there is always some one standing by to——

Brack (laughing). To look at your ankles, do you mean?

Hedda. Precisely.

Brack. Well but, dear me——

Hedda (with a gesture of repulsion). I won't have it. I would rather keep my seat where I happen to be—and continue the *tête-à-tête.*

Brack. But suppose a third person were to jump in and join the couple.

Hedda. Ah—that is quite another matter!

Brack. A trusted, sympathetic friend——

Hedda. ——with a fund of conversation on all sorts of lively topics——

Brack. ——and not the least bit of a specialist!

Hedda (with an audible sigh). Yes, that would be a relief indeed.

Brack (hears the front door open and glances in that direction). The triangle is completed.

Hedda (half aloud). And on goes the train.

[GEORGE TESMAN, *in a grey walking-suit, with a soft felt hat, enters from the hall. He has a number of unbound books under his arm and in his pockets.*

Tesman (goes up to the table beside the corner settee). Ouf—what a load for a warm day—all these books. *(Lays them on the table.)* I'm positively perspiring, Hedda. Hallo—are you there already, my dear Judge? Eh? Berta didn't tell me.

Brack (rising). I came in through the garden.

Hedda. What books have you got there?

Tesman (stands looking them through). Some new books on my special subjects—quite indispensable to me.

Hedda. Your special subjects?

Brack. Yes, books on his special subjects, Mrs. Tesman.

[BRACK *and* HEDDA *exchange a confidential smile.*

Hedda. Do you need still more books on your special subjects?

Tesman. Yes, my dear Hedda, one can never have too many of them. Of course one must keep up with all that is written and published.

Hedda. Yes, I suppose one must.

Tesman (searching among his books). And look here—I have got hold of Eilert Lövborg's new book, too. *(Offering it to her.)* Perhaps you would like to glance through it, Hedda? Eh?

Hedda. No, thank you. Or rather—afterwards perhaps.

Tesman. I looked into it a little on the way home.

Brack. Well, what do you think of it—as a specialist?

Tesman. I think it shows quite remarkable soundness of judgment. He never wrote like that before. *(Putting the books together.)* Now I shall take all these into my study. I'm longing to cut the leaves——! And then I must change my clothes. *(To* Brack.*)* I suppose we needn't start just yet? Eh?

Brack. Oh, dear no—there is not the slightest hurry.

Tesman. Well, then, I will take my time. *(Is going with his books, but stops in the doorway and turns.)* By-the-bye, Hedda—Aunt Julia is not coming this evening.

Hedda. Not coming? Is it that affair of the bonnet that keeps her away?

Tesman. Oh, not at all. How could you think such a thing of Aunt Julia? Just fancy——! The fact is, Aunt Rina is very ill.

Hedda. She always is.

Tesman. Yes, but to-day she is much worse than usual, poor dear.

Hedda. Oh, then it's only natural that her sister should remain with her. I must bear my disappointment.

Tesman. And you can't imagine, dear, how delighted Aunt Julia seemed to be—because you had come home looking so flourishing!

Hedda (half aloud, rising). Oh, those everlasting aunts!

Tesman. What?

Hedda (going to the glass door). Nothing.

Tesman. Oh, all right.

[*He goes through the inner room, out to the right.*

Brack. What bonnet were you talking about?

Hedda. Oh, it was a little episode with Miss Tesman this morning. She had laid down her bonnet on the chair there—*(looks at him and smiles.)*—And I pretended to think it was the servant's.

Brack (shaking his head). Now my dear Mrs. Hedda, how could you do such a thing? To that excellent old lady, too!

Hedda (nervously crossing the room). Well, you see—these impulses come over me all of a sudden; and I cannot resist them. *(Throws herself down in the easy-chair by the stove.)* Oh, I don't know how to explain it.

Brack (behind the easy-chair). You are not really happy —that is at the bottom of it.

Hedda (looking straight before her). I know of no reason why I should be—happy. Perhaps you can give me one?

Brack. Well—amongst other things, because you have got exactly the home you had set your heart on.

Hedda (looks up at him and laughs). Do you too believe in that legend?

Brack. Is there nothing in it, then?

Hedda. Oh, yes, there is something in it.

Brack. Well?

Hedda. There is this in it, that I made use of Tesman to see me home from evening parties last summer——

Brack. I, unfortunately, had to go quite a different way.

Hedda. That's true. I know you were going a different way last summer.

Brack (laughing). Oh fie, Mrs. Hedda! Well, then—you and Tesman——?

Hedda. Well, we happened to pass here one evening; Tesman, poor fellow, was writhing in the agony of having to find conversation; so I took pity on the learned man——

Brack (smiles doubtfully). You took pity? H'm——

Hedda. Yes, I really did. And so—to help him out of his torment—I happened to say, in pure thoughtlessness, that I should like to live in this villa.

Brack. No more than that?

Hedda. Not that evening.

Brack. But afterwards?

Hedda. Yes, my thoughtlessness had consequences, my dear Judge.

Brack. Unfortunately, that too often happens, Mrs. Hedda.

Hedda. Thanks! So you see it was this enthusiasm for Secretary's Falk's villa that first constituted a bond of sympathy between George Tesman and me. From that came our engagement and our marriage, and our wedding journey, and all the rest of it. Well, well, my dear Judge—as you make your bed so you must lie, I could almost say.

Brack. This is exquisite! And you really cared not a rap about it all the time?

Hedda. No, heaven knows I didn't.

Brack. But now? Now that we have made it so homelike for you?

Hedda. Uh—the rooms all seem to smell of lavender and dried rose-leaves.—But perhaps it's Aunt Julia that has brought that scent with her.

Brack (laughing). No, I think it must be a legacy from the late Mrs. Secretary Falk.

Hedda. Yes, there is an odour of mortality about it. It reminds me of a bouquet—the day after the ball. *(Clasps her hands behind her head, leans back in her chair and looks at him.)* Oh, my dear Judge—you cannot imagine how horribly I shall bore myself here.

Brack. Why should not you, too, find some sort of vocation in life, Mrs. Hedda?

Hedda. A vocation—that should attract me?

Brack. If possible, of course.

Hedda. Heaven knows what sort of vocation that could be. I often wonder whether—— *(Breaking off.)* But that would never do either.

Brack. Who can tell? Let me hear what it is.

Hedda. Whether I might not get Tesman to go into politics, I mean.

Brack (laughing). Tesman? No, really now, political life is not the thing for him—not at all in his line.

Hedda. No, I daresay not.—But if I could get him into it all the same?

Brack. Why—what satisfaction could you find in that? If he is not fitted for that sort of thing, why should you want to drive him into it?

Hedda. Because I am bored, I tell you! *(After a pause.)* So you think it quite out of the question that Tesman should ever get into the ministry?

Brack. H'm—you see, my dear Mrs. Hedda—to get into the ministry, he would have to be a tolerably rich man.

Hedda (rising impatiently). Yes, there we have it! It is this genteel poverty I have managed to drop into——! *(Crosses the room.)* That is what makes life so pitiable! So utterly ludicrous!—For that's what it is.

Brack. Now *I* should say the fault lay elsewhere.

Hedda. Where, then?

Brack. You have never gone through any really stimulating experience.

Hedda. Anything serious, you mean?

Brack. Yes, you may call it so. But now you may perhaps have one in store.

Hedda (tossing her head). Oh, you're thinking of the annoyances about this wretched professorship! But that must be Tesman's own affair. I assure you I shall not waste a thought upon it.

Brack. No, no, I daresay not. But suppose now that what people call—in elegant language—a solemn responsibility were to come upon you? *(Smiling.)* A new responsibility, Mrs. Hedda?

Hedda (angrily). Be quiet! Nothing of that sort will ever happen!

Brack (warily). We will speak of this again a year hence—at the very outside.

Hedda (curtly). I have no turn for anything of the sort, Judge Brack. No responsibilities for me!

Brack. Are you so unlike the generality of women as to have no turn for duties which——?

Hedda (beside the glass door). Oh, be quiet, I tell you!

—I often think there is only one thing in the world I have any turn for.

Brack (drawing near to her). And what is that, if I may ask?

Hedda (stands looking out). Boring myself to death. Now you know it. *(Turns, looks towards the inner room and laughs.)* Yes, as I thought! Here comes the Professor.

Brack (softly, in a tone of warning). Come, come, come, Mrs. Hedda!

[GEORGE TESMAN, *dressed for the party, with his gloves and hat in his hand, enters from the right through the inner room.*

Tesman. Hedda, has no message come from Eilert Lövborg? Eh?

Hedda. No.

Tesman. Then you'll see he'll be here presently.

Brack. Do you really think he will come?

Tesman. Yes, I am almost sure of it. For what you were telling us this morning must have been a mere floating rumour.

Brack. You think so?

Tesman. At any rate, Aunt Julia said she did not believe for a moment that he would ever stand in my way again. Fancy that!

Brack. Well, then, that's all right.

Tesman (placing his hat and gloves on a chair on the right.) Yes, but you must really let me wait for him as long as possible.

Brack. We have plenty of time yet. None of my guests will arrive before seven or half-past.

Tesman. Then meanwhile we can keep Hedda company and see what happens. Eh?

Hedda (placing BRACK'S *hat and overcoat upon the corner settee.)* And at the worst Mr. Lövborg can remain here with me.

Brack (offering to take his things). Oh, allow me, Mrs. Tesman!—What do you mean by "At the worst"?

Hedda. If he won't go with you and Tesman.

Tesman (looks dubiously at her). But, Hedda dear—do you think it would quite do for him to remain with you? Eh? Remember, Aunt Julia can't come.

Hedda. No, but Mrs. Elvsted is coming. We three can have a cup of tea together.

Tesman. Oh, yes, that will be all right.

Brack (smiling). And that would perhaps be the safest plan for him.

Hedda. Why so?

Brack. Well, you know, Mrs. Tesman, how you used to gird at my little bachelor parties. You declared they were adapted only for men of the strictest principles.

Hedda. But no doubt Mr. Lövborg's principles are strict enough now. A converted sinner——

[BERTA *appears at the hall door.*

Berta. There's a gentleman asking if you are at home, ma'am——

Hedda. Well, show him in.

Tesman (softly). I'm sure it is he! Fancy that!

[EILERT LÖVBORG *enters from the hall. He is slim and lean; of the same age as* TESMAN, *but looks older and somewhat worn-out. His hair and beard are of a blackish brown, his face long and pale, but with patches of colour on the cheek-bones. He is dressed in a well-cut black visiting suit, quite new. He has dark gloves and a silk hat. He stops near the door and makes a rapid bow, seeming somewhat embarrassed.*

Tesman (goes up to him and shakes him warmly by the hand). Well, my dear Eilert—so at last we meet again!

Eilert Lövborg (speaks in a subdued voice). Thanks for your letter, Tesman. *(Approaching* HEDDA.*)* Will you, too, shake hands with me, Mrs. Tesman?

Hedda (taking his hand). I am glad to see you, Mr. Lövborg. *(With a motion of her hand.)* I don't know whether you two gentlemen——?

Lövborg (bowing slightly). Judge Brack, I think.

Brack (doing likewise). Oh, yes,—in the old days——

Tesman (to LÖVBORG, *with his hands on his shoulders).* And now you must make yourself entirely at home, Eilert! Mustn't he, Hedda?—For I hear you are going to settle in town again? Eh?

Lövborg. Yes, I am.

Tesman. Quite right, quite right. Let me tell you, I have got hold of your new book; but I haven't had time to read it yet.

Lövborg. You may spare yourself the trouble.

Tesman. Why so?

Lövborg. Because there is very little in it.

Tesman. Just fancy—how can you say so?

Brack. But it has been very much praised, I hear.

Lövborg. That was what I wanted; so I put nothing into the book but what every one would agree with.

Brack. Very wise of you.

Tesman. Well but, my dear Eilert——!

Lövborg. For now I mean to win myself a position again—to make a fresh start.

Tesman (a little embarrassed). Ah, that is what you wish to do? Eh?

Lövborg (smiling, lays down his hat and draws a packet, wrapped in paper, from his coat pocket). But when this one appears, George Tesman, you will have to read it. For this is the real book—the book I have put my true self into.

Tesman. Indeed? And what is it?

Lövborg. It is the continuation.

Tesman. The continuation? Of what?

Lövborg. Of the book.

Tesman. Of the new book?

Lövborg. Of course.

Tesman. Why, my dear Eilert—does it not come down to our own days?

Lövborg. Yes, it does; and this one deals with the future.

Tesman. With the future! But, good heavens, we know nothing of the future!

Lövborg. No; but there is a thing or two to be said about it all the same. *(Opens the packet.)* Look here——

Tesman. Why, that's not your hand writing.

Lövborg. I dictated it. *(Turning over the pages.)* It falls into two sections. The first deals with the civilising forces of the future. And here is the second—*(running through the pages towards the end)*—forecasting the probable line of development.

Tesman. How odd now! I should never have thought of writing anything of that sort.

Hedda (at the glass door, drumming on the pane). H'm—I daresay not.

Lövborg (replacing the manuscript in its paper and laying the packet on the table). I brought it, thinking I might read you a little of it this evening.

Tesman. That was very good of you, Eilert. But this evening——? *(Looking at* Brack.*)* I don't quite see how we can manage it——

Lövborg. Well, then, some other time. There is no hurry.

Brack. I must tell you, Mr. Lövborg—there is a little gathering at my house this evening—mainly in honour of Tesman, you know——

Lövborg (looking for his hat). Oh—then I won't detain you——

Brack. No, but listen—will you not do me the favour of joining us?

Lövborg (curtly and decidedly). No, I can't—thank you very much.

Brack. Oh, nonsense—do! We shall be quite a select

little circle. And I assure you we shall have a "lively time," as Mrs. Hed—as Mrs. Tesman says.

Lövborg. I have no doubt of it. But nevertheless——

Brack. And then you might bring your manuscript with you and read it to Tesman at my house. I could give you a room to yourselves.

Tesman. Yes, think of that, Eilert,—why shouldn't you? Eh?

Hedda (interposing). But, Tesman, if Mr. Lövborg would really rather not! I am sure Mr. Lövborg is much more inclined to remain here and have supper with me.

Lövborg (looking at her). With you, Mrs. Tesman?

Hedda. And with Mrs. Elvsted.

Lövborg. Ah—— *(Lightly.)* I saw her for a moment this morning.

Hedda. Did you? Well, she is coming this evening. So you see you are almost bound to remain, Mr. Lövborg, or she will have no one to see her home.

Lövborg. That's true. Many thanks, Mrs. Tesman—in that case I will remain.

Hedda. Then I have one or two orders to give the servant——

[*She goes to the hall door and rings.* BERTA *enters.* HEDDA *talks to her in a whisper and points towards the inner room.* BERTA *nods and goes out again.*

Tesman (at the same time, to Lövborg). Tell me, Eilert—is it this new subject—the future—that you are going to lecture about?

Lövborg. Yes.

Tesman. They told me at the bookseller's that you are going to deliver a course of lectures this autumn.

Lövborg. That is my intention. I hope you won't take it ill, Tesman.

Tesman. Oh, no, not in the least! But——?

Lövborg. I can quite understand that it must be disagreeable to you.

Tesman (cast down). Oh, I can't expect you, out of consideration for me, to——

Lövborg. But I shall wait till you have received your appointment.

Tesman. Will you wait? Yes, but—yes, but—are you not going to compete with me? Eh?

Lövborg. No; it is only the moral victory I care for.

Tesman. Why, bless me—then Aunt Julia was right after all! Oh, yes—I knew it! Hedda! Just fancy—Eilert Lövborg is not going to stand in our way!

Hedda (curtly). Our way? Pray leave me out of the question.

[*She goes up towards the inner room, where* BERTA *is placing a tray with decanters and glasses on the table.* HEDDA *nods approval and comes forward again.* BERTA *goes out.*

Tesman (at the same time). And you, Judge Brack—what do you say to this? Eh?

Brack. Well, I say that a moral victory—h'm—may be all very fine——

Tesman. Yes, certainly. But all the same——

Hedda (looking at TESMAN *with a cold smile.)* You stand there looking as if you were thunderstruck——

Tesman. Yes—so I am—I almost think——

Brack. Don't you see, Mrs. Tesman, a thunderstorm has just passed over?

Hedda (pointing towards the inner room). Will you not take a glass of cold punch, gentlemen?

Brack (looking at his watch). A stirrup-cup? Yes, it wouldn't come amiss.

Tesman. A capital idea, Hedda! Just the thing! Now that the weight has been taken off my mind——

Hedda. Will you not join them, Mr. Lövborg?

Lövborg (with a gesture of refusal). No, thank you. Nothing for me.

Brack. Why, bless me—cold punch is surely not poison.

Lövborg. Perhaps not for every one.

Hedda. I will keep Mr. Lövborg company in the meantime.

Tesman. Yes, yes, Hedda dear, do.

[*He and* BRACK *go into the inner room, seat themselves, drink punch, smoke cigarettes and carry on a lively conversation during what follows.* EILERT LÖVBORG *remains standing beside the stove.* HEDDA *goes to the writing-table.*

Hedda (raising her voice a little). Do you care to look at some photographs, Mr. Lövborg? You know Tesman and I made a tour in the Tyrol on our way home?

[*She takes up an album, and places it on the table beside the sofa, in the further corner of which she seats herself.* EILERT LÖVBORG *approaches, stops and looks at her. Then he takes a chair and seats himself to her left, with his back towards the inner room.*

Hedda (opening the album). Do you see this range of mountains, Mr. Lövborg? It's the Ortler group. Tesman has written the name underneath. Here it is: "The Ortler group near Meran."

Lövborg (who has never taken his eyes off her, says softly and slowly:) Hedda—Gabler!

Hedda (glancing hastily at him). Ah! Hush!

Lövborg (repeats softly). Hedda Gabler!

Hedda (looking at the album). That was my name in the old days—when we two knew each other.

Lövborg. And I must teach myself never to say Hedda Gabler again—never, as long as I live.

Hedda (still turning over the pages). Yes, you must. And I think you ought to practise in time. The sooner the better, I should say.

Lövborg (in a tone of indignation). Hedda Gabler married? And married to—George Tesman!

Hedda. Yes—so the world goes.

Lövborg. Oh, Hedda, Hedda—how could you* throw yourself away!

Hedda (looks sharply at him). What? I can't allow this!

Lövborg. What do you mean?

[TESMAN *comes into the room and goes towards the sofa.*

Hedda (hears him coming and says in an indifferent tone). And this is a view from the Val d'Ampezzo, Mr. Lövborg. Just look at these peaks! *(Looks affectionately up at* TESMAN.*)* What's the name of these curious peaks, dear?

Tesman. Let me see. Oh, those are the Dolomites.

Hedda. Yes, that's it!—Those are the Dolomites, Mr. Lövborg.

Tesman. Hedda dear,—I only wanted to ask whether I shouldn't bring you a little punch after all? For yourself, at any rate—eh?

Hedda. Yes, do, please; and perhaps a few biscuits.

Tesman. No cigarettes?

Hedda. No.

Tesman. Very well.

[*He goes into the inner room and out to the right.* BRACK *sits in the inner room and keeps an eye from time to time on* HEDDA *and* LÖVBORG.

Lövborg (softly, as before). Answer me, Hedda—how could you go and do this?

Hedda (apparently absorbed in the album). If you continue to say *du* to me I won't talk to you.

Lövborg. May I not say *du* when we are alone?

Hedda. No. You may think it; but you mustn't say it.

* He uses the familiar *du.*

Lövborg. Ah, I understand. It is an offence against George Tesman, whom you*—love.

Hedda (glances at him and smiles). Love? What an idea!

Lövborg. You don't love him then!

Hedda. But I won't hear of any sort of unfaithfulness! Remember that.

Lövborg. Hedda—answer me one thing——

Hedda. Hush!

[TESMAN *enters with a small tray from the inner room.*

Tesman. Here you are! Isn't this tempting?

[*He puts the tray on the table.*

Hedda. Why do you bring it yourself?

Tesman (filling the glasses). Because I think it's such fun to wait upon you, Hedda.

Hedda. But you have poured out two glasses. Mr. Lövborg said he wouldn't have any——

Tesman. No, but Mrs. Elvsted will soon be here, won't she?

Hedda. Yes, by-the-bye—Mrs. Elvsted——

Tesman. Had you forgotten her? Eh?

Hedda. We were so absorbed in these photographs. *(Shows him a picture.)* Do you remember this little village?

Tesman. Oh, it's that one just below the Brenner Pass. It was there we passed the night——

Hedda. ——and met that lively party of tourists.

Tesman. Yes, that was the place. Fancy—if we could only have had you with us, Eilert! Eh?

[*He returns to the inner room and sits beside* BRACK.

Lövborg. Answer me this one thing, Hedda——

Hedda. Well?

* From this point onward Lövborg uses the formal *De.*

Lövborg. Was there no love in your friendship for me either? Not a spark—not a tinge of love in it?

Hedda. I wonder if there was? To me it seems as though we were two good comrades—two thoroughly intimate friends. *(Smilingly.)* You especially were frankness itself.

Lövborg. It was you that made me so.

Hedda. As I look back upon it all, I think there was really something beautiful, something fascinating—something daring—in—in that secret intimacy—that comradeship which no living creature so much as dreamed of.

Lövborg. Yes, yes, Hedda! Was there not?—When I used to come to your father's in the afternoon—and the General sat over at the window reading his papers—with his back towards us——

Hedda. And we two on the corner sofa——

Lövborg. Always with the same illustrated paper before us——

Hedda. For want of an album, yes.

Lövborg. Yes, Hedda, and when I made my confessions to you—told you about myself, things that at that time no one else knew! There I would sit and tell you of my escapades—my days and nights of devilment. Oh, Hedda—what was the power in you that forced me to confess these things?

Hedda. Do you think it was any power in me?

Lövborg. How else can I explain it? And all those—those roundabout questions you used to put to me——

Hedda. Which you understood so particularly well——

Lövborg. How could you sit and question me like that? Question me quite frankly——

Hedda. In roundabout terms, please observe.

Lövborg. Yes, but frankly nevertheless. Cross-question me about—all that sort of thing?

Hedda. And how could you answer, Mr. Lövborg?

Lövborg. Yes, that is just what I can't understand—in

looking back upon it. But tell me now, Hedda—was there not love at the bottom of our friendship? On your side, did you not feel as though you might purge my stains away—if I made you my confessor? Was it not so?

Hedda. No, not quite.

Lövborg. What was your motive, then?

Hedda. Do you think it quite incomprehensible that a young girl—when it can be done—without any one knowing——

Lövborg. Well?

Hedda. ——should be glad to have a peep, now and then, into a world which——

Lövborg. Which——?

Hedda. ——which she is forbidden to know anything about?

Lövborg. So that was it?

Hedda. Partly. Partly—I almost think.

Lövborg. Comradeship in the thirst for life. But why should not that, at any rate, have continued?

Hedda. The fault was yours.

Lövborg. It was you that broke with me.

Hedda. Yes, when our friendship threatened to develop into something more serious. Shame upon you, Eilert Lövborg! How could you think of wronging your—your frank comrade?

Lövborg (clenching his hands). Oh, why did you not carry out your threat? Why did you not shoot me down?

Hedda. Because I have such a dread of scandal.

Lövborg. Yes, Hedda, you are a coward at heart.

Hedda. A terrible coward. *(Changing her tone.)* But it was a lucky thing for you. And now you have found ample consolation at the Elvsteds'.

Lövborg. I know what Thea has confided to you.

Hedda. And perhaps you have confided to her something about us?

Lövborg. Not a word. She is too stupid to understand anything of that sort.

Hedda. Stupid?

Lövborg. She is stupid about matters of that sort.

Hedda. And I am cowardly. *(Bends over towards him, without looking him in the face, and says more softly:)* But now I will confide something to you.

Lövborg (eagerly). Well?

Hedda. The fact that I dared not shoot you down——

Lövborg. Yes!

Hedda. ——that was not my arrant cowardice—that evening.

Lövborg (looks at her a moment, understands and whispers passionately). Oh, Hedda! Hedda Gabler! Now I begin to see a hidden reason beneath our comradeship! You* and I——! After all, then, it was your craving for life——

Hedda (softly, with a sharp glance). Take care! Believe nothing of the sort!

[*Twilight has begun to fall. The hall door is opened from without by* BERTA.

Hedda. *(Closes the album with a bang and calls smilingly:)* Ah, at last! My darling Thea,—come along!

[MRS. ELVSTED *enters from the hall. She is in evening dress. The door is closed behind her.*

Hedda (on the sofa, stretches out her arms towards her). My sweet Thea—you can't think how I have been longing for you!

[MRS. ELVSTED, *in passing, exchanges slight salutations with the gentlemen in the inner room, then goes up to the table and gives* HEDDA *her hand.* EILERT LÖVBORG *has risen. He and* MRS. ELVSTED *greet each other with a silent nod.*

* In this speech he once more says *du.* Hedda addresses him throughout as *De.*

Mrs. Elvsted. Ought I to go in and talk to your husband for a moment?

Hedda. Oh, not at all. Leave those two alone. They will soon be going.

Mrs. Elvsted. Are they going out?

Hedda. Yes, to a supper-party.

Mrs. Elvsted (quickly, to LÖVBORG*).* Not you?

Lövborg. No.

Hedda. Mr. Lövborg remains with us.

Mrs. Elvsted (takes a chair and is about to seat herself at his side). Oh, how nice it is here!

Hedda. No, thank you, my little Thea! Not there! You'll be good enough to come over here to me. I will sit between you.

Mrs. Elvsted. Yes, just as you please.

[*She goes round the table and seats herself on the sofa on* HEDDA'S *right.* LÖVBORG *re-seats himself on his chair.*

Lövborg (after a short pause, to HEDDA*).* Is not she lovely to look at?

Hedda (lightly stroking her hair). Only to look at?

Lövborg. Yes. For we two—she and I—we are two real comrades. We have absolute faith in each other; so we can sit and talk with perfect frankness——

Hedda. Not round about, Mr. Lövborg?

Lövborg. Well——

Mrs. Elvsted (softly clinging close to HEDDA*).* Oh, how happy I am, Hedda; For, only think, he says I have inspired him, too.

Hedda (looks at her with a smile). Ah! Does he say that, dear?

Lövborg. And then she is so brave, Mrs. Tesman!

Mrs. Elvsted. Good heavens—am I brave?

Lövborg. Exceedingly—where your comrade is concerned.

Hedda. Ah yes—courage! If one only had that!

Lövborg. What then? What do you mean?

Hedda. Then life would perhaps be liveable, after all. *(With a sudden change of tone.)* But now, my dearest Thea, you really must have a glass of cold punch.

Mrs. Elvsted. No, thanks—I never take anything of that kind.

Hedda. Well, then, you, Mr. Lövborg.

Lövborg. Nor I, thank you.

Mrs. Elvsted. No, he doesn't either.

Hedda (looks fixedly at him). But if I say you shall?

Lövborg. It would be no use.

Hedda (laughing). Then I, poor creature, have no sort of power over you?

Lövborg. Not in that respect.

Hedda. But seriously, I think you ought to—for your own sake.

Mrs. Elvsted. Why, Hedda——!

Lövborg. How so?

Hedda. Or rather on account of other people.

Lövborg. Indeed?

Hedda. Otherwise people might be apt to suspect that —in your heart of hearts—you did not feel quite secure—quite confident in yourself.

Mrs. Elvsted (softly). Oh, please, Hedda——.

Lövborg. People may suspect what they like—for the present.

Mrs. Elvsted (joyfully). Yes, let them!

Hedda. I saw it plainly in Judge Brack's face a moment ago.

Lövborg. What did you see?

Hedda. His contemptuous smile, when you dared not go with them into the inner room.

Lövborg. Dared not? Of course I preferred to stop here and talk to you.

Mrs. Elvsted. What could be more natural, Hedda?

Hedda. But the Judge could not guess that. And I saw, too, the way he smiled and glanced at Tesman when you dared not accept his invitation to this wretched little supper-party of his.

Lövborg. Dared not! Do you say I dared not?

Hedda. *I* don't say so. But that was how Judge Brack understood it.

Lövborg. Well, let him.

Hedda. Then you are not going with them?

Lövborg. I will stay here with you and Thea.

Mrs. Elvsted. Yes, Hedda—how can you doubt that?

Hedda (smiles and nods approvingly to LÖVBORG*).* Firm as a rock! Faithful to your principles, now and for ever! Ah, that is how a man should be! *(Turns to* MRS. ELVSTED *and caresses her.)* Well, now, what did I tell you, when you came to us this morning in such a state of distraction——

Lövborg (surprised). Distraction!

Mrs. Elvsted (terrified). Hedda—oh Hedda——!

Hedda. You can see for yourself; You haven't the slightest reason to be in such mortal terror——*(Interrupting herself.)* There! Now we can all three enjoy ourselves!

Lövborg (who has given a start). Ah—what is all this, Mrs. Tesman?

Mrs. Elvsted. Oh, my God, Hedda! What are you saying? What are you doing?

Hedda. Don't get excited! That horrid Judge Brack is sitting watching you.

Lövborg. So she was in mortal terror! On my account!

Mrs. Elvsted (softly and piteously). Oh, Hedda—now you have ruined everything!

Lövborg (looks fixedly at her for a moment. His face is distorted). So that was my comrade's frank confidence in me?

Mrs. Elvsted (imploringly). Oh, my dearest friend—only let me tell you——

Lövborg (takes one of the glasses of punch, raises it to

his lips and says in a low, husky voice). Your health, Thea!

[*He empties the glass, puts it down and takes the second.*

Mrs. Elvsted (softly). Oh, Hedda, Hedda—how could you do this?

Hedda. *I* do it? *I?* Are you crazy?

Lövborg. Here's to your health, too, Mrs. Tesman. Thanks for the truth. Hurrah for the truth!

[*He empties the glass and is about to re-fill it.*

Hedda (lays her hand on his arm). Come, come—no more for the present. Remember you are going out to supper.

Mrs. Elvsted. No, no, no!

Hedda. Hush! They are sitting watching you.

Lövborg (putting down the glass). Now, Thea— tell me the truth——

Mrs. Elvsted. Yes.

Lövborg. Did your husband know that you had come after me?

Mrs. Elvsted (wringing her hands). Oh, Hedda—do you hear what he is asking?

Lövborg. Was it arranged between you and him that you were to come to town and look after me? Perhaps it was the Sheriff himself that urged you to come? Aha, my dear—no doubt he wanted my help in his office! Or was it at the card-table that he missed me?

Mrs. Elvsted (softly, in agony). Oh, Lövborg, Lövborg——!

Lövborg (seizes a glass and is on the point of filling it). Here's a glass for the old Sheriff, too!

Hedda (preventing him). No more just now. Remember you have to read your manuscript to Tesman.

Lövborg (calmly, putting down the glass). It was stupid of me all this, Thea—to take it in this way, I mean. Don't be angry with me, my dear, dear comrade. You shall see—

both you and the others—that if I was fallen once—now I have risen again! Thanks to you, Thea.

Mrs. Elvsted (radiant with joy). Oh, heaven be praised——!

[BRACK *has in the meantime looked at his watch. He and* TESMAN *rise and come into the drawing-room.*

Brack (takes his hat and overcoat). Well, Mrs. Tesman, our time has come.

Hedda. I suppose it has.

Lövborg (rising). Mine, too, Judge Brack.

Mrs. Elvsted (softly and imploringly). Oh, Lövborg, don't do it!

Hedda (pinching her arm). They can hear you!

Mrs. Elvsted (with a suppressed shriek). Ow!

Lövborg (to BRACK*).* You were good enough to invite me.

Brack. Well, are you coming after all?

Lövborg. Yes, many thanks.

Brack. I'm delighted——

Lövborg (to TESMAN, *putting the parcel of MS. in his pocket).* I should like to show you one or two things before I send it to the printers.

Tesman. Fancy—that will be delightful. But, Hedda dear, how is Mrs. Elvsted to get home? Eh?

Hedda. Oh, that can be managed somehow.

Lövborg (looking towards the ladies). Mrs. Elvsted? Of course, I'll come again and fetch her. *(Approaching.)* At ten or thereabouts, Mrs. Tesman? Will that do?

Hedda. Certainly. That will do capitally.

Tesman. Well, then, that's all right. But you must not expect me so early, Hedda.

Hedda.—Oh, you may stop as long—as long as ever you please.

Mrs. Elvsted (trying to conceal her anxiety). Well, then, Mr. Lövborg—I shall remain here until you come.

Lövborg (with his hat in his hand). Pray do, Mrs Elvsted.

Brack. And now off goes the excursion train, gentlemen! I hope we shall have a lively time, as a certain fair lady puts it.

Hedda. Ah, if only the fair lady could be present unseen——!

Brack. Why unseen?

Hedda. In order to hear a little of your liveliness at first hand, Judge Brack.

Brack (laughing). I should not advise the fair lady to try it.

Tesman (also laughing). Come, you're a nice one Hedda! Fancy that!

Brack. Well, good-bye, ladies.

Lövborg (bowing). About ten o'clock, then.

[BRACK, LÖVBORG *and* TESMAN *go out by the hall door. At the same time,* BERTA *enters from the inner room with a lighted lamp, which she places on the dining-room table; she goes out by the way she came.*

Mrs. Elvsted (who has risen and is wandering restlessly about the room). Hedda—Hedda—what will come of all this?

Hedda. At ten o'clock—he will be here. I can see him already—with vine-leaves in his hair—flushed and fearless——

Mrs. Elvsted. Oh, I hope he may.

Hedda. And then, you see—then he will have regained control over himself. Then he will be a free man for all his days.

Mrs. Elvsted. Oh, God!—if he would only come as you see him now!

Hedda. He will come as I see him—so, and not otherwise! *(Rises and approaches* THEA.*)* You may doubt him as long as you please; *I* believe in him. And now we will try——

Mrs. Elvsted. You have some hidden motive in this, Hedda!

Hedda. Yes, I have. I want for once in my life to have power to mould a human destiny.

Mrs. Elvsted. Have you not the power?

Hedda. I have not—and have never had it.

Mrs. Elvsted. Not your husband's?

Hedda. Do you think that is worth the trouble? Oh, if you could only understand how poor I am. And fate has made you so rich! *(Clasps her passionately in her arms.)* I think I must burn your hair off, after all.

Mrs. Elvsted. Let me go! Let me go! I am afraid of you, Hedda!

Berta (in the middle doorway). Tea is laid in the dining-room, ma'am.

Hedda. Very well. We are coming.

Mrs. Elvsted. No, no, no! I would rather go home alone! At once!

Hedda. Nonsense! First you shall have a cup of tea, you little stupid. And then—at ten o'clock—Eilert Lövborg will be here—with vine-leaves in his hair.

[*She drags* MRS. ELVSTED *almost by force towards the middle doorway.*

ACT III

The room at the TESMANS'. *The curtains are drawn over the middle doorway, and also over the glass door. The lamp, half turned down, and with a shade over it, is burning on the table. In the stove, the door of which stands open, there has been a fire, which is now nearly burnt out.*

MRS. ELVSTED, *wrapped in a large shawl, and with her feet upon a foot-rest, sits close to the stove, sunk back in the arm-chair.* HEDDA, *fully dressed, lies sleeping upon the sofa, with a sofa-blanket over her.*

Mrs. Elvsted (after a pause, suddenly sits up in her chair and listens eagerly. Then she sinks back again wearily, moaning to herself). Not yet!—Oh, God—oh, God—not yet!

[BERTA *slips cautiously in by the hall door. She has a letter in her hand.*

Mrs. Elvsted (turns and whispers eagerly). Well—has any one come?

Berta (softly). Yes, a girl has brought this letter.

Mrs. Elvsted (quickly, holding out her hand). A letter! Give it to me!

Berta. No, it's for Dr. Tesman, ma'am.

Mrs. Elvsted. Oh, indeed.

Berta. It was Miss Tesman's servant that brought it. I'll lay it here on the table.

Mrs. Elvsted. Yes, do.

Berta (laying down the letter). I think I had better put out the lamp. It's smoking.

Mrs. Elvested. Yes, put it out. It must soon be daylight now.

Berta (putting out the lamp). It is daylight already, ma'am.

Mrs. Elvested. Yes, broad day! And no one come back yet——!

Berta. Lord bless you, ma'am—I guessed how it would be.

Mrs. Elvested. You guessed?

Berta. Yes, when I saw that a certain person had come back to town—and that he went off with them. For we've heard enough about that gentleman before now.

Mrs. Elvsted. Don't speak so loud. You will waken Mrs. Tesman.

Berta (looks towards the sofa and sighs). No, no—let her sleep, poor thing. Shan't I put some wood on the fire?

Mrs. Elvsted. Thanks, not for me.

Berta. Oh, very well.

[*She goes softly out by the hall door.*

Hedda (is awakened by the shutting of the door and looks up). What's that——?

Mrs. Elvsted. It was only the servant——

Hedda (looking about her). Oh, we're here——! Yes now I remember. *(Sits erect upon the sofa, stretches her self and rubs her eyes.)* What o'clock is it, Thea?

Mrs. Elvsted (looks at her watch). It's past seven.

Hedda. When did Tesman come home?

Mrs. Elvsted. He has not come.

Hedda. Not come home yet?

Mrs. Elvsted (rising). No one has come.

Hedda. Think of our watching and waiting here till four in the morning——

Mrs. Elvsted (wringing her hands). And how I watched and waited for him!

Hedda (yawns and says with her hand before her

mouth). Well, well—we might have spared ourselves the trouble.

Mrs. Elvsted. Did you get a little sleep?

Hedda. Oh, yes; I believe I have slept pretty well. Have you not?

Mrs. Elvsted. Not for a moment. I couldn't, Hedda!—not to save my life.

Hedda (rises and goes towards her). There, there, there! There's nothing to be so alarmed about. I understand quite well what has happened.

Mrs. Elvsted. Well, what do you think? Won't you tell me?

Hedda. Why, of course it has been a very late affair at Judge Brack's——

Mrs. Elvsted. Yes, yes, that is clear enough. But all the same——

Hedda. And then, you see, Tesman hasn't cared to come home and ring us up in the middle of the night. *(Laughing.)* Perhaps he wasn't inclined to show himself either—immediately after a jollification.

Mrs. Elvsted. But in that case—where can he have gone?

Hedda. Of course he has gone to his aunts' and slept there. They have his old room ready for him.

Mrs. Elvsted. No, he can't be with them; for a letter has just come for him from Miss Tesman. There it lies.

Hedda. Indeed? *(Looks at the address.)* Why, yes, it's addressed in Aunt Julia's own hand. Well, then, he has remained at Judge Brack's. And as for Eilert Lövborg—he is sitting, with vine-leaves in his hair, reading his manuscript.

Mrs. Elvsted. Oh, Hedda, you are just saying things you don't believe a bit.

Hedda. You really are a little blockhead, Thea.

Mrs. Elvsted. Oh, yes, I suppose I am.

Hedda. And how mortally tired you look.

Mrs. Elvsted. Yes, I am mortally tired.

Hedda. Well, then, you must do as I tell you. You must go into my room and lie down for a little while.

Mrs. Elvsted. Oh, no, no—I shouldn't be able to sleep.

Hedda. I am sure you would.

Mrs. Elvsted. Well, but your husband is certain to come soon now; and then I want to know at once——

Hedda. I shall take care to let you know when he comes.

Mrs. Elvsted. Do you promise me, Hedda?

Hedda. Yes, rely upon me. Just you go in and have a sleep in the meantime.

Mrs. Elvsted. Thanks; then I'll try to.

[*She goes off through the inner room.*

[HEDDA *goes up to the glass door and draws back the curtains. The broad daylight streams into the room. Then she takes a little hand-glass from the writing-table, looks at herself in it and arranges her hair. Next she goes to the hall door and presses the bell-button.*

[BERTA *presently appears at the hall door.*

Berta. Did you want anything, ma'am?

Hedda. Yes; you must put some more wood in the stove. I am shivering.

Berta. Bless me—I'll make up the fire at once. *(She rakes the embers together and lays a piece of wood upon them; then stops and listens.)* That was a ring at the front door, ma'am.

Hedda. Then go to the door. I will look after the fire.

Berta. It'll soon burn up.

[*She goes out by the hall door.*

[HEDDA *kneels on the foot-rest and lays some more pieces of wood in the stove.*

[*After a short pause,* GEORGE TESMAN *enters from the hall. He looks tired and rather serious. He steals on tiptoe towards the middle doorway and is about to slip through the curtains.*

Hedda (at the stove, without looking up). Good morning.

Tesman (turns). Hedda! *(Approaching her.)* Good heavens—are you up so early? Eh?

Hedda. Yes, I am up very early this morning.

Tesman. And I never doubted you were still sound asleep! Fancy that, Hedda!

Hedda. Don't speak so loud. Mrs. Elvsted is resting in my room.

Tesman. Has Mrs. Elvsted been here all night?

Hedda. Yes, since no one came to fetch her.

Tesman. Ah, to be sure.

Hedda (closes the door of the stove and rises). Well, did you enjoy yourselves at Judge Brack's?

Tesman. Have you been anxious about me? Eh?

Hedda. No, I should never think of being anxious. But I asked if you had enjoyed yourself.

Tesman. Oh, yes,—for once in a way. Especially the beginning of the evening; for then Eilert read me part of his book. We arrived more than an hour too early—fancy that! And Brack had all sorts of arrangements to make—so Eilert read to me.

Hedda (seating herself by the table on the right). Well? Tell me, then—

Tesman (sitting on a footstool near the stove). Oh Hedda, you can't conceive what a book that is going to be! I believe it is one of the most remarkable things that have ever been written. Fancy that!

Hedda. Yes, yes; I don't care about that——

Tesman. I must make a confession to you, Hedda. When he had finished reading—a horrid feeling came over me.

Hedda. A horrid feeling?

Tesman. I felt jealous of Eilert for having had it in him to write such a book. Only think, Hedda!

Hedda. Yes, yes, I am thinking!

Tesman. And then how pitiful to think that he—with all his gifts—should be irreclaimable, after all.

Hedda. I suppose you mean that he has more courage than the rest?

Tesman. No, not at all—I mean that he is incapable of taking his pleasures in moderation.

Hedda. And what came of it all—in the end?

Tesman. Well, to tell the truth, I think it might best be described as an orgie, Hedda.

Hedda. Had he vine-leaves in his hair?

Tesman. Vine-leaves? No, I saw nothing of the sort. But he made a long, rambling speech in honour of the woman who had inspired him in his work—that was the phrase he used.

Hedda. Did he name her?

Tesman. No, he didn't; but I can't help thinking he meant Mrs. Elvsted. You may be sure he did.

Hedda. Well—where did you part from him?

Tesman. On the way to town. We broke up—the last of us at any rate—all together; and Brack came with us to get a breath of fresh air. And then, you see, we agreed to take Eilert home; for he had had far more than was good for him.

Hedda. I daresay.

Tesman. But now comes the strange part of it, Hedda; or, I should rather say, the melancholy part of it. I declare I am almost ashamed—on Eilert's account—to tell you——

Hedda. Oh, go on——

Tesman. Well, as we were getting near town, you see, I happened to drop a little behind the others. Only for a minute or two—fancy that!

Hedda. Yes, yes, yes, but——?

Tesman. And then, as I hurried after them—what do you think I found by the wayside? Eh?

Hedda. Oh, how should I know!

Tesman. You mustn't speak of it to a soul, Hedda! Do you hear! Promise me, for Eilert's sake. *(Draws a parcel, wrapped in paper, from his coat pocket.)* Fancy, dear —I found this.

Hedda. Is not that the parcel he had with him yesterday?

Tesman. Yes, it is the whole of his precious, irreplaceable manuscript! And he had gone and lost it and knew nothing about it. Only fancy, Hedda! So deplorably——

Hedda. But why did you not give him back the parcel at once?

Tesman. I didn't dare to—in the state he was then in——

Hedda. Did you not tell any of the others that you had found it?

Tesman. Oh, far from it! You can surely understand that, for Eilert's sake, I wouldn't do that.

Hedda. So no one knows that Eilert Lövborg's manuscript is in your possession?

Tesman. No. And no one must know it.

Hedda. Then what did you say to him afterwards?

Tesman. I didn't talk to him again at all; for when we got in among the streets, he and two or three of the others gave us the slip and disappeared. Fancy that!

Hedda. Indeed! They must have taken him home then.

Tesman. Yes, so it would appear. And Brack, too, left us.

Hedda. And what have you been doing with yourself since?

Tesman. Well, I and some of the others went home with one of the party, a jolly fellow, and took our morning coffee with him; or perhaps I should rather call it our night coffee —eh? But now, when I have rested a little, and given Eilert, poor fellow, time to have his sleep out, I must take this back to him.

Hedda (holds out her hand for the packet). No—don't give it to him! Not in such a hurry, I mean. Let me read it first.

Tesman. No, my dearest Hedda, I mustn't, I really mustn't.

Hedda. You must not?

Tesman. No—for you can imagine what a state of despair he will be in when he awakens and misses the manuscript. He has no copy of it, you must know! He told me so.

Hedda (looking searchingly at him). Can such a thing not be reproduced? Written over again?

Tesman. No, I don't think that would be possible. For the inspiration, you see——

Hedda. Yes, yes—I suppose it depends on that. *(Lightly.)* But, by-the-bye—here is a letter for you.

Tesman. Fancy——!

Hedda (handing it to him). It came early this morning.

Tesman. It's from Aunt Julia! What can it be? *(He lays the packet on the other footstool, opens the letter, runs his eye through it and jumps up.)* Oh, Hedda—she says that poor Aunt Rina is dying!

Hedda. Well, we were prepared for that.

Tesman. And that if I want to see her again, I must make haste. I'll run in to them at once.

Hedda (suppressing a smile). Will you run?

Tesman. Oh, dearest Hedda—if you could only make up your mind to come with me! Just think!

Hedda (rises and says wearily, repelling the idea). No, no, don't ask me. I will not look upon sickness and death. I loathe all sorts of ugliness.

Tesman. Well, well, then——! *(Bustling around.)* My hat—— My overcoat——? Oh, in the hall—— I do hope I mayn't come too late, Hedda! Eh?

Hedda. Oh, if you run——

[BERTA *appears at the hall door.*

Berta. Judge Brack is at the door and wishes to know if he may come in.

Tesman. At this time! No, I can't possibly see him.

Hedda. But I can. *(To* BERTA.*)* Ask Judge Brack to come in.

[BERTA *goes out.*

Hedda (quickly, whispering). The parcel, Tesman!

[*She snatches it up from the stool.*

Tesman. Yes, give it to me!

Hedda. No, no, I will keep it till you come back.

[*She goes to the writing-table and places it in the book-case.* TESMAN *stands in a flurry of haste and cannot get his gloves on.*

[JUDGE BRACK *enters from the hall.*

Hedda (nodding to him). You are an early bird, I must say.

Brack. Yes, don't you think so? *(To* TESMAN.*)* Are you on the move, too?

Tesman. Yes, I must rush off to my aunts'. Fancy—the invalid one is lying at death's door, poor creature.

Brack. Dear me, is she indeed? Then on no account let me detain you. At such a critical moment——

Tesman. Yes, I must really rush—— Good-bye! Good-bye!

[*He hastens out by the hall door.*

Hedda (approaching). You seem to have made a particularly lively night of it at your rooms, Judge Brack.

Brack. I assure you I have not had my clothes off, Mrs. Hedda.

Hedda. Not you, either?

Brack. No, as you may see. But what has Tesman been telling you of the night's adventures?

Hedda. Oh, some tiresome story. Only that they went and had coffee somewhere or other.

Brack. I have heard about that coffee-party already. Eilert Lövborg was not with them, I fancy?

Hedda. No, they had taken him home before that.

Brack. Tesman, too?

Hedda. No, but some of the others, he said.

Brack (smiling). George Tesman is really an ingenuous creature, Mrs. Hedda.

Hedda. Yes, heaven knows he is. Then is there something behind all this?

Brack. Yes, perhaps there may be.

Hedda. Well, then, sit down, my dear Judge, and tell your story in comfort.

[*She seats herself to the left of the table.* BRACK *sits near her, at the long side of the table.*

Hedda. Now then?

Brack. I had special reasons for keeping track of my guests—or rather of some of my guests—last night.

Hedda. Of Eilert Lövborg among the rest, perhaps?

Brack. Frankly, yes.

Hedda. Now you make me really curious——

Brack. Do you know where he and one or two of the others finished the night, Mrs. Hedda?

Hedda. If it is not quite unmentionable, tell me.

Brack. Oh, no, it's not at all unmentionable. Well, they put in an appearance at a particularly animated soirée.

Hedda. Of the lively kind?

Brack. Of the very liveliest——

Hedda. Tell me more of this, Judge Brack——

Brack. Lövborg, as well as the others, had been invited in advance. I knew all about it. But he had declined the invitation; for now, as you know, he has become a new man.

Hedda. Up at the Elvsteds', yes. But he went after all, then?

Brack. Well, you see, Mrs. Hedda—unhappily the spirit moved him at my rooms last evening——

Hedda. Yes, I hear he found inspiration.

Brack. Pretty violent inspiration. Well, I fancy that

altered his purpose; for we men folk are, unfortunately, not always so firm in our principles as we ought to be.

Hedda. Oh, I am sure you are an exception, Judge Brack. But as to Lövborg——?

Brack. To make a long story short—he landed at last in Mademoiselle Diana's rooms.

Hedda. Mademoiselle Diana's?

Brack. It was Mademoiselle Diana that was giving the soirée, to a select circle of her admirers and her lady friends.

Hedda. Is she a red-haired woman?

Brack. Precisely.

Hedda. A sort of a—singer?

Brack. Oh, yes—in her leisure moments. And moreover a mighty huntress—of men—Mrs. Hedda. You have no doubt heard of her. Eilert Lövborg was one of her most enthusiastic protectors—in the days of his glory.

Hedda. And how did all this end?

Brack. Far from amicably, it appears. After a most tender meeting, they seem to have come to blows——

Hedda. Lövborg and she?

Brack. Yes. He accused her or her friends of having robbed him. He declared that his pocket-book had disappeared—and other things as well. In short, he seems to have made a furious disturbance.

Hedda. And what came of it all?

Brack. It came to a general scrimmage, in which the ladies as well as the gentlemen took part. Fortunately the police at last appeared on the scene.

Hedda. The police, too?

Brack. Yes. I fancy it will prove a costly frolic for Eilert Lövborg, crazy being that he is.

Hedda. How so?

Brack. He seems to have made a violent resistance—to have hit one of the constables on the head and torn the coat off his back. So they had to march him off to the police-station with the rest.

Hedda. How have you learnt all this?

Brack. From the police themselves.

Hedda (gazing straight before her). So that is what happened. Then he had no vine-leaves in his hair.

Brack. Vine-leaves, Mrs. Hedda?

Hedda (changing her tone). But tell me now, Judge—what is your real reason for tracking out Eilert Lövborg's movements so carefully?

Brack. In the first place, it could not be entirely indifferent to me if it should appear in the police-court that he came straight from my house.

Hedda. Will the matter come into court, then?

Brack. Of course. However, I should scarcely have troubled so much about that. But I thought that, as a friend of the family, it was my duty to supply you and Tesman with a full account of his nocturnal exploits.

Hedda. Why so, Judge Brack?

Brack. Why, because I have a shrewd suspicion that he intends to use you as a sort of blind.

Hedda. Oh, how can you think such a thing!

Brack. Good heavens, Mrs. Hedda—we have eyes in our head. Mark my words! This Mrs. Elvsted will be in no hurry to leave town again.

Hedda. Well, even if there should be anything between them, I suppose there are plenty of other places where they could meet.

Brack. Not a single home. Henceforth, as before, every respectable house will be closed against Eilert Lövborg.

Hedda. And so ought mine to be, you mean?

Brack. Yes. I confess it would be more than painful to me if this personage were to be made free of your house. How superfluous, how intrusive, he would be, if he were to force his way into——

Hedda. —into the triangle?

Brack. Precisely. It would simply mean that I should find myself homeless.

Hedda (looks at him with a smile). So you want to be the one cock in the basket*—that is your aim.

Brack (nods slowly and lowers his voice). Yes, that is my aim. And for that I will fight—with every weapon I can command.

Hedda (her smile vanishing). I see you are a dangerous person—when it comes to the point.

Brack. Do you think so?

Hedda. I am beginning to think so. And I am exceedingly glad to think—that you have no sort of hold over me.

Brack (laughing equivocally). Well, well, Mrs. Hedda—perhaps you are right there. If I had, who knows what I might be capable of?

Hedda. Come, come now, Judge Brack! That sounds almost like a threat.

Brack (rising). Oh, not at all! The triangle, you know, ought, if possible, to be spontaneously constructed.

Hedda. There I agree with you.

Brack. Well, now I have said all I had to say; and I had better be getting back to town. Good-bye, Mrs. Hedda.

[*He goes towards the glass door.*

Hedda (rising). Are you going through the garden?

Brack. Yes, it's a short cut for me.

Hedda. And then it is a back way, too.

Brack. Quite so. I have no objection to back ways. They may be piquant enough at times.

Hedda. When there is ball practice going on, you mean?

Brack (in the doorway, laughing to her). Oh, people don't shoot their tame poultry, I fancy.

Hedda (also laughing). Oh, no, when there is only one cock in the basket——

[*They exchange laughing nods of farewell. He goes. She closes the door behind him.*

* "Eneste hane i kurven"—a proverbial saying.

[HEDDA, *who has become quite serious, stands for a moment looking out. Presently she goes and peeps through the curtain over the middle doorway. Then she goes to the writing-table, takes* LÖVBORG'S *packet out of the bookcase and is on the point of looking through its contents.* BERTA *is heard speaking loudly in the hall.* HEDDA *turns and listens. Then she hastily locks up the packet in the drawer and lays the key on the inkstand.*

[EILERT LÖVBORG, *with his greatcoat on and his hat in his hand, tears open the hall door. He looks somewhat confused and irritated.*

Lövborg (looking towards the hall). And I tell you I must and will come in! There!

[*He closes the door, turns, sees* HEDDA, *at once regains his self-control and bows.*

Hedda (at the writing-table). Well, Mr. Lövborg, this is rather a late hour to call for Thea.

Lövborg. You mean rather an early hour to call on you. Pray pardon me.

Hedda. How do you know that she is still here?

Lövborg. They told me at her lodgings that she had been out all night.

Hedda (going to the oval table). Did you notice anything about the people of the house when they said that?

Lövborg (looks inquiringly at her). Notice anything about them?

Hedda. I mean, did they seem to think it odd?

Lövborg (suddenly understanding). Oh, yes, of course! I am dragging her down with me! However, I didn't notice anything.——I suppose Tesman is not up yet?

Hedda. No—I think not——

Lövborg. When did he come home?

Hedda. Very late.

Lövborg. Did he tell you anything?

Hedda. Yes, I gathered that you had had an exceedingly jolly evening at Judge Brack's.

Lövborg. Nothing more?

Hedda. I don't think so. However, I was so dreadfully sleepy——

[MRS. ELVSTED *enters through the curtains of the middle doorway.*

Mrs. Elvsted (going towards him). Ah, Lövborg! At last——!

Lövborg. Yes, at last. And too late!

Mrs. Elvsted (looks anxiously at him). What is too late?

Lövborg. Everything is too late now. It is all over with me.

Mrs. Elvsted. Oh, no, no—don't say that!

Lövborg. You will say the same when you hear——

Mrs. Elvsted. I won't hear anything!

Hedda. Perhaps you would prefer to talk to her alone! If so, I will leave you.

Lövborg. No, stay—you, too. I beg you to stay.

Mrs. Elvsted. Yes, but I won't hear anything, I tell you.

Lövborg. It is not last night's adventures that I want to talk about.

Mrs. Elvsted. What is it then——?

Lövborg. I want to say that now our ways must part.

Mrs. Elvsted. Part!

Hedda (involuntarily). I knew it!

Lövborg. You can be of no more service to me, Thea.

Mrs. Elvsted. How can you stand there and say that! No more service to you! Am I not to help you now, as before? Are we not to go on working together?

Lövborg. Henceforward I shall do no work.

Mrs. Elvsted (despairingly). Then what am I to do with my life?

Lövborg. You must try to live your life as if you had never known me.

Mrs. Elvsted. But you know I cannot do that!

Lövborg. Try if you cannot, Thea. You must go home again——

Mrs. Elvsted (in vehement protest). Never in this world! Where you are, there will I be also! I will not let myself be driven away like this! I will remain here! I will be with you when the book appears.

Hedda (half aloud, in suspense). Ah, yes—the book!

Lövborg (looks at her). My book and Thea's; for that is what it is.

Mrs. Elvsted. Yes, I feel that it is. And that is why I have a right to be with you when it appears! I will see with my own eyes how respect and honour pour in upon you afresh. And the happiness—the happiness—oh, I must share it with you!

Lövborg. Thea—our book will never appear.

Hedda. Ah!

Mrs. Elvsted. Never appear!

Lövborg. Can never appear.

Mrs. Elvsted (in agonised foreboding). Lövberg—what have you done with the manuscript?

Hedda (looks anxiously at him). Yes, the manuscript——?

Mrs. Elvsted. Where is it?

Lövborg. Oh, Thea—don't ask me about it!

Mrs. Elvsted. Yes, yes, I will know. I demand to be told at once.

Lövborg. The manuscript—— Well, then—I have torn the manuscript into a thousand pieces.

Mrs. Elvsted (shrieks). Oh, no, no——!

Hedda (involuntarily). But that's not——

Lövborg (looks at her). Not true, you think?

Hedda (collecting herself). Oh, well, of course—since you say so. But it sounded so improbable——

Lövborg. It is true, all the same.

Mrs. Elvsted (wringing her hands). Oh, God—oh, God, Hedda—torn his own work to pieces!

Lövborg. I have torn my own life to pieces. So why should I not tear my life-work, too——?

Mrs. Elvsted. And you did this last night?

Lövborg. Yes, I tell you! Tore it into a thousand pieces and scattered them on the fiord—far out. There there is cool sea-water, at any rate—let them drift upon it —drift with the current and the wind. And then presently they will sink—deeper and deeper—as I shall, Thea.

Mrs. Elvsted. Do you know, Lövborg, that what you have done with the book—I shall think of it to my dying day as though you had killed a little child.

Lövborg. Yes, you are right. It is a sort of child-murder.

Mrs. Elvsted. How could you, then——! Did not the child belong to me, too?

Hedda (almost inaudibly). Ah, the child——

Mrs. Elvsted (breathing heavily). It is all over, then. Well, well, now I will go, Hedda.

Hedda. But you are not going away from town?

Mrs. Elvsted. Oh, I don't know what I shall do. I see nothing but darkness before me.

[*She goes out by the hall door.*

Hedda (stands waiting for a moment). So you are not going to see her home, Mr. Lövborg?

Lövborg. I? Through the streets? Would you have people see her walking with me?

Hedda. Of course I don't know what else may have happened last night. But is it so utterly irretrievable?

Lövborg. It will not end with last night—I know that perfectly well. And the thing is that now I have no taste for that sort of life either. I won't begin it anew. She has broken my courage and my power of braving life out.

Hedda (looking straight before her). So that pretty little fool has had her fingers in a man's destiny. *(Looks at him.)* But all the same, how could you treat her so heartlessly.

Lövborg. Oh, don't say that it was heartless!

Hedda. To go and destroy what has filled her whole soul for months and years! You do not call that heartless!

Lövborg. To you I can tell the truth, Hedda.

Hedda. The truth?

Lövborg. First promise me—give me your word—that what I now confide to you Thea shall never know.

Hedda. I give you my word.

Lövborg. Good. Then let me tell you that what I said just now was untrue.

Hedda. About the manuscript?

Lövborg. Yes. I have not torn it to pieces—nor thrown it into the fiord.

Hedda. No, n—— But—where is it then?

Lövborg. I have destroyed it none the less—utterly destroyed it, Hedda!

Hedda. I don't understand.

Lövborg. Thea said that what I had done seemed to her like a child-murder.

Hedda. Yes, so she said.

Lövborg. But to kill this child—that is not the worst thing a father can do to it.

Hedda. Not the worst?

Lövborg. No. I wanted to spare Thea from hearing the worst?

Hedda. Then what is the worst?

Lövborg. Suppose now, Hedda, that a man—in the small hours of the morning—came home to his child's mother after a night of riot and debauchery, and said: "Listen—I have been here and there—in this place and in that. And I have taken our child with me—to this place and to that. And I have lost the child—utterly lost it. The devil knows into what hands it may have fallen—who may have had their clutches on it."

Hedda. Well—but when all is said and done, you knor —this was only a book—

Lövborg. Thea's pure soul was in that book.

Hedda. Yes, so I understand.

Lövborg. And you can understand, too, that for her and me together no future is possible.

Hedda. What path do you mean to take, then?

Lövborg. None. I will only try to make an end of it all —the sooner the better

Hedda (a step nearer him). Eilert Lövborg—listen to me.——Will you not try to—to do it beautifully?

Lövborg. Beautifully? *(Smiling.)* With vine-leaves in my hair, as you used to dream in the old days——?

Hedda. No, no. I have lost my faith in the vine-leaves. But beautifully nevertheless! For once in a way!—Good-bye! You must go now—and do not come here any more.

Lövborg. Good-bye, Mrs. Tesman. And give George Tesman my love.

[*He is on the point of going.*

Hedda. No, wait! I must give you a memento to take with you.

[*She goes to the writing-table and opens the drawer and the pistol-case; then returns to* Lövborg *with one of the pistols.*

Lövborg (looks at her). This? Is this the memento?

Hedda (nodding slowly). Do you recognise it? It was aimed at you once.

Lövborg. You should have used it then.

Hedda. Take it—and do you use it now.

Lövborg (puts the pistol in his breast-pocket). Thanks!

Hedda. And beautifully, Eilert Lövborg. Promise me that!

Lövborg. Good-bye, Hedda Gabler.

[*He goes out by the hall door.*

[Hedda *listens for a moment at the door. Then she goes up to the writing-table, takes out the packet of manuscript, peeps under the cover, draws a few of the sheets half out and looks at them. Next she goes over and seats herself in the arm-chair beside the stove, with the packet in her lap. Presently she opens the stove door and then the packet.*

Hedda (throws one of the quires into the fire and whispers to herself). Now I am burning your child, Thea!——Burning it, curly-locks! *(Throwing one or two more quires into the stove.)* Your child and Eilert Lövborg's. *(Throws the rest in.)* I am burning—I am burning your child

ACT IV

The same rooms at the TESMANS'. *It is evening. The drawing-room is in darkness. The back room is lighted by the hanging lamp over the table. The curtains over the glass door are drawn close.*

HEDDA, *dressed in black, walks to and fro in the dark room. Then she goes into the back room and disappears for a moment to the left. She is heard to strike a few chords on the piano. Presently she comes in sight again and returns to the drawing-room.*

BERTA *enters from the right, through the inner room, with a lighted lamp, which she places on the table in front of the corner settee in the drawing-room. Her eyes are red with weeping, and she has black ribbons in her cap. She goes quietly and circumspectly out to the right.*

HEDDA *goes up to the glass door, lifts the curtain a little aside and looks out into the darkness.*

Shortly afterwards, MISS TESMAN, *in mourning, with a bonnet and veil on, comes in from the hall.* HEDDA *goes towards her and holds out her hand.*

Miss Tesman. Yes, Hedda, here I am, in mourning and forlorn; for now my poor sister has at last found peace.

Hedda. I have heard the news already, as you see. Tesman sent me a card.

Miss Tesman. Yes, he promised me he would. But nevertheless I thought that to Hedda—here in the house of life—I ought myself to bring the tidings of death.

Hedda. That was very kind of you.

Miss Tesman. Ah, Rina ought not to have left us just now. This is not the time for Hedda's house to be a house of mourning.

Hedda (changing the subject). She died quite peacefully, did she not, Miss Tesman?

Miss Tesman. Oh, her end was so calm, so beautiful. And then she had the unspeakable happiness of seeing George once more—and bidding him good-bye.—Has he come home yet?

Hedda. No. He wrote that he might be detained. But won't you sit down?

Miss Tesman. No thank you, my dear, dear Hedda. I should like to, but I have so much to do. I must prepare my dear one for her rest as well as I can. She shall go to her grave looking her best.

Hedda. Can I not help you in any way?

Miss Tesman. Oh, you must not think of it! Hedda Tesman must have no hand in such mournful work. Nor let her thoughts dwell on it either—not at this time.

Hedda. One is not always mistress of one's thoughts——

Miss Tesman (continuing). Ah, yes, it is the way of the world. At home we shall be sewing a shroud; and here there will soon be sewing, too, I suppose—but of another sort, thank God!

[GEORGE TESMAN *enters by the hall door.*

Hedda. Ah, you have come at last!

Tesman. You here, Aunt Julia? With Hedda? Fancy that!

Miss Tesman. I was just going, my dear boy. Well, have you done all you promised?

Tesman. No; I'm really afraid I have forgotten half of it. I must come to you again to-morrow. To-day my brain is all in a whirl. I can't keep my thoughts together.

Miss Tesman. Why, my dear George, you mustn't take it in this way.

Tesman. Mustn't——? How do you mean?

Miss Tesman. Even in your sorrow you must rejoice, as I do—rejoice that she is at rest.

Tesman. Oh, yes, yes—you are thinking of Aunt Rina.

Hedda. You will feel lonely now, Miss Tesman.

Miss Tesman. Just at first, yes. But that will not last very long, I hope. I daresay I shall soon find an occupant for poor Rina's little room.

Tesman. Indeed? Who do you think will take it? Eh?

Miss Tesman. Oh, there's always some poor invalid or other in want of nursing, unfortunately.

Hedda. Would you really take such a burden upon you again?

Miss Tesman. A burden! Heaven forgive you, child—it has been no burden to me.

Hedda. But suppose you had a total stranger on your hands——

Miss Tesman. Oh, one soon makes friends with sick folk; and it's such an absolute necessity for me to have some one to live for. Well, heaven be praised, there may soon be something in this house, too, to keep an old aunt busy.

Hedda. Oh, don't trouble about anything here.

Tesman. Yes, just fancy what a nice time we three might have together, if——?

Hedda. If——?

Tesman (uneasily). Oh, nothing. It will all come right. Let us hope so—eh?

Miss Tesman. Well, well, I daresay you two want to talk to each other. *(Smiling.)* And perhaps Hedda may have something to tell you, too, George. Good-bye! I must go home to Rina. *(Turning at the door.)* How strange it is to think that now Rina is with me and with my poor brother as well!

Tesman. Yes, fancy that, Aunt Julia! Eh?

[MISS TESMAN *goes out by the hall door.*

Hedda (follows TESMAN *coldly and searchingly with her eyes).* I almost believe your Aunt Rina's death affects you more than it does your Aunt Julia.

Tesman. Oh, it's not that alone. It's Eilert I am so terribly uneasy about.

Hedda (quickly). Is there anything new about him?

Tesman. I looked in at his rooms this afternoon, intending to tell him the manuscript was in safe keeping.

Hedda. Well, did you not find him?

Tesman. No. He wasn't at home. But afterwards I met Mrs. Elvsted, and she told me that he had been here early this morning.

Hedda. Yes, directly after you had gone.

Tesman. And he said that he had torn his manuscript to pieces—eh?

Hedda. Yes, so he declared.

Tesman. Why, good heavens, he must have been completely out of his mind! And I suppose you thought it best not to give it back to him, Hedda?

Hedda. No, he did not get it.

Tesman. But of course you told him that we had it?

Hedda. No. *(Quickly.)* Did you tell Mrs. Elvsted?

Tesman. No; I thought I had better not. But you ought to have told him. Fancy, if, in desperation, he should go and do himself some injury! Let me have the manuscript, Hedda! I will take it to him at once. Where is it?

Hedda (cold and immovable, leaning on the arm-chair). I have not got it.

Tesman. Have not got it? What in the world do you mean?

Hedda. I have burnt it—every line of it.

Tesman (with a violent movement of terror). Burnt! Burnt Eilert's manuscript!

Hedda. Don't scream so. The servant might hear you.

Tesman. Burnt! Why, good God——! No, no, no! It's impossible!

Hedda. It is so, nevertheless.

Tesman. Do you know what you have done, Hedda? It's unlawful appropriation of lost property. Fancy that! Just ask Judge Brack, and he'll tell you what it is.

Hedda. I advise you not to speak of it—either to Judge Brack, or to any one else.

Tesman. But how could you do anything so unheard-of? What put it into your head? What possessed you? Answer me that—eh?

Hedda (suppressing an almost imperceptible smile). I did it for your sake, George.

Tesman. For my sake!

Hedda. This morning, when you told me about what he had read to you——

Tesman. Yes, yes—what then?

Hedda. You acknowledged that you envied him his work.

Tesman. Oh, of course I didn't mean that literally.

Hedda. No matter—I could not bear the idea that any one should throw you into the shade.

Tesman (in an outburst of mingled doubt and joy). Hedda! Oh, is this true? But—but—I never knew you to show your love like that before. Fancy that!

Hedda. Well, I may as well tell you that—just at this time—— *(Impatiently, breaking off.)* No, no; you can ask Aunt Julia. She will tell you, fast enough.

Tesman. Oh, I almost think I understand you, Hedda! *(Clasps his hands together.)* Great heavens! do you really mean it! Eh?

Hedda. Don't shout so. The servant might hear.

Tesman (laughing in irrepressible glee). The servant! Why, how absurd you are, Hedda. It's only my old Berta! Why, I'll tell Berta myself.

Hedda (clenching her hands together in desperation). Oh, it is killing me,—it is killing me, all this!

Tesman. What is, Hedda? Eh?

Hedda (coldly, controlling herself). All this—absurdity—George.

Tesman. Absurdity! Do you see anything absurd in my being overjoyed at the news! But after all—perhaps I had better not say anything to Berta.

Hedda. Oh—why not that, too?

Tesman. No, no, not yet! But I must certainly tell Aunt Julia. And then that you have begun to call me George, too! Fancy that! Oh, Aunt Julia will be so happy—so happy!

Hedda. When she hears that I have burnt Eilert Lövborg's manuscript—for your sake?

Tesman. No, by-the-bye—that affair of the manuscript—of course nobody must know about that. But that you love me so much,* Hedda—Aunt Julia must really share my joy in that! I wonder, now, whether this sort of thing is usual in young wives? Eh?

Hedda. I think you had better ask Aunt Julia that question too.

Tesman. I will indeed, some time or other. *(Looks uneasy and downcast again.)* And yet the manuscript—the manuscript! Good God! it is terrible to think what will become of poor Eilert now.

[MRS. ELVSTED, *dressed as in the first Act, with hat and cloak, enters by the hall door.*

Mrs. Elvsted (greets them hurriedly and says in evident agitation). Oh, dear Hedda, forgive my coming again.

Hedda. What is the matter with you, Thea?

Tesman. Something about Eilert Lövborg again—eh?

Mrs. Elvsted. Yes! I am dreadfully afraid some misfortune has happened to him.

* Literally, "That you burn for me."

Hedda (seizes her arm). Ah.—do you think so?

Tesman. Why, good Lord—what makes you think that, Mrs. Elvsted?

Mrs. Elvsted. I heard them talking of him at my boarding-house—just as I came in. Oh, the most incredible rumours are afloat about him to-day.

Tesman. Yes, fancy, so I heard, too! And I can bear witness that he went straight home to bed last night. Fancy that!

Hedda. Well, what did they say at the boarding-house?

Mrs. Elvsted. Oh, I couldn't make out anything clearly. Either they knew nothing definite, or else—— They stopped talking when they saw me; and I did not dare to ask.

Tesman (moving about uneasily). We must hope—we must hope that you misunderstood them, Mrs. Elvsted.

Mrs. Elvsted. No, no; I am sure it was of him they were talking. And I heard something about the hospital or——

Tesman. The hospital?

Hedda. No—surely that cannot be!

Mrs. Elvsted. Oh, I was in such mortal terror! I went to his lodgings and asked for him there.

Hedda. You could make up your mind to that, Thea!

Mrs. Elvsted. What else could I do? I really could bear the suspense no longer.

Tesman. But you didn't find him either—eh?

Mrs. Elvsted. No. And the people knew nothing about him. He hadn't been home since yesterday afternoon, they said.

Tesman. Yesterday! Fancy, how could they say that?

Mrs. Elvsted. Oh, I am sure something terrible must have happened to him.

Tesman. Hedda dear—how would it be if I were to go and make inquiries——?

Hedda. No, no—don't you mix yourself up in this affair.

[JUDGE BRACK, *with his hat in his hand, enters by the hall door, which* BERTA *opens and closes behind him. He looks grave and bows in silence.*

Tesman. Oh, is that you, my dear Judge? Eh?

Brack. Yes. It was imperative I should see you this evening.

Tesman. I can see you have heard the news about Aunt Rina?

Brack. Yes, that among other things.

Tesman. Isn't it sad—eh?

Brack. Well, my dear Tesman, that depends on how you look at it.

Tesman (looks doubtfully at him). Has anything else happened?

Brack. Yes.

Hedda (in suspense). Anything sad, Judge Brack?

Brack. That, too, depends on how you look at it, Mrs. Tesman.

Mrs. Elvsted (unable to restrain her anxiety). Oh! it is something about Eilert Lövborg!

Brack (with a glance at her). What makes you think that, Madam? Perhaps you have already heard something——?

Mrs. Elvsted (in confusion). No, nothing at all, but——

Tesman. Oh, for heaven's sake, tell us!

Brack (shrugging his shoulders). Well, I regret to say Eilert Lövborg has been taken to the hospital. He is lying at the point of death.

Mrs. Elvsted (shrieks). Oh, God! Oh, God——!

Tesman. To the hospital! And at the point of death.

Hedda (involuntarily). So soon then——

Mrs. Elvsted (wailing). And we parted in anger, Hedda!

Hedda (whispers). Thea—Thea—be careful!

Mrs. Elvsted (not heeding her). I must go to him! I must see him alive!

Brack. It is useless, Madam. No one will be admitted.

Mrs. Elvsted. Oh, at least tell me what has happened to him? What is it?

Tesman. You don't mean to say that he has himself—— Eh?

Hedda. Yes, I am sure he has.

Tesman. Hedda, how can you——?

Brack (keeping his eyes fixed upon her). Unfortunately, you have guessed quite correctly, Mrs. Tesman.

Mrs. Elvsted. Oh, how horrible!

Tesman. Himself, then! Fancy that!

Hedda. Shot himself!

Brack. Rightly guessed again, Mrs. Tesman.

Mrs. Elvsted (with an effort at self-control). When did it happen, Mr. Brack?

Brack. This afternoon—between three and four.

Tesman. But, good Lord, where did he do it? Eh?

Brack (with some hesitation). Where? Well—I suppose at his lodgings.

Mrs. Elvsted. No, that cannot be; for I was there between six and seven.

Brack. Well, then, somewhere else. I don't know exactly. I only know that he was found——. He had shot himself—in the breast.

Mrs. Elvsted. Oh, how terrible! That he should die like that!

Hedda (to Brack). Was it in the breast?

Brack. Yes—as I told you.

Hedda. Not in the temple?

Brack. In the breast, Mrs. Tesman.

Hedda. Well, well—the breast is a good place, too.

Brack. How do you mean, Mrs. Tesman?

Hedda (evasively). Oh, nothing—nothing.

Tesman. And the wound is dangerous, you say—eh?

Brack. Absolutely mortal. The end has probably come by this time.

Mrs. Elvsted. Yes, yes, I feel it. The end! The end! Oh, Hedda——!

Tesman. But tell me, how have you learnt all this?

Brack (curtly). Through one of the police. A man I had some business with.

Hedda (in a clear voice). At last a deed worth doing!

Tesman (terrified). Good heavens, Hedda! what are you saying?

Hedda. I say there is beauty in this.

Brack. H'm, Mrs. Tesman——

Tesman. Beauty! Fancy that!

Mrs. Elvsted. Oh, Hedda, how can you talk of beauty in such an act!

Hedda. Eilert Lövborg has himself made up his account with life. He has had the courage to do—the one right thing.

Mrs. Elvsted. No, you must never think that was how it happened! It must have been in delirium that he did it.

Tesman. In despair!

Hedda. That he did not. I am certain of that.

Mrs. Elvsted. Yes, yes! In delirium! Just as when he tore up our manuscript.

Brack (starting). The manuscript? Has he torn that up?

Mrs. Elvsted. Yes, last night.

Tesman (whispers softly). Oh, Hedda, we shall never get over this.

Brack. H'm, very extraordinary.

Tesman (moving about the room). To think of Eilert going out of the world in this way! And not leaving behind him the book that would have immortalised his name——

Mrs. Elvsted. Oh, if only it could be put together again!

Tesman. Yes, if it only could! I don't know what I would not give——

Mrs. Elvsted. Perhaps it can, Mr. Tesman.

Tesman. What do you mean?

Mrs. Elvsted (searches in the pocket of her dress). Look here. I have kept all the loose notes he used to dictate from.

Hedda (a step forward). Ah——!

Tesman. You have kept them, Mrs. Elvsted! Eh?

Mrs. Elvsted. Yes, I have them here. I put them in my pocket when I left home. Here they still are——

Tesman. Oh, do let me see them!

Mrs. Elvsted (hands him a bundle of papers). But they are in such disorder—all mixed up.

Tesman. Fancy, if we could make something out of them, after all! Perhaps if we two put our heads together——

Mrs. Elvsted. Oh, yes, at least let us try——

Tesman. We will manage it! We must! I will dedicate my life to this task.

Hedda. You, George? Your life?

Tesman. Yes, or rather all the time I can spare. My own collections must wait in the meantime. Hedda—you understand, eh? I owe this to Eilert's memory.

Hedda. Perhaps.

Tesman. And so, my dear Mrs. Elvsted, we will give our whole minds to it. There is no use in brooding over what can't be undone—eh? We must try to control our grief as much as possible, and——

Mrs. Elvsted. Yes, yes, Mr. Tesman, I will do the best I can.

Tesman. Well, then, come here. I can't rest until we have looked through the notes. Where shall we sit? Here? No, in there, in the back room. Excuse me, my dear Judge. Come with me, Mrs. Elvsted.

Mrs. Elvsted. Oh, if only it were possible!

[TESMAN *and* MRS. ELVSTED *go into the back room. She takes off her hat and cloak. They both sit at the table under the hanging lamp and are soon deep in an eager examination of the papers.* HEDDA *crosses to the stove and sits in the arm-chair. Presently* BRACK *goes up to her.*

Hedda (in a low voice). Oh, what a sense of freedom it gives one, this act of Eilert Lövborg's.

Brack. Freedom, Mrs. Hedda? Well, of course, it is a release for him——

Hedda. I mean for me. It gives me a sense of freedom to know that a deed of deliberate courage is still possible in this world,—a deed of spontaneous beauty.

Brack (smiling). H'm—my dear Mrs. Hedda——

Hedda. Oh, I know what you are going to say. For you are a kind of specialist, too, like—you know!

Brack (looking hard at her). Eilert Lövborg was more to you than perhaps you are willing to admit to yourself. Am I wrong?

Hedda. I don't answer such questions. I only know that Eilert Lövborg has had the courage to live his life after his own fashion. And then—the last great act, with its beauty! Ah! that he should have the will and the strength to turn away from the banquet of life—so early.

Brack. I am sorry, Mrs. Hedda,—but I fear I must dispel an amiable illusion.

Hedda. Illusion?

Brack. Which could not have lasted long in any case.

Hedda. What do you mean?

Brack. Eilert Lövborg did not shoot himself—voluntarily.

Hedda. Not voluntarily?

Brack. No. The thing did not happen exactly as I told it.

Hedda (in suspense). Have you concealed something? What is it?

Brack. For poor Mrs. Elvsted's sake I idealised the facts a little.

Hedda. What are the facts?

Brack. First, that he is already dead.

Hedda. At the hospital?

Brack. Yes—without regaining consciousness.

Hedda. What more have you concealed?

Brack. This—the event did not happen at his lodgings.

Hedda. Oh, that can make no difference.

Brack. Perhaps it may. For I must tell you—Eilert Lövborg was found shot in—in Mademoiselle Diana's boudoir.

Hedda (makes a motion as if to rise, but sinks back again). That is impossible, Judge Brack! He cannot have been there again to-day.

Brack. He was there this afternoon. He went there, he said, to demand the return of something which they had taken from him. Talked wildly about a lost child——

Hedda. Ah—so that was why——

Brack. I thought probably he meant his manuscript! but now I hear he destroyed that himself. So I suppose it must have been his pocket-book.

Hedda. Yes, no doubt. And there—there he was found?

Brack. Yes, there. With a pistol in his breast-pocket, discharged. The ball had lodged in a vital part.

Hedda. In the breast—yes.

Brack. No—in the bowels.

Hedda (looks up at him with an expression of loathing). That, too! Oh, what curse is it that makes everything I touch turn ludicrous and mean?

Brack. There is one point more, Mrs. Hedda—another disagreeable feature in the affair.

Hedda. And what is that?

Brack. The pistol he carried——

Hedda (breathless). Well? What of it?

Brack. He must have stolen it.

Hedda (leaps up). Stolen it! That is not true! He did not steal it!

Brack. No other explanation is possible. He must have solen it—— Hush!

[TESMAN *and* MRS. ELVSTED *have risen from the table in the back room and come into the drawing room.*

Tesman (with the papers in both his hands). Hedda dear, it is almost impossible to see under that lamp. Think of that!

Hedda. Yes, I am thinking.

Tesman. Would you mind our sitting at your writing-table—eh?

Hedda. If you like. *(Quickly.)* No, wait! Let me clear it first!

Tesman. Oh, you needn't trouble, Hedda. There is plenty of room.

Hedda. No, no, let me clear it, I say! I will take these things in and put them on the piano. There!

(She has drawn out an object, covered with sheet music, from under the bookcase, places several other pieces of music upon it and carries the whole into the inner room, to the left. TESMAN *lays the scraps of paper on the writing-table and moves the lamp there from the corner table. He and* MRS. ELVSTED *sit down and proceed with their work.* HEDDA *returns.*

Hedda (behind MRS. ELVSTED'S *chair, gently ruffling her hair).* Well, my sweet Thea,—how goes it with Eilert Lövborg's monument?

Mrs. Elvsted (looks dispiritedly up at her). Oh, it will be terribly hard to put in order.

Tesman. We must manage it. I am determined. And arranging other people's papers is just the work for me.

[HEDDA *goes over to the stove and seats herself on one of the footstools.* BRACK *stands over her, leaning on the armchair.*

Hedda (whispers). What did you say about the pistol?

Brack (softly). That he must have stolen it.

Hedda. Why stolen it?

Brack. Because every other explanation ought to be impossible, Mrs. Hedda.

Hedda. Indeed?

Brack (glances at her). Of course Eilert Lövborg was here this morning. Was he not?

Hedda. Yes.

Brack. Were you alone with him?

Hedda. Part of the time.

Brack. Did you not leave the room whilst he was here?

Hedda. No.

Brack. Try to recollect. Were you not out of the room a moment?

Hedda. Yes, perhaps just a moment—out in the hall.

Brack. And where was your pistol-case during that time?

Hedda. I had it locked up in——

Brack. Well, Mrs. Hedda?

Hedda. The case stood there on the writing-table.

Brack. Have you looked since, to see whether both the pistols are there?

Hedda. No.

Brack. Well, you need not. I saw the pistol found in Lövborg's pocket, and I knew it at once as the one I had seen yesterday—and before, too.

Hedda. Have you it with you?

Brack. No; the police have it.

Hedda. What will the police do with it?

Brack. Search till they find the owner.

Hedda. Do you think they will succeed?

Brack (bends over her and whispers). No, Hedda Gabler—not so long as I say nothing.

Hedda (looks frightened at him). And if you do not say nothing,—what then?

Brack (shrugs his shoulders). There is always the possibility that the pistol was stolen.

Hedda (firmly). Death rather than that.

Brack (smiling). People say such things—but they don't do them.

Hedda (without replying). And supposing the pistol was not stolen, and the owner is discovered? What then?

Brack. Well, Hedda—then comes the scandal.

Hedda. The scandal!

Brack. Yes, the scandal—of which you are mortally afraid. You will, of course, be brought before the court—both you and Mademoiselle Diana. She will have to explain how the thing happened—whether it was an accidental shot or murder. Did the pistol go off as he was trying to take it out of his pocket, to threaten her with? Or did she tear the pistol out of his hand, shoot him and push it back into his pocket? That would be quite like her; for she is an able-bodied young person, this same Mademoiselle Diana.

Hedda. But *I* have nothing to do with all this repulsive business.

Brack. No. But you will have to answer the question: Why did you give Eilert Lövborg the pistol? And what conclusions will people draw from the fact that you did give it to him?

Hedda (lets her head sink). That is true. I did not think of that.

Brack. Well, fortunately, there is no danger, so long as I say nothing.

Hedda (looks up at him). So I am in your power, Judge Brack. You have me at your beck and call, from this time forward.

Brack (whispers softly). Dearest Hedda—believe me—I shall not abuse my advantage.

Hedda. I am in your power none the less. Subject to your will and your demands. A slave, a slave then! *(Rises impetuously.)* No, I cannot endure the thought of that! Never!

Brack (looks half-mockingly at her). People generally get used to the inevitable.

Hedda (returns his look). Yes, perhaps. *(She crosses to the writing-table. Suppressing an involuntary smile, she imitates* TESMAN'S *intonations.)* Well? Are you getting on, George? Eh?

Tesman. Heaven knows, dear. In any case it will be the work of months.

Hedda (as before). Fancy that! *(Passes her hands softly through* MRS. ELVSTED'S *hair.)* Doesn't it seem strange to you, Thea? Here are you sitting with Tesman—just as you used to sit with Eilert Lövborg?

Mrs. Elvsted. Ah, if I could only inspire your husband in the same way.

Hedda. Oh, that will come, too—in time.

Tesman. Yes, do you know, Hedda—I really think I begin to feel something of the sort. But won't you go and sit with Brack again?

Hedda. Is there nothing I can do to help you two?

Tesman. No, nothing in the world. *(Turning his head.)* I trust to you to keep Hedda company, my dear Brack.

Brack (with a glance at HEDDA*).* With the very greatest of pleasure.

Hedda. Thanks. But I am tired this evening. I will go in and lie down a little on the sofa.

Tesman. Yes, do dear—eh?

[HEDDA *goes into the back room and draws the curtains. A short pause. Suddenly she is heard playing a wild dance on the piano.*

Mrs. Elvsted (starts from her chair). Oh—what is that?

Tesman (runs to the doorway). Why, my dearest Hedda—don't play dance music to-night! Just think of Aunt Rina! And of Eilert, too!

Hedda (puts her head out between the curtains). And

of Aunt Julia. And of all the rest of them.—After this, I will be quiet. [*Closes the curtains again.*

Tesman (at the writing-table). It's not good for her to see us at this distressing work. I'll tell you what, Mrs. Elvsted,—you shall take the empty room at Aunt Julia's, and then I will come over in the evenings, and we can sit and work there—eh?

Hedda (in the inner room). I hear what you are saying, Tesman. But how am *I* to get through the evenings out here?

Tesman (turning over the papers). Oh, I daresay Judge Brack will be so kind as to look in now and then, even though I am out.

Brack (in the armchair, calls out gaily). Every blessed evening, with all the pleasure in life, Mrs. Tesman! We shall get on capitally together, we two!

Hedda (speaking loud and clear). Yes, don't you flatter yourself we will, Judge Brack? Now that you are the one cock in the basket——

[*A shot is heard within.* TESMAN, MRS. ELVSTED *and* BRACK *leap to their feet.*

Tesman. Oh, now she is playing with those pistols again.

[*He throws back the curtains and runs in, followed by* MRS. ELVSTED. HEDDA *lies stretched on the sofa, lifeless. Confusion and cries.* BERTA *enters in alarm from the right.*

Tesman (shrieks to BRACK*).* Shot herself! Shot herself in the temple! Fancy that!

Brack (half-fainting in the armchair). Good God!—people don't do such things.

JOHN GABRIEL BORKMAN
(1896)

CHARACTERS

JOHN GABRIEL BORKMAN, *formerly Managing Director of a Bank.*
MRS. GUNHILD BORKMAN, *his wife.*
ERHART BORKMAN, *their son, a student.*
MISS ELLA RENTHEIM, *Mrs. Borkman's twin sister.*
MRS. FANNY WILTON.
VILHELM FOLDAL, *subordinate clerk in a Government office.*
FRIDA FOLDAL, his daughter.
MRS. BORKMAN'S MAID.

A winter evening, at the Manor-house of the Rentheim family, in the neighbourhood of Christiania.

JOHN GABRIEL BORKMAN

ACT I

MRS. BORKMAN'S *drawing-room. It is furnished with old-fashioned, faded splendour. At the rear, an open sliding-door leads into a conservatory, with windows and a glass door, through which a view of the garden can be seen. A driving snow in the twilight. On the right, a door leading from the hall. Further forward, a large old-fashioned iron stove, the fire lighted. On the left, towards the back, a single smaller door. In front, on the same side, a window, covered with heavy curtains. A horsehair sofa stands between the window and the door. A table in front of the sofa is covered with a cloth. On the table, a shaded lamp. Beside the stove, an armchair with a high back.*

MRS. GUNHILD BORKMAN *sits on the sofa, knitting. She is an elderly lady, of cold, distinguished appearance, with stiff carriage and immobile features. Her hair is very grey, her delicate hands transparent. She is dressed in a gown of heavy dark silk, which had at one time been attractive, but is now somewhat worn and shabby. A woollen shawl is thrown over her shoulders.*

She sits for a time erect and rigid at her knitting. The bells of a passing sledge are heard.

Mrs. Borkman (listens; her eyes sparkle with enthusiasm and she whispers involuntarily). Erhart! At last!

[*She rises and draws the curtain a little aside to peer*

out. Seems disappointed and sits down on the sofa, resuming her work. Presently THE MAID *enters from the hall with a visiting card on a small tray.*

Mrs. Borkman (quickly). Has Mr. Erhart come after all?

The Maid. No, ma'am. But there's a lady——

Mrs. Borkman (putting aside her knitting). Oh, Mrs. Wilton, I suppose——

The Maid (coming nearer). No, it's a strange lady——

Mrs. Borkman (taking the card). Let me see—— *(Reads it; rises quickly and looks intently at the girl.)* Are you sure this is for me?

The Maid. Yes, I understand it was for you, ma'am.

Mrs. Borkman. Did she say she wanted to see Mrs. Borkman?

The Maid. Yes, she did.

Mrs. Borkman (abruptly, resolutely). Good. Then say I am at home.

[THE MAID *opens the door for the strange lady and goes out.* MISS ELLA RENTHEIM *enters. She resembles her sister; but her face reveals suffering rather than hardness of expression. It still shows signs of great beauty and strong character. She has luxuriant, snow-white hair, drawn back from the forehead in natural waves. She is dressed in black velvet, with a hat and a fur-lined cloak of the same material.*

The two sisters stand silent for a time, and look searchingly at each other. Each is evidently waiting for the other to speak first.

Ella Rentheim (still standing near the door). You are surprised to see me, Gunhild.

Mrs. Borkman (erect and immovable between the sofa and the table, resting her finger-tips upon the cloth). Have you not made a mistake? The bailiff lives in the side wing, you know.

Ella Rentheim. It is not the bailiff I want to see to-day.

Mrs. Borkman. Is it me you want, then?

Ella Rentheim. Yes. I have a few words to say to you.

Mrs. Borkman (advancing to the middle of the room). Well—then sit down.

Ella Rentheim. Thank you. I can stand just as well for the present.

Mrs. Borkman. As you please. But at least open your cloak.

Ella Rentheim (unbuttoning her cloak). Yes, it is very warm here.

Mrs. Borkman. I am always cold.

Ella Rentheim (looking at her for a time with her arms resting on the back of the armchair). Well, Gunhild, it is nearly eight years now since we saw each other last.

Mrs. Borkman (coldly). Since last we spoke to each other, at any rate.

Ella Rentheim. True, since we spoke to each other. I daresay you have seen me now and again—when I came on my yearly visit to the bailiff.

Mrs. Borkman. Once or twice, I have.

Ella Rentheim. I have caught one or two glimpses of you, too—there, at the window.

Mrs. Borkman. You must have seen me through the curtains, then. You have good eyes. *(Harshly and cuttingly.)* But the last time we spoke to each other—it was here in this room——

Ella Rentheim (trying to stop her). Yes, yes; I know, Gunhild!

Mrs. Borkman. —the week before he—before he was let out.

Ella Rentheim (moving towards the back). Oh, don't speak about that.

Mrs. Borkman (firmly, but in a low voice). It was the week before he—was set at liberty.

Ella Rentheim (coming down). Oh, yes, yes, yes! I shall never forget that time! But it is too terrible to think of! Only to recall it for a moment—oh!

Mrs. Borkman (gloomily). And yet one's thoughts can never get away from it! *(Vehemently; clenching her hands together.)* No, I can't understand it! I never shall! I can't understand how such a thing—how anything so horrible can come upon one single family! And then—that it should be our family! So old a family as ours! Think of its choosing us!

Ella Rentheim. Oh, Gunhild—there were many, many families besides ours upon whom that blow fell.

Mrs. Borkman. Oh, yes; but those others don't trouble me very much. In their case it was only a matter of a little money—or some papers. But for us—! For me! And then for Erhart! My little boy—as he then was! *(In rising excitement.)* The shame that fell upon us two innocent ones! The dishonour! The hateful, terrible dishonour! And then the utter ruin, too!

Ella Rentheim (cautiously). Tell me, Gunhild, how does he bear it?

Mrs. Borkman. Erhart, you mean?

Ella Rentheim. No—he himself. How does he bear it?

Mrs. Borkman (scornfully). Do you think I ever ask about that?

Ella Rentheim. Ask? Surely you do not have to ask——

Mrs. Borkman (looks at her surprised). You don't suppose I ever have anything to do with him? That I ever meet him? That I see anything of him?

Ella Rentheim. Not even that!

Mrs. Borkman. The man who was in gaol, in gaol for five years! *(Covers her face with her hands.)* Oh, the crushing shame of it! *(With rising vehemence.)* And then to think of all that the name of John Gabriel Borkman meant! No, no, no—I can never see him again! Never!

Ella Rentheim (looks at her for a moment). You have a hard heart, Gunhild.

Mrs. Borkman. Towards him, yes.

Ella Rentheim. After all, he is your husband.

Mrs. Borkman. Did he not say in court that it was I who began his ruin? That I spent money so recklessly?

Ella Rentheim (tentatively). But is there not some truth in that?

Mrs. Borkman. Why, he himself made me do it! He insisted on our living in such an absurdly lavish style——

Ella Rentheim. Yes, I know. But that is just where you should have restrained him; and apparently you didn't.

Mrs. Borkman. How was I to know that it was not his own money he gave me to squander? And that he himself used to squander, too—ten times more than I did!

Ella Rentheim (quietly). Well, I daresay his position forced him to do that—to some extent at any rate.

Mrs. Borkman (scornfully). Yes, it was always the same story—we had to "cut a figure." And he did "cut a figure" to some purpose! He used to drive about with a four-in-hand as if he were a king. And he had people bowing and scraping to him just as to a king. *(Laughing.)* And they always called him by his Christian names—all the country over—as if he had been the king himself. "John Gabriel," "John Gabriel." Every one knew what a great man "John Gabriel" was!

Ella Rentheim (warmly and emphatically). He was a great man then.

Mrs. Borkman. Yes, to all appearance. But he never breathed a single word to me as to his real position—never gave a hint as to where he got his wealth from.

Ella Rentheim. No, no; and other people did not dream of it either.

Mrs. Borkman. I don't care about other people. But it

was his duty to tell me the truth. And that he never did! He kept on lying to me—lying abominably——

Ella Rentheim (interrupting). Surely not, Gunhild. He withheld things, perhaps, but I am sure he did not lie.

Mrs. Borkman. Well, well; call it what you please; it makes no difference. And then it all collapsed—the whole thing.

Ella Rentheim (to herself). Yes, everything collapsed—for him—and for others.

Mrs. Borkman (drawing herself up menacingly). But I tell you this, Ella, I do not give up yet! I shall redeem myself yet—you may make up your mind to that!

Ella Rentheim (eagerly). Redeem yourself! What do you mean by that?

Mrs. Borkman. Redeem my name, and honour and fortune! Redeem my ruined life—that is what I mean! I have some one in reserve, let me tell you—one who will wash away every stain that he has left.

Ella Rentheim. Gunhild! Gunhild!

Mrs. Borkman (her excitement rising). There is an avenger living, I tell you! One who will make up to me for all his father's sins!

Ella Rentheim. Erhart, you mean.

Mrs. Borkman. Yes, Erhart, my own boy! He will redeem the family, the house, the name. All that can be redeemed.—And perhaps more besides.

Ella Rentheim. And how do you think that is to be done?

Mrs. Borkman. It must be done as best it can; I don't know how. But I know that it must and shall be done. *(Looks searchingly at her.)* Come now, Ella; isn't that really what you have had in mind, too, ever since he was a child?

Ella Rentheim. No, I can't exactly say that.

Mrs. Borkman. No? Then why did you take charge of him when the storm broke upon—upon this house?

Ella Rentheim. You could not look after him yourself at that time, Gunhild.

Mrs. Borkman. No, no, I could not. And his father—he had a valid enough excuse—while he was there—in safe keeping——

Ella Rentheim (indignant). Oh, how can you say such things!—You!

Mrs. Borkman (with a venomous expression). And how could you make up your mind to take charge of the child of a—a John Gabriel! Just as if he had been your own? To take the child away from me—home with you—and keep him there year after year, until the boy was nearly grown up. *(Looking suspiciously at her.)* What was your real reason, Ella? Why did you keep him with you?

Ella Rentheim. I came to love him so dearly——

Mrs. Borkman. More than I—his mother?

Ella Rentheim (evasively). I don't know about that. And then, you know, Erhart was rather delicate as a child——

Mrs. Borkman. Erhart—delicate!

Ella Rentheim. Yes, I thought so—at that time, at any rate. And you know the air of the west coast is so much milder than here.

Mrs. Borkman (smiling bitterly). H'm—is it indeed? *(Breaking off.)* Yes, it is true you have done a great deal for Erhart. *(Changing her tone.)* Well, of course, you could afford it. *(Smiling.)* You were so lucky, Ella; you managed to save all your money.

Ella Rentheim *(hurt).* I did not manage anything about it, I assure you. I had no idea—until long, long afterwards—that the securities belonging to me—that they had been left untouched.

Mrs. Borkman. Well, well; I don't understand anything about these things! I only say you were lucky. *(Looking inquiringly at her.)* But when you, of your own accord, unaertook to educate Erhart for me—what was your motive in that?

Ella Rentheim (staring at her). My motive?

Mrs. Borkman. Yes, some motive you must have had. What did you want to do with him? To make of him, I mean?

Ella Rentheim (deliberately). I wanted to smooth the way for Erhart to happiness in life.

Mrs. Borkman (contemptuously). Pooh—people situated as we are have something else than happiness to think of.

Ella Rentheim. What, then?

Mrs. Borkman (steadily and earnestly). Erhart has in the first place to make so brilliant a position for himself, that no trace shall be left of the shadow his father has cast upon my name—and my son's.

Ella Rentheim (searchingly). Tell me, Gunhild, is this what Erhart himself demands of his life?

Mrs. Borkman (slightly taken aback). Yes, I should hope so!

Ella Rentheim. Is it not rather what you demand of him?

Mrs. Borkman (curtly). Erhart and I always make the same demands upon ourselves.

Ella Rentheim (sadly and slowly). You are so very certain of your boy, then, Gunhild?

Mrs. Borkman (with veiled triumph). Yes, that I am—thank Heaven. You may be sure of that!

Ella Rentheim. Then I should think in reality you must be happy after all; in spite of all the rest.

Mrs. Borkman. So I am—so far as that goes. But then, every moment, all the rest comes rushing in upon me like a storm.

Ella Rentheim (changing her tone). Tell me—you may as well tell me at once—for that is really what I have come for——

Mrs. Borkman. What?

Ella Rentheim. Something I felt I must talk to you about.—Tell me—Erhart does not live out here with—with you others?

Mrs. Borkman (harshly). Erhart cannot live out here with me. He has to live in town——

Ella Rentheim. So he wrote to me.

Mrs. Borkman. He must, for the sake of his studies. But he comes out to me for a little while every evening.

Ella Rentheim. Well, may I see him then? May I speak to him at once?

Mrs. Borkman. He has not come yet; but I expect him any moment.

Ella Rentheim. Why, Gunhild, surely he must have come. I can hear his footsteps overhead.

Mrs. Borkman (with a rapid upward glance). Up in the long gallery?

Ella Rentheim. Yes. I have heard him walking up and down there ever since I came.

Mrs. Borkman (looking away from her). That is not Erhart, Ella.

Ella Rentheim (surprised). Not Erhart? *(Divining.)* Who is it then?

Mrs. Borkman. It is he.

Ella Rentheim (quietly, with suppressed pain). Borkman? John Gabriel Borkman?

Mrs. Borkman. He walks up and down like that—back and forth—from morning to night—day out and day in.

Ella Rentheim. I have heard something of this——

Mrs. Borkman. I daresay. People find plenty to say about us, no doubt.

Ella Rentheim. Erhart has spoken of it in his letters. He said that his father generally remained by himself—up there—and you alone down here.

Mrs. Borkman. Yes; that is how it has been, Ella, ever since they let him out and sent him home to me. All these long eight years.

Ella Rentheim. I never believed it could really be so. It seemed impossible!

Mrs. Borkman (nods). It is so; and it can never be otherwise.

Ella Rentheim (looking at her). This must be a terrible life, Gunhild.

Mrs. Borkman. Worse than terrible—almost unendurable.

Ella Rentheim. Yes, it must be.

Mrs. Borkman. Always to hear his footsteps up there —from early morning till far into the night. And everything sounds so clear in this house!

Ella Rentheim. Yes, it is strange how clear the sound is.

Mrs. Borkman. I often feel as if I had a sick wolf pacing his cage up there in the gallery, right over my head. *(Listens and whispers.)* Hark! Do you hear! Back and forth, up and down, goes the wolf.

Ella Rentheim (tentatively). Is no change possible, Gunhild?

Mrs. Borkman (with a gesture of repulsion). He has never made any movement towards a change.

Ella Rentheim. Could you not make the first movement, then?

Mrs. Borkman (indignantly). I! After all the wrong he has done me! No, thank you! Rather let the wolf go on prowling up there.

Ella Rentheim. This room is too hot for me. You must let me take off my things after all.

Mrs. Borkman. Yes, I asked you to.

[ELLA RENTHEIM *takes off her hat and cloak and lays them on a chair beside the door leading to hall.*

Ella Rentheim. Do you never happen to meet him, away from home?

Mrs. Borkman (with a bitter laugh). In society, do you mean?

Ella Rentheim. I mean, when he goes out walking. In the woods, or——

Mrs. Borkman. He never goes out.

Ella Rentheim. Not even in the twilight?

Mrs. Borkman. Never.

Ella Rentheim (with emotion). He cannot bring himself to go out?

Mrs. Borkman. I suppose not. He has his great cloak and his hat hanging in the cupboard—the cupboard in the hall, you know——

Ella Rentheim (to herself). The cupboard we used to hide in when we were little——

Mrs. Borkman (nods). And now and then—late in the evening—I can hear him come down as though to go out. But he always stops when he is halfway downstairs and turns back—straight back to the gallery.

Ella Rentheim (quietly). Do none of his old friends ever come up to see him?

Mrs. Borkman. He has no old friends.

Ella Rentheim. He had so many—once.

Mrs. Borkman. H'm! He took the best possible way to get rid of them. He was a dear friend to his friends, was John Gabriel.

Ella Rentheim. Oh, yes, that is true, Gunhild.

Mrs. Borkman (vehemently). All the same, I call it mean, petty, base, contemptible of them, to think so much of the paltry losses they may have suffered through him. They were only money losses, nothing more.

Ella Rentheim (not answering her). So he lives up there quite alone. Absolutely by himself.

Mrs. Borkman. Yes, practically so. They tell me an old clerk or copyist or something comes out to see him now and then.

Ella Rentheim. Ah, indeed; no doubt it is a man called Foldal. I know they were friends as young men.

Mrs. Borkman. Yes, I believe they were. But I know

nothing about him. He was quite outside our circle—when we had a circle——

Ella Rentheim. So he comes out to see Borkman now?

Mrs. Borkman. Yes, he condescends to. But of course he only comes when it is dark.

Ella Rentheim. This Foldal—he was one of those that suffered when the bank failed.

Mrs. Borkman (carelessly). Yes, I believe I heard he had lost some money. But no doubt it was something quite trifling.

Ella Rentheim (with slight emphasis). It was all he possessed.

Mrs. Borkman (smiling). Oh, well; what he possessed must have been little enough—nothing to speak of.

Ella Rentheim. And he did not speak of it—Foldal, I mean—during the investigation.

Mrs. Borkman. At all events, I can assure you Erhart has made ample amends for any little loss he may have suffered.

Ella Rentheim (with surprise). Erhart! How can Erhart have done that?

Mrs. Borkman. He has taken an interest in Foldal's youngest daughter. He has taught her things and put her in the way of getting employment, and some day providing for herself. I am sure that is a great deal more than her father could ever have done for her.

Ella Rentheim. Yes, I daresay her father can't afford to do much.

Mrs. Borkman. And then Erhart has arranged for her to have music lessons. She has made such progress already that she can come up to—to him in the gallery and play to him.

Ella Rentheim. So he is still fond of music?

Mrs. Borkman. Oh, yes, I suppose he is. Of course he has the piano you sent out here—when he was expected back——

Ella Rentheim. And she plays to him on it?

Mrs. Borkman. Yes, now and then—in the evenings. That is Erhart's doing, too.

Ella Rentheim. Has the poor girl to come all the long way out here and then back to town again?

Mrs. Borkman. No, she doesn't need to. Erhart has arranged for her to stay with a lady who lives near us—a Mrs. Wilton——

Ella Rentheim (with interest). Mrs. Wilton?

Mrs. Borkman. A very rich woman. You don't know her.

Ella Rentheim. I have heard her name. Mrs. Fanny Wilton, is it not——?

Mrs. Borkman. Yes, quite right.

Ella Rentheim. Erhart has mentioned her several times. Does she live out here now?

Mrs. Borkman. Yes, she has taken a villa here; she moved out from town some time ago.

Ella Rentheim (with slight hesitation). They say she is divorced from her husband.

Mrs. Borkman. Her husband has been dead for several years.

Ella Rentheim. Yes, but they were divorced. He got a divorce.

Mrs. Borkman. He deserted her, that is what he did. I am sure the fault wasn't hers.

Ella Rentheim. Do you know her at all intimately, Gunhild?

Mrs. Borkman. Oh, yes, pretty well. She lives close by here; and she looks in every now and then.

Ella Rentheim. And do you like her?

Mrs. Borkman. She is unusually intelligent; remarkably clear in her judgments.

Ella Rentheim. In her judgments of people, do you mean?

Mrs. Borkman. Yes, principally of people. She has

made quite a study of Erhart; looked deep into his character—into his soul. And the result is she idolises him, as she could not help doing.

Ella Rentheim (with a touch of finesse). Then perhaps she knows Erhart still better than she knows you?

Mrs. Borkman. Yes, Erhart saw a good deal of her in town, before she came out here.

Ella Rentheim (without thinking). And in spite of that she moved out of town?

Mrs. Borkman (taken aback, looking keenly at her). In spite of that! What do you mean?

Ella Rentheim (evasively). Oh, nothing particular.

Mrs. Borkman. You said it so strangely—you did mean something by it, Ella!

Ella Rentheim (looking her straight in the eyes). Yes, that is true, Gunhild! I did mean something by it.

Mrs. Borkman. Well, then, say it right out.

Ella Rentheim. First let me tell you, I think I, too, have a certain claim upon Erhart. Do you think I haven't?

Mrs. Borkman (glancing round the room). No doubt—after all the money you have spent upon him.

Ella Rentheim. Oh, not on that account, Gunhild. But because I love him.

Mrs. Borkman (smiling scornfully). Love my son? Is it possible? You? In spite of everything?

Ella Rentheim. Yes, it is possible—in spite of everything. And it is true. I love Erhart—as much as I can love any one—now—at my time of life.

Mrs. Borkman. Well, well, suppose you do: what then?

Ella Rentheim. Why, then, I am troubled as soon as I see anything threatening him.

Mrs. Borkman. Threatening Erhart! Why, what should threaten him? Or who?

Ella Rentheim. You in the first place—in your way.

Mrs. Borkman (vehemently). I!

Ella Rentheim. And then this Mrs. Wilton, too, I am afraid.

Mrs. Borkman (looks at her for a moment in speechless surprise). And you can think such things of Erhart! Of my own boy! He, who has his great mission to fulfil!

Ella Rentheim (lightly). Oh, his mission!

Mrs. Borkman (indignantly). How dare you say that so scornfully?

Ella Rentheim. Do you think a young man of Erhart's age, full of health and spirits—do you think he is going to sacrifice himself for—for such a thing as a "mission"?

Mrs. Borkman (emphatically). Erhart will! I know he will.

Ella Rentheim (shaking her head). You neither know it nor believe it, Gunhild.

Mrs. Borkman. I don't believe it!

Ella Rentheim. It is only a dream that you cherish. For if you hadn't that to cling to, you feel that you would utterly despair.

Mrs. Borkman. Yes, indeed I should despair. *(Vehemently.)* And I daresay that is what you would like to see, Ella!

Ella Rentheim (with head erect). Yes, I would rather see that than see you "redeem" yourself at Erhart's expense.

Mrs. Borkman (threateningly). You want to come between us? Between mother and son? You?

Ella Rentheim. I want to free him from your power—your will—your despotism.

Mrs. Borkman (triumphantly). You are too late! You had him in your nets all those years—until he was fifteen. But now I have won him again, you see!

Ella Rentheim. Then I will win him back from you! *(Hoarsely, half whispering.)* We two have fought a life-and-death battle before, Gunhild—for a man's soul!

Mrs. Borkman (looking at her in triumph). Yes, and I won the victory.

Ella Rentheim (with a smile of scorn). Do you still think that victory was worth the winning?

Mrs. Borkman (darkly). No; Heaven knows you are right there.

Ella Rentheim. You need look for no victory worth the winning this time either.

Mrs. Borkman. Not when I am fighting to preserve a mother's power over my son!

Ella Rentheim. No; for it is only power over him that you want.

Mrs. Borkman. And you?

Ella Rentheim (warmly). I want his affection—his soul—his whole heart!

Mrs. Borkman (with an outburst). That you shall never have in this world!

Ella Rentheim (staring at her). You have seen to that?

Mrs. Borkman (smiling). Yes, I have taken that liberty. Could you not see that in his letters?

Ella Rentheim (nods slowly). Yes. I could see you—the whole of you—in his letters of late.

Mrs. Borkman (provokingly). I have made the best use of these eight years. I have had him under my own eye, you see.

Ella Rentheim (controlling herself). What have you said to Erhart about me? Is it the sort of thing you can tell me?

Mrs. Borkman. Oh, yes, I can tell you well enough.

Ella Rentheim. Then please do.

Mrs. Borkman. I have only told him the truth.

Ella Rentheim. Well?

Mrs. Borkman. I have impressed upon him, every day of his life, that he must never forget that it is you we have to thank for being able to live as we do—for being able to live at all.

Ella Rentheim. Is that all?

Mrs. Borkman. Oh, that is the sort of thing that rankles; I feel that in my own heart.

Ella Rentheim. But that is very much what Erhart knew already.

Mrs. Borkman. When he came home to me, he imagined that you did it all out of goodness of heart. *(Looks malignly at her.)* Now he does not believe that any longer, Ella.

Ella Rentheim. Then what does he believe now?

Mrs. Borkman. He believes what is the truth. I asked him how he accounted for the fact that Aunt Ella never came here to visit us——

Ella Rentheim (interrupting). He knew my reasons already!

Mrs. Borkman. He knows them better now. You had got him to believe that it was to spare me and—and him up there in the gallery——

Ella Rentheim. And so it was.

Mrs. Borkman. Erhart does not believe that for a moment, now.

Ella Rentheim. What have you put in his head?

Mrs. Borkman. He thinks, what is the truth, that you are ashamed of us—that you despise us. And do you pretend that you don't? Were you not once planning to take him quite away from me? Think, Ella; you cannot have forgotten.

Ella Rentheim (with a gesture of denial). That was at the height of the scandal—when the case was before the courts. I have no such designs now.

Mrs. Borkman. And it would not matter if you had. For in that case what would become of his mission? No, thank you. It is me that Erhart needs—not you. And therefore he is as good as dead to you—and you to him.

Ella Rentheim (coldly and resolutely). We shall see. For now I shall remain out here.

Mrs. Borkman (stares at her). Here? In this house?

Ella Rentheim. Yes, here.

Mrs. Borkman. Here—with us? Remain all night?

Ella Rentheim. I shall remain here all the rest of my days if need be.

Mrs. Borkman (collecting herself). Very well, Ella; the house is yours——

Ella Rentheim. Oh, nonsense——

Mrs. Borkman. Everything is yours. The chair I am sitting in is yours. The bed I lie and toss in at night belongs to you. The food we eat comes to us from you.

Ella Rentheim. It can't be arranged otherwise, you know. Borkman can hold no property of his own; for some one would at once come and take it from him.

Mrs. Borkman. Yes, I know. We must be content to live upon your pity and charity.

Ella Rentheim (coldly). I cannot prevent you from looking at it in that light, Gunhild.

Mrs. Borkman. No, you cannot. When do you want us to move out?

Ella Rentheim (looking at her). Move out?

Mrs. Borkman (in great excitement). Yes; you don't imagine that I will go on living under the same roof with you! I tell you, I would rather go to the workhouse or tramp the roads!

Ella Rentheim Good. Then let me take Erhart with me——

Mrs. Borkman. Erhart? My own son? My child?

Ella Rentheim. Yes; for then I would go straight home again.

Mrs. Borkman (after reflecting a moment, firmly). Erhart himself shall choose between us.

Ella Rentheim (looking doubtfuly and hesitatingly at her). He choose? Dare you risk that, Gunhild?

Mrs Borkman (with a hard laugh). Dare I? Let my

boy choose between his mother and you? Yes, indeed I dare!

Ella Rentheim (listening). Is there some one coming? I thought I heard——

Mrs. Borkman. Then it must be Erhart.

[*There is a sharp knock at the door leading in from the hall, which is immediately opened.* MRS. WILTON *enters, in evening dress, and with outer wraps. She is followed by* THE MAID, *who has not had time to announce her, and looks bewildered. The door remains half open.* MRS. WILTON *is a strikingly handsome, well-developed woman in the thirties. Her lips are broad, red, smiling, her eyes sparkling. She has luxuriant dark hair.*

Mrs. Wilton. Good evening, my dearest Mrs. Borkman!

Mrs. Borkman (rather drily). Good evening, Mrs. Wilton. *(To* THE MAID, *pointing toward the conservatory.)* Take out the lamp that is in there and light it.

[THE MAID *takes the lamp and goes out with it.*]

Mrs. Wilton (seeing ELLA RENTHEIM*).* Oh, I beg your pardon—you have a visitor.

Mrs. Borkman. Only my sister, who has just arrived from——

[ERHART BORKMAN *flings the half-open door wide open and rushes in. He is a young man with bright cheerful eyes. He is well dressed; his moustache is beginning to grow.*

Erhart (radiant with joy; on the threshold). What is this! Is Aunt Ella here? *(Rushing up to her and seizing her hands.)* Aunt, aunt! Is it possible? Are you here?

Ella Rentheim (throws her arms round his neck). Erhart! My dear, dear boy! Why, how big you have grown! Oh, how good it is to see you again!

Mrs. Borkman (sharply). What does this mean, Erhart? Were you hiding out in the hall?

Mrs. Wilton (quickly). Erhart—Mr. Borkman came in with me.

Mrs. Borkman (looking hard at him). Indeed, Erhart! You don't come to your mother first.

Erhart. I had just to look in at Mrs. Wilton's for a moment—to call for little Frida.

Mrs. Borkman. Is that Miss Foldal with you, too?

Mrs. Wilton. Yes, we have left her in the hall.

Erhart (addressing some one through the open door). You can go right upstairs, Frida.

[*Pause.* Ella Rentheim *observes* Erhart. *He seems embarrassed and a little impatient; his face has assumed a nervous and colder expression.*

The Maid *brings the lighted lamp into the conservatory, goes out again and closes the door behind her.*

Mrs. Borkman (with forced politeness). Well, Mrs. Wilton, if you will give us the pleasure of your company this evening, won't you——

Mrs. Wilton. Many thanks, my dear lady, but I really can't. We have another invitation. We're going down to the Hinkels'.

Mrs. Borkman (staring at her). We? Whom do you mean by we?

Mrs. Wilton (laughing). Oh, I ought really to have said I. But I was commissioned by the ladies of the house to bring Mr. Borkman with me—if I happened to see him.

Mrs. Borkman. And you did happen to see him, it appears.

Mrs. Wilton. Yes, fortunately. He was good enough to look in at my house—to call for Frida.

Mrs. Borkman (drily). But, Erhart, I did not know that you knew that family—those Hinkels?

Erhart (irritated). No, I don't exactly know them.

(Adds rather impatiently.) You know better than anybody, mother, what people I know and don't know.

Mrs. Wilton. Oh, it doesn't matter! They soon put you at your ease in that house! They are such cheerful, hospitable people—the house swarms with young ladies.

Mrs. Borkman (with emphasis). If I know my son rightly, Mrs. Wilton, they are no fit company for him.

Mrs. Wilton. Why, good gracious, dear lady, he is young, too, you know!

Mrs. Borkman. Yes, fortunately, he's young. He would need to be young.

Erhart (concealing his impatience). Well, well, well, mother, it's quite clear I can't go to the Hinkels' this evening. Of course I shall remain here with you and Aunt Ella.

Mrs. Borkman. I knew you would, my dear Erhart.

Ella Rentheim. No, Erhart, you must not stop at home on my account——

Erhart. Yes, indeed, my dear aunt; I can't think of going. *(Looking doubtfully at* MRS. WILTON.*)* But how shall we manage? Can I get out of it? You have said "Yes" for me, haven't you?

Mrs. Wilton (gaily). What nonsense! Not get out of it! When I make my entrance into the festive halls—just imagine it!—deserted and forlorn—then I must simply say "No" for you.

Erhart (hesitatingly). Well, if you really think I can get out of it——

Mrs. Wilton (putting the matter lightly aside). I am quite used to saying both yes and no—on my own account. And you can't possibly think of leaving your aunt the moment she has arrived! For shame, Monsieur Erhart! Would that be behaving like a good son?

Mrs. Borkman (annoyed). Son?

Mrs. Wilton. Well, adopted son, then, Mrs. Borkman.

Mrs. Borkman. Yes, you may well add that.

Mrs. Wilton. Oh, it seems to me we have often more cause to be grateful to a foster-mother than to our own mother.

Mrs. Borkman. Has that been your experience?

Mrs. Wilton. I knew very little of my own mother, I am sorry to say. But if I had had a good foster-mother, perhaps I shouldn't have been so—so naughty, as people say I am. *(Turning towards* ERHART.*)* Well, then, we stop peaceably at home like a good boy and drink tea with mamma and auntie! *(To the ladies.)* Good-bye, good-bye, Mrs. Borkman! Good-bye, Miss Rentheim.

[*The ladies bow silently. She goes toward the door.*

Erhart (following her). Shan't I go a little bit of the way with you?

Mrs. Wilton (in the doorway, motioning him back). You shan't go a step with me. I am quite accustomed to taking my walks alone. *(Stops on the threshold, looks at him and nods.)* But now beware, Mr. Borkman—I warn you!

Erhart. What am I to beware of?

Mrs. Wilton (gaily). Why, as I go down the road—deserted and forlorn, as I said before—I shall try to cast a spell upon you.

Erhart (laughing). Oh, indeed! Are you going to try that again?

Mrs. Wilton (half seriously). Yes, just you beware! As I go down the road, I will say in my own mind—right from the very centre of my will—I will say: "Mr. Erhart Borkman, take your hat at once!"

Mrs. Borkman. And you think he will take it?

Mrs. Wilton (laughing). Good heavens, yes, he'll snatch up his hat instantly. And then I will say: "Now put on your overcoat, like a good boy, Erhart Borkman! And your goloshes! Be sure you don't forget the goloshes! And then follow me! Do as I bid you, as I bid you, as I bid you!"

Erhart (with forced gaiety). Oh, you may rely on that.

Mrs. Wilton (raising her forefinger). As I bid you! As I bid you! Good-night!

[*She laughs and nods to the ladies and closes the door behind her.*

Mrs. Borkman. Does she really play tricks of that sort?

Erhart. Oh, not at all. How can you think so! She only says it in fun. *(Breaking off.)* But don't let us talk about Mrs. Wilton. *(He forces* Ella Rentheim *to seat herself in the armchair beside the stove, then stands and looks at her.)* To think of your having taken all this long journey, Aunt Ella! And in winter, too!

Ella Rentheim. I found I had to, Erhart.

Erhart. Indeed? Why so?

Ella Rentheim. I had to come to town after all, to consult the doctors.

Erhart. Oh, I'm glad of that!

Ella Rentheim (smiling). Are you glad of that?

Erhart. I mean I am glad you made up your mind to it at last.

Mrs. Borkman (on the sofa, coldly). Are you ill, Ella?

Ella Rentheim (looking severely at her). You know quite well that I am ill.

Mrs. Borkman. I knew you were not strong and hadn't been for years.

Erhart. I told you before I left you that you ought to consult a doctor.

Ella Rentheim. There is no one in my neighbourhood that I have any real confidence in. And, besides, I did not feel it so much at that time.

Erhart. Are you worse, then, Aunt?

Ella Rentheim. Yes, my dear boy; I am worse now.

Erhart. But there's nothing dangerous?

Ella Rentheim. Oh, that depends how you look at it.

Erhart (emphatically). Well, then, I tell you what it is.

Aunt Ella; you mustn't think of going home again for the present.

Ella Rentheim. No, I am not thinking of it.

Erhart. You must remain in town; for here you can have your choice of all the best doctors.

Ella Rentheim. That was what I thought when I left home.

Erhart. And then you must be sure and find a really nice place to live—quiet, comfortable rooms.

Ella Rentheim. I went this morning to the old ones, where I used to stay before.

Erhart. Oh, well, you were comfortable enough there.

Ella Rentheim. Yes, but I shall not be staying there after all.

Erhart. Indeed? Why not?

Ella Rentheim. I changed my mind after coming out here.

Erhart (surprised). Really? Changed your mind?

Mrs. Borkman (knitting; without looking up). Your aunt will live here, in her own house, Erhart.

Erhart (looking from one to the other alternately). Here, with us? With us? Is this true, Aunt?

Ella Rentheim. Yes, that is what I have made up my mind to do.

Mrs. Borkman (as before). Everything here belongs to your aunt, you know.

Ella Rentheim. I intend to remain here, Erhart—just now—for the present. I shall set up a little establishment of my own, over in the bailiff's wing.

Erhart. Ah, that's a good idea. There are plenty of rooms there. *(With sudden vivacity.)* But, by-the-bye, Aunt—aren't you very tired after your journey?

Ella Rentheim. Oh, yes, rather tired.

Erhart. Well, then, I think you ought to go to bed early.

Ella Rentheim (looks at him smilingly). I mean to.

Erhart (eagerly). And then we could have a good long talk to-morrow—or some other day, of course—about this and that—about things in general—you and mother and I. Wouldn't that be much the best plan, Aunt Ella?

Mrs. Borkman (with an outburst, rising from the sofa). Erhart, I can see you are going to leave me!

Erhart (starts). What do you mean by that?

Mrs. Borkman. You are going down to—to the Hinkels'?

Erhart (involuntarily). Oh, that! *(Collecting himself.)* Well, you wouldn't have me sit here and keep Aunt Ella up half the night? Remember, she's an invalid, mother.

Mrs. Borkman. You are going to the Hinkels', Erhart!

Erhart (impatiently). Well, really, mother, I don't think I can well get out of it. What do you say, Aunt?

Ella Rentheim. I should like you to feel quite free Erhart.

Mrs. Borkman (goes up to her menacingly). You want to take him away from me!

Ella Rentheim (rising). Yes, if only I could, Gunhild!

[*Music is heard from above.*

Erhart (writhing as if in pain). Oh, I can't endure this! *(Looking round.)* What have I done with my hat? *(To* Ella Rentheim.*)* Do you know what she is playing up there?

Ella Rentheim. No. What is it?

Erhart. It's the *Danse Macabre*—the Dance of Death! Don't you know the Dance of Death, Aunt?

Ella Rentheim (smiling sadly). Not yet, Erhart.

Erhart (to Mrs. Borkman*).* Mother—I beg and implore you—let me go!

Mrs. Borkman (looks severely at him). Away from your mother? So that is what you want to do?

Erhart. Of course I'll come out again—to-morrow perhaps.

Mrs. Borkman (with passionate emotion). You want to go away from me! To be with those strange people! With—with—no, I will not even think of it!

Erhart. There are bright lights down there, and young, happy faces; and there's music there, mother!

Mrs. Borkman (pointing upwards). There is music here, too, Erhart.

Erhart. Yes, it's just that music that drives me out of the house.

Ella Rentheim. Do you grudge your father a moment of self-forgetfulness?

Erhart. No, I don't. I'm very, very glad that he should have it—if only *I* don't have to listen.

Mrs. Borkman (looks solemnly at him). Be strong, Erhart! Be strong, my son. Do not forget that you have your great mission.

Erhart. Oh, mother—do spare me these phrases! I wasn't born to be a "missionary."—Good-night, aunt dear! Good-night, mother!

[*He goes hastily out through the hall.*

Mrs. Borkman (after a short silence). It has not taken you long to recapture him, Ella, after all.

Ella Rentheim. I wish I could believe it.

Mrs. Borkman. But you shall see you won't be allowed to keep him long.

Ella Rentheim. Allowed? By you, do you mean?

Mrs. Borkman. By me or—by her, the other one——

Ella Rentheim. Then rather she than you.

Mrs. Borkman (nodding slowly). That I understand. I say the same. Rather she than you.

Ella Rentheim. Whatever should become of him in the end——

Mrs. Borkman. It wouldn't greatly matter, I should say.

Ella Rentheim (taking her outdoor things upon her arm). For the first time in our lives, we twin sisters are of one mind. Good-night, Gunhild.

[*She goes out by the hall. The music sounds louder from above.*

Mrs. Borkman (stands still for a moment, starts, shrinks together and whispers involuntarily). The wolf is whining again—the sick wolf. *(She stands still for a moment, then flings herself down on the floor, writhing in agony and whispering):* Erhart! Erhart—be true to me! Oh, come home and help your mother! I can bear this life no longer!

ACT II

The great gallery on the first floor of the Rentheim House. The walls are covered with old tapestries, representing hunting-scenes, shepherds and shepherdesses, all in faded colours. A folding-door to the left, and further forward a piano. In the left-hand corner, at the back, a door, cut in the tapestry, and covered with tapestry, without any frame. Against the middle of the right wall, a large writing-table of carved oak. There are many books and papers. Further forward on the same side, a sofa with a table and chairs in front of it. The furniture is all of a stiff Empire style. Lighted lamps on both tables.

JOHN GABRIEL BORKMAN *stands, his hands behind his back, beside the piano, listening to* FRIDA FOLDAL, *who is playing the last bars of the "Danse Macabre."*

BORKMAN *is of medium height, a well-knit, powerfully built man, well on in the sixties. His appearance is distinguished, his profile finely cut, his eyes piercing, his hair and beard curly and greyish-white. He is dressed in a slightly old-fashioned black coat and wears a white necktie.* FRIDA FOLDAL *is a pretty, pale girl of fifteen, with a somewhat weary and overstrained expression. She is cheaply dressed in light colours.*

[*The music ceases. A pause.*

Borkman. Can you guess where I first heard tones like these?

Frida (looking up at him). No, Mr. Borkman.

Borkman. It was down in the mines.

Frida (not understanding). Indeed. Down in the mines?

Borkman. I am a miner's son, you know. Or perhaps you did not know?

Frida. No, Mr. Borkman.

Borkman. A miner's son. And my father used sometimes to take me with him into the mines. The metal sings down there.

Frida. Really? Sings?

Borkman (nodding). When it is loosened. The hammer-strokes that loosen it are the midnight bell clanging to set it free; and that is why the metal sings—in its own way—for gladness.

Frida. Why does it do that, Mr. Borkman?

Borkman. It wants to come up into the light of day and serve mankind. *(He paces up and down the gallery, always with his hands behind his back.)*

Frida (sits waiting a little, then looks at her watch and rises). I beg your pardon, Mr. Borkman; but I am afraid I must go.

Borkman (stopping before her). Are you going already?

Frida (putting her music in its case). I really must. *(Visibly embarrassed.)* I have an engagement this evening.

Borkman. For a party?

Frida. Yes.

Borkman. And you are to play before the company?

Frida (biting her lip). No; at least I am only to play for dancing.

Borkman. Only for dancing?

Frida. Yes; there is to be a dance after supper.

Borkman (stands and looks at her). Do you like playing dance music? At parties, I mean?

Frida (putting on her outdoor clothes). Yes, when I can get an engagement. I can always earn a little in that way.

Borkman (interested). Is that the principal thing in your mind as you sit playing for the dancers?

Frida. No; I'm generally thinking how hard it is that I mayn't join in the dance myself.

Borkman (nodding). That is just what I wanted to know. *(Pacing restlessly about the room.)* Yes, yes, yes. That you must not join in the dance, that is the hardest thing of all. *(Stopping.)* But there is one thing that should make up to you for that, Frida.

Frida (looking questioningly at him). What is that, Mr. Borkman?

Borkman. The knowledge that you have ten times more music in you than all the dancers together.

Frida (smiling shyly). Oh, that's not at all so certain.

Borkman (holding up his fore-finger warningly). You must never be so mad as to have doubts of yourself!

Frida. But since no one knows it——

Borkman. So long as you know it yourself, that is enough. Where is it you are going to play this evening?

Frida. Over at Mr. Hinkel's.

Borkman (with a swift, keen glance at her). Hinkel's, you say!

Frida. Yes.

Borkman (with a cutting smile). Does that man give parties? Can he get people to visit him?

Frida. Yes, they have a great many people about them, Mrs. Wilton says.

Borkman (vehemently). But what sort of people? Can you tell me that?

Frida (a little nervously). No, I really don't know. Yes, by-the-bye, I know that young Mr. Borkman is to be there this evening.

Borkman (taken aback). Erhart? My son?

Frida. Yes, he is going there.

Borkman. How do you know that?

Frida. He said so himself—an hour ago.

Borkman. Is he out here to-day?

Frida. Yes, he has been at Mrs. Wilton's all the afternoon.

Borkman (inquiringly). Do you know if he called here, too? I mean, did he see any one downstairs?

Frida. Yes, he looked in to see Mrs. Borkman.

Borkman (bitterly). Aha—I might have known it.

Frida. There was a strange lady calling upon her, I think.

Borkman. Indeed? Was there? Oh, yes, I suppose people do come now and then to see Mrs. Borkman.

Frida. If I meet young Mr. Borkman this evening, shall I ask him to come up and see you, too?

Borkman (harshly). You shall do nothing of the sort! I won't have it on any account. The people who want to see me can come of their own accord. I ask no one.

Frida. Oh, very well; I shan't say anything then. Good-night, Mr. Borkman.

Borkman (pacing up and down and growling). Good-night.

Frida. Do you mind if I run down by the winding stair? It's the shortest way.

Borkman. Oh, by all means; take whatever stair you please, so far as I am concerned. Good-night to you!

Frida. Good-night, Mr. Borkman.

[*She goes out by the little tapestry door in the back on the left.*

BORKMAN, *lost in thought, goes up to the piano, and is about to close it, but changes his mind. Looks around the great empty room and sets to pacing up and down it from the corner beside the piano to the corner at the back on the right—pacing backward and forward nervously and incessantly. At last he goes up to the writing-table, listens in the direction of the folding-door, hastily snatches up a hand-mirror, looks at himself in it and straightens his necktie.*

A knock at the folding-door. BORKMAN *hears it, looks rapidly towards the door, but remains silent.*

In a little while there comes another knock, this time louder.

Borkman (standing beside the writing table with his left hand resting upon it, and his right thrust in the breast of his coat). Come in!

[VILHELM FOLDAL *comes softly into the room. He is a bent and worn man with mild blue eyes and long, thin grey hair straggling down over his coat collar. He has a portfolio under his arm, a soft felt hat and large horn spectacles, which he pushes up his forehead.*

Borkman (changes his attitude and looks at FOLDAL *with a half-disappointed, half-pleased expression).* Oh, is it only you?

Foldal. Good evening, John Gabriel. Yes, you see it is me.

Borkman (with a stern glance). I must say you are rather a late visitor.

Foldal. Well, you know, it's a good bit of a way, especially when you have to trudge it on foot.

Borkman. But why do you always walk, Vilhelm? The tramway passes your door.

Foldal. It's better for you to walk—and then you always save twopence. Well, has Frida been playing to you lately?

Borkman. She has just this moment gone. Did you not meet her outside?

Foldal. No, I have seen nothing of her for a long time; not since she went to live with this Mrs. Wilton.

Borkman (seating himself on the sofa and motioning toward a chair). You may sit down, Vilhelm.

Foldal (seating himself on the edge of a chair). Many thanks. *(Looks mournfully at him).* You can't think how lonely I feel since Frida left home.

Borkman. Oh, come—you have plenty left.

Foldal. Yes, God knows I have—five of them. But Frida was the only one who at all understood me. *(Shaking his head sadly.)* The others don't understand me a bit.

Borkman (gloomily, gazing straight before him and drumming on the table with his fingers). No, that's just it. That is the curse we exceptional, chosen people have to bear. The common herd—the average man and woman—they do not understand us, Vilhelm.

Foldal (with resignation). If it were only the lack of understanding—with a little patience, one could manage to wait for that awhile yet. *(His voice choked with tears.)* But there is something still bitterer.

Borkman (vehemently). There is nothing bitterer than that.

Foldal. Yes, there is, John Gabriel. I have gone through a domestic scene to-night—just before I started.

Borkman. Indeed? What about?

Foldal (with an outburst). My people at home—they despise me.

Borkman (indignantly). Despise——!

Foldal (wiping his eyes). I have long known it; but today it came out unmistakably.

Borkman (after a short pause). You made an unwise choice, I fear, when you married.

Foldal. I had practically no choice in the matter. And, you see, one feels a need for companionship as one begins to get on in years. And so crushed as I then was—so utterly broken down——

Borkman (jumping up in anger). Is this meant for me? A reproach——!

Foldal (alarmed). No, no, for Heaven's sake, John Gabriel——!

Borkman. Yes, you are thinking of the disaster to the bank; I can see you are!

Foldal (soothingly). But I don't blame you for that! Heaven forbid!

Borkman (growling, resumes his seat). Well, that is a good thing, at any rate.

Foldal. Besides, you mustn't think it is my wife that I complain of. It is true she has not much polish, poor thing; but she is a good sort of woman all the same. No, it's the children.

Borkman. I thought as much.

Foldal. For the children—well, they have more culture, and therefore they expect more of life.

Borkman (looking at him sympathetically). And so your children despise you, Vilhelm?

Foldal (shrugging his shouldiers). I haven't made much of a career, you see—there is no denying that.

Borkman (moving nearer to him and laying his hand upon his arm). Do they not know, then, that in your younger days you wrote a tragedy?

Foldal. Yes, of course they know that. But it doesn't seem to make much impression on them.

Borkman. Then they don't understand these things. For your tragedy is good. I am firmly convinced of that.

Foldal (brightening up). Yes, don't you think there are some good things in it, John Gabriel? Good God, if I could only manage to get it placed——! *(Opens his portfolio and begins eagerly turning over the contents.)* Look here. Just let me show you one or two alterations I have made.

Borkman. Have you it with you?

Foldal. Yes, I thought I would bring it. It's so long now since I have read it to you. And I thought perhaps it might amuse you to hear an act or two.

Borkman (rising, with a negative gesture). No, no, we will keep that for another time.

Foldal. Well, well, as you please.

[BORKMAN *paces up and down the room.* FOLDAL *puts the manuscript away.*

Borkman (stopping in front of him). You are quite right in what you said just now—you have not made any career.

But I promise you this, Vilhelm, that when once the hour of my restoration strikes——

Foldal (making a movement to rise). Oh, thanks, thanks!

Borkman (waving his hand). No, please be seated. *(With increasing excitement.)* When the hour of my restoration strikes—when they see that they cannot get on without me—when they come to me, here in the gallery, and crawl to my feet and beseech me to take the reins of the bank again——! The new bank, that they have founded and can't carry on—— *(Taking a position beside the writing-table in the same attitude as before and striking his breast.)* Here I shall stand, and receive them! And it shall be known far and wide, all the country over, what conditions John Gabriel Borkman imposes before he will—— *(Stopping suddenly and staring at* Foldal.*)* You're looking so doubtfully at me! Perhaps you do not believe that they will come? That they must, must, must come to me some day? Do you not believe it?

Foldal. Yes, Heaven knows I do, John Gabriel.

Borkman (seating himself again on the sofa). I firmly believe it. I am immovably convinced—I know that they will come. If I had not been certain of that, I would have put a bullet through my head long ago.

Foldal (anxiously). Oh, no, for Heaven's sake——!

Borkman (exultantly). But they will come! They will come sure enough! You shall see! I expect them any day, any moment. And you see, I hold myself in readiness to receive them.

Foldal (with a sigh). If only they would come quickly.

Borkman (restlessly). Yes, time flies: the years slip away; life—— Ah, no—I dare not think of it! *(Looking at him.)* Do you know what I sometimes feel like?

Foldal. What?

Borkman. I feel like a Napoleon who has been maimed in his first battle.

Foldal (placing his hand upon his portfolio). I have that feeling, too.

Borkman. Oh, well, that is on a smaller scale, of course.

Foldal (quietly). My little world of poetry is very precious to me, John Gabriel.

Borkman (vehemently). Yes, but think of me, who could have created millions! All the mines I should have controlled! New veins innumerable! And the water-falls! And the quarries! And the trade routes, and steamship-lines all the wide world over! I would have organised it all—I alone!

Foldal. Yes, I know, I know. There was nothing in the world you would have shrunk from.

Borkman (clenching his hands together). And now I have to sit here, like a wounded eagle, and look on while others pass me in the race and take everything away from me, piece by piece!

Foldal. That is my fate, too.

Borkman (not noticing him). Only to think of it; so near to the goal as I was! If I had only had another week to look about me! All the deposits would have been covered. All the securities I had dealt with so daringly should have been in their places again as before. Vast companies were within a hair's-breadth of being floated. Not a soul should have lost a half-penny.

Foldal. Yes, yes; you were on the very verge of success.

Borkman (with suppressed fury). And then treachery overtook me! Just at the critical moment! *(Looking at him.)* Do you know what I hold to be the most infamous crime a man can be guilty of?

Foldal. No, tell me.

Borkman. It is not murder. It is not robbery or house-breaking. It is not even perjury. For all these things people do to those they hate, or who are indifferent to them, and do not matter.

Foldal. What is the worst of all, then, John Gabriel?

Borkman (with emphasis). The most infamous of crimes is a friend's betrayal of his friend's confidence.

Foldal (somewhat doubtfully). Yes, but you know——

Borkman (firing up). What are you going to say? I see it in your face. But it is of no use. The people who had their securities in the bank should have got them all back again—every farthing. No; I tell you the most infamous crime a man can commit is to misuse a friend's letters; to publish to all the world what has been confided to him alone, in the closest secrecy, like a whisper in an empty, dark, double-locked room. The man who can do such things is infected and poisoned in every fibre with the morals of the higher rascality. And such a friend was mine—and it was he who crushed me.

Foldal. I can guess whom you mean.

Borkman. There was not a nook or cranny of my life that I hesitated to lay open to him. And, then, when the moment came, he turned against me the weapons I myself had placed in his hands.

Foldal. I have never been able to understand why he—— Of course, there were whispers of all sorts at the time.

Borkman. What were the whispers? Tell me. You see I know nothing. For I had to go straight into—into isolation. What did people whisper, Vilhelm.

Foldal. You were to have gone into the Cabinet, they said.

Borkman. I was offered a portfolio, but I refused it.

Foldal. Then it wasn't there you stood in his way?

Borkman. Oh, no; that was not the reason he betrayed me.

Foldal. Then I really can't understand——

Borkman. I may as well tell you, Vilhelm——

Foldal. Well?

Borkman. There was—in fact, there was a woman in the case.

Foldal. A woman in the case? Well, but, John Gabriel ——

Borkman (interrupting). Well, well—let us say no more of these stupid old stories. After all, neither of us got into the Cabinet, neither he nor I.

Foldal. But he rose high in the world.

Borkman. And I fell into the abyss.

Foldal. Oh, it's a terrible tragedy——

Borkman (nodding to him). Almost as terrible as yours, I fancy, when I come to think of it.

Foldal (naively). Yes, at least as terrible.

Borkman (laughing quietly). But looked at from another point of view, it is really a sort of comedy as well.

Foldal. A comedy? The story of your life?

Borkman. Yes, it seems to be taking a turn in that direction. For let me tell you——

Foldal. What?

Borkman. You say you did not meet Frida as you came in?

Foldal. No.

Borkman. At this moment, as we sit here, she is playing waltzes for the guests of the man who betrayed and ruined me.

Foldal. I hadn't the least idea of that.

Borkman. Yes, she took her music and went straight from me to—to the great house.

Foldal (apologetically). Well, you see, poor child——

Borkman. And can you guess for whom she is playing —among the rest?

Foldal. No.

Borkman. For my son.

Foldal. What?

Borkman. What do you think of that, Vilhelm? My son is down there in the whirl of the dance this evening. Am I not right in calling it a comedy?

Foldal. But in that case you may be sure he knows nothing about it.

Borkman. What does he not know?

Foldal. You may be sure he doesn't know how he—that man——

Borkman. Do not shrink from his name. I can quite well bear it now.

Foldal. I'm certain your son doesn't know the circumstances, John Gabriel.

Borkman (gloomily, sitting and striking the table). Yes, he knows, as surely as I am sitting here.

Foldal. Then how can he possibly be a guest in that house?

Borkman (shaking his head). My son probably does not see things with my eyes. I'll take my oath he is on my enemies' side! No doubt he thinks, as they do, that Hinkel only did his confounded duty when he went and betrayed me.

Foldal. But, my dear friend, who can have got him to see things in that light?

Borkman. Who? Do you forget who has brought him up? First his aunt, from the time he was six or seven years old; and now, of late years, his mother!

Foldal. I believe you are doing them an injustice.

Borkman (firing up). I never do any one injustice! Both of them have poisoned his mind against me, I tell you!

Foldal (soothingly). Well, well, well, I suppose they have.

Borkman (indignantly). Oh, these women! They wreck and ruin life for us! Play the devil with our whole destiny—our triumphal progress.

Foldal. Not all of them!

Borkman. Indeed? Can you tell me of a single one that is good for anything?

Foldal. No, that is the trouble. The few that I know are good for nothing.

Borkman (with a snort of scorn). Well, then, what is the good of it? What is the good of such women existing—if you never know them?

Foldal (warmly). Yes, John Gabriel, there is good in it, I assure you. It is such a blessed, beneficent thought that here or there in the world, somewhere, far away—the true woman exists after all.

Borkman (moving impatiently on the sofa). Oh, do spare me that poetical nonsense.

Foldal (looks at him, deeply wounded). Do you call my holiest faith poetical nonsense?

Borkman (harshly). Yes, I do! That is what has always prevented you from getting on in the world. If you would get all that out of your head, I could still help you on in life—help you to rise.

Foldal (boiling inwardly). Oh, you can't do that.

Borkman. I can, when once I come into power again.

Foldal. That won't be for many a day.

Borkman (vehemently). Perhaps you think that day will never come? Answer me!

Foldal. I don't know what to answer.

Borkman (rising, cold and dignified, and waving his hand towards the door). Then I no longer have any use for you.

Foldal (starting up). No use——!

Borkman. Since you do not believe that the tide will turn for me——

Foldal. How can I believe in the teeth of all reason? You would have to be legally rehabilitated——

Borkman. Go on! go on!

Foldal. It's true I never passed my examination; but I have read enough law to know that——

Borkman (quickly). It is impossible, you mean?

Foldal. There is no precedent for such a thing.

Borkman. Exceptional men are above precedents.

Foldal. The law knows nothing of such distinctions.

Borkman (harshly and decisively). You are no poet, Vilhelm.

Foldal (unconsciously folding his hands). Do you say that in sober earnest?

Borkman (dismissing the subject, without answering). We are only wasting each other's time. You had better not come here again.

Foldal. Then you really want me to leave you?

Borkman (without looking at him). I have no longer any use for you.

Foldal (softly, taking his portfolio). No, no, no; I daresay not.

Borkman. Here you have been lying to me all the time

Foldal (shaking his head). Never lying, John Gabriel.

Borkman. Have you not sat here feeding me with hope, and trust and confidence—that was all a lie?

Foldal. It wasn't a lie so long as you believed in my vocation. So long as you believed in me, I believed in you.

Borkman. Then we have been all the time deceiving each other. And perhaps deceiving ourselves—both of us.

Foldal. But isn't that just the essence of friendship, John Gabriel?

Borkman (smiling bitterly). Yes, you are right there. Friendship means—deception. I have learnt that once before.

Foldal (looking at him). I have no poetic vocation! And you could actually say it to me so bluntly.

Borkman (in a gentler tone). Well, you know, I don't pretend to know much about these matters.

Foldal. Perhaps you know more than you think.

Borkman. I?

Foldal (softly). Yes, you. For I myself have had my doubts, now and then, I may tell you. The horrible doubt that I may have bungled my life for the sake of a delusion.

Borkman. If you have no faith in yourself, you are on the downward path indeed.

Foldal. That was why I found such comfort in coming here to lean upon your faith in me. *(Taking his hat.)* But now you have become a stranger to me.

Borkman. And you to me.

Foldal. Good night, John Gabriel.

Borkman. Good night, Vilhelm.

[FOLDAL *goes out to the left.*

[BORKMAN *stands for a moment gazing at the closed door. He makes a movement as though to call* FOLDAL *back, but changes his mind, and begins to pace the floor with his hands behind his back. Then he stops at the table beside the sofa and puts out the lamp. The room becomes half dark. After a short pause, there comes a knock at the tapestry door.*

Borkman (at the table, starts, turns and asks in a loud voice). Who is that knocking?

[*No answer; another knock.*

Borkman (without moving). Who is it? Come in!

[ELLA RENTHEIM, *with a lighted candle in her hand, appears in the doorway. She wears her black dress, as before, with her cloak thrown loosely over her shoulders.*

Borkman (staring at her). Who are you? What do you want with me?

Ella Rentheim (closes the door and advances). It is I, Borkman.

[*She puts down the candle on the piano and remains standing beside it.*

Borkman (stands as though thunderstruck, stares fixedly at her and says in a half-whisper). Is it—is it Ella? Is it Ella Rentheim?

Ella Rentheim. Yes, it's "your" Ella, as you used to call me in the old days; many, many years ago.

Borkman (as before). Yes, it is you, Ella, I can see you now.

Ella Rentheim. Can you recognise me?

Borkman. Yes, now I begin to——

Ella Rentheim. The years have told on me and brought winter with them, Borkman. Do you not think so?

Borkman (in a forced voice). You are a good deal changed—just at the first glance.

Ella Rentheim. There are no dark curls on my neck now—the curls you once loved so to twist round your fingers.

Borkman (quickly). True! I can see now, Ella, you have done your hair differently.

Ella Rentheim (with a sad smile). Precisely; it is the way I do my hair that makes the difference.

Borkman (changing the subject). I had no idea that you were in this part of the world.

Ella Rentheim. I have only just arrived.

Borkman. Why have you come all this way now, in winter?

Ella Rentheim. That you shall hear.

Borkman. Is it me you have come to see?

Ella Rentheim. You among others. But if I am to tell you my errand, I must begin far back.

Borkman. You look tired.

Ella Rentheim. Yes, I am tired.

Borkman. Won't you sit down? There, on the sofa.

Ella Rentheim. Yes, thank you; I need rest.

[*She crosses to the right and seats herself in the extreme forward corner of the sofa.* BORKMAN *stands beside the table with his hands behind his back looking at her. A short silence.*

Ella Rentheim. It seems an endless time since we two met, Borkman, face to face.

Borkman (gloomily). It is a long, long time. And terrible things have passed since then.

Ella Rentheim. A whole lifetime has passed—a wasted lifetime.

Borkman (looking keenly at her). Wasted!

Ella Rentheim. Yes, I say wasted—for both of us.

Borkman (in a cold tone). I cannot regard my life as wasted, yet.

Ella Rentheim. And what about mine?

Borkman. There you have yourself to blame, Ella.

Ella Rentheim (with a start). And you can say that?

Borkman. You could quite well have been happy without me.

Ella Rentheim. Do you believe that?

Borkman. If you had made up your mind to.

Ella Rentheim (bitterly). Oh, yes, I know well enough there was some one else ready to marry me.

Borkman. But you rejected him.

Ella Rentheim. Yes, I did.

Borkman. Time after time you rejected him. Year after year——

Ella Rentheim (scornfully). Year after year I rejected happiness, I suppose you think?

Borkman. You might perfectly well have been happy with him. And then I should have been saved.

Ella Rentheim. You?

Borkman. Yes, you would have saved me, Ella.

Ella Rentheim. How do you mean?

Borkman. He thought I was at the bottom of your obstinacy—of your perpetual refusals. And then he took his revenge. It was so easy for him; he had all my frank, confiding letters in his keeping. He made his own use of them; and then it was all over with me—for the time, that is to say. So you see it is all your doing, Ella!

Ella Rentheim. Oh, indeed, Borkman. If we look into the matter, it appears that it is I who owe you reparation.

Borkman. It depends how you look at it. I know quite well all that you have done for us. You bought in this house, and the whole property, at the auction. You placed the house entirely at my disposal—and your sister's. You took charge of Erhart and cared for him in every way——

Ella Rentheim. As long as I was allowed to——

Borkman. By your sister, you mean. I have never interfered in these domestic affairs. As I was saying, I know all the sacrifices you have made for me and for your sister. But you were in a position to do so, Ella; and you must not forget that it was I who placed you in that position.

Ella Rentheim (indignantly). There you make a great mistake, Borkman! It was the love of my inmost heart for Erhart—and for you, too—that made me do it!

Borkman (interrupting). My dear Ella, do not let us get upon questions of sentiment and that sort of thing. I mean, of course, that if you acted generously, it was I that put it in your power to do so.

Ella Rentheim (smiling). H'm! In my power——

Borkman (warmly). Yes, put it in your power, I say! On the eve of the great decisive battle—when I could not afford to spare either kith or kin—when I had to grasp at—when I did grasp at the millions that were entrusted to me—then I spared all that was yours, every farthing, although I could have taken it, and made use of it, as I did of all the rest!

Ella Rentheim (coldly and quietly). That is quite true, Borkman.

Borkman. Yes, it is. And that was why, when they came and took me, they found all your securities untouched in the strong-room of the bank.

Ella Rentheim (looking at him). I have often and often wondered what was your real reason for sparing all my property? That, and that alone?

Borkman. My reason?

Ella Rentheim. Yes, your reason. Tell me.

Borkman (harshly and scornfully). Perhaps you think it was that I might have something to fall back upon, if things went wrong?

Ella Rentheim. Oh, no, I am sure you did not think of that in those days.

Borkman. Never! I was so absolutely certain of victory.

Ella Rentheim. Well, then, why was it that——?

Borkman (shrugging his shoulders). Upon my soul, Ella, it is not so easy to remember one's motives of twenty years ago. I only know that when I used to grapple, silently and alone, with all the great projects I had in my mind, I had something like the feeling of a man who is starting on a balloon-voyage. All through my sleepless nights I was inflating my giant balloon and preparing to soar away into perilous, unknown regions.

Ella Rentheim (smiling). You, who never had the least doubt of victory?

Borkman (impatiently). Men are made so, Ella. They both doubt and believe at the same time. *(Looking straight ahead.)* And I suppose that was why I would not take you and yours with me in the balloon.

Ella Rentheim (eagerly). Why, I ask you? Tell me why!

Borkman (without looking at her). One shrinks from risking what one holds dearest on such a voyage.

Ella Rentheim. You had risked what was dearest to you on that voyage. Your whole future life——

Borkman. Life is not always what one holds dearest.

Ella Rentheim (breathlessly). Was that how you felt at that time?

Borkman. I fancy it was.

Ella Rentheim. I was the dearest thing in the world to you?

Borkman. I seem to remember something of the sort.

Ella Rentheim. And yet years and years had passed since you had deserted me—and married—married another!

Borkman. Deserted you, you say? You must know very well that it was higher motives—well, then, other motives that compelled me. Without his support I could not have done anything.

Ella Rentheim (controlling herself). So you deserted me from—higher motives.

Borkman. I could not get on without his help. And he made you the price of helping me.

Ella Rentheim. And you paid the price. Paid it in full —without haggling.

Borkman. I had no choice. I had to conquer or fall.

Ella Rentheim (in a trembling voice, looking at him). Can what you tell me be true——that I was then the dearest thing in the world to you?

Borkman. Both then and afterwards—long, long after.

Ella Rentheim. But you bartered me away none the less; drove a bargain with another man for your love. Sold my love for a—for a directorship.

Borkman (gloomily and bowed down). I was driven by inexorable necessity, Ella.

Ella Rentheim (rises from the sofa, quivering with passion). Criminal!

Borkamn (starts, but controls himself). I have heard that word before.

Ella Rentheim. Oh, don't imagine I'm thinking of anything you may have done against the law of the land! The use you made of all those vouchers and securities, or whatever you call them—do you think I care a straw about that! If I could have stood at your side when the crash came——

Borkman (eagerly). What then, Ella?

Ella Rentheim. Trust me, I should have borne it all so gladly along with you. The shame, the ruin—I would have helped you to bear it all—all!

Borkman. Would you have had the will—the strength?

Ella Rentheim. Both the will and the strength. For then I did not know of your great, your terrible crime.

Borkman. What crime? What are you speaking of?

Ella Rentheim. I am speaking of that crime for which there is no forgiveness.

Borkman (staring at her) You must be out of your mind.

Ella Rentheim (approaching him). You are a murderer! You have committed the one mortal sin!

Borkman (falling back towards the piano). You are raving, Ella!

Ella Rentheim. You have killed the love-life in me. *(Still nearer him.)* Do you understand what that means? The Bible speaks of a mysterious sin for which there is no forgiveness. I have never understood what it could be; but now I understand. The great, unpardonable sin is to murder the love-life in a human soul.

Borkman. And you say I have done that?

Ella Rentheim. You have done that. I have never rightly understood until this evening what had really happened to me. That you deserted me and turned to Gunhild instead—I took that to be mere common fickleness on your part, and the result of heartless scheming on hers. I almost think I despised you a little, in spite of everything. But now I see it! You deserted the woman you loved! Me, me, me! What you held dearest in the world you were ready to barter away for gain. That is the double murder you have committed! The murder of your own soul and of mine!

Borkman (with cold self-control). How well I recognise your passionate, ungovernable spirit, Ella. No doubt it is natural enough that you should look at the thing in this light. Of course, you are a woman, and therefore it would seem that your own heart is the one thing you know or care about in the world.

Ella Rentheim. Yes, yes, it is.

Borkman. Your own heart is the only thing that exists for you.

Ella Rentheim. The only thing! The only thing! You are right there.

Borkman. But you must remember that I am a man. As a woman, you were the dearest thing in the world to me. But if the worst comes to the worst, one woman can always take the place of another.

Ella Rentheim (looks at him with a smile). Was that your experience when you had made Gunhild your wife?

Borkman. No. But the great aims I had in life helped me to bear even that. I wanted to have at my command all the sources of power in this country. All the wealth that lay hidden in the soil, and the rocks, and the forests and the sea—— I wanted to gather it all into my hands, to make myself master of it all, and so to promote the well-being of many, many thousands.

Ella Rentheim (lost in recollection). I know it. Think of all the evenings we spent in talking over your projects.

Borkman. Yes, I could talk to you, Ella.

Ella Rentheim. I jested with your plans and asked whether you wanted to awaken all the sleeping spirits of the mine.

Borkman (nodding). I remember that phrase. *(Slowly.)* All the sleeping spirits of the mine.

Ella Rentheim. But you did not take it as a jest. You said: "Yes, yes, Ella, that is just what I want to do."

Borkman. And so it was. If only I could get my foot into the stirrup—— And that depended on that one man. He could and would secure me the control of the bank—if I on my side——

Ella Rentheim. Yes, just so! If you on your side would renounce the woman you loved—and who loved you beyond words in return.

Borkman. I knew his consuming passion for you. I knew that on no other condition would he——

Ella Rentheim. And so you struck the bargain.

Borkman (vehemently). Yes, I did, Ella! For the love of power is uncontrollable in me, you see! So I struck the bargain; I had to. And he helped me half-way up towards the beckoning heights that I was bent on reaching. And I mounted and mounted; year by year I mounted——

Ella Rentheim. And I was as though wiped out of your life.

Borkman. And after all he hurled me into the abyss again. On account of you, Ella.

Ella Rentheim (after a short, thoughtful silence). Borkman, does it not seem to you as if there had been a sort of curse on our whole relation?

Borkman (looking at her). A curse?

Ella Rentheim. Yes. Don't you think so?

Borkman (uneasily). Yes. But why is it? *(With an outburst.)* Oh, Ella, I begin to wonder who is in the right—you or I!

Ella Rentheim. It is you who have sinned. You have done to death all the gladness of life in me.

Borkman (anxiously). Do not say that, Ella!

Ella Rentheim. All a woman's gladness at any rate. From the day when your image began to dwindle in my mind, I have lived my life as though under an eclipse. During all these years it has grown harder and harder for me—and at last utterly impossible—to love any living creature. Human beings, animals, plants: I shrank from all—from all but one——

Borkman. What one?

Ella Rentheim. Erhart, of course.

Borkman. Erhart?

Ella Rentheim. Erhart—your son, Borkman.

Borkman. Has he really been so close to your heart?

Ella Rentheim. Why else should I have taken him to me and kept him as long as ever I could? Why?

Borkman. I thought it was out of pity, like all the rest that you did.

Ella Rentheim (with strong inward emotion). Pity! Ha, ha! I have never known pity, since you deserted me.

I was incapable of feeling it. If a poor starved child came into my kitchen, shivering, and crying and begging for a morsel of food, I let the servants look to it. I never felt any desire to take the child to myself, to warm it at my own hearth, to have the pleasure of seeing it eat and be satisfied. And yet I was not like that when I was young; that I remember clearly! It is you that have created an empty, barren desert within me—and without me, too!

Borkman. Except only for Erhart.

Ella Rentheim. Yes, except for your son. But I am hardened to every other living thing. You have cheated me of a mother's joy and happiness in life—and of a mother's sorrows and tears as well. And perhaps that is the heaviest part of the loss to me.

Borkman. Do you say that, Ella?

Ella Rentheim. Who knows? It may be that a mother's sorrows and tears were what I needed most. *(With still deeper emotion.)* But at that time I could not resign myself to my loss; and that was why I took Erhart to me. I won him entirely. Won his whole warm, trustful, childish heart—until—— Oh!

Borkman. Until what?

Ella Rentheim. Until his mother—his mother in the flesh, I mean—took him from me again.

Borkman. He had to leave you in any case; he had to come to town.

Ella Rentheim (wringing her hands). Yes, but I cannot bear the solitude—the emptiness! I cannot bear the loss of your son's heart!

Borkman (an evil expression in his eyes). H'm—I doubt whether you have lost it, Ella. Hearts are not so easily lost to a certain person—in the room below.

Ella Rentheim. I have lost Erhart here, and she has won him back again. Or if not she, some one else. That is plain enough in the letters he writes me from time to time.

Borkman. Then it is to take him back with you that you have come here?

Ella Rentheim. Yes, if only it were possible——!

Borkman. It is possible enough, if you have set your heart upon it. For you have the first and strongest claims upon him.

Ella Rentheim. Oh, claims, claims! What is the use of claims? If he is not mine of his own free will, he is not mine at all. And have him I must! I must have my boy's heart, whole and undivided—now!

Borkman. You must remember that Erhart is well into his twenties. You could scarcely reckon on keeping his heart very long undivided, as you express it.

Ella Rentheim (with a melancholy smile). It would not need to be for so very long.

Borkman. Indeed? I should have thought that when you want a thing, you want it to the end of your days.

Ella Rentheim. So I do. But that need not mean for very long.

Borkman (taken aback). What do you mean by that?

Ella Rentheim. I suppose you know I have been in bad health for many years past?

Borkman. Have you?

Ella Rentheim. Do you not know that?

Borkman. No, I cannot say I did——

Ella Rentheim (looking at him in surprise). Has Erhart not told you so?

Borkman. I really don't remember at the moment.

Ella Rentheim. Perhaps he has not spoken of me at all?

Borkman. Oh, yes, I believe he has spoken of you. But the fact is, I so seldom see anything of him—scarcely ever. There is a certain person below that keeps him away from me. Keeps him away, you understand?

Ella Rentheim. Are you quite sure of that, Borkman?

Borkman. Yes, absolutely sure. *(Changing his tone.)* And so you have been in bad health, Ella?

Ella Rentheim. Yes, I have. And this autumn I grew so much worse that I had to come to town and take better medical advice.

Borkman. And you have seen the doctors already?

Ella Rentheim. Yes, this morning.

Borkman. And what did they say to you?

Ella Rentheim. They gave me full assurance of what I had long suspected.

Borkman. Well?

Ella Rentheim (calmly and quietly). My illness will never be cured, Borkman.

Borkman. Oh, you must not believe that, Ella.

Ella Rentheim. It is a disease that there is no help or cure for. The doctors can do nothing with it. They must just let it take its course. They cannot possibly check it; at most, they can allay the suffering. And that is always something.

Borkman. Oh, but it will take a long time to run its course. I am sure it will.

Ella Rentheim. I may perhaps last out the winter, they told me.

Borkman (without thinking). Oh, well, the winter is long.

Ella Rentheim (quietly). Long enough for me, at any rate.

Borkman (eagerly, changing the subject). But what in all the world can have brought on this illness? You, who have always lived such a healthy and regular life? What can have brought it on?

Ella Rentheim (looking at him). The doctors thought that perhaps at one time in my life I had had to go through some great stress of emotion.

Borkman (firing up). Emotion! Aha, I understand! You mean that it is my fault?

Ella Rentheim (with increasing inward agitation). It is too late to go into that now! But I must have my heart's own child again before I go! It is so unspeakably sad for me to think that I must go away from all that is called life —away from sun, and light and air—and not leave behind me one single human being who will think of me—who will remember me lovingly and mournfully—as a son remembers and thinks of the mother he has lost.

Borkman (after a short pause). Take him, Ella, if you can win him.

Ella Rentheim (with animation). Do you give your consent? Can you?

Borkman (gloomily). Yes. And it is no great sacrifice either. For in any case he is not mine.

Ella Rentheim. Thank you, thank you all the same for the sacrifice! But I have one thing more to beg of you— a great thing for me, Borkman.

Borkman. Well, what is it?

Ella Rentheim. I daresay you will think it childish of me—you will not understand——

Borkman. Go on—tell me what it is.

Ella Rentheim. When I die—as I must soon—I shall have a fair amount to leave behind me.

Borkman. Yes, I suppose so.

Ella Rentheim. And I intend to leave it all to Erhart.

Borkman. Well, you have really no one nearer to you than he.

Ella Rentheim (warmly). No, indeed, I have no one nearer me than he.

Borkman. No one of your own family. You are the last.

Ella Rentheim (nodding slowly). Yes, that is just it. When I die, the name of Rentheim dies with me. And that is such a torturing thought to me. To be wiped out of existence—even to your very name——

Borkman (firing up). Ah, I see what you are driving at!

Ella Rentheim (passionately). Let Erhart bear my name after me!

Borkman (looking harshly at her). I understand you well enough. You want to save my son from having to bear his father's name. That is your meaning.

Ella Rentheim. No, no, not that! I myself would have borne it proudly and gladly along with you! But a mother who is at the point of death—— There is more binding force in a name than you think or believe, Borkman.

Borkman (coldly and proudly). Well and good, Ella. I am man enough to bear my own name alone.

Ella Rentheim (seizing and pressing his hand). Thank you, thank you! Now there has been a full settlement between us! Yes, yes, let it be so! You have made all the atonement in your power. For when I have gone from the world, I shall leave Erhart Rentheim behind me!

[*The tapestry door is thrown open.* MRS. BORKMAN, *with the large shawl over her head, stands in the doorway.*

Mrs. Borkman (violently agitated). Never to his dying day shall Erhart be called by that name!

Ella Rentheim (shrinking back). Gunhild!

Borkman (harshly and threateningly). I allow no one to come up to my room!

Mrs. Borkman (advancing a step). I do not ask your permission.

Borkman (going towards her). What do you want with me?

Mrs. Borkman. I will fight with all my might for you. I will protect you from the powers of evil.

Ella Rentheim. The worst "powers of evil" are in yourself, Gunhild!

Mrs. Borkman (harshly). So be it then. *(Menacingly, with upstretched arm.)* But this I tell you—he shall bear his father's name! And bear it aloft in honour again. And I will be his mother! I alone! My son's heart shall be mine—mine, and no other's.

[*She goes out by the tapestry door and shuts it behind her.*

Ella Rentheim (shaken and shattered). Borkman, Erhart's life will be wrecked in this storm. There must be an understanding between you and Gunhild. We must go down to her at once.

Borkman (looking at her). We? I, too, do you mean?

Ella Rentheim. Both you and I.

Borkman (shaking his head). She is hard, I tell you. Hard as the metal I once dreamed of hewing out of the rocks.

Ella Rentheim. Then try it now.

[BORKMAN *does not answer, but stands looking doubtfully at her.*

ACT III

Mrs. Borkman's *drawing-room. The lamp is still burning on the table beside the sofa. The conservatory at the back is quite dark.*

Mrs. Borkman, *with the shawl still over her head, enters, in violent agitation, by the hall door, goes up to the window, draws the curtain a little aside, and looks out; then she seats herself beside the stove, but immediately springs up again, goes to the bell-cord and rings. Stands beside the sofa and waits a moment. No one comes. Then she rings again, this time more violently.*

The Maid *presently enters from the hall. She looks sleepy and out of temper and appears to have dressed in great haste.*

Mrs. Borkman (impatiently). What has become of you, Malena? I have rung for you twice!

The Maid. Yes, ma'am, I heard you.

Mrs. Borkman. And yet you didn't come?

The Maid (sulkily). I had to put some clothes on first, I suppose.

Mrs. Borkman. Yes, you must dress yourself properly, and then you must run at once and fetch my son.

The Maid (looking at her in astonishment). You want me to fetch Mr. Erhart?

Mrs. Borkman. Yes; tell him he must come home to me at once; I want to speak to him.

The Maid (grumbling). Then I'd better go to the bailiff's and call up the coachman.

Mrs. Borkman. Why?

The Maid. To get him to harness the sledge. The snow's dreadful to-night.

Mrs. Borkman. Oh, that doesn't matter; only make haste and go. It's just round the corner.

The Maid. Why, ma'am, you can't call that just round the corner!

Mrs. Borkman. Of course it is. Don't you know Mr. Hinkel's villa?

The Maid (maliciously). Oh, indeed! It's there Mr. Erhart is this evening?

Mrs. Borkman (taken aback). Why, where else should he be?

The Maid (with a slight smile). Well, I only thought he might be where he usually is.

Mrs. Borkman. Where do you mean?

The Maid. At that Mrs. Wilton's, as they call her.

Mrs. Borkman. Mrs. Wilton's? My son isn't so often there.

The Maid (half muttering). I've heard say as he's there every day of his life.

Mrs. Borkman. That's all nonsense, Malena. Go straight to Mr. Hinkel's and try to get hold of him.

The Maid (with a toss of her head). Oh, very well; I'm going.

[*She is on the point of going out by the hall, but just at that moment the hall door is opened, and* ELLA RENTHEIM *and* BORKMAN *appear on the threshold.*

Mrs. Borkman (staggers a step backwards). What does this mean?

The Maid (terrified, instinctively folding her hands). Lord save us!

Mrs. Borkman (whispers to THE MAID*).* Tell him he must come this instant.

The Maid (softly). Yes, ma'am.

[ELLA RENTHEIM *and, after her,* BORKMAN *enter*

the room. THE MAID *sidles behind them to the door, goes out and closes it after her.*

[*A short silence.*

Mrs. Borkman (having recovered her self-control, turns to ELLA). What does he want down here in my room?

Ella Rentheim. He wants to come to an understanding with you, Gunhild.

Mrs. Borkman. He has never tried that before.

Ella Rentheim. He is going to, this evening.

Mrs. Borkman. The last time we stood face to face—it was in the Court, when I was summoned to give an account——

Borkman (coming nearer). And this evening it is *I* who will give an account of myself.

Mrs. Borkman (staring at him). You?

Borkman. Not of what I have done amiss. All the world knows that.

Mrs. Borkman (sighing bitterly). Yes, that is true; all the world knows that.

Borkman. But it does not know why I did it; why I had to do it. People do not understand that I had to, because I was myself—because I was John Gabriel Borkman—myself, and not another. And that is what I will try to explain to you.

Mrs. Borkman (shaking her head). It is no use. Temptations and promptings acquit no one.

Borkman. They may acquit one in one's own eyes.

Mrs. Borkman (with a gesture of repulsion). Oh, let all that alone! I have thought over that black business of yours enough and to spare.

Borkman. I, too. During those five endless years in my cell—and elsewhere—I had time to think it over. And during the eight years up there in the gallery I have had still more ample time. I have re-tried the whole case—by myself. Time after time I have re-tried it. I have been my own accuser, my own defender and my own judge. I have been more impartial than any one else could be—that I venture to say. I have paced up and down the gallery there, turning every one of my actions upside down and inside out. I have examined them from all sides as unsparingly, as pitilessly, as any lawyer of them all. And the final judgment I have always come to is this: the one person I have sinned against is—myself.

Mrs. Borkman. And what about me? What about your son?

Borkman. You and he are included in what I mean when I say myself.

Mrs. Borkman. And what about the hundreds of others, then—the people you are said to have ruined?

Borkman (more vehemently). I had power in my hands! And then I felt the irresistible vocation within me! The prisoned millions lay all over the country, deep in the bowels of the earth, calling aloud to me! They shrieked to me to free them! But no one else heard their cry—I alone had ears for it.

Mrs. Borkman. Yes, to the branding of the name of Borkman.

Borkman. If the others had had the power, do you think they would not have acted exactly as I did?

Mrs. Borkman. No one, no one but you would have done it!

Borkman. Perhaps not. But that would have been because they had not my brains. And if they had done it, it would not have been with my aims in view. The act would have been a different act. In short, I have acquitted myself.

Ella Rentheim (quietly and appealingly). Oh, can you say that so confidently, Borkman?

Borkman (nodding). Acquitted myself on that score. But then comes the great, crushing self-accusation.

Mrs. Borkman. What is that?

Borkman. I have skulked up there and wasted eight precious years of my life! The very day I was set free, I should have gone forth into the world—out into the steel-hard, dreamless world of reality! I should have begun at the bottom and swung myself up to the heights anew—higher than ever before—in spite of all that lay between.

Mrs. Borkman. Oh, it would only have been the same thing over again; take my word for that.

Borkman (shakes his head and looks at her with a sententious air). It is true that nothing new happens; but what has happened does not repeat itself either. It is the eye that transforms the action. The eye, born anew, transforms the old action. *(Breaking off.)* But you do not understand this.

Mrs. Borkman (curtly). No, I do not understand it.

Borkman. Ah, that is just the curse—I have never found one single soul to understand me.

Ella Rentheim (looking at him). Never, Borkman?

Borkman. Except one—perhaps. Long, long ago. In the days when I did not think I needed understanding. Since then, at any rate, no one has understood me! There has been no one alive enough to my needs to be afoot and rouse me—to ring the morning bell for me—to call me up to manful work anew. And to impress upon me that I had done nothing inexpiable.

Mrs. Borkman (with a scornful laugh). So, after all, you require to have that impressed on you from without?

Borkman (with increasing indignation). Yes, when the whole world hisses in chorus that I have sunk never to rise again, there come moments when I almost believe it myself. *(Raising his head).* But then my inmost assurance rises again triumphant; and that acquits me.

Mrs. Borkman (looking harshly at him). Why have you never come and asked me for what you call understanding?

Borkman. What use would it have been to come to you?

Mrs. Borkman (with a gesture of repulsion). You have never loved anything outside yourself; that is the secret of the whole matter.

Borkman (proudly). I have loved power.

Mrs. Borkman. Yes, power!

Borkman. The power to create human happiness in wide, wide circles around me!

Mrs. Borkman. You had once the power to make me happy. Have you used it to that end?

Borkman (without looking at her). Some one must generally go down in a shipwreck.

Mrs. Borkman. And your own son! Have you used your power—have you lived and laboured—to make him happy?

Borkman. I do not know him.

Mrs. Borkman. No, that is true. You do not even know him.

Borkman (harshly). You, his mother, have taken care of that!

Mrs. Borkman (looking at him with a lofty air). Oh, you do not know what I have taken care of!

Borkman. You?

Mrs. Borkman. Yes, I. I alone.

Borkman. Then tell me.

Mrs. Borkman. I have taken care of your memory.

Borkman (with a short dry laugh). My memory? Oh, indeed! It sounds almost as if I were dead already.

Mrs. Borkman (emphatically). And so you are.

Borkman (slowly). Yes, perhaps you are right. *(Flaring up.)* But no, no! Not yet! I have been close to the verge of death. But now I have awakened. I have come to myself. A whole life lies before me yet. I can see it awaiting me, radiant and quickening. And you—you shall see it, too.

Mrs. Borkman (raising her hand). Never dream of life again! Lie quiet where you are.

Ella Rentheim (shocked). Gunhild! Gunhild, how can you——!

Mrs. Borkman (not listening to her). I will raise the monument over your grave.

Borkman. The pillar of shame, I suppose you mean?

Mrs. Borkman (with increasing excitement). Oh, no, it shall be no pillar of metal or stone. And no one shall be suffered to carve any scornful legend on the monument I shall raise. There shall be, as it were, a quickset hedge of trees and bushes, close, close around your tomb. They shall hide away all the darkness that has been. The eyes of men and the thoughts of men shall no longer dwell on John Gabriel Borkman!

Borkman (hoarsely and cuttingly). And this labour of love you will perform?

Mrs. Borkman. Not by my own strength. I cannot think of that. But I have brought up one to help me, who shall live for this alone. His life shall be so pure and high and bright, that your burrowing in the dark shall be as though it had never been!

Borkman (darkly and threateningly). If it is Erhard you mean, say so at once!

Mrs. Borkman (looking him straight in the eyes). Yes, it is Erhart; my son; he whom you are ready to renounce in atonement for your own acts.

Borkman (with a look towards Ella*).* In atonement for my blackest sin.

Mrs. Borkman (repelling the idea). A sin towards a stranger only. Remember the sin towards me! *(Looking triumphantly at them both.)* But he will not obey you! When I cry out to him in my need, he will come to me! It is with me that he will remain! With me, and never with any one else. *(Suddenly listens and cries.)* I hear him! He is here, he is here! Erhart!

[Erhart Borkman *hastily opens the hall door and enters the room. He is wearing an overcoat and has his hat on.*

Erhart (pale and anxious). Mother! What in Heaven's name——! *(Seeing* Borkman, *who is standing beside the doorway leading into the conservatory, he starts and takes off his hat. After a moment's silence, he asks:)* What do you want with me, mother? What has happened?

Mrs. Borkman (stretching out her arms towards him). I want to see you, Erhart! I want to have you with me, always!

Erhart (stammering). Have me——? Always? What do you mean by that?

Mrs. Borkman. I will have you, I say! There is some one who wants to take you from me!

Erhart (recoiling a step). Ah—so you know?

Mrs. Borkman. Yes. Do you know it, too?

Erhart (surprised, looking at her). Do *I* know it? Yes, of course.

Mrs. Borkman. Aha, so you have planned it all out! Behind my back! Erhart! Erhart!

Erhart (quickly). Mother, tell me what it is you know!

Mrs. Borkman. I know everything. I know that your aunt has come here to take you from me.

Erhart. Aunt Ella!

Ella Rentheim. Oh, listen to me a moment, Erhart!

Mrs. Borkman (continuing). She wants me to give you up to her. She wants to stand in your mother's place to you, Erhart! She wants you to be her son, and not mine, from now on. She wants you to inherit everything from her; to renounce your own name and take hers instead!

Erhart. Aunt Ella, is this true?

Ella Rentheim. Yes, it is true.

Erhart. I knew nothing of this. Why do you want to have me with you again?

Ella Rentheim. Because I feel that I am losing you here.

Mrs. Borkman (harshly). You are losing him to me—yes. And that is just as it should be.

Ella Rentheim (looks beseechingly at him). Erhart, I

cannot afford to lose you. For, I must tell you, I am a lonely—dying woman.

Erhart. Dying—?

Ella Rentheim. Yes, dying. Will you come and be with me to the end? Attach yourself wholly to me? Be to me, as though you were my own child——?

Mrs. Borkman (interrupting). And forsake your mother, and perhaps your mission in life as well? Will you, Erhart?

Ella Rentheim. I am condemned to death. Answer me, Erhart.

Erhart (warmly, with emotion). Aunt Ella, you have been unspeakably good to me. With you I grew up in as perfect happiness as any boy can ever have known——

Mrs. Borkman. Erhart, Erhart!

Ella Rentheim. Oh, how glad I am that you can still say that!

Erhart. But I cannot sacrifice myself to you now. It is not possible for me to devote myself wholly to taking a son's place towards you.

Mrs. Borkman (triumphantly). Ah, I knew it! You shall not have him! You shall not have him, Ella!

Ella Rentheim (sadly). I see it. You have won him back.

Mrs. Borkman. Yes, yes! Mine he is, and mine he shall remain! Erhart, say it is so, dear; we two have still a long way to go together, have we not?

Erhart (struggling with himself). Mother, I may as well tell you plainly——

Mrs. Borkman (eagerly). What?

Erhart. I am afraid it is only a very little way you and I can go together.

Mrs. Borkman (as though thunderstruck). What do you mean by that?

Erhart (summoning up spirit). Good heavens, mother, I am young, after all! I feel as if the close air of this room must stifle me in the end.

Mrs. Borkman. Close air? Here—with me?

Erhart. Yes, here with you, mother.

Ella Rentheim. Then come with me, Erhart.

Erhart. Oh, Aunt Ella, it's not a whit better with you. It's different, but no better—no better for me. It smells of rose-leaves and lavender there, too; it is as airless there as here.

Mrs. Borkman (shaken, but having recovered her composure with an effort). Airless in your mother's room, you say!

Erhart (with growing impatience). Yes, I don't know how else to express it. All this morbid watchfulness and —and idolisation, or whatever you like to call it—— I can't endure it any longer!

Mrs. Borkman (with deep solemnity). Have you forgotten what you have consecrated your life to, Erhart?

Erhart (in an outbrust). Oh, say rather what you have consecrated my life to. You, you have been my will. You have never given me leave to have any of my own. But now I cannot bear this yoke any longer. I am young; remember that, mother. *(With a polite, considerate glance towards* BORKMAN.*)* I cannot consecrate my life to making atonement for another—whoever that other may be.

Mrs. Borkman (seized with a growing anxiety). Who has transformed you, Erhart?

Erhart. Who? Can you not conceive that it is I myself?

Mrs. Borkman. No, no, no! You have come under some strange power. You are not in your mother's power any longer; nor in your—your foster-mother's either.

Erhart (with laboured defiance). I am in my own power, mother! And working my own will!

Borkman (advancing towards ERHART*).* Then perhaps my hour has come at last.

Erhart (distantly and with calculated politeness). How so? How do you mean, sir?

Mrs. Borkman (scornfully). Yes, you may well ask that.

Borkman (proceeding undisturbed). Listen, Erhart—will you not cast in your lot with your father? It is not through any other man's life that a man who has fallen can be raised up again. These are only empty fables that have been told to you down here in the airless room. If you were to set yourself to live your life like all the saints together, it would be of no use whatever to me.

Erhart (with measured respectfulness). That is very true indeed.

Borkman. Yes, it is. And it would be of no use either if I should resign myself to wither away in abject penitence. I have tried to feed myself upon hopes and dreams, all through these years. But I am not the man to be content with that; and now I mean to have done with dreaming.

Erhart (with a slight bow). And what will—what will you do, sir?

Borkman. I will work out my own redemption, that is what I will do. I will begin at the bottom again. It is only through his present and his future that a man can atone for his past. Through work, indefatigable work, for all that, in my youth, seemed to give life its meaning—and that now seems a thousand times greater than it did then. Erhart, will you join with me and help me in this new life?

Mrs. Borkman (raising her hand warningly). Do not do it, Erhart!

Ella Rentheim (warmly). Yes, yes, do it! Oh, help him, Erhart!

Mrs. Borkman. And you advise him to do that? You, the lonely, dying woman.

Ella Rentheim. I don't care about myself.

Mrs. Borkman. No, so long as it is not I that take him from you.

Ella Rentheim. Precisely so, Gunhild.

Borkman. Will you, Erhart?

Erhart (torn with pain). Father, I cannot now. It is utterly impossible.

Borkman. What do you want to do then?

Erhart (with a sudden glow). I am young! I want to live, for once in a way, as well as other people! I want to live my own life!

Ella Rentheim. You cannot give up two or three little months to brighten the close of a poor waning life?

Erhart. I cannot, Aunt, however much I may wish to.

Ella Rentheim. Not for the sake of one who loves you so dearly?

Erhart. I solemnly assure you, Aunt Ella, I cannot.

Mrs. Borkman (looking intently at him). And your mother has no power over you either, any more?

Erhart. I will always love you, mother; but I cannot go on living for you alone. This is no life for me.

Borkman. Then come and join with me, after all! For life, life means work, Erhart. Come, we two will go forth into life and work together!

Erhart (passionately). Yes, but I don't want to work now! For I am young! That's what I never realised before; but now the knowledge is tingling through every vein in my body. I will not work! I will only live, live, live!

Mrs. Borkman (with a cry of divination). Erhart, what will you live for?

Erhart (with sparkling eyes). For happiness, mother!

Mrs. Borkman. And where do you think you can find that?

Erhart. I have found it, already!

Mrs. Borkman (shrieks). Erhart!

[ERHART *goes quickly to the hall door and throws it open.*

Erhart (calls out). Fanny, you can come in now!

[MRS. WILTON, *in outdoor wraps, appears on the threshold.*

Mrs. Borkman (with hands aloft). Mrs. Wilton!

Mrs. Wilton (hesitating, with an enquiring glance at ERHART*).* Do you want me to——?

Erhart. Yes, now you can come in. I have told them everything.

[MRS. WILTON *comes forward into the room.* ERHART *closes the door behind her. She bows formally to* BORKMAN, *who returns her bow in silence. A short pause.*

Mrs. Wilton (in a subdued firm voice). So the word has been spoken—and I suppose you all think I have brought a great calamity upon this house?

Mrs. Borkman (slowly, looking hard at her). You have crushed the last remnant of interest in life for me. *(With an outburst.)* But all this—all this is utterly impossible!

Mrs. Wilton. I can quite understand that it must appear impossible to you, Mrs. Borkman.

Mrs. Borkman. Yes, you can surely see for yourself that it is impossible. Or what——?

Mrs. Wilton. I should rather say that it seems highly improbable. But it's so, none the less.

Mrs. Borkman (turning). Are you really in earnest about this, Erhart?

Erhart. This means happiness for me, mother—all the beauty and happiness of life. That is all I can say to you.

Mrs. Borkman (clenching her hands together; to MRS. WILTON*).* Oh, how you have cajoled and deluded my unhappy son!

Mrs. Wilton (raising her head proudly). I have done nothing of the sort.

Mrs. Borkman. You have not, you say!

Mrs. Wilton. No. I have neither cajoled nor deluded him. Erhart came to me of his own free will. And of my own free will I went out half-way to meet him.

Mrs. Borkman (measuring her scornfully with her eye). Yes, indeed! That I can easily believe.

Mrs. Wilton (with self-control). Mrs. Borkman, there

are forces in human life that you seem to know very little about.

Mrs. Borkman. What forces, may I ask?

Mrs. Wilton. The forces which ordain that two people shall join their lives together, indissolubly—and fearlessly.

Mrs. Borkman (with a smile). I thought you were already indissolubly bound—to another.

Mrs. Wilton (abruptly). That other has deserted me.

Mrs. Borkman. But he is still living, they say.

Mrs. Wilton. He's dead to me.

Erhart (insistently). Yes, mother, he is dead to Fanny. And besides, this other makes no difference to me!

Mrs. Borkman (looking sternly at him). So you know all this—about the other.

Erhart. Yes, mother, I know quite well—all about it!

Mrs. Borkman. And yet you can say that it makes no difference to you?

Erhart (with defiant petulance). I can only tell you that it is happiness I must have! I am young! I want to live, live, live!

Mrs. Borkman. Yes, you are young, Erhart. Too young for this.

Mrs. Wilton (firmly and earnestly). You must not think, Mrs. Borkman, that I haven't said the same to him. I have laid my whole life before him. Again and again I have reminded him that I am seven years older than he——

Erhart (interrupting). Oh, nonsense, Fanny—I knew that all the time.

Mrs. Wilton. But nothing—nothing was of any use.

Mrs. Borkman. Indeed? Nothing? Then why did you not dismiss him without more ado? Close your door to him? You should have done that, and done it in time!

Mrs. Wilton (looks at her and says in a low voice). I could not do that, Mrs. Borkman.

Mrs. Borkman. Why could you not?

Mrs. Wilton. Because for me, too, this meant happiness.

Mrs. Borkman (scornfully). H'm, happiness, happiness——

Mrs. Wilton. I have never before known happiness in life. And I cannot possibly drive happiness away from me, merely because it comes so late.

Mrs. Borkman. And how long do you think this happiness will last?

Erhart (interrupting). Whether it lasts or does not last, mother, it doesn't matter now!

Mrs. Borkman (angrily). Blind boy that you are! Do you not see where all this is leading you?

Erhart. I don't want to look into the future. I don't want to look around me in any direction; I am only determined to live my own life—at last!

Mrs. Borkman (with anguish). And you call this life, Erhart!

Erhart. Don't you see how lovely she is!

Mrs. Borkman (wringing her hands). And I have to bear this load of shame as well!

Borkman (at the back, harshly and cuttingly). Ho—you are used to bearing things of that sort, Gunhild!

Ella Rentheim (imploringly). Borkman!

Erhart. Father!

Mrs. Borkman. Day after day I shall have to see my own son linked to a—a——

Erhart (interrupting her harshly). You shall see nothing of the kind, mother! You may make your mind easy on that point. I shall not remain here.

Mrs. Wilton (quickly and decisively). We are going away, Mrs. Borkman.

Mrs. Borkman (turning pale). Are you going away, too? Together, no doubt?

Mrs. Wilton (nodding). Yes, I am going abroad, to the South. I am taking a young girl with me. And Erhart is going along with us.

Mrs. Borkman. With you—and a young girl?

Mrs. Wilton. Yes. It is little Frida Foldal, whom I have had living with me. I want her to go abroad and get more instruction in music.

Mrs. Borkman. So you are taking her with you?

Mrs. Wilton. Yes; I can't well send her out into the world alone.

Mrs. Borkman (suppressing a smile). What do you say to this, Erhart?

Erhart (embarrassed, shrugging his shoulders). Well, mother, since Fanny will have it so——

Mrs. Borkman (coldly). And when does this distinguished party set out, if one may ask?

Mrs. Wilton. We are going at once—to-night. My covered sledge is waiting on the road, outside the Hinkels'.

Mrs. Borkman (appraising her from head to foot). Aha! so that was what the party meant?

Mrs. Wilton (smiling). Yes, Erhart and I were the whole party. And little Frida, of course.

Mrs. Borkman. And where is she now?

Mrs. Wilton. She is sitting in the sledge waiting for us.

Erhart (in painful embarrassment). Mother, surely you can understand? I would have spared you all this—you and every one.

Mrs. Borkman (looks at him, deeply pained). You would have gone away from me without saying good-bye?

Erhart. Yes, I thought that would be best; best for all of us. Our boxes were packed and everything settled. But of course when you sent for me, I—— *(Holding out his hands to her.)* Good-bye, mother.

Mrs. Borkman (with a gesture of repulsion). Don't touch me!

Erhart (gently). Is that your last word?

Mrs. Borkman (sternly). Yes.

Erhart (turning). Good-bye to you, then, Aunt Ella.

Ella Rentheim (clasping his hands). Good-bye, Erhart!

And live your life—and be as happy—as happy as ever you can.

Erhart. Thanks, Aunt. *(Bowing to* BORKMAN.*)* Good-bye, father. *(Whispers to* MRS. WILTON.*)* Let us get away, the sooner the better.

Mrs. Wilton (in a whisper). Yes, let us.

Mrs. Borkman (with a malignant smile). Mrs. Wi'ton, do you think you are acting quite wisely in taking that girl with you?

Mrs. Wilton (returning the smile, half ironically, half seriously). Men are so unstable, Mrs. Borkman. And women, too. When Erhart is done with me—and I with him—then it will be well for us both that he, poor fellow, should have some one to fall back upon.

Mrs. Borkman. But you yourself?

Mrs. Wilton. Oh, I shall know what to do, I assure you. Good-bye to you all!

[*She bows and goes out by the hall door.* ERHART *stands for a moment as though wavering; then he turns and follows her.*

Mrs. Borkman (dropping her folded hands). Childless.

Borkman (as though awakened to a resolution). Then out into the storm alone! My hat! My cloak!

[*He goes hastily towards the door.*

Ella Rentheim (in terror, stopping him). John Gabriel, where are you going?

Borkman. Out into the storm of life, I tell you. Let me go, Ella!

Ella Rentheim (restraining him). No, no, I won't let you out! You are ill. I can see it in your face!

Borkman. Let me go, I tell you!

[*He tears himself away from her and goes out by the hall.*

Ella Rentheim (in the doorway). Help me to hold him, Gunhild!

Mrs. Borkman (coldly and sharply, standing in the middle of the room). I will not try to hold any one in all the world. Let them go away from me—both the one and the other! As far—as far as ever they please. *(Suddenly, with a piercing shriek.)* Erhart, don't leave me!

[*She rushes with outstretched arms towards the door.* ELLA RENTHEIM *stops her.*

ACT IV

An open space outside the main building, which lies to the right. A projecting corner of it is visible, with a door approached by a flight of low stone steps. The background consists of steep fir-clad slopes, quite near. On the left a fringe of trees, forming the margin of a wood. The snowstorm has ceased; but the newly fallen snow has drifted deep around. The fir-branches droop under heavy loads of snow. The night is dark, with drifting clouds. Now and then the moon gleams out faintly. Only a dim light is reflected from the snow.

BORKMAN, MRS. BORKMAN *and* ELLA RENTHEIM *are standing upon the steps,* BORKMAN *leaning wearily against the wall of the house. He has an old-fashioned cape thrown over his shoulders, holds a soft grey felt hat in one hand and a thick knotted stick in the other.* ELLA RENTHEIM *carries her cloak over her arm.* MRS. BORKMAN'S *great shawl has slipped down over her shoulders, so that her hair is uncovered.*

Ella Rentheim (barring the way for MRS. BORKMAN*).* Don't go after him, Gunhild!

Mrs. Borkman (in fear and agitation). Let me pass, I say! He must not go away from me!

Ella Rentheim. It is utterly useless, I tell you! You will never overtake him.

Mrs. Borkman. Let me go, Ella! I will cry aloud after him all down the road. And he must hear his mother's cry!

Ella Rentheim. He cannot hear you. You may be sure he is in the sledge already.

Mrs. Borkman. No, no; he can't be in the sledge yet!

Ella Rentheim. The doors are closed upon him long ago, believe me.

Mrs. Borkman (despairingly). If he is in the sledge, then he is there with her, with her—her!

Borkman laughing (gloomily). Then he probably won't hear his mother's cry.

Mrs. Borkman. No, he will not hear it. *(Listening.)* Hark! what is that?

Ella Rentheim (also listening). It sounds like sledge-bells.

Mrs. Borkman (with a suppressed scream). It is her sledge!

Ella Rentheim. Perhaps it's another.

Mrs. Borkman. No, no, it is Mrs. Wilton's covered sledge! I know the silver bells! Hark! Now they are driving right past here, at the foot of the hill!

Ella Rentheim (quickly). Gunhild, if you want to cry out to him, now is the time! Perhaps after all——! *(The tinkle of the bells sounds close at hand, in the wood.)* Make haste, Gunhild! Now they are right under us!

Mrs. Borkman (stands for a moment undecided, then she stiffens and says sternly and coldly). No. I will not cry out to him. Let Erhart Borkman pass away from me—far, far away—to what he calls life and happiness.

[*The sound of the bells dies away in the distance.*

Ella Rentheim (after a pause) Now the bells are out of hearing.

Mrs. Borkman. They sounded like funeral bells.

Borkman (with a dry laugh). Oho—it is not for me they are ringing to-night!

Mrs. Borkman. No, but for me—and for him who has gone from me.

Ella Rentheim (nodding thoughtfully). Who knows if, after all, they may not be ringing in life and happiness for him, Gunhild.

Mrs. Borkman (suddenly animated, looking hard at her). Life and happiness, you say!

Ella Rentheim. For a little while at any rate.

Mrs. Borkman. Could you endure to let him know life and happiness, with her?

Ella Rentheim (with warmth and feeling). Indeed I could, with all my heart and soul!

Mrs. Borkman (coldly). Then you must be richer than I am in the power of love.

Ella Rentheim (looking far away). Perhaps it is the lack of love that keeps that power alive.

Mrs. Borkman (fixing her eyes on her). If that is so, then I shall soon be as rich as you, Ella.

[*She turns and goes into the house.*

Ella Rentheim (stands for a time looking with a troubled expression at Borkman; *then lays her hand cautiously upon his shoulder).* Come, John—you must come in, too.

Borkman (as if awakening). I?

Ella Rentheim. Yes, this winter air is too keen for you; I can see that, John. So come—come in with me—into the house, into the warmth.

Borkman (angrily). Up to the gallery again, I suppose.

Ella Rentheim. No, rather into the room below.

Borkman (his anger flaming). Never will I set foot under that roof again!

Ella Rentheim. Where will you go then? So late, and in the dark, John?

Borkman (putting on his hat). First of all, I will go out and see to all my buried treasures.

Ella Rentheim (looking anxiously at him). John—I don't understand you.

Borkman (with laughter, interrupted by coughing). Oh, it is not hidden plunder I mean; don't be afraid of that, Ella. *(Stopping, and pointing.)* Do you see that man there? Who is it?

[Vilhelm Foldal, *in an old cape, covered with*

snow, with his hat-brim turned down, and a large umbrella in his hand, advances towards the corner of the house, laboriously stumbling through the snow. He is noticeably lame in his left foot.

Borkman. Vilhelm! What do you want with me again?

Foldal (looking up). Good heavens, are you out on the steps, John Gabriel? *(Bowing.)* And Mrs. Borkman, too, I see.

Borkman (abruptly). This is not Mrs. Borkman.

Foldal. Oh, I beg pardon. You see, I have lost my spectacles in the snow. But how is it that you, who never put your foot out of doors——?

Borkman (carelessly and gaily). It is high time I should come out into the open air again, don't you see? Nearly three years in detention—five years in prison—eight years in the gallery up there——

Ella Rentheim (distressed). Borkman, I beg you——

Foldal. Ah, yes, yes, yes!

Borkman. But I want to know what has brought you here.

Foldal (still standing at the foot of the steps). I wanted to come up to you, John Gabriel. I felt I must come to you, in the gallery. Ah, me, that gallery——!

Borkman. Did you want to come up to me after I had shown you the door?

Foldal. Oh, I couldn't let that stand in the way.

Borkman. What have you done to your foot? I see you are limping?

Foldal. Yes, what do you think—I have been run over.

Ella Rentheim. Run over!

Foldal. Yes, by a covered sledge.

Borkman. Oho!

Foldal. With two horses. They came down the hill at a tearing gallop. I couldn't get out of the way quick enough; and so——

Ella Rentheim. And so they ran over you?

Foldal. They came right down upon me, madam—or miss. They came right upon me and sent me rolling over and over in the snow—so that I lost my spectacles and got my umbrella broken. *(Rubbing his leg.)* And my ankle a little hurt, too.

Borkman (laughing inwardly). Do you know who was in that sledge, Vilhelm?

Foldal. No, how could I see? It was a covered sledge, and the curtains were down. And the driver didn't stop a moment after he had sent me spinning. But it doesn't matter a bit, for—— *(With an outburst.)* Oh, I am so happy, so happy!

Borkman. Happy?

Foldal. Well, I don't exactly know what to call it. But I think happy is the nearest word. For something so wonderful has happened! And that is why I couldn't help—I had to come out and share my happiness with you, John Gabriel.

Borkman (harshly). Well, share away then!

Ella Rentheim. Oh, but first take your friend indoors with you, Borkman.

Borkman (sternly). I have told you I will not go into the house.

Ella Rentheim. But don't you hear, he has been run over!

Borkman. Oh, we are all of us run over, sometime or other in life. The thing is to jump up again and let no one see you are hurt.

Foldal. That is a profound saying, John Gabriel. But I can easily tell you my story out here, in a few words.

Borkman (more mildly). Yes, please do, Vilhelm.

Foldal. Well, now you shall hear! Only think, when I got home this evening after I had been with you, what did I find but a letter. Can you guess who it was from?

Borkman. Possibly from your little Frida?

Foldal. Precisely! Think of your hitting on it at once!

Yes, it was a long—a pretty long letter from Frida. A footman had brought it. And can you imagine what was in it?

Borkman. Perhaps it was to say good-bye to her mother and you?

Foldal. Exactly! How good you are at guessing, John Gabriel. Yes, she tells me that Mrs. Wilton has taken such a fancy to her, and she is to go abroad with her and study music. And Mrs. Wilton has engaged a first-rate teacher who is to accompany them on the journey—and to read with Frida, too. For, unfortunately, she has been a good deal neglected in some branches, you see.

Borkman (shaken with inward laughter). Of course, of course—I see it all quite clearly, Vilhelm.

Foldal (continuing eagerly). And only think, she knew nothing about the arrangement until this evening; at that party, you know, h'm! And yet she found time to write to me. And the letter is such a beautiful one—so warm and affectionate, I assure you. There is not a trace of contempt for her father in it. And then what a delicate thought it was to say good-bye to us by letter—before she started. *(Laughing.)* But of course I can't let her go like that.

Borkman (looks inquiringly at him). How so?

Foldal. She tells me that they start early to-morrow morning; quite early.

Borkman. Oh, indeed—to-morrow? Does she tell you that?

Foldal (laughing and rubbing his hands). Yes; but I know a trick worth two of that, you see! I am going straight up to Mrs. Wilton's——

Borkman. This evening?

Foldal. Oh, it's not so very late yet. And even if the house is shut up, I shall ring; without hesitation. For I must and will see Frida before she starts. Good-night, good-night!

[*Makes a movement to go.*

Borkman. Stop a moment, my poor Vilhelm; you may spare yourself that heavy bit of road.

Foldal. Oh, you are thinking of my ankle——

Borkman. Yes; and in any case you won't get in at Mrs. Wilton's.

Foldal. Yes, indeed I will. I'll ring and knock till some one comes and lets me in. For I must and will see Frida

Ella Rentheim. Your daughter has gone already, Mr. Foldal.

Foldal (thunderstruck). Has Frida gone already! Are you quite sure? Who told you?

Borkman. We had it from her future teacher.

Foldal. Indeed? And who is he?

Borkman. A certain Mr. Erhart Borkman.

Foldal (beaming with joy). Your son, John Gabriel! Is he going with them?

Borkman. Yes; it is he that is to help Mrs. Wilton with little Frida's education.

Foldal. Oh, Heaven be praised! Then the child is in the best of hands. But is it quite certain that they have started with her already?

Borkman. They took her away in that sledge which ran over you on the road.

Foldal (clasping his hands). To think that my little Frida was in that magnificent sledge!

Borkman (nodding). Yes, yes, Vilhelm, your daughter has come to drive in her carriage. And Master Erhart, too. Tell me, did you notice the silver bells?

Foldal. Yes, indeed. Silver bells did you say? Were they silver? Real, genuine silver bells?

Borkman. You may be quite sure of that. Everything was genuine—both outside and in.

Foldal (with quiet intensity). Isn't it strange how fortune can sometimes befriend one? It is my—my little gift of song that has transmuted itself into music in Frida. So after all, it is not for nothing that I was born a poet. Fonow she is going forth into the great wide world, that I once yearned so passionately to see. Little Frida sets out in a splendid covered sledge with silver bells on the harness——

Borkman. And runs over her father.

Foldal (happily). Oh, pooh! What does it matter about me, if only the child——! Well, so I am too late, then, after all. I must just go home and comfort her mother. I left her crying in the kitchen.

Borkman. Crying?

Foldal (smiling). Yes, would you believe it, she was crying her eyes out when I came away.

Borkman. And you are laughing, Vilhelm?

Foldal. Yes, *I* am, of course. But she, poor thing, she doesn't know any better, you see. Well, good-bye! It's a good thing I have the tramway so handy. Good-bye, good-bye, John Gabriel. Good-bye, Madam.

[*He bows and limps laboriously out the way he came.*

Borkman (stands silent for a moment, gazing before him). Good-bye, Vilhelm! It is not the first time in your life that you've been run over, old friend.

Ella Rentheim (looking at him with suppressed anxiety). You are so pale, John, so very pale.

Borkman. That is the effect of the prison air up yonder.

Ella Rentheim. I have never seen you like this before.

Borkman. No, for I suppose you have never seen an escaped convict before.

Ella Rentheim. Oh, do come into the house with me, John!

Borkman. It is no use trying to lure me in. I have told you——

Ella Rentheim. But when I beg and implore you——? For your own sake——

[THE MAID *opens the door, and stands in the doorway.*

The Maid. I beg pardon. Mrs. Borkman told me to lock the front door now.

Borkman (in a low voice, to Ella*).* You see, they want to lock me up again!

Ella Rentheim (to The Maid*).* Mr. Borkman is not quite well. He wants to have a little fresh air before coming in.

The Maid. But Mrs. Borkman told me to——

Ella Rentheim. I shall lock the door. Just leave the key in the lock.

The Maid. Oh, very well; I'll leave it.

[*She goes into the house again.*

Borkman (stands silent for a moment and listens; then goes hastily down the steps and out into the open space). Now I am outside the walls, Ella! Now they will never get hold of me again!

Ella Rentheim (who has gone down to him). But you are a free man in there, too, John. You can come and go just as you please.

Borkman (softly, as though in terror). Never under a roof again! It is so good to be out here in the night. If I went up into the gallery now, ceiling and walls would shrink together and crush me—crush me flat as a fly.

Ella Rentheim. But where will you go, then?

Borkman. I will simply go on, and on and on. I will try if I cannot make my way to freedom, and life and human beings again. Will you go with me, Ella?

Ella Rentheim. I? Now?

Borkman. Yes, at once!

Ella Rentheim. But how far?

Borkman. As far as ever I can.

Ella Rentheim. Oh, but think what you are doing! Out in this raw, cold winter night——

Borkman (in a very hoarse voice). Oho—my lady is concerned about her health? Yes, yes—I know it is delicate.

Ella Rentheim. It is your health I am concerned about.

Borkman. Hohoho! A dead man's health! I can't help laughing at you, Ella!

[*He moves onwards.*

Ella Rentheim (following him, holding him back). What did you call yourself?

Borkman. A dead man, I said. Don't you remember, Gunhild told me to lie quiet where I was?

Ella Rentheim (with resolution, throwing her cloak around her). I will go with you, John.

Borkman. Yes, we two belong to each other, Ella. *(Advancing.)* So come!

[*They have gradually passed into the low wood on the left. It conceals them little by little, until they are quite lost to sight. The house and the open space disappear. The landscape, consisting of wooded slopes and ridges, slowly changes and grows wilder and wilder.*

Ella Rentheim's Voice (is heard in the wood to the right). Where are we going, John? I don't recognise this place.

Borkman's Voice (higher up). Just follow my footprints in the snow!

Ella Rentheim's Voice. But why need we climb so high?

Borkman's Voice (nearer at hand). We must go up the winding path.

Ella Rentheim (still hidden). Oh, but I can't go much further.

Borkman (on the edge of the wood to the right). Come, come! We are not far from the view now. There used to be a seat there.

Ella Rentheim (appearing among the trees). Do you remember it?

Borkman. You can rest there.

[*They have emerged upon a small high-lying, open plateau in the wood. The mountain rises abruptly behind them. To the left, far below, an extensive fiord landscape, with high ranges in the distance, towering one above the other. On the plateau, to the left, a dead fir-tree with a bench under it. The snow lies deep upon the plateau.*

BORKMAN *and, after him,* ELLA RENTHEIM *enter from the right and wade with difficulty through the snow.*

Borkman (stopping at the verge of the steep declivity on the left). Come here, Ella, and you shall see.

Ella Rentheim (coming up to him). What do you want to show me, John?

Borkman (pointing outwards). Do you see how free and open the country lies before us—away to the far horizon?

Ella Rentheim. We have often sat on this bench before and looked out into a much, much further distance.

Borkman. It was a dreamland we then looked out over.

Ella Rentheim (nodding sadly). It was the dreamland of our life, yes. And now that land is buried in snow. And the old tree is dead.

Borkman (not listening to her). Can you see the smoke of the great steamships out on the fiord?

Ella Rentheim. No.

Borkman. I can. They come and they go. They weave a network of fellowship all round the world. They shed light and warmth over the souls of men in many thousands of homes. That was what I dreamed of doing.

Ella Rentheim (softly). And it remained a dream.

Borkman. It remained a dream, yes. *(Listening.)* And hark, down by the river, dear! The factories are working! My factories! All those that I would have created! Listen! Do you hear them humming? The night shift is on—so they are working night and day. Hark! hark! the wheels are whirling and the bands are flashing—round and round and round. Can't you hear, Ella?

Ella Rentheim. No.

Borkman. I can hear it.

Ella Rentheim (anxiously). I think you are mistaken, John.

Borkman (more and more inspired). Oh, but all these—they are only like the outworks around the kingdom, I tell you!

Ella Rentheim. The kingdom, you say? What kingdom?

Borkman. My kingdom, of course! The kingdom I was on the point of conquering when I—when I died.

Ella Rentheim (shaken, in a low voice). Oh, John, John!

Borkman. And now there it lies—defenceless, masterless—exposed to all the robbers and plunderers. Ella, do you see the mountain chains there—far away? They soar, they tower aloft, one behind the other! That is my vast, my infinite, inexhaustible kingdom!

Ella Rentheim. Oh, but there comes an icy blast from that kingdom, John!

Borkman. That blast is the breath of life to me. That blast comes to me like a greeting from subject spirits. I seem to touch them, the prisoned millions; I can see the veins of metal stretch out their winding, branching, luring arms to me. I saw them before my eyes like living shapes, that night when I stood in the strong-room with the candle in my hand. You begged to be liberated, and I tried to free you. But my strength failed me; and the treasure sank back into the deep again. *(With outstretched hands.)* But I will whisper it to you here in the stillness of the night: I love you, as you lie there spellbound in the deeps and the darkness! I love you, unborn treasures, yearning for the light! I love you, with all your shining train of power and glory! I love you, love you, love you!

Ella Rentheim (in suppressed but rising agitation). Yes, your love is still down there, John. It has always been rooted there. But here, in the light of day, here there was a living, warm, human heart that throbbed and glowed for you. And this heart you crushed. Oh, worse than that! Ten times worse! You sold it for—for——

Borkman (trembles; a cold shudder seems to go through him). For the kingdom—and the power—and the glory—you mean?

Ella Rentheim. Yes, that is what I mean. I have said it once before to-night: you have murdered the love-life in the woman who loved you. And whom you loved in return, so far as you could love any one. *(With uplifted arm.)* And therefore I prophesy to you, John Gabriel Borkman—you will never touch the price you demanded for the murder. You will never enter in triumph into your cold, dark kingdom!

Borkman (staggers to the bench and seats himself heavily). I almost fear your prophecy will come true, Ella.

Ella Rentheim (going up to him). You must not fear it, John. That is the best thing that can happen to you.

Borkman (with a shriek; clutching at his breast). Ah——! *(Feebly.)* Now it let me go again.

Ella Rentheim (shaking him). What was it, John?

Borkman (sinking down against the back of the seat). It was a hand of ice that clutched at my heart.

Ella Rentheim. John! Did you feel the ice-hand again!

Borkman (murmurs). No. No ice-hand. It was a metal hand.

[*He sinks down upon the bench.*

Ella Rentheim (tears off her cloak and throws it over him). Lie still where you are! I will go and bring help for you.

[*She goes a step or two towards the right; then she stops, returns and carefully feels his pulse and touches his face.*

Ella Rentheim (softly and firmly). No. It is best so, John Borkman. Best so for you.

[*She spreads the cloak tighter around him and*

sinks down in the snow in front of the porch. A short silence.

[MRS. BORKMAN, *wrapped in a mantle, comes through the wood on the right.* THE MAID *goes before her carrying a lantern.*

The Maid (throwing the light upon the snow). Yes, yes, ma'am, here are their tracks.

Mrs. Borkman (peering around). Yes, here they are! They are sitting there on the bench. *(Calls.)* Ella!

Ella Rentheim (rising). Are you looking for us?

Mrs. Borkman (sternly). Yes, you see I have to.

Ella Rentheim (pointing). Look, there he lies, Gunhild.

Mrs. Borkman. Sleeping?

Ella Rentheim. A long, deep sleep, I think.

Mrs. Borkman (with an outburst). Ella! *(Controls herself and asks in a low voice.)* Did he do it—of his own accord?

Ella Rentheim. No.

Mrs. Borkman (relieved). Not by his own hand then?

Ella Rentheim. No. It was an ice-cold metal hand that gripped him by the heart.

Mrs. Borkman (to THE MAID*).* Go for help. Get the men to come up from the farm.

The Maid. Yes, I will, ma'am. *(To herself.)* Lord save us!

[*She goes out through the wood to the right.*

Mrs. Borkman (standing behind the bench). So the night air has killed him——

Ella Rentheim. So it appears.

Mrs. Borkman. ——strong man that he was.

Ella Rentheim (coming in front of the bench). Will you not look at him, Gunhild?

Mrs. Borkman (with a gesture of repulsion). No, no, no. *(Lowering her voice.)* He was a miner's son, John Gabriel Borkman. He could not live in the fresh air.

Ella Rentheim. It was rather the cold that killed him.

Mrs. Borkman (shakes her head). The cold, you say? The cold—that had killed him long ago.

Ella Rentheim (nodding to her). Yes—and changed us two into shadows.

Mrs. Borkman. You are right there.

Ella Rentheim (with a painful smile). A dead man and two shadows—that is what the cold has made of us.

Mrs. Borkman. Yes, the coldness of heart.—And now I think we two may hold out our hands to each other, Ella.

Ella Rentheim. I think we may, now.

Mrs. Borkman. We twin sisters—over him we have both loved.

Ella Rentheim. We two shadows—over the dead man.

[MRS. BORKMAN *behind the bench, and* ELLA RENTHEIM *in front of it, take each other's hand.*

THE WILD DUCK
(1884)

CHARACTERS

WERLE, *a merchant, manufacturer, etc.*
GREGERS WERLE, *his son.*
OLD EKDAL.
HIALMAR EKDAL, *his son, a photographer.*
GINA EKDAL, *Hjalmar's wife.*
HEDVIG, *their daughter, a girl of fourteen.*
MRS. SÖRBY, *Werle's housekeeper.*
RELLING, *a doctor.*
MOLVIK, *student of theology.*
GRÅBERG, *Werle's bookkeeper.*
PETTERSEN, *Werle's servant.*
JENSEN, *a hired waiter.*
A FLABBY GENTLEMAN.
A THIN-HAIRED GENTLEMAN.
A SHORT-SIGHTED GENTLEMAN.
SIX OTHER GENTLEMEN, *guests at Werle's dinner-party.*
SEVERAL HIRED WAITERS.

The first act passes in WERLE'S *house, the remaining acts at* HJALMAR EKDAL'S.

Pronunciation of Names: GREGERS WERLE = Grayghers Verlë; HIALMAR EKDAL = Yalmar Aykdal; GINA = Cheena; GRÅBERG = Groberg; JENSEN = Yensen.

THE WILD DUCK

ACT I

At Werle's *house. A richly and comfortably furnished study; bookcases and upholstered furniture; a writing-table, with papers and documents, in the centre of the room; lighted lamps with green shades, giving a subdued light. At the back, open folding-doors with curtains drawn back. Within is seen a large and handsome room, brilliantly lighted with lamps and branching candlesticks. In front, on the right (in the study), a small baize door leads into* Werle's *office. On the left, in front, a fireplace with a glowing coal fire, and farther back a double door leading into the dining-room.*

Werle's *servant,* Pettersen, *in livery, and* Jensen, *the hired waiter, in black, are putting the study in order. In the large room, two or three other hired waiters are moving about, arranging things and lighting more candles. From the dining-room, the hum of conversation and laughter of many voices are heard; a glass is tapped with a knife; silence follows, and a toast is proposed; shouts of "Bravo!" and then again a buzz of conversation.*

Pettersen (lights a lamp on the chimney-place and places a shade over it). Hark to them, Jensen! now the old man's on his legs holding a long palaver about Mrs. Sörby.

Jensen (pushing forward an armchair). Is it true, what folks say, that they're—very good friends, eh?

Pettersen. Lord knows.

Jensen. I've heard tell as he's been a lively customer in his day.

Pettersen. May be.

Jensen. And he's giving this spread in honour of his son, they say.

Pettersen. Yes. His son came home yesterday.

Jensen. This is the first time I ever heard as Mr. Werle had a son.

Pettersen. Oh, yes, he has a son, right enough. But he's a fixture, as you might say, up at the Höidal works. He's never once come to town all the years I've been in service here.

A Waiter (in the doorway of the other room). Pettersen, here's an old fellow wanting——

Pettersen (mutters). The devil—who's this now?

OLD EKDAL *appears from the right, in the inner room. He is dressed in a threadbare overcoat with a high collar; he wears woollen mittens and carries in his hand a stick and a fur cap. Under his arm, a brown paper parcel. Dirty red-brown wig and small grey moustache.*

Pettersen (goes towards him). Good Lord—what do you want here?

Ekdal (in the doorway). Must get into the office, Pettersen.

Pettersen. The office was closed an hour ago, and——

Ekdal. So they told me at the front door. But Gråberg's in there still. Let me slip in this way, Pettersen; there's a good fellow. *(Points towards the baize door.)* It's not the first time I've come this way.

Pettersen. Well, you may pass. *(Opens the door.)* But mind you go out again the proper way, for we've got company.

Ekdal. I know, I know—h'm! Thanks, Pettersen, good old friend! Thanks! *(Mutters softly.)* Ass!

[*He goes into the office;* PETTERSEN *shuts the door after him.*

Jensen. Is he one of the office people?

Pettersen. No he's only an outside hand that does odd jobs of copying. But he's been a tip-topper in his day, has old Ekdal.

Jensen. You can see he's been through a lot.

Pettersen. Yes; he was an army officer, you know.

Jensen. You don't say so?

Pettersen. No mistake about it. But then he went into the timber trade or something of the sort. They say he once played Mr. Werle a very nasty trick. They were partners in the Höidal works at the time. Oh, I know old Ekdal well, I do. Many a nip of bitters and bottle of ale we two have drunk at Madam Eriksen's.

Jensen. He don't look as if he'd much to stand treat with.

Pettersen. Why, bless you, Jensen, it's me that stands treat. I always think there's no harm in being a bit civil to folks that have seen better days.

Jensen. Did he go bankrupt, then?

Pettersen. Worse than that. He went to prison.

Jensen. To prison!

Pettersen. Or perhaps it was the Penitentiary. *(Listens.)* Sh! They're leaving the table.

The dining-room door is thrown open from within by a couple of waiters. MRS. SÖRBY *comes out conversing with two gentlemen. Gradually the whole company follows, amongst them* WERLE. *Last come* HIALMAR EKDAL *and* GREGERS WERLE.

Mrs. Sörby (in passing, to the servant). Tell them to serve the coffee in the music-room, Pettersen.

Pettersen. Very well, Madam.

[*She goes with the two Gentlemen into the inner room and thence out to the right.* PETTERSEN *and* JENSEN *go out the same way.*

A Flabby Gentleman (to a THIN-HAIRED GENTLEMAN*).* Whew! What a dinner!—It was no joke to do it justice!

The Thin-haired Gentleman. Oh, with a little good-will one can get through a lot in three hours.

The Flabby Gentleman. Yes, but afterwards, afterwards, my dear Chamberlain!

A Third Gentleman. I hear the coffee and maraschino are to be served in the music-room.

The Flabby Gentleman. Bravo! Then perhaps Mrs. Sörby will play us something.

The Thin-haired Gentleman (in a low voice). I hope Mrs. Sörby mayn't play us a tune we don't like, one of these days!

The Flabby Gentleman. Oh, no, not she! Bertha will never turn against her old friends.

[*They laugh and pass into the inner room.*

Werle (in a low voice, dejectedly). I don't think anybody noticed it, Gregers.

Gregers (looks at him). Noticed what?

Werle. Did you not notice it either?

Gregers. What do you mean?

Werle. We were thirteen at table.

Gregers. Indeed? Were there thirteen of us?

Werle (glances towards HIALMAR EKDAL*).* Our usual party is twelve. *(To the others.)* This way, gentlemen!

[WERLE *and the others, all except* HIALMAR *and* GREGERS, *go out by the back, to the right.*

Hialmar (who has overhead the conversation). You ought not to have invited me, Gregers.

Gregers. What! Not ask my best and only friend to a party supposed to be in my honour——?

Hialmar. But I don't think your father likes it. You see I am quite outside his circle.

Gregers. So I hear. But I wanted to see you and have a talk with you, and I certainly shan't be staying long.—Ah, we two old schoolfellows have drifted far apart from each other. It must be sixteen or seventeen years since we met.

Hialmar. Is it so long?

Gregers. It is indeed. Well, how goes it with you? You look well. You have put on flesh and grown almost stout.

Hialmar. Well, "stout" is scarcely the word; but I dare-say I look a little more of a man than I used to.

Gregers. Yes, you do; your outer man is in first-rate condition.

Hialmar (in a tone of gloom). Ah, but the inner man! That is a very different matter, I can tell you! Of course you know of the terrible catastrophe that has befallen me and mine since last we met.

Gregers (more softly). How are things going with your father now?

Hialmar. Don't let us talk of it, old fellow. Of course my poor unhappy father lives with me. He hasn't another soul in the world to care for him. But you can understand that this is a miserable subject for me.—Tell me, rather, how you have been getting on up at the works.

Gregers. I have had a delightfully lonely time of it—plenty of leisure to think and think about things. Come over here; we may as well make ourselves comfortable.

[*He seats himself in an armchair by the fire and draws* HIALMAR *down into another alongside of it.*

Hialmar (sentimentally). After all, Gregers, I thank you for inviting me to your father's table; for I take it as a sign that you have got over your feeling against me.

Gregers (surprised). How could you imagine I had any feeling against you?

Hialmar. You had at first, you know.

Gregers. How at first?

Hialmar. After the great misfortune. It was natural enough that you should. Your father was within an ace of being drawn into that—well, that terrible business.

Gregers. Why should that give me any feeling against you? Who can have put that into your head?

Hialmar. I know it did, Gregers; your father told me so himself.

Gregers (starts). My father! Oh, indeed. H'm.—Was that why you never let me hear from you?—not a single word.

Hialmar. Yes.

Gregers. Not even when you made up your mind to become a photographer?

Hialmar. Your father said I had better not write to you at all, about anything.

Gregers (looking straight before him). Well, well, perhaps he was right.—But tell me, now, Hialmar: are you pretty well satisfied with your present position?

Hialmar (with a little sigh). Oh, yes, I am; I have really no cause to complain. At first, as you may guess, I felt it a little strange. It was such a totally new state of things for me. But of course my whole circumstances were totally changed. Father's utter, irretrievable ruin,—the shame and disgrace of it, Gregers——

Gregers (affected). Yes, yes; I understand.

Hialmar. I couldn't think of remaining at college; there wasn't a shilling to spare; on the contrary, there were debts —mainly to your father, I believe——

Gregers. H'm——

Hialmar. In short, I thought it best to break, once for all, with my old surroundings and associations. It was your father that specially urged me to it; and since he interested himself so much in me——

Gregers. My father did?

Hialmar. Yes, you surely knew that, didn't you? Where do you suppose I found the money to learn photography, and to furnish a studio and make a start? All that cost a pretty penny, I can tell you.

Gregers. And my father provided the money?

Hialmar. Yes, my dear fellow, didn't you know? I understood him to say he had written to you about it.

Gregers. Not a word about his part in the business. He must have forgotten it. Our correspondence has always been purely a business one. So it was my father that——!

Hialmar. Yes, certainly. He didn't wish it to be generally known; but he it was. And of course it was he, too, that put me in a position to marry. Don't you—don't you know about that either?

Gregers. No, I haven't heard a word of it. *(Shakes him by the arm.)* But, my dear Hialmar, I can't tell you what pleasure all this gives me—pleasure, and self-reproach. I have perhaps done my father injustice after all—in some things. This proves that he has a heart. It shows a sort of compunction——

Hialmar. Compunction——?

Gregers. Yes, yes—whatever you like to call it. Oh, I can't tell you how glad I am to hear this of father.—So you are a married man, Hialmar! That is further than I shall ever get. Well, I hope you are happy in your married life?

Hialmar. Yes, thoroughly happy. She is as good and capable a wife as any man could wish for. And she is by no means without culture.

Gregers (rather surprised). No, of course not.

Hialmar. You see, life is itself an education. Her daily intercourse with me—— And then we know one or two rather remarkable men, who come a good deal about us. I assure you, you would hardly know Gina again.

Gregers. Gina?

Hialmar. Yes; had you forgotten that her name was Gina?

Gregers. Whose name? I haven't the slightest idea——

Hialmar. Don't you remember that she used to be in service here?

Gregers (looks at him). Is it Gina Hansen——?

Hialmar. Yes, of course it is Gina Hansen.

Gregers. ——who kept house for us during the last year of my mother's illness?

Hialmar. Yes, exactly. But, my dear friend, I'm quite sure your father told you that I was married.

Gregers (who has risen). Oh, yes, he mentioned it; but not that—— *(Walking about the room.)* Stay—perhaps he did—now that I think of it. My father always writes such short letters. *(Half seats himself on the arm of the chair.)* Now tell me, Hialmar—this is interesting—how did you come to know Gina—your wife?

Hialmar. The simplest thing in the world. You know Gina did not stay here long, everything was so much upset at that time, owing to your mother's illness and so forth, that Gina was not equal to it all; so she gave notice and left. That was the year before your mother died—or it may have been the same year.

Gregers. It was the same year. I was up at the works then. But afterwards——?

Hialmar. Well, Gina lived at home with her mother, Madam Hansen, an excellent hard-working woman, who kept a little eating-house. She had a room to let, too; a very nice comfortable room.

Gregers. And I suppose you were lucky enough to secure it?

Hialmar. Yes; in fact, it was your father that recommended it to me. So it was there, you see, that I really came to know Gina.

Gregers. And then you got engaged?

Hialmar. Yes. It doesn't take young people long to fall in love——; h'm——

Gregers (rises and moves about a little). Tell me: was it after your engagement—was it then that my father—I mean was it then that you began to take up photography?

Hialmar. Yes, precisely. I wanted to make a start and to set up house as soon as possible; and your father and I agreed that this photography business was the readiest way.

Gina thought so, too. Oh, and there was another thing in its favour, by-the-bye: it happened, luckily, that Gina had learnt to retouch.

Gregers. That chimed in marvellously.

Hialmar (pleased, rises). Yes, didn't it? Don't you think it was a marvellous piece of luck?

Gregers. Oh, unquestionably. My father seems to have been almost a kind of providence for you.

Hialmar (with emotion). He did not forsake his old friend's son in the hour of his need. For he has a heart, you see.

Mrs. Sörby (enters, arm-in-arm with WERLE*).* Nonsense, my dear Mr. Werle; you mustn't stop there any longer staring at all the lights. It's very bad for you.

Werle (lets go her arm and passes his hand over his eyes). I daresay you are right.

[PETTERSEN *and* JENSEN *carry round refreshment trays.*

Mrs. Sörby (to the Guests in the other room). This way, if you please, gentlemen. Whoever wants a glass of punch must be so good as to come in here.

The Flabby Gentleman (comes up to MRS. SÖRBY*).* Surely, it isn't possible that you have suspended our cherished right to smoke?

Mrs. Sörby. Yes. No smoking here, in Mr. Werle's sanctum, Chamberlain.

The Thin-haired Gentleman. When did you enact these stringent amendments on the cigar law, Mrs. Sörby?

Mrs. Sörby. After the last dinner, Chamberlain, when certain persons permitted themselves to overstep the mark.

The Thin-haired Gentleman. And may one never overstep the mark a little bit, Madame Bertha? Not the least little bit?

Mrs. Sörby. Not in any respect whatsoever, Mr. Balle

[*Most of the Guests have assembled in the study; servants hand round glasses of punch.*

Werle (to Hialmar, *who is standing beside a table).* What are you studying so intently, Ekdal?

Hialmar. Only an album, Mr. Werle.

The Thin-haired Gentleman (who is wandering about). Ah, photographs! They are quite in your line, of course.

The Flabby Gentleman (in an armchair). Haven't you brought any of your own with you?

Hialmar. No, I haven't.

The Flabby Gentleman. You ought to have; it's very good for the digestion to sit and look at pictures.

The Thin-haired Gentleman. And it contributes to the entertainment, you know.

The Short-sighted Gentleman. And all contributions are thankfully received.

Mrs. Sörby. The Chamberlains think that when one is invited out to dinner, one ought to exert oneself a little in return, Mr. Ekdal.

The Flabby Gentleman. Where one dines so well, that duty becomes a pleasure.

The Thin-haired Gentleman. And when it's a case of the struggle for existence, you know——

Mrs. Sörby. I quite agree with you!

[*They continue the conversation, with laughter and joking.*

Gregers (softly). You must join in, Hialmar.

Hialmar (writhing). What am I to talk about?

The Flabby Gentleman. Don't you think, Mr. Werle, that Tokay may be considered one of the more wholesome sorts of wine?

Werle (by the fire). I can answer for the Tokay you had to-day, at any rate; it's one of the very finest seasons. Of course you would notice that.

The Flabby Gentleman. Yes, it had a remarkably delicate flavour.

Hialmar (shyly). Is there any difference between the seasons?

The Flabby Gentleman (laughs). Come! That's good!

Werle (smiles). It really doesn't pay to set fine wine before you.

The Thin-haired Gentleman. Tokay is like photographs, Mr. Ekdal: they both need sunshine. Am I not right?

Hialmar. Yes, light is important no doubt.

Mrs. Sörby. And it's exactly the same with Chamberlains—they, too, depend very much on sunshine,* as the saying is.

The Thin-haired Gentleman. Oh, fie! That's a very threadbare sarcasm!

The Short-sighted Gentleman. Mrs. Sörby is coming out——

The Flabby Gentleman. ——and at our expense, too. *(Holds up his finger reprovingly.)* Oh, Madame Bertha, Madame Bertha!

Mrs. Sörby. Yes, and there's not the least doubt that the seasons differ greatly. The old vintages are the finest.

The Short-sighted Gentleman. Do you reckon me among the old vintages?

Mrs. Sörby. Oh, far from it.

The Thin-haired Gentleman. There now! But me, dear Mrs. Sörby——?

The Flabby Gentleman. Yes, and me? What vintage should you say that we belong to?

Mrs. Sörby. Why, to the sweet vintages, gentlemen.

[*She sips a glass of punch. The gentlemen laugh and flirt with her.*

Werle. Mrs. Sörby can always find a loop-hole—when she wants to. Fill your glasses, gentlemen! Pettersen, will you see to it——! Gregers, suppose we have a glass together. *(Gregers does not move.)* Won't you join us, Ekdal? I found no opportunity of drinking with you at table.

* The "sunshine" of court favour.

[GRÅBERG, *the Bookkeeper, looks in at the baize door.*

Gråberg. Excuse me, sir, but I can't get out.

Werle. Have you been locked in again?

Gråberg. Yes, and Flakstad has carried off the keys.

Werle. Well, you can pass out this way.

Gråberg. But there's some one else——

Werle. All right; come through, both of you. Don't be afraid.

[GRÅBERG *and* OLD EKDAL *come out of the office.*

Werle (involuntarily). Ugh!

[*The laughter and talk among the Guests cease.* HIALMAR *starts at the sight of his father, puts down his glass and turns towards the fireplace.*

Ekdal (does not look up, but makes little bows to both sides as he passes, murmuring). Beg pardon, come the wrong way. Dook locked—door locked. Beg pardon.

[*He and* GRÅBERG *go out by the back, to the right.*

Werle (between his teeth). That idiot Gråberg.

Gregers (open-mouthed and staring, to HIALMAR*).* Why surely that wasn't——!

The Flabby Gentleman. What's the matter? Who was it?

Gregers. Oh, nobody, only the bookkeeper and some one with him.

The Short-sighted Gentleman (to HIALMAR*).* Did you know that man?

Hialmar. I don't know—I didn't notice——

The Flabby Gentleman. What the deuce has come over every one?

[*He joins another group who are talking softly.*

Mrs. Sörby (whispers to the Servant). Give him something to take with him;—something good, mind.

Pettersen (nods). I'll see to it. [*Goes out.*

Gregers (softly and with emotion, to HIALMAR*).* So that was really he!

Hialmar. Yes.

Gregers. And you could stand there and deny that you knew him!

Hialmar (whispers vehemently). But how could I——!

Gregers. ——acknowledge your own father?

Hialmar (with pain). Oh, if you were in my place——

[*The conversation amongst the Guests, which has been carried on in a low tone, now swells into constrained joviality.*

The Thin-haired Gentleman (approaching HIALMAR *and* GREGERS *in a friendly manner).* Aha! Reviving old college memories, eh? Don't you smoke, Mr. Ekdal? May I give you a light? Oh, by-the-bye, we mustn't——

Hialmar. No, thank you, I won't——

The Flabby Gentleman. Haven't you a nice little poem you could recite to us, Mr. Ekdal? You used to recite so charmingly.

Hialmar. I am sorry I can't remember anything.

The Flabby Gentleman. Oh, that's a pity. Well, what shall we do, Balle?

[*Both Gentlemen move away and pass into the other room.*

Hialmar (gloomily). Gregers—I am going! When a man has felt the crushing hand of Fate, you see—— Say good-bye to your father for me.

Gregers. Yes, yes. Are you going straight home?

Hialmar. Yes. Why?

Gregers. Oh, because I may perhaps look in on you later.

Hialmar. No, you mustn't do that. You must not come to my home. Mine is a melancholy abode, Gregers; especially after a splendid banquet like this. We can always arrange to meet somewhere in the town.

Mrs. Sörby (who has quietly approached). Are you going, Ekdal?

Hialmar. Yes.

Mrs. Sörby. Remember me to Gina.

Hialmar. Thanks.

Mrs. Sörby. And say I am coming up to see her one of these days.

Hialmar. Yes, thank you. *(To* GREGERS*).* Stay here; I will slip out unobserved.

[*He saunters away, then into the other room, and so out to the right.*

Mrs. Sörby (softly to the Servant, who has come back). Well, did you give the old man something?

Pettersen. Yes; I sent him off with a bottle of cognac.

Mrs. Sörby. Oh, you might have thought of something better than that.

Pettersen. Oh, no, Mrs. Sörby; cognac is what he likes best in the world.

The Flabby Gentleman (in the doorway with a sheet of music in his hand). Shall we play a duet, Mrs. Sörby?

Mrs. Sörby. Yes, suppose we do.

The Guests. Bravo, bravo!

[*She goes with all the Guests through the back room, out to the right.* GREGERS *remains standing by the fire.* WERLE *is looking for something on the writing-table and appears to wish that* GREGERS *would go; as* GREGERS *does not move,* WERLE *goes towards the door.*

Gregers. Father, won't you stay a moment?

Werle (stops). What is it?

Gregers. I must have a word with you.

Werle. Can it not wait till we are alone?

Gregers. No, it cannot; for perhaps we shall never be alone together.

Werle (drawing nearer). What do you mean by that?

[*During what follows, the pianoforte is faintly heard from the distant music-room.*

Gregers. How has that family been allowed to go so miserably to the wall?

Werle. You mean the Ekdals, I suppose.

Gregers. Yes, I mean the Ekdals. Lieutenant Ekdal was once so closely associated with you.

Werle. Much too closely; I have felt that to my cost for many a year. It is thanks to him that I—yes *I*—have had a kind of slur cast upon my reputation.

Gregers (softly). Are you sure that he alone was to blame?

Werle. Who else do you suppose——?

Gregers. You and he acted together in that affair of the forests——

Werle. But was it not Ekdal that drew the map of the tracts we had bought—that fraudulent map! It was he who felled all that timber illegally on Government ground. In fact, the whole management was in his hands. I was quite in the dark as to what Lieutenant Ekdal was doing.

Gregers. Lieutenant Ekdal himself seems to have been very much in the dark as to what he was doing.

Werle. That may be. But the fact remains that he was found guilty and I acquitted.

Gregers. Yes, I know that nothing was proved against you.

Werle. Acquittal is acquittal. Why do you rake up these old miseries that turned my hair grey before its time? Is that the sort of thing you have been brooding over up there, all these years? I can assure you, Gregers, here in the town the whole story has been forgotten long ago—so far as *I* am concerned.

Gregers. But that unhappy Ekdal family——

Werle. What would you have had me do for the people? When Ekdal came out of prison he was a broken-down being, past all help. There are people in the world who dive to the bottom the moment they get a couple of slugs in their body and never come to the surface again. You may take my word for it, Gregers, I have done all I could without positively laying myself open to all sorts of suspicion and gossip——

Gregers. Suspicion——? Oh, I see.

Werle. I have given Ekdal copying to do for the office, and I pay him far, far more for it than his work is worth——

Gregers (without looking at him). H'm; that I don't doubt.

Werle. You laugh? Do you think I am not telling you the truth? Well, I certainly can't refer you to my books, for I never enter payments of that sort.

Gregers (smiles coldly). No, there are certain payments it is best to keep no account of.

Werle (taken aback). What do you mean by that?

Gregers (mustering up courage). Have you entered what it cost you to have Hialmar Ekdal taught photography?

Werle. I? How "entered" it?

Gregers. I have learnt that it was you who paid for his training. And I have learnt, too, that it was you who enabled him to set up house so comfortably.

Werle. Well, and yet you talk as though I had done nothing for the Ekdals! I can assure you these people have cost me enough in all conscience.

Gregers. Have you entered any of these expenses in your books?

Werle. Why do you ask?

Gregers. Oh, I have my reasons. Now tell me: when you interested yourself so warmly in your old friend's son—it was just before his marriage, was it not?

Werle. Why, deuce take it—after all these years, how can I——?

Gregers. You wrote me a letter about that time—a business letter, of course; and in a postscript you mentioned—quite briefly—that Hialmar Ekdal had married a Miss Hansen.

Werle. Yes, that was quite right. That was her name.

Gregers. But you did not mention that this Miss Hansen was Gina Hansen—our former housekeeper.

Werle (with a forced laugh of derision). No; to tell the truth, it didn't occur to me that you were so particularly interested in our former housekeeper.

Gregers. No more I was. But *(lowers his voice.)* there were others in this house who were particularly interested in her.

Werle. What do you mean by that? *(Flaring up.)* You are not alluding to me, I hope?

Gregers (softly but firmly). Yes, I am alluding to you.

Werle. And you dare——! You presume to——! How can that ungrateful hound—that photographer fellow—how dare he go making such insinuations!

Gregers. Hialmar has never breathed a word about this. I don't believe he has the faintest suspicion of such a thing.

Werle. Then where have you got it from? Who can have put such notions in your head?

Gregers. My poor unhappy mother told me; and that the very last time I saw her.

Werle. Your mother! I might have known as much! You and she—you always held together. It was she who turned you against me, from the first.

Gregers. No, it was all that she had to suffer and submit to, until she broke down and came to such a pitiful end.

Werle. Oh, she had nothing to suffer or submit to; not more than most people, at all events. But there's no getting on with morbid, overstrained creatures—that I have learnt to my cost.—And you could go on nursing such a suspicion—burrowing into all sorts of old rumours and slanders against your own father! I must say, Gregers, I really think that at your age you might find something more useful to do.

Gregers. Yes, it is high time.

Werle. Then perhaps your mind would be easier than it

seems to be now. What can be your object in remaining up at the works, year out and year in, drudging away like a common clerk, and not drawing a farthing more than the ordinary monthly wage? It is downright folly.

Gregers. Ah, if I were only sure of that.

Werle. I understand you well enough. You want to be independent; you won't be beholden to me for anything. Well, now there happens to be an opportunity for you to become independent, your own master in everything.

Gregers. Indeed? In what way——?

Werle. When I wrote you insisting on your coming to town at once—h'm——

Gregers. Yes, what is it you really want of me? I have been waiting all day to know.

Werle. I want to propose that you should enter the firm, as partner.

Gregers. I! Join your firm? As partner?

Werle. Yes. It would not involve our being constantly together. You could take over the business here in town, and I should move up to the works.

Gregers. You would?

Werle. The fact is, I am not so fit for work as I once was. I am obliged to spare my eyes, Gregers; they have begun to trouble me.

Gregers. They have always been weak.

Werle. Not as they are now. And, besides, circumstances might possibly make it desirable for me to live up there—for a time, at any rate.

Gregers. That is certainly quite a new idea to me.

Werle. Listen, Gregers: there are many things that stand between us; but we are father and son after all. We ought surely to be able to come to some sort of understanding with each other.

Gregers. Outwardly, you mean, of course?

Werle. Well, even that would be something. Think it over, Gregers. Don't you think it ought to be possible? Eh?

Gregers (looking at him coldly). There is something behind all this.

Werle. How so?

Gregers. You want to make use of me in some way.

Werle. In such a close relationship as ours, the one can always be useful to the other.

Gregers. Yes, so people say.

Werle. I want very much to have you at home with me for a time. I am a lonely man, Gregers; I have always felt lonely, all my life through; but most of all now that I am getting up in years. I feel the need of some one about me——

Gregers. You have Mrs. Sörby.

Werle. Yes, I have her; and she has become, I may say, almost indispensable to me. She is lively and even-tempered; she brightens up the house; and that is a very great thing for me.

Gregers. Well, then, you have everything just as you wish it.

Werle. Yes, but I am afraid it can't last. A woman so situated may easily find herself in a false position, in the eyes of the world. For that matter it does a man no good, either.

Gregers. Oh, when a man gives such dinners as you give, he can risk a great deal.

Werle. Yes, but how about the woman, Gregers? I fear she won't accept the situation much longer; and even if she did—even if, out of attachment to me, she were to take her chance of gossip and scandal and all that——? Do you think, Gregers—you with your strong sense of justice——

Gregers (interrupts him). Tell me in one word: are you thinking of marrying her?

Werle. Suppose I were thinking of it? What then?

Gregers. That's what I say: what then?

Werle. Should you be inflexibly opposed to it!

Gregers.—Not at all. Not by any means.

Werle. I was not sure whether your devotion to your mother's memory——

Gregers. I am not overstrained.

Werle. Well, whatever you may or may not be, at all events you have lifted a great weight from my mind. I am extremely pleased that I can reckon on your concurrence in this matter.

Gregers (looking intently at him). Now I see the use you want to put me to.

Werle. Use to put you to? What an expression!

Gregers. Oh, don't let us be nice in our choice of words —not when we are alone together, at any rate. *(With a short laugh.)* Well, well. So this is what made it absolutely essential that I should come to town in person. For the sake of Mrs. Sörby, we are to get up a pretence at family life in the house—a tableau of filial affection! That will be something new indeed.

Werle. How dare you speak in that tone!

Gregers. Was there ever any family life here? Never since I can remember. But now, forsooth, your plans demand something of the sort. No doubt it will have an excellent effect when it is reported that the son has hastened home, on the wings of filial piety, to the grey-haired father's wedding-feast. What will then remain of all the rumours as to the wrongs the poor dead mother had to submit to? Not a vestige. Her son annihilates them at one stroke.

Werle. Gregers—I believe there is no one in the world you detest as you do me.

Gregers (softly). I have seen you at too close quarters.

Werle. You have seen me with your mother's eyes. *(Lowers his voice a little.)* But you should remember that her eyes were—clouded now and then.

Gregers (quivering). I see what you are hinting at. But who was to blame for mother's unfortunate weakness? Why you, and all those——! The last of them was this woman that you palmed off upon Hialmar Ekdal, when you were —— Ugh!

Werle (shrugs his shoulders). Word for word as if it were your mother speaking!

Gregers (without heeding). And there he is now, with his great, confiding, childlike mind, compassed about with all this treachery—living under the same roof with such a creature and never dreaming that what he calls his home is built upon a lie! *(Comes a step nearer.)* When I look back upon your past, I seem to see a battle-field with shattered lives on every hand.

Werle. I begin to think the chasm that divides us is too wide.

Gregers (bowing, with self-command). So I have observed; and therefore I take my hat and go.

Werle. You are going! Out of the house?

Gregers. Yes. For at last I see my mission in life.

Werle. What mission?

Gregers. You would only laugh if I told you.

Werle. A lonely man doesn't laugh so easily, Gregers.

Gregers (pointing towards the background). Look, father,—the Chamberlains are playing blind-man's-buff with Mrs. Sörby.—Good-night and good-bye.

[*He goes out by the back to the right. Sounds of laughter and merriment from the Company, who are now visible in the outer room.*

Werle (muttering contemptuously after GREGERS*).* Ha ——! Poor wretch—and he says he is not overstrained!

ACT II

HIALMAR EKDAL'S *studio, a good-sized room, evidently in the top story of the building. On the right, a sloping roof of large panes of glass, half-covered by a blue curtain. In the right-hand corner, at the back, the entrance door; farther forward, on the same side, a door leading to the sitting-room. Two doors on the opposite side, and between them an iron stove. At the back, a wide double sliding-door. The studio is plainly but comfortably fitted up and furnished. Between the doors on the right, standing out a little from the wall, a sofa with a table and some chairs; on the table a lighted lamp with a shade; beside the stove an old armchair. Photographic instruments and apparatus of different kinds lying about the room. Against the back wall, to the left of the double door, stands a bookcase containing a few books, boxes, and bottles of chemicals, instruments, tools, and other objects. Photographs and small articles, such as camel's-hair pencils, paper, and so forth, lie on the table.*

GINA EKDAL *sits on a chair by the table, sewing.* HEDVIG *is sitting on the sofa, with her hands shading her eyes and her thumbs in her ears, reading a book.*

Gina (glances once or twice at HEDVIG, *as if with secret anxiety; then says):* Hedvig!

Hedvig (does not hear).

Gina (repeats more loudly). Hedvig!

Hedvig (takes away her hands and looks up). Yes, mother?

Gina. Hedvig dear, you mustn't sit reading any longer now.

Hedvig. Oh, mother, mayn't I read a little more? Just a little bit?

Gina. No, no, you must put away your book now. Father doesn't like it; he never reads hisself in the evening.

Hedvig (shuts the book). No, father doesn't care much about reading.

Gina (puts aside her sewing and takes up a lead pencil and a little account-book from the table). Can you remember how much we paid for the butter to-day?

Hedvig. It was one crown sixty-five.

Gina. That's right. *(Puts it down.)* It's terrible what a lot of butter we get through in this house. Then there was the smoked sausage, and the cheese—let me see—*(Writes)*—and the ham—*(Adds up.)* Yes, that makes just——

Hedvig. And then the beer.

Gina. Yes, to be sure. *(Writes.)* How it do mount up! But we can't manage with no less.

Hedvig. And then you and I didn't need anything hot for dinner, as father was out.

Gina. No; that was so much to the good. And then I took eight crowns fifty for the photographs.

Hedvig. Really! So much as that?

Gina. Exactly eight crowns fifty.

[*Silence.* GINA *takes up her sewing again,* HEDVIG *takes paper and pencil and begins to draw, shading her eyes with her left hand.*

Hedvig. Isn't it jolly to think that father is at Mr. Werle's big dinner-party?

Gina. You know he's not really Mr. Werle's guest. It was the son invited him. *(After a pause.)* We have nothing to do with that Mr. Werle.

Hedvig. I'm longing for father to come home. He promised to ask Mrs. Sörby for something nice for me.

Gina. Yes, there's plenty of good things going in that house, I can tell you.

Hedvig (goes on drawing). And I believe I'm a little hungry, too.

[OLD EKDAL, *with the paper parcel under his arm and another parcel in his coat pocket, comes in by the entrance door.*

Gina. How late you are to-day, grandfather!

Ekdal. They had locked the office door. Had to wait in Gråberg's room. And then they let me through—h'm.

Hedvig. Did you get some more copying to do, grandfather?

Ekdal. This whole packet. Just look.

Gina. That's capital.

Hedvig. And you have another parcel in your pocket.

Ekdal. Eh? Oh, never mind, that's nothing. *(Puts his stick away in a corner.)* This work will keep me going a long time, Gina. *(Opens one of the sliding-doors in the back wall a little.)* Hush! *(Peeps into the room for a moment, then pushes the door carefully to again.)* Hee-hee! They're fast asleep, all the lot of them. And she's gone into the basket herself. Hee-hee!

Hedvig. Are you sure she isn't cold in that basket, grandfather?

Ekdal. Not a bit of it! Cold? With all that straw? *(Goes towards the farther door on the left.)* There are matches in here, I suppose.

Gina. The matches is on the drawers.

[EKDAL *goes into his room.*

Hedvig. It's nice that grandfather has got all that copying.

Gina. Yes, poor old father; it means a bit of pocket-money for him.

Hedvig. And he won't be able to sit the whole forenoon down at that horrid Madam Eriksen's.

Gina. No more he won't. [*Short silence.*

Hedvig. Do you suppose they are still at the dinner-table?

Gina. Goodness knows; as like as not.

Hedvig. Think of all the delicious things father is having to eat! I'm certain he'll be in splendid spirits when he comes. Don't you think so, mother?

Gina. Yes; and if only we could tell him that we'd got the room let——

Hedvig. But we don't need that this evening.

Gina. Oh, we'd be none the worst of it, I can tell you. It's no use to us as it is.

Hedvig. I mean we don't need it this evening, for father will be in a good humour at any rate. It is best to keep the letting of the room for another time.

Gina (looks across at her). You like having some good news to tell father when he comes home in the evening?

Hedvig. Yes; for then things are pleasanter somehow.

Gina (thinking to herself). Yes, yes, there's something in that.

[OLD EKDAL *comes in again and is going out by the foremost door to the left.*

Gina (half turning in her chair). Do you want something out of the kitchen, grandfather?

Ekdal. Yes, yes, I do. Don't you trouble. [*Goes out.*

Gina. He's not poking away at the fire, is he? *(Waits a moment.)* Hedvig, go and see what he's about.

[EKDAL *comes in again with a small jug of steaming hot water.*

Hedvig. Have you been getting some hot water, grandfather?

Ekdal. Yes, hot water. Want it for something. Want to write, and the ink has got as thick as porridge—h'm.

Gina. But you'd best have your supper, first, grandfather. It's laid in there.

Ekdal. Can't be bothered with supper, Gina. Very

busy, I tell you. No one's to come to my room. No one—h'm.

[*He goes into his room;* GINA *and* HEDVIG *look at each other.*

Gina (softly). Can you imagine where he's got money from?

Hedvig. From Gråberg, perhaps.

Gina. Not a bit of it. Gråberg always sends the money to me.

Hedvig. Then he must have got a bottle on credit somewhere.

Gina. Poor grandfather, who'd give him credit?

[HIALMAR EKDAL, *in an overcoat and grey felt hat, comes in from the right.*

Gina (throws down her sewing and rises). Why, Ekdal, is that you already?

Hedvig (at the same time jumping up). Fancy your coming so soon, father!

Hialmar (taking off his hat). Yes, most of the people were coming away.

Hedvig. So early?

Hialmar. Yes, it was a dinner-party, you know.

[*Is taking off his overcoat.*

Gina. Let me help you.

Hedvig. Me, too.

[*They draw off his coat;* GINA *hangs it up on the back wall.*

Hedvig. Were there many people there, father?

Hialmar. Oh, no, not many. We were about twelve or fourteen at table.

Gina. And you had some talk with them all?

Hialmar. Oh, yes, a little; but Gregers took me up most of the time.

Gina. Is Gregers as ugly as ever?

Hialmar. Well, he's not very much to look at. Hasn't the old man come home?

Hedvig. Yes, grandfather is in his room, writing.

Hialmar. Did he say anything?

Gina. No, what should he say?

Hialmar. Didn't he say anything about——? I heard something about his having been with Gråberg. I'll go in and see him for a moment.

Gina. No, no, better not.

Hialmar. Why not? Did he say he didn't want me to go in?

Gina. I don't think he wants to see nobody this evening——

Hedvig (making signs). H'm—h'm!

Gina (not noticing). ——he has been in to fetch hot water——

Hialmar. Aha! Then he's——

Gina. Yes, I suppose so.

Hialmar. Oh, God! my poor old white-haired father!——Well, well; there let him sit and get all the enjoyment he can.

[OLD EKDAL, *in an indoor coat and with a lighted pipe, comes from his room.*

Ekdal. Got home? Thought it was you I heard talking.

Hialmar. Yes, I have just come.

Ekdal. You didn't see me, did you?

Hialmar. No, but they told me you had passed through—so I thought I would follow you.

Ekdal. H'm, good of you, Hialmar.—Who were they, all those fellows?

Hialmar.—Oh, all sorts of people. There was Chamberlain Flor, and Chamberlain Balle, and Chamberlain Kaspersen and Chamberlain—this, that, and the other—I don't know who all——

Ekdal (nodding). Hear that, Gina! Chamberlains every one of them!

Gina. Yes, I hear as they're terrible genteel in that house nowadays.

Hedvig. Did the Chamberlains sing, father? Or did they read aloud?

Hialmar. No, they only talked nonsense. They wanted me to recite something for them; but I knew better than that.

Ekdal. You weren't to be persuaded, eh?

Gina. Oh, you might have done it.

Hialmar. No; one mustn't be at everybody's beck and call. *(Walks about the room.)* That's not my way, at any rate.

Ekdal. No, no; Hialmar's not to be had for the asking, he isn't.

Hialmar. I don't see why *I* should bother myself to entertain people on the rare occasions when I go into society. Let the others exert themselves. These fellows go from one great dinner-table to the next and gorge and guzzle day out and day in. It's for them to bestir themselves and do something in return for all the good feeding they get.

Gina. But you didn't say that?

Hialmar (humming). Ho-ho-ho——; faith, I gave them a bit of my mind.

Ekdal. Not the Chamberlains?

Hialmar. Oh, why not? *(Lightly.)* After that, we had a little discussion about Tokay.

Ekdal. Tokay! There's a fine wine for you!

Hialmar (comes to a standstill). It may be a fine wine. But of course you know the vintages differ; it all depends on how much sunshine the grapes have had.

Gina. Why, you know everything, Ekdal.

Ekdal. And did they dispute that?

Hialmar. They tried to; but they were requested to observe that it was just the same with Chamberlains—that with them, too, different batches were of different qualities.

Gina. What things you do think of!

Ekdal. Hee-hee! So they got that in their pipes, too?

Hialmar. Right in their teeth.

Ekdal. Do you hear that, Gina? He said it right in the very teeth of all the Chamberlains.

Gina. Fancy——! Right in their teeth!

Hialmar. Yes, but I don't want it talked about. One doesn't speak of such things. The whole affair passed off quite amicably of course. They were nice, genial fellows; I didn't want to wound them—not I!

Ekdal. Right in their teeth, though——!

Hedvig (caressingly). How nice it is to see you in a dress-coat! It suits you so well, father.

Hialmar. Yes, don't you think so? And this one really sits to perfection. It fits almost as if it had been made for me;—a little tight in the arm-holes perhaps;—help me, Hedvig *(takes off the coat).* I think I'll put on my jacket. Where is my jacket, Gina?

Gina. Here it is. *(Brings the jacket and helps him.)*

Hialmar. That's it! Don't forget to send the coat back to Molvik first thing to-morrow morning.

Gina (laying it away). I'll be sure and see to it.

Hialmar (stretching himself). After all, there's a more homely feeling about this. A free-and-easy indoor costume suits my whole personality better. Don't you think so, Hedvig?

Hedvig. Yes, father.

Hialmar. When I loosen my necktie into a pair of flowing ends—like this—eh?

Hedvig. Yes, that goes so well with your moustache and the sweep of your curls.

Hialmar. I should not call them curls exactly; I should rather say locks.

Hedvig. Yes, they are too big for curls.

Hialmar. Locks describes them better.

Hedvig (after a pause, twitching his jacket). Father!

Hialmar. Well, what is it?

Hedvig. Oh, you know very well.

Hialmar. No, really I don't——

Hedvig (half laughing, half whispering). Oh, yes, father; now don't tease me any longer!

Hialmar. Why, what do you mean?

Hedvig (shaking him). Oh, what nonsense; come, where are they, father? All the good things you promised me, you know?

Hialmar. Oh—if I haven't forgotten all about them!

Hedvig. Now you're only teasing me, father! Oh, it's too bad of you! Where have you put them?

Hialmar. No, I positively forgot to get anything. But wait a little! I have something else for you, Hedvig.

[*Goes and searches in the pockets of the coat.*

Hedvig (skipping and clapping her hands). Oh, mother, mother!

Gina. There, you see; if you only give him time——

Hialmar (with a paper). Look, here it is.

Hedvig. That? Why, that's only a paper.

Hialmar. That is the bill of fare, my dear; the whole bill of fare. Here you see: "Menu"—that means bill of fare.

Hedvig. Haven't you anything else?

Hialmar. I forgot the other things, I tell you. But you may take my word for it, these dainties are very unsatisfying. Sit down at the table and read the bill of fare, and then I'll describe to you how the dishes taste. Here you are, Hedvig.

Hedvig (gulping down her tears). Thank you. *(She seats herself, but does not read;* GINA *makes signs to her;* HIALMAR *notices it.)*

Hialmar (pacing up and down the room). It's monstrous what absurd things the father of a family is expected to think of; and if he forgets the smallest trifle, he is treated to sour faces at once. Well, well, one gets used to that, too. *(Stops near the stove, by the old man's chair.)* Have you peeped in there this evening, father?

Ekdal. Yes, to be sure I have. She's gone into the basket.

Hialmar. Ah, she has gone into the basket. Then she's beginning to get used to it.

Ekdal. Yes; just as I prophesied. But you know there are still a few little things——

Hialmar. A few improvements, yes.

Ekdal. They've got to be made, you know.

Hialmar. Yes, let us have a talk about the improvements, father. Come, let us sit on the sofa.

Ekdal. All right. H'm—think I'll just fill my pipe first. Must clean it out, too. H'm. [*He goes into his room.*

Gina (smiling to HIALMAR*).* His pipe!

Hialmar. Oh, yes, yes, Gina; let him alone—the poor shipwrecked old man.—Yes, these improvements—we had better get them out of hand to-morrow.

Gina. You'll hardly have time to-morrow, Ekdal.

Hedvig (interposing). Oh, yes he will, mother!

Gina. ——for remember them prints that has to be retouched; they've sent for them time after time.

Hialmar. There now! those prints again! I shall get them finished all right! Have any new orders come in?

Gina. No, worse luck; to-morrow I have nothing but those two sittings, you know.

Hialmar. Nothing else? Oh, no, if people won't set about things with a will——

Gina. But what more can I do? Don't I advertise ir the papers as much as we can afford?

Hialmar. Yes, the papers, the papers; you see how much good they do. And I suppose no one has been to look at the room either?

Gina. No, not yet.

Hialmar. That was only to be expected. If people won't keep their eyes open——. Nothing can be done without a real effort, Gina!

Hedvig (going towards him). Shall I fetch you the flute, father?

Hialmar. No; no flute for me; *I* want no pleasures in

this world. *(Pacing about.)* Yes, indeed I will work to-morrow; you shall see if I don't. You may be sure I shall work as long as my strength holds out.

Gina. But my dear, good Ekdal, I didn't mean it in that way.

Hedvig. Father, mayn't I bring in a bottle of beer?

Hialmar. No, certainly not. I require nothing, nothing—— *(Comes to a standstill.)* Beer? Was it beer you were talking about?

Hedvig (cheerfully). Yes, father; beautiful, fresh beer.

Hialmar. Well—since you insist upon it, you may bring in a bottle.

Gina. Yes, do; and we'll be nice and cosy.

[HEDVIG *runs towards the kitchen door.*

Hialmar (by the stove, stops her, looks at her, puts his arm round her neck and presses her to him). Hedvig, Hedvig!

Hedvig (with tears of joy). My dear, kind father!

Hialmar. No, don't call me that. Here have I been feasting at the rich man's table,—battening at the groaning board——! And I couldn't even——!

Gina (sitting at the table). Oh, nonsense, nonsense, Ekdal.

Hialmar. It's not nonsense! And yet you mustn't be too hard upon me. You know that I love you for all that.

Hedvig (throwing her arms round him). And we love you, oh, so dearly, father!

Hialmar. And if I am unreasonable once in a while,—why then—you must remember that I am a man beset by a host of cares. There, there! *(Dries his eyes.)* No beer at such a moment as this. Give me the flute.

[HEDVIG *runs to the bookcase and fetches it.*

Hialmar. Thanks! That's right. With my flute in my hand and you two at my side——ah——!

[HEDVIG *seats herself at the table near* GINA; HIALMAR *paces backwards and forwards, pipes up vigorously and plays a Bohemian peasant dance, but in a slow plaintive tempo, and with sentimental expression.*

Hialmar (breaking off the melody, holds out his left hand to GINA *and says with emotion):* Our roof may be poor and humble, Gina; but it is home. And with all my heart I say: here dwells my happiness.

(He begins to play again; almost immediately after, a knocking is heard at the entrance door.

Gina (rising). Hush, Ekdal,—I think there's some one at the door.

Hialmar (laying the flute on the bookcase). There! Again! [GINA *goes and opens the door.*

Gregers Werle (in the passage). Excuse me——

Gina (starting back slightly). Oh!

Gregers. ——does not Mr. Ekdal, the photographer, live here?

Gina. Yes, he does.

Hialmar (going towards the door). Gregers! You here after all? Well, come in then.

Gregers (coming in). I told you I would come and look you up.

Hialmar. But this evening——? Have you left the party?

Gregers. I have left both the party and my father's house.—Good evening, Mrs. Ekdal. I don't know whether you recognise me?

Gina. Oh, yes; it's not difficult to know young Mr. Werle again.

Gregers. No, I am like my mother; and no doubt you remember her.

Hialmar. Left your father's house, did you say?

Gregers. Yes, I have gone to a hotel.

Hialmar. Indeed. Well, since you're here, take off your coat and sit down.

Gregers. Thanks.

[*He takes off his overcoat. He is now dressed in a plain grey suit of a countrified cut.*

Hialmar. Here, on the sofa. Make yourself comfortable.

[GREGERS *seat himself on the sofa;* HIALMAR *takes a chair at the table.*

Gregers (looking around him). So these are your quarters, Hialmar—this is your home.

Hialmar. This is the studio, as you see——

Gina. But it's the largest of our rooms, so we generally sit here.

Hialmar. We used to live in a better place; but this flat has one great advantage: there are such capital outer rooms——

Gina. And we have a room on the other side of the passage that we can let.

Gregers (to HIALMAR*).* Ah—so you have lodgers, too?

Hialmar. No, not yet. They're not so easy to find, you see; you have to keep your eyes open. *(To* HEDVIG.*)* What about the beer, eh?

[HEDVIG *nods and goes out into the kitchen.*

Gregers. So that is your daughter?

Hialmar. Yes, that is Hedvig.

Gregers. And she is your only child?

Hialmar. Yes, the only one. She is the joy of our lives, and—*(lowering his voice)*—at the same time our deepest sorrow, Gregers.

Gregers. What do you mean?

Hialmar. She is in serious danger of losing her eyesight.

Gregers. Becoming blind?

Hialmar. Yes. Only the first symptoms have appeared as yet, and she may not feel it much for some time. But the doctor has warned us. It is coming, inexorably.

Gregers. What a terrible misfortune! How do you account for it?

Hialmar (sighs). Hereditary, no doubt.

Gregers (starting). Hereditary?

Gina. Ekdal's mother had weak eyes.

Hialmar. Yes, so my father says; I can't remember her.

Gregers. Poor child! And how does she take it?

Hialmar. Oh, you can imagine we haven't the heart to tell her of it. She dreams of no danger. Gay and careless and chirping like a little bird, she flutters onward into a life of endless night. *(Overcome.)* Oh, it is cruelly hard on me, Gregers.

[HEDVIG *brings a tray with beer and glasses, which she sets upon the table.*

Hialmar (stroking her hair). Thanks, thanks, Hedvig.

[HEDVIG *puts her arm around his neck and whispers in his ear.*

Hialmar. No, no bread and butter just now. *(Looks up).* But perhaps you would like some, Gregers.

Gregers (with a gesture of refusal). No, no thank you.

Hialmar (still melancholy). Well, you can bring in a little all the same. If you have a crust, that is all I want And plenty of butter on it, mind.

[HEDVIG *nods gaily and goes out into the kitchen again.*

Gregers (who has been following her with his eyes). She seems quite strong and healthy otherwise.

Gina. Yes. In other ways there's nothing amiss with her, thank goodness.

Gregers. She promises to be very like you, Mrs. Ekdal. How old is she now?

Gina. Hedvig is close on fourteen; her birthday is the day after to-morrow.

Gregers. She is pretty tall for her age, then.

Gina. Yes, she's shot up wonderful this last year.

Gregers. It makes one realise one's own age to see these young people growing up.—How long is it now since you were married?

Gina. We've been married—let me see—just on fifteen years.

Gregers. Is it so long as that?

Gina (becomes attentive; looks at him). Yes, it is indeed.

Hialmar. Yes, so it is. Fifteen years all but a few months. *(Changing his tone.)* They must have been long years for you, up at the works, Gregers.

Gregers. They seemed long while I was living them; now they are over, I hardly know how the time has gone.

[OLD EKDAL *comes from his room without his pipe, but with his old-fashioned uniform cap on his head; his gait is somewhat unsteady.*

Ekdal. Come now, Hialmar, let's sit down and have a good talk about this—h'm—what was it again?

Hialmar (going towards him). Father, we have a visitor here—Gregers Werle.—I don't know if you remember him.

Ekdal (looking at GREGERS, *who has risen).* Werle? Is that the son? What does he want with me?

Hialmar. Nothing; it's me he has come to see.

Ekdal. Oh! Then there's nothing wrong?

Hialmar. No, no, of course not.

Ekdal (with a large gesture). Not that I'm afraid, you know; but——

Gregers (goes over to him). I bring you a greeting from your old hunting-grounds, Lieutenant Ekdal.

Ekdal. Hunting-grounds?

Gregers. Yes, up in Höidal, about the works, you know.

Ekdal. Oh, up there. Yes, I knew all those places well in the old days.

Gregers. You were a great sportsman then.

Ekdal. So I was, I don't deny it. You're looking at my uniform cap. I don't ask anybody's leave to wear it in the house. So long as I don't go out in the streets with it——

[HEDVIG *brings a plate of bread and butter, which she puts upon the table.*

Hialmar. Sit down, father, and have a glass of beer. Help yourself, Gregers.

[EKDAL *mutters and stumbles over to the sofa.* GREGERS *seats himself on the chair nearest to him,* HIALMAR *on the other side of* GREGERS. GINA *sits a little way from the table, sewing;* HEDVIG *stands beside her father.*

Gregers. Can you remember, Lieutenant Ekdal, how Hialmar and I used to come up and visit you in the summer and at Christmas?

Ekdal. Did you? No, no, no; I don't remember it. But sure enough I've been a tidy bit of a sportsman in my day. I've shot bears, too. I've shot nine of 'em, no less.

Gregers (looking sympathetically at him). And now you never get any shooting?

Ekdal. Can't just say that, sir. Get a shot now and then perhaps. Of course not in the old way. For the woods you see—the woods, the woods——! *(Drinks.)* Are the woods fine up there now?

Gregers. Not so fine as in your time. They have been thinned a good deal.

Ekdal. Thinned? *(More softly, and as if afraid.)* It's dangerous work that. Bad things come of it. The woods revenge themselves.

Hialmar (filling up his glass). Come—a little more, father.

Gregers. How can a man like you—such a man for the open air—live in the midst of a stuffy town, boxed within four walls?

Ekdal (laughs quietly and glances at HIALMAR*)*. Oh, it's not so bad here. Not at all so bad.

Gregers. But don't you miss all the things that used to be a part of your very being—the cool sweeping breezes, the free life in the woods and on the uplands, among beasts and birds——?

Ekdal (smiling). Hialmar, shall we let him see it?

Hialmar (hastily and a little embarrassed). Oh, no, no, father; not this evening.

Gregers. What does he want to show me?

Hialmar. Oh, it's only something—you can see it another time.

Gregers (continues, to the old man). You see I have been thinking, Lieutenant Ekdal, that you should come up with me to the works; I am sure to be going back soon. No doubt you could get some copying there, too. And here, you have nothing on earth to interest you—nothing to liven you up.

Ekdal (stares in astonishment at him). Have *I* nothing on earth to——!

Gregers. Of course you have Hialmar; but then he has his own family. And a man like you, who has always had such a passion for what is free and wild——

Ekdal (thumps the table). Hialmar, he shall see it!

Hialmar. Oh, do you think it's worth while, father? It's all dark.

Ekdal. Nonsense; it's moonlight. *(Rises).* He shall see it, I tell you. Let me pass! Come and help me, Hialmar.

Hedvig. Oh, yes, do, father!

Hialmar (rising). Very well then.

Gregers (to GINA*).* What is it?

Gina. Oh, nothing so very wonderful, after all.

[EKDAL *and* HIALMAR *have gone to the back wall and are each pushing back a side of the sliding door;* HEDVIG *helps the old man;* GREGERS *remains standing by the sofa;* GINA *sits still and sews. Through the open doorway a large, deep irregular garret is seen with odd nooks and corners; a couple of stove-pipes running through it, from rooms below. There are skylights through which clear moonbeams shine in on some parts of the great room; others lie in deep shadow.*

Ekdal (to GREGERS*).* You may come close up if you like.

Gregers (going over to them). Why, what is it?

Ekdal. Look for yourself. H'm.

Hialmar (somewhat embarrassed). This belongs to father, you understand.

Gregers (at the door, looks into the garret). Why, you keep poultry, Lieutenant Ekdal.

Ekdal. Should think we did keep poultry. They've gone to roost now. But you should just see our fowls by daylight, sir!

Hedvig. And there's a——

Ekdal. Sh—sh! don't say anything about it yet.

Gregers. And you have pigeons, too, I see.

Ekdal. Oh, yes, haven't we just got pigeons! They have their nest-boxes up there under the roof-tree; for pigeons like to roost high, you see.

Hialmar. They aren't all common pigeons.

Ekdal. Common! Should think not indeed! We have tumblers and a pair of pouters, too. But come here! Can you see that hutch down there by the wall?

Gregers. Yes; what do you use it for?

Ekdal. That's where the rabbits sleep, sir.

Gregers. Dear me; so you have rabbits, too?

Ekdal. Yes, you may take my word for it, we have rabbits! He wants to know if we have rabbits, Hialmar! H'm! But now comes the thing, let me tell you! Here we have it! Move away, Hedvig. Stand here; that's right,—and now look down there.—Don't you see a basket with straw in it?

Gregers. Yes. And I can see a fowl lying in the basket.

Ekdal. H'm—"a fowl"——

Gregers. Isn't it a duck?

Ekdal (hurt). Why, of course it's a duck.

Hialmar. But what kind of duck, do you think?

Hedvig. It's not just a common duck——

Ekdal. Sh!

Gregers. And it's not a Muscovy duck either.

Ekdal. No, Mr.—Werle; it's not a Muscovy duck; for it's a wild duck!

Gregers. Is it really? A wild duck?

Ekdal. Yes, that's what it is. That "fowl" as you call it—is the wild duck. It's our wild duck, sir.

Hedvig. My wild duck. It belongs to me.

Gregers. And can it live up here in the garret? Does it thrive?

Ekdal. Of course it has a trough of water to splash about in, you know.

Hialmar. Fresh water every other day.

Gina (turning towards HIALMAR*).* But my dear Ekdal, it's getting icy cold here.

Ekdal. H'm, we had better shut up then. It's as well not to disturb their night's rest, too. Close up, Hedvig.

[HIALMAR *and* HEDVIG *push the garret doors together.*

Ekdal. Another time you shall see her properly. *(Seats himself in the armchair by the stove.)* Oh, they're curious things, these wild ducks, I can tell you.

Gregers. How did you manage to catch it, Lieutenant Ekdal?

Ekdal. *I* didn't catch it. There's a certain man in this town whom we have to thank for it.

Gregers (starts slightly). That man was not my father, was he?

Ekdal. You've hit it. Your father and no one else. H'm.

Hialmar. Strange that you should guess that, Gregers.

Gregers. You were telling me that you owed so many things to my father; and so I thought perhaps——

Gina. But we didn't get the duck from Mr. Werle himself——

Ekdal. It's Håkon Werle we have to thank for her, all the same, Gina. *(To* GREGERS.*)* He was shooting from a boat, you see, and he brought her down. But your father's sight is not very good now. H'm; she was only wounded.

Gregers. Ah! She got a couple of slugs in her body, I suppose.

Hialmar. Yes, two or three.

Hedvig. She was hit under the wing, so that she couldn't fly.

Gregers. And I suppose she dived to the bottom, eh?

Ekdal (sleepily, in a thick voice). Of course. Always do that, wild ducks do. They shoot to the bottom as deep as they can get, sir—and bite themselves fast in the tangle and seaweed—and all the devil's own mess that grows down there. And they never come up again.

Gregers. But your wild duck came up again, Lieutenant Ekdal.

Ekdal. He had such an amazingly clever dog, your father had. And that dog—he dived in after the duck and fetched her up again.

Gregers (who has turned to HIALMAR*).* And then she was sent to you here?

Hialmar. Not at once; at first your father took her home. But she wouldn't thrive there; so Pettersen was told to put an end to her——

Ekdal (half asleep). H'm—yes—Pettersen—that ass——

Hialmar (speaking more softly). That was how we got her, you see; for father knows Pettersen a little; and when he heard about the wild duck he got him to hand her over to us.

Gregers. And now she thrives as well as possible in the garret there?

Hialmar. Yes, wonderfully well. She has got fat. You see, she has lived in there so long now that she has forgotten her natural wild life; and it all depends on that.

Gregers. You are right there, Hialmar. Be sure you never let her get a glimpse of the sky and the sea——. But I mustn't stay any longer; I think your father is asleep.

Hialmar. Oh, as for that——

Gregers. But, by-the-bye—you said you had a room to let—a spare room?

Hialmar. Yes; what then? Do you know of anybody——?

Gregers. Can *I* have that room?

Hialmar. You?

Gina. Oh, no, Mr. Werle, you——

Gregers. May I have the room? If so, I'll take possession first thing to-morrow morning.

Hialmar. Yes, with the greatest pleasure— —

Gina. But, Mr. Werle, I'm sure it's not at all the sort of room for you.

Hialmar. Why, Gina! how can you say that?

Gina. Why, because the room's neither large enough nor light enough, and——

Gregers. That really doesn't matter, Mrs. Ekdal.

Hialmar. I call it quite a nice room, and not at all badly furnished either.

Gina. But remember the pair of them underneath.

Gregers. What pair?

Gina. Well, there's one as has been a tutor——

Hialmar. That's Molvik—Mr. Molvik, B.A.

Gina. And then there's a doctor, by the name of Relling.

Gregers. Relling? I know him a little; he practised for a time up in Höidal.

Gina. They're a regular rackety pair, they are. As often as not, they're out on the loose in the evenings; and then they come home at all hours, and they're not always just——

Gregers. One soon gets used to that sort of thing. I daresay I shall be like the wild duck——

Gina. H'm; I think you ought to sleep upon it first, anyway.

Gregers. You seem very unwilling to have me in the house, Mrs. Ekdal.

Gina. Oh, no! What makes you think that?

Hialmar. Well, you really behave strangely about it,

Gina. *(To* Gregers.*)* Then I suppose you intend to remain in the town for the present?

Gregers (putting on his overcoat). Yes, now I intend to remain here.

Hialmar. And yet not at your father's? What do you propose to do, then?

Gregers. Ah, if I only knew that, Hialmar, I shouldn't be so badly off! But when one has the misfortune to be called Gregers—! "Gregers"—and then "Werle" after it: did you ever hear anything so hideous?

Hialmar. Oh, I don't think so at all.

Gregers. Ugh! Bah! I feel I should like to spit upon the fellow that answers to such a name. But when a man is once for all doomed to be Gregers—Werle in this world, as I am——

Hialmar (laughs). Ha, ha! If you weren't Gregers Werle, what would you like to be?

Gregers. If I should choose, I should like best to be a clever dog.

Gina. A dog!

Hedvig (involuntarily). Oh, no!

Gregers. Yes, an amazingly clever dog; one that goes to the bottom after wild ducks when they dive and bite themselves fast in tangle and sea-weed, down among the ooze.

Hialmar. Upon my word now, Gregers—I don't in the least know what you're driving at.

Gregers. Oh, well, you might not be much the wiser if you did. It's understood, then, that I move in early to-morrow morning. *(To* Gina.*)* I won't give you any trouble; I do everything for myself. *(To* Hialmar*).* We can talk about the rest to-morrow.—Good-night, Mrs. Ekdal. *(Nods to* Hedvig.*)* Good-night.

Gina. Good-night, Mr. Werle.

Hedvig. Good-night.

Hialmar (who has lighted a candle). Wait a moment; I must show you a light; the stairs are sure to be dark.

[GREGERS *and* HIALMAR *go out by the passage door.*

Gina (looking straight before her, with her sewing in her lap). Wasn't that queer-like talk about wanting to be a dog?

Hedvig. Do you know, mother—I believe he meant something quite different by that.

Gina. Why, what should he mean?

Hedvig. Oh, I don't know; but it seemed to me he meant something different from what he said—all the time.

Gina. Do you think so? Yes, it was sort of queer.

Hialmar (comes back). The lamp was still burning. *(Puts out the candle and sets it down).* Ah, now one can get a mouthful of food at last. *(Begins to eat the bread and butter.)* Well, you see, Gina—if only you keep your eyes open——

Gina. How, keep your eyes open——?

Hialmar. Why, haven't we at last had the luck to get the room let? And just think—to a person like Gregers—a good old friend.

Gina. Well, I don't know what to say about it.

Hedvig. Oh, mother, you'll see; it'll be such fun!

Hialmar. You're very strange. You were so bent upon getting the room let before; and now you don't like it.

Gina. Yes, I do, Ekdal; if it had only been to some one else—— But what do you suppose Mr. Werle will say?

Hialmar. Old Werle? It doesn't concern him.

Gina. But surely you can see that there's something amiss between them again, or the young man wouldn't be leaving home. You know very well those two can't get on with each other.

Hialmar. Very likely not, but——

Gina. And now Mr. Werle may fancy it's you that has egged him on——

Hialmar. Let him fancy so, then! Mr. Werle has done

a great deal for me; far be it from me to deny it. But that doesn't make me everlastingly dependent upon him.

Gina. But, my dear Ekdal, maybe grandfather'll suffer for it. He may lose the little bit of work he gets from Gråberg.

Hialmar. I could almost say: so much the better! Is it not humiliating for a man like me to see his grey-haired father treated as a pariah? But now I believe the fulness of time is at hand. *(Takes a fresh piece of bread and butter.)* As sure as I have a mission in life, I mean to fulfil it now!

Hedvig. Oh, yes, father, do!

Gina. Hush! Don't wake him!

Hialmar (more softly). I will fulfil it, I say. The day shall come when—— And that is why I say it's a good thing we have let the room; for that makes me more independent. The man who has a mission in life must be independent. *(By the armchair, with emotion.)* Poor old white-haired father! Rely on your Hialmar. He has broad shoulders—strong shoulders, at any rate. You shall yet wake up some fine day and—— *(To* GINA.*)* Do you not believe it?

Gina (rising). Yes, of course I do; but in the meantime suppose we see about getting him to bed.

Hialmar. Yes, come.

[*They take hold of the old man carefully.*

ACT III

HIALMAR EKDAL'S *studio. It is morning: the daylight shines through the large window in the slanting roof; the curtain is drawn back.*

HIALMAR *is sitting at the table, busy retouching a photograph; several others lie before him. Presently* GINA, *wearing her hat and cloak, enters by the passage door; she has a covered basket on her arm.*

Hialmar. Back already, Gina?

Gina. Oh, yes, one can't let the grass grow under one's feet.

[*Sets her basket on a chair and takes off her things.*

Hialmar. Did you look in at Gregers' room?

Gina. Yes, that I did. It's a rare sight, I can tell you; he's made a pretty mess to start off with.

Hialmar. How so?

Gina. He was determined to do everything for himself, he said; so he sets to work to light the stove, and what must he do but screw down the damper till the whole room is full of smoke. Ugh! There was a smell fit to——

Hialmar. Well, really!

Gina. But that's not the worst of it; for then he thinks he'll put out the fire, and goes and empties his water-jug into the stove and so makes the whole floor one filthy puddle.

Hialmar. How annoying!

Gina. I've got the porter's wife to clear up after him, pig that he is! But the room won't be fit to live in till the afternoon.

Hialmar. What's he doing with himself in the meantime?

Gina. He said he was going out for a little while.

Hialmar. I looked in upon him, too, for a moment—after you had gone.

Gina. So I heard. You've asked him to lunch.

Hialmar. Just to a little bit of early lunch, you know. It's his first day—we can hardly do less. You've got something in the house, I suppose?

Gina. I shall have to find something or other.

Hialmar. And don't cut it too fine, for I fancy Relling and Molvik are coming up, too. I just happened to meet Relling on the stairs, you see; so I had to——

Gina. Oh, are we to have those two as well?

Hialmar. Good Lord—couple more or less can't make any difference.

Old Ekdal (opens his door and looks in). I say, Hialmar—— *(Sees* GINA.*)* Oh!

Gina. Do you want anything, grandfather?

Ekdal. Oh, no, it doesn't matter. H'm!

[*Retires again.*

Gina (takes up the basket). Be sure you see that he doesn't go out.

Hialmar. All right, all right. And, Gina, a little herring-salad wouldn't be a bad idea; Relling and Molvik were out on the loose again last night.

Gina. If only they don't come before I'm ready for them——

Hialmar. No, of course they won't; take your own time.

Gina. Very well; and meanwhile you can be working a bit.

Hialmar. Well, I am working! I am working as hard as I can!

Gina. Then you'll have that job off your hands, you see.

[*She goes out to the kitchen with her basket.* HIALMAR *sits for a time penciling away at the photograph, in an indolent and listless manner.*

Ekdal (peeps in, looks round the studio and says softly): Are you busy?

Hialmar. Yes, I'm toiling at these wretched pictures——

Ekdal. Well, well, never mind,—since you're so busy—h'm! [*He goes out again; the door stands open.*

Hialmar (continues for some time in silence; then he lays down his brush and goes over to the door). Are you busy, father?

Ekdal (in a grumbling tone, within). If you're busy, I'm busy, too. H'm!

Hialmar. Oh, very well, then.

[*Goes to his work again.*

Ekdal (presently, coming to the door again). H'm; I say, Hialmar, I'm not so very busy, you know.

Hialmar. I thought you were writing.

Ekdal. Oh, the devil take it! can't Gråberg wait a day or two? After all, it's not a matter of life and death.

Hialmar. No; and you're not his slave either.

Ekdal. And about that other business in there——

Hialmar. Just what I was thinking of. Do you want to go in? Shall I open the door for you?

Ekdal. Well, it wouldn't be a bad notion.

Hialmar (rises). Then we'd have that off our hands.

Ekdal. Yes, exactly. It's got to be ready first thing to-morrow. It is to-morrow, isn't it? H'm?

Hialmar. Yes, of course it's to-morrow.

[HIALMAR *and* EKDAL *push aside each his half of the sliding door. The morning sun is shining in through the skylights; some doves are flying about; others sit cooing, upon the perches; the hens are heard clucking now and then, further back in the garret.*

Hialmar. There; now you can get to work, father.

Ekdal (goes in). Aren't you coming, too?

Hialmar. Well, really, do you know——; I almost think—— *(Sees* GINA *at the kitchen door.)* I? No; I haven't time; I must work.—But now for our new contrivance——

[*He pulls a cord, a curtain slips down inside, the lower part consisting of a piece of old sailcloth, the upper part of a stretched fishing net. The floor of the garret is thus no longer visible.*

Hialmar (goes to the table). So! Now, perhaps I can sit in peace for a little while.

Gina. Is he rampaging in there again?

Hialmar. Would you rather have had him slip down to Madam Eriksen's? *(Seats himself.)* Do you want anything? You know you said——

Gina. I only wanted to ask if you think we can lay the table for lunch here?

Hialmar. Yes; we have no early appointment, I suppose?

Gina. No, I expect no one to-day except those two sweethearts that are to be taken together.

Hialmar. Why the deuce couldn't they be taken together another day!

Gina. Don't you know, I told them to come in the afternoon, when you are having your nap.

Hialmar. Oh, that's capital. Very well, let us have lunch here then.

Gina. All right; but there's no hurry about laying the cloth; you can have the table for a good while yet.

Hialmar. Do you think I am not sticking at my work? I'm at it as hard as I can!

Gina. Then you'll be free later on, you know.

[*Goes out into the kitchen again. Short pause.*

Ekdal (in the garret doorway, behind the net). Hialmar!

Hialmar. Well?

Ekdal. Afraid we shall have to move the water-trough, after all.

Hialmar. What else have I been saying all along?

Ekdal. H'm—h'm—h'm.

[*Goes away from the door again.* HIALMAR *goes on working a little; glances towards the garret and half rises.* HEDVIG *comes in from the kitchen.*

Hialmar (sits down again hurriedly). What do you want?

Hedvig. I only wanted to come in beside you, father.

Hialmar (after a pause). What makes you go prying around like that? Perhaps you are told off to watch me?

Hedvig. No, no.

Hialmar. What is your mother doing out there?

Hedvig. Oh, mother's in the middle of making the herring-salad. *(Goes to the table).* Isn't there any little thing I could help you with, father?

Hialmar. Oh, no. It is right that I should bear the whole burden—so long as my strength holds out. Set your mind at rest, Hedvig; if only your father keeps his health——

Hedvig. Oh, no, father! You mustn't talk in that horrid way.

[*She wanders about a little, stops by the doorway and looks into the garret.*

Hialmar. Tell me, what is he doing?

Hedvig. I think he's making a new path to the water-trough.

Hialmar. He can never manage that by himself! And here am I doomed to sit——!

Hedvig (goes to him). Let me take the brush, father; I can do it, quite well.

Hialmar. Oh, nonsense; you will only hurt your eyes.

Hedvig. Not a bit. Give me the brush.

Hialmar (rising). Well, it won't take more than a minute or two.

Hedvig. Pooh, what harm can it do then? *(Takes the brush.)* There! *(Seats herself.)* I can begin upon this one.

Hialmar. But mind you don't hurt your eyes! Do you hear? *I* won't be answerable; you do it on your own responsibility—understand that.

Hedvig (retouching). Yes, yes, I understand.

Hialmar. You are quite clever at it, Hedvig. Only a minute or two, you know.

[*He slips through by the edge of the curtain into the garret.* HEDVIG *sits at her work.* HIALMAR *and* EKDAL *are heard disputing inside.*

Hialmar (appears behind the net). I say, Hedvig—give me those pincers that are lying on the shelf. And the chisel. *(Turns away inside.)* Now you shall see, father. Just let me show you first what I mean!

[HEDVIG *has fetched the required tools from the shelf and hands them to him through the net.*

Hialmar. Ah, thanks. I didn't come a moment too soon.

[*Goes back from the curtain again; they are heard carpentering and talking inside.* HEDVIG *stands looking in at them. A moment later there is a knock at the passage door; she does not notice it.*

Gregers Werle (bareheaded, in indoor dress, enters and stops near the door). H'm——!

Hedvig (turns and goes towards him). Good morning. Please come in.

Gregers. Thank you. *(Looking towards the garret.)* You seem to have workpeople in the house.

Hedvig. No, it is only father and grandfather. I'll tell them you are here.

Gregers. No, no, don't do that; I would rather wait a little. [*Seats himself on the sofa.*

Hedvig. It looks so untidy here——

[*Begins to clear away the photographs.*

Gregers. Oh, don't take them away. Are those prints that have to be finished off?

Hedvig. Yes, they are a few I was helping father with.

Gregers. Please don't let me disturb you.

Hedvig. Oh, no.

[*She gathers the things to her and sits down to work;* GREGERS *looks at her, meanwhile, in silence.*

Gregers. Did the wild duck sleep well last night?

Hedvig. Yes, I think so, thanks.

Gregers (turning towards the garret). It looks quite different by day from what it did last night in the moonlight.

Hedvig. Yes, it changes ever so much. It looks different in the morning and in the afternoon; and it's different on rainy days from what it is in fine weather.

Gregers. Have you noticed that?

Hedvig. Yes, how could I help it?

Gregers. Are you, too, fond of being in there with the wild duck?

Hedvig. Yes, when I can manage it——

Gregers. But I suppose you haven't much spare time; you go to school, no doubt.

Hedvig. No, not now; father is afraid of my hurting my eyes.

Gregers. Oh; then he reads with you himself?

Hedvig. Father has promised to read with me; but he has never had time yet.

Gregers. Then is there nobody else to give you a little help?

Hedvig. Yes, there is Mr. Molvik; but he is not always exactly—quite——

Gregers. Sober?

Hedvig. Yes, I suppose that's it!

Gregers. Why, then you must have any amount of time

on your hands. And in there I suppose it is a sort of world by itself?

Hedvig. Oh, yes, quite. And there are such lots of wonderful things.

Gregers. Indeed?

Hedvig. Yes, there are big cupboards full of books; and a great many of the books have pictures in them.

Gregers. Aha!

Hedvig. And there's an old bureau with drawers and flaps, and a big clock with figures that go out and in. But the clock isn't going now.

Gregers. So time has come to a standstill in there—in the wild duck's domain.

Hedvig. Yes. And then there's an old paint-box and things of that sort; and all the books.

Gregers. And you read the books, I suppose?

Hedvig. Oh, yes, when I get the chance. Most of them are English though, and I don't understand English. But then I look at the pictures.—There is one great big book called "Harrison's History of London." * It must be a hundred years old; and there are such heaps of pictures in it. At the beginning there is Death with an hour-glass and a woman. I think that is horrid. But then there are all the other pictures of churches, and castles, and streets and great ships sailing on the sea.

Gregers. But tell me, where did all those wonderful things come from?

Hedvig. Oh, an old sea captain once lived here, and he brought them home with him. They used to call him "The Flying Dutchman." That was curious, because he wasn't a Dutchman at all.

Gregers. Was he not?

Hedvig. No. But at last he was drowned at sea; and so he left all those things behind him.

* *A New and Universal History of the Cities of London and Westminster,* by Walter Harrison. London, 1775, folio.

Gregers. Tell me now—when you are sitting in there looking at the pictures, don't you wish you could travel and see the real world for yourself?

Hedvig. Oh, no! I mean always to stay at home and help father and mother.

Gregers. To retouch photographs?

Hedvig. No, not only that. I should love above everything to learn to engrave pictures like those in the English books.

Gregers. H'm. What does your father say to that?

Hedvig. I don't think father likes it; father is strange about such things. Only think, he talks of my learning basket-making and straw-plaiting! But I don't think that would be much good.

Gregers. Oh, no, I don't think so either.

Hedvig. But father was right in saying that if I had learnt basket-making I could have made the new basket for the wild duck.

Gregers. So you could; and it was you that ought to have done it, wasn't it?

Hedvig. Yes, for it's my wild duck.

Gregers. Of course it is.

Hedvig. Yes, it belongs to me. But I lend it to father and grandfather as often as they please.

Gregers. Indeed? What do they do with it?

Hedvig. Oh, they look after it, and build places for it, and so on.

Gregers. I see; for no doubt the wild duck is by far the most distinguished inhabitant of the garret?

Hedvig. Yes, indeed she is; for she is a real wild fowl, you know. And then she is so much to be pitied; she has no one to care for, poor thing.

Gregers. She has no family, as the rabbits have——

Hedvig. No. The hens, too, many of them, were chickens together; but she has been taken right away from all her friends. And then there is so much that is strange about the wild duck. Nobody knows her, and nobody knows where she came from either.

Gregers. And she has been down in the depths of the sea.

Hedvig (with a quick glance at him, represses a smile and asks): Why do you say "depths of the sea"?

Gregers. What else should I say?

Hedvig. You could say "the bottom of the sea." *

Gregers. Oh, mayn't I just as well say the depths of the sea?

Hedvig. Yes; but it sounds so strange to me when other people speak of the depths of the sea.

Gregers. Why so? Tell me why?

Hedvig. No, I won't; it's so stupid.

Gregers. Oh, no, I am sure it's not. Do tell me why you smiled.

Hedvig. Well, this is the reason: whenever I come to realise suddenly—in a flash—what is in there, it always seems to me that the whole room and everything in it should be called "the depths of the sea."—But that is so stupid.

Gregers. You mustn't say that.

Hedvig. Oh, yes, for you know it is only a garret.

Gregers (looks fixedly at her). Are you so sure of that?

Hedvig (astonished). That it's a garret?

Gregers. Are you quite certain of it?

[HEDVIG *is silent, and looks at him open-mouthed.* GINA *comes in from the kitchen with the table things.*

Gregers (rising). I have come in upon you too early.

Gina. Oh, you must be somewhere; and we're nearly ready now, anyway. Clear the table, Hedvig.

[HEDVIG *clears away her things; she and* GINA *lay the cloth during what follows.* GREGERS *seats*

* Gregers here uses the old-fashioned expression "havsens bund," while Hedvig would have him use the more commonplace "havets bund" or "havbunden."

himself in the armchair and turns over an album.

Gregers. I hear you can retouch, Mrs. Ekdal.

Gina (with a side glance). Yes, I can.

Gregers. That was exceedingly lucky.

Gina. How—lucky?

Gregers. Since Ekdal took to photography, I mean.

Hedvig. Mother can take photographs, too.

Gina. Oh, yes; I was bound to learn that.

Gregers. So it is really you that carry on the business, I suppose?

Gina. Yes, when Ekdal hasn't time himself——

Gregers. He is a great deal taken up with his old father, I daresay.

Gina. Yes; and then you can't expect a man like Ekdal to do nothing but take car-de-visits of Dick, Tom and Harry.

Gregers. I quite agree with you; but having once gone in for the thing——

Gina. You can surely understand, Mr. Werle, that Ekdal's not like one of your common photographers.

Gregers. Of course not; but still——

[*A shot is fired within the garret.*

Gregers (starting up). What's that?

Gina. Ugh! now they're firing again!

Gregers. Have they firearms in there?

Hedvig. They are out shooting.

Gregers. What! *(At the door of the garret.)* Are you shooting, Hialmar?

Hialmar (inside the net). Are you there? I didn't know; I was so taken up—— *(To* HEDVIG.*)* Why did you not let us know? [*Comes into the studio.*

Gregers. Do you go shooting in the garret?

Hialmar (showing a double-barrelled pistol). Oh, only with this thing.

Gina. Yes, you and grandfather will do yourselves a mischief some day with that there pigstol.

Hialmar (with irritation). I believe I have told you that this kind of firearm is called a pistol.

Gina. Oh, that doesn't make it much better, that I can see.

Gregers. So you have become a sportsman, too, Hialmar?

Hialmar. Only a little rabbit-shooting now and then Mostly to please father, you understand.

Gina. Men are strange beings; they must always have something to pervert theirselves with.

Hialmar (snappishly). Just so; we must always have something to divert ourselves with.

Gina. Yes, that's just what I say.

Hialmar. H'm. *(To* GREGERS.*)* You see the garret is fortunately so situated that no one can hear us shooting. *(Lays the pistol on the top shelf of the bookcase.)* Don't touch the pistol, Hedvig! One of the barrels is loaded; remember that.

Gregers (looking through the net). You have a fowling-piece, too, I see.

Hialmar. That is father's old gun. It's of no use now; something has gone wrong with the lock. But it's fun to have it all the same; for we can take it to pieces now and then, and clean and grease it, and screw it together again.—Of course, it's mostly father that fiddle-faddles with all that sort of thing.

Hedvig (beside GREGERS*).* Now you can see the wild duck properly.

Gregers. I was just looking at her. One of her wings seems to me to droop a bit.

Hedvig. Well, no wonder; her wing was broken, you know.

Gregers. And she trails one foot a little. Isn't that so?

Hialmar. Perhaps a very little bit.

Hedvig. Yes, it was by that foot the dog took hold of her.

Hialmar. But otherwise she hasn't the least thing the

matter with her; and that is simply marvellous for a creature that has a charge of shot in her body and has been between a dog's teeth——

Gregers (with a glance at HEDVIG*).* ——and that has lain in the depths of the sea—so long.

Hedvig (smiling). Yes.

Gina (laying the table). That blessed wild duck! What a lot of fuss you do make over her.

Hialmar. H'm;—will lunch soon be ready?

Gina. Yes, directly. Hedvig, you must come and help me now.

[GINA *and* HEDVIG *go out into the kitchen.*

Hialmar (in a low voice). I think you had better not stand there looking in at father; he doesn't like it. *(*GREGERS *moves away from the garret door.)* Besides, I may as well shut up before the others come. *(Claps his hands to drive the fowls back.)* Shh—shh, in with you! *(Draws up the curtain and pulls the doors together.)* All the contrivances are my own invention. It's really quite amusing to have things of this sort to potter with and to put to rights when they get out of order. And it's absolutely necessary, too; for Gina objects to having rabbits and fowls in the studio.

Gregers. To be sure; and I suppose the studio is your wife's special department?

Hialmar. As a rule, I leave the everyday details of business to her; for then I can take refuge in the parlour and give my mind to more important things.

Gregers. What things may they be, Hialmar?

Hialmar. I wonder you have not asked that question sooner. But perhaps you haven't heard of the invention?

Gregers. The invention? No.

Hialmar. Really? Have you not? Oh, no, out there in the wilds——

Gregers. So you have invented something, have you?

Hialmar. It is not quite completed yet; but I am working at it. You can easily imagine that when I resolved to devote myself to photography, it wasn't simply with the idea of taking likenesses of all sorts of commonplace people.

Gregers. No; your wife was saying the same thing just now.

Hialmar. I swore that if I consecrated my powers to this handicraft, I would so exalt it that it should become both an art and a science. And to that end I determined to make this great invention.

Gregers. And what is the nature of the invention? What purpose does it serve?

Hialmar. Oh, my dear fellow, you mustn't ask for details yet. It takes time, you see. And you must not think that my motive is vanity. It is not for my own sake that I am working. Oh, no; it is my life's mission that stands before me night and day.

Gregers. What is your life's mission?

Hialmar. Do you forget the old man with the silver hair?

Gregers. Your poor father? Well, but what can you do for him?

Hialmar. I can raise up his self-respect from the dead, by restoring the name of Ekdal to honour and dignity.

Gregers. Then that is your life's mission?

Hialmar. Yes. I will rescue the shipwrecked man. For shipwrecked he was, by the very first blast of the storm. Even while those terrible investigations were going on, he was no longer himself. That pistol there—the one we use to shoot rabbits with—has played its part in the tragedy of the house of Ekdal.

Gregers. The pistol? Indeed?

Hialmar. When the sentence of imprisonment was passed —he had the pistol in his hand——

Gregers. Had he——?

Hialmar. Yes; but he dared not use it. His courage failed him. So broken, so demoralised was he even then! Oh, can you understand it? He, a soldier; he, who had shot nine bears, and who was descended from two lieutenant-colonels—one after the other, of course. Can you understand it, Gregers?

Gregers. Yes, I understand it well enough.

Hialmar. I cannot. And once more the pistol played a part in the history of our house. When he had put on the grey clothes and was under lock and key—oh, that was a terrible time for me, I can tell you. I kept the blinds drawn down over both my windows. When I peeped out, I saw the sun shining as if nothing had happened. I could not understand it. I saw people going along the street, laughing and talking about indifferent things. I could not understand it. It seemed to me that the whole of existence must be at a standstill—as if under an eclipse.

Gregers. I felt that, too, when my mother died.

Hialmar. It was in such an hour that Hialmar Ekdal pointed the pistol at his own breast.

Gregers. You, too, thought of——!

Hialmar. Yes.

Gregers. But you did not fire?

Hialmar. No. At the decisive moment I won the victory over myself. I remained in life. But I can assure you it takes some courage to choose life under circumstances like those.

Gregers. Well, that depends on how you look at it.

Hialmar. Yes, indeed, it takes courage. But I am glad I was firm: for now I shall soon perfect my invention; and Dr. Relling thinks, as I do myself, that father may be allowed to wear his uniform again. I will demand that as my sole reward.

Gregers. So that is what he meant about his uniform——?

Hialmar. Yes, that is what he most yearns for. You can't think how my heart bleeds for him. Every time we celebrate any little family festival—Gina's and my wedding-day, or whatever it may be—in comes the old man in the lieutenant's uniform of happier days. But if he only hears a knock at the door—for he daren't show himself to strangers, you know—he hurries back to his room again as fast as his old legs can carry him. Oh, it's heart-rending for a son to see such things!

Gregers. How long do you think it will take you to finish your invention?

Hialmar. Come now, you mustn't expect me to enter into particulars like that. An invention is not a thing completely under one's own control. It depends largely on inspiration—on intuition—and it is almost impossible to predict when the inspiration may come.

Gregers. But it's advancing?

Hialmar. Yes, certainly, it is advancing. I turn it over in my mind every day; I am full of it. Every afternoon, when I have had my dinner, I shut myself up in the parlour, where I can ponder undisturbed. But I can't be goaded to it; it's not a bit of good; Relling says so, too.

Gregers. And you don't think that all that business in the garret draws you off and distracts you too much?

Hialmar. No, no, no; quite the contrary. You mustn't say that. I cannot be everlastingly absorbed in the same laborious train of thought. I must have something alongside of it to fill up the time of waiting. The inspiration, the intuition, you see—when it comes, it comes, and there's an end of it.

Gregers. My dear Hialmar, I almost think you have something of the wild duck in you.

Hialmar. Something of the wild duck? How do you mean?

Gregers. You have dived down and bitten yourself fast in the undergrowth.

Hialmar. Are you alluding to the well-nigh fatal shot that has broken my father's wing—and mine, too?

Gregers. Not exactly to that. I don't say that your wing has been broken; but you have strayed into a poisonous marsh, Hialmar; an insidious disease has taken hold of you, and you have sunk down to die in the dark.

Hialmar. I? To die in the dark? Look here, Gregers, you must really leave off talking such nonsense.

Gregers. Don't be afraid; I shall find a way to help you up again. I, too, have a mission in life now; I found it yesterday.

Hialmar. That's all very well; but you will please leave me out of it. I can assure you that—apart from my very natural melancholy, of course—I am as contented as any one can wish to be.

Gregers. Your contentment is an effect of the marsh poison.

Hialmar. Now, my dear Gregers, pray do not go on about disease and poison; I am not used to that sort of talk. In my house nobody ever speaks to me about unpleasant things.

Gregers. Ah, that I can easily believe.

Hialmar. It's not good for me, you see. And there are no marsh poisons here, as you express it. The poor photographer's roof is lowly, I know—and my circumstances are narrow. But I am an inventor, and I am the breadwinner of a family. That exalts me above my mean surroundings.—Ah, here comes lunch!

[GINA *and* HEDVIG *bring bottles of ale, a decanter of brandy, glasses, etc. At the same time,* RELLING *and* MOLVIK *enter from the passage; they are both without hat or overcoat.* MOLVIK *is dressed in black.*

Gina (placing the things upon the table). Ah, you two have come in the nick of time.

Relling. Molvik got it into his head that he could smell herring-salad, and then there was no holding him.—Good morning again, Ekdal.

Hialmar. Gregers, let me introduce you to Mr. Molvik. Doctor—— Oh, you know Relling, don't you?

Gregers. Yes, slightly.

Relling. Oh, Mr. Werle, junior! Yes, we two have had one or two little skirmishes up at the Höidal works. You've just moved in?

Gregers. I moved in this morning.

Relling. Molvik and I live right under you; so you haven't far to go for the doctor and the clergyman, if you should need anything in that line.

Gregers. Thanks, it's not quite unlikely; for yesterday we were thirteen at table.

Hialmar. Oh, come now, don't let us get upon unpleasant subjects again!

Relling. You may make your mind easy, Ekdal; I'll be hanged if the finger of fate points to you.

Hialmar. I should hope not, for the sake of my family. But let us sit down now, and eat and drink and be merry.

Gregers. Shall we not wait for your father?

Hialmar. No, his lunch will be taken in to him later. Come along!

[*The men seat themselves at table, and eat and drink.* GINA *and* HEDVIG *go in and out and wait upon them.*

Relling. Molvik was frightfully screwed yesterday, Mrs. Ekdal.

Gina. Really? Yesterday again?

Relling. Didn't you hear him when I brought him home last night?

Gina. No, I can't say I did.

Relling. That was a good thing, for Molvik was disgusting last night.

Gina. Is that true, Molvik?

Molvik. Let us draw a veil over last night's proceedings. That sort of thing is totally foreign to my better self.

Relling (to GREGERS*).* It comes over him like a sort of possession, and then I have to go out on the loose with him. Mr. Molvik is dæmonic, you see.

Gregers. Dæmonic?

Relling. Molvik is dæmonic, yes.

Gregers. H'm.

Relling. And dæmonic natures are not made to walk straight through the world; they must meander a little now and then.—Well, so you still stick up there at those horrible grimy works?

Gregers. I have stuck there until now.

Relling. And did you ever manage to collect that claim you went about presenting?

Gregers. Claim? *(Understands him.)* Ah, I see.

Hialmar. Have you been presenting claims, Gregers?

Gregers. Oh, nonsense.

Relling. Faith, but he has, though! He went around to all the cottars' cabins presenting something he called "the claim of the ideal."

Gregers. I was young then.

Relling. You're right; you were very young. And as for the claim of the ideal—you never got it honoured while *I* was up there.

Gregers. Nor since either.

Relling. Ah, then you've learnt to knock a little discount off, I expect.

Gregers. Never, when I have a true man to deal with.

Hialmar. No, I should think not, indeed. A little butter, Gina.

Relling. And a slice of bacon for Molvik.

Molvik. Ugh; not bacon!

[*A knock at the garret door.*

Hialmar. Open the door, Hedvig; father wants to come out.

[HEDVIG *goes over and opens the door a little way;* EKDAL *enters with a fresh rabbit-skin; she closes the door after him.*

Ekdal. Good morning, gentlemen! Good sport to-day. Shot a big one.

Hialmar. And you've gone and skinned it without waiting for me——!

Ekdal. Salted it, too. It's good tender meat, is rabbit; it's sweet; it tastes like sugar. Good appetite to you, gentlemen! [*Goes into his room.*

Molvik (rising). Excuse me——; I can't——; I must get downstairs immediately——

Relling. Drink some soda water, man!

Molvik (hurrying away). Ugh—ugh!

[*Goes out by the passage door.*

Relling (to HIALMAR*).* Let us drain a glass to the old hunter.

Hialmar (clinks glasses with him). To the undaunted sportsman who has looked death in the face!

Relling. To the grey-haired—— *(Drinks.)* By-the-bye, is his hair grey or white?

Hialmar. Something between the two, I fancy; for that matter, he has very few hairs left of any colour.

Relling. Well, well, one can get through the world with a wig. After all, you are a happy man, Ekdal; you have your noble mission to labour for——

Hialmar. And I do labour, I can tell you.

Relling. And then you have your excellent wife, shuffling quietly in and out in her felt slippers, and that see-saw walk of hers, and making everything cosy and comfortable about you.

Hialmar. Yes, Gina—*(nods to her)*—you were a good helpmate on the path of life.

Gina. Oh, don't sit there cricketising me.

Relling. And your Hedvig, too, Ekdal!

Hialmar (affected). The child, yes! The child before everything! Hedvig, come here to me. *(Strokes her hair.)* What day is it to-morrow, eh?

Hedvig (shaking him). Oh, no, you're not to say anything, father.

Hialmar. It cuts me to the heart when I think what a

poor affair it will be; only a little festivity in the garret——

Hedvig. Oh, but that's just what I like!

Relling. Just you wait till the wonderful invention sees the light, Hedvig!

Hialmar. Yes, indeed—then you shall see——! Hedvig, I have resolved to make your future secure. You shall live in comfort all your days. I will demand—something or other—on your behalf. That shall be the poor inventor's sole reward.

Hedvig (whispering, with her arms round his neck). Oh, you dear, kind father!

Relling (to Gregers*).* Come now, don't you find it pleasant, for once in a way, to sit at a well-spread table in a happy family circle?

Hialmar. Ah, yes, I really prize these social hours.

Gregers. For my part, I don't thrive in marsh vapours.

Relling. Marsh vapours?

Hialmar. Oh, don't begin with that stuff again!

Gina. Goodness knows there's no vapours in this house, Mr. Werle; I give the place a good airing every blessed day.

Gregers (leaves the table). No airing you can give will drive out the taint I mean.

Hialmar. Taint!

Gina. Yes, what do you say to that, Ekdal!

Relling. Excuse me—may it not be you yourself that have brought the taint from those mines up there?

Gregers. It is like you to call what I bring into this house a taint.

Relling (goes up to him). Look here, Mr. Werle, junior: I have a strong suspicion that you are still carrying about that "claim of the ideal" large as life, in your coat-tail pocket.

Gregers. I carry it in my breast.

Relling. Well, wherever you carry it, I advise you not to come dunning us with it here, so long as *I* am on the premises.

Gregers. And if I do so nonetheless?

Relling. Then you'll go head-foremost down the stairs; now I've warned you.

Hialmar (rising). Oh, but Relling——!

Gregers. Yes, you may turn me out——

Gina (interposing between them). We can't have that, Relling. But I must say, Mr. Werle, it ill becomes you to talk about vapours and taints, after all the mess you made with your stove. [*A knock at the passage door.*

Hedvig. Mother, there's somebody knocking.

Hialmar. There now, we're going to have a whole lot of people!

Gina. I'll go—— (*Goes over and opens the door, starts, and draws back.*) Oh—oh, dear!

[WERLE, *in a fur coat, advances one step into the room.*

Werle. Excuse me; but I think my son is staying here.

Gina (with a gulp). Yes.

Hialmar (approaching him). Won't you do us the honour to——?

Werle. Thank you, I merely wish to speak to my son.

Gregers. What is it? Here I am.

Werle. I want a few words with you, in your room.

Gregers. In my room? Very well—— [*About to go.*

Gina. No, no, your room's not in a fit state——

Werle. Well then, out in the passage here; I want to have a few words with you alone.

Hialmar. You can have them here, sir. Come into the parlour, Relling.

[HIALMAR *and* RELLING *go off to the right.* GINA *takes* HEDVIG *with her into the kitchen.*

Gregers (after a short pause). Well, now we are alone.

Werle. From something you let fall last evening, and from your coming to lodge with the Ekdals, I can't help inferring that you intend to make yourself unpleasant to me, in one way or another.

Gregers. I intend to open Hialmar Ekdal's eyes. He shall see his position as it really is—that is all.

Werle. Is that the mission in life you spoke of yesterday?

Gregers. Yes. You have left me no other.

Werle. Is it I, then, that have crippled your mind, Gregers?

Gregers. You have crippled my whole life. I am not thinking of all that about mother—— But it's thanks to you that I am continually haunted and harassed by a guilty conscience.

Werle. Indeed! It is your conscience that troubles you, is it?

Gregers. I ought to have taken a stand against you when the trap was set for Lieutenant Ekdal. I ought to have cautioned him; for I had a misgiving as to what was in the wind.

Werle. Yes, that was the time to have spoken.

Gregers. I did not dare to, I was so cowed and spiritless. I was mortally afraid of you—not only then, but long afterwards.

Werle. You have got over that fear now, it appears.

Gregers. Yes, fortunately. The wrong done to old Ekdal, both by me and by—others, can never be undone; but Hialmar I can rescue from all the falsehood and deception that are bringing him to ruin.

Werle. Do you think that will be doing him a kindness?

Gregers. I have not the least doubt of it.

Werle. You think our worthy photographer is the sort of man to appreciate such friendly offices?

Gregers. Yes, I do.

Werle. H'm—we shall see.

Gregers. Besides, if I am to go on living, I must try to find some cure for my sick conscience.

Werle. It will never be sound. Your conscience has been

sickly from childhood. That is a legacy from your mother, Gregers—the only one she left you.

Gregers (with a scornful half-smile). Have you not yet forgiven her for the mistake you made in supposing she would bring you a fortune?

Werle. Don't let us wander from the point.—Then you hold to your purpose of setting young Ekdal upon what you imagine to be the right scent?

Gregers. Yes, that is my fixed resolve.

Werle. Well, in that case I might have spared myself this visit; for, of course, it is useless to ask whether you will return home with me?

Gregers. Quite useless.

Werle. And I suppose you won't enter the firm either?

Gregers. No.

Werle. Very good. But as I am thinking of marrying again, your share in the property will fall to you at once.*

Gregers (quickly). No, I do not want that.

Werle. You don't want it?

Gregers. No, I dare not take it, for conscience' sake.

Werle (after a pause). Are you going up to the works again?

Gregers. No; I consider myself released from your service.

Werle. But what are you going to do?

Gregers. Only to fulfil my mission; nothing more.

Werle. Well, but afterwards? What are you going to live upon?

Gregers. I have laid by a little out of my salary.

Werle. How long will that last?

Gregers. I think it will last my time.

Werle. What do you mean?

* By Norwegian law, before a widower can marry again, a certain proportion of his property must be settled on his children by his former marriage.

Gregers. I shall answer no more questions.

Werle. Good-bye then, Gregers.

Gregers. Good-bye. [WERLE *goes.*

Hialmar (peeping in). He's gone, isn't he?

Gregers. Yes.

[HIALMAR *and* RELLING *enter; also* GINA *and* HEDVIG *from the kitchen.*

Relling. That luncheon-party was a failure.

Gregers. Put on your coat, Hialmar; I want you to come for a long walk with me.

Hialmar. With pleasure. What was it your father wanted? Had it anything to do with me?

Gregers. Come along. We must have a talk. I'll go and put on my overcoat.

[*Goes out by the passage door.*

Gina. You shouldn't go out with him, Ekdal.

Relling. No, don't you do it. Stay where you are.

Hialmar (gets his hat and overcoat). Oh, nonsense! When a friend of my youth feels impelled to open his mind to me in private——

Relling. But devil take it—don't you see that the fellow's mad, cracked, demented!

Gina. There, what did I tell you! His mother before him had crazy fits like that sometimes.

Hialmar. The more need for a friend's watchful eye. *(To* GINA.*)* Be sure you have dinner ready in good time. Good-bye for the present.

[*Goes out by the passage door.*

Relling. It's a thousand pities the fellow didn't go to hell through one of the Höidal mines.

Gina. Good Lord! what makes you say that?

Relling (muttering). Oh, I have my own reasons.

Gina. Do you think young Werle is really mad?

Relling. No, worse luck; he's no madder than most other people. But one disease he has certainly got in his system.

Gina. What is it that's the matter with him?

Relling. Well, I'll tell you, Mrs. Ekdal. He is suffering from an acute attack of integrity.

Gina. Integrity?

Hedvig. Is that a kind of disease?

Relling. Yes, it's a national disease; but it only appears sporadically. (*Nods to* GINA.) Thanks for your hospitality. [*He goes out by the passage door.*

Gina (moving restlessly to and fro). Ugh, that Gregers Werle—he was always a wretched creature.

Hedvig (standing by the table and looking searchingly at her). I think all this is very strange.

ACT IV

HIALMAR EKDAL'S *studio. A photograph has just been taken; a camera with the cloth over it, a pedestal, two chairs, a folding table, etc., are standing out in the room. Afternoon light; the sun is going down; a little later it begins to grow dusk.*

GINA *stands in the passage doorway, with a little box and a wet glass plate in her hand, and is speaking to somebody outside.*

Gina. Yes, certainly. When I make a promise I keep it. The first dozen shall be ready on Monday. Good afternoon.

[*Someone is heard going downstairs.* GINA *shuts the door, slips the plate into the box and puts it into the covered camera.*

Hedvig (comes in from the kitchen). Are they gone?

Gina (tidying up). Yes, thank goodness, I've got rid of them at last.

Hedvig. But can you imagine why father hasn't come home yet?

Gina. Are you sure he's not down in Relling's room?

Hedvig. No, he's not; I ran down the kitchen stair just now and asked.

Gina. And his dinner standing and getting cold, too.

Hedvig. Yes, I can't understand it. Father's always so careful to be home to dinner!

Gina. Oh, he'll be here directly, you'll see.

Hedvig. I wish he would come; everything seems so queer to-day.

Gina (calls out). There he is!

[HIALMAR EKDAL *comes in at the passage door.*

Hedvig (going to him). Father! Oh, what a time we've been waiting for you!

Gina (glancing sidelong at him). You've been out a long time, Ekdal.

Hialmar (without looking at her). Rather long, yes.

[*He takes off his overcoat;* GINA *and* HEDVIG *go to help him; he motions them away.*

Gina. Perhaps you've had dinner with Werle?

Hialmar (hanging up his coat). No.

Gina (going towards the kitchen door). Then I'll bring some in for you.

Hialmar. No; let the dinner alone. I want nothing to eat.

Hedvig (going nearer to him). Are you not well, father?

Hialmar. Well? Oh, yes, well enough. We have had a tiring walk, Gregers and I.

Gina. You didn't ought to have gone so far, Ekdal; you're not used to it.

Hialmar. H'm; there's many a thing a man must get used to in this world. *(Wanders about the room.)* Has any one been here whilst I was out?

Gina. Nobody but the two sweethearts.

Hialmar. No new orders?

Gina. No, not to-day.

Hedvig. There will be some to-morrow, father, you'll see.

Hialmar. I hope there will; for to-morrow I am going to set to work in real earnest.

Hedvig. To-morrow! Don't you remember what day it is to-morrow?

Hialmar. Oh, yes, by-the-bye——. Well, the day after, then. Henceforth I mean to do everything myself; I shall take all the work into my own hands.

Gina. Why, what can be the good of that, Ekdal? It'll

only make your life a burden to you. I can manage the photography all right; and you can go on working at your invention.

Hedvig. And think of the wild duck, father,—and all the hens and rabbits and——!

Hialmar. Don't talk to me of all that trash! From to-morrow I will never set foot in the garret again.

Hedvig. Oh, but father, you promised that we should have a little party——

Hialmar. H'm, true. Well, then, from the day after to-morrow. I should almost like to wring that cursed wild duck's neck!

Hedvig (shrieks). The wild duck!

Gina. Well, I never!

Hedvig (shaking him). Oh, no, father; you know it's my wild duck!

Hialmar. That is why I don't do it. I haven't the heart to—for your sake, Hedvig. But in my inmost soul I feel that I ought to do it. I ought not to tolerate under my roof a creature that has been through those hands.

Gina. Why, good gracious, even if grandfather did get it from that poor creature, Pettersen——

Hialmar (wandering about). There are certain claims—what shall I call them?—let me say claims of the ideal—certain obligations, which a man cannot disregard without injury to his soul.

Hedvig (going after him). But think of the wild duck,—the poor wild duck!

Hialmar (stops). I tell you I will spare it—for your sake. Not a hair of its head shall be—I mean, it shall be spared. There are greater problems than that to be dealt with. But you should go out a little now, Hedvig, as usual; it is getting dusk enough for you now.

Hedvig. No, I don't care about going out now.

Hialmar. Yes, do; it seems to me your eyes are blinking a

great deal; all these vapours in here are bad for you. The air is heavy under this roof.

Hedvig. Very well, then, I'll run down the kitchen stair and go for a little walk. My cloak and hat?—oh, they're in my own room. Father—be sure you don't do the wild duck any harm whilst I'm out.

Hialmar. Not a feather of its head shall be touched. *(Draws her to him.)* You and I, Hedvig—we two——! Well, go along.

[HEDVIG *nods to her parents and goes out through the kitchen.*

Hialmar (walks about without looking up). Gina.

Gina. Yes?

Hialmar. From to-morrow—or, say, from the day after to-morrow—I should like to keep the household account-book myself.

Gina. Do you want to keep the accounts, too, now?

Hialmar. Yes; or to check the receipts at any rate.

Gina. Lord help us! that's soon done.

Hialmar. One would hardly think so; at any rate, you seem to make the money go a very long way. *(Stops and looks at her.)* How do you manage it?

Gina. It's because me and Hedvig, we need so little.

Hialmar. Is it the case that father is very liberally paid for the copying he does for Mr. Werle?

Gina. I don't know as he gets anything out of the way. I don't know the rates for that sort of work.

Hialmar. Well, what does he get, about? Let me hear!

Gina. Oh, it varies; I daresay it'll come to about as much as he costs us, with a little pocket-money over.

Hialmar. As much as he costs us! And you have never told me this before!

Gina. No, how could I tell you? It pleased you so much to think he got everything from you.

Hialmar. And he gets it from Mr. Werle.

Gina. Oh, well, he has plenty and to spare, he has.

Hialmar. Light the lamp for me, please!

Gina (lighting the lamp). And, of course, we don't know as it's Mr. Werle himself; it may be Gråberg——

Hialmar. Why attempt such an evasion?

Gina. I don't know; I only thought——

Hialmar. H'm.

Gina. It wasn't me that got grandfather that copying. It was Bertha, when she used to come about us.

Hialmar. It seems to me your voice is trembling.

Gina (putting the lamp-shade on). Is it?

Hialmar. And your hands are shaking, are they not?

Gina (firmly). Come right out with it, Ekdal. What has he been saying about me?

Hialmar. Is it true—can it be true that—that there was an—an understanding between you and Mr. Werle, while you were in service there?

Gina. That's not true. Not at that time. Mr. Werle did come after me, that's a fact. And his wife thought there was something in it, and then she made such a hocus-pocus and hurly-burly, and she hustled me and bustled me about so that I left her service.

Hialmar. But afterwards, then?

Gina. Well, then I went home. And mother—well, she wasn't the woman you took her for, Ekdal; she kept on worrying and worrying at me about one thing and another—for Mr. Werle was a widower by that time.

Hialmar. Well, and then?

Gina. I suppose you've got to know it. He gave me no peace until he'd had his way.

Hialmar (striking his hands together). And this is the mother of my child! How could you hide this from me?

Gina. Yes, it was wrong of me; I ought certainly to have told you long ago.

Hialmar. You should have told me at the very first;—then I should have known the sort of woman you were.

Gina. But would you have married me all the same?

Hialmar. How can you dream that I would?

Gina. That's just why I didn't dare tell you anything, then. For I'd come to care for you so much, you see; and I couldn't go and make myself utterly miserable——

Hialmar (walks about). And this is my Hedvig's mother. And to know that all I see before me—*(kicks a chair)*—all that I call my home—I owe to a favoured predecessor! Oh, that scoundrel Werle!

Gina. Do you repent of the fourteen—the fifteen years we've lived together?

Hialmar (placing himself in front of her). Have you not every day, every hour, repented of the spider's-web of deceit you have spun around me? Answer me that! How could you help writhing with penitence and remorse?

Gina. Oh, my dear Ekdal, I've had all I could do to look after the house and get through the day's work——

Hialmar. Then you never think of reviewing your past?

Gina. No; Heaven knows I'd almost forgotten those old stories.

Hialmar. Oh, this dull, callous contentment! To me there is something revolting about it. Think of it—never so much as a twinge of remorse!

Gina. But tell me, Ekdal—what would have become of you if you hadn't had a wife like me?

Hialmar. Like you——!

Gina. Yes; for you know I've always been a bit more practical and wide-awake than you. Of course I'm a year or two older.

Hialmar. What would have become of me!

Gina. You'd got into all sorts of bad ways when first you met me; that you can't deny.

Hialmar. "Bad ways" do you call them? Little do you know what a man goes through when he is in grief and despair—especially a man of my fiery temperament.

Gina. Well, well, that may be so. And I've no reason

to crow over you, neither; for you turned a moral of a husband, that you did, as soon as ever you had a house and home of your own.—And now we'd got everything so nice and cosy about us; and me and Hedvig was just thinking we'd soon be able to let ourselves go a bit, in the way of both food and clothes.

Hialmar. In the swamp of deceit, yes.

Gina. I wish to goodness that detestable thing had never set his foot inside our doors!

Hilamar. And I, too, thought my home such a pleasant one. That was a delusion. Where shall I now find the elasticity of spirit to bring my invention into the world of reality? Perhaps it will die with me; and then it will be your past, Gina, that will have killed it.

Gina (nearly crying). You mustn't say such things, Ekdal. Me, that has only wanted to do the best I could for you, all my days!

Hialmar. I ask you, what becomes of the breadwinner's dream? When I used to lie in there on the sofa and brood over my invention, I had a clear enough presentiment that it would sap my vitality to the last drop. I felt even then that the day when I held the patent in my hand—that day—would bring my—release. And then it was my dream that you should live on after me, the dead inventor's well-to-do widow.

Gina (drying her tears). No, you mustn't talk like that, Ekdal. May the Lord never let me see the day I am left a widow!

Hialmar. Oh, the whole dream has vanished. It is all over now. All over!

[GREGERS WERLE *opens the passage door cautiously and looks in.*

Gregers. May I come in?

Hialmar. Yes, come in.

Gregers (comes forward, his face beaming with satisfaction, and holds out both his hands to them). Well, dear friends——! *(Looks from one to the other and whispers to* Hialmar.*)* Have you not done it yet?

Hialmar (aloud). It is done.

Gregers. It is?

Hialmar. I have passed through the bitterest moments of my life.

Gregers. But also, I trust, the most ennobiing.

Hialmar. Well, at any rate, we have got through it for the present.

Gina. God forgive you, Mr. Werle.

Gregers (in great surprise). But I don't understand this.

Hialmar. What don't you understand?

Gregers. After so great a crisis—a crisis that is to be the starting-point of an entirely new life—of a communion founded on truth, and free from all taint of deception——

Hialmar. Yes, yes, I know; I know that quite well.

Gregers. I confidently expected, when I entered the room, to find the light of transfiguration shining upon me from both husband and wife. And now I see nothing but dulness, oppression, gloom——

Gina. Oh, is that it? [*Takes off the lamp-shade.*

Gregers. You will not understand me, Mrs. Ekdal. Ah, well, you, I suppose, need time to——. But you, Hialmar? Surely you feel a new consecration after the great crisis.

Hialmar. Yes, of course I do. That is—in a sort of way.

Gregers. For surely nothing in the world can compare with the joy of forgiving one who has erred and raising her up to oneself in love.

Hialmar. Do you think a man can so easily throw off the bitter cup I have drained?

Gregers. No, not a common man, perhaps. But a man like you——!

Hialmar. Good God! I know that well enough. But you must keep me up to it, Gregers. It takes time, you know.

Gregers. You have much of the wild duck in you, Hialmar. [RELLING *has come in at the passage door.*

Relling. Oho! is the wild duck to the fore again?

Hialmar. Yes; Mr. Werle's wing-broken victim.

Relling. Mr. Werle's——? So it's him you are talking about?

Hialmar. Him and—ourselves.

Relling (in an undertone to GREGERS*).* May the devil fly away with you!

Hialmar. What is that you are saying?

Relling. Only uttering a heartfelt wish that this quacksalver would take himself off. If he stays here, he is quite equal to making an utter mess of life, for both of you.

Gregers. These two will not make a mess of life, Mr. Relling. Of course I won't speak of Hialmar—him we know. But she, too, in her innermost heart, has certainly something loyal and sincere——

Gina (almost crying). You might have let me alone for what I was, then.

Relling (to GREGERS*).* Is it rude to ask what you really want in this house?

Gregers. To lay the foundations of a true marriage.

Relling. So you don't think Ekdal's marriage is good enough as it is?

Gregers. No doubt it is as good a marriage as most others, worse luck. But a true marriage it has yet to become.

Hialmar. You have never had eyes for the claims of the ideal, Relling.

Relling. Rubbish, my boy!—but excuse me, Mr. Werle: how many—in round numbers—how many true marriages have you seen in the course of your life?

Gregers. Scarcely a single one.

Relling. Nor I either.

Gregers. But I have seen innumerable marriages of the opposite kind. And it has been my fate to see at close quarters what ruin such a marriage can work in two human souls.

Hialmar. A man's whole moral basis may give away beneath his feet; that is the terrible part of it.

Relling. Well, I can't say I've ever been exactly married, so I don't pretend to speak with authority. But this I know, that the child enters into the marriage problem. And you must leave the child in peace.

Hialmar. Oh—Hedvig! my poor Hedvig!

Relling. Yes, you must be good enough to keep Hedvig outside of all this. You two are grown-up people; you are free, in God's name, to make what mess and muddle you please of your life. But you must deal cautiously with Hedvig, I tell you; else you may do her a great injury.

Hialmar. An injury!

Relling. Yes, or she may do herself an injury—and perhaps others, too.

Gina. How can you know that, Relling?

Hialmar. Her sight is in no immediate danger, is it?

Relling. I am not talking about her sight. Hedvig is at a critical age. She may be getting all sorts of mischief into her head.

Gina. That's true—I've noticed it already! She's taken to carrying on with the fire, out in the kitchen. She calls it playing at house-on-fire. I'm often scared for fear she really sets fire to the house.

Relling. You see; I thought as much.

Gregers (to RELLING*).* But how do you account for that?

Relling (sullenly). Her constitution's changing, sir.

Hialmar. So long as the child has me——! So long as I am above ground——! [*A knock at the door.*

Gina. Hush, Ekdal; there's some one in the passage. *(Calls out.)* Come in!

[MRS. SÖRBY, *in walking dress, comes in.*

Mrs. Sörby. Good evening.

Gina (going towards her). Is it really you, Bertha?

Mrs. Sörby. Yes, of course it is. But I'm disturbing you, I'm afraid?

Hialmar. No, not at all; an emissary from that house——

Mrs. Sörby (to GINA*).* To tell the truth, I hoped your men-folk would be out at this time. I just ran up to have a little chat with you, and to say good-bye.

Gina. Good-bye? Are you going away, then?

Mrs. Sörby. Yes, to-morrow morning,—up to Höidal. Mr. Werle started this afternoon. *(Lightly to* GREGERS.*)* He asked me to say good-bye for him.

Gina. Only fancy——!

Hialmar. So Mr. Werle has gone? And now you are going after him?

Mrs. Sörby. Yes, what do you say to that, Ekdal?

Hialmar. I say: beware!

Gregers. I must explain the situation. My father and Mrs. Sörby are going to be married.

Hialmar. Going to be married!

Gina. Oh, Bertha! So it's come to that at last!

Relling (his voice quivering a little). This is surely not true?

Mrs. Sörby. Yes, my dear Relling, it's true enough.

Relling. You are going to marry again?

Mrs. Sörby. Yes, it looks like it. Werle has got a special licence, and we are going to be married quite quietly, up at the works.

Gregers. Then I must wish you all happiness, like a dutiful stepson.

Mrs. Sörby. Thank you very much—if you mean what you say. I certainly hope it will lead to happiness, both for Werle and for me.

Relling. You have every reason to hope that. Mr. Werle never gets drunk—so far as I know; and I don't suppose he's in the habit of thrashing his wives, like the late lamented horse-doctor.

Mrs. Sörby. Come now, let Sörby rest in peace. He had his good points, too.

Relling. Mr. Werle has better ones, I have no doubt.

Mrs. Sörby. He hasn't frittered away all that was good in him, at any rate. The man who does that must take the consequences.

Relling. I shall go out with Molvik this evening.

Mrs. Sörby. You mustn't do that, Relling. Don't do it —for my sake.

Relling. There's nothing else for it. *(To* HIALMAR.*)* If you're going with us, come along.

Gina. No, thank you. Ekdal doesn't go in for that sort of dissertation.

Hialmar (half aloud, in vexation). Oh, do hold your tongue!

Relling. Good-bye, Mrs.—Werle.

[*Goes out through the passage door.*

Gregers (to MRS. SÖRBY*).* You seem to know Dr. Relling pretty intimately.

Mrs. Sörby. Yes, we have known each other for many years. At one time it seemed as if things might have gone further between us.

Gregers. It was surely lucky for you that they did not.

Mrs. Sörby. You may well say that. But I have always been wary of acting on impulse. A woman can't afford absolutely to throw herself away.

Gregers. Are you not in the least afraid that I may let my father know about this old friendship?

Mrs. Sörby. Why, of course, I have told him all about it myself.

Gregers. Indeed?

Mrs. Sörby. Your father knows every single thing that can, with any truth, be said about me. I have told him all;

it was the first thing I did when I saw what was in his mind.

Gregers. Then you have been franker than most people, I think.

Mrs. Sörby. I have always been frank. We women find that the best policy.

Hialmar. What do you say to that, Gina?

Gina. Oh, we're not all alike, us women aren't. Some are made one way, some another.

Mrs. Sörby. Well, for my part, Gina, I believe it's wisest to do as I've done. And Werle has no secrets either, on his side. That's really the great bond between us, you see. Now he can talk to me as openly as a child. He has never had the chance to do that before. Fancy a man like him, full of health and vigour, passing his whole youth and the best years of his life in listening to nothing but penitential sermons! And very often the sermons had for their text the most imaginary offences—at least so I understand.

Gina. That's true enough.

Gregers. If you ladies are going to follow up this topic, I had better withdraw.

Mrs. Sörby. You can stay as far as that's concerned. I shan't say a word more. But I wanted you to know that I had done nothing secretly or in an underhand way. I may seem to have come in for a great piece of luck; and so I have, in a sense. But after all, I don't think I am getting any more than I am giving. I shall stand by him always, and I can tend and care for him as no one else can, now that he is getting helpless.

Hialmar. Getting helpless?

Gregers (to Mrs. Sörby*).* Hush, don't speak of that here.

Mrs. Sörby. There is no disguising it any longer, however much he would like to. He is going blind.

Hialmar (starts). Going blind? That's strange. He, too, going blind!

Gina. Lots of people do.

Mrs. Sörby. And you can imagine what that means to a business man. Well, I shall try as well as I can to make my eyes take the place of his. But I mustn't stay any longer; I have heaps of things to do.—Oh, by-the-bye, Ekdal, I was to tell you that if there is anything Werle can do for you, you must just apply to Gråberg.

Gregers. That offer I am sure Hialmar Ekdal will decline with thanks.

Mrs. Sörby. Indeed? I don't think he used to be so——

Gina. No, Bertha, Ekdal doesn't need anything from Mr. Werle now.

Hialmar (slowly, and with emphasis). Will you present my compliments to your future husband and say that I intend very shortly to call upon Mr. Gråberg——

Gregers. What! You don't really mean that?

Hialmar. To call upon Mr. Gråberg, I say, and obtain an account of the sum I owe his principal. I will pay that debt of honour—ha ha ha! a debt of honour, let us call it! In any case, I will pay the whole with five per cent. interest.

Gina. But, my dear Ekdal, God knows we haven't got the money to do it.

Hialmar. Be good enough to tell your future husband that I am working assiduously at my invention. Please tell him that what sustains me in this laborious task is the wish to free myself from a torturing burden of debt. That is my reason for proceeding with the invention. The entire profits shall be devoted to releasing me from my pecuniary obligations to your future husband.

Mrs. Sörby. Something has happened here.

Hialmar. Yes, you are right.

Mrs. Sörby. Well, good-bye. I had something else to speak to you about, Gina; but it must keep till another time. Good-bye.

[HIALMAR *and* GREGERS *bow silently.* GINA *follows* MRS. SÖRBY *to the door.*

Hialmar. Not beyond the threshold, Gina!

[Mrs. Sörby *goes;* Gina *shuts the door after her.*

Hialmar. There now, Gregers; I have got that burden of debt off my mind.

Gregers. You soon will, at all events.

Hialmar. I think my attitude may be called correct.

Gregers. You are the man I have always taken you for.

Hialmar. In certain cases, it is impossible to disregard the claim of the ideal. Yet, as the breadwinner of a family, I cannot but writhe and groan under it. I can tell you it is no joke for a man without capital to attempt the repayment of a long-standing obligation, over which, so to speak, the dust of oblivion had gathered. But it cannot be helped: the Man in me demands his rights.

Gregers (laying his hand on Hialmar's *shoulder).* My dear Hialmar—was it not a good thing I came?

Hialmar. Yes.

Gregers. Are you not glad to have had your true position made clear to you?

Hialmar (somewhat impatiently). Yes, of course I am. But there is one thing that is revolting to my sense of justice.

Gregers. And what is that?

Hialmar. It is that—but I don't know whether I ought to express myself so unreservedly about your father.

Gregers. Say what you please, so far as I am concerned.

Hialmar. Well, then, is it not exasperating to think that it is not I, but he, who will realise the true marriage?

Gregers. How can you say such a thing?

Hialmar. Because it is clearly the case. Isn't the marriage between your father and Mrs. Sörby founded upon complete confidence, upon entire and unreserved candour on both sides? They hide nothing from each other, they keep no secrets in the background; their relation is based, if I may put it so, on mutual confession and absolution.

Gregers. Well, what then?

Hialmar. Well, is not that the whole thing? Did you not

yourself say that this was precisely the difficulty that had to be overcome in order to found a true marriage?

Gregers. But this is a totally different matter, Hialmar. You surely don't compare either yourself or your wife with those two——? Oh, you understand me well enough.

Hialmar. Say what you like, there is something in all this that hurts and offends my sense of justice. It really looks as if there were no just providence to rule the world.

Gina. Oh, no, Ekdal; for God's sake don't say such things.

Gregers. H'm; don't let us get upon those questions.

Hialmar. And yet, after all, I cannot but recognise the guiding finger of fate. He is going blind.

Gina. Oh, you can't be sure of that.

Hialmar. There is no doubt about it. At all events there ought not to be; for in that very fact lies the righteous retribution. He has hoodwinked a confiding fellow creature in days gone by——

Gregers. I fear he has hoodwinked many.

Hialmar. And now comes inexorable, mysterious Fate and demands Werle's own eyes.

Gina. Oh, how dare you say such dreadful things! You make me quite scared.

Hialmar. It is profitable, now and then, to plunge deep into the night side of existence.

[HEDVIG, *in her hat and cloak, comes in by the passage door. She is pleasurably excited and out of breath.*

Gina. Are you back already?

Hedvig. Yes, I didn't care to go any farther. It was a good thing, too; for I've just met some one at the door.

Hialmar. It must have been that Mrs. Sörby.

Hedvig. Yes.

Hialmar (walks up and down). I hope you have seen her for the last time.

[*Silence.* HEDVIG, *discouraged, looks first at one*

and then at the other, trying to divine their frame of mind.

Hedvig (approaching, coaxingly). Father.

Hialmar. Well—what is it, Hedvig?

Hedvig. Mrs. Sörby had something with her for me.

Hialmar (stops). For you?

Hedvig. Yes. Something for to-morrow.

Gina. Bertha has always given you some little thing on your birthday.

Hialmar. What is it?

Hedvig. Oh, you mustn't see it now. Mother is to give it to me to-morrow morning before I'm up.

Hialmar. What is all this hocus-pocus that I am to be in the dark about!

Hedvig (quickly). Oh, no, you may see it if you like. It's a big letter.

[*Takes the letter out of her cloak pocket.*

Hialmar. A letter, too?

Hedvig. Yes, it is only a letter. The rest will come afterwards, I suppose. But fancy—a letter! I've never had a letter before. And there's "Miss" written upon it. *(Reads.)* "Miss Hedvig Ekdal." Only fancy—that's me!

Hialmar. Let me see that letter.

Hedvig (hands it to him). There it is.

Hialmar. That is Mr. Werle's hand.

Gina. Are you sure of that, Ekdal?

Hialmar. Look for yourself.

Gina. Oh, what do *I* know about such-like things?

Hialmar. Hedvig, may I open the letter—and read it?

Hedvig. Yes, of course you may, if you want to.

Gina. No, not to-night, Ekdal; it's to be kept till to-morrow.

Hedvig (softly). Oh, can't you let him read it! It's sure to be something good; and then father will be glad, and everything will be nice again.

Hialmar. I may open it, then?

Hedvig. Yes, do, father. I'm so anxious to know what it is.

Hialmar. Well and good. *(Opens the letter, takes out a paper, reads it through and appears bewildered.)* What is this——!

Gina. What does it say?

Hedvig. Oh, yes, father—tell us!

Hialmar. Be quiet. *(Reads it through again; he has turned pale, but says with self-control:)* It is a deed of gift, Hedvig.

Hedvig. Is it? What sort of gift am I to have?

Hialmar. Read for yourself.

[Hedvig *goes over and reads for a time by the lamp.*

Hialmar (half-aloud, clenching his hands). The eyes! The eyes—and then that letter!

Hedvig (leaves off reading). Yes, but it seems to me that it's grandfather that's to have it.

Hialmar (takes letter from her). Gina—can you understand this?

Gina. I know nothing whatever about it; tell me what's the matter.

Hialmar. Mr. Werle writes to Hedvig that her old grandfather need not trouble himself any longer with the copying, but that he can henceforth draw on the office for a hundred crowns a month——

Gregers. Aha!

Hedvig. A hundred crowns, mother! I read that.

Gina. What a good thing for grandfather!

Hialmar. ——a hundred crowns a month so long as he needs it—that means, of course, so long as he lives.

Gina. Well, so he's provided for, poor dear.

Hialmar. But there is more to come. You didn't read that, Hedvig. Afterwards this gift is to pass on to you.

Hedvig. To me! The whole of it?

Hialmar. He says that the same amount is assured to you for the whole of your life. Do you hear that, Gina?

Gina. Yes, I hear.

Hedvig. Fancy—all that money for me! *(Shakes him.)* Father, father, aren't you glad——?

Hialmar (eluding her). Glad! *(Walks about.)* Oh what vistas—what perspectives open up before me! It is Hedvig, Hedvig that he showers these benefactions upon!

Gina. Yes, because it's Hedvig's birthday——

Hedvig. And you'll get it all the same, father! You know quite well I shall give all the money to you and mother.

Hialmar. To mother, yes! There we have it.

Gregers. Hialmar, this is a trap he is setting for you.

Hialmar. Do you think it's another trap?

Gregers. When he was here this morning he said: Hialmar Ekdal is not the man you imagine him to be.

Hialmar. Not the man——!

Gregers. That you shall see, he said.

Hialmar. He meant you should see that I would let myself be bought off——!

Hedvig. Oh, mother, what does all this mean?

Gina. Go and take off your things.

[HEDVIG *goes out by the kitchen door, half-crying.*

Gregers. Yes, Hialmar—now is the time to show who was right, he or I.

Hialmar (slowly tears the paper across, lays both pieces on the table and says): Here is my answer.

Gregers. Just what I expected.

Hialmar (goes over to GINA, *who stands by the stove, and says in a low voice):* Now please make a clean breast of it. If the connection between you and him was quite over when you—came to care for me, as you call it—why did he place us in a position to marry?

Gina. I suppose he thought as he could come and go in our house.

Hialmar. Only that? Was not he afraid of a possible contingency?

Gina. I don't know what you mean.

Hialmar. I want to know whether—your child has the right to live under my roof.

Gina (draws herself up; her eyes flash). You ask that!

Hialmar. You shall answer me this one question: Does Hedvig belong to me—or——? Well!

Gina (looking at him with cold defiance). I don't know.

Hialmar (quivering a little). You don't know!

Gina. How should *I* know. A creature like me——

Hialmar (quietly turning away from her). Then I have nothing more to do in this house.

Gregers. Take care, Hialmar! Think what you are doing!

Hialmar (puts on his overcoat). In this case, there is nothing for a man like me to think twice about.

Gregers. Yes, indeed, there are endless things to be considered. You three must be together if you are to attain the true frame of mind for self-sacrifice and forgiveness.

Hialmar. I don't want to attain it. Never, never! My hat! *(Takes his hat.)* My home has fallen in ruins about me. *(Bursts into tears.)* Gregers, I have no child!

Hedvig (who has opened the kitchen door). What is that you're saying? *(Coming to him.)* Father, father!

Gina. There, you see!

Hialmar. Don't come near me, Hedvig! Keep far away. I cannot bear to see you. Oh! those eyes——! Good-bye.

[*Makes for the door.*

Hedvig (clinging close to him and screaming loudly). No! no! Don't leave me!

Gina (cries out). Look at the child, Ekdal! Look at the child!

Hialmar. I will not! I cannot! I must get out—away from all this!

[*He tears himself away from* HEDVIG *and goes out by the passage door.*

Hedvig (with despairing eyes). He is going away from us, mother! He is going away from us! He will never come back again!

Gina. Don't cry, Hedvig. Father's sure to come back again.

Hedvig (throws herself sobbing on the sofa). No, no, he'll never come home to us any more.

Gregers. Do you believe I meant all for the best, Mrs. Ekdal?

Gina. Yes, I daresay you did; but God forgive you, all the same.

Hedvig (lying on the sofa). Oh, this will kill me! What have I done to him? Mother, you must fetch him home again!

Gina. Yes, yes yes; only be quiet, and I'll go out and look for him. *(Puts on her outdoor things.)* Perhaps he's gone in to Relling's. But you mustn't lie there and cry. Promise me!

Hedvig (weeping convulsively). Yes, I'll stop, I'll stop; if only father comes back!

Gregers (to Gina, who is going). After all, had you not better leave him to fight out his bitter fight to the end?

Gina. Oh, he can do that afterwards. First of all, we must get the child quieted. [*Goes out by the passage door.*

Hedvig (sits up and dries her tears). Now you must tell me what all this means. Why doesn't father want me any more?

Gregers. You mustn't ask that till you are a big girl—quite grown-up.

Hedvig (sobs). But I can't go on being as miserable as this till I'm grown-up.—I think I know what it is.—Perhaps I'm not really father's child.

Gregers (uneasily). How could that be?

Hedvig. Mother might have found me. And perhaps father has just got to know it; I've read of such things.

Gregers. Well, but if it were so——

Hedvig. I think he might be just as fond of me for all that. Yes, fonder almost. We got the wild duck in a present, you know, and I love it so dearly all the same.

Gregers (turning the conversation). Ah, the wild duck, by-the-bye! Let us talk about the wild duck a little, Hedvig.

Hedvig. The poor wild duck! He doesn't want to see it any more either. Only think, he wanted to wring its neck!

Gregers. Oh, he won't do that.

Hedvig. No; but he said he would like to. And I think it was horrid of father to say it; for I pray for the wild duck every night and ask that it may be preserved from death and all that is evil.

Gregers (looking at her). Do you say your prayers every night?

Hedvig. Yes.

Gregers. Who taught you to do that?

Hedvig. I myself; one time when father was very ill, and had leeches on his neck and said that death was staring him in the face.

Gregers. Well?

Hedvig. Then I prayed for him as I lay in bed; and since then I have always kept it up.

Gregers. And now you pray for the wild duck, too?

Hedvig. I thought it was best to bring in the wild duck; for she was so weakly at first.

Gregers. Do you pray in the morning, too?

Hedvig. No, of course not.

Gregers. Why not in the morning as well?

Hedvig. In the morning it's light, you know, and there's nothing in particular to be afraid of.

Gregers. And your father was going to wring the neck of the wild duck that you love so dearly?

Hedvig. No; he said he ought to wring its neck, but he would spare it for my sake; and that was kind of father.

Gregers (coming a little nearer). But suppose you were to sacrifice the wild duck of your own free will for his sake.

Hedvig (rising). The wild duck!

Gregers. Suppose you were to make a free-will offering, for his sake, of the dearest treasure you have in the world!

Hedvig. Do you think that would do any good?

Gregers. Try it, Hedvig.

Hedvig. (softly, with flashing eyes). Yes, I will try it.

Gregers. Have you really the courage for it, do you think?

Hedvig. I'll ask grandfather to shoot the wild duck for me.

Gregers. Yes, do. But not a word to your mother about it.

Hedvig. Why not?

Gregers. She doesn't understand us.

Hedvig. The wild duck! I'll try it to-morrow morning.

[GINA *comes in by the passage door.*

Hedvig (going towards her). Did you find him, mother?

Gina. No, but I heard as he had called and taken Relling with him.

Gregers. Are you sure of that?

Gina. Yes, the porter's wife said so. Molvik went with them, too, she said.

Gregers. This evening, when his mind so sorely needs to wrestle in solitude——!

Gina (takes off her things). Yes, men are strange creatures, so they are. The Lord only knows where Relling has dragged him to! I ran over to Madam Eriksen's, but they weren't there.

Hedvig (struggling to keep back her tears). Oh, if he should never come home any more!

Gregers. He will come home again. I shall have news to give him to-morrow; and then you shall see how he comes home. You may relay upon that, Hedvig, and sleep in peace. Good-night.

[*He goes out by the passage door.*

Hedvig (throws herself sobbing on GINA'S *neck).* Mother, mother!

Gina (pats her shoulder and sighs). Ah, yes; Relling was right, he was. That's what comes of it when crazy creatures go about presenting the claims of the—what-you-may-call-it.

ACT V

HIALMAR EKDAL'S *studio. Cold, grey morning light. Wet snow lies upon the large panes of the sloping roof-window.*

GINA *comes from the kitchen with an apron and bib on, and carrying a dusting-brush and a duster; she goes towards the sitting-room door. At the same moment* HEDVIG *comes hurriedly in from the passage.*

Gina (stops). Well?

Hedvig. Oh, mother, I almost think he's down at Relling's——

Gina. There, you see!

Hedvig. ——because the porter's wife says she could hear that Relling had two people with him when he came home last night.

Gina. That's just what I thought.

Hedvig. But it's no use his being there, if he won't come up to us.

Gina. I'll go down and speak to him at all events.

[OLD EKDAL, *in dressing-gown and slippers, and with a lighted pipe, appears at the door of his room.*

Ekdal. Hialmar—— Isn't Hialmar at home?

Gina. No, he's gone out.

Ekdal. So early? And in such a tearing snowstorm? Well, well; just as he pleases; I can take my morning walk alone.

[*He slides the garret door aside;* HEDVIG *helps him; he goes in; she closes it after him.*

Hedvig (in an undertone). Only think, mother, when poor grandfather hears that father is going to leave us.

Gina. Oh, nonsense; grandfather mustn't hear anything about it. It was a heaven's mercy he wasn't at home yesterday in all that hurly-burly.

Hedvig. Yes, but——

[GREGERS *comes in by the passage door.*

Gregers. Well, have you any news of him?

Gina. They say he's down at Relling's.

Gregers. At Relling's! Has he really been out with those creatures?

Gina. Yes, like enough.

Gregers. When he ought to have been yearning for solitude, to collect and clear his thoughts——

Gina. Yes, you may well say so.

[RELLING *enters from the passage.*

Hedvig (going to him). Is father in your room?

Gina (at the same time). Is he there?

Relling. Yes, to be sure he is.

Hedvig. And you never let us know!

Relling. Yes, I'm a brute. But in the first place I had to look after the other brute; I mean our dæmonic friend, of course; and then I fell so dead asleep that——

Gina. What does Ekdal say to-day?

Relling. He says nothing whatever.

Hedvig. Doesn't he speak?

Relling. Not a blessed word.

Gregers. No, no; I can understand that very well.

Gina. But what's he doing then?

Relling. He's lying on the sofa, snoring.

Gina. Oh, is he? Yes, Ekdal's a rare one to snore.

Hedvig. Asleep? Can he sleep?

Relling. Well, it certainly looks like it.

Gregers. No wonder, after the spiritual conflict that has rent him——

Gina. And then he's never been used to gadding about out of doors at night.

Hedvig. Perhaps it's a good thing that he's getting sleep, mother.

Gina. Of course it is; and we must take care we don't wake him up too early. Thank you, Relling. I must get the house cleaned up a bit now, and then—— Come and help me, Hedvig.

[GINA *and* HEDVIG *go into the sitting-room.*

Gregers (turning to RELLING*).* What is your explanation of the spiritual tumult that is now going on in Hialmar Ekdal?

Relling. Devil a bit of a spiritual tumult have *I* noticed in him.

Gregers. What! Not at such a crisis, when his whole life has been placed on a new foundation——? How can you think that such an individuality as Hialmar's——?

Relling. Oh, individuality—he! If he ever had any tendency to the abnormal developments you call individuality, I can assure you it was rooted out of him while he was still in his teens.

Gregers. That would be strange indeed,—considering the loving care with which he was brought up.

Relling. By those two high-flown, hysterical maiden aunts, you mean?

Gregers. Let me tell you that they were women who never forgot the claim of the ideal—but of course you will only jeer at me again.

Relling. No, I'm in no humour for that. I know all about those ladies; for he has ladled out no end of rhetoric on the subject of his "two soul-mothers." But I don't think he has much to thank them for. Ekdal's misfortune is that in his own circle he has always been looked upon as a shining light——

Gregers. Not without reason, surely. Look at the depth of his mind!

Relling. *I* have never discovered it. That his father believed in it I don't so much wonder; the old lieutenant has been an ass all his days.

Gregers. He has had a child-like mind all his days; that is what you cannot understand.

Relling. Well, so be it. But then, when our dear, sweet Hialmar went to college, he at once passed for the great light of the future amongst his comrades, too! He was handsome, the rascal—red and white—a shop-girl's dream of manly beauty; and with his superficially emotional temperament, and his sympathetic voice and his talent for declaiming other people's verses and other people's thoughts——

Gregers (indignantly). Is it Hialmar Ekdal you are talking about in this strain?

Relling. Yes, with your permission; I am simply giving you an inside view of the idol you are grovelling before.

Gregers. I should hardly have thought I was quite stone blind.

Relling. Yes, you are—or not far from it. You are a sick man, too, you see.

Gregers. You are right there.

Relling. Yes. Yours is a complicated case. First of all there is that plaguy integrity-fever; and then—what's worse—you are always in a delirium of hero-worship; you must always have something to adore, outside yourself.

Gregers. Yes, I must certainly seek it outside myself.

Relling. But you make such shocking mistakes about every new phœnix you think you have discovered. Here again you have come to a cotter's cabin with your claim of the ideal; and the people of the house are insolvent.

Gregers. If you don't think better than that of Hialmar Ekdal, what pleasure can you find in being everlastingly with him?

Relling. Well, you see, I'm supposed to be a sort of a doctor—save the mark! I can't but give a hand to the poor sick folk who live under the same roof with me.

Gregers. Oh, indeed! Hialmar Ekdal is sick, too, is he!

Relling. Most people are, worse luck.

Gregers. And what remedy are you applying in Hialmar's case?

Relling. My usual one. I am cultivating the life-illusion* in him.

Gregers. Life—illusion? I didn't catch what you said.

Relling. Yes, I said illusion. For illusion, you know, is the stimulating principle.

Gregers. May I ask with what illusion Hialmar is inoculated?

Relling. No, thank you; I don't betray professional secrets to quacksalvers. You would probably go and muddle his case still more than you have already. But my method is infallible. I have applied it to Molvik as well. I have made him "dæmonic." That's the blister I have to put on his neck.

Gregers. Is he not really dæmonic, then?

Relling. What the devil do you mean by dæmonic! It's only a piece of gibberish I've invented to keep up a spark of life in him. But for that, the poor harmles creature would have succumbed to self-contempt and despair many a long year ago. And then the old lieutenant! But he has hit upon his own cure, you see.

Gregers. Lieutenant Ekdal? What of him?

Relling. Just think of the old bear-hunter shutting himself up in that dark garret to shoot rabbits! I tell you there is not a happier sportsman in the world than that old man pottering about in there among all that rubbish. The four or five withered Christmas trees he has saved up are the same to him as the whole great fresh Höidal forest; the cock and the hens are big game-birds in the fir-tops; and the rabbits that flop about the garret floor are the bears he has to battle with—the mighty hunter of the mountains!

* "Livslögnen," literally "the life-lie."

Gregers. Poor unfortunate old man! Yes; he has indeed had to narrow the ideals of his youth.

Relling. While I think of it, Mr. Werle, junior—don't use that foreign word: ideals. We have the excellent native word: lies.

Gregers. Do you think the two things are related?

Relling. Yes, just about as closely as typhus and putrid fever.

Gregers. Dr. Relling, I shall not give up the struggle until I have rescued Hialmar from your clutches!

Relling. So much the worse for him. Rob the average man of his life-illusion, and you rob him of his happiness at the same stroke. *(To* HEDVIG, *who comes in from the sitting-room.)* Well, little wild-duck-mother, I'm just going down to see whether papa is still lying meditating upon that wonderful invention of his. [*Goes out by passage door.*

Gregers (approaches HEDVIG*).* I can see by your face that you have not yet done it.

Hedvig. What? Oh, that about the wild duck! No.

Gregers. I suppose your courage failed when the time came.

Hedvig. No, that wasn't it. But when I awoke this morning and remembered what we had been talking about, it seemed so strange.

Gregers. Strange?

Hedvig. Yes, I don't know—— Yesterday evening, at the moment, I thought there was something so delightful about it; but since I have slept and thought of it again, it somehow doesn't seem worth while.

Gregers. Ah, I thought you could not have grown up quite unharmed in this house.

Hedvig. I don't care about that, if only father would come up——

Gregers. Oh, if only your eyes had been opened to that which gives life its value—if you possessed the true, joyous, fearless spirit of sacrifice, you would soon see how he would come up to you.—But I believe in you still, Hedvig.

[*He goes out by the passage door.* HEDVIG *wanders about the room for a time; she is on the point of going into the kitchen when a knock is heard at the garret door.* HEDVIG *goes over and opens it a little; old* EKDAL *comes out; she pushes the door to again.*

Ekdal. H'm, it's not much fun to take one's morning walk alone.

Hedvig. Wouldn't you like to go shooting, grandfather?

Ekdal. It's not the weather for it to-day. It's so dark there, you can scarcely see where you're going.

Hedvig. Do you never want to shoot anything besides the rabbits?

Ekdal. Do you think the rabbits aren't good enough?

Hedvig. Yes, but what about the wild duck?

Ekdal. Ho-ho! are you afraid I shall shoot your wild duck? Never in the world. Never.

Hedvig. No, I suppose you couldn't; they say it's very difficult to shoot wild ducks.

Ekdal. Couldn't! Should rather think I could.

Hedvig. How would you set about it, grandfather?—I don't mean with my wild duck, but with others?

Ekdal. I should take care to shoot them in the breast, you know; that's the surest place. And then you must shoot against the feathers, you see—not the way of the feathers.

Hedvig. Do they die then, grandfather?

Ekdal. Yes, they die right enough—when you shoot properly. Well, I must go and brush up a bit. H'm—understand—h'm. [*Goes into his room.*

[HEDVIG *waits a little, glances towards the sitting-room door, goes over to the book-case, stands on tip-toe, takes the double-barrelled pistol down from the shelf and looks at it.* GINA, *with brush and duster, comes from the sitting-room.* HEDVIG *hastily lays down the pistol, unobserved.*

Gina. Don't stand raking amongst father's things, Hedvig.

Hedvig (goes away from the bookcase). I was only going to tidy up a little.

Gina. You'd better go into the kitchen and see if the coffee's keeping hot: I'll take his breakfast on a tray, when I go down to him.

[HEDVIG *goes out.* GINA *begins to sweep and clean up the studio. Presently the passage door is opened with hesitation, and* HIALMAR EKDAL *looks in. He has on his overcoat, but not his hat; he is unwashed, and his hair is dishevelled and unkempt. His eyes are dull and heavy.*

Gina (standing with the brush in her hand and looking at him). Oh, there now, Ekdal—so you've come after all!

Hialmar (comes in and answers in a toneless voice). I come—only to depart again immediately.

Gina. Yes, yes, I suppose so. But, Lord help us! what a sight you are!

Hialmar. A sight?

Gina. And your nice winter coat, too! Well, that's done for.

Hedvig (at the kitchen door). Mother, hadn't I better——? *(Sees* HIALMAR, *gives a loud scream of joy and runs to him.)* Oh, father, father!

Hialmar (turns away and makes a gesture of repulsion). Away, away, away! *(To* GINA*)* Keep her away from me, I say!

Gina (in a low tone). Go into the sitting-room, Hedvig.

[HEDVIG *does so without a word.*

Hialmar (fussily pulls out the table-drawer). I must have my books with me. Where are my books?

Gina. Which books?

Hialmar. My scientific books, of course; the technical magazines I require for my invention.

Gina (searches in the bookcase). Is it these here paper-covered ones?

Hialmar. Yes, of course.

Gina (lays a heap of magazines on the table). Shan't I get Hedvig to cut them for you?

Hialmar. I don't require to have them cut for me.

[*Short silence.*

Gina. Then you're still set on leaving us, Ekdal?

Hialmar (rummaging amonst the books). Yes, that is a matter of course, I should think.

Gina. Well, well.

Hialmar (vehemently). How can I live here, to be stabbed to the heart every hour of the day?

Gina. God forgive you for thinking such vile things of me.

Hialmar. Prove——!

Gina. I think it's you as has got to prove.

Hialmar. After a past like yours? There are certain claims—I may almost call them claims of the ideal——

Gina. But what about grandfather? What's to become of him, poor dear!

Hialmar. I know my duty; my helpless father will come with me. I am going out into the town to make arrangements—— H'm—*(hesitatingly)*—has any one found my hat on the stairs?

Gina. No. Have you lost your hat?

Hialmar. Of course I had it on when I came in last night; there's no doubt about that; but I couldn't find it this morning.

Gina. Lord help us! where have you been to with those two ne'er-do-wells?

Hialmar. Oh, don't bother me about trifles. Do you suppose I am in the mood to remember details?

Gina. If only you haven't caught cold, Ekdal——

[*Goes out into the kitchen.*

Hialmar (talks to himself in a low tone of irritation, whilst he empties the table-drawer). You're a scoundrel, Relling! —You're a low fellow!—Ah, you shameless tempter!—I wish I could get some one to stick a knife into you!

[*He lays some old letters on one side, finds the torn document of yesterday, takes it up and looks at the pieces; puts it down hurriedly as* GINA *enters.*

Gina (sets a tray with coffee, etc., on the table). Here's a drop of something hot, if you'd fancy it. And there's some bread and butter and a snack of salt meat.

Hialmar (glancing at the tray). Salt meat? Never under this roof! It's true I have not had a mouthful of solid food for nearly twenty-four hours; but no matter.—My memoranda! The commencement of my autobiography! What has become of my diary, and all my important papers? *(Opens the sitting-room door but draws back.)* She is there, too!

Gina. Good Lord! the child must be somewhere!

Hialmar. Come out.

[*He makes room,* HEDVIG *comes, scared, into the studio.*

Hialmar (with his hand upon the door-handle, says to GINA*):* In these, the last moments I spend in my former home, I wish to be spared from interlopers——

[*Goes into the room.*

Hedvig (with a bound towards her mother, asks softly, trembling). Does that mean me?

Gina. Stay out in the kitchen, Hedvig; or, no—you'd best go into your own room. *(Speaks to* HIALMAR *as she goes in to him.)* Wait a bit, Ekdal; don't rummage so in the drawers; *I* know where everything is.

Hedvig (stands a moment immovable, in terror and perplexity, biting her lips to keep back the tears; then she clenches her hands convulsively and says softly): The wild duck.

[*She steals over and takes the pistol from the shelf, opens the garret door a little way, creeps in and draws the door to after her.*

[HIALMAR *and* GINA *can be heard disputing in the sitting-room.*

Hialmar (comes in with some manuscript books and old loose papers, which he lays upon the table). That portmanteau is of no use! There are a thousand and one things I must drag with me.

Gina (following with the portmanteau). Why not leave all the rest for the present and only take a shirt and a pair of woollen drawers with you?

Hialmar Whew!—all these exhausting preparations——!

[*Pulls off his overcoat and throws it upon the sofa.*

Gina. And there's the coffee getting cold.

Hialmar. H'm.

[*Drinks a mouthful without thinking of it and then another.*

Gina (dusting the backs of the chairs). A nice job you'll have to find such another big garret for the rabbits.

Hialmar. What! Am I to drag all those rabbits with me, too?

Gina. You don't suppose grandfather can get on without his rabbits.

Hialmar. He must just get used to doing without them. Have not *I* to sacrifice very much greater things than rabbits!

Gina (dusting the bookcase). Shall I put the flute in the portmanteau for you?

Hialmar. No. No flute for me. But give me the pistol!

Gina. Do you want to take the pistol with you?

Hialmar. Yes. My loaded pistol.

Gina (searching for it). It's gone. He must have taken it in with him.

Hialmar. Is he in the garret?

Gina. Yes, of course he's in the garret.

Hialmar. H'm—poor lonely old man.

[*He takes a piece of bread and butter, eats it and finishes his cup of coffee.*

Gina. If we hadn't have let that room, you could have moved in there.

Hialmar. And continued to live under the same roof with——! Never,—never!

Gina. But couldn't you put up with the sitting-room for a day or two? You could have it all to yourself.

Hialmar. Never within these walls!

Gina. Well, then, down with Relling and Molvik.

Hialmar. Don't mention those wretches' names to me! The very thought of them almost takes away my appetite.—Oh, no, I must go out into the storm and the snow-drift,—go from house to house and seek shelter for my father and myself.

Gina. But you've got no hat, Ekdal! You've been and lost your hat, you know.

Hialmar. Oh, those two brutes, those slaves of all the vices! A hat must be procured. *(Takes another piece of bread and butter.)* Some arrangements must be made. For I have no mind to throw away my life, either.

[*Looks for something on the tray.*

Gina. What are you looking for?

Hialmar. Butter.

Gina. I'll get some at once. [*Goes out into the kitchen.*

Hialmar (calls after her). Oh, it doesn't matter; dry bread is good enough for me.

Gina (brings a dish of butter.) Look here; this is fresh churned.

[*She pours out another cup of coffee for him; he seats himself on the sofa, spreads more butter on the already buttered bread and eats and drinks awhile in silence.*

Hialmar. Could I, without being subject to intrusion—intrusion of any sort—could I live in the sitting-room there for a day or two?

Gina. Yes, to be sure you could, if you only would.

Hialmar. For I see no possibility of getting all father's things out in such a hurry.

Gina. And, besides, you've surely got to tell him first as you don't mean to live with us others no more.

Hialmar (pushes away his coffee cup). Yes, there is that, too; I shall have to lay bare the whole tangled story to him—— I must turn matters over; I must have breathing-time; I cannot take all these burdens on my shoulders in a single day.

Gina. No, especially in such horrible weather as it is outside.

Hialmar (touching WERLE'S *letter).* I see that paper is still lying about here.

Gina. Yes, *I* haven't touched it.

Hialmar. So far as I am concerned it is mere waste paper——

Gina. Well, *I* have certainly no notion of making any use of it.

Hialmar. ——but we had better not let it get lost all the same;—in all the upset when I move, it might easily——

Gina. I'll take good care of it, Ekdal.

Hialmar. The donation is in the first instance made to father, and it rests with him to accept or decline it.

Gina (sighs). Yes, poor old father——

Hialmar. To make quite safe—— Where shall I find some gum?

Gina (goes to the bookcase). Here's the gum-pot.

Hialmar. And a brush?

Gina. The brush is here, too. [*Brings him the things.*

Hialmar (takes a pair of scissors). Just a strip of paper at the back——*(clips and gums.)* Far be it from me to lay hands upon what is not my own—and least of all upon what belongs to a destitute old man—and to—the other as well.—There now. Let it lie there for a time; and when it is dry, take it away. I wish never to see that document again. Never!

[GREGERS WERLE *enters from the passage.*

Gregers (somewhat surprised). What,—are you sitting here, Hialmar?

Hialmar (rises hurriedly). I had sunk down from fatigue.

Gregers. You have been having breakfast, I see.

Hialmar. The body sometimes makes its claims felt, too.

Gregers. What have you decided to do?

Hialmar. For a man like me, there is only one course possible. I am just putting my most important things together. But it takes time, you know.

Gina (with a touch of impatience). Am I to get the room ready for you, or am I to pack your portmanteau?

Hialmar (after a glance of annoyance at GREGERS*).* Pack —and get the room ready!

Gina (takes the portmanteau). Very well; then I'll put in the shirt and the other things.

[*Goes into the sitting-room and draws the door to after her.*

Gregers (after a short silence). I never dreamed that this would be the end of it. Do you really feel it a necessity to leave house and home?

Hialmar (wanders about restlessly). What would you have me do?—I am not fitted to bear unhappiness, Gregers. I must feel secure and at peace in my surroundings.

Gregers. But can you not feel that here? Just try it. I should have thought you had firm ground to build upon now—if only you start afresh. And, remember, you have your invention to live for.

Hialmar. Oh, don't talk about my invention. It's perhaps still in the dim distance.

Gregers. Indeed!

Hialmar. Why, great heavens, what would you have me

invent? Other people have invented almost everything already. It becomes more and more difficult every day——

Gregers. And you have devoted so much labour to it.

Hialmar. It was that blackguard Relling that urged me to it.

Gregers. Relling?

Hialmar. Yes, it was he that first made me realise my aptitude for making some notable discovery in photography.

Gregers. Aha—it was Relling!

Hialmar. Oh, I have been so truly happy over it! Not so much for the sake of the invention itself, as because Hedvig believed in it—believed in it with a child's whole eagerness of faith.—At least, I have been fool enough to go and imagine that she believed in it.

Gregers. Can you really think Hedvig has been false towards you?

Hialmar. I can think anything now. It is Hedvig that stands in my way. She will blot out the sunlight from my whole life.

Gregers. Hedvig! Is it Hedvig you are talking of? How should she blot out your sunlight?

Hialmar (without answering). How unutterably I have loved that child! How unutterably happy I have felt every time I came home to my humble room, and she flew to meet me, with her sweet little blinking eyes. Oh, confiding fool that I have been! I loved her unutterably;—and I yielded myself up to the dream, the delusion, that she loved me unutterably in return.

Gregers. Do you call that a delusion?

Hialmar. How should I know? I can get nothing out of Gina; and besides, she is totally blind to the ideal side of these complications. But to you I feel impelled to open my mind, Gregers. I cannot shake off this frightful doubt—perhaps Hedvig has never really and honestly loved me.

Gregers. What would you say if she were to give you a

proof of her love? *(Listens.)* What's that? I thought I heard the wild duck——?

Hialmar. It's the wild duck quacking. Father's in the garret.

Gregers. Is he? *(His face lights up with joy).* I say, you may yet have proof that your poor misunderstood Hedvig loves you!

Hialmar. Oh, what proof can she give me? I dare not believe in any assurance from that quarter.

Gregers. Hedvig does not know what deceit means.

Hialmar. Oh, Gregers, that is just what I cannot be sure of. Who knows what Gina and that Mrs. Sörby may many a time have sat here whispering and tattling about? And Hedvig usually has her ears open, I can tell you. Perhaps the deed of gift was not such a surprise to her, after all. In fact, I'm not sure but that I noticed something of the sort.

Gregers. What spirt is this that has taken possession of you?

Hialmar. I have had my eyes opened. Just you notice; —you'll see, the deed of gift is only a beginning. Mrs. Sörby has always been a good deal taken up with Hedvig; and now she has the power to do whatever she likes for the child. They can take her from me whenever they please.

Gregers. Hedvig will never, never leave you.

Hialmar. Don't be so sure of that. If only they beckon to her and throw out a golden bait——! And, oh! I have loved her so unspeakably! I would have counted it my highest happiness to take her tenderly by the hand and lead her, as one leads a timid child through a great dark empty room!—I am cruelly certain now that the poor photographer in his humble attic has never really and truly been anything to her. She has only cunningly contrived to keep on a good footing with him until the time came.

Gregers. You don't believe that yourself, Hialmar.

Hialmar. That is just the terrible part of it—I don't know what to believe,—I never can know it. But can you really doubt that it must be as I say? Ho-ho, you have far too much faith in the claim of the ideal, my good Gregers! If those others came, with the glamour of wealth about them, and called to the child:—"Leave him: come to us: here life awaits you——!"

Gregers (quickly). Well, what then?

Hialmar. If I then asked her: Hedvig, are you willing to renounce that life for me? *(Laughs scornfully.)* No thank you! You would soon hear what answer I should get. [*A pistol shot is heard from within the garret.*

Gregers (loudly and joyfully). Hialmar!

Hialmar. There now; he must needs go shooting, too.

Gina (comes in). Oh, Ekdal, I can hear grandfather blazing away in the garret by hisself.

Hialmar. I'll look in——

Gregers (eagerly, with emotion). Wait a moment! Do you know what that was?

Hialmar. Yes, of course I know.

Gregers. No, you don't know. But *I* do. That was the proof!

Hialmar. What proof?

Gregers. It was a child's free-will offering. She has got your father to shoot the wild duck.

Hialmar. To shoot the wild duck!

Gina. Oh, think of that——!

Hialmar. What was that for?

Gregers. She wanted to sacrifice to you her most cherished possession; for then she thought you would surely come to love her again.

Hialmar (tenderly, with emotion). Oh, poor child!

Gina. What things she does think of!

Gregers. She only wanted your love again, Hialmar. She could not live without it.

Gina (struggling with her tears). There, you can see for yourself, Ekdal.

Hialmar. Gina, where is she?

Gina (sniffs). Poor dear, she's sitting out in the kitchen, I dare say.

Hialmar (goes over, tears open the kitchen door and says): Hedvig, come, come in to me! *(Looks around.)* No, she's not here.

Gina. Then she must be in her own little room.

Hialmar (without). No, she's not here either. *(Comes in.)* She must have gone out.

Gina. Yes, you wouldn't have her anywheres in the house.

Hialmer. Oh, if she would only come home quickly, so that I can tell her—— Everything will come right now, Gregers; now I believe we can begin life afresh.

Gregers (quietly). I knew it; I knew the child would make amends.

[OLD EKDAL *appears at the door of his room; he is in full uniform and is busy buckling on his sword.*

Hialmar (astonished). Father! Are you there?

Gina. Have you been firing in your room?

Ekdal (resentfully, approaching). So you go shooting alone, do you, Hialmar?

Hialmar (excited and confused). Then it wasn't you that fired that shot in the garret?

Ekdal. Me that fired? H'm.

Gregers (calls out to HIALMAR*).* She has shot the wild duck herself!

Hialmar. What can it mean? *(Hastens to the garret door, tears it aside, looks in and calls loudly):* Hedvig!

Gina (runs to the door). Good God, what's that!

Hialmar (goes in). She's lying on the floor!

Gregers. Hedvig! lying on the floor!

[*Goes in to* HIALMAR.

Gina (at the same time). Hedvig! *(Inside the garret.)* No, no, no!

Ekdal. Ho-ho! does she go shooting, too, now?

[HIALMAR, GINA *and* GREGERS *carry* HEDVIG *into the studio; in her dangling right hand she holds the pistol fast clasped in her fingers.*

Hialmar (distracted). The pistol has gone off. She has wounded herself. Call for help! Help!

Gina (runs into the passage and calls down). Relling! Relling! Doctor Relling; come up as quick as you can!

[HIALMAR *and* GREGERS *lay* HEDVIG *down on the sofa.*

Ekdal (quietly). The woods avenge themselves.

Hialmar (on his knees beside HEDVIG*).* She'll soon come to now. She's coming to——; yes, yes, yes.

Gina (who has come in again). Where has she hurt herself? I can't see anything——

[RELLING *comes hurriedly, and immediately after him* MOLVIK; *the latter without his waistcoat and necktie, and with his coat open.*

Relling. What's the matter here?

Gina. They say Hedvig has shot herself.

Hialmar. Come and help us!

Relling. Shot herself!

[*He pushes the table aside and begins to examine her.*

Hialmar (kneeling and looking anxiously up at him). It can't be dangerous? Speak, Relling! She is scarcely bleeding at all. It can't be dangerous?

Relling. How did it happen?

Hialmar. Oh, we don't know——

Gina. She wanted to shoot the wild duck.

Relling. The wild duck?

Hialmar. The pistol must have gone off.

Relling. H'm. Indeed.

Ekdal The woods avenge themselves. But I'm not afraid, all the same.

[*Goes into the garret and closes the door after him.*

Hialmar. Well, Relling,—why don't you say something?

Relling. The ball has entered the breast.

Hialmar. Yes, but she's coming to!

Relling. Surely you can see that Hedvig is dead.

Gina (bursts into tears). Oh, my child, my child——

Gregers (huskily). In the depths of the sea——

Hialmar (jumps up). No, no, she must live! Oh, for God's sake, Relling—only a moment—only just till I can tell her how unspeakably I loved her all the time!

Relling. The bullet has gone through her heart. Internal hemorrhage. Death must have been instantaneous.

Hialmar. And I! I hunted her from me like an animal! And she crept terrified into the garret and died for love of me! *(Sobbing.)* I can never atone to her! I can never tell her——! *(Clenches his hands and cries, upwards.)* O thou above——! If thou be indeed! Why hast thou done this thing to me?

Gina. Hush, hush, you mustn't go on that awful way. We had no right to keep her, I suppose.

Molvik. The child is not dead, but sleepeth.

Relling. Bosh.

Hialmar (becomes calm, goes over to the sofa, folds his arms and looks at HEDVIG*).* There she lies so stiff and still.

Relling (tries to loosen the pistol). She's holding it so tight, so tight.

Gina. No, no, Relling, don't break her fingers; let the pistol be.

Hialmar. She shall take it with her.

Gina. Yes, let her. But the child mustn't lie here for a show. She shall go to her own room, so she shall. Help me, Ekdal. [HIALMAR *and* GINA *take* HEDVIG *between them.*

Hialmar (as they are carrying her). Oh, Gina, Gina, can you survive this!

Gina. We must help each other to bear it. For now at least she belongs to both of us.

Molvik (stretches out his arms and mumbles.) Blessed be the Lord; to earth thou shalt return; to earth thou shalt return——

Relling (whispers). Hold your tongue, you fool; you're drunk.

[HIALMAR *and* GINA *carry the body out through the kitchen door.* RELLING *shuts it after them.* MOLVIK *slinks out into the passage.*

Relling (goes over to GREGERS *and says):* No one shall ever convince me that the pistol went off by accident.

Gregers (who has stood terrified, with convulsive twitchings). Who can say how the dreadful thing happened?

Relling. The powder has burnt the body of her dress. She must have pressed the pistol right against her breast and fired.

Gregers. Hedvig has not died in vain. Did you not see how sorrow set free what is noble in him?

Relling. Most people are ennobled by the actual presence of death. But how long do you suppose this nobility will last in him?

Gregers. Why should it not endure and increase throughout his life?

Relling. Before a year is over, little Hedvig will be nothing to him but a pretty theme for declamation.

Gregers. How dare you say that of Hialmar Edkal?

Relling. We will talk of this again, when the grass has first withered on her grave. Then you'll hear him spouting about "the child too early torn from her father's heart;" then you'll see him steep himself in a syrup of sentiment and self-admiration and self-pity. Just you wait!

Gregers. If you are right and I am wrong, then life is not worth living.

Relling. Oh, life would be quite tolerable, after all, if

only we could be rid of the confounded duns that keep on pestering us, in our poverty, with the claim of the ideal.

Gregers (looking straight before him). In that case, I am glad that my destiny is what is.

Relling. May I inquire,—what is your destiny?

Gregers (going). To be the thirteenth at table.

Relling. The devil it is.

THE LEAGUE OF YOUTH
(1869)

CHARACTERS

CHAMBERLAIN BRATSBERG,* *owner of iron-works.*
ERIK BRATSBERG, *his son, a merchant.*
THORA, *his daughter.*
SELMA, *Erik's wife.*
DOCTOR FIELDBO, *physician at the Chamberlain's works.*
STENSGÅRD,† *a lawyer.*
MONS MONSEN, *of Stonelee.*‡
BASTIAN MONSEN, *his son.*
RAGNA, *his daughter.*
HELLE,§ *student of theology, tutor at Stonelee.*
RINGDAL, *manager of the iron-works.*
ANDERS LUNDESTAD, *landowner.*
DANIEL HEIRE.¶
MADAM|| RUNDHOLMEN, *widow of a storekeeper and publican.*
ASLAKSEN, a printer.
A MAID-SERVANT AT THE CHAMBERLAIN'S.
A WAITER.
A WAITRESS AT MADAM RUNDHOLMEN'S.
Townspeople, Guests at the Chamberlain's, etc., etc.

The action takes place in the neighbourhood of the iron-works, not far from a market town in Southern Norway.

* "Chamberlain" (Kammerherre) is a title conferred by the King of Norway upon men of wealth and position. Hereditary nobility was abolished in 1821. † Pronounce *Staynsgore.* ‡ In the original "Storli." § Pronounce *Hellë.* ¶ Heire (pronounce *Heirë*) = Heron. || Married women and widows of the lower middle-class are addressed as Madam in Norway.

THE LEAGUE OF YOUTH

ACT I

The Seventeenth of May. A popular fête in the Chamberlain's grounds. Music and dancing in the background. Coloured lights among the trees. In the middle, somewhat towards the back, a rostrum. To the right, the entrance to a large refreshment-tent; before it, a table with benches. In the foreground on the left, another table, decorated with flowers and surrounded with lounging-chairs.*

A Crowd of People. LUNDESTAD, *with a committee-badge at his button-hole, stands on the rostrum.* RINGDAL, *also with a committee-badge, at the table on the left.*

Lundestad. . . . Therefore, friends and fellow-citizens, I drink to our freedom! As we have inherited it from our fathers, so will we preserve it for ourselves and for our children! Three cheers for the day! Three cheers for the Seventeenth of May!

The Crowd. Hurrah! hurrah! hurrah!

Ringdal (as LUNDESTAD *descends from the rostrum).* And one cheer more for old Lundestad!

Some of the Crowd (hissing). Ss! Ss!

Many Voices (drowning the others). Hurrah for Lundestad! Long live old Lundestad! Hurrah!

[*The* CROWD *gradually disperses.* MONSEN, *his*

* The Norwegian "Independence Day."

son BASTIAN, STENSGÅRD *and* ASLAKSEN *make their way forward through the throng.*

Monsen. 'Pon my soul, it's time he was laid on the shelf!

Aslaksen. It was the local situation* he was talking about! Ho-ho!

Monsen. He has made the same speech year after year as long as I can remember. Come over here.

Stensgård. No, no, not that way, Mr. Monsen. We are quite deserting your daughter.

Monsen. Oh, Ragna will find us again.

Bastian. She's all right; young Helle is with her.

Stensgård. Helle?

Monsen. Yes, Helle. But *(nudging* STENSGÅRD *familiarly)* you have me here, you see, and the rest of us. Come on! Here we shall be out of the crowd and can discuss more fully what——

[*Has meanwhile taken a seat beside the table on the left.*

Ringdal (approaching). Excuse me, Mr. Monsen—that table is reserved——

Stensgård. Reserved? For whom?

Ringdal. For the Chamberlain's party.

Stensgård. Oh, confound the Chamberlain's party! There's none of them here.

Ringdal. No, but we expect them every minute.

Stensgård. Then let them sit somewhere else.

[*Takes a chair.*

Lundestad (laying his hand on the chair). No, the table is reserved, and there's an end of it.

Monsen (rising). Come, Mr. Stensgård; there are just as good seats over there. *(Crosses to the right.)* Waiter!

* "Local situation" is a very ineffectual rendering of Aslaksen's phrase, "lokale forholde"—German, *Verkältnisse*—but there seems to be no other which will fit into all the different contexts in which it occurs. It reappears in *An Enemy of the People*, Act v.

Ha, no waiters either. The Committee should have seen to that in time. Oh, Aslaksen, just go in and get us four bottles of champagne. Order the dearest; tell them to put it down to Monsen!

[ASLAKSEN *goes into the tent; the three others seat themselves.*

Lundestad (goes quietly over to them and addresses Stensgård). I hope you won't take it ill——

Monsen. Take it ill! Good gracious, no! Not in the least.

Lundestad (still to STENSGÅRD*).* It's not my doing; it's the Committee that decided——

Monsen. Of course. The Committee orders, and we must obey.

Lundestad (as before). You see, we are on the Chamberlain's own ground here. He has been so kind as to throw open his park and garden for this evening; so we thought——

Stensgård. We're extremely comfortable here, Mr. Lundestad—if only people would leave us in peace—the crowd, I mean.

Lundestad (unruffled). Very well; then it's all right.

[*Goes towards the back.*

Aslaksen (entering from the tent). The waiter is just coming with the wine. [*Sits.*

Monsen. A table apart, under special care of the Committee! And on our Independence Day of all others! There you have a specimen of the way things go.

Stensgård. But why on earth do you put up with all this, you good people?

Monsen. The habit of generations, you see.

Aslaksen. You're new to the district, Mr. Stensgård. If only you knew a little of the local situation——

A Waiter (brings champagne). Was it you that ordered——?

Aslaksen. Yes, certainly; open the bottle.

The Waiter (pouring out the wine). It goes to your account, Mr. Monsen?

Monsen. The whole thing; don't be afraid.

[*The* WAITER *goes.*

Monsen (clinks glasses with STENSGÅRD*).* Here's welcome among us, Mr. Stensgård! It gives me great pleasure to have made your acquaintance; I cannot but call it an honour to the district that such a man should settle here. The newspapers have made us familiar with your name, on all sorts of public occasions. You have great gifts of oratory, Mr. Stensgård, and a warm heart for the public weal. I trust you will enter with life and vigour into the—h'm, into the——

Aslaksen. The local situation.

Monsen. Oh, yes, the local situation. I drink to that.

[*They drink.*

Stensgård. Whatever I do, I shall certainly put life and vigour into it.

Monsen. Bravo! Hear, hear! Another glass in honour of that promise.

Stensgård. No, stop; I've already——

Monsen. Oh, nonsense! Another glass, I say—to seal the bond!

[*They clink glasses and drink. During what follows* BASTIAN *keeps on filling the glasses as soon as they are empty.*

Monsen. However—since we have got upon the subject —I must tell you that it's not the Chamberlain himself that keeps everything under his thumb. No, sir—old Lundestad is the man that stands behind and drives the sledge.

Stensgård. So I am told in many quarters. I can't understand how a Liberal like him——

Monsen. Lundestad? Do you call Anders Lundestad a Liberal? To be sure, he professed Liberalism in his young days, when he was still at the foot of the ladder. And then he inherited his seat in Parliament from his father. Good Lord! everything runs in families here.

Stensgård. But there must be some means of putting a stop to all these abuses.

Aslaksen. Yes, damn it all, Mr. Stensgård—see if you can't put a stop to them!

Stensgård. I don't say that I——

Aslaksen. Yes, you! You are just the man. You have the gift of gab, as the saying goes; and what's more: you have the pen of a ready writer. My paper's at your disposal, you know.

Monsen. If anything is to be done, it must be done quickly. The preliminary election* comes on in three days now.

Stensgård. And if you were elected, your private affairs would not prevent your accepting the charge?

Monsen. My private affairs would suffer, of course; but if it appeared that the good of the community demanded the sacrifice, I should have to put aside all personal considerations.

Stensgård. Good; that's good. And you have a party already: that I can see clearly.

Monsen. I flatter myself the majority of the younger, go-ahead generation——

Aslaksen. H'm, h'm! 'ware spies!

[DANIEL HEIRE *enters from the tent; he peers about short-sightedly and approaches.*

Heire. May I beg for the loan of a spare seat; I want to sit over there.

Monsen. The benches are fastened here, you see; but won't you take a place at this table?

* The system of indirect election obtains in Norway. The constituencies choose a College of Electors, who, in turn, choose the Members of the Storthing or Parliament. It is the preliminary "Election of Electors" to which Monsen refers.

Heire. Here? At this table? Oh, yes, with pleasure. *(Sits.)* Dear, dear! Champagne, I believe.

Monsen. Yes; won't you join us in a glass?

Heire. No, thank you! Madam Rundholmen's champagne—— Well, well, just half a glass to keep you company. If only one had a glass, now.

Monsen. Bastian, go and get one.

Bastian. Oh, Aslaksen, just go and fetch a glass.

[ASLAKSEN *goes into the tent. A pause.*

Heire. Don't let me interrupt you, gentlemen. I wouldn't for the world——! Thanks, Aslaksen. *(Bows to* STENSGÅRD.*)* A strange face—a recent arrival! Have I the pleasure of addressing our new legal luminary, Mr. Stensgård?

Monsen. Quite right. *(Introducing them.)* Mr. Stensgård, Mr. Daniel Heire——

Bastian. Capitalist.

Heire. Ex-capitalist, you should rather say. It's all gone now; slipped through my fingers, so to speak. Not that I'm bankrupt—for goodness' sake don't think that.

Monsen. Drink, drink, while the froth is on it.

Heire. But rascality, you understand—sharp practice and so forth—— I say no more. Well, well, I am confident it is only temporary. When I get my outstanding law-suits and some other little matters off my hands, I shall soon be on the track of our aristocratic old Reynard the Fox. Let us drink to that—— You won't, eh?

Stensgård. I should like to know first who your aristocratic old Reynard the Fox may be.

Heire. Hee-hee; you needn't look so uncomfortable, man. You don't suppose I'm alluding to Mr. Monsen. No one can accuse Mr. Monsen of being aristocratic. No; it's Chamberlain Bratsberg, my dear young friend.

Stensgård. What! In money matters the Chamberlain is surely above reproach.

Heire. You think so, young man? H'm; I say no more. *(Draws nearer.)* Twenty years ago I was worth no end of money. My father left me a great fortune. You've heard of my father, I daresay? No? Old Hans Heire? They called him Gold Hans. He was a shipowner: made heaps of money in the blockade time; had his window-frames and door-posts gilded; he could afford it—— I say no more; so they called him Gold Hans.

Aslaksen. Didn't he gild his chimney-pots, too?

Heire. No; that was only a penny-a-liner's lie; invented long before your time, however. But he made the money fly; and so did I in my time. My visit to London, for instance—haven't you heard of my visit to London? I took a prince's retinue with me. Have you really not heard of it, eh? And the sums I have lavished on art and science! And on bringing rising talent to the front!

Aslaksen (rises). Well, good-bye, gentlemen.

Monsen. What? Are you leaving us?

Aslaksen. Yes; I want to stretch my legs a bit. [*Goes.*

Heire (speaking low). He was one of them—just as grateful as the rest, hee-hee! Do you know, I kept him a whole year at college?

Stensgård. Indeed? Has Aslaksen been to college?

Heire. Like young Monsen. He made nothing of it; also like—— I say no more. Had to give him up, you see; he had already developed his unhappy taste for spirits——

Monsen. But you've forgotten what you were going to tell Mr. Stensgård about the Chamberlain.

Heire. Oh, it's a complicated business. When my father was in his glory, things were going downhill with the old Chamberlain—this one's father, you understand; he was a Chamberlain, too.

Bastian. Of course; everything runs in families here.

Heire. Including the social graces—— I say no more.

The conversion of the currency, rash speculations, extravagances he launched out into, in the year 1816 or thereabouts, forced him to sell some of his land.

Stensgård. And your father bought it?

Heire. Bought and paid for it. Well, what then? I came into my property; I make improvements by the thousand——

Bastian. Of course.

Heire. Your health, my young friend!—Improvements by the thousand, I say—thinning the woods, and so forth. Years pass; and then comes Master Reynard—the present one, I mean—and repudiates the bargain!

Stensgård. But, my dear Mr. Heire, you could surely have snapped your fingers at him.

Heire. Not so easily! Some small formalities had been overlooked, he declared. Besides, I happened then to be in temporary difficulties, which afterwards became permanent. And what can a man do nowadays without capital?

Monsen. You're right there, by God! And in many ways you can't do very much with capital either. That I know to my cost. Why, even my innocent children——

Bastian (thumps the table). Ugh, father! if I only had certain people here!

Stensgård. Your children, you say?

Monsen. Yes; take Bastian, for example. Perhaps I haven't given him a good education?

Heire. A threefold education! First for the University; then for painting; and then for—what is it?—it's a civil engineer he is now, isn't it?

Bastian. Yes, that I am, by the Lord!

Monsen. Yes, that he is; I can produce his bills and his certificates to prove it! But who gets the town business? Who has got the local road-making—especially these last two years? Foreigners, or at any rate strangers—in short, people no one knows anything about!

Heire. Yes; it's shameful the way things go on. Only

last New Year, when the managership of the Savings Bank fell vacant, what must they do but give Monsen the go-by and choose an individual that knew—*(Coughs)*—that knew how to keep his purse-strings drawn—which our princely host obviously does not. Whenever there's a post of confidence going, it's always the same! Never Monsen—always some one that enjoys the confidence—of the people in power. Well, well; *commune suffragium*, as the Roman Law puts it; that means shipwreck in the Common Council, sir.* It's a shame! Your health!

Monsen. Thanks! But, to change the subject—how are all your law-suits getting on?

Heire. They are still pending; I can say no more for the present. What endless annoyance they do give me! Next week I shall have to summon the whole Town Council before the Arbitration Commission.†

Bastian. Is it true that you once summoned yourself before the Arbitration Commission?

Heire. Myself? Yes; but I didn't put in an appearance.

Monsen. Ha, ha! You didn't, eh?

Heire. I had a sufficient excuse: had to cross the river, and it was unfortunately the very year of Bastian's bridge—plump! down it went, you know——

Bastian. Why, confound it all——!

Heire. Take it coolly, young man! You are not the first that has bent the bow till it breaks. Everything runs in families, you know—— I say no more.

Monsen. Ho, ho, ho! You say no more, eh? Well, drink, then, and say no more! *(To* STENSGARD.*)* You see, Mr. Heire's tongue is licensed to wag as it pleases.

* In this untranslatable passage Daniel Heire seems to be making a sort of pun on *suffragium* and *naufragium*.

† In Norway, before an action comes into Court, the parties are bound to appear in person before a commission of Arbitration or Conciliation. If the Commission can suggest an arrangement acceptable to both sides, this arrangement has the validity of a judgment, and the case goes no further. Counsel are not allowed to appear before the Commision.

Heire. Yes, freedom of speech is the only civic right I really value.

Stensgård. What a pity the law should restrict it.

Heire. Hee-hee! Our legal friend's mouth is watering for a nice action for slander, eh? Make your mind easy, my dear sir! I'm an old hand, let me tell you!

Stensgård. Especially at slander?

Heire. Your pardon, young man! That outburst of indignation does honour to your heart. I beg you to forget an old man's untimely frankness about your absent friends.

Stensgård. Absent friends?

Heire. I have nothing to say against the son, of course —nor against the daughter. And if I happened to cast a passing slur upon the Chamberlain's character——

Stensgård. The Chamberlain's? Is it the Chamberlain's family you call my friends?

Heire. Well, you don't pay visits to your enemies, I presume?

Bastian. Visits?

Monsen. What?

Heire. Ow, ow, ow! Here am I letting cats out of bags——!

Monsen. Have you been paying visits at the Chamberlain's?

Stensgård. Nonsense! A misunderstanding——

Heire. A most unhappy slip on my part. But how was I to know it was a secret? *(To* MONSEN.*)* Besides, you mustn't take my expressions too literally. When I say a visit, I mean only a sort of formal call; a frock-coat and yellow gloves affair——

Stensgård. I tell you I haven't exchanged a single word with any of that family!

Heire. Is it possible? Were *you* not received the second time either? I know they were "not at home" the first time.

Stensgård (to MONSEN*).* I had a letter to deliver from a friend in Christiania—that was all.

Heire (rising). I'll be hanged if it isn't positively revolting! Here is a young man at the outset of his career; full of simple-minded confidence, he seeks out the experienced man-of-the-world and knocks at his door; turns to him, who has brought his ship to port, to beg for—— I say no more! The man-of-the-world shuts the door in his face; is not at home; never is at home when it's his duty to be—— I say no more! *(With indignation.)* Was there ever such shameful insolence!

Stensgård. Oh, never mind that stupid business.

Heire. Not at home! He, who goes about professing that he is always at home to reputable people!

Stensgård. Does he say that?

Heire. A mere empty phrase. He's not at home to Mr. Monsen either. But I can't think what has made him hate you so much. Yes, hate you, I say; for what do you think I heard yesterday?

Stensgård. I don't want to know what you heard yesterday.

Heire. Then I say no more. Besides, the expressions didn't surprise me—coming from the Chamberlain, I mean. Only I can't understand why he should have added "demagogue."

Stensgård. Demagogue!

Heire. Well, since you insist upon it, I must confess that the Chamberlain called you an adventurer and demagogue.

Stensgård (jumps up). What!

Heire. Adventurer and demagogue—or demagogue and adventurer; I won't answer for the order.

Stensgård. And you heard that?

Heire. I? If I had been present, Mr. Stensgård, you may be sure I should have stood up for you as you deserve.

Monsen. There, you see what comes of——

Stensgård. How dare the old scoundrel——?

Heire. Come, come, come! Keep your temper. Very likely it was a mere figure of speech—a harmless little joke, I have no doubt. You can demand an explanation to-morrow; for I suppose you are going to the great dinner-party, eh?

Stensgård. I am not going to any dinner-party.

Heire. Two calls and no invitation——!

Stensgård. Demagogue and adventurer! What can he be thinking of?

Monsen. Look here! Talk of the devil——! Come, Bastian. [*Goes off with* BASTIAN.

Stensgård. What did he mean by it, Mr. Heire?

Heire. Haven't the ghost of an idea.—It pains you? Your hand, young man! Pardon me if my frankness has wounded you. Believe me, you have yet many bitter lessons to learn in this life. You are young; you are confiding; you are trustful. It is beautiful; it is even touching; but—but—trustfulness is silver, experience is gold: that's a proverb of my own invention, sir! God bless you! [*Goes.*

[CHAMBERLAIN BRATSBERG, *his daughter* THORA *and* DOCTOR FIELDBO *enter from the left.*

Lundestad (strikes the bell on the rostrum). Silence for Mr. Ringdal's speech!

Stensgård (shouts). Mr. Lundestad, I demand to be heard.

Lundestad. Afterwards.

Stensgård. No, now! at once!

Lundestad. You can't speak just now. Silence for Mr. Ringdal!

Ringdal (on the rostrum). Ladies and gentlemen! We have at this moment the honour of seeing in our midst the man with the warm heart and the open hand—the man we have all looked up to for many a year, as to a father—the man who is always ready to help us, both in word and deed—the man whose door is never closed to any reputable citizen—the man who—who—ladies and gentlemen, our honoured guest is no lover of long speeches; so, without more words, I call for three cheers for Chamberlain Bratsberg and his family! Long life to them! Hurrah!

The Crowd. Hurrah! hurrah! hurrah!

[*Great enthusiasm; people press around the* CHAMBERLAIN, *who thanks them and shakes hands with those nearest him.*

Stensgård. Now may I speak?

Lundestad. By all means. The platform is at your service.

Stensgård (jumps upon the table). I shall choose my own platform!

The Young Men (crowding around him). Hurrah!

The Chamberlain (to the DOCTOR*).* Who is this obstreperous personage?

Fieldbo. Mr. Stensgård.

The Chamberlain. Oh, it's he, is it?

Stensgård. Listen to me, my glad-hearted brothers and sisters! Hear me, all you who have in your souls—though it may not reach your lips—the exultant song of the day, the day of our freedom! I am a stranger among you——

Aslaksen. No!

Stensgård. Thanks for that "No!" I take it as the utterance of a longing, an aspiration. A stranger I am, however; but this I swear, that I come among you with a great and open-hearted sympathy for your sorrows and your joys, your victories and defeats. If it lay in my power——

Aslaksen. It does, it does!

Lundestad. No interruptions! You have no right to speak.

Stensgård. You still less! I abolish the Committee! Freedom on the day of freedom, boys!

The Young Men. Hurrah for freedom!

Stensgård. They deny you the right of speech! You hear it—they want to gag you! Away with this tyranny!

I won't stand here declaiming to a flock of dumb animals. I will talk; but you shall talk, too. We will talk to each other, from the heart!

The Crowd (with growing enthusiasm). Hurrah!

Stensgård. We will have no more of these barren, white-chokered festivities! A golden harvest of deeds shall hereafter shoot up from each Seventeenth of May. May! Is it not the season of bud and blossom, the blushing maiden-month of the year? On the first of June I shall have been just two months among you; and in that time what greatness and littleness, what beauty and deformity, have I not seen?

The Chamberlain. What on earth is he talking about, Doctor?

Fieldbo. Aslaksen says it's the local situation.

Stensgård. I have seen great and brilliant possibilities among the masses; but I have seen, too, a spirit of corruption brooding over the germs of promise and bringing them to nought. I have seen ardent and trustful youth rush yearning forth—and I have seen the door shut in its face.

Thora. Oh, Heaven!

The Chamberlain. What does he mean by that?

Stensgård. Yes, my brothers and sisters in rejoicing! There hovers in the air an Influence, a Spectre from the dead and rotten past, which spreads darkness and oppression where there should be nothing but buoyancy and light. We must lay that Spectre; down with it!

The Crowd. Hurrah! Hurrah for the Seventeenth of May!

Thora. Come away, father——!

The Chamberlain. What the deuce does he mean by a spectre? Who is he talking about, Doctor?

Fieldbo (quickly). Oh, it's about——

[*Whispers a word or two.*

The Chamberlain. Aha! So that's it!

Thoma (softly to FIELDBO*).* Thanks!

Stensgård. If no one else will crush the dragon, I will! But we must hold together, boys!

Many Voices. Yes! yes!

Stensgård. We are young! The time belongs to us; but we also belong to the time. Our right is our duty! Elbow-room for faculty, for will, for power! Listen to me! We must form a League. The money-bag has ceased to rule among us!

The Chamberlain. Bravo! *(To the* DOCTOR*).* He said the money-bag; so no doubt you're right——

Stensgård. Yes, boys; we, we are the wealth of the country, if only there's metal in us. Our will is the ringing gold that shall pass from man to man. War to the knife against whoever shall deny its currency!

The Crowd. Hurrah!

Stensgård. A scornful "bravo" has been flung in my teeth——

The Chamberlain. No, no!

Stensgård. What care I! Thanks and threats alike are powerless over the perfect will. And now, God be with us! For we are going about His work, with youth and faith to help us. Come, then, into the refreshment-tent—our League shall be baptised this very hour.

The Crowd. Hurrah! Carry him! Shoulder high with him! [*He is lifted shoulder high.*

Voices. Speak on! More! More!

Stensgård. Let us hold together, I say! Providence is on the side of the League of Youth. It lies with us to rule the world—here in the district!

[*He is carried into the tent amid wild enthusiasm.*

Madam Rundholmen (wiping her eyes). Oh, Lord, how beautifully he does speak! Don't you feel as if you could kiss him, Mr. Heire?

Heire. Thank you, I'd rather not.

Madam Rundholmen. Oh, you! I daresay not.

Heire. Perhaps you would like to kiss him, Madam Rundholmen.

Madam Rundholmen. Ugh, how horrid you are!

[*She goes into the tent;* HEIRE *follows her.*

The Chamberlain. Spectre—and dragon—and money-bag! It was horribly rude—but well deserved!

Lundestad (approaching). I'm heartily sorry, Chamberlain——

The Chamberlain. Yes, where was your knowledge of character, Lundestad? Well, well; we are none of us infallible. Good-night, and thanks for a pleasant evening. (*Turns to* THORA *and the* DOCTOR.) But bless me, I've been positively rude to that fine young fellow!

Fieldbo. How so?

Thora. His call, you mean——?

The Chamberlain. He called twice. It's really Lundestad's fault. He told me he was an adventurer and—and I forget what else. Fortunately I can make up for it.

Thora. How?

The Chamberlain. Come, Thora; let us see to it at once——

Fieldbo. Oh, do you think it's worth while, Chamberlain——?

Thora (softly). Hush!

The Chamberlain. When one has done an injustice one should lose no time in undoing it; that's a plain matter of duty. Good-night, Doctor. After all, I've spent an amusing hour; and that's more than I have to thank you for to-day.

Fieldbo. Me, Chamberlain?

The Chamberlain. Yes, yes, yes—you and others.

Fieldbo. May I ask what I——?

The Chamberlain. Don't be curious, Doctor. I am never curious. Come, come—no offence—good-night!

[THE CHAMBERLAIN *and* THORA *go out to the left;* FIELDBO *gazes thoughtfully after them.*

Aslaksen (from the tent). Hei, waiter! Pen and ink! Things are getting lively, Doctor!

Fieldbo. What things?

Aslaksen. He's founding the League. It's nearly founded.

Lundestad (who has quietly drawn near). Are many putting down their names?

Aslaksen. We've enrolled about seven-and-thirty, not counting widows and so forth. Pen and ink, I say! No waiters to be found!—that's the fault of the local situation.

[*Goes off behind the tent.*

Lundestad. Puh! It has been hot to-day.

Fieldbo. I'm afraid we have hotter days to come.

Lundestad. Do you think the Chamberlain was very angry?

Fieldbo. Oh, not in the least; you could see that, couldn't you? But what do you say to the new League?

Lundestad. H'm; I say nothing. What is there to be said?

Fieldbo. It's the beginning of a struggle for power here in the district.

Lundestad. Well, well; no harm in a fight. He has great gifts, that Stensgård.

Fieldbo. He is determined to make his way.

Lundestad. Youth is always determined to make its way. I was, when I was young; no one can object to that. But mightn't we look in and see——

Heire (from the tent). Well, Mr. Lundestad, are you going to move the previous question, eh? To head the opposition? Hee-hee! You must make haste!

Lundestad. Oh, I daresay I shall be in time.

Heire. Too late, sir! Unless you want to stand godfather. *(Cheering from the tent.)* There, they're chanting Amen; the baptism is over.

Lundestad. I suppose one may be permitted to listen; I shall keep quiet. [*Enters the tent.*

Heire. There goes one of the falling trees! There will be a rare uprooting, I can tell you! The place will soon look like a wood after a tornado. Won't I chuckle over it!

Fieldbo. Tell me, Mr. Heire, what interest have you in the matter?

Heire. Interest? I am entirely disinterested, Doctor! If I chuckle, it is on behalf of my fellow-citizens. There will be life, spirit, go, in things. For my own part—good Lord, it's all the same to me; I say, as the Grand Turk said of the Emperor of Austria and the King of France—I don't care whether the pig eats the dog or the dog the pig.

[*Goes toward the back on the right.*

The Crowd (in the tent). Long live Stensgård! Hurrah! Hurrah for the League of Youth! Wine! Punch! Hei, hei! Beer! Hurrah!

Bastian (comes from the tent). God bless you and every one. *(With tears in his voice.)* Oh, Doctor, I feel so strong this evening; I must do something.

Fieldbo. Don't mind me. What would you like to do?

Bastian. I think I'll go down to the dancing-room and fight one or two fellows. [*Goes out behind the tent.*

Stensgård (comes from the tent without his hat and greatly excited). My dear Fieldbo, is that you?

Fieldbo. At your service, Tribune of the People! For I suppose you've been elected——?

Stensgård. Of course; but——

Fieldbo. And what is to come of it all? What nice little post are you to have? The management of the Bank? Or perhaps——

Stensgård. Oh, don't talk to me like that! I know you don't mean it. You are not so empty and wooden as you like to appear.

Fieldbo. Empty and wooden, eh?

Stensgård. Fieldbo! Be my friend as you used to be!

We have not understood each other of late. You have wounded and repelled me with your ridicule and irony. Believe me, it was wrong of you. *(Embraces him.)* Oh, my great God! how happy I am!

Fieldbo. You, too? So am I, so am I!

Stensgård. Yes, I should be the meanest hound on earth if all heaven's bounty didn't make me good and true. How have I deserved it, Fieldbo? What have I, sinner that I am, done to be so richly blessed?

Fieldbo. There is my hand! This evening I am your friend indeed!

Stensgård. Thanks! Be faithful and true, as I shall be! —Oh, isn't it an unspeakable joy to carry all that multitude away and along with you? How can you help becoming good from mere thankfulness? And how it makes you love all your fellow-creatures! I feel as if I could clasp them all in one embrace, and weep and beg their forgiveness because God has been so partial as to give me more than them.

Fieldbo (quietly). Yes, treasures without price may fall to one man's lot. This evening I would not crush an insect, not a green leaf upon my path.

Stensgård. You?

Fieldbo. Never mind. That's apart from the question. I only mean that I understand you.

Stensgård. What a lovely night! Listen to the music and merriment floating out over the meadows. And how still it is in the valley! I tell you the man whose life is not reconsecrated in such an hour does not deserve to live on God's earth!

Fieldbo. Yes; but tell me now: what do you mean to build up out of it—to-morrow, and through the working-days to come?

Stensgård. To build up? We have to tear down first.— Fieldbo, I had once a dream—or did I see it? No; it was a dream, but such a vivid one! I thought the Day of Judgment was come upon the world. I could see the whole curve of the hemisphere. There was no sun, only a livid storm-light. A tempest arose; it came rushing from the west and swept everything before it: first withered leaves, then men; but they kept on their feet all the time, and their garments clung fast to them, so that they seemed to be hurried along sitting. At first they looked like townspeople running after their hats in a wind; but when they came nearer they were emperors and kings; and it was their crowns and orbs they were chasing and catching at, and seemed always on the point of grasping, but never grasped. Oh, there were hundreds and hundreds of them, and none of them understood in the least what was happening; but many bewailed themselves and asked: "Whence can it come, this terrible storm?" Then there came the answer: "One Voice spoke, and the storm is the echo of that one Voice."

Fieldbo. When did you dream that?

Stensgård. Oh, I don't remember when; several years ago.

Fieldbo. There were probably disturbances somewhere in Europe, and you had been reading the newspapers after a heavy supper.

Stensgård. The same shiver, the same thrill, that then ran down my back, I felt again to-night. Yes, I will give my whole soul utterance. I will be the Voice——

Fieldbo. Come, my dear Stensgård, pause and reflect. You will be the Voice, you say. Good! But where will you be the Voice? Here in the parish? Or at most here in the county! And who will echo you and raise the storm? Why, people like Monsen and Aslaksen and that fat-headed genius, Mr. Bastian. And instead of the flying emperors and kings, we shall see old Lundestad rushing about after his lost seat in Parliament. Then what will it all amount to? Just what you at first saw in your dream—townsfolk in a wind.

Stensgård. In the beginning, yes. But who knows how far the storm may sweep?

Fieldbo. Fiddlesticks with you and your storm! And the first thing you go and do, hoodwinked and blinded and gulled as you are, is to turn your weapons precisely against all that is worthy and capable among us——

Stensgård. That is not true.

Fieldbo. It is true! Monsen and the Stonelee gang got hold of you the moment you came here; and if you don't shake him off it will be your ruin. Chamberlain Bratsberg is a man of honour; that you may rely on. Do you know why the great Monsen hates him? Why, because——

Stensgård. Not a word more! I won't hear a word against my friends!

Fieldbo. Look into yourself, Stensgård! Is Mr. Mons Monsen really your friend?

Stensgård. Mr. Monsen has most kindly opened his doors to me——

Fieldbo. To people of the better sort he opens his doors in vain.

Stensgård. Oh, whom do you call the better sort? A few stuck-up officials! I know all about it. As for me, I have been received at Stonelee with so much cordiality and appreciation——

Fieldbo. Appreciation? Yes, unfortunately—there we are at the root of the matter.

Stensgård. Not at all! I can see with unprejudiced eyes. Mr. Monsen has abilities, he has reading, he has a keen sense for public affairs.

Fieldbo. Abilities? Oh, yes, in a way. Reading, too: he takes in the papers and has read your speeches and articles. And his sense for public affairs he has, of course, proved by applauding the said articles and speeches.

Stensgård. Now, Fieldbo, up come the dregs of your nature again. Can you never shake off that polluting habit of thought? Why must you always assume mean or ridiculous motives for everything? Oh, you are not serious!

Now you look good and true again. I'll tell you the real root of the matter. Do you know Ragna?

Fieldbo. Ragna Monsen? Oh, after a fashion—at second hand.

Stensgård. Yes, I know she is sometimes at the Chamberlain's.

Fieldbo. In a quiet way, yes. She and Miss Bratsberg are old schoolfellows.

Stensgård. And what do you think of her?

Fieldbo. Why, from all I have heard she seems to be a very good girl.

Stensgård. Oh, you should see her in her home! She thinks of nothing but her two little sisters. And how devotedly she must have nursed her mother! You know the mother was out of her mind for some years before she died.

Fieldbo. Yes; I was their doctor at one time. But surely, my dear fellow, you don't mean that——

Stensgård. Yes, Fieldbo, I love her truly; to you I can confess it. Oh, I know what you are surprised at. You think it strange that so soon after—of course you know that I was engaged to Christiania?

Fieldbo. Yes, so I was told.

Stensgård. The whole thing was a disappointment. I had to break it off; it was best for all parties. Oh, how I suffered in that affair! The torture, the sense of oppression I endured——! Now, thank heaven, I am out of it all. That was my reason for leaving town.

Fieldbo. And with regard to Ragna Monsen, are you quite sure of yourself?

Stensgård. Yes, I am, indeed. There's no mistake possible in this case.

Fieldbo. Well, then, in heaven's name, go in and win! It means your life's happiness! Oh, there's so much I could say to you——

Stensgård. Really? Has she said anything? Has she confided in Miss Bratsberg?

Fieldbo. No; that's not what I mean. But how can you, in the midst of your happiness, go and fuddle yourself in these political orgies? How can town tattle take any hold upon a mind that is——

Stensgård. Why not? Man is a complex machine—I am, at any rate. Besides, my way to her lies through these very party turmoils.

Fieldbo. A terribly prosaic way.

Stensgård. Fieldbo, I am ambitious; you know I am. I must make my way in the world. When I remember that I'm thirty and am still on the first round of the ladder, I feel my conscience gnawing at me.

Fieldbo. Not with its wisdom teeth.

Stensgård. It's of no use talking to you. You have never felt the spur of ambition. You have dawdled and drifted all your days—first at college, then abroad, now here.

Fieldbo. Perhaps; but at least it has been delightful. And no reaction follows, like what you feel when you get down from the table after——

Stensgård. Stop that! I can bear anything but that. You are doing a bad action—you are damping my ardour.

Fieldbo. Oh, come! If your ardour is so easily damped——

Stensgård. Stop, I say! What right have you to break in upon my happiness? Do you think I am not sincere?

Fieldbo. Yes, I am sure you are.

Stensgård. Well, then, why go and make me feel empty, and disgusted and suspicious of myself? *(Shouts and cheers from the tent.)* There—listen! They are drinking my health. An idea that can take such hold upon people —by God, it must have truth in it!

[THORA BRATSBERG, RAGNA MONSEN *and* MR. HELLE *enter from the left and cross, half-way back.*

Helle. Look, Miss Bratsberg; there is Mr. Stensgård.

Thora. Then I won't go any further. Good-night, Ragna dear.

Helle and Miss Monsen. Good-night, good-night.

[*They go out to the right.*

Thora (advancing). I am Miss Bratsberg. I have a letter for you, from my father.

Stensgård. For me?

Thora. Yes; here it is. [*Going.*

Fieldbo. May I not see you home?

Thora. No, thank you. I can go alone. Good-night.

[*Goes out to the left.*

Stensgård (reading the letter by a Chinese lantern). What is this!

Fieldbo. Well—what has the Chamberlain to say to you?

Stensgård (bursts into loud laughter). I must say I didn't expect this!

Fieldbo. Tell me——?

Stensgård. Chamberlain Bratsberg is a pitiful creature.

Fieldbo. You dare to——

Stensgård. Pitiful! Pitiful. Tell any one you please that I said so. Or rather, say nothing about it—— *(Puts the letter in his pocket.)* Don't mention this to any one!

[*The* COMPANY *come out from the tent.*

Monsen. Mr. President! Where is Mr. Stensgård?

The Crowd. There he is! Hurrah!

Lundestad. Mr. President has forgotten his hat.

[*Hands it to him.*

Aslaksen. Here; have some punch! Here's a whole bowlful!

Stensgård. Thanks, no more.

Monsen. And the members of the League will recollect that we meet to-morrow at Stonelee——

Stensgård. To-morrow? It wasn't to-morrow, was it——?

Monsen. Yes, certainly; to draw up the manifesto——

Stensgård. No, I really can't to-morrow—I shall see about it the day after to-morrow, or the day after that. Well, good-night, gentlemen; hearty thanks all round, and hurrah for the future!

The Crowd. Hurrah! Let's take him home in triumph!

Stensgård. Thanks, thanks! But you really mustn't——

Aslaksen. We'll all go with you.

Stensgård. Very well, come along. Good-night, Fieldbo; you're not coming with us?

Fieldbo. No; but let me tell you, what you said about Chamberlain Bratsberg——

Stensgård. Hush, hush! It was an exaggeration—I withdraw it! Well, my friends, if you're coming, come; I'll take the lead.

Monsen. You arm, Stensgård!

Bastian. A song! Strike up! Something thoroughly patriotic!

The Crowd. A song! A song! Music!

[*A popular air is played and sunk. The procession marches out by the back to the right.*

Fieldbo (to LUNDESTAD, *who remains behind).* A gallant procession.

Lundestad. Yes—and with a gallant leader.

Fieldbo. And where are you going, Mr. Lundestad?

Lundestad. I? I'm going home to bed.

[*He nods and goes off.* DOCTOR FIELDBO *remains behind alone.*

ACT II

A garden-room of the CHAMBERLAIN'S, *elegantly furnished with a piano, flowers, and rare plants. Entrance door at the back. On the left, a door leading to the dining-room; on the right, several glass doors lead out to the garden.*

ASLAKSEN *stands at the entrance door.* A MAID-SERVANT *is carrying some dishes of fruit into the dining-room.*

The Maid. Yes, but I tell you they're still at table; you must call again.

Aslaksen. I'd rather wait, if I may.

The Maid. Oh, yes, if you like. You can sit there for the present.

[*She goes into the dining-room.* ASLAKSEN *takes a seat near the door. Pause.* DR. FIELDBO *enters from the back.*

Fieldbo. Ah, good evening, Aslaksen: are you here?

The Maid (returning). You're late this evening, sir.

Fieldbo. I was called to see a patient.

The Maid. The Chamberlain and Miss Bratsberg have both been inquiring about you.

Fieldbo. Indeed?

The Maid. Yes. Won't you go in at once, sir; or shall I say that——?

Fieldbo. No, no; never mind. I can have a snack afterwards; I shall wait here in the meantime.

The Maid. Dinner will soon be over.

[*She goes out by the back.*

Aslaksen (after a pause). How can you resist such a

dinner, Doctor—with dessert, and fine wines and all sorts of good things?

Fieldbo. Why, man, it seems to me we get too many good things hereabouts, rather than too few.

Aslaksen. There I can't agree with you.

Fieldbo. H'm. I suppose you are waiting for some one.

Aslaksen. Yes, I am.

Fieldbo. And are things going tolerably at home? Your wife——?

Aslaksen. In bed, as usual; coughing and wasting away.

Fieldbo. And your second child?

Aslaksen. Oh, he's a cripple for the rest of his days; you know that. That's our luck, you see; what the devil's the use of talking about it?

Fieldbo. Let me look at you, Aslaksen!

Aslaksen. Well; what do you want to see?

Fieldbo. You've been drinking to-day.

Aslaksen. Yes, and yesterday, too.

Fieldbo. Well, yesterday there was some excuse for it; but to-day——

Aslaksen. What about your friends in there, then? Aren't they drinking, too?

Fieldbo. Yes, my dear Aslaksen; that's a fair retort; but circumstances differ so in this world.

Aslaksen. I didn't choose my circumstances.

Fieldbo. No; God chose them for you.

Aslaksen. No, he didn't—men chose them. Daniel Heire chose, when he took me from the printing-house and sent me to college. And Chamberlain Bratsberg chose, when he ruined Daniel Heire and sent me back to the printing-house.

Fieldbo. Now you know that's not true. The Chamberlain did not ruin Daniel Heire; Daniel Heire ruined himself.

Aslaksen. Perhaps! But how dared Daniel Heire ruin himself, in the face of his responsibilities towards me? God's partly to blame, too, of course. Why should he give me talent and ability? Well, of course, I could have turned them to account as a respectable handicraftsman; but then comes that tattling old fool——

Fieldbo. It's base of you to say that. Daniel Heire acted with the best intentions.

Aslaksen. What good do his "best intentions" do me? You hear them in there, clinking glasses and drinking healths? Well, I, too, have sat at that table in my day, dressed in purple and fine linen, like the best of them——! That was just the thing for me, that was—for me, that has read so much and had thirsted so long to have my share in all the good things of life. Well, well; how long was Jeppe in Paradise?* Smash, crash! down you go—and my fine fortunes fell to pi, as we printers say.

Fieldbo. But, after all, you were not so badly off; you had your trade to fall back upon.

Aslaksen. That's easily said. After getting out of your class you can't get into it again. They took the ground from under my feet and shoved me out on the slippery ice—and then they abuse me because I stumble.

Fieldbo. Well, far be it from me to judge you harshly——

Aslaksen. No; you have no right to.—What a queer jumble it is! Daniel Heire, and Providence, and the Chamberlain, and Destiny and Circumstance—and I myself in the middle of it! I've often thought of unravelling it all and writing a book about it; but it's so cursedly entangled that—— *(Glances towards the door on the left.)* Ah! They're rising from table.

[*The party, ladies and gentlemen, pass from the dining-room into the garden, in lively conversa-*

* An allusion to Holberg's comedy, *Jeppe pa Bierget,* which deals with the theme of Abou Hassan, treated by Shakespeare in the Induction to *The Taming of the Shrew,* and by Hauptmann in *Schluck und Iau.*

tion. Among the guests is STENSGÅRD, *with* THORA *on his left arm and* SELMA *on his right* FIELDBO *and* ASLAKSEN *stand beside the door at the back.*

Stensgård. I don't know my way here yet; you must tell me where I am to take you, ladies.

Selma. Out into the air; you must see the garden.

Stensgård. Oh, that will be delightful.

[*They go out by the foremost glass door on the right.*

Fieldbo. Why, by all that's wonderful, there's Stensgård!

Aslaksen. It's him I want to speak to. I've had a fine chase after him; fortunately I met Daniel Heire——

[DANIEL HEIRE *and* ERIK BRATSBERG *enter from the dining-room.*

Heire. Hee-hee! Excellent sherry, upon my word. I've tasted nothing like it since I was in London.

Erik. Yes, it's good, isn't it? It puts life into you.

Heire. Well, well—it's a real pleasure to see one's money so well spent.

Erik. How so? *(Laughing.)* Oh, yes; I see, I see.

[*They go into the garden.*

Fieldbo. You want to speak to Stensgård, you say?

Aslaksen. Yes.

Fieldbo. On business?

Aslaksen. Of course; the report of the fête——

Fieldbo. Well, then, you must wait out there in the meantime.

Aslaksen. In the passage?

Fieldbo. In the anteroom. This is scarcely the time or place—but the moment I see Stensgård alone, I'll tell him——

Aslaksen. Very well; I'll bide my time.

[*Goes out by the back.*

[CHAMBERLAIN BRATSBERG, LUNDESTAD, RINGDAL *and one or two other gentlemen come out of the dining-room.*

The Chamberlain (conversing with LUNDESTAD*).* Violent, you say? Well, perhaps the form wasn't all that could be desired; but there were real gems in the speech, I can assure you.

Lundestad. Well, if you are satisfied, Chamberlain, I have no right to complain.

The Chamberlain. Why should you? Ah, here's the Doctor! Starving, I'll be bound.

Fieldbo. It doesn't matter, Chamberlain. The servants will attend to me. I feel myself almost at home here, you know.

The Chamberlain. Oh, you do, do you? I wouldn't be in too great a hurry.

Fieldbo. What? Am I taking too great a liberty? You yourself permitted me to——

The Chamberlain. What I permitted, I permitted. Well, well, make yourself at home and forage for something to eat. *(Slaps him lightly on the shoulder and turns to* LUNDESTAD.*)* Now, here's one you may call an adventurer and —and the other thing I can't remember.

Fieldbo. Why, Chamberlain——!

Lundestad. No, I assure you——

The Chamberlain. No arguments after dinner; it's bad for the digestion. They'll serve the coffee outside presently.

[*Goes with the guests into the garden.*

Lundestad (to FIELDBO*).* Did you ever see the Chamberlain so strange as he is to-day?

Fieldbo. I noticed it yesterday evening.

Lundestad. He will have it that I called Mr. Stensgård an adventurer and something else of that sort.

Fieldbo. Oh, well, Mr. Lundestad, what if you did? Excuse me; I must go and talk to the ladies.

[*Goes out to the right.*

Lundestad (to RINGDAL, *who is arranging a card table).* How do you account for Mr. Stengård's appearance here to-day?

Ringdal. Yes, how? He wasn't on the original list.

Lundestad. An afterthought, then? After his attack on the Chamberlain yesterday——?

Ringdal. Yes, can you understand it?

Lundestad. Understand it? Oh, yes, I suppose I can.

Ringdal (more softly). You think the Chamberlain is afraid of him?

Lundestad. I think he is prudent—that's what I think.

[*They go up to the back conversing, and so out into the garden. At the same time* SELMA *and* STENSGÅRD *enter by the foremost door on the right.*

Selma. Yes, just look—over the tops of the trees you can see the church tower and all the upper part of the town.

Stensgård. So you can; I shouldn't have thought so.

Selma. Don't you think it's a beautiful view?

Stensgård. Everything is beautiful here: the garden, and the view, and the sunshine and the people! Great heaven, how beautiful it all is! And you live here all the summer?

Selma. No, not my husband and I; we come and go. We have a big, showy house in town, much finer than this; you'll see it soon.

Stensgård. Perhaps your family live in town?

Selma. My family? Who are my family?

Stensgård. Oh, I didn't know——

Selma. We fairy princesses have no family.

Stensgård. Fairy princesses?

Selma. At most we have a wicked stepmother——

Stensgård. A witch, yes! So you are a princess!

Selma. Princess of all the sunken palaces, whence you hear the soft music on midsummer nights. Doctor Fieldbo thinks it must be pleasant to be a princess; but I must tell you——

Erik Bratsberg (coming from the garden). Ah, at last I find the little lady!

Selma. The little lady is telling Mr. Stensgård the story of her life.

Erik. Oh, indeed. And what part does the husband play in the little lady's story?

Selma. The Prince, of course. *(To* STENSGÅRD.*)* You know the prince always comes and breaks the spell, and then all ends happily, and every one calls and congratulates, and the fairy-tale is over.

Stensgård. Oh, it's too short.

Selma. Perhaps—in a way.

Erik (putting his arm around her waist). But a new fairy-tale grows out of the old one, and in it the Princess becomes a Queen!

Selma. On the same conditions as real Princesses?

Erik. What condition?

Selma. They must go into exile—to a foreign kingdom.

Erik. A cigar, Mr. Stensgård?

Stensgård. Thank you, not just now.

[DOCTOR FIELDBO *and* THORA *enter from the garden.*

Selma (going toward them). Is that you, Thora dear? I hope you're not ill?

Thora. I? No.

Selma. Oh, but I'm sure you must be; you seem to be always consulting the doctor of late.

Thora. No, I assure you——

Selma. Nonsense; let me feel your pulse! You are burning. My dear Doctor, don't you think the fever will pass over?

Fieldbo. Everything has its time.

Thora. Would you rather have me freezing——?

Selma. No, a medium temperature is the best—ask my husband.

The Chamberlain (enters from the garden). The whole

family gathered in secret conclave? That's not very polite to the guests.

Thora. I am just going, father dear——

The Chamberlain. Aha, it is you the ladies are paying court to, Mr. Stensgård! I must look to this.

Thora (softly to FIELDBO*).* Remain here!

[*She goes into the garden.*

Erik (offers SELMA *his arm).* Has Madame any objection——?

Selma. Come! [*They go out to the right.*

The Chamberlain (looking after them). It's impossible to get these two separated.

Fieldbo. It would be sinful to try.

The Chamberlain. Fools that we are! How Providence blesses us in spite of ourselves. *(Calls out.)* Thora, Thora, do look after Selma! Get a shawl for her and don't let her run about so: she'll catch cold! How short-sighted we mortals are, Doctor! Do you know any cure for that disease?

Fieldbo. The spectacles of experience; through them you will see more clearly a second time.

The Chamberlain. You don't say so! Thanks for the advice. But since you feel yourself at home here, you must really pay a little attention to your guests.

Fieldbo. Certainly; come, Stensgård, shall we——?

The Chamberlain. Oh, no, no—there's my old friend Heire out there——

Fieldbo. He thinks himself at home here, too.

The Chamberlain. Ha, ha, ha! So he does.

Fieldbo. Well, we two will join forces, and do our best.

[*Goes into the garden.*

Stensgård. You were speaking of Daniel Heire, Chamberlain. I must say I was rather surprised to see him here.

The Chamberlain. Were you? Mr. Heire and I are old school and college friends. Besides, we have had a good deal to do with each other in many ways since——

Stensgård. Yes, Mr. Heire was good enough to give his own account of some of these transactions, yesterday evening.

The Chamberlain. H'm!

Stensgård. Had it not been for him, I certainly should not have let myself boil over as I did. But he has a way of speaking of people and things, that—in short, he has a vile tongue in his head.

The Chamberlain. My dear young friend—Mr. Heire is my guest; you must not forget that. My house is liberty hall, with only one reservation: my guests must not be discussed to their disadvantage.

Stensgård. I beg your pardon, I'm sure——!

The Chamberlain. Oh, never mind; you belong to the younger generation, that's not so punctilious. As for Mr. Heire, I don't think you really know him. I, at any rate, owe Mr. Heire a great deal.

Stensgård. Yes, he gave one to understand; but I didn't think——

The Chamberlain. I owe him the best part of our domestic happiness, Mr. Stensgård! I owe him my daughter-in-law. Yes, that is really so. Daniel Heire was kind to her in her childhood. She was a youthful prodigy; she gave concerts when she was only ten years old. I daresay you have heard her spoken of—Selma Sjöblom.*

Stensgård. Sjöblom? Yes, of course; her father was Swedish?

The Chamberlain. Yes, a music-teacher. He came here many years ago. Musicians, you know, are seldom millionaires; and their habits are not always calculated to——; in short, Mr. Heire has always had an eye for talent; he was struck with the child, and had her sent to Berlin; and then, when her father was dead and Heire's fortunes were on the

* Pronounce "Shöblom"—the modified "ö" much as in German.

wane, she returned to Christiania, where she was, of course, taken up by the best people. That was how my son happened to fall in with her.

Stensgård. Then in that way old Daniel Heire has indeed been an instrument for good——

The Chamberlain. That is how one thing leads to another in this life, you see. We are all instruments, Mr. Stensgård; you, like the rest of us; an instrument of wrath, I suppose——

Stensgård. Oh, don't speak of it, Chamberlain. I am utterly ashamed——

The Chamberlain. Ashamed?

Stensgård. It was most unbecoming——

The Chamberlain. The form was perhaps open to criticism, but the intention was excellent. And now I want to ask you, in future, when you are contemplating any move of the sort, just to come to me and tell me of it openly, and without reserve. You know we all want to act for the best; and it is my duty——

Stensgård. You will permit me to speak frankly to you?

The Chamberlain. Of course I will. Do you think I haven't long realised that matters here have in some ways taken a most undesirable turn? But what was I to do? In the late King's time I lived for the most part in Stockholm. I am old now; and besides, it is not in my nature to take the lead in reforms, or to throw myself personally into the turmoil of public affairs. You, on the other hand, Mr. Stensgård, have every qualification for them; so let us hold together.

Stensgård. Thanks, Chamberlain; many, many thanks!

[RINGDAL *and* DANIEL HEIRE *enter from the garden.*

Ringdal. And I tell you it must be a misunderstanding.

Heire. Indeed? I like that! How should I misunderstand my own ears?

The Chamberlain. Anything new, Heire?

Heire. Only that Anders Lundestad is going over to the Stonelee party.

The Chamberlain. Oh, you're joking!

Heire. I beg your pardon, my dear sir; I have it from his own lips. Mr. Lundestad intends, on account of failing health, to retire from political life; you can draw your own conclusions from that.

Stensgård. He told you so himself?

Heire. Of course he did. He made the momentous announcement to an awe-struck circle down in the garden; hee-hee!

The Chamberlain. Why, my dear Ringdal, what can be the meaning of this?

Heire. Oh, it's not difficult to guess.

The Chamberlain. Indeed it is, though. This is a most important affair for the district. Come along, Ringdal; we must find the man himself.

[*He and* RINGDAL *go down the garden.*

Fieldbo (entering by the furthest back garden-door). Has the Chamberlain gone out?

Heire. Sh! The sages are deliberating! Great news Doctor! Lundestad is going to resign.

Fieldbo. Oh, impossible!

Stensgård. Can you understand it?

Heire. Ah, now we may look out for real sport. It's the League of Youth that's beginning to work, Mr. Stensgård. Do you know what you should call your League? I'll tell you some other time.

Stensgård. Do you think it's really our League——?

Heire. Not the least doubt about it. So we're to have the pleasure of sending our respected friend Mr. Mons Monsen to Parliament! I wish he were off already;—I'd give him a lift with pleasure—— I say no more; hee-hee!

[*Goes into the garden.*

Stensgård. Tell me, Fieldbo—how do you explain all this?

Fieldbo. There are other things still more difficult to explain. How come you to be here?

Stensgård. I? Like the rest, of course—by invitation.

Fieldbo. I hear you were invited yesterday evening—after your speech——

Stensgård. What then?

Fieldbo. How could you accept the invitation?

Stensgård. What the deuce was I to do? I couldn't insult these good people.

Fieldbo. Indeed! You couldn't? What about your speech then?

Stensgård. Nonsense! It was principles I attacked in my speech, not persons.

Fieldbo. And how do you account for the Chamberlain's invitation?

Stensgård. Why, my dear friend, there can only be one way of accounting for it.

Fieldbo. Namely, that the Chamberlain is afraid of you?

Stensgård. By heaven, he shall have no reason to be! He is a gentleman.

Fieldbo. That he is.

Stensgård. Isn't it touching the way the old man has taken this affair? And how lovely Miss Bratsberg looked when she brought me the letter!

Fieldbo. But look here—they haven't mentioned the scene of yesterday, have they?

Stensgård. Not a word; they have far too much tact for that. But I am filled with remorse; I must find an opportunity of apologising——

Fieldbo. I strongly advise you not to! You don't know the Chamberlain——

Stensgård. Very well; then my acts shall speak for me.

Fieldbo. You won't break with the Stonelee party?

Stensgård. I shall bring about a reconciliation. I have my League; it's a power already, you see.

Fieldbo. By-the-bye, while I remember—we were speaking of Miss Monsen—I advised you to go in and win——

Stensgård. Oh, there's no hurry——

Fieldbo. But listen; I have been thinking it over: you had better put all that out of your head.

Stensgård. I believe you are right. If you marry into an underbred family, you marry the whole tribe of them.

Fieldbo. Yes, and there are other reasons——

Stensgård. Monsen is an underbred fellow; I see that now.

Fieldbo. Well, polish is not his strong point.

Stensgård. No, indeed it's not! He goes and speaks ill of his guests; that's ungentlemanly. His rooms all reek of stale tobacco——

Fieldbo. My dear fellow, how is it you haven't noticed the stale tobacco before?

Stensgård. It's the contrast that does it. I made a false start when I settled here. I fell into the clutches of a clique, and they bewildered me with their clamour. But there shall be an end to that! I won't go and wear my life out as a tool in the hands of self-interest or coarse stupidity.

Fieldbo. But what will you do with your League?

Stensgård. The League shall remain as it is; it's founded on a pretty broad basis. Its purpose is to counteract noxious influences; and I am just beginning to realise what side the noxious influences come from.

Fieldbo. But do you think the "Youth" will see it in the same light?

Stensgård. They shall! I have surely a right to expect fellows like that to bow before my superior insight.

Fieldbo. But if they won't?

Stensgård. Then they can go their own way. I have done with them. You don't suppose I am going to let my life slip into a wrong groove and never reach the goal, for the sake of mere blind, pig-headed consistency!

Fieldbo. What do you call the goal?

Stensgård. A career that gives scope for my talents and fulfils my aspirations.

Fieldbo. No vague phrases! What do you mean by your goal?

Stensgård. Well, to you I can make a clean breast of it. My goal is this: in the course of time to get into Parliament, perhaps into the Ministry, and to marry happily into a family of means and position.

Fieldbo. Oh, indeed! And by help of the Chamberlain's social connections you intend to——?

Stensgård. I intend to reach the goal by my own exertions! I must and will reach it; and without help from any one. It will take time, I daresay; but never mind! Meanwhile I shall enjoy life here, drinking in beauty and sunshine——

Fieldbo. Here?

Stensgård. Yes, here! Here there are fine manners; life moves gracefully here; the very floors seem laid to be trodden only by lacquered shoes. Here the armchairs are deep and the ladies sink exquisitely into them. Here conversation moves lightly and elegantly, like a game at battledore; here no blunders come plumping in to make an awkward silence. Oh, Fieldbo—here I feel for the first time what distinction means! Yes, we have indeed an aristocracy of our own; a little circle; an aristocracy of culture; and to it I will belong. Don't you yourself feel the refining influence of this place? Don't you feel that wealth here loses its grossness? When I think of Monsen's money, I seem to see piles of fetid bank-notes and greasy mortgages—but here! here it is shimmering silver! And the people are the same. Look at the Chamberlain—what a fine high-bred old fellow!

Fieldbo. He is, indeed.

Stensgård. And the son—alert, straightforward, capable!

Fieldbo. Certainly.

Stensgård. And then the daughter-in-law! Isn't she a pearl? Good God, what a rich, what a fascinating nature!

Fieldbo. Thora—Miss Bratsberg has that, too.

Stensgård. Oh, yes; but she is less remarkable.

Fieldbo. Oh, you don't know her. You don't know how deep, and steadfast and true her nature is.

Stensgård. But, oh, the daughter-in-law! So frank, almost reckless; and yet so appreciative, so irresistible——

Fieldbo. Why, I really believe you're in love with her.

Stensgård. With a married woman? Are you crazy? What good would that do me? No, but I am falling in love—I can feel that plainly. Yes, she is indeed deep, and steadfast and true.

Fieldbo. Who?

Stensgård. Miss Bratsberg, of course.

Fieldbo. What? You're never thinking of——?

Stensgård. Yes, by heaven I am!

Fieldbo. I assure you it's quite out of the question.

Stensgård. Ho-ho! Will rules the world, my dear fellow! We shall see if it doesn't.

Fieldbo. Why, this is the merest extravagance! Yesterday it was Miss Monsen——

Stensgård. Oh, I was too hasty about that; besides, you yourself advised me not to——

Fieldbo. I advise you most emphatically to dismiss all thought of either of them.

Stensgård. Indeed! Perhaps you yourself think of throwing the handkerchief to one of them?

Fieldbo. I? No, I assure you——

Stensgård. Well, it wouldn't have mattered if you had. If people stand in my way and want to balk me of my future, why, I stick at nothing.

Fieldbo. Take care I don't say the same!

Stensgård. You! What right have you to pose as guardian and protector to Chamberlain Bratsberg's family?

Fieldbo. I have at least the right of a friend.

Stensgård. Pooh! that sort of talk won't do with me. Your motive is mere self-interest! It gratifies your petty vanity to imagine yourself cock-of-the-walk in this house; and so I am to be kept outside the pale.

Fieldbo. That is the best thing that could happen to you. Here you are standing on hollow ground.

Stensgård. Am I indeed? Many thanks. I shall manage to prop it up.

Fieldbo. Try; but I warn you, it will fall through with you first.

Stensgård. Ho-ho! So you are intriguing against me, are you? I'm glad I have found it out. I know you now; you are my enemy, the only one I have here.

Fieldbo. Indeed I am not.

Stensgård. Indeed you are! You have always been so, ever since our school-days. Just look around here and see how every one appreciates me, stranger as I am. You, on the other hand, you who know me, have never appreciated me. That is the radical weakness of your character—you can never appreciate any one. What did you do in Christiania but go about from tea-party to tea-party, spreading yourself out in little witticisms? That sort of thing brings its own punishment! You dull your sense for all that makes life worth living, for all that is ennobling and inspiring; and presently you get left behind, fit for nothing.

Fieldbo. Am I fit for nothing?

Stensgård. Have you ever been fit to appreciate me?

Fieldbo. What was I to appreciate in you?

Stensgård. My will, if nothing else. Every one else appreciates it—the crowd at the fête yesterday—Chamberlain Bratsberg and his family——

Fieldbo. Mr. Mons Monsen and his ditto——! And by-the-bye, that reminds me—there's some one out here waiting for you——

Stensgård. Who?

Fieldbo (going towards the back). One who appreciates you. *(Opens the door and calls.)* Aslaksen, come in!

Stensgård. Aslaksen?

Aslaksen (entering). Ah, at last!

Fieldbo. Good-bye for the present; I won't intrude upon friends in council. [*Goes into the garden.*

Stensgård. What in the devil's name do you want here?

Aslaksen. I must speak to you. You promised me yesterday an account of the founding of the League, and——

Stensgård. I can't give it you; it must wait till another time.

Aslaksen. Impossible, Mr. Stensgård; the paper appears to-morrow morning.

Stensgård. Nonsense! It has all to be altered. The matter has entered on a new phase; new forces have come into play. What I said about Chamberlain Bratsberg must be entirely recast before it can appear.

Aslaksen. Oh, that about the Chamberlain, that's in type already.

Stensgård. Then it must come out of type again.

Aslaksen. Not go in?

Stensgård. I won't have it published in that form. Why do you stare at me? Do you think I don't know how to manage the affairs of the League?

Aslaksen. Oh, certainly; but you must let me tell you——

Stensgård. No arguing, Aslaksen; that I can't stand and won't stand!

Aslaksen. Do you know, Mr. Stensgård, that you are doing your best to take the bread out of my mouth? Do you know that?

Stensgård. No; I know nothing of the sort.

Aslaksen. But you are. Last winter, before you came here, my paper was looking up. I edited it myself, I must tell you, and I edited it on a principle.

Stensgård. You?

Aslaksen. Yes, I!—I said to myself: it's the great public that supports a paper; now the great public is the bad public—that comes of the local situation; and the bad public will have a bad paper. So, you see, I edited it——

Stensgård. Badly! Yes, that's undeniable.

Aslaksen. Well, and I prospered by it. But then you came and brought ideas into the district. The paper took on a colour, and then Lundestad's supporters all fell away. The subscribers that are left won't pay their subscriptions——

Stensgård. Ah, but the paper has become a good one.

Aslaksen. I can't live on a good paper. You were to make things lively; you were to grapple with abuses, as you promised yesterday. The bigwigs were to be pilloried; the paper was to be filled with things people were bound to read—and now, you leave me in the lurch——

Stensgård. Ho-ho! You think I am going to keep you supplied with libels! No, thank you, my good sir!

Aslaksen. Mr. Stensgård, you mustn't drive me to desperation, or you'll repent it.

Stensgård. What do you mean?

Aslaksen. I mean that I must make the paper pay in another way. Heaven knows I should be sorry to do it. Before you came I made an honest living out of accidents and suicides and other harmless things, that often hadn't even happened. But now you have turned everything topsy-turvy; people now want very different fare——

Stensgård. Just let me tell you this: if you break loose in any way, if you go a single step beyond my orders, and try to exploit the movement in your own dirty interests, I'll go to the opposition printer and start a new paper. We have money, you must know! We can bring your rag to ruin in a fortnight.

Aslaksen (pale). You wouldn't do that!

Stensgård. Yes, I would; and you'll see I can edit a paper so as to appeal to the great public.

Aslaksen. Then I'll go this instant to Chamberlain Bratsberg——

Stensgård. You? What have you to do with him?

Aslaksen. What have you to do with him? Do you think I don't know why you are invited here? It's because he is afraid of you, and of what you may do; and you are making capital of that. But if he's afraid of what you may do, he'll be no less afraid of what I may print; and *I* will make capital of that!

Stensgård. Would you dare to? A wretched creature like you——!

Aslaksen. I'll soon show you. If your speech is to be kept out of the paper, the Chamberlain shall pay me for keeping it out.

Stensgård. Try it; just try it! You're drunk, fellow——!

Aslaksen. Only in moderation. But I'll fight like a lion if you try to take my poor crust out of my mouth. Little you know what sort of a home mine is: a bedridden wife, a crippled child——

Stensgård. Off with you! Do you think I want to be soiled with your squalor? What are your bedridden wives and deformed brats to me? If you stand in my way, if you dare so much as to obstruct a single one of my prospects, you shall be on the parish before the year's out!

Aslaksen. I'll wait one day——

Stensgård. Ah, you're coming to your senses.

Aslaksen. I shall announce to the subscribers in a handbill that in consequence of an indisposition contracted at the fête, the editor——

Stensgård. Yes, do so; I daresay, later on, we shall come to an understanding.

Aslaksen. I trust we may.—Remember this, Mr. Stensgård: that paper is my one ewe lamb.

[*Goes out by the back.*

Lundestad (at the foremost garden door). Ah, Mr. Stensgård!

Stensgård. Ah, Mr. Lundestad!

Lundestad. You here alone? If you have no objection, I should like to have a little talk with you.

Stensgård. With pleasure.

Lundestad. In the first place, let me say that if any one has told you that I have said anything to your disadvantage, you mustn't believe it.

Stensgård. To my disadvantage? What do you mean?

Lundestad. Oh, nothing; nothing, I assure you. You see, there are so many busybodies here, that go about doing nothing but setting people by the ears.

Stensgård. Well, on the whole—I'm afraid our relations are a little strained.

Lundestad. They are quite natural relations, Mr. Stensgård: the relation of the old to the new; it is always so.

Stensgård. Oh, come, Mr. Lundestad, you are not so old as all that.

Lundestad. Yes, indeed, I'm getting old. I have held my seat ever since 1839. It's time I should be relieved.

Stensgård. Relieved?

Lundestad. Times change, you see. New problems arise, and for their solution we want new forces.

Stensgård. Now, frankly, Mr. Lundestad—are you really going to give up your seat to Monsen?

Lundestad. To Monsen? No, certainly not to Monsen.

Stensgård. Then I don't understand——

Lundestad. Suppose, now, I did retire in Monsen's favour: do you think he would be elected?

Stensgård. It's hard to say. As the preliminary election comes on the day after to-morrow, there may scarcely be time to prepare the public mind; but——

Lundestad. I don't believe he would manage it. The Chamberlain's party, my party, would not vote for him. Of course "my party" is a figure of speech; I mean the men of property, the old families, who are settled on their own land and belong to it. They won't have anything to do with Monsen. Monsen is a newcomer; no one really knows anything about Monsen and his affairs. And then he has had to cut down so much to clear a place for himself—to fell both tiees and men, you may say.

Stensgård. Well, then, if you think he has no chance——

Lundestad. H'm! You are a man of rare gifts, Mr. Stensgård. Providence has dealt lavishly with you. But it has made one little oversight: it ought to have given you one thing more.

Stensgård. And what might that be?

Lundestad. Tell me—why do you never think of yourself? Why have you no ambition?

Stensgård. Ambition? I?

Lundestad. Why do you waste all your strength on other people? In one word—why not go into Parliament yourself?

Stensgård. I? You are not serious?

Lundestad. Why not? You have qualified, I hear. And if you don't seize this opportunity, then some one else will come in; and when once he is firm in the saddle, it may not be so easy to unseat him.

Stensgård. Great heavens, Mr. Lundestad! do you really mean what you say?

Lundestad. Oh, I don't want to commit you; if you don't care about it——

Stensgård. Not care about it! Well, I must confess I'm not so utterly devoid of ambition as you suppose. But do you really think it possible?

Lundestad. Oh, there's nothing impossible about it. I should do my best, and so, no doubt, would the Chamberlain; he knows your oratorical gifts. You have the young men on your side——

Stensgård. Mr. Lundestad, by heaven, you are my true friend!

Lundestad. Oh, you don't mean much by that. If you really looked upon me as a friend, you would relieve me of this burden. You have young shoulders; you could bear it so easily.

Stensgård. I place myself entirely at your disposal; I will not fail you.

Lundestad. Then you are really not disinclined to——

Stensgård. Here's my hand on it!

Lundestad. Thanks! Believe me, Mr. Stensgård, you will not regret it. But now we must go warily to work. We must both of us take care to be on the electoral college—I to propose you as my successor and put you through your facings before the rest; and you to give an account of your views——

Stensgård. If we once get so far, we are safe. In the electoral college you are omnipotent.

Lundestad. There is a limit to omnipotence. You must of course bring your oratory into play; you must take care to explain away anything that might seem really awkward or objectionable——

Stensgård. You don't mean that I am to break with my party?

Lundestad. Now just look at the thing reasonably. What do we mean when we talk of two parties? We have, on the one hand, certain men or families who are in possession of the common civic advantages—I mean property, independence and power. That is the party I belong to. On the other hand, we have the mass of our younger fellow-citizens who want to share in these advantages. That is your party. But that party you will quite naturally and properly pass out of when you get into power—to say nothing of taking up a solid position as a man of property—for, of course, that is essential, Mr. Stensgård.

Stensgård. Yes, I believe it is. But the time is short; and such a position is not to be attained in a day.

Lundestad. That's true; but perhaps the prospect of such a position would be enough——

Stensgård. The prospect——?

Lundestad. Have you any rooted objection to a good marriage, Mr. Stensgård? Their are heiresses in the country-side. A man like you, with a future before him—a man who can reckon on attaining the highest offices—believe me, you needn't fear a repulse if you play your cards neatly.

Stensgård. Then, for heaven's sake, help me in the game! You open wide vistas to me—great visions! All that I have hoped and longed for, and that seemed so dreamlike and far away, stands suddenly before me in living reality—to lead the people forward towards emancipation, to——

Lundestad. Yes, we must keep our eyes open, Mr. Stensgård. I see your ambition is already on the alert. That's well. The rest will come of itself.—In the meantime, thanks! I shall never forget your readiness to take the burden of office from my shoulders.

[*The whole party gradually enters from the garden. Two maid-servants bring in candles and hand round refreshments during the following scene.*

Selma (goes towards the piano at the back, left). Mr. Stensgård, you must join us; we are going to have a game of forfeits.

Stensgård. With pleasure; I am just in the mood.

[*Follows her towards the back, makes arrangements with her, places chairs, etc., etc.*

Erik Bratsberg (in an undertone). What the deuce is this my father is saying, Mr. Heire? What speech has Mr. Stensgård been making yesterday?

Heire. Hee-hee! Don't you know about it?

Erik. No; we townspeople had our dinner and ball at the Club. My father declares Mr. Stensgård has entirely broken with the Stonelee gang—that he was frightfully rude to Monsen——

Heire. To Monsen! No, you must have misunderstood him, my dear sir.

Erik. Well, there were a whole lot of people about, so that I couldn't quite follow what he said; but I certainly heard——

Heire. Wait till to-morrow—— I say no more. You'll have the whole story with your coffee, in Aslaksen's paper.

[*They separate.*

The Chamberlain. Well, my dear Lundestad, are you sticking to those crotchets of yours?

Lundestad. They are no crotchets, Chamberlain; rather than be ousted, one should give way gracefully.

The Chamberlain. Nonsense; who is dreaming of ousting you?

Lundestad. H'm; I'm an old weather-prophet. There has been a change in the wind. Besides, I have my successor ready. Mr. Stensgård is willing——

The Chamberlain. Mr. Stensgård?

Lundestad. Wasn't that what you meant? I took it for a hint when you said he was a man we must make friends with and support.

The Chamberlain. I meant in his onslaught upon all the corruption and swindling that goes on at Stonelee.

Lundestad. But how could you count so confidently upon his breaking with that crew?

The Chamberlain. He did it openly enough last evening, my dear fellow.

Lundestad. Last evening?

The Chamberlain. Yes, when he spoke of Monsen's deplorable influence in the district.

Lundestad (open-mouthed). Of Monsen's——?

The Chamberlain. Of course; that time on the table——

Lundestad. On the table? Yes?

The Chamberlain. He was frightfully rude; called him a money-bag, and a griffin or a basilisk, or something. Ha-ha!—it was great sport to hear him.

Lundestad. Great sport, was it?

The Chamberlain. Yes, I own I'm not sorry to see these people a little roughly handled. But now we must back him up; for after such a savage attack——

Lundestad. As that of yesterday, you mean?

The Chamberlain. Of course.

Lundestad. Upon the table?

The Chamberlain. Yes, upon the table.

Lundestad. Against Monsen?

The Chamberlain. Yes, against Monsen and his set. Of course they'll try to have their revenge; you can't blame them——

Lundestad (decidedly). Mr. Stensgård must be supported—that is clear.

Thora. Father dear, you must join in the game.

The Chamberlain. Oh, nonsense, child——

Thora. Yes, indeed you must; Selma insists upon it.

The Chamberlain. Very well, I suppose I must give in. *(In an undertone as they go towards the back.)* I'm quite distressed about Lundestad; he is really failing; fancy, he didn't in the least understand what Stensgård——

Thora. Oh, come, come; they've begun the game.

[*She drags him into the circle of young people where the game is in full swing.*

Erik (calls from his place). Mr. Heire, you are appointed forfeit-judge.

Heire. Hee-hee! It's the first appointment I ever had.

Stensgård (also in the circle). On account of your legal experience, Mr. Heire.

Heire. Oh, my amiable young friends, I should be delighted to sentence you all—— I say no more!

Stensgård (slips up to LUNDESTAD, *who stands in front on the left).* You were speaking to the Chamberlain. What about? Was it about me?

Lundestad. Unfortunately, it was—about that affair of yesterday evening——

Stensgård (writhing). Oh, confound it all!

Lundestad. He said you had been frightfully rude.

Stensgård. Do you think it isn't a torture to me?

Lundestad. Now is your chance to atone for it.

Erik (calls). Mr. Stensgård, it's your turn.

Stensgård. Coming. *(Quickly to* LUNDESTAD.*)* What do you mean?

Lundestad. Find an opportunity and apologise to the Chamberlain.

Stensgård. By heaven, I will!

Selma. Make haste, make haste!

Stensgård. I'm coming! Here I am!

[*The game goes on with noise and laughter. Some elderly gentlemen play cards on the right.* LUNDESTAD *takes a seat on the left;* DANIEL HEIRE *near him.*

Heire. That whelp twits me with my legal experience, does he?

Lundestad. He's rather free with his tongue, that's certain.

Heire. And so the whole family goes and fawns upon him. Hee-hee! They're pitifully afraid of him.

Lundestad. No, there you are wrong, Mr. Heire; the Chamberlain is not afraid of him.

Heire. Not afraid? Do you think I'm blind, my good sir?

Lundestad. No, but—I can trust you to keep the secret? Well, I'll tell you all about it. The Chamberlain thinks it was Monsen he was attacking.

Heire. Monsen? Oh, absurd!

Lundestad. Fact, Mr. Heire! Ringdal or Miss Thora must have got him persuaded that——

Heire. And so he goes and asks him to a state dinner-party! Deuce take me, if that isn't the best thing I've heard for long! No, really now, I can't keep that bottled up.

Lundestad. Sh, sh! Remember your promise. The Chamberlain's your old school-fellow; and even if he has been a little hard upon you——

Heire. Hee-hee! I'll pay him back with interest!

Lundestad. Take care! The Chamberlain is powerful. Don't play tricks in the lion's den!

Heire. Bratsberg a lion? Pooh, he's a blockhead, sir, and I am not. Oh, won't I get a rare crop of taunts, and jibes and innuendoes out of this, when once our great suit comes on!

Selma (calls from the circle). Learned judge, what shall the owner of this forfeit do?

Erik (unnoticed, to HEIRE*).* It's Stengård's! Think of something amusing.

Heire. That forfeit? Hee-hee, let me see; he might, for example—yes—he shall make a speech!

Selma. It's Mr. Stensgård's forfeit.

Erik. Mr. Stensgård is to make a speech.

Stensgård. Oh, no, spare me that; I came off badly enough last night.

The Chamberlain. Excellently, Mr. Stensgård; I know something of public speaking.

Lundestad (to HEIRE*).* If only he doesn't put his foot in it now.

Heire. Put his foot in it? Hee-hee! You're a sharp one! That's an inspiration! *(In an undertone to* STENSGÅRD.*)* If you came off badly last night, why not put yourself right again to-night?

Stensgård (seized with a sudden idea). Lundestad, here is the opportunity!

Lundestad (evasively). Play your cards neatly.

[*Looks for his hat and slips quietly towards the door.*

Stensgård. Yes, I will make a speech!

The Young Ladies. Bravo! Bravo!

Stensgård. Fill your glasses, ladies and gentlemen! I am going to make a speech which shall begin with a fable; for here I seem to breathe the finer air of fable-land.

Erik (to the Ladies*).* Hush! Listen!

[*The* Chamberlain *takes his glass from the card-table on the right, beside which he remains standing.* Ringdal, Fieldbo *and one or two other gentlemen come in from the garden.*

Stensgård. It was in the spring time. There came a young cuckoo flying over the uplands. Now the cuckoo is an adventurer. There was a great Bird-Parliament on the meadow beneath him, and both wild and tame fowl flocked to it. They came tripping out of the hen-yards; they waddled up from the goose-ponds; down from Stonelee hulked a fat capercailzie, flying low and noisily; he settled down, and ruffled his feathers and flapped his wings, and made himself even broader than he was; and every now and then he crowed, "Krak, krak, krak!" as much as to say: I'm the game-cock from Stonelee, I am!

The Chamberlain. Capital! Hear, hear!

Stensgård. And then there was an old woodpecker. He bustled up and down the tree-trunks, pecking with his pointed beak and gorging himself with grubs and everything that turns to gall. To right and left you heard him going: prik, prik, prik! And that was the woodpecker.

Erik. Excuse me, wasn't it a stork, or a——? *

Heire. Say no more!

Stensgård. That was the old woodpecker. But now there

* As before stated, "Heire" means a heron.

came life into the crew; for they found something to cackle evil about. And they flustered together and cackled in chorus, until at last the young cuckoo began to join in the cackling——

Fieldbo (unnoticed). For God's sake, man, be quiet!

Stensgård. Now it was an eagle they cackled about—an eagle who dwelt in lonely dignity upon a beetling cliff.* They were all agreed about him. "He's a bugbear to the neighbourhood," croaked a hoarse raven. But the eagle swooped down into their midst, seized the cuckoo and bore him aloft to his eyrie.—Heart conquered heart! From that clear summit the adventurer-cuckoo looked far and wide over the lowlands; there he found sunshine and peace; and there he learned to judge aright the swarm from the hen-yards and the clearings——

Fieldbo (loudly). Bravo, bravo! And now some music.

The Chamberlain. Hush! Don't interrupt him.

Stensgård. Chamberlain Bratsberg—here my fable ends; and here I stand before you, in the presence of every one, to beg your forgiveness for last night.

The Chamberlain (falls a step backwards). Mine——?

Stensgård. I thank you for the magnanimous vengeance you have taken for my senseless words. In me you have henceforth a faithful champion. And now, ladies and gentlemen, I drink the health of the eagle on the mountain-top —the health of Chamberlain Bratsberg.

The Chamberlain (clutching at the table). Thank you, Mr.—Mr. Stensgård.

The Guests (for the most part in painful embarrassment). The Chamberlain! Chamberlain Bratsberg!

The Chamberlain. Ladies! Gentlemen! *(Softly.)* Thora!

Thora. Father!

The Chamberlain. Oh, Doctor, Doctor, what have you done——?

* "Et brat fjeld"—an allusion to the name Bratsberg.

Stensgård (with his glass in his hand, radiant with self-satisfaction). Now to our places again! Hullo, Fieldbo! Come, join in—join in the League of Youth! The game's going merrily!

Heire (in front, on the left). Yes, on my soul, the game's going merrily!

[LUNDESTAD *slips out by the door in the back.*

ACT III

An elegant morning-room, with entrance door in the back. On the left, the door of the CHAMBERLAIN'S *study; further back, a door leading to the drawing-room. On the right, a door leading to* RINGDAL'S *offices; further forward, a window.*

THORA *is seated on the sofa, left, weeping. The* CHAMBERLAIN *paces angrily up and down.*

The Chamberlain. Yes, now we have the epilogue—tears and lamentations——

Thora. Oh, that we had never seen that man!

The Chamberlain. What man?

Thora. That wretched Mr. Stensgård, of course.

The Chamberlain. You should rather say: Oh, that we had never seen that wretched Doctor.

Thora. Doctor Fieldbo?

The Chamberlain. Yes, Fieldbo, Fieldbo! Wasn't it he that palmed off a parcel of lies upon me——?

Thora. No, my dear father, it was I.

The Chamberlain. You? Well, then, both of you! You were his accomplice—behind my back. A nice state of affairs!

Thora. Oh, father, if you only knew——

The Chamberlain. Oh, I know enough; more than enough; much more!

[DR. FIELDBO *enters from the back.*

Fieldbo. Good morning, Chamberlain! Good morning, Miss Bratsberg!

The Chamberlain (still pacing the room). So you are there, are you—bird of evil omen!

Fieldbo. Yes, it was a very unpleasant affair.

The Chamberlain (looking out at the window). Oh, you think so?

Fieldbo. You must have noticed how I kept my eye upon Stensgård all the evening. Unfortunately, when I heard there was to be a game of forfeits, I thought there was no danger——

The Chamberlain (stamping on the floor). To be made a laughing-stock by such a windbag! What must my guests have thought of me? That I was mean enough to want to buy this creature, this—this —— as Lundestad calls him!

Fieldbo. Yes, but——

Thora (unnoticed by her father). Don't speak.

The Chamberlain (after a short pause, turns to Fieldbo*).* Tell me frankly, Doctor:—Am I really denser than the general run of people?

Fieldbo. How can you ask such a question, Chamberlain?

The Chamberlain. Then how did it happen that I was probably the only person there who didn't understand that that confounded speech was meant for me?

Fieldbo. Shall I tell you why?

The Chamberlain. Certainly.

Fieldbo. It is because you yourself regard your position in the district differently from other people.

The Chamberlain. I regard my position as my father before me regarded his. No one would ever have ventured to treat him so.

Fieldbo. Your father died about the year 1830.

The Chamberlain. Oh, yes; many a barrier has broken down since that time. But, after all, it's my own fault. I have mixed myself up too much with these good people. So now I must be content to have my name coupled with Anders Lundestad's!

Fieldbo. Well, frankly, I see no disgrace in that.

The Chamberlain. Oh, you know quite well what I mean. Of course, I don't plume myself on rank, or titles, or anything of that sort. But what I hold in honour, and expect others to hold in honour, is the integrity handed down in our family from generation to generation. What I mean is that when a man like Lundestad goes into public life, he cannot keep his character and his conduct entirely free from stain. In the general mud-throwing, he is sure to find himself bespattered. But they might leave me in peace; I stand outside their parties.

Fieldbo. Not so entirely, Chamberlain; at least you were delighted so long as you thought it was Monsen that was attacked.

The Chamberlain. Don't mention that fellow!—It is he that has relaxed the moral sense of the district. And now he has gone and turned my son's head, confound him!

Thora. Erik's?

Fieldbo. Your son's?

The Chamberlain. Yes; what tempted him to go and set up in business? It leads to nothing.

Fieldbo. Why, my dear Chamberlain, he must live and——

The Chamberlain. Oh, with economy he could quite well live on the money that came to him from his mother.

Fieldbo. He might perhaps live on it; but what could he live for?

The Chamberlain. For? Well, if he absolutely must have something to live for, hasn't he qualified as a lawyer? He might live for his profession.

Fieldbo. No, that he couldn't do; it is against his nature. Then there was no official appointment he could well hope for; you have kept the management of your property in your own hands; and your son has no children to educate. Under these circumstances, when he sees tempting examples around him—people who have started from nothing and are worth their half million——

The Chamberlain. Their half million! Oh, come now, let us keep to the hundred thousands. But neither the half million nor the hundred thousands can be scraped together with perfectly clean hands:—I don't mean in the eyes of the world; Heaven knows it is easy enough to keep within the law; but in respect to one's own conscience. Of course my son cannot descend to anything questionable; so you may be quite sure Mr. Erik Bratsberg's financial operations won't bring in any half millions.

[SELMA, *in walking dress, enters from the back.*

Selma. Good morning! Is Erik not here?

The Chamberlain. Good morning, child! Are you looking for your husband?

Selma. Yes, he said he was coming here. Mr. Monsen called upon him early this morning, and then——

The Chamberlain. Monsen? Does Monsen come to your house?

Selma. Now and then; generally on business. Why, my dear Thora, what's the matter? Have you been crying?

Thora. Oh, it's nothing.

Selma. No, it's not nothing! At home Erik was out of humour, and here—— I can see it in your looks: there is something wrong. What is it?

The Chamberlain. Nothing you need trouble about, at any rate. You are too dainty to carry burdens, my little Selma. Go into the drawing-room for the present. If Erik said he was coming, he will be here soon, no doubt.

Selma. Come, Thora—and be sure you don't let me sit in a draught! *(Embracing her.)* Oh, I could hug the life out of you, my sweet Thora!

[*The two ladies go off to the left.*

The Chamberlain. So they are hand in glove, are they, the two speculators! They should go into partnership.

Monsen and Bratsberg—how nice it would sound! *(A knock at the door in the back.)* Come in!

[STENSGÅRD *enters.*

The Chamberlain (recoiling a step). What is this?

Stensgård. Yes, here I am again, Chamberlain!

The Chamberlain. So I see.

Fieldbo. Are you mad, Stensgård?

Stensgård. You retired early yesterday evening. When Fieldbo had explained to me how matters stood, you had already——

The Chamberlain. Excuse me—all explanations are superfluous——

Stensgård. I understand that; therefore I have not come to make any.

The Chamberlain. Oh, indeed?

Stensgård. I know I have insulted you.

The Chamberlain. I know that, too; and before I have you turned out, perhaps you will be good enough to tell me why you are here.

Stensgård. Because I love your daughter, Chamberlain.

Fieldbo. What——!

The Chamberlain. What does he say, Doctor?

Stensgård. Ah, you can't grasp the idea, Chamberlain. You are an old man; you have nothing to fight for——

The Chamberlain. And you presume to——?

Stensgård. I am here to ask for your daughter's hand, Chamberlain.

The Chamberlain. You—— you——? Won't you sit down?

Stensgård. Thanks, I prefer to stand.

The Chamberlain. What do you say to this, Doctor?

Stensgård. Oh, Fieldbo is on my side; he is my friend; the only true friend I have.

Fieldbo. No, no, man! Never in this world, if you——

The Chamberlain. Perhaps it was with this view that

Doctor Fieldbo secured his friend's introduction into my house?

Stensgård. You know me only by my exploits of yesterday and the day before. That is not enough. Besides, I am not the same man to-day that I was then. My intercourse with you and yours has fallen like spring showers upon my spirit, making it put forth new blossoms in a single night! You must not hurl me back into my sordid past. Till now, I have never been at home with the beautiful in life; it has always been beyond my reach——

The Chamberlain. But my daughter——?

Stensgård. Oh, I shall win her.

The Chamberlain. Indeed? H'm!

Stensgård. Yes, for I have will on my side. Remember what you told me yesterday. You were opposed to your son's marriage—and see how it has turned out! You must put on the glasses of experience, as Fieldbo said——

The Chamberlain. Ah, that was what you meant?

Fieldbo. Not in the least! My dear Chamberlain, let me speak to him alone——

Stensgård. Nonsense; I have nothing to speak to you about. Now, pray be reasonable, Chamberlain! A family like yours needs new alliances, or its brains stagnate——

The Chamberlain. Oh, this is too much!

Stensgård. Now, now, don't be angry! These high-and-mighty airs are unworthy of you—of course you know they are all nonsense at bottom. You shall see how much you'll value me when you come to know me. Yes, yes; you shall value me—both you and your daughter! I will make her——

The Chamberlain. What do you think of this, Doctor?

Fieldbo. I think it's madness.

Stensgård. Yes, it would be in you; but I, you see—I have a mission to fulfil on God's beautiful earth;—I am not to be deterred by nonsensical prejudices——

The Chamberlain. Mr. Stensgård, there is the door.

Stensgård. You show me——?

The Chamberlain. The door!

Stensgård. Don't do that!

The Chamberlain. Out with you! You are an adventurer, an a—a—confound my memory! You're a——

Stensgård. What am I?

The Chamberlain. You are—that other thing—it's on the tip of my tongue——

Stensgård. Beware how you block my career!

The Chamberlain. Beware? Of what?

Stensgård. I will attack you in the papers, persecute you, libel you, do all I can to undermine your reputation. You shall shriek under the lash. You shall seem to see spirits in the air raining blows upon you. You shall huddle together in dread and crouch with your arms bent over your head to ward off the strokes—you shall try to creep into shelter——

The Chamberlain. Creep into shelter yourself—in a madhouse; that is the proper place for you!

Stensgård. Ha-ha; that is a cheap retort; but you know no better, Mr. Bratsberg! I tell you the wrath of the Lord is in me. It is His will you are opposing. He has destined me for the light—beware how you cast a shadow!—Well, I see I shall make no way with you to-day; but that matters nothing. I only ask you to speak to your daughter—to prepare her—to give her the opportunity of choosing! Reflect and look around you. Where can you expect to find a son-in-law among these plodding dunces? Fieldbo says she is deep and steadfast and true. So now you know just how matters stand. Good-bye, Chamberlain—I leave you to choose between my friendship and my enmity. Good-bye!

[*Goes out by the back.*

The Chamberlain. So it has come to this! This is how they dare to treat me in my own house!

Fieldbo. Stensgård dares; no one else would.

The Chamberlain. He to-day; others to-morrow.

Fieldbo. Let them come; I shall keep them off; I would go through fire and water for you——

The Chamberlain. Yes, you who have caused all the mischief!—H'm; that Stensgård is the most impudent scoundrel I have ever known! And yet, after all—deuce take me if there isn't something I like about him.

Fieldbo. He has possibilities——

The Chamberlain. He has openness, Dr. Fieldbo! He doesn't go playing his own game behind one's back, like so many other people; he-he——!

Fieldbo. It's not worth disputing about. Only be firm, Chamberlain; no, and no again, to Stensgård——!

The Chamberlain. Oh, keep your advice to yourself! You may rely upon it that neither he nor anyone else——

Ringdal (enters by the door on the right). Excuse me, Chamberlain; one word—— [*Whispers.*

The Chamberlain. What? In your room?

Ringdal. He came in by the back way and begs you to see him.

The Chamberlain. H'm.—Oh, Doctor, just go into the drawing-room for a moment; there's some one here who—— But don't say a word to Selma of Mr. Stensgård and his visit. She must be kept outside all this business. As for my daughter, I should prefer that you should say nothing to her either; but—— Oh, what's the use——? Please go now.

[FIELDBO *goes into the drawing-room.* RINGDAL *has, in the meantime, gone back to his office, whence* MONSEN *presently enters.*

Monsen (at the door). I beg ten thousand pardons, sir——

The Chamberlain. Oh, come in, come in!

Monsen. I trust your family is in good health?

The Chamberlain. Thank you. Is there anything you want?

Monsen. I can't quite put it that way. Thank heaven,

I'm one of those that have got pretty nearly all they can want.

The Chamberlain. Oh, indeed? That is a good deal to say.

Monsen. But I've had to work for it, Chamberlain. Oh, I know you regard my work with no very friendly eye.

The Chamberlain. I cannot suppose that your work is in any way affected by my way of regarding it.

Monsen. Who knows? At any rate, I'm thinking of gradually withdrawing from business.

The Chamberlain. Really?

Monsen. The luck has been on my side, I may tell you. I've gone ahead as far as I care to; so now I think it's about time to slack off a little——

The Chamberlain. Well, I congratulate both you—and other people.

Monsen. And if I could at the same time do you a service, Chamberlain——

The Chamberlain. Me?

Monsen. When the Langerud woods were put up to auction five years ago, you made a bid for them——

The Chamberlain. Yes, but you outbade me, and they were knocked down to you.

Monsen. You can have them now, with the saw-mills and all appurtenances——

The Chamberlain. After all your sinful cutting and hacking——!

Monsen. Oh, they're worth a good deal still; and with your method of working, in a few years——

The Chamberlain. Thank you; unfortunately, I must decline the proposal.

Monsen. There's a great deal of money in it, Chamberlain. As for me,—I may tell you I have a great speculation on hand; the stakes are large; I mean there's a big haul to be made—a hundred thousand or so——

The Chamberlain. A hundred thousand? That is certainly no trifle.

Monsen. Ha, ha, ha! A nice round sum to add to the pile. But when you're going into a great battle you need reserve forces, as the saying goes. There's not much ready money about; the names that are worth anything are rather used up——

The Chamberlain. Yes, certain people have taken care of that.

Monsen. It's a case of you scratch me, I scratch you. Well, Chamberlain, is it to be a bargain? You shall have the woods at your own figure——

The Chamberlain. I will not have them at any figure, Mr. Monsen.

Monsen. Well, one good offer deserves another. Will you help me, sir?

The Chamberlain. What do you mean?

Monsen. Of course I'll give good security. I have plenty of property. Look here—these papers—just let me explain my position to you.

The Chamberlain (waving the papers aside). Is it pecuniary aid you want?

Monsen. Not ready money; oh, no! But your support, Chamberlain. Of course I'll pay for it—and give security, and——

The Chamberlain. And you come to me with such a proposal as this?

Monsen. Yes, precisely to you. I know you've often let bygones be bygones when a man was in real straits.

The Chamberlain. Well, in a way, I must thank you for your good opinion—especially at a time like this; but nevertheless——

Monsen. Won't you tell me, Chamberlain, what sets you against me?

The Chamberlain. Oh, what would be the use?

Monsen. It might lead to a better understanding between us. I've never stood in your way that I know of.

The Chamberlain. You think not? Then let me tell you of one case in which you have stood in my way. I founded the Iron-works Savings Bank for the benefit of my employees and others. But then you must needs set up as a banker; people take their savings to you——

Monsen. Naturally, sir, for I give higher interest.

The Chamberlain. Yes, but you charge higher interest on loans.

Monsen. But I don't make so many difficulties about security and so forth.

The Chamberlain. That is just the mischief of it; for now we have people making bargains to the tune of ten or twenty thousand dollars,* though neither of the parties has so much as a brass farthing. That is what sets me against you, Mr. Monsen. And there is another thing, too, that touches me still more nearly. Do you think it was with my good will that my son flung himself into all these wild speculations?

Monsen. But how can I help that?

The Chamberlain. It was your example that infected him, as it did the others. Why could you not stick to your last?

Monsen. Remain a lumberman, like my father?

The Chamberlain. Was it a disgrace to be in my employment? Your father made his bread honourably and was respected in his own class.

Monsen. Yes, until he'd almost worked his life out and at last went over the waterfall with his raft. Do you know anything of life in that class, Chamberlain? Have you ever realized what the men have to endure who toil for you deep in the forests and along the river-reaches, while you sit

* The dollar—four crowns—four-and-sixpence, was the unit of coinage at the time this play was written. It has since been replaced by the crown.

comfortably at home and fatten on the profits? Can you blame such a man for struggling to rise in the world? I had had a little more schooling than my father; perhaps I had rather more brains, too——

The Chamberlain. Very likely. But by what means have you risen in the world? You began by selling brandy. Then you bought up doubtful debts and enforced them mercilessly;—and so you got on and on. How many people have you not ruined to push yourself forward!

Monsen. That's the course of business; one up, another down.

The Chamberlain. But there are different methods of business. I know of respectable families whom you have brought to the workhouse.

Monsen. Daniel Heire is not very far from the workhouse.

The Chamberlain. I understand you; but I can justify my conduct before God and man! When the country was in distress, after the separation from Denmark, my father made sacrifices beyond his means. Thus part of our property came into the hands of the Heire family. What was the result? The people who lived upon the property suffered under Daniel Heire's incompetent management. He cut down timber to the injury, I may even say to the ruin, of the district. Was it not my obvious duty to put a stop to it if I was able? And it happened that I was able; I had the law on my side; I was well within my rights when I re-entered upon my family property.

Monsen. I, too, have always had the law on my side.

The Chamberlain. But what about your sense of right, your conscience, if you have such a thing? And how you have broken down all social order! How you have impaired the respect that should attach to wealth! People never think of asking nowadays how such and such a fortune was made, or how long it has been in such and such a family; they only ask: how much is so-and-so worth?—and they esteem him accordingly. Now I suffer by all this; I find myself regarded as a sort of associate of yours; people speak of us in one breath, because we are the two largest proprietors in the neighbourhood. This state of things I cannot endure! I tell you once for all: that is why I am set against you.

Monsen. This state of things shall come to an end, sir; I will give up business and make way for you at every point; but I beg you, I implore you, to help me!

The Chamberlain. I will not.

Monsen. I'm willing to pay you what you like——

The Chamberlain. To pay! And you dare to——!

Monsen. If not for my sake, then for your son's!

The Chamberlain. My son's!

Monsen. Yes, he's in it. I reckon he stands to win some twenty thousand dollars.

The Chamberlain. Stands to win?

Monsen. Yes.

The Chamberlain. Then, good God, who stands to lose all this money?

Monsen. How do you mean?

The Chamberlain. If my son wins, some one or other must lose!

Monsen. It's a good stroke of business; I'm not in a position to say more. But I need a solid name; only just your endorsement——

The Chamberlain. Endorsement! On a bill——?

Monsen. Only for ten or fifteen thousand dollars.

The Chamberlain. Do you suppose for a moment that ——? My name! In such an affair! My name? As surety, no doubt?

Monsen. A mere matter of form——

The Chamberlain. A matter of swindling! My name! Not upon any consideration. I have never put my name on other men's paper.

Monsen. Never? That's an exaggeration, Chamberlain.

The Chamberlain. It is the literal truth.

Monsen. No, not literal; I've seen it with my own eyes.

The Chamberlain. What have you seen?

Monsen. Your name—on one bill at least.

The Chamberlain. It is false, I tell you! You have never seen it!

Monsen. I have! On a bill for two thousand dollars. Think again!

The Chamberlain. Neither for two thousand nor for ten thousand! On my sacred word of honour, never!

Monsen. Then it's a forgery.

The Chamberlain. Forgery?

Monsen. Yes, a forgery—for I have seen it.

The Chamberlain. Forgery? Forgery! Where did you see it? In whose hands?

Monsen. That I won't tell you.

The Chamberlain. Ha-ha! We shall soon find that out——

Monsen. Listen to me——!

The Chamberlain. Silence! It has come to this then! Forgery. They must mix me up in their abominations! No wonder, then, that people bracket me with the rest of you. But it is my turn now!

Monsen. Chamberlain—for your own sake and for the sake of others——

The Chamberlain. Off with you! Out of my sight! It is you that are at the root of it all!—Yes you are! Woe unto him from whom offences come. Your home-life is scandalous. What sort of society do you get about you? Persons from Christiania and elsewhere, who think only of eating and drinking, and do not care in what company they gorge themselves. Silence! I have seen with my own eyes your distinguished guests tearing along the roads at Christmas-time like a pack of howling wolves. And there is worse behind. You have had scandals with your own maid-servants. You drove your wife out of her mind by your ill-treatment and debauchery.

Monsen. Come, this is going too far! You shall pay for these words!

The Chamberlain. Oh, to the deuce with your threats! What harm can you do to me? Me? You asked what I had to say against you. Well, I have said it. Now you know why I have kept you out of decent society.

Monsen. Yes, and now I'll drag your decent society down——

The Chamberlain. That way!

Monsen. I know my way, Chamberlain!

[*Goes out by the back.*

The Chamberlain (opens the door on the right and calls). Ringdal, Ringdal—come here!

Ringdal. What is it, sir?

The Chamberlain (calls into the drawing-room). Doctor, please come this way!—Now, Ringdal, now you shall see my prophecies fulfilled.

Fieldbo (entering). What can I do for you, Chamberlain?

Ringdal. What prophecies, sir?

The Chamberlain. What do you say to this, Doctor? You have always accused me of exaggerating when I said that Monsen was corrupting the neighbourhood.

Fieldbo. Well, what then?

The Chamberlain. We are getting on, I can tell you! What do you think? There are forgeries going about.

Ringdal. Forgeries?

The Chamberlain. Yes, forgeries! And whose name do you think they have forged? Why, mine!

Fieldbo. Who in the world can have done it?

The Chamberlain. How can I tell? I don't know all the scoundrels in the district. But we shall soon find out.—Doctor, do me a service. The papers must have come into the hands either of the Savings Bank or the Iron-works Bank. Drive up to Lundestad; he is the director who knows most about things. Find out whether there is any such paper——

Fieldbo. Certainly; at once.

Ringdal. Lundestad is here at the works to-day; there's a meeting of the school committee.

The Chamberlain. So much the better. Find him; bring him here.

Fieldbo. I'll go at once. [*Goes out at the back.*

The Chamberlain. And you, Ringdal, make inquiries at the Iron-works. As soon as we have got to the bottom of the matter, we'll lay an information. No mercy to the scoundrels!

Ringdal. Very good, sir. Bless me, who'd have thought of such a thing? [*Goes out to the right.*

[*The* CHAMBERLAIN *paces the room once or twice and is then about to go into his study. At that instant* ERIK BRATSBERG *enters from the back.*

Erik. My dear father——!

The Chamberlain. Oh, are you there?

Erik. I want so much to speak to you.

The Chamberlain. H'm; I'm not much in the humour for speaking to any one. What do you want?

Erik. You know I have never mixed you up in my affairs, father.

The Chamberlain. No; that is an honour I should certainly have declined.

Erik. But now I am forced to——

The Chamberlain. What are you forced to do?

Erik. Father, you must help me!

The Chamberlain. With money! You may be very sure that——

Erik. Only this once! I swear I'll never again—— The fact is, I am under certain engagements to Monsen of Stonelee——

The Chamberlain. I know that. You have a brilliant speculation on hand.

Erik. A speculation? We? No! Who told you so?

The Chamberlain. Monsen himself.

Erik. Has Monsen been here?

The Chamberlain. He has just gone. I showed him the door.

Erik. If you don't help me, father, I am ruined.

The Chamberlain. You?

Erik. Yes. Monsen has advanced me money. I had to pay terribly dear for it; and now the bills have fallen due——

The Chamberlain. There we have it! What did I tell you——?

Erik. Yes, yes; it's too late now——

The Chamberlain. Ruined! In two years! But how could you expect anything else? What had you to do among these charlatans that go about dazzling people's eyes with wealth that never existed! They were no company for you. Among people of that sort you must meet cunning with cunning, or you'll go to the wall; you have learnt that now.

Erik. Father, will you save me or will you not?

The Chamberlain. No; for the last time, no. I will not.

Erik. My honour is at stake——

The Chamberlain. Oh, let us have no big phrases! There's no honour involved in commercial success nowadays; quite the opposite, I had almost said. Go home and make up your accounts; pay every man his due and have done with it, the sooner the better.

Erik. Oh, you don't know——

[SELMA *and* THORA *enter from the drawing-room.*

Selma. Is that Erik's voice?—Good heavens, what is the matter?

The Chamberlain. Nothing. Go into the drawing-room again.

Selma. No, I won't go. I will know. Erik, what is it? Tell me!

Erik. It's only that I am ruined!

Thora. Ruined!

The Chamberlain. There, you see!

Selma. What is ruined?

Erik. Everything.

Selma. Do you mean you have lost your money?

Erik. Money, house, inheritance—everything!

Selma. Is that what you call everything?

Erik. Come, let us go, Selma. You are all I have left me. We must bear the blow together.

Selma. The blow? Bear it together? *(With a cry.)* Do you think I am fit for that, now?

The Chamberlain. For heaven's sake——!

Erik. What do you mean?

Thora. Oh, Selma, take care!

Selma. No, I won't take care! I cannot go on lying and shamming any longer! I must speak the truth. I will not "bear" anything!

Erik. Selma!

The Chamberlain. Child, what are you saying?

Selma. Oh, how cruel you have been to me! Shamefully—all of you! It was my part always to accept—never to give. I have been like a pauper among you. You never came and demanded a sacrifice of me; I was not fit to bear anything. I hate you! I loathe you!

Erik. What can this mean?

The Chamberlain. She is ill; she is out of her mind!

Selma. How I have thirsted for a single drop of your troubles, your anxieties! But when I begged for it you only laughed me off. You have dressed me up like a doll; you have played with me as you would play with a child. Oh, what a joy it would have been to me to take my share in your burdens! How I longed, how I yearned, for a large, and high and strenuous part in life! Now you come to me, Erik, now that you have nothing else left. But I will not be treated simply as a last resource. I will have nothing to do with your troubles now. I won't stay with you! I will rather play and sing in the streets——! Let me be! Let me be! [*She rushes out by the back.*

The Chamberlain. Thora, was there any meaning in all that, or——

Thora. Oh, yes, there was meaning in it; if only I had seen it sooner. [*Goes out by the back.*

Erik. No! All else I can lose, but not her! Selma, Selma! [*Follows* THORA *and* SELMA.

Ringdal (enters from the right). Chamberlain!

The Chamberlain. Well, what is it?

Ringdal. I have been to the Bank——

The Chamberlain. The Bank? Oh, yes, about the bill——

Ringdal. It's all right; they have never had any bill endorsed by you——

[FIELDBO *and* LUNDESTAD *enter by the back.*

Fieldbo. False alarm, Chamberlain!

The Chamberlain. Indeed? Not at the Savings Bank either?

Lundestad. Certainly not. During all the years I've been a director I have never once seen your name; except, of course, on your son's bill.

The Chamberlain. My son's bill?

Lundestad. Yes, the bill you accepted for him early this spring.

The Chamberlain. My son? My son? Do you dare to tell me——?

Lundestad. Why, bless me, just think a moment; the bill for two thousand dollars drawn by your son——

The Chamberlain (groping for a chair). Oh, my God——!

Fieldbo. For heaven's sake——!

Ringdal. It's not possible that——!

The Chamberlain (who has sunk down on a chair). Quietly, quietly! Drawn by my son, you say? Accepted by me? For two thousand dollars?

Fieldbo (to LUNDESTAD*).* And this bill is in the Savings Bank?

Lundestad. Not now; it was redeemed last week by Monsen——

The Chamberlain. By Monsen——?

Ringdal. Monsen may still be at the works; I'll go——

The Chamberlain. Stop here!

[DANIEL HEIRE *enters by the back.*

Heire. Good morning, gentlemen! Good morning, Chamberlain! Thank you so much for the delightful evening we spent yesterday. What do you think I've just heard——?

Ringdal. Excuse me; we are busy——

Heire. So are other people, I can tell you; our friend from Stonelee, for example——

The Chamberlain. Monsen?

Heire. Hee-hee; it's a pretty story! The electioneering intrigues are in full swing. And what do you think is the last idea? They are going to bribe you, Chamberlain!

Lundestad. To bribe——?

The Chamberlain. They judge the tree by its fruit.

Heire. Deuce take me if it isn't the most impudent thing I ever heard of! I just looked in at Madam Rundholmen's to have a glass of bitters. There sat Messrs. Monsen and Stensgård drinking port—filthy stuff! I wouldn't touch it; but they might have had the decency to offer me a glass, all the same. However, Monsen turned to me and said, "What do you bet that Chamberlain Bratsberg won't go with our party at the preliminary election to-morrow?" "Indeed," said I, "how's that to be managed?" "Oh," he said, "this bill will persuade him——"

Fieldbo. Bill——?

Lundestad. At the election——?

The Chamberlain. Well? What then?

Heire. Oh, I know no more. They said something about two thousand dollars. That's the figure they rate a gentleman's conscience at! Oh, it's abominable, I say!

The Chamberlain. A bill for two thousand dollars?

Ringdal. And Monsen has it?

Heire. No, he handed it over to Stensgård.

Lundestad. Indeed!

Fieldbo. To Stensgård?

The Chamberlain. Are you sure of that?

Heire. Quite certain. "You can make what use you please of it," he said. But I don't understand——

Lundestad. I want to speak to you, Mr. Heire—and you too, Ringdal.

[*The three converse in a whisper at the back.*

Fieldbo. Chamberlain!

The Chamberlain. Well?

Fieldbo. Your son's bill is genuine, of course——?

The Chamberlain. One would suppose so.

Fieldbo. Of course. But now if the forged bill were to turn up——?

The Chamberlain. I will lay no information.

Fieldbo. Naturally not;—but you must do more.

The Chamberlain (rising). I can do no more.

Fieldbo. Yes, for heaven's sake, you can and must. You must save the poor fellow——

The Chamberlain. In what way?

Fieldbo. Quite simply: by acknowledging the signature.

The Chamberlain. Then you think, Doctor, that we stick at nothing in our family?

Fieldbo. I am trying to think for the best, Chamberlain.

The Chamberlain. And do you believe for a moment that I can tell a tie?—that I can play into the hands of forgers?

Fieldbo. And do you realise what will be the consequences if you do not?

The Chamberlain. The offender must settle that with the law. [*He goes out to the left.*

ACT IV

A public room in MADAM RUNDHOLMEN'S *hotel. Entrance door in the back; a smaller door on either side. A window on the right; before it, a table with writing materials; further back, in the middle of the room, another table.*

Madam Rundholmen (within, on the left, heard talking loudly). Oh, let them go about their business! Tell them they've come here to vote and not to drink. If they won't wait, they can do the other thing.

Stensgård (enters by the back). Good morning! H'm, h'm, Madam Rundholmen! *(Goes to the door on the left and knocks.)* Good morning, Madam Rundholmen!

Madam Rundholmen (within). Oh! Who's there?

Stensgård. It is I—Stensgård. May I come in?

Madam Rundholmen. No, indeed, you mustn't! No! I'm not dress'd.

Stensgård. What? Are you so late to-day?

Madam Rundholmen. Oh, I can tell you I've been up since all hours; but one must look a little decent, you know. *(Peeps out, with a kerchief over her head.)* Well, what is it? No, you really mustn't look at me, Mr. Stensgård.—Oh, there's some one else!

[*Disappears, slamming the door to.*

Aslaksen (enters from the back with a bundle of papers). Good morning, Mr. Stensgård.

Stensgård. Well, is it in?

Aslaksen. Yes, here it is. Look—"The Independence

Day Celebrations—From our Special Correspondent." Here's the founding of the League on the other side and your speech up here. I've leaded all the abuse.

Stensgård. It seems to me it's all leaded.

Aslaksen. Pretty nearly.

Stensgård. And the extra number was of course distributed yesterday?

Aslaksen. Of course; all over the district, both to subscribers and others. Would you like to see it?

[*Hands him a copy.*

Stensgård (running his eye over the paper). "Our respected member, Mr. Lundestad, proposes to resign . . . long and faithful service . . . in the words of the poet: 'Rest, patriot, it is thy due!'" H'm! "The association founded on Independence Day!: the League of Youth . . . Mr. Stensgård, the guiding intelligence of the League . . . timely reforms, credit on easier terms." Ah, that's very good. Has the polling begun?

Aslaksen. It's in full swing. The whole League is on the spot—both voters and others.

Stensgård. Oh, deuce take the others—between ourselves, of course. Well, you go down and talk to the waverers.

Aslaksen. All right.

Stensgård. You can tell them that I am pretty much at one with Lundestad——

Aslaksen. Trust to me; I know the local situation.

Stensgård. One thing more; just to oblige me, Aslaksen, don't drink to-day.

Aslaksen. Oh, what do you mean——!

Stensgård. We'll have a jolly evening when it's all over; but remember what you, as well as I, have at stake; your paper—— Come, now, my good fellow, let me see that you can——

Aslaksen. There, that's enough now; I'm old enough to look after myself. [*Goes out to the right.*

Madam Rundholmen (enters from the left, elaborately dressed). Now, Mr. Stensgård, I'm at your service. Is it anything of importance——?

Stensgård. No, only that I want you to be good enough to let me know when Mr. Monsen comes.

Madam Rundholmen. He won't be here to-day.

Stensgård. Not to-day?

Madam Rundholmen. No; he drove past here at four this morning; he's always driving about nowadays. What's more, he came in and roused me out of bed—he wanted to borrow money, you must know.

Stensgård. Monsen did?

Madam Rundholmen. Yes. He's a tremendous man to get through money is Monsen. I hope things may turn out all right for him. And I say the same to you; for I hear you're going into Parliament.

Stensgård. I? Nonsense. Who told you so?

Madam Rundholmen. Oh, some of Mr. Lundestad's people.

Daniel Heire (enters from the back). Hee-hee! Good morning! I'm not in the way, am I?

Madam Rundholmen. Gracious, no!

Heire. Good God, how resplendent! Can it be for me that you've got yourself up like this?

Madam Rundholmen. Of course. It's for you bachelors we get ourselves up, isn't it?

Heire. For marrying men, Madam Rundholmen; for marrying men! Unfortunately, my law-suits take up all my time——

Madam Rundholmen. Oh, nonsense; you've always plenty of time to get married.

Heire. No; deuce take me if I have! Marriage is a thing you've got to give your whole mind to. Well, well—if you can't have me, you must put up with somebody else. For you ought to marry again.

Madam Rundholmen. Now, do you know, I'm sometimes of the same opinion.

Heire. Naturally; when once one has tasted the joys of matrimony—— Of course, poor Rundholmen was one in a thousand——

Madam Rundholmen. Well, I won't go so far as that; he was a bit rough and rather too fond of his glass; but a husband's always a husband.

Heire. Very true, Madam Rundholmen; a husband's a husband, and a widow's a widow——

Madam Rundholmen. And business is business. Oh, when I think of all I've got to attend to, I don't know whether I'm on my heels or my head. Every one wants to buy; but when it comes to paying, I've got to go in for summonses and executions, and Lord knows what. Upon my word, I'll soon have to engage a lawyer all to myself.

Heire. I'll tell you what, Madam Rundholmen, you should retain Mr. Stensgård; he's a bachelor.

Madam Rundholmen. Oh, how you do talk! I won't listen to a word more. [*Goes out to the right.*

Heire. A substantial woman, sir! Comfortable and well preserved; no children up to date; money well invested. Education, too; she's widely read, sir.

Stensgård. Widely read, eh?

Heire. Hee-hee; she ought to be; she had charge of Alm's circulating library for a couple of years. But your head's full of other things to-day, I daresay.

Stensgård. Not at all; I don't even know that I shall vote. Who are you going to vote for, Mr. Heire?

Heire. Haven't got a vote, sir. There was only one kennel that would qualify in the market, and that you bought.

Stensgård. If you're at a loss for a lodging, I'll give it up to you.

Heire. Hee-hee, you're joking . Ah, youth, youth! What

a pleasant humour it has! But now I must be off and have a look at the menagerie. I'm told your whole League is afoot. *(Sees* FIELDBO, *who enters from the back.)* Here's the Doctor, too! I suppose you have come on a scientific mission?

Fieldbo. A scientific mission?

Heire. Yes, to study the epidemic; you've heard of the virulent *rabies agitatoria* that has broken out? God be with you, my dear young friends? [*Goes out to the right.*

Stensgård. Tell me quickly—have you seen the Chamberlain to-day?

Fieldbo. Yes.

Stensgård. And what did he say?

Fieldbo. What did he say?

Stensgård. Yes; you know I have written to him.

Fieldbo. Have you? What did you write?

Stensgård. That I am still of the same mind about his daughter; that I want to talk the matter over with him; and that I propose to call on him to-morrow.

Fieldbo. If I were you, I should at least defer my visit. It is the Chamberlain's birthday to-morrow; a crowd of people will be there——

Stensgård. That's all right; the more the better. I hold big cards in my hand, let me tell you.

Fieldbo. And perhaps you have bluffed a little with your big cards?

Stensgård. How do you mean?

Fieldbo. I mean you have perhaps embellished your declaration of love with a few little threats or so?

Stensgård. Fieldbo, you have seen the letter!

Fieldbo. No, I assure you——

Stensgård. Well, then, frankly—I have threatened him.

Fieldbo. Ah! Then I have, in a way, an answer to your letter.

Stensgård. An answer? Out with it, man!

Fieldbo (shows him a sealed paper). Look here—the Chamberlain's proxy.

Stensgård. And who does he vote for?

Fieldbo. Not for you, at any rate.

Stensgård. For whom then? For whom?

Fieldbo. For the Sheriff and the Provost.*

Stensgård. What! Not even for Lundestad?

Fieldbo. No. And do you know why? Because Lundestad is going to propose you as his successor.

Stensgård. He dares to do this!

Fieldbo. Yes, he does. And he added: "If you see Stensgård, you can tell him how I am voting; it will show him on what footing we stand."

Stensgård. Good; since he will have it so!

Fieldbo. Take care; it's dangerous to tug at an old tower—it may come down on your head.

Stensgård. Oh, I have learnt wisdom in these two days.

Fieldbo. Indeed? You're not so wise but that you let old Lundestad lead you by the nose.

Stensgård. Do you think I haven't seen through Lundestad? Do you think I don't understand that he took me up because he thought I had won over the Chamberlain, and because he wanted to break up our League and keep Monsen out?

Fieldbo. But now that he knows you haven't won over the Chamberlain——

Stensgård. He has gone too far to draw back; and I've made good use of the time and scattered announcements broadcast. Most of his supporters will abstain from voting; mine are all here——

Fieldbo. It's a big stride from the preliminary election to the final election.

* "Amtmanden og provsten." The "Amtmand" is the chief magistrate of an "Amt" or county; the "Provst" is an ecclesiastical functionary, perhaps equivalent to a rural dean.

Stensgård. Lundestad knows very well that if he fails me in the College of Electors, I'll soon agitate him out of the town Council.

Fieldbo. Not a bad calculation. And to succeed in all this, you feel that you must strike root here more firmly than you have as yet done?

Stensgård. Yes, these people always demand material guarantees, community of interests——

Fieldbo. Just so; and therefore Miss Bratsberg is to be sacrificed?

Stensgård. Sacrificed? If that were so, I should be no better than a scoundrel. But it will be for her happiness, that I'm convinced. What now? Fieldbo, why do you look like that? You have some underhand scheme of your own——

Fieldbo. I?

Stensgård. Yes, you have! You are intriguing against me, behind my back. Why do you do that? Be open with me—will you?

Fieldbo. Frankly, I won't. You are so dangerous, so unscrupulous—well, so reckless at any rate, that one dare not be open with you. Whatever you know, you make use of without hesitation. But this I say to you as a friend: put Miss Bratsberg out of your head.

Stensgård. I cannot. I must extricate myself from these sordid surroundings. I can't go on living in this hugger-mugger way. Here have I got to be hail-fellow-well-met with Dick, Tom and Harry; to whisper in corners with them, to hob-nob with them, to laugh at their beery witticisms; to be hand in glove with hobbledehoys and unlicked cubs. How can I keep my love of the People untarnished in the midst of all this? I feel as if all the electricity went out of my words. I have no elbow-room, no fresh air to breathe. Oh, a longing comes over me at times for exquisite women! I want something that brings beauty with it! I lie here in a sort of turbid eddy, while out there the clear blue current sweeps past me—— But what can you understand of all this!

Lundestad (enters from the back). Ah, here we are. Good morning, gentlemen.

Stensgård. I have news for you, Mr. Lundestad! Do you know who the Chamberlain is voting for?

Fieldbo. Silence! It's dishonourable of you.

Stensgård. What do I care? He is voting for the Sheriff and the Provost.

Lundestad. Oh, that was to be expected. You went and ruined your chances with him—though I implored you to play your cards neatly.

Stensgård. I shall play them neatly enough—in future.

Fieldbo. Take care—two can play at that game.

[*Goes out to the right.*

Stensgård. That fellow has something up his sleeve. Have you any idea what it can be?

Lundestad. No, I haven't. But, by-the-bye, I see you are flourishing in the paper to-day.

Stensgård. I?

Lundestad. Yes, with a nice little epitaph on me.

Stensgård. Oh, that's that beast Aslaksen, of course——

Lundestad. Your attack on the Chamberlain is in, too.

Stensgård. I don't know anything about that. If it's to be war between the Chamberlain and me, I have sharper weapons.

Lundestad. Indeed!

Stensgård. Have you ever seen this bill? Look at it. Is it good?

Lundestad. Good, you say? This bill here?

Stensgård. Yes; look closely at it.

Heire (enters from the right). Why, what the deuce can be the meaning of—— Ah, how interesting! Do remain as you are, gentlemen, I beg! Do you know what you irresistibly remind me of? Of a summer night in the Far North.

Lundestad. That's a curious simile.

Heire. A very obvious one—the setting and the rising sun together. Delightful, delightful! But, talking of that, what the deuce is the matter outside there? Your fellow-citizens are scuttling about like frightened fowls, cackling and crowing and not knowing what perch to settle on.

Stensgård. Well, it's an occasion of great importance.

Heire. Oh, you and your importance! No, it's something quite different, my dear friends. There are whispers of a great failure; a bankruptcy—oh, not political, Mr. Lundestad; I don't mean that!

Stensgård. A bankruptcy?

Heire. Hee-hee! That puts life into our legal friend. Yes, a bankruptcy; some one is on his last legs; the axe is laid to the root of the tree—— I say no more! Two strange gentlemen have been seen driving past; but where to? To whose address? Do you know anything, Mr. Lundestad?

Lundestad. I know how to hold my tongue, Mr. Heire.

Heire. Of course; you are a statesman, a diplomatist. But I must be off and find out all I can about it. It's such sport with these heroes of finance: they are like beads on a string—when one slips off, all the rest follow.

[*Goes out by the back.*

Stensgård. Is there any truth in all this gossip?

Lundestad. You showed me a bill; I thought I saw young Mr. Bratsberg's name upon it?

Stensgård. The Chamberlain's, too.

Lundestad. And you asked me if it was good?

Stensgård. Yes; just look at it.

Lundestad. It's perhaps not so good as it might be.

Stensgård. You see it, then?

Lundestad. What?

Stensgård. That it is a forgery.

Lundestad. A forgery? Forged bills are often the safest; people redeem them first.

Stensgård. But what do you think? Isn't it a forgery?

Lundestad. I don't much like the look of it.

Stensgård. How so?

Lundestad. I'm afraid there are too many of these about, Mr. Stensgard.

Stensgård. What! It's not possible that——?

Lundestad. If young Mr. Bratsberg slips off the string, those nearest him are only too likely to follow.

Stensgård (seizes his arm). What do you mean by those nearest him?

Lundestad. Who can be nearer than father and son?

Stensgård. Why, good God——!

Lundestad. Remember, I say nothing! It was Daniel Heire that was talking of failure and bankruptcy and——

Stensgård. This is a thunderbolt to me.

Lundestad. Oh, many a man that seemed solid enough has gone to the wall before now. Perhaps he's too good-natured; goes and backs bills; ready money isn't always to be had; property has to be sold for an old song——

Stensgård. And of course this falls on—falls on the chil dren as well.

Lundestad. Yes, I'm heartily grieved for Miss Bratsberg. She didn't get much from her mother; and heaven knows if even the little she has is secured.

Stensgård. Oh, now I understand Fieldbo's advice! He's a true friend, after all.

Lundestad. What did Doctor Fieldbo say?

Stensgård. He was too loyal to say anything, but I understand him all the same. And now I understand you, too, Mr. Lundestad.

Lundestad. Have you not understood me before?

Stensgård. Not thoroughly. I forget the proverb about the rats and the sinking ship.

Lundestad. That's not a very nice way to put it. But what's the matter with you? You look quite ill. Good God, I haven't gone and blasted your hopes, have I?

Stensgård. How do you mean?

Lundestad. Yes, yes—I see it all. Old fool that I am! My dear Mr. Stensgård, if you really love the girl, what does it matter whether she is rich or poor?

Stensgård. Matter? No, of course——

Lundestad. Good Lord, we all know happiness isn't a matter of money.

Stensgård. Of course not.

Lundestad. And with industry and determination you'll soon be on your feet again. Don't let poverty frighten you. I know what love is; I went into all that in my young days. A happy home; a faithful woman——! My dear young friend, beware how you take any step that may involve you in life-long self-reproach.

Stensgård. But what will become of your plans?

Lundestad. Oh, they must go as best they can. I couldn't think of demanding the sacrifice of your heart!

Stensgård. But I will make the sacrifice. Yes, I will show you that I have the strength for it. Think of the longing multitude out there: they claim me with a sort of voiceless pathos. I cannot, I dare not, fail them!

Lundestad. Yes, but the stake in the district——?

Stensgård. I shall take measures to fulfil the demands of my fellow-citizens in that respect, Mr. Lundestad. I see a way, a new way; and I will follow it up. I renounce the happiness of toiling in obscurity for the woman I love. I say to my fellow-countrymen: "Here I am—take me!"

Lundestad (looks at him in quiet admiration and presses his hand.) You are indeed a man of rare gifts, Mr. Stensgård. [*Goes out to the right.*

[STENSGÅRD *paces the room several times, now stopping for a moment at the window, now running his fingers through his hair. Presently* BASTIAN MONSEN *enters from the back.*

Bastian. Here I am, my dear friend.*

* Bastian now says "thou" (du) to Stensgard—*il le tutoie.*

Stensgård. Where have you come from?

Bastian. From the Nation.

Stensgård. The Nation? What does that mean?

Bastian. Don't you know what the Nation means? It means the People; the common people; those who have nothing and are nothing; those who lie chained——

Stensgård. What monkey-tricks are these, I should like to know?

Bastian. Monkey-tricks?

Stensgård. I have noticed lately that you go about mimicking me; you imitate even my clothes and my handwriting. Be kind enough to stop that.

Bastian. What do you mean? Don't we belong to the same party?

Stensgård. Yes, but I won't put up with this—you make yourself ridiculous——

Bastian. By being like you?

Stensgård. By aping me. Be sensible now, Monsen, and give it up. It's quite disgusting. But look here—can you tell me when your father is coming back?

Bastian. I have no idea. I believe he's gone to Christiania; he may not be back for a week or so.

Stensgård. Indeed? I'm sorry for that. He has a big stroke of business on hand, I hear.

Bastian. I have a big stroke of business on hand, too. Look here, Stensgård, you must do me a service.

Stensgård. Willingly. What is it?

Bastian. I feel so full of energy. I have to thank you for that; you have stimulated me. I feel I must do something, Stensgård:—I want to get married.

Stensgård. To get married? To whom?

Bastian. Sh! Some one in this house.

Stensgård. Madam Rundholmen?

Bastian. Sh! Yes, it's her. Put in a good word for me, do! This sort of thing is just the thing for me. She's in the swim, you know; she's on the best of terms with the

Chamberlain's people, ever since her sister was housekeeper there. If I get her, perhaps I shall get the town-contracts, too. So that on the whole—damn it, I love her!

Stensgård. Oh, love, love! Have done with that sickening hypocrisy.

Bastian. Hypocrisy!

Stensgård. Yes; you are lying to yourself, at any rate. You talk in one breath of town-contracts and of love. Why not call a spade a spade? There's something sordid about all this; I will have nothing to do with it.

Bastian. But listen——!

Stensgård. Do your dirty work yourself, I say! *(To* FIELDBO, *who enters from the right.)* Well, how goes the election?

Fieldbo. Excellently for you, it appears. I saw Lundestad just now; he said you were getting all the votes.

Stensgård. Am I indeed?

Fieldbo. But what good will they do you? Since you're not a man of property——

Stensgård (between his teeth). Isn't it confounded!

Fieldbo. Well, you can't do two things at once. If you win on the one side, you must be content to lose on the other. Good-bye! [*Goes out by the back.*

Bastian. What did he mean by winning and losing?

Stensgård. I'll tell you afterwards. But now, my dear Monsen—to return to what we were talking about—I promised to put in a good word for you——

Bastian. You promised? On the contrary, I thought you said——?

Stensgård. Oh, nonsense; you didn't let me explain myself fully. What I meant was that there is something sordid in mixing up your love with town-contracts and so forth; it is an offence against all that is noblest in your nature. So, my dear friend, if you really love the girl——

Bastian. The widow——

Stensgård. Yes, yes; it's all the same. I mean when one

really loves a woman, that in itself should be a conclusive reason——

Bastian. Yes, that's just what I think. So you'll speak for me, will you?

Stensgård. Yes, with great pleasure—but on one condition.

Bastian. What's that?

Stensgård. Tit for tat, my dear Bastian—you must put in a word for me, too.

Bastian. I? With whom?

Stensgård. Have you really not noticed anything? Yet it's before your very nose.

Bastian. You surely don't mean——?

Stensgård. Your sister Ragna? Yes, it is she. Oh, you don't know how I have been moved by the sight of her quiet, self-sacrificing devotion to her home——

Bastian. Do you really mean to say so?

Stensgård. And you, with your penetrating eye, have suspected nothing?

Bastiar. Yes, at one time I did think——; but now people are talking of your hanging about the Chamberlain's——

Stensgård. Oh, the Chamberlain's! Well, Monsen, I'll tell you frankly that for a moment I did hesitate; but, thank goodness, that is over; now I see my way quite clear before me.

Bastian. There's my hand. I'll back you up, you may be sure. And as for Ragna—why, she daren't do anything but what I and father wish.

Stensgård. Yes, but your father—that's just what I wanted to say——

Bastian. Sh! There—I hear Madam Rundholmen. Now's your chance to speak for me, if she's not too busy; for then she's apt to be snappish. You do your best, my dear fellow, and leave the rest to me. Do you happen to have seen Aslaksen?

Stensgård. He's probably at the polling-booth.

[BASTIAN *goes out by the back, as* MADAM RUNDHOLMEN *enters from the right.*

Madam Rundholmen. Things are going as smooth as possible, Mr. Stensgård; every one is voting for you.

Stensgård. That's very odd.

Madam Rundholmen. Goodness knows what Monsen of Stonelee will say.

Stensgård. I want a word with you, Madam Rundholmen.

Madam Rundholmen. Well, what is it?

Stensgård. Will you listen to me?

Madam Rundholmen. Lord, yes, that I will.

Stensgård. Well, then: you were talking just now about being alone in the world——

Madam Rundholmen. Oh, it was that horrid old Heire——

Stensgård. You were saying how hard it is for an unprotected widow——

Madam Rundholmen. Yes, indeed; you should just try it, Mr. Stensgård!

Stensgård. But now if there came a fine young man——

Madam Rundholmen. A fine young man?

Stensgård. One who had long loved you in secret——

Madam Rundholmen. Oh, come now, Mr. Stensgård, I won't hear any more of your nonsense.

Stensgård. You must! A young man who, like yourself, finds it hard to be alone in the world——

Madam Rundholmen. Well, what then? I don't understand you at all.

Stensgård. If you could make two people happy, Madam Rundholmen—yourself and——

Madam Rundholmen. And a fine young man?

Stensgård. Just so; now, answer me——

Madam Rundholmen. Mr. Stensgård, you can't be in earnest?

Stensgård. You don't suppose I would jest on such a subject? Should you be disposed——?

Madam Rundholmen. Yes, that I am, the Lord knows! Oh, you dear, sweet——

Stensgård (recoiling a step). What is this?

Madam Rundholmen. Bother, here comes some one!

[RAGNA MONSEN *enters hastily, and in evident disquietude, from the back.*

Ragna. I beg your pardon—isn't my father here?

Madam Rundholmen. Your father? Yes; no;—I—I don't know—excuse me——

Ragna. Where is he?

Madam Rundholmen. Your father? Oh, he drove past here——

Stensgård. Towards Christiania.

Ragna. No; it's impossible——

Madam Rundholmen. Yes, I know for certain he drove down the road. Oh, my dear Miss Monsen, you can't think how happy I am! Wait a moment—I'll just run to the cellar and fetch up a bottle of the real thing.

[*Goes out to the left.*

Stensgård. Tell me, Miss Monsen—is it really your father you are looking for?

Ragna. Yes, of course it is.

Stensgård. And you didn't know that he had gone away?

Ragna. Oh, how should I know? They tell me nothing. But to Christiania——? That's impossible; they would have met him. Good-bye!

Stensgård (intercepts her). Ragna! Tell me! Why are you so changed towards me?

Ragna. I? Let me pass! Let me go!

Stensgård. No, you shall not go! I believe Providence guided you here at this moment. Oh, why do you shrink from me? You used not to.

Ragna. Ah, that is all over, thank God!

Stensgård. But why?

Ragna. I have learnt to know you better; it is well that I learned in time.

Stensgård. Oh, that is it? People have been lying about me? Perhaps I am to blame, too; I have been lost in a maze of perplexities. But that is past now. Oh, the very sight of you makes a better man of me. It is you I care for, deeply and truly; it is you I love, Ragna—you and no other!

Ragna. Let me pass! I am afraid of you——

Stensgård. Oh, but to-morrow, Ragna—may I come and speak to you to-morrow?

Ragna. Yes, yes, if you must; only for heaven's sake not to-day.

Stensgård. Only not to-day! Hurrah! I have won; now I am happy!

Madam Rundholmen (enters from the left with cake and wine). Come now, we must drink a glass for luck.

Stensgård. For luck in love! Here's to love and happiness! Hurrah for to-morrow! [*He drinks.*

Helle (entering, from the right, to RAGNA*).* Have you found him?

Ragna. No, he is not here. Come, come!

Madam Rundholmen. Heaven help us, what's the matter?

Helle. Nothing; only some visitors have arrived at Stonelee——

Ragna. Thanks for all your kindness, Madam Rundholmen——

Madam Rundholmen. Oh, have you got visitors on your hands again?

Ragna. Yes, yes; excuse me; I must go home. Good-bye!

Stensgård. Good-bye—till to-morrow!

[RAGNA *and* HELLE *go out by the back.*

[DANIEL HEIRE *enters from the right.*

Heire. Ha-ha! It's going like a house on fire! They're all cackling Stensgård, Stensgård, Stensgård! They're all plumping for you. Now you should plump for him, too, Madam Rundholmen!

Madam Rundholmen. Hey, that's an idea! Are they all voting for him?

Heire. Unanimously—Mr. Stensgård enjoys the confidence of the constituency, as the saying is. Old Lundestad is going about with a face like a pickled cucumber. Oh, it's a pleasure to see it all.

Madam Rundholmen. They shan't regret having voted for him. If I can't vote, I can stand treat.

[*Goes out to the left.*

Heire. Ah, you are the man for the widows, Mr. Stensgård! I'll tell you what—if you can only get hold of her, you're a made man, sir!

Stensgård. Get hold of Madam Rundholmen?

Heire. Yes, why not? She's a substantial woman in every sense of the word. She'll be mistress of the situation as soon as the Stonelee card-castle has come to grief.

Stensgård. There's nothing wrong at Stonelee, is there?

Heire. Isn't there? You have a short memory, my dear sir. Didn't I tell you there were rumours of failure, and bankruptcy, and——?

Stensgård. Well, what then?

Heire. What then? That's just what we want to know. There's a hue and cry after Monsen; two men have come to Stonelee——

Stensgård. Yes, I know—a couple of visitors——

Heire. Uninvited visitors, my dear young friend; there are whispers of the police and infuriated creditors—there's something queer about the accounts, you must know! Talking of that—what paper was that Monsen gave you yesterday?

Stensgård. Oh, just a paper—— Something queer about the accounts, you say? Look here! you know Chamberlain Bratsberg's signature?

Heire. Hee-hee! I should rather think I did.

Stensgård (produces the bill). Well, look at this.

Heire. Give it here—I'm rather short-sighted, you know. *(After examining it.)* That, my dear sir? That's not the Chamberlain's hand.

Stensgård. Not? Then it is——?

Heire. And it's drawn by Monsen?

Stensgård. No, by young Mr. Bratsberg.

Heire. Nonsense! Let me see. *(Looks at the paper and hands it back again.)* You can light your cigar with this.

Stensgård. What! The drawer's name, too——?

Heire. A forgery, young man; a forgery, as sure as my name's Daniel. You have only to look at it with the keen eye of suspicion——

Stensgård. But how can that be? Monsen can't have known——

Heire. Monsen? No, he knows nothing about either his own paper or other people's. But I'm glad it has come to an end, Mr. Stensgård!—It's a satisfaction to one's moral sense. Ah, I have often glowed with a noble indignation, if I may say so, at having to stand by and see—— I say no more! But the best of it all is that now Monsen is down he'll drag young Bratsberg after him; and the son will bring the father down——

Stensgård. Yes, so Lundestad said.

Heire. But of course there's method even in bankruptcy. You'll see; I am an old hand at prophecy. Monsen will go to prison; young Bratsberg will compound with his creditors; and the Chamberlain will be placed under trustees; that's to say, his creditors will present him with an annuity of a couple of thousand dollars. That's how things go, Mr. Stensgård; I know it, I know it! What says the classic? *Fiat justitia, pereat mundus;* which means: Fie on what's called justice in this wicked world, sir!

Stensgård (pacing the room). One after the other! Both ways barred!

Heire. What the deuce——?

Stensgård. And now, too! Just at this moment!

Aslaksen (enters from the right). I congratulate you, chosen of the people!

Stensgård. Elected!

Aslaksen. Elected by 117 votes, and Lundestad by 53. The rest all nowhere.

Heire. Your first step on the path of glory, Mr. Stensgård.

Aslaksen. And it shall cost you a bowl of punch——

Heire. Well, it's the first step that costs, they say.

Aslaksen (goes off to the left, shouting). Punch, Madam Rundholmen! A bowl of punch! The chosen of the people stands treat!

[LUNDESTAD, *and after him several* ELECTORS, *enter from the right.*

Heire (in a tone of condolence to LUNDESTAD*).* Fifty-three! That's the grey-haired patriot's reward!

Lundestad (whispers to STENSGÅRD*).* Are you firm in your resolve?

Stensgård. What's the use of being firm when everything is tumbling about your ears?

Lundestad. Do you think the game is lost?

Aslaksen (returning by the left). Madam Rundholmen stands treat herself. She says she has the best right to.

Stensgård (struck by an idea). Madam Rundholmen!—has the best right to——!

Lundestad. What?

Stensgård. The game is not lost, Mr. Lundestad!

[*Sits at the right-hand table and writes.*

Lundestad (in a low voice). Oh, Aslaksen—can you get something into your next paper for me?

Aslaksen. Of course I can. Is it libellous?

Lundestad. No, certainly not!

Aslaksen. Well, never mind; I'll take it all the same.

Lundestad. It is my political last will and testament; I shall write it to-night.

A Maid-servant (enters from the left). The punch, with Madam Rundholmen's compliments.

Aslaksen. Hurrah! Now there's some life in the local situation.

[*He places the punch-bowl on the middle table, serves the others and drinks freely himself during the following scene.* BASTIAN MONSEN *has meanwhile entered from the right.*

Bastian (softly). You won't forget my letter?

Aslaksen. Don't be afraid. *(Taps his breast-pocket.)* I have it here.

Bastian. You'll deliver it as soon as you can—when you see she's disengaged, you understand.

Aslaksen. I understand. *(Calls.)* Come, now, the glasses are filled.

Bastian. You shan't do it for nothing, I promise you.

Aslaksen. All right, all right. *(To the servant.)* A lemon, Karen—quick as the wind! [BASTIAN *retires.*

Stensgård. A word, Aslaksen; shall you be passing here to-morrow evening?

Aslaksen. To-morrow evening? I can, if you like.

Stensgård. Then you might look in and give Madam Rundholmen this letter.

Aslaksen. From you?

Stensgård. Yes. Put it in your pocket. There now. To-morrow evening, then?

Aslaksen. All right; trust to me.

[*The servant brings the lemon;* STENSGARD *goes towards the window.*

Bastian. Well—have you spoken to Madam Rundholmen?

Stensgård. Spoken? Oh, yes, I said a word or two——

Bastian. And what do you think?

Stensgård. Oh—well—we were interrupted. I can't say anything definite.

Bastian. I'll take my chance all the same; she's always complaining of her loneliness. My fate shall be sealed within an hour.

Stensgård. Within an hour?

Bastian (sees MADAM RUNDHOLMEN, *who enters from the left).* Sh! Not a word to any one!

[*Goes towards the back.*

Stensgård (whispers to ASLAKSEN*).* Give me back the letter.

Aslaksen. Do you want it back?

Stensgård. Yes, at once; I shall deliver it myself.

Aslaksen. Very well; here it is.

[STENSGÅRD *thrusts the letter into his pocket and mixes with the rest.*

Madam Rundholmen (to BASTIAN). What do you say to the election, Mr. Bastian?

Bastian. I'm delighted. Stensgård and I are bosom friends, you know. I shouldn't be surprised if he got into Parliament.

Madam Rundholmen. But your father wouldn't much like that.

Bastian. Oh, father has so many irons in the fire. Besides, if Stensgård's elected, it will still be all in the family, I daresay.

Madam Rundholmen. How so?

Bastian. He wants to marry——

Madam Rundholmen. Lord! Has he said anything?

Bastian. Yes; and I've promised to put in a word for him. It'll be all right. I'm sure Ragna likes him.

Madam Rundholmen. Ragna!

Lundestad (approaching). What is interesting you so deeply, Madam Rundholmen?

Madam Rundholmen. What do you think he says? Why, that Mr. Stensgård's making up to——

Lundestad. Yes, but he won't find the Chamberlain so easy to deal with.

Bastian. The Chamberlain?

Lundestad. He probably thinks her too good a match for a mere lawyer——

Madam Rundholmen. Who? Who?

Lundestad. Why, his daughter, Miss Bratsberg, of course.

Bastian. He's surely not making love to Miss Bratsberg?

Lundestad. Yes, indeed he is.

Madam Rundholmen. You are quite sure of that?

Bastian. And he told me——! Oh, I want to say a word to you!

[LUNDESTAD *and* BASTIAN *go towards the back.*

Madam Rundholmen (approaching STENSGÅRD*).* You must be on your guard, Mr. Stensgård.

Stensgård. Against whom?

Madam Rundholmen. Against malicious people who are slandering you.

Stensgård. Why, let them—so long as one person doesn't believe their slanders.

Madam Rundholmen. And who may that one person be?

Stensgård (slips the letter into her hand). Take this; read it when you are alone.

Madam Rundholmen. Ah, I knew it!

[*Goes off to the left.*

Ringdal (enters from the right). Well, I hear you have won a brilliant victory, Mr. Stensgård.

Stensgård. Yes, I have, Mr. Ringdal, in spite of your noble chief's endeavours.

Ringdal. His endeavours? What to do?

Stensgård. To keep me out.

Ringdal. Like other people, he has a right to vote as he pleases.

Stensgård. It's a pity he is not likely to retain that right for long.

Ringdal. What do you mean?

Stensgård. I mean, since his affairs are not so straight as they might be——

Ringdal. His affairs! What affairs! What have you got into your head?

Stensgård. Oh, you needn't pretend ignorance. Isn't there a storm brewing?—a great crash impending?

Ringdal. Yes, so I hear on all sides.

Stensgård. And aren't both the Bratsbergs involved in it?

Ringdal. My dear sir, are you crazy?

Stensgård. Oh, you naturally want to keep it dark.

Ringdal. What good would that be? That sort of thing can't be kept dark.

Stensgård. Is it not true, then?

Ringdal. Not a word of it, so far as the Chamberlain is concerned. How could you believe such nonsense? Who has been humbugging you?

Stensgård. I won't tell you just yet.

Ringdal. Well, you needn't; but whoever it was must have had a motive.

Stensgård. A motive——!

Ringdal. Yes, just think: is there no one who has an interest in keeping you and the Chamberlain apart?

Stensgård. Yes, on my soul, but there is though!

Ringdal. The Chamberlain in reality thinks very highly of you——

Stensgård. Does he?

Ringdal. Yes, and that's why people want to make mischief between you. They reckon on your ignorance of the situation, on your impulsiveness and your confiding disposition——

Stensgård. Oh, the vipers! And Madam Rundholmen has my letter!

Ringdal. What letter?

Stensgård. Oh, nothing. But it's not too late! My dear Mr. Ringdal, shall you see the Chamberlain this evening?

Ringdal. In all probability.

Stensgård. Then tell him to think no more of those threats—he will understand; tell him I shall call to-morrow and explain everything.

Ringdal. You'll call?

Stensgård. Yes, to prove to him—— Ah, a proof! Look here, Mr. Ringdal; will you give the Chamberlain this bill from me?

Ringdal. This bill——?

Stensgård. Yes; it's a matter I can't explain to you; but just you give it to him——

Ringdal. Upon my word, Mr. Stensgård——

Stensgård. And just add these words from me: This is how I treat those who vote against me!

Ringdal. I shan't forget. [*Goes out at the back.*

Stensgård. I say, Mr. Heire—how could you go and palm off that story about the Chamberlain upon me?

Heire. How could I palm it off on you——?

Stensgård. Yes—it's a lie from beginning to end.

Heire. No! Is it indeed? I'm delighted to hear it. Do you hear, Mr. Lundestad? It's all a lie about the Chamberlain.

Lundestad. Sh! We were on a false scent; it's nearer at hand.

Stensgård. How nearer at hand?

Lundestad. I know nothing for certain; but they talk of Madam Rundholmen——

Stensgård. What!

Heire. Haven't I prophesied it! She has been too much mixed up with our friend at Stonelee——

Lundestad. He drove off this morning before daylight——

Heire. And his family is out hunting for him——

Lundestad. And the son has been doing all he knows to get his sister provided for——

Stensgård. Provided for! "To-morrow" she said; and then her anxiety about her father——!

Heire. Hee-hee! You'll see he's gone and hanged himself, sir!

Aslaksen. Has any one hanged himself?

Lundestad. Mr. Heire says Monsen of Stonelee——

Monsen (enters from the back). A dozen of champagne!

Aslaksen and Others. Monsen!

Monsen. Yes, Monsen! Champagne-Monsen! Money-Monsen! Let's have the wine, confound it all!

Heire. But, my dear sir——

Stensgård. Why, where have you dropped from?

Monsen. I've been doing a stroke of business, sir! Cleared a hundred thousand! Hei! To-morrow I'll give a thundering dinner at Stonelee. I invite you all. Champagne, I say! I congratulate you, Stensgård! I hear you're elected.

Stensgård. Yes; I must explain to you——

Monsen. Pooh; what does it matter to me? Wine, I say! Where is Madam Rundholmen?

[*Makes a motion to go out to the left.*

The Maid-servant (who has just entered, intercepts him). No one can see the mistress just now; she's got a letter——

Bastian. Oh, damn it all! [*Goes out by the back.*

Stensgård. Is she reading it?

Servant. Yes; and it seems quite to have upset her.

Stensgård. Good-bye, Mr. Monsen; dinner at Stonelee to-morrow——?

Monsen. Yes, to-morrow. Good-bye!

Stensgård (whispers). Mr. Heire, will you do me a service?

Heire. Certainly, certainly.

Stensgård. Then just run me down a little to Madam

Rundholmen; indulge in an innuendo or two at my expense. You are so good at that sort of thing.

Heire. What the deuce is the meaning of this?

Stensgård. I have my reasons. It's a joke, you know—a wager with—with some one you have a grudge against.

Heire. Aha, I understand. I say no more!

Stensgård. Don't go too far, you know. Just place me in a more or less equivocal light—make her a little suspicious of me, for the moment.

Heire. Rely upon me; it will be a real pleasure to me.

Stensgård. Thanks, thanks in advance. *(Goes towards the table.)* Mr. Lundestad, we shall meet to-morrow forenoon at the Chamberlain's.

Lundestad. Have you hopes?

Stensgård. A three-fold hope.

Lundestad. Threefold? I don't understand——

Stensgård. You needn't. Henceforth, I will be my own counsellor. [*Goes out by the back.*

Monsen (at the punch-bowl). Another glass, Aslaksen! Where's Bastian?

Aslaksen. He's just gone out. But I have a letter to deliver for him.

Monsen. Have you?

Aslaksen. To Madam Rundholmen.

Monsen. Ah, at last!

Aslaksen. But not till to-morrow evening, he said; to-morrow evening, neither sooner nor later. Here's to you!

Heire (to LUNDESTAD*).* What the deuce is all this business between Stensgård and Madam Rundholmen?

Lundestad (whispers). He's courting her.

Heire. I suspected as much! But he asked me to run him down a bit—to cast a slur on his character——

Lundestad. And you said you would?

Heire. Yes, of course.

Lundestad. I believe he says of you that your word is as good as your bond—and no better.

Heire. Hee-hee—the dear fellow! He shall find out his mistake this time.

Madam Rundholmen (with an open letter in her hand, at the door on the left). Where is Mr. Stensgård?

Heire. He kissed your chambermaid and went, Madam Rundholmen!

ACT V

Large reception-room at the CHAMBERLAIN'S. *Entrance door at the back. Doors right and left.*

RINGDAL *stands at a table looking through some papers. A knock.*

Ringdal. Come in.

Fieldbo (from the back). Good morning.

Ringdal. Good morning, Doctor.

Fieldbo. All well, eh?

Ringdal. Oh, yes, well enough; but——

Fieldbo. What?

Ringdal. Of course you've heard the great news?

Fieldbo. No. What is it?

Ringdal. Do you mean to say you haven't heard what has happened at Stonelee?

Fieldbo. No.

Ringdal. Monsen has absconded!

Fieldbo. Absconded! Monsen?

Ringdal. Absconded.

Fieldbo. Great heavens——!

Ringdal. There were ugly rumours yesterday; but then Monsen turned up again; he managed to throw dust in people's eyes——

Fieldbo. But the reason? The reason?

Ringdal. Enormous losses in timber, they say. Several houses in Christiania have stopped payment, and so——

Fieldbo. And so he has gone off!

Ringdal. To Sweden, probably. The authorities took

possession at Stonelee this morning. Things are being inventoried and sealed up——

Fieldbo. And the unfortunate children——?

Ringdal. The son seems to have kept clear of the business; at least I hear he puts a bold face on it.

Fieldbo. But the daughter?

Ringdal. Sh! The daughter is here.

Fieldbo. Here?

Ringdal. The tutor brought her and the two little ones here this morning. Miss Bratsberg is looking after them, quietly you know.

Fieldbo. And how does she bear it?

Ringdal. Oh, pretty well, I fancy. You may guess, after the treatment she has met with at home—— And, besides, I may tell you she is—— Ah, here's the Chamberlain.

The Chamberlain (from the left). So you are there, my dear Doctor?

Fieldbo. Yes, I am pretty early astir. Let me wish you many happy returns of the day, Chamberlain.

The Chamberlain. Oh, as for happiness——! But thank you, all the same; I know you mean it kindly.

Fieldbo. And may I ask, Chamberlain——?

The Chamberlain. One word: be good enough to drop that title.

Fieldbo. What do you mean?

The Chamberlain. I am an ironmaster, and nothing more.

Fieldbo. Why, what strange notion is this?

The Chamberlain. I have renounced my post and my title. I am sending in my resignation to-day.

Fieldbo. You should sleep upon that.

The Chamberlain. When his Majesty was graciously pleased to assign me a place in his immediate circle, he did so because of the unblemished honour of my family through long generations.

Fieldbo. Well, what then?

The Chamberlain. My family is disgraced, just as much as Mr. Monsen's. Of course, you have heard about Monsen?

Fieldbo. Yes, I have.

The Chamberlain (to RINGDAL*).* Any further news about him?

Ringdal. Only that he brings down with him a good many of the younger men.

The Chamberlain. And my son?

Ringdal. Your son has sent me his balance-sheet. He will be able to pay in full; but there will be nothing over.

The Chamberlain. H'm. Then will you get my resignation copied?

Ringdal. I'll see to it.

[*Goes out by the foremost door on the right.*

Fieldbo. Have you reflected what you are doing? Things can be arranged without any one being a bit the wiser.

The Chamberlain. Indeed! Can I make myself ignorant of what has happened?

Fieldbo. Oh, after all, what has happened? Has not he written to you, acknowledged his fault and begged for your forgiveness? This is the only time he has done anything of the sort; why not simply blot it out?

The Chamberlain. Would you do what my son has done?

Fieldbo. He won't repeat it; that is the main point.

The Chamberlain. How do you know he will not repeat it?

Fieldbo. If for no other reason, because of what you yourself told me—the scene with your daughter-in-law. Whatever else comes of it, that will steady him.

The Chamberlain (pacing the room). My poor Selma! Our peace and happiness gone!

Fieldbo. There are higher things than peace and happiness. Your happiness has been an illusion. Yes, I must speak frankly to you: in that, as in many other things, you have built on a hollow foundation. You have been short-sighted and over-weening, Chamberlain!

The Chamberlain (stops short). I?

Fieldbo. Yes, you! You have plumed yourself on your family honour; but when has that honour been tried? Are you sure it would have stood the test?

The Chamberlain. You can spare your sermons, Doctor. Do you think I have not learnt a lesson from the events of these days?

Fieldbo. I daresay you have; but prove it, by showing greater tolerance and clearer insight. You reproach your son; but what have you done for him? You have taken care to develop his faculties, but not to form his character. You have lectured him on what he owed to the honour of his family; but you have not guided and moulded him so that honour became to him an irresistible instinct.

The Chamberlain. Do you think so?

Fieldbo. I not only think, I know it. But that is generally the way here: people are bent on learning, not on living. And you see what comes of it; you see hundreds of men with great gifts, who never seem to be more than half ripe; who are one thing in their ideas and feelings, and something quite different in their habits and acts. Just look at Stensgård——

The Chamberlain. Ah, Stensgård now! What do you make of Stensgård?

Fieldbo. A patchwork. I have known him from childhood. His father was a mere rag of a man, a withered weed, a nobody. He kept a little huckster's shop and eked things out with pawnbroking; or rather his wife did for him. She was a coarse-grained woman, the most unwomanly I ever knew. She had her husband declared incapable;* she had not an ounce of heart in her. And in that home Stensgård passed his childhood. Then he went to the grammar-school.

* "Gjort umyndig"=placed under a legal interdict.

"He shall go to college," said his mother; "I'll make a smart solicitor of him." Squalor at home, high-pressure at school; soul, temperament, will, talents, all pulling in different ways —what could it lead to but disintegration of character?

The Chamberlain. What could it lead to, eh? I should like to know what is good enough for you. We are to expect nothing of Stensgård; nothing of my son; but we may look to you, I suppose—to you——?

Fieldbo. Yes, to me—precisely. Oh, you needn't laugh; I take no credit to myself; but my lot has been one that begets equilibrium and firmness of character. I was brought up amid the peace and harmony of a modest middle-class home. My mother is a woman of the finest type; in our home we had no desires that outstripped our opportunities, no cravings that were wrecked on the rocks of circumstance; and death did not break in upon our circle, leaving emptiness and longing behind it. We were brought up in the love of beauty, but it informed our whole view of life, instead of being a side-interest, a thing apart. We were taught to shun excesses, whether of the intellect or of the feelings——

The Chamberlain. Bless me! So that accounts for your being the pink of perfection?

Fieldbo. I am far from thinking so. I only say that fate has been infinitely kind to me, and that I regard its favours in the light of obligations.

The Chamberlain. Very well; but if Stensgård is under no such obligations, it is all the more to his credit that he——

Fieldbo. What? What is to his credit?

The Chamberlain. You have misjudged him, my good Doctor. Look here. What do you say to this?

Fieldbo. Your son's bill!

The Chamberlain. Yes; he has sent it to me.

Fieldbo. Of his own accord?

The Chamberlain. Of his own accord, and unconditionally. It is fine; it is noble. From this day forth, my house is open to him.

Fieldbo. Think again! For your own sake, for your daughter's——

The Chamberlain. Oh, let me alone! He is better than you in many ways. At any rate he is straightforward, while you are underhand in your dealings.

Fieldbo. I?

The Chamberlain. Yes, you! You have made yourself the master of this house; you come and go as you please; I consult you about everything—and yet——

Fieldbo. Well?—And yet?

The Chamberlain. And yet there's always something confoundedly close about you; yes, and something—something uppish that I cannot endure!

Fieldbo. Please explain yourself!

The Chamberlain. I? No, it is you that ought to explain yourself! But now you must take the consequences.

Fieldbo. We don't understand each other, Chamberlain. I have no bill to give up to you; yet, who knows but I may be making a greater sacrifice for your sake?

The Chamberlain. Indeed! How so?

Fieldbo. By holding my tongue.

The Chamberlain. Holding your tongue, indeed! Shall I tell you what I am tempted to do? To forget my manners, use bad language and join the League of Youth. You are a stiff-necked Pharisee, my good Doctor; and that sort of thing is out of place in our free society. Look at Stensgård; he is not like that; so he shall come here whenever he likes; he shall—he shall——! Oh, what's the use of talking——! You must take the consequences; as you make your bed, so you must lie.

Lundestad (enters from the back). My congratulations, Chamberlain! May you long enjoy the respect and——

The Chamberlain. Oh. go to the devil—I'm almost inclined to say! That's all humbug, my dear Lundestad. There's nothing but humbug in this world.

Lundestad. That is what Mr. Monsen's creditors are saying.

The Chamberlain. Ah, about Monsen—didn't it come upon you like a thunderbolt?

Lundestad. Oh, you have often prophesied it, Chamberlain.

The Chamberlain. H'm, h'm;—yes, to be sure I have. I prophesied it only the day before yesterday; he came here trying to get money out of me——

Fieldbo. It might have saved him.

Lundestad. Impossible; he was too deep in the mire; and whatever is, is for the best.

The Chamberlain. That is your opinion? Was it for the best, then, that you were beaten at the poll yesterday?

Lundestad. I wasn't beaten; everything went just as I wanted. Stensgård is not a man to make an enemy of; he has got what we others have to whistle for.

The Chamberlain. I don't quite understand what you mean——?

Lundestad. He has the power of carrying people away with him. And then he has the luck to be unhampered by either character, or conviction, or social position; so that Liberalism is the easiest thing in the world to him.

The Chamberlain. Well, really, I should have thought we were all Liberals.

Lundestad. Yes, of course we are Liberals, Chamberlain; not a doubt of it. But the thing is that we are Liberal only on our own behalf, whereas Stensgård's Liberalism extends to other people. That's the novelty of the thing.

The Chamberlain. And you are going over to these subversive ideas?

Lundestad. I've read in old story-books about people who could summon up spirits, but could not lay them again.

The Chamberlain. Why, my dear Lundestad, how can a man of your enlightenment——?

Lundestad. I know it's mere popish superstition, Chamberlain. But new ideas are like those spirits: it's not so easy to lay them; the best plan is to compromise with them as best you can.

The Chamberlain. But now that Monsen has fallen, and no doubt his crew of agitators with him——

Lundestad. If Monsen's fall had come two or three days ago, things would have been very different.

The Chamberlain. Yes, unfortunately. You have been too hasty.

Lundestad. Partly out of consideration for you, Chamberlain.

The Chamberlain. For me?

Lundestad. Our party must keep up its reputation in the eyes of the people. We represent the old, deep-rooted Norse sense of honour. If I had deserted Stensgård, you know he holds a paper——

The Chamberlain. Not now.

Lundestad. What?

The Chamberlain. Here it is.

Lundestad. He has given it up to you?

The Chamberlain. Yes. Personally, he *is* a gentleman; so much I must say for him.

Lundestad (thoughtfully). Mr. Stensgård has rare abilities.

Stensgård (at the back, standing in the doorway). May I come in?

The Chamberlain (going to meet him). I am delighted to see you.

Stensgård. And you will accept my congratulations?

The Chamberlain. With all my heart.

Stensgård. Then with all my heart I wish you happiness! And you must forget all the stupid things I have written.

The Chamberlain. I go by deeds, not words, Mr. Stensgård.

Stensgård. How good of you to say so!

The Chamberlain. And henceforth—since you wish it—you must consider yourself at home here.

Stensgård. May I? May I really?

[*A knock at the door.*

The Chamberlain. Come in.

[*Several* LEADING MEN *of the neighbourhood,* TOWN COUNCILLORS, *etc., enter.* THE CHAMBERLAIN *goes to receive them, accepts their congratulations and converses with them.*

Thora (who has meantime entered by the second door on the left). Mr. Stensgård, let me thank you.

Stensgård. You, Miss Bratsberg!

Thora. My father has told me how nobly you have acted.

Stensgård. But——?

Thora. Oh, how we have misjudged you!

Stensgård. Have you——?

Thora. It was your own fault—— No, no; it was ours. Oh, what would I not do to atone for our error.

Stensgård. Would you? You yourself? Would you really——?

Thora. All of us would; if we only knew——

The Chamberlain. Refreshments for these gentlemen, my child.

Thora. They are just coming.

[*She retires towards the door again, where a* SERVANT *at the same moment appears with cake and wine, which are handed round.*

Stensgård. Oh, my dear Lundestad! I feel like a conquering god.

Lundestad. So you must have felt yesterday, I suppose.

Stensgård. Pooh! This is something quite different; the final triumph; the crown of all! There is a glory, a halo, over my life.

Lundestad. Oho; dreams of love!

Stensgård. Not dreams! Realities, glorious realities!

Lundestad. So brother Bastian has brought you the answer?

Stensgård. Bastian——?

Lundestad. Yes, he gave me a hint yesterday; he had promised to plead your cause with a certain young lady.

Stensgård. Oh, what nonsense——

Lundestad. Why make a mystery of it? If you haven't heard already, I can give you the news. You have won the day, Mr. Stensgård; I have it from Ringdal.

Stensgård. What have you from Ringdal?

Lundestad. Miss Monsen has accepted you.

Stensgård. What!

Lundestad. Accepted you, I say.

Stensgård. Accepted me! And the father has bolted!

Lundestad. But the daughter hasn't.

Stensgård. Accepted me! In the midst of all this family trouble! How unwomanly! How repellant to any man with the least delicacy of feeling! But the whole thing is a misunderstanding. I never commissioned Bastian—— How could that idiot——? However, it doesn't matter to me; he must answer for his follies himself.

Daniel Heire (enters from the back). Hee-hee! Quite a gathering! Of course, of course! We are paying our respects, propitiating the powers that be, as the saying goes. May I, too——

The Chamberlain. Thanks, thanks, old friend!

Heire. Oh, I protest, my dear sir? That is too much condescension. *(New* GUESTS *arrive.)* Ah, here we have the myrmidons of justice—the executive—— I say no more. *(Goes over to* STENSGÅRD.*)* Ah, my dear fortunate youth, are you there? Your hand! Accept the assurance of an old man's unfeigned rejoicing.

Stensgård. At what?

Heire. You asked me yesterday to run you down a little to her—you know——

Stensgård. Yes, yes; what then?

Heire. It was a heartfelt pleasure to me to oblige you——

Stensgård. Well—and what happened then? How did she take it?

Heire. Like a loving woman, of course—burst into tears; locked herself into her room; would neither answer nor show herself——

Stensgård. Ah, thank goodness!

Heire. It's barbarous to subject a widow's heart to such cruel tests, to go and gloat over her jealous agonies! But love has cat's eyes—— I say no more! For to-day, as I drove past, there stood Madam Rundholmen, brisk and buxom, at her open window, combing her hair. She looked like a mermaid, if you'll allow me to say so. Oh, she's a fine woman!

Stensgård. Well, and then?

Heire. Why, she laughed like one possessed, sir, and waved a letter in the air, and called out "A proposal, Mr. Heire! I'm engaged to be married."

Stensgård. What! Engaged?

Heire. My hearty congratulations, young man; I'm inexpressibly pleased to be the first to announce to you——

Stensgård. It's all rubbish! It's nonsense!

Heire. What is nonsense?

Stensgård. You have misunderstood her; or else she has misunderstood—— Engaged! Preposterous! Now that Monsen's down, she'll probably——

Heire. Not at all, sir, not at all! Madam Rundholmen has solid legs to stand on.

Stensgård. No matter! I have quite other intentions. All that about the letter was only a joke—a wager, as I told you. My dear Mr. Heire, do oblige me by not saying a word to anyone of this silly affair.

Heire. I see, I see! It's to be kept secret; it's to be a romance. Ah, youth, youth! it's nothing if not poetical.

Stensgård. Yes, yes; mum's the word. You shan't regret it—I'll take up the cases—— Sh! I rely upon you.

[*He retires.*

The Chamberlain (who has meanwhile been talking to LUNDESTAD*).* No, Lundestad—that I really cannot believe!

Lundestad. I assure you, Chamberlain—Daniel Heire told me so himself.

Heire. What did I tell you, may I inquire?

The Chamberlain. Did Mr. Stensgård show you a bill yesterday?

Heire. Yes, by-the-bye——! What on earth was the meaning of all that?

The Chamberlain. I'll tell you afterwards. And you told him——

Lundestad. You persuaded him it was a forgery?

Heire. Pooh, a mere innocent jest, to bewilder him a little in the hour of triumph.

Lundestad. And you told him both signatures were forged?

Heire. Oh, yes; why not both while I was about it?

The Chamberlain. So that was it!

Lundestad (to the CHAMBERLAIN*).* And when he heard that——

The Chamberlain. He gave the bill to Ringdal!

Lundestad. The bill that was useless as a weapon of offence.

The Chamberlain. He shams magnanimity! Makes a fool of me a second time! Gains admission to my house, and makes me welcome him and thank him—this—this——! And this is the fellow——

Heire. Why, what are you going on about, my dear sir?

The Chamberlain. I'll tell you all about it afterwards

(Takes LUNDESTAD *apart.)* And this is the fellow you protect, push forward, help to rise!

Lundestad. Well, he took you in, too!

The Chamberlain. Oh, I should like to——!

Lundestad (pointing to STENSGÅRD, *who is speaking to* THORA*).* Look there! What will people be fancying!

The Chamberlain. I shall soon put a stop to these fancies.

Lundestad. Too late, Chamberlain; he'll worm himself forward by dint of promises and general plausibility——

The Chamberlain. I, too, can manœuvre, Mr. Lundestad.

Lundestad. What will you do?

The Chamberlain. Just watch. *(Goes over to* FIELDBO.*)* Doctor Fieldbo, will you do me a service?

Fieldbo. With pleasure.

The Chamberlain. Then turn that fellow out of my house.

Fieldbo. Stensgård?

The Chamberlain. Yes, the adventurer; I hate his very name; turn him out!

Fieldbo. But how can I——?

The Chamberlain. This is your affair; I give you a free hand.

Fieldbo. A free hand! Do you mean it? Entirely free?

The Chamberlain. Yes, yes, by all means.

Fieldbo. Your hand on it, Chamberlain!

The Chamberlain. Here it is.

Fieldbo. So be it, then; now or never! *(Loudly.)* May I request the attention of the company for a moment?

The Chamberlain. Silence for Doctor Fieldbo!

Fieldbo. With Chamberlain Bratsberg's consent, I have the pleasure of announcing my engagement to his daughter.

[*An outburst of astonishment.* THORA *utters a slight scream.* THE CHAMBERLAIN *is on the point of speaking, but refrains. Loud talk and congratulations.*

Stensgård. Engagement! Your engagement——

Heire. With the Chamberlain's——? With your—— What does it mean?

Lundestad. Is the Doctor out of his mind?

Stensgård. But, Chamberlain——?

The Chamberlain. What can I do? I am a Liberal. I join the League of Youth!

Fieldbo. Thanks, thanks—and forgive me!

The Chamberlain. Associations are the order of the day, Mr. Stensgård. There is nothing like free competition!

Thora. Oh, my dear father!

Lundestad. Yes, and engagements are the order of the day. I have another to announce.

Stensgård. A mere invention!

Lundestad. No, not a bit of it; Miss Monsen is engaged to——

Stensgård. False, false, I say!

Thora. No, father, it's true; they are both here.

The Chamberlain. Who? Where?

Thora. Ragna and Mr. Helle. They are in here——

[*Goes towards the second door on the right.*

Lundestad. Mr. Helle! Then it's he——!

The Chamberlain. Here? In my house? *(Goes towards the door.)* Come in, my dear child.

Ragna (shrinking back shyly). Oh, no, no; there are so many people.

The Chamberlain. Don't be bashful; you couldn't help what has happened.

Helle. She is homeless now, Chamberlain.

Ragna. Oh, you must help us!

The Chamberlain. I will, indeed; and thank you for giving me the opportunity.

Heire. You may well say engagements are the order of the day. I have one to add to the list.

The Chamberlain. What? You? At your age?—How rash of you!

Heire. Oh——! I say no more.

Lundestad. The game is up, Mr. Stensgård.

Stensgård. Indeed? *(Loudly.) I* have one to add to the list, Mr. Heire! An announcement, gentlemen: I, too, have cast anchor for life.

The Chamberlain. What?

Stensgård. One is now and then forced to play a double game, to conceal one's true intentions. I regard this as permissible when the general weal is at stake. My life-work lies clear before me and is all in all to me. I consecrate my whole energies to this district; I find here a ferment of ideas which I must strive to clarify. But this task cannot be accomplished by a mere adventurer. The men of the district must gather round one of themselves. Therefore I have determined to unite my interests indissolubly with yours—to unite them by a bond of affection. If I have awakened any false hopes, I must plead for forgiveness. I, too, am engaged.

The Chamberlain. You?

Fieldbo. Engaged?

Heire. I can bear witness.

The Chamberlain. But how——?

Fieldbo. Engaged? To whom?

Lundestad. It surely can't be——?

Stensgård. It is a union both of the heart and of the understanding. Yes, my fellow-citizens, I am engaged to Madam Rundholmen.

Fieldbo. To Madam Rundholmen!

The Chamberlain. The storekeeper's widow!

Lundestad. H'm. Indeed!

The Chamberlain. Why, my head's going round! How could you——?

Stensgård. A manœuvre, Mr. Bratsberg!

Lundestad. He has rare abilities!

Aslaksen (looks in at the door, back). I humbly beg pardon——

The Chamberlain. Oh, come in, Aslaksen! A visit of congratulation, eh?

Aslaksen. Oh, not at all; I wouldn't presume—— But I have something very important to say to Mr. Stensgård.

Stensgård. Another time; you can wait outside.

Aslaksen. No, confound it; I must tell you——

Stensgård. Hold your tongue! What intrusiveness is this?—Yes, gentlemen, strange are the ways of destiny. The district and I required a bond that should bind us firmly together; and I found on my path a woman of ripened character who could make a home for me. I have put off the adventurer, gentlemen, and here I stand in your midst, as one of yourselves. Take me; I am ready to stand or fall in any post your confidence may assign me.

Lundestad. You have won.

The Chamberlain. Well, really, I must say—— *(To the* MAID, *who has entered from the back.)* Well, what is it? What are you giggling about?

The Servant. Madam Rundholmen——?

The Company. Madam Rundholmen?

The Chamberlain. What about her?

The Servant. Madam Rundholmen is waiting outside with her young man——

The Company (to each other). Her young man? Madam Rundholmen! How's this?

The Chamberlain (at the door). Come along, come along!

[BASTIAN MONSEN, *with* MADAM RUNDHOLMEN *on his arm, enters from the back. A general movement.*

Madam Rundholmen. I hope I'm not intruding, sir——

The Chamberlain. Not at all, not at all.

Madam Rundholmen. But I couldn't resist bringing up my young man to show him to you and Miss Bratsberg.

The Chamberlain. Yes, I hear you are engaged; but——

Thora. We didn't know——

Stensgård (to Aslaksen*).* How is all this——?

Aslaksen. I had so much in my head yesterday; so much to think about, I mean——

Stensgård. But I gave her my letter, and——

Aslaksen. No, you gave her Bastian Monsen's; here is yours.

Stensgård. Bastian's? And here——? *(Glances at the address, crumples the letter together and crams it into his pocket.)* Oh, curse you for a blunderer!

Madam Rundholmen. Of course I was willing enough. There's no trusting the men-folk, I know; but when you have it in black and white that their intentions are honourable—— Why, there's Mr. Stensgård, I declare. Well, Mr. Stensgård, won't you congratulate me?

Heire (to Lundestad*).* How hungrily she glares at him.

The Chamberlain. Of course he will, Madam Rundholmen; but won't you congratulate your sister-in-law to be?

Madam Rundholmen. Who?

Thora. Ragna; she is engaged, too.

Bastian. Are you, Ragna?

Madam Rundholmen. Indeed? Yes, Bastian told me there was something in the wind. I wish you both joy; and welcome into the family, Mr. Stensgård!

Fieldbo. No, no; not Stensgård!

The Chamberlain. No, it's Mr. Helle; an excellent choice. And, by-the-bye, you may congratulate my daughter, too.

Madam Rundholmen. Miss Bratsberg! Ah, so Lundestad was right, after all. I congratulate you, Miss Thora; and you, too, Mr. Stensgård.

Fieldbo. You mean Doctor Fieldbo.

Madam Rundholmen. What?

Fieldbo. I am the happy man.

Madam Rundholmen. Well, now, I don't in the least know where I am.

The Chamberlain. And we have just found out where we are.

Stensgård. Excuse me; I have an appointment——

The Chamberlain (aside). Lundestad, what was the other word?

Lundestad. What other?

The Chamberlain. Not adventurer, but the other——?

Lundestad. Demagogue.

Stensgård.—I take my leave.

The Chamberlain. One word—only one word, Mr. Stensgård—a word which has long been on the tip of my tongue

Stensgård (at the door). Excuse me; I'm in a hurry.

The Chamberlain (following him). Demagogue!

Stensgård. Good-bye; good-bye!

[*Goes out by the back*

The Chamberlain (coming forward again). Now the air is pure again, my friends.

Bastian. I hope you don't blame me, sir, for what has happened at home?

The Chamberlain. Every one must bear his own burden.

Bastian. I had really no part in it.

Selma (who, during the preceding scene, has been listening at the second door on the right). Father! Now you are happy;—may he come now?

The Chamberlain. Selma! You! You plead for him? After what happened two days ago——

Selma. Oh, two days are a long time. All is well now. I know now that he can go astray——

The Chamberlain. And that pleases you?

Selma. Yes, that he can; but in future I won't let him.

The Chamberlain. Bring him in then.

[SELMA *goes out again to the right.*

Ringdal (enters by the foremost door on the right). Here is your resignation.

The Chamberlain. Thanks; but you can tear it up.

Ringdal. Tear it up?

The Chamberlain. Yes, Ringdal; I have found another

way. I can make atonement without that; I shall set to work in earnest— —

Erik (enters with Selma *from the right).* Can you forgive me?

The Chamberlain (hands him the bill). I cannot be less merciful than fate.

Erik. Father! I shall retire this very day from the business you dislike so much.

The Chamberlain. No, indeed; you must stick to it. No cowardice! No running away from temptation! But I will stand at your side. *(Loudly.)* News for you, gentlemen! I have entered into partnership with my son.

Several Gentlemen. What? You, Chamberlain?

Heire. You, my dear sir?

The Chamberlain. Yes; it is a useful and honourable calling; or at any rate it can be made so. And now I have no reason to hold aloof any longer.

Lundestad. Well, I'll tell you what, Chamberlain—since you are going to set to work for the good of the district, it would be a shame and disgrace if an old soldier like me were to sulk in his tent.

Erik. Ah, what is this?

Lundestad. I cannot, in fact. After the disappointments in love that have befallen Mr. Stensgård to-day, Heaven forbid we should force the poor fellow into the political mill. He must rest and recover; a change of air is what he wants, and I shall see that he gets it. So if my constituents want me, why, they can have me.

The Gentlemen (shaking hands with him enthusiastically). Thanks, Lundestad! That's a good fellow! You won't fail us!

The Chamberlain. Now, this is as it should be; things are settling down again. But whom have we to thank for all this?

Fieldbo. Come, Aslaksen, you can explain——?

Aslaksen (alarmed). I, Doctor? I'm as innocent as the babe unborn!

Fieldbo. What about that letter, then——?

Aslaksen. It wasn't my fault, I tell you! It was the election and Bastian Monsen, and chance, and destiny, and Madam Rundholmen's punch—there was no lemon in it—and there was I, with the whole responsibility of the press upon me——

The Chamberlain (approaching). What? What's that?

Aslaksen. The press, sir?

The Chamberlain. The press! That's just it! Haven't I always said that the press has marvellous influence these days?

Aslaksen. Oh, Chamberlain——

The Chamberlain. No false modesty, Mr. Aslaksen! I haven't hitherto been in the habit of reading your paper, but henceforth I will. I shall subscribe for ten copies.

Aslaksen. Oh, you can have twenty, Chamberlain!

The Chamberlain. Very well, then; let me have twenty. And if you need money, come to me; I mean to support the press; but I tell you once for all—I won't write for it.

Ringdal. What's this I hear? Your daughter engaged?

The Chamberlain. Yes; what do you say to that?

Ringdal. I am delighted! But when was it arranged?

Fieldbo (quickly). I'll tell you afterwards——

The Chamberlain. Why, it was arranged on the Seventeenth of May.

Fieldbo. What?

The Chamberlain. The day little Miss Ragna was here.

Thora. Father, father; did you know——?

The Chamberlain. Yes, my dear; I have known all along.

Fieldbo. Oh, Chamberlain——!

Thora. Who can have——?

The Chamberlain. Another time, I should advise you young ladies not to talk so loud when I am taking my siesta in the bay window.

Thora. Oh! so you were behind the curtains?

Fieldbo. Now I understand!

The Chamberlain. Yes, you are the one to keep your own counsel——

Fieldbo. Would it have been of any use for me to speak earlier?

The Chamberlain. You are right, Fieldbo. These days have taught me a lesson.

Thora (aside to Fieldbo*).* Yes, you can keep your own counsel. All this about Mr. Stensgård—why did you tell me nothing?

Fieldbo. When a hawk is hovering over the dove-cote, one watches and shields his little dove—one does not alarm her.

[*They are interrupted by* Madam Rundholmen.

Heire (to the Chamberlain*).* I'm sorry to tell you, Chamberlain, that the settlement of our little legal differences will have to be adjourned indefinitely.

The Chamberlain. Indeed; why so?

Heire. You must know I've accepted a post as society reporter on Aslaksen's paper.

The Chamberlain. I am glad to hear it.

Heire. And of course you'll understand—with so much business on hand——

Madam Rundholmen (to Thora*).* Yes, I can tell you he's cost me many a tear, that bad man. But now I thank the Lord for Bastian. The other was false as the sea-foam; and then he's a terrible smoker, Miss Bratsberg, and frightfully particular about his meals. I found him a regular gourmand.

A Servant (enters from the left). Dinner is on the table.

The Chamberlain. Come along, then, all of you. Mr. Lundestad, you shall sit beside me; and you, too, Mr. Aslaksen.

Ringdal. We shall have a lot of toasts to drink after dinner!

Heire. Yes; and perhaps an old man may be allowed to put in a claim for the toast of "Absent Friends."

Lundestad. One absent friend will return, Mr. Heire.

Heire. Stensgård?

Lundestad. Yes; you'll see, gentlemen! In ten or fifteen years, Stensgård will either be in Parliament or in the Ministry—perhaps in both at once.*

Fieldbo. In ten or fifteen years? Perhaps; but then he can scarcely stand at the head of the League of Youth.

Heire. Why not?

Fieldbo. Why, because by that time his youth will be—questionable.

Heire. Then he can stand at the head of the Questionable League, sir. That's what Lundestad means. He says like Napoleon—"It's the questionable people that make politicians"; hee-hee!

Fieldbo. Well, after all is said and done, our League shall last through young days and questionable days as well; and it shall continue to be the League of Youth. When Stensgård founded his League and was carried shoulder-high amid all the enthusiasm of Independence Day, he said—"Providence is on the side of the League of Youth." I think even Mr. Helle, theologian as he is, will let us apply that saying to ourselves.

The Chamberlain. I think so, too, my friends; for truly we have been groping and stumbling in darkness; but good angels guided us.

Lundestad. Oh, for that matter, I think the angels were only middling.

Aslaksen. Yes; that comes of the local situation, Mr. Lundestad.

* When this play was written, Ministers did not sit in the Storthing, and were not responsible to it. This state of things was altered—as Ibsen here predicts—in the great constitutional struggle of 1872-84, which ended in the victory of the Liberal party, their leader, Johan Sverdrup, becoming Prime Minister.

ROSMERSHOLM
(1886)

CHARACTERS

JOHANNES ROSMER, *of Rosmersholm, formerly clergyman of the parish.*
REBECCA WEST, *in charge of Rosmer's household.*
RECTOR* KROLL, *Rosmer's brother-in-law.*
ULRIC BRENDEL.
PETER MORTENSGÅRD.†
MADAM HELSETH, *housekeeper at Rosmersholm.*

The action takes place at Rosmersholm, an old family seat near a small coast town in the west of Norway.

* "Rector" in the Scotch Continental sense of headmaster of a school, not in the English sense of a beneficed clergyman.
† Pronounce *Mortensgore.*

ROSMERSHOLM

PLAY IN FOUR ACTS

ACT I

Sitting-room at Rosmersholm; spacious, old-fashioned and comfortable. In front, on the right, a stove decked with fresh birch-branches and wild flowers. Farther back, on the same side, a door. In the back wall, folding-doors opening into the hall. To the left, a window, and before it a stand with flowers and plants. Beside the stove a table with a sofa and easy chairs. On the walls, old and more recent portraits of clergymen, officers and government officials in uniform. The window is open; so are the door into the hall and the house door beyond. Outside can be seen an avenue of fine old trees, leading up to the house. It is a summer evening, after sunset.

REBECCA WEST *is sitting in an easy-chair by the window and crocheting a large white woollen shawl, which is nearly finished. She now and then looks out expectantly through the leaves of the plants.* MADAM HELSETH *presently enters from the right.*

Madam Helseth. I suppose I had better begin to lay the table, Miss?

Rebecca West. Yes, please do. The Pastor must soon be in now.

Madam Helseth. Don't you feel the draught, Miss, where you're sitting?

Rebecca. Yes, there is a little draught. Perhaps you had better shut the window.

[MADAM HELSETH *shuts the door into the hall and then comes to the window.*

Madam Helseth (about to shut the window, looks out). Why, isn't that the Pastor over there?

Rebecca (hastily). Where? *(Rises.)* Yes, it is he. *(Behind the curtain.)* Stand aside—don't let him see us.

Madam Helseth (keeping back from the window). Only think, Miss—he's beginning to take the path by the mill again.

Rebecca. He went that way the day before yesterday, too. *(Peeps out between the curtains and the window-frame.)* But let us see whether——

Madam Helseth. Will he venture across the foot-bridge?

Rebecca. That is what I want to see. *(After a pause.)* No, he is turning. He is going by the upper road again. *(Leaves the window.)* A long way round.

Madam Helseth. Dear Lord, yes. No wonder the Pastor thinks twice about setting foot on that bridge. A place where a thing like that has happened——

Rebecca (folding up her work). They cling to their dead here at Rosmersholm.

Madam Helseth. Now *I* would say, Miss, that it's the dead that clings to Rosmersholm.

Rebecca (looks at her). The dead?

Madam Helseth. Yes, it's almost as if they couldn't tear themselves away from the folk that are left.

Rebecca. What makes you fancy that?

Madam Helseth. Well, if it wasn't for that, there would be no White Horse, I suppose.

Rebecca. Now what is all this about the White Horse, Madam Helseth?

Madam Helseth. Oh, I don't like to talk about it. And, besides, you don't believe in such things.

Rebecca. Do you believe in it, then?

Madam Helseth (goes and shuts the window). Oh, you'd only be for laughing at me, Miss. *(Looks out.)* Why, isn't that Mr. Rosmer on the mill-path again——?

Rebecca (looks out). That man there? *(Goes to the window.)* No, that's the Rector!

Madam Helseth. Yes, so it is.

Rebecca. This is delightful. You may be sure he's coming here.

Madam Helseth. He goes straight over the foot-bridge, he does. And yet she was his sister, his own flesh and blood. Well, I'll go and lay the table then, Miss West.

[*She goes out to the right.* REBECCA *stands at the window for a short time; then smiles and nods to some one outside. It begins to grow dark.*

Rebecca (goes to the door on the right). Oh, Madam Helseth, you might let us have some little extra dish for supper. You know what the Rector likes best.

Madam Helseth (outside). Oh, yes, Miss, I'll see to it.

Rebecca (opens the door to the hall). At last—! How glad I am to see you, my dear Rector.

Rector Kroll (in the hall, laying down his stick). Thanks Then I am not disturbing you?

Rebecca. You? How can you ask?

Kroll (comes in). Amiable as ever. *(Looks round.)* Is Rosmer upstairs in his room?

Rebecca. No, he is out walking. He has stayed out rather longer than usual; but he is sure to be in directly. *(Motioning him to sit on the sofa.)* Won't you sit down till he comes?

Kroll (laying down his hat). Many thanks. *(Sits down and looks about him.)* Why, how you have brightened up the old room! Flowers everywhere!

Rebecca. Mr. Rosmer is so fond of having fresh, growing flowers about him.

Kroll. And you are, too, are you not?

Rebecca. Yes; they have a delightfully soothing effect on me. We had to do without them, though, till lately.

Kroll (nods sadly). Yes, their scent was too much for poor Beata.

Rebecca. Their colours, too. They quite bewildered her——

Kroll. I remember, I remember. *(In a lighter tone.)* Well, how are things going out here?

Rebecca. Oh, everything is going its quiet, jog-trot way. One day is just like another.—And with you? Your wife——?

Kroll. Ah, my dear Miss West, don't let us talk about my affairs. There is always something or other amiss in a family; especially in times like these.

Rebecca (after a pause, sitting down in an easy-chair beside the sofa). How is it you haven't once been near us during the whole of the holidays?

Kroll. Oh, it doesn't do to make oneself a nuisance——

Rebecca. If you knew how we have missed you——

Kroll. And then I have been away——

Rebecca. Yes, for the last week or two. We have heard of you at political meetings.

Kroll (nods). Yes what do you say to that? Did you think I would turn political agitator in my old age, eh?

Rebecca (smiling). Well, you have always been a bit of an agitator, Rector Kroll.

Kroll. Why, yes, just for my private amusement. But henceforth it is to be no laughing matter, I can tell you.—Do you ever see those radical newspapers?

Rebecca. Well, yes, my dear Rector, I can't deny that——

Kroll. My dear Miss West, I have nothing to say against it—nothing in your case.

Rebecca. No, surely not. One likes to know what's going on—to keep up with the time——

Kroll. And of course I should not think of expecting you, as a woman, to side actively with either party in the civil contest—I might almost say the civil war—that is raging among us.—But you have seen then, I suppose, how these gentlemen of "the people" have been pleased to treat me? What infamous abuse they have had the audacity to heap on me?

Rebecca. Yes; but it seems to me you gave as good as you got.

Kroll. So I did, though I say it that shouldn't. For now I have tasted blood; and they shall soon find to their cost that I am not the man to turn the other cheek—— *(Breaks off.)* But, come, come—don't let us get upon that subject this evening—it's too painful and irritating.

Rebecca. Oh, no, don't let us talk of it.

Kroll. Tell me now—how do you get on at Rosmersholm, now that you are alone? Since our poor Beata——

Rebecca. Thank you, I get on very well. Of course one feels a great blank in many ways—a great sorrow and longing. But otherwise——

Kroll. And do you think of remaining here?—permanently, I mean.

Rebecca. My dear Rector, I really haven't thought about it, one way or the other. I have got so used to the place now, that I feel almost as if I belonged to it.

Kroll. Why, of course you belong to it.

Rebecca. And so long as Mr. Rosmer finds that I am of any use or comfort to him—why, so long, I suppose, I shall stay here.

Kroll (looks at her with emotion). Do you know,—it is really fine for a woman to sacrifice her whole youth to others as you have done.

Rebecca. Oh, what else should I have had to live for?

Kroll. First, there was your untiring devotion to your paralytic and exacting foster-father——

Rebecca. You mustn't suppose that Dr. West was such a charge when we were up in Finmark. It was those terrible boat-voyages up there that broke him down. But after we came here—well, yes, the two years before he found rest were certainly hard enough.

Kroll. And the years that followed—were they not even harder for you?

Rebecca. Oh, how can you say such a thing? When I was so fond of Beata—and when she, poor dear, stood so sadly in need of care and forbearance.

Kroll. How good it is of you to think of her with so much kindness!

Rebecca (moves a little nearer). My dear Rector, you say that with such a ring of sincerity that I cannot think there is any ill-feeling lurking in the background.

Kroll. Ill-feeling? Why, what do you mean?

Rebecca. Well, it would be only natural if you felt it painful to see a stranger managing the household here at Rosmersholm.

Kroll. Why, how on earth——!

Rebecca. But you have no such feeling? *(Takes his hand.)* Thanks, my dear Rector; thank you again and again.

Kroll. How on earth did you get such an idea into your head?

Rebecca. I began to be a little afraid when your visits became so rare.

Kroll. Then you have been on a totally wrong scent, Miss West. Besides—after all, there has been no essential change. Even while poor Beata was alive—in her last unhappy days—it was you, and you alone, that managed everything.

Rebecca. That was only a sort of regency in Beata's name.

Kroll. Be that as it may——. Do you know, Miss West —for my part, I should have no objection whatever if you——. But I suppose I mustn't say such a thing.

Rebecca. What must you not say?

Kroll. If matters were to shape so that you took the empty place——

Rebecca. I have the only place I want, Rector.

Kroll. In fact, yes; but not in——

Rebecca (interrupting gravely). For shame, Rector Kroll. How can you joke about such things?

Kroll. Oh, well, our good Johannes Rosmer very likely thinks he has had more than enough of married life already. But nevertheless——

Rebecca. You are really too absurd, Rector.

Kroll. Nevertheless——. Tell me, Miss West—if you will forgive the question—what is your age?

Rebecca. I'm sorry to say I am over nine-and-twenty, Rector; I am in my thirtieth year.

Kroll. Indeed. And Rosmer—how old is he? Let me see: he is five years younger than I am, so that makes him well over forty-three. I think it would be most suitable.

Rebecca (rises). Of course, of course; most suitable.— Will you stay to supper this evening?

Kroll. Yes, many thanks; I thought of staying. There is a matter I want to discuss with our good friend.—And I suppose, Miss West, in case you should take fancies into your head again, I had better come out pretty often for the future—as I used to in the old days.

Rebecca. Oh, yes, do—do. *(Shakes both his hands.)* Many thanks—how kind and good you are!

Kroll (gruffly). Am I? Well, that's not what they tell me at home.

[JOHANNES ROSMER *enters by the door on the right.*

Rebecca. Mr. Rosmer, do you see who is here?

Johannes Rosmer. Madam Helseth told me.

[RECTOR KROLL *has risen.*

Rosmer (gently and softly, pressing his hands). Welcome back to this house, my dear Kroll. *(Lays his hands on* KROLL'S *shoulders and looks into his eyes.)* My dear old friend! I knew that sooner or later things would come all right between us.

Kroll. Why, my dear fellow—do you mean to say you, too, have been so foolish as to fancy there was anything wrong?

Rebecca (to ROSMER*).* Yes, only think,—it was nothing but fancy after all!

Rosmer. Is that really the case, Kroll? Then why did you desert us so entirely?

Kroll (gravely, in a low voice). Because my presence would always have been reminding you of the years of your happiness, and of—the life that ended in the mill-race.

Rosmer. Well, it was a kind thought—you were always considerate. But it was quite unnecessary to remain away on that account.—Come, sit here on the sofa. *(They sit down.)* No, I assure you, the thought of Beata has no pain for me. We speak of her every day. We feel almost as if she were still one of the household.

Kroll. Do you really?

Rebecca (lighting the lamp). Yes, indeed we do.

Rosmer. It is quite natural. We were both so deeply attached to her. And both Rebec—both Miss West and I know that we did all that was possible for her in her affliction. We have nothing to reproach ourselves with.—So I feel nothing but a tranquil tenderness now at the thought of Beata.

Kroll. You dear, good people! Henceforward, I declare I shall come out and see you every day.

Rebecca (seats herself in an armchair). Mind, we shall expect you to keep your word.

Rosmer (with some hesitation). My dear Kroll—I wish

very much that our intercourse had never been interrupted. Ever since we have known each other, you have seemed predestined to be my adviser—ever since I went to the University.

Kroll. Yes, and I have always been proud of the office. But is there anything particular just now——?

Rosmer. There are many things that I would give a great deal to talk over with you, quite frankly—straight from the heart.

Rebecca. Ah, yes, Mr. Rosmer—that must be such a comfort—between old friends——

Kroll. Oh, I can tell you I have still more to talk to you about. I suppose you know I have turned a militant politician?

Rosmer. Yes, so you have. How did that come about?

Kroll. I was forced into it in spite of myself. It is impossible to stand idly looking on any longer. Now that the Radicals have unhappily come into power, it is high time something should be done,—so I have got our little group of friends in the town to close up their ranks. I tell you it is high time!

Rebecca (with a faint smile). Don't you think it may even be a little late?

Kroll. Unquestionably it would have been better if we had checked the stream at an earlier point in its course. But who could foresee what was going to happen? Certainly not I. *(Rises and walks up and down.)* But now I have had my eyes opened once and for all; for now the spirit of revolt has crept into the school itself.

Rosmer. Into the school? Surely not into your school?

Kroll. I tell you it has—into my own school. What do you think? It has come to my knowledge that the sixth-form boys—a number of them at any rate—have been keeping up a secret society for over six months; and they take in Mortensgård's paper!

Rebecca. The "Beacon"?

Kroll. Yes; nice mental sustenance for future government officials, is it not? But the worst of it is that it's all the cleverest boys in the form that have banded together in his conspiracy against me. Only the dunces at the bottom of the class have kept out of it.

Rebecca. Do you take this so very much to heart, Rector?

Kroll. Do I take it to heart! To be so thwarted and opposed in the work of my whole life! *(Lower.)* But I could almost say I don't care about the school—for there is worse behind. *(Looks around.)* I suppose no one can hear us?

Rebecca. Oh, no, of course not.

Kroll. Well, then, I must tell you that dissension and revolt have crept into my own house—into my own quiet home. They have destroyed the peace of my family life.

Rosmer (rises). What! Into your own house——?

Rebecca (goes over to the Rector*).* My dear Rector, what has happened?

Kroll. Would you believe that my own children—— In short, it is Laurits that is the ringleader of the school conspiracy; and Hilda has embroidered a red portfolio to keep the "Beacon" in.

Rosmer. I should certainly never have dreamt that, in your own house——

Kroll. No, who would have dreamt of such a thing? In my house, the very home of obedience and order—where one will, and one only, has always prevailed——

Rebecca. How does your wife take all this?

Kroll. Why, that is the most incredible part of it. My wife, who all her life long has shared my opinions and concurred in my views, both in great things and small—she is actually inclined to side with the children on many points. And she blames me for what has happened. She says I tyrannise over the children. As if it weren't necessary to——. Well, you see how my house is divided against itself. But of course I say as little about it as possible. Such things are best kept quiet. *(Wanders up the room.)* Ah, well, well, well.

[*Stands at the window with his hands behind his back and looks out.*

Rebecca (comes up close to Rosmer *and says rapidly and in a low voice, so that the* Rector *does not hear her).* Do it now!

Rosmer (also in a low voice). Not this evening.

Rebecca (as before). Yes, just this evening.

[*Goes to the table and busies herself with the lamp.*

Kroll (comes forward). Well, my dear Rosmer, now you know how the spirit of the age has overshadowed both my domestic and my official life. And am I to refrain from combating this pernicious, subversive, anarchic spirit, with any weapons I can lay my hands on? Fight it I will, trust me for that; both with tongue and pen.

Rosmer. Have you any hope of stemming the tide in that way?

Kroll. At any rate, I shall have done my duty as a citizen in defence of the State. And I hold it the duty of every right-minded man with an atom of patriotism to do likewise. In fact—that was my principal reason for coming out here this evening.

Rosmer. Why, my dear Kroll, what do you mean——? What can I——?

Kroll. You can stand by your old friends. Do as we do. Lend a hand, with all your might.

Rebecca. But, Rector Kroll, you know Mr. Rosmer's distaste for public life.

Kroll. He must get over his distaste.—You don't keep abreast of things, Rosmer. You bury yourself alive here, with your historical collections. Far be it from me to speak disrespectfully of family trees, and so forth; but, unfortunately, this is no time for hobbies of that sort. You cannot imaginc the state things are in, all over the country. There is hardly a single accepted idea that hasn't been turned topsy-turvy. It will be a gigantic task to get all the errors rooted out again.

Rosmer. I have no doubt of it. But I am the last man to undertake such a task.

Rebecca. And besides, I think Mr. Rosmer has come to take a wider view of life than he used to.

Kroll (with surprise). Wider?

Rebecca. Yes; or freer, if you like—less one-sided.

Kroll. What is the meaning of this? Rosmer—surely you are not so weak as to be influenced by the accident that the leaders of the mob have won a temporary advantage?

Rosmer. My dear Kroll, you know how little I understand of politics. But I confess it seems to me that within the last few years people are beginning to show greater independence of thought.

Kroll. Indeed! And you take it for granted that that must be an improvement! But in any case you are quite mistaken, my friend. Just inquire a little into the opinions that are current among the Radicals, both out here and in the town. They are neither more nor less than the wisdom that's retailed in the "Beacon."

Rebecca. Yes; Mortensgård has great influence over many people hereabouts.

Kroll. Yes, just think of it! A man of his foul antecedents—a creature that was turned out of his place as a schoolmaster on account of his immoral life! A fellow like that sets himself up as a leader of the people! And succeeds, too! Actually succeeds! I hear he is going to enlarge his paper. I know on good authority that he is on the lookout for a capable assistant.

Rebecca. I wonder that you and your friends don't set up an opposition to him.

Kroll. That is the very thing we are going to do. We have to-day bought the "County News"; there was no difficulty about the money question. But—— *(Turns to* ROSMER.*)* Now I come to my real errand. The difficulty lies in the conduct of the paper—the editing—— Tell me, Rosmer,—don't you feel it your duty to undertake it, for the sake of the good cause?

Rosmer (almost in consternation). I?

Rebecca. Oh, how can you think of such a thing?

Kroll. I can quite understand your horror of public meetings and your reluctance to expose yourself to their tender mercies. But an editor's work is less conspicuous, or rather——

Rosmer. No, no my dear friend, you must not ask me to do this.

Kroll. I should be quite willing to try my own hand at that style of work, too; but I couldn't possibly manage it. I have such a multitude of irons in the fire already. But for you, with no profession to tie you down—— Of course the rest of us would give you as much help as we could.

Rosmer. I cannot, Kroll. I am not fitted for it.

Kroll. Not fitted? You said the same thing when your father preferred you to the living here——

Rosmer. And I was right. That was why I resigned it.

Kroll. Oh, if only you are as good an editor as you were a clergyman, we shall not complain.

Rosmer. My dear Kroll—I tell you once for all—I cannot do it.

Kroll. Well, at any rate, you will lend us your name.

Rosmer. My name?

Kroll. Yes, the mere name, Johannes Rosmer, will be a great thing for the paper. We others are looked upon as confirmed partisans—indeed I hear I am denounced as a desperate fanatic—so that if we work the paper in our own names, we can't reckon upon its making much way among the misguided masses. You, on the contrary, have always kept out of the fight. Everybody knows and values your humanity and uprightness—your delicacy of mind—your unimpeachable honour. And then the prestige of your former position as a clergyman still clings to you; and, to crown all, you have your grand old family name!

Rosmer. Oh, my name——

Kroll (points to the portraits). Rosmers of Rosmersholm—clergymen and soldiers; government officials of high place and trust; gentlemen to the finger-tips, every man of them—a family that for nearly two centuries has held its place as the first in the district. *(Lays his hand on* ROSMER'S *shoulder.)* Rosmer—you owe it to yourself and to the traditions of your race to take your share in guarding all that has hitherto been held sacred in our society. *(Turns round.)* What do you say, Miss West?

Rebecca (laughing softly, as if to herself). My dear Rector—I can't tell you how ludicrous all this seems to me.

Kroll. What do you say? Ludicrous?

Rebecca. Yes, ludicrous. For you must let me tell you frankly——

Rosmer (quickly). No, no—be quiet! Not just now!

Kroll (looks from one to the other). My dear friends, what on earth——? *(Interrupting himself.)* H'm.

[MADAM HELSETH *appears in the doorway on the right.*

Madam Helseth. There's a man out in the kitchen passage that says he wants to see the Pastor.

Rosmer (relieved). Ah, very well. Ask him to come in.

Madam Helseth. Into the sitting-room?

Rosmer. Yes, of course.

Madam Helseth. But he looks scarcely the sort of man to bring into the sitting-room.

Rebecca. Why, what does he look like, Madam Helseth?

Madam Helseth. Well, he's not much to look at, Miss, and that's a fact.

Rosmer. Did he not give his name?

Madam Helseth. Yes—I think he said his name was Hekman or something of the sort.

Rosmer. I know nobody of that name.

Madam Helseth. And then he said he was called Uldric, too.

Rosmer (in surprise). Ulric Hetman! Was that it?

Madam Helseth. Yes, so it was—Hetman.

Kroll. I've surely heard that name before——

Rebecca. Wasn't that the name he used to write under—that strange being——

Rosmer (to Kroll*).* It is Ulric Brendel's pseudonym.

Kroll. That black sheep Ulric Brendel's—of course it is.

Rebecca. Then he is still alive.

Rosmer. I heard he had joined a company of strolling players.

Kroll. When last *I* heard of him, he was in the House of Correction.

Rosmer. Ask him to come in, Madam Helseth.

Madam Helseth. Oh, very well. [*She goes out.*

Kroll. Are you really going to let a man like that into your house?

Rosmer. You know he was once my tutor.

Kroll. Yes, I know he went and crammed your head full of revolutionary ideas, until your father showed him the door—with his horsewhip.

Rosmer (with a touch of bitterness). Father was a martinet at home as well as in his regiment.

Kroll. Thank him in his grave for that, my dear Rosmer.—Well!

[Madam Helseth *opens the door on the right for* Ulric Brendel *and then withdraws, shutting the door behind him. He is a handsome man, with grey hair and beard; somewhat gaunt, but active and well set up. He is dressed like a common tramp; threadbare frock-coat; worn-out shoes; no shirt visible. He wears an old pair of black gloves, and carries a soft, greasy felt hat under his arm, and a walking-stick in his hand.*

Ulric Brendel (hesitates at first, then goes quickly up to the RECTOR *and holds out his hand).* Good evening, Johannes!

Kroll. Excuse me——

Brendel. Did you expect to see me again? And within these hated walls, too?

Kroll. Excuse me—— *(Pointing.)* There——

Brendel (turns). Right. There he is. Johannes—my boy—my best-beloved——!

Rosmer (takes his hand). My old teacher.

Brendel. Notwithstanding certain painful memories, I could not pass by Rosmersholm without paying you a flying visit.

Rosmer. You are heartily welcome here now. Be sure of that.

Brendel. Ah, this charming lady——? *(Bows.)* Mrs. Rosmer, of course.

Rosmer. Miss West.

Brendel. A near relation, no doubt. And yonder unknown——? A brother of the cloth, I see.

Rosmer. Rector Kroll.

Brendel. Kroll? Kroll? Wait a bit?—Weren't you a student of philology in your young days?

Kroll. Of course I was.

Brendel. Why *Donnerwetter,* then I knew you!

Kroll. Pardon me——

Brendel. Weren't you——

Kroll. Pardon me——

Brendel. ——one of those myrmidons of morality that got me turned out of the Debating Club?

Kroll. Very likely. But I disclaim any closer acquaintanceship.

Brendel. Well, well! *Nach Belieben, Herr Doctor.* It's all one to me. Ulric Brendel remains the man he is for all that.

Rebecca. You are on your way into town, Mr. Brendel?

Brendel. You have hit it, gracious lady. At certain intervals, I am constrained to strike a blow for existence. It goes against the grain; but—*enfin*—imperious necessity——

Rosmer. Oh, but, my dear Mr. Brendel, you must allow me to help you. In one way or another, I am sure——

Brendel. Ha, such a proposal to me! Would you desecrate the bond that unites us? Never, Johannes, never!

Rosmer. But what do you think of doing in town? Believe me, you won't find it easy to——

Brendel. Leave that to me, my boy. The die is cast. Simple as I stand here before you, I am engaged in a comprehensive campaign—more comprehensive than all my previous excursions put together. *(To* RECTOR KROLL.*)* Dare I ask the Herr Professor—*unter uns*—have you a tolerably decent, reputable and commodious Public Hall in your estimable city?

Kroll. The hall of the Workmen's Society is the largest.

Brendel. And has the Herr Professor any official influence in this doubtless most beneficent Society?

Kroll. I have nothing to do with it.

Rebecca (to BRENDEL*).* You should apply to Peter Mortensgård.

Brendel. Pardon, madame—what sort of an idiot is he?

Rosmer. What makes you take him for an idiot?

Brendel. Can't I tell at once by the name that it belongs to a plebeian?

Kroll. I did not expect that answer.

Brendel. But I will conquer my reluctance. There is no alternative. When a man stands—as I do—at a turning-point in his career——. It is settled. I will approach this individual—will open personal negotiations——

Rosmer. Are you really and seriously standing at a turning-point?

Brendel. Surely my own boy knows that, stand he where

he may, Ulric Brendel always stands really and seriously.—Yes, Johannes, I am going to put on a new man—to throw off the modest reserve I have hitherto maintained——

Rosmer. How——?

Brendel. I am about to take hold of life with a strong hand; to step forth; to assert myself. We live in a tempestuous, an equinoctial age.—I am about to lay my mite on the altar of Emancipation.

Kroll. You, too?

Brendel (to them all). Is the local public at all familiar with my occasional writings?

Kroll. No, I must candidly confess that——

Rebecca. I have read several of them. My adopted father had them in his library.

Brendel. Fair lady, then you have wasted your time. For, let me tell you, they are so much rubbish.

Rebecca. Indeed!

Brendel. What you have read, yes. My really important works no man or woman knows. No one—except myself.

Rebecca. How does that happen?

Brendel. Because they are not written.

Rosmer. But, my dear Mr. Brendel——

Brendel. You know, my Johannes, that I am a bit of a Sybarite—a *Feinschmecker*. I have been so all my days. I like to take my pleasures in solitude; for then I enjoy them doubly—tenfold. So, you see when golden dreams descended and enwrapped me—when new, dizzy, far-reaching thoughts were born in me and wafted me aloft on their sustaining pinions—I bodied them forth in poems, visions, pictures—in the rough, as it were, you understand.

Rosmer. Yes, yes.

Brendel. Oh, what pleasures, what intoxications I have enjoyed in my time! The mysterious bliss of creation—in the rough, as I said—applause, gratitude, renown, the wreath of bays—all these I have garnered with full hands quivering with joy. I have sated myself, in my secret thoughts, with a rapture—oh! so intense, so inebriating——!

Kroll. H'm.

Rosmer. But you have written nothing down?

Brendel. Not a word. The soulless toil of the scrivener has always aroused a sickening aversion in me. And besides, why should I profane my own ideals, when I could enjoy them in their purity by myself? But now they shall be offered up. I assure you I feel like a mother who delivers her tender daughters into their bridegrooms' arms. But I will offer them up, nonetheless. I will sacrifice them on the altar of Emancipation. A series of carefully elaborated lectures—over the whole country——!

Rebecca (with animation). This is noble of you, Mr. Brendel! You are yielding up the dearest thing you possess.

Rosmer. The only thing.

Rebecca (looking significantly at Rosmer*).* How many are there who do as much—who dare do as much?

Rosmer (returning the look). Who knows?

Brendel. My audience is touched. That does my heart good—and steels my will. So now I will proceed to action. Stay—one thing more. *(To the* Rector.*)* Can you tell me, Herr Preceptor,—is there such a thing as a Temperance Society in the town? A Total Abstinence Society? I need scarcely ask.

Kroll. Yes, there is. I am the president, at your service.

Brendel. I saw it in your face! Well, it is by no means impossible that I may come to you and enrol myself as a member for a week.

Kroll. Excuse me—we don't receive members by the week.

Brendel. A la bonne heure, Herr Pedagogue. Ulric Brendel has never forced himself into that sort of Society. *(Turns.)* But I must not prolong my stay in this house, so rich in memories. I must get on to the town and select a suitable lodging. I presume there is a decent hotel in the place.

Rebecca. Mayn't I offer you anything before you go?

Brendel. Of what sort, gracious lady?

Rebecca. A cup of tea, or——

Brendel. I thank my bountiful hostess—but I am always loath to trespass on private hospitality. *(Waves his hand.)* Farewell, gentlefolks all! *(Goes towards the door, but turns again.)* Oh, by the way—Johannes—Pastor Rosmer—for the sake of our ancient friendship, will you do your former teacher a service?

Rosmer. Yes, with all my heart.

Brendel. Good. Then lend me—for a day or two—a starched shirt—with cuffs.

Rosmer. Nothing else?

Brendel. For you see I am travelling on foot—at present. My trunk is being sent after me.

Rosmer. Quite so. But is there nothing else?

Brendel. Well, do you know—perhaps you could spare me an oldish, well-worn summer overcoat.

Rosmer. Yes, yes; certainly I can.

Brendel. And if a respectable pair of boots happened to go along with the coat——

Rosmer. That we can manage, too. As soon as you let us know your address, we will send the things in.

Brendel. Not on any account. Pray do not let me give you any trouble! I will take the bagatelles with me.

Rosmer. As you please. Come upstairs with me, then.

Rebecca. Let me go. Madam Helseth and I will see to it.

Brendel. I cannot think of suffering this distinguished lady to——

Rebecca. Oh, nonsense! Come along, Mr. Brendel.

[*She goes out to the right.*

Rosmer (detaining him). Tell me—is there nothing else I can do for you?

Brendel. Upon my word, I know of nothing more. Well, yes, damn it all—now that I think of it——! Johannes, do you happen to have eight crowns in your pocket?

Rosmer. Let me see. *(Opens his purse.)* Here are two ten-crown notes.

Brendel. Well, well, never mind! I can take them. I can always get them changed in town. Thanks in the meantime. Remember it was two tenners you lent me. Good-night my own dear boy. Good-night, respected Sir.

[*Goes out to the right.* ROSMER *takes leave of him and shuts the door behind him.*

Kroll. Merciful Heaven—so that is the Ulric Brendel people once expected such great things of.

Rosmer (quietly). At least he has had the courage to live his life his own way. I don't think that is such a small matter either.

Kroll. What? A life like his! I almost believe he has it in him to turn your head afresh.

Rosmer. Oh, no. My mind is quite clear now, upon all points.

Kroll. I wish I could believe it, my dear Rosmer. You are so terribly impressionable.

Rosmer. Let us sit down. I want to talk to you.

Kroll. Yes, let us.

[*They seat themselves on the sofa.*

Rosmer (after a slight pause). Don't you think we lead a pleasant and comfortable life here?

Kroll. Yes, your life is pleasant and comfortable now—and peaceful. You have found yourself a home, Rosmer. And I have lost mine.

Rosmer. My dear friend, don't say that. The wound will heal again in time.

Kroll. Never; never. The barb will always rankle. Things can never be as they were.

Rosmer. Listen to me, Kroll. We have been fast friends for many and many a year. Does it seem to you conceivable that our friendship should ever go to wreck?

Kroll. I know of nothing in the world that could estrange us. What puts that into your head?

Rosmer. You attach such paramount importance to uniformity of opinions and views.

Kroll. No doubt; but we two are in practical agreement, at any rate, on the great essential questions.

Rosmer (in a low voice). No; not now.

Kroll (tries to spring up). What is this?

Rosmer (holding him). No, you must sit still—I entreat you, Kroll.

Kroll. What can this mean? I don't understand you. Speak plainly.

Rosmer. A new summer has blossomed in my soul. I see with eyes grown young again. And so now I stand——

Kroll. Where—where, Rosmer?

Rosmer. Where your children stand.

Kroll. You? You! Impossible! Where do you say you stand?

Rosmer. On the same side as Laurits and Hilda.

Kroll (bows his head). An apostate! Johannes Rosmer an apostate!

Rosmer. I should have felt so happy—so intensely happy, in what you call my apostasy. But, nevertheless, I suffered deeply; for I knew it would be a bitter sorrow to you.

Kroll. Rosmer—Rosmer! I shall never get over this! *(Looks gloomily at him.)* To think that you, too, can find it in your heart to help on the work of corruption and ruin in this unhappy land.

Rosmer. It is the work of emancipation I wish to help on.

Kroll. Oh, yes, I know. That is what both the tempters and their victims call it. But do you think there is any emancipation to be expected from the spirit that is now poisoning our social life?

Rosmer. I am not in love with the spirit that is in the ascendant, nor with either of the contending parties. I will try to bring together men from both sides—as many as I can—and to unite them as closely as possible. I will devote my life and all my energies to this one thing—the creation of a true democracy in this country.

Kroll. So you don't think we have democracy enough already! For my part it seems to me we are all in a fair way to be dragged down into the mire, where hitherto only the mob have been able to thrive.

Rosmer. That is just why I want to awaken the democracy to its true task.

Kroll. What task?

Rosmer. That of making all the people of this country noble——

Kroll. All the people——?

Rosmer. As many as possible, at any rate.

Kroll. By what means?

Rosmer. By freeing their minds and purifying their wills.

Kroll. You are a dreamer, Rosmer. Will you free them? Will you purify them?

Rosmer. No, my dear friend—I will only try to arouse them to their task. They themselves must accomplish it.

Kroll. And you think they can?

Rosmer. Yes.

Kroll. By their own strength?

Rosmer. Yes, precisely by their own strength. There is no other.

Kroll (rises). Is this becoming language for a priest?

Rosmer. I am no longer a priest.

Kroll. Well but—the faith of your fathers——?

Rosmer. It is mine no more.

Kroll. No more——!

Rosmer (rises). I have given it up. I had to give it up, Kroll.

Kroll (controlling his agitation). Oh, indeed—— Yes, yes, yes. I suppose one thing goes with another. Was this, then, your reason for leaving the Church?

Rosmer. Yes. As soon as my mind was clear—as soon as I was quite certain that this was no passing attack of scepticism, but a conviction I neither could nor would shake off—then I at once left the Church.

Kroll. So this has been your state of mind all this time! And we—your friends—have heard nothing of it. Rosmer—Rosmer—how could you hide the miserable truth from us!

Rosmer. Because it seemed to me a matter that concerned myself alone. And besides, I did not wish to give you and my other friends any needless pain. I thought I might live on here, as before, quietly, serenely, happily. I wanted to read, to bury myself in all the studies that until then had been sealed books to me. I wanted to make myself thoroughly at home in the great world of truth and freedom that has been revealed to me.

Kroll. Apostate! Every word proves it. But why, then, do you confess your secret apostasy after all? And why just at this time?

Rosmer. You yourself have driven me to it, Kroll.

Kroll. I? Have I driven you——?

Rosmer. When I heard of your violence on the platform—when I read all the rancorous speeches you made—your bitter onslaughts on your opponents—the contemptuous invectives you heaped on them—oh, Kroll, to think that you—you—could come to this!—then my duty stood imperatively before me. Men are growing evil in this struggle. Peace and joy and mutual forbearance must once more enter into our souls. That is why I now intend to step forward and openly avow myself for what I am. I, too, will try my strength. Could not you—from your side—help me in this, Kroll?

Kroll. Never so long as I live will I make peace with the subversive forces in society.

Rosmer. Then at least let us fight with honourable weapons—since fight we must.

Kroll. Whoever is not with me in the essential things of life, him I no longer know. I owe him no consideration.

Rosmer. Does that apply to me, too?

Kroll. It is you that have broken with me, Rosmer.

Rosmer. Is this a breach, then?

Kroll. This! It is a breach with all who have hitherto been your friends. You must take the consequences.

[REBECCA WEST *enters from the right and opens the door wide.*

Rebecca. There now; he is on his way to his great sacrifice. And now we can go to supper. Will you come in, Rector?

Kroll (takes up his hat). Good-night, Miss West. I have nothing more to do here.

Rebecca (eagerly). What is this? *(Shuts the door and comes forward.)* Have you spoken?

Rosmer. He knows everything.

Kroll. We will not let you go, Rosmer. We will force you to come back to us.

Rosmer. I can never stand where I did.

Kroll. We shall see. You are not the man to endure standing alone.

Rosmer. I shall not be so completely alone after all.—There are two of us to bear the loneliness together.

Kroll. Ah——. *(A suspicion appears in his face.)* That, too! Beata's words——!

Rosmer. Beata's——?

Kroll (shaking off the thought). No, no—that was vile. Forgive me.

Rosmer. What? What do you mean?

Kroll. Don't ask. Bah! Forgive me! Good-bye!

[*Goes towards the entrance door.*

Rosmer (follows him). Kroll! Our friendship must not end like this. I will come and see you to-morrow.

Kroll (in the hall, turns). You shall never cross my threshold again.

[*He takes up his stick and goes out.*

[ROSMER *stands for a moment in the doorway; then shuts the door and walks up to the table.*

Rosmer. It does not matter, Rebecca. We will see it out, we two faithful friends—you* and I.

Rebecca. What do you think he meant when he said "That was vile"?

Rosmer. Don't trouble about that, dear. He himself didn't believe what was in his mind. To-morrow I will go and see him. Good-night!

Rebecca. Are you going upstairs so early to-night? After this?

Rosmer. To-night as usual. I feel so relieved, now it is over. You see—I am quite calm, Rebecca. Do you, too, take it calmly. Good-night!

Rebecca. Good-night, dear friend! Sleep well!

[ROSMER *goes out by the hall door; his steps are heard ascending the staircase.*

[REBECCA *goes and pulls a bell-rope near the stove. Shortly after,* MADAM HELSETH *enters from the right.*

Rebecca. You can take away the supper things, Madam Helseth. Mr. Rosmer doesn't want anything, and the Rector has gone home.

Madam Helseth. Has the Rector gone? What was the matter with him?

* From this point, and throughout when alone, Rosmer and Rebecca use the *du* of intimate friendship in speaking to each other.

Rebecca (takes up her crochet work). He said he thought there was a heavy storm brewing——

Madam Helseth. What a strange notion! There's not a cloud in the sky this evening.

Rebecca. Let us hope he mayn't meet the White Horse! I'm afraid we shall soon be hearing something from the bogies now.

Madam Helseth. Lord forgive you, Miss! Don't say such awful things.

Rebecca. Well, well, well——

Madam Helseth (softly). Do you really think some one is to go soon, Miss?

Rebecca. No; why should I think so? But there are so many sorts of white horses in this world, Madam Helseth.— Well, good-night. I shall go to my room now.

Madam Helseth. Good-night, Miss.

[REBECCA *goes out to the right, with her crochet work.*

Madam Helseth (turns the lamp down, shaking her head and muttering to herself). Lord—Lord! That Miss West! The things she does say!

ACT II

JOHANNES ROSMER'S *study. Entrance door on the left. At the back, a doorway with a curtain drawn aside, leading into* ROSMER'S *bedroom. On the right a window, and in front of it a writing-table covered with books and papers. Book-shelves and cases round the room. The furniture is simple. On the left, an old-fashioned sofa, with a table in front of it.*

JOHANNES ROSMER, *in an indoor jacket, is sitting in a high-backed chair at the writing-table. He is cutting and turning over the leaves of a pamphlet, and reading a little here and there.*

There is a knock at the door on the left.

Rosmer (without moving). Come in.

Rebecca West (enters, dressed in a morning gown). Good morning.

Rosmer (turning the leaves of the pamphlet). Good morning, dear. Do you want anything?

Rebecca. I only wanted to hear if you had slept well.

Rosmer. Oh, I have had a beautiful, peaceful night. *(Turns.)* And you?

Rebecca. Oh, yes, thanks—towards morning——

Rosmer. I don't know when I have felt so light-hearted as I do now. I am so glad I managed to speak out at last.

Rebecca. Yes, it is a pity you remained silent so long, Rosmer.

Rosmer. I don't understand myself how I could be such a coward.

Rebecca. It wasn't precisely cowardice——

Rosmer. Oh, yes, dear—when I think the thing out, I can see there was a touch of cowardice at the bottom of it.

Rebecca. All the braver, then, to make the plunge at last. *(Sits on a chair at the writing-table, close to him.)* But now I want to tell you of something I have done—and you mustn't be vexed with me about it.

Rosmer. Vexed? How can you think——?

Rebecca. Well, it was perhaps rather indiscreet of me but——

Rosmer. Let me hear what it was.

Rebecca. Yesterday evening, when Ulric Brendel was leaving—I gave him a note to Peter Mortensgård.

Rosmer (a little doubtful). Why, my dear Rebecca—— Well, what did you say?

Rebecca. I said that he would be doing you a service if he would look after that unfortunate creature a little and help him in any way he could.

Rosmer. Dear, you shouldn't have done that. You have only done Brendel harm. And Mortensgård is not a man I care to have anything to do with. You know of that old episode between us.

Rebecca. But don't you think it would be as well to make it up with him again?

Rosmer. I? With Mortensgård? In what way do you mean?

Rebecca. Well, you know you can't feel absolutely secure now—after this breach with your old friends.

Rosmer (looks at her and shakes his head). Can you really believe that Kroll or any of the others would try to take revenge on me? That they would be capable of——?

Rebecca. In the first heat of anger, dear——. No one can be sure. I think—after the way the Rector took it——

Rosmer. Oh, you ought surely to know him better than that. Kroll is a gentleman, to the backbone. I am going into town this afternoon to talk to him. I will talk to them all. Oh, you shall see how easily it will all go——

[MADAM HELSETH *appears at the door on the left.*

Rebecca (rises). What is it, Madam Helseth?

Madam Helseth. Rector Kroll is downstairs in the hall.

Rosmer (rises hastily). Kroll!

Rebecca. The Rector! Is it possible——

Madam Helseth. He wants to know if he may come upstairs, Mr. Rosmer.

Rosmer (to REBECCA*).* What did I tell you?—Of course he may. *(Goes to the door and calls down the stairs.)* Come up, dear friend! I am delighted to see you.

[ROSMER *stands holding the door open.* MADAM HELSETH *goes out.* REBECCA *draws the curtain before the doorway at the back and then begins arranging things in the room.*

[RECTOR KROLL *enters, with his hat in his hand.*

Rosmer (with quiet emotion). I knew it couldn't be the last time——

Kroll. I see things to-day in quite a different light from yesterday.

Rosmer. Ah, yes, Kroll; I was sure you would, now that you have had time to reflect.

Kroll. You misunderstand me completely. *(Lays his hat on the table beside the sofa.)* It is of the utmost importance that I should speak to you, alone.

Rosmer. Why may not Miss West——?

Rebecca. No, no, Mr. Rosmer. I will go.

Kroll (looks at her from head to foot). And I must ask Miss West to excuse my coming at such an untimely hour—taking her unawares before she has had time to——

Rebecca (surprised). What do you mean? Do you see any harm in my wearing a morning gown about the house?

Kroll. Heaven forbid! I know nothing of what may now be customary at Rosmersholm.

Rosmer. Why, Kroll—you are not yourself to-day!

Rebecca. Allow me to wish you good morning, Rector Kroll. [*She goes out to the left.*

Kroll. By your leave—— [*Sits on the sofa.*

Rosmer. Yes, Kroll, sit down, and let us talk things out amicably.

[*He seats himself in a chair directly opposite to the* RECTOR.

Kroll. I haven't closed an eye since yesterday. I have been lying thinking and thinking all night.

Rosmer. And what do you say to things to-day?

Kroll. It will be a long story, Rosmer. Let me begin with a sort of introduction. I can give you news of Ulric Brendel.

Rosmer. Has he called on you?

Kroll. No. He took up his quarters in a low public-house—in the lowest company of course—and drank and stood treat as long as he had any money. Then he began abusing the whole company as a set of disreputable blackguards—and so far he was quite right—whereupon they thrashed him and pitched him out into the gutter.

Rosmer. So he is incorrigible after all.

Kroll. He had pawned the coat, too; but I am told that has been redeemed for him. Can you guess by whom?

Rosmer. Perhaps by you?

Kroll. No; by the distinguished Mr. Mortensgård.

Rosmer. Ah, indeed.

Kroll. I understand that Mr. Brendel's first visit was to the "idiot" and "plebeian."

Rosmer. Well, it was lucky for him——

Kroll. To be sure it was. (*Leans over the table towards* ROSMER.) And that brings me to a matter it is my duty to warn you about, for our old—for our former friendship's sake.

Rosmer. My dear Kroll, what can that be?

Kroll. It is this: there are things going on behind your back in this house.

Rosmer. How can you think so? Is it Reb—is it Miss West you are aiming at?

Kroll. Precisely. I can quite understand it on her part. She has so long been accustomed to have everything her own way here. But nevertheless——

Rosmer. My dear Kroll, you are utterly mistaken. She and I—we have no concealments from each other on any subject whatever.

Kroll. Has she told you, then, that she has entered into correspondence with the editor of the "Beacon"?

Rosmer. Oh, you are thinking of the few lines she sent by Ulric Brendel?

Kroll. Then you have found it out. And do you approve of her entering into relations with a scurrilous scribbler, who never lets a week pass without holding me up to ridicule, both as a schoolmaster and as a public man?

Rosmer. My dear Kroll, I don't suppose that side of the matter ever entered her head. And besides, of course she has full liberty of action, just as I have.

Kroll. Indeed? Ah, no doubt that follows from your new line of thought. For Miss West presumably shares your present standpoint?

Rosmer. Yes, she does. We two have worked our way forward in faithful comradeship.

Kroll (looks at him and slowly shakes his head). Oh, you blind, deluded being!

Rosmer. I? Why do you say that?

Kroll. Because I dare not—I will not think the worst. No, no, let me say my say out.—You really do value my friendship, Rosmer? And my respect, too? Do you not?

Rosmer. I surely need not answer that question.

Kroll. Well, but there are other questions that do require an answer—a full explanation on your part.—Will you submit to a sort of investigation——?

Rosmer. Investigation?

Kroll. Yes; will you let me question you about certain things it may pain you to be reminded of? You see—this apostasy of yours—well, this emancipation, as you call it—is bound up with many other things that for your own sake you must explain to me.

Rosmer. My dear Kroll, ask what questions you please. I have nothing to conceal.

Kroll. Then tell me—what do you think was the real, the ultimate reason why Beata put an end to her life?

Rosmer. Can you have any doubt on the subject? Or, rather, can you ask for reasons for what an unhappy, irresponsible invalid may do?

Kroll. Are you certain that Beata was completely irresponsible for her actions? The doctors, at any rate, were by no means convinced of it.

Rosmer. If the doctors had ever seen her as I have so often seen her, for days and nights together, they would have had no doubts.

Kroll. I had no doubts either—then.

Rosmer. Oh, no, unhappily, there wasn't the smallest room for doubt. I have told you of her wild frenzies of passion—which she expected me to return. Oh, how they appalled me! And then her causeless, consuming self-reproaches during the last few years.

Kroll. Yes, when she had learnt that she must remain childless all her life.

Rosmer. Yes, just think of that! Such terrible, haunting agony of mind about a thing utterly beyond her control——! How could you call her responsible for her actions?

Kroll. H'm——. Can you remember whether you had any books in the house at that time treating of the rationale of marriage—according to the "advanced" ideas of the day?

Rosmer. I remember Miss West lending me a work of the kind. The Doctor left her his library, you know. But, my dear Kroll, you surely cannot suppose we were so reckless as to let my poor sick wife get hold of any such ideas?

I can solemnly assure you that the fault was not ours. It was her own distempered brain that drove her into these wild aberrations.

Kroll. One thing at any rate I can tell you; and that is, that poor, overstrung, tortured Beata put an end to her life in order that you might live happily—live freely, and—after your own heart.

Rosmer (starts half up from his chair). What do you mean by that?

Kroll. Listen to me quietly, Rosmer; for now I can speak of it. In the last year of her life she came to me twice to pour forth all her anguish and despair.

Rosmer. On this same subject?

Kroll. No. The first time she came, it was to declare that you were on the road to perversion—that you were going to break with the faith of your fathers.

Rosmer (eagerly). What you say is impossible, Kroll. Absolutely impossible! You must be mistaken.

Kroll. And why?

Rosmer. Because while Beata was alive I was still wrestling with myself in doubt. And that fight I fought out alone and in utter silence. I don't think even Rebecca——

Kroll. Rebecca?

Rosmer. Oh, well—Miss West. I call her Rebecca for convenience' sake.

Kroll. So I have remarked.

Rosmer. So it is inconceivable to me how Beata could have got hold of the idea. And why did she not speak to me about it? She never did—she never said a single word.

Kroll. Poor creature—she begged and implored me to talk to you.

Rosmer. And why did you not?

Kroll. At that time I never for a moment doubted that she was out of her mind. Such an accusation against a man like you!—And then she came again—about a month later. This time she seemed outwardly calmer; but as she was going she said: "They may soon expect the White Horse at Rosmersholm now."

Rosmer. Yes, yes. The White Horse—she often spoke of it.

Kroll. And when I tried to divert her mind from such melancholy fancies, she only answered: "I have not long to live; for Johannes must marry Rebecca at once."

Rosmer (almost speechless). What do you say? I marry——?

Kroll. That was on a Thursday afternoon——. On the Saturday evening she threw herself from the bridge into the mill-race.

Rosmer. And you never warned us——!

Kroll. You know very well how often she used to say that she felt her end was near.

Rosmer. Yes, I know. But nevertheless—you should have warned us!

Kroll. I did think of it; but not till too late.

Rosmer. But afterwards, why did you not——? Why have you said nothing about all this?

Kroll. What good would it have done for me to come torturing and harassing you still further? I took all she said for mere wild, empty ravings—until yesterday evening.

Rosmer. Then you have now changed your opinion?

Kroll. Did not Beata see quite clearly when she declared you were about to desert the faith of your fathers?

Rosmer (looks fixedly, straight before him). I cannot understand it. It is the most incomprehensible thing in the world.

Kroll. Incomprehensible or not—there it is. And now I ask you, Rosmer,—how much truth is there in her other accusation? The last one, I mean.

Rosmer. Accusation? Was that an accusation?

Kroll. Perhaps you did not notice the way she worded it. She had to go, she said—why?

Rosmer. In order that I might marry Rebecca——

Kroll. These were not precisely her words. Beata used a different expression. She said: "I have not long to live; for Johannes must marry Rebecca at once."

Rosmer (looks at him for a moment; then rises). Now I understand you, Kroll.

Kroll. And what then? What is your answer?

Rosmer (still quiet and self-restrained). To such an unheard-of——? The only fitting answer would be to point to the door.

Kroll (rises). Well and good.

Rosmer (stands in front of him). Listen to me. For more than a year—ever since Beata left us—Rebecca West and I have lived alone here at Rosmersholm. During all that time you have known of Beata's accusation against us. But I have never for a moment noticed that you disapproved of Rebecca's living in my house.

Kroll. I did not know till yesterday evening that it was an unbelieving man who was living with an—emancipated woman.

Rosmer. Ah——! Then you do not believe that purity of mind is to be found among the unbelieving and the emancipated? You do not believe that morality may be an instinctive law of their nature!

Kroll. I have no great faith in the morality that is not founded on the teachings of the Church.

Rosmer. And you mean this to apply to Rebecca and me? To the relation between us two——?

Kroll. Not even out of consideration for you two can I depart from my opinion that there is no unfathomable gulf between free thought and—h'm——

Rosmer. And what?

Kroll. ——and free love,—since you will have it.

Rosmer (in a low voice). And you are not ashamed to say this to me! You, who have known me from my earliest youth!

Kroll. For that very reason. I know how easily you

are influenced by the people you associate with. And this Rebecca of yours—well, Miss West, then—we really know little or nothing about her. In short, Rosmer—I will not give you up. And you—you must try to save yourself in time.

Rosmer. Save myself? How——?

[MADAM HELSETH *peeps in at the door on the left.*

Rosmer. What do you want?

Madam Helseth. I wanted to ask Miss West to step downstairs.

Rosmer. Miss West is not up here.

Madam Helseth. Isn't she? *(Looks round the room.)* Well, that's strange. [*She goes.*

Rosmer. You were saying——?

Kroll. Listen to me. I am not going to inquire too closely into the secret history of what went on here in Beata's lifetime—and may still be going on. I know that your marriage was a most unhappy one; and I suppose that must be taken as some sort of excuse——

Rosmer. Oh, how little you really know me——!

Kroll. Don't interrupt me. What I mean is this: if your present mode of life with Miss West is to continue, it is absolutely necessary that the change of views—the unhappy backsliding—brought about by her evil influence, should be hushed up. Let me speak! Let me speak! I say, if the worst comes to the worst, in Heaven's name think and believe whatever you like about everything under the sun. But you must keep your views to yourself. These things are purely personal matters, after all. There is no need to proclaim them from the housetops.

Rosmer. I feel it an absolute necessity to get out of a false and equivocal position.

Kroll. But you have a duty towards the traditions of your race, Rosmer! Remember that! Rosmersholm has, so to speak, radiated morality and order from time immemorial—yes, and respectful conformity to all that is accepted and sanctioned by the best people. The whole district has taken its stamp from Rosmersholm. It would lead to deplorable, irremediable confusion if it were known that you had broken with what I may call the hereditary idea of the house of Rosmer.

Rosmer. My dear Kroll, I cannot see the matter in that light. I look upon it as my imperative duty to spread a little light and gladness here, where the Rosmer family has from generation to generation been a centre of darkness and oppression.

Kroll (looks at him severely). Yes, that would be a worthy life-work for the last of your race! No, Rosmer; let such things alone; you are the last man for such a task. You were born to be a quiet student.

Rosmer. Perhaps so. But for once in a way I mean to bear my part in the battle of life.

Kroll. And do you know what that battle of life will mean for you? It will mean a life-and-death struggle with all your friends.

Rosmer (quietly). They cannot all be such fanatics as you.

Kroll. You are a credulous creature, Rosmer. An inexperienced creature, too. You have no conception of the overwhelming storm that will burst upon you.

[MADAM HELSETH *looks in at the door on the left.*

Madam Helseth. Miss West wants to know——

Rosmer. What is it?

Madam Helseth. There's a man downstairs wanting to have a word with the Pastor.

Rosmer. Is it the man who was here yesterday evening?

Madam Helseth. No, it's that Mortensgård.

Rosmer. Mortensgård?

Kroll. Aha! So it has come to this, has it?—Already!

Rosmer. What does he want with me? Why didn't you send him away?

Madam Helseth. Miss West said I was to ask if he might come upstairs.

Rosmer. Tell him I'm engaged——

Kroll (to MADAM HELSETH*).* Let him come up, Madam Helseth. [MADAM HELSETH *goes.*

Kroll (takes up his hat). I retire from the field—for the moment. But the main battle has yet to be fought.

Rosmer. On my honour, Kroll—I have nothing whatever to do with Mortensgård.

Kroll. I do not believe you. On no subject and in no relation whatever will I henceforth believe you. It is war to the knife now. We will try whether we cannot disarm you.

Rosmer. Oh, Kroll—how low—how very low you have sunk!

Kroll. I? And you think you have the right to say that to me! Remember Beata!

Rosmer. Still harping upon that?

Kroll. No. You must solve the enigma of the mill-race according to your own conscience—if you have anything of the sort left.

[PETER MORTENSGÅRD *enters softly and quietly from the left. He is a small, wiry man with thin reddish hair and beard.*

Kroll (with a look of hatred). Ah, here we have the "Beacon"—burning at Rosmersholm! *(Buttons his coat.)* Well, now I can no longer hesitate what course to steer.

Mortensgård (deferentially). The "Beacon" may always be relied upon to light the Rector home.

Kroll. Yes; you have long shown your goodwill. To be sure there's a commandment about bearing false witness against your neighbour——

Mortensgård. Rector Kroll need not instruct me in the commandments.

Kroll. Not even in the seventh?

Rosmer. —Kroll——!

Mortensgård. If I needed instruction, it would rather be the Pastor's business.

Kroll (with covert sarcasm). The Pastor's? Oh, yes, unquestionably Pastor Rosmer is the man for that.—Good luck to your conference, gentlemen!

[*Goes out and slams the door behind him.*

Rosmer (keeps his eyes fixed on the closed door and says to himself). Well, well—so be it then. *(Turns.)* Will you be good enough to tell me, Mr. Mortensgård, what brings you out here to me?

Mortensgård. It was really Miss West I came to see. I wanted to thank her for the friendly note I received from her yesterday.

Rosmer. I know she wrote to you. Have you seen her, then?

Mortensgård. Yes, for a short time. *(Smiles slightly.)* I hear there has been a certain change of views out here at Rosmersholm.

Rosmer. My views are altered in many respects. I might almost say in all.

Mortensgård. So Miss West told me; and that's why she thought I had better come up and talk things over with the Pastor.

Rosmer. What things, Mr. Mortensgård.

Mortensgård. May I announce in the "Beacon" that there has been a change in your views—that you have joined the party of freedom and progress?

Rosmer. Certainly you may. In fact, I beg you to make the announcement.

Mortensgård. Then it shall appear in to-morrow's paper. It will cause a great sensation when it's known that Pastor Rosmer of Rosmersholm is prepared to take up arms for the cause of light, in that sense, too.

Rosmer. I don't quite understand you.

Mortensgård. I mean that the moral position of our

party is greatly strengthened whenever we gain an adherent of serious, Christian principles.

Rosmer (with some surprise). Then you do not know——? Did not Miss West tell you that, too?

Mortensgård. What, Pastor Rosmer? Miss West was in a great hurry. She said I was to go upstairs and hear the rest from yourself.

Rosmer. Well, in that case I may tell you that I have emancipated myself entirely, and on every side. I have broken with all the dogmas of the Church. Henceforth they are nothing to me.

Mortensgård (looks at him in amazement). Well—if the skies were to fall I couldn't be more——! Pastor Rosmer himself announces——.

Rosmer. Yes, I now stand where you have stood for many years. That, too, you may announce in the "Beacon" to-morrow.

Mortensgård. That, too? No, my dear Pastor—excuse me—— I don't think it would be wise to touch on that side of the matter.

Rosmer. Not touch on it?

Mortensgård. Not at present, I mean.

Rosmer. I don't understand——

Mortensgård. Well, you see, Pastor Rosmer—you probably don't know the ins and outs of things so well as I do. But, since you have come over to the party of freedom—and, as I hear from Miss West, you intend to take an active share in the movement—I presume you would like to be of as much service as possible, both to the cause in general and to this particular agitation.

Rosmer. Yes, that is my earnest wish.

Mortensgård. Good. But now I must tell you, Pastor Rosmer, that if you openly declare your defection from the Church, you tie your own hands at the very outset.

Rosmer. Do you think so?

Mortensgård. Yes; believe me, you won't be able to do

much for the cause, in this part of the country at any rate. And besides—we have plenty of free-thinkers already, Pastor Rosmer—I might almost say too many. What the party requires, is a Christian element—something that every one must respect. That is what we are sadly in need of. And, therefore, I advise you to keep your own counsel about what doesn't concern the public. That's my view of the matter, at least.

Rosmer. I understand. Then if I openly confess my apostasy, you dare not have anything to do with me?

Mortensgård (shaking his head). I scarcely like to risk it, Pastor Rosmer. I have made it a rule for some time past not to support any one or anything that is actively opposed to the Church.

Rosmer. Then you have yourself returned to the Church?

Mortensgård. That concerns no one but myself.

Rosmer. Ah, so that is it. Now I understand you.

Mortensgård. Pastor Rosmer—you ought to remember that I—I in particular—have not full liberty of action.

Rosmer What hampers you?

Mortensgård. The fact that I am a marked man.

Rosmer. Ah—indeed.

Mortensgård. A marked man, Pastor Rosmer. You, above all men, should remember that; for I have chiefly you to thank for the scandal that branded me.

Rosmer. If I had then stood where I stand now, I should have dealt more gently with your offence.

Mortensgård. That I don't doubt. But it is too late now. You have branded me once for all—branded me for life. I suppose you can scarcely understand what that means. But now you may perhaps come to feel the smart of it yourself, Pastor Rosmer.

Rosmer. I?

Mortensgård. Yes. You surely don't suppose that Rector Kroll and his set will ever forgive a desertion like yours?

I hear the "County News" is going to be very savage in future. You, too, may find yourself a marked man before long.

Rosmer. In personal matters, Mr. Mortensgård, I feel myself secure from attack. My life is beyond reproach.

Mortensgård (with a sly smile). That's a large word, Mr. Rosmer.

Rosmer. Perhaps; but I have a right to use it.

Mortensgård. Even if you were to scrutinise your conduct as closely as you once scrutinised mine?

Rosmer. Your tone is very curious. What are you hinting at? Anything definite?

Mortensgård. Yes, something definite. Only one thing. But that might be bad enough, if malicious opponents got wind of it.

Rosmer. Will you have the kindness to let me hear what it is?

Mortensgård. Cannot you guess for yourself, Pastor?

Rosmer. No, certainly not. I have not the slightest idea.

Mortensgård. Well, well, I suppose I must come out with it, then.—I have in my possession a strange letter, dated from Rosmersholm.

Rosmer. Miss West's letter, do you mean? Is it so strange?

Mortensgård. No, there's nothing strange about that. But I once received another letter from this house.

Rosmer. Also from Miss West?

Mortensgård. No, Mr. Rosmer.

Rosmer. Well, then, from whom? From whom?

Mortensgård. From the late Mrs. Rosmer.

Rosmer. From my wife! You received a letter from my wife!

Mortensgård. I did.

Rosmer. When?

Mortensgård. Towards the close of Mrs. Rosmer's life.

Perhaps about a year and a half ago. That is the letter I call strange.

Rosmer. I suppose you know that my wife's mind was affected at that time.

Mortensgård. Yes; I know many people thought so. But I don't think there was anything in the letter to show it. When I call it strange, I mean in another sense.

Rosmer. And what in the world did my poor wife take it into her head to write to you about?

Mortensgård. I have the letter at home. She begins to the effect that she is living in great anxiety and fear; there are so many malicious people about here, she says; and they think of nothing but causing you trouble and injury.

Rosmer. Me?

Mortensgård. Yes, so she says. And then comes the strangest part of all. Shall I go on, Pastor Rosmer?

Rosmer. Assuredly! Tell me everything, without reserve.

Mortensgård. The deceased lady begs and implores me to be magnanimous. She knows, she says, that it was her husband that had me dismissed from my post as teacher; and she conjured me by all that's sacred not to avenge myself.

Rosmer. How did she suppose you could avenge yourself?

Mortensgård. The letter says that if I should hear rumours of sinful doings at Rosmersholm, I am not to believe them; they are only spread abroad by wicked people who wish to make you unhappy.

Rosmer. Is all that in the letter?

Mortensgård. You may read it for yourself, sir, when you please.

Rosmer. But I don't understand——! What did she imagine the rumour to be about?

Mortensgård. Firstly, that the Pastor had deserted the

faith of his fathers. Your wife denied that absolutely—then. And next—h'm——

Rosmer. Next?

Mortensgård. Well, next she writes—rather confusedly—that she knows nothing of any sinful intrigue at Rosmersholm; that she has never been wronged in any way. And if any such rumours should get about, she implores me to say nothing of the matter in the "Beacon."

Rosmer. Is no name mentioned?

Mortensgård. None.

Rosmer. Who brought you the letter?

Mortensgård. I have promised not to say. It was handed to me one evening, at dusk.

Rosmer. If you had made inquiries at the time, you would have learnt that my poor, unhappy wife was not fully accountable for her actions.

Mortensgård. I did make inquiries, Pastor Rosmer. But I must say that was not the impression I received.

Rosmer. Was it not?—But what is your precise reason for telling me now about this incomprehensible old letter?

Mortensgård. To impress on you the necessity for extreme prudence, Pastor Rosmer.

Rosmer. In my life, do you mean?

Mortensgård. Yes. You must remember that from today you have ceased to be a neutral.

Rosmer. Then you have quite made up your mind that I must have something to conceal?

Mortensgård. I don't know why an emancipated man should refrain from living his life out as fully as possible. But, as I said before, be exceedingly cautious in future. If anything should get abroad that conflicts with current prejudices, you may be sure the whole liberal movement will have to suffer for it.—Good-bye, Pastor Rosmer.

Rosmer. Good-bye.

Mortensgård. I shall go straight to the office and have the great news put into the "Beacon."

Rosmer. Yes; omit nothing.

Mortensgård. I shall omit nothing that the public need know.

[*He bows and goes out.* ROSMER *remains standing in the doorway while he goes down the stairs. The outer door is heard to close.*

Rosmer (in the doorway, calls softly). Rebecca! Re——H'm. *(Aloud.)* Madam Helseth,—is Miss West not there?

Madam Helseth (from the hall). No, Pastor Rosmer, she's not here.

[*The curtain at the back is drawn aside.* REBECCA *appears in the doorway.*

Rebecca. Rosmer!

Rosmer. (turns). What! Were you in my room? My dear, what were you doing there?

Rebecca (goes up to him). I was listening.

Rosmer. Oh, Rebecca, how could you?

Rebecca. I could not help it. He said it so hatefully—that about my morning gown——

Rosmer. Then you were there wnen Kroll——?

Rebecca. Yes. I wanted to know what was lurking in his mind.

Rosmer. I would have told you.

Rebecca. You would scarcely have told me all. And certainly not in his own words.

Rosmer. Did you hear everything, then?

Rebecca. Nearly everything, I think. I had to go downstairs for a moment when Mortensgård came.

Rosmer. And then you came back again——?

Rebecca. Don't be vexed with me, dear friend!

Rosmer. Do whatever you think right. You are mistress of your own actions.—But what do you say to all this, Rebecca——? Oh, I seem never to have needed you so much before!

Rebecca. Both you and I have been prepared for what must happen some time.

Rosmer. No, no—not for this.

Rebecca. Not for this?

Rosmer. I knew well enough that sooner or later our beautiful, pure friendship might be misinterpreted and sordid. Not by Kroll—I could never have believed such a thing of him—but by all those other people with the coarse souls and the ignoble eyes. Oh, yes—I had reason enough for keeping our alliance so jealously concealed. It was a dangerous secret.

Rebecca. Oh, why should we care what all those people think! We know in our own hearts that we are blameless.

Rosmer. Blameless? Yes, I thought so—till to-day. But now—now, Rebecca——?

Rebecca. Well, what now?

Rosmer. How am I to explain Beata's terrible accusation?

Rebecca (vehemently). Oh, don't speak of Beata! Don't think of Beata any more! You were just beginning to shake off the hold she has upon you, even in the grave.

Rosmer. Since I have heard all this, she seems, in a ghastly sort of way, to be alive again.

Rebecca. Oh, no—not that, Rosmer! Not that!

Rosmer. Yes, I tell you. We must try to get to the bottom of this. What can possibly have led her to misinterpret things so fatally?

Rebecca. You are surely not beginning to doubt that she was on the very verge of insanity?

Rosmer. Oh, yes—that is just what I can't feel quite certain of any longer. And besides—even if she was——

Rebecca. If she was? Well, what then?

Rosmer. I mean—where are we to look for the determining cause that drove her morbid spirit over the borderline of madness?

Rebecca. Oh, why brood over problems no one can solve?

Rosmer. I cannot help it, Rebecca. I cannot shake off these gnawing doubts, however much I may wish to.

Rebecca. But it may become dangerous—this eternal dwelling upon one miserable subject.

Rosmer (walks about restlessly, in thought). I must have betrayed myself in one way or another. She must have noticed how happy I began to feel from the time you came to us.

Rebecca. Yes but, dear, even if she did——?

Rosmer. Be sure it didn't escape her that we read the same books—that the interest of discussing all the new ideas drew us together. Yet I cannot understand it! I was so careful to spare her. As I look back, it seems to me I made it the business of my life to keep her in ignorance of all our interests. Did I not, Rebecca?

Rebecca. Yes, yes; certainly you did.

Rosmer. And you, too. And yet——! Oh, it's terrible to think of! She must have gone about here—full of her morbid passion—saying never a word—watching us—noting everything—and misinterpreting everything.

Rebecca (pressing her hands together). Oh, I should never have come to Rosmersholm!

Rosmer. To think of all she must have suffered in silence! All the foulness her sick brain must have conjured up around us! Did she never say anything to you to put you at all on the alert?

Rebecca (as if startled). To me! Do you think I should have stayed a day longer if she had?

Rosmer. No, no, of course not.—Oh, what a battle she must have fought! And alone, too, Rebecca; desperate and quite alone!—and then, at last, that heart-breaking, accusing victory—in the mill-race.

[*Throws himself into the chair by the writing-table, with his elbows on the table and his face in his hands.*

Rebecca (approaches him cautiously from behind). Listen, Rosmer. If it were in your power to call Beata back—to you—to Rosmersholm—would you do it?

Rosmer. Oh, how do I know what I would or would not do? I can think of nothing but this one thing—that cannot be recalled.

Rebecca. You were just beginning to live, Rosmer. You had begun. You had freed yourself—on every side. You felt so buoyant and happy——

Rosmer. Oh, yes—I did indeed.—And now this crushing blow falls on me.

Rebecca (behind him, rests her arms on the chair-back). How beautiful it was when we sat in the twilight, in the room downstairs, helping each other to lay out our new life-plans! You were to set resolutely to work in the world—the living world of to-day, as you said. You were to go as a messenger of emancipation from home to home; to win over minds and wills; to create noble-men around you in wider and wider circles. Noble-men.

Rosmer. Happy noble-men.

Rebecca. Yes—happy.

Rosmer. For it is happiness that ennobles, Rebecca.

Rebecca. Should you not say—sorrow as well? A great sorrow?

Rosmer. Yes—if one can get through it—over it—away from it.

Rebecca. That is what you must do.

Rosmer (shakes his head gloomily). I shall never get over this—wholly. There will always be a doubt—a question left. I can never again know that luxury of the soul which makes life so marvellously sweet to live!

Rebecca (bends over his chair-back, and says more softly). What is it you mean, Rosmer?

Rosmer (looking up at her). Peaceful, happy innocence.

Rebecca (recoils a step). Yes. Innocence.

[*A short pause.*

Rosmer (with his elbow on the table, leaning his head on his hand and looking straight before him). And what extraordinary penetration she showed! How systematically she put all this together! First she begins to doubt my orthodoxy—— How could that occur to her? But it did occur to her; and then it grew to be a certainty. And, then—yes, then of course it was easy for her to think all the rest possible. *(Sits up in his chair and runs his hands through his hair.)* Oh, all these horrible imaginings! I shall never get rid of them. I feel it. I know it. At any moment they will come rushing in upon me and bring back the thought of the dead!

Rebecca. Like the White Horse of Rosmersholm.

Rosmer. Yes, like that. Rushing forth in the darkness—in the silence.

Rebecca. And because of this miserable figment of the brain, you will let slip the hold you were beginning to take upon the living world?

Rosmer. You may well think it hard. Yes, hard, Rebecca. But I have no choice. How could I ever leave this behind me?

Rebecca (behind his chair). By entering into new relations.

Rosmer. (surprised, looks up). New relations?

Rebecca. Yes, new relations to the outside world. Live, work, act. Don't sit here brooding and groping among insoluble enigmas.

Rosmer (rises). New relations? *(Walks across the floor, stops at the door and then comes back.)* One question occurs to me. Has it not occurred to you, too, Rebecca?

Rebecca (drawing breath with difficulty). Let me—hear—what it is.

Rosmer. What form do you think our relations will take after to-day?

Rebecca. I believe our friendship will endure—come what may.

Rosmer. That is not exactly what I meant. The thing that first brought us together, and that unites us so closely —our common faith in a pure comradeship between man and woman——

Rebecca. Yes, yes—what of that?

Rosmer. I mean, that such a relation—as this of ours—does it not presuppose a quiet, happy, peaceful life——?

Rebecca. What then?

Rosmer. But the life I must now look forward to is one of struggle and unrest and strong agitations. For I will live my life, Rebecca! I will not be crushed to earth by horrible possibilities. I will not have my course of life forced upon me, either by the living or by—any one else.

Rebecca. No, no—do not! Be an absolutely free man, Rosmer!

Rosmer. But can you not guess what is in my mind? Do you not know? Don't you see how I can best shake off all gnawing memories—all the unhappy past?

Rebecca. How?

Rosmer. By opposing to it a new, a living reality.

Rebecca (feeling for the chair-back). A living—— What do you mean?

Rosmer (comes nearer). Rebecca—if I were to ask you —will you be my second wife?

Rebecca (for a moment speechless, then cries out with joy). Your wife! Your——! I!

Rosmer. Come; let us try it. We two will be one. The place of the dead must stand empty no longer.

Rebecca. I—in Beata's place——!

Rosmer. Then she will be out of the saga—completely —for ever and ever.

Rebecca (softly, trembling). Do you believe that, Rosmer?

Rosmer. It must be so! It must! I cannot—I will not go through life with a dead body on my back. Help me to cast it off, Rebecca. And let us stifle all memories in freedom, in joy, in passion. You shall be to me the only wife I have ever had.

Rebecca (with self-command). Never speak of this again. I will never be your wife.

Rosmer. What! Never! Do you not think you could come to love me? Is there not already a strain of love in our friendship?

Rebecca (puts her hands over her ears as if in terror). Don't speak so, Rosmer! Don't say such things!

Rosmer (seizes her arm). Yes, yes—there is a growing promise in our relation. Oh, I can see that you feel it, too. Do you not, Rebecca?

Rebecca (once more firm and calm). Listen to me. I tell you—if you persist in this, I will go away from Rosmersholm.

Rosmer. Go away! You! You cannot. It is impossible.

Rebecca. It is still more impossible that I should be your wife. Never in this world can I marry you.

Rosmer (looks at her in surprise). You say "can"; and you say it so strangely. Why can you not?

Rebecca (seizes both his hands). Dear friend—both for your own sake and for mine—do not ask why. *(Lets go his hands).* Do not, Rosmer.

[*Goes towards the door on the left.*

Rosmer. Henceforth I can think of nothing but that one question—why?

Rebecca (turns and looks at him). Then it is all over.

Rosmer. Between you and me?

Rebecca. Yes.

Rosmer. It will never be all over between us two. You will never leave Rosmersholm.

Rebecca (with her hand on the door-handle). No, perhaps I shall not. But if you ask me again—it is all over.

Rosmer. All over? How——?

Rebecca. For then I will go the way that Beata went. Now you know it, Rosmer.

Rosmer. Rebecca——?

Rebecca (in the doorway, nods slowly). Now you know it. [*She goes out.*

Rosmer (stares, thunderstruck, at the door and says to himself). What—is—this?

ACT III

The sitting-room at Rosmersholm. The window and the entrance door are open. The sun is shining outside. Forenoon.

REBECCA WEST, *dressed as in the first Act, stands at the window, watering and arranging the flowers. Her crochet work lies in the armchair.* MADAM HELSETH *is moving about, dusting the furniture with a feather-brush.*

Rebecca (after a short silence). I can't understand the Pastor remaining so long upstairs to-day.

Madam Helseth. Oh, he often does that. But he'll soon be down now, I should think.

Rebecca. Have you seen anything of him?

Madam Helseth. I caught a glimpse of him when I went upstairs with his coffee. He was in his bedroom, dressing.

Rebecca. I asked because he was a little out of sorts yesterday.

Madam Helseth. He didn't look well. I wonder if there isn't something amiss between him and his brother-in-law.

Rebecca. What do you think it can be?

Madam Helseth. I couldn't say. Perhaps it's that Mortensgård that has been setting them against each other.

Rebecca. Likely enough.—Do you know anything of this Peter Mortensgård?

Madam Helseth. No indeed. How could you think so, Miss? A fellow like him?

Rebecca. Do you mean because he edits such a low paper?

Madam Helseth. Oh, it's not only that.—You must have heard, Miss, that he had a child by a married woman that had been deserted by her husband?

Rebecca. Yes, I have heard of it. But it must have been long before I came here.

Madam Helseth. It's true he was very young at the time; and she should have known better. He wanted to marry her, too; but of course he couldn't do that. And I don't say he hasn't paid dear for it.—But, good Lord, Mortensgård has got on in the world since those days. There's a many people run after him now.

Rebecca. Yes, most of the poor people bring their affairs to him when they're in any trouble.

Madam Helseth. Ah, and others, too, perhaps, besides the poor folk——

Rebecca (looks at her furtively). Indeed.

Madam Helseth (by the sofa, dusting away vigorously). Perhaps the last people you would think likely to, Miss.

Rebecca (busy with the flowers). Come, now, that's only an idea of yours, Madam Helseth. You can't be sure of what you're saying.

Madam Helseth. You think I can't, Miss? But I can tell you I am. Why—if you must know it—I once took a letter in to Mortensgård myself.

Rebecca (turning). No—did you?

Madam Helseth. Yes, indeed I did. And a letter that was written here at Rosmersholm, too.

Rebecca. Really, Madam Helseth?

Madam Helseth. Yes, that it was. And it was on fine paper, and there was a fine red seal on it, too.

Rebecca. And it was given to you to deliver? Then, my dear Madam Helseth, it's not difficult to guess who wrote it.

Madam Helseth. Well?

Rebecca. It must have been something that poor Mrs. Rosmer, in her morbid state——

Madam Helseth. It's you that say that, Miss, not me.

Rebecca. But what was in the letter? Oh, I forgot—— you can't know that.

Madam Helseth. H'm; what if I did know it, all the same?

Rebecca. Did she tell you what she was writing about?

Madam Helseth. No, she didn't exactly do that. But Mortensgård, when he'd read it, he began questioning me backwards and forwards and up and down, so that I soon guessed what was in it.

Rebecca. Then what do you think it was? Oh, my dear good Madam Helseth, do tell me.

Madam Helseth. Oh, no, Miss. Not for the whole world.

Rebecca. Oh, you can surely tell me. We two are such good friends.

Madam Helseth. Lord preserve me from telling you anything about that, Miss. I can only tell you that it was something horrible that they'd got the poor sick lady to believe.

Rebecca. Who had got her to believe it?

Madam Helseth. Wicked people, Miss West. Wicked people.

Rebecca. Wicked——?

Madam Helseth. Yes, I say it again. They must have been real wicked people.

Rebecca. And who do you think it could have been?

Madama Helseth. Oh, I know well enough what to think. But Lord forbid *I* should say anything. To be sure there's a certain lady in the town—h'm!

Rebecca. I can see that you mean Mrs. Kroll.

Madam Helseth. Ah, she's a fine one, she is. She has always been the great lady with me. And she's never had any too much love for you neither.

Rebecca. Do you think Mrs. Rosmer was in her right mind when she wrote that letter to Mortensgård?

Madam Helseth. It's a queer thing a person's mind, Miss. Clean out of her mind I don't think she was.

Rebecca. But she seemed to go distracted when she learned that she must always be childless. It was that that unsettled her reason.

Madam Helseth. Yes, poor lady, that was a dreadful blow to her.

Rebecca (takes up her crochet and sits in a chair by the window). But after all—don't you think it was a good thing for the Pastor, Madam Helseth?

Madam Helseth. What, Miss?

Rebecca. That there were no children. Don't you think so?

Madam Helseth. H'm, I'm sure I don't know what to say about that.

Rebecca. Oh, yes, believe me, it was fortunate for him. Pastor Rosmer is not the man to have crying children about his house.

Madam Helseth. Ah, Miss, little children don't cry at Rosmersholm.

Rebecca (looks at her). Don't cry?

Madam Helseth. No. As long as people can remember, children have never been known to cry in this house.

Rebecca. That's very strange.

Madam Helseth. Yes; isn't it? But it runs in the family. And then there's another strange thing. When they grow up, they never laugh. Never, as long as they live.

Rebecca. Why, how extraordinary——

Madam Helseth. Have you ever once heard or seen the Pastor laugh, Miss?

Rebecca. No—now that I think of it, I almost believe you are right. But I don't think any one laughs much in this part of the country.

Madam Helseth. No, they don't. They say it began at Rosmersholm. And then I suppose it spread round about, as if it was catching-like.

Rebecca. You are a very wise woman, Madam Helseth.

Madam Helseth. Oh, Miss, you musn't sit there and make fun of me. *(Listens.)* Hush, hush—here's the Pastor coming down. He doesn't like to see dusting going on.

[*She goes out to the right.*

[JOHANNES ROSMER, *with his hat and stick in his hand, enters from the hall.*

Rosmer. Good morning, Rebecca.

Rebecca. Good morning, dear. *(A moment after—crocheting.)* Are you going out?

Rosmer. Yes.

Rebecca. It's a beautiful day.

Rosmer. You didn't look in on me this morning.

Rebecca. No, I didn't. Not to-day.

Rosmer. Do you not intend to in future?

Rebecca. Oh, I don't know yet, dear.

Rosmer. Has anything come for me?

Rebecca. The "County News" has come.

Rosmer. The "County News"?

Rebecca. There it is on the table.

Rosmer (puts down his hat and stick). Is there anything——?

Rebecca. Yes.

Rosmer. And you didn't send it up?

Rebecca. You will read it soon enough.

Rosmer. Oh, indeed? *(Takes the paper and reads, standing by the table.)*—What!—"We cannot warn our readers too earnestly against unprincipled renegades." *(Looks at her.)* They call me a renegade, Rebecca.

Rebecca. They mention no names.

Rosmer. That makes no difference. *(Reads on.)* "Secret traitors to the good cause."—"Judas-natures, who make brazen confession of their apostasy as soon as they think the most convenient and—profitable moment has arrived." "Ruthless befouling of a name honoured through generations"—"in the confident hope of a suitable reward from the party in momentary power." *(Lays down the paper on the table.)* And they can say such things of me! —Men who have known me so long and so well! Things they themselves don't believe. Things they know there is not a word of truth in—they print them all the same.

Rebecca. That is not all.

Rosmer (takes up the paper again). "Inexperience and lack of judgment the only excuse"—"pernicious influence—possibly extending to matters which, for the present, we do not wish to make subjects of public discussion or accusation." *(Looks at her.)* What is this?

Rebecca. It is aimed at me, plainly enough.

Rosmer (lays down the paper). Rebecca,—this is the conduct of dishonourable men.

Rebecca. Yes, they need scarcely be so contemptuous of Mortensgård.

Rosmer (walks about the room). Something must be done. All that is good in human nature will go to ruin, if this is allowed to go on. But it shall not go on! Oh, what a joy—what a joy it would be to me to let a little light into all this gloom and ugliness!

Rebecca (rises). Ah, yes, Rosmer. In that you have a great and glorious object to live for.

Rosmer. Only think, if I could rouse them to see themselves as they are; teach them to repent and blush before their better natures; bring them together in mutal forbearance—in love, Rebecca!

Rebecca. Yes, put your whole strength into that, and you must succeed.

Rosmer. I think success must be possible. Oh, what a delight it would be then to live one's life! No more malignant wrangling; only emulation. All eyes fixed on the same goal. Every mind, every will pressing forward—upward—each by the path its nature prescribes for it. Happiness for all—through all. *(Happens to look out of the window, starts and says sadly.)* Ah! Not through me.

Rebecca. Not——? Not through you?

Rosmer. Nor for me.

Rebecca. Oh, Rosmer, do not let such doubts take hold of you.

Rosmer. Happiness—dear Rebecca—happiness is above all things the calm, glad certainty of innocence.

Rebecca (looks straight before her). Yes, innocence——

Rosmer. Oh, you cannot know what guilt means. But I——

Rebecca. You least of all!

Rosmer (points out of the window). The mill-race.

Rebecca. Oh, Rosmer——!

[MADAM HELSETH *looks in at the door.*

Madam Helseth. Miss West!

Rebecca. Presently, presently. Not now.

Madam Helseth. Only a word, Miss.

[REBECCA *goes to the door.* MADAM HELSETH *tells her something. They whisper together for a few moments.* MADAM HELSETH *nods and goes out.*

Rosmer (uneasily). Was it anything for me?

Rebecca. No, only something about the house-work.—You ought to go out into the fresh air, dear Rosmer. You should take a good long walk.

Rosmer (takes up his hat). Yes, come. Let us go together.

Rebecca. No, dear, I can't just now. You must go alone. But shake off all these gloomy thoughts. Promise me.

Rosmer. I am afraid I shall never shake them off.

Rebecca. Oh, that such baseless fancies should take so strong a hold of you——!

Rosmer. Not so baseless I am afraid, Rebecca. I lay awake all night thinking it over and over. Perhaps Beata saw clearly after all.

Rebecca. In what?

Rosmer. In her belief that I loved you, Rebecca.

Rebecca. Right in that!

Rosmer (lays his hat down on the table). The question that haunts me is this: were we two not deceiving ourselves all the time—when we called our relation friendship?

Rebecca. You mean that it might as well have been called——?

Rosmer. ——love. Yes, Rebecca, that is what I mean. Even while Beata was alive, all my thoughts were for you. It was you alone I longed for. It was when you were by my side that I felt the calm gladness of utter content. If you think it over, Rebecca—did we not feel for each other from the first a sort of sweet, secret child-love—desireless, dreamless? Was it not so with you? Tell me.

Rebecca (struggling with herself). Oh—I don't know what to answer.

Rosmer. And it was this close-linked life in and for each other that we took for friendship. No, Rebecca—our bond has been a spiritual marriage—perhaps from the very first. That is why there is guilt on my soul. I had no right to such happiness—it was a sin against Beata.

Rebecca. No right to live happily? Do you believe that, Rosmer?

Rosmer. She looked at our relation with the eyes of her love—judged it after the fashion of her love. Inevitably. Beata could not have judged otherwise than she did.

Rebecca. But how can you accuse yourself because of Beata's delusion?

Rosmer. It was love for me—her kind of love—that drove her into the mill-race. That is an immovable fact, Rebecca. And that is what I can never get over.

Rebecca. Oh, think of nothing but the great, beautiful task you have devoted your life to.

Rosmer (shakes his head). It can never be accomplished, dear. Not by me. Not after what I have come to know.

Rebecca. Why not by you?

Rosmer. Because no cause ever triumphs that has its origin in sin.

Rebecca (vehemently). Oh, these are only ancestral doubts—ancestral fears—ancestral scruples. They say the dead come back to Rosmersholm in the shape of rushing white horses. I think this shows that it is true.

Rosmer. Be that as it may; what does it matter, so long as I cannot rid myself of the feeling? And believe me, Rebecca, it is as I tell you. The cause that is to win a lasting victory must have for its champion a happy and innocent man.

Rebecca. Is happiness so indispensable to you, Rosmer?

Rosmer. Happiness? Yes, dear,—it is.

Rebecca. To you, who can never laugh?

Rosmer. Yes, in spite of that. Believe me, I have a great capacity for happiness.

Rebecca. Now go for your walk, dear. A good long walk. Do you hear?—See, here is your hat. And your stick, too.

Rosmer (takes both). Thanks. And you won't come with me?

Rebecca. No, no; I can't just now.

Rosmer. Very well, then. You are with me nonetheless.

[*He goes out by the entrance door.* REBECCA *waits a moment, cautiously watching his departure from behind the open door; then she goes to the door on the right.*

Rebecca (opens the door, and says in a low tone). Now, Madam Helseth. You can show him in now.

[*Goes towards the window.*

[*A moment after* RECTOR KROLL *enters from the right. He bows silently and formally, and keeps his hat in his hand.*

Kroll. He has gone out?

Rebecca. Yes.

Kroll. Does he usually stay out long?

Rebecca. Yes, he does. But one cannot count on him to-day. So if you don't care to meet him——

Kroll. No, no. It is you I want to speak to,—quite alone.

Rebecca. Then we had better not lose time. Sit down, Rector.

[*She sits in the easy-chair by the window.* RECTOR KROLL *sits on a chair beside her.*

Kroll. Miss West—you can scarcely imagine how deeply and painfully I have taken this to heart—this change in Johannes Rosmer.

Rebecca. We expected it would be so—at first.

Kroll. Only at first?

Rebecca. Rosmer was confident that sooner or later you would join him.

Kroll. I?

Rebecca. You and all his other friends.

Kroll. Ah, there you see! That shows the infirmity of his judgment in all that concerns men and practical life.

Rebecca. But after all—since he feels it a necessity to emancipate himself on all sides——

Kroll. Yes, but wait—that is just what I do not believe.

Rebecca. What do you believe, then?

Kroll. I believe that you are at the bottom of it all.

Rebecca. It is your wife who has put that in your head, Rector Kroll.

Kroll. No matter who has put it in my head. What is certain is that I feel a strong suspicion—an exceedingly strong suspicion—when I think things over and piece together all I know of your behaviour ever since you came here.

Rebecca (looks at him). I seem to recollect a time when you felt an exceedingly strong faith in me, dear Rector. I might almost call it a warm faith.

Kroll (in a subdued voice). Whom could you not bewitch—if you tried?

Rebecca. Did I try——?

Kroll. Yes, you did. I am no longer such a fool as to believe that there was any feeling in the matter. You simply wanted to get a footing at Rosmersholm—to strike root here—and in that I was to serve you. Now I see it.

Rebecca. You seem utterly to have forgotten that it was Beata who begged and implored me to come out here?

Kroll. Yes, when you had bewitched her to. Can the feeling she came to entertain for you be called friendship? It was adoration—almost idolatry. It developed into—what shall I call it?—a sort of desperate passion.—Yes, that is the right word for it.

Rebecca. Be so good as to recollect the state your sister was in. So far as I am concerned, I don't think any one can accuse me of being hysterical.

Kroll. No; that you certainly are not. But that makes you all the more dangerous to the people you want to get into your power. It is easy for you to weigh your acts and calculate consequences—just because your heart is cold.

Rebecca. Cold? Are you so sure of that?

Kroll. I am quite certain of it now. Otherwise you could never have lived here year after year without faltering in the pursuit of your object. Well, well—you have gained your end. You have got him and everything into your power. But in order to do so, you have not scrupled to make him unhappy.

Rebecca. That is not true. It is not I—it is you yourself that have made him unhappy.

Kroll. I?

Rebecca. Yes, when you led him to imagine that he was responsible for Beata's terrible end.

Kroll. Does he feel that so deeply, then?

Rebecca. How can you doubt it? A mind so sensitive as his——

Kroll. I thought that an emancipated man, so-called, was above all such scruples.—But there we have it! Oh, yes—I admit I knew how it would be. The descendant of the men that look down on us from these walls—how could we hope to cut himself adrift from all that has been handed down without a break from generation to generation?

Rebecca (looks down thoughtfully). Johannes Rosmer's spirit is deeply rooted in his ancestry. That is very certain.

Kroll. Yes, and you should have taken that fact into consideration, if you had felt any affection for him. But that sort of consideration was no doubt beyond you. There is such an immeasurable difference between your antecedents and his.

Rebecca. What antecedents do you mean?

Kross. I am speaking of your origin—your family antecedents, Miss West.

Rebecca. Oh, indeed! Yes, it is quite true that I come of very humble folk. Nevertheless——

Kroll. I am not thinking of rank and position. I allude to your moral antecedents.

Rebecca. Moral——? In what sense?

Kroll. The circumstances of your birth.

Rebecca. What do you mean?

Kroll. I only mention the matter because it accounts for your whole conduct.

Rebecca. I do not understand this. You must explain.

Kroll. I really did not suppose you could require an explanation. Otherwise it would have been very odd that you should have let Dr. West adopt you——

Rebecca (rises). Ah! Now I understand.

Kroll. ——and that you should have taken his name. Your mother's name was Gamvik.

Rebecca (walks across the room). My father's name was Gamvik, Rector Kroll.

Kroll. Your mother's business must have brought her very frequently into contact with the parish doctor.

Rebecca. Yes, it did.

Kroll. And then he takes you into his house—as soon as your mother dies. He treats you harshly; and yet you stay with him. You know that he won't leave you a half-penny—as a matter of fact, you only got a case full of books—and yet you stay on; you bear with him; you nurse him to the last.

Rebecca (stands by the table, looking scornfully at him). And you account for all this by assuming that there was something immoral—something criminal about my birth?

Kroll. I attribute your care for him to involuntary filial instinct. Indeed I believe your whole conduct is determined by your origin.

Rebecca (vehemently). But there is not a single word of truth in what you say! And I can prove it! Dr. West did not come to Finmark till after I was born.

Kroll. Excuse me, Miss West. He settled there the year before. I have assured myself of that.

Rebecca. You are mistaken, I say! You are utterly mistaken.

Kroll. You told me the day before yesterday that you were nine-and-twenty—in your thirtieth year.

Rebecca. Indeed! Did I say so?

Kroll. Yes, you did. And I can calculate from that——

Rebecca. Stop! You needn't calculate. I may as well tell you at once: I am a year older than I give myself out to be.

Kroll (smiles incredulously). Really! I am surprised! What can be the reason of that?

Rebecca. When I had passed twenty-five, it seemed to me I was getting altogether too old for an unmarried woman. And so I began to lie about my age.

Kroll. You? An emancipated woman! Have you prejudices about the age for marriage?

Rebecca. Yes, it was idiotic of me—idiotic and absurd,

But some folly or other will always cling to us, not to be shaken off. We are made so.

Kroll. Well, so be it; but my calculation may be right, nonetheless. For Dr. West was up there on a short visit the year before he got the appointment.

Rebecca (with a vehement outburst). It is not true!

Kroll. Is it not true?

Rebecca. No. My mother never spoke of any such visit.

Kroll. Did she not?

Rebecca. No, never. Nor Dr. West either; not a word about it.

Kroll. Might not that be because they both had reasons for suppressing a year? Just as you have done, Miss West. Perhaps it is a family foible.

Rebecca (walks about clenching and wringing her hands). It is impossible. You want to cheat me into believing it. This can never, never be true. It cannot! Never in this world——

Kroll (rises). My dear Miss West—why in heaven's name are you so terribly excited? You quite frighten me! What am I to think—to believe——?

Rebecca. Nothing! You are to think and believe nothing.

Kroll. Then you must really tell me how you can take this affair—this possibility—so terribly to heart.

Rebecca (controlling herself). It is perfectly simple, Rector Kroll. I have no wish to be taken for an illegitimate child.

Kroll. Indeed! Well, well, let us be satisfied with that explanation—in the meantime. But in that case you must still have a certain—prejudice on that point, too?

Rebecca. Yes, I suppose I have.

Kroll. Ah, I fancy it is much the same with most of what you call your "emancipation." You have read your self into a number of new ideas and opinions. You have got a sort of smattering of recent discoveries in various fields—discoveries that seem to overthrow certain principles which have hitherto been held impregnable and unassailable. But all this has only been a matter of the intellect, Miss West—a superficial acquisition. It has not passed into your blood.

Rebecca (thoughtfully). Perhaps you are right.

Kroll. Yes, look into your own mind, and you will see! And if this is the case with you, one may easily guess how it must be with Johannes Rosmer. It is sheer, unmitigated madness—it is running blindfold to destruction—for him to think of coming openly forward and confessing himself an apostate! Only think—a man of his sensitive nature! Imagine him disowned and persecuted by the circle of which he has always formed a part—exposed to ruthless attacks from all the best people in the community! He is not—he never can be the man to endure all that.

Rebecca. He must endure it! It is too late now for him to retreat.

Kroll. Not at all too late. By no means. What has happened can be hushed up—or at least explained away as a mere temporary aberration, however deplorable. But—one measure is certainly indispensable.

Rebecca. And what is that?

Kroll. You must get him to legalise the position, Miss West.

Rebecca. His position towards me?

Kroll. Yes. You must make him do that.

Rebecca. Then you absolutely cannot clear your mind of the idea that our position requires to be—legalised, as you call it?

Kroll. I would rather not go into the matter too closely. But I believe I have noticed that it is nowhere easier to break through all so-called prejudices than in—h'm——

Rebecca. In the relation between man and woman, you mean?

Kroll. Yes—to speak plainly—I think so.

Rebecca (wanders across the room and looks out at the window). I could almost say—I wish you were right, Rector Kroll.

Kroll. What do you mean by that? You say it so strangely.

Rebecca. Oh, well—please let us drop the subject. Ah,—there he comes.

Kroll. Already! Then I will go.

Rebecca (goes towards him). No—please stay. There is something I want you to hear.

Kroll. Not now. I don't feel as if I could bear to see him.

Rebecca. I beg you to stay. Do! If not, you will regret it by-and-by. It is the last time I shall ask you for anything.

Kroll (looks at her in surprise and puts down his hat). Very well, Miss West—so be it, then.

[*A short silence. Then* JOHANNES ROSMER *enters from the hall.*

Rosmer (sees the RECTOR, *and stops in the doorway).* What!—Are you here?

Rebecca. He did not wish to meet you, dear.*

Kroll (involuntarily). "Dear!"

Rebecca. Yes, Rector Kroll, Rosmer and I say "dear" to each other. That is one result of our "position."

Kroll. Was that what you wanted me to hear?

Rebecca. That—and a little more.

Rosmer (comes forward). What is the object of this visit?

* In the original, Rebecca here addresses Rosmer as *"du"* for the first time in Kroll's presence.

Kroll. I wanted to try once more to stop you and win you back to us.

Rosmer (points to the newspaper). After what appears in that paper?

Kroll. I did not write it.

Rosmer. Did you make the slightest effort to prevent its appearance?

Kroll. That would have been to betray the cause I serve. And, besides, it was not in my power.

Rebecca (tears the paper into shreds, crushes up the pieces and throws them behind the stove). There! Now it is out of sight. And let it be out of mind, too. For there will be nothing more of that sort, Rosmer.

Kroll. Ah, if you could only make sure of that!

Rebecca. Come, let us sit down, dear. All three of us. And then I will tell you everything.

Rosmer (seats himself mechanically). What has come over you, Rebecca? This unnatural calmness—what is it?

Rebecca. The calmness of resolution. *(Seats herself.)* Pray sit down, too, Rector.

[RECTOR KROLL *seats himself on the sofa.*

Rosmer. Resolution, you say? What resolution?

Rebecca. I am going to give you back what you require in order to live your life. Dear friend, you shall have your happy innocence back again!

Rosmer. What can you mean?

Rebecca. I have only to tell you something. That will be enough.

Rosmer. Well!

Rebecca. When I came down here from Finmark—along with Dr. West—it seemed to me that a great, wide new world was opening up before me. The Doctor had taught me all sorts of things—all the fragmentary knowledge of life that I possessed in those days. *(With a struggle and in a scarcely audible voice.)* And then——

Kroll. And then?

Rosmer. But Rebecca—I know all this.

Rebecca (mastering herself). Yes, yes—you are right. You know enough about this.

Kroll (looks hard at her). Perhaps I had better go.

Rebecca. No, please stay where you are, my dear Rector. *(To* ROSMER.*)* Well, you see, this was how it was—I wanted to take my share in the life of the new era that was dawning, with all its new ideas.—Rector Kroll told me one day that Ulric Brendel had had great influence over you while you were still a boy. I thought it must surely be possible for me to carry on his work.

Rosmer. You came here with a secret design——?

Rebecca. We two, I thought, should march onward in freedom, side by side. Ever onward. Ever farther and farther to the front. But between you and perfect emancipation there rose that dismal, insurmountable barrier.

Rosmer. What barrier do you mean?

Rebecca. I mean this, Rosmer: You could grow into freedom only in the clear, fresh sunshine—and here you were pining, sickening in the gloom of such a marriage.

Rosmer. You have never before spoken to me of my marriage in that tone.

Rebecca. No, I did not dare to, for I should have frightened you.

Kroll (nods to ROSMER*).* Do you hear that?

Rebecca (goes on). But I saw quite well where your deliverance lay—your only deliverance. And then I went to work.

Rosmer. Went to work? In what way?

Kroll. Do you mean that——?

Rebecca. Yes, Rosmer—— *(Rises.)* Sit still. You, too, Rector Kroll. But now it must out. It was not you, Rosmer. You are innocent. It was I that lured—that ended in luring Beata out into the paths of delusion——

Rosmer (springs up). Rebecca!

Kroll (rises from the sofa). The paths of delusion!

Rebecca. The paths—that led to the mill-race. Now you know it, both of you.

Rosmer (as if stunned). But I don't understand—— What is it she is saying? I don't understand a word——!

Kroll. Oh, yes, Rosmer, I am beginning to understand.

Rosmer. But what did you do? What can you possibly have told her? There was nothing—absolutely nothing to tell!

Rebecca. She came to know that you were working yourself free from all the old prejudices.

Rosmer. Yes, but that was not the case at that time.

Rebecca. I knew that it soon would be.

Kroll (nods to Rosmer*).* Aha!

Rosmer. And then? What more? I must know all now.

Rebecca. Some time after—I begged and implored her to let me go away from Rosmersholm.

Rosmer. Why did you want to go—then?

Rebecca. I did not want to go; I wanted to stay here, where I was. But I told her that it would be best for us all—that I should go away in time. I gave her to understand that if I stayed here any longer, I could not—I could not tell—what might happen.

Rosmer. Then this is what you said and did!

Rebecca. Yes, Rosmer.

Rosmer. This is what you call "going to work."

Rebecca (in a broken voice). I called it so, yes.

Rosmer (after a pause). Have you confessed all now, Rebecca?

Rebecca. Yes.

Kroll. Not all.

Rebecca (looks at him in fear). What more should there be?

Kroll. Did you not at last give Beata to understand that it was necessary—not only that it would be wisest, but that it was necessary—both for your own sake and Rosmer's, that you should go away somewhere—as soon as possible? Well?

Rebecca (low and indistinctly). Perhaps I did say something of the sort.

Rosmer (sinks into the armchair by the window). And this tissue of lies and deceit she—my unhappy, sick wife believed in! Believed in it so firmly! So immovably! *(Looks up at* Rebecca.*)* And she never turned to me. Never said one word to me! Oh, Rebecca,—I can see it in your face—you dissuaded her from it!

Rebecca. She had conceived a fixed idea that she, as a childless wife, had no right to be here. And then she imagined that it was her duty to you to efface herself.

Rosmer. And you—you did nothing to disabuse her of the idea?

Rebecca. No.

Kroll. Perhaps you confirmed her in it? Answer me! Did you not?

Rebecca. I believe she may have understood me so.

Rosmer. Yes, yes—and in everything she bowed before your will. And she did efface herself! *(Springs up.)* How could you—how could you play this ghastly game!

Rebecca. It seemed to me I had to choose between your life and hers, Rosmer.

Kroll (severely and impressively). That choice was not for you to make.

Rebecca (vehemently). You think then that I was cool and calculating and self-possessed all the time! I was not the same woman then that I am now, as I stand here telling it all. Besides, there are two sorts of will in us I believe! I wanted Beata away, by one means or another; but I never really believed that it would come to pass. As I felt my way forward, at each step I ventured, I seemed to hear something within me cry out: No farther! Not a step farther! And yet I could not stop. I had to venture the least little bit farther. Only one hair's-breadth more. And then one more—and always one more.—And then it happened.—That is the way such things come about.

[*A short silence.*

Rosmer (to Rebecca*).* What do you think lies before you now? After this?

Rebecca. Things must go with me as they will. It doesn't greatly matter.

Kroll. Not a word of remorse! Is it possible you feel none?

Rebecca (coldly putting aside his question). Excuse me, Rector Kroll—that is a matter which concerns no one but me. I must settle it with myself.

Kroll (to Rosmer*).* And this is the woman you are living under the same roof with—in the closest intimacy! *(Looks round at the pictures.)* Oh, if those that are gone could see us now!

Rosmer. Are you going back to town?

Kroll (takes up his hat). Yes. The sooner the better.

Rosmer (does the same). Then I will go with you.

Kroll. Will you? Ah, yes, I was sure we had not lost you for good.

Rosmer. Come then, Kroll! Come!

[*Both go out through the hall without looking at* Rebecca.

[*After a moment,* Rebecca *goes cautiously to the window and looks out through the flowers.*

Rebecca (speaks to herself under her breath). Not over the foot-bridge to-day either. He goes round. Never across the mill-race. Never. *(Leaves window.)* Well, well, well!

[*Goes and pulls the bell-rope; a moment after,* Madam Helseth *enters from the right.*

Madam Helseth. What is it, Miss?

Rebecca. Madam Helseth, would you be so good as to have my trunk brought down from the garret?

Madam Helseth. Your trunk?

Rebecca. Yes—the brown sealskin trunk, you know.

Madam Helseth. Yes, yes. But, Lord preserve us—are you going on a journey, Miss?

Rebecca. Yes—now I am going on a journey, Madam Helseth.

Madam Helseth. And immediately!

Rebecca. As soon as I have packed up.

Madam Helseth. Well, I've never heard the like of that! But you'll come back again soon, Miss, of course?

Rebecca. I shall never come back again.

Madam Helseth. Never! Dear Lord, what will things be like at Rosmersholm when you're gone, Miss? And the poor Pastor was just beginning to be so happy and comfortable.

Rebecca. Yes, but I have taken fright to-day, Madam Helseth.

Madam Helseth. Taken fright! Dear, dear! how was that?

Rebecca. I thought I saw something like a glimpse of white horses.

Madam Helseth. White horses! In broad daylight!

Rebecca. Oh, they are abroad early and late—the white horses of Rosmersholm. *(With a change of tone.)* Well, about the trunk, Madam Helseth.

Madam Helseth. Yes, yes. The trunk.

[*Both go out to the right.*

ACT IV

The sitting-room at Rosmersholm. Late evening. A lighted lamp, with a shade over it, on the table.
REBECCA WEST *stands by the table, packing some small articles in a hand-bag. Her cloak, hat and the white crocheted shawl are hanging over the back of the sofa.*
MADAM HELSETH *enters from the right.*

Madam Helseth (speaks in a low voice and appears ill at ease). All your things have been taken down, Miss. They are in the kitchen passage.

Rebecca. Very well. You have ordered the carriage?

Madam Helseth. Yes. The coachman wants to know what time he ought to be here.

Rebecca. About eleven o'clock, I think. The steamer starts at midnight.

Madam Helseth (hesitates a little). But the Pastor? If he shouldn't be home by that time?

Rebecca. I shall go all the same. If I don't see him, you can tell him that I will write to him—a long letter. Tell him that.

Madam Helseth. Yes, writing—that may be all very well. But, poor Miss West—I do think you should try to speak to him once more.

Rebecca. Perhaps so. And yet—perhaps not.

Madam Helseth. Well—that I should live to see this! I never thought of such a thing.

Rebecca. What did you think then, Madam Helseth?

Madam Helseth. Well, I certainly thought Pastor Rosmer was a more dependable man than this.

Rebecca. Dependable?

Madam Helseth. Yes, that's what *I* say.

Rebecca. Why, my dear Madam Helseth, what do you mean?

Madam Helseth. I mean what's right and true, Miss He shouldn't get out of it in this way, that he shouldn't.

Rebecca (looks at her). Come now, Madam Helseth, tell me plainly: what do you think is the reason I am going away?

Madam Helseth. Well, Heaven forgive us, I suppose it can't be helped, Miss. Ah, well, well, well! But I certainly don't think the Pastor's behaving handsome-like. Mortensgård had some excuse; for her husband was alive, so that they two couldn't marry, however much they wanted to. But as for the Pastor—h'm!

Rebecca (with a faint smile). Could you have believed such a thing of Pastor Rosmer and me?

Madam Helseth. No, never in this world. At least, I mean—not until to-day.

Rebecca. But to-day, then——?

Madam Helseth. Well,—after all the horrible things that they tell me the papers are saying about the Pastor——

Rebecca. Aha!

Madam Helseth. For the man that can go over to Mortensgård's religion—good Lord, I can believe anything of him.

Rebecca. Oh, yes, I suppose so. But what about me? What have you to say about me?

Madam Helseth. Lord preserve us, Miss—I don't see that there's much to be said against you. It's not so easy for a lone woman to be always on her guard, that's certain. —We're all of us human, Miss West.

Rebecca. That's very true, Madam Helseth. We are all of us human.—What are you listening to?

Madam Helseth (in a low voice). Oh, Lord,—if I don't believe that's him coming.

Rebecca (starts). After all then——? *(Resolutely.)* Well, well; so be it.

[JOHANNES ROSMER *enters from the hall.*

Rosmer (sees the hand-bag, etc., turns to REBECCA *and asks).* What does this mean?

Rebecca. I am going.

Rosmer. At once?

Rebecca. Yes. *(To* MADAM HELSETH.*)* Eleven o'clock, then.

Madam Helseth. Very well, Miss.

[*Goes out to the right.*

Rosmer (after a short pause). Where are you going to, Rebecca?

Rebecca. North, by the steamer.

Rosmer. North? What takes you to the North?

Rebecca. It was there I came from.

Rosmer. But you have no ties there now.

Rebecca. I have none here either.

Rosmer. What do you think of doing?

Rebecca. I don't know. I only want to have done with it all.

Rosmer. To have done with it?

Rebecca. Rosmersholm has broken me.

Rosmer (his attention aroused). Do you say that?

Rebecca. Broken me utterly and hopelessly.—I had a free and fearless will when I came here. Now I have bent my neck under a strange law.—From this day forth, I feel as if I had no courage for anything in the world.

Rosmer. Why not? What is the law that you say you have——?

Rebecca. Dear, don't let us talk of that just now.—What happened between you and the Rector?

Rosmer. We have made peace.

Rebecca. Ah, yes; so that was the end.

Rosmer. He gathered all our old friends together at his house. They have made it clear to me that the work of ennobling the minds of men—is not for me.—And besides, it is hopeless in itself, Rebecca.—I shall let it alone.

Rebecca. Yes, yes—perhaps it is best so.

Rosmer. Is that what you say now? Do you think so now?

Rebecca. I have come to think so—in the last few days.

Rosmer. You are lying, Rebecca.

Rebecca. Lying——!

Rosmer. Yes, you are lying. You have never believed in me. You have never believed that I was man enough to carry the cause through to victory.

Rebecca. I believed that we two together could do it.

Rosmer. That is not true. You thought that you yourself could do something great in life; and that you could use me to further your ends. I was to be a serviceable instrument to you—that is what you thought.

Rebecca. Listen to me, Rosmer——

Rosmer (seats himself listlessly on the sofa). Oh, what is the use? I see through it all now—I have been like a glove in your hands.

Rebecca. Listen, Rosmer. Hear what I have to say. It will be for the last time. *(Sits in a chair close to the sofa.)* I intended to write you all about it—when I was back in the North. But I daresay it is best that you should hear it at once.

Rosmer. Have you more confessions to make?

Rebecca. The greatest of all is to come.

Rosmer. The greatest?

Rebecca. What you have never suspected. What gives light and shade to all the rest.

Rosmer (shakes his head). I don't understand you at all.

Rebecca. It is perfectly true that I once schemed to gain a footing at Rosmersholm. I thought I could not fail to turn things to good account here. In one way or the other—you understand.

Rosmer. Well, you accomplished your ends.

Rebecca. I believe I could have accomplished anything, anything in the world—at that time. For I had still my fearless, free-born will. I knew no scruples—I stood in awe of no human tie.—But then began what has broken my will—and cowed me so pitiably for all my days.

Rosmer. What began? Do not speak in riddles.

Rebecca. It came over me,—this wild, uncontrollable passion——. Oh, Rosmer——!

Rosmer. Passion? You——! For what?

Rebecca. For you.

Rosmer (tries to spring up). What is this?

Rebecca (stops him). Sit still, dear; there is more to tell.

Rosmer. And you mean to say—that you have loved me—in that way!

Rebecca. I thought that it should be called love—then. Yes, I thought it was love. But it was not. It was what I said. It was a wild, uncontrollable passion.

Rosmer (with difficulty). Rebecca, is it really you—you yourself—that you are speaking of?

Rebecca. Yes, would you believe it, Rosmer?

Rosmer. Then it was because of this—under the influence of this—that you—that you "went to work," as you call it?

Rebecca. It came upon me like a storm on the sea. It was like one of the storms we sometimes have in the North in the winter time. It seizes you—and whirls you along with it—wherever it will. There is no resisting it.

Rosmer. And so it swept the unhappy Beata into the mill-race.

Rebecca. Yes; for it was a life-and-death struggle between Beata and me at that time.

Rosmer. Assuredly you were the strongest at Rosmersholm. Stronger than Beata and I together.

Rebecca. I judged you rightly in so far that I was sure I

could never reach you until you were a free man, both in circumstances—and in spirit.

Rosmer. But I don't understand you, Rebecca. You—yourself—your whole conduct is an insoluble riddle to me. I am free now—both in spirit and in circumstances. You have reached the very goal you aimed at from the first. And yet——

Rebecca. I have never stood farther from my goal than now.

Rosmer. And yet I say—when I asked you yesterday—begged you to be my wife—you cried out, as if in fear, that it could never be.

Rebecca. I cried out in despair, Rosmer.

Rosmer. Why?

Rebecca. Because Rosmersholm has sapped my strength. My old fearless will has had its wings clipped here. It is crippled! The time is past when I had courage for anything in the world. I have lost the power of action, Rosmer.

Rosmer. Tell me how this has come about.

Rebecca. It has come about through my life with you.

Rosmer. But how? How?

Rebecca. When I was left alone with you here,—and when you had become yourself again——

Rosmer. Yes, yes?

Rebecca. ——for you were never quite yourself so long as Beata lived——

Rosmer. I am afraid you are right there.

Rebecca. But when I found myself sharing your life here,—in quiet—in solitude,—when you showed me all your thoughts without reserve—every tender and delicate feeling, just as it came to you—then the great change came over me. Little by little, you understand. Almost imperceptibly—but at last with such overwhelming force that it reached to the depths of my soul.

Rosmer. Oh, is this true, Rebecca?

Rebecca. All the rest—the horrible sense-intoxicated desire—passed far, far away from me. All the whirling passions settled down into quiet and silence. Rest descended on my soul—a stillness as on one of our northern bird-cliffs under the midnight sun.

Rosmer. Tell me more of this. Tell me all you can.

Rebecca. There is not much more, dear. Only this—it was love that was born in me. The great self-denying love, that is content with life, as we two have lived it together.

Rosmer. Oh, if I had only had the faintest suspicion of all this!

Rebecca. It is best as it is. Yesterday—when you asked me if I would be your wife—I cried out with joy——

Rosmer. Yes, did you not, Rebecca! I thought that was the meaning of your cry.

Rebecca. For a moment, yes. I had forgotten myself. It was my old buoyant will that was struggling to be free. But it has no energy left now—no power of endurance.

Rosmer. How do you account for what has happened to you?

Rebecca. It is the Rosmer view of life—or your view of life, at any rate—that has infected my will.

Rosmer. Infected?

Rebecca. And made it sick. Enslaved it to laws that had no power over me before. You—life with you—has ennobled my mind——

Rosmer. Oh, that I could believe it!

Rebecca. You may safely believe it! The Rosmer view of life ennobles. But—— *(Shaking her head.)* But—but——

Rosmer. But——? Well?

Rebecca. ——but it kills happiness.

Rosmer. Do you think so, Rebecca?

Rebecca. My happiness, at any rate.

Rosmer. Yes, but are you so certain of that? If I were to ask you again now——? If I were to beg and entreat you——?

Rebecca. Dear,—never speak of this again! It is impossible——! For you must know, Rosmer, I have a—a past behind me.

Rosmer. More than what you have told me?

Rebecca. Yes. Something different and something more.

Rosmer (with a faint smile). Is it not strange, Rebecca? Some such idea has crossed my mind now and then.

Rebecca. It has? And yet——? Even so——?

Rosmer. I never believed it. I only played with it—in my thoughts, you understand.

Rebecca. If you wish it, I will tell you all, at once.

Rosmer (turning it off). No, no! I will not hear a word. Whatever it may be—I can forget it.

Rebecca. But I cannot.

Rosmer. Oh, Rebecca——!

Rebecca. Yes, Rosmer—this is the terrible part of it: that now, when all life's happiness is within my grasp—my heart is changed, and my own past cuts me off from it.

Rosmer. Your past is dead, Rebecca. It has no hold on you any more—it is no part of you—as you are now.

Rebecca. Oh, you know that these are only phrases, dear. And innocence? Where am I to get that from?

Rosmer (sadly). Ah,—innocence.

Rebecca. Yes, innocence. That is the source of peace and happiness. That was the vital truth you were to implant in the coming generation of happy noble-men——

Rosmer. Oh, don't remind me of that. It was only an abortive dream, Rebecca—an immature idea, that I myself no longer believe in.—Ah, no, we cannot be ennobled from without, Rebecca.

Rebecca (softly). Not even by tranquil love, Rosmer?

Rosmer (thoughtfully). Yes—that would be the great thing—the most glorious in life, almost—if it were so. *(Moves uneasily.)* But how can I be certain of that? How convince myself?

Rebecca. Do you not believe me, Rosmer?

Rosmer. Oh, Rebecca—how can I believe in you, fully? You who have all this while been cloaking, concealing such a multitude of things!—Now you come forward with something new. If you have a secret purpose in all this, tell me plainly what it is. Is there anything you want to gain by it? You know that I will gladly do everything I can for you.

Rebecca (wringing her hands). Oh this killing doubt——! Rosmer—Rosmer——!

Rosmer. Yes, is it not terrible, Rebecca? But I cannot help it. I shall never be able to shake off the doubt. I can never be absolutely sure that you are mine in pure and perfect love.

Rebecca. Is there nothing in the depths of your own heart that bears witness to the transformation in me? And tells you that it is due to you—and you alone?

Rosmer. Oh, Rebecca—I no longer believe in my power of transforming any one. My faith in myself is utterly dead. I believe neither in myself nor in you.

Rebecca (looks darkly at him). Then how will you be able to live your life?

Rosmer. That I don't know. I cannot imagine how. I don't think I can live it.—And I know of nothing in the world that is worth living for.

Rebecca. Oh, life—life will renew itself. Let us hold fast to it, Rosmer.—We shall leave it soon enough.

Rosmer (springs up restlessly). Then give me my faith again! My faith in you, Rebecca! My faith in your love! Proof! I must have proof!

Rebecca. Proof? How can I give you proof——?

Rosmer. You must! *(Walks across the room.)* I cannot bear this desolation—this horrible emptiness—this—this—— [*A loud knock at the hall door.*

Rebecca (starts up from her chair). Ah—did you hear that?

[*The door opens.* Ulric Brendel *enters. He has a white shirt on, a black coat and a good pair of boots, with his trousers tucked into them. Otherwise he is dressed as in the first Act. He looks excited.*

Rosmer. Ah, is it you, Mr. Brendel?

Brendel. Johannes, my boy—hail—and farewell!

Rosmer. Where are you going so late?

Brendel. Downhill.

Rosmer. How——?

Brendel. I am going homewards, my beloved pupil. I am home-sick for the mighty Nothingness.

Rosmer. Something has happened to you, Mr. Brendel! What is it?

Brendel. So you observe the transformation? Yes—well you may. When I last set foot in these halls—I stood before you as a man of substance and slapped my breast-pocket.

Rosmer. Indeed! I don't quite understand——

Brendel. But as you see me this night, I am a deposed monarch on the ash-heap that was my palace.

Rosmer. If there is anything *I* can do for you——

Brendel. You have preserved your child-like heart, Johannes. Can you grant me a loan?

Rosmer. Yes, yes, most willingly!

Brendel. Can you spare me an ideal or two?

Rosmer. What do you say?

Brendel. One or two cast-off ideals. It would be an act of charity. For I'm cleaned out, my boy. Ruined, beggared.

Rebecca. Have you not delivered your lecture?

Brendel. No, seductive lady. What do you think? Just as I am standing ready to pour forth the horn of plenty, I make the painful discovery that I am bankrupt.

Rebecca. But all your unwritten works——?

Brendel. For five-and-twenty years I have sat like a

miser on his double-locked treasure-chest. And then yesterday—when I open it and want to display the treasure—there's none there! The teeth of time had ground it into dust. There was nix and nothing in the whole concern.

Rosmer. But are you so sure of that?

Brendel. There's no room for doubt, my dear fellow. The President has convinced me of it.

Rosmer. The President?

Brendel. Well, well—His Excellency then. *Ganz nach Belieben.*

Rosmer. What do you mean?

Brendel. Peter Mortensgård, of course.

Rosmer. What?

Brendel (mysteriously). Hush, hush, hush! Peter Mortensgård is the lord and leader of the future. Never have I stood in a more august presence. Peter Mortensgård has the secret of omnipotence. He can do whatever he will.

Rosmer. Oh, don't believe that.

Brendel. Yes, my boy! For Peter Mortensgård never wills more than he can do. Peter Mortensgård is capable of living his life without ideals. And that, do you see—that is just the mighty secret of action and of victory. It is the sum of the whole world's wisdom. *Basta!*

Rosmer (in a low voice). Now I understand—why you leave here poorer than you came.

Brendel. Bien! Then take a *Beispiel* by your ancient teacher. Rub out all that he once imprinted on your mind. Build not thy house on shifting sand. And look ahead—and feel your way—before you build on this exquisite creature, who here lends sweetness to your life.

Rebecca. Is it me you mean?

Brendel. Yes, my fascinating mermaid.

Rebecca. Why am I not to be built on?

Brendel (comes a step nearer). I gather that my former pupil has a great cause to carry forward to victory.

Rebecca. What then——?

Brendel. Victory is assured. But—mark me well—on one indispensable condition.

Rebecca. Which is——?

Brendel (taking her gently by the wrist). That the woman who loves him shall gladly go out into the kitchen and hack off her tender, rosy-white little finger—here—just here at the middle joint. Item, that the aforesaid loving woman—again gladly—shall slice off her incomparably-moulded left ear. *(Lets her go and turns to* ROSMER.*)* Farewell, my conquering Johannes.

Rosmer. Are you going now? In the dark night?

Brendel. The dark night is best. Peace be with you.

[*He goes. There is a short silence in the room.*

Rebecca (breathes heavily). Oh, how close and sultry it is here!

[*Goes to the window, opens it and remains standing by it.*

Rosmer (sits down in the armchair by the stove). There is nothing else for it after all, Rebecca. I see it. You must go away.

Rebecca. Yes, I see no choice.

Rosmer. Let us make the most of our last hour. Come here and sit by me.

Rebecca (goes and sits on the sofa). What do you want to say to me, Rosmer?

Rosmer. First, I want to tell you that you need not feel any anxiety about your future.

Rebecca (smiles). H'm, my future.

Rosmer. I have long ago arranged for everything. Whatever may happen, you are provided for.

Rebecca. That, too, my dear one?

Rosmer. You might surely have known that.

Rebecca. It is many a long day since I have given a thought to such things.

Rosmer. Yes, yes—you thought things would always remain as they were between us.

Rebecca. Yes, I thought so.

Rosmer. So did I. But if I were to go——

Rebecca. Oh, Rosmer—you will live longer than I.

Rosmer. Surely my worthless life lies in my own hands.

Rebecca. What is this? You are never thinking of——!

Rosmer. Do you think it would be so strange? After this pitiful, lamentable defeat! I, who was to have borne a great cause on to victory—have I not fled from the battle before it was well begun?

Rebecca. Take up the fight again, Rosmer! Only try —and you shall see, you will conquer. You will ennoble hundreds—thousands of minds. Only try!

Rosmer. Oh, Rebecca—I, who no longer believe in my own mission!

Rebecca. But your mission has stood the test already. You have ennobled one human being at least—me you have ennobled for the rest of my days.

Rosmer. Oh—if I dared believe you.

Rebecca (pressing her hands together). Oh, Rosmer,—do you know of nothing—nothing that could make you believe it?

Rosmer (starts as if in fear). Don't speak of that! Keep away from that, Rebecca! Not a word more.

Rebecca. Yes, this is precisely what we must speak about. Do you know of anything that would kill the doubt? For *I* know of nothing in the world.

Rosmer. It is well for you that you do not know.—It is well for both of us.

Rebecca. No, no, no.—I will not be put off in this way! If you know of anything that would absolve me in your eyes, I claim as my right to be told of it.

Rosmer (as if impelled against his will to speak). Then let us see. You say that a great love is in you; that through me your mind has been ennobled. Is it so? Is your reckoning just, Rebecca? Shall we try to prove the sum? Say?

Rebecca. I am ready.

Rosmer. At any time?

Rebecca. Whenever you please. The sooner the better.

Rosmer. Then let me see, Rebecca,—if you for my sake —this very evening—— *(Breaks off.)* Oh, no, no, no!

Rebecca. Yes, Rosmer! Yes! Tell me, and you shall see.

Rosmer. Have you the courage—have you the will—gladly, as Ulric Brendel said—for my sake, to-night—gladly —to go the same way that Beata went?

Rebecca (rises slowly from the sofa; almost voiceless). Rosmer——!

Rosmer. Yes, Rebecca—that is the question that will for ever haunt me—when you are gone. Every hour in the day it will return upon me. Oh, I seem to see you before my very eyes. You are standing out on the foot-bridge—right in the middle. Now you are bending forward over the railing—drawn dizzily downwards, downwards towards the rushing water! No—you recoil. You have not the heart to do what she dared.

Rebecca. But if I had the heart to do it? And the will to do it gladly? What then?

Rosmer. I should have to believe you then. I should recover my faith in my mission. Faith in my power to ennoble human souls. Faith in the human soul's power to attain nobility.

Rebecca (takes up her shawl slowly and puts it over her head; says with composure). You shall have your faith again.

Rosmer. Have you the will and the courage—for this, Rebecca?

Rebecca. That you shall see to-morrow—or afterwards —when they find my body.

Rosmer (puts his hand to his forehead). There is a horrible fascination in this——!

Rebecca. For I don't want to remain down there. Not longer than necessary. You must see that they find me.

Rosmer (springs up). But all this—is nothing but madness. Go—or stay! I will take your bare word this time, too.

Rebecca. Phrases, Rosmer! Let us have no more cowardly subterfuges, dear! How can you believe me on my bare word after this day?

Rosmer. I shrink from seeing your defeat, Rebecca!

Rebecca. It will be no defeat.

Rosmer. Yes, it will. You will never bring yourself to go Beata's way.

Rebecca. Do you think not?

Rosmer. Never. You are not like Beata. You are not under the dominion of a distorted view of life.

Rebecca. But I am under the dominion of the Rosmersholm view of life—now. What I have sinned—it is fit that I should expiate.

Rosmer (looks at her fixedly). Is that your point of view?

Rebecca. Yes.

Rosmer (with resolution). Well, then, *I* stand firm in our emancipated view of life, Rebecca. There is no judge over us; and therefore we must do justice upon ourselves.

Rebecca (misunderstanding him). Yes, that is true—that, too. My going away will save what is best in you.

Rosmer. Oh, there is nothing left to save in me.

Rebecca. Yes, there is. But I—after to-day, I should only be a sea-troll dragging down the ship that is to carry you forward. I must go overboard. Why should I remain here in the world, trailing after me my own crippled life? Why brood and brood over the happiness that my past has forfeited for ever? I must give up the game, Rosmer.

Rosmer. If you go—I go with you.

Rebecca (smiles almost imperceptibly, looks at him and says more softly). Yes, come with me—and see——

Rosmer. I go with you, I say.

Rebecca. To the foot-bridge, yes. You know you never dare go out upon it.

Rosmer. Have you noticed that?

Rebecca (sadly and brokenly). Yes.—It was that that made my love hopeless.

Rosmer. Rebecca,—now I lay my hand on your head—*(Does so)*—and I wed you as my true wife.

Rebecca (takes both his hands and bows her head towards his breast). Thanks, Rosmer. *(Lets him go.)* And now I will go—gladly.

Rosmer. Man and wife should go together.

Rebecca. Only to the bridge, Rosmer.

Rosmer. Out on to it, too. As far as you go—so far shall I go with you. For now I dare.

Rebecca. Are you absolutely certain—that this way is the best for you?

Rosmer. I am certain that it is the only way.

Rebecca. If you were deceiving yourself? If it were only a delusion? One of those white horses of Rosmersholm.

Rosmer. It may be so. For we can never escape from them—we of this house.

Rebecca. Then stay, Rosmer!

Rosmer. The husband shall go with his wife, as the wife with her husband.

Rebecca. Yes, but first tell me this: Is it you who follow me? Or is it I who follow you?

Rosmer. We shall never think that question out.

Rebecca. But I should like to know.

Rosmer. We go with each other, Rebecca—I with you and you with me.

Rebecca. I almost think that is the truth.

Rosmer. For now we two are one.

Rebecca. Yes. We are one. Come! We go gladly.

[*They go out hand in hand through the hall and are seen to turn to the left. The door remains open. The room stands empty for a little while. Then the door to the right is opened by* MADAM HELSETH.

Madam Helseth. Miss West—the carriage is—— *(Looks round.)* Not here? Out together at this time of night? Well—I must say——! H'm! *(Goes out into the hall, looks round and comes in again.)* Not on the garden seat. Ah, well, well. *(Goes to the window and looks out.)* Oh, good God! that white thing there——! My soul! They're both of them out on the bridge! God forgive the sinful creatures—if they're not in each other's arms! *(Shrieks aloud.)* Oh—down—both of them! Out into the mill-race! Help! Help! *(Her knees tremble; she holds on to the chair-back, shaking all over; she can scarcely get the words out.)* No. No help here.—The dead wife has taken them.

PEER GYNT
(1867)

CHARACTERS

AASE, *widow of John Gynt, a peasant.*
PEER GYNT, *her son.*
Two Old Women with corn-sacks.
ASLAK, *a blacksmith.*
Wedding Guests, a Steward at the Wedding, a Fiddler, etc.
A Stranger and his Wife.
SOLVEIG *and little* HELGA, *their daughters.*
The Owner of Hægstad Farm.
INGRID, *his daughter.*
The Bridegroom and his Parents.
Three Cowherd Girls. A Woman in Green.
The TROLL KING. *Several Trolls of his Court.*
Troll Boys and Girls. Two Witches. Hobgoblins, Brownies, Elves, etc.
An Ugly Urchin. A Voice in the Gloom. Birds' Cries.
KARI, *a cotter's wife.*
MR. COTTON, MONSIEUR BALLON, HERR VON EBERKOPF, HERR TRUMPETERSTRAALE, *tourists.*
A Thief and a Receiver of Stolen Goods.
ANITRA, *daughter of a Bedouin Chief.*
Arabs, Female Slaves, Dancing Girls, etc.
The Statue of Memnon (with song). The Sphinx at Gizeh (dumb).
PROFESSOR BEGRIFFENFELDT, *Ph.D., in charge of the Lunatic Asylum at Cairo.*
Lunatics with their Keepers.

HUHU, *a language-reformer from the Malabar coast.*
HUSSEIN, *an Eastern Secretary of State.*
A Fellah, carrying a royal mummy.
A Norwegian Skipper and his Crew.
A Strange Passenger.
A Priest.
A Funeral Party.
A Button-Moulder.
A Thin Man.

The action, which begins in the early years of the century and ends somewhere about our own day [1867], takes place partly in the Gudbrandsdal and on the surrounding mountain-tops, partly on the coast of Morocco, in the Sahara Desert, in the Cairo Lunatic Asylum, at Sea, etc.

ACT I

SCENE I

SCENE.—*The wooded mountain-side near* AASE'S *farm, with a stream rushing past. On the farther bank stands an old mill. It is a hot summer's day.* PEER GYNT, *a sturdy youth of twenty, comes down the path, followed by his mother* AASE, *who is short and slight. She is scolding him angrily.*

Aase. Peer, you're lying!

Peer Gynt (without stopping). No, I'm not!

Aase. Well, then, will you swear it's true?

Peer Gynt. Swear? Why should I?

Aase. Ah, you daren't! Your whole tale's a pack of lies!

Peer Gynt. Every blessed word is true!

Aase (facing him). I wonder you can face your mother! First of all, just when the work is at busiest, off you go to prowl about the hills for weeks after reindeer in the snow; come back with your clothes in rags, game-bag empty—and no gun! Then you have the cheek to think you can make your mother swallow such a pack of lies as this about your hunting!—Tell me, then, where you found this precious buck?

Peer Gynt. West of Gendin.

Aase (with a scornful laugh). I dare say!

Peer Gynt. I was leeward of the blast, and behind a clump of trees he was scraping in the snow for some moss——

Aase (as before). Oh, yes, no doubt!

Peer Gynt. I stood and listened, held my breath, heard the scraping of his hoof, saw the antlers of his horns; then upon my belly crawled carefully between the rocks; peeped from cover of the stones— Such a buck, so sleek and fat, I suppose was never seen!

Aase. I expect not!

Peer Gynt. Then I fired! Down the buck came on the ground! But the moment he had fallen I was up astride his back, on his left ear got my grip and was just in act of thrusting with my knife into his gullet just behind his head —when, hi! with a scream the ugly beggar scrambled up upon his feet. From my hand his sudden back-throw jerked my hunting-knife and scabbard, pinned me to his loins and held me by the legs between his antlers like a pair of mighty pincers; then he rushed with bounds gigantic right along the ridge of Gendin!

Aase (involuntarily). Christ in Heaven——!

Peer Gynt. Have you ever been upon the ridge at Gendin? Fully half a mile it stretches, at the top as sheer and narrow as a scythe-blade. Looking downward—past the slopes and past the glaciers, past the grey ravines and gullies —either side you see the water wrapped in dark and gloomy slumber half a mile at least beneath you. Right along it he and I clove our passage through the air. Never rode I such a steed! Far ahead the peaks were sparkling as we rushed along. Beneath us in the void the dusky eagles fell away like motes in sunshine; you could see the ice-floes breaking on the banks, yet hear no murmur. But the sprites that turn us dizzy danced and sang and circled round us—I could hear and seemed to see them!

Aase (swaying as if giddy). Heaven help us!

Peer Gynt. On a sudden, on the precipice's edge, from the hole where it lay hidden almost at the reindeer's feet, up a ptarmigan rose, cackling, flapping with its wings in terror. Then the reindeer, madly swerving, gave a bound sky-high that sent us plunging o'er the edge and downwards. *(*AASE *totters and grasps a tree-trunk.* PEER GYNT *continues.)* Gloomy precipice behind us!—Fathomless abyss below us! First through clouds of mist we hurtled, then a flock of gulls we scattered wheeling through the air and screaming. Downward still and ever downwards! But beneath us something glistened whitish, like a reindeer's belly. Mother, 'twas our own reflection mirrored in the lake beneath us, rushing up, it seemed, to meet us just as swiftly and as madly as we downwards rushed towards it.

Aase (gasping for breath). Peer! God help me——! Tell me quickly!

Peer Gynt. Buck from air and buck from water met with mighty splash together, scattering the foam around us. Then at last we somehow managed to the northern shore to struggle; Buck, he swam and dragged me after—so I got home——

Aase. But where's the reindeer?

Peer Gynt. I expect he's where I left him—— *(Snaps his fingers, turns on his heel and adds):* If you find him, you may keep him!

Aase. And your neck you haven't broken? Nor your legs? Nor smashed your backbone? Praise and thanks to God be given for His goodness that has saved you! There's a rent across your breeches, it is true; but that is scarcely worth a mention when one thinks what the harm might well have been from a leap like that of yours—— *(She suddenly pauses, stares at him with open mouth, seems to struggle for speech and at last breaks out.)* Oh, you lying little devil!—Christ above us, what a liar! All that rigmarole you told me is the tale of Gudbrand Glesnë that I heard when I was twenty. 'Twas to him that all this happened, not to you, you——

Peer Gynt. Yes, it did; history repeats itself.

Aase. Lies, I know, can be so furbished and disguised in gorgeous wrappings that their skinny carcasses not a soul would recognize. That's what you've been doing now, with your wonderful adventures—eagles' wings, and all that nonsense—making up a pack of lies, tales of breathless risk and danger, till one can no longer tell what one knows and what one doesn't.

Peer Gynt. If a man said that to me, I would beat him to a jelly.

Aase (in tears). Would to God that I were dead and buried in the cold black earth! Prayers and tears have no effect. You're a hopeless ne'er-do-well!

Peer Gynt (in tears). Dearest pretty little mother, every word you say is true; so be gay and happy——

Aase. Pshaw! Don't talk nonsense. How could I be happy, if I wanted to, with such a pig as you for son? Don't you think it's pretty hard for a poor weak widow never to feel anything but shame? *(Weeps again.)* How much is there left of all that your grandfather enjoyed in his days of comfort? Where are the well-filled money-bags left by good old Rasmus Gynt? 'Twas your father emptied them, pouring money out like sand—buying land in all directions—gilded coach to ride about in. Where's the stuff so freely wasted at the famous winter banquet, when each guest sent glass and bottle crash against the wall behind him?

Peer Gynt. Where are the snows of yesteryear?

Aase. Hold your tongue when I am speaking! See the farm-house—scarce a window but is smashed and stuffed with dish-clout; scarce a hedge or fence is standing; no protection for the cattle from the wind and wet; the meadows and the fields all lying fallow; every month distraint on something——

Peer Gynt. That's enough of dismal wailing! Often when our luck's been drooping it has grown as strong as ever.

Aase. Where it grew, the soil is poisoned. Peer, you certainly don't lack good opinion of yourself. You are just as brisk and bumptious, just as pert, as when the Parson who had come from Copenhagen asked you what your Christian name was, telling you that where he came from lots of men of highest station would be glad to be as clever; and your father was so grateful for his amiable praises that a horse and sledge he gave him. Ah, me! All went well in those days. Parsons, Captains and such people, dropping in to see us daily—filling up with drink and victuals until they were nearly bursting. But it's when your fortunes alter that you get to know your neighbours. Since the day when "rich John Gynt" took the road with pedlar's pack, not a soul has e'er been near us. *(Wipes her eyes with her apron.)* You're a stout and strapping fellow—you should be a staff supporting your old mother in her troubles. You should work the farm for profit and look after all the little that your father left behind him. *(Weeps again.)* Heaven knows, it's precious little use you've been to me, you rascal. When you are at home, you're loafing by the fire, or grubbing idly in the ashes and the embers; when you're in the town you frighten all the girls you meet at dances, so that I'm ashamed to own you—fighting with the lowest tramps——

Peer Gynt (moving away from her). Let me be!

Aase (following him). Can you deny you were foremost in the brawling in that dog-fight of a scrimmage down at Lundë? Who but you cracked the blacksmith Aslak's arm? Or at any rate disjointed one of his ten fingers for him?

Peer Gynt. Who has stuffed you up with that?

Aase (hotly). Why, the cotter heard his howls!

Peer Gynt (rubbing his elbow). Yes—but it was I that howled.

Aase. What!

Peer Gynt. Yes, mother, *I* got thrashed.

Aase. What?

Peer Gynt. Well, he's a lusty chap.

Aase. Who is?

Peer Gynt. Aslak—as I felt!

Aase. Shame! I'd like to spit upon you! To let such a scurvy swiller, such a worthless drunken rascal, beat you! *(Weeps again.)* Often I've endured shame and scorn on your account, but that this disgrace should happen is the very worst of all. If he *is* a lusty fellow, need that mean you're a weakling?

Peer Gynt (with a laugh). Well, it doesn't seem to matter if I beat, or if I'm beaten—either way you start your wailing. You may cheer up——

Aase. Are you lying now again?

Peer Gynt. Yes, just this once; so you may as well stop crying. *(Clenches his left hand.)* See, 'twas with this pair of pincers that I bent the blacksmith double, while my right hand was my hammer——

Aase. Oh, you brawler! You will bring me to my grave by your behaviour!

Peer Gynt. Nonsense! You're worth something better—better twenty thousand times! Little, homely, dainty mother, just believe what I am saying. All the town shall do you honour; only wait till I have done something—something really great!

Aase (contemptuously). You!

Peer Gynt. Who knows what lies before him!

Aase. If you ever know enough to mend your breeches when they're torn, 'tis the most that I could hope for!

Peer Gynt (hotly). I'll be a King, an Emperor!

Aase. Oh, God help me! Now he's losing what was left him of his wits!

Peer Gynt. Yes, I shall! Just give me time!

Aase. Of course! As the old proverb runs, "Everything comes to him that waits."

Peer Gynt. Mother, you shall see.

Aase. Be quiet! You are as mad as mad can be. After all, it's true enough something might have come of you if you'd thought of something else but your stupid lies and nonsense. Hægstad's daughter fancied you, and you might have won the game if you'd rightly gone to work——

Peer Gynt. Do you think so?

Aase. The old man is too weak to stand against her. He is obstinate enough in a way; but in the end it is Ingrid takes the lead, and where *she* goes, step by step the old hunks comes stumbling after. *(Begins to cry again.)* Ah, Peer—a richly dowered girl, heir to his lands, just think of it. You might, if only you had liked, in bridegroom's finery be dressed instead of in these dirty rags!

Peer Gynt (quickly). Come on, I'll be a suitor now.

Aase. Where?

Peer Gynt. Why, at Hægstad!

Aase. Ah, poor boy, the right of way is barred to you.

Peer Gynt. What do you mean?

Aase. Alas, alas! You've lost the moment—lost your chance——

Peer Gynt. How's that?

Aase (sobbing). While you were on the hills, riding your reindeer through the air, Mads Moen went and won the girl.

Peer Gynt. What? He? That guy the girls all laugh at?

Aase. Yes. Now she's betrothed to him.

Peer Gynt. Just wait till I have harnessed up the cart—— *(Turns to go.)*

Aase. You needn't take the trouble. The wedding is to-morrow.

Peer Gynt. Pooh! I'll get there by this evening.

Aase. Fie! Do you want to make things worse? Just think how everyone will mock us!

Peer Gynt. Cheer up! All will turn our right. *(Shouting and laughing at the same time.)* No, mother! We won't take the cart; we haven't time to put the mare in.

[*Lifts her off her feet.*

Aase. Let me alone!

Peer Gynt. No, in my arms you shall be carried to the wedding! [*Wades out into the water.*

Aase. Help! Help! Oh, Heaven protect me!—Peer, we'll drown——

Peer Gynt. Oh, no, we shan't—I'm born to meet a better death.

Aase. That's true; you'll probably be hanged. *(Pulls his hair.)* You beast!

Peer Gynt. You'd best keep quiet, for just here the bottom's smooth and slippery.

Aase. Ass!

Peer Gynt. Yes, abuse me if you like, words don't do any harm. Aha! The bottom's sloping upwards now——

Aase. Don't lose your hold of me!

Peer Gynt. Gee up! We'll play at Peer and Reindeer now! *(Prances.)* I am the reindeer, you are Peer!

Aase. I'm sure I don't know what I am!

Peer Gynt. See here, now—here's an even bottom. *(Wades to the bank.)* Now give your steed a pretty kiss to thank him for the ride you've had.

Aase (boxing his ears). That's the thanks I'll give him!

Peer Gynt. Wow! That's a scurvy sort of tip.

Aase. Put me down!

Peer Gynt. Not till we get to where the wedding is afoot. You are so clever, you must be my spokesman—talk to the old fool—tell him Mads Moen is a sot——

Aase. Put me down!

Peer Gynt. And tell him, too, the sort of lad that Peer Gynt is.

Aase. Yes, you may take your oath I will! A pretty character I'll give you! I'll draw a faithful portrait, too,—and all your devil's pranks and antics I'll tell them of—in every detail——

Peer Gynt. Oh, will you!

Aase (kicking him in her temper). I won't hold my

tongue till the old man sets his dog upon you, as upon a tramp!

Peer Gynt. Ah, then I think I'll go alone.

Aase. All right, but I shall follow you!

Peer Gynt. Dear mother, you're not strong enough.

Aase. Not strong enough? I'm so worked up that I could smash a heap of stones! Oh, I could make a meal of flints! So put me down!

Peer Gynt. Yes, if you promise——

Aase. Nothing! I'm going there with you, and they shall know the sort you are!

Peer Gynt. Oh, no, you won't; you'll stay behind.

Aase. Never! I'm going there with you.

Peer Gynt. Oh, no, you aren't.

Aase. What will you do?

Peer Gynt. I'll put you on the mill-house roof!

[*Puts her up there. She screams.*

Aase. Lift me down!

Peer Gynt. If you will listen——

Aase. Bah!

Peer Gynt. Now, little mother, listen——

Aase (throwing a bit of turf thatch at him). Lift me down this moment, Peer!

Peer Gynt. If I dared I would, indeed. *(Goes nearer to her.)* Remember to sit still and quiet—not to kick your legs about, nor the tiles to break or loosen—or an accident may happen, and you might fall off.

Aase. You beast!

Peer Gynt. Don't shift!

Aase. I wish you'd been shifted up the chimney, like a changeling!

Peer Gynt. Mother! Shame!

Aase. Pooh!

Peer Gynt. You should rather give your blessing on my journey. Will you?

Aase. I'll give you a thrashing, big as your are!

Peer Gynt. Oh, well, good-bye! Only have patience, mother dear; I shan't be long *(Is going; but turns, lifts a warning finger and says):* But don't forget you mustn't try to move from there! [*Goes.*

Aase. Peer!—Heaven help me, he is gone! Reindeer-rider! Liar! Hi! Will you listen?—No, he's off over the meadows. *(Screams.)* Help! I'm giddy!

[*Two* Old Women, *with sacks on their backs, come down the path towards the mill.*

First Old Woman. Who's that screaming?

Aase. Me!

Second Old Woman. Why, Aase, you have had a lift in life!

Aase. One that won't do me much good—I'll be booked for heaven directly!

First Old Woman. Pleasant journey!

Aase. Fetch a ladder! Get me down! That devil Peer——

Second Old Woman. What, your son?

Aase. Now you can say you have seen how he behaves.

First Old Woman. We'll bear witness.

Aase. Only help me—help me to get straight to Hægstad——

Second Old Woman. Is he there?

First Old Woman. You'll be revenged; the blacksmith's going to the party.

Aase (wringing her hands). Oh, God help me! My poor boy! They will murder him between them!

First Old Woman. Ah, we know that lot quite well; you may bet that's what will happen!

Second Old Woman. You can see she's lost her senses. *(Calls up the hill.)* Eivind! Anders! Hi! come here!

A Man's Voice. What?

Second Old Woman. Peer Gynt has put his mother up upon the mill-house roof!

SCENE II

SCENE.—*A little hill covered with bushes and heather. The high-road, shut off by a fence, runs at the back.* PEER GYNT *comes down a foot-path, goes quickly up to the fence, and stands looking out over the landscape beyond.*

Peer Gynt. Yonder lies Hægstad. I shall soon be at it. *(Climbs half over the fence, then stops and considers.)* I wonder if Ingrid's sitting all alone there? *(Shades his eyes and looks along the road.)* No, folk with gifts are swarming up like midges. Perhaps I had better turn and go no farther. *(Draws his leg back over the fence.)* There'll be their grins behind my back for certain—whispers that seem to burn their way right through you. *(Moves a few steps away from the fence and begins absently plucking leaves.)* If only I'd a good strong drink inside me—or could just slip into the house unnoticed—— Or if no one knew me——. No, some good strong liquor would be best; their laughter wouldn't hurt then.

[*Looks round suddenly as if startled, then hides among the bushes. Some* COUNTRY FOLK, *carrying presents, pass along the road on their way to the wedding.*

A Man (in conversation). With a drunkard for father, and a poor thing of a mother——

A Woman. Yes, it's no wonder the boy is such a wastrel.

[*They pass on. After a little,* PEER GYNT *comes forward, blushing with shame, and peeps after them.*

Peer Gynt (softly). Was it of me they gossiped? *(With a forced shrug.)* Oh, well, let them! Anyway they can't kill me with their gossip. *(Throws himself down on the heather slope and for some time lies on his back with his hands under his head, staring up into the sky.)* What a curious cloud! That bit's like a horse, and there is its rider and saddle and bridle, and behind them an old crone is riding a broomstick. *(Laughs quietly to himself.)* That's mother! She's scolding and screaming "You beast! Hi! Peer, come back!" *(Gradually closes his eyes.)* Yes, now she is frightened.—There rides Peer Gynt at the head of his henchmen, his charger gold-shod, silver-crested his harness. Peer carries gauntlets and sabre and scabbard, wears a long coat with a fine silky lining. Splendid the men in his retinue following; but there's not one sits his charger as proudly, not one that glitters like him in the sunshine. The people in groups by the wayside are gathered, lifting their hats as they stare up in wonder; the women are curtseying, everyone knows it is Kaiser Peer Gynt and his thousand retainers. Half-guinea pieces and glittering shillings are strewn on the roadway as if they were pebbles; rich as a lord is each man in the parish. Peer Gynt rides over the seas in his glory; Engelland's Prince on the shore is awaiting, and Engelland's maidens all ready to welcome him. Engelland's nobles and Engelland's Kaiser rise from their seats as he deigns to approach them. Lifting his crown, speaks the Kaiser in welcome——

Aslak the Smith (to some others, as they pass by on the other side of the fence). Hullo! Look here! Why, it's Peer Gynt the drunkard!

Peer Gynt (half rising). What, Kaiser——!

Aslak (leaning on the fence and grinning). Get up on your feet, my young fellow!

Peer Gynt. What the devil——? The blacksmith! Well, pray, what do *you* want?

Aslak (to the others). He hasn't got over our spree down at Lundë.

Peer Gynt (springing up). Just let me alone!

Aslak. That I will. But, young fellow, what have you done with yourself since we parted? It's six weeks ago Have the troll-folk been at you?

Peer Gynt. I can tell you I've done something wonderful, Aslak.

Aslak (winking to the others). Let's hear it then, Peer!

Peer Gynt. No, it won't interest you.

Aslak. Shall we see you at Hægstad?

Peer Gynt. You won't.

Aslak. Why, the gossip says there was a time you were fancied by Ingrid.

Peer Gynt. You dirty-faced crow!

Aslak. Now don't get in a temper! If the girl *has* refused you, there surely are others. Remember the goodly John Gynt was your father! Come along to the farm! There'll be girls at the wedding as tender as lambkins and widows well seasoned——

Peer Gynt. Go to hell!

Aslak. You'll be sure to find someone who'll have you. Good evening. I'll give the bride all your good wishes!

[*They go off, laughing and whispering.* PEER *stands for a moment looking after them, then tosses his head and turns half round.*

Peer Gynt. Well, Ingrid at Hægstad may wed whom she pleases, for all that I care! I shall be just as happy! *(Looks down at his clothes.)* Breeches all torn—all dirty and tattered. If only I had something new to put on me—— *(Stamps his foot on the slope.)* If I only could carve at their breasts like a butcher and tear out the scorn and contempt that they show me! *(Looks round suddenly.)* What was that? Who is it that's laughing behind there? I certainly thought that I heard——. No, there's no one. I'll go home to mother. *(Moves off, but stops again and listens in the direction of Hægstad.)* The dance is beginning! *(Stares and listens; moves step by step towards the fence; his eyes glisten; he rubs his hands down his legs.)* How the girls swarm! Seven or eight of them there for each man! Oh, death and damnation, I must go to the party!—But what about mother, sitting up there on the roof of the mill-house——? *(His eyes wander towards the fence again; he skips and laughs.)* Haha! I can hear them out dancing a Halling! Guttorm's the boy—how he handles his fiddle! Hear it sparkle and flash like a stream at a waterfall! And think of the girls—all the pick of the neighbourhood—— Yes, death and damnation, I'm off to the party!

[*Vaults over the fence and goes off down the road.*

SCENE III

SCENE.—*The courtyard of the farm at Hægstad. The farm buildings are at the back. A number of guests are assembled, and a lively dance is in progress on the grass. The* FIDDLER *is seated on a table. The* STEWARD *stands in the doorway. Cookmaids pass to and fro between the buildings. The older folk are sitting about, gossiping.*

A Woman (joining a group of guests who are sitting on some logs). The bride? To be sure she is crying a little, but that's not a thing that is out of the usual.

The Steward (to another group). Now then, my friends, you must empty your noggins!

A Man. Ah, thank you kindly—you fill up too quickly!

A Youth (as he flies past the FIDDLER, *holding a girl by the hand).* That's the way, Guttorm! Don't spare your fiddle-strings!

The Girl. Scrape till it echoes out over the meadows!

Other Girls (standing in a ring round a youth who is dancing). That's a good step!

A Girl. He's lusty and nimble!

The Youth (dancing). The roof here is high and the walls far apart, you know!

[*The* BRIDEGROOM *comes up whimpering to his* FATHER, *who is standing talking to some others, and pulls at his jacket.*

The Bridegroom. Father, she won't! She is not being nice to me!

His Father. What won't she do?

The Bridegroom. She has locked herself in.

His Father. Well, you must see if you can't find the key.

The Bridegroom. But I don't know how.

His Father. Oh, you are a nuisance!

[*Turns to the others again. The* BRIDEGROOM *drifts across the courtyard.*

A Boy (coming from behind the house). I say, you girls! Now things will be livelier! Peer Gynt's arrived!

Aslak (who has just come on the scene). Who invited him?

The Steward. No one did. [*Goes into the house.*

Aslak (to the girls). If he should speak to you, don't seem to hear him.

A Girl (to the others). No, we'll pretend that we don't even see him.

[PEER GYNT *comes in, hot and eager, stops in front of the group and rubs his hands.*

Peer Gynt. Who is the nimblest girl of the lot of you?

A Girl (whom he has approached). Not I.

Another. Nor I.

A Third. No, nor I either.

Peer Gynt (to a fourth). Then *you* dance with me, for want of a better.

The Girl (turning away). I haven't time.

Peer Gynt (to a fifth). You, then.

The Girl (moving away). I'm off homeward.

Peer Gynt. Homeward to-night? Are you out of your senses?

Aslak (after a little in a low voice). Peer, she has taken an old man to dance with.

Peer Gynt (turning quickly to another man). Where are the disengaged girls?

The Man. Go and look for them.

[*He moves away from* PEER GYNT, *who has suddenly become subdued. He glances furtively and shyly at the group. They all look at him, but no one speaks. He approaches other groups. Wherever he goes there is a sudden silence; when he moves away, they smile and look after him.*

Peer Gynt (in a low voice). Glances—and thoughts and smiles that are cutting—jarring on one like a file on a saw-blade!

[*He sidles along by the palings.* SOLVEIG, *holding little* HELGA *by the hand, comes into the courtyard with her* PARENTS.

A Man (to another, close to PEER GYNT*).* These are the newcomers.

The Other. Living out westward?

First Man. Yes, out at Hedal.

The Other. Ah, yes—of course they are.

[PEER GYNT *advances to meet the newcomers, points to* SOLVEIG *and addresses her* FATHER.

Peer Gynt. May I dance with your daughter?

The Father. You may; but before that we must go indoors and give our hosts greetings. [*They go in.*

The Steward (to PEER GYNT, *offering him a drink).* As you're here, I suppose you must wet your whistle.

Peer Gynt (looking fixedly after the newcomers). Thanks, I'm for dancing. I don't feel thirsty. *(The* STEWARD *leaves him.* PEER GYNT *looks towards the house and laughs.)* How fair she is! Was there ever a fairer? Eyes glancing down at her shoes and white apron—and the way she held on to her mother's skirt, too—and carried her prayer-book wrapped in a kerchief——! I must have a look at her!

[*Is going into the house, but is met by several* YOUTHS *coming out.*

A Youth. What, off already? Away from the dance?

Peer Gynt. No.

The Youth. You're on the wrong road, then!

[*Takes him by the shoulders to turn him round.*

Peer Gynt. Let me get past!

The Youth. Are you frightened of Aslak?

Peer Gynt. I, frightened?

The Youth. Remember what happened at Lundë!

[*The group laugh and move off to where the dancing is going on.* SOLVEIG *comes to the door.*

Solveig. Are you the boy who wanted to dance with me?

Peer Gynt. Of course I am. Can't you tell by the look of me? Come on!

Solveig. But I mustn't go far—mother said so.

Peer Gynt. Mother said? mother said? Were you only born yesterday?

Solveig. Don't laugh——

Peer Gynt. It is true you are almost a kiddie still. Are you grown up?

Solveig. I shall soon be confirmed, you know.

Peer Gynt. Tell me your name—then we can talk easier.

Solveig. My name is Solveig. Tell me what yours is.

Peer Gynt. Peer Gynt.

Solveig (drawing back her hand from his). Oh, heavens!

Peer Gynt. Why, what is the matter?

Solveig. My garter's come loose; I must tie it more carefully. *(Leaves him.)*

The Bridegroom (pulling at his MOTHER'S *sleeve).* Mother, she won't——

His Mother. She won't? What won't she do?

The Bridegroom. Mother, she won't——

His Mother. What?

The Bridegroom. Unbar the door to me!

His Father (in a low and angry voice). You're only fit to be tied in a stable, sir!

His Mother. Poor boy, don't scold him—he'll be all right presently.

[*A* YOUTH *comes in, with a crowd of others who have been dancing.*

The Youth. Brandy, Peer?

Peer Gynt. No.

Youth. Just a drop!

Peer Gynt. Have you got any?

Youth. Maybe I have. *(Pulls out a flask and drinks.)* Ah, that's got a bite to it! Well?

Peter Gynt. Let me try it. *(Drinks.)*

Second Youth. And now have a pull at mine!

Peer Gynt. No.

Youth. Oh, what rubbish! Don't be a simpleton! Have a drink, Peer!

Peer Gynt. Well, give me a drop of it. *(Drinks again.)*

A Girl (in an undertone). Come, let's be off.

Peer Gynt. Why, are you afraid of me?

Youth. Do you think there is any that isn't afraid of you? You showed us what you could do, down at Lundë.

Peer Gynt. I can do better than that if I'm roused, you know!

Youth (whispering). Now he is getting on!

Others (making a ring round PEER*).* Come on, now—tell us, Peer, what you can do?

Peer Gynt. Oh, I'll tell you to-morrow——

Others. No! Tell us to-night!

A Girl. Can you show us some witchcraft, Peer?

Peer Gynt. Ah, I can conjure the Devil!

A Man. My grandmother, she could do that long before I was born, they say.

Peer Gynt. Liar! What *I* can do, no one alive can do. Why, once I conjured him into a nutshell, right through a worm-hole!

Others (laughing). Of course—we can guess that!

Peer Gynt. He swore and he wept and promised to give me all sorts of things——

One of the Group. But had to go into it?

Peer Gynt. Yes; and then, when I'd stopped up the worm-hole, Lord! if you'd heard him buzzing and rumbling!

A Girl. Fancy!

Peer Gynt. 'Twas like a great bumble-bee buzzing.

The Girl. And pray have you got him still in the nutshell?

Peer Gynt. No, the old Devil got right clean away again. It is his fault the blacksmith dislikes me.

A Boy. How's that?

Peer Gynt. Because I took him to the smithy and asked the smith to crack the nutshell for me. He said he would. I laid it on the anvil; but you know Aslak's very heavy-handed, and with a will he laid on the hammer——

A Voice from the Group. Did he kill the Devil?

Peer Gynt. No; he laid on stoutly, but the Devil looked after himself and just vanished through ceiling and walls in a flame of fire.

Several Voices. And Aslak——?

Peer Gynt. Stood there with his hands well roasted. And since that day we have never been friendly.

[*General laughter.*

Voices. That's a fine rigmarole!

Others. Easily his best one!

Peer Gynt. Do you suggest that I made it up?

A Man. Oh, no, I know you didn't; for I've heard the story told by my grandfather——

Peer Gynt. Liar! It happened to me, I tell you!

The Man. Oh, well—that's all right.

Peer Gynt (tossing his head). Pooh! I can ride through the clouds on horseback! There are lots of fine things I can do, I tell you! [*Roars of laughter again.*

One of the Group. Peer, let us see you ride clouds!

Others. Yes, dear Peer——!

Peer Gynt. Oh, you won't need to beg me so humbly—one day I'll ride like a storm o'er the lot of you! The whole countryside shall fall at my feet!

An Older Man. Why, now he's raving!

Another. Yes, the great booby!

A Third. The braggart!

A Fourth. The liar!

Peer Gynt (threatening them). Just wait and you'll see, then!

A Man (half drunk). Yes, wait and you'll get your jacket well dusted!

Others. A good sound drubbing! A nice black eye, too!

[*The crowd disperses, the older ones angry and the younger ones laughing and mocking him.*

The Bridegroom (edging up to Peer*).* Peer, is it true you can ride through the clouds, then?

Peer Gynt (shortly). Anything, Mads! I'm the boy, I can tell you!

The Bridegroom. I suppose you've a coat that will make you invisible?

Peer Gynt. An invisible hat, do you mean? Yes, I have one. *(Turns away from him.* Solveig *comes across the courtyard leading* Helga *by the hand.* Peer Gynt *goes to meet them, looking happier.)* Solveig! Ah, I am glad you have come to me! *(Grasps her wrists.)* Now I shall swing you round most nimbly!

Solveig. Oh, let me go!

Peer Gynt. Why?

Solveig. You look so wildly.

Peer Gynt. The reindeer grows wild when summer's approaching. Come along, girl! Come, don't be sullen!

Solveig (drawing back her arm). No—no, I daren't.

Peer Gynt. Why?

Solveig. No, you've been drinking.

[*Moves away a little, with* HELGA.

Peer Gynt. I wish I had stuck my knife in the lot of them!

The Bridegroom (nudging PEER'S *elbow).* Can't you help me to get in there where the bride is?

Peer Gynt (absently). The bride? Where is she?

The Bridegroom. In the loft.

Peer Gynt. Oh, is she?

The Bridegroom. Oh, come, Peer—dear Peer—you might try to!

Peer Gynt. No, you must manage to do without me. *(A thought strikes him. He says, softly and meaningly):* Ingrid! The loft! *(Goes up to* SOLVEIG.*)* Have you made up your mind, then? *(*SOLVEIG *turns to get away, but he bars her path.)* I look like a tramp, and so you're ashamed of me.

Solveig (hastily). Oh, no, you don't; that isn't the truth.

Peer Gynt. It is. And it's because you think I am fuddled; but that was for spite, because you had hurt me. Come along, then!

Solveig. I daren't, if I wanted to.

Peer Gynt. Who are you frightened of?

Solveig. Mostly of father.

Peer Gynt. Your father? Oh, yes—he's one of the solemn ones! Sanctimonious, isn't he? Answer me!

Solveig. What shall I say?

Peer Gynt. Perhaps he's a preacher? And you and your mother the same, I dare say? Are you going to answer me?

Solveig. Let me alone.

Peer Gynt. I won't! *(In a low but hard and threatening voice.)* I can turn myself into a troll! I shall come and stand by your bed at midnight; and if you hear something that's hissing and spitting, don't you suppose it's your cat you are hearing. It is I! And I'll drain your life-blood out of you; and your little sister—I'll eat her up, for I turn to a werewolf whenever the night falls, your loins and your back I'll bite all over—— *(Changes his tone suddenly and entreats her anxiously.)* Dance with me, Solveig!

Solveig (looking darkly at him). Ah—now you are horrid.

[*Goes into the house.*

The Bridegroom (drifting up to PEER *again).* I'll give you an ox, if you'll help me!

Peer Gynt. Come!

[*They go behind the house. At the same moment a crowd comes back from dancing, most of them drunk. Noise and confusion.* SOLVEIG, HELGA *and their* PARENTS *come out to the door.*

The Steward (to ASLAK, *who is in the front of the crowd).* Be quiet!

Aslak (pulling off his coat). No, here we'll settle the matter. Peer Gynt or I shall get a thrashing.

Some of the Crowd. Yes, let them fight!

Others. No, no, let them argue!

Aslak. No, we must fight; we want no arguing.

Solveig's Father. Be quiet, man!

Helga. Will he hit him, mother?

A Boy. It's better fun with his lies to tease him!

Another. Kick him out, I say!

A Third. No, spit in his face!

A Fourth (to ASLAK*).* Are you backing out?

Aslak (throwing away his coat). I'll murder the beggar!

Solveig's Mother (to SOLVEIG*).* You see now what they think of the booby.

[AASE *comes in, with a cudgel in her hand.*

Aase. Is my son here? He shall have such a drubbing! Just wait and you'll see what a thrashing I'll give him!

Aslak (turning up his shirt-sleeves). No, *your* little body's too weak for that.

Voices. Aslak will thrash him!

Others. Slash him!

Aslak (spitting on his hands and nodding to Aase*).* Hang him!

Aase. What? Hang my Peer? Just try, if you dare! This old Aase's got teeth and claws!—Where is he? *(Calls across the courtyard.)* Peer!

The Bridegroom (running in). Oh, God in Heaven! Come, father! Mother!

His Father. Why, what's the matter?

The Bridegroom. Oh, Peer Gynt! I——!

Aase (with a scream). What? What? Have you killed him?

The Bridegroom. No, Peer Gynt——! Look, up there on the hillside!

Voices. With the bride!

Aase (letting her cudgel fall). The beast!

Aslak (in amazement). Where the hill is steepest he's climbing, by God—like a mountain goat!

The Bridegroom (in tears). And carrying her under his arm like a pig!

Aase (shaking her fist at Peer*).* I wish he would fall and——! *(Screams anxiously.)* Take care of your footing!

Ingrid's Father (coming out bareheaded and white with rage). I'll have his life for his rape of the bride!

Aase. No, may God punish me if I let you!

ACT II

SCENE I

SCENE.—*A narrow track high up on the mountain-side. It is early morning.* PEER GYNT *comes hurriedly and sulkily along the path.* INGRID, *wearing some of her bridal ornaments, is trying to hold him back.*

Peer Gynt. Get away!

Ingrid (in tears). What, after this? Where to?

Peer Gynt. Anywhere you like.

Ingrid (wringing her hands). What deceit!

Peer Gynt. It's no use railing. We must go our own ways—both.

Ingrid. Think what binds us two together!

Peer Gynt. Oh, the devil take all thinking! And the devil take all women—except one——!

Ingrid. And who is she?

Peer Gynt. She's not you.

Ingrid. Who is it, then?

Peer Gynt. Get you back to where you came from! Go back to your father!

Ingrid. Dearest——

Peer Gynt. Pshaw!

Ingrid. You surely can't be meaning what you say.

Peer Gynt. I can and do.

Ingrid. To ruin me and then forsake me?

Peer Gynt. Well, what have you got to offer?

Ingrid. Hægstad farm, and something more.

Peer Gynt. Is your prayer-book in your kerchief? Where's your mane of hair all golden? Do you glance down at your apron? Do you hold on to your mother by her skirt? Come, answer!

Ingrid. No; but——

Peter Gynt. Shall you go to Confirmation very shortly?

Ingrid. No, but, dearest——

Peer Gynt. Are your glances always bashful? If I beg, can you deny me?

Ingrid. Christ! I think he's lost his senses——!

Peer Gynt. Does one feel a holy feeling when one sees you? Answer!

Ingrid. No, but——

Peer Gynt. Then what matter what you offer?

[*Turns to go.*

Ingrid (confronting him). Remember it's a hanging matter to forsake me now.

Peer Gynt. So be it.

Ingrid. Rich you may be, and respected, if you take me——

Peer Gynt. I can't do it.

Ingrid (bursting into tears). Oh, you tempted——

Peer Gynt. You were willing.

Ingrid. I was wretched.

Peer Gynt. I was mad.

Ingrid (threateningly). You'll pay a heavy price for this!

Peer Gynt. I should call the heaviest cheap.

Ingrid. Is your mind made up?

Peer Gynt. Like stone.

Ingrid. Very well. You'll see who'll win.

[*Goes down the hill.*

Peer Gynt (is silent for a little; then suddenly calls out). Oh, the devil take all thinking! And the devil take all women!

Ingrid (turns head and calls up mockingly). All but one!

Peer Gynt. Yes, all but one!

[*They each go their way.*

SCENE II

SCENE.—*By a mountain lake, on boggy moorland. A storm is blowing up.* AASE, *in despair, is calling and searchin every direction.* SOLVEIG *can scarcely keep pace with her. Her* PARENTS *and* HELGA *are a little way behind.* AASE *beats the air with her arms and tears her hair.*

Aase. Everything's against me with the might of anger! The skies and the water and the hateful mountains! Fogs from the skies are rolling to mislead him—treacherous waters will delude and drown him—mountains will crush or slip away beneath him——! And all these people! They are out to kill him! By God, they shall not! I can't do without him! The oaf! To think the devil thus should tempt him! *(Turns to* SOLVEIG.*)* Ah, my girl, one simply can't believe it. He, who was always full of lies and nonsense—he, who was only clever with his talking—he, who had never done a thing worth telling—he——! Oh, I want to laugh and cry together! We were such friends in our needs and troubles. For, you must know, my husband was a drunkard, made us a byword in the neighbours' gossip, brought all our good estate to rack and ruin, while I and Peerkin sat at home together—tried to forget—we knew no better counsel; I was too weak to stand up stoutly to it. It is so hard to face the fate that's coming; and so one tries to shake one's sorrows off one, or do one's best to rid one's mind of thinking. Some fly to brandy, others try romancing; so we found comfort in the fairy stories all about trolls and princes and such cattle—tales, too, of stolen brides—but who would ever think that such stories in his mind would linger? *(Becomes terrified again.)* Ah, what a screech! A nixie or a kelpie! Peer! Oh, my Peer!—Up there upon the hillock ——! *(Runs up on to a little hillock and looks over the* *lake.* SOLVEIG'S PARENTS *come up to her.)* Not a thing to be seen!

The Husband (quietly). It is worst for him.

Aase (in tears). Oh, Peer! my Peer! My own lost lamb!

The Husband (nodding his head gently). Aye, lost indeed.

Aase. Say no such thing! He is so clever; there's no one like him.

The Husband. You foolish woman!

Aase. Oh, yes, oh, yes, I may be foolish, but he is fine!

The Husband (always quietly and with a gentle expression). His heart is stubborn; his soul is lost.

Aase (anxiously). No, no! God's not so hard as that!

The Husband. Do you think he feels the weight of his sinning?

Aase (hastily). No—he can ride through the air on a reindeer!

The Wife. Christ! Are you mad?

The Husband. What are you saying?

Aase. There's nothing that is too great for him. You'll see, if only he live to do it——

The Husband. 'Twould be best to see him hang on the gallows.

Aase (with a scream). Good God!

The Husband. When he's in the hangman's clutches perhaps his heart may turn to repentance.

Aase (confusedly). Your talk will make me dazed and giddy! We must find him!

The Husband. Save his soul.

Aase. And body! We must drag him out if he's in the marshes, and ring church bells if the trolls have got him.

The Husband. Ah! Here's a track——

Aase. May God repay you if you help me aright!

The Husband. 'Tis our Christian duty.

Aase. All the others are naught but heathens! There was only one that would come and wander——

The Husband. They knew him too well.

Aase. He was too good for them. *(Wrings her hands.)* And to think—to think his life is in danger!

The Husband. Here's a footprint.

Aase. That's the way we must go, then!

The Husband. We'll scatter and search below the pastures. [*He and his wife go on.*

Solveig (to AASE*).* Tell me some more.

Aase (wiping her eyes). About my son?

Solveig. Yes. Tell me everything!

Aase (smiling and holding her head up). Everything? 'Twould weary you!

Solveig. You'd be sooner wearied with telling me, than I with hearing.

SCENE III

SCENE.—*Low treeless hills below the higher mountains, whose peaks show in the distance. It is late in the day, and long shadows are falling.* PEER *comes running in at full speed, and stops on a slope.*

Peer Gynt. They're after me now—the whole of the parish! And everyone's taken his stick or his rifle. The old man from Hægstad is leading them, howling. It has soon got abroad that Peer Gynt is the quarry! A different thing from a fight with the blacksmith! This is life! All my muscles are strong as a bear's. *(Swings his arms about and leaps into the air.)* To overthrow everything! Breast a waterfall! Strike! Pull a fir-tree up by the roots! This is life! It can harden and it can exalt! To hell with all my trumpery lying!

[THREE COWHERD GIRLS *run across the hill, shouting and singing.*

The Girls. Trond of Valfjeld! Baard and Kaare! Listen, trolls! Would you sleep in our arms?

Peer Gynt. Who are you shouting for?

The Girls. Trolls! Trolls! Trolls!

First Girl. Trond, come lovingly!

Second Girl. Come, lusty Baard!

Third Girl. All the beds in our hut are empty!

First Girl. Love is lusty!

Second Girl. And lustiness love!

Third Girl. When boys are lacking, one plays with trolls!

Peer Gynt. Where are your boys, then?

The Girls (with a burst of laughter). They can't come!

First Girl. Mine called me dearest sweetheart, too, now he is wed to an elderly widow.

Second Girl. Mine met a gipsy wench up at Lien, now they are both on the road together.

Third Girl. Mine made an end of our bastard brat, now on a stake his head is grinning.

All Three. Trond of Valfjeld! Baard and Kaare! Listen, trolls! Would you sleep in our arms?

Peer Gynt (leaping suddenly among them). I'm a three-headed troll, and the boy for three girls!

The Girls. Can you tackle the job?

Peer Gynt. You shall see if I can!

First Girl. To the hut! To the hut!

Second Girl. We have mead!

Peer Gynt. Let it flow!

Third Girl. This Saturday night not a bed shall be empty!

Second Girl (kissing Peer). He gleams and glitters like glowing iron!

Third Girl (kissing Peer). Like a baby's eyes from the blackest tarn!

Peer Gynt (dancing with them). Dismal bodings and wanton thoughts, laughter in eyes and tears in throat!

The Girls (making long noses at the mountain-tops, and shouting and singing.) Trond of Valfjeld! Baard and Kaare! Listen, trolls! Did you sleep in our arms?

[*They dance away over the hills with* PEER GYNT *between them.*

SCENE IV

SCENE.—*Among the mountains. The snowy peaks are gleaming in the sunset.* PEER GYNT *comes in, looking wild and distraught.*

Peer Gynt. Palace o'er palace is rising! See, what a glittering gate! Stop! Will you stop!—It is moving farther and farther away! The cock on the weather-vane's lifting its wings as if for a flight—into rifts of rock it has vanished, and the mountain's barred and locked. What are these roots and tree trunks that grow from the clefts of the ridge? They are heroes with feet of herons—and now they are vanished away. A shimmer like strips of rainbow my sight and mind assails. Are they bells that I hear in the distance? What's weighing my eyebrows down? Oh, how my forehead's aching—as if I'd a red-hot band pressing—! But who the devil put it there I don't know! *(Sinks down.)* A flight o'er the ridge at Gendin—romancing and damned lies! Over the steepest walls with the bride—and drunk for a day—hawks and kites to fight with—threatened by trolls and the like—sporting with crazy lasses—damned romancing and lies! *(Gazes upwards for a long time.)* There hover two brown eagles; the wild geese fly to the south; and I have to trudge and stumble knee-deep in mud and mire. *(Springs up.)* I'll go with them! Cleanse my foulness in a bath of the keenest wind! Up aloft I'll lave my stains in that glittering christening-font! I'll away out over the pastures; I'll fly till I'm pure and clean—fly o'er the ocean waters, o'er the Prince of Engelland's head! Ah, you may stare, you maidens; I'm flying, but not to you. It's no use your waiting——! Yet I might swoop below —— Why, where are the two brown eagles? They've gone to the devil, I think! See, there's the end of a gable, it's rising bit by bit; it's growing out of the rubbish—see, now the door stands wide! Aha! I recognize it, grandfather's farm new built! Gone are the clouts from the casements and the fence that was tumbling down; lights gleam from every window; they are feasting there within. Listen! The Parson's tapping his knife upon his glass; the Captain's hurled his bottle and broken the mirror to smash. Let them waste and let them squander! Hush, mother—there's plenty more! It's rich John Gynt that is feasting; hurrah for the race of Gynt! What's all the bustle and rumpus? What are the cries and shouts? "Where's Peer?" the Captain is calling—the Parson would drink my health—go in, then, Peer, for the verdict; you shall have it in songs of praise: Great, Peer, were thy beginnings, and in great things thou shalt end.

[*He leaps forward, but runs his nose against a rock, falls and remains lying on the ground.*

SCENE V

SCENE.—*A mountain-side, with trees in full leaf through which the wind is whispering. Stars are twinkling through the branches. Birds are singing in the treetops. A* WOMAN IN GREEN *crosses the slope. After her follows* PEER GYNT, *performing all sorts of amorous antics.*

The Woman in Green (stopping and turning round). Is it true?

Peer Gynt (drawing his finger across his throat.) As true

as my name is Peer; as true as that you are a lovely woman! Will you have me? You'll see how nice I can be; you shall never have to weave or to spin; you shall be fed till you're ready to burst; I promise I never will pull your hair——

The Woman in Green. Nor strike me, either?

Peer Gynt. No; is it likely? We sons of kings don't strike our women.

The Woman in Green. A king's son?

Peer Gynt. Yes.

The Woman in Green. I'm the Dovrë-King's daughter.

Peer Gynt. Are you really? Well, well! How suitable!

The Woman in Green. In the mountains my father has his castle.

Peer Gynt. And my mother a larger one, let me tell you.

The Woman in Green. Do you know my father? His name's King Brosë.

Peer Gynt. Do you know my mother? Her name's Queen Aase.

The Woman in Green. The mountains reel when my father's angry.

Peer Gynt. If my mother begins to scold, they totter.

The Woman in Green. My father can kick to the highest rafters.

Peer Gynt. My mother can ride through the fiercest river.

The Woman in Green. Besides those rags have you other clothing?

Peer Gynt. Ah, you should see my Sunday garments!

The Woman in Green. My week-day garments are gold and silver.

Peer Gynt. It looks to me more like tow and grasses.

The Woman in Green. Yes. There's just one thing to remember: we mountain folk have an ancient custom; all that we have has a double shape. So when you come to my father's palace it would not be in the least surprising if you were inclined to think it merely a heap of ugly stones and rubbish.

Peer Gynt. That's just the same as it is with us! You may think our gold all rust and mildew and mistake each glittering window-pane for a bundle of worn-out clouts and stockings.

The Woman in Green. Black looks like white, and ugly like fair.

Peer Gynt. Big looks like little, and filthy like clean.

The Woman in Green (falling on his neck). Oh, Peer, I see we are splendidly suited!

Peer Gynt. Like the hair to the comb—or the leg to the breeches.

The Woman in Green (calling over the hillside.) My steed! My steed! My wedding steed!

[*A gigantic pig comes running in, with a rope's end for a halter and an old sack for a saddle.* PEER GYNT *swings himself on to its back and seats the* WOMAN IN GREEN *in front of him.*

Peer Gynt. Houp-là! We'll gallop right into the palace! Come up! Come up, my noble charger!

The Woman in Green (caressingly). And to think I was feeling so sad and lonely—one never can tell what is going to happen!

Peer Gynt (whipping up the pig, which trots off). Great folk are known by the steeds they ride!

SCENE VI

SCENE.—*The Royal Hall of the King of the Trolls. A great assembly of* TROLL COURTIERS, BROWNIES *and* GNOMES. *The* TROLL KING *is seated on his throne, with crown and sceptre. His children and nearest relations sit on either side of him.* PEER GYNT *is standing before him. There is a great uproar in the hall.*

Troll Courtiers. Slay him! The Christian's son has tempted the fairest daughter of our King!

A Young Troll. Let me slash him on the fingers!

Another. May I tear his hair out for him?

A Troll Maiden. Let me bite him on the buttocks!

Troll Witch (with a ladle). Let me boil him down for broth!

Another (holding a chopper). Shall he toast on a spit or be browned in a kettle?

The Kroll King. Quiet! Keep calm! *(Beckons to his counsellors to approach him.)* We must not be too boastful. Things have been going badly with us lately; we don't feel sure if we shall last or perish, and can't afford to throw away assistance. Besides, the lad is almost without blemish, and well-built, too, as far as I can gather. It's true enough that he has only *one* head; but then my daughter hasn't more than one. Three-headed Trolls are going out of fashion; two-headed even, nowadays aren't common, and *their* heads usually are not up to much. *(To* PEER GYNT.*)* And so, my lad, it's my daughter you're after?

Peer Gynt. Yes, if she comes with a kingdom for dowry.

The Troll King. You shall have half while I am living and the other half when I am done for.

Peer Gynt. I'm content with that.

The Troll King. But stop, young fellow, *you've* got to give some pledges also. Break one of them, and our bargain's off and you don't get out of here alive. First, you must promise never to give thought to aught except what within these hills is bounded; shun the day, its deeds, and all the sunlit places.

Peer Gynt. If I'm called King, 'twill not be hard to do it.

The Troll King. Secondly—now I'll see how far you're clever—— [*Rises from his seat.*

The Oldest Troll Courtier (to PEER GYNT*).* Let's see if you've got a wisdom tooth that can crack the nut of our monarch's riddle!

The Troll King. What is the difference between Trolls and Men?

Peer Gynt. There isn't any, as far as I can gather; big trolls would roast and little ones would claw you—just as with us if only we dared do it.

The Troll King. True; we're alike in that and other things, too. Still, just as morning's different from evening, so there's a real difference between us, and I will tell you what it is. Out yonder under the skies, men have a common saying: "Man, to thyself be true!" But here, 'mongst Trolls, "Troll, to theyself be—enough!" it runs.

Troll Courtier (to PEER GYNT*).* Well, do you fathom it?

Peer Gynt. It seem rather hazy.

The Troll King. "Enough," my son—that word so fraught with meaning—must be the motto written on your buckler.

Peer Gynt (scratching his head). Well, but——

The Troll King. It *must,* if you're to be a king here!

Peer Gynt. All right; so be it. It is not much worse than——

The Troll King. Next you must learn to value rightly our simple, homely way of living. *(He beckons. Two* TROLLS *with pigs' heads, wearing white nightcaps, bring food and drink.)* Our cows give cakes and our oxen mead; no matter whether their taste is sour or sweet; the great thing to remember is that they're home-made and home-brewed.

Peer Gynt (pushing the things away from him). The devil take your home-brewed drink! I'll never get used to your country's habits.

The Troll King. The bowl goes with it, and it is golden. Who takes the bowl gets my daughter, too.

Peer Gynt (thoughtfully). Of course we're told that a man should master his disposition, and in the long run perhaps the drink will taste less sour. So, here goes! [*Drinks.*

The Troll King. Now that was sensibly said. But you spit?

Peer Gynt. I must trust to the force of habit.

The Troll King. Next, you must take off all your Christian clothing; for you must know we boast that in the Dovrë all's mountain-made; we've nothing from the valleys except the bows of silk that deck our tail-tips.

Peer Gynt (angrily). I haven't got a tail!

The Troll King. Then you shall have one. *(To one of the courtiers.)* See that my Sunday tail is fastened on him.

Peer Gynt. No, that he shan't! Do you want to make a fool of me?

The Troll King. Don't try with tail-less rump to court my daughter.

Peer Gynt. Making a beast of a man!

The Troll King. My son, you're wrong there; I'd only make a courtly wooer of you. And, as a mark of very highest honour, the bow you wear shall be of bright flame-colour.

Peer Gynt (reflectively). We're taught, of course, that man is but a shadow; and one must pay some heed to use and wont, too. So, tie away!

The Troll King. You're coming to your senses.

Troll Courtier. Just see how nicely you can wag and wave it!

Peer Gynt (angrily). Now, do you mean to ask anything more of me? Do you want me to give up my Christian faith?

The Troll King. No, to keep that you are perfectly welcome. Faith is quite free and pays no duty; it's his dress and its cut that a Troll should be known by. If we're of one mind as to manners and costume you're free to believe what would give us the horrors.

Peer Gynt. You are really, in spite of your many conditions, more reasonable than one might have expected.

The Troll King. We Trolls are better than our reputation, my son; and that is another difference between you and us. But now we have finished the serious part of the present assembly. Our ears and our eyes shall now be delighted. Let the harp-maid waken the Dovrë-harp's strings, let the dance-maiden tread the Dovrë-hall's floor. *(Music and a dance.)* What do you think of it?

Peer Gynt. Think of it? H'm——

The Troll King. Tell me quite openly. What did you see?

Peer Gynt. See? What I saw was impossibly ugly. A bell-cow thrumming her hoof on a gut-string, a sow in short stockings pretending to dance to it.

The Troll Courtiers. Eat him!

The Troll King. Remember his understanding is only human.

Troll Maidens. Oh, tear his eyes out and cut off his ears!

The Woman in Green (weeping). Are we to endure it, my sister and I, when we've played and danced?

Peer Gynt. Oho, was it you? Well, you know, at a banquet a joke is a joke—no offence was intended.

The Woman in Green. Will you swear to me you were only joking?

Peer Gynt. The dance and the music were both delightful.

The Troll King. It's a funny thing, this human nature; it clings to a man with such persistence. Suppose we fight it and it is wounded, there may be a scar, but it heals up quickly. My son-in-law's now most accommodating; he has willingly cast off his Christian breeches, willingly drunk of the mead-filled goblet, willingly tied on a tail behind him—is so willing, in fact, to do all we ask him that I certainly thought the old Adam banished for good and all; then, all of a sudden, we find him uppermost. Yes, my son, you certainly must undergo some treatment to cure this troublesome human nature.

Peer Gynt. What will you do?

The Troll King. I'll scratch you slightly in the left eye, and then your vision will be oblique, and all you look on will seem to you to be perfection. Then I'll cut out your right-hand window——

Peer Gynt. You're drunk!

The Troll King (laying some sharp instruments on the table). See, here are the glazier's tools. You must be tamed like a raging bullock; then you'll perceive that your bride is lovely, and never again will your sight deceive you with dancing sows or bell-cows thrumming——

Peer Gynt. That's fool's talk.

The Oldest Courtier. It's the Troll King's word; he is the wise man and you the fool.

The Troll King. Just think what a lot of trouble and worry you will be rid of for good and all. Remember, too, that the eye is the source of the bitter, searing flood of tears.

Peer Gynt. That's true; and it says in the family Bible: "If thine eye offend thee, pluck it out." But, tell me, when will my sight recover and be as it is now?

The Troll King. Never, my friend.

Peer Gynt. Oh, really! Then I must decline with thanks.

The Troll King. But what do you mean to do?

Peer Gynt. To leave you.

The Troll King. Softly! It's easy to get within here; but the Troll King's gate doesn't open outwards.

Peer Gynt. You surely don't mean to detain me by force?

The Troll King. Now listen, Prince Peer, and give way to reason. You're cut out for a Troll. Why, look, already you bear yourself quite in a Troll-like fashion! And you want to become one, don't you?

Peer Gynt. Of course. In return for a bride and a well-founded kingdom I'm not unwilling to sacrifice something; but all things have their natural limit. I have taken a tail, it is true; but then I can undo the knots that our friend has tied and take the thing off. I have shed my breeches; they were old and patched; but that won't prevent me from putting them on if I have a mind to. I shall probably find it just as easy to deal with your Trollish way of living. I can easily swear that a cow's a maiden; an oath's not a difficult thing to swallow. But to know that one never can get one's freedom—not even to die as a human being—to end one's days as a Troll of the mountains—never go back, as you tell me plainly—that is a thing that I'll not submit to.

The Troll King. Now, on my sins, I'm getting angry; I'm not in the mood to be made a fool of. You scurvy lout! Do you know who I am? To begin with, you made too free with my daughter——

Peer Gynt. That's a lie in your throat!

The Troll King. And you have to marry her.

Peer Gynt. Do you dare accuse me of——?

The Troll King. Can you deny that she was the object of all your desire?

Peer Gynt (whistles). But no more than that. What the deuce does that matter?

The Troll King. You human beings are always the same. You are always ready to talk of your souls, but heed nothing really save what is tangible. You think desires are things that don't matter? Wait; your own eyes will prove to you shortly——

Peer Gynt. It's no use baiting your hook with lies!

The Troll King. My Peer, ere the year's out you'll be a father.

Peer Gynt. Unlock the doors. I'm going.

The Troll King. We'll send you the brat in a goat-skin.

Peer Gynt (wiping the sweat from his brow). I wish I could wake up!

The Troll King. Shall we send to your Palace?

Peer Gynt. Oh, send to the Parish!

The Troll King. As you like, Prince Peer; it's your affair solely. But one thing is certain—what's done can't be undone, and you will see how your offspring will grow up! Mongrels like that grow remarkably quickly——

Peer Gynt. Oh, come, old chap, don't go at me like a

bullock! Fair maiden, be reasonable! Let's come to terms. I have to confess that I'm neither a prince nor rich; and, however you take my measure, I'm sure you won't find you've made much of a bargain.

[*The* WOMAN IN GREEN *faints and is carried out by the* TROLL MAIDENS.

The Troll King (looks at him for a while with a contemptuous expression, then says): Dash him to bits on the rocks, my good children!

Young Trolls. Dad, mayn't we first play at Owls and Eagles? Or the Wolf-Game? Or Grey Mouse and Red-Eyed Pussy?

The Troll King. Yes, but be quick. I'm angry and sleepy. Good night! [*Goes.*

Peer Gynt (hunted by the YOUNG TROLLS*).* Let me go, you young devils! [*Tries to climb up the chimney.*

Young Trolls. Hobgoblins! Brownies! Come, bite him!

Peer Gynt. Ow!

[*Tries to get away through the cellar-flap.*

Young Trolls. Stop all the holes up!

Troll Courtier. How the youngsters enjoy it!

Peer Gynt (fighting with a little TROLL *who has bitten deep into his ear).* You filth, let go!

Troll Courtier (rapping PEER GYNT *over the knuckles).* A little respect for a king's son, you scoundrel!

Peer Gynt. Ah! A rat hole! [*Runs towards it.*

Young Trolls. Stop up the holes, Brownie brothers!

Peer Gynt. The old man was foul, but the young ones are worse!

Young Trolls. Flay him!

Peer Gynt. I wish I were small as a mouse!

Young Trolls (swarming about him). Don't let him escape!

Peer Gynt. I wish I were a louse!

Young Trolls. Now jump on his face!

Peer Gynt (smothered in Trolls). Help, mother, I'm dying! [*Church bells are heard afar off.*

Young Trolls. Bells in the Valley! The Blackfrock's Cows!

[*The* TROLLS *disperse in a turmoil and wild shrieks. The Hall falls to pieces. Everything disappears.*

SCENE VII

Pitch darkness, PEER GYNT *is heard slashing and hitting about him with a branch of a tree.*

Peer Gynt. Answer! Who are you?

A Voice in the Darkness. Myself!

Peer Gynt. Let me pass, then!

Voice. Go round about, Peer! Room enough on the mountain.

[PEER GYNT *tries to pass another way, but runs up against something.*

Peer Gynt. Who are you?

Voice. Myself. Can you say as much?

Peer Gynt. I can say what I like, and my sword can strike! Look out for yourself! I'm going to smash you! King Saul slew hundreds; Peer Gynt slays thousands! *(Hits about him wildly.)* Who are you?

Voice. Myself.

Peer Gynt. That's a silly answer, and you can keep it. It tells me nothing. What are you?

Voice. The great Boyg.

Peer Gynt. No, are you really? Things were black before! now some grey is showing. Out of my way, Boyg!

Voice. Go round about, Peer!

Peer Gynt. No, through you! *(Hits out wildly.)* He's down! *(Tries to get on, but always runs up against something.)* Ha, ha! Are there more of you?

Voice. The Boyg, Peer Gynt. The one and only. The Boyg that's unwounded, the Boyg that was hurt. The Boyg that was dead and the Boyg that's alive.

Peer Gynt (throwing away his branch.) My weapon's bewitched; but I have my fists!

[*Strikes out in front of him.*

Voice. Yes, put your trust in your fists and strength! Ho, ho! Peer Gynt, they'll bring you out top!

Peer Gynt. Backward or forward, it's just as far.—Out or in, the way's as narrow. It's there!—and there!—and all about me! I think I've got out, and I'm back in the midst of it. What's your name! Let me see you! Say what you are!

Voice. The Boyg.

Peer Gynt (feeling round him). Neither dead, nor alive; slime and mistiness; no shape or form! It's as if one were smothered amidst any number of bears that are growling at being waked up! *(Shrieks.)* Why don't you hit out at me!

Voice. The Boyg's not so foolish as that.

Peer Gynt. Oh, strike at me!

Voice. The Boyg doesn't strike.

Peer Gynt. Come, fight! You *shall* fight with me!

Voice. The great Boyg can triumph without any fighting.

Peer Gynt. I'd far rather it were the Brownies tormenting me! Or even as much as a one-year-old Troll! Just something to fight with—and not this blank nothingness! It's snoring now! Boyg!

Voice. What is it?

Peer Gynt. Show fight, will you!

Voice. The great Boyg can get all he wishes by gentleness.

Peer Gynt (biting his own hands and arms). Oh, for

claws and teeth that would tear my flesh! I must see a drop of my own blood flow!

[*A Sound is heard like the beating of wings of great birds.*

Birds' Cries. Is he coming, Boyg?

Voice. Yes, foot by foot.

Birds' Cries. Sisters afar off, fly to meet us!

Peer Gynt. If you mean to save me, girl, be quick! Don't hang your head and look down blushing. Your prayer-book! Hit him straight in the eye with it!

Birds' Cries. He's failing!

Voice. He's ours.

Birds' Cries. Come, sisters, quickly!

Peer Gynt. An hour of torture such as this is too dear a price to pay for life. [*Sinks down.*

Birds' Cries. Boyg, he is down! Boyg, seize him! Seize him!

[*Church bells and the singing of psalms are heard in the distance.*

Voice (with a gasp, as the Boyg gradually dwindles away to nothing). He was too strong. There were women behind him.

SCENE VIII

SCENE.—*On the hillside outside a hut on Aase's mountain pasture. It is sunrise. The door of the hut is barred. Everything is empty and still.* PEER GYNT *lies asleep by the hut. Presently he wakes and looks around him with listless and heavy eyes.*

Peer Gynt (spitting). I'd give the world for a pickled herring! *(He spits again; then he sees* HELGA *approaching, carrying a basket of food.)* You here, youngster? What do you want?

Helga. It was Solveig——

Peer Gynt (springing up). Where is she?

Helga. Behind the hut.

Solveig (from behind the hut). If you come any nearer, I'll run away!

Peer Gynt (standing still). Perhaps you're afraid I shall carry you off?

Solveig. For shame!

Peer Gynt. Do you know where I was last night? The Troll King's daughter is hunting me down.

Solveig. 'Twas well done, then, that we rang the bells.

Peer Gynt. Oh, Peer Gynt's not quite the lad to get caught—What's that you say?

Helga (crying). She's running away. *(Runs after Solveig.)* Wait for me!

Peer Gynt (gripping her by the arm). See what I've got in my pocket! A fine silver button! And you shall have it if you speak up for me!

Helga. Oh, let me go!

Peer Gynt. Take it, then.

Helga. Oh, let me go!—and my basket!

Peer Gynt. You had better look out if you don't——!

Helga. Oh, you frighten me!

Peer Gynt (quietly, as he lets her go). No; all I meant was: don't let her forget me! [HELGA *runs off.*

ACT III

SCENE I

SCENE.—*The depths of a pine-wood. It is a grey autumn day, and snow is falling.* PEER GYNT *is in his shirt-sleeves, felling timber. He has just tackled a tall tree with crooked branches.*

Peer Gynt. Oh, yes, you're tough, my ancient friend, but that won't help you; you're coming down! *(Sets to work again.)* I know you're wearing a coat of mail; but I'll slash through, were it never so strong. Yes, you may shake your crooked arms; I daresay you're both fierce and angry, but all the same you shall bow to me——! *(Suddenly breaks off sullenly.)* What lies! It's only an ancient tree. What lies! I'm fighting no mail-clad foe; it's only a fir with its bark all cracked. It's toilsome work, this felling timber; but the devil's own job when all the time one's dreams get mixed up with one's working. All that must stop——this daytime dreaming and always being in the clouds. My lad, remember that you're an outlaw! Your only shelter's in this forest. *(Works again hurriedly for a while.)* An outlaw, yes. You have no mother to bring you food and spread your table. If you want to eat, you must help yourself; get what you can from the woods and the stream, forage for sticks if you want a fire, look to yourself for everything. If you need clothes, you must skin a deer; if you want a wall to put round your house, you must break the stones; if you want to build, you must fell the timber and shoulder it and carry it to the spot you've chosen. *(He lets his axe fall and stares in front of him.)* I'll build a beauty! Up on the roof I'll have a tower and weather-vane, and on the gable-end I'll carve a lovely mermaid. Vane and locks shall be of brass, and window-panes shall shine so bright that from afar people shall wonder what it is that they see gleaming in the sun. *(Laughs bitterly.)* Damned lies! Why, there I go again! Remember that you're an outlaw, boy! *(Sets to work feverishly.)* A well-thatched hut is quite enough to keep out both the frost and rain. *(Looks up at the tree.)* It's giving way. One more stroke! There! He's down and fallen all his length, and all the undergrowth is quivering. *(Sets to work to lop off the branches, all at once he stops and listens, with uplifted axe.)* There's some-one coming! Ingrid's father—— Trying to catch me treacherously! *(Hides behind a tree and peeps out.)* A boy! Just one. And he looks frightened. He's glancing round him. What is that he's hiding underneath his jacket? A sickle. Now he stands and looks—— He lays his hand upon a log—— What now? Why does he brace himself ——? Ugh! He has chopped a finger off! And now he's bleeding like a pig—— And now he runs off with his hand wrapped in a clout. *(Comes forward.)* He must be mad! Chopped it right off!—a precious finger! And did it, too, as if he meant it. Oho, I see! If one's not anxious to serve His Gracious Majesty that is the only way. So that's it! They would have called him for the army, but he, I see, would be exempted. Still, to cut off——? To lose for ever——? The thought, perhaps—the wish—the will—— Those I could understand; but really to *do* the deed! Ah, no—that beats me!

[*Shakes his head a little; then resumes his work.*

SCENE II

SCENE.—*A room in* AASE'S *house. Everything is in disorder. The clothes-chest is standing open; clothes lie scattered about; a cat is lying on the bed.* AASE *and* KARI *are trying to put things in order.*

Aase (running to one side of the room). Kari, tell me——

Kari. What is it?

Aase. Tell me—— Where is——? Where shall I find——? Oh, tell me, where is——? What am I looking for? I'm going crazy! Where's the chest key?

Kari. It's in the keyhole.

Aase. What's that rumbling?

Kari. The last load going off to Hægstad.

Aase (weeping). I wish they were taking me in my coffin! What we poor creatures have to suffer! God pity me! The whole house emptied! What Hægstad left, the Judge has taken. They've scarcely left me with a rag to put upon my back. It's shameful to have pronounced so hard a sentence! *(Sits down on the edge of the bed.)* The farm's gone now, and all our land. He's a hard man, but the Law was harder; no one to help me—none showed mercy—— Peer gone, and no one to advise me.

Kari. You've got this house until you die.

Aase. Oh, yes—the bread of charity, for me and for my cat!

Kari. Old mother, God help you! Peer has cost you dear.

Aase. My Peer? I think you've lost your senses! They got their Ingrid, safe and sound. They should have rightly blamed the Devil; he is the culprit, and no other; 'twas he, the ugly beast, that tempted my poor dear boy!

Kari. Had you not better send for the priest? For all you know, things may be worse than you believe.

Aase. Send for the priest? Perhaps I'd better. *(Gets up.)* No, no—I cannot! I'm his mother; I must help the boy—it's only my duty; I must do my best, when everyone fails me. They've left him that coat. I must get it patched. I wish I had dared to keep the bed-cover! Where are the stockings?

Kari. There, with that rubbish.

Aase (fumbling among the things). What's this? Look here! An old casting-ladle! He used to pretent to mould buttons with this, melt them and shape them and stamp them, too. Once, when we'd company, in came the boy and begged of his father a bit of tin. "Not tin," said John, "King Christian's coin! A silver coin to melt and show that you're the son of rich John Gynt." May God forgive him, for he was drunk; and when he was drunk it was all the same, tin or gold. Ah, here are the stockings! They are all in holes; I must darn them, Kari.

Kari. They certainly need it.

Aase. When that is done, I must go to bed. I feel so bad, so wretchedly ill. *(Joyfully.)* Oh, look here, Kari! Two flannel shirts that they have forgotten!

Kari. Aye, so they have.

Aase. That's a lucky find. You might put one of them aside. Or—no, I think we'll take them both; the one he has on is so thin and worn.

Kari. But, Aase, you know that it's a sin!

Aase. Oh, yes; but you know the parson tells us that all our sins may be forgiven.

SCENE III

SCENE.—*Outside a newly built hut in the forest. Reindeer horns over the door. Deep snow everywhere. It is nightfall.* PEER GYNT *is standing fixing a heavy wooden bolt to the door.*

Peer Gynt (laughing now and then). There must be a bolt, to fasten my door against the Troll-folk and men and women. There must be a bolt, to keep me safe from all the plaguy crowd of goblins. They'll come when it's dark, and I'll hear them knocking: "Open, Peer, we are quick as thoughts! Under the bed, on the hearth in the ashes, you'll hear us creeping and crawling about; we'll fly down the chimney like fiery dragons. Hee-hee! Do you think your nails and planks can save you from plaguy goblin-thoughts?"

[SOLVEIG *comes over the snow on skis; she has a shawl over her head and a bundle in her hand.*

Solveig. God bless your work. You must not reject me. I had your message, and you must take me.

Peer Gynt. Solveig! It can't be——! Yes, it is! And not afraid to come so near me!

Solveig. I had your message from little Helga, and others I had from the winds and the silence. There was one in all that your mother told me, and others that came to me in my dreams. The dreary nights and the empty days brought me the message that I must come. All light had gone from my life down yonder; I had neither the heart to laugh nor to weep. I could not tell what was in your mind; I could only tell what I needs must do.

Peer Gynt. But your father?

Solveig. I've no one on God's wide earth that I can call father or mother now; I've left them for ever.

Peer Gynt. Solveig, my dear—— To come to me?

Solveig. Yes, to you alone; you must be all to me—friend and comfort. *(In tears.)* The worst was leaving my little sister; and worse than that, to leave my father; and worst of all to leave her who carried me at her breast; no, God forgive me, the worst indeed was the bitter sorrow that I must part from all my dear ones!

Peer Gynt. And do you know the heavy sentence the law pronounced? They've taken from me everything that I had or might have.

Solveig. 'Twas not for what you had or might have I give up what was dearest to me.

Peer Gynt. And do you know that if I venture beyond this forest I am forfeit if any man can lay hand on me?

Solveig. When I asked my way as I came hither, they questioned me—where was I going? "I'm going home": that was my answer.

Peer Gynt. Ah, then I need no bolts to guard me, no locks against the powers of evil! My hunter's hut is consecrated if you deign enter it and live there. Dear, let me look at you! Not too near you—— I'd only look at you! How lovely, how pure you are! Let my arms lift you! How slim and light you are, my Solveig! I'd carry you for ever, dearest, and never weary! I'll not soil you; I'll hold your warm and lovely body at arms' length from me! Ah, my Solveig, can I believe I've made you love me? Both night and day 'tis what I've longed for. See, I have built this little dwelling—— It shall come down; it's cramped and ugly——

Solveig. Little or big, I'm happy here. Here one can breathe, in the buffeting wind. Down yonder 'twas sultry; I felt hemmed in; it was partly that, that drove me away. But here, where one hears the fir-trees soughing—— Such song and silence!—I feel at home.

Peer Gynt. But, dear, are you sure? It means for ever!

Solveig. There's no way back on the road I have trodden.

Peer Gynt. You're mine, then! Go in! I would see you within! Go in! I will fetch some wood for a fire, to warm you snugly and flicker brightly; you shall sit soft and never shiver. *(He unbars the door, and* SOLVEIG *goes in. He stands silent for a moment, then laughs aloud for joy and leaps into the air.)* My princess! Now she is found and won! Now my palace shall spring into being!

[*Seizes his axe and crosses over towards the trees. At the same moment an elderly woman in a tattered green gown advances out of the wood; an ugly child with a flagon in his hand limps after her, holding on to her skirt.*

The Woman. Good evening, Peer Light-Foot!

Peer Gynt. What is it? Who are you?

The Woman. Old friends, Peer Gynt! My hut is quite near here. We're neighbours.

Peer Gynt. Indeed? I was not aware of it.

The Woman. As your hut grew up, so mine grew beside it.

Peer Gynt (trying to get away). I'm in a great hurry.

The Woman. You always were that; but, trudging along, in the end I come up with you.

Peer Gynt. Old dame, you're mistaken!

The Woman. I know I was once; that day when you made me such wonderful promises.

Peer Gynt. I made you promises? Why, what the devil——?

The Woman. Do you mean you've forgotten the night when you drank at my father's? Do you mean you've forgotten——

Peer Gynt. I mean I've forgotten what never took place to remember! What nonsense is this? And when last did we meet?

The Woman. The last time we met was the first time we met. *(To the child.)* Give your father a drink; I think he is thirsty.

Peer Gynt. His father? You're drunk! Do you mean that this urchin——?

The Woman. You're not going to say that you can't

recognize him? Have you eyes? Can't you see that he's lame in the shanks as you're lame in your mind?

Peer Gynt. Do you mean to pretend——?

The Woman. You can't wriggle out of it!

Peer Gynt. That long-legged brat——?

The Woman. He has grown very fast.

Peer Gynt. Why, you ugly old hag, do you dare to assert that this——?

The Woman. Listen, Peer Gynt; you're as coarse as a bullock. *(Weeps.)* Oh, how can I help it if I'm not as fair as I was when you tempted me out on the hill-side up there in the mountains? And when in the autumn my travail came on me, I'd only the Devil to act as a midwife; so it isn't surprising I lost all my beauty. But if you would see me as fair as before, you've only to turn out that girl that's in there, out of your house and your mind and your sight; do that, dearest lad, and my ill-looks will vanish!

Peer Gynt. Get away, you old witch!

The Woman. You shall see if I will!

Peer Gynt. I'll break your head for you!

The Woman. Try, if you dare! You'll find me, Peer, a hard nut to crack! Every day I shall be back again, peeping at doors and spying on both of you. When you and your girl are sitting together, and you are inclined for cuddling and fondling, you'll find me beside you, claiming my share of it. She and I will share you—turn about. Good-bye, dear boy. If you like the prospect, then wed her to-morrow!

Peer Gynt. You devil's nightmare!

The Woman. But I had forgotten! You've got to look after your little son—this graceful urchin! Come on, little imp, will you go to your father?

The Boy (spitting at PEER*).* If I had an axe, I'd split you in two with it! Just wait!

The Woman (kissing the BOY*).* What a head he's got on

his shoulders! When you've grown up you'll be just like your father!

Peer Gynt (stamping his foot). I wish you——

The Woman. As far off as now we are near you?

Peer Gynt (clinching his fists). And all this comes——

The Woman. Just of thoughts and desires! Hard luck for you, Peer!

Peer Gynt. It's hardest for her—for Solveig—my loveliest, purest treasure!

The Woman. Oh, yes; the innocent always suffer—as the Devil said when his mother thrashed him because his father had come home drunk!

[*She moves off into the wood with the* Boy, *who throws the flagon behind him.*

Peer Gynt (after a long silence). "Round about," said the Boyg; that's how I must go.—My palace has tumbled about my ears! She was so near me; and now there has risen a wall between us, and all in a moment my joy is gone and everything's ugly. "Round about"—ah, yes; there's no straight road that leads through this from me to her. No straight road? All the same, there might be. If I remember aright, the Bible says something somewhere about repentance—but I've no Bible, and I've forgotten the most of it, and in this forest there's not a thing that will give me guidance. Repent? It might take years to do it before I found the way. And, meanwhile, a life that's empty, ugly, dreary; and in the end from shreds and fragments to try and patch the thing together? One can patch up a broken fiddle, but not a watch-spring. If one tramples on growing things they're spoiled for ever.—But, surely, the old witch was lying! I can put all those ugly doings out of my sight! But—can I put them out of my mind? I shall be haunted by lurking memories—of Ingrid—of those three girls upon the hillside. Will they come, too, and jeer and threaten, and beg of me to hold them closely or lift them tenderly at arms' length? It's no use! Were my arms as long as fir-trees' stems or pine-trees' branches, I should be holding *her* too near to set her down again unsullied. I must find some way round about, without a thought of gain or loss; some way to free me from such thoughts and shut them from my mind for ever. *(Takes a few steps towards the hut, then stops.)* But—go in now? Disgraced and soiled? With all these Troll-folk at my heels? Speak, and yet not tell all? Confess, and still be hiding something from her? *(Throws away his axe.)* No, no—to go and meet her now, such as I am, were sacrilege.

[SOLVEIG *appears at the door of the hut.*

Solveig. Are you coming, dear?

Peer Gynt (below his breath). "Go round about"!

Solveig. What do you say?

Peer Gynt. Dear, you must wait. It's dark, and I've a heavy load.

Solveig. I'll come and help you bear the load.

Peer Gynt. No, do not come! Stay where you are! I'll bear the whole of it.

Solveig. But, dear, don't be too long.

Peer Gynt. Be patient, child; whether the time is long or short, you must just wait.

Solveig (nodding to him). Yes, I will wait.

[PEER GYNT *goes off along the forest path.* SOLVEIG *remains standing at the half-open door.*

SCENE IV

SCENE.—AASE'S *house. It is evening. A log fire is burning on the hearth and lights up the room. A cat is lying on a chair at the foot of a bed on which* AASE *is lying, fumbling restlessly with the sheets.*

Aase. Ah me, is my son never coming? The nights are so weary and long. I've no one to take him a message, and so much to say to him now, my time's running short—oh, how quickly! To think that the end should be this! If only I'd known, I would never have said a hard word to the boy! [PEER GYNT *comes in.*

Peer Gynt. Good evening!

Aase. My boy! Oh, God bless you! My dearest, at last you have come! But how have you dared to come hither? Your life is in danger, you know.

Peer Gynt. My life?—oh, my life doesn't matter. I had to come down to you now.

Aase. And Kari!—she said that you wouldn't! Ah, now I can leave you in peace.

Peer Gynt. Leave me? Why, what are you saying? And where do you think you can go?

Aase. Ah, Peer, it's the end that's approaching; I haven't much longer to live.

Peer Gynt (turning away abruptly and walking across the room). I was running away from my sorrows and thought at least here I'd be free——! Are you cold? Are your hands and your feet cold?

Aase. Yes, Peer; you'll be done with me soon. When my eyes lose their light you must close them—but tenderly, carefully, Peer. And then you must get me a coffin and see that it's handsome and fine. Ah, no, I forgot——

Peer Gynt. Do be quiet! Time enough for all that by-and-by.

Aase. Yes, yes. *(Looks uneasily round the room.)* Do you see what a little they've left me? It's all one to them.

Peer Gynt (with a grimace). There you go! *(Harshly.)* Yes, I know I am guilty. But what do you think is the good of raking it up to remind me?

Aase. No! It was the drink was to blame. That damnable drink that destroyed you, my boy; for you know you were drunk and didn't know what you were doing. Besides—that wild ride on the buck!—I'm sure it was not to be wondered if you were not right in your head.

Peer Gynt. Never mind all that nonsense and rubbish; never mind about anything now. Let's put off serious thinking till later—another day. *(Sits down on the edge of the bed.)* Now, mother, let's have a gossip and talk of all sorts of things, except what's ugly and horrid and hurts—let's forget all that. Bless me! Why, there's old pussy! To think that he's still alive!

Aase. At night he seems so uneasy; and we all know what that means!

Peer Gynt (turning away). What is the news in the district?

Aase (smiling). They do say that hereabouts there's a girl that longs for the mountains——

Peer Gynt (hastily). Mads Moen—is he content?

Aase. They say that she will not listen to the old folks' prayers and tears. You ought to go and see her; maybe you could find a way——

Peer Gynt. And what's become of the blacksmith?

Aase. Oh, bother the dirty smith! I'd so much rather tell you her name—that girl's, you know——

Peer Gynt. No, we're going to have a gossip and talk of all sorts of things, except what's ugly and horrid and hurts—let's forget all that. Shall I fetch you a drink? Are you thirsty? Can you stretch in that little bed? Let me look—why, this is surely the bed I had as a boy! Do you remember your sitting beside my bed at night smoothing the bed-spread over and singing me rhymes and songs?

Aase. Yes, and we played at sleighing, when your father had gone away—the bed-spread was our apron, and the floor an ice-bound fjord.

Peer Gynt. Yes, but do you remember the finest bit of it all—our pair of prancing horses?

Aase. Why, yes—of course I do. 'Twas Kari's cat we borrowed and put up on a stool.

Peer Gynt. To Soria-Moria Castle, that's westward of the moon and eastward of the sunrise, o'er hill and dale we flew. A stick that we found in the cupboard made you a splendid whip.

Aase. I sat up like the driver——

Peer Gynt. Yes, and you shook the reins; and turned round as we galloped, to ask if I were cold. God bless you, you old scolder! You were a dear to me—— Why do you groan?

Aase. It's my back, Peer; it's sore from lying here.

Peer Gynt. Stretch up and I'll support you. There—now you're lying snug.

Aase (uneasily). I want to get away, Peer.

Peer Gynt. To get away?

Aase. Ah, yes—it's what I'm always longing.

Peer Gynt. What senseless talk is that? See, let me smooth the bed-clothes and then sit on the bed,—now, we will make the time fly with singing rhymes and songs.

Aase. No, let me have my prayer-book; my mind is ill at ease.

Peer Gynt. In Soria-Moria Castle they're having a splendid feast. Rest back upon the cushions; I'll drive you quickly there——

Aase. But, dear, am I invited?

Peer Gynt. Of course—and I am, too. *(He throws a cord round the back of the chair on which the cat is lying, takes a stick in his hand and sits down on the foot of the bed.)* Gee up! Get on with you, Blackie! Mother, you're sure you're not cold? Aha! Now we shall be moving, when Granë kicks up his heels!

Aase. But, Peer—I hear something ringing——

Peer Gynt. It's the glittering sleigh-bells, dear.

Aase. They sound so strange and hollow!

Peer Gynt. We're driving over a fjord.

Aase. I'm frightened! What is it, that sighing and moaning so wild and drear?

Peer Gynt. It's only the firs on the hillside whispering. Just sit still.

Aase. I seem to see lights in the distance. What is it that's glistening there?

Peer Gynt. It's the window and gates of the Castle. Can you hear the dancers?

Aase. Yes.

Peer Gynt. And outside stands Saint Peter asking you to come in.

Aase. Does he greet me?

Peer Gynt. Yes, with honour, and offers you sweetest wine.

Aase. Wine! Does he offer cakes, too?

Peer Gynt. A plateful of them, yes! And our parson's wife preparing your coffee and your dessert.

Aase. What! Shall I really meet her?

Peer Gynt. As soon and as oft as you please.

Aase. You're driving your poor old mother to a splendid party, Peer!

Peer Gynt (smacking his whip). Gee up! Get on with you, Blackie!

Aase. Are you sure that you know the way?

Peer Gynt (smacking his whip again). I can see the road.

Aase. But the journey makes me feel ill and tired.

Peer Gynt. I can see the Castle before me; the drive will soon be done.

Aase. I'll lie back with my eyes shut and trust to you, my boy!

Peer Gynt. Now show your paces, Granë! The Castle is all agog; the folk all swarm to the gateway; Peer Gynt and his mother arrive! Why, what's that, Mister Saint Peter? You won't let my mother in? You must look far, I can tell you, to find a worthier soul. Of myself I will say nothing; I can turn back to the gate. I'll take pot-luck, if you'll have me; if not, it's all one to me. Like the Devil in the pulpit, I've told a heap of lies and have called my dear old mother a silly old hen, I know, because she cackled and scolded; but things must be different here. You must respect and revere her, sincerely and honestly; you'll not get anyone better from our parts nowadays.—Oho! Here's God the father! Saint Peter, you'll catch it now! *(Speaks in a deep voice.)* "Just stop that bullying, will you! Mother Aase is welcome here!" *(Laughs aloud and turns to his mother.)* I knew how 'twould be! Saint Peter is singing small enough now! *(His voice takes on an anxious tone.)* Why do you stare so, mother? Have you lost your senses, dear? *(Goes to the head of the bed.)* You mustn't lie and stare so——! Speak, mother; it's I, your boy! *(Feels her forehead and hands cautiously; then throws the cord away on to the chair and says in a low voice):* So it's that!—You may rest now, Granë; our journey's over and done. *(Shuts her eyes and bends over her.)* Thanks, dear, for all you gave me, thrashings and kisses alike! And now it's for you to thank me—— *(Presses his cheek against her lips.)* There—that was the driver's fee. [KARI *comes in.*

Kari. What? Peer! Then her deepest sorrow and grieving will be forgot! Good Lord, how sound she is sleeping! Or is she——?

Peer Gynt. Hush, she is dead.

[KARI *weeps by* AASE'S *body.* PEER GYNT *walks to and fro in the room; at last he stops by the bedside.*

Peer Gynt. See that she's decently buried. I must try to escape from here.

Kari. Where shall you go?

Peer Gynt. To the sea-coast.

Kari. So far! Aye, and farther still. [*Goes out.*

ACT IV

SCENE I

SCENE.—*A grove of palm-trees, on the south-west coast of Morocco. A dining-table is spread under an awning; rush matting underfoot. Farther back in the grove hammocks are hanging. A steam yacht, flying the Norwegian and American flags, is flying off the shore. A jolly-boat is drawn up on the beach. It is nearly sundown.* PEER GYNT, *now a good-looking middle-aged man, dressed in a neat travelling-suit, with a pair of gold-mounted eyeglasses dangling on his breast, is presiding at table as host to* MR. COTTON, MONSIEUR BALLON, HERR VON EBERKOPF, *and* HERR TRUMPETERSTRAALE. *The party have just finished a meal.* PEER GYNT *is passing the wine.*

Peer Gynt. Drink, gentlemen! If man is meant for pleasure, let him take his pleasure. The past's the past—what's done is done—so we are taught. What may I give you?

Herr Trumpeterstraale. As host, dear brother Gynt, you're splendid!

Peer Gynt. The credit's just as much my purse's, my cook's and steward's——

Mr. Cotton. Very well, then here's a health to all the four!

Monsieur Ballon. Monsieur, your taste—your *ton*—is such as nowadays one seldom meets with amongst men living *en garçon*—a certain *je ne sais quoi*——

Herr von Eberkopf. Quite so; a breath, a gleam of introspection—world-citizenship's inspiration; a glance that pierces clouds, that's free from any narrow prejudices; a glimpse of higher criticism; a simple nature coupled with a life's experience and thereby uplifted to the highest power. I think that's what you meant—eh, Monsieur?

Monsieur Ballon. Yes, very possibly. In French it doesn't sound quite so impressive.

Herr von Eberkopf. Of course not. French is somewhat cramped. But if we want to trace the source of this phenomenon——

Peer Gynt. That's easy; it's just because I've never married. Why, gentlemen, the thing's as clear as daylight. What's a man's first duty? The answer's brief: To be himself—to take good care of all that touches himself and what is his. But how can he do this if his existence is that of a pack-camel laden with someone else's weal and woe?

Herr von Eberkopf. But I dare say you've had to fight for this self-centred concentration?

Peer Gynt. Oh, yes, I've had to fight for it, but I have always won the honours; though once I very nearly fell into a trap, for all my cunning. I was a wild, good-looking spark and let my roving fancy capture a girl who was of royal blood——

Monsieur Ballon. Of royal blood?

Peer Gynt (carelessly). Or very nearly. You know——

Herr Trumpeterstraale (thumping on the table). These damned aristocrats!

Peer Gynt (shrugging his shoulders). These bogus Highnesses, whose pride is to keep off from their escutcheon the slightest speck of what's plebeian.

Mr. Cotton. And so it came to nothing, then?

Monsieur Ballon. The family opposed the match?

Peer Gynt. Quite the reverse!

Monsieur Ballon. Ah!

Peer Gynt (discreetly). Well, you see, things took a turn which made them think that it was high time we were married. But, to be candid, the affair from first to last was most distasteful. In certain things I'm very dainty, and also like my independence; and when her father came and hinted that he would make it a condition that I should change my name and status and lose my own nobility—with lots of similar conditions I could not stomach or accept—I gracefully retired from it, refused the father's ultimatum and gave my youthful bride her congé. *(Drums on the table with his fingers and says with a pious air.)* Ah, yes, there is a Hand that guides us, and we poor men can trust to that. It's very comforting to know it.

Monsieur Ballon. So the affair went by the board?

Peer Gynt. No, it took on another aspect. Outsiders meddled in the game and raised an unexpected pother. The youngsters of the family were much the worst. I had to battle with seven of them all at once. I never shall forget that time, though I emerged from it the victor. Some blood was spilt; but still that blood sealed my certificate of valour and proved what I remarked just now—that there's a Hand that guides us wisely.

Herr von Eberkopf. You have an outlook upon life that proves you a philosopher. For, while an ordinary thinker sees every detail separately and never grasps the whole completely, your vision covers all together. You have a universal standard to measure life with. Your perceptions, like rays of sunlight, emanating from a great central contemplation, pierce every fallacy.—And yet you say you had no education?

Peer Gynt. I am, as I've already told you, a self-taught man in every way. I've never learnt methodically, but I have thought and speculated and read a bit on every subject. I was not young when I began; and so, of course, it wasn't easy to plough the field of knowledge up and do the thing at all completely. I've learnt my history in scraps; for more than that I've had no leisure. And since, when evil days assail, a man needs certain things to trust in, I fitfully absorbed religion; I found that it assimilated much easier if taken that way. No use to glut one's self with reading, but to select what may be useful——

Mr. Cotton. Ah, now, that's practical!

Peer Gynt. Dear friends, just think what my career has been. What was I when I first went westwards? Quite penniless and empty-handed. I had to work hard for my food—— No easy job, believe me, often; but life, my friends, is always sweet, and death, as we all know, is bitter. Well! Luck, you see, did not desert me, and good old Fate was always kindly. Things moved, and I was always careful, and so things went from good to better; and, ten years after that, they called me the Crœsus of the Charlestown traders; my name was known in every port and luck pursued me with my shipping——

Mr. Cotton. What was your trade?

Peer Gynt. I trafficked most in negro slaves for Carolina and idols that were sent to China.

Monsieur Ballon. Oh, fie, for shame!

Herr Trumpeterstraale. Friend Gynt, how could you?

Peer Gynt. You think my enterprise was passing beyond the bounds of what was lawful? I felt the same thing very keenly; I found it hateful in the end. But, once begun, you may believe me 'twas difficult enough to end it. In any case, so big a business affected others by the thousand; to break it off too suddenly would have, of course, been most disastrous. I never like to break things off; but all the same, I must admit I've always fully been alive to what you'd call the consequences; and, when I've overstepped the bounds, it's always made me feel uneasy. Besides, I wasn't growing younger. By that time I was nearly fifty, and by degrees my hair was greying; and, though my health was always perfect, thoughts such as this cropped up to plague me; "who knows how short the time may be before the Great Assize is summoned and sheep from goats are separated?" What could I do? To cease my trade with China was impossible. I found a way. I opened up a second traffic to those waters; and, though each spring I sent to China shiploads of idols, every autumn I sent out Missionaries furnished with everything that could be needful to work conversion—stockings, rum, Bibles and rice——

Mr. Cotton. All at a profit?

Peer Gynt. Oh, well, of course.—The plan worked well. For every idol sold out yonder there was a duly baptized coolie, so one thing neutralized the other. We kept the Missionaries busy, because they had to counteract the idols that we were exporting.

Mr. Cotton. But what about the negro traffic?

Peer Gynt. Why, there my morals triumphed also. I felt the trade was scarcely suited to one whose years were fast increasing; you never know when death may claim you. And then there were the thousand pitfalls dug by our philanthropic friends, besides the chance of being caught and daily risks from wind and weather. By taking thought I found a way. "You'll have to reef your sails, friend Peter, and see" —so I said to myself—"how you can best retrieve your error!" I bought land in a southern state and held back my last load of niggers (which was of first-class quality) and settled them on the plantation. They throve apace, grew fat and sleek, and they, as well as I, were happy. Yes, without bragging I may say I treated them like any father —— And the result was handsome profit. I built them schools, so as to set a standard of morality to be maintained, and saw to it that it was kept well up to mark. And then, to make the change complete, out of the business I retired, and sold, with livestock, as it stood, the whole plantation. When I left, to all alike, both young and old, a gratis gift of grog was issued, and every nigger got a skinful. The widows, as an extra gift, were given snuff. And so I hope—unless the Word is merely froth which says one's deeds are surely good if they are not as surely evil—that all my errors are forgot, and that perhaps in greater measure than in most people's case, my deeds will more than balance out my sins.

Herr von Eberkopf (clinking glasses with him). How edifying 'tis to hear a scheme of life worked out so deftly, freed from the fog of theories and undisturbed by outer clamour!

Peer Gynt (who during the foregoing conversation has been applying steadily to the bottle). We northern men are famous hands at planning a campaign! The secret of life's success is very simple—merely to keep one's ears shut tight to the insidious advances of a pernicious reptile.

Mr. Cotton. Aye, but what's the reptile, my dear friend?

Peer Gynt. A small one, always tempting men to take irrevocable steps. *(Drinks again.)* A man can venture without fear and keep his courage, if he's careful not to get definitely caught in any of life's cunning pitfalls—if he looks forward and beyond the present moment and its chances, and always carefully preserves a bridge behind him to retire on. That theory has held me up and always coloured all my conduct—a theory I inherited and learnt at home from early childhood.

Monsieur Ballon. You're a Norwegian, I believe?

Peer Gynt. By birth, yes; but by disposition I am a citizen of the world. For the good fortune I've enjoyed, I have to thank America; my well-stocked library I owe to Germany's advanced young thinkers; from France I get my taste in dress, my manners, and whatever turn I have for subtleness of mind; England has taught me industry and care for my own interests; the Jews have taught me how to wait; from Italy I've caught a dash of taste for *dolce far niente;* and once, when in a sorry fix, I reached the goal of my desire by trusting to good Swedish steel.

Herr Trumpeterstraale (lifting his glass). Ah, Swedish steel——!

Herr von Eberkopf. Yes, first and foremost we offer homage to the man who is a swordsman.

[*They clink glasses and drink with* PEER GYNT *who is beginning to get heated with wine.*

Mr. Cotton. All you've said is excellent; but now, sir, pray tell us what you propose to do with all your wealth.

Peer Gynt (smiling). Do with it, eh?

All (drawing nearer to him). Yes, let us hear!

Peer Gynt. Well, first of all, to travel; and that's why, you see, I took you all on board my yacht as company. I had a mind to have a choir to worship at my Altar of the Golden Calf——

Herr von Eberkopf. How witty!

Mr. Cotton. Yes, but no one sails for the mere pleasure of a journey. You have an object, without doubt; what is it?

Peer Gynt. To be Emperor.

All. What!

Peer Gynt (nodding his head). To be Emperor.

All. But where?

Peer Gynt. Of the whole world.

Monsieur Ballon. But how, my friend——?

Peer Gynt. Just simply by the power of gold! It's not a new idea at all; it has inspired my every effort. In boyish dreams I used to travel over the sea upon a cloud; I tried to soar to fancied grandeurs and then dropped down on to all-fours; but to its goal my mind was constant. Somewhere—I can't remember where—it says that if a man shall win the whole wide world, but lose *himself*, all that he gains is only like a wreath upon an empty skull. That's what it says—or something like it—and, trust me, it is pretty true.

Herr von Eberkopf. But what, then, is the Gyntian Self?

Peer Gynt. The world which lies within my brain; which makes me *me*, and no one else—no more than God can be the Devil.

Herr Trumpeterstraale. Now I can see at what you're driving!

Monsieur Ballon. Sublime philosopher!

Herr von Eberkopf. Great poet!

Peer Gynt (with growing exaltation). The Gyntian Self! —An army, that, of wishes, appetites, desires! The Gyntian Self! It is a sea of fancies, claims and aspirations; in fact, it's all that swells within my breast and makes it come about that I am I and live as such. But, just as our Good Lord has need of earthly mould to be earth's God, so I have need of lots of gold if I'm to be an Emperor.

Monsieur Ballon. But you are rich!

Peer Gynt. Not rich enough. Enough, perhaps, for me to pose for two or three days as a princeling in some such place as Lippe-Detmold; but I must be *myself*—complete—A Gynt fit for the universe—Sir Peter Gynt from head to heels!

Monsieur Ballon (in transports). To purchase all the loveliest things the world can offer!

Herr von Eberkopf. All the bins of century-old Johannisberger!

Herr Trumpeterstraale. The armoury of Charles the Twelfth!

Mr. Cotton. But, before all, to seize the chance of profitable business.

Peer Gynt. Well, I've found a way to get them all, and that is why we're anchored here! to-night our course will be to northward. The newspapers I've just received have brought me some important news. *(Rises and lifts his glass.)* It shows that fortune always favours those who have confidence to grasp it——

All. Well? Tell us——!

Peer Gynt. Greece is in an uproar.

All. (springing to their feet). What, have the Greeks ——?

Peer Gynt. They have revolted.

All. Hurrah!

Peer Gynt. And Turkey's in a hole.

Monsieur Ballon. To Greece! The way to glory's open! I'll help them with my sword of France!

Herr von Eberkopf. I with my voice—but at a distance!

Mr. Cotton. I'll get a contract to supply them!

Herr Trumpeterstraale. Let us away! I'll find at Bender Charles the Twelfth's famous spur-buckles!

Monsieur Ballon (falling on PEER GYNT'S *neck).* Forgive me, friend, if for a moment I had misjudged you!

Herr von Eberkopf (grasping PEER GYNT *by the hand).* I'm a fool! I almost took you for a scoundrel!

Mr. Cotton. That's much too strong—say, rather, for a simpleton——

Herr Trumpeterstraale (embracing PEER GYNT*).* And I, dear friend, had put you down as an example of the worst type of Yankee rascal! Forgive me!

Herr von Eberkopf. We were all mistaken——

Peer Gynt. What do you mean?

Herr von Eberkopf. We now can glimpse the banners of the Gyntian army of wishes, appetites, desires——!

Monsieur Ballon (admiringly). That's what you meant by "being a Gynt"!

Herr von Eberkopf (in the same tone). A Gynt that's worthy of all honour!

Peer Gynt. But tell me——?

Monsieur Ballon. Don't you understand?

Peer Gynt. I'm hanged if I can take your meaning.

Monsieur Ballon. Why, aren't you going to help the Greeks with money and with ships?

Peer Gynt (whistling). No, thank you! I'm going to help the stronger side and lend my money to the Turks.

Monsieur Ballon. Impossible!

Herr von Eberkopf. That's very funny!—But you, of course, must have your joke!

[PEER GYNT *is silent for a moment, then leans on a chair and assumes an air of importance.*

Peer Gynt. Gentlemen, we had better part before the last remains of friendship dissolve like wreaths of smoke. The man who hasn't anything may lightly take any chances; those whose all is no more than the scrap of earth they stand on, are the fittest far for sacrifice and cannon-fodder. But when a man's well off, as I am, he risks a greater stake than they. Pray go to Greece. I'll land you there and furnish you with weapons gratis; the more you fan the flame of strife, the better it will be for me. Strike hard for Freedom and the Right! Attack the Turks and give them hell; and meet a glorious end upon a janissary's spear-point.—But, excuse me if I don't come with you. *(Slaps his pockets.)* I've money in my pockets, and I am Myself—Sir Peer Gynt.

[*Puts up his umbrella and goes into the grove where the hammocks are hanging.*

Herr Trumpeterstraale. The swine!

Monsieur Ballon. He has no sense of honour!

Mr. Cotton. Oh, honour—let that pass. But think what splendid profits we could make if only Greece could free herself——

Monsieur Ballon. I saw myself acclaimed a victor by crowds of lovely Grecian women!

Herr Trumpeterstraale. I felt those famous buckles safe within my Swedish grasp!

Herr von Eberkopf. I saw my glorious fatherland's *Kultur* spread widely over land and sea——

Mr. Cotton. The actual loss is worst of all. Goddam!—I feel inclined to cry! I saw myself proprietor of Mount Olympus, which contains (unless what men have said is false) rich veins of copper to be worked; and the renowned Castalian stream—its many waterfalls would yield a thousand horsepower, easily!

Herr Trumpeterstraale. I shall go, all the same! My sword is worth more, still, than Yankee gold.

Mr. Cotton. Perhaps; but, fighting in the ranks, we

should be merely swamped by numbers. What profit should we get from that?

Monsieur Ballon. Curse it! So near the heights of fortune—and then to be dashed down again.

Mr. Cotton (shaking his fist at the yacht). To think that all this nabob's gold, that he has sweated from his niggers, is in that ship!

Herr von Eberkopf. An inspiration! Come on, and let us act! His empire shall come to nothing now! Hurrah!

Monsieur Ballon. What will you do?

Herr von Eberkopf. I'll seize his power! The crew will easily be bought. On board! I'll commandeer his yacht!

Mr. Cotton. You'll—what?

Herr von Eberkopf. I mean to bag the lot.

[*Goes towards the jolly-boat.*

Mr. Cotton. It's clearly to my interest to share with you.

[*Follows him.*

Herr Trumpeterstraale. There goes a scamp!

Monsieur Ballon. A proper scoundrel! But—*enfin!*

[*Follows the others.*

Herr Trumpeterstraale. Well, I suppose I may as well go with them—under protest, though! [*Follows.*

SCENE II

SCENE.—*Another part of the coast. Moonlight and passing clouds. Out at sea the yacht is seen steaming at full speed.* PEER GYNT *is running along the shore, now pinching himself in the arm, now staring out to sea.*

Peer Gynt. It's nightmare!—Illusion!—I soon shall wake up! It's heading to sea! And at top of its speed! It's a dream, and I'm sleeping! I'm drunk or I'm mad! *(Wrings his hands.)* It's impossible that I should perish like this! *(Tears his hair.)* It's a dream! It *must* be—it *shall* be—a dream! It's terrible! Ah, but alas it is true! My scoundrelly friends——! Oh, hear me, Good Lord! You are Wisdom and Justice—oh, punish them, Lord! *(Stretches up his arms.)* It is I—Peer Gynt! Do look after me, Lord! Take care of me, Father, or else I shall die! Make them slacken the engines—or cast off the gig! Stop the robbers! Make something go wrong with the works! Do listen! Leave other folk's matters alone! The world will look after itself while You do.—He's not listening. He is as deaf as a post! It's too much! A God that can't think what to do! *(Beckons up to the sky.)* I say! I've disposed of my negro plantation, and sent heaps of Missionaries out to Asia. Don't You think that one good turn's deserving another? Oh, help me to get on the ship——! *(A sudden glare rises into the sky from the yacht, followed by a thick cloud of smoke. A dull explosion is heard.* PEER GYNT *utters a shriek and sinks down on the sand. The smoke gradually disperses and the yacht is seen to have disappeared.* PEER GYNT *looks up, with a pale face, and says in a low voice.)* 'Twas a judgment! Sunk with all hands in a moment of time! All thanks to the chances of fortune. *(Emotionally.)* No, no! There was more than the chance of fortune in this, that I should be saved while the rest of them perish. Thanks be to Thee who hast been my protector and kept an eye on me in spite of my failings! *(Takes a deep breath.)* What a wonderful feeling of safety and comfort it gives you to know that you're specially guarded! But where shall I find meat and drink in the desert? I don't know, I'm sure. But He will understand. It *can't* be so dangerous.—— *(In a loud and insinuating voice.)* He will not suffer such a poor little sparrow as I am to perish! I must humble myself—and allow Him some time. The Lord will provide; I must not be downhearted.—— *(Springs to his feet with a cry of terror.)* Did I hear a lion? That growl in the rushes——? *(His teeth chatter.)* No, it was no lion. *(Pulls himself together.)* I'm certain it was! Those creatures, of course, know to keep at a distance; they dare not take bites at a lord of creation. They have instinct, of course; it's by instinct they feel that an elephant's not a safe thing to attack. —All the same, I will see if I can't find a tree. Ah, there I see palms and acacias waving; if I climb one of them, I'll get safety and shelter—especially if I can only remember some psalms to repeat.—— *(Climbs up a tree.)* "Lo, morning and evening are different things"—that's a verse that is often discussed and examined. *(Settles himself in the tree.)* How pleasant it is to feel that one's soul is so nobly uplifted! Thoughts that ennoble are worth more than riches. I'll trust myself to Him. He knows just how far I am able to drink of the cup of affliction. He takes a most fatherly interest in me—— *(Looks out over the sea, and whispers with a sigh:)* but He's not what you'd call economical over it!

SCENE III

SCENE.—*A Moroccan camp on the edge of the desert, at night.* WARRIORS *are resting by a watch-fire.*

A Slave (running in and tearing his hair). Gone is the Emperor's white charger!

Another Slave. The Emperor's sacred garb is stolen!

A Chief of the Warriors (coming in). A hundred strokes of the bastinado to all of you, if the thieves escape!

[*The* WARRIORS *spring on to their steeds and gallop off in all directions.*

SCENE IV

SCENE.—*A clump of palm-trees and acacias. It is dawn.* PEER GYNT, *in a tree, is trying to defend himself with a broken-off branch against a swarm of Apes.*

Peter Gynt. I've spent an extremely uncomfortable night. *(Hits about him.)* Is that them again? The infernal creatures! They're throwing down fruit. No, it's something else. Apes are the most disgusting beasts! It is written that one must watch and fight; but I can't do it—I'm wearied out. *(Is disturbed again. Speaks impatiently.)* I must make an end of all this discomfort—try and get hold of one of these creatures, hang him and flay him and dress myself up from head to foot in his shaggy hide; then the others will think I am one of them.—We men are but nothing, after all, and must bow to the force of circumstances.—Another lot! Why they swarm like flies! Away with you! Shoo! They act like madmen. If only I could get a false tail—or something to make me look like a beast—what's that up there above my head? *(Looks up.)* An old one—his paws chock-full of filth! *(Crouches down nervously and keeps still for a little. The* APE *makes a movement;* PEER GYNT *tries to coax him, as one would a dog.)* Hullo, old man! Is that you up there? He's a good chap, if you speak to him kindly. *He* won't throw things down—will he? No! It's I! Good dog! We're the best of friends. Wuff, wuff! Do you hear, I can speak your language: old man and I are as good as cousins! Would he like a nice bit of sugar——? The dirty beast! He's thrown the lot all over me! Disgusting brute!—Or was it food, perhaps? Its taste was unfamiliar, certainly. But taste is mostly a thing of habit. What is it that some philosopher has said: You must just spit and trust to force of habit.—Here's the crowd of youngsters now! *(Hits about him.)* This is too much! That man, who's his Creator's image, should have to suffer.—

Murder! Help! The old one's foul, but the youngsters fouler!

SCENE V

SCENE.—*A rocky spot overlooking the desert. It is early morning. On one side, a ravine with the entrance to a cave. A* THIEF *and a* RECEIVER OF STOLEN GOODS *are standing in the ravine, with the Emperor's charger and robe. The charger, richly caparisoned, is tied to a rock.* HORSEMEN *are seen in the distance.*

Thief. Spear-points, gleaming in the sunshine! See! see!

Receiver. I hear them galloping over the sand! Woe! Woe!

Thief (folding his arms on his breast). My father thieved; his son must steal.

Receiver. My father received; and so must I.

Thief. We must bear our lot and be ourselves.

Receiver (listening). Footsteps in the thicket! Away! But where?

Thief. The cave is deep and the Prophet great!

[*They fly, leaving the stolen goods behind them. The* HORSEMEN *disappear in the distance.* PEER GYNT *comes in, whittling a reed.*

Peer Gynt. Really a most enchanting morning! The beetles are busy at work in the sand; out of their shells the snails are peeping. Morning! Ah, morning's worth more than gold! It's strange what a very remarkable power there is in daylight. In its beams you feel so safe—your courage waxes—you're ready to fight wild bulls, if need be. What silence around me! These rural joys—it's strange that I never appreciated these things so much till now. To think that men live cooped up in great cities, just to be pestered and plagued by people. Look at those lizards, bustling about enjoying the air and thinking of nothing. What innocence in the life of beasts! They perform the behest of their great Creator, their character stamped indelibly on them; they are *themselves,* whether playing or fighting—themselves, as they were when He first said "Be." *(Puts on his eye-glasses.)* A toad—looking out of a piece of sandstone, only his head peeping out of his chamber. He sits, as if looking out of a window at the world; to himself he is—enough. *(Thoughtfully.)* Enough? Where have I read that before? Most probably in the Great Book I read as a boy. Or perhaps it was in the Prayer-book? Or else set down in Solomon's Proverbs? Dear me—I notice, as years go on, I cannot remember times and places as once I used. *(Sits down in the shade.)* Here's a spot that's cool; I'll sit and rest my bones awhile. Ah, here are ferns—one can eat the roots. *(Tastes one.)* It's really food for beasts; but then the Book says we must subdue our nature, and, further, that pride must be abased. "Who humbleth himself, shall be exalted." *(Uneasily.)* Exalted? Of course that will happen to me—the contrary's quite unthinkable. Fate surely will help me away from here and set my feet on the road to fortune. This is but a test; if the Lord will grant me strength to endure, I'll be rescued later. *(Shakes off such thoughts, lights a cigar, stretches himself out and gazes over the desert.)* What an enormous, boundless waste!—Far off, there, I can see an ostrich.—It is hard to perceive the Almighty's purpose in all this dead and empty desert, where there is nothing that is life-giving; a burnt-up waste that profits no one, this bit of the world that's for ever sterile; a corpse that never, since it was shaped, has brought its Creator anything—not even thanks. Why was it made? Nature is ever extravagant.—Is that the sea that glitters yonder, away in the east? No—only mirage. The sea's to the west, where, like a dam, sandhills protect the desert from it. *(An idea strikes him.)* A dam! Then I might——! The hills are low. A dam! Then a cutting—a canal—and through the gap the rushing waters would fill the desert with a life-flood, and all this empty burnt-up grave become a fresh and rippling ocean! Islands would show in it where now there are oases; to the north, Atlas would fringe the shore with verdure; and to the south, like heedless birds, white sails would skim along, where now the caravans plod painfully; a lively breeze would dissipate this stuffy air, and from the clouds a gentle dew would fall. In time town after town would be established, and grass grow round the swaying palm-trees. The country beyond the Sahara's edge, away in the south, would become a land of busy trade and seamen's ventures. Steam should drive works in Tombuktu, new colonies arise in Bornu, and the explorer should be carried safe in his waggon through the land of Habes to the Upper Nile. Then in the middle of my sea, on the most fertile, rich oasis, I'll settle Norsemen—for the blood of dalesmen is the nearest thing to that of royalty; a cross with Arab blood will do the rest. And on a cape with sloping shore I'll build Peeropolis, the capital! The old world's out of date; and now it is the turn of Gyntiana, my new-born land! *(Springs up.)* I only need some capital, and the thing is done—a golden key, and the ocean's gate is open! A crusade 'gainst death! That grisly miser shall disgorge the hidden treasure that he's hoarding. There is a world-wide wish for freedom. Like Noah's donkey in the Ark, I'll bray my message to the world; Liberty's baptism I will pour over these prisoned shores, till they grow lovely in their freedom!—Forward! In east or west I'll have to seek the money for the work! My kingdom—or half my kingdom—for a horse! *(The horse in the ravine neighs.)* A horse! And robes! And ornaments! And weapons! *(Goes nearer.)* It's impossible—and yet it's true!—I know I've read somewhere that faith can move a mountain, but never thought that it could bring a horse! I must be dreaming—— No, it is a fact—there stands the horse! *Ab esse ad posse,* etcetera.—— *(Puts on the robe and looks himself over.)* Sir Peter—and Turk from head to foot! Well, truly one can never tell what's going to happen to one! Come up, Granë, my steed! *(Climbs into the saddle.)* Gold stirrups, too! Great folk are known by the steeds they ride!

[*Gallops away across the desert.*

SCENE VI

SCENE.—*The tent of an Arab Chieftain, on an oasis.* PEER GYNT, *in his oriental robes, is taking his ease on a divan, drinking coffee and smoking a long pipe.* ANITRA *and a troupe of* GIRLS *are dancing and singing to him.*

Chorus of Girls. The Prophet is come! The Prophet, the Lord, the All-Wise One, to us, to us he has come, riding over the sea of sand! The Prophet, the Lord, the Infallible, to us, to us he has come sailing over the sea of sand! Blow flute! Sound drum! The Prophet, the Prophet is come!

Anitra. His charger is white as milk in the streams of Paradise! Bend the knee! Bow low! His eyes are stars that flash and yet are full of love. No earth-born eyes can meet the flashing of those stars! Across the desert he came, decked with gold and pearls. Where he rode it was light; behind him all was dark, drought and the dread simoom. The Mighty One has come! Over the desert he came, clothed in mortal shape. Kaaba is empty now! Himself has told us so.

Chorus of Girls. Blow flute! Sound drum! The Prophet, the Prophet is come.

[*The girls dance to soft music.*

Peer Gynt. I have read in a book, and the saying's true, that no man's a prophet in his own country.—This life's a deal more to my liking than that which I led as a Charlestown trader. There was something false about it all, something foreign to me and shady; I never could feel myself at home, or feel I had chosen the right profession, *Qu'allais-je faire dans cette galère,* grubbing about with business matters? I can't understand it, the more I try—it simply happened, and that is all. To climb up the world on money-bags is just like building a house on sand. If you wear rings and a watch, and so forth, people will curtsey and bow to you, take off their hats if you wear a breast-pin; but the rings and the pin are not yourself. Now a Prophet—he has a definite status; you know exactly where you're standing, if a man salutes you, it's for *yourself,* and not because of your pounds and shillings. You are what you are without pretence. Owing nothing to chance or accident, independent of patents or concessions. A Prophet—yes, that's the life for me. And it happened so unexpectedly—simply from riding across the desert and coming upon these children of nature. The Prophet had come; it was clear to them. But indeed it was not my design to deceive them—an official reply from a Prophet is one thing, and a lie quite another; in any case, too, I can always retire from my present position. I'm in no way bound; so it's not so bad. It's all, so to speak, like a private arrangement. I can go as I came; my steed's standing ready; in short, I am master of the situation.

Anitra (at the door of the tent). Prophet and Master!

Peer Gynt. What is it, my slave?

Anitra. At the door of the tent stand sons of the desert, craving to look on the face of the Prophet——

Peer Gynt. Stop! You can tell them they must keep their distance; I will receive their petitions at a distance. Tell them no man may set his foot within here! Menfolk, my child, are but a set of scoundrels—they are, in fact, a filthy lot of rascals. You, my Anitra, cannot well imagine with what barefaced impertinence they cheat one—h'm!—I should say, how grievously they sin. Now, no more of that!

Come, dance for me, my children! I would forget these thoughts that make me angry.

The Girls (as they dance). The Prophet is good! His heart is distressed for the sins that the sons of earth have committed. The Prophet is kind! All praise to his kindness which leads such poor sinners to Paradise!

Peer Gynt (whose eyes have followed Anitra *through the dance).* Her legs flit about like nimble drumsticks! She's really a tasty morsel, the baggage! It's true her figure's pronounced in some ways—not quite in accord with the standards of beauty; but what is beauty? A mere convention, a currency coined for a special purpose. And it's just these extravagances that tickle a palate that's sated with what is normal. In marriage there's always something wanting; she's either too fat or else too scraggy, annoyingly young or alarmingly ancient; and if she's between the two, she's insipid.—Her feet, it is true, might well be cleaner, also her arms—especially that one. But, after all, that's nothing to matter; one might rather call it a qualification.—Anitra, come here!

Anitra. Thy slave, my Master!

Peer Gynt. You attract me, child! The Prophet is moved. If you don't believe me, I'll prove it to you—I'll make you a Houri in Paradise!

Anitra. Impossible, Master!

Peer Gynt. You don't believe me? As I am alive, I'm in real earnest!

Anitra. But I've no soul!

Peer Gynt. Then you shall have one!

Anitra. How shall I, Master?

Peer Gynt. That's my affair. I shall look after your education. No soul? It's true you are pretty stupid; I've noticed that fact with some regret; but there's room enough in you for a soul. Come here! Let me measure your head. Oh, yes, there's plenty of room, as I knew there was. True enough, you'll never be anything much; a great soul will be quite beyond you. But, pshaw! it really doesn't matter; you'll have enough to prevent your feeling ashamed of it——

Anitra. My Lord is kind——

Peer Gynt. You're hesitating? What is the matter?

Anitra. I'd rather have——

Peer Gynt. Speak out, at once!

Anitra. I don't care so much about having a soul; I'd rather have——

Peer Gynt. What?

Anitra (pointing to his turban). That lovely opal!

Peer Gynt (in raptures, as he hands her the jewel). Anitra, you're one of Eve's true daughters! Your charm attracts me—for I am a man; and, as a noted writer puts it: "*Das ewig weibliche zeihet uns an.*"

SCENE VII

SCENE.—*A grove of palm-trees outside* ANITRA'S *tent. The moon is shining.* PEER GYNT, *with an Arabian lute in his hands, is sitting under a tree. His beard and hair have been trimmed, which makes him look considerably younger.*

PEER GYNT *(plays and sings).*

I locked the gate of Paradise
And took away the key.
  My bark afar the north wind bore,
  While lovely women on the shore
Were weeping there for me.

Southward I sailed the salty depths
Before the die was cast;
  Where palms were waving proud
      and free

Around an inlet of the sea,
I burned my ship at last.

A desert-ship I mounted then—
A four-legged ship, I trow—
To bear me o'er the desert dark.
I am a bird of passage! Hark!
I'm twittering on a bough!

Anitra, thou art like the wine
Of palm-trees, sparkling clear!
Angora-goats'-milk cheese is good,
But it's not half so sweet a food
As thou, Anitra dear!

(Slings the lute over his shoulder and approaches the tent.) All is silent! Now I wonder if she heard my little song? Is she there behind the curtain, peeping out with nothing on? What's that sound? It's like a bottle someone is uncorking!—There! There again I heard it—Is it sighs of love?—a lover's song?—No, it's clearly someone snoring. Lovely sound! Anitra sleeps! Nightingales, desist from singing! You shall suffer if you dare with your silly cluck and gurgle.—Oh, well, after all—sing on! Every nightingale's a songster, just as I am one myself; with their notes, like me, they capture tender, delicate young hearts. Night's cool hours are meant for singing; singing is our common sphere; singing is the art of being *us*—Peer Gynt and nightingale. And to hear Anitra sleeping is the topmost bliss of love; it's like lifting up a goblet to the lips, but drinking naught.—Oh, but here she comes! Well, really, after all that is the best.

Anitra (at her tent door). Did I hear my Master calling?

Peer Gynt. Yes, my dear, the Prophet called. I was wakened by a hubbub; cats were fighting all around——

Anitra. Ah, they were not fighting, Master. It was something worse than that.

Peer Gynt. What was it?

Anitra. Oh, spare me!

Peer Gynt. Tell me!

Anitra. I am blushing!

Peer Gynt (going close to her). Do you mean the emotion I was feeling when you had my opal, dear?

Anitra (horrified). Don't compare yourself, great Master, to an old disgusting cat!

Peer Gynt. Child—considered just as lovers, there's perhaps not much to choose 'twixt a tom-cat and a Prophet.

Anitra. Honeyed jests, great Master, fall from your lips.

Peer Gynt. My little friend, you, like other girls, pass judgment solely by a great man's looks, I am really very playful—especially when *tête-à-tête.* My position makes it needful for me to put on a mask of most serious behaviour; I'm constrained by daily duties and the nature of the business relative to my great office, to assume a weighty manner, and at times may seem to others too prophetically abrupt; but 'tis all upon the surface.—Away with all that bosh! In private I am Peer—that's who I am. Come, now, I will drop the Prophet; you shall know my very self! *(Sits down under a tree and draws* ANITRA *closer to him.)* Come, Anitra, let us dally underneath this waving palm! You shall smile and I shall whisper nothings in your ear; and then we'll reverse the parts we're playing, your sweet lips shall whisper love in my ear while I sit smiling!

Anitra (lying at his feet). All you say is sweet as music, though I don't quite understand. Tell me, Master, can your daughter get a soul by listening?

Peer Gynt. Presently you shall be dowered with the light of life—a soul; when upon the rosy portals of the dawn we see in gold "I am daybreak" clearly written,—then it will be time enough to begin your education. But for me to play schoolmaster and to waste this lovely night trying to collect together weatherbeaten bits of lore, would be stupid altogether, even if I wanted to. And, besides, considered rightly, souls are not the chiefest things in our lives; it's hearts that matter.

Anitra. Speak on, Master! When you speak, it's like opals flashing fire.

Peer Gynt. Too much cleverness is folly; and the fruit of cowardice pushed too far, is cruelty. Truth, if it's exaggerated, is no more than wisdom's self turned hind-foremost.—Yes, my child, you may take my word for it, there are people in the world gorged with soul but dull of vision. I once knew a chap like that; he seemed brighter than his fellows; yet he let resounding phrases which he did not understand quite mislead him from his business.—Look around this fair oasis, at the desert; if my turban I took off and fluttered gently once or twice, the mighty ocean at my bidding would invade it, filling up its every corner. But I'd be a silly cuckoo if I set about creating seas and continents. Do you know, my child, what life is?

Anitra. No, instruct me.

Peer Gynt. Life means passing safe and dry-shod down the rushing stream of time. Manly strength is what is needed to be what I am, my dear. Age makes eagles lose their feathers, makes old fogies' footsteps fail, sets an old crone's teeth decaying, gives an old man withered hands,—and they all get withered souls. Give me youth! I mean as Sultan, ardent and vigorous, to rule—not the realms of Gyntiana with their palm-trees and their vines—but the realm of fresh young beauty that lies in a maiden's thoughts. So you see, my child, the reason why I graciously was pleased to bestow my love upon you; why I chose your little heart, so to speak, to be the empire that shall be my caliphate. None but I shall know your longings; in the empire of my love I must reign supreme, unquestioned! For you must be mine alone. I shall be your gentle gaoler, binding you with gold and gems. If we part, life will be empty—or, at any rate, for you! Not a fibre of your being, not an instinct of your will, but shall know me as their master—you shall be so filled with me. And your raven locks—your beauty—all in you that can allure—these shall be a pleasant garden for your Sultan's foot to tread. And that's why it's really lucky you've an empty little head. Souls are apt to make their owners too absorbed about themselves. And—while we're upon the topic—if you like, I'll seal the pact by bestowing on your ankle this fine bangle. That, I think, fairly meets the situation. Me—instead of soul—you'll have; otherwise, the *status quo.* *(*ANITRA *snores.)* What? Is she sleeping? Have my words fallen on unheeding ears? No; it shows the power lying in my words—that, like a stream, they transport her gently with them to the land of dreams. *(Gets up and puts some jewels in her lap.)* Anitra! Here are jewels! Here are more! Sleep, Anitra! Dream of Peer! Sleep, for in your sleep you've set a crown upon your Emperor's head! Peer Gynt has won a victory of personality to-night.

SCENE VIII

SCENE.—*A caravan route. The oasis is visible in the remote background.* PEER GYNT, *on his white horse, is galloping over the desert, holding* ANITRA *before him on the pommel of his saddle.*

Anitra. Let go! I'll bite you!

Peer Gynt. You little rogue!

Anitra. What do you want to do?

Peer Gynt. To play at love and falcon! To carry you off and do all sorts of reckless things!

Anitra. For shame! An old Prophet, too!

Peer Gynt. Oh, bosh! The Prophet is not old, you goose! Do you think this looks as if he were old?

Anitra. Let me go! I want to go home!

Peer Gynt. You flirt! Home! To father-in-law! That's

good! We birds that have flown out of our cage dare not be seen by him again. Besides, my child, no one should stay too long in the same place; he's apt to lose as much in estimation as he can gain by making friends; and this is especially the case when he's a Prophet, or the like. His should be flying visits—seen as snatches of a song are heard. It was time that my visit should come to an end; these sons of the desert are shifty creatures,—incense and gifts have both been lacking for some days.

Anitra. Yes, but *are* you a Prophet?

Peer Gynt. I am your Emperor! *(Tries to kiss her, but she draws back.)* Oh, come! Don't be a proud little birdie, now!

Anitra. Give me the ring that's on your finger.

Peer Gynt. Take the lot if you wish, dear!

Anitra. Your words are like life-giving music!

Peer Gynt. What happiness 'tis to be loved like this! Let me dismount! I will lead the horse and be your slave! *(Hands her the whip and dismounts.)* See now, my pretty, my beautiful rose—here am I now, and here I'll tread the sands until I get a sunstroke and have to stop. I am young, Anitra! Remember that! You mustn't look at my deeds too closely; jokes and fun are what youth is known by! And, if you were not quite so stupid, my graceful flower, you'd understand that, since your lover is full of fun, *ergo* he's young!

Anitra. Yes, you are young. Have you any more rings?

Peer Gynt. Of course I'm young! Look, I am bounding like a deer! If there was any green-stuff handy, I'd make myself a wreath! Aha! Of course I'm young! Just see me dance! [*Dances and sings.*

I am a happy little cock!
Peck me, my little pullet!
Houp-là! Just see me foot it!
I am a happy little cock!

Anitra. You're sweating, my Prophet; I'm afraid you will melt. Let me carry that bag that weighs down on your belt.

Peer Gynt. What tender concern! You shall carry the purse; hearts that are loving have no need of gold!

[*Dances and sings again.*

He is a madcap, your little Peer!
He doesn't know what he is doing!
And doesn't care—if he keeps going!
He is a madcap, your little Peer!

Anitra. How joyful 'tis to see the Prophet dancing!

Peer Gynt. Oh, drop that "Prophet" nonsense! Let's put on each other's clothes! Come on! You take yours off!

Anitra. Your caftan is too long, your belt too roomy, your stockings much too small.

Peer Gynt. *Eh bien!* Instead, inflict some pain upon me; for 'tis sweet for loving hearts to suffer for their love! And, when we come to where my castle stands——

Anitra. Your Paradise? Have we got far to ride?

Peer Gynt. A thousand miles or so!

Anitra. Oh, what a way!

Peer Gynt. Then you shall have the soul I promised you——

Anitra. No, thanks; I think I'll do without the soul. But you were asking for some pain——

Peer Gynt. Ah, yes! Something severe but brief—a passing pang——!

Anitra. Anitra must obey the Prophet! So—farewell!

[*Hits him smartly over the fingers with the whip and gallops back over the desert at full speed.*

Peer Gynt (after standing for a long time as if thunderstruck). Well, I am——!

SCENE IX

SCENE. *The same as the preceding, an hour later.* PEER GYNT *is taking off his Turkish dress bit by bit, deliberately and thoughtfully. When he has finished, he takes a travelling-cap out of his coat pocket, puts it on and stands once more in European dress. He flings the turban far away from him.*

Peer Gynt. There lies the Turk, and here stand I! A pagan existence is no good at all. It's lucky that I can throw it away with the clothes, and that it's not bred in the bone. *Qu'allais-je faire dans cette galère?* It's certainly best to live as a Christian, avoid the temptation of sumptuous garments, fashion your life by what's lawful and moral; in fact, be yourself—and deserve at the last a funeral oration and wreaths on your coffin. *(Takes a few steps.)* The baggage!—Only a little more, and I believe she'd have turned my head. But I'll be hanged if I understand what it was in her that so upset me. I am well out of it! If the joke had been pursued a little farther, it would have made me ridiculous.—I have erred, no doubt; but it's comforting to feel that my erring was the result of the position I had assumed; it was not I, myself, that erred. It was, as a fact, the prophetic life—devoid of any savouring salt of active work—that caused in me these lapses into want of taste. It's a sorry business being a Prophet! In the course of your duties you're apt to get heedless. You're sober and dignified; all of a sudden you find you're nothing of the sort. I certainly gave proof of it by paying homage to that goose, still, all the same—— *(Bursts out laughing.)* Just think of it! Spending the time in wanton dancing! Trying to stem the stream of life by fooling like that!—sweet music, caresses, sighs—and in the end be plucked like any silly hen! Prophetically wild behaviour!—Plucked!—To my shame

I've been plucked badly! Still, I've a little left in hand,—some in America, and some safe in my pocket; so I'm not quite on the rocks. And, after all, a moderate amount of wealth is best. I am no longer tied by horses, coachmen and the like; I've neither carriages nor luggage to give me trouble. In a word, I'm master of the situation.—Which way shall I choose? Many are open. It's in such choice that wisdom counts. My business life is a finished chapter; my love affairs, discarded garments; and I have no mind to retrace my steps. "Forward or back it's just as far; out or in, it's just as narrow"—as I think it says in some clever book. I must find some new, some ennobling task; an object that's worth my pains and money. Suppose I wrote, without concealment, the story of my life—a book to serve as a guide and an example to others after me? Or, wait——! I've lots of time at my command—suppose I become a travelling scholar, making a study of bygone ages? That, I believe, is the thing for me! I'd always a fancy for history, and lately I've improved my knowledge. I'll trace the story of mankind! Float like a feather upon the stream of history; and live again, as in a dream, the days of old; see the fierce fights the heroes waged—but from a vantage-point that's safe, that of an onlooker; see how thinkers were slaughtered, martyrs bled; how kingdoms rose and kingdoms fell; watch epochs of world-history grow from their birth; and, in a word, skim all the cream of history.—I must try and get hold of a book of Becker's and go chronologically about it. It's true that my previous knowledge is sketchy, and history's rather an intricate matter,—but what is the odds! It frequently happens that very unusual methods of starting lead to the most original outcome.—To see one's goal and drive towards it, steeling one's heart, is most uplifting! *(With restrained emotion.)* Breaking through every bond that hinders, sundering ties of home and friendship, bidding adieu to love's soft promptings, to solve the mystery of truth! *(Wipes a tear from his eye.)* *That* is the test of a real enquirer! It makes me happy beyond measure to feel I have solved the great enigma of my destiny. I've only, now, to hold my course through thick and thin! I think I may be well forgiven if I feel proud, and call Peer Gynt a Man, and Manhood's Emperor! The Past shall be a lock to which I have the key; I will desert the sordid paths of modern life. The Present is not worth a shoe-lace. The ways of men are empty, faithless; their minds are dull, their deeds are futile —*(Shrugs his shoulders.)* And women—well their name is frailty! *(Moves on.)*

SCENE X

SCENE. *Outside a hut in a forest in the far north of Norway. It is a summer's day. The door, which stands open, is furnished with a massive wooden bolt; above the door a pair of reindeer horns is fixed. A herd of goats are feeding by the wall.* Solveig, *now a fair and handsome middle-aged woman, is sitting spinning in the sunshine.*

Solveig (looks down the path and sings).

It may not be till winter's past,
And spring and summer—the whole long year;
But I know that you will come at last,
And I shall wait, for I promised you, dear.

[*Calls to her goats, then resumes her spinning and singing.*

God guard you, dear, where'er you be!
If in Heaven, God have you in His care!
I shall wait till you come back to me;
If you're waiting above, I shall meet you there!

SCENE XI

SCENE. *In Egypt, at the foot of the statue of Memnon, at dawn.* PEER GYNT *comes walking along, stops and looks around him.*

Peer Gynt. I think that this place will do for a start.—Now, for a change, I'm an Egyptian; but Egyptian always upon the basis of the Gyntian Self. I'll wander later into Assyria. I'll stop short of going back to the Creation, for that would only lead to danger. I'll skirt the edges of Bible history. No doubt I'll discover certain traces that will confirm it; but to go minutely into it is not according to my plan of action. *(Sits down on a stone.)* I'll rest awhile and wait with patience until I've heard the Statue singing its customary morning song; and, after I have had my breakfast, I'll climb the Pyramid, and then, if I have time I'll look inside it. Then to the Red Sea, where perhaps I shall discover King Potiphar's grave. Then I will be an Asiatic; in Babylon I'll seek the famous Hanging Gardens and Concubines—the fairest products, that's to say, of civilization. Then a leap, and I'll be at the walls of Troy; and then the sea-route is direct to beautiful old Athens. There, I shall examine, stone by stone, the pass Leonidas defended; I'll make myself familiar with all the best philosophies; find out the gaol where Socrates laid down his life as sacrifice—but, stop a minute, I forgot——! Greece is at war, so for the present I must put Hellenism aside. *(Looks at his watch.)* What a ridiculous time the sun takes in rising! My time's precious. Well, then,—from Troy—that's where I'd got to—*(Gets up and listens.)* I wonder what that curious murmur——?

[*The sun rises.*

The Memnon Statue (singing).

From the demi-god's ashes arise new-born

Singing birds.
Zeus, the all-knowing,
Shaped them for conflict.
Owl of Wisdom,
Where sleep my birds?
You must die if you read not
The Riddle of the Song!

Peer Gynt. I really do believe I heard sounds from the Statue! That would be the music of the past. I heard the rise and fall of the Statue's voice. I'll note that down for consideration at experts' hands. *(Makes a note in his pocket-book.)* "The Statue sang. I heard the sounds quite plainly, but could not completely understand the words. I have, of course, no doubt the whole thing was hallucination. Otherwise, I have not observed anything of importance so far." [*He moves on.*

SCENE XII

SCENE. *Near the village of Gizeh, by the great Sphinx carved out of the rocks. In the distance are seen the spires and minarets of Cairo.* PEER GYNT *arrives; he examines the Sphinx carefully, sometimes through his eye-glass, sometimes through the hollow of his hand.*

Peer Gynt. Now where in the world have I met before something I only half remember that this ugly thing reminds me of? For met it I have—either north or south. Was it a man? And, in that case, who? The Memnon Statue reminded me of the Troll King of our fairy tales, sitting like that, all stiff and rigid, resting his rump on a piece of rock; but this remarkable mongrel here, this monster, half lion and half woman—have I known it, too, in a fairy tale? Or have I some real recollection of it? A fairy tale?—No, I know the chap! It's the Boyg, if you please, whose skull I cracked—I meant to say that I dreamt I did, for I was lying ill of a fever. *(Goes nearer to the Sphinx.)* The selfsame eyes, the selfsame lips! Not quite so sluggish—a bit more cunning—but in the main points just the same. Well, Boyg, old fellow, you're like a lion, seen from behind and in the daylight! Are you still full of riddles? We'll try and see; we'll see if you answer as you did before. *(Calls to the Sphinx.)* Hi, Boyg! Who are you?

Voice (from behind the Sphinx). Ach, Sfinx, wer bist du?

Peer Gynt. What's that? An echo in German? Astounding!

Voice. Wer bist du?

Peer Gynt. It's got a perfect accent! The observation's new, and my own. *(Makes a note in his book.)* "Echo in German—with Berlin accent."

[BEGRIFFENFELDT *comes from behind the Sphinx.*

Begriffenfeldt. A man!

Peer Gynt. Oh—it was *he* that was talking. *(Makes a further note.)* "Came later to another conclusion."

Begriffenfeldt (with signs of great excitement). Excuse me, sir——! A vital question——! What was it brought you here to-day?

Peer Gynt. A visit. I'm greeting a friend of my youth.

Begriffenfeldt. The Sphinx?

Peer Gynt. Yes, I knew him in days gone by.

Begriffenfeldt. Splendid!—And after the night I've spent! My forehead is throbbing as if it would burst!—You know him, sir? Then speak! What is he? Can you tell me that?

Peer Gynt. What is he? Yes, I can tell you that. He is *himself*.

Begriffenfeldt (with a start). Ha! Like a flash I see the answer to life's enigma!—Is it certain that he's himself?

Peer Gynt. Yes; at least, he said so.

Begriffenfeldt. Himself! The great awakening's come! *(Takes off his hat.)* Your name, sir?

Peer Gynt. I am called Peer Gynt.

Begriffenfeldt (with an air of quiet amazement). Peer Gynt! Allegorical! What one expected. Peer Gynt? That means: the Great Unknown—the Messiah that was announced to me——

Peer Gynt. No—really? And you came here to find him——?

Begriffenfeldt. Peer Gynt! Profound! Enigmatic! Incisive! Each word is full of deepest teaching! What are you?

Peer Gynt (modestly). I have always tried to be myself. And, for the rest, my passport——

Begriffenfeldt. Enigmatic, too! All an enigma! *(Grasps him by the hand.)* Come to Cairo! Come! I have found the Emperor of Exegesis!

Peer Gynt. Emperor?

Begriffenfeldt. Come!

Peer Gynt. Am I really known——?

Begriffenfeldt (dragging him away with him). The Emperor of Exegesis—based on Self!

SCENE XIII

SCENE. *In a lunatic asylum at Cairo. A big courtyard surrounded by high walls and buildings with barred windows. Iron cages on the ground level. Three of the* KEEPERS *are in the courtyard. A fourth comes in.*

Fourth Keeper. I say, Schafmann—where's the Director?

Another Keeper. He went out this morning, long before dawn.

Fourth Keeper. I'm afraid something's happened that has upset him, because in the night——

Another. Hush! Here he comes!

[BEGRIFFENFELDT *shows* PEER GYNT *in, locks the gate and puts the key in his pocket.*

Peer Gynt (aside). He is a remarkably learned man; almost all that he says is beyond understanding. *(Looks round him.)* So this, then, is your Savants' Club?

Begriffenfeldt. Yes, here you'll find them, bag and baggage—the coterie of seventy professors of Exegesis. Lately a hundred and three new ones joined them.—*(Calls to the* KEEPERS.*)* Mikkel, Schlingelberg, Schafmann, Fuchs—into the cages with you! Quick!

The Keepers. We!

Begriffenfeldt. Yes—who else? Get on! get on! As the world's topsy-turvy, we must follow suit! *(Shuts them up in the cage.)* The mighty Peer has come to us to-day; so you can join the others.—I will say no more.

[*Locks the cage and throws the key into a well.*

Peer Gynt. But why—my dear Director——?

Begriffenfeldt. Don't call me that! I *was* Director until—— Sir, can you keep a secret? I must unburden myself——

Peer Gynt. What is it?

Begriffenfeldt. Promise me that you will not tremble.

Peer Gynt. I will try not to.

Begriffenfeldt (takes him into a corner and whispers). Absolute reason expired at eleven o'clock last night!

Peer Gynt. God help us——!

Begriffenfeldt. Yes, it's a great disaster. In *my* position, too, you see, it's doubly disagreeable; because this place, until it happened, was known as a lunatic asylum.

Peer Gynt. A lunatic asylum!

Begriffenfeldt. Ah, not *now,* you understand!

Peer Gynt (aside, growing pale). I see exactly how it is; this fellow is mad--and not a soul suspects it.

[*Moves away.*

Begriffenfeldt (following him). I hope you have really understood me? To say it's dead is not accurate. It has left itself—got out of its skin like my friend Baron Munchausen's fox.

Peer Gynt (trying to get away). Excuse me——

Begriffenfeldt (holding on to him). No, it was like an eel, not a fox. A nail right through its eye—and there it was, squirming on the wall——

Peer Gynt. How on earth am I to save myself?

Begriffenfeldt. Just one slit round the neck—and pop! Out of its pelt it came!

Peer Gynt. Quite mad!

Begriffenfeldt. And now the fact is evident that this same exit-from-itself entails a revolution in all the world. All persons who up to that time were known as mad at eleven o'clock last night became normal; this, in conformity with Reason in its newest phase. And, if you consider the matter farther, it's clear that from the selfsame hour our so-called wise men all went mad.

Peer Gynt. Speaking of time, my time is precious——

Begriffenfeldt. Your time? You've jogged my memory! *(Opens a door and calls out.)* Come out! The appointed time has come! Reason is dead. Long live Peer Gynt!

Peer Gynt. No, my dear friend——!

[*The mad folk come one after another into the courtyard.*

Begriffenfeldt. Good morning to you! Come out and greet the dawn of freedom! Your Emperor's here!

Peer Gynt. Their Emperor?

Begriffenfeldt. Certainly!

Peer Gynt. It's too great an honour—far more than——

Begriffenfeldt. No false modesty at such a time as this!

Peer Gynt. At least give me some respite!—I'm not fit for such a task; I'm quite dumbfounded!

Begriffenfeldt. The man who guessed the Sphinx's riddle! Who is himself!

Peer Gynt. That's just my trouble. I am myself in every way! but here, so far as I can see, everyone gets outside themselves.

Begriffenfeldt. Outside themselves? Oh, no, you're wrong. It's here that men are most themselves—themselves and nothing but themselves—sailing with outspread sails of self. Each shuts himself in a cask of self, the cask stopped with a bung of self and seasoned in a well of self. None has a tear for others' woes or cares what any other thinks. We are ourselves in thought and voice—ourselves up to the very limit; and, consequently, if we want an Emperor, it's very clear that you're the man.

Peer Gynt. I wish to goodness——!

Begriffenfeldt. Don't be downhearted; everything that's new, at first seems strange to one. "One's self"—well, as a specimen, I'll choose the first that comes to hand. *(To a gloomy figure that is passing.)* Good morning, Huhu! Still, my lad, looking the picture of misery?

Huhu (a Language-Reformer from Malabar). What can I do, when generation after generation dies lacking an interpreter? *(To Peer Gynt.)* You're a stranger; will you listen?

Peer Gynt (bowing). By all means.

Huhu. Then pay attention.—Away in the East, like a bridal crown, lie the shores of Malabar. Portuguese and Hollanders try to civilize the place, where there still survive a lot of original Malabari. These good folk have muddled up their language and now rule supreme in that land. But, long ago, that same countryside was ruled by Orang-outangs. The woods were all theirs; and they could fight, growl and snarl to hearts' content—live, in fact, as Nature made them; they could screech without permission and were lords of all the country. Then there came this horde of strangers and disturbed the primal language that was spoken in the forests. Now four hundred years have passed—that means many generations—and so long a time as that, as one knows, can easily stamp out aborigines. The forest cries have long been dumb, not a growl is ever heard; if we want to speak our minds, we must have recourse to words. It applies to all alike—Portuguese and Hollanders, Hybrid races, Malabari—all are equally affected. I have tried my best to fight for our real forest-tongue; tried to bring its corpse to life; upheld people's right to screech, screeched myself and pointed out the necessity of screeching in our folk-songs. But my efforts met with no result whatever.—Now I think you understand what my grievance is. I thank you for your courtesy in listening. If you think you can advise me what to do, I beg you'll tell me!

Peer Gynt (aside). They say that when you are in Rome you should do as the Romans do. *(Aloud.)* My friend, if I remember rightly, there are forests in Morocco where there are Orang-outangs that have neither songs nor teacher; and their language much resembles that of Malabar; if you were, like many other statesmen, to expatriate yourself for the good of these same people, it would be a noble action and a fine example also.

Huhu. Let me thank you, sir, for listening; I will follow your advice. *(With an impressive gesture.)* In the east they flout their singer! The west has its Orang-outangs!

[*Goes out.*

Begriffenfeldt. Now, surely you'll say that *he's* himself! He's full of himself and nothing else; himself in every word he says—himself when he's beside himself. Come here! I want to show you another, who's been no less conformable to Reason since last night's occurrence. *(To a* FELLAH *who is carrying about a Mummy on his back.)* King Apis, how goes it, my noble sir?

Fellah (fiercely, to PEER GYNT*).* Am I King Apis?

Peer Gynt (getting behind BEGRIFFENFELDT*).* I'm afraid I'm not quite qualified to say; but I should think, if I may judge from what your voice suggests to me——

Fellah. Now you are lying, too!

Begriffenfeldt. Your Highness must kindly deign to let us have an explanation.

Fellah. Well, I will. *(Turns to* PEER GYNT.*)* You see this man I'm carrying? King Apis was his name. They call him now a Mummy; and, what is more, he's dead. He built up all the Pyramids, and carved the mighty Sphinx, and fought—so the Director says—with Turks on every side. And therefore the Egyptians worshipped him as a God and set up in their temples his statue as a bull. But *I* am that King Apis—it's just as clear as day; if you don't understand it, I'll make you very soon. King Apis was out a-hunting, and got down from his horse and stepped aside for a moment in my grandfather's field. The soil King Apis fertilized has nourished *me* with corn; and, if more proof is needed, I have invisible horns. Then don't you think it's damnable that I can't get my due? By my birth I am King Apis, but only a Fellah here. If you think you can advise me, tell me, without delay, what I'm to do to make myself like Apis, the great king.

Peer Gynt. Your Highness must build Pyramids and carve a mighty Sphinx, and fight—as the Director says—with Turks on every side.

Fellah. Yes, that's a likely story! A Fellah! A hungry louse! It's all I can do to keep my hut clear of the rats and mice. Come, think of something better, to make me great and safe, and also make me look like King Apis that's on my back.

Peer Gynt. Suppose your Highness hanged yourself, and then, deep in the ground, within a coffin's sheltering walls, behaved like one that's dead——

Fellah. I'll do it! Let me have a rope! To the gallows

with my head! I'll not be quite like him at first, but time will alter that.

[*Goes away and makes preparations to hang himself.*

Begriffenfeldt. A great personality that, my friend—a man with method——

Peer Gynt. Yes, so I see.—But he really *is* hanging himself! God help us! I feel quite sick—and my brain is turning!

Begriffenfeldt. A transitional stage; it won't last long.

Peer Gynt. Transition? To what? I really must go——

Begriffenfeldt (holding him back). Are you mad?

Peer Gynt. Not yet! Mad? God forbid!

[*Amidst an uproar,* HUSSEIN, *a Minister of State, pushes his way through the other lunatics.*

Hussein. They tell me an Emperor's come to-day. *(To* PEER GYNT.*)* Is it you?

Peer Gynt (desperately). They've settled that it is!

Hussein. Good.—Here are papers that need an answer.

Peer Gynt (tearing his hair). Aha! Go on! The more the merrier!

Hussein. Perhaps you will honour me with a dip? *(Bows low.)* I am a pen.

Peer Gynt (bowing still lower). And I am merely a trumpery imperial parchment.

Hussein. My history, sir, is briefly this: they think me a sand-box, and not a pen.

Peer Gynt. And mine, Sir Pen, succinctly told: I'm a paper that's never been written on.

Hussein. They never will understand what I'm meant for; they all want to use me to sprinkle sand!

Peer Gynt. I was a book with silver clasps, when I belonged to a woman once. Madness or wisdom is merely a misprint.

Hussein. But, think—how wretched to be a pen that never has tasted the edge of a knife!

Peer Gynt (leaping into the air). Think what it is to be a reindeer that's always jumping down from a height and never reaching solid ground!

Hussein. A knife! I am blunt; I need repairing! The world will perish if I'm not mended!

Peer Gynt. That would be sad when, like all that He made, our Heavenly Father admired it so much.

Begriffenfeldt. Here's a knife!

Hussein (grasping it). Ah, how I shall lick up the ink! How lovely to cut one's self!

[*Cuts his throat.*

Begriffenfeldt (moving to one side). Don't splash me!

Peer Gynt (with growing terror). Hold him!

Hussein. Yes, hold me! That's the word! Hold! Hold the Pen! Is the paper there——? *(Falls.)* I'm worn out. A postscript—don't forget it: He was a pen in the hands of others.

Peer Gynt. What shall I——? What am I? Oh, Thou—keep hold! I am what Thou wilt—a Turk, a Sinner, a Troll; only help me! Something has burst within me! *(Shrieks.)* I cannot remember Thy name—help me, Thou—Guardian of all madmen!

[*Sinks down in a swoon.* BEGRIFFENFELDT, *holding a straw crown in his hand, leaps on to* PEER GYNT *and sits astride of him.*

Begriffenfeldt. See how he sits enthroned in the mud!—He's out of himself! Let us crown him now! *(Puts the crown on* PEER GYNT'S *head and shouts)* Long live the Emperor of Self!

Schafmann (in the cage). Es lebe hoch der grosse Peer!

ACT V

SCENE I

SCENE. *On board a ship in the North Sea, off the coast of Norway. Sunset and a threatening sky.* PEER GYNT, *now a vigorous old man with grey hair and beard, is on the poop. His clothes, which are somewhat the worse for wear, are half sailor-like; he wears a pilot-jacket and sea-boots. He looks weatherbeaten, and his expression has hardened. The* CAPTAIN *is at the wheel with the* HELMSMAN. *The crew is forward.* PEER GYNT *is leaning his arms on the gunwale and gazing at the land.*

Peer Gynt. There's Hallingskarven in winter dress; he shows up well in the evening light. And there's his brother Jöklen behind, still wearing his ice-green glacier cap; and, like a lady dressed in white, lies Folgefond behind them both.—Don't try any follies, my ancient friends! Stay where you are—you are made of stone.

Captain (calling forward). Two men to the wheel—and hoist the light!

Peer Gynt. It's blowing.

Captain. Aye, we'll have a storm.

Peer Gynt. Can one see Rondë from the sea?

Captain. No—it lies hidden behind Faanen.

Peer Gynt. Or Blaahö?

Captain. No; but, from aloft, Galdhöpiggen when the weather's clear.

Peer Gynt. Which way's Harteigen?

Captain (pointing). Over there.

Peer Gynt. Of course.

Captain. You seem to know the country.

Peer Gynt. I passed this way when I sailed from home; and early impressions, as they say, last longest. *(Spits over the side and continues gazing at the coast.)* It is over there—where the hillside glens are blue, in the dark and narrow valleys, and along the open fjords—that is where the people live. *(Looks at the* CAPTAIN.*)* Not many houses on this coast.

Captain. No, they are few and far between.

Peer Gynt. Shall we be in by morning?

Captain. Aye, I hope so, if the night is not too bad.

Peer Gynt. It's gathering in the west.

Captain. It is.

Peer Gynt. Oh, by the way, look here—remind me, when we're settling up, that I intend to make a present to the crew——

Captain. You're very good.

Peer Gynt. It will only be a small one. I made money, but I've lost it; Fate and I have fallen out. You know what I have got on board; well, that's the lot. The rest of it has taken wings and flown away.

Captain. Oh, what you've got is quite enough to win respect from folk at home.

Peer Gynt. I have no folk. There's no one waiting for this rich ugly uncle.—Well, I shall be spared some fuss at landing.

Captain. The storm is brewing.

Peer Gynt. Now remember, if any of you need it badly I'm not close-fisted with my money.

Captain. That's kind. They're mostly badly off; they all have wives and families—can scarcely live upon their pay—and, if your kindness sends them home with something extra in their pockets, to-morrow's home-coming will never be forgotten.

Peer Gynt. What's all that? Do you say they've wives and children? Married?

Captain. Yes, married—all the lot. The poorest of them all's the Cook; his house is never free from hunger.

Peer Gynt. Married? And someone waiting there to greet them when they come? Is that it?

Captain. Of course, like all poor folk.

Peer Gynt. Supposing it's evening when they come—what then?

Captain. Then I expect that something tasty will have been got for the occasion——

Peer Gynt. A lamp upon the table?

Captain. Aye, and maybe two; a dram to drink——

Peer Gynt. They'll sit at ease, in warmth and comfort, with children round them? And such hubbub in the room that no one hears half the other says to them, just because they are so happy?

Captain. Very likely; and that's why it's so kind of you to promise they shall have a little present.

Peer Gynt (banging his fist on the gunwale). No, I'm damned if they shall have it! Do you think me such a fool as to fork out for the pleasure of helping other people's children? I've worked too hard to get my money! No one's waiting for old Peer Gynt.

Captain. Just as you please; it's your own money.

Peer Gynt. Quite so. It's mine and no one else's. Directly you have cast your anchor I'll settle up for what I owe you for my cabin passage hither from Panama; and then I'll give you something for a dram of brandy for the crew; but not a penny more than that. You may have leave to knock me down if I give more!

Captain. You'll get my receipt, and nothing else. Now please excuse me; the storm is rising.

[*He crosses the deck. It has become dark, and the cabin lamps are being lit. The sea grows rougher. Fog and thick clouds gather.*

Peer Gynt. Provide for a crowd of others' children——? Fill others' hearts with happiness and so be always in their thoughts——? There's no one wasting thoughts on me. Lamps on their tables? I'll put them out! I'll find some way——! I will make them drunk; not one of these fellows shall go home sober. They shall go drunk to their wives and children; they shall swear—bang loudly on the table—frighten their families out of their wits! Their wives shall scream and run out of the house, and their children, too! I'll spoil their pleasure! *(The ship rolls heavily; he stumbles and has difficulty in holding on.)* That was a bad one! The sea's as busy as if it were paid for what it's doing. It's the same always, up here in the north; the sea to fight with, fierce and angry——*(Listens.)* What was that cry?

The Watch (forward). A wreck to leeward!

Captain (amidships). Starboard the helm! Keep her close to the wind!

Helmsman. Are there men on the wreck?

The Watch. I can make out three.

Peer Gynt. Lower a boat——!

Captain. It would only capsize. [*Goes forward.*

Peer Gynt. Who thinks of that? *(To the crew.)* If you're men, you'll save them! You're surely not afraid of a wetting?

Boatswain. It's impossible in such a sea as this.

Peer Gynt. They're calling again! The wind is raging.—Cook, won't you try? Come on! I'll pay you——

Cook. Not if you gave me twenty guineas.

Peer Gynt. You dogs! You cowards! Don't you know that these are men that have wives and children who are waiting——?

Boatswain. Patience will do them good.

Captain. Keep her stern to the breakers!

Helmsman. The wreck's gone under.

Peer Gynt. Was that sudden silence——?

Boatswain. If they are married, as you suggest, then the world's the richer by three newly-created widows.

[*The storm increases in violence.* PETER GYNT *goes aft.*

Peer Gynt. There's no more Faith among men any longer—no more Christianity worth the name; there's little that's good in their words or their deeds, and they pay no heed to the Powers Above. In a storm like to-night's, one may very well be afraid of God; these brutes should cower and remember that, as the saying goes, it's risky to play with elephants,—and then they defy Him openly! *I'm* guiltless enough; if it comes to judgment, I can prove that I made an offer to pay them. But what do I get in return for that? I know they say that your head lies easy if your conscience is clear. That may be true on *terra firma;* but on the sea, where an honest man's quite the exception, I don't consider it worth a rush. At sea you never can be yourself; you simply sink or swim with the others; should the hour of vengeance chance to strike for the Cook and the Boatswain, I most likely should be swept along to perdition with them: there's no respect for individuals,—you're nothing more than one of the crowd. My mistake has been that I've been too meek and get the blame for all that has happened. If I were younger, I do believe I'd change my tune and play the boss. There's time for it yet! It shall get abroad that Peer has come overseas a winner! By hook or crook I'll get back the farm; I'll build on it—it shall look like a castle. But not a soul shall come into my house! They shall stand at the door and twiddle their caps, they shall beg—I'll let them do *that* with pleasure—but I'll not give them a single farthing. If I've had to smart from the lash of fortune, they'll find out that I can hit back again——

[*A* STRANGER *is seen standing beside* PEER GYNT *in the gloom, bowing politely to him.*

Stranger. Good evening!

Peer Gynt. Good evening! What——? Who are you?

Stranger. Your fellow-passenger, at your service.

Peer Gynt. Indeed? I thought I was the only one.

Stranger. A wrong impression, corrected now.

Peer Gynt. But it's very strange I have never seen you until this evening——

Stranger. I don't go out in daytime.

Peer Gynt. Perhaps you are not well? You're as white as a sheet——

Stranger. I'm quite well, thank you.

Peer Gynt. What a storm!

Stranger. Yes, what a blessing, man!

Peer Gynt. A blessing?

Stranger. The waves are mountains high. It makes one's mouth water to think of the wrecks that there will be tonight!—of the corpses that will be washed ashore.

Peer Gynt. God forbid!

Stranger. Have you ever seen a man that has been strangled—or hanged—or drowned?

Peer Gynt. What on earth do you mean?

Stranger. There's a grin on their faces; but the grin is ghastly, and for the most part they've bitten their tongues.

Peer Gynt. Do go away!

Stranger. Only one question! Suppose, for instance, that the ship should run aground to-night and sink——

Peer Gynt. Then do you think there's danger?

Stranger. I really don't know what to answer. Suppose I'm saved and you get drowned——

Peer Gynt. Oh, bosh——!

Stranger. Well, it's just possible. With one foot in the grave, a man inclines to charitable thoughts——

Peer Gynt (putting his hand in his pocket). I see, it's money that you want!

Stranger. No; but if you would be so kind as to present me with your corpse——?

Peer Gynt. This is too much!

Stranger. Merely your corpse! It's for a scientific purpose——

Peer Gynt. Get out!

Stranger. But, my dear friend, consider—the thing would be to your advantage! I'd have you opened and laid bare. It really is the seat of dreaming that I am seeking; but, besides, I'd have you thoroughly examined——

Peer Gynt. Get out!

Stranger. But, sir—a mere drowned corpse!

Peer Gynt. Blasphemous man! You encourage the storm! What folly! In all this wind and rain and heavy seas and every sign that some fatality may happen—here are you asking for something worse!

Stranger. I see that you're not disposed, for the moment, to carry the matter farther. But time so very often will alter things. *(Bows politely.)* We shall meet when you're sinking, if not before; then, perhaps, you'll be in a better humour. [*Goes into the cabin.*

Peer Gynt. Unpleasant fellows, these men of science! Freethinkers, too—— *(To the* BOATSWAIN *who is passing.)* A word, my friend! Who is that lunatic passenger?

Boatswain. I did not know we had any but you.

Peer Gynt. No other? Why, this gets worse and worse. *(To a* SAILOR *who comes out of the cabin.)* Who went into the cabin just now?

Sailor. The ship's dog, sir! [*Passes on.*

The Watch (calling out). Land close ahead!

Peer Gynt. My trunk! My box! Bring them up on deck!

Boatswain. We have something else to think about now.

Peer Gynt. Captain, I wasn't serious in what I said! I was only joking! Of course I'm going to help the Cook——!

Captain. The jib has gone!

Mate. There went the foresail!

Boatswain (calling from forward). Breakers ahead!

Captain. She'll go to pieces!

[*The ship strikes. Noise and confusion.*

SCENE II

SCENE. *Off the coast, amongst rocks and breakers. The ship is sinking. Through the mist, glimpses are caught of a boat with two men in it. A breaking wave fills it; it capsizes; a scream is heard, then all is still for a while. Soon afterwards the boat comes into sight, floating keel uppermost.* PEER GYNT *comes to the surface near the boat.*

Peer Gynt. Help! Help! A boat!—Help! I shall sink! God save me—as the Bible says!

[*Clings tight to the keel of the boat. The* COOK *comes to the surface on the other side of the boat.*

Cook. Oh, God—for my dear children's sake be pitiful! Let me be saved! [*Holds on to the keel.*

Peer Gynt. Let go!

Cook. Let go!

Peer Gynt. I'll push you off!

Cook. I'll push *you* off!

Peer Gynt. I'll kick you off! Let go your hold! It won't bear two!

Cook. I know. Get off!

Peer Gynt. Get off yourself!

Cook. Not likely!

[*They fight. The* COOK *gets one hand hurt, but clings fast to the boat with the other hand.*

Peer Gynt. Take your hand away!

Cook. Be kind! Be merciful!—Just think of my young children there at home!

Peer Gynt. I have more need to live than you, for I have got no children yet.

Cook. Let go! You've had your life; I'm young!

Peer Gynt. Be quick and sink; you're much too heavy.

Cook. Have mercy! For God's sake let go! There's no one that will mourn for you—*(Shrieks and slips down.)* I'm drowning!

Peer Gynt (catching hold of the COOK'S *hair).* No, I've got you tight by your back hair; repeat "Our Father"!

Cook. I can't remember—all seems dark——

Peer Gynt. Say what is most essential! Quick!

Cook. "Give us this day"——

Peer Gynt. Oh, skip all that; you have got all that you will need.

Cook. "Give us this day"——

Peer Gynt. The same old song! It's easy seen you were a cook—— [*His grip gives way.*

Cook (sinking). "Give us this day our"——

[*Goes under.*

Peer Gynt. Amen, lad! You were yourself up to the end. *(Swings himself up on to the keel of the boat.)* Where there is life there's always hope——

[*The* STRANGER *is seen in the water, catching hold of the boat.*

Stranger. Good morning!

Peer Gynt. Eh!

Stranger. I heard a cry; it's funny I should find you here. Well? Do you see I spoke the truth?

Peer Gynt. Let go! There's barely room for one!

Stranger. I'll swim quite well with my left leg. I'll float if only I insert my finger-tip into this crack. But what about your corpse?

Peer Gynt. Be quiet!

Stranger. The rest is absolutely done for——

Peer Gynt. Do hold your tongue!

Stranger. Just as you wish. [*Silence.*

Peer Gynt. Well?

Stranger. I am silent.

Peer Gynt. Devil's tricks!—What are you doing?

Stranger. I am waiting.

Peer Gynt (tearing his hair). I shall go mad! What are you?

Stranger (nodding to him). Friendly!

Peer Gynt. Go on! What more?

Stranger. What do you think? Don't you know anyone that's like me?

Peer Gynt. I know the Devil——

Stranger (lowering his voice). Is he wont to light us on the darkest paths of life when we're beset by fear?

Peer Gynt. Oh! So it seems, on explanation, that you're a messenger of the light?

Stranger. Friend, have you known—say, twice a year—what terror really means?

Peer Gynt. Of course. One is afraid when danger threatens; but your words are ambiguous——

Stranger. Well, have you ever, even once, triumphed as the result of terror?

Peer Gynt (looking at him). If you have come to guide my steps, 'twas stupid not to come before. It's not much good to choose the time when I'm most likely to be drowned.

Stranger. And would your triumph be more likely if you sat snugly by your fire?

Peer Gynt. Perhaps not; but your talk was foolish. How could you think it would affect me?

Stranger. Where I come from, they think a smile worth quite as much as any pathos.

Peer Gynt. There is a time for everything. Things which a publican may do are most disgraceful in a bishop.

Stranger. The souls of those bygone days whose ashes rest in funeral urns aren't always in a solemn humour.

Peer Gynt. Leave me, you bugbear! Get away! I won't die! I must get to land!

Stranger. As far as that goes, make your mind quite easy; no one ever dies until he's seen the fifth act through.

[*Disappears.*

Peer Gynt. Ah, it slipped out of him at last;—he was a wretched Moralist.

SCENE III

SCENE. *A churchyard high up in the mountains. A funeral is going on. The* PRIEST *and the* MOURNERS *are just finishing the last verse of a hymn.* PEER GYNT *is passing on the road and stops at the churchyard gate.*

Peer Gynt. Here's another man going the way of all flesh. Well, God be praised that it isn't me!

[*Goes into the churchyard.*

Priest. Now that his soul has gone to meet its God, and this poor dust waits like an empty husk,—let us, dear friends, in a few words recall the dead man's journey on this earth of ours. He wasn't rich, nor was he very clever; his voice was weak, his bearings scarcely manly; he had no strength of mind, nor much decision; nor in his own home did he seem the master. His manner when he came to church was such as if he felt he must request permission to take his seat among the congregation. Of Gudbrandsdal he was, you know, a native, and he was scarce a boy when he came hither; and, to the last, as you no doubt have noticed, he always kept his right hand in his pocket. That same peculiarity I mention was probably the only thing that stamped his picture on our minds; that, and the shyness—the almost shamefaced diffidence—with which he bore himself when he came in amongst us. But, though he was so diffident and quiet, and to the last was almost like a stranger, you know quite well, in spite of his concealment, the hand he hid had no more than four fingers.—I well remember, many years ago, during the war, one morning a Conscription was held at Lundë. Everyone was full of Norway's troubles and her doubtful future. Behind a table, I remember, sat a Captain and the Mayor, and several Sergeants; and one by one our lads came in, were measured, enrolled and duly sworn in to the army. The room was full; and outside in the courtyard was heard the noise of the young people's laughter. A name was called out, and a lad came in with face as white as snow upon the hilltops. They told him to come forward to the table. His right hand was all swathed up in a napkin; he gasped and swallowed—tried to find his voice—but seemed as if he had no words to answer the Captain's questions. Still, at last, he did; and then, with crimson face and faltering tongue that sometimes let the words out with a rush, he mumbled some tale of an accident—a reaping-hook that slipped and cut his finger clean off his hand. There was a sudden silence. Men exchanged glances; lips were curled in scorn; looks of disdain were flashed upon the lad, who stood there staring with unseeing eyes; he felt their scorn although he did not see it. And then the Captain, an old grey-haired man, stood up, and spat, and pointed to the door and said: "Begone!"—and so the lad went out. Those in the room divided to make way, so that he ran the gauntlet of them all. He reached the door and then took to his heels; ran up the hillside—through the woods and pastures, up over rocks and stones, stumbling and slipping—to where his home was, far up in the mountains. 'Twas six months after that when he came hither, bringing his mother, children and betrothed. He leased some land upon the mountain-side near to where Lomb is bounded by the moor. As soon as it was possible, he married the mother of his children; built a house; broke up the stony ground with such success that yellow grain in patches soon appeared amidst the rocks. It's true that when he went to church he kept his right hand in his pocket; but on his farm I know he worked as well with nine fingers as others with their ten.—Then, one wet spring, a flood swept all away. They saved their lives, but nothing else; and, poor and naked as he was, he set to work to clear the soil afresh; and by the autumn he'd built himself a house on safer ground. Safer? Yes, from the flood but not the mountains. For, two years later, in an avalanche all that he had was overwhelmed again. But even avalanches had no power to daunt his soul. He set to work to dig and clear the snow and save what might be left; and, ere the winter's snow had come again, he'd built his little house a third time up. Three sons he had—three fine young lads—and they must go to school, and school was far away; and so, from where the public roadway ended, he had to cut a steep and narrow path through the hard snow. And then—what did he do? The eldest boy had to climb up and scramble as best he could; and where it was too steep his father roped him to him for support. The other two he carried in his arms and on his back. And thus, year after year, he drudged; and his three sons grew to be men. Then came a time when he might surely ask for something in return from them; but they, three prosperous men in far America, had quite forgotten their Norwegian father and how he used to help them to the school. He was a man whose vision never saw farther than what lay nearest to his hand. Words which resound in other people's hearts were meaningless to him as tinkling bells; Family, Country—all that's best and brightest—was blurred and hidden by a veil of tears. But never did I know a man so humble. From that Conscription Day he carried with him the sense of guilt, which showed as plainly on him as did the blush of shame upon his cheek and his four fingers hidden in his pocket. A breaker of his country's laws? Perhaps! But there is something that outshines the law as certainly as Glittertinde's peaks stand gleaming in the sun above the clouds. He was a bad citizen, no doubt; for Church and State alike, a sterile tree; but up there on the rocky mountainside, in the small circle of his hearth and home, where his work lay, *there* I say he was great, because he was himself. 'Twas only there the metal he was made of could ring true. His life was like a melody that's played on muted strings.—And therefore, peace be with you, poor silent warrior, who fought and fell waging the little war of peasant's life! We will not seek to search the heart and reins; that's not a task for us, but for his Maker. Still, this I hope—and hope with confidence: that this man, as he stands before the Throne, is not a cripple in the eyes of God!

[*The congregation disperses.* PEER GYNT *remains alone.*

Peer Gynt. Well, *that's* what I call Christianity! Nothing in it to make one feel uneasy. Indeed the theme of the Priest's address—that we should all strive to be ourselves—is really extremely edifying. *(Looks into the grave.)* Was it he, I wonder, who slashed his knuckles when I was felling trees in the forest? Who knows? If I were not standing here by the grave of this congenial spirit, I might believe that it was myself that was sleeping there and was listening in dreams to praises that I deserved. It's really a beautiful Christian practice to take a kindly retrospect of the whole life of the departed. I'd readily accept a verdict from this most worthy priest.—However, I've still some time left, I expect, before the sexton comes and claims me; and, as the Scripture says: "The best is still the best"; and, in like manner: "Sufficient for the day is the evil thereof"; and, further: "Do not borrow trouble."—The Church is the only comforter. Up till now I have never given the credit to it that is its due; but now I know what good it does you to hear authority proclaim: "As you have sowed, so must you reap." We must be ourselves; in everything, both great and small, we must look after ourselves and what concerns ourselves. Though Fortune fail us we shall win respect, if our careers have been shaped in accordance with this doctrine.—And now for home! What though the way be steep and narrow—what though Fortune be still malicious—old Peer Gynt will go his own way, and remain, as always: poor but virtuous. [*Goes.*

SCENE IV

SCENE. *A hillside showing the dried-up bed of a stream, by which stands a ruined mill. The ground is torn up, and everything is in a ruinous state. Outside the mill an auction is taking place; there is a large and noisy gathering of people, and drinking is going on.* PEER GYNT *is sitting on a heap of rubbish near the mill.*

Peer Gynt. Backward or forward, it's just as far; out or in, the way's as narrow. Time destroys and the stream cuts through. "Round about," said the Boyg; and we needs must, here.

A Man in Mourning. Now there's nothing left but the rubbish. *(Looks at* PEER GYNT.*)* Strangers, too? God save you, sir!

Peer Gynt. Well met! This is a merry scene; is it a chistening, or a wedding?

Man in Mourning. I should rather say a house-warming; the bride, poor thing, is food for worms.

Peer Gynt. And worms are fighting for rags and scraps.

Man in Mourning. It's a finished story, and this is the end.

Peer Gynt. Every story ends the same; I've known them all since I was a boy.

A Young Boy (holding a casting-ladle). Look what a fine thing I have bought! Peer Gynt used to mould buttons with this.

Another. I got a fine purse for a farthing!

A Third. A pedlar's pack for twopence halfpenny!

Peer Gynt. Peer Gynt? Who was he?

Man in Mourning. I only know he was brother-in-law to the bridegroom, Death, and also to the blacksmith Aslak.

A Man in Grey. You're forgetting me; you must be drunk!

Man in Mourning. You're forgetting the loft-door at Hægstad.

Man in Grey. So I was; but you were never dainty.

Man in Mourning. If only she doesn't play Death a trick——

Man in Grey. Come on! Have a drink with your relation!

Man in Mourning. Relation be damned! Your drunken fancies——

Man in Grey. Oh, nonsense! Blood is thicker than that; at least we're both Peer Gynt's relations.

[*They go off together.*

Peer Gynt (aside). I'm meeting old friends.

A Boy (calling after the MAN IN MOURNING*).* My poor dead mother will come after you, Aslak, if you get drinking.

Peer Gynt (getting up). The Agriculturalists are wrong; it doesn't smell better the deeper you dig.

A Boy (with a bearskin). Here's the Dovrë-Cat!—or at least his skin! It was he chased the Troll on Christmas Eve.

Another (with a pair of reindeer-horns). Here's the fine buck on which Peer Gynt rode right along the ridge of Gendin.

A Third (with a hammer, calls to the MAN IN MOURNING*).* Hi! Aslak! Do you know this hammer? Was it this you used when the Devil escaped?

A Fourth (showing his empty hands). Mads Moen, here's the invisible cloak in which Peer Gynt and Ingrid vanished.

Peer Gynt. Some brandy, boys! I'm feeling old; I'll hold an auction of all my rubbish.

A Boy. What have you got to sell?

Peer Gynt. A castle; it's up at Rondë, and solidly built.

Boy. I bid one button!

Peer Gynt. A drink with it, then; it's a sin and a shame to offer less.

Another Boy. He's a merry old chap!

[*The crowd gathers round* PEER GYNT.

Peer Gynt. Granë, my horse!—Who bids?

One of the Crowd. Where is he?

Peer Gynt. Away in the West! Near the sunset, boys! He can trot as fast as Peer Gynt could make up his lies.

Voices. What more have you?

Peer Gynt. Both gold and rubbish! I bought them at a loss, and now I'll sell them at a sacrifice.

A Boy. Put them up!

Peer Gynt. A vision of a prayer-book! You may have it for a hook and eye.

Boy. Deuce take your visions!

Peer Gynt. Then—my Empire! I throw it to you; you may scramble for it!

Boy. Does a crown go with it?

Peer Gynt. A lovely crown of straw, and it will fit the first that puts it on.—Here's something more! An empty egg! Grey hair of a madman! The Prophet's beard!—You may have them all, if you'll only show me on the hill-side a signpost marked: "This is the way"!

The Mayor (who has come up). The way you're going on, my man, I think will lead you to the lock-up.

Peer Gynt (with his hat in his hand). Very likely. But, tell me, who was Peer Gynt?

The Mayor. Oh, bother——!

Peer Gynt. Excuse me—I want to know——!

The Mayor. Well,—they say, an incurable romancer.

Peer Gynt. Romancer?

The Mayor. Yes; romanced about all sorts of glorious deeds as if he had done all of them himself. Excuse me now, my friend, I'm busy—— [*Goes away*

Peer Gynt. And where's this wonderful fellow now?

An Elderly Man. He went oversea to a foreign land and came to grief as one might have expected. It's many years now since he was hanged.

Peer Gynt. Hanged? Dear me! I was sure of it; the late Peer Gynt was himself to the last. *(Bows.)* Goodbye. I'm much obliged to you all! *(Takes a few steps, then stops.)* You merry boys and lovely women, may I tell you a story in return?

Voices. Yes, if you know one!

Peer Gynt. Certainly. *(Comes back to them. His face takes on an altered expression.)* I was in San Francisco, gold-digging, and the whole town was full of freaks; one played the fiddle with his toes, one danced fandangoes on his knees, a third, I heard, kept making verses while holes were bored right through his skull. To this freak-show the Devil came, to try his luck like so many others. His line was this: he could imitate the grunting of a pig exactly. His personality attracted although he was not recognized. The house was full and on tenterhooks of expectation. In he strode, dressed in a cape with flowing wings; *Man muss sich drappieren,* as the Germans say. But no one knew that in his cape he had a little pig concealed. And now he started his performance. The Devil pinched; the pig gave tongue. The whole was a fantasia on a pig's life, from birth to slaughter, ending up with a shriek like that which follows on the slaughterer's stroke; with which, the artist bowed and went.—Then there arose a keen discussion among the experts in the audience. The noises were both praised and censured; some found the tone of them too thin. Others declared the dying shriek was far too studied; but they all were of the same mind on one point: That the performance was, *qua* grunt, exceedingly exaggerated. You see, that's what the Devil got, because he'd made the sad mistake of reckoning without his public.

[*Bows and goes away. An uneasy silence falls on the crowd.*

SCENE V

SCENE. *A clearing in a great forest, on the Eve of Pentecost. In the background is seen a hut, with a pair of reindeer-horns over the door.* PEER GYNT *is on all-fours on the ground, grubbing up wild onions.*

Peer Gynt. This is one standpoint. Where is the next? One should try all things and choose the best. I have done that; I've been a Cæsar, and now I'm behaving like Nebuchadnezzar. So I might go through Bible history. This old boy's back to mother earth. I remember the Book says: "Dust thou art." The great thing in life is to fill your belly. Fill it with onions? It matters little; I'll fit some cunning traps and snares. There is a brook; I'll not go thirsty; and all wild things shall do my bidding. And, suppose I die—which perhaps may happen—I'll creep beneath a fallen tree; like the bear, I'll cover myself with leaves and scratch in the bark, in great big letters: "Here lies Peer Gynt, a decent chap, who was Emperor of all the Beasts."—Emperor? *(Laughs to himself.)* You absurd old humbug! You're not an emperor, you're an onion! Now, my dear Peer, I'm going to peel you, however little you may enjoy it. *(Takes an onion and peels it, layer by layer.)* There's the untidy outer husk; that's the shipwrecked man on the wreck of the boat; next layer's the Passenger, thin and skinny—still smacking of Peer Gynt a little. Next we come to the gold-digger self; the pith of it's gone—someone's seen to that. This layer with a hardened edge is the fur-hunter of Hudson's Bay. The next one's like a crown. No, thank you! We'll throw it away without further question. Here's the

Antiquarian, short and sturdy; and here is the Prophet, fresh and juicy; he stinks, as the saying goes, of lies enough to bring water to your eyes. This layer, effeminately curled, is the man who lived a life of pleasure. The next looks sickly. It's streaked with black. Black may mean missionaries or negroes. *(Pulls off several layers together.)* There's a most surprising lot of layers! Are we never coming to the kernel? *(Pulls all that is left to pieces.)* There isn't one! To the innermost bit it's nothing but layers, smaller and smaller. Nature's a joker! *(Throws the bits away from him.)* Deuce take all thinking! If you begin that, you may miss your footing. Well, anyway, *I* don't run that risk as long as I'm down on all-fours here. *(Scratches the back of his head.)* Life's an uncommonly odd contraption; it plays an underhand game with us; if you try to catch hold of it, it eludes you, and you get what you didn't expect—or nothing. *(Goes closer to the hut, looks at it and starts.)* That hut? In the forest——! Eh? *(Rubs his eyes.)* I'm certain I must have seen that hut before. The reindeer-horns there, over the door——! A mermaid carved on the end of the gable——! That's a lie! No mermaid—just logs and nails—and the bolt that should keep out plaguy thoughts——!

[SOLVEIG'S *voice is heard from the hut.*

Solveig (singing).

Now all is ready for Pentecost.
Dear lad far away, are you coming near?
If your burden's heavy, then rest awhile;
I shall wait, because I promised you, dear.

[PEER GYNT *rises to his feet, deathly pale and quiet.*

Peer Gynt. One who remembered—and one who forgot; one who has kept what the other has lost. Life's serious, not a foolish jest! Ah, misery! *Here* my Empire lay!

[*Runs into the wood.*

SCENE VI

SCENE. *A moor with firs, at night. A forest fire has laid it waste. Charred tree-trunks for miles around. Patches of white mist are lying here and there over the ground.* PEER GYNT *comes running over the moor.*

Peer Gynt. Ashes, mists and dust clouds flying—fine material to build with! Stench and rottenness within them; all a whited sepulchre. Fancies, dreams and still-born wisdom for a base, while lies shall serve for a staircase for the building of a lofty pyramid. Flight from everything that's worthy; no repentance—only terror; these shall cap a building labelled: "Petruf Gyntus Cæsar fecit"! *(Listens.)* What is that sound like children's weeping?—Weeping that is half a song? What are these that I see rolling at my feet, like balls of thread? *(Kicks his feet about.)* Get away! You block the path up!

The Threadballs (on the ground).

We are thoughts;
You should have thought us;
Little feet, to life
You should have brought us!

Peer Gynt (going round them). I've only brought *one* thought to life,—and it was wry and bandy-legged!

The Threadballs.

We should have risen
With glorious sound;
But here like threadballs
We are earth-bound.

Peer Gynt (stumbling). Threadballs! You infernal rascals! Are you tripping up your father? [*Runs away.*

Withered Leaves (flying before the wind).

We are a watchword;
You should have used us!

Life, by your sloth,
Has been refused us.
By worms we're eaten
All up and down;
No fruit will have us
For spreading crown.

Peer Gynt. Still, you have not been born for nothing; lie still, and you will serve for manure.

A Sighing in the Air.

We are songs;
You should have sung us!
In the depths of your heart
Despair has wrung us!
We lay and waited;
You called us not.
May your throat and voice
With poison rot!

Peer Gynt. Poison yourselves, you silly doggerel! Had I any time for verse and twaddle? [*Goes to one side.*

Dewdrops (dropping from the branches).

We are tears
Which were never shed.
The cutting ice
Which all hearts dread
We could have melted;
But now its dart
Is frozen into
A stubborn heart.
The wound is closed;
Our power is lost.

Peer Gynt. Thanks!—I wept at Rondesvalen and got a thrashing on the backside!

Broken Straws.

We are deeds
You have left undone;
Strangled by doubt,

Spoiled ere begun.
At the Judgment Day
We shall be there
To tell our tale;
How will you fare?

Peer Gynt. Rubbish! You can't condemn a man for actions that he *hasn't* done!

Aase's Voice (from afar off).

Fi, what a driver!
Ugh! You've upset me
Into a snowdrift,
Muddied and wet me.
Peer, where's the Castle?
You've driven madly;
The whip in your hand
The Devil's used badly!

Peer Gynt. I'd best be off while I am able. If I have to bear the burden of the Devil's sins, I'll sink into the ground. I find my own quite a heavy enough load. [*Runs off.*

SCENE VII

SCENE. *Another part of the moor.*

Peer Gynt (singing).

A sexton! a sexton! Where are you all?
Open your bleating mouths and sing!
We've bands of crape tied round our hats,
And plenty of corpses for burying!

[*The* BUTTON MOULDER, *carrying his box of tools and a big casting-ladle, comes in by a side path.*

Button Moulder. Well met, gaffer!

Peer Gynt. Good evening, my friend!

Button Moulder. You seem in a hurry. Where are you going?

Peer Gynt. To a funeral.

Button Moulder. Really? My sight's not good—excuse me—is your name by any chance Peer?

Peer Gynt. Peer Gynt's my name.

Button Moulder. What a piece of luck! It was just Peer Gynt I was looking for.

Peer Gynt. Were you? What for?

Button Moulder. Well, as you see, I am a button moulder; and you must be popped into my Castle-ladle.

Peer Gynt. What for?

Button Moulder. So as to be melted down.

Peer Gynt. Melted?

Button Moulder. Yes; it's clean and it's empty. Your grave is dug and your coffin ordered; your body will make fine food for worms; but the Master's orders bid me fetch your soul at once.

Peer Gynt. Impossible! Like this?—without the slightest warning?

Button Moulder. Alike for funerals and confinements the custom is to choose the day without giving the slightest warning to the chief guest of the occasion.

Peer Gynt. Quite so. My head is going round! You are——?

Button Moulder. You heard; a button moulder.

Peer Gynt. I understand! A favourite child is called by lots of names.—Well, Peer, so *that's* to be the end of your journey!—Still, it's a scurvy trick to play me. I deserved something a little kinder. I'm not so bad as perhaps you think; I've done some little good in the world. At worst I might be called a bungler, but certainly not an out-and-out sinner.

Button Moulder. But that is just the point, my man. In the highest sense you're not a sinner; so you escape the pangs of torment and come into the Casting-ladle.

Peer Gynt. Oh, call it what you like—a ladle or the bottomless pit—it's just the same! Ginger is always hot in the mouth, whatever you may be pleased to call it. Satan, away!

Button Moulder. You are not so rude as to think that I've a cloven hoof?

Peer Gynt. Cloven hoof or fox's claws—whichever you like. So now pack off! Mind your own business and be off!

Button Moulder. My friend, you're under a great delusion. We're both in a hurry; so, to save time, I'll try to explain the matter to you. You are, as you yourself have said, nothing great in the way of a sinner—scarcely a middling one, perhaps——

Peer Gynt. Now you are talking reasonably.

Button Moulder. Wait a bit!—I think it would be going too far to call you virtuous——

Peer Gynt. I certainly don't lay claim to that.

Button Moulder. Well, then, say, something betwixt and between. Sinners in the true grand style are seldom met with nowadays; that style of sin needs power of mind—it's something more than dabbling in mud.

Peer Gynt. That's perfectly true; one should go at it with something of a Berserk's fury.

Button Moulder. You, on the contrary, my friend, took sinning lightly.

Peer Gynt. Just, my friend, a little mud-splashed, so to speak.

Button Moulder. Now we're agreed. The bottomless pit is not for you who played with mud.

Peer Gynt. Consequently, my friend, I take it that I may have your leave to go just as I came?

Button Moulder. Oh, no, my friend—consequently you'll be melted down.

Peer Gynt. What's this new game that you've invented while I have been abroad?

Button Moulder. The practice is just as old as the Creation and was invented for the purpose of keeping things up to the standard. You know in metal work, for instance, it sometimes happens that a casting turns out a failure, absolutely—buttons are turned out without loops. What would you do in such a case?

Peer Gynt. I'd throw the trash away.

Button Moulder. Exactly. Your father had the reputation of reckless wastefulness as long as he had anything to waste. The Master, on the other hand, is economical, you see, and therefore is a man of substance. He never throws away as useless a single thing that may be dealt with as raw material.—Now, *you* were meant to be a gleaming button on the world's waistcoat, but your loop was missing; so you've got to go into the scrap-heap, to be merged into the mass.

Peer Gynt. But do you mean that I've got to be melted down with any Tom and Dick and Harry and moulded fresh?

Button Moulder. That's what I mean. That's what we've done to not a few, it's what they do at the mint with the money when the coin is too much worn with use.

Peer Gynt. But it's simply disgusting niggardliness! My dear friend, won't you let me go? A loopless button—a smooth-worn coin—what are they to a man of your master's substance?

Button Moulder. The fact of your having a soul's enough to give you a certain intrinsic value.

Peer Gynt. No, I say! No! With tooth and nail I'll fight against it! I'd rather, far, put up with anything than that!

Button Moulder. But what do you mean by "anything"? You must be reasonable, you know; you're not the sort that goes to heaven——

Peer Gynt. I'm humble; I don't aim so high as that; but I'm not going to lose a single jot of what's myself. Let me be sentenced in ancient fashion; Send me to Him with the Cloven Hoof for a certain time—say, a hundred years, if the sentence must be a very severe one. That's a thing I dare say one might put up with; the torture would then be only moral, and perhaps, after all, not so very tremendous. It would be a transition, so to speak, as the fox said. If you wait, there comes deliverance and you may get back; meanwhile you hope for better days. But the other idea—to be swallowed up like a speck in a mass of strange material—this ladle business—losing all the attributes that make a Gynt—*that* fills my inmost soul with horror!

Button Moulder. But, my dear Peer, there is no need for you to make so great a fuss about so small a thing; because you never yet have been yourself. What difference can it make to you if, when you die, you disappear?

Peer Gynt. *I*'ve never been myself! Haha! You almost make me laugh. Peer Gynt anything but himself!—No, no, friend Button Moulder, you are wrong; you're judging blindly. If you searched my inmost being, you would find I'm Peer right through, and nothing else.

Button Moulder. Impossible. Here are my orders. See, they say: "You will fetch Peer Gynt. He has defied his destiny. He is a failure, and must go straight into the Casting-ladle."

Peer Gynt. What nonsense! It must surely mean some other Gynt. Are you quite sure that it says Peer?—not John, or Rasmus?

Button Moulder. I melted them down long ago. Now, come along and don't waste time.

Peer Gynt. No, that I won't! Suppose to-morrow you found that it meant someone else? That would be pleasant! My good man, you must be careful, and remember what a responsibility——

Button Moulder. I've got my orders to protect me.

Peer Gynt. Give me a little respite, then!

Button Moulder. What for?

Peer Gynt. I will find means to prove that, all my life, I've been myself; that is, of course, the point at issue.

Button Moulder. Prove it? But how?

Peer Gynt. With witnesses and testimonials.

Button Moulder. I fear that you won't satisfy the Master.

Peer Gynt. I'm quite sure that I shall! Besides, we'll talk about that when the time comes. Dear man, just let me have myself on loan for quite a little while. I will come back to you. We men are not born more than once, you know, and naturally we make a fight to keep the self with which we came into the world.—Are we agreed?

Button Moulder. So be it. But, remember this: At the next crossroads we shall meet. [PEER GYNT *runs off.*

SCENE VIII

SCENE. *Another part of the moor.*

Peer Gynt (running in). Time is money, as people say. If I only knew where the crossroads are—it may be near, or it may be far. The ground seems to burn my feet like fire. A witness! A witness! Where shall I find one? It's next to impossible, here in the forest. The world's a bungle! It's managed wrong, if it's necessary for a man to prove his rights that are clear as the noonday sun!

[*A bent* OLD MAN, *with a staff in his hand and a bag on his back, hobbles up to* PEER GYNT.

Old Man. Kind sir, give a homeless old man a penny!

Peer Gynt. I'm sorry—I have no change about me——

Old Man. Prince Peer! Can it be that we meet at last?

Peer Gynt. Why, who——?

Old Man. He's forgotten the old man at Rondë!

Peer Gynt. You surely are never——?

Old Man. The King of the Dovrë.

Peer Gynt. The Troll King? Really? The Troll King?—Answer!

Old Man. I'm he, but in different circumstances.

Peer Gynt. Ruined?

Old Man. Aye, robbed of everything; a tramp, and as hungry as a wolf.

Peer Gynt. Hurrah! Such witnesses as this don't grow on every tree!

Old Man. Your Highness has grown grey too since last we met.

Peer Gynt. Worry and age, dear father-in-law. Well, let's forget our private affairs; and, above all, our family squabbles. I was a foolish youth——

Old Man. Yes, yes; you were young, and youth must have its fling. And it's lucky for you that you jilted your bride; you've escaped a lot of shame and bother, for afterwards she went clean to the bad——

Peer Gynt. Dear me!

Old Man. Now she may look after herself. Just think —she and Trond have gone off together.

Peer Gynt. What Trond?

Old Man. Of the Valfjeld.

Peer Gynt. He? Aha, I robbed him of the cowherd girls.

Old Man. But my grandson's grown a fine big fellow and has bouncing babies all over the country.

Peer Gynt. Now, my dear man, I must cut you short: I am full of quite a different matter.—I'm in rather a difficult position and have to get a certificate or a testimonial from someone; and I think you'll be the very person. I can always raise the wind enough to stand you a drink——

Old Man. Oh! Can I really be of assistance to Your Highness? Perhaps, if that is so, you'll give me a character in return?

Peer Gynt. With pleasure. I'm a little short of ready money and have to be careful in every way.—Now, listen to me. Of course you remember how I came that night to woo your daughter——

Old Man. Of course, Your Highness!

Peer Gynt. Oh, drop the title! Well, you wanted to do me violence—to spoil my sight by cutting my eyeball and turn Peer Gynt into a Troll. What did I do? I strongly objected; swore I would stand on my own feet; gave up my love, and power and honours, simply and solely to be myself. I want you to swear to that in court——

Old Man. I can't do that!

Peer Gynt. What's that you're saying?

Old Man. You'll surely not force me to swear a lie? Remember that you put on Troll breeches and tasted our mead——

Peer Gynt. Yes, you tempted me. But I resolutely made up my mind that I would not give in. And *that's* the way a man shows what he's worth. A song depends on its concluding verse.

Old Man. But the conclusion, Peer, was just the opposite of what you think.

Peer Gynt. What do you mean?

Old Man. You took away my motto graven on your heart.

Peer Gynt. What motto?

Old Man. That compelling word——

Peer Gynt. Word——?

Old Man. ——that distinguishes a Troll from Mankind: "Troll, to thyself be—*Enough*"!

Peer Gynt (with a shriek). Enough!

Old Man. And, ever since, with all the energy you have, you've lived according to that motto.

Peer Gynt. I? I? Peer Gynt?

Old Man (weeping). You're most ungrateful. You've lived like a Troll, but have kept it secret. The word I taught has enabled you to move in the world like a well-to-do man; and now you begin abusing me and the word to which you owe gratitude.

Peer Gynt. Enough!—A mere Troll! An egoist! It must be nonsense—it can't be true!

Old Man (producing a bundle of newspapers). Don't you suppose that we have our papers? Wait; I will show you in black and white how the *Bloksberg Post* has sung your praises; the *Heklefjeld News* has done the same ever since the winter you went abroad. Will you read them, Peer? I'll be pleased to let you. Here's an article signed: "Stallion's Hoof." Here's one: "On the National Spirit of Trolldom"; the writer shows how true it is that it doesn't depend upon horns or tails, but on having the spirit of Trollhood in one. "Our 'Enough,' " he concludes, "is what gives the stamp of Troll to Man"; and he mentions you as a striking instance.

Peer Gynt. I—a Troll?

Old Man. It seems quite clear.

Peer Gynt. Then I might have stayed where I was and lived in peace and comfort at Rondë! I might have saved shoe leather and spared myself much toil and trouble! Peer Gynt—a Troll! It's a pack of lies! Good-bye! Here's a penny to buy tobacco.

Old Man. But, dear Prince Peer——!

Peer Gynt. Oh, drop this nonsense! You're mad, or else you're in your dotage. Go to a hospital.

Old Man. Aye, it's that I'm looking for. But, as I told you, my grandson's very influential in all this part and tells the people I don't exist except in legends. The saying goes that one's relations are always the worst; and now, alas, I feel the truth of it. It's sad to be looked on as being merely a legendary personage——

Peer Gynt. Dear man, you're not the only one to suffer that mishap.

Old Man. And then, we Trolls have nothing in the way of Charities or Savings Banks or Alms-boxes; such institutions would never be acceptable at Rondë.

Peer Gynt. No; and there you see the work of your confounded motto—your fine "To thyself be *enough*"!

Old Man. Your Highness has no need to grumble. And if, in some way or another——?

Peer Gynt. You're on the wrong scent altogether; I'm at the end of my resources.

Old Man. Impossible! Your Highness ruined?

Peer Gynt. Cleared out. Even my princely self is now in pawn. And that's your fault, you cursed Trolls! It only shows what comes of evil company.

Old Man. So there's another of my hopes destroyed!—Good-bye! I'd better try and beg my way down to the town——

Peer Gynt. And when you're there, what will you do?

Old Man. I'll try and go upon the stage. They're advertising for National Types in the papers.

Peer Gynt. Well, good luck to you!—And give my kind regards to them! If I can only free myself, I'll go the same way, too. I'll write a farce that shall be both profound and entertaining, and its title shall be: "Sic Transit Gloria Mundi."

[*Runs off along the path, leaving the* OLD MAN *calling after him.*

SCENE IX

SCENE. *At crossroads.*

Peer Gynt. This is the tightest corner, Peer, you've ever been in. The Trolls' "Enough" has done for you. Your ship's a wreck; you must cling to the wreckage—anything—to avoid the general rubbish heap.

Button Moulder (at the parting of the ways). Well Peer Gynt? And your witnesses?

Peer Gynt. What, crossroads here? This is quick work.

Button Moulder. I can read your face as easily as I can a book and know your thoughts.

Peer Gynt. I'm tired from running—one goes astray——

Button Moulder. Yes; and, besides, what does it lead to?

Peer Gynt. True enough; in the woods, in this failing light——

Button Moulder. There's an old man trudging alone; shall we call him?

Peer Gynt. No, let him alone; he's a drunken scamp.

Button Moulder. But perhaps he could——

Peer Gynt. Hush! No—don't call him!

Button Moulder. Is that the way of it?

Peer Gynt. Just one question: What is it really to "be one's self"?

Button Moulder. That's a strange question for a man who just now——

Peer Gynt. Tell me what I ask you.

Button Moulder. To be one's self is to slay one's self. But as perhaps that explanation is thrown away on you, let's say: to follow out, in everything, what the Master's intention was.

Peer Gynt. But suppose a man was never told what the Master's intention was?

Button Moulder. Insight should tell him.

Peer Gynt. But our insight so often is at fault, and then we're thrown out of our stride completely.

Button Moulder. Quite so, Peer Gynt. And lack of insight gives to our friend with the Cloven Hoof his strongest weapon, let me tell you.

Peer Gynt. It's all an extremely subtle problem.—But, listen; I give up my claim to have been myself; it very likely would be too difficult to prove it. I'll not attempt to fight the point. But, as I was wandering all alone over the moor just now, I felt a sudden prick from the spur of conscience. I said to myself: "You are a sinner——"

Button Moulder. Oh, now you're back to where you started——

Peer Gynt. No, not at all; I mean a *great* one,—not only in deed, but in thought and word. I lived a dreadful life abroad——

Button Moulder. May be; but have you anything to show to prove it?

Peer Gynt. Give me time; I'll find a priest and get it all in writing, properly attested.

Button Moulder. If you can do that, it will clear things up, and you will be spared the Casting-ladle. But my orders, Peer——

Peer Gynt. They're on very old paper; it certainly dates from a long time back, when the life I lived was loose and foolish. I posed as a Prophet and Fatalist.—Well, may I try?

Button Moulder. But——

Peer Gynt. Be obliging! I'm sure you have no great press of business. It's excellent air in this part of the country; they say it adds years to the people's lives. The parson at Justedal used to say: "It is seldom that anyone dies in this valley."

Button Moulder. As far as the next crossroads—no farther.

Peer Gynt. I must find a parson, if I have to go through fire and water to get him!

SCENE X

SCENE *A heathery slope. A winding path leads up to the hills.*

Peer Gynt. You never can tell what will come in useful as Esben said of the magpie's wing. Who would have thought that one's sinfulness would, in the end, prove one's salvation? The whole affair is a ticklish business, for it's out of the frying-pan into the fire; but still there's a saying that's very true—namely, that while there's life there's hope. *(A* THIN PERSON, *dressed in a priest's cassock which is well tucked up, and carrying a bird-catcher's net over his shoulder, comes running down the hill.)* Who's that with the bird-net? It's a parson! Hurrah! I am really in luck to-day!—Good afternoon, sir! The path is rough——

Thin Person. It is; but what would not one put up with to win a soul?

Peer Gynt. Oh, then there's someone who's bound for heaven?

Thin Person. Not at all; I hope he's bound for another place.

Peer Gynt. May I walk with you a little way?

Thin Person. By all means; I'm glad of company.

Peer Gynt. Something is on my mind——

Thin Person. Speak on!

Peer Gynt. You have the look of an honest man. I have always kept my country's laws and have never been put under lock and key; still, a man misses his footing sometimes and stumbles——

Thin Person. That's so, with the best of us.

Peer Gynt. These trifles, you know——

Thin Person. Only trifles?

Peer Gynt. Yes; I have never gone in for wholesale sinning.

Thin Person. Then, my dear man, don't bother me. I'm not the man you seem to think. I see you're looking at my fingers; what do you think of them?

Peer Gynt. Your nails seem most remarkably developed.

Thin Person. And now you're glancing at my feet?

Peer Gynt (pointing). Is that hoof natural?

Thin Person. Of course.

Peer Gynt (lifting his hat). I would have sworn you were a parson. And so I have the honour to meet——?

What luck! If the front door is open, one doesn't use the servants' entrance; if one should meet the King himself, one need not seek approach through lackeys.

Thin Person. Shake hands! You seem unprejudiced. My dear sir, what can I do to serve you? You must not ask me for wealth or power; I haven't such a thing to give you, however willing I might be. You wouldn't believe how bad things are with us just now; nothing goes right; souls are so scarce—just now and then a single one——

Peer Gynt. Have people, then, improved so wonderfully?

Thin Person. No, just the reverse,—deteriorated shamefully; the most of them end in the Casting-ladle.

Peer Gynt. Ah! I've heard a little about that; it really was on that account that I approached you.

Thin Person. Speak quite freely!

Peer Gynt. Well, if it's not too much to ask, I'm very anxious to secure——

Thin Person. A snug retreat, eh?

Peer Gynt. You have guessed what I would say before I said it. You say you're not doing much business, and so perhaps my small suggestion may not be irksome——

Thin Person. But, my friend——

Peer Gynt. I do not ask for much. Of course I shouldn't look for any wages, but only as far as possible to be treated as one of the family.

Thin Person. A nice warm room?

Peer Gynt. But not too warm. And, preferably, I should like an easy access, in and out, so that I could retrace my steps if opportunity should offer for something better.

Thin Person. My dear friend, I really am extremely sorry, but you can't think how very often exactly similar requests are made to me by people leaving the scene of all their earthly labours.

Peer Gynt. But when I call to mind my conduct in days

gone by, it seems to me I am just suited for admittance——

Thin Person. But they were trifles——

Peer Gynt. In a sense still, now that I remember it, I did some trade in negro slaves——

Thin Person. I have had folk who carried on a trade in minds and wills, but still did it half-heartedly,—and they didn't get in.

Peer Gynt. Well—I've exported idols of Buddha out to China.

Thin Person. Rubbish! We only laugh at those. I have known folk disseminating uglier idols, far—in sermons, in art and literature—and yet not getting in.

Peer Gynt. Yes, but—look here! I've passed myself off as a Prophet!

Thin Person. Abroad? That's nothing! Such escapades end mostly in the Casting-ladle. If you've no stronger claim than that, I can't admit you, however much I'd like to do it.

Peer Gynt. Well, but—listen! I had been shipwrecked, and was clinging fast to a boat that had been capsized. "A drowning man clings to a straw," the saying goes; but there's another; "Everyone for himself";—and so the fact that the ship's cook was drowned was certainly half due to me.

Thin Person. It would have been more to the point if you had been responsible for stealing half a cook-maid's virtue. Begging your pardon, what's the good of all this talk of half a sin? Who do you think, in these hard times, is going to waste expensive fuel on worthless rubbish such as that? Now, don't be angry; it's your sins and not yourself I'm sneering at. Excuse my speaking out so plainly. Be wise, my friend, and give it up; resign yourself to the Casting-ladle. Suppose I gave you board and lodging, what would you gain by that? Consider—you are a reasonable man; your memory's good, it's very true; but everything you can recall, whether you judge it with your head or with your heart, is nothing more than what our Swedish friends would call "Very poor sport." There's nothing in it that's worth a tear or worth a smile, worth boasting or despairing of, nothing to make one hot or cold—only, perhaps, to make one angry.

Peer Gynt. You can't tell where the shoe is pinching unless you've got it on, you know.

Thin Person. That's true; and—thanks to so-and-so—I only need one odd one. Still, I'm glad you mentioned shoes, because it has reminded me that I must push along. I've got to fetch a joint I hope will prove a fat one. I haven't any time to spare to stand here gossiping like this——

Peer Gynt. And may I ask what sort of brew of sin this fellow has concocted?

Thin Person. As far as I can gather, he has been persistently himself by day and night; and that is what is at the root of the whole matter.

Peer Gynt. Himself? Does your domain include people like *that?*

Thin Person. Just as it happens; the door is always left ajar. Remember that there are two ways a man can be himself; a cloth has both a right side and a wrong. You know they've lately invented in Paris a method by which they can take a portrait by means of the sun. They can either make a picture like the original, or else what is called a negative, the latter reverses the light and shade; to the casual eye it's far from pretty; but the likeness is in it, all the same, and to bring it out is all that is needed. If in the conduct of its life a soul has photographed itself so as to make a negative, they don't on that account destroy the plate; they send it on to me. I take in hand the rest of the process and proceed to effect a transformation. I steam it, dip it, burn it, clean it, with sulphur and other ingredients, till I get the likeness the plate should give,—that's to say, what is called a positive. But when, as in your case, it's half rubbed out, no sulphur or lye is of any use.

Peer Gynt. So, then, one may come to you like soot and depart like snow?—May I ask what name is on the particular negative that you're on the point of converting now into a positive?

Thin Person. Yes—Peer Gynt.

Peer Gynt. Peer Gynt? Indeed! Is Peer Gynt himself?

Thin Person. He swears he is.

Peer Gynt. He's a truthful man.

Thin Person. You know him, perhaps?

Peer Gynt. Just as one knows so many people.

Thin Person. I've not much time; where did you see him last?

Peer Gynt. At the Cape.

Thin Person. The Cape of Good Hope?

Peer Gynt. Yes—but I think he's just on the point of leaving there.

Thin Person. Then I must start for there at once. I only hope I'm in time to catch him! I've always had bad luck at the Cape—it's full of Missionaries from Stavanger.
[*Goes off southwards.*

Peer Gynt. The silly creature! He's off at a run; on a wrong scent, too. He'll be disappointed. It was quite a pleasure to fool such a donkey. A nice chap, he, to give himself airs and come the superior over me! He has nothing to give himself airs about! He won't grow fat on his trade, I'll warrant; he'll lose his job if he isn't careful. H'm! *I*'m not so very secure in the saddle; I am out of the "self"-aristocracy for good and all, as it seems to me. *(A shooting-star flashes across the sky. He nods to it.)* Peer Gynt salutes you, Brother Star! To shine,—to be quenched, and lost in the void——. *(Pulls himself together apprehensively and plunges deeper into the mist. After a short silence he calls out)* Is there no one in the universe—nor in the abyss, nor yet in heaven——? *(Retraces his steps, throws his hat on the ground and tears his hair. By de-*

grees he grows calmer.) So poor, so miserably poor may a soul return to the darkling mists and become as nothing. Beautiful earth, forgive me for having trodden thee all to no purpose. Beautiful sun, thy glorious rays have shone upon an empty shell—no one within to receive warmth and comfort from thee, the owner never in his house. Beautiful sun, beautiful earth, 'twas but for naught you warmed and nourished my mother. Nature is a spendthrift, and the Spirit but a greedy miser. One's life's a heavy price to pay for being born.—I will go up, up to the highest mountain-tops; I'll see the sun rise once again and gaze upon the promised land until my eyes are weary. Then the snow may fall and cover me, and on my resting-place be written as epitaph: "The Tomb of *No One*"! And—after that—well, come what may.

Churchfolk (singing on the road).

Oh, blessed day when the Gift of Tongues
Descended on earth in rays of fire!
O'er all the world creation sings
The language of the heavenly choir!

Peer Gynt (crouching down in terror). I will not look! There's nothing there but desert waste.—I am in terror of being dead long ere my death.

[*Tries to steal into the thickets, but finds himself standing at crossroads.*

SCENE XI

SCENE.—*Crossroads.* PEER GYNT *is confronted by the Button Moulder.*

Button Moulder. Good morning, Peer Gynt! Where's your list of sins?

Peer Gynt. I assure you that I have shouted and whistled for all I knew!

Button Moulder. But you found no one?

Peer Gynt. Only a travelling photographer.

Button Moulder. Well, your time is up.

Peer Gynt. Everything's up. The owl smells a rat. Do you hear him hooting?

Button Moulder. That's the matins bell——

Peer Gynt (pointing). What's that, that's shining?

Button Moulder. Only a light in a house.

Peer Gynt. That sound like wailing?

Button Moulder. Only a woman's song.

Peer Gynt. 'Tis there—there I shall find my list of sins!

Button Moulder (grasping him by the arm). Come, set your house in order.

[*They have come out of the wood and are standing near* SOLVEIG'S *hut. Day is dawning.*

Peer Gynt. Set my house in order? That's it!—Go! Be off! Were your ladle as big as a coffin, I tell you 'twould not hold me and my list!

Button Moulder. To the third crossroads, Peer; but *then——!* [*Moves aside and disappears.*

Peer Gynt (approaching the hut). Backward or forward, it's just as far; out or in, the way's as narrow. *(Stops.)* No! Like a wild unceasing cry I seem to hear a voice that bids me go in—go back—back to my home. *(Takes a few steps, then stops again.)* "Round about," said the Boyg! *(Hears the sound of singing from the hut.)* No; this time it's straight ahead in spite of all, however narrow be the way!

[*Runs towards the hut. At the same time* SOLVEIG *comes to the door, guiding her steps with a stick (for she is nearly blind). She is dressed for church and carries a prayer-book wrapped up in a handkerchief. She stands still, erect and gentle.*

Peer Gynt (throwing himself down on the threshold). Pronounce the sentence of a sinner!

Solevig. 'Tis he! 'Tis he! Thanks be to God. *(Gropes for him.)*

Peer Gynt. Tell me how sinfully I have offended!

Solveig. You have sinned in nothing, my own dear lad! *(Gropes for him again and finds him.)*

Button Moulder (from behind the hut). Where is that list of sin, Peer Gynt?

Peer Gynt. Cry out, cry out my sins aloud!

Solveig (sitting down beside him). You have made my life a beautiful song. Bless you for having come back to me! And blest be this morn of Pentecost!

Peer Gynt. Then I am lost!

Solveig. There is One who will help.

Peer Gynt (with a laugh). Lost! Unless you can solve a riddle!

Solveig. What is it?

Peer Gynt. What is it? You shall hear. Can you tell me where Peer Gynt has been since last we met?

Solveig. Where he has been?

Peer Gynt. With the mark of destiny on his brow—the man that he was when a thought of God's created him! Can you tell me that? If not, I must go to my last home in the land of shadows.

Solveig (smiling). That riddle's easy.

Peer Gynt. Tell me, then—where was my real self, complete and true—the Peer who bore the stamp of God upon his brow?

Solveig. In my faith, in my hope and in my love.

Peer Gynt. What are you saying? It is a riddle that you are speaking now. So speaks a mother of her child.

Solveig. Ah, yes; and that is what I am; but He who grants a pardon for the sake of a mother's prayers, He is his father.

[*A ray of light seems to flash on* PEER GYNT. *He cries out.*